Managing

Managing
Organizations

Organizations

William D. Brinckloe
University of Pittsburgh

Mary T. Coughlin
H. B. Maynard & Co., Inc.

Drawings by Julie Brinckloe

GLENCOE PRESS
A division of Benziger Bruce & Glencoe, Inc.
Encino, California

Collier Macmillan Publishers
London

Copyright © 1977 by Benziger Bruce & Glencoe, Inc.

Printed in the United States of America

All rights reserved. No part of this book may be reproduced or transmitted in any form or by any means, electronic or mechanical, including photocopying, recording, or by any information storage and retrieval system, without permission in writing from the Publisher.

Glencoe Press
A division of Benziger Bruce & Glencoe, Inc.
17337 Ventura Boulevard
Encino, California 91316

Collier Macmillan Canada, Ltd.

Library of Congress catalog card number: 76–4021

First printing 1977

ISBN 0-02-471200-0

ACKNOWLEDGMENTS

Acknowledgment is gratefully made to the following authors, publishers, and organizations who have granted permission to use selections from their publications.

AFL-CIO, for: "AFL-CIO Organization Chart."

American Management Association, for: "Dale's Classification of Organizational Problems at Seven Stages of Growth," from E. Dale, "Planning and Developing the Company Organization Structure," *AMA Research Report* 20 (1952): 22.

Association of National Advertisers, for: "Regression Analysis of Advertising Impact," from R.S. Weinberg, *An Analytical Approach to Advertising Expenditure Strategy* (New York, 1960), p. 24.

Booz, Allen and Hamilton, Inc., for: "Old and New Product Share of Sales."

Business Publications, Inc., for: "Typical Employee Behavior Rules," from William F. Glueck, *Personnel: A Diagnostic Approach* (Dallas, 1974), p. 608.

Business Week Magazine for: "Price Growth for Producers and Consumers," reprinted from the 6 April 1974 issue of *Business Week* by special permission. © 1974 by McGraw-Hill, Inc.

"Beef Consumption Trends," reprinted from the 13 April 1974 issue of *Business Week* by special permission. © 1974 by McGraw-Hill, Inc.

"Factors Used by FTC in Choosing Cases," reprinted from the 11 March 1972 issue of *Business Week* by special permission. © 1972 by McGraw-Hill, Inc.

"Personnel Recruitment Guidelines," reprinted from the 26 May 1975 issue of *Business Week* by special permission. © 1975 by McGraw-Hill, Inc.

"Corporate Financial Performance," reprinted from the 10 August 1974 *Business Week Quarterly Report* by special permission. © 1974 by McGraw-Hill, Inc.

"Debt Status of Selected Corporations," reprinted from the 12 October 1974 issue of *Business Week* by special permission. © 1974 by McGraw-Hill, Inc.

Communications Satellite Corporation, for: "Five-Year Income and Earnings Analysis."

The Conference Board, for: "Research Distribution for Various Industry Categories," from "The Role and Organization of Marketing Research," *Experiences in Marketing Management* (New York, 1969), p. 5.

Chris W. Ford and Frederick C. Dyer, for: "Sample Personal Balance Sheet," from Chris W. Ford and Frederick C. Dyer, "What, Me an Executive?" *The Retired Officer* (October 1974).

Fortune Magazine, for: "Nonverbal Communication at Work," from "The Science of Telling Executives How They're Doing," *Fortune* (January 1974): 111. Courtesy also Tom Cardamone.

"Trends that Guide Economic Planners," from *Fortune* (January 1974): 68. Courtesy also Tom Cardamone.

"Financial Implications of Capital Leasing," from "The Powerful Logic of the Leasing Boom," *Fortune* (November 1973): 133. Courtesy also Tom Cardamone.

"A Computer May Be Deciding What You Get Paid," from article by same title in *Fortune* (November 1973): 168.

"Regional Shopping Locational Patterns," from " 'Downtown' Has Fled to the Suburbs," *Fortune* (October 1972): 82-83. Courtesy also Gabor Kiss.

General Electric Company, for: "Distribution of Completion Times."

Harvard College, for: "Continuum of Management Styles," from Robert Tannenbaum and Warren H. Schmidt, "How to Choose a Leadership Pattern," *Harvard Business Review* (May-June 1973): 164. Copyright © 1973 by the President and Fellows of Harvard College. All rights reserved.

Heinz U.S.A., division of H.J. Heinz Company, for: "Assembly Line Monotony."

Indiana Telephone Corporation, for: "Impact of Price-Level Accounting on Balance Sheet."

Industry Week Magazine, for: "Product Line Manager Organization," from "Bridging the Gap Between Manufacturing and Marketing," *Industry Week* (August 5, 1974): 36. Courtesy also Richard S. Sloma.

Mallinckrodt, Inc., for: "Ten-Year Earnings Growth."

A.H. McCollough, Publisher, for: "Product Life Cycle," from Jordan P. Yale, "The Strategy of Nylon's Growth: Create New Markets," *Modern Textiles* (February 1964): 33. Copyright © 1962 by Jordan P. Yale. Reprinted also by permission of Jordan P. Yale.

McGraw-Hill Book Company, for: "Management Styles and Worker Performance Questionnaire," from Rensis Likert, *The Human Organization*. Copyright ©1967 by McGraw-Hill, Inc.

"Questionnaire Results" and "Perceptions of Communication Freedom," from Rensis Likert, *New Patterns of Management*. Copyright ©1961 by McGraw-Hill, Inc.

"Traditional vs. Self-Management Role Definitions" and "Correlation of Manager's Age and Attitudes with Growth Potential," from M. Scott Myers, *Every Employee a Manager*. Copyright ©1970 by McGraw-Hill, Inc.

"The Lower-Middle-Income Worker," from *Blue Collar Workers*, ed. Sar A. Levitan. Copyright © 1976 by McGraw-Hill, Inc.

MTM Association for Standards and Research, for: "Basic Elements in Methods-Time Management." Copyrighted by the MTM Association for Standards and Research. No reprint permission without written consent from the MTM Association, 9-10 Saddle River Road, Fairlawn, NJ 07410.

National Association of Accountants, for: "Typical Balance Sheet and Income Statement," from Robert F. Randall, "People Are Capital Investments at R.G. Barry Corp.," *Management Accounting* (November 1971): 55.

Newsweek Magazine, for: "Results of Magazine Readership Studies," from a recent (1975) *Newsweek* advertisement in several trade papers.

Opinion Research Corporation, for: "How Shareholders Rate Accountants."

Reliance Group, Inc., for: "Combine Leasing Companies Balance Sheet."

Leonard Sayles, for: Excerpt in chapter 2 from Leonard R. Sayles, *Behavior of Industrial Work Groups: Prediction and Control* (New York: John Wiley & Sons, Inc., 1958), pp. 7-9, 11-14, 18-19, 32-35, 38-39.

Scott, Foresman, for: "Performance Determinants," from L.L. Cummings and Donald P. Schwab, *Performance in Organizations: Determinants and Appraisal*. Copyright © 1973 by Scott, Foresman and Company.

Starch INRA Hooper, for: "Ranking of Attitudes Toward Publications."

Tiger International, Inc., for: "Quarterly Corporate Income Statement" and "Quarterly Corporate Balance Sheet."

United Steelworkers of America, for: "Timetable for Key Basic Steel Benefits."

John Wiley & Sons, Inc., for: "Operation Chart for Assembly Process," from R.M. Barnes, *Motion and Time Study*, 4th ed. (New York, 1958), p. 94.

Contents

Preface   xi

PART ONE / THE BUILDING BLOCKS OF ORGANIZATIONS

1. **THE INDIVIDUAL AT WORK**   2
   - North Star Prologue   2
   - A Look Ahead   5
   - Principles of Self-Management   5
   - Motivation: Stimulation for Individual Action   12
   - Planning Your Career   13
   - The Individual as Proprietor   14
   - The Individual Within the Organization   21

2. **GROUPS AT WORK**   27
   - North Star Prologue   27
   - The Individual and the Group   30
   - Role of Groups in the Organization   42
   - The Manager and the Group   53

3. **DESIGN AND DEVELOPMENT OF ORGANIZATIONS**   64
   - North Star Prologue   64
   - Principles of Organization   68
   - Organizations as People-Systems   78
   - Organizational Development and Growth   86
   - Describing Organizations   92

PART TWO / MANAGEMENT PROCESSES

4. **LEADERSHIP**   100
   - North Star Prologue   100
   - The Environment and Purpose of Leadership   103
   - Leadership in Action   117
   - Developing Leadership   124
   - Changing Patterns in Leadership   129

5. **COMMUNICATION**   141
   - North Star Prologue   141
   - Concepts of Communication   145

Organizations as Communication Systems	157
Techniques of Organizational Communication	164
Problems in Communication Systems	169
6. PLANNING	**179**
North Star Prologue	179
Nature and Purpose of Planning	182
Types and Levels of Planning	188
The Planning Process	204
Self-Planning	208
7. DECISION MAKING	**214**
North Star Prologue	214
What Is Decision Making?	217
Who Makes Decisions?	228
How Are Decisions Made?	233

PART THREE / MANAGERS AT WORK

8. GETTING THINGS DONE	**256**
North Star Prologue	256
Directing	260
Producing	275
Monitoring	286
Selecting	289
9. CONTROLLING	**294**
North Star Prologue	294
The Control Process	297
Types of Control	313
Methods of Control	329
10. PERSONNEL MANAGEMENT	**339**
North Star Prologue	339
The Role of Line and Staff	342
A Systems View of Personnel Management	351
Managing Conflict	366
The Changing Scene in Personnel Management	369
11. MANAGING FINANCES	**380**
North Star Prologue	380
Financial Planning	383
Managing Funds	397
Raising Funds	403
Investing Funds	411
12. HANDLING AND USING INFORMATION	**420**
North Star Prologue	420
The Concept and Purpose of Information	423
Information Needs	431
Information Systems	453

Information Problems	461
Appendix: Manufacturing Analogy	465

PART FOUR / MANAGEMENT AND ITS ENVIRONMENT

13. FACING THE MARKET — 474
- North Star Prologue — 474
- Organizing the Marketing Function — 477
- Determining Public Needs — 496
- Dealing with Public Needs — 508
- Today's Consumer — 515

14. THE IMPACT OF LAWS AND REGULATIONS — 525
- North Star Prologue — 525
- The Elements of Business Law — 529
- Administrative Law — 535
- Regulatory Agencies — 549
- Consumer Movements — 557

15. LABOR-MANAGEMENT RELATIONS — 566
- North Star Prologue — 566
- The Role of Unions in Society — 569
- The Work Force — 582
- Dealing with Unions — 596
- The Changing Labor Environment — 604

16. MANAGEMENT AND THE PUBLIC — 614
- North Star Prologue — 614
- Management in the Urban Setting — 619
- The Public as Partner — 631
- Social Responsibility of Business — 639
- Business and Ethics — 649

PART FIVE / MANAGEMENT THEORY

17. DEVELOPMENT OF MANAGEMENT THEORY — 662
- North Star Prologue — 662
- Background of Management Theory — 665
- Schools of Management Theory — 671
- Current Issues in Management Theory — 688

Epilogue — 697
Index — 701

Preface

In recent years, the role of management in a successful organization has become increasingly complex as the organizations themselves have expanded and diversified. At the same time, the duties of the modern manager have been complicated by the growing responsiveness of organizations to the needs of employees and the public. Reconciling the demands of these groups with organizational goals is a challenge unique to our time. Today's managers have few if any precedents to rely on, but cannot afford the risk of trial-and-error decision making. Thus, they must be trained professionals who possess the skills and flexibility to handle a wide range of fluctuating responsibilities.

The primary objective of *Managing Organizations* is to explain the nature of the manager's job so that students, as prospective managers, can begin to develop this professional awareness and ability. The book focuses on key managerial functions—planning, organizing, directing, and controlling. The best way to understand these tasks is to perform them, but numerous pitfalls can be avoided by studying each in the context of the manager/employee relationship. While stressing functions, the text does not overlook managerial concepts, because a sound grasp of theory encourages a thoughtful, adaptive response to the changing organizational environment.

The emphasis, however, is on the *practice* of management—the application of managerial techniques to a variety of situations. Text examples, drawn from actual management crises in organizations of different types and sizes, are followed by analyses of successful and unsuccessful solutions. To further underscore the relevance of the text material, the book includes a running narrative about the development of a fictitious organization—North Star Associates—from a one-person enterprise to a large and thriving corporation. Each chapter opens with an excerpt from the story that illustrates the principles discussed in that chapter. While the text can be used without the story, North Star does offer students a useful preview of the obstacles and triumphs the new manager and the growing organization are likely to encounter.

With the North Star story as an ongoing illustration, the chapter sequence corresponds to the management needs that face an organization in successive stages of growth. Part One (The Building Blocks of Management) covers principles crucial to small enterprises, from one-person firms to growing companies encountering multiple-management problems for the first time. Part Two (Management Processes) presents general management techniques for leadership, communication, planning, and decision making—essential skills for any manager in any organization. Part Three (Managers at Work) explores the functional techniques and principles for managing separate divisions of a larger organization—production, control, personnel, finance, and information. Part Four (Management and Its Environment) deals with the impact of external forces on the organization, including government regulations, labor unions, and the public. Part Five (Management Theory) introduces the historical background for the theoretical framework implied in the preceding chapters. Throughout the text, theory is offered as a prescription for action, not as a valid substitute.

To supplement the North Star chapter prologues, marginal questions within each chapter link different aspects of the story to the principles introduced in the text; in addition, marginal subject headings highlight important terms and concepts as they arise. Each chapter ends with a summary of salient points, straightforward review questions, and more difficult discussion questions. Finally, each chapter includes a detailed case problem based on the North Star story with accompanying questions, and a bibliography listing sources of more detailed information on the chapter materials.

The book is illustrated with numerous charts, tables, and diagrams that clarify and expand on major themes and ideas; in addition, lively cartoons provide a lighter commentary on the text material.

With its comprehensive approach and emphasis on practical situations, *Managing Organizations* is suitable for any principles of management course. Students using this text should gain a broad understanding of basic managerial concepts and techniques that apply to dealing with and meeting specific goals in any organization.

PART ONE

The Building Blocks of Management

The Individual at Work

North Star Prologue

Henry North enlisted in the Navy during the Korean War, and was sent to the Philippines as a member of the Seabees, the Navy's overseas construction organization. He worked on the construction of the airfield in Subic Bay, an imaginative project that carved a runway out of the mountains and the landfilled harbor in an earth-moving operation vaster than the building of the Panama Canal. His boss was Lieutenant Richard Boyer, the Navy civil engineer in charge of the earth moving, and under that officer's influence Henry decided to become a civil engineer himself. When his enlistment was up he entered college under the G.I. Bill and majored in civil engineering.

During his university days he became close friends with his academic advisor, Professor Millard Jameson, who supplemented his university salary by serving as consultant and city engineer for the town of Blackridge, near the university. Henry did many interesting jobs for Blackridge under Jameson's tutelage, and eventually the city manager got to know and like him. Shortly before Henry graduated, Professor Jameson's health failed and he was forced to retire; the city manager of Blackridge invited Henry to take Jameson's place, with the understanding that the latter would be available for guidance and counsel when needed. The town offered to pay Henry one day a week as retainer, and expected to give him work from time to time on a fee basis.

Henry accepted eagerly, and after graduating he opened a small office in Blackridge as a full-fledged (though fledgling) consulting engineer. He did a very challenging and extensive job for Blackridge on flood plain layouts, drew plans for extension of city services to new developments on the edge of town, and did most of the design for the city's proposed sewage treatment plant. The Blackridge work was not enough for full-time employment, but through the help of Jameson and the recommendations of the city manager he began to get small additional assignments from other sources. It began to appear that he would be able to exist as a lone entrepreneur, even though he was that rarity as a consultant—a brand-new graduate. He regretted having to devote a large slice of his time to selling his services, keeping the books, making financial reports, and handling the details of his small office; but he realized that these tasks were necessary evils of operating independently. The part he liked was that he didn't need to get permission or approval from anyone before he took an action. On the whole, he was quite content.

His contentment did not last. Now and then Henry saw requests issued by the county, the university, city, or a federal agency in the area calling for design and analysis proposals from engineering firms. These projects were quite substantial, and Henry sometimes submitted proposals, but he found that his one-

This is a book about management.

We will be discussing the way managers apply various sophisticated and not-so-sophisticated tools to organizational processes to ensure that decisions will be based on rational and precise premises (as often as possible). There are different approaches to almost any task; given the proper information, analytical methods, and prior experience, the manager is expected to select the most efficient alternatives. Since time is limited (managers never have enough), and false starts are costly in many ways, potential managers are well advised to make a formal study of management (as you are doing) to improve their chances of making wise decisions.

In a sense, management of self parallels management of others. You must learn to manage your own affairs before you can be entrusted with the precious right to manage the group efforts of those whose performance levels depend on your skills.

Of the organizational "building blocks" discussed in Part One, the individual is the key block. As this first chapter will demonstrate, you are already gaining priceless experience in the art of effective management by planning, organizing, and directing your own activities. You can view the way a single individual applies management principles to his or her personal life from three perspectives:

1. *Management for self-guidance.* Managerial tools within an organization may be considered analogous to the individual's self-management processes.

2. *The individual as a proprietor.* In a one-man or one-woman operation, the individual carries out the different management tasks by donning several different "hats."

3. *The individual within the organization.* As the individual joins forces with others to achieve ends, a new pattern of interrelated goals and values may emerge.

As you read more and more about management, you may often find yourself enjoying an "A-ha!" experience when you relate the various principles and cases to your personal experiences. You may even pick up a few pointers with regard to planning your own daily schedule or your future. No matter what your occupation, you will find that managers dominate much of the scene; without their skills, the organization could not flourish. Indeed, there would be no organization, but only a grab bag of uncoordinated fragments blundering about in all directions.

On an individual level, you will find part of your efforts directed toward managing your own actions—using many of the same skills that the manager of a large operation such as General Motors needs to keep the company going. Management, of self or of others, is an exciting game; but to become a skillful player, you must learn to channel your efforts productively.

man organization was far too limited for him to receive any consideration. It occurred to him that his livelihood was almost totally dependent on the good will of Blackridge, and at any time the town council might decide that he was too inexperienced for the work he was doing. Indeed, he admitted privately, he *was* too inexperienced for the variety of tasks he was called upon to do. If anything were to happen to Jameson, it seemed obvious that the city manager could no longer justify doing business with a new graduate who had not yet taken his professional engineering examination. He concluded that he would have to establish a firmer base, to guard against being put out of business overnight.

Henry had started attending the monthly meetings of the local engineering society chapter, and at one of these he met an environmental engineer, Bertram Starr, who seemed to share several of his own interests. Bert, who had graduated shortly before Henry, shared his liking and admiration for Jameson. Bert had stayed on at the university for a master's degree in public health, and had worked part time for the state department of environmental health while he completed his thesis. This emphasis had given him something of a head start in the new field of environmental engineering, and since receiving his degree he had worked for large engineering firms which had not yet formed environmental staffs. Occasionally, in fact, he found himself providing the environmental expertise for firms that would bid on, and win, the same projects that attracted Henry. Bert had received some job offers to associate full time with these firms, and realized that it was only a matter of time until they would hire their own staffs to handle the environmental aspects, after which they would have no more need for him.

Henry and Bert found that each had been chafing under the limitation of not being able to bid directly on these attractive projects because each was a one-man operation. They decided that a partnership would provide more strength than the sum of their separate capabilities. Bert would provide environmental know-how, and Henry would bring his experience in municipal engineering. They decided to team up, using Henry's office as headquarters; each would contribute the work he had been doing already, and together they would seek additional jobs.

For their new name, they thought of Starr & North, or North & Starr, but finally settled on the obvious "North Star Associates." It was this name that they registered with the state—and they were in business.

What Henry North Can Learn from Chapter 1

1. The awareness that management principles apply to his own life and the realization that practicing self-management prepares one for becoming a manager

2. The central role which planning, organizing, and decision making play in managing both self and organizations

3. The role which motivation plays in stimulating individuals to action (whether they are alone or in groups) and the realization that individuals have different needs and consequently require different motivators

4. How a sole proprietor like himself must be both specialist and generalist

5. How the personal freedom which comes from being one's own boss comes only at a price: the sole proprietor assumes *total responsibility* for the organization and risks his or her entire personal fortune

6. How individual and organizational goals are not always compatible, but an individual who assumes an active role in planning his or her career can follow the desired course through an organization

A Look Ahead

Some of the management tools described in the pages that follow may seem unfamiliar to you. Unless you are an accounting major, for example, the financial jargon of the balance sheet and income statement—"net worth," "equity," "liquidity," "liability," and so on—will be confusing at first. Without realizing it, however, you have already used all these principles to keep your own finances in shape. You are keenly aware of the state of your personal balance sheet, whether you actually get it down on paper or not. Similarly, you may assume that a section on data processing is not for you. But when you begin to grasp the *function* of a computer—to break down information into its simplest components and reassemble it in the most logical pattern, just as your own mind does—the task of reading the section doesn't seem so formidable after all.

Although management techniques can be complex, for the most part managing boils down to applying a set of common principles practiced by every human being who leads a reasonably organized life. The essence of good management is knowing what method to apply to each of the vast array of problems that confront a manager—many in the course of a single day. Throughout this chapter, we will discuss the process of making such decisions, which applies equally to managing one's personal life, running a small business, or surviving as part of an organization.

Principles of Self-Management

Some 40 years ago, management theorist Luther Gulick[1] made up the acronym POSDCORB from the first letters of the key management functions: *P*lanning, *O*rganizing, *S*taffing, *D*irecting, *CO*ordinating, *Re*porting, and *B*udgeting. Modern management writers may rephrase the list a bit, but Gulick's functions still constitute the essence of management—and each must be addressed when you manage yourself. You plan your efforts, organize your daily affairs, decide which of your selves can do which tasks and assign the remainder to outside people (the garage mechanic, doctor, teacher, etc.), force yourself to get on with distasteful tasks, keep a desk calendar or scraps of paper to itemize what has been done already and what remains, coordinate your various responsibilities so you can fulfill them in the most efficient sequence (e.g., when you drive to the library for a book, you stop at the grocery for supplies en route), and apportion your resources so you can meet all your bills when they come due (more or less).

POSDCORB

Think back to the days when you first contemplated college. Daydreams of life in a dorm or a rented pad, with the freedom to cut classes now and then, were exciting but probably vague as well, because you really didn't know what college was like. Few high school seniors hit college "cold," however, for they have been planning their schoolwork and organizing their activities around the goal of college for a long time—much as managers must plan, organize, and make decisions based on a calculated projection of future developments.

planning

Planning

Let's go through the major management tasks (roughly paralleling Gulick's scenario) to carry the analogy further. Each aspect of planning, a basic tool of management, is thoroughly explored in chapter 6: setting objectives, mapping out alternatives, determining workloads and how they will be accomplished, and conducting research to reduce the uncertainty of future events. (As Winston Churchill once said, the tough part about predicting the future is that it hasn't happened yet.) Unless an organization or an individual plans ahead, any turn of events that wasn't almost painfully obvious can result in disaster.

Probably your college planning started shortly after you entered high school. With the help of your guidance counselor, you chose the academic or vocational curriculum that would prepare you for college or a job on graduation. Assuming that college was your goal, you took the college board examinations or perhaps the preliminary examinations during junior year, and senior year you took the college boards for the first or second time. Hearing that colleges prefer applicants who take part in extracurricular activities, you joined a few clubs and the like. You also sent for the catalogs of schools you hoped to attend, to make sure you would meet the entrance requirements.

By the time you actually applied to individual colleges (perhaps after visiting them and being interviewed), your planning had been under way for several years; the application was visible evidence that the goal was in sight. But since every ending is a beginning, acceptance by a college shifted your attention to planning for your life in college. What should you take with you? Where would you live? What programs might you be interested in?

Unless an organization or an individual plans, any turn of events that wasn't painfully obvious can catch one off guard and totally unprepared.

6
THE BUILDING BLOCKS OF MANAGEMENT

So the planning cycle goes on. Everything we do involves planning, whether long- or short-term. Your college planning was long-term (in a sense it was preparation for the rest of your life). You are involved in short-term planning when you lay out daily and weekly schedules, select a route to work, or decide what appointments to make today. Some of this planning may be unconscious, yet you have a firm idea of where you are going. If you had *no* plans, conscious or unconscious, much of your activity would be purposeless.

As chapter 6 points out, some managers are similarly remiss in organizational planning. There are specific planning aids for the aspiring manager, but one of the best preparations is to incorporate planning into personal life. These guidelines may prove useful:

- What is (are) my basic objective(s)?
- What are alternative ways to reach this objective (or these objectives)?
- What are the costs and benefits of each alternative?
- What are the direct consequences of each alternative?
- What may be some unintended side effects of each alternative?

How did Henry North incorporate planning into his personal life prior to forming North Star?

planning guidelines

Once these questions are answered to the best of your ability (perhaps realizing that you lack answers to some of them and doing some more research), you will be ready to *decide* which alternative to go with—another crucial step in the management process, whether individual or organizational.

Organizing

Before moving on to decision making, let's turn to the consideration of *organizing* in self-management. In order to activate your plan (whatever it may be), you must systematize the tasks that it entails. An integrated whole in management is usually far more than the sum of its parts, just as an automobile is a functioning system, in contrast to a bin of auto parts. On an organizational level, it is necessary to build a structure in which people can work well together and really get things done. Chapter 3, "Design and Development of Organizations," discusses this structural procedure. Self-organizing may be an easier task than coordinating different people, but the individual faces many of the same tasks the organization faces.

organizing

How often have you had to cram for an important examination when you might have studied more effectively over a three-day period, or had to ask for an extension of an important deadline? It is not easy to lay out a set of activities and then convince yourself to do what you ought to do; yet the individual who succeeds finds that the rewards are sweet. Organizing makes life less helter-skelter and harried, and helps us accomplish what we set out to do. (In some ways, disciplining yourself to finish a certain distasteful task is a sign of self-leadership even more than self-organization.)

Organization is the first step in turning plans into action. A plan is nothing unless it can be implemented; but without planning your organizing will not be meaningful, for the consequences of many of your actions will not have been analyzed. The two concepts go hand in hand, and in self-management it is often hard to tell where planning stops and organizing starts.

Scheduling

scheduling

You organize when you decide what to do, how you will do it, and what tools you will use. You schedule when you put your various tasks in sequence and determine the times when each will be done. Organizing to study for an exam involves getting your notes in order, lining up the books you will use, and determining your priorities (which subjects need the most time). Scheduling involves deciding to study for Course A on Monday and Tuesday evening, for Course B on Monday afternoon, and so on.

Getting Things Done

getting things done

Everything that has gone before, while essential, is preparation. No wheel turns until your getting-things-done self actually sits down and bites the bullet. The first step in getting things done (chapter 8 is devoted to this crucial activity) is to lay out the specific steps for the task (before tuning your car, for example, you buy the tuneup kit and read the auto manual to ascertain the steps you must follow to do the job right).

In the 1940s bestseller *Cheaper by the Dozen,* two children of pioneer industrial engineer Frank B. Gilbreth described his passion for efficiency in everything, down to the most simple personal activities. After concluding that the usual bath was a very wasteful operation, taking much longer than it should, Gilbreth designed a path for soaping that went up one side, across the top, down the other side—and the task was done. In the movie version of the book, Gilbreth takes one of his children to a new school and the headmistress asks what he does for a living. In the process of explaining, he sits down on the floor to demonstrate how the principles of motion economy can be applied to the everyday operation of bathing. Suddenly the superintendent enters the office, showing obvious surprise at the sight of Mr. Gilbreth sitting on the floor waving his arms. "Mr. Gilbreth is showing me how to take a bath," the headmistress remarks dryly.

Whether you need preparation to take an efficient bath or not, many things you do could be done equally well in less time. The principles of chapter 8 can be profitably applied to your personal affairs, just as they can to those of a large organization.

Decision Making

decision making

Each day you are confronted with the need to make dozens of decisions, as simple as whether to run a yellow light and as complex as whether to take a part-time job. There are many types of decisions and many ways to make them, as shown in chapter 7, "Decision Making." When you pass through a cafeteria line, you almost instinctively decide what to buy; your decision will influence your immediate satisfaction but not the shape of your life. When the stakes (or steaks?) are high, however, you must base your decisions on more serious considerations. You cannot choose the right alternative in any important matter until you have set out your goals and traced the effects of each alternative on those goals.

What was the pattern you used in selecting your college? If you are a rational person, you thought out your life objective and decided which jobs might best help you attain it. Then you assessed each college you thought of attending in terms of how well it would prepare you for such jobs. You cranked in a dose of realism, in terms of what you could afford (whether to live at home or on campus, whether to go out of state, and so on). Perhaps you decided that certain goals conflicted—a college best suited to the attainment of one goal was not best for another; so you had to rank your goals in some priority order.

A key rule in decision making is that once the proper framework has been set up, the decision must be *made*. Too many individuals and managers like to put decisions off, hoping the problem will somehow go away, but usually it won't. (Napoleon is said to have kept all of his incoming mail a month or longer, declaring that by that time most of it didn't need to be answered anymore. Only unusually gifted leaders, however, can afford that kind of indulgence.) Life for such procrastinators is a merry-go-round, for they run around in circles without getting anywhere, even missing out on the brass ring. In your college career, there comes a point where you must choose a major and stick with it, or you run the risk of being the perennial student with 200 assorted credits but nothing solid enough to help you graduate (or find a job).

If you step back and examine the reasons for not deciding, you may see evidence of insufficient planning at the outset, or simply no understanding of how one converts a disordered array of inputs into a decision. Sometimes it is the risk that causes managers to delay, feeling that as long as they haven't decided, they are safe. Good planning lowers the risk by assessing all of the possible outcomes, but inevitably a good measure of risk will remain. Life is inherently risky. Every time we step outdoors or even into the bathtub we encounter risk, but just as we don't stop bathing we cannot avoid attacking an issue and putting it behind us.

nondeciding

How did Henry North go about deciding whether or not to take on a partner? What impact might the decision to take on a partner have on his organization? the decision to choose Bert Starr as the partner?

Communication

Communication plays a large role in our personal lives, just as it does in the activities of a large organization, and the individual must guard against many of the obstacles that plague organizational communication. We all continuously communicate with friends, family, store clerks, service workers, professors, and everyone else we deal with. (Some claim you must talk to your plants, if you want them to thrive.) The process is complex, as chapter 5 points out, and unless the receiver clearly understands the intent of the sender no communication takes place. When we communicate with professors, we often hesitate to ask questions for fear of looking stupid or embarrassing them; the hierarchical structure of many organizations represents a similar handicap for managers.

communication

We also communicate with ourselves. We tell ourselves to get a certain job done. We occasionally read a passage out loud to stress its meaning and help us remember it. We chide ourselves for stupid actions. We raise questions with ourselves and heed the answers. We are creatures of many facets, and internal communication keeps all the sides of our personalities in tune.

Managing Finances

managing finances

An important tool in your individual survival kit is the ability to handle your money. No doubt you would be delighted to run up your net worth, but at this point you must settle for keeping within a safe debt limit. These are equally important goals for companies, and though they use more sophisticated techniques to stay solvent, an individual with some appreciation for his or her balance sheet and income statement has passed the first test for understanding organizational accounting.

The Need for Information

information channels

To function effectively, individuals and organizations need a continuous and accurate supply of information. Just as the manager must be attuned to numerous incoming information channels to ensure good decisions, the individual must keep informed on events in his or her nation, community, organization, group, and family. The daily decisions of government bodies, college administrators, corporations, and so on have an impact on all of us. Unless we are aware of their meaning and ramifications, we may miss out on benefits or fail to perform an obligation. By the same token, we must avoid being drowned in information, and must insure that the information on which we act is timely and reliable.

Selling Yourself

selling yourself

Your public relations constitute your marketing function. You must sell yourself again and again: to get into college, to be admitted to a closed

We must recognize that we also communicate with ourselves.

10
THE BUILDING BLOCKS OF MANAGEMENT

course, to get part-time work, to get a scholarship or fellowship, and to get your job after graduation.

To get into college, you had to present your prior record, including perhaps an essay that you wrote. Your activities had to be put in the best possible light. If you were seeking membership in a student club, perhaps you had to focus on a different set of activities, or at least to present your past experience in a different light. Perhaps a personal interview was required for admission to your college; that involved another kind of selling.

To get a job, you may have to conduct an active campaign to sell yourself to the potential employer. You may have to do the same thing to get a date. Often, the intended "buyer" in such cases will later remark, "He came on too strong," in describing why the date or the job didn't materialize. In other words, the seller's advertising campaign bombed; he chose the wrong technique in trying to create a demand for the product. That seller needs a better understanding of the marketing principles—how to present a product, why people buy, and so on—discussed in chapter 13, "Facing the Market."

Laws and Regulations

Much of what we do and want to do is shaped by external rules. Whether we are managing a corporation or simply our own lives, we must be aware of the powerful presence of laws and regulations and understand their significance to us. The law enters virtually every aspect of our lives—when we were born, marry, have children, or pass on, to whatever reward we have earned. Uncle Sam and his local relatives take the first bite from our

laws and regulations

Individuals and organizations would perish if placed in an informational vacuum for very long.

THE INDIVIDUAL AT WORK

paychecks, and may come back for more at year's end. Government ordinance may dictate how I must repair or renovate my house, or even what color I can paint it (Charleston, S.C., recently passed an ordinance requiring homeowners in the historic section to get permission before altering the appearance of their homes in any way). The significance of any law lies in the government's power of enforcement; it is essential to know the relevant laws and regulations before engaging in any unfamiliar ventures. Chapter 14, "The Impact of Laws and Regulations," discusses the pervasive influence of the various government agencies and the courts on the corporation, and the need for corporations to have large legal staffs. Similarly, the individual in business is responsible for fulfilling whatever requirements the law imposes and avoiding any violations.

Motivation: Stimulation for Individual Action

motivational tools

How often have you sworn solemnly to stay in the entire weekend and study for an upcoming quiz, only to be lured from your books by a friend's invitation to go to a show? Life is filled with conflicting demands upon our time; in order to survive, we must learn to sort out our values and focus on those that provide the greatest satisfaction. Since many essential tasks conflict with highly valued activities, management theorists have devised various tools to stimulate people to do what they *ought* to do but don't *want* to do. These range from the relatively straightforward carrot-and-stick approach to such complex psychological prods as emulation of our hero figures or conformance to group norms. As we discuss in later chapters, the appropriate motivational device must be based on an individual's needs, and these differ sharply from one individual to the next. One of the basic tasks of management is to know the members of an organization well enough to determine which motivational tools are most appropriate in a given case.

know yourself

What served as motivational devices for Henry North, proprietor?

As a self-manager, your first step toward a productive course is to *know yourself*. What are your priorities and what will best motivate you to accomplish them? You won't be able to come up with the answer immediately, but take a little time to reflect. If you don't know what drives you to achieve, how can you be expected to know what drives others?

Have you ever found your room getting messier and messier, until you despair of ever getting it tidy? Under such circumstances, you may be so disheartened that you don't even make your bed in the morning. Then something happens, and you decide to take the big step: you go all out and get it straightened up completely, and shining like a pin. For the next week or so, it is easy to tidy up, because you are inspired by the condition of the place.

Similarly, you may find yourself slipping behind in your studies. Perhaps four hours of study a day will keep you afloat, but you have been skidding a bit, and you're now three or four papers and quite a bit of reading behind. The right thing to do is put *six* hours of study a day into the task of getting caught up, but oddly enough you don't even put *two* hours into it. Just when your need is greatest, your effort is least. Rational? Hardly. But understandable? Of course. The task looks so insurmountable that you just don't have any incentive to tackle it, and without incentive you can't stir yourself to do what has to be done.

If you could effectively "manage" yourself, you would exercise the proper amount of discipline and control, mixed with a bit of inspiration and praise, to see that you never got into this fix. Once in it, however, you would take yourself in hand and exercise the sort of tough discipline that puts everything else on the back burner until things are straightened out. Oddly enough (perhaps not so oddly), most individuals find self-discipline a chore, even though their rational selves see clearly how important it is. That explains why people with serious debts will pay financial counselors to lay out a repayment plan that will get them out of trouble. The debtors could have done it themselves, but the counselor provided the essential motivation by making them feel that they *had* to do it or they would be wasting the money they had paid for professional advice. The counselor told them what they already knew, and they were grateful for it.

If you are a good self-manager, you have built-in motivation to organize your life wisely. In any case, if you plan to be a good manager of others you must practice on yourself first. Focus on the good results that will flow from your decision to be conscientious and budget your time. Praise yourself a bit for every bit of progress. Be tough with yourself. *Manage* yourself.

self-manager

Planning Your Career

A first step to applying management skills in a long-term sense is to plan your own career. No task could be more important, yet no task is more neglected, or approached more haphazardly.

career planning

Turn ahead at this point to page 208 at the end of chapter 6, and read the brief section on self-planning in an organization. So many people drop into a job, and ultimately a whole career, on the basis of hearsay, casual recommendations of friends, or simply the accident of whatever strikes their fancy (or whatever company makes them an offer) first. Certain factors are important to you (lifetime goals, aspirations, interests, localities, friends) and you possess certain skills (meeting people, making friends, analyzing sets of numbers, arguing, singing, planning). Sometimes goals and skills are not related; usually, however, they are (because we learn to do well the things that interest us). It makes sense, then, to set out your goals and match them with the characteristics of various possible professions. It also makes sense to go one step further and determine your personal chances for success in the various professions. Perhaps "opera singer" or "rock star" fits well with what you *want* to do, but if you have a voice like a crow you had better consider alternative professions in the musical world.

As another step, you must match desirable professions with the academic programs that prepare you for them. Every course you take should have a recognizable connection with one of your lifetime goals. If it doesn't, you aren't planning. Assuming you have matched your goals and skills accurately, of course, the subjects that relate to your chosen profession will *also* coincide with your interests.

The sole proprietor goes around with a perpetual headache from wearing so many hats at once.

The Individual as Proprietor

The One-Person Band

People who (like Henry North) decide to go into business for themselves eventually draw on most of the management skills we discuss in this book. Just as self-management involves performing many management functions, so the sole proprietor goes around with a perpetual headache from wearing so many hats at once. He or she must be both *specialist* and *generalist* at the same time. While concentrating on a specialty—engineering, writing, or merchandising, for example—the owner also keeps the books, markets the company and the product, orders supplies, provides and maintains the office, writes letters, fulfills legal requirements, and plans for future business, among other chores. The sole proprietor must shoulder a heavy load of responsibilities, which may leave less time for the special work he or she cares most about.

In addition, the business is probably the proprietor's only source of income; perhaps it has already devoured personal savings. This manager literally can't afford to fail (though all too often such businesses do collapse, for reasons that you may begin to see). By contrast, most of the managers in a large corporation are simply hired hands, and if the firm goes under they can step nimbly into the lifeboats to seek other jobs. They

specialist
generalist

sole proprietor

will collect whatever severance pay is due them; they may take a modest loss on stock acquired through various options or purchase plans, but the blow is not fatal. The poor sole proprietor, by contrast, may be completely wiped out if the business fails. Since the government does not separate a sole proprietor's business from personal assets, everything is forfeited if the business's debts exceed its assets. Creditors may and will appropriate personal assets; indeed, the knowledge that this step was possible may have induced them to grant the proprietor credit in the first place.

There are solutions to this dilemma, but they are not ideal. The internal revenue laws provide for a special sort of mini-corporation known as a "Subchapter S" corporation. This kind of small corporation has all the protection against personal property loss that a regular corporation provides, without the double taxation that characterizes the regular corporation. The individual who wants to take this route simply sets up friends and relations as fellow stockholders, and the business is under way. Two disadvantages are involved. One is that savvy creditors understand Subchapter S quite well and are unlikely to grant the proprietor much credit unless he or she countersigns the notes personally. The other is that however small, the Subchapter S corporation *is* a real corporation, and the other stockholders may get together and decide to throw out the proprietor and find someone else to run the business.

Subchapter S corporation

stockholders

An individual who takes the step of becoming his or her own boss in a business must have a good grasp of management skills and be fully aware of the problems that may arise. With so much at stake in a one-person band, the sole proprietor must possess at least a smattering of all the skills described in this book.

Setting Up Shop

There are a number of preliminary steps an individual should take before setting out to organize a company. In *You, Incorporated*, Peter Weaver describes "a detailed escape route to being your own boss,"[2] but warns potential proprietors not to be too hasty in breaking away to begin on their own. The individual must *plan* what he or she wants to do, and must gain some expertise in the chosen area, before diving in headfirst.

What are the differences in the planning processes between an organization like Henry North's and one designed to market retail products?

Planning extends beyond preparing yourself to assessing the market for your product or skill, selecting a site (closely related to marketability), seeking legal and financial advice and assistance, planning market strategy, finding enough money to keep afloat, estimating realistic cash flows by avoiding the "rule of ten" (new business owners usually estimate their costs ten times too low and their receipts ten times too high), and learning all the necessary skills outside your specialty required to keep a business going.

rule of ten

Your Personal Balance Sheet

Figure 1-1 illustrates an important step in setting up your own business— taking stock of your own assets and liabilities. Creating a simple balance sheet like the one shown would seem a minimal preparation for the momentous step of going into business for yourself, but many people are

personal balance sheet

THE INDIVIDUAL AT WORK

What were Henry North's resources on his personal balance sheet? What were his difficulties? Was he right to take the gamble of starting out on his own?

so mesmerized by the very thought of being their own bosses that they overlook many fundamental precautions.

The sample illustrates a number of factors you should consider, but does not indicate whether you have a handle on a potentially profitable business. This question requires a "Personal Income and Expense Statement," a companion piece to the balance sheet, as you will see in chapter 11. Eager to get the shop open and start doing business, the new proprietor may be like the old park superintendent, one of whose duties was to polish the brass cannon on the hilltop. For years he polished it; then one day he up and quit. When friends asked him why, he said he had bought his own brass cannon and was going to go into business for himself.

Running the Shop

Once you have set up shop, your one-person operation has begun, and you must keep yourself properly organized. You must spread your various selves over many tasks, and the amount of time you allocate to each is an important factor in deciding how successful you are. If all your time goes into chasing business (essential as that is), you have no time left to fill the orders. But if your nose is constantly kept to the production grindstone, you will have no innovating or marketing time, and so will get no business. Schedules are vital: if you forget to order something, no one is there to remind you. In short, if you spread your efforts too thin, or concentrate on certain interesting areas at the expense of the dull work, you will inevitably fall behind.

Figure 1-1.
Sample Personal Balance Sheet

MY BALANCE SHEET AT THE START OF MY HOME BUSINESS

Strengths and Resources

1. Age 35 with 35 years of experience
2. House—half paid for
3. Equivalent of 1 year college
4. Willing to learn
5. Have five good neighbors; three will really help in a pinch
6. Aunt Tillie will loan $500.00
7. Get $35.00 each month from an inheritance
8. Typewriter on hand in good condition
9. Have 28 friends and relatives who send Christmas cards; can provide five more contacts
10. Have car and access to bus transportation
11. Know how to_____
12. _____
13. _____
14. _____
15. _____

Etc. to at least 20. Force yourself to brainstorm at least that many.

Difficulties and Problems

1. Need at least $_____ a week to live on
2. Debt of $_____
3. Lack _____ education
4. Handicapped by _____
5. Children tie me down four hours a day
6. Afraid to meet people
7. Don't like to ask people to buy
8. Back hurts when I stand
9. Have only evenings free
10. Nobody likes me . . .

Stop, you can't have that many! Restudy all after number 5 to see if they can't be turned into opportunities.

Of course, if a sole proprietor makes any money at all, assistants will soon be hired to help in such areas as selling, keeping the books, doing the clerical chores, and so on. As sole proprietor, you have many decisions to make: how much inventory to keep on hand, what to do about contracts, how to handle advertising, how much working capital is needed, how to assess the future, and a pack of others. Since you are both generalist and specialist, at times you will have to call in professionals such as lawyers, accountants, bankers, or real estate consultants to guide you in difficult decisions. No one can be an expert in everything, and it is not a sign of weakness to know when you don't know.

The sole proprietor is both manager and employee. Thus, you may feel freer than the individual who works for an organization, but you have not eliminated the boss. You must be manager over yourself, and if you manage poorly the cost can be heavy. The failure rate for new mini-businesses runs as high as 80%, and most of the failures can be traced to poor management. This is a tragic waste, for management skills can be learned. Sole proprietors have so much to lose (often their life savings) that they feel compelled to press ahead every instant with whatever seems to be the "job at hand." They would think it ridiculous to "waste time" on management study or perhaps even on asking for help. But the *real* job at hand is to stay afloat, and if they fail to grasp this priority any one of several reefs could do them in.

Sometimes help is available and the sole proprietor doesn't know it. The federal government provides assistance for minority small businesses through the Office of Minority Business Enterprise of the Department of Commerce, with consultants in various cities who are available at no charge. Universities often will help in specialized areas. Department of Commerce field offices can steer fledgling enterprises to sources of help. Often large corporations will lend a hand. It is never harmful to ask.

The Record Shop

Let's peer behind the scenes at a single proprietorship about to get going. Suppose your friends keep suggesting to you that a lot of money can be made by opening a record shop in a particular location near the college. You have enough money saved from working during the summers to enable you to invest in a small business, provided you get your money back in time to pay for your remaining education in a couple of years. And it would be fun to be your own boss in a real enterprise!

You, wise soul, have enough good sense not to leap in with both feet before you look, so you make an analysis of the costs and benefits of setting up such a shop, getting help from knowledgeable people. After you have analyzed your personal "balance sheet" as described in the previous section, you assess the demand for a record shop (perhaps using some of the demand forecasting and locational analysis techniques discussed in chapter 13, "Facing the Market"). Your friends are right about the need for a record shop near the college—but not where they suggest you put it. The vacant store they want you to grab up has gone out of business for a reason: though it is close at hand, it is the wrong hand. The student traffic is heavier in the other direction, toward the neighborhood shopping center, as a brief traffic survey quickly discloses. The only businesses near the vacant building are a barber shop and a bar, neither a very good source of "interchange" customers for a record shop.

You do, however, find a hole-in-the-wall location in the shopping center, where a news dealer is willing to share space and rent with you. After lengthy consultation with your banker, who sends you to a lawyer forthwith, you are ready to set up shop. Fortunately, you worked in a record shop once, so you are familiar with certain elements of the business: identifying the popular numbers, ordering, keeping inventory, arranging displays, establishing credit policies, and advertising. At least, you think you are. After being in business for a time, however, you find that there are a few surprises: the rate of theft, the growth in overhead, deciding when and why to have a clearance sale, and learning to spot trends in record demand.

Tough as things are, you are one of the lucky ones, and you might just make it. You have used a few analytical tools to find things out, rather than going on hearsay or hopes, and you have a little prior experience to draw on during these rocky early months. (Peter Weaver suggests that before you take the plunge into your own business, you should indulge in a little "creative moonlighting" by apprenticing yourself to an experienced person in the same kind of business and keeping your eyes and ears open.) You have started well, but your finances and fortune are close to the line, and a little tough luck before you build up momentum can do you in. More management savvy is needed if you are to keep on running the shop successfully.

creative moonlighting

Coping with the Need for Specialization

Henry North did not remain a sole proprietor for very long, because he discovered that his realm of expertise was far too limited to bring him any sizable contracts. He and Bert were very conscious of the merits of two heads instead of one. Acting alone, each was limited in what he could accomplish, for each was qualified in only one field. Their combined efforts proved more productive than the sum of each working separately, because their specialty as a team covered a reasonably broad field. This team operation proved fruitful in attracting additional and better customers, because they had improved the joint product.

One of the primary differences between a proprietorship and a large corporation is the degree of specialization. Corporations grow as they add more products and tasks to their menu, and must hire specialized personnel to handle the broadened job assortment. The single proprietor, by contrast, is jack of all trades (and sometimes master of few). But single proprietors have one significant advantage: having done everything, they acquire a broad, comprehensive view of an organization that their more sheltered brethren in individual slots of a large corporation never manage (though in most areas, the view tends to lack depth).

Before taking the relatively irreversible step of adding a partner, the proprietor should take inventory of his or her personal strengths and weaknesses. The best strategy is not to choose someone exactly like yourself, as much fun as that would be, for then you simply reinforce what you already have and still leave the holes unfilled. If your first and only love is dirtying your hands in the shop, you'd better join forces with a personable individual who can bring in those orders. If you are always brainstorming (people admire your million-dollar ideas), but somehow don't quite make the translation to results, you need a partner who is adept at organizing. Being your own boss means you have the freedom to join forces with whomever you want, but then you are stuck with what you have chosen; so you'd better use some management tools in selecting the individual you hire or team up with.

The individual proprietor may add a partner for reasons other than the need for additional expertise or help. Expanding the business, for example, requires additional capital, which calls for a partner with funds to invest—who then, of course, gets a share of the original pie. Or a desire for contacts in a different field may indicate a partner with an entree into that field. Maybe, although more help is needed, the proprietor can't afford to pay any salary at this time; a partner who sees the golden prospects for the future will trade pay now for the hope of later gains, whereas a hired hand will want wages on the spot. When hired help is taken on, the overhead shoots up, and the curse of small businesses is too much overhead too soon. At least four dollars in sales are needed to carry every dollar spent for such fixed costs as rent and salary. Thus, when the record shop entrepreneur accepted the idea of sharing the tiny shop with the newsdealer, the rent was cut in half, and the chances of a successful business increased accordingly.

overhead

fixed costs

Expressways and Roadblocks

Personal Freedom

Ask any person who owns a business what is the greatest advantage of ownership, and you will probably get the answer "Being my own boss." Solo employment offers the great satisfaction of the freedom to answer to no one else (except, of course, the customer—a very demanding boss indeed). Although the chief executive officer of a corporation may appear to be alone at the top of the hierarchy, he or she must please the stockholders, through their representatives on the board of directors.

Those who venture out on their own give up many real benefits of working in a large corporation or government agency: a guaranteed salary in good times and bad, many fringe benefits, and job security. But organization workers pay for these amenities by surrendering at least some of their loyalties to the organization, and by adhering to organizational standards which may gall them at times. Sometimes a large organization can stifle an individual's creativity, as good ideas filter at a snail's pace through the many layers of its cumbersome screening mechanism. When we are working on our own, we have the chance to follow our creative impulses and observe the results (or lack of results, if the fates are unkind). A small outfit can literally move thousands of times faster than a large one, acting while the big outfit is still preparing the first position paper on the pros and cons—a great plus for the person who likes action.

If you run your own show, you can make all the decisions and rejoice or grieve over the outcomes. As your own boss, you know very well what you have accomplished (managers in big companies often go to their graves wondering whether they ever really got anything done), and the rewards flow in to you if the business prospers. You don't have to wait for some senior executive to pat you on the shoulder.

As you will see in chapter 5, "Communication," interchange of ideas and information in a large organization can be very cumbersome. Not so in the one-person operation. In a large outfit, one department may simply not know whether its performance is helping or hurting the whole company; even worse, sometimes that department really doesn't care about overall goals, but only about its own subgoals. Your operation won't have this kind of trouble, because coordination is one thing you have plenty of.

Motivation is seldom a problem for sole proprietors, because they see quite clearly that things would go to pot if they gave less than their best. They probably are doing something they really want to do, and no thrill exceeds that of watching a business that you have started pick up and take off. They identify fully with the job, and usually it has their fullest loyalty. Even their families get involved at times, and this support and guidance is exhilarating.

The Costs of Freedom

The "freedom" of a self-proprietorship is not quite "free," for the owner-manager pays for it in many ways. The show must go on in fair weather or foul, whether you are tired or not, and sometimes this constant burden of responsibility becomes almost too heavy. Often it seems unduly difficult to reach decisions alone, even after careful study, and you may long for a colleague with equal interest in the business to share in the problem-solving effort. If times get hard, it is you alone who must endure the sleepless nights of worry. If you want to get out for an afternoon of golf, you must close the shop—a reality perhaps omitted from your dreams when you were planning the business. In many ways, a one-person business is like a dairy cow: someone must be there twice a day to do the milking, in sickness and in health, and at times the milk just doesn't seem worth the price.

Vacations are nice things, and of course the owner-manager can take one anytime—provided he or she can accept the temporary stoppage of income. The owner of a travel agency was asked recently if it wasn't delightful to go on those great tours, and she said she had never had the least bit of fun on one, because she was deluged with work and problems night and day until it was over. When asked what she did on a vacation, she said she rented a small cottage in the woods with her family—but only stayed two days herself, because she had to get back to the agency.

There is a widespread belief that owners in certain businesses can get the best outputs of those businesses for their families and themselves. But it never seems to work that way. The old saying that the shoemaker's children never get shod is closer to the truth. The best products and prime time are devoted to the customers who can pay, and often the home team takes what is left over.

Another price of freedom for the lone wolf is that small businesses can't do big things. On a certain scale, this is quite obvious: it takes a large company to come up with the resources to drill an oil well, for example. But even in smaller things, the rule applies; a one-person engineering firm is unlikely to be entrusted with (or able to handle) anything larger than a very modest consulting contract.

If you, as proprietor, hire an assistant, you will unconsciously expect the same dedication that you feel yourself, but you are not likely to command it. This situation is not so much a disadvantage of entrepreneurship as a fact of organizational life, but the large-company manager knows about divided loyalties and plans backup systems to cover for the hired hand who fails him. The individual proprietor hiring an assistant doesn't have those backup systems, and the inevitable shortcomings of nondedicated employees are likely to cause problems.

The Individual within the Organization

A very few people start their own businesses on graduation, but most will go to work for an organization. If you do the latter, your goal is to become a manager—*after* you have learned to manage your own relationship to the organization. Organizations have goals, just as individuals do, and the efforts of many individuals are required to meet them. As we shall discuss in later chapters, however, individuals behave differently: because of their varied backgrounds and experiences, individuals perceive things differently and are driven by different forces[3] For organizational goals to be met, the range of individual efforts must be coordinated; usually the organization is arranged hierarchically, as discussed in chapter 3, with ascending levels of management to ensure that things function harmoniously.

individual goals

organizational goals

The individual must drop into a slot in this organizational hierarchy, sacrificing a good deal of independence and individuality to the will of the organization. If you were a General Motors employee, and had a strong conviction that a certain engineering feature of a popular foreign car should be adapted to the General Motors models (perhaps even a firm belief that the present designs were unsafe), you might find it very hard to get anyone in the company to listen to you. If, after listening, they disagreed with you, there would be nothing you could do about it but leave the company and fight it out from outside.

organization hierarchy

Individual versus Organizational Goals

Chester Barnard, a senior corporate executive turned management writer, has observed that the individual loses preeminence when viewed from within the organization and that another, nonpersonal entity becomes dominant[4] As we shall see in the next chapter, human beings are the most social of animals, and most of their activities occur in groups. The group performs many useful and satisfying functions for the individual, but in the process some autonomy is submerged in group norms. You were reminded of that the last time you went with your friends to see Movie A when you really wanted to see Movie B. True, you say, but when I go to work I want to be *noticed* and fulfill my own needs, because that's what I'm all about. Brave words, and more power to you—but companies have only begun to acknowledge this viewpoint, and very few of them actually accept it.

THE INDIVIDUAL AT WORK

classical management theory

Classical management theory (sometimes called "scientific management") holds that work is separate from satisfaction; Adam's fall doomed us to work, and because we do not enjoy it we must be driven to the work place by our need to earn a living. Frederick Taylor, father of scientific management, advocated setting pay rates on piecework output. In this way, Taylor believed, high output would result even though worker and management goals were far apart, and both sides would attain their goals.

human relations theory

A more recent approach, the human relations theory (advanced in various writings by Elton Mayo and Douglas McGregor, among others), asserts that money will not motivate completely because men and women do not inherently dislike work. On the basis of experiments by Mayo and McGregor which appeared to show that workers treated as partners respond favorably and produce better, managers were advised to cater to "higher order" individual needs such as esteem and self-actualization. These researchers concluded that organizational and individual goals could be in harmony if management recognized these needs.

structuralist theory

conflict

The human relations theory reshaped management thought in many quarters, with the qualification that complete harmony is not attainable in the real world. A third theory, the structuralist approach,[5] synthesized the two schools—acknowledging that individual and organizational goals must in fact often conflict. When you work for a company, you want as much pay as possible; the company wants to pay you as little as possible, so profits will be maximized; and no "harmonizing of objectives" can wipe out these elemental differences. Conflict, say the structuralists, is a normal occurrence of life. Though it cannot be eliminated, it can be reduced through techniques such as those discussed in chapters 2 and 5, "Groups at Work" and "Communication."

How would adding a partner affect the personal goal of Henry? of Bert? What strategy should each employ to maintain his own identity in the newly formed organization, yet promote the organizational goal?

Recognizing that individual and organizational goals are never completely compatible, how should you, the individual, act to insure that your needs are fulfilled? And how should you at the same time (as a potential manager) proceed to ensure that organizational goals get a fair shake as well? This dilemma may not be as tough as it appears. An individual ought to assess personal needs before seeking a job, and avoid places where personal and organizational needs appear incompatible. When times are hard, any job will do if the alternative is unemployment, but times are seldom quite that hard. Most job seekers know next to nothing about the companies they select, yet all sorts of information sources exist. One of the best is the group of college graduates who joined the company last year or the year before. Another is the personnel of competing companies, who are exposed to your company when they battle for the same customers. Another is the group of managers at middle level, the kind you would be working for if you were hired. Seldom do you need to join a company whose goals are in active opposition to yours.

passive approach

active approach

Once you are in an organization, you can take an active or a passive approach to your path within that organization. The passive approach says in effect, "Here I am, do what you will with me." Sometimes you may take that approach, but get lucky. If you are a computer expert who comes along just as computers get important in the company, you can grow as the computer applications grow—with minimal effort on your part but a lot of help from lady luck. The active approach looks for targets of

THE BUILDING BLOCKS OF MANAGEMENT

opportunity. It says: What do I have? What does the organization need? Where is there a beachhead, where the organization and I can grow together? This individual tries to dope out where the organization, or at least some part of it, is headed, and prepares; or better yet, sees where the organization should go and tries to encourage it.

Suppose you were selling steel for a steel company. Suppose you have been reading up on the business and conclude that steel as an office construction material is going to have a future by bonding directly with plastic to form a two-part sheet that can be used directly for office partitions. You prepare by learning what you can about plastic, about the bonding process, about the characteristics of this "sandwich" material, and so on. When things develop as you anticipated, you may show up as the only person in the sales department who really understands the new product you are called upon to sell.

There is nothing sneaky about this technique. It is good for you, and certainly good for the company. It doesn't even require a great deal of prophetic vision. Such future directions are common knowledge within certain parts of the company long before they take place. But they may not be common knowledge in the sales office, or wherever you work—you have to do a little digging to uncover them. The digging can be well worth the effort.

Suppose you are one of several new trainees being rotated through different departments before permanent assignment to one of them. You don't know which one you will get, and don't even know what selection system will be used. But you do know that the people doing the selecting are human, and want to do as good a job at it as possible. Say you hit one department that you really enjoy, and you want above all to be assigned there. Don't fall all over yourself during the training session trying to make an impression, because it won't work. But during the rest of the training period, spend all of your spare time back in that section. Talk to the people there. Find out what they do, and learn enough so that you could do it, too. Show the enthusiasm you feel for their work, and show by your questions that you understand what is going on there. When the selection process takes place, you will be the one person the head of that department remembers by name, and it is highly likely that you will be requested. Why not? You are the only one who indicated a real interest, and who already has a good understanding of the work there.

There is nothing sneaky about this technique either. You *are* interested, or you wouldn't have put in all your spare time hanging about. You probably are the best bet for that department. Why not devote some thought and effort to being assigned where you want to be and probably should be? Why not exert some control over your path through the organization?

Summary

This is a book about management, in which we will discuss the way managers apply sophisticated and not-so-sophisticated tools to organizational processes to ensure that decisions will be based on rational and precise premises (as often as possible). In a sense, management of self parallels management of others. You must learn to manage your own affairs before you can be entrusted with the precious right to manage the group efforts of those whose performance levels depend on your skills. The key management functions can be utilized in self-management as well as the management of organizations: planning, organizing, staffing, directing, coordinating, reporting, and budgeting (POSDCORB).

Planning is a basic tool of management which involves setting objectives, mapping out alternatives, determining workloads and how they will be accomplished, and conducting research to reduce the uncertainty of future events. Planning is the prerequisite to organizing and to making good decisions; whether you are mapping your weekly schedule, your lifetime career, or a prospective business, you should not begin without a plan.

Just as organizing, scheduling, getting things done, decision making, communicating, managing finances, getting information, staffing, marketing, and coping with laws and regulations are "essentials" in running an organization, so too are they necessary for managing yourself. Each of us operates on a smaller scale than a business, of course, and our problems may not be as complex, but we must make use of the same concepts in order to survive.

Motivation is the driving force behind individual activity. As we discuss in later chapters, the appropriate motivational device for each individual must be based on personal needs—needs which are different for everyone. One of the basic tasks of a manager is to know the members of an organization well enough to determine which motivational tools to use with each person. As a self-manager, your first step toward getting onto a productive course is to *know yourself;* if you don't know what drives you to achieve, how can you know what drives others?

A sole proprietor must be both generalist and specialist. There are both advantages and disadvantages to "being your own boss," for the cost of personal freedom can sometimes be high. A sole proprietor should invest in some "creative moonlighting" before jumping in headfirst, and add some management training as additional stability insurance.

Individual and organizational goals are not always compatible. Several management theories postulate the ideal situation, the most plausible being the structuralist theory, which recognizes the inherent conflicts. An individual who takes an active approach, looking for targets of opportunity within the organization, can take a major role in shaping his or her future.

Notes

1. Luther Gulick and Lyndall Urwick, eds., "Notes on the Theory of Organization," in *Papers on the Science of Administration* (New York: Institute of Public Administration, 1937), p. 13.

2. Peter Weaver, *You, Incorporated: A Detailed Escape Route to Being Your Own Boss* (Garden City, N.Y.: Doubleday & Co., Inc., 1975).

3. Psychological theorists have long studied individual differences and have classified needs in order of importance, ranging from basic physiological requirements to desire for self-esteem and self-actualization. Organizations try to meet these individual needs, but their techniques are imperfect and most

managers are trained only in the school of experience, so they rarely succeed completely. We will discuss these questions in detail in chapter 4, "Leadership."

4. Chester I. Barnard, *The Functions of the Executive* (Cambridge, Mass.: Harvard University Press, 1938).

5. Amitai Etzioni, *Modern Organizations* (Englewood Cliffs, N.J.: Prentice-Hall, Inc., 1964).

Review Questions

1. What are the key management functions and how does each apply to self-management?
2. What are the guidelines to assist in self-planning?
3. How does planning relate to organizing and decision making?
4. Why do individuals often procrastinate instead of making key decisions?
5. What is a balance sheet? an income statement?
6. Why does the control of information play a key role in the management process?
7. In what areas do laws and regulations affect your personal life? Is ignorance of the law an acceptable excuse for an individual who is shortsighted?
8. What role does motivation play in self-management and in managing organizations?
9. How should a rational individual plan his career?
10. What is a specialist? a generalist? Why must the sole proprietor combine the two functions?
11. What steps should an individual take before starting his own business?
12. What are the advantages of being your own boss? disadvantages?
13. What are the advantages of taking on a partner? disadvantages?
14. What is the individual's role within the organization? How have theorists defined the ideal individual/organization relationship?

Discussion Questions

1. Suppose a friend came to you and said she was having difficulty trying to decide whether to attend art school or a liberal arts college in the fall or maybe even take off and work for a while. Her dad, she said, thought it would be a good idea for her to get a taste of life while her brother insisted she was a "born artist." Since you are a "sound person," she says, she'd like your opinion. How would you tell her to structure the problem?

2. What are some barriers to interpersonal communication? How do you think these apply to communication in organizations?

3. Fortunately, you have only two term papers to do your last term of college and you vow to begin both of them the first week since both professors gave you the subjects early. Professor A assigned due dates for an outline and progress report, which would form part of the paper grade; Professor B listed only his office hours and the final due date. What are the differences in their motivational techniques? Which method would most inspire you to fulfill your self-promise of starting early? Why?

4. How would you advise a friend just out of school with no savings who wants to borrow money and start a pizza parlor?

5. As a student, which of your goals are compatible with those of the college? Which are not? If you were your own student adviser, how could you improve their meshing?

6. How have organizations been changing to account more for individual worker attitudes? Have individuals been moving closer to organizational goals?

North Star Case Study

Suppose Henry had gone to work for a construction firm and was asked to supervise a field job erecting transmission towers. The company sent with him an estimator and materials expert, a timekeeper, and a foreman, with instructions for Henry to hire the work force on-site in accordance with the company's usual practice for doing field work. Henry was very dependent on the experienced cadre who accompanied him and he recognized that dependence.

When the job was finished, the president of the utility who had contracted with them told Henry there were numerous other jobs coming along and suggested that Henry become an independent contractor in that city and perform similar jobs himself. The president promised that there would be plenty of work to keep him busy. The only reason he would not hire Henry directly was that it was simpler to contract the work out because of possible union conflicts that might arise with "in-house" jobs.

1. If Henry accepts the proposition, what unforeseen problems might he face?
2. How much can he depend on the utility president's promise that there will be plenty of work in the future?
3. If the work does not reach the level predicted by the utility president, what are Henry's chances for receiving additional business from other sources, given his lack of experience?
4. How would he provide for the experience of the three "old hands"?
5. How would his personal balance sheet look (corresponding to Figure 1-1)?
6. Do you think there are any ethical questions involved in Henry's taking a job with a customer of his present employer?
7. Should Henry take the job?

Suggestions for Further Reading

Buck, C.G. "So You Want To Go into Business for Yourself?" *Fortune,* April 1972.

Fiore, M.V. *Promotable Now! A Guide to Achieving Personal and Corporate Success.* New York: John Wiley & Sons, Inc., 1972.

Jennings, E. *Routes to the Executive Suite.* New York: McGraw-Hill Book Co., 1971.

"Plotting a Route to the Top." *Business Week,* October 12, 1974.

Weaver, P. *You, Inc: A Detailed Escape Route to Being Your Own Boss.* Garden City, N.Y.: Doubleday & Co., Inc., 1975.

Groups at Work

North Star Prologue

Upon graduation from college, Henry North became the sole proprietor of his own consulting firm. He soon learned that the company's growth potential was restricted by his personal limitations, so he took on a partner, Bertram Starr. They named the company North Star Associates and set out to seek additional contracts with their expanded team.

They still did not have enough skills to ensure successful proposals on the projects that had attracted them in the first place. Their inadequacy was particularly evident in two vital areas: large projects that involved earth moving and heavy structural work, and the engineering economics and systems analysis required to forecast traffic flow or to calculate the benefits and costs of public projects. For the second area, Jameson came to their rescue by putting them in touch with an assistant professor in his department who had negotiated a half-time teaching load with the understanding that the rest of her time would be devoted to a government research project—until the president vetoed the funds and the project disappeared. She had just the credentials they needed, and was delighted to come in as a partner on an as-needed basis, and to work more steadily for them if and when more work materialized.

For the first post—the large-project civil engineer—Henry thought at once of Lieutenant Boyer, who had been his boss during the Navy tour. With no real hope of success, he wrote to Boyer—and was surprised and delighted when Boyer wrote back immediately to say he was just leaving the Navy, with a bit of money socked away, and was interested enough to come and talk it over. The talk was fruitful, and Boyer came aboard.

The newly registered company name seemed inappropriate in view of the enlarged slate of partners, but it turned out to be all right after all. The assistant professor—an easygoing extrovert who had been christened Josephine Alkire Parnela but seldom answered to anything other than "Jo"—said it didn't matter to her what they called it. Dick Boyer thought the name was important, but with his Navy background he liked the connotations of steadfastness and direction implicit in "North Star." So they kept the name, and brought Dick Boyer in as a full partner and Jo Parnela as a limited partner.

It was not until the group won its first bid contract—a highway routing study that was limited to small business participation, so that most of the large engineering firms were ineligible to compete—that some small but rather fundamental differences in viewpoints came to light. From the first, Dick was the highly structured administrator; he insisted that close attention be paid to the progress of costs, and that none of the partners make any charges against the project until it was authorized or exceed any time estimate without changing the estimate. Bert was the public conscience, insisting that environmental factors be given paramount consideration, even when the terms of the contract definition did not so require—a position the other partners feared would give North Star Associates a reputation as a group of young radicals antagonistic to the establishment. Henry found himself cast as the champion of the smaller municipalities, so often overlooked when the state planned a highway; his experiences in Blackridge made him almost antagonistic to the viewpoint of the state, which in this case was their client. And Jo was the complete opposite of Dick Boyer: she cared nothing for the status of funds or schedules, but only for the intellectual stimulation the study might yield; she was perfectly prepared to go beyond the required work and undertake unauthorized explorations if she considered it in the interest of scholarly attainment. In short, Bert saw the project as a chance to help the environment, Henry as a chance to help the towns, Jo as a chance to break new ground in her profession—and only Dick felt an overriding responsibility to deliver the product requested.

The problem was that their organization had no boss. Everyone was equal, and there was no device except discussion to settle differences among them. Even so, the project was completed—only a little late, but considerably over cost (the state had required that most of the benefit-cost analysis be redone in accordance with their specifications, which dictated a modification of the route through the urban sections of the highway). As a result, the partners had to drop their rates of payment to themselves in order not to show a loss on the contract. In a post-mortem on the contract, the four partners discussed what had happened and why. On the plus side, their organization had many things going for it. Each partner had a special area of competence, ensuring the absence of professional jealousy or disagreement on technical issues. All clearly wanted the enterprise to succeed, and they mutually agreed that each was an extremely conscientious person according to his or her own lights. All were hard workers, and the issue of one partner claiming pay for work he or she had not completed never arose; on the contrary, each would put in extra hours to make sure the job was done properly. Their little organization possessed new areas of competence which the old-line engineering firms were slow to achieve—particularly the environmental and systems analysis skills currently in great demand—and they felt quite competitive in a number of potential job contract areas.

The trouble lay in the minus side. When a difference of opinion arose, it was invariably settled via time-consuming and sometimes emotionally wearing discussion. The fact that each partner was conscientious and strong-willed made things even worse. Henry privately concluded that he probably was the least "value-prone" member of the group, in that he often reconciled views by being the first to give in on points that seemed important to others but were secondary to him. He concluded further—and on this point all the partners agreed with him—that North Star needed some sort of decision-making hierarchy to prevent time-consuming hassles over such trivial questions as the design of their report covers or the format of a bid proposal.

Although the partners were less than delighted with their performance on the highway routing project, because they had finished late and had to redo part of the work, the state was entirely satisfied with the product. Indeed, soon after they were approached by an official in the State Department's Agency for International Development (AID). He told them that a foreign engineering firm was being hired by the agency for an overseas project to design and construct a new seaport complex, with highway links to the capital city of the firm's country and an area planned for an industrial center. The country in question was quite anxious to employ that particular firm, but AID did not consider it qualified to handle all aspects of the design and analysis task. It had suggested a large U.S. engineering firm as partner, but this idea was resisted by the foreign nation for prestige reasons. What was needed was a firm with a low profile but the necessary competence to serve as a subcontractor to the foreign firm. The chief engineer of the state highway department, who had been technical representative for North Star's just-completed project, had happened to recommend North Star to the AID official. The contract would last some three years, and the partners would have to expand their company to four times its present size to do the work. About half the work would be done overseas, and the other half would be done at the North Star home office in the U.S.

The partners jumped at the opportunity, which seemed to be manna from heaven for a struggling young firm, and started to make plans for the project. Immediately they realized that their days of informal operations were over. For one thing, AID required a detailed statement of their organizational structure, something they had never formulated. For another, it *was* going to take some organization to run this major overseas project, and still keep their home fires burning against the day when this job would be completed and they would need other work. They sat down to consider the ramifications of this remarkable opportunity and work out a managerial strategy.

What North Star Can Learn from Chapter 2

1. The various types of groups which form in the organization
2. The reasons why groups form in an organization and the role they play in the organization
3. The vitality of informal groups and the way they interact with the formal organization
4. The advantages and disadvantages which groups have for the organization
5. How groups affect individual members and the ramifications of this influence for the organization
6. How management can deal with groups to achieve the goals of both group members and the organization

Organizations have both a formal and an informal structure. The formal structure consists of the hierarchy and procedures established by management to accomplish the goals of the enterprise. But since we are social beings, the formal, management-structured groups are supplemented by informal groups, which take shape almost automatically as a result of employee interaction. Depending on the nature of these groups and the managerial problems of the moment, the "informal organization" can be either an asset or a liability. In working to achieve organizational goals, the manager must not underestimate the importance of informal groups as a source of guidance—positive or negative—for the individual member.

This chapter is divided into three sections: (1) the individual and the group, (2) the role of the informal group in the organization, and (3) the manager and the group. The first section explains why groups form, how an individual functions within the group, and how the group influences the individual's behavior patterns. The second describes the functions of the group within the organization, the types of groups in an organization, and the advantages and disadvantages of groups relative to organizational goals. The third explains how managers deal with groups: enlisting their support, dealing with hostility, negotiating, using them as decision makers, and drawing on the techniques of group dynamics.

A group is much more than the sum of its individual members. Like a swarm of bees, it can take on a life of its own, far more significant as an entity than are its members as individuals. Picture the power of a destructive mob, or, in a pleasanter vein, of a symphony orchestra.

Try to think of an organization you know of that has no groups. If you can, chances are it is either very new or very passive. Managers can no more ignore the positive and negative potential of groups than they can ignore physical facilities, financial resources, or employee skills. But the organization chart makes no allowance for informal groups; the manager must look for more subtle clues in order to determine their nature.

The Individual and the Group

The 747 jetliner, flying the great circle route from Seattle to Tokyo, was totally unprepared for the sudden hammer blow of the typhoon's first strike when it hit the plane. There had been reports of weather coming in from the Aleutians, but nothing even approaching the severity of the mad storm that was buffeting the huge plane about as a terrier shakes a rat. The extent of the damage was not clear, but all radio and radar were out, the controls were ominously sluggish, and the port engine was showing an alarming rip in the fabric which suggested that it might not be operable, or even secure in its mount, much longer. The captain paled at the thought of what might happen if the massive engine were to rip loose and impact the fuselage in the cabin area as it hurtled aft. The aircraft appeared to be caught in a gigantic jet stream that was thrusting it at a tremendous rate of speed in a generally southerly direction, though with the gyrocompass out and the magnetic compass swinging wildly this was only a guess.

How long they were caught in the grip of this massive turbulent force the captain did not know, because the flight deck crew was busy fighting to keep the plane aloft and in something resembling a flying attitude. The altimeter was useless, but gradually he realized that they were losing altitude steadily, falling inexorably toward the dark seas below. At once he knew that they would have to ditch in the sea, with not the slightest notion of where they were or what land might be near. Peering desperately into the gloom, he finally made out a shadowy mass that suggested land of some sort—what sort, he could not tell. He circled once, using up the last precious bit of altitude, and came in for a belly landing on the heaving water. The shock of the impact made the whole plane shudder, but he thought he sensed an additional force—perhaps the lower fuselage tearing as the plane thrust itself over the coral heads rimming the beach.

* * *

It is morning. The aircraft is aground in shallow water just off the wide sandy beach, and the passengers have been evacuated to land, where they are gathered in a disorganized group between the sea and the thick forest bordering the beach. The plane is working and pounding in the light ground swell, even in the relatively calm weather, and it is apparent that it will start to break up as soon as the weather worsens, possibly before. The captain has organized the removal of everything useful from the plane, a process now under way. Within a short time the great plane will be nothing but rubble, and the 160 castaways will be on their own.

What now?

Obviously the captain will take charge initially, as he is trained and expected to do. He is the only figure of authority in the group at present. But his aircraft—his command—is no more, and thus he has no institutional right to lead. His leadership now derives from the continuity effect of his former status and the inertia of the others, but if he is to keep the job he will have to earn it by virtue of superior knowledge or performance. Otherwise, he will eventually be replaced by a leader who better displays these attributes.

To examine this process, let's begin by summarizing the various power centers that will spring up on the beach, based on the unfamiliar new needs of the small community:

- leadership (initially captain and crew)
- medical and public health (to tend to any injuries from the landing, see to the sanitation of the water and food supplies, dispose of garbage, etc.)
- woodcraft and hunting (to monitor survival in the forest, avoid dangerous animals or reptiles, catch animals for food, etc.)
- construction (to build shelter, making use of materials left from the plane and found in the forest)
- fishing, marine life (to find food in the sea, identify dangerous species, etc.)
- farming, botany (to recognize edible plant species and ultimately to plant crops if the stay is that extended)
- radio repair, etc. (to endeavor to repair the radio, and perhaps other instruments)

- weather (to forecast the weather)
- boat building, seamanship (to arrange for escape craft and to pilot them, if it comes to that)
- science (for general knowledge about the environment, such as minerals, fire, explosives, and other needed technology)
- strength (to assist in keeping order, performing heavy tasks, etc.)

What groups will develop in the island community, both immediately and as time goes on? The initial management group, consisting of the captain and flight crew, already exists. Very shortly the captain will develop an advisory "cabinet" of those who approach him with useful suggestions and appear to possess valuable leadership qualities. Shortly thereafter he will designate something on the order of a security force, ostensibly to safeguard against potential hazards from the forest but also to maintain order among the community (for there is no law except that of the jungle until a police structure is established). As the various needs arise, he will assign volunteers and others to work groups to handle the tasks involved. Probably he will soon find that he needs an administrative staff to coordinate the various activities. Thus certain *formal* groups will be established.

formal groups

- top management group
- board of directors
- security force
- administrative staff
- working groups

informal groups

Inevitably, since no formal institutions can meet all the needs of the community, various informal groups will emerge, perhaps along the following lines:

- "let's get out of here" group, advocating pushing off through the jungle, launching a raft and heading out to sea, setting fire to the jungle in hopes that someone will see it, or simply criticizing the management for "doing nothing"

- parent-child clique, initially huddling for comfort and joint support in their special problems, but shortly petitioning the management for special attention to their needs (a bigger share in the scarce foods for the kids, etc.)

- teen-age group, initially hanging around the "corner drugstore" for companionship, but later pushing for attention to their recreational and other needs (probably including pressure for more share in the decision making)

- malcontents of every stripe (any advocates whose plans are not being heeded, who unite to reinforce one another in their arguments and perhaps actions to force their views on management)

- elderly group, with same thrusts as the teen group

- spokespersons for any work groups that feel they are having to work too hard with too little reward or say in the decisions, etc.

(These complaints may cut across more than one work group, provided common interests are involved.)

- lawless elements (groups that organize for theft, intimidation, rape, murder, etc.)

If any of these groups manage to break into the formal power structure, they will create a dynamically changing situation, producing still more informal groups. Suppose the lawless element manages to gain control, more or less terrorizing the community. It will thus become a formal group; it will stimulate the development of an informal "vigilante group" of normally law-abiding citizens, who will meet secretly to combat the "formal" actions of the lawless management group. And of course, if the vigilantes succeed in overthrowing the outlaws and gaining control, still other informal groups will develop.

This island situation displays in miniature the significant elements of all group behavior. When a formal organization is established, any structural gaps are filled by informal groups. And if any of these informal groups become formalized (which is the usual trend over time), other informal groups spring up to meet any new needs that arise. The cycle never ends.

Think of all the groups to which you belong. No doubt the first you would name is the family unit. Perhaps you are also a member of a student or professional association, a religious organization, a recreational group, or a community association. If you have a job, you are a member of your employer's organization automatically, and thus also part of smaller task forces within the company. You have a special group of friends who work in the organization, and a group of teammates who work in your section. If you have had to join a union, the local has become an important factor in your work.

Although our Constitution stresses individuality and personal freedom, the fact remains that much of what we do takes place in groups. Regardless of our social position, each of us depends on others to help in accomplishing necessary tasks, to provide encouragement and support when the going gets rough, to render praise for a job well done, to share in the pleasure of a small triumph, or to create strength in numbers for support of a particular position. Seventeenth-century poet John Donne said it most effectively: "No man is an island, entire of itself." The hermit who lives in complete isolation is a rarity.

Why Groups Form

Groups are composed of individuals who share a common interest. Perhaps the simplest example (though the relationship is far from simple) is the husband-wife team. In earlier times a man could hardly survive without the helping hand of his wife, for it was she who performed the necessary tasks of weaving and sewing the clothes, preparing (and sometimes growing) the food, repairing and readying the hunting weapons, and rearing the children who would care for him in his old age, while he was hunting for food, raiding the camps of hostile tribes, or defending against raids of others. Peter Freuchen, in his *Book of the*

What groups are likely to form in a new organization such as North Star?

Groups are composed of individuals who share a common interest.

Eskimos, observes that in some Eskimo tribes a man who loses his wife cannot survive alone, and must move in with another married couple or perish.[1] Today, although it can hardly be said that a single man or woman could not survive, husband-wife teams provide a great deal of mutual support in more intangible ways.

Of almost equal strength to the husband-wife tie (and in some cases of greater strength) is the work-team tie at the work place. The work group is intensely important to most individuals, because such a large part of their lives is spent in the work environment.

work group

In these and other situations, groups perform a number of functions for their individual members. They provide a basis of mutual support, they divide up the tasks so that individuals do what they can do best, and they supply a great deal of necessary security or protection.

Groups as Moral Support

As already established, we spend most of our lives as members of various groups. Each group to which we belong has a great deal to do with forming our values and beliefs, and we are markedly dependent on our particular groups to provide guidance and support in our daily lives. Think of the last time you had a significant problem. Did you wrestle with it entirely alone, or did you perhaps turn to a trusted friend for some advice? Think of the last time you passed an important examination, the time you took home your first paycheck, or the times you got a date with one of your favorite people. You had cause for celebration, and in the act of sharing the good news with others you allowed the group reaction to enhance your feeling of satisfaction.

Studies of soldiers in combat have shown that the soldier's closest associates—squad, patrol group, or gun crew—are his greatest source of support, providing the encouragement and will to endure danger and hardship without caving in. Loyalty to the group takes precedence over more abstract goals such as freedom, patriotism, or altruism, because it is a more immediate morale-builder and a concrete source of reward and consolation.

The Green Berets, an elite army group whose members were assigned to dangerous assignments for no more pay or material rewards than the regular troops, performed up to the high expectations accorded them because each was supported by the example set by the others. They may have been quite cynical about the overall justification of the Vietnam War, but they had the expectations of the group when they undertook a task, and the approval of the group when they performed it. Similarly, athletes in a sport such as baseball like to perform well individually, but most prefer to strive for team accomplishment before personal stardom. For it is the team that supports the individual players and draws the fans into the ballpark.

Group solidarity played an important role in building morale in prisoner-of-war camps, and the lack of group solidarity was responsible for tearing down morale. American soldiers captured by the Germans during World War II were able to maintain tightly knit groups, arrange successful escapes, and hold up well under sometimes arduous Nazi questioning and even torture. By contrast, Americans captured by the Chinese during the Korean War completely lacked this kind of spirit. Many died, few escaped, and far more broke down under questioning. Edgar Schein's comparison study shows that the primary differences between the two situations lay in the differing structures of the Chinese and German prison camps.[2] The Germans adhered to the normal military hierarchical system, and placed officer prisoners in charge of keeping order among the prisoners; they fed the prisoners inferior food; and they always returned each prisoner to his group after questioning. Thus the group was able to maintain its identity, derive some solidarity from the knowledge that the inferior food made its members "brothers in misery," and could act as a source of moral support for a member who had withstood the questioning (or apply sanctions to one who had caved in under pressure). The Chinese violated the hierarchical system by placing lower ranking soldiers in charge; they gave the prisoners the same food they ate; and they never returned individuals to the same unit after questioning. Thus the precapture hierarchical strength was broken down, the excuse of inferior food was missing (bad though it was by Western standards), and questioned prisoners knew they stood alone when they were being interrogated. As a result, many American prisoners fared badly in prison, there were few escapes because they were not able to organize to plan escapes, and they could not present much united opposition to prison camp conditions.

group solidarity

Specialization of Tasks

The group which formed North Star served a very useful purpose by dividing up the tasks into components based on the skills of the different individuals, as the chapter prologue describes. Few individuals could tackle every job in an organization (or even very many of them) alone, so a division of labor is necessary in all but the simplest enterprises. In the case of North Star, Bert provided the environmental skills, Henry the civil engineering training, Dick the project management experience, and Jo the systems analysis expertise. (The aircraft castaways, similarly, would need to stratify the tasks to match the expertise of the various passengers as closely as possible.) Together the four North Star partners were able to function smoothly and produce an output far superior to the capabilities of any one of them.

division of labor

Even in social groups that develop on the job, specialization of a sort takes place. Management theorist Donald Roy has described the informal social group that developed in a small factory work team.[3] One individual was made responsible for providing fruit for morning snacks, another for initiating daily horseplay, another for bringing afternoon snacks, and another for providing leadership. When Roy joined the group, he was assigned the task of going out for drinks in the afternoons.

social groups

Work groups perform educative tasks for newcomers, with the various specialists in the group contributing their separate skills. A new assembler will be taken in hand by one of the old assemblers and given tips on how to do the job right and how to shorten the repetitive tasks; it would be almost unthinkable for someone other than an assembler to provide this guidance. If the supervisor asks to see the newcomer, perhaps to discuss a rule violation, the group "leader" will offer clues on how to behave during the session with the supervisor. (If newcomers should request such information from someone else in the group, chances are they would be directed to the "leader" for guidance.) After some time with the group, the newcomer too will slip into some specialization niche, perhaps as the one who thinks up the jokes or passes on the front office gossip.

Within work assignments, specialization is equally clear-cut. Management assigns tasks, of course, and the union has a great deal to say about who does what; but these requirements aside, work group lines are still fairly rigid. When a telephone company team arrives at a new house to install the telephones, the team might consist of the linemen in their heavy truck for running the lines in from the road, the installer in a panel truck to put in the telephone and connect it up, and the supervisor in a pickup truck (if the job is in any way out of the ordinary). Either the linemen or the installer would be able to connect the line at the street end, but the installer has the specific information as to which of the connections at the street end to use. If the installer has told the linemen which connections will be used, the latter could make the connection, and if the installer is not there the linemen will do so. But if both are there, the linemen are almost sure to defer to the installer, who will then make the connection. This arrangement persists even though one of the linemen must climb the pole at the street end to run the line and could easily make the connection while up there. The question of union jurisdiction is not involved, since both job descriptions include making connections; but the group functions more smoothly if such overlapping tasks are assigned more specifically.

The Group as a Protective Mechanism

One of the primary advantages a group provides for its individual members is the protective function. Workers quickly discovered that bargaining strength with management came only after they organized into groups and presented a united front in their demands. The voice of a single individual simply went unheard. Thus the new managerial structure spawned by the Industrial Revolution was soon followed by the union movement. Indeed, it produced the union movement. The union was not an entirely new institution, of course, for its precursor was the craft guild of the Middle Ages. These guilds protected craftsmen of the various towns from competition by outsiders and restricted entry into their professions through the imposition of stringent apprenticeship requirements. The guilds' social network, which included religious services, often had features assuring members that their families would be provided for in time of need.

protective function

Individual entrepreneurs form partnerships for several reasons, including the pooling of financial resources and special skills. But no less significant is the mutual protection thus afforded, reassuring all partners that, should they become seriously ill or die, the business will go on providing for their families. Corporations provide protection of another sort; since the corporation is itself a legal "person," it stands between its stockholder-owners and the world, and no creditor can reach through the corporation and seize the assets of an owner to satisfy corporate liabilities.[4] An unscrupulous owner can erect several corporations for various purposes; if one should be sued for damages, it can be cut loose while the owner steps nimbly aside. (In the early days of strip mining, a marginal operator might have a different corporation for each site. When one site was about played out, that corporation would pay profits to the owner as dividends, leaving it an empty shell that could not be sued to restore the land because it had no assets.)

Neighbors in a community that has suffered robberies may provide mutual protection by jointly hiring a night watchman to guard all of their homes. Members of street gangs sometimes find protection by wearing the distinctive jacket that marks them as belonging to a particular group, because of the fear that harassment will bring down the wrath of the gang on the attacker.

Sometimes groups form for protection but change their function when that need disappears. The Military Order of the Loyal Legion was a group of Union army officers who banded together when President Lincoln was assassinated after the Civil War and swore to prevent unlawful takeover of the government by the organization thought to have arranged the assassination. The emergency (if emergency it was) passed soon, and the reins of government were transferred in an orderly way to the vice-president, but the Loyal Legion endures to this day as a patriotic and social organization. It appears in the limelight briefly each February, when it hosts a gathering on the steps of the Lincoln Memorial at which the president speaks.

Functioning within the Group

Certain demands are made upon the individual as the "price of admission" to a group. The first step generally involves gaining group acceptance. Walking into a party where every guest is a stranger to you is not the easiest thing in the world. To have a good time, you must make your way into one of the many groups which have already formed; and unless it is a mixer, where strangers are expected and planned for, none of the groups may want to let you in. Probably, however, you will find a reasonably congenial group before long, because the groups are only temporary and their bonds (and "tickets of admission") are not very great.

The difficulty of acceptance is much greater with the informal groups which form in an organization, or in the related professional or social associations, because these structures are permanent and the admission implies a permanent acceptance which is not given lightly.[5] Often a new employee will have to eat lunch alone the first week or so on the job, for he or she is not a member of any "eating" group. Gradually the newcomer becomes known, learns the norms of the group, and is included in their talk and lunch sessions.

A businessman who moved to an eastern city applied for membership in a prestigious downtown business club, and after a wait of several years was finally admitted. He was then rather chagrined to find that he had only cracked the outer circle—separate eating clubs had formed about each of the large tables in the main dining room, and he had to start all over again to gain acceptance by one of these.

Sociologist E.E. LeMasters observed an informal group of blue-collar construction workers who habitually frequented a particular neighborhood bar.[6] This neighborhood tavern, he observed, was a blue-collar country club where the stranger was made to feel unwelcome. In this comfortable atmosphere, surrounded by their peers, these men exchanged views on life, discussed their jobs (which most found quite fulfilling), denigrated the paper-pushing white-collarites, and celebrated one another's accomplishments. LeMasters called the bar "The Oasis," to signify its drawing power over group members who seek a refuge from the outside world.

Group Norms

What group norms are likely to be established fairly quickly in North Star?

Groups establish rather strict standards of conduct, or norms, for their members. The group has the power of administering rewards and punishments, for if it is to survive members must conform to its dictates. Teenagers look to their peer group to decide how to dress, how to wear their hair, what records to buy, and how to behave in school. If they violate these norms, they are held up to painful ridicule which few of them have the strength to buck. A new employee looks to the group for guidelines on how much work to do, how to react to the boss, and how much time to take for coffee breaks. An eager beaver who outproduces everyone else on the line or in the shop is pulled quickly aside by the informal group leader and given the rules of the game. Usually, the rule is to restrict the level of output, as an expression of the survival needs of the workers; if they raise the standards, they fear that management will raise the quotas, thus upping the work pace and making it more difficult to earn additional incentive pay. (Managers sometimes deride these fears as unreasonable, but the history of work incentives and production standards is full of cases where such fears were realized.)

If an individual refuses to observe the norms, other members of the group will quickly invoke sanctions to force compliance. These can range from warnings and ridicule to violent acts against the individual or social ostracism of his or her family. The deviant who persists in ignoring these warnings will ultimately become an outcast, completely discarded by the group. It is even possible that management, having sensed that the individual is not a "team player" and observed that the work organization constantly runs down his or her performance and behavior (possibly aided by occasional sabotage of the individual's work or machine), will assist the group by firing the nonconformist.

Thus, an individual must learn to gauge how much deviation from the norms is permissible in order to retain the status of a loyal group member. In general, the group will be more tolerant of workers who have proven themselves over time than of relative newcomers.

group norms

deviant

Submergence within the Group

We have seen that the group exerts powerful pressure on the individual. What effect does this have on the individual feeling the pressure? Many critics of group conformity within an organization assert that the individual loses creativity by kowtowing to the group's norms. Others refute these charges by observing that groups reward faithful members and often stimulate new courses of action that a single individual could not have projected.

effect on individuals

What impact did the North Star group have upon the individual members? What impact did the individuals have upon the group?

An eager beaver who outproduces workmates is quickly given the rules of the game.

Experiments have shown that individuals do indeed change their judgments when in the presence of a group. For example, in the 1930s group theorist Muzafer Sherif performed an experiment that sought to determine individual versus group perceptions of the "autokinetic effect."[7] This effect is defined as follows: As a subject peering into a darkened box sees a beam of light, the light will appear to waver, though it is actually motionless. Subjects individually reported how much the light moved; then they were placed in groups of twos and threes and were again asked to state what they saw, in the presence of the others. As the individuals heard and responded to estimates differing from their own, a group norm gradually emerged, from which the individuals did not deviate after being separated from the group. This experiment illustrates the power that group opinion can exert over an individual's personal perceptions.

More recently, behaviorist Solomon Asch used similar experiments to confirm Sherif's finding that individuals tend to substitute group opinions for their own.[8] Subjects were asked to compare and match lines of various lengths. In these experiments, the scientist purposely arranged for all but one of the subjects in the groups of seven or eight to be plants, who purposely and unanimously gave wrong estimates—thereby exposing the unsuspecting subject to a conflict between his or her senses and the majority opinion. A fourth of the 50 subjects never wavered from their own opinions throughout the set of 18 trials; a third went with the majority more than half the time; the remainder fell midway between these two extremes. Asch cites three reasons for yielding to this group pressure, subtle though it was:

1. *Distortion of perception,* whereby subjects perceive the majority estimates as correct and are unaware that their estimates have been distorted by the majority view.

2. *Distortion of judgment,* whereby subjects who suffer from lack of confidence decide that their perceptions must be inaccurate and that those of the majority must be correct.

3. *Distortion of action,* whereby subjects continue to believe their own judgments are correct but have an overwhelming need not to appear different and thus "inferior" to the others.

The majority of Asch's subjects who yielded to the group pressure fell in the distorted judgment category.

Experiments such as these confirm that the group exerts real pressures toward a group consensus, and does indeed have a marked impact on both the opinions and the actions of the individual.

Groups as Mutual Supporters

A significant example of this submergence within the group and individual change under group stimuli occurs when an individual rises above normal abilities or takes action totally foreign to his or her usual nature, under the "intoxication" of group approval. In groups of city dwellers taken on arduous mountain treks involving difficult obstacle courses or frightening terrain, where the price of refusing any venture was abandonment of the trek by the individual and return to the base, individuals have found themselves scaling sheer precipices or clambering over high walls, strengthened both by the support of the group and the fear of being found wanting if they balked. Coast Guard cadets, asked to climb to dizzy heights in the rigging of their training ship, must put aside their fear of heights when faced with the greater fear of being found wanting by their peers. Properly used, such a spur can be of great advantage to both the individual and the organization. Improperly used, it can produce tragic situations like that of the shy student invited by members of the football team to a fund-raising rally. Intoxicated by the apparent acceptance of these campus heroes, the student pledges away his tuition money.

Group Cohesion

Group cohesion is an important factor in determining how much power the group holds over its individual members. Cohesiveness is the composite of attractive forces which makes the group stay together; it is measured by the display of group loyalty, the willingness to defend the group against attack, and the feeling of unity exhibited by the members. If your lawnmower slices off the top of a large anthill, or if you expose an ant's nest by turning over an old log, you may see a sprinkling of small white eggs and a wild turmoil of ants trying to take the eggs to safety. Their actions are utterly selfless: regardless of the danger to them as individuals, they think only of protecting the eggs. If you take a twig and push an ant aside again and again, tumbling it over, it will not flee, but will keep returning to the task of safeguarding the group as long as it is alive. For the ants, submergence of self within the group is a matter of instinct; for humans, it is a matter of habit, derived from the specific emotional need for acceptance.

Management theorist Leonard R. Sayles cites a number of factors which determine the amount of group cohesion: high versus low status of the group as a whole; small versus large departments within which the group forms; homogeneity (similarity) among the members; physical isolation from other groups; ease in communicating among the members; supervisory behavior that minimizes intragroup competition; and outside pressure, particularly if it is perceived as a threat to the group.[9]

In a truly cohesive group, it is "us against the world." This kind of unity has been known to occur on construction jobs where management was attempting to install work measurement. The time-and-motion analysts would find themselves threatened by heavy wrenches "accidentally" dropped near or even on them, to give them the hint that their operations were threatening the workers. Similarly, during a trucker work stoppage to protest fuel cost increases and the imposition of 55 mph speed limits as an energy conservation measure, drivers who ignored the suggestions to get off the highways were shot at from overpasses, and some were seriously wounded by gunfire.

In our complex world, divided into nation states which are often hostile to one another, it has been said that only an attack by Martians could create a worldwide feeling of mutual support and cohesion. The competing American steel companies are hardly warring nations, but in recent years the threat of low-priced Japanese steel imports has brought them unusually close together in facing this outside attack.

group cohesion

What conditions existed to make North Star's partnership a cohesive group?

Role of Groups in the Organization

Look at any organization in detail, and you will manage to isolate a number of different groups. There are the groups and committees formed by management to get the work done (formal groups). Organizational components themselves are groups: the president's staff, the departments, etc. There are informal peer groups of employees, organized groups such as unions and credit unions, opposition groups dedicated to effecting change, recreational groups such as the company baseball team or bowling league, and the myriad spontaneous groups that spring up in response to various stimuli in the environment. Informal groups are as natural to an organization as swimming is to a duck. They arise to fill the voids left by the formal organization, and to fulfill the unmet needs of the employees. You can see that as the airplane castaways began to organize themselves as a community, the leadership would be unlikely to think of every need, and you can appreciate how natural it is for segments of the community with some common need or interest to be drawn together to provide whatever is missing.

Many managers, unlikely as it may seem, are scarcely aware of this informal network of groups. Other managers, though realizing they exist, attempt to counteract their formation and influence, fearing the powerful impact that groups can have on individual employees and recognizing that strength lies in numbers. Yet groups are a perfectly natural phenomenon. Indeed, organizations would not work at all if there were no informal groups. When people are thrown together, they have an affinity for interacting with one another, and for seeking mutual satisfaction from the task at hand. If the job itself is not intrinsically satisfying, the group becomes an even more important vehicle to provide that ingredient of satisfaction to the work environment. Although some groups clearly are detrimental to the organization (as was the lawless element in the castaway community), most groups accept the basic goals of their organization and are not out to destroy it (though they certainly may be out to negotiate with it). They simply constitute a part of the organization which the manager must recognize and understand in order to harness their activities for the best interests of employees and organization alike.

Functions of Groups in the Organization

Early management writers, failing to recognize the importance of groups in the organization, focused their attention on its formal aspects even when trying to stimulate workers to produce more output. The role of informal groups in the organization was first publicized by Elton Mayo in his studies of Western Electric Company employees in the 1920s and 1930s.[10] These studies helped give birth to the human relations movement, in which emphasis shifted from formal structures to elements that affected "human relationships" in the organization. These studies at Western Electric's Hawthorne plant had a great deal of impact on management theory, and we shall refer to them throughout the book. One important finding of the Hawthorne studies (confirming the suspicions of some theorists) was that informal relationships among workers contribute

human relations movement

massively to worker satisfaction, which in turn can positively affect worker productivity.

The Group as a Stimulus to Productivity

As we have seen, it is only human to affiliate oneself with others. A major source of human satisfaction comes from sharing our lives with friends and associates. Clearly, if we are happier in groups our dispositions and willingness to cooperate in organizational goals will improve. In the relay assembly test room at Western Electric, six girls were separated from the other workers so that researchers could test the effects of different variables on their production rate. No matter what experimental variation was applied (rest pauses, length of working day, group incentives, and others), the rate of productivity rose steadily. A second group of relay assembly workers was left in the regular workroom but received the same incentives as the test group. Their production rate increased, but at a markedly lower rate than the former group. Thus, Mayo concluded that the incentive rates only partially accounted for the productivity increase; improved human relationships explained the rest.[11]

effects on productivity

As a result of these findings, researchers began to view organizations in terms of groups rather than as a composite of individuals. Other studies have reinforced Mayo's discovery that worker productivity increases when employees are able to form groups. Researchers Trist and Bainforth convincingly illustrated this point in their study of the longwall method of coal mining in Britain.[12] When the English coal mines were mechanized, the traditional teams of two to four men who performed all the operations at the mine face were replaced by a continuous mining machine utilizing the longwall method. The new system divided the work into three shifts, differentiating tasks according to the shifts and breaking up the old groups. This dissolution of the face-to-face group relationship resulted in serious problems of absenteeism, high turnover, and sickness among the miners. It was necessary to modify the rigorous reorganization in order to function effectively and reestablish elements of group solidarity without completely abandoning the longwall method.

In the Volvo Company's innovative Kalmar plant in Sweden, the regular automotive assembly line has been changed drastically. Instead of a line, component sub-assembly takes place in detached bays, with a group made responsible for turning out a certain number of such units in a day, but at its own pace and in its own way. If it wishes to speed up in the morning and take it easier in the afternoon, fine. The group can arrange its own techniques and job divisions to a large extent. It is too early to draw broad conclusions from the innovation, but experience to date suggests that the increased group solidarity thus introduced may be improving productivity and work quality.

The well-publicized work slowdowns and unofficial strikes at General Motors' highly automated Lordstown, Pennsylvania, Vega plant (the causes of which are discussed in chapter 15) certainly had something to do with the highly impersonal job structure. GM is doing what it can to alter the situation, but the design of the plant precludes any innovations like those practiced at the Volvo plant.[13]

The approach of trying to obtain the benefits of group solidarity and work satisfaction in automobile production is not new. Henry Kaiser tried to introduce it in the plants manufacturing his postwar Kaiser and Frazer automobiles, but time was running out for those cars, and the operation ceased production before the group system had a chance to be effective.

Other organizations, such as Japan's Sony Corporation, have recognized the important role of groups and have patterned their operations around such task teams. Sony allows group members considerable autonomy within the organization and gives them many opportunities to influence top company policy. Disciplinary action against individuals is a group process, as is the responsibility for getting the job completed.

task teams

In an automobile mirror plant housed in three "elephant" quonset huts in Bolivar, Tennessee, the United Automobile Workers and Harmon International Industries are undertaking a novel experiment. They are changing the entire atmosphere of an industrial plant, which involves increasing productivity and work quality by revising the whole relationship between workers and management.[14] The basic spur for initiating change is small groups of workers and supervisors, who sit around a big table with a professional psychologist and talk about things that get in the way of progress. In one such session, a woman whose job is to wipe and pack mirrors describes a recurring situation where the wipers run out of work because the painters have no paint and the production line stops. The wipers would offer to help, but the painters don't want any help. "We don't all work together as we should," she says. "What the problem is, I don't know." The group discusses the problem for half an hour, and finally decides to see if the painters want some help in getting resupplied.

As a result of these sessions, small groups of workers have decided to work in teams, rotating jobs and making desirable changes in the work situation—and supervising themselves. A lot of attention is focused on these few workers, because it is a pilot test for the U.A.W. in improving the quality of life in automobile plants. Irving Bluestone, head of the General Motors Department of the U.A.W. and one of the key people in this project, says, "If this experiment is successful, it will give us a lever to present to other companies [an idea] of what direction to take. If these efforts are going to spread, they've got to spread in the old plant [and not in a brand-new plant with a new work force]."

Promising as this experiment is, it is not without problems. The U.A.W. leaders are learning how to handle the challenges that these initiatives bring. For instance, when some workers who form groups complete their quotas by noon, should they be allowed to go home, made to stay at the plant so other workers will not be upset, or given additional work and rewarded with raises for their productivity? If changes make far more production possible, can work standards eventually be changed? Questions aside, the experiment itself represents strong encouragement for joint worker-management efforts to harness the potential benefits of group solidarity.

Obstacles to Productivity

Since informal groups exist to support the members rather than the organization, it is not surprising that group objectives often can conflict with organizational goals—with reduced productivity as a result.

One of the most time-honored institutions engendered by groups in an industrial plant is the work norm. In a major shipyard (now defunct) in the northeast, the widely accepted norm called for "four hours' work for eight hours' pay," and it was freely circulated to new employees as a mandatory unofficial rule. In many factory departments there is a well-understood limit on how many items will be produced in a shift, and exceeding the limit would be a dangerous mistake for any worker. If executives of different companies get together and decide to limit production to keep prices up, they are committing a felony (collusion for restraint of trade, discussed in chapter 14). Though self-imposed work limits by plant employees are presumably no less collusive, the difficulties of prosecution would be overwhelming.

Cumshaw is almost as old and "honored" an institution as limitation of output. The term refers to appropriation of company property for personal use or performance of personal work on company time with company equipment. The practice is widespread and very difficult to stop; in some companies, it extends all the way to the executive suite. (It is much harder to stamp out, of course, if top management participates. A boss who misappropriates puts himself in hock to his subordinates, who can blow the whistle on him if they are caught, and establishes an atmosphere of permissiveness which encourages such behavior at all levels.) Cumshaw can be a serious drag on productivity because it involves so much diversion of labor and material. In one dramatic case, an employee who had made himself an elaborate TV antenna at his work bench over a period of weeks was caught. The company estimated what they would have charged for a handmade piece of equipment of that complexity, and billed him for labor, materials, and profit: about $375 in all.

Sometimes a group will establish some form of institutionalized though unauthorized recreation, such as a crap game every evening after "lunch" on the night shift. Lookouts are posted to warn of the arrival of management representatives, and the game may take up an hour or more every night. Since it is a regular event, production stays relatively steady (though well below potential levels), and it can go on for years without detection. Supervisors sometimes suspect the existence of these enterprises, but prefer not to have their suspicions confirmed, and consequently perform their inspections on a highly regularized basis.

Some groups with substantial clout in the organization can arrange to have their size increased out of proportion to their workload, particularly if they are "prestige" groups doing highly regarded work. When they succeed, the very prestige that gave them this power guarantees that their productivity will go down.

Lack of productivity is not restricted to the factory floor; it can exist in the executive suite as well. When a corporation gets into financial difficulties, the senior executives may be so preoccupied with planning alternate futures (for themselves) that they neglect their jobs and make the corporation's troubles even worse. In such a case, discussions among the executives can reinforce their individual resolves.

Group-Think

A related phenomenon is that of "group-think," where the members of a group will appear to be exploring all aspects of a situation to reach the best decision when they are actually steering each other toward a previously determined path. An example would be a conference to determine

group-think

whether it would pay to install a new machine that would require the supervisors to learn a new process and would involve major changes in production practices. It is clear that the shop superintendent, the foremen, and the lead mechanics are not anxious to undertake all of this retraining—but if production might be improved, the option has to be considered. There is an excellent chance that the question will *appear* to be talked out analytically, but that every point will be slanted to give the present situation the edge. The industrial engineer may say, "The unit time will go down from 5 to 3½ minutes with the new machine." A foreman will say, "Yes, but are you allowing for the time to troubleshoot when it breaks down?" The industrial engineer may reply, "Yeah, that's true." Note that there was no accurate analysis of what this time amounts to. Careful study might reveal only an extra quarter-minute per unit, still giving the new machine a substantial edge; or perhaps the new machine will break down no more than the old one. By avoiding hard data and sticking to superficial opinions, the supervisors can comfortably conclude that they have considered the unit time reduction and discarded it on valid grounds.

The result of this exercise can be predicted in advance, if the composition and predilections of the group are known well enough. The new machine has no chance, and the "productivity committee" has just struck another group-think blow at productivity improvement. The industrial engineer and several other participants know full well that the new machine would enhance productivity. But the foremen and lead mechanics are unwilling to pay the price of changing old habits, and the shop superintendent and industrial engineer are unwilling to risk the consequences of arousing their opposition.

Factors Affecting Functioning of Groups

Thus we see that the formation of teams is an important factor in organizational productivity. Whether the presence of groups raises or lowers productivity, however, varies depending on other factors. For example, a study by S. E. Seashore determined that if members of a highly cohesive group felt secure in their relations with the company, productivity tended to be high, but if they did not it tended to be low.[15] Overall, Seashore found no direct relationship between cohesiveness of work groups and productivity, suggesting that other variables make it difficult to analyze the performance of work groups. Throughout this book we shall discuss such factors as motivation, communication, organizational and group goals, and leadership, all of which influence the performance of the group in the organization.

One important focus of group analyses has been the study of interaction among group members, or *group dynamics*. Psychologists and sociologists who have examined the behavior of small groups cite many factors that affect the morale, satisfaction, effectiveness, and longevity of various groups in the organization. The results of such studies are important to the manager, for they provide clues that may be useful in dealing with these groups, as we discuss later in the chapter.

group processes

Group norms are extremely important in determining and homogenizing the output of individual members. About 20 years ago, management researcher B. S. Georgeopoulos discovered that variations in productivity among different groups run nearly six times as great as variations in productivity among individual members within the groups.[16] (That is, Group B may have six times the productive output of Group A, but within Group B and within Group A there are no individual differences anywhere near this great.) Clearly the group norm for productivity affects every member in the group, forcing a conformity that does not reflect the difficulty of a particular job.

These findings have been supported by the Hospital Utilization Project in Pittsburgh, a cooperative nonprofit venture that analyzes and promulgates operating statistics for the 22 major hospitals in the metropolitan area. The Project compared such variables as the length of preoperative and postoperative stays for a relatively standardized operation such as a cholosystectomy (gall bladder removal). These comparisons showed that while differences among hospitals were substantial, one averaging more than three times as long as another, differences among individual surgeons in any one hospital were relatively small. In other studies of the Pittsburgh hospitals (which are probably fairly representative of most hospitals), the great effect which the group norm exerted on individual physicians was noted. A doctor practicing in one hospital and conforming generally to its procedures would move to another hospital and in a short time adopt the new procedures, which might be markedly different from those in the first hospital.[17]

When an organization falls on hard times, its groups may display one of two diametrically opposed responses, depending on the magnitude of the trouble. If the problem is serious, but not enough to threaten organizational survival, the groups are likely to put aside lower priority

Group norms are extremely important in determining the output of individual members.

considerations and concentrate on protecting the parent organization. But if the danger is perceived as a strong threat to the company's survival, group priorities shift from aiding the organization to self-preservation. The loss of ships at sea illustrates this phenomenon. Many ships go down slowly, with plenty of time to get the lifeboats off and radio for other ships to come to the scene; in such cases, the performance of the ship's officers will be correct and often exemplary. But if the sinking is rapid, or other complicating factors are present, the ship's officers may commandeer the lifeboats for themselves and leave the passengers to go down with the ship.

Synthesis of Formal and Informal Groups

As we have emphasized, groups are the essence of the organization. If the organization depended solely on its formal structure to meet its objectives, many key tasks that require worker interaction, informal communication between workers and managers, and adherence to group norms would be left undone. Often, important decisions are made around the lunch table, on the golf course, or during coffee break discussions. The executive gets chief billing as decision maker, but high-level decisions evolve from interaction with many groups: plant supervisors, informal group leaders, union stewards, customers, and so on.

A leading home appliance maker has its offices and plants in a small midwestern city, where it is by far the major corporate presence. A small group of the top executives and their wives meet together socially, almost to the exclusion of noncompany members. Although the group does not make a conscious effort to discuss company affairs at these parties, the topic is always present, and most major decisions are shaped by preliminary analyses in one or another living room. At the plant supervisor level, and again at the senior mechanic level, similar social groups meet throughout the community, and lower-level company decisions are made by the same process. Note that if a particular officer, plant supervisor, or senior mechanic is not represented in one of these informal social groups, that individual will make no contribution to the decisions involved, and will pay the price of reduced stature within the formal structure.

Imagine that one of these informal groups becomes formalized. Suppose, for example, that the benefits of plant supervisor interaction outside the plant become so apparent that a decision is made to have a monthly dinner at a local restaurant. Inevitably the dinner would become organized, with a speaker now and then, an agenda, and rules of order for bringing up items. Moreover, those supervisors who were formerly excluded would have to be included now. Obviously, the very formality of these get-togethers would stimulate the need for *other* meetings, informal in nature, to fill in the inevitable gaps.

School boards illustrate this process. In the past, they were accustomed to meeting privately, a tradition that permitted uninhibited discussion of sensitive matters. More recently, pressures for public disclosure have forced school boards to hold open sessions. But the continued need for private discussion of some matters has forced members to meet for informal preliminary talks where they can formulate a position on sensitive matters in advance.

Multinational corporations, under pressure to conform to the laws of their home country while surviving in the competitive atmosphere of their host countries, find groups forming in the latter countries to cope with the perceived needs there. The U.S. representatives of various companies in some foreign country will tend to band together, meet socially, and assist each other in many ways—far more than they would at home—because they feel less than comfortable in the unfamiliar environment of the strange land. Executives of normally fiercely competitive companies will work very closely together in such a situation. Not only do they think of foreign customers and officials as outsiders; they come to feel that way about colleagues in their own company back home.

Types of Groups in the Organization

Work groups are a most important element in the organization, for they constitute management's primary vehicle for getting work done. Also, formal work groups are the source of the informal groups that eventually determine overall worker productivity and willingness to support organizational goals. What are some basic types of informal groups and how can they be recognized and dealt with?

Leonard R. Sayles, after studying 300 work groups under different supervisors, established four classifications: apathetic groups, erratic groups, strategic groups, and conservative groups.[18] Their behavior characteristics were defined as follows:

1. *Apathetic groups.* These were least likely to develop grievances or engage in any concerted opposition, unlikely to pressure management in order to gain advantages, and relatively uninterested in union activity. However, they did not rank high in cooperativeness or productivity. Leaders occasionally existed, but their power was limited, and they could not invariably swing the whole group behind them. Also, the apathetic groups were not immune to internal friction and suppressed discontent. They were likely to include low-skilled and low-paid workers, though not exclusively.

apathetic groups

2. *Erratic groups.* These were characterized by management as the "most dangerous" groups because their behavior was unpredictable. Deep-seated grievances could exist for a long time with no overt reaction, but an apparently trivial incident could trigger a wildcat strike or mass demonstration. Strong individualized leadership was likely, with the same person often serving both as social leader and as external negotiator with management. Workers in these groups held nearly identical jobs, primarily worker-controlled, such as stevedoring. They were active in union relationships. Oddly enough, their behavior could swing from antagonistic to friendly, and back again, without warning.

erratic groups

3. *Strategic groups.* These groups were the shrewdly calculating pressure points, whose leaders never tired of watching every management action and seeking loopholes that would benefit their interests. They would put the same pressure on the union officers, keeping close track of how well they were tending to member interests. They demanded constant attention to their problems and had the sophistication and power

strategic groups

to harness group action to reinforce their demands. However, the pressure they exerted was predictable and never exceeded the amount required to attain their ends; in that sense, their behavior was seen as reasonably acceptable to both management and union. Departments containing such groups were highly cohesive, with specialized and influential leadership; the work was both important and skillfully performed. The production record of these groups was usually good, but not always.

4. *Conservative groups.* These were the most stable and least likely to use concerted action or to participate in union affairs. They constituted the reservoir of critical and scarce skills in the company. Their position in the company was so secure that they had developed special privileges over the years, almost placing the company in the position of negotiating with them. Their skills were in demand in the labor market, and they were not dependent on the present company for their livelihood. These groups were at the top rung in both job titles and intangible status. Most of their pressure had been exerted in the past, and they had little need to show their strength to obtain their wishes.

That such differences exist among informal work groups is not surprising, for they are composed of individuals with varying interests and abilities, are formed for different purposes, exist in different environments, and receive varying degrees of encouragement from supervisors. As we shall see, the attitude of management toward groups plays a large role in deciding how the groups behave.

Researchers have found that workers in small departments and organizations develop more cohesive groups than those in larger organizations and departments, and are generally more satisfied. The small department is more able to support such groups since physical proximity, ease in communicating, and commonality of interest are essential ingredients in maintaining cohesive groups. The small community of castaways from the airplane wreck was itself a cohesive group, brought together by an intense common bond of survival needs and mutual adversity. Moreover, the community as a whole was small enough so that a small subgroup would have an appreciable chance of being heard, which would not be the case in a large corporation.

The castaway community serves as a useful model of the types of groups that would form in any organization. Each of the *management* groups would be devoted to running some part of the community. Various *social* groups would be devoted to exploring social interests (parents, teenagers, young children, outdoor types, discussion types, etc.). The *work* groups would be high-prestige groups, in view of the great importance of work for community survival. Note that the prestige associated with certain occupations, such as those of the hunter (and farmer), would be much greater than it was in the technological society left behind because the efficiency of these workers would be crucial to group survival. There would be *protest* or *negotiating* groups, to present the views and demands of people outside the management power structure, and perhaps to "strike" to gain their ends. Within the work groups themselves would develop the same sort of informal groups discussed earlier.

Overlapping of Groups

Groups gain strength through the linkages they develop with other groups, often through common membership. If a golfing group in a company includes the chief executive, the group itself picks up strength and prestige from that fact alone—and its other members will lend strength to their other groups because of this linkage to power.

Figure 2-1 shows one small segment of the group linkages that might emanate from this golf foursome. One of the players is the superintendent of Shop A. This golfer lunches with three foremen (out of perhaps ten foremen in the shop); the three foremen, in turn, fish together. They are in a bowling league with a foreman from Shop B, the chief timekeeper, and the business agent of the union. Similar overlapping groups connected with the golf foursome exist all over the organization, and draw some strength and cooperative effectiveness from that connection. For example, if the union business agent cannot contact the chief executive directly (for the union president of the local would want to be involved before that happened), she might talk it over between frames at a bowling match with the foreman of Department 2 who was her bowling partner. He in turn would mention it at lunch to the superintendent of Shop A, who would pass it on to the chief executive. Ultimately, the president of the local would become aware of this path through interlocking groups, and might decide to use it instead of a formal approach. When the

overlapping groups

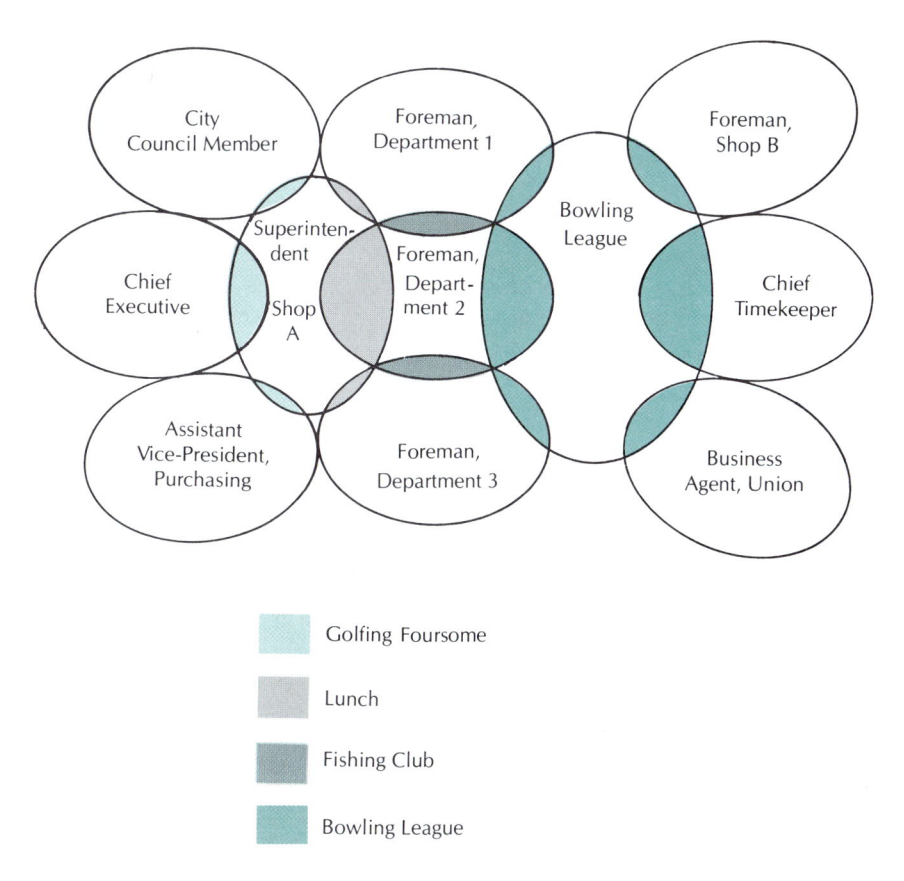

Figure 2-1.
Overlapping Organizational Groups

51
GROUPS AT WORK

president makes that decision, the business agent's prestige goes up somewhat in his eyes. Thus groups build up their strength through their complex of overlaps and linkages.

Advantages and Disadvantages of Groups for the Organization

As discussed in the case outlined earlier, you can see that social groups benefit the organization for the most part, for they increase efficiency by occasionally bypassing the formal chain of communication and command. If the chief executive thinks a matter is important, action can be initiated. If it does not seem important, or if the executive disagrees with the point the business agent is making, it can be dismissed as casually as it apparently was broached by the agent, and no harm has been done. The business agent has floated a trial balloon to see if it will fly, but if she is rebuffed everyone can act as if it was not brought up at all. For this reason, companies encourage social interchange at managerial levels, and encourage it at and among all levels.

Problems can arise with this informal channel. The superintendent of Shop A has a boss who is subordinate to the chief executive, perhaps by two or three levels. If both the chief executive and the superintendent of Shop A are not very careful in their relationships, they run the risk of unthinkingly bypassing this person in the middle, making him or her both uncertain and angry. The informal groups are helpful in supplementing the formal group structure, but harmful if they supplant it.

Some of the advantages and disadvantages of groups in an organization can be itemized as follows:

group advantages

1. *Advantages*
   - create a more pleasant work environment for the "ins"
   - moderate individual conflict by the restraining effect of group norms and pressures
   - establish a viable social system that facilitates communication
   - set forth group norms which make behavior predictable and avoid possibly unpleasant surprises
   - establish group standards of performance which may be higher than management would have demanded
   - facilitate group willingness to undertake difficult or dangerous tasks
   - mobilize group cooperation so that the whole can be greater than the sum of its parts
   - occasionally innovate new production methods through group interaction
   - provide informal channels of communication that occasionally "grease the wheels" and facilitate cooperation
   - provide essential support to the individual and mutual stimulation from interaction with the group
   - provide an informal management to cope with roadblocks and facilitate the performance of work
   - greatly extend the span of control past the formal span, by networks of informal linkages

- give management an "ear to the ground," bringing it information and suggestions it would not get through formal channels
- keep managers on their toes, by providing in effect a substitute or alternate structure that will handle things if the manager does not act

2. *Disadvantages*
   - create a more unpleasant work environment for the "outs"
   - may contribute to favoritism by increasing the rewards to members
   - group conflict can make the environment unpleasant
   - groups can work at cross-purposes, impairing productivity
   - group goals may diverge violently from organizational goals, as in work limitation compacts, theft rings, groups set up to see that their members are promoted over others, etc.
   - groups may obstruct progress by holding out for the old ways (opposition to computerizing a function, etc.)
   - group linkages can improperly bypass and undercut management
   - supervisory effectiveness may be undercut if the group is strong
   - jurisdictional fights over what group gets to do a new job may become so severe that management is unable to install the new operation—if structural fiberglass comes in as an improved material for some applications, the painters may want jurisdiction because it is painted on, the structural workers because it is a structural material, and the sheetmetal workers because it is a sheathing material; the jurisdictional fights between groups may lead management to forget about its advantages and avoid using it
   - groups usually demand something in return for their organizations—what Edwin B. Flippo has called the costs of "lubricating the informal organization"[19]
   - may make it hard for management to shift personnel around, for fear of disturbing existing groups
   - many group activities work against managerial policy

The Manager and the Group

Managers simply cannot be effective if they cannot deal with groups or if they are unaware of the group structure within their organizations. In the previous sections, we have seen the powerful force that groups exert over their members and the good and harmful consequences this force implies for the organization. A manager must be adept at harnessing these group forces to work for the goals of the organization, or at least at preventing adverse forces from overwhelming it. An organization can succeed only if it has the support of its members, for a group at odds with the organization can virtually close it down—through formalized group opposition, spontaneous resistance, or overall nonactivity. (When a municipal police force comes down with the "blue flu"—a euphemism for purposeful absenteeism to make a point in labor negotiations—the police

> **group disadvantages**
>
> What are the advantages and disadvantages of groups in a new, small company such as North Star?

chief is virtually powerless to prove that they are not really sick. When air controllers decide to enforce the regulations on spacing between incoming aircraft rigorously and unreasonably, as they did at Kennedy International Airport during a recent labor disagreement, their group action can throw the operation into turmoil and cause impossible traffic delays without management being able to do much about it.)

Enlisting the Support of the Group

Some managers forget that they need to enlist group support in order to make their ventures succeed. Consequently, they neglect to recognize and deal with the informal group leaders who have the power to sway group members toward or against organizational objectives. Groups have a structure just as other organizations do, and the manager must understand that structure in order to know whom to approach and how to deal. As we shall see in chapter 4, "Leadership," groups often have more than one leader—perhaps a task leader to provide the cues for getting the job done and a social leader to maintain group harmony and morale. The true leaders of the group may not be the ones formally recognized by management, for they wear no badges or special attire. To identify these leaders, the manager must be thoroughly familiar with the employees. Thus the manager who develops contact at the "grass roots" is far more likely to succeed than the manager who remains remote from the workers. Although a manager may be familiar with sophisticated management tools (and should be, to make the organization carry out its many tasks), these tools will not replace the need to nourish human relationships within the rank and file.

In a highly technological society, it is easy to forget that without the willing collaboration of the machine operators the shop won't run. Groups are the dynamic element in any organization, and the manager can stand or fall on his or her ability to deal with them. For example, it is prudent to check with the union representative before introducing any new process, equipment, or working conditions; it is well to clear it informally with the group leader as well. Probably the new innovation will not provoke objections and it might even improve the group's situation; but if it comes as a surprise (or if the group is not the first to hear about it), it might create a hostility which appears unreasonable to the manager. Also it is a good idea to inform the group leader of the situation before taking disciplinary action against an individual in that group. This action is not cleared with the leader, for that would appear a sign of weakness and encourage disrespect. But it is useful for the manager to anticipate any possible disagreements as to the justice of the penalty. Similarly, work standards must be established with the cooperation and tacit approval of group leaders. If management is considering installing an employee convenience, such as a fast-food center with lunch tables, it would not be sensible to do something so intimately involved with employee preferences without being satisfied that the group really wants it. Common courtesy would dictate that they be consulted, but too many managers adopt an impersonal approach of thinking they know what is "good for the workers." They don't.

work standards

There are cases where informal group action can be taken with the tacit consent of the management, when management cannot take the action directly. Suppose, for example, that the shop superintendent has announced an examination to replace a retiring foreman, and has announced that the post will go to the person who receives the highest mark on the examination. The logical choice is John Oldhand, well-liked by the men and with a good knowledge of the practical work. Young Bill Upstart, who joined the group only a year or two before and is generally thought to be well versed in theory but lacking in practical experience, can qualify for the examination. The workers (and the department supervisor who supervises several foremen under the shop superintendent) are afraid he will get the higher mark on the examination and thus be selected—which all agree would be a disaster. The department supervisor might comment to one of the group leaders that he sure hopes Upstart doesn't take the examination, because the damn fool just might luck out and score highest. The group gets the message, and the next day Upstart comes to the department supervisor and says he has decided not to take the examination. The latter does not know exactly what caused Upstart to decline, but he recognizes group power when he sees it.

In another example, a municipal personnel department once wrote job standards for garbage collectors, specifying that they did not have to pick up loads weighing in excess of 50 pounds. The union contract thus automatically incorporated this provision as a condition of work. One of the employees announced that he was going to blow the whistle on management because many loads exceeded 50 pounds slightly, and they would have to send out a crane to pick up these loads. The foreman knew what this plan would do to their productivity, and recognized that the city council would be pressured to consider an outside garbage contractor as a result. He put the word out to the workers, and the employee said no more about the plan to file a grievance.

Groups as Decision Makers

In chapter 4, we discuss many styles of leadership and their varying effects on group morale and cooperation. As we shall see, a participative leadership style is more successful in creating group support and enhancing productivity than is an authoritarian style. Although there are some exceptions, most people want to have a say in matters which directly affect their jobs, and feel more fulfilled if they believe they have had a role in making decisions. The manager who perceives this trait and takes it into account will be better accepted by the group.

participative leadership style

authoritarian leadership style

The participative management style inherently places a certain amount of trust in the group, reflecting management's belief in the group's importance. The group in turn appreciates this fact, and is likely to reward the manager by performing in a manner worthy of the trust. Sony and Volvo, among other companies, have built participative decision making into their organizational structures, and thus far both managements have been pleased with the results. As more companies realize the possible benefits of actively enlisting group participation in decision making, they too will adopt the team approach to management.

In some environments, obviously, the participative approach is bound to fail. A company where the worker-management relationship was rife with suspicion could not suddenly introduce group involvement of this sort, because no one would believe the gesture was sincere.

group decision making

Decisions by a group take more time. When a quick decision is needed, participation may not be a workable technique. Groups may fall into the "group-think" syndrome discussed earlier, whereby every member of the group ends by acceding to a predetermined course of action even though some individuals originally opposed it. Pressured in a subtle fashion to concur with a group opinion (which in reality was never reached), all members are hesitant to express their reservations. Thus the group comes up with an apparently unanimous decision, which many would not have adopted on their own and still do not really favor.

Studies have shown that group decision making is usually a fruitful exercise, despite these caveats. It allows for the possibility of generating alternatives and lessens the chance of being confined to a single train of thought. One type of manager, however, likes to bring in advisors whose ideas parallel his or hers and weed out all nonsympathizers. This practice is unhealthy for the organization because it limits the forward vision of the policymaker to the biases of these top subordinates (who essentially mirror management's biases). Such "tunnel vision" can make trouble for the organization because management cannot wisely anticipate or evaluate the course of events.

Final decisions made by groups often are no better than those of top management acting individually. Whether a decision is better or worse if made in a group depends on the circumstances. If the solution depends critically on information gathering, more of that is available from a group than from an individual. If the quality of the decision is not so important as its acceptability, the latter will be enhanced in a group decision. If group members disagree on fundamental principles, the final decision is likely to be a watered-down compromise that pleases no one. Group decision making is useful for defining problems, generating a number of alternatives, and brainstorming different situations. Often, however, the final solution may best be arrived at by the manager acting alone.

Delphi technique

The Delphi technique is a modified form of group decision making where the group never meets face to face but interacts indirectly. In this technique, each member of the group is asked individually for an opinion or a decision on a matter, then shown the written responses from the others and asked to modify his or her response if desired. Obviously the answers from the others will have some influence, possibly as a memory prod or a reminder of overlooked points; but the individual is not subject to inordinate group pressures to conform. This technique seems to offer some of the advantages of group decision making without the dangers of the group-think syndrome.

Coping with Group Opposition

group conflict

In a world where resources are scarce and there is a variety of interests, conflict is inevitable, either among competing groups or between some groups and management. We have seen that group objectives often compete or conflict with those of other groups or of the larger organization. Conflict is normal between production and sales groups, since one seeks ease of manufacture and the other wants to please the customer—goals that don't always go together. Conflicts over trade jurisdiction can be very bitter, since job security is involved. All conflict of this sort is not unhealthy for an organization, for when groups compete the level of effort of all members tends to be high. When two departments are competing for additional funds for the coming year, each will attempt to produce outstanding work and demonstrate worthiness for the additional grant.

Too much conflict can be detrimental, especially if group members concentrate more on winning the battle than on accomplishing management goals. For instance, when unions compete to represent employees of a company, the latter can become a battlefield where one group sabotages the other and everyone loses. Unions may make promises they know are not realistic or are harmful to everyone's interests. A manager must know when to stimulate conflict or instill the competitive spirit among groups and when to seek the elimination of unproductive conflict.

Once the manager pinpoints such a potential trouble spot in the organization, there are several courses of action that may alleviate the situation. A broader, more wide-ranging (superordinate) goal can be devised that will transcend the separate goals of competing factions without contradicting them. In an experiment, Sherif created two competing groups among young male campers.[20] The intensity of the competition in all events produced strong hostility between the two groups, which was alleviated only by creating situations where the two teams were forced to work together toward a common goal (such as repairing a broken-down camp truck). As chapter 15 (on labor-management relations) explains, the threat of cut-rate Japanese steel imports in the early '70s enabled labor and management representatives to sign an Experimental Negotiating Agreement (ENA) in 1973, which guaranteed that a settlement would occur without a strike and that the company and union would work together to increase productivity.

superordinate goals

Another approach to conflict settlement is alteration of the organization structure. Transferring the troublemakers, assimilating smaller opposition groups, transferring supervisors around to create greater understanding and empathy—all these methods have been employed successfully to reduce conflict, and almost certainly it will spring up again. This approach simply creates new actors for the same old problems.

Although some conflicts (such as jurisdictional issues) spring from the desire to make one group dominant over another, other conflicts spring from misunderstanding. If the latter is the case, it is helpful for management to get at the roots of the conflict through discussion and arbitration, if possible. If the source of the conflict is indeed a misunderstanding, then full information will clarify the situation. Group dynamics techniques are very helpful toward this end.

Thus far we have discussed conflicts among different groups. In the conflict between group and manager, the manager is not an arbiter but one of the conflicting parties. This situation, the focus of chapter 4, "Leadership," is analyzed more briefly on the following pages.

Negotiating with Groups

bargaining

In a discussion between management and any group, the process is a bargaining one. Each side starts from several premises, makes certain assumptions, and is in possession of certain presumed facts. One of the first steps is to explore these together, to see how much air can be cleared by agreeing as much as possible on these basics. What are the facts? Does either party have them wrong in a way that can be demonstrated to be wrong? Why are the present assumptions made? Perhaps a discussion team can be assigned to explore these basic matters, and come up with a joint report that at least will clear up these questions.

third party mediation

Perhaps a third party should be brought in, whether or not the two conflicting parties are willing to make that party's decision binding. At least he or she will be considered impartial (if both groups take part in the choice) and should clear the air a bit more. Perhaps management can give a bit on inessentials (from the management viewpoint); these items may turn out to be the important ones to the group. Perhaps some prestige or other rewards can be offered the group, to provide status (which, again, may be the very thing that is wanted, but pride prevents the group from saying so). Perhaps the group can be co-opted, in the sense of being made to share the goals of management for a larger project. Perhaps, in a longer range approach, some of the group leaders can be educated in management principles (through training seminars or, in appropriate cases, graduate courses), a procedure that will recast the composition of the group. (This action involves management taking former blue-collar workers who have been promoted to management slots but still retain many instinctive beliefs about the industrial environment, and widening their perspectives through extended management education.) In some cases management may be the side that needs more education, to learn what it's really like down there on the line. Perhaps leaders of the group, or all its members, can be given certain perquisites such as parking privileges or freedom from clocking in and out (though management must then be prepared for requests for similar privileges from other informal organizational groups).

Dealing with Group Hostility

In this situation, management is dealing not with relatively open-minded group members, but with hostile and suspicious people who are not likely to believe in management's sincerity. The same recipes apply, but in a more complex form.

encounter sessions

Perhaps encounter sessions are needed, to provide an opportunity for open exploration of hostilities. Perhaps a common ground may still be found, starting with the common competitor and enemy, and working back from there. More information and better communication are still valuable tools. Here is where an "ombudsman" is needed—a company employee who has been so selected, and whose job tenure is so guaranteed, that it is apparent he or she exists to hear and act on employee complaints. The ombudsman must be freely accessible to employees, must safeguard their confidences completely, and must have significant access to top management. Perhaps the problem is that management really has *not* been open and honest; it might help to start by introducing policies that clearly reflect these traits. If a situation reaches the point where it is

ombudsman

undercutting organizational operations as a whole, perhaps a firing is indicated, on either the management or the worker side.

Group Dynamics

An essential element of dealing with groups is to understand the processes by which they operate. Sociologists and psychologists use the term *group dynamics* to describe the interactive processes of small groups. The techniques managers employ to facilitate group harmony, then, are known as group dynamics techniques, though the term can have a wider meaning. Small group studies have sought to isolate those factors that contribute to the smooth functioning of groups, such as size, membership, structure, problem-solving capacities, cohesiveness, and the role of the individual with regard to the group. Specialists in group dynamics devote much time trying to make managers aware of the interactive processes at work in groups. By participating in "T-groups" (*T* for *training*), sensitivity analysis, and management development courses, managers actually become part of a group process where the members participate wholeheartedly. They watch a group emerge from a melting pot of individuals involved in a particular situation (again, such as the air crash castaway situation) and take positions that harden into prejudices and policy. They see the effect of showing the individuals why they are doing what they are doing. And the trainers hope that this enlightenment will somehow bring greater understanding and flexibility of behavior all around.

group dynamics

T-groups

Summary

Organizations are composed of both formal and informal groups which determine the pace, style, and modus operandi of organizational activity. The key to understanding groups in organizations lies in knowing the ground rules for any group interaction. No matter where they spring up, groups form for essentially the same purposes: to provide a source of moral support for their members, to afford expertise in getting a job done, and to serve as a protective mechanism against outsiders. In return for these benefits, however, members must sacrifice some of their individuality and conform to group norms. Norms set the standards for group behavior and, in an organizational setting, provide guidelines on how much work employees should do, how they should react to the boss, and how long they should take for coffee breaks. If an individual fails to abide by the rules, the group will invoke sanctions ranging from warning and ridicule to violent acts against the individual or the individual's family to make the point.

Group cohesiveness—the feeling of unity among group members—is an important factor in determining how much power the group holds over its individual members. A tightly knit cohesive group possesses a feeling of togetherness that often impels members to undertake great risks or perform astounding feats for the benefit of the group. Such a group can be a tremendous asset for management—if it is on management's side. If, however, members of a close-knit cohesive group see their own goals and those of management as divergent, they will adopt a set of norms that run counter to what management stands for. A wise manager always strives to win the favor of the various groups in the organization—especially those most likely to affect productivity and morale.

The Hawthorne studies at Western Electric first illustrated the impact of informal groups within the organization on worker morale and productivity. Other studies have shown that productivity increases with improved human relationships (although workers can also decide to restrict productivity). As a result, many modern plants are adopting task team work methods to heighten worker job satisfaction and productivity.

Many important decisions in the organization are made through the informal channels that develop through the interaction of informal groups. Although the chief executive may be given primary billing as decision maker, final management decisions evolve from interaction with many groups, both formal and informal: plant supervisors, union stewards, informal team leaders, customers, etc. In essence, informal groups in the organization serve the vital function of filling in the gaps left by the formal structure and facilitate communication among the various organizational elements.

Groups offer both advantages and disadvantages to the organization. Overall they serve a vital, necessary function, yet they are a potential source of conflict unless a manager learns to deal effectively with the groups and their informal leaders. A wise manager attempts to enlist the support of groups by acknowledging their existence, recognizing their leaders, and gaining familiarity with group members by frequent cooperation and consultation. Although there are some pitfalls to group decision making, an experienced manager knows when to use this potential asset.

A manager must also be able to pinpoint when conflict between groups has surpassed the healthy stage and take steps to manage the conflict effectively. Often discussing the problem with the group or imposing a more comprehensive goal will suffice, but sometimes more drastic means of conflict settlement are necessary, such as altering structure or personnel or calling in a third party for arbitration. When conflict occurs between management and labor, the groups enter into labor negotiations, a step that implies a range of settlement procedures.

The study of group interaction is referred to as *group dynamics.* Group dynamics has become a popular phrase among organization specialists who have explored a range of techniques to facilitate group communication and to explain the various and complex elements of group interaction. Since groups play such a vital role in organization activity, it is not surprising that much recent research has centered on the small group. Managers should carefully study the results of this research, for by more thoroughly understanding group processes, they can better understand how their organizations function.

Notes

1. Peter Freuchen, *Book of the Eskimos* (Cleveland, Ohio: Collins & World, 1961), p. 100.
2. Cited in David R. Hampton, Charles E. Summer, and Ross Webber, *Organizational Behavior and the Practice of Management* (Glenview, Ill.: Scott, Foresman & Co., 1973).
3. Ibid.

4. The corporation does not provide protection against individual violation of law by corporate officers, however.

5. Eric Berne's best seller, *Games People Play* (New York: Grove Press, 1964), discusses the shenanigans involved in gaining acceptance into various groups and situations.

6. E. E. LeMasters, *The Blue-Collar Aristocrats* (Madison, Wis.: University of Wisconsin Press, 1975).

7. Muzafer Sherif, *The Psychology of Social Norms* (New York: Harper & Row, Pubs., 1936).

8. Solomon Asch, "Opinions & Social Pressure," *Scientific American* 193 (November 1955): 31-35.

9. Leonard R. Sayles, *Human Behavior in Organizations* (Englewood Cliffs, N.J.: Prentice-Hall, Inc., 1966), pp. 102-04.

10. F. J. Roethlisberger and W. J. Dickson, *Management and the Worker* (Cambridge, Mass.: Harvard University Press, 1939).

11. Roethlisberger and Dickson, *Management and the Worker*, p. 75.

12. E. L. Trist and K. W. Bamforth, "Some Social and Psychological Consequences of the Longwall Method of Coal-getting," *Human Relations* 4, 1951.

13. General Motors sent a group of six workers to Volvo's Kalmar plant in order to study the innovative system. It is interesting to note that they reported upon their return, almost unanimously, that they preferred the American specialized method.

14. This and the following paragraph are based on an article in the New York *Times,* April 9, 1975, p. 24.

15. S. E. Seashore, *Group Cohesiveness in the Industrial Work Group* (Ann Arbor, Mich.: Institute for Social Research, 1954).

16. B. S. Georgeopoulos and A. S. Tannenbaum, "A Study of Organizational Effectiveness," *American Sociological Review* 22 (1957): 534-40.

17. Results of these studies are discussed by Morris London in "Variations in Postoperative Stay Among Appendectomy Patients," *Hospital Management* 96 (Nov. 1963 and Dec. 1963): 49-52 and 45-47, respectively.

18. Leonard R. Sayles, "Informal Work Groups and the Formal Organization," in *Human Relations in Administration,* ed. Robert Dubin, 4th ed. (Englewood Cliffs, N.J.: Prentice-Hall, Inc., 1974), pp.144-49.

19. Edwin B. Flippo, *Management: A Behavioral Approach* (Boston: Allyn & Bacon, Inc., 1970), pp. 194-208.

20. Muzafer Sherif, "Experiments in Group Conflict," *Scientific American* 195 (1956).

Review Questions

1. Why do individuals join groups?
2. What role do groups play in an organization?
3. What are group norms? How do they affect employee behavior?
4. What impact did the Hawthorne studies have upon management?
5. What impact does a group have upon individual behavior? What impact do individuals have upon group behavior?
6. What is cohesiveness? What factors contribute to group cohesion?
7. What effect does cohesiveness have upon group behavior?
8. How does the existence of groups in the organization affect productivity?
9. What is the relationship between formal and informal groups in an organization?
10. What is group-think? What effects does it have on decision making?
11. What types of work groups exist in an organization, as cited by Sayles?

12. What are advantages and disadvantages of groups in an organization?
13. What are benefits of participative decision making? What are some disadvantages?
14. What is the Delphi technique? How is it useful to an organization?
15. How can management control conflict within an organization?
16. What is group dynamics? How are group dynamics techniques useful to an organization?

Discussion Questions

1. If you were an American senior officer in a Chinese prison camp, what steps could you and your colleagues take to maintain group solidarity?
2. What are common group norms that are beneficial to fulfillment of company goals? detrimental to company goals? How can a manager encourage the development of norms which are attuned to the goals of the company?
3. See if you can think of some functions of management in a company organized on a task team approach.
4. How can management counteract the work norm, cumshaw, and similar obstacles to productivity?
5. Draw a picture like Figure 2-1 which shows the overlapping of groups in our castaway community.
6. What steps can an organization take to avoid "group-think"?

North Star Case Study

The AID project required close cooperation between Dick's group of project engineers stationed abroad and Bert's environmental design specialists at home. As you have seen, Dick had a great deal of practical experience and was concerned with cost factors and getting the work out on time. The members of Bert's group, however, were more concerned with building a name for North Star and themselves as professionals by focusing much attention on elegance, efficiency, and perfection in environmental systems design. As specialists, cost and time factors were not their greatest concern; rather, they wanted to develop the optimum, or best possible, system.

Dick's major projects required the approval of Bert's section members, who scrutinized the technical specifications for environmental impact, making alternative and substitute suggestions to improve the plan where needed. In a period of three months, Bert's section rejected and delayed three of Dick's projects, trying to arrive at a more suitable design that would satisfy both engineering and environmental standards.

Dick wrote an angry letter to Henry complaining that Bert and his boy scout enthusiasts were holding up the works by being overly concerned with good design. So far, Bert's dilatory responses and unfounded nitpicking scruples had pushed back his time schedule one month and were threatening to violate his budget constraints. Furthermore, when he invited Bert to come out immediately to discuss their differences and to meet the foreign contractor, Bert had offered the unlikely excuse of a commitment to chair a panel at an engineering conference. Dick proposed that he hire his own environmental specialist for the overseas project, who would be accountable to him alone, so that progress would no longer be forestalled; and he urged Henry to persuade the others to approve the action forthwith.

1. What were the various group interests in this situation?
2. How were individual and organizational goals incompatible? How were group and organizational goals incompatible? compatible?
3. What steps could be taken to draw the organizational, group, and individual goals into greater harmony?
4. Assuming that Henry is president of the company, what can he do to ameliorate the conflict between Dick and Bert?
5. Do you approve of Dick's suggestion that he hire his own environmental specialist? What ramifications might this entail for the organization?

Suggestions for Further Reading

Berne, E. *Games People Play: The Psychology of Human Relationships.* New York: Grove Press, 1964.

Blau, P. M. and W. R. Scott. *Formal Organizations: A Comparative Approach.* New York: Thomas Y. Crowell Co., 1962.

Bobbitt, H. R., et al. *Organizational Behavior: Understanding and Predicting.* Englewood Cliffs, N.J.: Prentice-Hall, Inc., 1974.

Cartwright, D., and A. Zander. *Group Dynamics.* New York: Harper & Row, Pubs., 1968.

Cathcart, S., and A. Samovar. *Small Group Communication.* Dubuque, Iowa: William C. Brown Co., Pubs., 1970.

Hampton, David R.; C. E. Summer; and R. Webber. *Organizational Behavior and the Practice of Management.* Glenview, Ill.: Scott, Foresman & Co., 1973.

Hare, A. P. *Handbook of Small Group Research.* New York: The Free Press, 1962.

Homans, G. *The Human Group.* New York: Harcourt Brace Jovanovich, Inc., 1950.

Janis, L. "Groupthink." In *Psychology Today,* November 1971.

Kobanashi, S. *Creative Management.* New York: American Management Association, Inc., 1971.

LeMasters, E. E. *The Blue-Collar Aristocrats.* Madison, Wis.: University of Wisconsin Press, 1975.

Likert, R. *New Patterns of Management.* New York: McGraw-Hill Book Co., Inc., 1961.

———. *The Human Side of Enterprise.* New York: McGraw-Hill Book Co., Inc., 1967.

Robbins, P. *Managing Organizational Conflict.* Englewood Cliffs, N.J.: Prentice-Hall, Inc., 1974.

Shepherd, C.R. *Small Groups: Some Sociological Perspectives.* New York: Thomas Y. Crowell Co., 1964.

Whyte, W. F. *Organizational Behavior: Theory and Application.* Homewood, Ill.: Richard D. Irwin, Inc., 1969.

Design and Development of Organizations

3

North Star Prologue

The recently formed North Star Associates has been an informal association of four equal partners, each contributing what he or she could do best. When the successful completion of a state contract brought them the opportunity for a three-year contract overseas, they realized the shortcomings of their informal managerial style and the inadequacies of their organization structure. So they set to work to design a suitable organization for their new task.

One necessity arose at the outset: Jo Parnela would have to spend most of her time at the overseas site, because a very important segment of the work was analysis of the economic consequences of the project and selection of the alternatives that would create the best industrial and social development. This requirement meant that Jo would have to sever her relationship with the university; after a lot of agonized soul-searching, she did in fact take an indefinite leave of absence (which had the same effect as resignation but left the door open for an eventual return). Jo put her foot down, however, at the suggestion that she run the overseas office, for the prospect of playing nursemaid to a group of engineers and draftsmen adrift in a foreign country did not exactly appeal to her. So another partner would have to be billeted at the overseas site, charged with running the North Star office and with responsibility for production, cost control, and liaison with Natal Engineers, Limited—the foreign engineering firm with the prime contract.

Jo Parnela said there was really no problem with an organization chart: she quickly sketched one showing a president and three vice-presidents, as in Figure 3-1, and said they could draw straws for the title of presi-

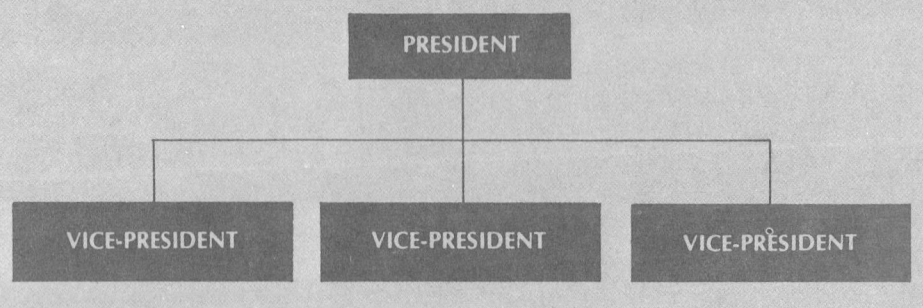

Figure 3-1. Jo's North Star Organization Chart

dent—provided they left her out of the competition. Bert said the structure needed more complexity: if the president was to be a figurehead, someone else would have to run the administrative details—sort of an "executive director"; and the chart ought to show their four specialties, rather than leaving out the specialty of whoever happened to win the toss and get the "president" box. He sketched the chart shown in Figure 3-2. Dick Boyer said they were seriously underestimating the difficulties involved in running a major project, particularly one that combined work outside the country and work for a foreign firm; even their recent experience with the highway routing job suggested the necessity for someone to be in charge of projects. He sketched another chart, showing the four partners on one line and the director of project management separately, commenting that the latter job could be rotated depending on the qualifications needed. Before Dick finished his sketch, Jo said anything was okay with her provided she had no administrative duties; so Dick modified the sketch to locate Jo in a "staff" block, indicating that she was working only as an individual. When he added the executive director block, the final sketch resembled Figure 3-3. Dick explained that both the president and the director of project management amounted to "double-hatted" jobs, meaning that the holders of these positions appeared more than once on the organization chart.

The partners finally sent Dick's version of the organization chart to AID, and back it came. There were several things wrong with it, said their advisor. First of all, if the president was going to remain in the home office, another officer would have to be empowered

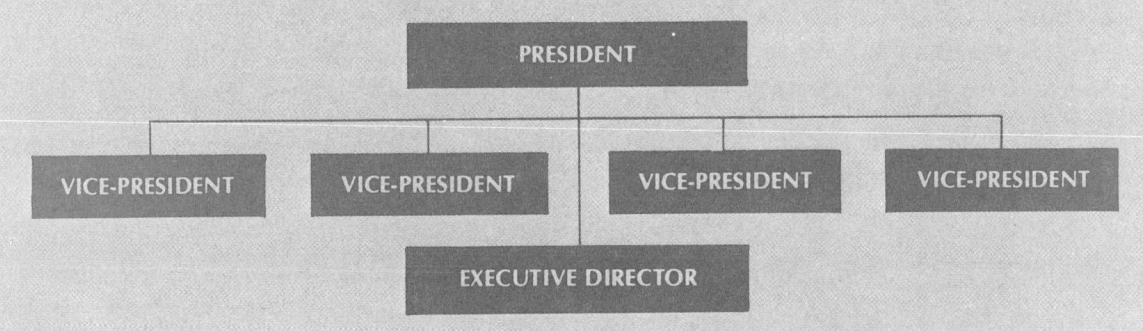

Figure 3-2. North Star Chart as Revised by Bert

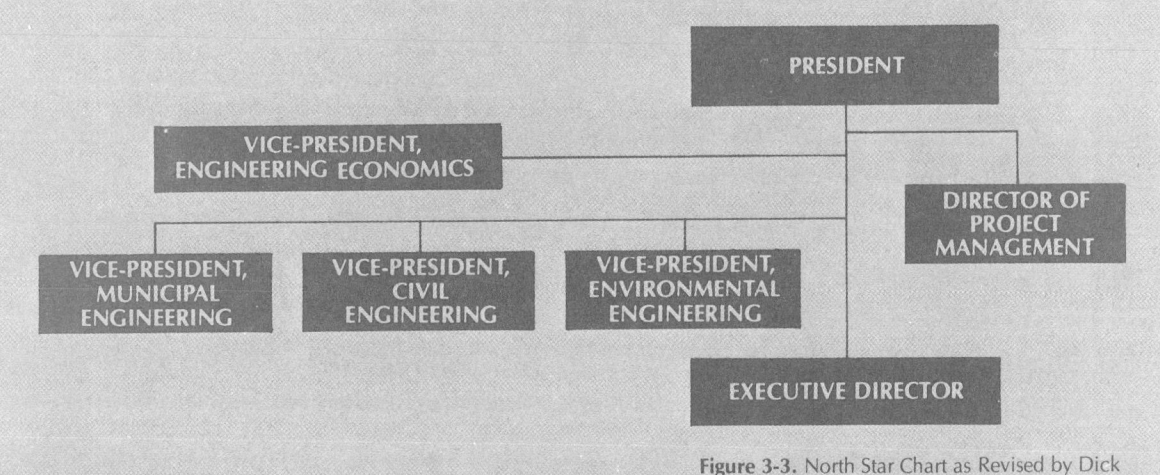

Figure 3-3. North Star Chart as Revised by Dick

DESIGN AND DEVELOPMENT OF ORGANIZATIONS

to commit the company on site overseas—so they needed an executive vice-president (whoever was selected to assist Jo at the overseas job site.) Second, they needed a chief engineer or equivalent to sign the plans and be generally responsible for the technical correctness of all plans and analyses; this officer, a registered engineer, should be based at the home office. Third, a relatively senior individual should be responsible for keeping track of funds and insuring contract compliance. An "Executive Director" title would be confusing since the proposed structure already included an executive vice-president, but a business manager would be ideal, reporting outside the chain of technical or project management responsibility in order to maintain independence of financial management and contract administration. And fourth, the advisor heartily approved of the project director post (managerial rather than technical), superior to the project manager for this AID project (and to other project managers for any other projects the company had on the string). If they would prepare such an organization chart and submit it to AID, the advisor would approve it and forward it to the overseas company for setting up the contract. Include the names for each block, he added. The chart he enclosed looked like Figure 3-4.

So the partners caucused and decided that the AID organization plan made a good deal of sense. None of the partners wanted (or felt qualified) to serve as business manager, so they decided to recruit for that. Jo Parnela, the vice-president for economics, would be required to locate overseas on site; Dick Boyer, with his overseas Navy construction experience, seemed the logical person to accompany her as project manager, and he reluctantly agreed with this logic. Since the technical director should be located at the home office, that meant Bert or Henry—but Henry was not yet a registered professional engineer, which gave Bert the job by default. The nominal post of executive vice-president fell in Dick's lap, since the AID country officer had said the on-site project manager should take that responsibility.

Only one block remained unfilled—that of president. It was Jo, who had originally suggested drawing straws, who proposed Henry since he was the only one left without a major title. As she reminded the others when they seemed hesitant, the structure was to serve only for this one project anyway. No one could think of a better solution, and the organization chart had to be sent along promptly, so it was filled in accordingly and mailed off. Bert pointed out ruefully that it was the first time in his experience that

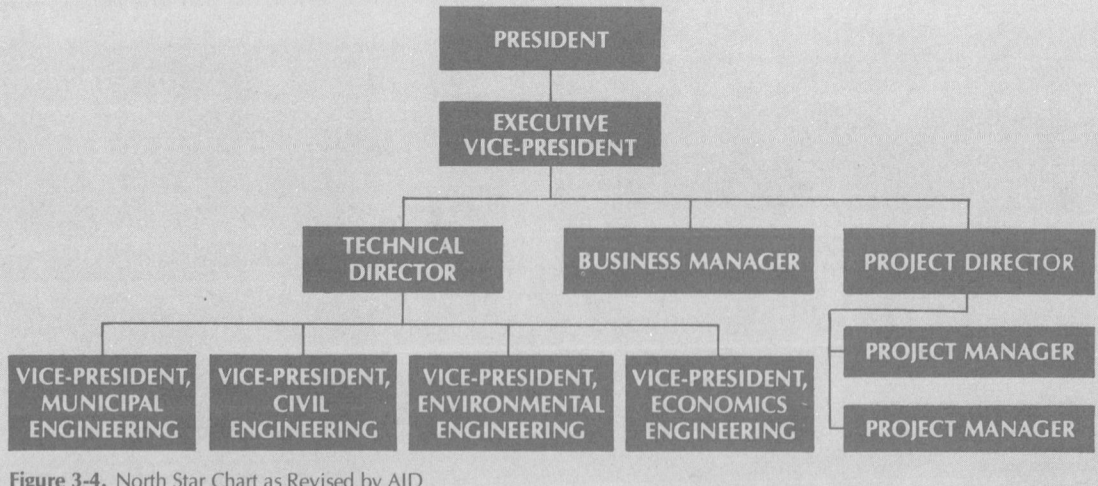

Figure 3-4. North Star Chart as Revised by AID

someone had qualified as head of an engineering firm because he did *not* have a professional registration. Dick said it was a bit irregular, but after all it was only temporary, and to that they all agreed. Except for the AID contract, it didn't mean a thing.

None of the partners suspected how wrong that assumption would prove to be.

The overseas job started well. Dick Boyer and his wife moved to the site, digging in for a long stay as project manager (and executive vice-president for protocol purposes). The organization chart that went to AID also showed Dick as director of project management for the company, but since none of the other North Star work was of a project nature the latter title had little meaning. Jo Parnela wanted to keep her apartment at home; she stayed in a hotel for the periods on site. Dick did the necessary hiring of engineers and other personnel, with help from the AID representative who put him in touch with companies finishing up overseas projects and letting people go. All of the draftsmen and three of the five engineers he hired were local people. Of the two U.S. engineers, one was a young man working for the Army Engineers in Washington, who came because he and his wife wanted the overseas experience before they started raising a family. The other was an overseas veteran in his fifties, a goldmine of knowledge and experience when sober but seldom able to resist the bottle for more than a few days at a time.

The business manager practically fell into their laps. They had been advertising in the paper and interviewing for two weeks with no success, when Henry happened to go to the university to see the director of maintenance for some help on a Blackridge job. Henry casually mentioned their search for a business manager, and his friend told him that he had just turned down a likely applicant a moment before—in fact, the man had just gotten into the elevator to leave. The two men rushed down and caught him in the parking lot, and before the day was over Zebulon Shehan was on the North Star payroll. Zeb had been administrator of a university-affiliated research institute in another city, but a change in university policy caused its sale to a private corporation which cut back the staff and he was one of those let go. He was returning to the Blackridge area because his wife's family lived there. Zeb's qualifications closely paralleled North Star's requirements, and he brought much-needed financial experience to the firm. At 45, he was far and away the oldest member of the North Star team.

Henry explained to Zeb that the company was operating on very limited funding, although the AID job promised to take care of its financial needs for the near future. Zeb was not at all disturbed by the nearly empty treasury; he assured Henry that he had operated from hand to mouth at his former job for ten years, and knew how to stall creditors until funds came.

---

1. General rules for successful organizations
2. Steps in designing the organization structure
3. What the organization chart shows—and doesn't show
4. The differences between line and staff
5. Alternate types of organizations: advantages and disadvantages
6. The place for formalism in organizations
7. Benefits and problems of decentralization
8. The practical meaning of "managing by consent"
9. How growth changes the organization
10. Ways to describe organizations, and why they are useful

In this chapter we discuss how people are brought together into organizations, and how organizations grow or change in response to differences in their tasks. Four major facets of organizational structure and purpose are examined:

1. *Principles of organization*—basic elements and rules for organizing, principal types of formal organization, and methods of departmentalizing or dividing the work
2. *Organizations as people-systems*—alternative approaches to managing, organizations as complex and interrelated entities, and the interplay between the organization and its individual members and sub-groups
3. *Organizational development and growth*—how tasks engender compatible organizational structures, how organizations grow and change, and the problems of excessive stability in an environment of change
4. *Techniques for describing organizations and making them work*—charts, manuals, position descriptions, standing instructions

These principles and relationships apply to all organizations; they are as valid for government agencies as for private enterprises. While they take on particular force in larger organizations, conceptually they are valid for the smallest of undertakings.

Principles of Organization

Newly formed companies often pay little attention to organizational structure, devoting the bulk of their time to turning out the product or service they were created to provide. This emphasis can be an invitation to disaster, however, for few companies have product lines so unique that they can afford to utilize their resources carelessly and still succeed. A one-person firm has no need for an organization, and perhaps a group of five or six can parcel out tasks informally; but when a company gets much larger, the reverse of organization is likely to occur. Without clear assignment of responsibilities, tasks are not properly executed: some jobs are done twice while others are overlooked, promises made by one person are not kept by another, standards start to slip, and one part of the group does not know what the other parts are doing. Even so small an organization as a husband-and-wife team experiences these problems ("I thought you were going to pay that bill!" "I thought *you* were!"). So it is not surprising that they occur frequently when the group is much larger than two.

Fundamental Rules of Organizing

bureaucratic elements

Early in this century, German sociologist and economist Max Weber set forth the elements he considered to be essential to a bureaucratic organization:[1]

1. Specialization of workers by skills
2. A clear hierarchy of authority
3. Detailed operating rules
4. An impersonal method of operation
5. Managers specially trained for their jobs

How many of these elements exist for North Star?

Weber reasoned that managers in this sort of organization would know what orders to give, and subordinates would do as they were told. They would know what to expect, would understand their roles, and would realize how they contributed. No one would encounter the problem of receiving orders from two or more superiors, since Weber's structure gives each individual a single supervisor for everything.

This set of elements is satisfactory for describing large and stable units such as church, military, and government operations, where employees are used to looking to a single authority for all orders and decisions—and where that authority has a reasonable chance to develop the necessary competence for making all decisions. It must be modified to handle complex or rapidly changing organizations, where one superior cannot qualify in all necessary areas and employees must take direction from various specialists for different aspects of their jobs. For example, a shop foreman in an electronics firm might get guidance from Engineering on technical matters, Scheduling on sequencing jobs through the plant, Personnel on employee benefits and labor relations, and Inspection on the quality of output. It would be quite time-consuming if each of these groups dealt only with the plant superintendent, who in turn had to advise the foreman about each issue. Similarly, a county road maintenance foreman would feel free to consult the fire marshal, pollution control office, sewage department, and parks naturalist about matters within their special purview without directing each question through the chief highway engineer.

Weber envisioned a stable organization where there would be plenty of time to adjust to new conditions and where new questions would seldom arise. In contemporary organizations, however, a subordinate may not have time to consult a superior on an urgent problem and may have to assume the necessary authority to handle it. Weber's concepts make sense when applied to the organizations he studied, but they are too rigid for most modern undertakings. Today's young manager is expected to use initiative to stretch the rules when this approach supports the organization's real goals; the servile subordinate who does exactly—and only—what he or she is told, like Ebenezer Scrooge's clerk Bob Cratchit in Dickens' *A Christmas Carol*, will not make the grade.

A French contemporary of Weber's, engineer Henri Fayol, who served illustriously as director-general of a large iron and coal combine for 30 years, summarized his rules for organizing in terms that hold up well today:

1. The organization should have a clear *objective*, and each group or individual should have a compatible sub-objective that supports the overall organizational objective.
2. The work of each person should be *specialized* to a single function, with like functions grouped under a single head.

organizing rules

3. The structure should contain means for *coordinating* the efforts of all parts toward this overall objective.
4. There should be a single overall *authority*, with clear chains of command that extend to, and are understood by, everyone in the organization.
5. When a person or group is assigned *responsibility*, corresponding authority must be given to that person or group.²

<small>Does North Star meet these rules?</small>

Organizational Guidelines

When the young partners in North Star Associates found it necessary to establish some sort of organizational structure, they were operating largely from intuition, with relatively little practical experience to draw on. They could have used some straightforward procedural lines, like those described below.

Steps in Organizing

The objectives of the organization must be known. The type of organization differs depending on its goals and the organizational structure should be determined in accordance with these objectives.

<small>organizing steps</small>

- Work must be broken down into specific tasks, so that it can be fitted to the specialized skills of the people in the organization.
- Activities must be grouped into units of workable size: no unit should be so large that it is unmanageable or so small that it is inefficient.
- Duties of every unit and every employee category must be defined; employees may not live up to management expectations otherwise.
- Resources must be provided, and responsibility delegated, commensurate with the stated objectives of each unit. It is a sign of managerial inexperience to expect results from a person or group when the necessary tools for such results have not been supplied.
- Personnel must be assigned to the units to flesh out the organization, which until then is simply a paper structure.
- Tasks and relationships must be specified in detail. This can be the most difficult of all, because in any organization there are overlapping areas where two or more groups seek jurisdiction. (If Personnel is to handle all disciplinary actions, this delegation must be made very specific, because line supervisors may feel discipline is traditionally their responsibility and tend to exercise it in the absence of clear and unmistakable instructions to the contrary.)

Guidelines for Structure

<small>structure guidelines</small>

- Activities must be balanced. For example, a group manager supervising five departments should endeavor to assign roughly a fifth of the total group load to each department.
- Duplication of work must be minimized, or some of the benefits sought from organization will be lost as two groups try to do the same job. A small amount of duplication may be useful in ensuring that different viewpoints are brought to a problem, but too much of it is wasteful and destructive.

Assign people only to tasks that they are qualified to perform.

- Assign people only to tasks they are qualified to perform. Young organizations, particularly those experiencing some confusion in settling down to their tasks, tend to think of each new individual as superhuman; they sketch out a set of duties for the position, and just assume that somehow the person appointed will perform these duties, regardless of their extent or complexity.
- Establish clear lines of authority. Battles between a project manager and an engineering supervisor to decide who will approve the plans for the new project waste time and talent and injure the morale of both groups, whose members sit in the stands cheering on their leaders while cooperation goes down the drain. And this situation is confusing and disillusioning to customers, who see an organization that doesn't know enough to handle its own affairs.
- Provide controls—and use them. Rules, guidelines, and standards are not enough; someone must see that they are carried out. The organization needs constant surveillance to stay on the track.

Has North Star done this?

Organizational Structures

Activities may be grouped within an organization in several different ways, depending on how authority relationships are established. A structure may be primarily *internal,* reflecting traditional line and/or staff management patterns; or primarily *external,* reflecting the nature of the products, processes, or markets with which a company is involved. The extent to which authority is centralized or decentralized within a company varies according to the type of structure and the company's objectives.

Internal Management Structure

One of the oldest ways to categorize managers is by dividing them into two groups: "line" and "staff." The division seems simple, but it can be confusing. A military organization provides a clear-cut example of these categories: the general commanding a division in the field is *line,* in direct control of all operations; intelligence, supply, and planning subordinates are *staff,* because they exist only to advise and support the general's efforts and have no direct control over operations. This division of management responsibilities becomes confusing when a manager is "staff" in some respects and "line" in others. The general's subordinate in the area of supply is *staff* when advising the general on supply matters and supporting the general's operational needs by providing supplies; but the same person is *line* when handling logistics vehicles and commanding supply personnel who are moving the material.

Nevertheless, the concept is useful in establishing overall concepts of managerial structure. An organization may be principally *line,* which implies that its major executives run all aspects of their operations, and look *within their own units* for staff help; or it may be *line-and-staff,* implying that these executives run the major aspects of their operations, but look *outside to centralized corporate staff groups* for staff help. Figure 3-5 illustrates a basic line organization; the district managers shown on the third line have complete control of all their staff functions. Figure 3-6 shows a simple line-and-staff organization chart; the line vice-presidents (connected by solid lines to the chief executive) run the operating aspects of their jobs, but they look to the corporate staff offices (connected by dotted lines to the chief executive) for guidance in such specialty areas as engineering and legal matters. Some chartists would show dotted lines from each staff block to each line block, indicating technical advice and guidance flowing from the staff officers to the line activities.

The disadvantage of the strictly line arrangement is that each small line operation must contain within itself all necessary expertise in the various staff areas. Thus, in Figure 3-5 each of four district managers would have to hire a personnel specialist, a legal specialist, and so on; but the manager might not have enough work in each specialty to keep these staff people busy, and couldn't afford the same level of talent and experience that would be found in centralized staff offices. The advantage, of course, is the quick and flexible action possible in each district office because the district manager need not communicate with several corporate offices.

Small organizations can operate solely as line organizations, provided the managers have sufficiently broad experience and understanding to furnish the necessary staff expertise. Large organizations, however, almost invariably use some version of the line-and-staff structure. A very large organization often has line executives at the top, so that the major subdivisions are headed by line officers. But each of these large units (each as large as a major company, perhaps) contains line-and-staff elements similar to those in Figure 3-6. Even in these giant enterprises, some staff officers report directly to the president or chairman to ensure that the top executive has the necessary information to control major aspects of policy.

The question of who is "staff" often arises in line-and-staff organizations. The classical notion that staff officers only advise and plan does not apply to the many staff managers with action responsibility in broad areas. But in some large corporations the differentiation is very clear. The French combine BSN-Gervais Danone, a glass, food, and beverage group that is one of Europe's largest, has just three product divisions and two staff departments—a classic line-and-staff organization.

The fact that staff departments do not have authority to run the organization does not mean that they are less important. Frequently, the opposite is true. Growing interest in environmental and social legislation and the increased tendency of consumers and public interest groups to sue corporations has vastly enhanced the importance of legal staff members, for example; the president of American Can recently estimated that he spends 60% of his time on legal problems. As to their importance, he added that "we are fighting for our lives."

A third sort of composite structure, which extends the staff concept, is called a *functional* organization because the main managerial divisions are designated by the functions they are to perform. Figure 3-7 shows how a functional structure might be applied to a large automotive dealership with branch offices. The chart shows the central organization as it relates to one of the branch offices. The president has a central organization

functional

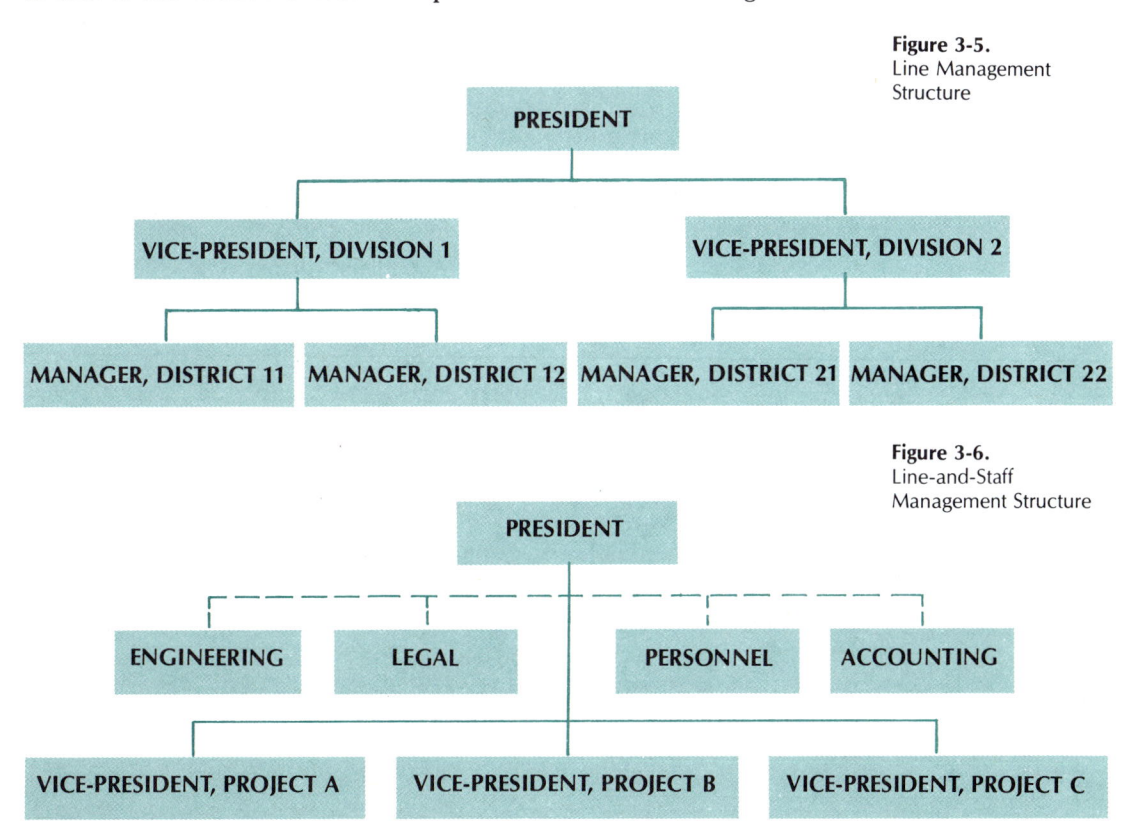

Figure 3-5.
Line Management Structure

Figure 3-6.
Line-and-Staff Management Structure

73
DESIGN AND DEVELOPMENT OF ORGANIZATIONS

divided into functional groups: Personnel, Accounting, Repair and Servicing, Body and Paint, Sales and Leasing. Each of these six managers reports directly to the president. A branch manager for each branch (only one shown) also reports directly to the president. Traditionally, the six functional managers would be considered staff, and the branch managers would be considered line. Within each branch are the same six functional groups, and the head of each group in a branch office reports to the branch manager for line control. But the vertical dotted lines within each function indicate technical control—a form of coordination. Thus the central vice-president for leasing establishes company-wide policies on leasing, decides on the number of lease cars to be purchased, sets rates, and may even tell each branch manager how many lease cars that branch will get. The leasing manager in a branch office can be excused for a little schizophrenia at times, for clearly he or she serves two bosses. One significant factor identifies the real boss: the one with firing power. In most organizations, that would be the branch manager. Consequently, when the chips are down it is the branch manager whose dictates the leasing manager follows.

The extraordinarily successful International Telephone & Telegraph Corporation, one of the United States' ten largest industrial corporations, requires that the chief financial officer in each subsidiary corporation report directly to the corporate financial officer—and look to that source for raises and promotions. Avis Corporation, when it was an ITT subsidiary company, protested strenuously against this arrangement as an infringement on the authority of Avis's president—until ITT learned that Avis itself had adopted the system by having the chief financial officer in each of its divisions report directly to the Avis controller. Such arrangements make the line-staff differentiation difficult to pin down; many organizations do not even attempt to do so.

Structure Based on Product, Process, or Market

Organizations do not always evolve in accordance with systematic managerial principles. Sometimes their development is affected critically

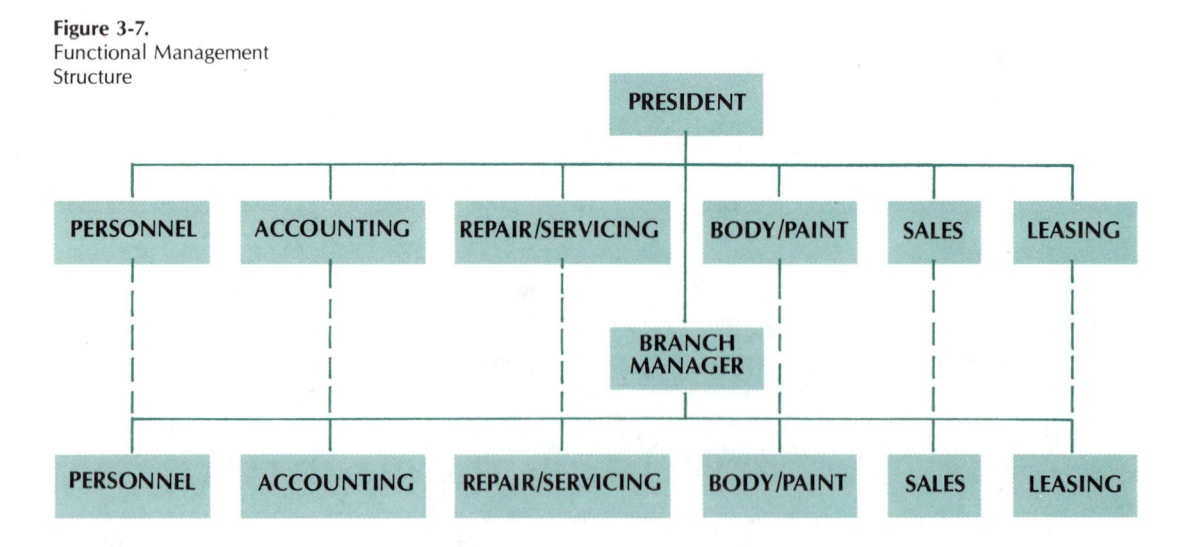

Figure 3-7.
Functional Management Structure

by the accident of where they start operating, who their customers are, or what special skills their initial members possess. North Star's first efforts at laying out an organization focused on the areas of expertise of the four partners, but when the first formal organization chart took shape it was influenced both by the fact of a major customer and the fact of an important overseas project. Thus it was inevitable that the partners would devise an organizational unit tied in with Natal Engineers, their most important customer, and it was almost as inevitable that their technical operations would fall into four divisions—one for each skill represented by the partners.

North Star, then, illustrates the way an organization can be structured in accordance with such factors as *territory, customer, product,* or *process.* A nationwide retail chain is quite likely to have a western division, a southern division, and so on; its operations are repetitive in the various locations, and geography usually is the most important point of differentiation. A company like Rockwell International, for which the automobile, the airplane, and the nation's cities are all key customer areas, probably is well advised to have divisions corresponding to automotive, aerospace, and municipal customers. A conglomerate, which may turn out such varied items as sporting goods, meats, and steel, will make best use of its management skills by separating these dissimilar products into separate divisions. And a technologically oriented company, working on the frontiers of scientific knowledge in such areas as holography, matrix isolation, and solid state electronics, will make the best use of valuable technical talent by organizing according to each research field.

When a U.S. corporation first branches out overseas, not only will it set up a relatively independent overseas subsidiary, it will also recognize that foreign laws, personnel practices, and marketing systems may require a different organizational structure. In this case, *territorial* organization makes the most sense.

territorial

If the same corporation decides that its product experience could be extended into a totally new field in the U.S.—say into security equipment of the sort bought by police and fire departments—it will recognize that it has a great deal to learn about the needs and practices in this new market (even though it anticipates that many of the technical or manufacturing processes will be unfamiliar). Selling to such customers will be so different from its past experience, and product applications will be so unknown to it, that it will be almost forced to utilize a *customer* organization in order to succeed in this new field.

customer

Is North Star a territorial or customer organization?

Perhaps, on the other hand, the corporation hopes to sell to this new market the same equipment it has successfully sold in other markets. Say it has long manufactured industrial pumps, wishes to extend this market into fire-fighting pumps, and believes that the customer's needs in the fire-fighting area will not be substantially different from those of other market sectors where pumps are used. Moreover, it does not expect that a detailed knowledge of fire department administration and practice will be required. The product is more central to its operations than the customer, so it probably will stick to a *product* organization.

product

Perhaps the corporation is selling a highly specialized product line, where technical expertise and scientific excellence are essential to a first-class product. Say it is building heat and smoke detection equipment

process

on advanced scientific principles, a process that depends on constant research. Since it has little fear of successful competition from a company which simply sells "everything for the fire fighter," it will place primary emphasis on keeping the technology up-to-date. Thus, a *process* organization may be most suitable.

You can see that no one of these systems of organization is better than any other until you take into account the conditions under which the organization will operate. What is good for one is cumbersome for another. An organizational structure is not inherently efficient or inefficient; rather its usefulness depends on how well it meets the special needs of the organization in question. Only after the goals of an organization are known and its business style and environment described in detail are we ready to build the organization structure that will work best.

Extent of Centralization or Decentralization

When Dick Boyer went to his overseas site as project manager and Bert Starr assumed the post of technical director, with Henry North nominally in charge of both, the stage was set for some troublesome arguments (described in the chapter prologue) on just how decentralized this organization was. Dick clearly expected to run his show on the project site, and all he wanted from the home office was engineering support plus any stateside chores he might need. Henry wanted (or should have wanted) a good deal more policy control than that. For one thing, North Star Associates as a company did not want Dick negotiating contract changes that were financially undesirable, or working in a way that would endanger profits or financial liquidity. The company did not want him taking any personnel actions that could lead to a charge of improper labor practices against the home office. The company was vitally interested in the reputation for good work and professional conduct which Dick's operations could establish or tear down, because of its impact on other jobs in other areas. And so forth.

decentralization

The extent of decentralization—delegation of authority below the central figure—is an important policy matter. The typical small enterprise is highly centralized because it tends to be a sole proprietorship, with one principal owner who is the boss in all matters. As a company grows, regardless of its basic organizational structure, the question constantly arises as to how much authority to delegate. A major defect of extensive decentralization (say, for a company with separate divisions) is that one division can lose enough money to drag down other divisions with it. The conglomerate corporations that have sprung up in recent years, where dissimilar companies were acquired and often left to operate almost independently because the central management had little experience in the various special fields, are good examples. In many cases heavy losses by subsidiaries have blighted the earnings performance of the parent corporations.

In contrast to many of the ailing conglomerates, which acquired operating companies and skilled executives but often failed to make them mesh for the benefit of the whole, is giant General Motors Corporation. Its success story has been a management classic. Alfred P. Sloan, Jr., who headed GM for nearly 30 years, brought the company from an ailing enterprise one-fifth the size of Ford to an industrial colossus that makes over half the cars and trucks in the U.S. plus a wide range of other products. To accomplish this feat, Sloan introduced a structure he termed "decentralized organization with centralized control."[3] He gave division heads wide latitude over operations, design, sales, and distribution, but retained tight control over financial reporting and expenditures. Where it was profitable for the corporation to carry out an operation centrally, Sloan permitted that arrangement. Otherwise, however, he left the divisions free to exercise the maximum initiative, and even to compete energetically with each other when the corporate well-being was not harmed thereby.

Advantages and disadvantages. A major advantage of centralization is that divisions rarely get far off the track without headquarters learning of it. Another is central control over company policies and practices, which helps ensure that operations in one division will not harm those in another. A third is the possibility for economic gain and improved communications resulting from use of centralized specialist groups for all divisions. And a fourth, as the conglomerates have learned, is avoidance of the need for elaborate reporting and control systems to keep the chief executive informed of what the divisions are doing—systems that often fail just when they are most needed.

A major advantage of decentralization is that decision power is closer to the scene of operations, where more and better information for decision is available. As a corollary, the amount of "detail work" borne by the chief executive is reduced. A third advantage is that the enthusiasm and initiative of divisional officers may be harnessed by giving them the authority to stand or fall on their own efforts. And a fourth is the improved ability to separate all costs and earnings of each decentralized division from those of the others, so divisional profit performance stands out clearly and elaborate accounting adjustments are not necessary.

Guidelines for centralization-decentralization. Often the divisional or departmental structure of an organization will help determine how much authority to decentralize. North Star's project organization overseas made it essential to decentralize the project operation, since the home office was too far away to play any important role except in providing detailed engineering design, and the questions that arose on site were too individualized for absentee decision making. Other organizations with territorial structure but more routinized operations might centralize decisions far more. Thus, a branch bank in a remote site would have its decisions on loan policy, interest rates, and trust practices determined at the home office.

It is possible to set forth some principles for determining the desirable extent of decentralization in accordance with the organizational structure, as follows:

1. It is desirable to centralize policy, but to decentralize operations within this policy framework.
2. It is desirable to lighten the decision load of the chief executive so that he or she delegates as much as possible, and manages "by exception"—handling only those matters that fall outside previously established guidelines.

3. It is well to centralize matters where corporate coordination is important, such as labor negotiations or legal actions at corporate level.
4. It is economical to centralize (or at least coordinate) matters where division operations can support one another, such as institutional advertising, joint purchasing, or mutual servicing.
5. There should be enough decentralization so all divisions decide those things they are best equipped to decide, and develop to the fullest a sense of achievement and pride.
6. There should be enough centralization so the chief executive receives timely and adequate information, particularly as to trouble.
7. The organization's structure should be such that collaboration among divisions is encouraged and facilitated.

Organizations as People-Systems

The manager does not, of course, operate precisely as the strict authority relationships on the organization chart might suggest: getting orders from above and transmitting them below, receiving information from below and passing it up, all the while making decisions and turning them into instructions for subordinates who will carry them out. Organizations are far more complex than this. A manager's world is not divided neatly into people who must obey and people who must be obeyed. Rather, it consists of a confusing jumble of people involved in every conceivable authority relationship. The manager's authority is shared by people *not* in the same chain of command, and often lower in the hierarchy, whose decisions—with regard to personnel policies, safety rules, legal prohibitions, financial limitations, engineering limits, public relations guidelines, and so on—must be heeded. The manager's authority is also shared by people *lower* in the same chain of command, because of limitations on what they can be ordered to do: an order may violate overtime limits, safety policies, or informal norms of what is legitimate and proper. And the manager's authority is shared by managers at the *same* level, who individually can make the task easy or impossible by cooperation or opposition, and to some extent by *subordinates* of those managers, whose assistance or supporting work is essential to timely completion of the job.

Span of Control

In many ways, the simplest of the relationships described above is that of managing subordinates, since the manager is formally *empowered* to issue orders to them and they are formally *required* to carry out legitimate orders (whether they *do* carry out the orders or not is another matter). Let us examine the management/subordinates element of the organizational structure.

span of control

The ideal number of subordinates has been estimated by various management authorities at somewhere between three and ten. Forty years ago Lyndall Urwick, in his "Axioms of Organization," observed that it "appears to be four, [although] at the lowest level [it] may be eight or twelve....Centralization of authority should always be regarded as a necessary evil, to be kept at a minimum."[4] One obvious objection to a large span of control or authority is the rapid increase in the number of interpersonal relationships as the number of subordinates goes up. If a manager has two subordinates—say Ms. X has Mr. A and Mr. B under her—she must be concerned with six relationships:

interpersonal relationships

| X with A | X with B | X with A & B |
| A alone | B alone | A with B |

If she has three subordinates, she has 14 relationships to worry about:

X with A	X with B	X with C
X with A & B	X with B & C	X with A & C
X with A & B & C		
A alone	B alone	C alone
A with B & C	B with A & C	C with A & B
A with B with C		

With five subordinates this grows to 62 relationships, with seven it burgeons to 254, and by ten it has exploded to 2,046 different relationships to be considered—each with its own subtle interpersonal implications that can absorb managerial time and energy.[5]

A manager who supervises groups doing similar work, such as branch income tax offices spread around a metropolitan region, can handle more subordinates because the operating and marketing problems will be much the same for each. By contrast, a manager supervising different sorts of units—legal, research, accounting, production, planning, and so on—will find little technical overlap between the areas and thus must develop a far wider span of professional knowledge. Even in the former situation, however, the manager must still cope with the proliferation of interpersonal problems discussed above, and often it is these matters that chew up time and levy a heavy toll on managerial stamina. It probably is true that any time one manager is directly in charge of more than ten or twelve subordinates, that supervisor is overloaded and the organization is suffering.

The Spectrum of Management Systems

Management students are often surprised at the wide variety of management styles that appear to achieve success—or, conversely, at the fact that the same management system can succeed in one environment and fail in another. A family company operating in a small and close-knit community may use a paternalistic style (in which management acts as a benevolent parent in deciding what benefits and rewards its employees need) with great success to achieve high morale and strong company support; a large corporation in an industrial community that tried to behave similarly would have its work force out on strike in no time. An organization with a tradition of fortitude and personal stamina or courage (such as a team of oil well fire fighters or a coast guard ocean rescue unit) will put up with extraordinary hardships and truly miserable working conditions and take pride in the very discomforts and hazards that surround its tasks; the same individuals, transported to softer surroundings, might object strenuously if they had to walk up a few flights when the elevator was out of commission.

Such differences in environments, social settings, and levels of commitment produce many different approaches in seeking to weld people into smoothly functioning units. By the same token, these approaches share a fundamental goal: to persuade the people in an organization that their well-being is closely related to that of the organization.

Alternative Approaches to Managing

formalism

Formalism in an organization consists of doing everything "by the book," within strict lines of authority. Early government bureaucracies were extremely formal organizations, and in some countries they still are. There are certain advantages to a rigid structure: all members of the group know exactly where they stand and what is expected of them; more importantly, subordinates are never disconcerted by the need to assume unfamiliar responsibilities. It surprises young college-bred managers to encounter older employees who refuse higher-paying posts for which they appear qualified, because they are more comfortable in familiar tasks and shun unfamiliar duties where there may be risk of failure. It is probable that Dick Boyer found a very formal organization existing at Natal Engineers, and that as a result his own overseas operations for North Star took on a formalism that would have seemed quite artificial at home.

participation

At the other extreme is a *participatory* organization, with everyone concerned adding input to organizational decisions and the final actions arising more or less out of consensus or popular vote. The four-person North Star team was so much a participatory group that its members found little significance in the matter of who was chosen to be president. In participatory organizations every effort is made to bring as many

Formalism in an organization consists of doing everything by the book.

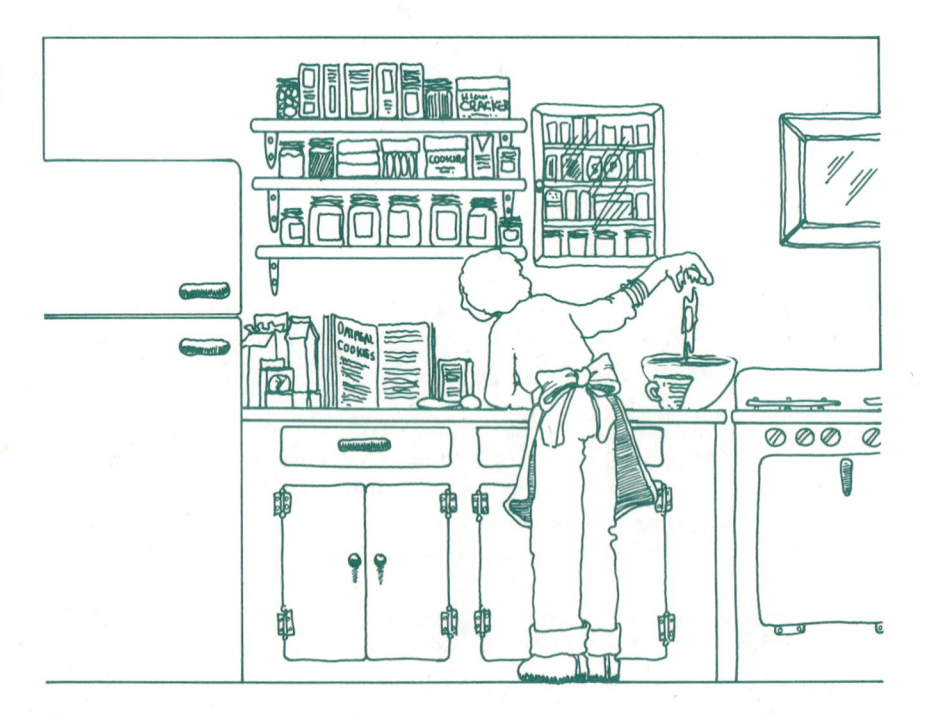

THE BUILDING BLOCKS OF MANAGEMENT

members as possible into the decision-making process, much in the manner of New England town meetings. The principal advantage is the feeling engendered in the members that it is *their* organization, which leads to strong loyalty. The principal disadvantages are that it takes much time and compromise to reach decisions (which usually fail to satisfy everyone), and that many members simply don't have the knowledge or experience to make good decisions.

The *human relations* school of organization, while not going so far as to involve every participant in the decision process, sees human satisfaction as a vital factor in organizational success and pays more attention to achieving personal fulfillment of employees than to striving for operating efficiency. Indeed, human relations advocates would deny any such choice, for they would claim that an organization that helps each member to satisfy personal needs for fulfillment and happiness *will* be efficient, because every member will work to capacity.

Checks and balances in an organization imply an administrative design with built-in conflict points between administrators, or the notion of "countervailing power." No one element can become too strong, because it will be held in check by other elements that have power to prevent excesses. The U.S. government, with its executive, legislative, and judicial power centers, is a classic example of such checks and balances. Sometimes a chief executive will assign overlapping areas of jurisdiction to subordinate executives with the deliberate aim of keeping them constantly competing with (and thus checking on) one another. Such an environment may not be a peaceful or pleasant one, but some people thrive in a competitive atmosphere, and for them it may be an effective managerial climate.

Centralization bears some relation to formalism, but there are important differences. A centralized organization is one where all vital decisions are made at the top, and where subordinate managers have clear-cut limitations to their discretionary authority. As in a formalized organization, clear channels of authority exist and subordinates know the limits of their jurisdiction. In contrast to a formalized organization, however, rapid changes in direction and thrust can occur. A formalized structure resists change, while the concentration of decision power in a centralized organization may be designed to facilitate new ventures and policy shifts in the first place. Rockwell International, a corporation that heavily reflects the policies and decisions of its chief executive, Willard Rockwell, Jr., is quite centralized in that all significant decisions are made at headquarters, but it is far from formalized; its subordinate executives have become accustomed to unexpected acquisitions and joint venture announcements as a way of life.

Decentralized organizations are those where a conscious effort is made to parcel out the decision process to the field, and maintain only policy control and overall review of operations at the top level. It is easy to centralize, but decentralization takes a great deal of careful design to insure that enough authority is delegated to permit effective operations without delegating so much that divisions work at cross-purposes. The United States government is a decentralized organization, with extensive powers delegated to the 50 states, as compared to France, where vast powers are administered by the central government.[6]

Requirements for Managing

Regardless of the management style, any group of people must exhibit certain unifying elements to rise above the level of a mob and become a manageable entity which can act productively. These elements are *authority, responsibility, loyalty,* and *communication.*

authority

Authority implies that someone is in charge, to resolve differences and make effective decisions so the organization can move ahead. It is a widely held belief that a large mass of people, stirred by a common goal, can achieve great things with no apparent leader; in real life, however, it doesn't work that way. The many conflicting demands of different individuals and small-group goals and needs must be resolved by a compromiser with the authority to make decisions stick.

responsibility

Responsibility is the lodestar that gives managers direction, and harnesses their energies for effective accomplishment of objectives. When the leader of the band of settlers says, "You take a patrol and watch from that hill," "You unhitch the horses," "You see to the cooking fire," responsibilities are being assigned so that everyone won't run in all directions and produce only confusion. If managers do not have a clear picture of their responsibilities—and in some organizations they may not—the organization cannot produce as a unit.

loyalty

Could Dick Boyer develop more loyalty to Natal than to North Star? Why?

Loyalty is the glue that holds an organization together. A subordinate who receives an order will not obey it automatically (though inexperienced managers may expect that result), but will comply only if that brings more satisfaction than ignoring the order. This obedience may stem from fear of the consequences of disobeying. It may come from pleasure—the act is inherently attractive (perhaps the company orders the subordinate to take the family and open an office in Switzerland). Or, more frequently, it may come from organizational loyalty—the subordinate neither likes nor dislikes the act, but likes the notion of being part of a valuable organization performing useful work. Such loyalty may be strong enough to stimulate performance of the act even though it is personally distasteful. When this sort of loyalty disappears, the organization is in danger of disintegrating soon after.

communication

Communication is the essential ingredient of spreading the word. Subordinates must know what their superiors want, and what company policy is; superiors must know what is happening down in the organization, and what their subordinates think, want, and recommend. In the heat of battle, the army that loses its lines of communication loses the fight. In organizational behavior the same thing happens, though far less dramatically. Inexperienced managers believe they need only tell the troops *what* to do, without telling them *why*; they also believe there is no need to hear what the troops *think* about the orders they receive. This element of communication is so vital that chapter 5 is entirely devoted to it.

Management by Consent

consent

The notion of obtaining "consent" for policies and practices from employees or other subordinates seems so foreign to managing that it sounds more like a cooperative than a conventional organization. But a little thought will show that any instruction must be acceptable to the recipient before it will be carried out. Extreme cases are obvious: when you tell an employee to stick a hand in the fire, or attack a policeman inspecting your premises, or steal supplies for the office, refusal is almost certain because these actions are contrary to basic notions of expected or useful behavior. Other cases are less clear: when you tell an employee to produce 80 units in a day, despite an existing informal "shop standard" of 70 units, you are asking for rejection of an extremely powerful unofficial social norm. The worker is almost certain to find a way to demonstrate that 70 units cannot be exceeded.

Chester Barnard, once president of New Jersey Bell Telephone Company and a prominent management writer, has set forth four conditions which must be met before a communication is accepted and carried out by a subordinate:

1. He or she understands the communication (order).
2. He or she believes it is consistent with the purpose of the organization.
3. He or she believes it is compatible with personal interests.
4. He or she is capable of complying with it.[7]

conditions for consent

Some years ago, several of the nation's largest electrical equipment manufacturers were charged with illegal price fixing, and several senior officers (though not the chief executives) were convicted and sentenced. In such a situation, imagine that the senior officers of the company are brought together for a staff meeting. First the chief executive comes in, and sternly advises one and all that they are to obey the antitrust laws and avoid price-fixing practices. Then the chief leaves and two executive vice-presidents take over, to describe graphically the conditions in the industry (with ruinous competition among companies resulting in such low bids to electric utilities that no company can make any money) and to point out to the other officers something everyone there already knows: that if the operation is not made profitable, the officers will be fired and replaced with people who can make a profit. They are warned not to complain that ruinous competition is making it impossible for any company to make money. Just before the session ends, the chief executive rejoins the group, reminds them all that the corporation will not tolerate violation of antitrust laws, and adjourns the meeting with a hope that the industry will see better times soon.

The chief executive has issued a clear and uncomplicated order. At least one of the companies involved can cite an occasion when the chief executive did issue such an order. Yet the order is disregarded. Why?

Organizational Complexity

Modern organization is a highly complex people-system. Responsibilities overlap, regardless of efforts to purify relationships. For example, a sales group may be responsible for improving product acceptance, a design group for product safety, and a production group for product economy. When sales tries to improve the acceptance of a product by changing its design, safety and production costs may be affected adversely; conversely, if production changes are made the acceptance may decrease even further. Such a situation is ripe for controversy.

complexity

83

DESIGN AND DEVELOPMENT OF ORGANIZATIONS

Simple moves in an organization are found to have very wide effects. Say a manager allows a secretary to arrive ten minutes late and leave on time (but take ten minutes less for lunch hour) because the secretary's bus arrives a little late. That action could be the subject of a union grievance because everyone in the company does not have the same privilege. Or say a modest change in billing procedures brings in all payments at the end of the month rather than throughout the month as before. Thus, bookkeeping must work overtime (and purchasing, which shares the same office, demands an equal "share" of overtime work), the treasurer must increase the line of credit to meet the company's financial needs, the corporation's position on the annual statement is altered...and so on. This potential for disastrous "ripple effects" explains many management rules that might otherwise seem capricious.

Almost everyone in a complex organization has more than one boss. A subordinate may be directed from one point on technical matters, from another on personnel rules, from another on legal niceties, and from still another on market performance. Moreover, these bosses don't see their own jurisdictions too clearly, and often attempt to overlap into each other's backyards, with still more pulling and tugging at the hapless subordinate in the center. More precise job descriptions can ease these pressures, but since organizational complexity is the root cause the job descriptions won't really cure the problem. Moreover, too much detail in prescribing jobs can stifle initiative and needed freedom of action.

What are the indirect relationships of North Star's Technical Director?

And the manager has even more relationships to worry about—bosses, semibosses, subordinates, semisubordinates, colleagues, clients, and outright enemies in all directions. A manager cannot even afford the luxury of arguing with a complete stranger, because the stranger may have secondary connections that affect the manager's job. Some years ago the president of a respected old-line firm in a midwestern town came to Washington as a Cabinet officer. By the time he had spent three months trying to get results in this multi-dimensional arena, where every decision had to be checked in a dozen unsuspected directions, all of his natural confidence born of years operating in his uncomplicated home territory had evaporated. He quit and went home, certainly a sadder and quite probably a much wiser man.

Supervisors have a particular dilemma. They need to be liked, but they also need to make unpopular decisions. There is an old Navy saw that a good ship needs a popular skipper and an executive officer who is a martinet—or a skipper who is a martinet and a popular executive officer. The point, of course, is that workers like to rally 'round a popular leader but organizations must have the power to say no. When an election has thrown out one party and brought to power the other party, whose representatives have made numerous promises in seeking to be popular, the most pressing need is for a mechanism that can make unpopular decisions. The leadership, to shield itself from this onerous task, sets up a cumbersome structure of committees and departments to carry the unwelcome load. Once in a great while a truly talented leader emerges with the courage to say no when needed, with surgical simplicity—and everyone is surprised at how easy it looks. It is *not* easy to make unpopular decisions, but it is necessary. A good manager must learn not to avoid the duty.

saying no

Almost everyone in a complex organization has more than one boss.

Systems Analysis

Because organizations are so complex, techniques have grown up to deal with complexity and make it more understandable. One such technique, known as *systems analysis,* first divides a complex mechanism into its component parts so that each component may be understood, and then fits the components into a complex whole in a way that explains how they interact with each other. A symphony orchestra seems an impossibly complicated mechanism from which to extract stirring music, and so it would be if the conductor just called together a group of assorted musicians, handed out instruments, and told them to start playing. The composer is the systems analyst, who knows the capabilities of strings, brass, woodwinds, percussion, and so on—and moreover, understands the theory behind the harmonies these various instruments can produce. An automotive assembly line is vastly complex, with all sorts of subordinate lines feeding in parts and subassemblies, and with the work of a hundred specialties beautifully balanced so that the line flows smoothly from start to finished product. Such a line doesn't just happen; it is the result of painstaking study of the various systems and their interactions, by industrial engineers who have learned their skills over the years as Detroit grew from its handcraft machine shops to the mechanized and automated marvel it is today.

systems analysis

DESIGN AND DEVELOPMENT OF ORGANIZATIONS

As complex as an assembly line is, people-systems are far more complex. Even on the assembly line, the auto makers have learned that efficiency isn't enough—the workers have to like what they do, and often an industrial process that seems efficient on paper fails miserably if the workers find the monotony deadening and respond by absenteeism and excessive errors. A modern organization can benefit from a systematic effort to understand its component parts and how they mesh, but people must be considered along with engineering, finance, and marketing. The behavioral scientist must join forces with the management scientist if this complex art, now in its infancy, is to live up to its promise.

Organizational Development and Growth

Patterns of Growth

growth

Growth is essential for a new organization if it is not to stagnate or die. And organizational change is a necessary corollary to growth. What works for a small organization cannot work for a larger one, primarily because people do not grow as fast as responsibilities do. The chief executive of a large firm may be twice as effective as the chief executive of a small firm, but the tasks to be carried out are a hundred times as demanding. Thus, the executive needs an entirely different type of help from subordinates. Aside from the matter of size, a complete change in priorities may be involved. Think back on the history of the Ford Motor Company. Henry Ford was first of all a gifted "tinkerer" or mechanical designer, and his early cars were built in the machine shops of the Dodge brothers. Later on, as the business grew, the problem-solving focus moved from design and mechanical areas to manufacturing—how to produce economically at high volumes. Henry Ford weathered that shift well; indeed, he became the mass production genius of the age. But with further growth (and tough competition from Chevrolet) the problem shifted to one of marketing, and Henry Ford proved markedly insensitive to the changing needs of that era.[8] World War II production requirements gave the company both a breathing spell and a new infusion of capital, but it took a change of management and several years of tough sledding before Ford regained its competitive strength.

Service Specialization

When a one-person organization starts to grow, the jobs to be done rapidly outstrip the ability of the sole owner to handle everything personally. The usual reaction to this pleasant dilemma is to hire an assistant on whom the owner can dump the routine tasks while continuing to concentrate on the complex ones. A storekeeper will hire someone to make deliveries, with additional duties in handling stock, cleaning up, and doing odd jobs. The proprietor then has time for the more demanding tasks of ordering and arranging stock, keeping the books, and satisfying customers. With continued growth a clerk or two may be hired, but the vital tasks remain the owner's responsibility.

service expansion

As the business continues to grow, the owner will find other special tasks for subordinates—bookkeeping, inventory control, ordering stock, perhaps even writing advertising copy—but will retain the management functions as long as possible.

If the entrepreneur opens a second store in another part of town, in all probability purchasing, bookkeeping, advertising, and other service functions for both stores will be handled in one place, to get the advantages of "centralized" service. There is no reason to duplicate the same function in two places when it can be done more economically in one. But if the business keeps on growing, perhaps opening a large store in another city, the time may come when the owner will give in to the demands of growth and let the distant branch handle its own ordering, bookkeeping, and so on.

Assuming the successful expansion continues, eventually the proprietor will own so many stores that it will be profitable to install a centralized bookkeeping headquarters and put the bookkeeper of each branch under the technical control of this central unit. By this time the service organization for bookkeeping has expanded to the point that its head is the Manager of Accounting Services; also, other service supervisors may be located at headquarters to serve the needs of the branch stores.

How does this apply to North Star's overseas operation?

Functional Expansion

Now let the organization really begin to grow, and the original proprietor will have to let go of many managerial tasks as well as service chores. (If the business is as successful as described above, this stage will actually occur much earlier.) Since it is hard to give up control of what seem the most vital operations, the owner will try to hold off, but eventually some functions must be delegated or the enterprise will bog down in delay and indecision. So a principal function, such as sales, will be separated; then purchasing, then finance, until a completely functional organization is created and the days of the owner dealing directly with the branch managers are over. Note that to this point the assistants have been in the area of *service,* but now *line management* is being shared with subordinate executives.

functional expansion

These phases are illustrated in Figure 3-8. In section A, the first store has grown to the point where a bookkeeper is hired as well as clerks. In B, the first branch store is opened, but the service function is retained at the main store. At C, additional branch stores are opened and it is necessary for each to have its own bookkeeper, etc. However, continued growth, represented by D, has reached the point where service functions need a centralized head, and an accounting manager is added at headquarters for technical control of all bookkeeping functions in the branches. Finally, at E, expansion reaches the point where the owner must share line management functions, and a wholesale reorganization of the enterprise takes place.

How is North Star's business manager similar to the accounting manager (Figure 3-8)?

Decentralization Expansion

All is well for the time being, and the owner of the enterprise is confident that the operation is well under control with the functional managers at headquarters. Their offices are next door to the proprietor's, who can see them ten times a day if need be. Experts in every functional area have been hired, and efficient service is provided to the branches, avoiding duplication and reaping the benefits of a sort of mass production of service and management. All is not equally well from the branch managers' viewpoints. They see a bureaucracy at headquarters, keeping the chief happy but not always responsive to branch store needs. They object to having all their purchases handled by the centralized purchasing office, and they find the centralized marketing office unable to keep up with the special marketing opportunities and needs of a different city. They see local stores, unencumbered by a distant bureaucratic supervision, moving dynamically to compete with them, and they feel handicapped when they try to respond energetically or swiftly.

decentralized expansion

The time is coming, if it has not already, for the functional organization to give way to a territorial organization, where each city (perhaps with three or four branches by now) handles its own affairs as though its group of stores were a small company. Suppose the parent company has expanded even more, going beyond the retail business. If it has a food-packing plant and a grain elevator in a farm community, these probably will be "spun off" as a separate division (or even a separate subsidiary corporation, if they are large enough), and the various service and managerial functions formerly run from headquarters will now be run entirely within the division. The central corporate office will maintain policy and coordination control, but day-to-day operations will be completely decentralized.

Dynamics of Development

dynamics of development

The above idealized growth pattern implies that no problems accompany this growth. As the owner started more and more stores, the move from service specialization to functional expansion to decentralized expansion (probably territorial) took place with never a jolt. That picture is idealized, however. One of the most painful shifts for a company is the change of its organization in the process of successful growth. It is difficult for management to replace the very style that has brought it success with an unproven system that may bring more problems than it solves. Some managements cannot bring themselves to make the shift, and a previously strong company starts running into hard times.

Outgrowing the Founders

A typical horror story in managerial folklore is that of the brilliant but aging founder of a company who is fired by scoundrels who have nefariously seized control of the organization. Horror story it may be, but often because of the horrible position the obsolete executive forced upon the organization before the salvagers could wrest the helm away and apply the needed first aid. Managers change (usually through age) and organizations change; it is not surprising that a growing organization can outgrow its earlier management.

When the retail chain described in the preceding section began to grow, it probably met its needs for growth capital by finding investors who thus became part owners in the firm. While they no doubt had confidence in the founder initially (or the investment would not have looked promising to them), their enthusiasm may have diminished if expansion problems were handled poorly. Perhaps the owner waited too long to give the branch managers any initiative, or tried to make all decisions

Figure 3-8.
Five Phases of Organizational Growth

A

- BOSS
  - Clerks
  - Bookkeeper
  - Helpers

B

- BOSS
  - Bookkeeper
  - Main Store
  - Branch Store

C

- BOSS
  - Branch Store
    - Bookkeeper
  - Main Store
    - Bookkeeper
  - Branch Store
    - Bookkeeper

D

- BOSS
  - Accounting Manager
  - Branch Store
  - Branch Store
  - Main Store
  - Branch Store
  - Branch Store

E

- BOSS
  - Vice-President Marketing
  - Vice-President Branches
    - Branch
    - Branch
    - Branch
    - Branch
  - Vice-President Purchasing
  - Vice-President Finance

DESIGN AND DEVELOPMENT OF ORGANIZATIONS

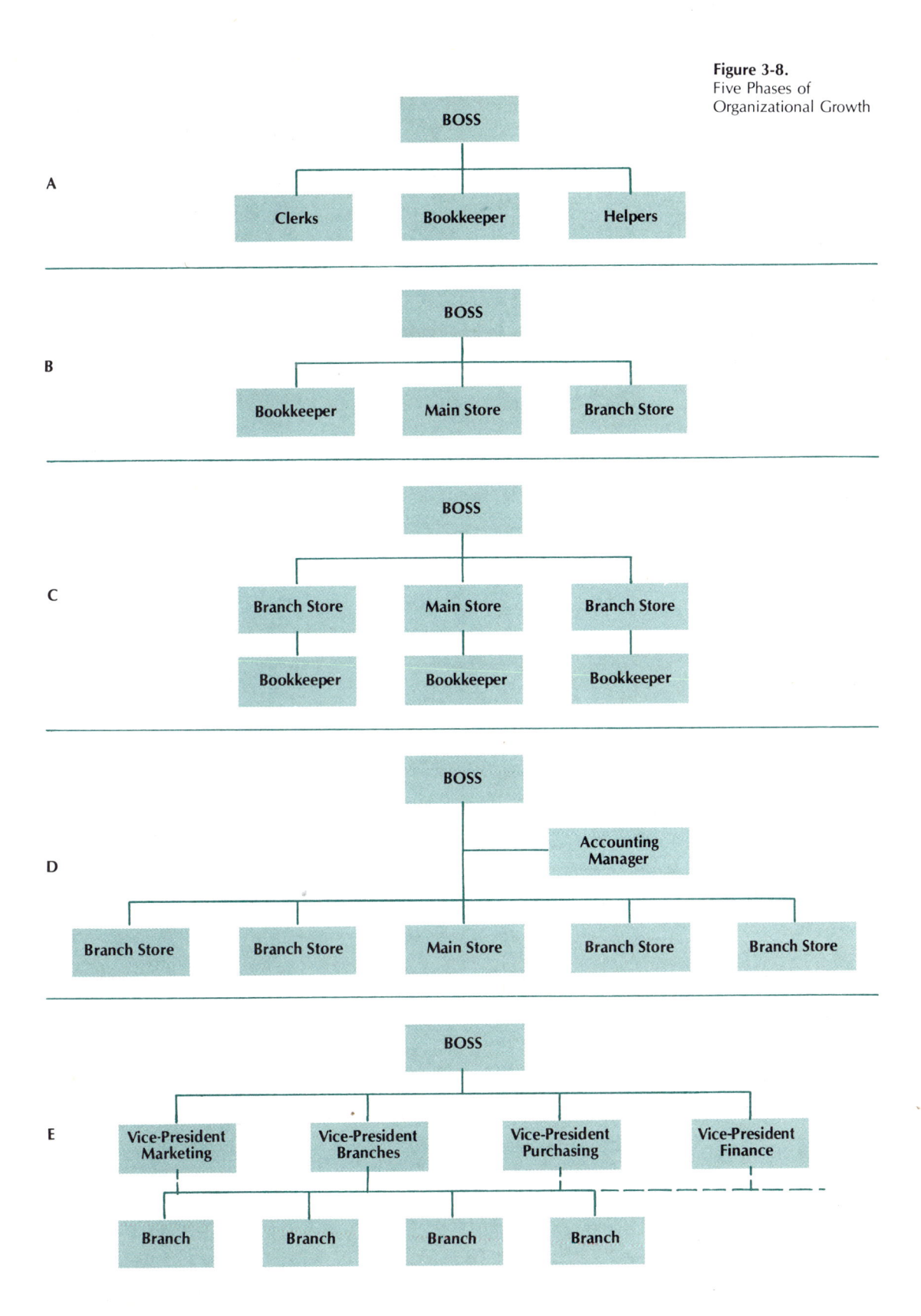

personally. It is not at all unusual for senior executives to be fired or shifted when a company is doing poorly, but it can also happen when a company is growing.

<aside>Who would do this in North Star if Henry were incompetent?</aside>

The best course of action is to face matters openly with the overtaxed executive[9] and try to ease the load by providing help or transferring some duties elsewhere. If this approach does not work, perhaps the original chief executive may be willing to move to an honorary post of "chairperson," free to supply advice but relieved of the pressure of daily decisions. But if these methods do not work, or if the executive refuses to face the situation and insists on staying put, there is probably no alternative to a graceful retirement.

It need not be the chief executive who becomes obsolete. Quite often the whole executive team is out of date, and strong leadership must be brought in. Wholesale removals of executives take place when a company is acquired by another company, and the latter believes that a new team would do better with the expanding operation. This procedure is by no means customary, but it happens frequently enough to suggest that new owners often believe the old management team is not capable of handling the new environment brought about by growth.

Before managerial shifts of this sort are made, there must be a careful analysis of where the organization is going and what management skills it needs. The difference between the organization as it has been and as you want it to be must be made clear. Simply discarding experienced managers is not only uncharitable, it is wasteful. The people who have faithfully brought the organization to its present point have many valuable characteristics, and the most effective approach is to analyze their skills and the organization's needs so that the two can be matched with overall benefit.

Timing of Change

<aside>timing of change</aside>

When change appears called for, there are two general approaches: (1) the "new broom" or drastic change, and (2) the gradual or evolutionary change. And there are two corresponding durations for change: (1) short-range (including temporary) change, and (2) long-range or fundamental change.

When an organization is seriously ailing, and it is obvious that many in the organization know it, there is merit in making the entire change with almost surgical speed. While some wrong decisions may be made along with the right ones (because of insufficient time for study), and a certain degree of employee shock is inevitable, at least the painful action will be over with all at once, avoiding the worry of waiting for the axe to fall. If a new manager is brought in, and things need to be modified (but not drastically), it is extremely wise for the manager to wait several months before accomplishing any organizational shifts. For one thing, the organization will not believe that the proper action can be determined without an understanding of the environment, and the manager will lose their respect. For another thing, they are right: it is essential to consult with subordinates so they will know the new boss wants two-way communication, and so their counsel will be available in a complex situation. This is not to say that the manager should wait when the proper action is obvious to almost everyone—but usually it is not.

THE BUILDING BLOCKS OF MANAGEMENT

When an organization is seriously ailing, there is merit in making the indicated changes with almost surgical speed.

Short-range changes are corrective in nature, whereas long-range changes are curative. The former involve meeting particular problems by modifying procedures or by temporary personnel changes. They may require consulting with other departments and obtaining agreement for waiving rules or changing standards. If such a change is made to get a rush job done early, perhaps by varying regular scheduling, the benefits must be weighed carefully against the price you pay for such variances. Are all rush jobs going to require such changes hereafter? If so, maybe some more fundamental change is required, or your regular procedure will end up in a shambles. If fundamental problems related to growth or change are handled mostly by short-range changes, the real disease may not be treated at all.

Long-range changes involve (usually) making organizational changes. If short-term problems recur repeatedly, a long-range modification is indicated. If superiors must depart from their regular duties and "put out fires" frequently, this is a warning signal that the organization does not have the right "fire-fighting" organization. Long-term changes need not be instituted quickly or all at once; there are advantages to making the change in phases, so the effectiveness of a new organization can be assessed during the process.

A good manager is almost constantly involved in effecting long-range change, because a people-system is an evolving mechanism. Old ways tend to become careless ways, people who are not inspired and pushed tend to accept less than their best, and customers establish undesirable relationships that work to the disadvantage of the organization. And, of course, the outside environment is changing—technology, social customs, environmental standards, markets. An organization that accepts the status quo too comfortably is starting to die.

Describing Organizations

It is not enough for an organization to be given the proper structure and staffed with the right people. The members of the organization need to understand how the organization is intended to work. This process can involve organization charts, manuals of operation, standing instructions, current orders, and position descriptions.

Organization Charts

organization charts

The five different charts shown in Figure 3-8 tell five different stories of how the company is supposed to operate. Chart A is crystal clear: every individual in the company works for the boss in everything he or she does. Chart C is equally clear: the store managers work totally for the boss, and the bookkeepers work totally for the store managers. Chart D leaves some questions unanswered: is the accounting manager only a staff assistant to the boss, or does the job include some supervision over the branch store managers—or does it include technical review over branch store bookkeepers but no authority over the managers? Chart E suggests with its solid lines that the vice-president for branches has direct line management over each branch, and with its dotted lines that the other vice-presidents have technical control or staff guidance over their respective functions in the branches.

This is useful information, which illustrates the organizational structure in general terms. But it leaves us in doubt as to the details. Can a branch manager fire the purchasing staff, or does that group report for hiring and firing to the vice-president of purchasing? Can a branch manager go against the purchasing "advice" of the latter? Can the vice-president for branches override technical advice from the other vice-presidents? And so on.[10]

Manuals of Operation

operations manuals

These questions require more detailed definition of relationships than is possible in a chart (even such an elaborate chart as that in Figure 3-9). A company of any size requires a written description of relationships, usually called a manual of operations or organization manual. This document attempts to define all the authority and responsibility relationships of the key individuals in the organization structure. A manual of operations is a permanent company document, changed only when responsibilities change or the structure is modified. When the boss decided to centralize bookkeeping control, as in Chart D, the manual of operations would have to explain just what the responsibilities of the new accounting manager would be and exactly how that officer could deal with the bookkeepers in each branch.

Position Descriptions

The manual describes how people relate to one another. Position descriptions set forth the responsibilities and duties that accompany specific jobs. The position description for accounting manager would explain what that officer is expected to know, what work he or she performs, and what goals must be met. It overlaps the manual of operations in that it states who works for whom, but these relationships are not set forth in as much detail as in the former; they are not intended to establish authority interrelations as much as to define the level of responsibility and hence the job complexity. Position descriptions are used to establish the difficulty of a job and hence the salary range; they are also used to evaluate job applicants for suitability.

Other Documents

A great many more systems of orders and instructions are used to manage organizations, but most of these deal with how the organization *works*. The three just cited are of more interest to us here, since they deal with how the organization is structured.

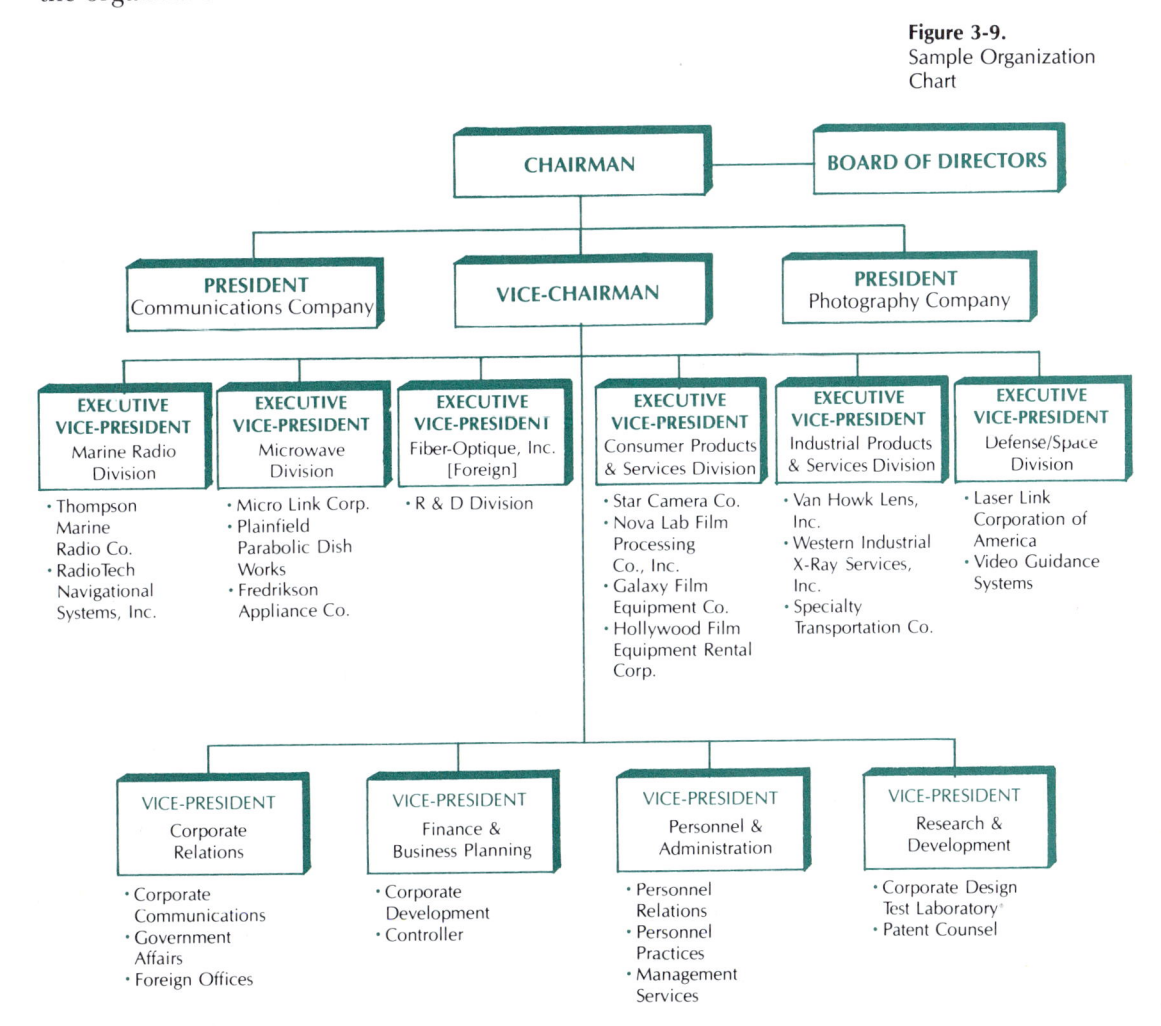

Figure 3-9. Sample Organization Chart

```
                              CHAIRMAN ─── BOARD OF DIRECTORS
         ┌───────────────────────┼───────────────────────┐
    PRESIDENT              VICE-CHAIRMAN              PRESIDENT
Communications Company                            Photography Company
```

EXECUTIVE VICE-PRESIDENT Marine Radio Division	EXECUTIVE VICE-PRESIDENT Microwave Division	EXECUTIVE VICE-PRESIDENT Fiber-Optique, Inc. [Foreign]	EXECUTIVE VICE-PRESIDENT Consumer Products & Services Division	EXECUTIVE VICE-PRESIDENT Industrial Products & Services Division	EXECUTIVE VICE-PRESIDENT Defense/Space Division
• Thompson Marine Radio Co. • RadioTech Navigational Systems, Inc.	• Micro Link Corp. • Plainfield Parabolic Dish Works • Fredrikson Appliance Co.	• R & D Division	• Star Camera Co. • Nova Lab Film Processing Co., Inc. • Galaxy Film Equipment Co. • Hollywood Film Equipment Rental Corp.	• Van Howk Lens, Inc. • Western Industrial X-Ray Services, Inc. • Specialty Transportation Co.	• Laser Link Corporation of America • Video Guidance Systems

VICE-PRESIDENT Corporate Relations	VICE-PRESIDENT Finance & Business Planning	VICE-PRESIDENT Personnel & Administration	VICE-PRESIDENT Research & Development
• Corporate Communications • Government Affairs • Foreign Offices	• Corporate Development • Controller	• Personnel Relations • Personnel Practices • Management Services	• Corporate Design Test Laboratory • Patent Counsel

DESIGN AND DEVELOPMENT OF ORGANIZATIONS

Summary

The fundamental rules for organizing are: there should be a clear objective, work functions should be specialized, there must be means for coordination, there must be well-understood chains of authority, and responsibility must be accompanied by the necessary authority.

Activities may be grouped in an organization by management line and/or staff patterns or by type of product, process, or market. Organizational structure and objectives help determine the appropriate degree of decentralization. If authority is either too centralized or too decentralized, the organization will suffer.

A key concept in designing organizations is the span of control of a manager—how many subordinates are supervised directly. While this depends on the diversity of subordinate tasks, it is unlikely that a supervisor can handle more than ten or twelve subordinates well. In addition to the individuals in the direct chain of command up and down, any manager encounters a complex assortment of interconnecting lines of information, authority, and action with people outside the direct chain but vitally important to the performance of the job.

A wide variety of management styles may be utilized—formalism, participation, human relations, centralization, decentralization—depending principally on the environment and social structure of the organization. It is not feasible to establish a managerial style without regard to the organization's tasks and environment.

Regardless of the type of organization, no superior can manage for long without at least the implied consent of subordinates. Before a subordinate will accept an order, he or she must understand it, believe it fits the organization's purpose, believe it is in his or her personal interest, and be capable of carrying it out.

A modern organization is highly complex. It is rare for an individual to have only one boss; frequently many people have some control over different aspects of one person's work. The complexity of organizations makes it essential to view them as integrated systems, so that actions in one part of the organization can be understood in terms of their secondary effects in other parts.

When an organization grows, it characteristically changes its structure. A very small organization has a vertical structure, with everyone subject to the direction of a single superior. As it grows, various functions formerly performed by the single superior are split off, and management is thus divided into these functions. With continued growth, the enterprise is likely to be split into territorial or divisional units, each of which is nearly as complete as a single independent organization. When managers fail to grow with the organization, they must be reassigned or replaced.

Devices used to describe organizations include organization charts, manuals of operation, standing instructions, and position descriptions.

Notes

1. H. H. Gerth and C. W. Mills, *From Max Weber: Essays in Sociology* (New York: Oxford University Press, 1958), pp. 196-98.
2. Henri Fayol, *General and Industrial Management,* trans. Constance Starrs (London: Sir Isaac Pitman & Sons, 1940).

3. *My Years with General Motors* (Garden City, N.Y.: Doubleday & Co., Inc., 1964).

4. Cited in E. Peterson and E. G. Plowman, *Business Organization and Management*, 3d ed. (Homewood, Ill.: Richard D. Irwin, Inc., 1953), p. 117.

5. The formula used to calculate these figures is $\left[\sum_{n=0}^{s} C(s,n) \right] \times 2$, where "s" = number of coordinates. Thus, for a manager with a group of five subordinates the computation would be: $(2^5 - 1) \times 2 = 62$. Some analysts compute even more, seeing a difference between A with B and B with A (perhaps one is in charge of a joint undertaking). V. A. Graicunas, in a French management treatise published in 1933, calculates direct, cross, and direct-group relationships which would total 100 for a manager with five subordinates.

6. One reason for this, of course, is that the U.S. began as separate states which joined together reluctantly, and only after erecting safeguards to see that "states' rights" would be protected from a powerful central government attempting to act as a monarchy.

7. Chester I. Barnard, *The Functions of the Executive* (Cambridge, Mass.: Harvard University Press, 1938), p. 165.

8. His famous slogan that the customers could have any color car they desired as long as it was black, which enabled him to attain great initial economies of standardization, later proved a great handicap when the customers no longer were satisfied with black.

9. See "The Science of Telling Executives How They're Doing," *Fortune*, January 1974, p. 102.

10. Additionally, of course, the organization chart shows what management thinks or hopes the relationships will be. As this book explains later, there are informal relationships not shown on the chart that round out the relationships.

Review Questions

1. What are the objections to a large span of control? Under what circumstances is it satisfactory to supervise more people than would be acceptable in the typical organization?
2. What are the advantages and disadvantages of participatory management?
3. What managerial element might make an employee perform a personally distasteful act for the organization? What is the potential harm in this situation?
4. What conditions must be present before a subordinate carries out an order?
5. Subordinates work for their superiors directly; whom do they work for indirectly? How do you think they are made aware of this situation?
6. Why should work be specialized? When should it not be specialized?
7. Why are clear lines of authority important? Is it always possible to achieve them? Why not?
8. Why is it difficult to determine whether a job is "line" or "staff"?
9. What are organization charts for? What are their shortcomings? How are their shortcomings compensated for in describing organization structure?
10. When would it be wise for an organization to be structured by customer? by process?
11. Why is growth likely to bring changes in organizational structure?

Discussion Questions

1. When might the basic guidelines for organizational structure be violated? For example, in what sort of organization might controls be harmful? When might imbalance be desirable?

2. How would you change the functional organization of Figure 3-3 to a pure line organization? Would this improve operations or make them worse? Why?

3. Describe the sort of company, operating in several cities, that should be essentially centralized. What sort of government agency operating in several cities should be essentially centralized? Why?

4. How might a participatory organization include checks and balances? Could this also be a decentralized organization?

5. How could the chief executive insure that an order would be obeyed in a case where other officers clearly intended to violate it "for the good of the organization"? Discuss in terms of Barnard's four conditions.

6. In Figure 3-4, when the organization changes from functional (Chart E) to divisional, what will happen to the vice-presidents? Will they oppose the shift? How might they we won over?

North Star Case Study

Suppose that, instead of having a single overseas job and a small volume of consulting engineering work at home, North Star Associates was bought by an Arab financial group which not only invested heavily in the company but obtained engineering design jobs for it in eight locations in the Arab countries, with a promise of more to come. The Arab group is not interested in managing North Star, but clearly will be impatient with poor financial performance. Thus Dick Boyer suddenly becomes "project director" over nine important projects, all involving major design work at the home office, and employing 800 men, which force will expand rapidly to nearly 2,000 on overseas assignment alone.

Moreover, it is clear that the Arab owners expect that the company will expand equally in the U.S., and intend to provide the necessary investment capital to make that possible.

1. What changes do you envision in the North Star organization chart shown in Figure 3-4?
2. What are the implications of the increased "span of control" for Dick Boyer?
3. What steps will the company have to take to give the new employees who are coming on board so rapidly a sense of participation?
4. What management style would be most suitable for the overseas project sites? Why?
5. What can Henry do, from headquarters, to satisfy the four management requirements of authority, responsibility, loyalty, and communication when such a major part of his organization is thousands of miles away?
6. If the decision is made to break up the project director concept (which, after all, was established at a time when it was thought there would be only one project under Dick Boyer), how can this be done without making Dick think he is being demoted? What should his new job be?

Suggestions for Further Reading

Argyris, C. *Organization and Motivation.* Homewood, Ill.: Richard D. Irwin, Inc., 1965.

Barnard, C. I. *Organization and Management: Selected Papers.* Cambridge, Mass.: Harvard University Press, 1948.

Bennis, W. G. *Organizational Development: Its Nature, Origins, and Prospects.* Reading, Mass.: Addison-Wesley Pub. Co., Inc., 1969.

Blau, P. M. *The Structure of Organizations.* New York: Basic Books, Inc., Pubs., 1971.

Etzioni, A. *Modern Organizations.* Englewood Cliffs, N.J.: Prentice-Hall, Inc, 1964.

———, ed. *A Sociological Reader on Complex Organizations.* New York: Holt, Rinehart & Winston, Inc., 1969.

Franklin, J. L. *Organizational Development: An Annotated Bibliography.* Ann Arbor, Mich.: University of Michigan Institute for Social Research, 1973.

Golembiewski, R., et al., eds. *Public Administration, Institutions, and Processes.* Chicago: Rand McNally & Co., 1973.

Gulick, L. H., and L. Urwick, eds. *Papers on the Science of Administration.* Clifton, N. J.: Augustus M. Kelley, Pubs., 1969.

Henry, N. *Public Administration and Public Affairs.* Englewood Cliffs, N.J.: Prentice-Hall, Inc., 1975.

Hicks, H. G. *Management, Organizations, and Human Resources.* New York: McGraw-Hill Book Co., 1972.

March, J. G. *Handbook of Organizations.* Chicago: Rand McNally & Co., 1965.

———, and H. A. Simon. *Organizations.* New York: John Wiley & Sons, Inc., 1965.

Scott, W. G. *Organization Theory: A Structural and Behavioral Analysis.* Homewood, Ill.: Richard D. Irwin, Inc., 1972.

Steiglitz, H., and C. D. Wilkerson. *Corporate Organization Structures.* New York: National Industrial Conference Board, Inc., 1968.

Tausky, C. *Work Organizations: Major Theoretical Perspectives.* Itasca, Ill.: F. T. Peacock Pubs., Inc., 1970.

Thompson, J. D., ed. *Approaches to Organizational Design.* Pittsburgh, Pa.: University of Pittsburgh Press, 1966.

Williamson, O. E. *Corporate Control and Business Behavior.* Englewood Cliffs, N.J.: Prentice-Hall, Inc., 1970.

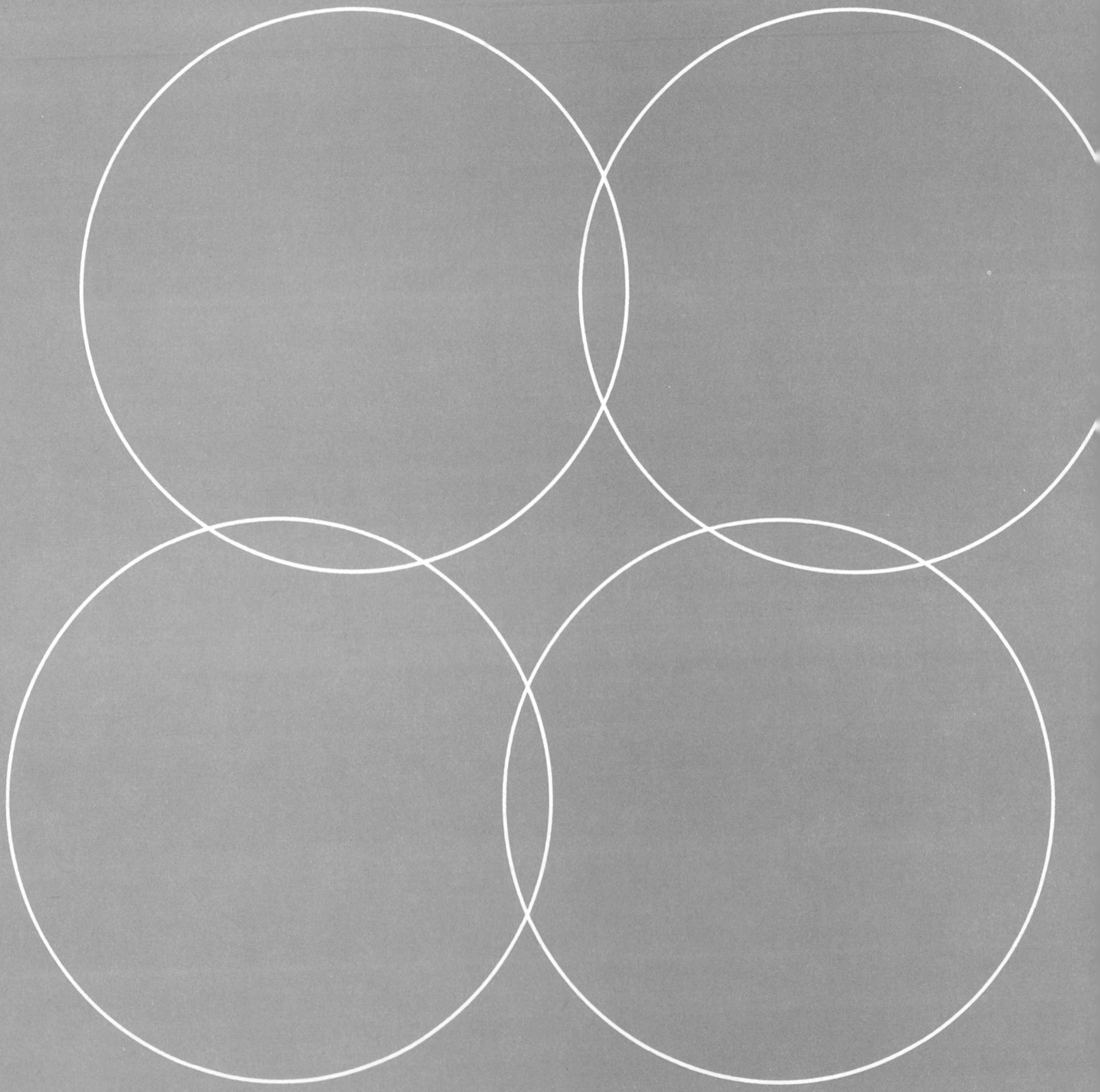

PART TWO

Management Processes

Leadership

North Star Prologue

Henry North, returned from the Navy and graduated from engineering school, started in as a consultant to a municipality—a post obtained with the help of his faculty advisor. Finding a one-man shop quite limited, he joined in partnership with Bert Starr, who was in similar circumstances. Even two partners left the company too small to undertake many potential jobs, so they enlarged the company to four. When they took on their first significant contract, they discovered substantial differences of viewpoint as to how they should proceed and what they ought to emphasize and began to see the need for some organizational structure. They were inclined to underrate the importance of how they were organized, and indeed Henry was given the job of president almost by default—because everyone else seemed to fit in with another job. Nonetheless, they did get an organization set up, and began functioning under it.

The home office contingent soon established basic working relationships among themselves, with Dick gone full time and Jo returning to the States about once a month to bring design information and keep in touch with her old haunts. Bert had to sign all the plans, as technical director and moreover the only registered engineer in the home office, so gradually he began to assume all responsibility for the Natal project. Henry, with Blackridge work occupying only a small part of his time, and with Bert doing most of the supervision of the eight engineers and semiprofessional people now on board for the Natal job, found himself cast in the role of prospector for new work. It didn't really suit him, and he found himself reluctant to press clients to buy North Star Associates and their service.

He spoke to Zeb about his distaste for the chore and lack of success at it, and the latter suggested that he accompany Henry on the next foray. It happened to be a visit to a large forge shop, proposing a noise analysis and reduction study; Henry had made his technical presentation and the plant engineer was thanking him and saying he'd be in touch, when Zeb broke in to request that a purchase order be issued on the spot. He asked if there was any more information the plant engineer needed, pointed out that they could start in the morning if authorized right away, and argued that prompt correction of conditions might just prevent a disability suit or two in addition to improving production. The plant engineer agreed with Zeb that time was indeed money, and Henry was amazed to see what to him seemed a crude and overly importuning approach succeed so completely.

As they walked out with the purchase order in their pockets, Zeb told Henry that the two of them might make a pretty good team—Henry to carry the technical load (the "brains," as he called it) and Zeb to do the closing when it was clear that further technical discussion would be useless. Henry agreed with alacrity, coupled with a good deal of admiration, and from then on the two of them went as a pair on all marketing excursions. This approach was quite successful, and within a year after Zeb had joined the firm he was able to inform Henry that home office billings on local jobs were starting to exceed those on the Natal project. When the overseas billings were added in, Natal still provided the majority of North Star's volume, but the other work was picking up comfortably, in a way neither Bert nor Henry would have predicted a year earlier.

North Star was bursting at the seams for space. When the AID job first started, Henry took the office adjacent to his in Blackridge, and later they were able to get the upstairs loft over both offices, but the crowding was both unpleasant and unproductive. Henry convened Bert, Zeb, and Jo (who happened to be in the city) for a conference on what to do. Bert was all for taking space in the newly completed Engineers' Building, which was modern, stylish, and "where the action is." Jo had no real objection to that, but preferred space adjacent to the university, convenient to the library and the computer center; when told that the university area was short of space, and as a result had the highest rates and worst accommodations in the city, she did not press the point. Zeb favored neither location; he said all they needed was comfortable and adequate space, and reminded them that clients virtually never visited their offices. As to being "where the action is" with the rest of the engineering firms, he observed that other engineers were not usually their clients. Bert did not agree that the Engineers' Building offered no advantages, and Henry could see that he seemed to resent Zeb's taking a strong position. There was more than a trace of professional snobbery in the way Bert phrased his argument, almost as though he felt that a nonengineer shouldn't be consulted on a topic dealing with the firm's professional status.

All three of them looked at Henry for his opinion: Bert looking tense and with his face unnaturally red, Zeb with an unexpectedly firm jut to his jaw, and Jo quietly amused at the argument. It struck Henry that the argument had escalated into a battle of principles, with Bert wanting a prestige location and convinced that a nonengineer just didn't appreciate why this was important, and with Zeb ready to fight for the idea that the business manager should be involved in any decision involving a substantial recurring expense. Some instinct told Henry that there was no way he could avoid seriously offending Bert or Zeb if he took sides at that point, so he said he'd like to think about it.

After the meeting he talked separately with each of the two adversaries, asking them to outline their positions in more detail. Zeb's boiled down to two points: first, it would be foolish to spend a dime more for rent than they had to; second, the issue was primarily a business matter, which he had the experience to take care of. Bert also made two points: first, if they didn't "hang out their shingle" in proper surroundings they would project the image of a two-bit outfit; and second, location was more than just a question of buying the most economical carbon paper or typewriter ribbon, so the "office manager" ought to keep out of the discussion.

Henry was tempted to tell them both to act their age, but again he held his tongue. He recalled hearing of new office space available in an industrial park the county was building to entice new industry into the area, and a check with the director indicated that North Star would qualify as a new professional company. He went out to look, and was shown a small building with office space in front and the balance of the building unfinished, designed for a company doing light manufacturing. The front was well landscaped, as was the surrounding area, and the whole impression was one of modernity and professionalism. The director told him that North Star would qualify for a 90% loan at 2% interest under the state's science and engineering program, which would produce a very low equivalent rent—and North Star would own its building. Henry saw an opportunity to resolve his dilemma. He could promote this site to Bert on the basis that the location was professional, the building itself externally impressive, and the option of a "North Star Building" address available to them. As to the uncompleted interior, they could use it at present without modification, since clients would never see it, and they could complete the floor plan to the precise specifications to suit their needs at a later date. He could sell Zeb on the basis that the rent was as low as they would get anywhere and the interior could remain unfinished until they were well able to finish it.

And so it worked out. Bert went out to pass on the building from the standpoint of appearance and location, while Zeb stayed home and enjoyed the fact of the low cost. When Bert returned with his approval, Henry breathed a sigh of relief. It was not until later that he realized that the others were actually treating him as the president, in that they were looking to him to ratify the final decision. He pondered the fact that his authority had flowed from the fact that he had leaned over backwards to avoid the appearance of exercising any authority. It struck him that perhaps the best way to get compliance with a necessary decision was to give everyone a piece of the action, so that the decision when finally taken would appear the result of circumstances rather than the conscious choice of a boss. He wondered why this useful notion, so at variance with the traditional idea of the decisive manager, had never been presented in any of his university classes.

What North Star Can Learn from Chapter 4

1. The realization that good leaders pay close attention to individual needs and aspirations

2. The various ways that leaders acquire formal and informal power

3. The different styles of leadership, depending on the leader's characteristics, the situation, and the characteristics of those led

4. How the previous point might apply when Henry attempts to lead someone like Dick Boyer, formerly his Navy supervisor

5. How leadership is developed (though the partners are likely to think this a bit premature at the company's present stage)

6. How leadership patterns are changing today, and the impact this might have on their present and near-future leadership problems

This chapter describes the element of management that makes it possible for managers to harness the talents and energies of their subordinates to achieve the goals of the organization. Leadership spells the intangible but vital difference between passable and excellent organizational performance. Since few managers are trained explicitly in leading—and indeed, many managers feel that it is an unimportant skill, or one they possess instinctively—it is perhaps the single most neglected aspect of running an organization.

The chapter is divided into four sections:

1. *The environment and purpose of leadership*—the role of leadership, leading individuals and groups, and sources of power.
2. *Leadership in action*—leadership styles, the process of matching the style with the environment, and characteristics of proven leaders.
3. *Developing leadership*—self-development and formal approaches to leadership training of both supervisors and managers.
4. *Changing patterns in leadership*—emerging problems at both blue-collar and managerial levels and the actions organizations are taking to cope with them.

At first, the idea of consciously trying to influence employee behavior may seem distasteful and even unprincipled. On the contrary, however, true leadership is inspirational, and members of an organization pulling together in productive achievement are fulfilled in their work. The exhilaration you have seen in a well-coached winning team, or the heady enthusiasm you may have experienced in the cast and crew of a well-directed school play, have their counterpart in the solid satisfaction exhibited by the members of a well-led organization doing any worthwhile task successfully. Leadership is the means by which this organizational environment is achieved; the tragedy is that leadership, unlike bookkeeping or dancing or stunt flying, is rarely taught. Managers are generally left to learn it for themselves, and all too often they never do.

The Environment and Purpose of Leadership

The environment of an organization involves many complex interactions, and the success of a manager depends on the ability to deal effectively with these, singly and as a whole. For example, each employee must be viewed as two different people: an *individual,* whose highly personal needs and goals must be guessed at and fulfilled if possible, and a *group member,* whose often perplexing collective behavior presents the supervisor with a complex new dimension. The essence of leadership is coordination of these overlapping demands in a way that will achieve organizational goals.

External and internal elements of the organizational environment play important roles in determining how the goals will be met, and a wise manager must spot short- and long-run changes (or see the need for changes that are overdue), and use this knowledge to build the organization. At any management level, a leader must be sensitive to this environment, and must act in the manner that fits it best.

The Role of Leadership

Organizations accomplish their tasks through people. The leadership of an organization coordinates all of its functions to ensure that its goals will be attained. Henry North did not feel much like a leader when he was tapped for the president's job at North Star, but he was startled to learn that the others were looking to him for direction when he assumed the leader's mantle. (And perhaps a bit unnerved as well; in the words of Shakespeare's King Henry IV, "Uneasy lies the head that wears a crown.") It suddenly became his job to maintain harmony and productivity, and to map future paths for the organization to follow. Perhaps Henry sensed that he had three principal leadership tasks to carry out:

leadership tasks

1. To set priorities and goals for the organization, and to devise procedures to attain these goals
2. To establish a work environment producing a convergence of individual and organizational goals
3. To stimulate employees and inspire good performance in the pursuit of these goals

Good leaders are in short supply at all levels in an organization, although their precise responsibilities vary with their positions. But from chief executive to bench foreman, the primary need is skill in dealing with people. Many management writers define leadership as the art of getting things done through people. John D. Rockefeller, who created the giant Standard Oil Company,[1] commented on the primacy of this element: "I will pay more for the ability to deal with people than any other ability under the sun."

scientific management

In order to deal effectively with people, the manager must put them first, instead of concentrating on the technical aspects of the job at hand. It is *people* who will get the job done. At the beginning of this century, when the scientific management school was born, managers focused on mechanical factors—time and motion studies, assembly lines, division and specialization of labor, and piecework wages—in seeking to raise worker productivity. But human beings refused to respond by rote as machines do, and this approach proved far from the final answer. In some plants, where scientific management was exercised like a fine art, productivity levels seemed to wane, absenteeism increased despite piecework pay, and an unexpected climate of alienation developed before the scientific managers' astonished eyes.

human relations

This failure of scientific management to achieve the millenium stimulated a revised approach that recognized the employee as an *individual*. It seemed abundantly clear that the earlier reward system had major flaws, and some managers decided that consideration of individual needs would be the direction of the future. Such *human relations* writers as Abraham Maslow, Frederick Herzberg, and Douglas McGregor believe the answer lies in the area of employee motivation which develops a feeling of kinship with the organization, more than in seeking increased efficiency through methods manipulation. It seems to be true, as a sort of unexpected dividend, that in the process of attending to human needs the managers find themselves changing, and looking at workers through newly humanized eyes.

The Worker as an Individual

What motivates you to keep reading this book on management? Do you aspire to run an organization one day, and thus feel you must learn the basics? Maybe you don't really know your career goals, but simply want to fulfill the class assignment. Perhaps a chance comment by your instructor stimulated you to seek additional information on this topic of leadership. Or perhaps you feel this reading will help extract a good grade. Whatever your reasons, you (unlike the student who dropped the course last week) continue to read on. Something, obviously, is motivating you, or you would have lost enthusiasm and dropped out yourself.

No matter what the task at hand, motivation plays a key role in its successful accomplishment. Motivation can be internal, can be stimulated by the organization, or can be generated by interaction between an internal force and an organizational stimulus. Since leaders get little done on their own, but rather, work through people, they must concentrate on seeing that the task at hand provides enough stimulus to ensure its successful accomplishment. It is useful, in designing tasks, to consider how well each contains its own driving fuel of motivation, just as though you were organizing a hill climb and were insuring that each motorcycle had its own supply of gasoline.

motivation

No less important than the task at hand is the organizational environment, which determines who does what. The leadership of an organization is an important part of this environment; the leader's direction and style play a vital role in influencing employee behavior. The leader's own values, goals, and beliefs are by no means the same as those of the workers; the leader must be aware that this difference in personal goals implies a difference in outlook on organizational goals. Each employee is different, even though they usually interact as a cohesive group. Common needs may impel them to act together on some occasions, like passengers on the same airplane, but their individual goals and aspirations will soon take precedence again, just as the passengers have a wide variety of destinations in mind after the plane lands. These varying needs and aspirations, influenced by numerous environmental factors, determine the attitudes of employees toward their work and the level of effort they put forth.

Determinants of Individual Performance

Walk through a factory or construction site where the pace is not set by an assembly line, and you will notice that some workers get twice as much done as others. The difference in performance may be traced to two factors: individual ability and worker motivation. Both of these factors are products of internal and organizational influences. Obviously the manager wants to hire workers with the greatest innate or learned ability to do the job, but judicious use of training can add markedly to such ability. Similarly, a worker can come to the job already motivated by the need to earn a living, the desire to advance in the field, and so on, but the level of output depends heavily on individual perception of the reward system. Figure 4-1 demonstrates this relationship between environmental and individual factors.

performance determinants

> How does each of these serve as motivator for Henry and Bert?

Three key issues influence a worker's motivation to perform:

1. The intensity of individual persistence in engaging in certain behavior
2. The mechanisms through which motivation is channeled toward the task
3. The mechanisms which sustain motivation over a period of time

Motivational Strength

Motivation has no meaning if it is not related to the needs of those whose attention, loyalty, or performance you are trying to affect. An incentive must be appropriate to the need structure of the person involved, or results will be zero. (Try offering a beautiful new suit to a man dying of thirst on the desert, or tempting with an offer of a free trip to Las Vegas a mother whose son is coming up for trial on a dope charge.) An individual's behavior at any given moment is prompted by his or her strongest need.

> hierarchy of human needs

Abraham Maslow arranges human needs in hierarchical fashion.[2] The most important are *life needs,* followed in descending order by *security, affiliation* (acceptance), *esteem* (recognition), and *self-actualization.* Once a basic need has been satisfied, it is no longer important, and the individual is able to concentrate on fulfilling higher order needs. For example, once basic life needs such as food, shelter, and clothing are provided for, and reasonable job security has been assured through unions, pension plans, etc., salary raises or fringe benefits no longer serve as complete motivators. Rather, the worker will respond more favorably to such incentives as praise (acceptance), promotion (recognition), and other perquisites which symbolize greater status and stature within the organization.

Since every individual is different, employees are forever endeavoring to fulfill different orders of needs. And since people are complex, they do not concentrate on just one need. A pay raise will inspire an employee to strive for further increases that will support an even higher standard of living or will help achieve the status a higher wage represents. Recent studies show, however, that traditional rewards such as money do not

Figure 4-1. Performance Determinants

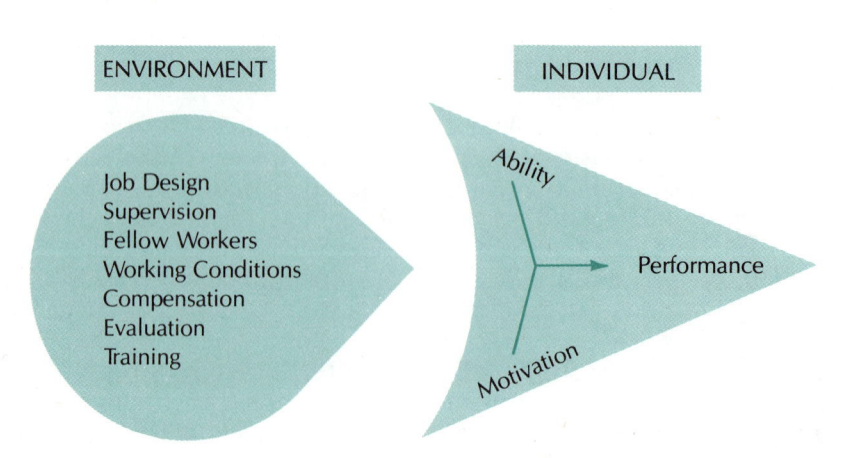

ENVIRONMENT

Job Design
Supervision
Fellow Workers
Working Conditions
Compensation
Evaluation
Training

INDIVIDUAL

Ability
Motivation
Performance

command the same attraction as they did once. Most workers in the U.S. have provided adequately for their physiological and safety needs (and many for their security needs as well), and now seek a higher order of fulfillment.

This trend is confirmed by a study conducted by the Survey Research Center of the University of Michigan.[3] When asked to rank twenty-five work-related needs in order of importance to them, 1533 American workers (from a variety of occupations and job levels) ordered their priorities as follows:

1. Interesting work
2. Enough help and equipment to get the job done
3. Enough information to get the job done
4. Enough authority to get the job done
5. Good pay
6. Opportunities to develop special abilities
7. Job security
8. Seeing the results of one's work

In essence, these results indicate that workers want, first, to enjoy what they do; second, to do their jobs competently; and third, to feel that they and their work are important.

Unfortunately, management has often been slow to recognize the impact of these higher order needs in motivating workers. In an era of increasing worker sophistication, however, managers must seek to provide rewards that correspond to the abovementioned priorities—incentives that really work.

The level of output depends on the perceived reward.

Hygiene Factors as Motivators

In the 1960s, psychologist Frederick Herzberg conducted a series of studies to enhance his knowledge about the nature of motivation in organizations by isolating the applicable factors.[4] He concluded that people have two different categories of needs which are essentially independent of each other and are fulfilled by different rewards. When people are dissatisfied with their jobs, they evince concern about the environment in which they work. Herzberg defined the issues raised in these complaints as "hygiene factors," because they describe the environment as the key to worker dissatisfaction. Hygiene factors include such environmental conditions as wages, security, administration, supervisory policies, and working conditions. Although provision of the appropriate hygiene rewards prevents actual job dissatisfaction, it has little positive motivating effect. When workers are satisfied with their jobs, Herzberg found, the stimulus is the work itself, which involves such benefits as achievement, recognition, increased responsibility, challenging work, and growth and development. Herzberg labeled these factors as "motivators," concluding that increased job productivity results when a worker focuses on job-related rewards.

hygiene factors

Although more recent studies question Herzberg's sharp distinction between hygiene and motivating factors, his contribution is important for contemporary managers. Individuals do have a hierarchy of needs, to which they assign shifting priorities. Managers who concentrate on the bottom (or basic) rung of the ladder fail to recognize that workers want and deserve personal rewards *from* their jobs as well as tangible and material payoffs *for* their jobs.

As we shall see, the structure of rewards within the organization is an important element in sustaining motivation over time. If the individuals do not perceive that their needs are being fulfilled through adequate rewards, their levels of productivity will stagnate and may fall. Psychologists have termed the individual's perception of rewards "expectancy theory." Many management writers contend that these expectations, as well as the priority values which individuals place on the available rewards, are the primary determinants of worker motivation.

expectancy theory

Leading the Group

As we discussed in chapter 2, "Groups at Work," the group is a force to be reckoned with in any organization. It behooves the leader to harness this powerful force as much as possible, in a direction that is positive for both the group and the organization. This is no easy task, for groups are formed for many purposes, and often their goals are quite different from those of the leader or the organization. It is not always simple to locate the informal group's leader or leaders, since different individuals can lead different aspects of the group activities. When group/organization cooperation can be achieved, even in part, it is a most productive and rewarding phenomenon, and a leader who manages to win the respect and confidence of the major groups within a particular sphere of operations is well on the way to a successful performance. Obviously there are many demands on a supervisor's time, and personnel administration is only one of these, but a manager who fails here will fail altogether

informal groups

Think of some area in which Dick would be the group leader for North Star. In which would Jo be?

before long. Groups are the essence of any complex organization, and energy directed toward earning their willing collaboration will have a significant payoff.

Creating a Team Effort

Although most groups are not formed through any management initiative, all effective managers try to influence group behavior to work for the organization. Group behavior is an integral part of the job. People want to be proud of the work they do, and thus of the organization where they work. They want to be needed by the organization, and valuable to it. Recognition by the group partially fulfills this need, and positive affirmation by management of the group's worth reinforces the benefits of such recognition.

Some groups are formed by management, or with close management support, such as sports teams and company unions. Some groups may be quite antagonistic to management, such as informal compacts to restrict work output to some given comfortable level ("no more than five hours work for eight hours pay"). At times, management may even coexist with antagonistic groups, as when the company as a whole is in trouble. In mid-1975, many Pan-American Airlines employees worked without pay until the company obtained government financial help to compensate for losses due to ruinous competition on the North Atlantic air routes. The truce is only temporary, but while it lasts a good deal of supportive work gets done.

When a company team has a winning season, this group triumph spills over into improved organization spirit. The demonstrated cooperative effort on the ball field creates excitement which can translate into improved company achievement, if the manager provides opportunities to channel this potential into the work situation. The organization is a team, too, and it wins or loses its "games." Pride in one's organization is a powerful motivator, and a team that thinks "we make the best damned roller bearings going" has a strong incentive to continue doing so.

One way for a manager to build group morale and pride is to make an extra effort in going to bat for the group. In one such instance, a company foremen's group was in the habit of holding a monthly luncheon with the production manager at a private club of which the latter was a member. When they arrived for one of their luncheons, they were told with no advance notice and with scant courtesy that the club had decided nonmembers could no longer use the facilities and were turned away forthwith. The production manager promptly converted an unused warehouse to a handsomely appointed luncheon room, not only to continue the monthly luncheon but for other affairs the foremen wished to hold, and made it clear to all that he was responding vigorously to the apparent "put-down" of the foremen group. Such actions show the group that the leader takes a personal interest in their welfare, and they respond positively. The group's conviction that the leader will at least try to consider their needs is essential for developing a solid group/organization relationship.

If individual worker efforts are to be channeled for management, some meshing of goals must occur. Figure 4-2 shows in rather simple fashion why goals need not be identical to have more in common than the

Figure 4-2.
Consensus

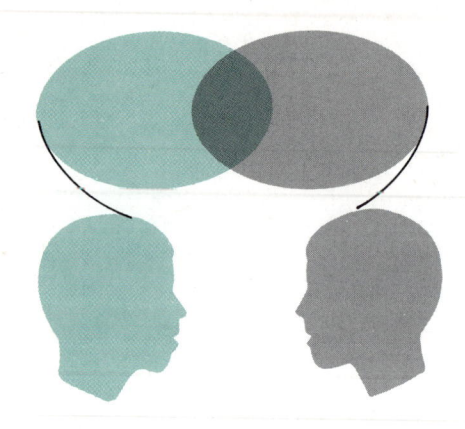

group-organization consensus

single point of doing a job and getting paid. The leader treats the consensus area as a beachhead, a place to establish a landing point, so to speak, which can be broadened through continued supportive relationships.

A striking case of this process—and the source of today's emphasis on group behavior—was the Hawthorne Study in a Western Electric plant near Chicago in the 1930s. It began as a National Research Council investigation of the way lighting affected worker efficiency, but the results were startling. A relay assembly test room team of six women was used to test the effect of lighting (and ultimately other factors such as length of day, number of rest periods, etc.) on output. As conditions were improved, production went up; but as conditions were worsened, production continued to improve regardless. The lighting had to be reduced to conditions approaching bright moonlight before production finally began to turn down. This totally unexpected result was diagnosed as a triumph of group morale over environmental hardships: the six girls were identified as a special group, and their performance reflected their pride and excitement in being singled out.

The Hawthorne experiment showed management theorists and practitioners the great importance of the social organization in a company and the rewards a worker obtains from the personal relationships with the group. It led to several years of additional research at the Hawthorne plant,[5] generally emphasizing the importance of group norms and leadership. A six-month study of fourteen men in the bank wiring room disclosed strong group pressures to restrict output to what the group thought was a "right" day's work, despite the fact that piecework incentive rates meant a reduction in possible earnings. Not only did the work group restrict output, but it was observed to establish the "proper" roles that various workers and even supervisors could play.

The Informal Group Leader

Leadership is not unique to the formal organization. Informal groups working within the organization appoint their own leaders, though the process is not at all clear-cut and may not even be recognized by the actors concerned. A leader may arise in response to a special situation, and either maintain that position after the situation ends or relinquish it to another.

An informal group may have different leaders for different purposes. In a manufacturing plant, a group that forms in a certain work center may have its muscle man who can lick anyone in the outfit, its intelligence expert who manages to tune in the company grapevine better than anyone else, and its work arbiter who sets the pace for job-related matters and tends to do the negotiating with supervisors. Figure 4-3 illustrates the structure of such a group, indicating the shared leadership arrangements. A hierarchy of leadership can exist in each jurisdiction, as shown—and there are group members who exert no leadership of any sort, but just respond to group pressures.

leadership of groups

Sometimes a distraught manager may say, "If only I could get rid of that guy Robertson, everything would be fine." The manager is mistaken. If Robertson goes, Struthers or Harris or someone else will take over. Groups abhor a vacuum just as nature does. If by chance a group should remain leaderless for a time, it will turn lethargic, which is not a plus for the individuals or the organization.

Companies are turning more and more to the conference, the "T-group," management by objectives, and job enrichment programs to shorten the distance between manager and subordinate. It doesn't take a theorist to recognize that when people have a hand in decisions—and therefore, a personal stake in the outcome—performance will improve accordingly. In one case a small branch plant had to shut down for a changeover that had taken 14 days or more at the corporation's other plants. Although this branch was allowed 21 days for the task, because of

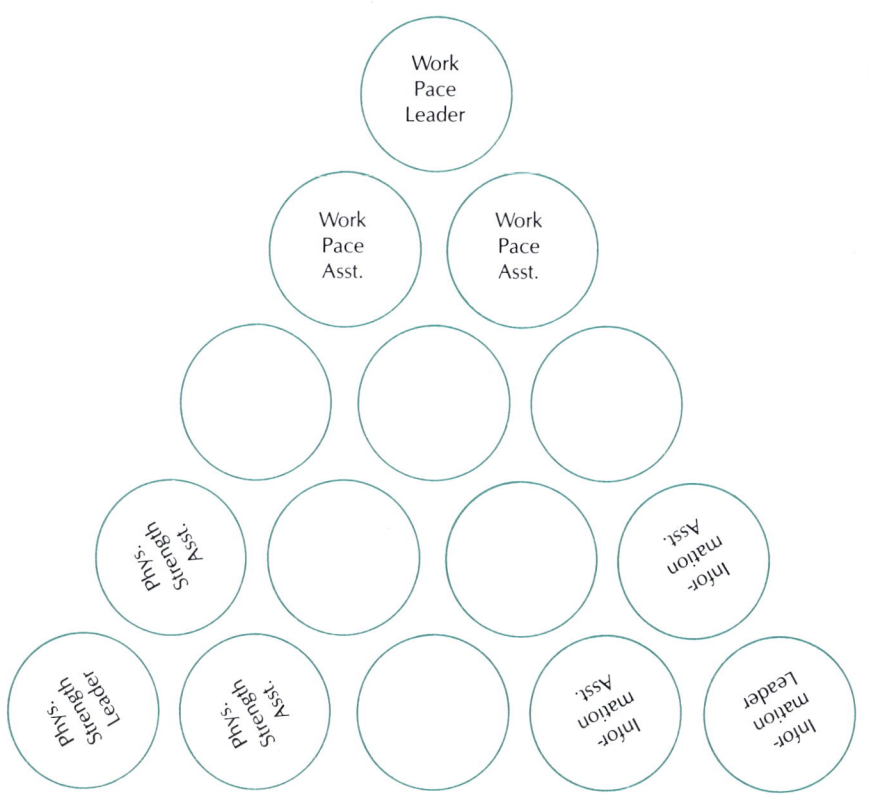

Figure 4-3.
Tripartite Group Leadership

its limited facilities and lack of familiarity with the job, management called the workers together and they jointly set a target date of 10 days—which they bettered by more than a day. There were many worker suggestions about how to save time, people worked through the quit-work whistle, and beating the deadline became a highly desired goal on the part of the entire plant—including office workers, warehouse workers, security guards, and others who had little or nothing to do with the project but wanted to participate anyway.

participation

Participation comes in all shapes and sizes, as we will discuss below. Workers are skilled at sensing whether management is employing human relations techniques for manipulative purposes, without having any real intention of establishing participation or delivering on the implied promises; the results of such manipulation predictably are negative. In a sense, of course, all attempts by one person to influence another can be termed manipulative, but the motive and objectivity behind the manipulation must be assessed in order to determine its validity. Outright exploitation is not only morally wrong but probably bad business as well (because it doesn't often work). But when all parties involved stand to gain through the leadership effort, the motivating process *is* beneficial. Indeed, workers are entitled to have leaders who motivate, just as they are entitled to a good work environment and high-quality equipment.

In some respects this is Henry's situation, as the youngest member in the company. Does any of this apply to his situation?

The new college graduate who reports to a first job and is introduced to a work group—perhaps a group of subordinates—may perceive its members as strange and apparently hostile people who appear to be waiting only for the new boss to make a mistake. But this approach puts the emphasis in the wrong place. A leader should worry, not about gaining the friendship of subordinates, but about what can be done for them. They may have some curiosity about the new supervisor, but their strongest doubts are about themselves: what will his or her arrival mean to them? A real leader will start learning about the needs of the "troops." This group contains a complex mixture of individuals, on the order of Figure 4-3, and each individual has motivators that can be dealt with. Also, the group as a whole has motivators, and the leader must find out what they are. As far as possible, the leader must identify each group that exists and seek to become part of it.

Sources of Power

All great leaders have developed the power to command the respect and dedication of those around them. Winston Churchill, discredited after the ill-starred Gallipoli Campaign of World War I and thrust aside during the 1930s, drove Britain to victory in World War II by inspiring an indomitable spirit of resistance and sacrifice in the entire nation. Eleanor Roosevelt, perhaps the most controversial First Lady in history, was responsible for many major social reforms during three turbulent decades—from the '30s through the '50s. The changes she worked for have touched virtually all Americans, yet she never ran for public office. What enables people like these to harness and wield such power? Is it some mysterious inner spark, an external force, or some happy combination of both that confers this miraculous cloak of legitimacy upon the leader?

Types of Authority

The word *leadership* connotes followers, suggesting that the basis of the leader's position lies in power and authority over those within the organization who must follow or choose to follow. The leader's authority can be created in two ways: as *formal authority*, denoted by position on the organization chart, and *acceptance authority*, which arises from worker acceptance of the leader's preeminence. The importance and impact of these two forces differs according to the organization. In a tightly structured organization such as the military or the Catholic church, position (formal authority) commands far more obedience from subordinates than in a more individualistic organization such as a research laboratory. In the latter case, each scientist works at his or her own pace to get the job done; in effect, individuals drive themselves, and a rigid structure would be both superfluous and counterproductive.

formal authority
acceptance authority

Formal authority is conferred from above, but acceptance authority can be won only by earning the respect of the group. How does a leader earn this respect? Perhaps by demonstrating superior knowledge; soldiers will follow a clearly able patrol leader on very hazardous missions, but there is little future in tagging along after a sergeant who might blunder straight into an ambush. Perhaps the leader has the kind of charisma that inspires the admittedly weaker tug-of-war team to rise above its puny muscles and take first place at the Fourth of July picnic. Perhaps the leader always stands behind the group in a pinch, ready to take the blame when things go wrong and to give them the credit when things go well. Or perhaps the leader exudes confidence, seemingly a match for any emergency and always making subordinates feel that everything is well in hand. A leader who lacks self-confidence cannot inspire confidence in others.

Authority versus Power

Power is by no means synonymous with authority, though the two attributes often go hand-in-hand. The ice-calm stranger who quiets the screaming passengers in the airplane crash, setting one group to tending the wounded, dispatching another to find water, and ordering a third to start rigging shelter against the winds, may have no authority but is well on the way to developing de facto (acceptance) power.

Anyone who influences the behavior of others is exerting power, whether formal authority is an intervening element or not. The head of your organization has power over you (if you have a job) when instructing you to carry out certain tasks. Your neighbor who caught ten beautiful fish last Saturday certainly has a sort of power over you—that catch will influence your choice of fishing holes this Saturday. The exercise of power permeates all levels of the organization. The leader of an informal group in the motor pool may command as much influence with the drivers as does their supervisor—and a smart supervisor is keenly aware that these alignments of power may be channeled toward useful goals. Otherwise, opposition of group leaders may generate intense competition between group and supervisor, to the latter's inevitable detriment.

power

Within the informal group itself, there is a total absence of formal authority, but there can be a highly structured hierarchy of power. The "pecking order" may be less immediately evident than in a chicken yard, but it does exist.

Types of Power

Sometimes the word *power* connotes coercion or force. In sterner times managers resorted to coercive tactics such as suspension, reduction in pay, or firing to maintain authority and command obedience. Employees were ridiculed or shamed to keep them in line. In a case known to the authors, a woman replaced a man in charge of a largely male office, and almost immediately a test of strength ensued between her and an assertive man who showed contempt for her authority by almost openly ridiculing her and flouting her instructions. Having been a matron in a jail, she was no stranger to confrontation, and elected to meet the situation head-on. When the office cleared for the night, she moved her antagonist's desk up front immediately opposite hers. When he came in the next morning she told him publicly that he was acting like a child, and she was going to act like a teacher by putting him right up where she could watch him until he "learned to behave." The tactic worked: short of total insubordination, which he could not risk without fear of dismissal, there was nothing he could do. In order to prevent absolute and continuing loss of face with his colleagues, he accepted the lesser evil and backed down. The woman's approach was successful, but it involved the use of power in a way that runs directly counter to modern human relations principles. As many of today's managers have found, positive rewards are often more effective than negative sanctions in achieving the desired results with subordinates.

Some management theorists define the source of the leader's influence as authority, power, or status, depending on the legitimizing force.

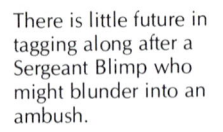

There is little future in tagging along after a Sergeant Blimp who might blunder into an ambush.

Employees may be ridiculed or shamed to keep them in line.

Figure 4-4 represents this interplay of leadership determinants schematically. "Authority" is derived from a legal source ("you are hereby placed in charge of Project X") and "status" from the organizational structure ("section heads work for the branch head, branch heads for the department head, department heads for the division head"). "Power" stems from either of these legitimizers or is simply assumed ("I've planned our work schedules for the next month"; "If you have any trouble with the supervisor, let me know"; etc.)

French and Raven[6] cite five bases of power that emerge in superior/subordinate relations: coercion, reward, expertise, reference, and legitimacy.

Coercive power focuses on deprivation of a worker's needs as a punishing force. The manager using this power basis believes that the threat of retribution will act as a catalyst in extracting worker compliance. Of course it will produce initial compliance, and perhaps in some organizations it will work as a regular technique; but it develops nothing in the way of loyalty or other positive support elements.

Reward power draws on the intangible and tangible benefits available to the worker who performs according to the supervisor's wishes. Consider

coercive power

reward power

the rewards at the leader's command: judicious use of praise, delegation of desired responsibility, recognition of accomplishment, increase in pay, sincere interest in the worker's well-being, informal privileges or other fringe benefits, etc. Since each worker is different and responds to different stimuli, the leader must heed both individual and group needs and be discriminating in the selection of rewards. Moreover, rewards for small returns must be carefully allocated to ensure that motivation for large efforts will be available.

expert power

Expert power comes from the leader's display of superior knowledge or ability. The workers feel that the boss is extremely competent; thus, they are more willing to carry out orders, convinced that they will produce results. Note that the boss must be not just as good but *better* than subordinates at the work in question, or they will have no incentive to follow their supervisor instead of their own inclinations.

referent power

Referent power occurs when the subordinates identify with the boss and attempt to shape their behavior in the same pattern, either consciously or unconsciously. This approach is most conspicuous when a small child imitates a parent, but a careful observer can see it in many other situations: a college student may select a teaching career because of admiration for a favorite professor rather than teaching ability, or a worker may adopt the mannerisms of a foreman because of an unconscious feeling that such actions will confer prestige or status.

legitimate power

Legitimate power has three sources:

1. Legal power, arising from a formal mandate to assume the post
2. Traditional power, based on the historical right (the "godfather" post, the "divine right" of kings, and so on)
3. Charismatic power, arising from a compelling personality (the follower finds the leader so magnetic that his or her authority is accepted with little question)

In an effort to link these theories with actual situations, workers in five different settings were asked which of the five power bases explained why they complied with their bosses' requests. In all of the five settings (kinds

Figure 4-4. Leadership Determinants

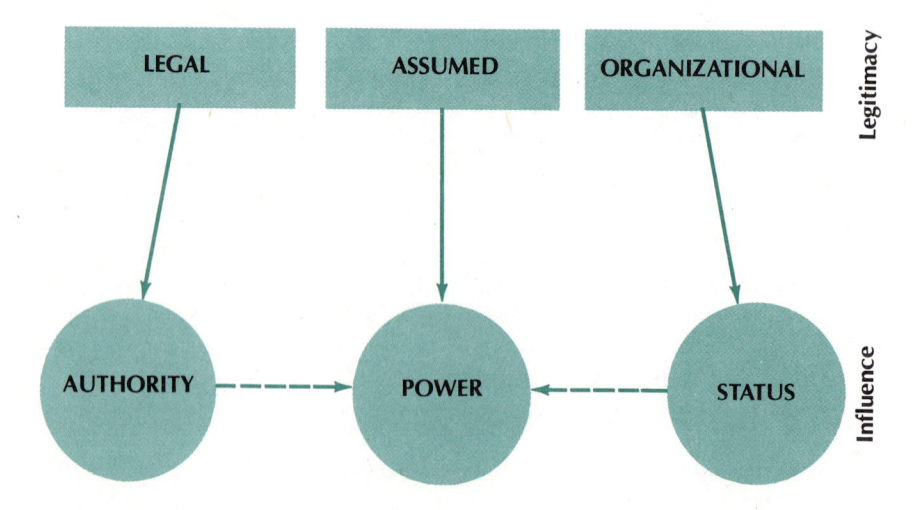

of job environment), the most common reasons were related to *expert power* and *legitimate power*. ("She's the boss, isn't she?"; "God made managers to tell people like me what to do"; "He's been around since year one, he ought to know something"; "Where the hell would I be, putting the old man down?") Coercive power was the least important reason for accepting the leader's authority. When the same workers were asked which of the five power bases related positively or negatively to satisfaction on the job, they were most influenced by *expert power* and *referent power*, and least influenced (that is, most dissatisfied) by coercive power.[7]

Which (if any) of these five bases of power applies to Dick? To Henry?

Leadership in Action

Seldom is there one best way to do anything. We are creative beings, continually seeking out better ways to channel our energies. Different tasks involve different priorities, and people select different actions to reach the same end. Sometimes a manager goes for maximum profit; at other times maximum output, or minimum layoffs, or highest market share may be the goal. As priorities shift, so does the approach. A few years ago we thought private enterprise far superior to government "meddling"; today government regulation and even intervention is widespread, to the point that the line between public and private interests is becoming blurred.

Even when the objective remains constant, we can find different ways to do a job without great differences in efficiency. Consider the construction of an office building. One contractor erects stairwells, bathrooms, and utility spaces as completed modules, prefabricated elsewhere and almost ready for use when they reach the site; another proceeds more traditionally by putting up the floors and walls and doing the interior finishing in place. But when the costs are totaled, there is little to choose between the two approaches. Similarly, when two individuals tackle the same job their particular skills and experience will dictate their methods. In one instance, an operations research analyst and a conventional accountant each analyzed a case under litigation where an automobile distributor was suing a manufacturer for alleged changes in distributorship contract benefits. Despite the sharp difference in their approaches, the two arrived at virtually identical results. A husky foreman breaks up a fight by pulling the contestants apart, while a slight foreman appeals to reason; as long as the fight ends, it probably makes little difference which method was used.

This same diversity applies in the practice of leadership. Many studies have sought the "best" approach, but it remains elusive, for good leaders are observed to use many styles. Leadership style depends on three factors and the interplay between them:

leadership factors

- the leader's characteristics
- the followers' characteristics, individually and as a group
- the situation

One organization may need radically different leaders at various stages in its development. Probably history is full of examples where "the right person at the right time" would have been a disgruntled misfit if born 50 years earlier or later. During the early rise of major corporations, tough entrepreneurs such as Jim Fisk in railroads, John D. Rockefeller in oil, William C. Durant in automobiles, Andrew Carnegie in steel, and J. Pierpont Morgan in banking had the stamina and occasionally the ruthlessness to carve out enduring industrial empires, but none of these rugged individualists would be elected by a modern board of directors. Durant's replacement, Alfred Sloan, supplanted Durant's bold financial wizardry (which initially created the General Motors Corporation) with a far less autocratic style and the patient administrative skills needed to consolidate the original concept into an integrated company.[8] Both men had a powerful impact on the company—probably, both were essential—but each was peculiarly suited to his times and the situation he faced.

One condition management faces today is the great new pressures from outside the organization: pressures to exercise social responsibility and meet consumer demands. The successful leader will be the individual who can mesh organizational goals with these strong public demands.

Leadership Styles

There are as many different leadership styles as there are leaders, for every individual brings to his or her position a unique combination of background, values, perceptions, goals, and experiences. During this century, numerous studies have analyzed various facets of leadership and the corresponding reactions of those led. The *human relations approach* has found widespread acceptance in recent years, and most theories of leadership discussed today contrast the authoritative and participative approaches.

human relations approach

Theory X-Theory Y

Theory X - Theory Y was the contribution of Douglas McGregor, an early member of the human relations school. Inspired by the Hawthorne studies, he theorized that management behavior is governed by the leader's assumptions about human nature. Under *Theory X,* the leader assumes that people lack ambition and dislike work, so they must be controlled closely and often coerced to achieve management goals; moreover, they have little creativity and actually prefer direction rather than welcome responsibility. Thus, the Theory X leader runs a tightly controlled unit, using lower order rewards on Maslow's scale. Frederick W. Taylor, an early twentieth-century management innovator who became known as the "father of scientific management," clearly subscribed to Theory X. In explaining how to increase production in handling pig iron at the Bethlehem Steel Company, Taylor stated that "one of the first requirements for a man fit to handle pig iron as a regular occupation is that he shall be so stupid that he more nearly resembles in his mental makeup the ox than any other type...and he must consequently be trained by a man more intelligent than himself."[9] By contrast, *Theory Y* assumes that people are creative and that work is both natural and enjoyable. Authoritative managers stifle motivation and create the appearance of lethargy, but managers who motivate by appeal to higher order needs unleash the creative potential of their people.

McGregor's analysis ignited a fuse in management theory. The human relations approach caught on, and managers flocked to training sessions aimed at making them more "employee oriented." His model was still quite general, however, and offered few specific guides for managers. It was left to Rensis Likert, another management theorist, to qualify the notions McGregor had propounded.

Leadership Classification

Rensis Likert, expanding on McGregor's theory, classified management styles as *exploitative authoritative, benevolent authoritative, consultative,* and *participative group.* He first advanced these categories in 1961, in *Patterns of Management,* and developed his ideas in 1967 in *The Human Organization.* By the time the latter book came out, Likert had started referring to the various styles as Systems 1 through 4, so the managers to whom he administered test questionnaires would not place their own value judgments on his descriptive terms.

management style classification

Likert tested his ideas by asking hundreds of managers to fill out a classification questionnaire like that shown in Figure 4-5. The questionnaire listed the values corresponding to the four systems, and managers were asked to identify where their most productive and least productive units fell along the continuum. The results were quite encouraging: almost invariably, the high performance units ranked closer to 4 than 1.

In earlier studies, Likert contrasted the supervisory efforts in high and low performance units on the basis of whether they were "job-centered" (emphasizing production) or "employee-centered" (concentrating on building effective work groups and attending to employee problems). Figure 4-6 shows the distribution of seven high-productivity units and ten low-productivity units according to this classification of supervisory style; it suggests a good correlation between an employee-centered style and good unit performance.

Figure 4-5. Management Styles and Worker Performance Questionnaire

ORGANIZATIONAL VARIABLE	SYSTEM 1	SYSTEM 2	SYSTEM 3	SYSTEM 4
Leadership processes used Extent to which superiors have confidence and trust in *subordinates*	Have no confidence and trust in subordinates	Have condescending confidence and trust, such as master has to servant	Substantial but not complete confidence and trust; still wishes to keep control of decisions	Complete confidence and trust in all matters
Character of motivational forces. Manner in which motives are used	Fear, threats, punishment and occasional rewards	Rewards and some actual or potential punishment	Rewards, occasional punishment, and some involvement	Economic rewards based on compensation system developed through participation; group participation and involvement in setting goals, improving methods, appraising progress toward goals, etc.

119
LEADERSHIP

Likert and his colleagues in the Institute for Social Research at the University of Michigan have administered their questionnaires to hundreds of managers. Since no two situations are the same, it is unrealistic to assume that there is one most effective style, but the results from these and other studies give high marks to an employee-oriented approach.

The question is: how participative should management be? It must be answered in relation to the characteristics of the three primary variables—the leader, the subordinates, and the situation. In a 1958 *Harvard Business Review* article, "How to Choose a Leadership Pattern," Tannenbaum and Schmidt presented a continuum of management styles from authoritarian to almost that of interested observer.[10] At the right end of the continuum (Figure 4-7), employees lead the way in formulating policies, establishing work quotas, solving problems, and so on. This approach to leadership is aimed at giving the employee high motivation and a sense of true participation in the organization's tasks.

management style continuum

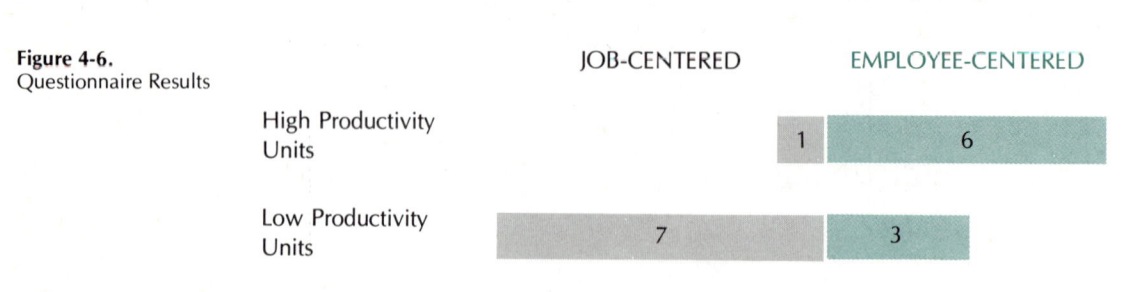

It is well, however, to heed McGregor's warning upon leaving a demanding management job as president of Antioch College (many years after he proposed Theory X-Theory Y): "It took a couple of years, but I finally began to realize that a leader can't avoid the exercise of authority any more than he can avoid the responsibility for what happens to his organization"[11] (or, in Harry Truman's famous words, "The buck stops here"). Someone has to make the tough decisions (including those that no employee would touch with a ten-foot pole), and that is the leader's job; it cannot be shirked under the cloak of participative management.

As a general rule, excessive participation is not a problem in U.S. management today. Studies show that managers are reluctant to give up much of their power to subordinates. A manager who has been taken advantage of by opportunistic employees is likely to harden his or her style to avoid a repeat performance. Certain employees are as well aware of the human relations philosophy as are managers, and seek to turn it to their own ends if they can. The inexperienced leader can be hazed in subtle ways, just like the new apprentice who is sent to find a bucket of striped paint or a left-handed monkey wrench. Sometimes the hazing is not so subtle. A new naval ensign (the lowest officer rank), just graduated from the Naval Academy and reporting to his first ship, was asked by an enlisted man in his division if the ensign could take a package ashore and mail it to the enlisted man's mother, since it was her birthday and he could not go ashore because he was on the duty section. Anxious to be a considerate leader, the ensign took it along and mailed it. The next day an electric sander turned up missing from the enlisted man's work station. The ensign recalled the size and weight of the supposed food mixer he had mailed, and realized that he had been conned into disposing of stolen

Figure 4-6.
Questionnaire Results

	JOB-CENTERED	EMPLOYEE-CENTERED
High Productivity Units	1	6
Low Productivity Units	7	3

goods. Since officers are not searched on leaving the ship, he was a safe courier. Moreover, he realized that the enlisted man knew he would guess what had been in the package, and that the members of his informal group were laughing at having taken the young officer in. He was helpless to prove anything or to take any action, beyond vowing to moderate his "participative approach" in the future.

Matching the Style with the Environment

Differences in work settings and the makeup of employee groups play a large role in determining the best possible leadership style. A manager will shift from participative to benevolent authoritative style as variables such as available time, need for secrecy, and degree of employee experience shift with the job to be done. If a flash flood threatens the plant, the boss raps out orders to take emergency action with no thought of asking the employees their views on the decisions; if asked by the front office to prepare secret contingency plans for a possible move into a close competitor's area, the supervisor can't let anyone else in on it for fear of a leak; and if a job involving utterly new technology is being considered, it would hardly be helpful to ask advice of employees who have never heard of the process.

Forces within the organization operate in ways that are not immediately obvious, and a newly arrived manager goes through a learning period with regard to group structure and size, local norms and taboos (is work measurement commonplace or intensely disliked?), and the orientation of top management. A manager should assess these things before taking a new job, if possible, to anticipate problems in adapting to a strange environment.

Fred E. Fiedler suggests that jobs should be tailored to fit leaders rather than the reverse, because every manager has a special set of competences and these do not fit every situation.[12] Fiedler's view is that a manager who avoids a situation where failure is likely and seeks a spot

fitting tasks to leaders

Figure 4-7.
Continuum of Management Styles

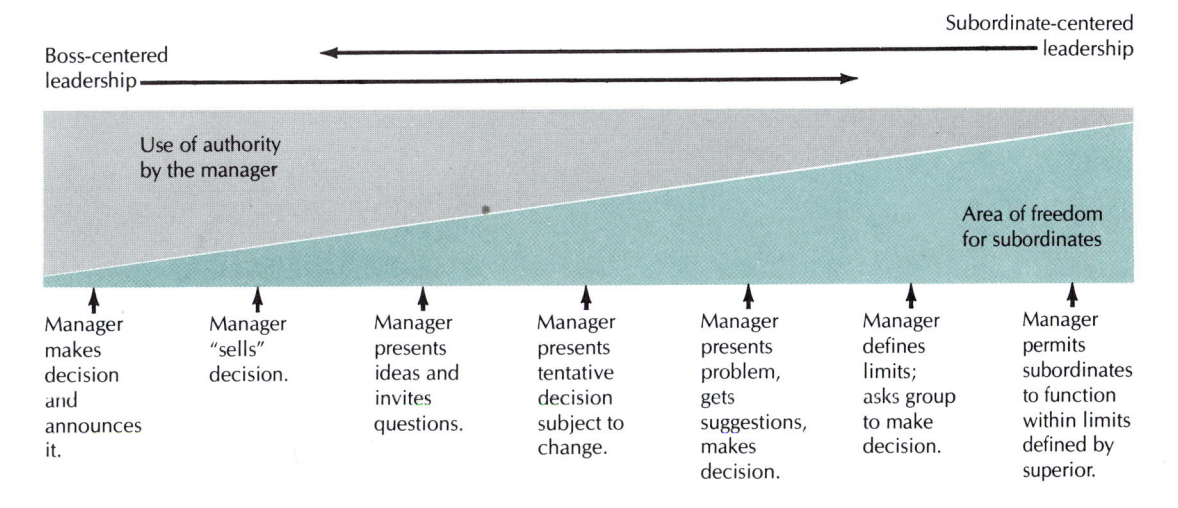

Boss-centered leadership ⟷ Subordinate-centered leadership

Use of authority by the manager

Area of freedom for subordinates

| Manager makes decision and announces it. | Manager "sells" decision. | Manager presents ideas and invites questions. | Manager presents tentative decision subject to change. | Manager presents problem, gets suggestions, makes decision. | Manager defines limits; asks group to make decision. | Manager permits subordinates to function within limits defined by superior. |

fitting personal leadership competences stands a good chance of becoming a successful leader. President Eisenhower, in organizing his White House assistants, wanted to make use of the exceptional organizational skills of Sherman Adams, former governor of Massachusetts. Therefore, he created the job of Chief of Staff to fit Adams' particular skills.

fitting approach to task structure

Do you think the partners did a good job in fitting the tasks to the available managers, or did they fit the people to existing tasks?

The structure of a task helps to determine a successful approach. A highly structured task presents no need for a participative style, for there are few decisions to be made. A highly individualized task suggests more concentration on the individual than the group. A task requiring close teamwork cannot be accomplished without the support of the job-group team. Similarly, the characteristics of the subordinates suggest the best approach. If they have a strong need for independence, and are competent to assume it, as with a group of new management trainees selected because of their drive and initiative, a participative style is the only way to go. If they are a group of untrained new immigrants hired for janitorial work in an office building, unfamiliar with both the language and the tools of the trade, it would be ridiculous to do other than set forth their duties in positive and explicit terms. Frederick W. Taylor's assessment of the employee's desire to be told exactly what to do, although far too undiscriminating, does fit the occasional employee who needs a structured environment and has no wish to assume any responsibility.

Characteristics of the Leader

Early leadership studies focused only on the leader, in an effort to pinpoint the various traits which managers do and should possess. Many lists were made up, and many tests correlating traits with results were conducted. To the surprise of many researchers, virtually no consistent patterns emerged. Charles Bird examined inventories of observed leadership traits from such studies, and found that of twenty such lists, *not one single trait* appeared on all of them.[13] Even such perennials as "honesty," "consideration for subordinates," or "initiative" were not considered essential in all the actual situations observed. William Jenkins reviewed additional studies a few years later, and confirmed this finding: "No single trait or group of characteristics...sets off the leader from the members of his group."[14]

leadership traits

Even though no absolute requirements were discerned, some traits did appear highly desirable in many different environments and cases. These were: *technical competence* (it is hard for a leader to manage a group without a thorough knowledge of the field); *initiative* (the ability to act when action is required, even though it appears easier to let things go for a bit and "see how the dust settles"); *self-confidence* (often the leader has to be a lonely person, taking action that everyone else thinks is wrong and believing in his or her own judgment); and *good judgment* (the ability to analyze a problem and reach at least reasonably good conclusions as to the proper action, with due regard for the framework within which the problem is being viewed by the workers). Unfortunately, from the viewpoint of those who would *learn* leadership, only the first of these four appears to be learnable—and when technical competence is being acquired, it is with very little reference to its use in leadership.

The redeeming feature of this apparently gloomy conclusion—implying that leaders are indeed "born and not made"—is that good leadership derives from the total set of positive traits, and even if *they* cannot be learned the erstwhile leader can concentrate on *emphasizing their application* in relation to employees and leadership situations. Initiative comes more naturally if the manager pushes to exercise it, thrusting aside laziness or procrastination to hunt for the action-oriented solution and adopt it. Good judgment is developed by exercising judgment and seeing the outcome. Self-confidence comes from experience. But most important is the mental state of consciously striving to apply leadership principles, to think of employees rather than oneself, and to maximize one's own plus factors.

Take stock of your individual characteristics. Your background will make certain environments easy for you and others difficult, requiring you to work on adapting to the latter. Your values may establish blocks to certain needed insights, and you must recognize this. (In the Senate hearings for his confirmation as vice-president, Nelson Rockefeller admitted that his lifelong background of great wealth might blind him to certain factors; but he commented that a candidate from a severely deprived background has blinders, too, of another sort.). Your perceptions may make it hard for you to understand the needs of employees with different perceptions, or to see why actions you take are resented at times. And your personality may influence your ability to deal with people. You cannot change your individual characteristics, but you can modify them to some degree, and you can understand how they help you in some cases and hinder you in others.

Some of these characteristics—technical ability, initiative, self-confidence, and judgment—are basic to all management situations. But others are important only in terms of those being led. Figure 4-8 suggests these relationships. For example, a supervisor's values may not be held particularly strongly (only slightly on the positive side of the scale), but they may be highly compatible with those of the workers, and hence the equivalent of a +4 Leadership Index (on an arbitrary basis). The supervisor is quite a perceptive individual within the usual frame of reference, but totally unable to see the harmful impact of certain practices on new and unsure employees; thus, the score of this factor is -2 on the Leadership Index. Situations of this sort can arise in such stressful situations as Marine boot camp, where the tough drill sergeant comes from the same background as the recruits and quite possibly shares their basic values, but in his zeal to indoctrinate them into the military verities does not see that he may be pushing the group beyond endurance. To him, the tough regimen is all in the day's work (as it will be to them later in their military careers); to them, now, it is virtually paralyzing. They are quite willing to accept his values—even eager to do so—but his approach is tying them in knots.

Leadership Compatibility Index

It may be hard for a leader to change because of background constraints, which was Fiedler's thesis. But training can make it easier to recognize limitations induced by background, and can encourage the leader to solicit and accept feedback from employees in the interest of improved adaptation.

Developing Leadership

Management analyst Robert H. Guest once stated that "you could dispose of almost all the leadership training courses for supervision in American industry today without anyone knowing the difference."[15] His point was not that leadership training itself lacks value, but that leadership *situations* vary to such an extent that ideas that make sense in one environment may fall flat in a different one. Most training in industry is aimed at concrete objectives—teaching workers how to assemble the Mark 5 Test Set, how to weld stainless steel, or how to operate a punch press. But training in "leadership" is often vaguely dismissed as "supervisory development" or "executive development" and turned over to staff training people who may have difficulty relating their generalizations to specific situations in the plant. Moreover, some leadership concepts may be "out of bounds" for the training supervisor, in particular any that seem to criticize managers, to hint at the merits of worker manipulation, or to acknowledge the existence of nonsupportive or destructive informal groups.

Another unresolved issue with regard to such educational efforts is whether every manager *can* be trained as a leader. There are enough horror stories of leadership training graduates who are less capable leaders after training than before to convince many managers that "you just have it or you don't." So few organizations make leadership training a primary objective that no tested body of practice is available. And too many managers confuse leadership with conferred authority, and think they already know how to be leaders simply because they wear the mantle.

Figure 4-8.
Leadership Compatibility Index

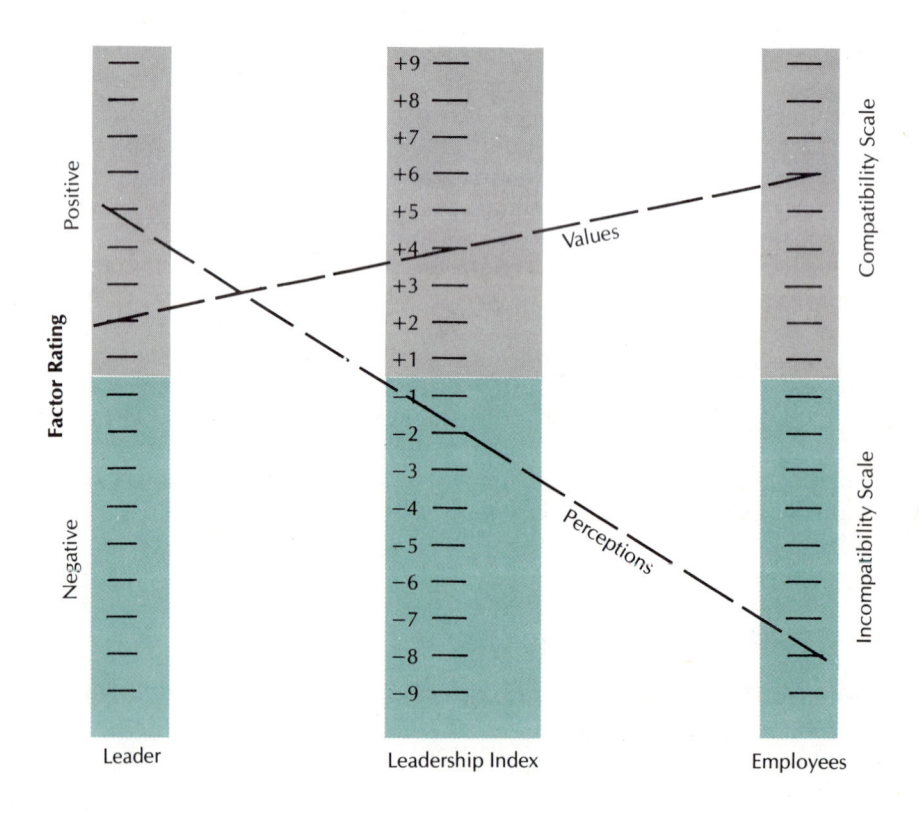

One recalls the successful businessman who bought a yacht, garbed himself in yachting uniform, and took his elderly parents for a spin on the bay one pleasant afternoon. "Look, Momma," he said, adjusting his cap at a rakish angle, "I'm a captain." His mother gave him a questioning look. "By me, you're a captain," she said. "And by Poppa, you're a captain. But by a *captain,* are you a captain?"

Developing leadership is tough. But the effort has to be made.

Self-Development

One of the most popular management clichés describes any good manager as "a born leader." This phrase is analogous to a common description of middle-aged people in trim condition: "They're lucky—they don't put on weight." In all probability, those described don't put on weight because they exercise willpower in the presence of fattening food; and it may be equally true that the "born leader" has put a great deal of time and thought into the question of how to do a good leadership job.

Leadership involves forming the habit of thinking of others before yourself, and there is nothing natural about this. A prominent executive with a national reputation as a leader was asked about his observed practice of being very generous with praise for his subordinates—specifically, whether this behavior came naturally or was learned. He responded that it had been a deliberate tactic in his younger years, and that only now, 20 years later, was it getting to be second nature. He said, "I have a sort of quota—ten favorable comments for every unfavorable one; but when I do have an unfavorable one, it might be a lulu." His criticisms were so rare that they had real impact: everyone knew he meant it, and responded accordingly.

self-training in leadership

The Basics of Leadership

Certain basic principles apply in almost any leadership situation. Other principles are *situational*—they may or may not apply, depending on the situation and the other actors. And still others are *personal*—they depend on the abilities and style of the leader.

The principle of careful explanation, so that employees understand as well as possible what your problems are and why you act as you do, hardly fits a situation where the building is about to explode and you want it evacuated immediately. The principle of always meeting a situation head-on, so your people will see that you are not the timid or hesitant type, will not match your capabilities if one of your crazy drunk 220-pound troops is breaking up a bar—and you weigh in at 135 pounds soaking wet. Situations and capabilities must modify your behavior as a leader, which is why many managers think leadership cannot be taught. But some aspects of leadership *are* universally applicable, regardless of job, age, environment, or social climate.

basic leadership principles

One such principle involves concentrating on the other person's joys and sorrows instead of your own. It is very pleasant to tell others about *your* achievements, of *your* troubles, but they don't want to hear it. Psychiatrists are quite honest about this: they charge you $50 an hour for the privilege of telling them. Others, however, *do* want to talk about *their* achievements and *their* troubles, if they think the listener is sincere. So another principle is that of sincerity. You can't just look interested—you have to *be* interested, which is much harder. But you can practice it everywhere, in any conversation, and the more you show an interest in others the more you actually become interested.

A third principle is that of honesty in your relations with others. If you say you have presented your subordinates' case to the boss and argued for them when actually you have told the boss something else, they will soon realize that your word means nothing. At first, this maneuver may seem harmless (perhaps what they are asking is unreasonable, and you know the boss will not go for it), but before long one of these "double-speak" cases will backfire and you will be found out. If you cannot recommend your subordinates' viewpoint to the boss, you must tell them so frankly, and take any flak that may result.

A fourth principle is that of dependability. If you say you will recommend someone for promotion or a training course, *do it.* Your people may give you a few extra chances if you disappoint them by forgetting to keep such a promise, but they won't put up with it for long. And once you get a reputation for undependability, it's hard to lose.

A final principle is to know your field. If you are running an operation, prepare yourself so you know how to do it. All too many supervisors try to get by without knowing their jobs, under the impression that their subordinates will know how and all they need to do is "supervise." Supervising *is* knowing. You may think you are fooling your people by pretending to know when you do not, but they are hard to fool.

How would Henry apply these principles to avoid "turning off" his partners when he takes some actions as president?

Maximizing Your Style
You do certain things well and others badly. If you are basically the quiet, modest type, don't try to be one of the boys at the company picnic, trying to run the volleyball team and the chow line simultaneously. You won't be able to pull it off, and you will look ridiculous. If you're not the intellectual type, don't tell the company brain trust how to do its job. You won't be thanked for it. Try to be available when skills like yours are needed.

If you are comfortable climbing out on slender scaffolding on a construction job, go to it. But if heights make you dizzy, say so and stay down on the ground. The workers will respect your human limitations; they have limitations, too. On the other hand, if you are asked a question in a technical area that calls for college training, and you know the answer—go ahead and answer it without trying to pretend that all that book learning is over your head. By the same token, if you really don't know, don't try to bluff it out under the impression that they don't know whether you're right anyway.

In short, be yourself. Don't try to pretend you are what you aren't, and don't try to pretend you aren't what you are.

Training for Leadership

Supervisory Training

supervisory leadership training

It is the supervisor who is closest to the production workers, and for whom leadership training can pay off most immediately in directing the largest body of labor in the organization. Since the first-line supervisor—

the foreman or equivalent—has probably worked up from the ranks of nonsupervisory labor rather than joining the company from outside, that individual probably knows the details of production work from firsthand experience but has had no training or indoctrination in management. An additional factor, which is often a handicap, is that the supervisor was formerly a union member (if it is a union shop). This implies close ties with the interest and viewpoint of the workers, but few ties with management and little prior opportunity to gain a management outlook. As supervisor, the former worker must take policies developed in the executive suite—where there is only one viewpoint and no articulated opposition—and put them into effect at a much lower level, where there *is* a highly vocal opposition. Since the new manager knows that uncertain performance or even a modest reduction in force could signal his return to the workbench and the union, it is scarcely easy to burn bridges with the subordinates who may be fellow workers again on very little notice.

There are some positive advantages. Having been *in* one or more groups, the supervisor is aware not only of their existence but of their leaders and many of their nuances. He or she knows the work force as individuals, in contrast to higher management levels who know them as various numbers of each trade and department. And the supervisor perceives the current obstacles to meeting production schedules—many of which probably stem from failures on the part of higher management and therefore cannot be resolved at the first-line level.

This supervisor approaches a supervisory training program with weary suspicion, and justifiably so. If a member of the training staff gives a course on leadership or human relations, it may well consist of platitudes such as: a good supervisor tries to get all the facts before deciding; a good supervisor must understand the needs of his subordinates; and so on. It may describe the work situation in terms the supervisor knows do not apply here. It may be a "safe" course that describes grievance procedures and other routines which the supervisor already knows. If an outside instructor is brought in, he or she may know too little about this plant to cover suitable material, or may try to run an entertaining session rather than a useful one. If a member of company management conducts the session, students will avoid many "dangerous" topics that should be aired.

Sometimes management's expectations for such a program are unrealistic. Having failed to get full supervisory cooperation, through their own shortcomings, they now demand that the training director "make these people understand their responsibility to back up management." They may give the training director a list of pie-in-the-sky demands, such as "tell them they have to increase productivity 50%," when many of the productivity deficiencies really should be laid at management's door.

It is possible, however, for supervisory training in leadership to be successful—if it is planned carefully, and not too much is expected of it. The following are some methods that have been useful when well planned.

The *case method* describes an actual or fictitious situation in detail and asks supervisor-students to solve the problem that situation presents for the manager. This approach permits airing of all possible solutions without real-life consequences, and lets the supervisors talk each situation

case method

over collectively and bring to bear their best combined judgment. If the case is a factual one, they can study the procedure actually used by the manager and discuss the results. Thus supervisors can prepare in advance for situations they have not yet encountered. Insights from an experienced instructor will further enrich the training session.

role-playing

Role-playing is an extension of the case method; instead of simply talking about a case, the students act it out. Participants are assigned various roles, and if the problem is realistic enough they may actually become emotionally involved. Since emotion is a key element in real leadership situations, this makes the role-playing approach superior to the unemotional atmosphere of the case study—but only if the problem is real and complex.

sensitivity training

Sensitivity training is a form of simulated group encounter designed ideally to create a feeling of openness, sincerity, and trust among the participants. The goal is not only to disclose unsuspected hostilities and human relations obstacles, but also to teach supervisors to use open discussion in actual work situations. Participants are encouraged to discuss both positive and negative reactions toward one another and the organization with a high degree of frankness. Although the intent of the T-group is to encourage free and uninhibited interaction among colleagues, sometimes these sessions get out of hand and hostilities erupt to a degree that can't be turned off when the sessions are over. Similarly, a successful T-group experience may create a feeling of euphoria, making participants feel they can achieve miracles. This state of mind often turns to cynicism when they return to the office atmosphere and encounter individuals who don't view the world that way.

Sensitivity training at its worst recalls the James Thurber fable about the lecturer who was telling the rabbits they were their own worst enemies because of their timidity. When a horrible but unreasonable fear swept over them, they ought to probe for that fear, drag the dreaded thing out into the light, look at it—and they would see that it was harmless. When the lecturer finished all the older rabbits applauded wildly, then went to their holes and firmly blocked the doors against danger—all but one impressionable young rabbit, who could be seen striding purposefully down the road to the dog kennels, repeating to himself, "Drag the dreaded thing out into the light."

leadership lectures

Lectures are no better and no worse than the lecturer. It is rare for a lecturer from within the company to be effective, partly because he or she is not likely to be a specialist in the field but perhaps even more because of audience reluctance to believe anyone within the same organization. Although outside lecturers are not as common in supervisory training as case studies (the most popular approach), some of the best can be very good indeed. Their particular strength lies in their contacts with a variety of different companies, giving them a broader perspective than trainers within one firm.

Executive Development

executive leadership training

Most executive training in leadership involves either young managers who are on the "fast track" and thought to be headed for more responsibility, or senior managers who are going back for "retreading" in a specialized university program for executives.

One risk of training programs for junior managers is the aura of elitism surrounding those selected for the course; the morale and loyalty of those who are not selected may be seriously damaged. To avoid this problem, the training can be made an option that managers apply for if they wish, or all managers can be sent for training at a certain stage in their careers. The former is likely to appeal to the professional course-attender, while the busy young manager whom you really want to contact may feel too busy and absorbed in current work to take time for the course. The latter approach is more costly but probably preferable. One advantage is that some managers who had not been considered prime candidates for promotion may profit substantially from training and merit a second look.

Training for senior managers is usually conducted away from the job, often for extended periods. When a training program is conducted on the regular job site, managers must keep up with their regular job responsibilities and the program is likely to be ineffective. The best situation is for managers to go off to a retreat, where they immerse themselves in their training program night and day. After all, the purpose of leadership training for senior managers is to *break their past habit patterns* and *implant new patterns*, which means devoting a week or two to the new propositions. Being able and alert individuals, they will criticize the ideas presented to them, pose tough questions designed to undermine the theories, think up situations where they don't appear to apply—and eventually retain some of what they hear. Discussion and sensitivity groups are among the popular techniques utilized in senior management training sessions.

Management training stands a better chance if carried out on a widespread basis, so the concepts taught in the training sessions have a sufficiently broad company audience to effect significant changes in personnel relations philosophy. Studies show that a single manager can return from a good course full of enthusiasm for change but quickly lose that enthusiasm when faced with the stone walls of existing practice.

Despite the current emphasis on both supervisory and management training, much of it focusing on leadership issues, we do not really know whether it is effective or not. There are no dependable ways to measure its payoff. Organizations that conduct such programs have to be contented with subjective measures, such as the impression that productivity and morale are bound to improve if managers are better leaders, and that leadership training is bound to have some positive effect. Until methods are developed for relating the results of training to the training programs themselves, we cannot really isolate the most effective ways to teach leadership.

Changing Patterns in Leadership

What does the future hold for leadership behavior? No one can be sure, but certain trends are developing that suggest a few patterns.

leadership trends

One clear trend is the unwillingness of young workers and managers to accept organizational patterns and goals without question, as their parents did. Workers are likely to rebel against the monotony of the assembly line and other highly structured industrial processes. Superficially, this rebellion is reflected in their less conventional dress and hair styles; more fundamentally, it is expressed in their frequent unwillingness to work required overtime, their occasional high rate of absenteeism, their refusal to work under dangerous or extreme hardship conditions, and their rejection at times of such traditional loyalties as union support. Managers are impatient at the traditional promotion rates and want to be featured players at an early age. They do not accept unquestioningly the goals and policies of the corporation, seeking only to fit in; rather, they hope to act as reformers, instituting important changes in the style and substance of corporate management. If they are in government agencies, they do not believe that their agency chief is entitled to unswerving loyalty, but are more inclined to assign their loyalty to the public interest and will ring the bell openly on the boss if he violates their standards of public service.

blue-collar leadership problems

Detroit is a good bellwether of the new trends. A third of the hourly employees of General Motors, Ford, and Chrysler are under 30. They average 12 years of school, compared with ten for the generation ahead of them—a truly major difference, since it means double the amount of high school. First-line managers who are proud of Detroit's past production triumphs don't understand what motivates these youngsters, who are mobile, demanding, restless, and united in their hatred of what the assembly line stands for. They do know that the angry young contingent forming a third of their work force is protesting through the avenues most readily available to them: excessive absenteeism, high turnover, erratic and careless work performance, and occasionally, sabotage.

One reason for the incipient rebellion is the monotony of the work. Figure 4-9 shows a repetitive factory-type task (stemming tomatoes in a packing plant) which can be done at a rate of 50 times a minute—or close to 20,000 times in an eight-hour shift, with allowance for rest periods. A more complex assembly line task in an automotive assembly line (attaching brake tubing to junction blocks) will be repeated about 350 times in an eight-hour shift. Probably a significant reason why these situations have not erupted into a wave of union protests, particularly in the automotive plant, is that the young workers distrust the United Automobile Workers nearly as much as they do the companies.

Management is approaching this mounting problem in genuine bewilderment, but attempting in a number of ways to tune in to the leadership needs of the younger generation. The new General Motors plant in Lordstown, Ohio, is far more automated than existing plants, in an effort to eliminate some of the more mind-deadening repetitive tasks. Sensitivity training for the older supervisors has been instituted in an effort to close the generation gap between supervisors and managers, to some extent at least. Older managers, brought up for 30 to 40 years in a highly structured and mature industry with standardized practices, are reluctant to accept the notion that the work place is short on motivational elements, preferring to believe that the younger employees have simply been spoiled and are now getting their first taste of discipline. The present thrust of leadership training within the industry is to break down these strongly held but not very helpful viewpoints.

Walter Reuther, in a television interview shortly before his death, probably caught the essence of the dilemma. When the young workers get three or four days' pay, Reuther noted, they say, "Well, I can live on that.

I'm not really interested in these material things anyhow; I'm interested in a sense of fulfillment as a human being." The prospect of a lifetime spent doing the operation shown in Figure 4-9 "doesn't lift the human spirit." In such a job, the employee "is not master of his own destiny. He's going to run away from it every time he gets a chance."

Clearly, pay alone does not motivate. At General Motors, even the lowest paid hourly employees are in the top third of U.S. incomes. But the job resembles prison life in many ways. Workers cannot get time off for a telephone call, much less to stop at the post office, the bank, the motor vehicle bureau, the grocery store, a child's school, or any of the hundred other miscellaneous chores required by an increasingly bureaucratic

Figure 4-9.
Assembly Line Monotony

existence. When workers plan a stop immediately after work, an unexpected extra hour or two of overtime is unwelcome, even at time-and-a-half rates.

The automobile companies, deeply disturbed, have instituted major training programs for foremen (who supervise an average of thirty workers each, and who come from the assembly line or related work themselves). Foremen are being sent to weekend sensitivity training sessions, emphasizing the problems of young workers. There are role-playing sessions to acquaint these supervisors with the lifestyles of various unfamiliar cultures. There are human relations programs aimed at dealing with motivation and decreasing the tensions of new employees. General Motors has an unusually active suggestion program (most company suggestion programs are practically worthless), which brings in a third of a million suggestions and pays out some $20 million for the five out of six that are adopted. Various techniques are being used to personalize the worker's feeling of participation in company objectives, including systems for assuming personal responsibility for production units. The foremen are being encouraged to know their workers as individuals and to make them *want* to do their jobs well. Arrangements are being made to permit time off for personal chores (to keep a worker from taking a whole unauthorized day off for a half-hour chore). Green trading stamps have been tried as a reward for regular attendance. Letters are being written to employees and their families, explaining the terrible impact of even low absenteeism and tardiness on efficiency of the line, trying to bring the problem into the worker's home life. Experiments with such motivators as job rotation, team jobs, employee-set quotas, and "contract" assembly jobs will, hopefully, reinstate the feeling of craftsmanship and responsibility for work.

manager leadership problems

The problems with the young managers are different in detail, but perhaps not in substance. They, too, are strikingly different from their predecessors in the corporate scene. Judson Gooding, writing in the March 1971 issue of *Fortune,* compares them with the "organization man" of the 1950s and the "young executive" of the early 1960s. The former was reconciled to a role as executive cog in the corporation, willing to go along with management toward organizational goals. The latter was colder and more of a corporate automaton, absorbed in the company to the exclusion of everything else, and seldom doubted the worth of corporate aims. By contrast, today's junior managers exhibit the passionate concerns of the youth of the late '60s for individuality, participation, concern—and most of all, change. If they find inadequate response, their deep anger at what they see as callousness toward the imperfections of society could lead to a sort of industrial mutiny. They have a high degree of both competence and self-confidence; they are not as good as they think they are, and some have an unjustified intolerance for views that differ from theirs, but they are very good. They are naive about the social impact of business, expecting it to reform social ills in ways far beyond its ability no matter what it spends.

And sometimes, despite the corporate rewards, they simply leave. A former oil company junior executive earning $20,000 left to become business manager for a struggling youth-oriented magazine at "much, much less" salary. He said, "I felt I wasn't giving anything; only 2% of me was being used." In his second job, he commented that "in any group that gets together to accomplish things, you have to have a hierarchy, but ours is a horizontal hierarchy. The players own the team. We've humanized the job, so we enjoy it."[16]

These young managers demand personal and psychological values rather than material ones, although they expect a good salary as a matter of course. They want early responsibility, either to move up or to move out. They thirst for risk and challenge—the chance to give it a try, and if they hang themselves, so be it. And they demand to be treated as individuals. They will not accept irrational behavior by management, and they are concerned about the long-term implications of company policies. They are willing to work hard, even very hard, but not at tasks they think are trivial.

Corporate leaders are worried that any steps they take now may create frustration later. If you promote a young manager early, how can you keep up the pace when there are just so many billets? The leaders are learning, however, that they can be frank about the shortcomings of their companies without turning off the young managers. Ford Motor Company, in an indoctrination film,[17] has a worker say, "I got a good job—but it's pretty bad," and another describes his job by saying, "It's a drag." And Marine Midland Bank's recruiting ad[18] passes up the hard sell in favor of predicting "real jobs, real responsibilities, real problems"—and frankly telling the candidates what the problems are.

Corporations who take the trouble to investigate find that the first boss can make or break the candidate's marriage with the company and that sensitivity training for this first boss is essential. Such profound questions as the need for corporate profits may be passionately debated by new recruits, and the boss must be prepared to accept less than total allegiance to corporate goals. Corporations such as Cummins Engine are pioneering in job enrichment for both managers and blue-collar workers, at the behest of chairman J. Irwin Miller, a national leader in efforts to improve the way society works and lives. "We have been slow in accommodating people," he says. "We have to pay serious, dignified attention to individuals. We will stand or fall on how we handle this." And he adds, "The ethic of the young is to contribute. The best way to keep the ablest of the young people is to load them up a little beyond their capacity. That capacity then turns out to be very high."

Do you think this principle will operate in North Star at this stage in its development? How?

Young people are going to insist that the companies and agencies where they work make some meaningful responses to their intense demands for personal fulfillment, as well as to larger social problems. Traditional managers, whether first-line supervisors or chief executives, are in for some painful retreading if they don't know how to provide such responses or don't think them worth providing. One approach to this task has been set forth by Scott Myers, in charge of job enrichment for Texas Instruments, in a provocative book he wrote while on a "sabbatical leave" from the company at the Massachusetts Institute of Technology's Sloan School of Management.[19] Myers maintains that in a world of disappearing management prerogatives, competence is supplanting authority as a source of influence, and emphasizes the importance of building "self-managed" jobs wherever possible—jobs that provide a realistic opportunity for the incumbent to be responsible for the total plan/do/control phases

self-managed jobs

of the job. When this approach was instituted at Texas Instruments, one supervisor was disconcerted when a problem-solving group under his nominal jurisdiction casually informed him that he was free to attend to other matters and they would "keep him posted on progress."

When a group of similarly "disenfranchised" supervisors undertook the task of defining their bewildering new role, with the assistance of their training director, the result resembled the left column of Figure 4-10. Despite the fact that they were striving conscientiously to institute the new "self-management" approach, they opted for the traditional authority-oriented form—a sort of "we'll free you, but do it our way" prescription. When they perceived this dichotomy, they had another try at it, and produced the goal-oriented definition in the right column. Their definition of the new supervisory role worked out like this:

goal-oriented supervisory role

- Make company goals highly visible
- Provide budgets and facilities
- Mediate conflict
- Stay out of the way, to let people manage their own work

The goal-oriented person enlarges the job, in contrast to the authority-oriented person who feels managed by the job. According to Myers, goals replace conformity, responsibility replaces prerogatives, competence replaces authority, and neither the supervisor nor the employee becomes obsolescent.

Figure 4-10.
Traditional vs. Self-Management Role Definitions

AUTHORITY-ORIENTED	GOAL-ORIENTED
Set goals for subordinates, define standards and results expected.	Participate with people in problem solving and goal setting.
Give them information necessary to do their job.	Give them access to information which they want.
Train them how to do the job.	Create situations for optimum learning.
Explain rules and apply discipline to ensure conformity; suppress conflict.	Explain rules and consequences of violations; mediate conflict.
Stimulate subordinates through persuasive leadership.	Allow people to set challenging goals.
Develop and install new methods.	Teach methods improvement techniques to job incumbents.
Develop and free them for promotion.	Enable them to pursue and move into growth opportunities.
Reward achievements and punish failures.	Recognize achievements and help them learn from failures.

PLAN → LEAD → CONTROL → DO

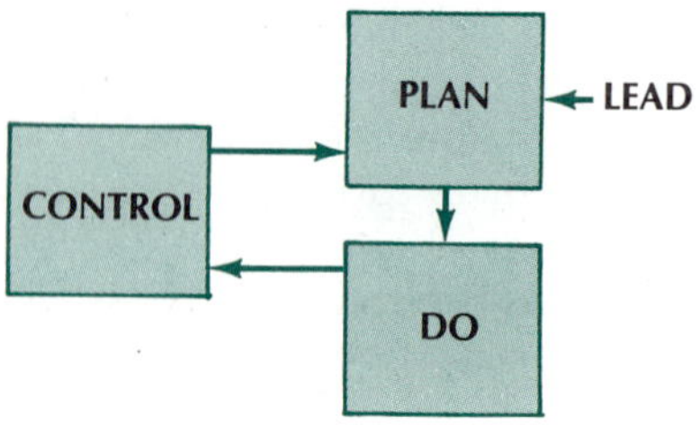

PLAN ← LEAD; CONTROL → PLAN → DO → CONTROL

134
MANAGEMENT PROCESSES

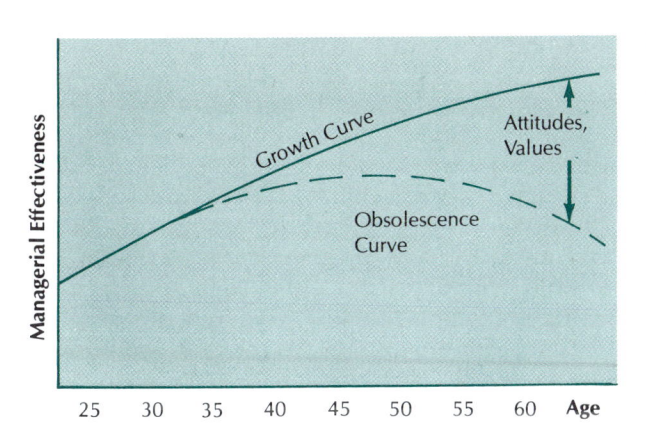

Figure 4-11.
Correlation of Manager's Age and Attitudes with Growth Potential

One of the significant elements in distinguishing between managerial growth and obsolescence is the question of changing values. Myers says the manager who attempts to manage from the foundation of authoritarian values tolerated in the past is out of date, because a manager's values establish the style of supervision. This manager will encounter increasing resistance and rebellion. Equally important is the manager's attitude, because it translates into the approach to subordinates, as Figure 4-11 illustrates.

We know very little about leadership and the apparent changes in leadership patterns and demands today. But evidence is accumulating, and it seems clear that what works in one era and in one situation will not work in another. A manager must be able to relate social changes to worker aspirations and adapt his or her management style accordingly.

managerial growth and obsolescence

Summary

The leader must view each employee both as an individual and as part of a group, in setting priorities and devising procedures to attain them, establishing a work environment meshing individual with organizational goals, and stimulating employees to good performance.

Motivation plays a major role in the individual's performance, as does innate ability; each of these is partly determined by external influences and partly modified on the job. Motivation determines the intensity and persistence with which a worker does a job, and this motivation must be channeled and sustained by the leader. Each individual has a hierarchy of needs, and workers respond only to those needs that are important to them at the time; a fulfilled need does not motivate. Depending on their incomes and the nature of their jobs, workers may rank appreciation, a feeling of being "in" on things, and understanding of their personal problems higher than job security or good wages; working conditions are far down the list of motivating factors.

Groups are extremely important to organizational achievement. Even when groups are antagonistic to management, there may be some common ground where the two can unite. A group may have several leaders for different purposes. Sensitivity training can help managers to understand what workers need and why they resort to groups to attain their needs.

Power can be attained in several ways. It can arise from formal authority, conferred by the organization in some specific fashion, or from acceptance authority, which exists when workers act as though leaders had power. It can be derived from status—a position in the organization that is understood to confer power. Or it can be assumed, without any delegation, but simply because a given set of circumstances lead to power. The old-fashioned notion of power implies coercive power, but other power bases exist as well: reward power, expertise power, reference power, and legitimacy. Expert and legitimate power are the usual sources of authority, but expert and reference power best contribute to job satisfaction.

Leadership style depends on the interplay of the leader's characteristics, the followers' characteristics (including group characteristics), and the situation. In recent years, the human relations leadership approach has gained popularity, with its assumption that people are basically creative and can enjoy work if it fits their aspirations. There is evidence that supervisors who are employee-centered achieve better productivity than those who are job-centered. Participatory leadership is still relatively uncommon in the United States.

Leaders who are successful appear to possess the traits of technical competence, initiative, self-confidence, and good judgment. Significant factors bearing on leadership performance are values, perceptions, personality, and background, with physical characteristics playing a small part.

Some principles in self-development for leadership are: concentrating on your workers instead of yourself and cultivating sincerity, honesty, dependability, and knowledge. Supervisory training is very important, since the supervisor is the only manager in direct contact with the main labor force; human relations training, using the case method or role-playing, probably fills the greatest need, though sensitivity training has some popularity. Management training also has concentrated more on human relations, seeking to break down old habit patterns and implant new ones. It is hard to be sure such training is effective, but indications are that it is.

The future of leadership training appears to lie in meeting the job needs of the articulate new generation which will not accept deadening work as inevitable and which demands to be more involved and find more job fulfillment. The most important element to change in old-line supervisors is their attitude toward the values and needs of this young labor force.

Notes

1. Now Exxon, second largest (after General Motors) industrial corporation in the U.S. in terms of sales; number one in assets and stockholder equity.

2. Abraham Maslow, *Toward a Psychology of Being* (Princeton, N.J.: D. Van Nostrand Co., Inc., 1962).

3. *Work in America,* Report of a Special Task Force to the Secretary of Health, Education and Welfare, submitted to the Senate Committee on Labor and Public Welfare (Washington, D.C., February 1973).

4. Frederick Herzberg, *Work and the Nature of Man* (New York: World Publishing Company, 1966).

5. For more information on these experiments, see F. J. Roethlisberger and W. J. Dickson, *Management and the Worker* (Cambridge, Mass.: Harvard University Press, 1939).

6. "The Bases of Social Power," in *Studies in Social Power,* ed. D. Cartwright (Ann Arbor, Mich.: University of Michigan Press, 1959), pp. 150–67.

7. J. G. Bachman, D. G. Bowers, and P. M. Marcus, "Bases of Supervisory Power: A Comparative Study in Five Organizational Settings," in A. S. Tannenbaum, *Control in Organizations* (New York: McGraw-Hill Book Co., 1968).

8. Ernest Dale, *The Great Organizers* (New York: McGraw-Hill Book Co., 1960), pp. 73–76.

9. Frederick W. Taylor, *The Principles of Scientific Management* (New York: Harper & Row, Inc., 1911).

10. Robert Tannenbaum and Warren H. Schmidt, "How to Choose a Leadership Pattern," *Harvard Business Review* 51 (May–June, 1973).

11. Douglas McGregor, *Leadership and Motivation* (Cambridge, Mass.: MIT Press, 1966).

12. Fred E. Fiedler, *A Theory of Leadership Effectiveness* (New York: McGraw-Hill Book Co., 1967).

13. Charles Bird, *Social Psychology* (New York: Appleton-Century Crofts, 1940), p. 378.

14. W. O. Jenkins, "Review of Leadership Studies with Particular Reference to Military Problems," *Psychological Bulletin* 44 (1947): 74–75.

15. Robert H. Guest, "Of Time and the Foreman," *Personnel* 32 (May 1956): 478.

16. "Two Who Rejected the Business World," *Fortune* (March 1971): 102.

17. "Don't Paint It Like Disneyland," Ford Motor Company training film.

18. "Here's a Great Opportunity to Fail," Marine Midland Bank recruiting brochure.

19. M. Scott Myers, *Every Employee a Manager* (New York: McGraw-Hill Book Co., 1970).

Review Questions

1. What are the three broad leadership tasks of the organizational manager?
2. What are three key issues in making workers perform to their maximum potential?
3. What are Maslow's human needs, and what do they mean?
4. How can group pressures assist in achieving organizational goals?
5. Explain how a group can have several leaders at the same time.
6. What are the sources of power?
7. Explain the five bases of power cited by French and Raven.
8. What factor does effective leadership style depend on?
9. Explain McGregor's "Theory X-Theory Y." How does it relate to "job-centered" and "employee-centered" supervisors?
10. How can leadership style be matched to the structure of a particular task?
11. What traits do successful leaders usually possess?
12. What is meant by "Leadership Compatibility Index"?
13. What are some basic leadership principles?
14. What four methods have been used in supervisory leadership training?
15. What is sensitivity training, or "T-group" training?

16. Why are today's automotive industry workers discontented? What is management trying to do about it?
17. What do young managers want from their jobs?
18. What does Myers mean by "self-managed" jobs?

Discussion Questions

1. What motivations do you think would influence you most strongly in each of the following three situations?
    a. You and your spouse have moved to a farm in a remote section of Newfoundland, where you will attempt to raise food initially but ultimately hope to found a commune.
    b. You have been selected at an unusually young age to manage a supermarket in a new community, where all the residents are almost as new to the area as you.
    c. You have been assigned a franchise to sell a new product in your area, with your profits coming entirely from commissions.

2. Frederick Taylor would assume that "Theory Y" could not possibly apply to the pig iron handlers he supervised. What do you think about this?

3. As the example of the naval ensign conned into mailing the stolen sander shows, there is a problem with being participative when employees stand ready to take advantage of you. Does this mean that participative approaches are nonsense in certain cases, or is there a way to get around this problem?

4. If you are challenged to go up on a high scaffolding, when you know it is likely to make you tremble or otherwise show your extreme nervousness, how would you handle this "damned if you do and damned if you don't" situation?

5. What are your thoughts about sensitivity training for yourself? Suppose you were in such a group, and after a few minutes it struck you that it was all talk and no results—so you said, "This is a bunch of nonsense; why don't we appoint a committee to work out a plan for what we are going to get done, and then we can proceed efficiently because we will know where we are going?" Suppose the group turned on you and attacked you for having old-fashioned hangups about having to "get things done," and asked what your anxieties were all about and why you couldn't stand anything that might disclose something about your feelings. How would you react to that? Do you think they might be right about your reasons for wanting a more orderly discussion? How would you answer their accusations?

6. What future problems might the worker's lack of a sense of personal direction and achievement produce on assembly lines? Will the big corporations be able to solve this leadership crisis and still keep the lines? If they do not, what happens to our production efficiency?

North Star Case Study

Eventually, North Star Associates acquires a drafting room divided into engineering specialties, plus a library, computer section, estimating unit, and certain other groups.

At that point, several of the draftsmen in one of the engineering units start wearing long flowing robes and beads, burning incense at their drawing tables, and at lunch time sitting around in a circle in the corner of the drafting room, hands clasped and chanting what apparently are prayers in a foreign tongue. The head of the group, an older engineer, is thoroughly disgusted, and orders them to straighten up and stop these crazy practices. They are very courteous, but ignore his orders. When he snatches up the incense and throws it out the window, they start a campaign of slowing down in their work and making excessive errors. He seems unable to deal with this practice, and only becomes more irritated.

Finally he goes to the head of the drafting room, the chief draftsman, who supports him but to no avail. The two of them present the matter to Bert Starr, then technical director. They tell Bert that if this sort of thing is not nipped in the bud the morale of the entire drafting room will be shot. Bert asks what the rest of the drafting room crew thinks of the situation, and is told that mostly they seem to be laughing at it.

1. What do you think of the action of the unit head in ordering the draftsmen to stop their unorthodox behavior?
2. What do you think of his method of tackling the problem?
3. Now that it has gone to Bert, what do you think he ought to do about it?
4. How are Bert's actions likely to come out?
5. What would you think of letting the whole group go, perhaps dismissing them with two weeks' pay? (There is no union or other contract, and they were hired with the understanding that they had no job tenure but were there only as long as they were needed).
6. How do you think firing them would affect the rest of the drafting room, who had basically taken the position that they were harmless freaks (though getting out plenty of work until the slowdown started)?
7. Assuming these practices developed slowly, should the supervisor have done anything about it earlier? What? Discuss.

Suggestions for Further Reading

Basil, D. C. *Leadership Skills for Executive Action.* New York: American Management Association, Inc., 1971.

Cartwright, D., ed. *Studies in Social Power.* Ann Arbor, Mich.: University of Michigan Press, 1959.

Cummings, L. L., and D. P. Schwab. *Performance in Organizations: Determinants and Appraisal.* Glenview, Ill.: Scott, Foresman & Co., 1973.

Dale, E. *The Great Organizers.* New York: McGraw-Hill Book Co., 1960.

Dubin, R. *Human Relations in Administration.* 4th ed. Englewood Cliffs, N.J.: Prentice-Hall, Inc., 1974.

Fiedler, F. E. *Leadership and Effective Management.* Glenview, Ill.: Scott, Foresman & Co., 1974.

Hersey, P. and K. H. Blanchard. *Management of Organizational Behavior: Utilizing Human Resources.* Englewood Cliffs, N.J.: Prentice-Hall, Inc., 1969.

Likert, R. *New Patterns of Management.* New York: McGraw-Hill Book Co., 1961.

———. *The Human Organization.* New York: McGraw-Hill Book Co., 1966.

McGregor, D. *Leadership and Motivation.* Cambridge, Mass.: M.I.T. Press, 1966.

Myers, M. *Every Employee a Manager.* New York: McGraw-Hill Book Co., 1970.

Roethlisberger, F. J., and W. J. Dickson. *Management and the Worker.* Cambridge, Mass.: Harvard University Press, 1939.

Selznick, P. *Leadership in Administration: A Sociological Interpretation.* Evanston, Ill.: Row, Peterson, 1957.

Stogdill, R. M. *Handbook of Leadership: A Survey of Theory and Research.* New York: The Free Press, 1974.

Tannenbaum, R. and W. Schmidt. "How to Choose a Leadership Pattern." *Harvard Business Review,* March 1958 (reprinted with foreword, May 1973).

Vroom, V. H., and P. W. Yetton. *Leadership and Decision Making.* Pittsburgh: University of Pittsburgh Press, 1973.

Communication

North Star Prologue

The fledgling North Star grew from a proprietorship to an organization of five principal members, with Henry North, founder, as president. When North Star became the recipient of an AID contract which required an overseas manager, Dick Boyer moved abroad to assume the post. As the workload increased, the group began to search for larger office facilities. The job of relocating became one of Henry's first tests as a leader, and he passed the test with flying colors. All the home team appeared to be well contented with the new location, and prepared to move.

The home office contingent was totally unprepared for the scorching letter they received from Dick Boyer shortly after Jo Parnela returned to the site. Apparently Jo had told him North Star had bought a new office building without explaining how that action was justified, so that it appeared to Dick as a senseless extravagance. Why, Henry asked the group plaintively, hadn't Jo told Dick how favorable the terms were, that the price per square foot actually was lower than in their previous inadequate quarters? And why, added Bert, hadn't she mentioned the unfinished bulk of the building, which provided flexibility as well as economy—and still gave the appearance of a prestige address? Probably, said Zeb dryly, because no one had given *Jo* that information.

They looked at one another, first in surprise and then in dismay. It was perfectly true—Jo had shown no interest, and consequently no one had bothered to do more than show her the industrial park's promotional pictures of the building, which represented it as a luxury structure on a prime site. The misunderstanding had done no harm as far as Jo was concerned, because she was relatively unconcerned about the financial side of the business, but the fragmentary information she transmitted to Dick—who was crucially concerned about finances, since he lived under the constant shadow of incurring a loss on the Natal project and bankrupting the company—had done all sorts of harm.

Two things worried Henry about the situation, and he communicated his worry to the others. One was the fact that Dick had used some rather intemperate language, and there was bound to be some embarrassment when he had to retract it in part, particularly with regard to charging the home office with extravagance. The other was their own error in judgment—they actually *had* taken this important step without any consultation at all with one of the partners. Indeed, they hadn't even thought about consulting him. Looking back, Henry was amazed that they could have overlooked so obvious a step. Clearly, they had to set up a more formal approval and consultative process to avoid a repeat performance.

Bert told Henry he ought to get off a letter to Dick promptly, but Henry answered that this was a letter they would both have to write. They informed Dick about the rationale for the new building and apologized for their failure to consult him. Things were smoothed over on the surface, but underneath they could sense that the matter rankled for a long time. And all the unpleasantness and hint of distrust could have been avoided, thought Henry, with better communication procedures.

Henry and Bert were quite busy for the next few weeks, and had little time to discuss the North Star communications gap in any formal way. When they finally forced themselves to sit down and draft a procedural memorandum on keeping one another informed, the exercise brought another information gap to light. Dick Boyer was completely on top of the Natal job, and doing what he liked best—but if anything were to happen to him the company would have precious little documentation as to where the job stood administratively, what technical agreements or job modifications had been made, what inspections had been performed and what waivers executed, and so on. Jo Parnela was hardly likely to be informed about such matters, and Dick had not made a practice of telling the home office anything except what design work to get out and when to submit billings to the prime contractor. Henry asked Bert if he would be in a position to take over smoothly if Dick were out of commission for one reason or another, and Bert left no doubt that he would not.

They wrote Dick about their worries, and he replied that he was in full agreement. He had been keeping a sketchy diary, which he duplicated and sent them, but he agreed to institute a monthly diary on a more formal basis which he would send back to the home office. It might even get Bert's drafting room off the dime once in a while, he said, if they could see where the requested work fitted into the whole picture. Dick mentioned another virtue of this practice which had not occurred to Bert or Henry: North Star was making inevitable mistakes on its first overseas project, some of them pretty costly, and if it ever obtained a second contract Dick's trial-and-error narrative would be required reading for the future project manager.

Shortly before they moved into the new building, Bert and Dick had jointly decided that they needed a teletypewriter installation, to speed up radio-telegraph queries and responses between the site and the home office and avoid expensive delays on site. When they moved into the new building and the machine was installed, Bert put it in his office for safekeeping, and saw that the office was locked whenever he was away. The drafting room was organized into four departments—civil and mechanical, architectural, electrical, and estimating—with the first three each headed by an engineer and the last by a draftsman with long years of experience in construction estimating. The senior civil and mechanical engineer, Abner Jenkins, was in charge of the drafting room as a whole, under Bert. Whenever an environmental engineering design was needed, Bert did it himself, and got in the habit of handling it in the estimating department to avoid setting up another department containing only himself. He gave the estimator the key to his office, so that he would have access to the environmental files if necessary. One day Bert was out of town when the teletypewriter started operating, and the estimator had to open the door so Henry could see what was coming in and take the needed action. In order to avoid a similar problem in the future, Bert told the estimator to check the teletypewriter every so often, if he wasn't in, to see if anything was awaiting action.

One day Ab Jenkins came to Bert and said the back room was close to mutiny, with a couple of the engineers threatening to quit. He said all the engineers had been upset to begin with when they learned that Jim Pozzi, the estimator, had access to the overseas messages when they did not. Lately, though, Pozzi had been rubbing it in by hinting at important happenings that would affect them all, but not giving any details. Then just yesterday the architect had seen a message on Pozzi's desk that said they were trying to put all the work overseas because of the lower wage rate and shut down the home office entirely on the Natal project. Ab said that the men resented being kept in the dark, particularly when Pozzi was in on things, and they were very upset at the news that North Star would try to do them out of work without telling them.

Bert was flabbergasted. As to pulling out the home office work, he said there was never any thought of such a move; the wire the architect had seen referred to some work to be done by the prime contractor, who of course would use in-country engineers. As to Pozzi having access to the teletypewriter, that was just an administrative convenience—but Bert suddenly perceived the potential for misunderstandings arising from that "convenience."

After he had reassured Ab Jenkins, Bert decided that the desire for confidentiality was not as important as the need for understanding and harmony in the back room, so he moved the teletypewriter into the back room by Ab's desk and told him he would have charge of it hereafter. And with Zeb's concurrence, another action was taken: the monthly chronological file of correspondence in and out, which had been kept in the secretary's desk, was moved to a table next to the teletypewriter; everyone could leaf through it periodically and review all phases of the firm's affairs.

A month after this episode, Ab Jenkins told Bert that in reading the correspondence, department heads had learned of several cases where the front office was saying things that were not quite correct, or was taking action that could have been improved if more consultation took place with the back room. He suggested that a weekly meeting of department heads and officers, where all pending business could be discussed, would help resolve such problems. Bert talked with Henry, who agreed at once, wondering why he hadn't thought of so obvious a device, and the weekly meetings were set up.

What North Star Can Learn from Chapter 5

1. Realization that an effective communications system doesn't come naturally, but must continually be nurtured to serve the organization well, although it is a central element in the management process

2. Understanding of the communication process and the opportunities for misunderstanding between message transmittal and reception

3. Importance of feedback in any good communication system (the element which makes the vital difference between one-way and two-way communications)

4. The difference between formal and unofficial communications, and the critical functions fulfilled by each

5. An awareness of the various techniques an organization should apply to ensure an effective communication system

6. The importance of promoting upward communication, as well as focusing on the downward element

7. The various problems which intervene to shortcut the flow of information and create obstacles to decision making

This chapter examines the element that enables the various groups within organizations to function harmoniously in accordance with overall goals and objectives. Just as arteries and veins sustain the flow of life-giving blood to the vital organs of the body, so communication is the lifeblood of an organization. Listen to the cacophony of typewriters, voices, and other reassuring office sounds—group meetings, individual conversations, orders, questions, telephone messages, papers rustling, pencils scratching—in short, communication at work. Now erase all these communication processes, and see what is left: the functionless shell of the organization. Suppose this office were the New York Stock Exchange, alive with teletypes and ticker-tape systems linking worldwide stock transactions and providing the information that makes such transactions happen. The Stock Exchange is communications technology in action, but a good system is much more than technology. The effectiveness of a communication system depends on the attitudes and perceptions of managers and workers, and their awareness of how these factors influence the communication process. (In the same manner, the quality of your personal life improves as you become attuned to the complexities inherent in communicating.) It is the manager's responsibility to build the proper atmosphere and establish appropriate channels for effective internal and external communication.

Communication is examined from four perspectives:

1. *Concepts of communication*—steps in the communication process from sender to receiver, and the many roadblocks that interfere with the sender's meaning.
2. *Organizations as communication systems*—exploring the importance of communications for organizational survival and channels and networks (formal and informal) in an organizational communication system.
3. *Techniques of organizational communication*—barriers to communication in organizations and the nuts and bolts of good communications practice for managers.
4. *Problems in communication systems*—the pitfalls caused by rejection of communications, overload and duplication of information, and incompleteness or omission of communications.

We shall see that too much information is as bad as not enough, because in either case the intended meaning is not conveyed.

Communication systems have been the focus of much recent research and discussion, often in connection with information systems. As our society and its organizations grow in complexity, few would question the increasing need for a mechanism to keep track of the information explosion and ensure a timely and effective organizational response to change. All too often, however, the high-speed computer is embraced as the ultimate solution to information and communication problems. Without question the computer is an extremely useful aid to handling and processing information, as we shall discuss in chapter 13, but it should only represent a single component of the overall communication system. The central purposes of the latter—to maintain the flow of accurate information within the organization, to stimulate good decisions and appropriate actions, and to provoke necessary change—are far broader than the capabilities of any computer system by itself. A good communication system is such a basic element in an organization's daily operations that managers tend to take its existence for granted. Such a casual attitude can lead to serious disruptions, for communication is a vital element of organizational success and it does not take place automatically.

Concepts of Communication

Importance of Communication

Communicating is one of the basic processes in any organism. Observe a colony of ants, and you will see in operation the communication system they have developed to fit their communal needs. Watch the "wagtail dance" of bees directing their hivemates toward the source of nectar. Listen to the mournful mating call of the coyote echoing eerily across the prairie night. Without some communication system, long-term survival for any living creature would be virtually impossible.

We cannot even do without communication when we plan and accomplish an entire task by ourselves. When we order material, get instructions, or dispose of something we have produced, obstacles will arise from poor communications. We can understand these obstacles better when we examine the communication process in detail.

The Communication Process

Communication requires a sender to originate (encode) the message and a receiver to understand (decode) it. An organization has a multiplicity of senders and receivers, based on its hierarchy and the relationships among its members. Regardless of the individuals involved, each message travels a route like that shown in Figure 5-1. Sometimes the information originates with the sender, but more often the sender is passing along information from other sources. A senior executive informs subordinates about policies formulated at directors' meetings on the basis of data the directors have received from various sources in and outside of the organization. Supervisors send information to the middle management level based on reports from their subordinates on the operating line. Cocktail party tidbits originate from newspaper items, office memoranda, the grapevine, statements by authorities, or comments from a friend. Such information, whatever its origin, passes through the sender's "filter" before it is prepared for transmittal to the intended recipient: the sender is encoding it in a personal style and with a personal axe to grind.

    sender
    receiver

    filter

Consider an example of Figure 5-1 in operation. The board of directors of a company determines as a policy that employees cannot be ordered to work overtime without 24 hours' notice, except in cases of bona fide emergency.

    1. *Information.* The company president passes this decision on to the personnel director with instructions to circulate orders accordingly.

encoding
perceptions

2. *Message preparation* (encoding). Based on the personnel director's *perceptions* ("If foremen planned properly, they wouldn't have to ask for overtime without notice; the new policy is a crutch to prop up poor management"), and *attitudes* ("Labor peace is the most important thing, to avoid grievances that can lead to crippling strikes"), the policy is translated into detailed instructions for the foremen.

message transmission

3. *Message transmission.* Because it is a policy matter, the personnel director prepares a detailed "standing instruction" to be added to the set of such instructions in the large book kept in each shop. At the various shops, the shop superintendent calls in the foremen from time to time as they are available, and has them read it. Because it must cover a wide variety of situations, its language is general; it uses the term "bona fide emergency" as the only justification for overtime that cannot be planned by noon of the previous day. Foremen do not get a copy of the instruction to keep, but can consult it in the shop office if needed.

4. *Message reception.* The foreman who reads the instruction—probably pointed out to him when he happens to visit the shop office with a question or problem, has his *perceptions* ("Management is transferring its dilemmas to us; it really wants to keep production levels up, but has to look good in print because of the union"), and his *attitudes* ("Production is crucial to the company, and that personnel director doesn't know what we're up against. I had to work when necessary, and these young kids must, too"). Moreover, after a brief discussion with the shop superintendent, it is clear to the foreman that the superintendent shares these views. He drops the instruction and gets on with the important question that brought him to the office in the first place (a form of *interference* with the communication).

message translation

5. *Translation.* Since anyone with production experience knows you can't "plan" overtime by noon Tuesday for 4 P.M. Wednesday, management is putting the bee on the foremen to use the "emergency" label whenever overtime is needed.

feedback

6. *Feedback.* While the personnel director is responsible for preparing and promulgating the instruction, he or she is not in the chain for compliance and therefore has little or no notion of how well the order is

Figure 5-1.
Communications Model

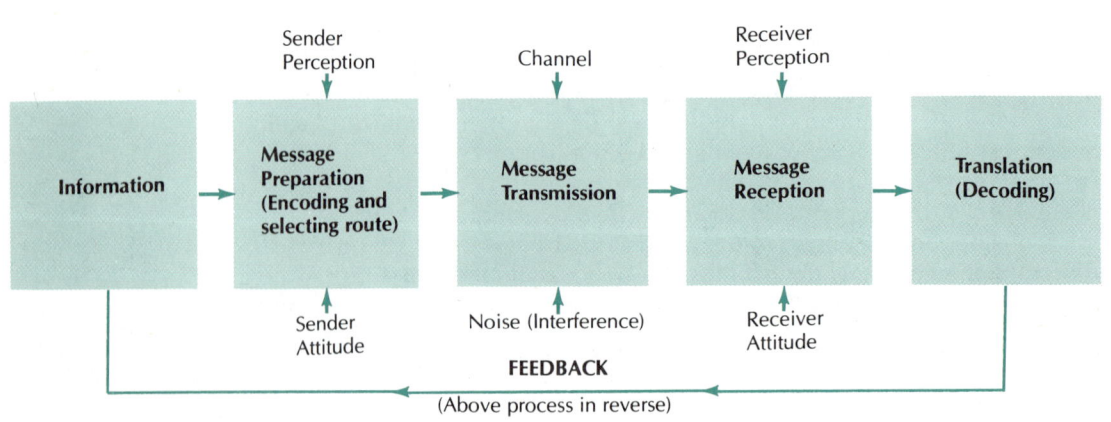

being executed. The foremen would not discuss the subject with personnel under any circumstances, since they regard the department as an unrealistic nuisance with no grasp of production problems. Therefore, when the president asks the director how the instruction is working, he receives a reassuring answer that reports no trouble with it. If the president should check with timekeeping, he will see that all overtime worked on short notice is for "bona fide emergencies." If the board of directors asks the president how the policy is working out, they will be told "fine."

Actually, as you can see, nothing has changed. If an employee should file a grievance, the union will have little difficulty in proving that management uses the "bona fide emergency" clause deceptively, and management will be genuinely surprised. Chances are the foremen will be blamed for failure to carry out an unworkable policy—but they had no access to real communication channels, to let management know the policy was unworkable, so that a better one could be worked out.

Thus, in any communication network, the sender selects the *encoding system*, which determines how the information will be set forth. It is perfectly possible to phrase an order in terms that absolutely guarantee misunderstanding, as when a professor informs a freshman composition class that their first assignment is to trace the literary antecedents of any Shakespeare play.

The sender also selects the *route*, which determines who will get the message and through what channels, an important step. If you have a boss named Smith, who in turn has a boss named Jones, and you route a complaint about Smith's treatment of you to Jones, with a copy to Smith, you are declaring war. If you send the complaint to Smith, with a direct copy to Jones, you have still established an adversary situation, as both Smith and Jones will realize (but it isn't quite as overt, because Smith is expected to take the action with Jones simply observing). If you send the complaint to Jones *via* Smith, your action is much more diplomatic, because Smith can annotate the complaint before Jones sees it—or deal with you first so the complaint need not go to Jones at all. If you send it only to Smith, the message is still less abrasive, for there is no hint that Jones will be brought into the problem.

message routing

The sender usually selects the *channel*—verbal, face-to-face, telephone, individual memorandum, published instruction to a group, telegram, bulletin board, messenger, or even the taking of an action which carries the message. The channel will play a significant role in how well the message is received. (If you give a nice wedding present, would you rather get an individual written note of thanks, a printed "thank you" card, or a mimeographed notice of "thanks to all our friends too numerous to contact in person"?) In sending a message about a major change in company policy—perhaps a notification that overtime, a common practice in the past, would not be used in the future—did every employee affected receive an explanatory memorandum? Was the information placed in the company newspaper, generally devoted to social chitchat such as employee marriages and company teams? Or was it simply stuck on a few crowded bulletin boards?

channel

The process of encoding decisions includes consideration of the *translation* problem. Just as it makes little sense for a North American manager in Latin America to give instructions in English, so it is useless for a manager in the U.S., addressing new and inexperienced workers, to say, "I practice the 'management by exception' principle" without explaining what that means. A supervisor telling workers they must tighten their work habits would achieve a more favorable translation by saying that they are expected to work a full eight-hour day than by demanding that they "keep their noses to the grindstone."

noise

Interference, or *noise,* can distort meaning or even block a channel completely. Some noise is almost inevitable, possibly originating within the channel itself, as in radio static, TV "snow," or hum in the telephone receiver. Noise can also occur outside the channel, as when an important message is mislaid or competing with other demands on the receiver's time. The ramifications of noise are so serious that the communication itself must be designed to counteract noise effects. Three methods for doing this are: *attention, redundancy,* and *repetition.*

A message attracts *attention* when it is different from competing demands on the recipient's time. The telephone company sends overdue bill notices to businesses in a distinctive envelope that shows a date a few days off and carries a notation in heavy type: "THIS DATE CAN BE VERY IMPORTANT TO YOU" (it is stated as the date when telephone service can be disconnected). Some firms trying to sell vacation properties send advertisements in window envelopes through which a check to the addressee seems to be visible—though it actually is a "free gift" come-on. Airmail envelopes have a distinctive red and blue border that demands attention. Western Union mailgrams come in the familiar color and format of telegrams, suggesting a priority message. Some executives send handwrit-

Communication requires a sender who originates the message and a receiver who gets it.

ten memos to subordinates on a recognizable format memorandum paper bearing a personal mark and thus of higher priority than a typed memo that someone else could have originated.[1] Innumerable devices are used to make a communication stand out from the crowd and obtain priority attention from the recipient.

Redundancy is formally defined as superfluity or excessiveness, but in communications this apparent excess is useful to insure that the meaning gets through the noise. The intent may be emphasized through a variety of methods, rephrasing the message two or more times, or summarizing the message in the final paragraph. A typical newspaper article carries the story in capsule form in the headline, repeats it in slightly more detail in the first paragraph, and covers it in full in the remaining paragraphs. A message with all the redundancy drained out may not convey the intended meaning. During World War II, a public relations officer in London needed to know General Mark Clark's age for a press release about the commander of the Italian invasion, so he sent a terse telegram to Clark's headquarters: "HOW OLD MARK CLARK?" Back came the equally terse reply: "HE FINE HOW YOU?" But too much redundancy is a hazard, and the sender must strike a happy balance between transmitting enough to make the point but not so much that the channels are unnecessarily cluttered.

redundancy

Repetition of a message occurs when the sender transmits the same information through more than one channel, or more than once through the same channel. Weather broadcasts for yacht crews are repeated over and over again, to insure that mariners will not miss one broadcast and set sail without the essential knowledge about the weather. If a group has reached agreement in a meeting, the leader usually sends each participant a memorandum summarizing the outcome, as a reinforcing mechanism. A supervisor may send telephone instructions to a subordinate and follow up with a written memo repeating the same instructions. Advertisers use repetition to emphasize the point they are making and drive it more firmly into the mind of the potential customer. In short, *repetition* implies *duplication* of the message, whereas redundancy implies an *alternate form* of the same message.

repetition

At the end of the message channel is the *receiver*—who has a filtering system, just as the sender does, to admit what is desired. The receiver decodes the message by using the same process the sender used in encoding it. The crucial question is whether the message was interpreted as the sender intended; all too often, it was not. If the sender is viewing the world through 3-D glasses, the receiver's bifocals won't show the same image. If your perspective is different from that of your receiver, you need to allow for this in the way you encode the message.

Feedback is the process through which the results of the communication are reported back to the sender. In face-to-face communication, feedback is usually simple and immediate—by indicating understanding, repeating the communication to the sender, or taking action that demonstrates accurate reception of the message. In organizations, this feedback function is carried out through formal and informal systems involving a number of cross-check points. The time frame may be immediate, as above, or may be of long duration if complicated directions or delayed actions are involved. Frequent feedback is important, so the sender can rectify a misinterpreted message before it is too late. When the hired boy returned from town where he had been sent with the horse to get it *shod,* and reported that it had been *shot,* feedback to the sender was significant but too late. To keep too many organizational horses from meeting such a fate, management must establish feedback points and see that the process is kept well-oiled.

Automatic feedback occurs in your home when the furnace thermostat picks up the rising temperature and turns off the burner. Automatic feedback takes place in an organization when a union-negotiated cost of living increase goes into effect upon a given rise in the consumer price index. Feedback should permeate the entire management process, for it is this monitoring device that enables management to discover what is really happening in the organization. Upward communication, a relatively neglected area in management, is a vital lifeline for the health of the organization.

Filters

In a society bombarding us with masses of wanted and unwanted information, we depend on filtering systems to select those messages which are relevant to our needs and interests. Within our cognitive processes, such systems are gates that let desired signals in and attempt to bar the way to others. Consider the operation of your filtering system when you pick up a newspaper. If you are a sports fan, you turn immediately to the sports page. If you are seeking a job, you open to the classified ads and then perhaps the business news. As you scan the news headlines, your filtering system is hard at work. If you have witnessed a traffic accident on your way to work, that story will catch your interest. If your family lives in Maine and a headline cites a cold wave with record low temperatures there, you may read that first.

Filtering systems may be conscious, unconscious, or some combination of the two. A physical example of a conscious filtering system is the radar in an aircraft. The signal sent out to bounce off other aircraft and echo back to the sender must compete with an atmosphere crammed with all sorts of confusing electromagnetic signals, so the radar designer invents an electronic "gate" that admits only signals of the same frequency as the one sent out. Thus the relatively weak echo stands out from the welter of other noise that may be much more intense, because it is the only signal allowed through the gate. An unconscious filtering system might be demonstrated by a politician working in his office with an unheeded radio droning on, when suddenly a mention of his name jerks him to attention. Consciously he was not even listening to the program, but his unconscious filter was at work tuning out insignificant material and letting in significant items.

Human filters are the product of all our life experiences. The accident of birth determines many of our values and thus our responses to certain cues. Our culture, religion, and early family lifestyle shape our thoughts and behavior as long as we live; contact with later groups modifies our viewpoints on many subjects, but studies show that political and religious beliefs are surprisingly persistent. Filters develop when the need arises. The parents who sleep through the screaming siren of a passing ambulance but awaken to their baby's faint cry are using a filter programmed to guard the infant.

Suppose that at the moment of birth you had traded homes with a baby on the Chinese mainland and had been raised in that household. Today you would speak a different language and have vastly different perceptions on such matters as authority and the role of the personal ego in society. In essence, you would be an entirely different person, viewing the world from a very different perspective.

These inbred filters are augmented by subjective filters conditioned by later associations. Enrollment in an engineering course, membership in the garden or yacht club or accounting association, status as a new parent, present occupation, or personal ambitions, all build interest and expertise and sensitize our filters accordingly. Long after a Peace Corps worker returns from a tour in Chad, news items on that country will be of interest; Chad has taken on a cognitive importance to that individual.

acquired filter

These intentional and unintentional filters coexist in an uneasy truce. We are well aware of our interests, but we may not be aware that they have fashioned a filter that automatically produces a hostile reaction to management—or even that our reaction *is* hostile. We may instinctively screen out arguments favoring management (or the union) without knowing it. When we select a political candidate, if we decide to support one who will work for a cause we favor, we may filter out information suggesting administrative incompetence and/or lack of moral fiber in that particular candidate.

Emotional state is an important filtering influence. If you had an unpleasant experience on the way to work, your outlook on the job will be less enthusiastic. In recession times, a company whose business is "recession-proof" will tend to take a cautious attitude toward ventures that would be considered conservative in normal times. When you are upset, you may tend to impute the wrong motives to people who approach you, like the motorist driving a country road late at night who found himself with a flat tire and no jack. He approached a nearby farmhouse, hesitant to wake the farmer, but telling himself the farmer would be unreasonable to be irritated since it was so vital to the motorist to have help. By the time his pounding at the door had brought the farmer to the window, he was so incensed at the thought that the farmer might be irritated that he screamed, "You can keep your damned jack!"

The first step in insuring that a communication is understood is to be aware of the recipient's filtering system *and of your own*. You must ask yourself, "How will that person view what I am saying?" If the message is not coded and transmitted in channels and language relevant to the receiver's needs and interests, it will be filtered out or misinterpreted. Just as you would not advertise to attract stamp collectors in *Popular Photography* magazine, so you cannot transmit to labor or management through channels or in language to which that audience is not attuned.

What role did filtering systems play in the misunderstanding between Dick and the home office? How did Jo's filter differ from Bert's? From Zeb's?

Meaning

Communication is conveyed by symbols, both verbal and nonverbal. Intonation, gestures, facial expression, degree of interest—all contribute to getting the message across. The English language often attaches a

meaning

variety of meanings to the same word (Wilfred Funk, in *Six Weeks to Words of Power,* tells us that "run" has over 382 different meanings in its noun and verb forms), and the same sentence or combination of words can have diametrically opposed meanings. The sentence "I will see that you get what's coming to you" can have vastly different meanings depending on whether it comes from your lawyer during a grievance session or from a supervisor who has caught you in an unauthorized act. Add to this problem the need to reconcile verbal and nonverbal signals that appear to conflict (like the supervisor's words of praise contrasting with a paycheck that never gets bigger), and it is easy to see how the intended meaning can be lost. Managers must learn to pay far more attention to nonverbal signals, for subordinates are heavily influenced by them—often to the point where they nullify the verbal messages management is trying to send.

Intepretation—A Personal Thing

interpretation

The filtering system discussed above plays an important role in the deciphering of the message by the receiver. The communication must have significance for the recipient, or it will not get through. A young manager who tells workers it is in their self-interest to exert extra effort to improve the company's profit level may as well talk to the wall. An increase in company profits has no visible significance to the workers (short of a bankruptcy situation), and unless the discussion is linked to some incentives workers can relate to, their filters will screen out the well-intended message—without the manager realizing it. For communication to occur, the receiver must understand the sender's message; for the receiver to *act* on the basis of a message, some sort of motivation must be provided. In Lewis Carroll's *Alice in Wonderland,* Humpty Dumpty tells Alice he let words mean whatever he wanted them to mean, and they came around on Saturday night to be paid for this privilege. Too often senders adopt this practice of letting words mean what they want them to mean, and then express surprise that they are misunderstood.

Levels of Abstraction

ladder of abstraction

Compare a modern painting with a Renaissance masterpiece; often, one difference involves the degree of abstraction. Language, like modern art, works on various levels of abstraction. To be understood, a speaker must plant the message on the proper rung of the listener's "ladder of abstraction." Figure 5-2 shows a continuum of abstraction, ranging from most specific to most abstract; the subject of the continuum is the knowledge a manager might have about the overtime authorization

Figure 5-2.
Abstraction Ladder

Most Specific				INCREASING LEVEL OF ABSTRACTION ➡				Most Abstract
Instruction on authorizing emergency overtime	Overtime Procedures	Administrative Procedures	Communication Topic	Management Course	College Education	Education	Knowledge

152
MANAGEMENT PROCESSES

described in Figure 5-1. The most specific knowledge, of course, relates to the particular instruction for authorizing overtime in bona fide emergencies. Somewhat less specific is knowledge of overtime procedures in general, and even less specific is general understanding of administrative procedures in published form. More abstract is knowledge on the overall topic of communications (this chapter, for example), and knowledge of management in general (this whole book), then college education as a whole (which might or might not include any study of management). Still more abstract is all forms of education, of which college is only a small part; at the highest level of abstraction is all knowledge, no matter how acquired.

It is a far cry from asking, "Do you have a body of knowledge?" to asking, "Do you know the details of XYZ Company's standing instruction on the authorization of emergency overtime, as described in the lecture on communications of the course in management at ABC College?" If we ask, "What knowledge do you have?" (and have the patience to stick around for the whole answer), we would hardly expect the specific information on overtime. On the other hand, if we wish to be more abstract (more general), too specific a focus will defeat our purpose. A financial reporter wishing to set forth the condition of the entire financial market cannot focus on the current stock price of Go Go Fund, Inc., and ignore all the other financial indicators.

The practical implications of level of abstraction for managers are obvious: when they plan to communicate to other members of the organization—upward, downward, or laterally—they must select the proper level of abstraction. If they are too specific, the receivers will be locked in tightly and perhaps excessively; but if they are too abstract, receivers may have more leeway than was intended or may simply misunderstand entirely.

Breadth and Shading of Meaning

The use of symbols and the meanings we attach to them reflect the range and diversity of our experiences. When we say it is "snowing," the word hardly pins down the wide variety of precipitation that might be taking place. By contrast, the Eskimo (to whom snow is a life-or-death commodity) is said to have 20 words or more to convey exactly the kind of snow in question. When we refer to objects at various distances, we have only two pronouns: this and that. The Tlinglit Indians, to whom the precise distance of a foe or game was crucial at times, differentiated between objects which were very close *(he)*, medium close *(ya)*, rather far off *(yu)*, and out of sight *(we)*. Similarly, when a senior manager speaks of "loyalty" in talking to employees, it is essential to consider the many shades of meaning that might be in the listeners' minds: loyalty to family, to country, to church, to professional or union organizations, to friends or members of working groups—and, perhaps well down the line, to the company. The manager's meaning must be specific. Thus, it might be wise to use an entirely different term that will be translated more accurately.

breadth and shading of meaning

Conflicting Meaning

It is easy for a communicator to prepare a message that may have meanings other than the intended one; the communicator, after all,

conflicting meaning

knows what is meant and thus may be blinded to the other (and perhaps more natural) interpretations of the message. If a sales manager tells people that the winner in the annual sales volume competition will be computed on the formula "volume of promoted sales (those where the company helps get the lead) plus volume of regular sales times two divided by the fraction of days during the period the salesman was out on the road (all in thousands)," at the end of the year Smith, Jones, and Brown may have an equal right to win. Figure 5-3 shows the sales volume for each of the three and the fraction of selling days during the period, and Figure 5-4 shows how each of the three computed the scores.

Now that the fat is in the fire, it will be extremely difficult for the sales manager to clarify which formula is correct, since the decision will appear to favor one of the three top salespeople. The time to make the communication clear is when it is first prepared.

Even a poorly punctuated sentence (or in speech, a sentence with an unintended inflection) can turn the meaning upside down. A few years ago, members of the Oklahoma legislature were astonished by a deluge of letters from organized teachers, urging passage of a bill granting tax exemptions to farmers who raised baby turkeys.[2] Lobbyists later discovered that the teachers had been asked, verbally, to back "House Bill 1320, too." So they wrote their letters supporting House Bill 1322, the turkey bill. (It passed.) And there is room for confusion when supervisor and workers belong to different generations, because of the "slang gap." When young employees use such terms as "tough," "heavy," "mother," "ripoff," and "split," the manager may be dismayed, annoyed, or simply perplexed. In this situation, repetition, redundancy, and feedback are essential for communication of the intended messages.

Misunderstanding

misunderstanding

We spend 75% of each day issuing or receiving communications (managers are said to spend 95%), but most of us still do it poorly because we fail to realize what a complex problem it is. When someone says, "But I thought you meant..." after a misunderstanding, it is likely that he heard the exact words of the sender but gave them his own interpretation. The manager who tells the material clerk to order (among other things) 12 boxes of pencils will be slightly stunned to find 12 cases of 48 boxes each filling the mailroom. The manager should have considered the material clerk's frame of reference: in the company, consumer quantity measures are seldom used, and a "box" almost invariably means a case. If the manager plaintively asks, "Why didn't the clerk *think*?", one could turn the question around and ask, "Why didn't the manager think?"

If your message is misunderstood, it is your fault. A manager who asks the foreman to turn in a report "before" an important meeting,

Figure 5-3.
Competition Statistics

Salesman	Promoted Volume	Regular Volume	Selling Fraction
Smith	$900	$500	.9
Jones	540	600	.8
Brown	200	650	.7

intending to study the report and perhaps take some corrective action before the meeting, will be very upset if it is handed in five minutes before the meeting begins. It is the sender's job to be sure the receiver has deciphered the real meaning, not just heard the *words* themselves.

Experiences and Culture

We can communicate only what we know, and can translate only in terms of our culture-bound past experiences. Many of the symbols and patterns of speech that we take for granted are laden with cultural inferences. An American manager in Asia may tell the plant manager, "I want you to hire the best supervisors you can get, with no favoritism." Later, discovering that the manager has given all the jobs to relatives, the American is furious—and the manager doesn't understand, for of course relatives are "best"—they will offer complete loyalty, whereas strangers will not.

When a large U.S. beverage company was planning an advertising campaign in Taiwan, showing a frosted bottle with the slogan "Baby, it's cold outside," someone took the precaution of having an independent translator retranslate the slogan back to English. It came back as "Small mosquito, outdoors it is very cold." "Small mosquito" is Chinese slang for infant or very small child—technically a correct translation, but the ad would certainly have mystified Taiwan consumers. One of the authors, delivering a hastily memorized greeting in an Asian dialect, discovered later that a scarcely perceptible change in inflection made him refer to his

culture-bound experience

Figure 5-4.
Competition Results

Smith's Analysis	$\dfrac{(900 + 500) \times 2}{.9} = 3111$ Smith	**(Smith Wins)**
	$\dfrac{(540 + 600) \times 2}{.8} = 2850$ Jones	
	$\dfrac{(200 + 650) \times 2}{.7} = 2429$ Brown	
Jones's Analysis	$\dfrac{900 + (500 \times 2)}{.9} = 2111$ Smith	
	$\dfrac{540 + (600 \times 2)}{.8} = 2175$ Jones	**(Jones Wins)**
	$\dfrac{200 + (650 \times 2)}{.7} = 2143$ Brown	
Brown's Analysis	$900 + \dfrac{(500 \times 2)}{.9} = 2011$ Smith	
	$540 + \dfrac{(600 \times 2)}{.8} = 2040$ Jones	
	$200 + \dfrac{(650 \times 2)}{.7} = 2057$ Brown	**(Brown Wins)**

audience as "my dear mangoes" instead of "my dear friends." Such mistakes occur not only in different languages but also when the language is the same and the cultures are different.

Value-Laden Symbols

value-laden symbols

Have you ever heard an argument between two people for whom the same words mean different things? Such words as "democracy," "fair," "profits," "evil," "justice," "strength," and so on always reflect the values of the user. Capitalist and communist peoples would agree that democracy is a form of government, but each group thinks its arrangement is the more democratic. Basically, we think the things we want are "just," and what our enemies want is "evil"; and they think the same, in reverse. The manager's concern for "profits" may seem more like "greediness" to the union representative who negotiates with him. Such words cause problems in communications unless they are very explicitly defined.

Context

context

A phrase has little meaning outside of the context of the entire paragraph. A few years ago, the chairman of the President's Council of Economic Advisors, Alan Greenspan, brought down the wrath of the press, Congress, and much of the public on his head when he said stockbrokers were the hardest hit by the 1974 inflation/recession. He meant that their incomes had declined at the fastest rate, and that more brokerage firms had gone under than any other major industry; but what came across was that they were closest to the poverty level, which clearly was not true. Theater advertisers sometimes take favorable quotes out of context to suggest that the reviewer liked the play, when just the opposite may be true; a devastating review saying, "You must attend this play if you want to see first-hand why the Broadway stage is dying," can be excerpted to "...you must attend this play...." This technique, of course, involves deliberate deception—but the same thing can happen accidentally, as with Greenspan's comment.

The receiver too can alter the context by filtering out unwanted parts of a communication. If an evaluation report describes a management trainee as "eager to do a good job, popular with colleagues, very agreeable in attitude and completely loyal," the trainee may overlook more critical comments such as "somewhat lacking in initiative, tends to be discouraged when things do not work out just right, could be more aggressive, and has some difficulty in dealing with subordinates." Actually, the first list covers relatively unimportant mangerial traits, while those on the second list are essential. Management has failed the trainee by de-emphasizing the critical problems, and the trainee has failed by indulging in self-deception, and is likely to be astonished when management takes the obvious next step—release.

Hidden Meanings

hidden meaning

Words do not always mean what they say. In some political campaigns a few years ago, the term "law and order" was widely interpreted as synonymous with oppression of individual rights. In some marriages, when the wife says, "I'll be there at eight o'clock," both she and her husband know she really means eight-thirty; and as long as both of them have the cues straight, the difference causes no problem.

Receivers themselves can filter out unwanted parts of a communication.

The Lubrizol Corporation manufactures the additives in one can of lubricating oil out of every three around the world. Near the bottom of the largest 500 U.S. corporations in size, it ranks about tenth in return on sales. President Thomas W. Mastin sees that ideas travel freely within his highly informal company; he knows a third of his 3,300 employees personally and spends three-fourths of his time talking with them. He says that many of the workers calling on him "are just people who think they have something interesting to tell me." Such wide-open communication channels, which encourage any employees with ideas for improvement to propose them, insure that there are few hidden meanings in the dialogue between management and the workers.

Organizations as Communication Systems

The modern company could not survive without an elaborate communication system to link the divisions and units which may be thousands of miles from headquarters. One major goal of such a corporate communication system is *coordination*, which brings information from all parts of the organization to the key decision centers rapidly and accurately. Communication aids decision making in three stages:

communication functions

- As a transmitter of policies, instructions, and information necessary for determining what must be done and scheduling it correctly,

from top levels or intermediate levels to the working level (downward communication)
- As a relayer of feedback from lower and intermediate levels to decision-making levels of management (upward communication)
- As an intelligence gathering mechanism, probing beneath the surface and looking beyond the routine or obvious for information that may not automatically find its way to the managerial level (secondary upward communication)

In order to control an organization, management needs vast quantities of information while it is still hot. Every organization has predetermined control mechanisms, such as financial reports, which stimulate corrective action; but they are not always working properly, and almost never are they as complete as they should be. President Mastin of Lubrizol undoubtedly picks up valuable suggestions and information in his informal contacts with employees at all levels—material a formal system would never ferret out, which certainly helps the company to be so fast on its feet. (Executive Vice-President Lester Coleman says, "We can go from testing and development to pilot plant and full production in three months if necessary"—a sequence that can take a less flexible company five to ten years.)

communication in decision making
A. W. Steiss, in *Public Management and Budgeting*,[3] has defined five kinds of organizational communication flows in decision-making processes:

1. *Expressive*—directed to the external audience, as in annual reports, releases, etc.
2. *Educative*—messages designed to elicit information, transmitted as questions directed at specific points within the organization
3. *Informative*—restricted to transmission of data and information at various levels of interpretation and analysis
4. *Influential*—containing advice, suggestions, recommendations
5. *Authoritative*—consisting of orders, commands, directives; designed to initiate action on the part of others

These functions are served through formal, informal, unofficial, and nonverbal communication.

Formal Communication

chain of command

The traditional notion of the manager is that of an order issuer in the chain of command—a structure so designed that every individual knows to whom he or she is accountable, and every individual has only one boss (eliminating the possible conflicts arising when more than one person has authority over a situation). Such a structure is depicted in Figure 3-1, with the lines defining the up-and-down routes for all communication. This hierarchical structure imposes direction on information flow. As information trickles upward, it is summarized by each higher level in turn, until a tightly capsuled version finally reaches top management. Because of the repeated filtering, there is no guarantee that what finally survives contains the most important information, or even correct information. Although the principle of "management by exception" is at work here, seeking to

management by exception

filter out less important information so that the top manager is not overloaded with data, it is likely that much important information never leaves the foremen's desks—or the workers' benches. Thus management may be starved for information, unless it takes conscious steps to design checks into the system that will fill in the blanks inevitably caused by hierarchical information flow.

Formal communication in a hierarchical organization flows downward from the chief executive, when policy decisions are issued to immediate subordinates. Each of these retransmits the information in revised form (to suit the intended receivers), and it proceeds downward as it fans out. If each person in the organization works for one superior in a clearly defined relationship, in theory the organization will ensure that each worker receives necessary information from that superior. Formal communication flows upward on the same basis, reporting on the performance of work and responses to prior instructions. Much of this information is sent in written form, although a large volume of verbal communication occurs among members of the hierarchy.

formal communication

Design of the formal communication system is very important. While it is necessary to dispense with formalities under urgent conditions, the heart of the organization is its underlying formal communication system, and if this is weak the entire structure is shaky. Too many levels of management will attenuate the communication reaching the top, and loss of information and duplication of effort are almost bound to result. Too few may leave certain areas untended, and some information needed for decision making will not be collected. In a formal system, even one with shortcomings, the route for and content of information are standardized, and at least some information will flow. In an ad hoc system with no standardization, the routing content will have to be worked out every time information is needed, which is not only a costly use of management effort but a virtual guarantee that something will be overlooked.

In chapter 3, "Design and Development of Organizations," we discussed the case for and against centralization. A decentralized organization will send only policy communications downward and receive broad measures of performance and operating results upward, thus using the corporate communication channels more for coordination than for day-to-day operations. A highly centralized organization, handling more details at headquarters, necessarily puts a tremendous load on its communication channels.

centralization vs. decentralization

Whatever the type of organization, the formal system must transmit company goals and policies through all levels down to the working ranks, and must provide receptive channels for feedback in return, as follows:

channels of formal communication

- *Policy manuals and procedural handbooks,* containing written statements of what the organization expects, how it is organized, and who does what in accordance with what procedures—including specifying upward information flows and procedures for using them.
- *Memoranda and orders,* covering special situations which are not part of regular organizational routine or occur too infrequently to be included in the permanent documentation. Generally speaking, memoranda contain information and orders contain instructions.

How did the lack of a formalized communication structure create problems for North Star? Which of these innovations would you recommend for North Star?

159
COMMUNICATION

- *Scheduled meetings and conferences,* at which progress is reviewed, problems discussed, and decisions reached. At the top level, these may result in development of policy; at lower levels, they deal with solving immediate problems. Meetings are a primary method of passing information upward, supplementing written reports.
- *Reports* of various sorts, either regular (weekly, monthly, etc.) or in response to events that trigger required reports (completion of a project, exceeding a predetermined expenditure level, etc.)
- *Unscheduled communications* proceeding through standard channels, such as a memorandum from a supervisor to an immediate superior reporting difficulties with material procurement and requesting permission to make a substitute purchase or use alternate materials. While these are not specifically scheduled in the formal system (and of course cannot be, since they arise in response to one-time situations), they are clearly provided for in communication policy, and it is expected that they will flow freely whenever necessary.
- *Person-to-person* supervisory and review contacts, constituting the routine relationships between levels in the organization, provided for in the description of duties and responsibilities in policy and procedural documents.

Figure 5-5 shows a simple organization that illustrates these steps. The manuals and handbooks are maintained by the president's office. Memoranda flow from president to vice-presidents or further down; and from the vice-presidents to their managers or further down. Each vice-president holds conferences with the managers, and the president in turn holds conferences with the vice-presidents. Reports are sent from districts to divisions, and consolidated reports are sent from the vice-presidents to the president. Unscheduled communications and person-to-person contacts occur through the channels where lines intersect.

Informal Communication

informal communications

No organization remains as formal or structured as Figure 5-5, however, because no operations are as smooth and free of trouble or obstruction as

Figure 5-5.
Formal Communication Flow

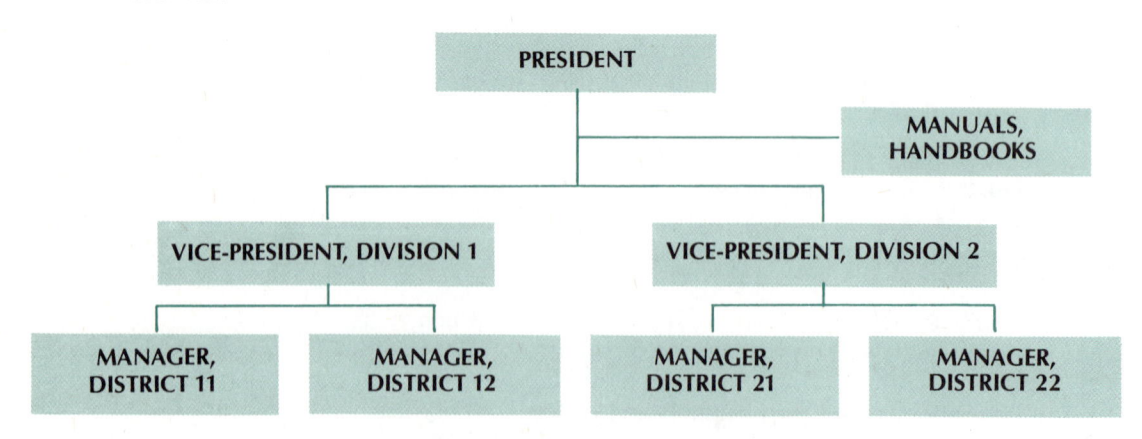

this simple set of connections implies. Figure 5-6 shows in dotted lines some communication channels that are likely to exist outside the hierarchical structure.

Communication outside formal lines of authority is necessary to maintain organizational linkages and fill in the gaps and omissions of the formal system. Imagine how difficult and distorted communication would be if the manager of district 11 had to go through formal channels to contact the manager of district 21 for advice on a problem the latter had previously encountered! When a manager who has just come from an important conference with subordinates asks one subordinate privately for an opinion on the meeting, the manager is communicating informally because there is no formal channel for supervisors to be evaluated by subordinates. Informal communication also occurs when a production supervisor calls a design engineer for suggestions on solving a technical problem. In each case the sender is going outside the formal channels to find the receiver who seems best able to provide the needed assistance, regardless of the organizational position of either party.

It is in management's best interest to encourage these informal links. On many construction projects, the foremen for various trades are required to submit progress reports each month or more frequently; but it is easy to leave out the cues warning of trouble ahead and report only items which are going well. Such reports are all too common, since it is human nature to want to look good before the boss and to postpone the day of reckoning in hopes that things will straighten out somehow. If numerous informal ties exist among the various managers, the reverberations of problems will be heard and all the resources of the organization can be put to the task of setting them right before it is too late.

Bypassing the Chain of Command

It is not good practice to circumvent the established lines of communication and authority as a regular thing, and the individual who does must take the responsibility for "cleaning up" after that action (informing the regular chain if necessary and making sure that no one is left out). But lateral communications such as (2), (3), and (4) on Figure 5-6 would be

What were the informal routes of communication in North Star?

bypassing the chain of command

Figure 5-6.
Informal Communication Flow

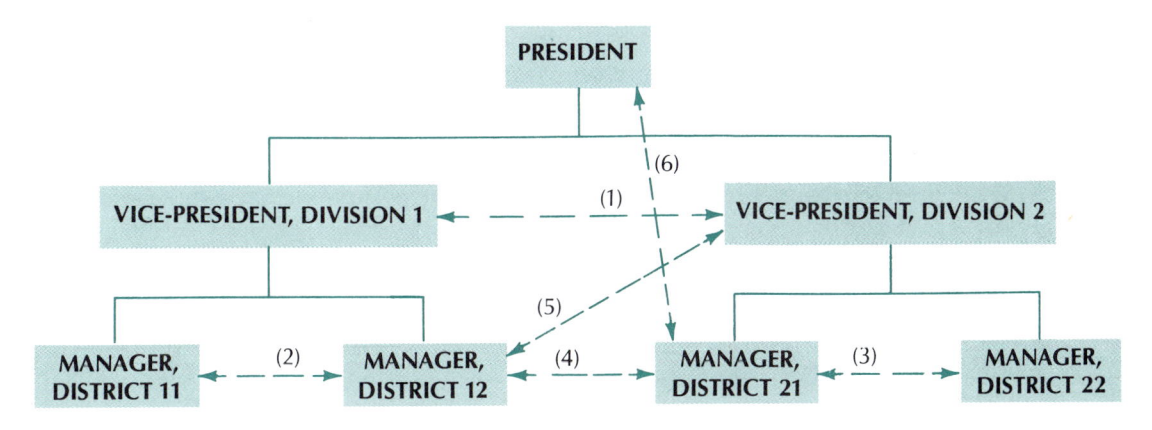

COMMUNICATION

delayed to the point of absurdity if every query or piece of information had to wait for the slow path up, over, and down the chain of command. There is a fine line between informal communications that expedite the work of the organization and needless bypassing of the chain of command. The former helps immeasurably to get things done; the latter is an irritant that leads to hard feelings and eventual change of personnel.

A systematic method of bypassing the chain of command upward is the *suggestion box*. Properly run, it gives every member of the organization a license to propose change in any procedure—and even to be paid for it, if the idea is accepted. In poor organizations, the suggestion system is handled at too low a level or ignored, which makes it a farce. Good organizations recognize that individual employees potentially can provide a wealth of valuable information, and a suggestion system that works may be a way to uncover some of it.

House organs (company magazines or newspapers, radio shows on the public address system, letters to employees, and so on) constitute a method of bypassing the chain of command downward. Top management, recognizing that policy statements do not always make the long and tortuous trip to the working level in their original form, may establish a *redundant channel* by restating the policy in the company paper. Such a publication does not have the force of an order; rather, it reports that an order is being issued, and thus alerts the workers to be on the watch for such an order. If the personnel director, shop superintendents, and foremen all read the company paper, and know that the workers will be reading it as well, there is a strong incentive for them not to take any action or issue any instructions that contravene what top management has published. This device must be used with care, because it can give intermediate levels of management the feeling that their authority is being eroded; but it is a good device to insure that the accurate word is getting out to all levels.

Unofficial Communication

Much organizational communication is interpersonal. Chapter 2, "Groups at Work," describes some of the complex interrelations in an organization. The unofficial communication within and among these social structures in the plant is heavily loaded with company business, since the company is a major element in the lives of employees. Company releases, orders of supervisors, and status of work are constant subjects of conversation—sharing the floor with sports news, politics, and gossip.

The device for promulgating gossip as well as news about the organization is the *grapevine*, a rumor mill that transmits information of highly varying accuracy at a remarkably high speed throughout the company. Employees are in the grapevine circuit to the extent that they are in groups; thus, workers who are not part of any groups are likely to be left out of the grapevine information system. A tells B, C, and D, each of whom tells two or three others, producing widespread dissemination but often highly inaccurate repetition. Topics that travel the grapevine are those which, in their correct or erroneously reported form, appear to be of general interest. The grapevine has a built-in magnifying property because of the desire of storytellers to tell a dramatic tale, but it serves a positive function as a barometer of employee feelings and attitudes. The danger lies in the communicator's propensity to blow up items into false or misleading messages, thus alarming employees unnecessarily. Management must be alert to stymie false rumors by providing a plentiful supply of accurate information to counteract false information in the unofficial network.

Nonverbal Communication

Nonverbal cues are important indicators for managers, since they provide good feedback for an alert observer. When an individual talks to you, eyes, eyebrows, facial expressions, hand positions, and body movements all suggest the real meaning of what is being said. A teacher who looks up to find half the class asleep has received some instant feedback that only a fool could misunderstand. The employee who says he has no questions after an order but stands with a puzzled expression, or the foreman who says the job is all completed but wears a quizzical look and speaks hesitatingly, are telling the manager something with nonverbal cues. In the former case, a repetition may produce the desired look of understanding. The latter case is more difficult, because the foreman is trying to let you think he knows the status of the job when it is fairly clear that he does not. (If you were to watch his actions as soon as the manager leaves, probably you would see him hurry to the job to check its actual status.) In the case of the foreman, the manager is partly at fault. His or her nonverbal cues implied that the foreman *should* know the answer, and invited a guess in reply. If the manager had asked, "Can you find out and let me know?" an accurate report would have been more likely.

"Body language" or personal appearance often distracts the receiver from the spoken message. No matter how well-qualified the mod job seeker in Figure 5-7 may be, he is communicating something else to his potential employer—and most of his job qualifications are being filtered out by the starchy gentleman in the straight-backed chair.

Unintended communication results when outside cues enter the channel to blur the intended transmission. If the job seeker in Figure 5-7 is serious

nonverbal cues

body language

unintended communication

Figure 5-7. Nonverbal Communication at Work

intended communication

When did Bert and Henry send unintended communications? What ramifications did these mistakes have for the organization?

in this endeavor, his appearance may act as an obstacle, counteracting the effect of his words. Sometimes, however, nonverbal actions that contradict verbal communications are *intended communication,* in that the sender wants the words disregarded and is signaling accordingly. Perhaps the casually dressed job seeker is applying for a job he doesn't want because of pressure from parents or wife, and is sending a nonverbal signal asking to be rejected. When the manager who has stayed with the company too long is told by the president's secretary that "Ms. Boss wants you to turn over your routine duties to Mr. Upandcoming and concentrate on our important planning study, and thought you'd like it better with an office over in the Annex where you can have more privacy," he recognizes the face-saving alternative to outright demotion.

Managers must realize that such cues may influence listeners when they are *not* intended, or they will be greeted after a misunderstanding with a comment such as, "I know you *said* it, but I didn't think you *meant* it." It makes no sense for you, as the manager, to reply that you always mean what you say; you don't.

Techniques of Organizational Communication

Communication as a Two-Way Process

two-way communication

Figure 5-8.
Communication Game

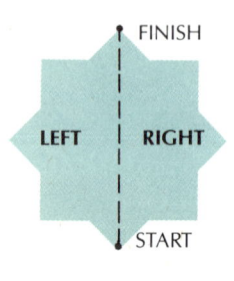

[Figure: Diamond/star shape with FINISH at top, START at bottom, labeled LEFT and RIGHT on either side of center dashed line]

one-way communication

In the first section of this chapter, we saw that communication links the sender and receiver both through the communication process itself and through *feedback*. If the latter is missing, misunderstanding is likely. Consider the parlor game figure shown in Figure 5-8. A sender has two receivers, each of whom starts at the bottom apex, one to draw the right half and the other the left half of the figure shown. Right and left sides of the paper are separated during the drawing. The sender first tells the right receiver how to draw the half-figure, step by step. Then the left paper is put in place, and the left receiver is told how to draw. The aim is to have the two top corners together at the completion of the exercise, when the two halves are placed together.

If the game is undertaken with no questions permitted by the two receivers, the results are ludicrous. If feedback is permitted, the receivers can check their understanding of the instructions they receive, and the results are much better. Try it.

One-way communication is faster and more orderly than two-way communication, but the latter is more accurate and the recipients have more confidence in the outcome. Sometimes the former is preferred: when the sender doesn't want any questioning of an order or lacks enough confidence to deal with questions, when speed of execution is paramount, or when the message is clearly unmistakable. A drill sergeant who calls out, "Right, face!" doesn't want to discuss the matter; nor does a football quarterback giving signals. An unsure manager, perhaps new to the environment and relaying half-understood orders from above, will try to avoid any feedback that would show up this uncertainty. An arbitrary manager who doesn't want any "back talk" believes that feedback is a sign of softness.

Usually two-way communication is preferred, particularly where the primary aim is to meet the organization's goals rather than to build up the managerial ego or cater to managerial insecurities. The manager will get the message across better by cultivating a dialogue and has a better chance of learning occasionally that an order was wrong and ought to be modified. It is not enough to *prefer* two-way communication; the manager must go out of the way to *cultivate* it. Just opening the boss's door and announcing an open door policy won't make people come in—they must be encouraged and persuaded and cajoled into doing so, because all the traditions of the work place militate against coming in and volunteering information. The old Army slogan "Keep your powder dry and never volunteer for nothin'" applies in many organizations. It is equally hard to get people to volunteer questions when they do not understand, particularly in groups where each individual hates to display ignorance. In the remainder of this section, we discuss how managers can encourage the dialogue so essential to circulation of reliable and timely information.

Communication Networks

In the previous section, we noted that communication must flow in all directions throughout an organization. Although the formal organizational structure does not strictly control the flow of information, it has a lot to do with facilitating or hampering communication. Consider the three possible arrangements of individuals within an organization shown in Figure 5-9. I represents a formal hierarchical system, with relatively few information channels. It allows for fast transmission from leader to each individual member, and fast feedback. II implies an organization with relative equality in status (although A may be the leader), where each member is free to express an opinion or otherwise transmit to other members. This structure allows a maximum of discussion but slows the speed of final transmission. II is a typical research organization. Studies show that when problems are at all complex, people are happier in II networks than in I networks, even though a final solution takes longer to reach.[4] The manager may be officially "in charge" but subscribes to group decision making, listening to the viewpoints of colleagues and involving them in the problem as well as the answer. In III, the top manager is insulated from the lower echelons, leaving the intermediate manager in a position to collect incoming information and filter out what he or she wishes, in both directions—a very powerful position. Sometimes this

communication networks

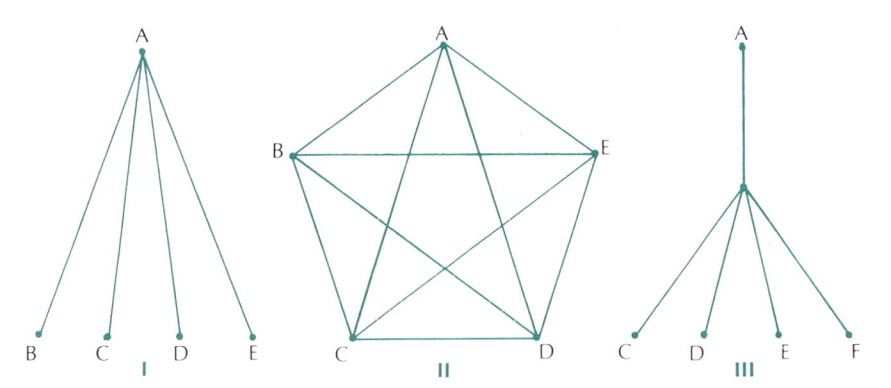

Figure 5-9.
Basic Communication Networks

Figure 5-10.
Formal Network with Safety Factor

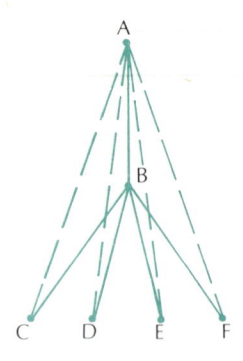

Do any of these networks describe North Star's policymaking process? The organization of the drafting room? Which best fits Bert's leadership style?

communication barriers

filtering is unconscious; B may filter out information in accordance with personal principles, without actually trying to do so. Numerous hazards are implicit in III, and many organizations have elements of such communications barriers built into the structure without the top management realizing it.

A variant of III that contains a safety factor is shown in Figure 5-10. Here B is the executive vice-president or senior vice-president for administration who coordinates matters that call for standard treatment (such as personnel actions, overtime rules, procurement, security, and running the plant in general). A is the president, and the individual vice-presidents (C, D, E, and F) deal with A directly on technical matters in their areas (C, the production vice-president, deals directly on questions of production, product quality, future planning for manufacturing, etc.). If some of the administrative rules established by B get in the way of production, C will discuss this with the president, A—and this prospect keeps B from acting arbitrarily.

Surmounting Barriers to Communication

Have you ever been in a group discussion where some members remained silent despite efforts to get them to participate? Even if a manager earnestly desires to promote communications with subordinates, many barriers may block the channel—and only an astute individual will be aware of them. Figure 5-11 depicts data developed by Rensis Likert at the University of Michigan's Institute for Social Research about the extent to which subordinates feel free to discuss important job items with the superior, as seen by superiors and by subordinates. Notice that in each case—top staff vs. foremen and foremen vs. workers—the superior thinks subordinates feel much freer to come through that open door than in fact they do. It is an astonishing fact of management that we have feelings of hesitancy in *our* dealings with *our* superior (we are not very likely to complain about management's actions, and the worse they are the less likely we are to say so), but we don't think our subordinates have the same feelings of hesitancy in *their* dealings with *us*.

A good supervisor must allow for this instinctive blindness and must be on the lookout for possible obstructions to effect upward communications by subordinates. In this section we will discuss some common barriers to effective communications, and suggest some preventive medicine.

Figure 5-11.
Perceptions of Communication Freedom

	Top staff says about foremen	Foremen say about themselves	Foremen say about the workers	Workers say about themselves
Feel very free to discuss key points with supervisor	90%	67%	85%	51%
Feel fairly free	10	23	15	29
Not very free	—	10	—	14
Not at all free	—	—	—	6

MANAGEMENT PROCESSES

Problems Created by Hierarchy

An effective organization is a beehive of communications: upward, downward, and laterally, with angle shots from one subordinate to another subordinate's boss, and so on. Yet the nature of the superior-subordinate relationship creates automatic stumbling blocks which interfere with this network and constrain it into insufficient channels. The natural desire of anyone to impress superiors with a good performance tends to distort the information an individual is willing to send up. Withholding information derogatory to oneself lessens the chance of reprimand or "demerit," and hopefully the situation will straighten out without the boss ever having to know. The pressures on an individual who feels promotion chances are good can be extremely strong in this regard, as that person is sometimes tempted to put personal welfare ahead of the organization's.

Another distortion that can arise is the temptation to tell the boss what he or she presumably wants to hear. It takes an exceptional superior to accept bad news without unconsciously blaming the bearer, and there is always the fear that a disappointment may be taken out on the person nearest at hand. (In ancient times it was the practice of Oriental princes to kill messengers bringing bad tidings, hoping thus to blunt the extent of the misfortune; some vestige of this technique remains in many business situations today.) Employees may even attempt to fulfill what are perceived to be the manager's personal goals over those of the organization, unless the manager sees the situation clearly and acts to prevent it. Bruce Harriman, vice-president of the Massachusetts area of New England Telephone, noted that department heads and staff members were reacting to his personal aversion to prolonged analysis of numbers by minimizing their use. Thus, although budgetary analysis and control were not his favorite pastimes, he insisted on budget reviews and commitments whenever he met with subordinates for performance review.[5]

Workers will gauge the extent of their communications to the boss according to whether the information is used "fairly" or not. If a manager seems to react to the detriment of subordinates, the line will be cut off. This is one of management's toughest choices: if a worker tells the boss about something improper that the former has done, the temptation is to "play fair" and take no action, and in a sense this approach is valid. But if the boss is seen as being a soft touch in this respect, he or she will receive "confessions" designed specifically to forestall corrective action.

The open-door policy is fine, but only if the boss puts forth a real effort to bypass personal filters and see things with the eyes of the workers. Not only must critics be dealt with fairly, and responses made to innovative suggestions, but the boss must go more than halfway in understanding what it is like "down there." In short, the management must learn to speak the subordinates' language. Clarence Day, in "Edible Workers," chiding humanity for failing to employ animals for many back-breaking tasks, notes that people have mastered many languages but yet cannot communicate with the beasts. "Why," Day asks, "should the poor creatures learn our language? Why don't we learn theirs?"[6] Too many managers make little or no effort to learn their subordinates' language, requiring all of the effort to be on the other side.

open-door policy

Does Bert maintain a true open-door policy? How has this contributed to the organization's effectiveness? What might have happened had Bert ignored Ab's problem?

Akin to language is the question of value. A manager must guard against forming predetermined value judgments before hearing out subordinates, and basing decisions on assumptions that may not be valid when applied to a situation where the subordinate has proceeded from different premises. Communication is not supposed to mean *agreement* between parties, but is predicated on reaching full *understanding*.

Promoting Upward Communication

upward communication

An effective upward communication system is much harder to achieve than a good downward system, because all of the effort in organization charting seems to run the other way. Managers always have the theoretical right of access to their subordinates: bursting in on them without warning to monitor operations, reading their correspondence, calling on them for reports and comments. But the subordinate has no theoretical rights the other way; the only access is what the manager specifically thinks to grant (or what the subordinate demands in confrontation tactics, something of a last resort). Organizations are always in danger of starving for lack of reliable and timely upward information, because of the many filters and barriers the managers erect without thinking.

Not only must the upward path be provided, in designs that are easier to use than not to use, but workers and lower levels of management must be convinced that their superiors are empathetic and fair—that they really and truly want to hear about it. This goal is not easy to achieve, since most upward information brings problems with it, but avoidance of the communication bypasses the chance of dealing with problems while they are small and manageable. A subordinate is unlikely to walk into the boss's office and denounce a policy or the manager, except when about to leave the company. But this information is just what the boss must have, somehow. Managers must provide both channels and incentive for the bad news to reach them.

tools of upward communication

Recently the New England Telephone Company hooked up what it called "private lines" to full-time staff, over which any employee can pass a question or register a complaint without disclosing his or her identity. The system assures that the matter will be referred to the right official and a reply will be put in the company newspaper. The reply column has turned out to be the most widely read column in the paper. Task groups of employees have been appointed to work out specific problems so raised. Not only do management and workers understand one another better, but management gets a wealth of information formerly denied it.

There are many other tools for upward communication: suggestion boxes, employee committees, attitudinal surveys by neutral parties, performance evaluations up and down the line, constant site visits by managers where there is opportunity for conversations on the job with workers, and regular meetings of management with "shop committee people" elected by workers.

Josef Stalin, manager of the world's most centralized planned economy, published a 1931 article emphasizing the need for upward communication. "To think that you can now direct by sitting in an office, far from the factories, is a delusion," he wrote; "in order to direct the factories, you must come into more frequent contact with the staffs in those factories, maintain live contact with them."[7] He warned managers not only to teach the local people, but also to learn from them. In effect, Stalin was proposing an upward communication system.

How did Bert encourage upward communication? What barriers prevented upward communication?

One caveat in dealing with upward communications: the manager has to consider the source, and the possible motivation of the sender, in deciding the credibility of the message. When the wolf proposed to the pig that they visit a field where he knew there were lots of juicy turnips, the pig was well advised to bear in mind that the wolf had a powerful motive in convincing him how delicious the turnips would be. Everyone has a point of view, conscious or unconscious, and the manager can be protected from biased information only by seeking a multiplicity of sources to produce a well-balanced picture.

Group Communication

A manager who calls a committee meeting under the impression that complete participation is being stressed should bear in mind some common barriers to group communication. The most frequent is managerial dominance at the meeting. Even the silent supervisory presence may prevent some people from talking at all. The manager needs to spot the people who are silent and encourage them to talk. The value of a contribution does not always correspond to the contributor's willingness to speak out.

barriers to group communication

What words of wisdom would you have for Henry as he prepares for the weekly meetings?

There are many forces tending to suppress comment in a committee meeting. Perhaps one or two of the participants clearly are experts in the topic of the meeting, and if they speak out early they tend to inhibit comment from others who are less expert—but whose opinions are needed. Perhaps there is a range of seniority in the group, and the more senior members tend to monopolize the conversation and eventually keep the less senior from speaking at all. This phenomenon can be seen at an auction: if one bidder wins the first three or four rounds of bidding, particularly if he tends to raise quickly and aggressively, there is a tendency for the remaining bidders to clam up and let him and a few other bidders take over all the action.

How does the committee chairperson persuade the "silent majority" to speak out? One way is to reduce each participant to a single unit, so to speak, by saying, "Now we'll go around the table, and ask every member to comment on _____." In this way, it is clear that the chairperson is not rating any particular individuals more highly than others. Another way is to divide the group into subgroups, making sure that hitherto silent members are in groups that do not include the most aggressive participants, so the silent ones will not have undue competition. The manager's actions should signal a desire for input from all those present, and they can be arranged to encourage widespread participation.

Problems in Communication Systems

We have seen that many barriers are inherent in the communication system, creating unfortunate distortions of the information transmitted. There are other problems as well, relating to the volume, content, and time frame of the information, which we will discuss below.

When your radio is tuned to two stations at once, you may receive a lot of information, but it does you very little good.

Overloading the Information Circuit

information overload

When your radio is tuned to two stations at once, you have lots of information but it does you very little good. Managers find this dilemma very familiar. Computers can spew forth masses of paper, but organization analysts often see most of it going unread into file cabinets. An individual who is flooded with information may scan it all in cursory fashion, read certain parts of it (perhaps not the most important parts), or give up and make decisions based on what is already known. Despite efforts to *manage by exception* (seeing only whatever information signals the need for action), the problems of overinformation still persist.

One cure for communication overkill is to reduce the flow from the top. President Thomas Mastin of Lubrizol once asked the company's financial vice-president to show him all the computer printouts that everyone in the company was receiving. As the vice-president remarked, when the president asks for printouts, anyone receiving data by computer makes sure it is really necessary information. Another cure is to make recipients pay for computer reports, just as you and I pay for magazine and newspaper subscriptions. But the best way is to see that managers *ask* for information they really want so they are not sent anything they haven't asked for.

There have been semiserious suggestions that managers be given tests from time to time, to pressure them to be selective in what they review.

One company took this suggestion seriously. Iroquois Brands, Limited, at a recent executive seminar, distributed twenty questions on pertinent facts contained in its annual report and other publications to its managers, with pocket calculators as the prize for the best scores. The exercise served to refocus everybody's attention on "the oneness of our company," according to a senior executive, and prompted vigorous discussions on the overall situation of the company.

One solution to the *communication* problem of communication overload is to treat it as an *organizational* problem. If too many communications are going to each manager, perhaps too many people are doing the same job—or trying to. The overload may be a signal that responsibilities should be assigned more precisely, so each manager can concentrate on primary responsibilities and cease reviewing the responsibilities of others. It may call for a heavier dose of management by exception, where senior managers cease trying to review *everything* their immediate subordinates are doing, but instead review their performance in more overall terms—which means fewer but more significant reports.

Barrier-Induced Errors

Try curling your right index finger around on itself so only a pinhole opening is left, then look at this page through the pinhole with your right eye and directly with your left eye; you will see the right eye image magnified by the diverging light rays, as in Figure 5-12. Similarly, communication barriers may result in completely erroneous information as to the origin of the signal, may change its form so that it is not recognizable, or may magnify it far beyond what was encoded by the sender. If the barrier is total, as in an ocean breakwater with no openings, the incoming signal may dash itself vainly against the outside but never penetrate at all.

The principal defense against errors produced by communication barriers is redundancy: sending the same message in another form or by

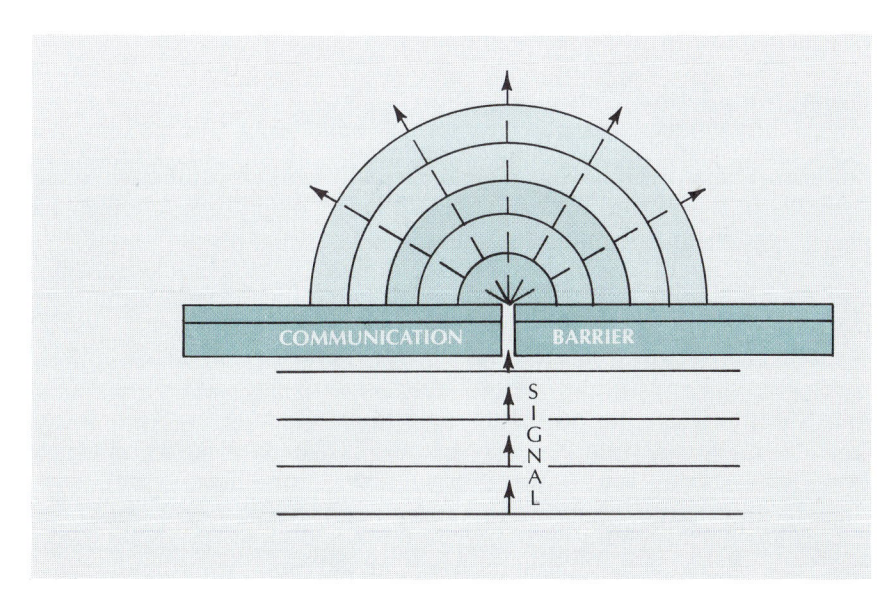

Figure 5-12.
Signal Distortion

another channel, so that at least one form gets through. The important thing for the manager is to recognize that the barrier exists, and to understand how completely it can distort the origin and meaning of a signal, so that more thorough communication coverage can be provided.

Confusing Reports with Reality

reports versus reality

A typical mistake made by managers is to treat the computer analysis as "the whole truth," forgetting that an error in sales forecasting will be perpetuated in every computer printout and will mar related forecasts of cash flow, production volume, profits, and so on. During the past decade, there was a strong trend toward industry diversification, with manufacturers going into unfamiliar product lines or acquiring different companies and forming them into conglomerate holding companies. The idea was that the nerve center would review computerized performance reports and monitor results. The payoff in many cases, however, was not as great as the manufacturers had expected. Computers have a great capacity for processing information, but problems in food processing, shipping, and steel making are inherently different, and comprehensive financial reports cannot carry the whole load of describing these diverse operations at a distance. Computer models of performance are useful, but they cannot portray turndowns which have not yet occurred or describe a loss of consumer confidence or product obsolescence not yet reflected in the balance sheet. While some conglomerates did well, many of them fell on unexpected hard times—a blow to the notion that centralized reports carry the whole story about operations.

The same thing is true in a single company. Not only can reports be slanted to paint a rosier picture than the reality warrants, but they can be entirely falsified. Even accurate reports cannot be comprehensive; many elements of a company, including such vital intangibles as morale and inventiveness, cannot possibly be incorporated into rows of figures. Managers must forever remind themselves that reports are only a pale imitation of reality, no substitute for constant study of the real thing.

Nonacceptance of Communication

nonacceptance of communication

A story about the 1938 hurricane, the most unexpected and disastrous in our history, tells of a suburban New Yorker who worked in the city buying a fine barometer from Abercrombie and Fitch. When he got home and unwrapped it, the barometer indicated HURRICANE. Irritated (the weather report said merely "rain"), he took it back to the store the next morning and got his money back. When he returned to his suburban community that evening, his house had been washed away.

This tale demonstrates our unwillingness to believe communications that run counter to our impressions of reality. Similarly, workers in a plant or office who receive an instruction that they don't want to carry out can convince themselves that management "really doesn't mean it," in which case the instruction will not be effective. If the instruction appears to do them harm (such as a requirement to sign out on leave without pay for short absences from the job), they are unlikely to comply. If there seem to be two possible interpretations, even though the favorable interpretation

We are unwilling to accept communications that do not coincide with our perceptions of reality.

requires a real stretching of management's probable meaning, the favorable one is likely to be adopted. If information on performance of a division has conflicting signals—say sales volume is up, but profits are down—managers responsible for the division are likely to take comfort from the improved sales volume, but discredit the profit signal on the basis that it comes from short-term or one-time items, such as excessive inventory write-offs. "After all," they will say, "sales volume is what really counts." (Let the two reports be reversed, though, and you would hear them say, "After all, profits are what really count.")

conflicting signals

If reports exist, their unpleasant tidings are as likely to be right as their pleasant ones, and should be investigated rather than shrugged off. Managers issuing instructions likely to be rejected must take extraordinary steps to explain, sell, and follow up; otherwise they must resign themselves to the probability that the "messenger bringing bad tidings" will be shot down.

Hoarding Information

"Knowledge is power," and all experienced managers know it. The possession of information that others do not have confers advantage in various ways. Knowledge that a mining company is about to announce a major find enables the possessor to buy stock in the company before it goes up. Knowledge that management is going to conduct an inspection

hoarding information

173
COMMUNICATION

of the plant enables the supervisor to prepare for the inspection. Knowledge of a technical process makes the possessor useful to those who lack the knowledge.

A few years ago, the owner of a rapidly growing company with a broad product line in specialty filters received an order for a model that had not been made for a year or so. When the order went to the plant, it developed that everyone who had manufactured that model previously had left the company; a surprising amount of investigating and cut-and-try was necessary before the manufacturing process was relearned. The owner-president got the message and promptly called in an industrial consultant to prepare process sheets covering all the company's current models. In that case, no intent was involved, but the situation would have been the same if individuals had elected not to release the key information they possessed.

Many supervisors hesitate instinctively to pass on information, feeling that possession of information their subordinates do not have sets them apart and lends prestige of a sort. This tendency is widespread, and does a good deal of harm to both morale and efficiency. When the information is administrative (leave schedules, time when next promotions will be made, etc.), withholding it leaves the organization uncertain, suspicious, and insecure. When it is technical, withholding it creates mistakes, delays, and increased costs. Management can buck this tendency by utilizing downward redundancy—sending the same information over several channels to ensure that it gets through. In addition, cultivating an atmosphere of openness will do a lot to dispel the felt pressures to hoard information.

Delay in Information

During the war, when overseas troops heard sporting events over the Armed Forces Radio Network, broadcasts were often delayed (perhaps to put them during daylight hours, because of the difference in time between home and overseas, or for other reasons). Occasionally a sharp operator would learn the outcome of an event before the broadcast and clean up by betting on the team he knew to be the winner. Compared with the timeliness of his knowledge, the delayed information represented by the broadcast was worse than useless.

Many organizational communications are of little value if not prompt. Management should see reports of worker job assignments the same day they occur, if it wishes to check their accuracy by on-site inspections. Corrections to construction plans must come out before the work is under way to avoid expensive modifications. Reports of material receipt must reach the shop swiftly, since received material the shop doesn't know about may as well not have come in yet. Safety inspection reports must reach management at once, so unsafe work can be stopped at the earliest possible moment. And so on.

Efforts to express a communication in precisely the right way usually slow it down. The advantages of precision must be weighed against the advantages of promptness—and the latter usually wins. Timely information is required for good decisions. This is another case where communication delay may be caused by organizational complexity, and simplifying organizational relationships will improve the speed of transmission.

timeliness of information

The Primacy of Communication

The abovementioned items reflect only a few of the many possible communication problems managers may encounter. But perhaps the overriding cause of inadequate communication in an organization is the fact that management takes communication for granted, and doesn't pay conscious attention to the problem of improving it—by structure, by organizational climate, and by participative management.

Summary

Communication is one of the most basic processes of life itself, but people are the only beings with the ability to express their feelings on a variety of subjects through an array of different symbols.

Communication requires a sender who originates the message and a receiver who gets its. Many pitfalls are inherent in the process, because every individual is a product of different experiences, and therefore the sender and receiver have different filtering systems through which the message must pass. Outside noise in the channel can further distort the transmission. Thus, meaning often is changed or lost. Although communication is a common phenomenon, it is rarely as clear as it might be. Redundancy, repetition, and feedback are mechanisms used to ensure correct transmission.

An organization has a multiplicity of senders and receivers, based on its hierarchy and the relationships among members. A major corporate communications goal is the coordination that makes good decision making possible, by seeing that information is collected from all organizational divisions and brought to the decision centers quickly and accurately. A good communication system should transmit policies, instructions, and information through the organization, relay feedback from lower and intermediate levels to decision-making levels, and probe beneath the surface for information that would not emerge automatically. Thus an effective system flows downward, upward, and laterally.

Three types of communication systems operate in every organization: formal, informal, and unofficial. The formal system transmits goals, policies, and instructions throughout the organization, and receives reports and feedback through manuals, policy papers, memoranda and orders, meetings, and reports of various sorts. The informal system provides necessary communication outside of these preestablished lines, to fill in the gaps, maintain linkages, and handle one-time situations. The unofficial system refers to that casual exchange which occurs on an interpersonal level and often includes discussion of company matters; the grapevine, with its built-in magnifying property, is the vehicle that transmits unofficial communications.

Management must be aware of the many barriers which can obstruct the communication process and take steps to ensure that the lines remain open. The superior-subordinate relationship sometimes hampers communication, as does the tendency to overlook the importance of upward communications. Although managers may believe that a committee meeting will produce dialogue, they must realize that this will not occur unless every individual is encouraged to air views through a number of devices.

There are other problems in communications. The computer will speak the truth only when it has accurate and comprehensive input, and when the data can be interpreted easily. Too much information is nearly as much of a problem as too little. Information that is delayed may be worthless. And a communication must be in a form that will be accepted by the recipient, or it will not get through.

Notes

1. President Theodore Roosevelt was said to have directed his secretary to leave a mistake or two in an important letter, so he could correct it in ink in his own handwriting, thus lending it additional importance through the recognition that the president had indeed read the letter thoroughly, rather than signing it perfunctorily as one of a thousand similar letters.
2. *Wall Street Journal,* November 11, 1975, p. 1.
3. (Lexington, Mass.: D. C. Heath & Co., 1972).
4. Harold J. Leavitt, *Managerial Psychology,* 3d ed. (Chicago: University of Chicago Press, 1972), p. 192.
5. Reported in "Up and Down the Communications Ladder," *Harvard Business Review,* September-October 1974.
6. In *After All* (New York: Alfred A. Knopf, Inc., 1936), pp. 23-27.
7. Josef Stalin, "New Methods of Work, New Methods of Management," *Pravda* 183 (July 5, 1931).

Review Questions

1. What are the basic elements of the communication process? What are the barriers to complete understanding of the message by the receiver?
2. Why is routing an important step in the communication process?
3. What is redundancy? Repetition? Why are these safeguards needed?
4. How does feedback fit into the communication process?
5. What are three types of filters? What is their significance in the communication process?
6. What distortions may blur the intended meaning of a communication?
7. What are five kinds of communication flows in decision-making processes?
8. What do we mean by formal communication?
9. What is "management by exception"?
10. What are the channels for formal communication in an organization?
11. How would you define informal communication? How is it manifested in an organization?
12. What is the "grapevine"? Is it helpful or harmful to an organization?
13. What is the significance of nonverbal communication?
14. What are the differences between one-way and two-way communication?
15. What difference does the form of the organizational network make in communication effectiveness? How is this related to the kind of message being communicated?
16. What barriers to effective communication are inherent in the superior-subordinate relationship?
17. What are the obstacles to upward communication in an organization?
18. What are the basic issues faced by management in deciding how centralized their communications system should be?
19. How has the computer contributed to communication problems in organizations? How can it be used effectively in promoting good communications?

Discussion Questions

1. Try to describe the kind of an overtime instruction system in which feedback would play an active role.
2. As a new manager of an American firm in Thailand, you tell your assistant, who is a native, to hire some employees under a fair system. As the new employees come in, you discover that all are friends and relatives of the assistant. How would you handle this situation?
3. Can you think of any other methods of upward communication aside from house organs, a suggestion box, and similar devices? Other methods of downward communication, aside from policy manuals, memoranda, orders, meetings, and so on?
4. Describe a situation in which each of the three communication networks portrayed in this chapter would work best.
5. Do you think that a plant in a democratic society would be likely to have a more open communication system than one in a communist society? Why or why not?
6. What might be the characteristics of a person who hoards information? What mechanisms might be built in to a communications system to forestall this occurrence?

North Star Case Study

Assume that the North Star drafting room is organized as shown in the sketch. Henry is president, Bert vice-president, and Ab chief engineer. Suppose that, in line with classical notions of the "chain of command," Henry is careful never to contact Ab directly in order to avoid upsetting Bert. Ab, as an old-line tough supervisor, is in the habit of maintaining firm control over the drafting room crowd.

One day, in the midst of employee unrest over one of Ab's policies, a group of engineers go directly to Henry, bypassing Bert and Ab, to voice their grievances. Rena, the spokesperson, says their problems are serious enough to warrant a "hot line" directly to the top. The group is tired of dealing with a muscle-bound supervisor with his head in the sand. Henry agrees to make himself more available to the employees and announces that he will maintain an open-door policy hereafter. Indeed, he says, he always had, and thought it was understood.

He asks Bert to join them, and Bert blows up. "I'm not going to listen to this when it comes to me this way," he announces. "If they have a problem in my area, they can come to me. Not once have they come to me with any of these grievances. My door is always open. Let them use it." At that, Bert turns and leaves the office. Nonplussed, Henry tells Rena the engineers had better take the issue up with Bert, and see how that works out.

When Ab hears of the action, he storms into Henry's office and says, "I'm quitting if I have to put up with this kind of stuff. Too many cooks spoil the broth, and you ought to know that." Henry tells him to cool off and go talk to Bert about it. As Ab walks out, Henry begins to wonder why his sincere efforts to get closer to the drafting room problems are met with such resistance.

1. What is the root of this problem?
2. Should Henry have listened to the group's grievances immediately? What implications will Henry's agreement to "make himself available" have for the subordinate managers' authority?

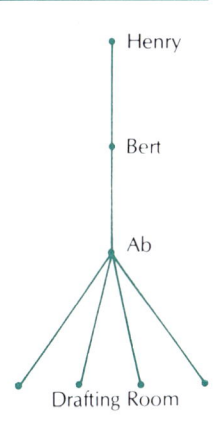

3. How can Henry become more informed of the organizational problems without undermining Bert's or Ab's authority?
4. What techniques can Ab employ to regain control of his group and reestablish a relationship of mutual confidence?
5. What should Bert's role be in the organization?
6. What changes might be made in the organizational structure to place Henry closer to the action?

Suggestions for Further Reading

Berlo, D. K. *Process of Communication: An Introduction to Theory and Practice.* New York: Holt, Rinehart & Winston, Inc., 1960.

Cathcart, R. S., and L. A. Samovar. *Small Group Communication.* Dubuque, Iowa: William C. Brown Co., 1970.

Cherry, C. *On Human Communication.* Cambridge, Mass.: M.I.T. Press, 1957.

Demare, G. *Communicating for Leadership: A Guide for Executives.* New York: The Ronald Press Co., 1968.

Foltz, R. G. *Management by Communication.* Philadelphia: Chilton Book Co., 1973.

Harriman, B. "Up and Down the Communications Ladder." *Harvard Business Review,* September-October 1974.

Kaufman, H. *Administrative Feedback: Monitoring Subordinates' Behavior.* Washington, D.C.: Brookings Institute, 1973.

Leavitt, H. *Managerial Psychology.* Chicago: University of Chicago Press, 1972.

Lesikar, K. K. *Business Communication: Theory and Application.* Homewood, Ill.: Richard D. Irwin, Inc., 1974.

Lesly, P. *The People Factor: Managing the Human Climate.* Homewood, Ill.: Dow Jones-Richard D. Irwin, Inc., 1974.

McMurray, R. N. "Clear Communications for Chief Executives." *Harvard Business Review,* September 1974.

Maier, Norman. *Superior-Subordinate Communication in Management.* New York: American Management Association, Inc., 1961.

Reusch, J., and W. Kees. *Nonverbal Communication: Notes on the Visual Perception of Human Relations.* Berkeley, Calif.: University of California Press, 1966.

Smith, A. G., ed. *Communication and Culture: Readings in the Code of Human Interaction.* New York: Holt, Rinehart & Winston, Inc., 1966.

Thayer, L. O. *Communication and Communication Systems in Organizations, Management, and Interpersonal Relations.* Homewood, Ill.: Richard D. Irwin, Inc., 1968.

Vardaman, G. T. *Effective Communication of Ideas.* New York: D. Van Nostrand Co., 1970.

Weitz, S., ed. *Nonverbal Communication: Readings with Commentary.* New York: Oxford University Press, 1974.

Planning 6

North Star Prologue

The new organization necessitated by the overseas operation included a business manager, who was the first executive to be added after the original four partners. When his marketing help led to more consulting work, they found it necessary to locate larger offices. Resolving the different preferences as to the type of accommodations called on all of Henry's leadership skills and disclosed shortcomings in communications among the partners. A near-mutiny in the drafting room shortly after the move disclosed communications problems at other levels as well, and the decision was made to shift to a more open style of operations. One result was the establishment of a weekly department head meeting.

After the first weekly meeting, Henry was congratulating himself on the smooth flow of communication and the emergence of useful give-and-take. He asked Zeb what he thought of the session, and was surprised when the latter seemed unimpressed. Zeb explained that there was no structure to the meeting —everyone simply brought up whatever occurred to him, and there was no assurance that important points would be covered. From a human relations viewpoint, it was great, but as a productive business session it left much to be desired. Zeb offered as a pattern the procedure they had used for weekly meetings at the university research center where he had worked previously. An agenda was prepared by the administrator, with three headings—current projects, prospective business, and administration—to insure that necessary business was not overlooked and control the conference schedule to avoid wasting time on unimportant topics. They tried Zeb's system for the next meeting, with the agenda distributed the day before the meeting, and Henry had to agree that it was an effective session. Preparing the agenda was a chore, but one that Zeb seemed glad to assume.

At the third meeting, the last item under the administration section was the one-word entry "Planning." When they arrive at that item, Zeb took the floor. He reminded them that the AID job was half over, and to date they had made no plans for replacing that segment of the business or for operating at the necessary reduced scale if it could not be replaced. In fact, they had no system for planning ahead at all, but simply did things as they thought about them. He suggested some issues they needed to consider:

1. What should they spend (in labor and other costs) on marketing?
2. What market areas represented their present competence?
   a. In which of these were they better than the competition?

    b. In which of these were they barely adequate?
3. Which promising new areas should they prepare to compete in?
4. What volume of work could they expect in three months? six months?
5. What would their approximate budget for next year look like? Could they meet it with expected revenues?
6. What were their plans for expansion?
    a. What rate of expansion seemed desirable?
    b. What jobs would fuel the expansion?
    c. What capabilities would they need that they did not have today?
7. What follow-up action should be taken with AID or Natal Engineers?

Bert said they certainly didn't have time for that sort of daydreaming; they had a job to do and they were behind with important work. Ab Jenkins said he was inclined to agree that all this was pretty theoretical. After all, they weren't a huge corporation. Bert rose to go, and his drafting room supervisors started to leave with him, when Zeb pulled out a financial chart. It represented, he told them, an income and expenditures statement for a period two years in the future, assuming that Natal was completed (and was as profitable as they hoped it would be) and that their other work stayed at its present level. Note, he said, that it showed a loss for every month, even with all the overseas employees terminated except Dick and Jo. At least, he added dryly, they ought to plan which members of the outfit to lay off so that they could afford to pay the rest. Bert sank back into his chair, as did the other engineers, and they listened to what Zeb had to say.

When he was finished, Henry asked if anyone was opposed to the idea of establishing a company plan. No one was. He asked Zeb if he could take on the task, and Zeb said he didn't mind doing the routine part, but the plan needed substantive input from all of them. He said that good planning really was a top management task, and therefore if they were serious about it Henry ought to give it a lot of personal attention. (Henry glanced quickly at Bert, to see if he was put off by the way Zeb called Henry "top management," but Bert didn't seem to have noticed.) OK, said Henry; just as an exercise, he would take a stab at assigning Zeb's question areas to people in the company. He assigned responsibility for information gathering on the seven points as follows:

1. Henry, Zeb
2. Technical Division
   (Bert and colleagues)
3. Bert
4. Henry, Zeb
5. Zeb
6. Henry and Bert
7. Dick, Jo

No one objected to the assignment, so it was agreed that all of them would bring the results of their research to the staff meeting the following week. To Henry, it was clear that the first point was fundamentally different from the rest because it involved an actual spending decision, as opposed to the forecasts implied by the rest; but again Bert did not seem to be put off. In fact, he commented that he and his people had all the interesting questions to work on.

The subject of planning wasn't disposed of at the next meeting. Instead it took six weeks of intense and often spirited discussion and work before the outlines of a future strategy began to take shape. Dick had been brought into the discussions, first by teletypewriter and then in greater detail by letter. Henry found that planning was not simply an exercise in peering sagely into the future, but rather called for much detailed basic information from which a rational plan could evolve. He and Zeb analyzed the jobs won by North Star to date, attempting to weigh the extent of the marketing effort demanded in each instance (in order to calculate which types of jobs cost more to pin down than they were worth and which came in more easily, thus meriting more intensive prospecting). They analyzed all jobs awarded in their area to any firm, and tried to estimate which of these reasonably could have been won by North Star Associates with a little more experience or a modest expansion of capability. They considered the sum of all possible jobs, and grouped them by the type of marketing effort most likely to be productive (brochures, letters, calls, proposals, or joint venture approaches with other firms). Meanwhile Bert was doing much the same thing in the drafting room, though with more of a technical orientation as befitted the subject areas he had been assigned.

Dick Boyer's planning effort was the first to bear fruit. He determined that the decision point for jobs such as the one with Natal was AID headquarters in Washington, so on his next trip back he stayed over for three days and made a detailed presentation of North Star capabilities and their likely contribution to the agency's goal of more in-country engineering work. When this approach paid off, with a subcontract for a country-wide transportation study in a nation near the Natal project, Dick came back to the home office to celebrate. It was the first time he had been home in two years, and for all of the group there was much catching up to do. Dick commented generously that if Zeb hadn't started them off on this planning kick he probably wouldn't have gotten around to his sales trip for another year—and that would have been too late to hold his overseas organization together.

The planning exercise at home showed that the associates had been devoting most of their promotional efforts to rather small jobs, which required a great deal of marketing effort for a rather small return. While these jobs had kept the municipal and industrial areas going, and probably were inevitable given the newness of North Star and its initial lack of experience, the time had come to aim for contracts where the marketing effort and cost could be spread over a much larger overall job. It took real self-restraint to keep from going after jobs that they were pretty sure they could get, but the data that went into their planning effort made it clear that such work did not encourage future growth.

What North Star Can Learn from Chapter 6

1. The difference between instinctive and purposeful planning
2. The necessity for setting objectives before starting to plan
3. The elements of job planning
4. The difference between variability and flexibility in plans
5. The interrelationships between planning, action, and control
6. Why managers need to plan and what planning does for them
7. The separate elements in activity planning
8. The major divisions of an institutional plan, and how they relate to the horizon of institutional planning
9. The various levels of forecasting for institutional planning and the methods utilized for each
10. A suitable sequence for the development of institutional plans
11. How to organize for planning
12. Why self-planning is important, both for individuals and the organization

In this chapter we discuss an essential yet generally slighted element of the management toolkit—deciding what the organization is going to do in the future, whether tomorrow or twenty years away. It may involve laying out a simple and easily comprehended sequence of tasks, or broad strategic planning that affects the overall posture of the organization. This neglected managerial process is analyzed in three segments:

1. *The nature and purpose of planning*—what it consists of, what it deals with, and why organizations must do it.
2. *Types and levels of planning*—from immediate to far in the future, and throughout the corporate hierarchy from top policy maker to junior clerk.
3. *The planning process*—the skills involved, the range of approaches to choose from, and the various organizational levels where planning occurs. As a postscript, we examine the planning you need to do as an individual to achieve your maximum potential with the organization.

Planning is generic to all organizations, large or small, public or private. A manager can appear to be completely on top of the job on a daily basis; yet if significant long- and short-term planning does not take place, the manager is undermining the organization's chances for success, and perhaps even sowing the seeds of ultimate disaster.

Nature and Purpose of Planning

Do you think their plan was a good one? Why?

When a group of individuals assembles to start an enterprise, as Bert and Henry did with North Star Associates, that action is *planning*. But as soon as the organization takes shape, the founders have real events to cope with, and planning is too often forgotten. To some extent, this lapse is understandable: the new partners are so busy filling all the organizational slots that they can scarcely keep their heads above water. Planning can wait, and it does. But it can't wait long.

The Concept of Planning

instinctive planning

Of necessity, we all do some planning every day. Almost instinctively, we decide what to put on in the morning, what to eat for breakfast, which route to take to work. On the way to work we may decide, a little more carefully, which tasks to complete today and which to defer. We may not weigh the alternatives systematically or "price out" the costs of putting off one job as against the costs of putting off another; probably we use a mixture of common sense, intuition, and the lessons of experience to make our decisions.

systematic planning

At the other end of the spectrum, too few of us actually carry out strategic planning with regard to our own affairs. Many people make no wills, thus leaving the planning of their affairs after death to chance or the caprice of often inapplicable laws. Only a very small fraction of the public (usually with huge incomes) makes detailed estate plans. Yet the reasons for such careful financial planning should be obvious. Similarly, it makes sense to take stock of personal assets and liabilities, and chart directions to fill in the gaps, to attain a high measure of personal fulfillment. But most of us neglect long-range planning in both financial affairs and personal goals; and many enterprises are equally negligent.

Setting Objectives

It is pointless to start planning until an organization knows its objectives, just as a family cannot start a trip until the destination has been determined. This simple fact often is overlooked, and a planning group may start building an institutional plan before reaching any agreement on the institution's goals. Imagine a planning committee for the U.S. Postal Service, assigned the task of developing a ten-year plan. One member notes that second-class mail is growing in volume but losing money, and so advocates raising the rates because apparently the demand will support a higher rate. Another member comments that small packages cost proportionately more to handle than large ones, and advocates a minimum allowed package size. A third proposes that, since special delivery is a heavy loss item compared with regular first class mail, it should be discontinued and more resources put into the profitable first-class product line. And a fourth suggests that post offices sell stationery and office supplies as tie-in items, since they have a large volume of walk-in customers who presumably are in the market for these things. Most of these proposals sound ridiculous. Why? Because the postal service has certain goals, and they will not be advanced by these steps. A private company can decide that a certain product line (small packages) is not profitable and discontinue it; the postal service emphatically cannot do the same. Second-class mail includes periodicals, and perhaps Congress intends that they be carried at a loss because of their value in advancing education and providing nationwide communications. These goals must be established with certainty before planning can start.

objectives

Perhaps the objectives of a commercial undertaking can be stated with less chance for error: they all boil down to making a profit. (Individuals within the commercial enterprise work toward numerous overlapping and often conflicting goals, of course, but for the firm as a whole, profit is the overriding objective.) But even that leaves a great deal of room for variation. Does the company seek a quick profit, or is it looking to the long pull (the sacrifice of some profitability now in favor of more profitability in a few years)? Perhaps it would rather build up strength in a particular field that promises continued growth, even at the cost of losses today. Perhaps the company has social goals that it will not sacrifice for increased profits. Relatively few companies will strive for profits at *any* cost.

It is the responsibility of top management (the board of directors for a corporation, Congress for a federal agency, the city council for a municipality, and so on) to establish the broad objectives of any organization it controls. Once established, these constitute the framework for lesser, supporting objectives.

What are North Star's objectives?

Allocating Resources

At intermediate levels in an organization, planning is the mechanism that allocates funds (or equivalent resources) to various projects and organizational units in whatever way will best accomplish organizational goals. If

resource allocation

one intermediate goal of the postal service is improvement of management (supporting a broader goal of effective operation), it favors a decision to send 100 executives to an advanced management school each year. If another is reduction of lost mail, the service favors installing costly mail-sorting machinery at some determined yearly rate. The planners must decide if full implementation of both these items is appropriate or if they should reduce outlays for one in order to emphasize the other (in addition to considering all other candidates for funds).

If funds were unlimited and planners could calculate with certainty what returns a given expenditure would produce, they would plan to spend in each division of the enterprise to the point where the last dollar invested would bring exactly one dollar in return. In reality, of course, this simple concept does not apply; planners are restricted by uncertainty as to what an investment will earn and how soon, difficulty in deciding how much it will cost to make an investment, and limits to available funds for such investing. Moreover, different planners will have different estimates of probable return and different opinions as to what sort of return the organization wants. But in theory, planners seek to apportion resources equally to all deserving areas, and as close to break-even points as their information and funding will permit.

Planning Jobs

job planning

By the time actual jobs are being planned in an organization, such questions as allotment of corporate resources have been resolved. Here the manager knows what product is desired, and the task is to create the detailed plans that will bring it into existence. The questions to answer here include *what* is to be produced, *how* it will be made, *who* will make it (usually several different specialists, each doing a part), *when* each part of the job will be completed, and *where* within the plant each step will take place. The planner must see that the necessary labor, materials, machines, and instructions are available when needed for this particular production job.

routing, scheduling, dispatching

In a manufacturing plant, these planning elements are embodied in processes of *routing* (detailing what steps will take place in what parts of the plant), *scheduling* (detailing when each step will take place and for how long), and *dispatching* (issuing the instructions that will put the plan into action). In mass production shops, the plans are laid out in great detail, leaving almost nothing to the discretion of the individual employee. This approach is particularly important for assembly lines, where the timing of operations must mesh very precisely.

Planning the Future

All planning (except perhaps job planning) deals with the future, and we can only guess at future events. We can collect useful information and evaluate it systematically, but much uncertainty remains, and the further into the future we attempt to plan the more uncertainty there is. Therefore, any plan must take into account two related factors: uncertainty

uncertainty, chance

and chance. To cope with both elements, a plan must contain some degree of built-in flexibility. We are uncertain about future demand for our product; it could vary from 5% less than last year to 10% more, and our production levels must be designed to tolerate this spread. We also know that *chance* (a drastic alteration in consumer tastes, a sudden raw material shortage, or a major technical discovery) might operate to wipe out a product line. If we depend on a costly and inflexible automated factory which can make only one product, we have provided no escape hatch for this sort of emergency.

One reason planning is so difficult is that administrators often confuse the future with the present. A builder may predict that young families are going to start moving to the suburbs, when in fact that trend is already under way. A true forecast analyzes developing social preferences in order to predict the trends that are likely to materialize in response to these forces. Accurate forecasting is not easy, but effective planning demands it.

Does forecast of future overseas work for North Star deal more with uncertainty or chance?

The Need for Planning

A recent study of some 250 small companies in a metropolitan area disclosed that soon after starting operations, 200 went out of business. In analyzing the firms, researchers learned that almost all the survivors kept good financial records, while almost none of the dropouts did. Let us imagine one such business, a small grocery store. The proprietor gets a start-up loan and stocks the store. As the receipts come in, the owner goes to the cash register and takes out living expenses. Suddenly bills come in from suppliers for reordered stock, and there isn't enough money in the register to pay them. Without a budget or financial plan, the owner failed to recognize that many of these receipts should have been earmarked for replenishing stock.

why companies plan

The chapter prologue relates how North Star had begun to follow this pattern when Zeb brought the partners up short by insisting that they needed a plan. They were living on the overseas funds as though all those receipts were theirs to spend, instead of realizing that some of that income had to cover marketing expenses for future business. No doubt they had a budget for the current year, but when Zeb showed them a projected budget for a period two years in the future they suddenly perceived how bleak their prospects would be if they did not plan.

Even at the highest levels of government, it is surprising how little planning is done except for the coming year. The essential facts leading to a shortage of energy in many nations were there for anyone to read, but they had to be pulled together in forecasts before their implications would be clear. Since no coherent forecasts were prepared, the follow-up step of developing an energy plan was not taken. Governments at all levels do far less planning than businesses, probably because elected officials feel pressured to achieve short-term results that will impress the voters. Business leaders, who retain their jobs for indefinite but generally longer periods, can pay more attention to planning for the future.

Planning and Control

In the previous section we pointed out that an organization cannot move effectively without clear objectives. In the same way, an organization

control

scheduling

Figure 6-1.
Organizational Planning Cycle

plan junctions

Where would Dick Boyer put a junction in his plan to expand overseas work?

cannot have any effective system of internal controls unless it has a plan. The plan establishes guidelines for progress, the control process steers the organization toward these guideposts and dictates operational changes when the organization deviates from the plan. This process is shown diagrammatically in Figure 6-1. An approved *plan* leads to *action* (perhaps the production of a line of goods for a certain market), with the imposition of *control* to see that the desired output is achieved. In the control phase, the output is compared with the *plan* (perhaps too many items are being manufactured for the market at present, and inventory is building up faster than the plan called for), which leads to further *action* (a reduced rate of production), and the cycle continues.

An important link between planning and control is *scheduling*. A detailed plan is usually expressed in terms of a schedule for completing the steps in the plan; control consists of seeing that the scheduled events take place on time and within the cost estimates. Any change from the planning figures is a *variance,* and constitutes a red flag for management to investigate. If a job is running late, or exceeding its costs, something is wrong, and management control must be exercised to set things right. This is not to say that jobs never run late or cost more than was planned. Indeed, major undertakings that involve new technologies or large uncertainties are quite likely to exceed original time and cost estimates. But without the element of planning associated with control of resources and operations when variances show up, these overages would be much greater and would occur without warning. (If a potential for such crises exists in a given project, plans usually reveal that potential, if not the exact nature of the problem.)

The Dynamics of Planning

Figure 6-1 describes a simple situation where the plan is correct and needs no changing, so that the only problem is to make actions conform to the plan. In reality, plans can never be fixed, since they are based on estimates of future events which are almost sure to be wrong in some particulars. Thus, plans must be reassessed constantly as the near future becomes the present and new information develops. Consider a plan for the sewage collection and treatment system for a municipality, shown in Table 6-1. As originally conceived, the plan covers 15 years.

As time passes, this plan will have to be revised. Part of the revision is anticipated, as shown in the notes. Another part cannot be anticipated: change in environmental standards that requires more expensive treatment of solid waste; legislation providing for 75% Federal funding of approved treatment plants; change in living habits that emphasizes apartments over single-family dwellings; and so forth. If the entire system is planned at the start, land acquired for the treatment plant, and surveys of the collection system completed, the plan will not be flexible enough to adjust to future events.

Since future events may change any plan, flexibility must be provided in advance by establishing "junctions" where the planners will stop and take stock; at these points, a change in direction is made as easy as possible. Funds should not be committed for any stage of the plan until the latest possible time, and when the commitment is made it should be in a form that retains maximum flexibility.

MANAGEMENT PROCESSES

Benefits of Planning

Without an overall plan, everyone in the organization simply moves in the direction he or she thinks best—that is, if individuals are planning at all. In the case of North Star, as the chapter prologue observes, Dick Boyer was so enmeshed in his daily problems overseas that the thought of planning for the future never entered his mind. If it had, perhaps he would have considered how he could expand his work for Natal Engineers, with very little consideration of what that would involve for the rest of the company. Henry, not being on site at the Natal operation, would have given more thought to other North Star matters. Bert probably would have thought of ways to improve the drafting room operations—improvements that could hamper efforts to expand overseas.

With proper coordination of planning for the whole organization, everyone directs efforts and assesses information with purposeful and orderly growth of the enterprise in mind. Any resource expenditures are considered on the basis of organizational objectives, and distracting operations are curtailed. Morever, the whole organization is apprised of the plan's impact on each organizational unit and determines what each unit must do to meet the group objectives. Tasks can be assigned to those best able to accomplish them for the overall good.

When a plan begins to take shape, the spotlight is on steps that must be taken to achieve it. Only when Zeb revealed the expected deficit budget two years down the road did the North Star group realize how essential it was to take action. As soon as a plan was under way, an assortment of possible corrective actions were presented: "What if we take follow-up action with AID?" "What if we explore this or that market area?" The answers to these questions are the basis of an acceptable strategy.

Managers are decision makers, but they need criteria in order to reach decisions. Planned targets and planned courses of action provide

Table 6-1.
Sewage System Development Schedule

Year (from present)	Action
0	Start accruing funds
5	Make general layout of system[1]
7	Get referendum approval from public
8	Start detailed plans of collection system[2]
9	Acquire site for new treatment plant[2]
10	Install collection system (first increment)[3]
12	Build new treatment plant on site[4]
14-15	Install collection system (second increment)[5]

1. Based on general estimates of probable expansion
2. Based on housing starts and developers' plans
3. Based on later information of developers' plans
4. Based on developers' plans and revised estimates of probable expansion, with excess capacity included
5. Based on still later information of developers' plans and long-range zoning plan for municipality

managers with guidelines against which to measure performance. There is a time for thinking ahead and a time for action; the separation of planning and operating functions helps the manager to use personal skills effectively, without the uncertainties of wondering whether the organization is headed in the right direction. With a properly prepared plan, information has been gathered systematically and placed at the disposal of the manager, who is thus spared the effort of collecting it personally or (more typically) of trying to estimate the necessary facts and figures.

assumptions

Every enterprise has to make certain assumptions about the future, its possible responses, and its preferences. When a plan has been prepared and agreed upon, these assumptions, responses, and preferences are stated, and managers can utilize them without further thought or effort. If you were a manager in a company utilizing petroleum products, it would be more useful for you to know the company's estimate of what the products will cost next year than to attempt your own estimates of petroleum costs; moreover, it is far more efficient for these estimates to be made once (and by the best authorities in the company) than several times by various company managers. If one division manager estimates a lower price than do other division managers, a strategy may be adopted for that division which does not coincide with other divisional strategies.

Proper planning will minimize costs by smoothing out workloads, preventing discontinuities in the work of one division while waiting for work to be completed in another. If production for sale occurs in spurts, with idle spots in between, a good plan will schedule production for stock during the slack periods. Planning will minimize the situation where too much work is piled on only one division, requiring costly overtime to get out of the bind. If a period of heavy work is coming up, good planning will prepare by rescheduling lower priority work, arranging for subcontracting, or taking other action to prevent the workload peak from causing avoidable difficulties.

Sometimes managers allege that planning requires more facts than are obtainable, and that they can do better by using experience and judgment. One benefit of planning is that it shows the need for such facts and makes it clear to managers that they have been deciding without sufficient information.

When a complex task is being undertaken, such as the construction of a plant, experienced supervisors are likely to believe that they know how to proceed without detailed work sequence schedules. Perhaps they do know enough to proceed without planning the schedule of events in advance, but often they do not. At the start of a task all options are open as to where to begin, but after the job is a year down the road it is too late to find that some other part of the work should have been started first. Experience is not a reason for omitting planning; it is a help to good planning.

Types and Levels of Planning

The word "planning" means different things to different people, because there are so many kinds and degrees of planning. To the operator of a turret lathe in a machine shop, it may mean arranging the operations of the machine in the proper order for a given job. To the stock clerk, it may mean scheduling orders so as not to run out of parts or overfill the bins. To the chief executive of an electric utility, it may mean scheduling the construction of new power plants so that there is enough generating capacity to meet customer needs but not so much that excessive borrowing is necessary. To the service manager of an automobile dealership, it may mean training mechanics on new models in time to be ready for the repairs that develop with a new model year. To the developer of a Disney World, it means assessing the tastes of the public for entertainment over the next twenty years or more.

These different viewpoints vary in two distinct ways: the organizational level at which they exist and the length of time involved in the projection. Job planning (the turret lathe operator) almost certainly means planning for the immediate future. Inventory planning (the stock clerk) looks a bit further into the future, but not much. In the above example, the chief executive of the utility is engaged in mid-range planning, but that is not to say that all top planning deals with the distant future; the chief executive is equally likely to plan the next day's board of directors meeting.

level of planning

When events are being planned for the very distant future, the uncertainty factor may render the plan nearly useless. An entrepreneur acquiring the food concession in a football stadium has little need to explore the long-range future for professional football, since anyone can get out of that business on a year's notice at little cost. But the entrepreneur building the stadium is vitally interested in the long-term future of professional football in that area, since that investment will not be recouped for many years. In general, the planning horizon should be at least as long as the useful life of company investments.

The Hierarchy of Planning

If we omit the extremely localized planning done by the machine operator or the clerk and concentrate on managerial planning, we can identify two main categories at opposite ends of the planning spectrum. One is *activity planning*, which guides the relatively short-range operations of a division or unit within an organization (such as manufacturing planning). The other is *institutional planning*, which determines what the whole organization will do as an independent entity, over both the short and the long range. In the short range, the institutional plan coordinates and guides the activity plans for all divisions so that they pull together in pursuit of common institutional objectives. In the long range, it forecasts the future environment, and sets a broad policy against which all planning in the organization will be measured.

Which of the tasks Zeb laid out would be activity planning? Which institutional planning?

Several intermediate levels of planning exist, but essentially they serve as channels for information to pass upward to the policy level (without which plans will not be realistic or properly oriented), and for direction to pass downward to the operating level (so that decisions can be based on correct premises). Figure 6-2 shows five levels of planning in an enterprise large enough to have a board of directors and several divisions or activities. In this organization, *institutional planning* is accomplished at

institutional planning

activity planning   levels II and III, and *activity planning* is accomplished at level IV. We will discuss each of these in turn.

Activity Planning

A principal activity in most modern enterprises is manufacturing. In many companies it occupies a principal position in the spectrum of activities, since it provides the product that represents the reason for the enterprise to exist. Thus, manufacturing planning will constitute a good illustration of planning at the activity level.

manufacturing planning

The planning process for a manufacturing activity incorporates seven separate but interrelated planning activities:

market planning

1. *Market planning* is the process of deciding what to make. Before a product line can be selected, the company has to know whether there is a market for it and exactly what type of product will sell best. In the long run, this process may involve analysis of social trends, probable action of regulatory agencies, long-term profit trends, and competition from products not yet developed. In the short run, with which activity planning is concerned, it deals mainly with evaluating markets for the coming year and selecting the products that will fare best in those markets.

design planning

2. *Design planning* is the process of determining what form the product line will take. If it is a television set, should it be plastic or wood, with disposable modules or with a chassis repairable piece by piece? Should the newest picture tube technology be employed or not? Should it be sold in decorator colors? What other design elements are important, and how should the questions be resolved?

Figure 6-2. Organizational Planning Hierarchy

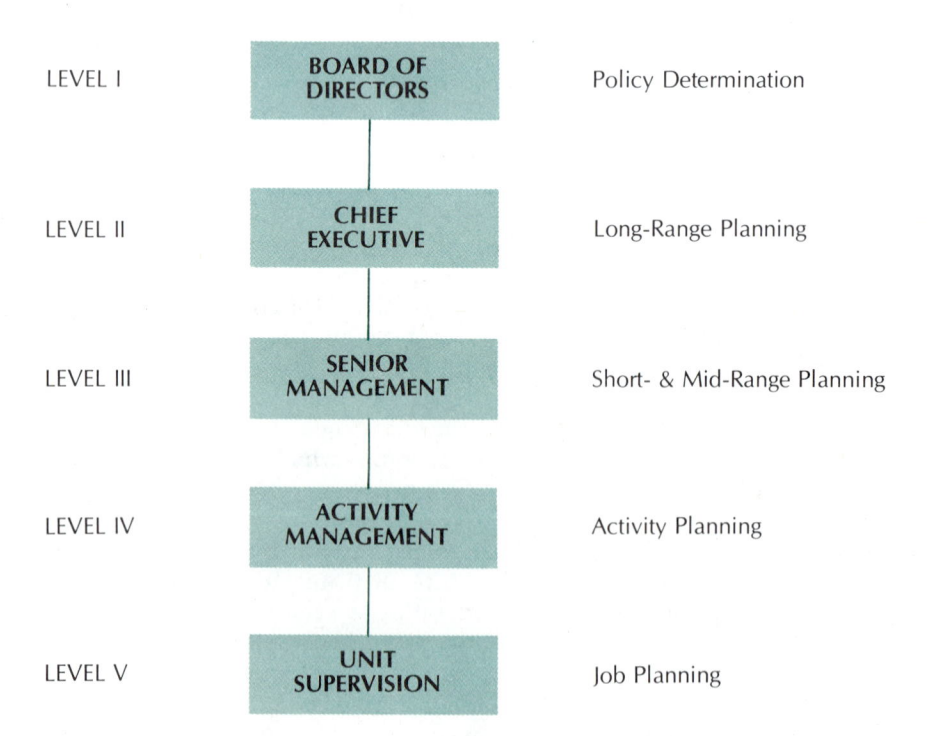

LEVEL I	BOARD OF DIRECTORS	Policy Determination
LEVEL II	CHIEF EXECUTIVE	Long-Range Planning
LEVEL III	SENIOR MANAGEMENT	Short- & Mid-Range Planning
LEVEL IV	ACTIVITY MANAGEMENT	Activity Planning
LEVEL V	UNIT SUPERVISION	Job Planning

3. *Material planning* is the process of arranging for the parts and raw materials needed to manufacture the end product. In the automobile industry, material planning and scheduling is a highly precise art, with components needed for the assembly line scheduled to arrive only hours before they are used. The planners must arrange to have enough so they will not run short, but not so much that they are spending needlessly for inventory and warehouse space. material planning

4. *Personnel planning* is the process of seeing that properly trained workers are available when needed. In an increasingly technological age, companies have to run elaborate training programs to provide the necessary competences where and when they need them. Many skills required by businesses cannot be found in the job market; these must be developed through in-house training programs. personnel planning

5. *Facility planning* sees that the equipment and plant required for the manufacturing effort are brought together to support the manufacturing process. With the modern emphasis on labor-saving machinery, it is essential that tooling and equipment be suited to the task and available when needed. facility planning

6. *Budget planning* insures that funds are allocated for the manufacturing expenditures as well as all the support items mentioned above. The development of a budget includes estimates of revenues and their timing, to get an idea of the profit and cash flow picture. If new facilities are required, funds must be made available and decisions reached as to the rate of amortization and cost sharing between this and other manufacturing projects. budget planning

7. *Production planning* "puts it all together," programming the details of routing jobs from machine to machine, scheduling jobs so that machines are kept occupied, estimating the length of jobs by evaluating the data on unit times through industrial engineering techniques, and so on. production planning

The activity need not be manufacturing. It might be advertising, or research, or purchasing, or bookkeeping. It may be staff or line. But each activity is required to plan its operations in the way that will best achieve its goals, subject always to the overall constraints of the organization as a whole. That is to say, the individual activity must not try so hard to improve its own operations that it injures the operations of another activity in the process.

Institutional Planning

At this end of the planning spectrum, the enterprise seeks to attain the best possible results as a total entity. When Zeb presented the need for planning to the North Star partners, he was speaking principally of institutional planning, necessary to keep the whole ship afloat. In the process of such team planning, it might very well happen that one activity or another would have to be curtailed or even discontinued for the good of the whole. If the company saw its future in expansion of overseas work, Ab Jenkins and his whole drafting room might have to be scattered to various overseas sites in support of that operation. Clearly this is not a plan that Ab would willingly develop at the activity level; so some device to provide an overriding institutional viewpoint is needed by organizations.

The institutional plan might be divided into the *capital budget,* the *operating budget,* and the *schedule* for implementation of planned events.

capital budget

Although these overlap in many ways, they can be understood best by discussing each in turn.

The capital budget expresses the company's plans for fixed expenditures during the planning period (usually the next year). *Capital* refers to items that will not be used up in the process of production (or whatever the function of the enterprise is). Capital items are essentially tools of a more or less permanent nature, required to produce the output of the enterprise but not consumed. A large machine tool that will last 20 years is a capital item, as is a truck that will last six years. Although it may not be so apparent, a research project needed to develop a product line is also a capital expenditure, because the benefits of the research will extend over several years as the product continues to be manufactured. Training of employees may be a capital expenditure, if the benefits of the training will spread over several years.

Some capital expenditure items are virtually *required,* while others fall in the *desirable* category. Required expenditures replace buildings or equipment destroyed by fire, worn out, damaged, or otherwise simply not available — provided the equipment is necessary to continuation of the operation. Almost equally important are items that will keep the enterprise competitive; perhaps a new process or technology has been developed, and companies that retain the old methods will lose their market share. All other capital investment candidates fall in the desirable category, and management must choose among these on the basis of what each will cost and what it will earn. One of the most perplexing elements of institutional planning is choosing among alternative capital expenditures, because of the many different factors to be considered in an atmosphere of uncertainty. Managers deal constantly with uncertainty (indeed, anyone who is uncomfortable making decisions on the basis of incomplete information probably should not seek a career in management), but nowhere is the uncertainty so pervasive as in choosing among large expenditures that will take many years to amortize.

Consider the relatively simple choice between two capital investment opportunities, represented in Figure 6-3. Reading down the columns, you see that Candidate A has an estimated "return if successful" that is 50% more than that of Candidate B ($1.8 million to $1.2 million), but its cost is more than 50% higher than Candidate B (50% higher would be $7.5 million, and it costs $8 million). So you are tempted to choose B over A. But you also note that B is more risky than A (only a 60% chance of success as against 80% for A). When you apply this percentage probability of success to the estimated "return if successful,"[1] Candidate A anticipates an average yearly payoff of $1,280,000 against $720,000 for Candidate B.

Figure 6-3.
Two Investment Opportunities

	Candidate A	Candidate B
Initial cost	$8,000,000	$5,000,000
Return/year if successful	1,800,000	1,200,000
Probability of success	80%	60%
Expected return/yr (Return x Proby)	1,280,000	720,000
Rate of return on investment	16%	14.4%

Thus the *rate of return on investment* for A is better than that for B—16% against 14.4%, ignoring "discounting," or the effect of interest rate. If that were figured in, say at 8%, the comparison after interest on the capital cost would be 8% for Candidate A against 6.4% for Candidate B.

Now it becomes a simple choice, and the obvious conclusion is to select A over B. Even in this case, however, A calls for a bigger investment than B, and normally when companies make larger investments they demand larger rates of return to compensate for risking a bigger slice of their capital. (This point is discussed in chapter 7, "Decision Making.") But few decisions are this simple. Perhaps A fits in better with the present product line, so selling it will be simpler; perhaps B fits the present manufacturing techniques better, so production will be easier; perhaps A involves some risk of a patent infringement suit from a competitor; perhaps B involves use of more hazardous raw materials. Maybe the chief executive is afraid that not enough time was spent on researching the information in Figure 6-3, and thus lacks complete confidence in it—but getting more information will be costly and time-consuming. Maybe Candidate B, although not as promising a profit maker, will strike the board of directors as a more conservative choice. If the chief executive selects A and it succeeds, all is well, but if it fails the directors will be highly critical. If the executive selects B, the directors will support the choice and in a sense will "share" in the misfortune if it fails. Perhaps A promises long life if it succeeds, whereas B is in a technical area where new developments are likely to come along in ten or 15 years and cut into its sales drastically.

Thus, choices are not usually so simple, and probably most capital investment planners would be happy to be right three-fourths of the time. But decisions must be made. And in order to make them, planners require estimates of the future environment for as long as the capital equipment is going to last—or at least for the period over which the company will depreciate it. This leads to the need for *forecasting*, discussed in a later section.

The *operating budget* demands far less ability to read the future, since it generally covers only a one-year period, and can be changed in response to developments during that year. In some respects operating costs can be substituted for capital costs; if you are considering a new machine that will save labor costs, you can "substitute" for this machine by spending more on labor during the year, or by contracting out that part of the work to a company that has such a machine, or by buying parts involving this work rather than making them. Plans are placed in effect through the medium of the budget, since the availability of operating funds makes it possible for divisions to expand or requires them to contract. If a decision has been made to increase the marketing effort for the coming year, it is expressed in the increased marketing budget.

Level budgeting means that each unit starts with the funds it received the previous year and adjusts up or down from this level in accordance with planning changes. A level budget is conservative in nature, implying that few changes are going to be made—and perhaps also implying that management has few real guidelines for deciding how to distribute the funds, so falls back on procedures that have succeeded in the past. On the other hand, level budgeting is less disruptive to personnel, since it leads to continuity of employment within each unit and engenders a feeling of security (possibly too much at times).

program budgeting

Program budgeting endeavors to charge against each operation all of the real costs of that operation, whether they are administratively borne by that unit or another. Under this concept, management tries to determine what part of equipment costs, research costs, marketing costs, and other overhead costs really are incurred for the benefit of a particular operation or product line, and thus should be considered in deciding whether or not to handle that operation or product. Many accounting difficulties arise with this process. For example, say you open a night shift for two operations, incurring the cost of guards and other second-shift administrative staff. Should the operation that initially needed the night shift be charged with all such costs and the operation that began later get a free ride, or should the costs be split? To the extent that program budgeting is possible, however, it gives management a better picture of all the costs for the various options being considered.

performance budgeting

The concept of *performance budgeting* is simple enough: what is a given operation earning on the funds allotted to it? The goal is to distribute funds so that the high earners get the money, but achieving this objective is much more complex than it sounds. How do you decide what a safety program earns, for example? What are the earnings of long-range research, or of the accounting department, or of the industrial health program? To the extent that figures can be determined, as in the case of program budgeting, this approach is quite useful, but it is far from a decision making cureall.

schedule

The *schedule* is the document that time-phases the expenditures authorized in the capital and operating budgets. A schedule may be as simple as establishing the rule that no more than 30% of a unit's operating budget can be expended in any quarter. It may be a detailed schedule by

Most capital investment planners would be happy to be right three-fourths of the time.

194
MANAGEMENT PROCESSES

days and operations, which seeks to mesh the operations of separate units into a unified whole. The advantage of a schedule is the thought it demands before it can be prepared — thought that imposes self-discipline on managers who may be inclined to skip over the tiresome details of seeing how a plan will be put in effect. Another advantage is that it gets everyone pulling in the same direction, and prevents the conflicts that occur when two groups try to use a resource at the same time. A carefully scheduled project is likely to be an efficient project, because the bottlenecks have been foreseen and avoided insofar as possible.

The Horizon of Planning

The preceding discussion of institutional planning mingled various planning horizons. Budgetary planning for operations generally involves the very short term, seldom more than the coming year, while capital planning by definition involves a longer period (since the definition of capital investment is one that is not consumed in the short run). But we did not try to pin down the planning period for capital items. In this section we will differentiate between *short-range*, *mid-range* and *long-range* planning, and discuss the fundamental differences among these concepts as well as the need for coordination.

The Range of Planning

There are several ways of differentiating between the characteristics of planning for the near future and planning for more distant futures. One way is simply by the time period involved. *Short-range* planning typically involves the next budget year — between one and two years into the future — and the process of short-range planning is nearly synonymous with developing next year's budget. *Mid-range* planning deals with the period two to five years in the future (perhaps somewhat longer for enterprises where future developments are of vital importance). *Long-range* planning peers into the hazy future extending from six or eight years to 15 or 20 years, and sometimes more.

Another way to differentiate is by the sort of uncertainty involved. Short-range planning basically involves the here and now, where you are using your present employees and materials, dealing with presently known products and processes, and encountering markets of the sort with which you are quite familiar. Mid-range planning introduces some troublesome uncertainties, because employee preferences and expectations are shifting, material costs and availability will change, new technologies will enter the equation, and markets may be shifting appreciably; but all of these developments are evolutionary rather than revolutionary. Long-range planning, however, is a totally different proposition, and the past is a very undependable guide. Social preferences and lifestyles may change markedly, with a drastic impact on companies whose success is subject to human foibles. Material costs may shift enough to make entire product lines uneconomic. Technology may shift the base of an entire industry (as in the move to solid state electronics), and companies that do not bet their research chips on the right squares in time can lose huge hunks of the market or go out of business entirely. Regulatory agencies may outlaw foods, medicines, tobaccos, industrial processes, or raw material extraction practices,

short-range planning

mid-range planning

long-range planning

What range is North Star looking at in its proposed planning activities? Explain.

throwing important industrial sectors out of business or at least putting a crimp in their operations.

The airline industry is an example of both the importance and difficulty of planning. Operational planning is extremely crucial to an airline. It must know where it will fly and how many passengers it will carry so it can buy the right aircraft, because wrong guesses can mean costly overcapacity or inability to fly the distances economically. It must know the seasonal peaks so it can schedule maintenance around the heavy demand periods. When schedules change, as during the 1974 petroleum embargo, the airline must let some pilots go and retrain others for their changed jobs, which is both costly and time-consuming.[2] When the total volume of air travel drops markedly, the airline is left with underutilized assets whose costs cannot be cut appreciably. (President F. C. Wiser, Jr., of Trans World Airlines recently estimated that over a third of TWA's costs would continue even if the company stopped flying completely; it might take many years to get out of facility agreements at airports all over the world and terminate interest payments on the idle aircraft.) Airlines must know years in advance what sort of aircraft they will need, but wrong guesses can lead to situations such as that recently experienced by American Airlines, where a decision to ground ten of its Boeing 747s cost it $2.5 million a year per plane in interest and depreciation.[3]

The Difficulty of Strategic Planning

strategic planning

Long-range planning, sometimes called *strategic planning,* is a very different undertaking from day-to-day managing, and calls for a completely different approach. Indeed, some of the very skills that make a good manager are likely to make a bad strategic planner. A manager is decisive, accustomed to making choices quickly and not taking time to look back or brood over spilt milk; a strategic planner must be deliberate and contemplative, thinking and rethinking issues as a dog worries a bone, forever alert to changing decisions in the light of new evidence. A manager watches the situation develop, and is trained to shift tactics quickly and drastically to adjust to events; a planner doesn't get such feedback because his or her environment is the dim future. Managers are trained in their profession, and it represents familiar ground; moreover, they associate with colleagues whose values they share, who provide plenty of reinforcement for their decisions. The lonely planner deals with a vague and unfamiliar future, with few colleagues who understand the hazy furrow he or she plows, so the decisions are lonely ones. They are worse than lonely—they are probably unpopular, because any planning choice is bound to threaten some operating division, and its head will protest it vigorously. And since operating managers ought to know more about their areas than a remote planner, chances are they can make the planner look silly in the front office.

How does this apply to Henry's planning assignment?

The above list could be extended in many directions. But there are other roadblocks as well. One important one is simply the *frame of mind* required for good strategic planning. It seems logical for a successful enterprise to start its planning by taking stock of its present strengths and resources, and to seek futures that will make the best use of these, but actually that is going at the task backwards. It really makes little difference what the enterprise knows how to make; the important thing is to concentrate on what will be needed in the future. A gold prospector would never say, "I have this equipment and these maps, so where would it be most convenient for me to look?" Rather, the question is "Never mind what areas would suit me best—where is gold likely to be?" If the direction where gold beckons, figuratively speaking, requires the company to make wholesale changes in its past way of life, so be it—that is the price of survival, and the company must stand ready to pay it.

If an open-minded attitude toward long-range planning may require the enterprise to scrap some existing operations—perhaps abandon whole divisions or activities which are profitable today—it is easy to see how unproductive it would be to put such long-range planning in the hands of division or activity chiefs. It is expecting superhuman selflessness to believe that such operating managers could preside objectively over their own funerals. Yet it would not be effective to assign such planning to a nonoperating staff, because such people will lack the detailed knowledge required for realistic assessments. Companies that do such planning most successfully are likely to have a centralized staff unit without operating responsibilities that *plans the planning*—assembles economic data, industry forecasts, and evidence on social shifts, and prepares planning agendas that keep the discussion on track. Thus, planning becomes a company-wide enterprise that draws in principal managers for their expertise but keeps them from steering the plan in parochial directions.

The federal government is not immune to these long-range planning problems. The increasing volume of foreign car imports into the United States has led the United Automobile Workers and its congressional allies to urge the restriction of small foreign car imports, because of the special claims of U.S. automobile producers. At a time when fuel conservation

I have this equipment and these maps, so where would it be most convenient for me to look?

has become more important than ever, reduction of vigorous competition in production of economical automobiles would not seem to mesh with the nation's long-term interests. Although these overseas manufacturers cut into sales of cars produced here in the short term, in the long run this competition forces U.S. car manufacturers to adjust energetically to changing conditions, and should both strengthen their competitive position and give the U.S. consumer a better chance at more economical transportation.

Forecasting

forecasting uncertainties

An essential input to effective planning is accurate estimates about future developments. The future is a jumble of uncertainties. There are uncertainties on the *supply* side: What technological developments are ahead? What will happen to material availability and price? Where is the labor market going? There are uncertainties on the *demand* side: What products will the public want? What prices will it pay? And in today's climate of consumer awareness there are uncertainties as to the *environment* of enterprise: What constraints will be applied to manufacturing processes? What limitations will be placed on saleable products? Over all of these forecasts stands the broad question about the economic climate: What will the situation be with regard to inflation, employment, international trade, and economic growth?

The pineapple has for years been synonymous with Hawaii. With pineapples its second largest crop, Hawaii used to produce more than two-thirds of the world's output. Yet today the two leading Hawaiian producers are cutting back sharply and virtually abandoning cannery operations. Dole's 1974 production of 220,000 tons compares with 520,000 tons in 1971. Production is shifting to Africa and Asia. Wage scales are one reason (Del Monte's Hawaiian manager states that production costs for canned sliced pineapple are more than double those in other major growing areas); another is U.S. laws requiring shipment from Hawaii to be in U.S. vessels (making shipping costs from Hawaii a third higher than from far-off Taiwan). Dole has recognized the onset of this situation, and has spent millions trying to improve mechanization and thus reduce high labor costs, but without success. It is probable that the present cutbacks were planned as much as ten years ago (although it is doubtful that the planning extended to exploring solutions for the Molokai labor force, now faced with a 75% unemployment rate for which it is largely unprepared). Comprehensive long-range planning by the companies, the union, and the state might have revealed the conditions leading to this cutback many years ago, and could have initiated energetic programs to find solutions for the displaced workers.

economy forecasting

Forecasting starts with an analysis of general business conditions. Since there are many agencies in the United States (and in other nations) that attempt to forecast the key factors of economic health, a company has many sources to draw upon. But even the best of forecasters can be wrong, and their errors can have drastic effects on individual companies. In recent years the President's Council of Economic Advisers has been rather consistently wrong in estimating the extent of inflation (along with much of the economic community)—always on the low side. Figure 6-4 shows the ten-year inflationary growth of prices for producers and consumers between 1964 and 1974. Notice the increase in the index cost of crude materials to producers during the first five years of this period: 97 to 110, or 13.4%. A similar growth during the second five years would have brought the index cost up from 110 to 125, and a forecaster might have been excused for making this estimate; in fact, however, the cost by February, 1974, had reached 200—a growth rate of not 13.4%, but 72%. Any company that made a ten-year forecast in 1964, and made a

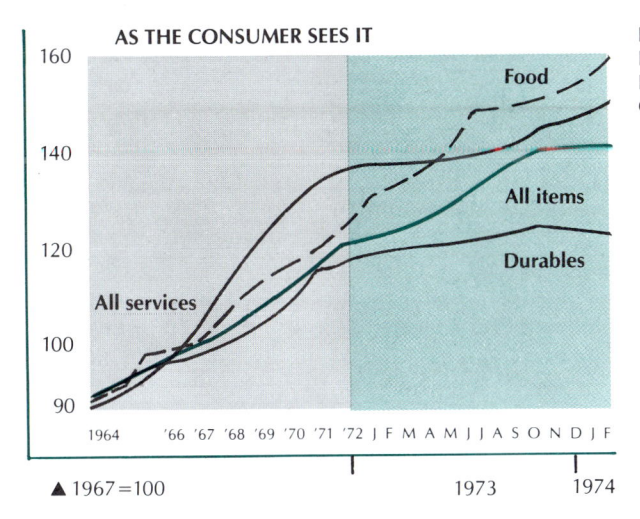

Figure 6-4.
Price Growth for Producers and Consumers

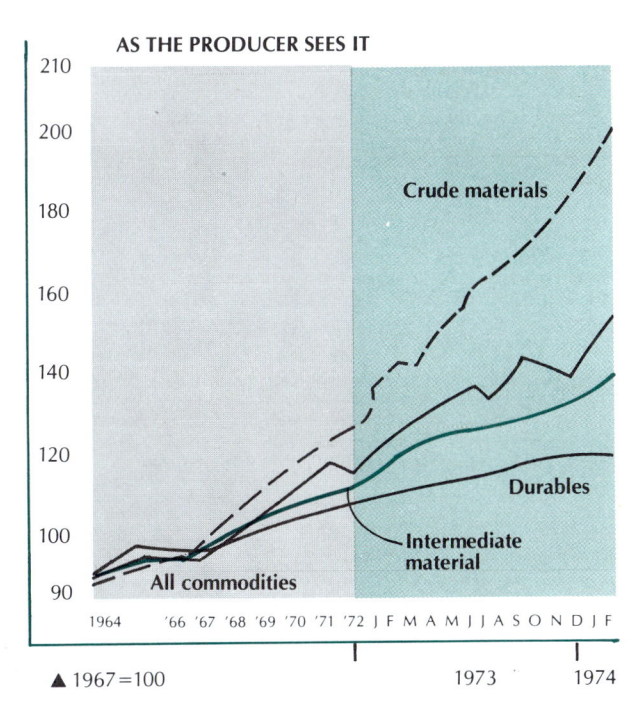

Data: Department of Labor

reasonable prediction of crude material prices based on their rate of growth prior to 1964, thus would have planned for a rate of 125 in 1974 instead of the 200 that actually resulted—a gross underestimate and quite possibly a disastrous one.

Figure 6-5 shows some of the many trends the economic planner must consider in deciding what the future has in store for the company—the labor and materials they use, the energy they consume, the buying power of their customers, the prospective strength of the dollar, the foreign trade situation, and so on.

industry forecasting

Industry forecasting is the next step. After the planners have decided what the general economy of the world and the nation is likely to be, they seek to derive from these general indicators the probable trends in their particular industry. North Star is a consulting firm, and if the nation's overall economic indicators point toward a slowdown it is reasonable to forecast that the slowdown for consulting firms will be even worse: a corporation facing hard times cuts back on its outside sources of help before it starts laying off its own employees. But even if there is no slowdown in sight, the industry planner must answer many questions. What direction will styles and technology take? What will happen to the present market—is it starting to take off, or is it on its last legs? What does the competition have in mind that will change tastes or prices? Is the product of some different industry starting to threaten us (maybe we

Figure 6-5.
Trends that Guide Economic Planners

IS LABOR TOUGHER?

The first inkling that the inflation of the late 1960's might be more intractable than those of the past was the extraordinary behavior of labor in the 1969-70 recession. There was practically no relaxation of labor's push for increased compensation this time—although in previous business cycles employees had always settled for less when the economy turned down.

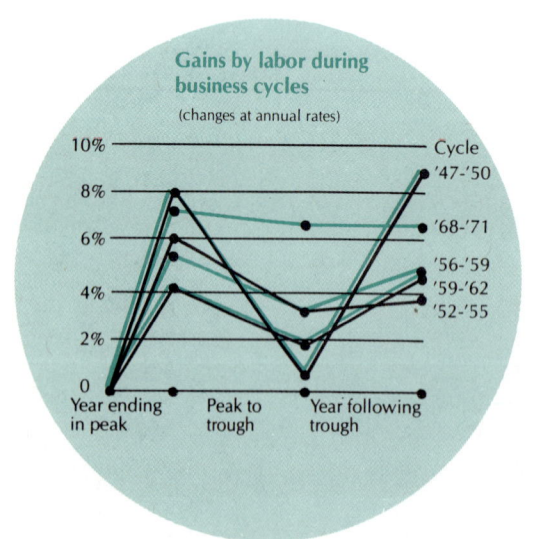

WILL ENERGY LIMIT G.N.P.?

The dimensions of our new energy crisis are still largely undefined, but there is a rather urgent question implied by the chart, which shows the upward sweep of gross national product being supported by a near-identical rise in consumption of energy (as measured in B.T.U.'s). We will soon be discovering whether energy cutbacks necessitate cuts in output.

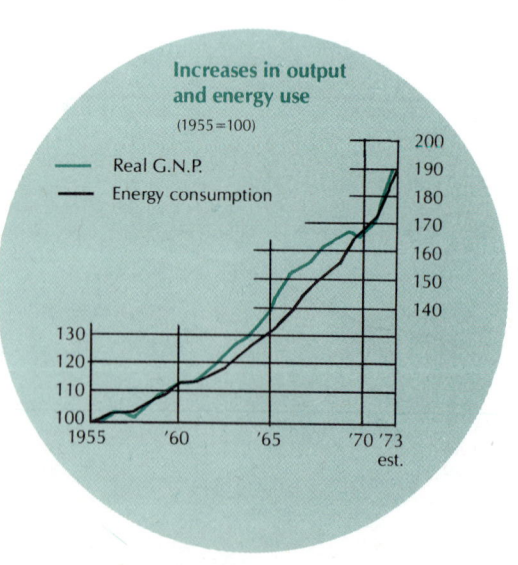

MANAGEMENT PROCESSES

build get-away-from-it-all boats, but get-away-from-it-all campers could capture the leisure time market for getting away)? There is lots of help to be had from trade associations, professional meetings, and industry journals, but lots of uncertainties remain.

Company forecasting is the point where the planners are on their own. Since they are forecasting for their enterprise only, essentially in competition with their industry colleagues, there is no outsider who is willing to help. Many outsiders *do* help, however. Your competitors help by their actions. If one company builds a new plant to produce plastics, that tells you that their market surveys give plastics a good mark for future business. If another opens an overseas office, that shows you where they think expansion is likely to come in the years ahead. Your customers help when they share their own future planning with you, enabling you to guess what sort of parts or materials they may be buying from suppliers like you. The many contacts your salesmen, engineers, and other employees have built up could be a mine of information about your public image and which way it is moving—provided you do far more than most companies to create a welcome atmosphere for such information to flow up to the planners.

company forecasting

It is not very hard for a company to forecast a year or two ahead; this can be done fairly successfully by extension of past trends, with a leavening of common sense that reminds you to pay attention to

WILL FOOD BE SCARCE?
For some time after the inflation rate accelerated in 1966, prices for food tended to rise only moderately. But in the last three years, and especially in 1973, food prices have gone up more than those of other consumer items. Assumptions about plentiful and cheap supplies of food are obviously called into question now.

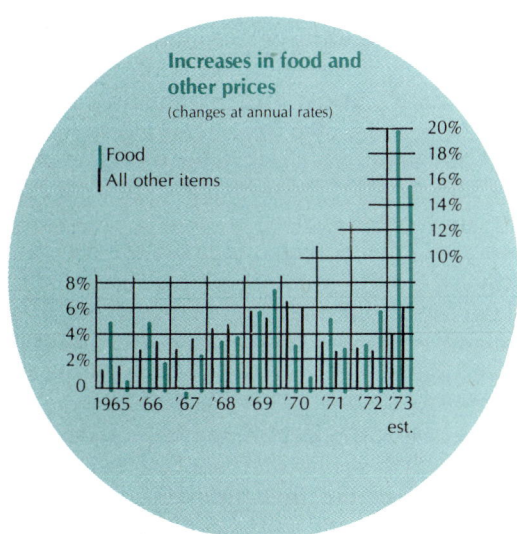

IS CAPACITY LAGGING?
If business had known about the data reflected in that red line, it might have been ready for the excruciating shortages of 1973. But the FRB did not make its "major materials" index available until last August; meanwhile, the Fed's manufacturing index was telling business it had capacity to spare. The lag in growth of materials capacity may be hard to cure.

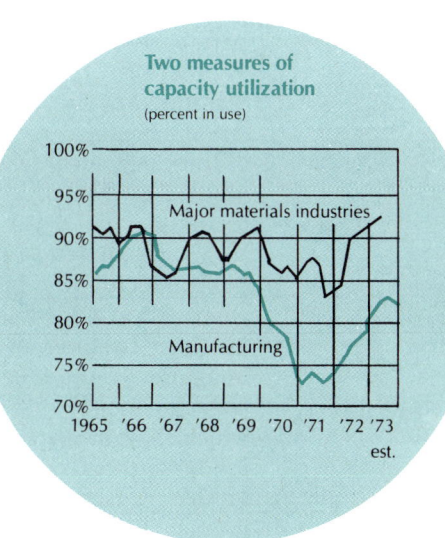

Increases in food and other prices
(changes at annual rates)

Two measures of capacity utilization
(percent in use)

significant developments in the industry and the economy as well. Mid-range forecasting calls for a great deal more skill. A useful technique for making forecasts several years into the future is that of *correlation analysis:* working out what factors have affected demand for your product (or supply of your raw materials, or whatever you are analyzing) in the past, and the relative weight of each factor. Suppose you were in charge of forecasting for one of the airlines and wanted to predict volume of air traffic at one of the cities on your route. You might decide, for starters, that the number of passengers would depend on *air fare* (F), *per capita income* (I), *population growth* (P), and a *time trend* (T).[4] Your statistician could set up for you a "forecasting equation" that examines the recent past in terms of all these variables and analyzes what effect each appeared to have on past passenger volume in that city. It might turn out that while increasing air fare tended to reduce volume, increasing per capita income tended to increase volume at a rate greater than the rate of reduction. Thus, a 10% increase in air fares coupled with a 10% increase in per capita income would not just allow air traffic volume to hold its own, but would cause it to grow at about 10% itself. Armed by your statistician with the separate contribution of each factor, and by your economist with forecasts of where factors F, I, and P are going in the next five to ten years (you already know where T is going), you can make realistic projections of air traffic volumes by combining all these elements in your "regression equation" or statistical forecast.

A forecast of this sort was made recently for the beef industry. The *Journal of Farm Economics* published a study disclosing that the demand for fed beef (fattened on grain in "feedlots") behaved as follows with respect to the impact of beef prices and of buyer income: if meat price and family income both rise by 10%, the family will still eat about 10% more beef because the "income effect" will more than balance the "price effect."[5] And a 10% drop in both price and income would reduce their beef consumption by roughly 10%. Figure 6-6 shows a regular and continuing increase from 1950–1973 in per capita consumption of beef by the American consumer, despite gradually rising beef prices during this period—because the consumer's income was going up too. But between 1973 and 1974, spendable earnings dropped nearly 5% while beef prices continued to rise, and the result was a marked drop in demand for beef. Another result was that feedlot operators, who were generally not aware of these statistical relationships, lost about $1 billion in the first six months of 1974 as they tried to cope with the glut of overweight cattle in their feedlots.

For truly long-range forecasts, even correlation analysis falls short. Several techniques have been used for this purpose. One is *brainstorming*, where knowledgeable people in the organization get together and try to let their imaginations range far and wide, to see if the futures they imagine—and the company responses they propose—strike responsive sparks with the other participants. Another method is *evolutionary analysis*, which examines areas of human activity where the demand for technological breakthroughs is intense (such as the polio vaccine of a few years ago or the "cancer cure" today), and concludes that the pent-up need will induce such activity that the breakthrough will occur. This approach might be called the "where there's a will there's a way" philosophy. The

brainstorming

evolutionary analysis

America's love affair with beef cools a bit

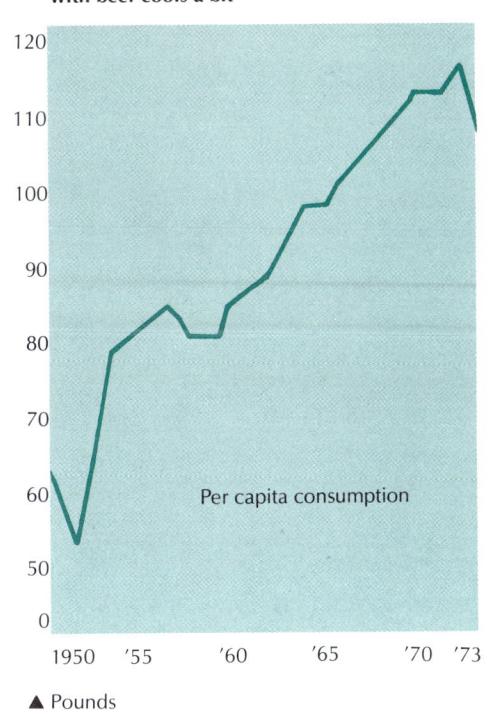

Figure 6-6.
Beef Consumption Trends

planner then says, "The breakthrough will occur; now how will that affect us, and what should we do to be ready to exploit it?"

A third technique is *dynamic forecasting,* which attempts to build a conceptual model of the environment that interests the company, looks at all the pressures operating on the environment, and tries to deduce logically how the environment will evolve as all those pressures act. This method is akin to the deductive system you might use if your cat stole the pincushion, and you tried to imagine where you would go with that pincushion if you were a cat. In its advanced forms, dynamic forecasting extends to elaborate mathematical models that can be simulated on a computer; models have been proposed that seek to plot the future path of mankind itself, though not without stirring up rather heated disagreement.[6] In a more practical application, an organization whose growth depends on the population of young people—say a large university— might try to analyze the demand for a high-rise dormitory with a 40-year life span that it planned to build. One input would be the total supply of such young people, which would depend directly upon the birth rate trends for some 18 years earlier. Figure 6-7 shows that the U.S. birth rate has been in a marked decline in recent years; indeed, for the last two years of the graph the rate has been below the figure of 2.1 births required to sustain a level population. So any planner for future youth business would have to take in account this decline in total expected population—and, for a long-term investment such as a dormitory, would have to project the trends for future years (whether social and demographic factors would be

dynamic forecasting

203
PLANNING

Figure 6-7.
Trends in Total Fertility Rate

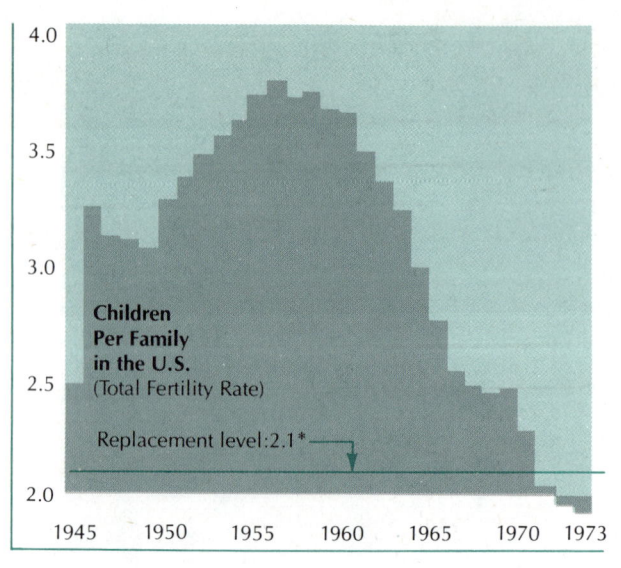

Children Per Family in the U.S. (Total Fertility Rate)

Replacement level: 2.1*

*Replacement level: The number of average births per woman over her lifetime necessary for the population eventually to reach zero population growth. This would take about 70 years.

Sources: National Center for Health Statistics, Census Bureau

expected to make the rate turn up again, level off, or continue down). The planner would have to analyze such social trends as whether future college students would prefer dormitories or other lifestyles and how many would attend college in the first place. Dynamic forecasting is a very uncertain art, but there are guidelines, and this procedure makes the best possible effort to put them all together in a meaningful projection.

Many of these techniques are executive mind-stretchers rather than complete forecasts in themselves. Nothing can take the place of a thorough understanding of the company and its environment when long-range planning is required. Regardless of the formal techniques available to assist in this task, peering into the company's future comes down largely to a judgmental assessment. The executive should use all possible aids, but cannot turn over complete forecasting responsibility to specialists.

Does North Star need to make long-range forecasts at this point? Why or why not?

The Planning Process

Peter Drucker, a well-known management writer and consultant, has described the proper planning attitude as follows:

- Build on the strength of your organization.
- Look for opportunities (not problems).
- Stress attainable results (not dangers).[7]

It is very useful for an organization to establish this kind of planning philosophy, to guard against becoming so enmeshed in the details of planning that the goals it hopes to achieve are lost in preoccupation with planning techniques. In this section we will explain how to *approach* planning and *organize* for planning, with Drucker's philosophy in mind.

Approaches to Planning

The *sequence of planning* in an organization should be systematic, so that no essential steps will be omitted. A logical sequence in developing institutional plans and phasing into activity plans is outlined below.

sequence of planning

1. *Set organizational objectives*—profit, survival, improvement in overall financial strength, attainment of a larger share in the company's field, and so on.

2. *Express institutional policies* as they apply to objectives. A tentative objective may be to capture a larger share of a certain market; if so, it is necessary to know whether the company's policy is to avoid certain types of competitive actions (such as price wars). Another objective may be to expand in certain fields; it will save much lost motion to be aware of corporate policy on acquiring other companies. Policies often are unwritten, and there may be considerable misunderstanding about them throughout the organization; such lack of policy guidance will result in misdirected planning and wasted time.

3. *Develop organizational strategies* that define the broad approach of the enterprise to attaining the goals. Such a strategy might be expressed by saying that the corporation plans to *integrate its product backwards* (make more of its basic parts and perhaps even extract and process its own raw materials, rather than continuing to buy these from other firms), in order to widen its profit margin and increase volume and perhaps also to protect its sources of supply in a period of projected material shortages. A corporation manufacturing mechanical equipment might plan to *expand*

Trying to imagine where you would go with a pincushion if you were a cat is a form of dynamic forecasting.

205
PLANNING

into electronic equipment for the same markets, in order to broaden its product line in these markets and perhaps reduce unit selling costs while it increases volume.

4. *Establish organizational assumptions* that insure that all members of the organizational family adopt the same premises as to the projected economic future, projected approaches to certain laws, regulations, or actions of competitors, and projected responses to certain future events (such as union organizing activities, attacks by consumer groups, or legislative hearings). Lacking such general agreements among various planning groups, the organization may find its components acting at cross-purposes.

5. *Develop programs* that are intended to implement selected strategies. If an adopted strategy is to integrate the product forward (taking a larger part in delivering the product to the final user, rather than manufacturing products which are sold through others), a specific program might be to acquire a corporation with a group of 25 stores in the northeast. Thus, the company would gain experience with retail marketing of the product as a first step, and rechart future program direction after a period of operating these stores and selling the company product through them.

6. *Construct budgets* that provide the funding to set adopted programs in motion and to mesh all activities in the corporation in furtherance of these programs.

7. *Develop schedules* that establish the timing and emphasis of the actions charted by the program plans and funded by the budget plans.

8. *Develop individual activity plans* to manufacture the items planned, to provide the services called for, or in other ways to support and execute the plans unfolded in the preceding steps of the sequence.

<aside>degree of centralization

Is this a problem with North Star?</aside>

The *degree of centralization* in the planning process is an important aspect of corporate planning policy. Centralized planning creates the danger of stifled initiative: middle managers will feel that they have no voice and their actions are unheeded, which is a step away from indifference. Centralized planning also entails the risk of missing essential information that is available only by tapping the many units within an organization. A centralized plan is likely to be inflexible, incapable of adjusting to unanticipated events throughout the organization. If planning is largely decentralized, on the other hand, localized departmental goals may be overemphasized at the expense of the overall organizational good. Individual departmental planners, with a narrow outlook, may not be competent at planning, and often their information will be too specialized. A decentralized plan is likely to be fragmented, failing to produce a unified thrust; indeed, the danger of divisions working at cross-purposes is very real under decentralized planning.

A successful planning process requires centralized direction, to insure a broad outlook and concentration on overall goals. But planners must also have access to decentralized information and recommendations in order to harness all corporate resources and make all members of the team feel that they are contributing and that the final plan deserves their support and loyalty.

<aside>currency of planning</aside>

The *currency of planning* is extremely critical. A plan represents the best decision at the time it was made, but an organization receives a steady flow of information, and no plan is worthwhile once the information on which it was based changes. Therefore, provisions must be incorporated in the plan to keep it *flexible;* this goal can be met by stating the information on which the plan is based, providing for specific times to review the information, and indicating in general how the plan will change if initial estimates are proven to be in error.

If a plan commits the organization to an investment for capital projects, based on certain information, and the information changes after the investment has been committed, the new information may come too late to recapture funds spent for the wrong purpose. In order to minimize this possibility, capital investment plans should provide for committing funds at the latest possible date, and for all possible "escape hatches" that will allow for withdrawing or changing direction as economically as possible if decisions change. For example, the building schedule for a manufacturing plant should provide for generalized construction first (so the building can be readily converted to other uses), and specialized construction at the latest date possible.

The *cost of planning* deserves mention here. Some companies and public organizations do too much planning. They spend more on detailed analysis of their future course of action than such planning is worth. In two circumstances, no planning should be done: (1) when the course of action is obvious and no planning is needed, and (2) when available information is so uncertain that no planning can be done successfully. Between these two poles some planning usually is justified and necessary, but planning expenditures must reflect the fact that planning, like any other organizational activity, must be worth more than it costs. Some organizations have complex and elaborate planning operations, whose original purpose of helping the organization deal with the future has evidently given way to the aim of keeping the planning staff in business.

cost of planning

Organizing for Planning

It is hard to know how to organize for successful institutional planning. When North Star decided that some planning was necessary, the first thought was that everyone would do a little bit of it. Henry divided up the planning duties, and asked each division to take part of the load. This approach has advantages, in that everyone is being brought into the act and opinions are being solicited from those likely to have current and complete information. But it also has disadvantages, in that the separate planning evolutions may be disconnected and pulling in several directions at once.

Some organizations, heeding the admonition that planning is a top management responsibility, make the chief executive the key planning officer. This seldom works, because the chief has pressing responsibilities which at any given time will appear to be more important than a long-term planning exercise. Moreover, the top executive lacks many details about the organization. If the chief plans a certain way, it will be very hard for subordinate executives, even with knowledge of the plan's deficiencies, to criticize it very strongly. Even with planning skills and the longest view on objectives and policy of anyone in the company, the executive is by no means a professional planner, but rather an aggressive doer who probably lacks the patience to make careful forecasts, collect volumes of economic information, and plot detailed trends of various sorts.

At the other end of the scale, it is tempting to put the planning responsibilities where the operating responsibilities are: with each activity head or divisional chief planning for his or her outfit. But this approach is likely to be a grave mistake. Suppose a multidivisional corporation has a manufacturing division and a retail division, and financial analysis discloses that most of the profits are being made on retail sales, with manufacturing operations generally running at a loss or close to it. If the manufacturing division head is developing plans for that division, it is highly unlikely that this person can take an objective look at the profit situation and dispassionately recommend abolition of the division. The head is far more likely to recommend a program of cost reduction involving the installation of new equipment, which could mean throwing good money after bad. Moreover, when divisional heads plan, it is very difficult for their planning to be meshed, because in a sense they are competing for corporate capital investment funds — a frame of mind that does not encourage mutually supportive action.

This situation poses a dilemma. Planning cannot be carried out by the top executive; neither can it be done by various subordinates acting separately. The solution is for planning to be *coordinated centrally*, but *carried out jointly*. Usually, some individual in the organization is made responsible for seeing that planning takes place, and for the tedious data collection needed to support it. That person develops the organizational assumptions or premises that will be agreed to by all during the planning, calls and runs the planning meetings, and establishes the annual "planning cycle" that provides the schedule within the year for each element of the planning and budget preparation process.[8] Each subordinate of the chief executive is given responsibility for developing information and recommendations on matters appropriate for each to handle. Note that this individual (possibly a vice-president for planning or someone at a similar level) does not personally build the plan, but rather establishes the system within which a wide cross-section of the organization builds it. Without specific divisional or departmental interests, the planning coordinator can appear objective to all participants. Freed from day-to-day operating responsibilities, this person can find the time to explore offbeat ideas and unusual areas and bring them to the attention of the planning group in a carefully researched format. As a direct subordinate of the chief executive, the coordinator can explore suggestions and innovations with the top level.

How is North Star organizing its planning effort?

Self-Planning

This is a chapter about planning in organizations, but it would be inappropriate to close without saying something about individual planning, for organizations are composed of individuals. If individual planning runs counter to organizational planning, the organization cannot succeed. Yet individuals and organizations do not necessarily have the same goals; often their goals are opposed, as when the organization wants to reduce production costs and the individual wants to maximize personal salary. Organizations succeed because most of the goals of organizations are not seriously incompatible with the individual goals of their members; in highly successful organizations there is very close correspondence between these two sets of goals.

Earlier, we mentioned the importance of personal estate planning. It is equally necessary for managers to plan their professional lives. Unfortunately, too few managers do planning of either sort—personal or professional.

Consider a young man or woman who has a technical education: accounting, engineering, computer programming, or public health. It is not hard to forecast that when this individual has been in the job a few years, and is performing well, the job specifications are going to shift in the direction of less technical and more managerial responsibilities. The principal of "up and out" is at work: success in doing the first type of job will lead to promotion into an entirely different type of job. The danger is that the incumbent will not recognize this change, and will think that the initial training provides sufficient qualifications for the new responsibilities. Even if the new responsibilities appear as technical as before—perhaps as project leader—the need to supervise the work of others and inspire them to high performance is a new responsibility *on top of* the need to keep up technically. There may be a need to retrain for supervision *and* to retrain for technical upgrading. Since it can confidently be predicted that success will bring such changes, what is the individual doing to plan for them?

In the great majority of cases—nothing.

Why not be as systematic in self-planning as in organizational planning? In the first place, assess the objectives and policies of the organization as realistically as you can. Do they fit your conceptions, and can you live with them comfortably? If not, recognize the mismatch, and get out now. Change to a career closer to your own aspirations. If they do match, go on to the next step. Look about you at individuals in various levels in the organization, and construct a series of possible paths for yourself that would put you on one or another of these career ladders at certain times during your organizational lifetime. These are possible career patterns that are realistic for you and realistic for this organization.

Now for another checkpoint. Are you having to wait too long for advancement, or do the paths take you into fields you actively dislike? If so, get out, and change to an organization with career paths that suit you better.

Are you still here? If so, it is time to analyze what this set of different jobs means in terms of your self-preparation. In today's world a successful individual may have to retrain for three or four jobs in a lifetime, so accept the fact and plan for it. Perhaps you like one of the career paths more than another; if so, prepare actively for that path, and you will stand a better chance of moving along it than those who trust to luck.

Some organizations make this sort of self-planning very easy. The military is a good example, with regularized steps of advancement. But all organizations have a good deal of structure to their advancement steps, though they may not publicize these structures. Good self-planning involves a thorough understanding of the structure for your organization, and sufficient follow-up so that you plan for yourself the necessary training (within the company as well as formal training) you will need in order to be ready when they are.

Don't trust to luck. Leave that to the others.

Summary

Some planning is associated with almost all activity, but much of it is either unconscious (such as selecting which streets you will take when you drive downtown) or obviously required (such as drawing plans for a house). However, many people and organizations fail to plan when they should.

Planning starts with setting objectives, since it is difficult to plan without knowing where you want to go. It is planning that decides how to allocate scarce funds among alternative projects.

At the job-planning level, detailed plans specify the what, how, who, when, and where of getting the job done. In job planning for manufacturing processes, these five elements are embodied in routing, scheduling, and dispatching. In job planning, little uncertainty or chance exist, but in any longer-range planning these elements become increasingly important.

Planning sets action in motion, and control monitors the results to see that the plan is being achieved. An important link between planning and control is scheduling; any change from the plan signals management to take corrective action. Plans must be reassessed constantly as time passes and new information becomes available, and "junctions" must be incorpo-

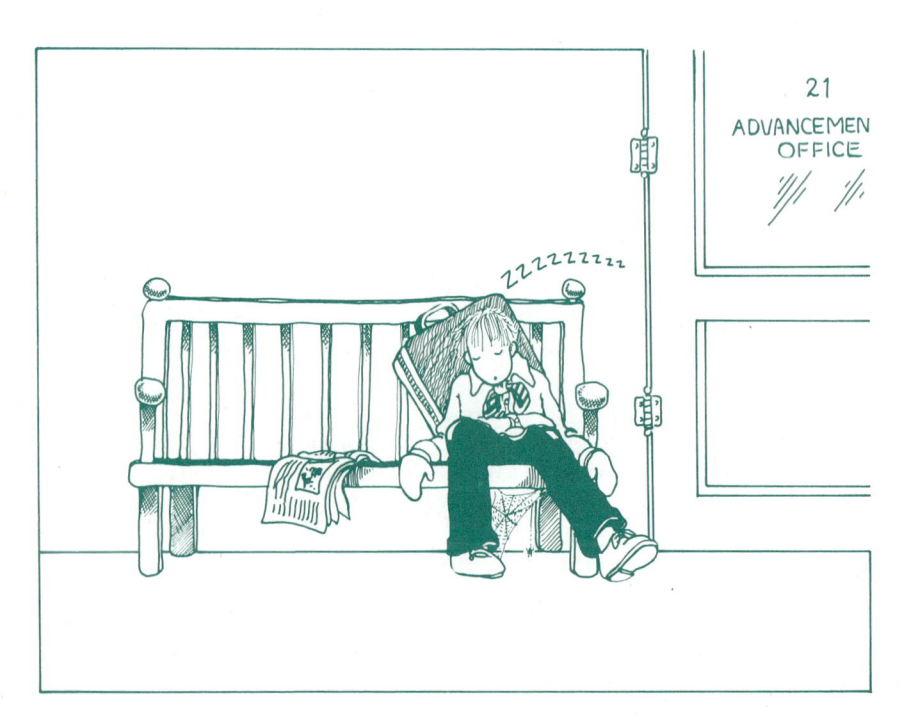

Are you having to wait too long for advancement?

rated in the plans to permit economical changes in direction based on changed information.

Without institutional planning, the separate parts of an organization are likely to move in different directions, with resulting confusion and inefficiency. Overall assumptions must be established by the organization for use by all planning groups, to ensure coordination and direction.

Planning takes place at several levels in an organization, and differs in scope as the level changes. At the higher levels, planning is institutional, while at the lower levels it is concerned with individual activity or particular jobs. Institutional planning may be short-range, mid-range, or long-range; activity planning is usually short-range. There is a logical sequence of events for activity planning: market, design, material, manpower, facility, budget, and production planning. There is also a logical sequence of events for institutional planning: set objectives, express policies, develop strategies, establish assumptions, develop programs, construct budgets, develop schedules, develop activity plans.

Institutional plans can be divided into capital budgets, operating budgets, and schedules. Forecasting is an essential element of institutional planning; there are uncertainties on the supply side, on the demand side, and concerning the environment of the enterprise. Forecasting starts with predictions about the economy, then the industry, and finally the company. Some techniques of forecasting are correlation analysis, brainstorming, evolutionary analysis, and dynamic forecasting.

Successful organization for planning requires centralized coordination with participatory inputs. Ideally, an individual or group is responsible for managing and expediting the planning operation, and bringing in all units of the organization to contribute their appropriate parts.

Individuals in an organization should also be involved in self-planning, to prepare themselves for the expected changes in their responsibilities during their professional lifetimes.

Notes

1. By multiplying the return if successful by the probability of success, just as you would in assessing a dice game: if you get $12 each time a "2" comes up, and its probability of coming up on any throw is 1/6, in the long run you expect to average $2 a toss ($12 x 1/6).

2. Schedule reductions caused by fuel shortages forced United Airlines to lay off 300 pilots—which meant retraining 1200 others to take over the available jobs, at a cost of $1,500,000 and a time lag of six months.

3. Story in *Business Week*, March 30, 1974, p. 55.

4. A recognition of the fact that in a developing industry some growth comes simply with the passing of time—as customers get more accustomed to the service, as technology improves safety and performance, and as industries develop in areas that come to depend on the service more and more.

5. Larry Langemeier and Russell Thompson, "Demand and Supply and Price Relationships for the Beef Sector: Post-World War II Period," *Journal of Farm Economics*, February 1967, p. 169.

6. See Donella H. Meadows et al., *The Limits to Growth* (New York: Universe Books, 1972).

7. Peter Drucker, *Managing for Results* (New York: Harper & Row, Pubs., 1964).

8. Budget preparation, however, would usually be coordinated by the controller.

Review Questions

1. Why is it essential to establish objectives before starting to plan? Why is this often a difficult and controversial task?
2. Why does failure to plan expose an enterprise to greater hazards of failure?
3. What are some benefits of planning for an organization of medium size? For a very small organization?
4. What separate planning activities are involved in the planning process for a manufacturing activity?
5. What elements should be considered in choosing between two competing capital expenditures? In what sense can operating expenditures be considered substitutes for capital expenditures?
6. Distinguish between program budgeting and performance budgeting.
7. Why might a good manager be a poor strategic planner?
8. How do outside activities help you with company forecasting?
9. Describe the concept of dynamic forecasting. Can you think of an example?
10. Where in the sequence of institutional planning does forecasting logically occur?
11. What is a good organizational system for institutional planning?

Discussion Questions

1. How would you test a forecast to see if it is truly an assessment of the future, or simply a statement of what is happening already?
2. We say organizations need to plan, yet it is often stated that the federal government does little broad planning. What do you think might be the reasons for this?
3. Suppose the organization of Figure 6-2 made only one product—rail cars. Would planning the production line for next year's car production involve both activity and institutional planning in this case? Explain.
4. It is said that the range of planning should be at least as long as your major capital investment items will last. If you don't make such investments (perhaps you rent all your equipment), is it therefore unnecessary for you to do anything more than short-range planning?
5. What factors might help you to make useful long-range forecasts if you were in charge of the expansion program for a large urban hospital?
6. If you were a consultant preparing a long-range comprehensive mass transit plan for a metropolitan community, how would you seek to avoid the hazards of centralized planning? What are the hazards?

North Star Case Study

Imagine that it is several years in the future and North Star has grown and prospered. It has an overseas engineering design subsidiary that operates in several countries and a labor force that goes as high as several thousand during peak periods.

The home office sees an opportunity in designing and building nuclear power plants overseas, although North Star has never done actual construction in the past. This new venture will require a large investment for construction equipment and for extensive training of personnel in the technology and exacting standards of nuclear plant construction.

The partners decide to develop a plan for taking this step and evaluate the plan critically before making the decision.

1. Refer to the questions suggested by Zeb, on pages 179-180 of the North Star prologue. Which of these are applicable to the problem just discussed? Explain.
2. What forecasts will the planning team need? (In what areas, of what kinds of trends?)
3. If the planners were to lay out two columns on a sheet of paper, one headed "Costs of Proceeding" and the other headed "Costs of Not Proceeding," what are some items that might appear under each heading?
4. How might a procedure such as that shown in Figure 6-3 be helpful?
5. What escape hatches might be put into the plan? Where?
6. How would you apply the sequence of planning set forth on pages 205-206 to this problem?

Suggestions for Further Reading

Ackoff, R. L. *A Concept of Corporate Planning.* New York: John Wiley & Sons, Inc., 1970.

Bacon, J. *Planning and Forecasting in the Smaller Company.* New York: National Industrial Conference Board, Inc., 1974.

Brown, J. K. *Planning and the Corporate Planning Director.* New York: National Industrial Conference Board, Inc., 1974.

Chambers, J. C. *An Executive's Guide to Forecasting.* New York: John Wiley & Sons, Inc., 1974.

Elliott-Jones, M. *Economic Forecasting and Corporate Planning.* New York: National Industrial Conference Board, Inc., 1973.

Ewing, D. W., ed. *Long-Range Planning for Management.* New York: Harper & Row, Pubs., 1972.

Jenkins, J. R., and J. F. Jay. *Planning the Advertising Campaign: A Player's Manual.* New York: Macmillan Pub. Co., Inc., 1971.

Judge, G. C., and T. Takayama. *Studies in Economic Planning Over Space and Time.* New York: American Elsevier Pub. Co., Inc., 1973.

Lightwood, M. B. *Public and Business Planning in the United States: A Bibliography.* Detroit: Gale Research Co., 1972.

Lyden, F. J. *Planning, Programming, Budgeting: A Systems Approach to Management.* Chicago: Markham Pub. Co., 1972.

Miller, E. C. *Advanced Techniques for Strategic Planning.* New York: American Management Association, Inc., 1971.

Mockler, R. J. *Business Planning and Policy Formulation.* New York: Appleton-Century-Crofts, 1971.

Schwendiman, J. S. *Strategic and Long-Range Planning for the Multinational Corporation.* New York: Praeger Pubs., Inc., 1973.

Walley, B. H. *How to Apply Strategy in Profile Planning.* London: Business Books, 1971.

Decision Making

North Star Prologue

The four North Star partners started with a fortunate overseas contract that brought with it the need to organize their efforts more formally. Business success and the consequent need to expand both in space and people disclosed problems with leadership and communications. Additionally, it highlighted the need for adequate planning, the lack of which threatened to tempt the fledgling company to overlook its financial limitations. As a result of systematic planning, the company's marketing efforts were directed into more fruitful areas – one of which presented a knotty decision problem.

When the Natal job was in its last year and the transportation study was well under way, Dick wired Henry and Bert to come to the site for an important discussion. Bert had been out twice, but this was Henry's first trip, and he eagerly accepted the invitation. On their arrival, Dick and Jo presented them with a fascinating dilemma. Two related events had taken place. The first was a request by Natal Engineers, Limited, for North Star to enter into a new contract on an entirely different project. The World Bank had approved a large loan to finance a nuclear power plant—the first in the country—and Natal Engineers was going to build it in a joint venture with a U.S. electrical firm that was providing the nuclear equipment. If they accepted the Natal offer, their role would be to provide the project management expertise, and to monitor the performance of Barnhard and Walker, the U.S. firm already involved in the joint venture. Barnhard and Walker's nuclear design and fabrication facilities were located in the same city as North Star's home office—one reason Natal Engineers thought it would be logical for them to perform the monitoring task.

The other event was a real thriller. The senior vice-president of Barnhard & Walker had heard of the Natal plans, and a few days later had come to Dick with a proposal that Barnhard & Walker acquire North Star and make it a wholly owned subsidiary. The four partners thus would sell their company to Barnhard & Walker in return for B&W stock, and thereafter would be employees of the large corporation. While they would stay on as officers of North Star Associates, there would be no guarantee that they would hold these jobs permanently. The agreement would, however, guarantee them each three years' employment in their North Star jobs "or in other equivalent positions with Barnhard & Walker Corporation." They would be used in substantially the same capacity as envisioned by Natal Engineers, but of course the monitoring role would have very little meaning, since Barnhard & Walker would in effect be monitoring itself.

The acquisition offer seemed too good to

believe. Bert and Henry recalled so vividly the creation of North Star barely five years before, when it amounted to little more than a prayer, that it was hard to believe someone would pay real money for the entity—particularly the substantial sum that had been offered. Bert asked how fast they could close the deal, and Henry felt in full agreement, but Dick said they ought to analyze it a bit. He and Jo had had a little time to think it over, and they should consider Jo's reaction. Jo took the floor. She said they were faced with a classic decision problem: a bit too big for intuition or unaided judgment, but quite amenable to systematic problem-solving techniques. First, what were their goals—as individuals and ultimately as members of the North Star team? They had to decide what each of them wanted in his or her professional life, and set it down as explicitly as possible. Second, what measures could they come up with to show the extent to which various probable outcomes contributed to those goals? Money was a pretty universal measure, of course, but by no means the only one; if it were, they should probably be robbing banks for a living. Next, what would the probable outcomes be under the two alternative options that appeared to be offered here? This question asked them to sketch out the probable futures, for North Star and for them as individuals, that would flow from the two decisions now presented. What variables were important under each of the two options—the elements that could fall one way or another, requiring some judgments as to probabilities? And finally, what were the "expected values" of the two courses of action?

Since the last was probably the easiest to analyze (at least the financial expected values—there were also nonfinancial values to be computed), they ought to take it first. The B&W offer amounted to $125,000 apiece for the four partners—a total of $500,000 for the company. This figure was exactly equivalent, using a 6% interest rate for the value of money, to a payment of $10,000 a year for 21 years. Since North Star's value had to be viewed in terms of what it would earn in managerial profits (not salary, but profits to the owners) over an extended period of years, the B&W offer should be converted to that form of expression in order to compare the two "profit streams." So from a financial point of view, the B&W offer was equivalent to having the company earn $10,000 a year for each of the partners until the twenty-first year, and at that time going suddenly out of existence with no salvage value. If at that twenty-first year the company was worth $1 million (and the partners could sell it for that amount then), they would be giving up the present value of this expectation of $1 million 21 years hence—and this present value at 6% would come to $312,000, or just $188,000 less than the B&W offer. And $188,000 today was equivalent to an annual profit income for each partner of about $3750 a year for 21 years. Looking at it in still another way, $500,000 now would be equivalent to $1,600,000 twenty-one years from now. And if North Star kept growing as it had been and would be expected to grow, it should be worth a good deal more than $1,600,000 in 20 years or so.

So much for the financial expected value of the Barnhard & Walker offer. They could probably compute a financial expected value of continuing on their present path, by working out the present trend of profitability and extending it 20 years or so into the future. Jo wasn't completely informed on the financial status, but she had a pretty good idea, and from a rough calculation the present trend would make the company worth close to $10 million by that time. If that figure was anything like correct, then Barnhard & Walker would be getting a steal if they bought the company now for half a million.

But even these figures, as conclusive as they now appeared to be, did not tell the whole story. The partners really had to get into the tough question of making their life goals explicit, and then analyzing how well these would be achieved under each of the two alternatives. For herself, said Jo, she prized independence to work in the professional area in which she had been trained, and sufficient control over the environment of her job so that she would never have to distort an outcome to meet corporate aims. She didn't know, but she suspected that both Bert and Henry valued the entrepreneurial freedom they had to run their own shows, and the excitement of making an organization grow. If they did, then Barnhard & Walker was not for them.

Bert was still thinking about the financial expected value, and he broke in to ask Jo if the B&W senior vice-president was estimating that North Star would be worth $10 million after 20 years. No, said Jo, because the vice-president was using a different criterion. He didn't give a hoot what North Star would be worth in 20 years by itself, but only what it would be worth to B&W if they bought it. There is plenty of room in a $300 million nuclear power plant contract to take a chance on a $500,000 company, particularly one experienced in working with the joint venture partner and doubtless able to lubricate relationships on many occasions. Finally, of course, the purchase of North Star would remove the annoyance of an independent monitor.

Jo Parnela went on with her analysis, but Henry had heard enough. It was remarkable, he mused, that he had been completely convinced of the overwhelming advantages of the sale, and an hour listening to a professor discuss decision theory had completely changed his mind. The four of them didn't need to take a vote; it was apparent to all of them that even a doubled offer from the big corporation would not have changed their minds.

That night, as he lay under his mosquito bar and listened to the drone of the fan, Henry thought how essentially simple Jo's analysis had been, and yet neither he nor Bert had thought to approach the problem that way. He realized again, as he did so often in North Star, how little he really knew about the whole mysterious concept known as management.

What North Star Can Learn from Chapter 7

1. The advantage of setting up a problem in quantitative terms, so that costs and benefits become apparent

2. The importance of developing all significant alternatives before making a decision, so no course of action will be left unconsidered

3. The concept of a sequential lottery in assessing the outcomes of decisions

4. The role of the group in decision making

5. The need for a systematic decision pattern for carrying out the decision process

6. The benefit of guidelines in assisting with decision making, to be sure no step has been overlooked

7. The use of a payoff table and probability in assessing outcomes

8. The value of establishing an overall framework against which to evaluate where the organization is going, what you want from it, and how the goals can best be met

This chapter reviews the process that some managers claim is the whole function of management: deciding what action to take, resolving conflicts, solving problems—all covered by the inclusive label of decision making. You will explore that function in three parts:

1. *What is decision making?* What creates the need for a decision, and how does the decision impinge on other functions of the organization, such as planning and organizing?
2. *Who makes decisions?* When does the individual decide, when does a group decide, and how are group views incorporated into management choices?
3. *How are decisions made?* What theories guide decision making, how are they converted into practice, and what elements enter into the decision process? This section concludes with suggestions for making good decisions and also describes certain aids which the alert manager can utilize in this process.

Decision making is generic to organizations of any sort and any size. A one-person organization must make decisions as surely, and perhaps as frequently, as the chief executive of a mighty corporation. Governmental organizations require decisions as surely as do commercial enterprises. While a manager needs other traits, of course (such as the ability to get along well with others, organizational expertise, and personal integrity), no one can be a successful manager without learning how to make decisions—rather than avoiding or postponing them—and how to make them effectively.

What Is Decision Making?

Most people hold one of two different views of the manager in the process of reaching organizational decisions. In one view, the confident executive determines all the alternatives, weighs the costs and benefits of each against the organization's goals, assesses the probabilities of various events, considers their impacts on the various alternative actions, and systematically ranks the various outcomes in order of preference. In another view, the bewildered executive cannot identify all the alternatives (as a result of ignorance or a lack of research resources), recognizes only a few of the costs and benefits of whatever alternatives are obvious, and has a highly imperfect understanding of the probable events and their relation to the choice in question. Since this manager has no accurate basis for choosing among the alternatives, the first one that seems satisfactory is likely to be accepted.

The first manager is "optimizing" and the second is "satisficing," which means settling for a *satisfactory* solution instead of hunting for the *best* solution. The management writers who first coined the term "satisfice"[1] justify it as rational executive behavior by likening it to the search for a needle in a haystack—the satisficer doesn't try to find the sharpest needle in the whole stack, but only one sharp enough to sew with. In some cases this approach may be rational, as when the additional search isn't worth the cost. More often, however, it simply reflects human frailty.

optimizing
satisficing

Have the North Star managers been optimizing or satisficing? Why do you think so?

The satisficing executive, when faced with the need to choose, defines the situation to fit previous experiences and ingrained prejudices and chooses solutions that have worked before. The search for alternatives never goes outside familiar territory, and the only acceptable alternative is a familiar one.

The organization may find itself encouraging satisficing behavior, unless it actively *discourages* that approach. Since most managers lean toward satisficing methods anyway, organizational standards must be established to counteract this tendency. As this chapter will demonstrate, the establishment of good decision-making practices is the best way to avoid managerial satisficing.

The Characteristics of Decision Making

It is hard to separate decision making from planning. You might argue that planning *is* making decisions, because it determines what will be done now, or next week, or next year, out of a set of many things that could be done. And you could just as well argue that deciding is planning, because the very act of choosing a course of action by reaching a decision creates a plan.

Many executives, however, separate the two functions. All executives consider themselves decision makers; but most, asked if they were planners, would probably respond by saying they were *doers*. Somehow, planning connotes contemplation and study, while decision making connotes action. What are the characteristics of this function that seems such an integral part of planning, yet is perceived almost instinctively as something quite different?

Levels of Deciding

levels of deciding

automatic decisions

The simplest form of decision making is one in which the information sought itself reveals the action that should be taken. If you are going for a ten-minute jog, the information that ten minutes are up leads automatically to the decision to stop. If you intend to hire candidates who pass an employment test, the information on which candidates passed automatically produces the decision on which candidates to hire.

expected-information decisions

Climbing one level higher in complexity, the result of a forecast (or "expected information") provides the decision on the action to take. In this case, you are not sure of the information—you or someone else must estimate it—but once the estimate is made, the decision is just as automatic as before. If you intend to introduce a new product, provided 30% of the prospective customers like it better than a competitive product, a survey of 100 people showing that 38% of those sampled prefer it (which would tell a statistician that 30% of the population would definitely prefer it) would mean an automatic decision to introduce the product.

factor-weighting decisions

At the next highest level in complexity, information is collected and analyzed before the decision can be made. Here, the process differs in that the factors involved must be *weighed*. If you are considering which of two pairs of shoes to buy, you consider the cost, quality, and appearance of each, and must know how important each of these factors is to you before you can make the selection. But there is no uncertainty as to the product characteristics.

At a fourth level of complexity—and the level at which most of the tough decisions must be made—uncertainty exists on both sides: as to the information and as to the weighting factors. If you are handling a discipline case, you may get stories from the employee, the supervisor, and bystanders, all differing in important respects, creating substantial uncertainty as to what really happened. In addition, you must consider the relative seriousness of the offense and the importance of supporting the supervisor, as compared with the importance of protecting the employee's dignity and rights. If you are hiring an employee, you are uncertain as to how much honesty, loyalty, intelligence, initiative, and skill that person will display; in addition, you must decide how important each of these traits is relative to the others. To complicate the matter still further, perhaps you are choosing among *three* prospective employees.

dual-uncertainty decisions

Degree of Structure

A structured decision is one that could be expressed on a flow chart—sometimes called an "if-then" decision sequence. Figure 7-1 illustrates such a decision sequence as it would be made by an airport limousine dispatcher. In the top line, the dispatcher asks whether a *limousine is available* at the airport to serve arriving passengers who wish to leave for some run—say, center city. If the answer is YES, no action is needed; if the answer is NO, the dispatcher continues. The next question asks whether any *passengers are waiting*. If NO, nothing is done, if YES, the dispatcher must ask if another limousine to serve them is *due within 30 minutes*, and so on. Inspection of the chart shows that three actions may be taken in the event of certain situations, indicated by the circles: HIRE CAB, if the number of waiting passengers is not too large; SEND STANDBY LIMO, if one is available in the airport standby garage; DIVERT A LIMO from another run, if it can get there fast enough. Otherwise, the dispatcher does nothing, even if passengers are waiting.

structured decisions

Structured decisions are particularly suitable for computer solution. As you can see, there is only a two-way choice at each decision point, and one decision is made and out of the way before the next arises. Computer flow charts (discussed in more detail later) are made in this way; when the problem can be narrowed down to this extent, all that remains is the rather mechanical task of programming the computer so that it will make the choices directed by the flow chart.

Unfortunately, most decisions made by managers do not display anything like this degree of structure. (Perhaps we should say fortunately, for many people dislike the notion that computers can take over managerial tasks.) The decision-making process described above appears to be the dispatcher's responsibility, but was actually structured in advance by the traffic manager who established the rules for taking the various actions. A typical management decision will involve far less structure than this, and chances are that the higher in the organization it occurs the less structure it will have. A relatively junior manager is influenced very heavily by what has been done in the past, and is unlikely to take actions that will appear novel or offbeat no matter how desirable they seem. Even more senior ranks often display a strong tendency to "follow the leader"; if the leading company in your line is bringing out a certain product, it seems safest to bring out such a product yourself.[2]

unstructured decisions

What are the uncertainties in the North Star merger decision? Which are most uncertain? least?

In general, however, top-level decisions are shot through with many kinds of uncertainties: you are trying to predict the future, and you do not know what customers will want (or even what sort of people future customers will be), what materials will be available or how much they will cost, what regulations will constrain your actions, what your financial position will be, or what your goals really are. You cannot be sure how long you will keep your job; the plan you set in motion may be carried out by another person who may not give it the sort of effort you would. (After all, if your successor fails it was *your* plan.) If you plan a government job (such as a municipal project), you cannot know whether the citizens will favor it or vote down the bond issue needed to put it into effect.

Search for Alternatives

No decision can be made unless the manager has alternatives to decide among. In its simplest form a decision can appear to be just the choice

Figure 7-1.
Sample Decision Sequence

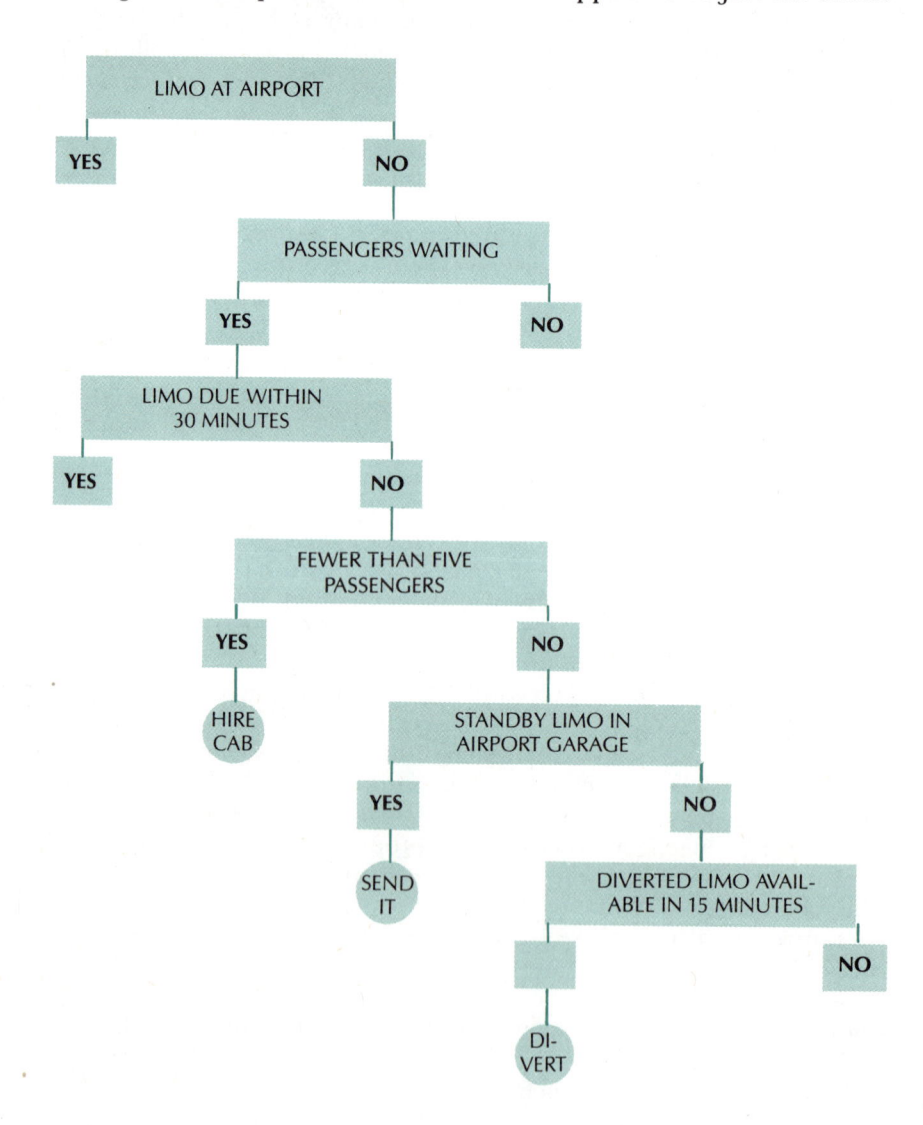

```
                    LIMO AT AIRPORT
                   /               \
                 YES                NO
                                    |
                            PASSENGERS WAITING
                           /                  \
                         YES                   NO
                          |
                  LIMO DUE WITHIN
                   30 MINUTES
                  /            \
                YES             NO
                                |
                        FEWER THAN FIVE
                          PASSENGERS
                         /            \
                       YES             NO
                        |               |
                      HIRE       STANDBY LIMO IN
                      CAB        AIRPORT GARAGE
                                /              \
                              YES               NO
                               |                 |
                             SEND        DIVERTED LIMO AVAIL-
                              IT         ABLE IN 15 MINUTES
                                              /        \
                                                        NO
                                          DI-
                                          VERT
```

220
MANAGEMENT PROCESSES

between saying yes or no: the decision maker grants permission for an act or withholds it, approves a course of action or vetoes it, proceeds or holds back. Even in this stripped-down situation, there is more to the choice than that. If employees ask for time off and are refused, they don't go back to the bench or desk and forget it; chances are they protest, or brood, or enter a grievance—they may even break something, consciously or unconsciously. If a course of action to develop a new product is disapproved, the old product must try to fill in the gap, and money may have to be spent on its improvement or redesign or accelerated marketing.

Almost as important as the ability to make good decisions is the ability to develop all the significant alternatives and trace through all of their implications. Seldom is the choice as simple as A or B, because if A is chosen a stream of consequences will lead to other choices down the road, and if B is chosen a different stream of consequences will lead to other choices. Consider a numerical example. You have $100, and are offered the following gamble, for a $10 fee: first a 50:50 coin toss, paying $66 if you win but costing $50 if you lose; and immediately after a second 50:50 coin toss, paying $82 if you win but costing $54 if you lose. You see at once that both are very favorable odds, but the second toss is much more favorable than the first—and if you play the first and lose you won't have enough money to play the second. You have two questions: Is this proposition worth the $10 admission fee? If it is, should you bet on the first toss or hold back to be sure you will have enough money to play the much higher-odds second toss?

alternative choice

This is a sequential lottery, and of course it is highly structured, but in concept it does illustrate the problem you face when you must choose between alternatives that have future consequences. Figure 7-2 shows a

sequential lottery

Unfortunately, most managerial decisions are relatively unstructured.

Could you set up the decision as a two-stage lottery? How?

method for analyzing the two courses of action: whether to bet on the first toss or to hold off and be sure of the second.

It is not enough, of course, simply to compare the obvious alternatives. An important part of managerial decision making is determining what alternatives are available. Thus, a company attempting to deal with an expected shortage of natural gas would want to investigate the feasibility of using fuel oil, coal, or electricity—not to mention ways of reducing the energy requirements of its present manufacturing processes. But only a creative decision maker would go beyond these straightforward possibilities to consider such options as shifting operations to a

Figure 7-2.
A Two-Stage Sequential Lottery

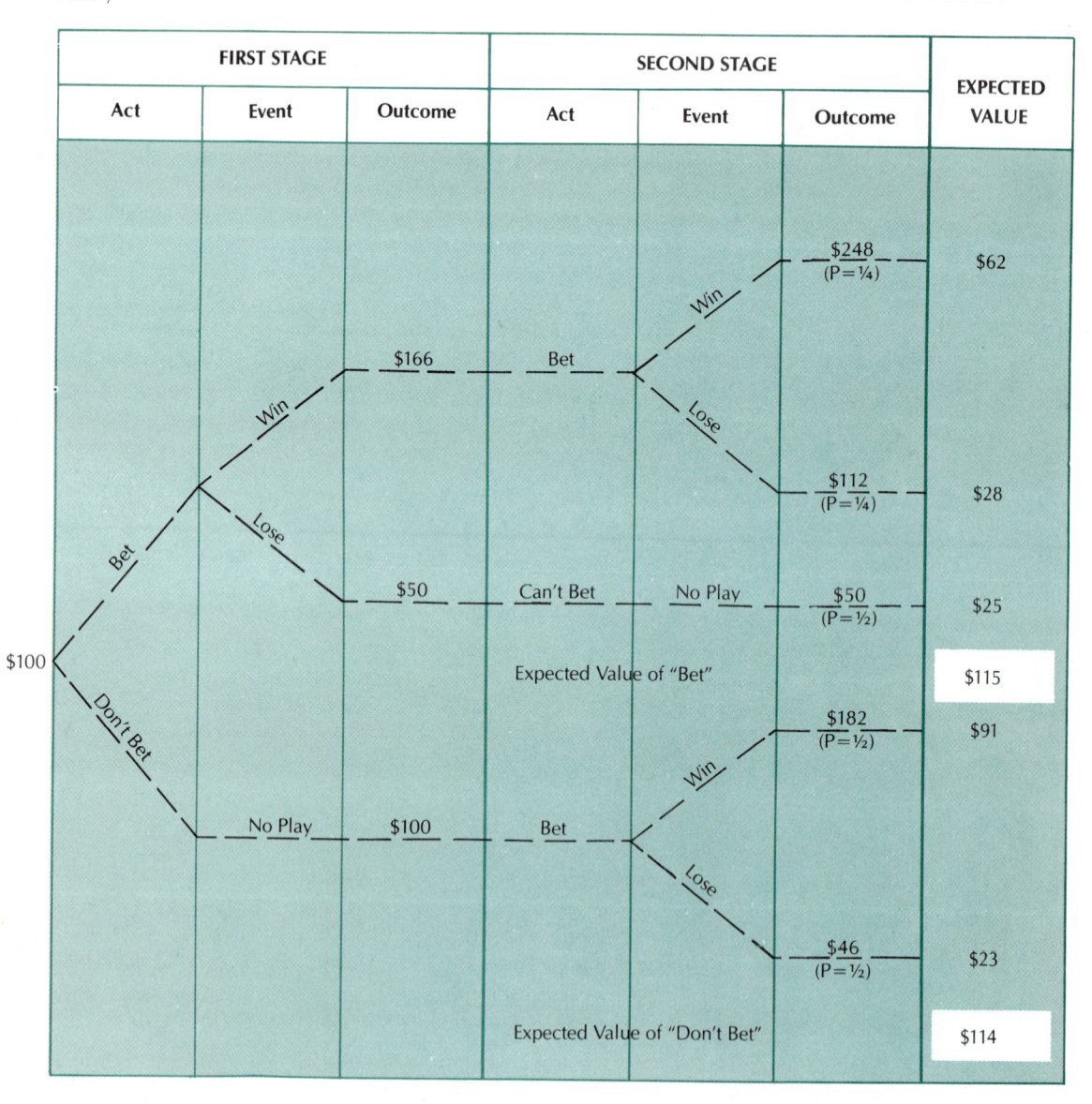

FIRST STAGE			SECOND STAGE			EXPECTED VALUE
Act	Event	Outcome	Act	Event	Outcome	

First Stage:
- Bet (starting $100)
  - Win → $166
    - Bet
      - Win → $248 (P=¼) → $62
      - Lose → $112 (P=¼) → $28
  - Lose → $50
    - Can't Bet → No Play → $50 (P=½) → $25
  - Expected Value of "Bet" → **$115**
- Don't Bet
  - No Play → $100
    - Bet
      - Win → $182 (P=½) → $91
      - Lose → $46 (P=½) → $23
  - Expected Value of "Don't Bet" → **$114**

222
MANAGEMENT PROCESSES

Mid-Eastern site, where fuel is both plentiful and cheap; merging with a company in a different business, where the necessary heat might be available as a presently discarded by-product; or even going out of the business entirely and starting another where energy was less of a problem. The most sophisticated analytical tools for choosing among alternatives are not much use if some of the best alternatives are not even presented.

Some companies advocate "brainstorming" during the preliminary phase of developing alternatives, conducting sessions where the wildest ideas are welcomed and given serious consideration. Most brainstorming ideas are fatally defective in some practical way, but the open attitude of such sessions encourages the occasional ingenious solution which the management of a more conservative company would miss entirely.

Most of us have experienced the pleasure of an unexpected windfall, perhaps by selling something or receiving a gift or tax refund. We consider all the possible ways of spending it, and revel in the unfamiliar power of having such an opportunity. But the moment we have spent it on one thing, all of the other buying opportunities disappear. It is the same in choosing among alternative business investments—the manager may choose the best of all the alternatives that come to mind, but there is the chance that a better alternative will appear as soon as the commitment is made and the company can no longer take advantage of it.

To guard against this hazard, managers often establish a "standard" investment choice, in terms of how much return it will bring on the money invested, and make a rule never to invest in any alternative unless it will return at least the standard amount. Thus a company may have a policy that it will not invest in a new product for manufacture unless the receipts from that product will pay off the initial investment in five years (or six, or whatever past experience shows to be realistic). This approach guards to some degree against the danger that a better new alternative is waiting around the corner.

standard choice

The manager must make every effort to consider all reasonable alternatives, not just those that are traditional or conventional. Perhaps too many will come to mind; in this case, the less promising ones must be eliminated because there just isn't time or money to analyze them all. Some simply won't surface at all. Some may lie outside the manager's area of discretion, and cannot be executed without extensive consultation and negotiation. Others may be impractical in view of the company's technical or managerial limitations. Some may violate company policy or ethics, or even a specific law or statute. For those that remain, the manager must determine the probable outcomes (including the secondary consequences and the unintended "spillovers"). The most important factors must be selected for analysis, because it would be impossible to analyze everything. And the various factors must be weighed for compatability with the goals of the organization. In a later section we will discuss the question of uncertainty, and how this factor will affect the manager's choice. Should a lower but more certain payoff be selected over a higher but chancier one?

The Basis of Decision Making

At the start of this chapter we described the two extremes of managerial decision making: the confident and highly systematic manager who looks at all the factors, weighs them accurately, and comes up with the *optimum* solution, and the bewildered manager with a very limited vision who skims the few alternatives nearest at hand and picks the first one that looks as though it will do. We commented on the fact that the organization has the power to influence the behavior of the latter executive; higher organizational standards will extract better decision performance.

In fact, organizational pressures affect managers at all levels, competent and incompetent. Decisions are not made in a vacuum or an ivory tower, but in the context of various groups with various interests and strengths; the interplay of these elements helps to shape the decision in the first place and serves to modify it as it is put into practice.

Organizational Factors in Decision Making

In chapter 3, when we discussed organizations as people-systems, we stated that the manager's world is not a neat organization but a confusing jumble of people, displaying all degrees of authority relationships. We pointed out that a manager takes instructions from many people other than an immediate superior, including at times people who are actually lower in the organizational hierarchy. Nowhere do these pressure points become so obvious as in the process of decision making. When a critical decision must be made, all sorts of special-interest groups start bringing pressure to bear on the manager. Some of this input is couched in terms of specialist advice—the production manager points out how hard it will be to make a new product and describes the changes that should be introduced for efficiency; the sales manager advises modifications to increase customer acceptance (and perhaps make the selling job easier); the safety engineer objects to a manufacturing technique as too hazardous; and so forth. But for most decisions there are many factors to consider, and none of the specialist viewpoints stands alone. The manager has to weigh all of these special pleadings and decide where the golden mean lies.

Unfortunately, no decision of any consequence pleases everyone. There will always be an injured party, and usually that party has weapons to strike back with when the injury seems objectionable. The manager cannot ignore these objections and hostilities, whether they are "justified" or not, because they come from members of the organization. Thus, decisions must balance the demands of the various competing groups that make up the manager's environment.

We think of the compromise approach in political terms; we expect municipal officials to "horse trade" in their decisions, trying to please as many pressure groups as possible, and sounding like "all things to all people." But we expect more detachment from managers. We shouldn't, however, because the manager faces many of the same pressures as the politician. Both evaluate alternative projects on their merits as far as possible, but both must decide how much support they can sacrifice in one area in order to gain support in another.

Suppose a production manager, under pressure of deadlines from a key customer, finds it necessary to start welding operations before an area has been completely tested for explosive gases (knowing that, although this procedure violates a written safety regulation, the danger is more apparent than real). The safety engineer will not approve, and may

decision pressure points

express this displeasure by more meticulous enforcement on other jobs or by reporting the production manager's action to the vice-president for manufacturing. Similarly, other units can pressure the production manager for violating their norms, even though the manager is not subordinate to these units and may be superior to some of them.

Almost all managers must violate rules to get results at times, and every time they do they become, in a sense, hostages of units who catch them at it. If union rules require that truck drivers have helpers to lift off loads, the driver may go along with the shop supervisor in ignoring this rule for small loads in the interest of cost-saving. As a result, however, the supervisor may be less able to discipline the driver for some minor offense because of the risk that the driver will stop cooperating in this practice and a helper will be required for every trip. A widely publicized example concerns air traffic controllers slowing down air travel by "enforcing the rules" on spacing between planes, to dramatize their feeling that they were serving as scapegoats for numerous airport problems. *Before* they decided they were being exploited, clearly, the controllers had been helping management shave the rules in the interest of improved aircraft volume.

violation of norms

An organization that never shaves corners or breaks rules is a bureaucratic organization, more interested in procedure than results, and in all probability is an inefficient organization. But the very presence of so many hands in the decision-making process probably sharpens managerial performance. Too many cooks do not spoil the broth in this case (though they may add substantially to their own frustrations); rather, they improve it by requiring it to pass muster in so many ways.

Programmed vs. Unprogrammed Decisions

Thus far we have considered three elements of decision making: the level involved (available information and weighting factors); the degree of structure involved; and the impact of the organization on the decision maker.

Another way to analyze decisions is by the extent to which they are programmable, or contain predictable elements. The cost factor is so crucial in such management decisions as selection of projects (perhaps in developing the corporate capital investment plan for the coming year) that cost analysis has been reduced to a rather systematic process. A new building can be priced out quite accurately by drawing on past cost records and extending them into the future; managers can delegate this job to cost technicians. If a manager must decide whether to change a distribution system for company products, mathematical formulas can be used to calculate the most economical combination of routes in a fraction of the time an experienced manager would need, and more accurately as well.

programmable decisions

This programming process draws on past records and relationships, and uses statistical or similar techniques to project them into the future. If machines provided by supplier X have required less maintenance in the past than those from suppliers Y and Z, it is reasonable in the absence of other factors to predict that this trend will continue. If maintenance of company trucks has been cheapest when they get annual overhauls (with other maintenance only when breakdowns occur), as compared with either semiannual overhauls or biennial overhauls, this is the way to go henceforth.

statistical inference

Programmable decisions are made by analyzing statistical relationships and drawing reasonable inferences based on the data. One of the most necessary assumptions to be made is that a pattern established in the past will not suddenly change in the future. A related assumption is that events have some underlying pattern, and if this can be discovered one can forecast events with good reliability. Physical science abounds with such underlying patterns, which are referred to as "theories" (e.g., Einstein's general theory of relativity) and even, if extremely reliable, as "laws." The law of gravity tells us that objects dropped in free fall (unencumbered by air resistance) will attain speeds by a given time precisely predictable by the following formula:

speed = acceleration of gravity x *time*

and will cover distances precisely predictable by the following formula:

distance = ½ acceleration of gravity x *(time)^2*.

Management scientists try to find similar underlying patterns, though the process is less rigorous and accurate than in physical science. Sometimes a pattern *seems* to be established, but is not reliable for prediction. Figure 7-3 shows a series of circles with an increasing number of points as you go from left to right, and with all points connected in each circle. The upper row of figures gives the number of *points,* increasing *arithmetically* from left to right; the lower row gives the number of *spaces* partitioned off by the lines connecting the points, apparently increasing *geometrically* from left to right.

Given this pattern, we predict 32 spaces in the six-point figure. But, in fact, there are only 30 spaces. The pattern we assumed does not exist, and the prediction we made from it is erroneous. This hazard is present when you try to detect underlying patterns to help with your decision-making forecasts. It is well, when trying to develop patterns and relationships, to think your model through and see if theory (or common sense) supports it.

Figure 7-3.
An Unreliable Pattern

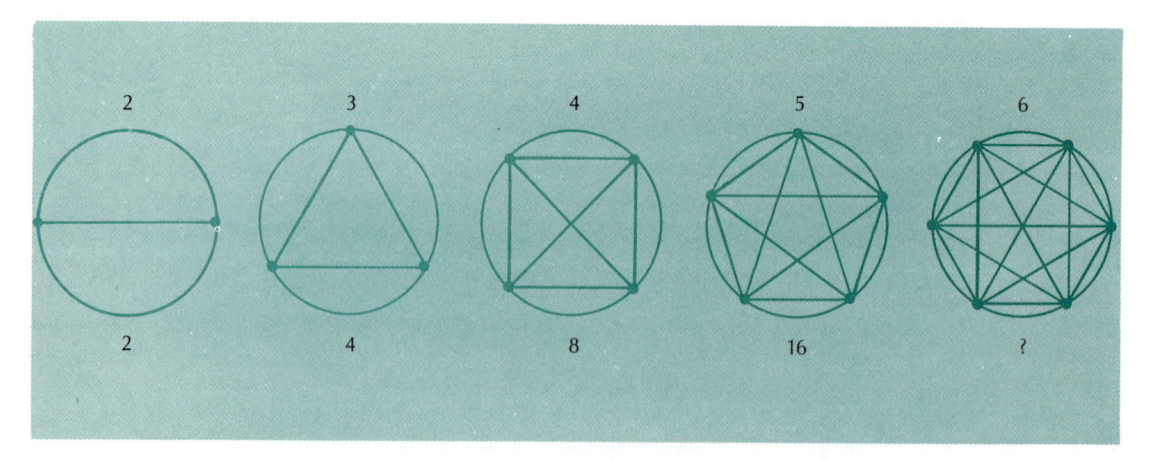

Suppose you are trying to determine the relationship between the amount you spend for advertising and the net profit from the product line you are advertising, to help you decide how large the advertising budget will be next year. You get figures on advertising expenditures and net profit for the past 12 years, and plot them on Figure 7-4. When you sketch a line through the points as best you can, it seems to indicate that profit goes up faster than advertising. That is, if you double your advertising budget, net profit nearly triples. Are you going to act on the basis of this pattern, and run the advertising budget right out the roof?

Stop a moment, and theorize about the way advertising and profit *should* relate. When a company does relatively little advertising, perhaps it is hardly enough to make any impression on customers at all. Somewhat more, and the message starts getting through at last: repetition begins paying off. Advertise at a still higher level, and this increasing rate begins to taper off. Keep going still higher, and eventually you are buying ads to convey your message to people who are your customers already, and who may be turned off with so much repetition, to the point where additional advertising expenditures don't buy you a thing. There is an empirical theory—the "law of diminishing returns"—that describes this pattern: at some point, additional input inevitably produces less and less output. According to this commonsense theory, advertising should be related to profit about as shown in Figure 7-5, and the data you collected was for a level of advertising shown in the little dotted box of Figure 7-5. Now Figure 7-4 makes sense, and you can build a theory that is confirmed by actual facts from your past operations.

Most decision problems contain both programmable and unprogrammable elements. When you drive a car, many of the movements you make are repeated so many times that you have been "programmed" to perform them almost automatically: steering to stay in lane, braking as you approach a light, signaling a turn, and so on. Your brain doesn't consciously report that the car is straying off to the right and then demand that you turn the wheel a bit to the left. Other elements in driving are unprogrammable: deciding where to go, whether to buy gasoline, whether to pass before or after the curve, and so on. Managerial decisions have this same mix, and the more a manager can be free of the need to

correlation

Figure 7-4.
Advertising/Profit Relationship

Figure 7-5.
Law of Diminishing Returns

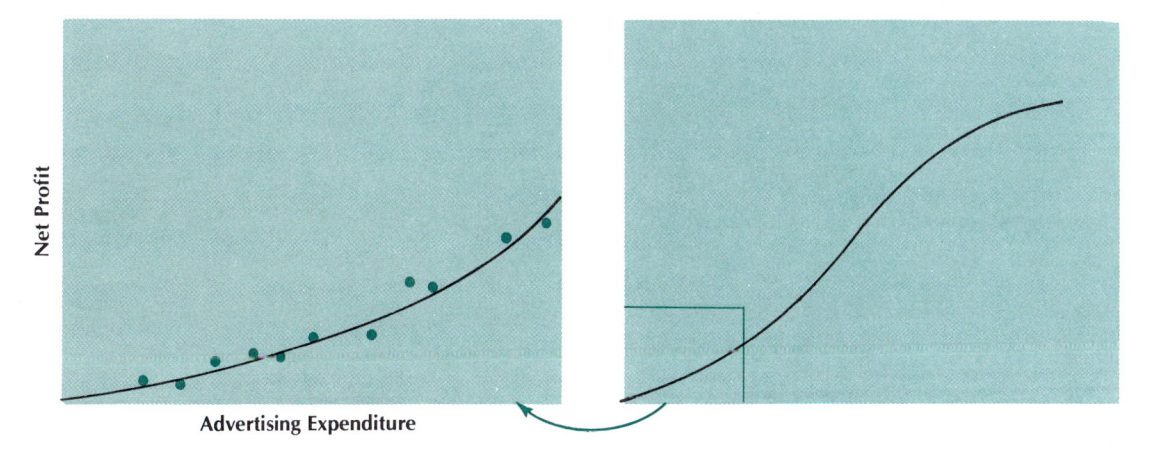

consider the programmable elements of a decision, the more time there will be for the unprogrammable fraction.

A great deal of nonsense has been written about computers taking over management functions, especially for middle managers. If the computer can take over a chore, great! But in that case, the chore hardly involved "management" in the first place. Look back at the flow chart of Figure 7-1. Computers can do that sort of deciding, and in fact quite a bit more, but managers have to set up the problem in rather simplified if-then form before the computers can handle it. The mark of a mature manager is a willingness to turn over the programmable aspects of a decision problem to technicians (human or computer), and to give personal attention to the untidy and unstructured remainder.

The Key Factors

Many factors affect a desired outcome—usually far too many to consider. Fortunately, most have only a marginal effect on the outcome, and for practical purposes can be ignored. Golfers spend a good deal of money on golf bags, but most of them would score just as high if they carried their clubs in a burlap sack. Other factors make a great difference to the outcome, and the decision maker must take them into account. If you were asked to predict the scores of ten golfers, ask yourself how you would rank the following factors as to their usefulness in your prediction:

1. number of clubs,
2. weight,
3. make of ball,
4. head down or not,
5. size of bag,
6. clothing,
7. height,
8. grip,
9. swing, and
10. age.

All of these probably have some effect on score (it would be hard to make a good score in a deep-sea diving rig, for instance), but after you consider 4, 8, and 9 the other factors don't have very much predictive power.

key variables

What are the key factors in the merger decision? Which of them do you consider most important?

When you collect information for a decision, concentrate on the key factors, and generally you can neglect the remainder. When you are taking action, perform the key steps and the others will tend to take care of themselves (or someone else will take care of them).

Who Makes Decisions?

There are several ways to approach the question of who makes management decisions. One way is to consider *specialist* decisions that often (though not always) affect only particular groups and *generalist* decisions that have broad application. Another way is to consider the differences in decisions because of the organizational level at which they are made. A third way is to consider the differences in decisions made by individuals and decisions made by groups, with many shadings in between. Let us consider the factors involved.

Who Should Make Decisions?

level of decisions

Certainly decisions should be made at the lowest possible level, because senior management cannot function unless it can delegate all the decisions that any subordinate manager can handle. This does not mean that any subordinate manager who feels competent to decide always *is* competent; perhaps unavailable information would dictate a different decision, or perhaps the manager's perspective is not broad enough to ensure decisions made with the whole organization in mind. Perhaps, in addition, the manager really isn't competent; many junior managers think they could do better than the boss, when in fact they have little notion of the complexities involved in making good decisions. (An inexperienced decision maker is likely to overlook the issue of setting a precedent: if you let office personnel use the office typewriter for personal chores when they are not busy, you will have little excuse to turn down everyone else who wants to use company equipment at idle times.)

Decisions should be made at the lowest level where an *informed* and *impartial* decision maker exists. That individual must be informed in order to make decisions on a rational basis and impartial so that the decisions will be fair. In a baseball game, the catcher is not the one to decide whether the pitch was a ball or strike, because the decision would not be made objectively; the umpire, by contrast, has no personal stake in the outcome but plenty of interest in a reputation for fairness.

Decisions made in one division can force action on other divisions, and therefore must be made only after broad consideration of consequences. The sales manager cannot unilaterally agree to speed up deliveries, no matter how much that improves sales, without consulting with the production manager and the traffic manager who will have to make the promises come true. The third-grade teacher cannot release the class early for recess if the students are likely to disrupt the fourth-grade physical education class taking place in the schoolyard. In general, if a particular decision will affect two or more divisions, the person in charge of all the divisions affected will be the best one to decide.

side consequences

If a decision is technical, the generalist usually is not equipped to make it. A question concerning contract provisions must be referred to the legal counsel, one of safety to the safety engineer, and one of occupational health to the industrial hygienist. Often generalist executives may appear decisive when they come up with an answer in such cases, but the appearance is misleading. In the case of occupational health questions, the executive should call the qualified expert to determine *if there is a hazard;* once that is determined, the executive then decides *what to do about it.* Otherwise, the procedure will be based on guesswork.

Individual vs. Group Decisions

The question of when decisions should be made by the *group* which is affected, and when they should be made by the *boss*, is a difficult one. One viewpoint—the participative one—holds that individuals carry out decisions much better when they have had a hand in making them; and the decisions may be better ones because more inputs have been provided. Another viewpoint—the efficiency one—holds that there simply isn't time to refer every decision to the group. Moreover, the group may be unwilling to consider painful alternatives (such as a layoff), and group decisions often involve so much compromise that all the good alternatives are voted down and the final decision pleases no one.

participation

efficiency

Seldom is it a question of one viewpoint or the other. Even when the boss reserves the right to make the final decision, subordinates should be consulted for suggestions and information. This approach will help them feel that their opinions and inputs can influence the organization. For routine decisions, regular meetings can be arranged with subordinates (the chief executive meets with immediate subordinates, they meet with their immediate subordinates, and so on), where two-way communication is encouraged. Thus, when decisions are made, the subordinates know that the boss was informed as to their views. For nonroutine decisions—perhaps a question as to whether to meet reduced sales by laying off the junior employees or shortening hours for all—special efforts must be made to explain things to the organization and solicit the viewpoint of its members.

Sometimes a manager must make a critical decision without consulting subordinates, usually because there was no time for consultation. Perhaps a contract has been signed calling for delivery of a product in an unusually short time, or the organization has agreed to transfer some responsibilities to another organization, or a new program has been initiated. Whatever the decision, it is essential for subordinates to be informed of it as soon as possible after the fact, and to understand why the action was necessary. They must know that the executive gave full consideration to their desires and rights and concluded that the decision was right under the circumstances. In effect, since there was no way to get their approval in advance, it must be sought after the fact. It is particularly important that the decision not reach subordinates through the company grapevine, or they will pick up inaccurate or incomplete information which may generate a negative response before the executive has a chance to explain the decision personally.

Group Decision Making

group decisions

When group decision making is undertaken, two separate elements are involved: making a decision that is *more acceptable,* and making a decision that is *better.* A more acceptable decision is one that the group favors, usually because it was involved during the decision-making process and has a feeling of participation. A better decision, in the sense of being more nearly the correct response to a problem, is one that has benefited from information available to different members of the group. A group decision may be simultaneously more acceptable than if it was made by the boss and better than if it had utilized only the information available to the boss; indeed, most group decisions, when properly made, reflect both elements.

In chapter 2, "Groups at Work," we explained how group members and leaders can influence group behavior to facilitate effective group performance. When groups are trying to develop information for a decision, they can behave in two rather different ways. One way is to seek *consensus,* a process by which individual members compromise so that the final result will be more acceptable to all (but perhaps not entirely acceptable to any one member). Another way is to seek *facts,* under the assumption that when the relevant facts are known the wisest decision will be obvious to reasonable people. The former is a horse-trading process, where the group is less interested in the facts than in what decision the individual members will *accept.* For a group to seek facts, the members

consensus

facts

must have a high degree of confidence that everyone in the group wants to seek for the truth regardless of who it helps or hurts. When a compatible group seeks to extract the best information from its members, they weigh the facts and refine their views in an atmosphere of mutual trust.

nominal group technique

The "nominal group technique" is a structured format for group decision making. Individuals in the group develop their own thoughts on the problem at hand, and each in turn then presents these ideas or solution to the group. The ideas are written around the wall, on blackboard or chart paper. This process is followed by a group discussion of the various presentations; each member then votes privately on the alternative to be selected. Final selection is by majority vote.

Delphi method

A somewhat similar technique (but not face-to-face) is the "Delphi method." Participants are asked individually for their input on a particular topic, then presented privately with the suggestions made by the other participants (whom they never see), and given the opportunity to adjust their responses based on their reactions to this additional input. A properly run Delphi session usually extracts relatively accurate data from a group, in part because individuals who have been guessing or using intuition are willing to modify their responses when faced with information from others who appear better informed.

Who Should Not Make Decisions

responsibility for outcome

Chapter 3, "Design and Development of Organizations," discusses the need to relate authority to responsibility so that no manager is given responsibility for a task who lacks the necessary authority to carry it out. It works the other way as well: no one should have authority over an area who is not also responsible for performance in that area. In other words, those who hold decision-making power should be responsible for the success or failure of their decisions. Politics clearly illustrates the rationale behind this assumption. Public officials have the unfortunate opportunity to take actions whose effects will not be felt while they are in office (e.g., negotiating for pensions and other retirement benefits that won't raise taxes for several years, to buy labor peace in the present).

Quite often in an organization a staff officer makes decisions that will affect line officers, although the decision making is not always apparent. A comptroller, in preparing the organization's budget, specifies the level of operations of each department but will not be held responsible for the performance of these departments. Thus, the company should permit line departments to air their reactions to the budget, and the ultimate decision must be made by a senior officer who *is* in charge of the line departments and responsible for their performance. The same warning applies to staff personnel who decide on space allocation, secretarial help, and other resources; they can propose, but it is a violation of good management principles if they make final decisions that significantly affect the performance of divisions or units not under their jurisdiction.

Scope and Importance of Decisions

Every decision involves the exercise of some judgment, even when it appears that all the facts are known and any fool could decide, because there are hidden factors that bear on the decision. But some decisions involve far less important matters than others, and clearly some decisions demand far less judgment than others. A common guidepost for allocating decision authority involves the total amount of money involved. A corporation may allow department heads to commit up to $10,000 of nonroutine expenditures, division heads up to $25,000, and the chief executive up to $60,000, reserving the decision for sums up to $150,000 to the board of directors (and referring to the stockholders if the sum involved exceeds that figure).

Such restrictions place a dollar limit on the degree of judgment called for. An expenditure decision of $10,000 involves more routine elements than an expenditure decision of $25,000, and a higher order of judgment is required to deal with the greater complexities of the latter.

spectrum of decisions

Figure 7-6 shows this spectrum of decision making graphically. The left side of the curve involves decisions of a sort the organization has often faced before, where the major question is whether the facts are understood. By contrast, the right side deals more and more with uncertain factors that fall outside past experience and must be interpreted by study of many unfamiliar areas. Not only does the penalty for being wrong increase as the sum invested goes up; the chance of being wrong increases as well. The organization wants to put such risks in the hands of the very best decision makers it has.

Figure 7-6.
Decision-Making Spectrum

Routine problems; much guidance from past experience ←

Complex problems; environment of high uncertainty →

Expenditure authorization limit (degree of judgment demanded)

$150,000
125,000
100,000
75,000
50,000
25,000
0

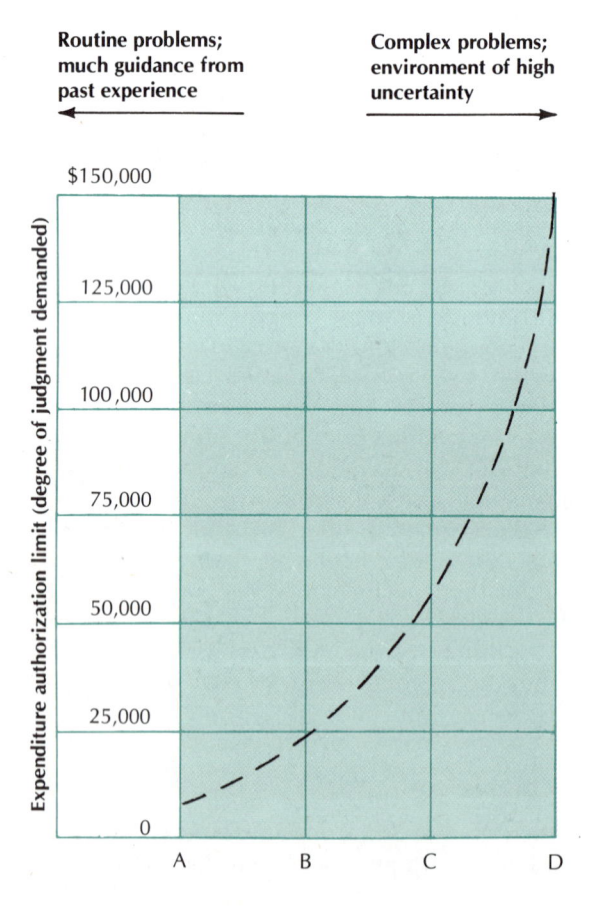

A — Department Head
B — Division Head
C — Chief Executive
D — Board of Directors

How Decisions Are Made

Every specialist tends to say that decisions are made through the application of his or her special bag of tricks. The behavioral scientist points out that *what* the manager decides may not be as important as *how* the decision is made—bringing all important personnel into the act, reacting to organizational pressures in a way that will cause the least pain, watching for shifts in support from subordinates, colleagues, and outsiders. The management scientist parades all the systematic techniques for making better decisions—decision theory, programming, simulation, the whole arsenal of systems analysis—and notes how frequently managers err by ignoring these useful tools. The pragmatic executive emphasizes the value of experience—learning by doing, and by making mistakes—and of being quick on one's feet so that a bad decision can be changed if it doesn't work out in practice. And the astrologer might throw in the importance of luck.

Managers differ almost as much as specialists. Some managers use a great deal of structure in their decision processes, while others seem to carry out the whole process informally, with little preliminary consideration of their actions. The disconcerting thing is that good decision makers are found in all categories. However, few managers could not improve their decisions by giving some thought to elements they normally overlook.

The Decision Process

Even if an executive seems to prefer an unstructured decision-making approach, chances are that at least some rational process is involved. Let us examine some different techniques, and try to develop an effective decision pattern.

Approaches to Decision Making

1. *Facts.* The systematic manager seeks to assemble all the facts about a problem, after which, presumably, the decision will make itself. This inference sounds reasonable, and certainly facts are necessary for a good decision, but it isn't really that simple. For one thing, the available facts are seldom as clear or complete as one would wish. Sometimes two "facts" may signal directly opposite decisions, and the manager cannot tell which to heed. Even without this sort of confusion, there usually are not enough facts at hand, and it is expensive and time-consuming to get more, so the manager who deals only with "facts" often does not have enough to solve the problem. Moreover, the manager must acknowledge that many decisions fall in areas where facts are at best a general guide, such as predictions of future events. Facts are useful in avoiding trial-and-error decision making (based on past experience, a certain set of facts will indicate a certain decision), but over-reliance on facts may cause the executive to miss important considerations that cannot be supported by facts.

2. *Experience.* There is no question that the manager who has been over the course many times in the past has an edge over the new executive.

facts

Consider which of these methods Jo Parnela was using in her analysis. Which was Henry using when he made his decision?

experience

We learn from mistakes (or should), and old hands can refer to many past mistakes to warn them away from the shoals. Even though past events never coincide precisely with current problems, a good manager generalizes from experience and builds up an informal body of do's and don'ts. One hazard in relying on experience is that the manager may reject one kind of action when in fact it is appropriate, on grounds that "We tried that five years ago, and it didn't work." In 1936 the Chrysler Corporation came out with an "Airflow" design which was the forerunner of the modern streamlined car, and the public rejected it in droves. An "experienced" executive who ignored the causes for changing tastes might have concluded that such a car would never succeed. Too often, "experienced" is synonymous with "over-conservative"; it is no accident that imaginative new enterprises are often started by young managers who are not hemmed in by past notions of what will or won't work.

intuition

3. *Intuition.* Intuition has been praised as the indispensable trait for good managers and criticized as practically immoral. In a way it is both. When good managers use intuition, they probably summarize hundreds of experiences into an unconscious pattern of action that draws from experience but also goes beyond it. A bad manager, however, may use "intuition" as a basis for very superficial decisions. The chief criticism of intuitive decision making is the lack of any disciplined analysis, which can lead to deciding on the basis of a few obvious facts while overlooking many important elements. When there is no evident reason for a particular decision — when even the executive cannot review the decision process and perceive a logical basis for the decision or a relationship between the facts and the action — the intuitive approach is not working as it should.

logic

4. *Logic.* There is more to logical decision making than just "being logical." It implies a rational study of all elements on each side, considering the importance of each, weighing the reliability of the information (perhaps delaying to get more facts when the available information seems inconclusive), and analyzing the costs and benefits of each course of action. It requires the decision maker to put aside personal preferences and whims and choose the preferred alternative in an open and consistent way, such that any other executive examining the same information would be likely to make the same choice. A logical decision process can be set down on paper, with the evidence weighed much in the manner of a court trial, and with as little as possible left to chance. It is never "logical" to steer the information in a way that will enable the prejudices or selfish wishes of the manager to show through.

systems analysis

5. *Systems analysis.* The magic of the computer has led many commentators to conclude that quantitative decision making has some higher power that makes it superior to human judgment. This approach is ill-advised, because by overstating the real benefits of quantitative aids to management it risks discrediting the whole field of systems analysis. There are many aspects of a manager's job where the numbers are too numerous or their interrelations too complex for unaided comprehension, and in such cases a mathematical summary of what is happening can be extremely useful. As Dr. Tukey of Bell Laboratories has said, you need to "listen to what the numbers are trying to tell you." If the traffic manager has been using two makes of tires, and the statistician reports that one make has gotten 8% better mileage than the other, this is useful

information that the manager would be an idiot to ignore. If a production manager builds a "mathematical model" of a manufacturing process, which reveals that bottlenecks will occur in the milling machine department when the production line gets under way, the manager can proceed to revise the process or get another machine. When the president is selecting a location for a regional warehouse, a linear programming analysis of the shipping network can develop the least-cost solution to this geographical problem by considering thousands of alternatives that would absolutely overwhelm the president's unaided judgment. Systems analysis is not an alternative way to manage — it is an additional tool that no manager can afford to ignore in its proper sphere, but one that becomes ridiculous and dangerous when used outside its proper sphere.

Indeed, none of the techniques listed above is an *alternative* way of managing. Many managers take the eclectic approach, selecting from any or all of these aids in response to the situation or their personal styles. Thus, every manager will try to assemble at least some facts and will bring to bear whatever epxerience seems applicable. In a relatively simple situation, the manager might lean almost entirely on intuition, while the elements of a more complicated problem would be arranged in a logical decision-making framework. And so on.

Some managers and writers would add a sixth approach: *politics*. The modern corporation has many competing masters, or at least constituencies: employees, unions, customers, suppliers, bankers, stockholders, competitors, public interest groups, and the government. Many actions it takes are governed not so much by rational choice as by a judgmental assessment of how best to balance the competing demands of these groups. A corporation may undertake an agricultural project not because it looks more profitable than alternative investment opportunities, but because it may convey the favorable image of "feeding the hungry of the world," and thus give the corporation a "good press" at a time when possibly undesirable regulatory steps are being considered.[3]

The guidelines that follow suggest factors that a manager must consider in making any decision, regardless of the specific approach that seems most appropriate.

Guidelines for Decision Making

1. *Be clear on the goals of the operation.* It is impossible to make a choice of actions when you haven't decided clearly what the action is intended to achieve. Goals may not be obvious at all. If you are the public works director of a city, deciding whether to pave a road through the park, the goal of that road may be more to maintain an atmosphere of rustic charm than to carry heavy traffic — and paving would spoil the flavor of the park.

2. *Decide exactly how this action will contribute to goals.* Many a company has spent heavily to build a new office building which makes little or no contribution to profits, but serves mainly as a corporate monument or gratifies the ego of the chief executive. The discipline of describing the proposed building in profit-and-loss terms might serve to kill a project that never should have been carried through.

3. *Analyze the sequence of events the action will produce.* For how long a period will you be paying out money but getting no return, and what will

guidelines

What do you think the goals of the partners are, and how might the merger contribute to them? Try to consider more than one.

the deficit be before you turn a profit? What changes will be required in procedures, and who might get hurt? If the plan does not seem to be working out, how expensive will it be to modify plans? At what planned "decision points" can you stop and take stock of whether to go ahead or change course? What might go wrong, and how wrong can things go? When the action has been completed, and things are on an even course again, what have the benefits been? How large a gamble are you taking in case the worst happens, and is the risk disproportionate to the gains if the best happens? Are you and the organization ready to make the inevitable changes this new decision requires? There are many questions of this sort to consider, and too often the enthusiasm for a new plan causes management to brush these distasteful issues aside. Every important decision should be subjected to a professional criticizer (or consultant) who tries to find flaws in it, and management should explore each criticism carefully while it still costs nothing to modify or abandon the plan.

4. *Test the action by carrying it out in a small way, if possible.* It is almost unheard-of for manufacturers of high-volume consumer products to introduce new items without test marketing them in selected cities known to reflect the buying patterns of the nation as a whole. Management's first notion of what ought to be done may involve important omissions or misconceptions that such a test can disclose.

5. *Once committed, be consistent.* Nothing is more demoralizing to an organization than constant uncertainty as to what has been decided. Take plenty of time to decide, but once the facts are in, don't change every time an insignificant criticism arises, or the organization will be in an uproar and unable to settle down to good work.

6. *Stick with the decision, and carry through.* It is wrong to be too timid, just as it is to be too hasty. If a decision is needed, make it. Once it is made, take all the related actions needed to see that it is carried out and doesn't die from neglect. And after it is in effect, follow up to see how well it is working and what adjustments need to be made. A new operation is a fragile and unfamiliar flower, and needs a helping hand to gain acceptance.

7. *Learn from the decision.* When the results of the action start to come in, they should be appraised to see if they meet expectations. Only in this way can useful experience be collected that will help not only the company but the managers concerned.

8. *If the decision was a poor one, scrap it.* If the decision did not pan out, the only correct action is to admit it and get out. This approach takes remarkable courage, and many managers don't have it. Such an action is a direct confession that the manager was wrong in the first place, and a storm is likely to descend when it is taken, but in the long run companies that cut their losses early can recover from a bad choice; companies that hope a bad decision will work out somehow are asking for heavy trouble.

Theories of Decision Making

Since decision making is such a central element in management, in some respects theories of decision making relate closely to theories of management. Thus we have the *bureaucratic* school, which places heavy emphasis on operating within a rigid organization structure; in this school the subordinates feed information and problems up to the boss at the apex of the pyramid, who has both the information and ability to solve all problems from the organization's nerve center. The *scientific management* school believes that tasks can be broken into logical elements, which can be engineered scientifically for most efficient performance, and that management alone possesses the skills to analyze problems and outline detailed solutions.[4] The *human relations* school believes that organizations work better when more attention is paid to the human side—job satisfaction, participation in decisions, treating the organization as a social group with aims other than sheer efficiency—and members' wants and needs are weighed in deciding on courses of action. The *economic rationality* school holds that an organization is an economic unit that converts inputs to outputs, and should be organized to do this most efficiently; in this school, a course of action is continued as long as it is worth more than it costs. The *satisficing* school despairs of achieving any sort of perfection, believing that most managers are so beset by problems that they do well to make decisions that are even reasonably rational; this school requires the manager to accept the first option with a fighting chance of success, thus making time to "decide" all the other problems. The *systems analysis* school believes that every problem exists within a system composed of subsystems fitted together like pieces in a jigsaw puzzle, and which is itself a subsystem of a larger system, all of which have some impact on each other. (Reminding one of the old rhyme: "The smallest fleas we see today, have smaller fleas which on them prey; and these have smaller still to bite 'em, and so proceed ad infinitem.") In this school, a problem must be probed exhaustively to analyze its effects on other problems; in effect, you must build a conceptual model of a large system before you make decisions within your small system.

Categories of Theories

Most theories of decision making reduce to one of the following categories: *judgmental, quantitative,* or *psychological.* Of course, all decision making involves judgments; but the first category here implies primary reliance on judgment and experience at the expense of other methods.

Bureaucratic organizations depend heavily on the *judgment* of the man at the top. Bureaucratic managers tend to assume that consultation with subordinates is a sign of weakness. Consequently, one sign of a "strong-man" organization is lack of consultation with others and failure to draw on factual data or statistical studies which could provide a broader base for the decision. A prime industry for judgmental decision making by the top executive is the independent oil tanker business. In 1973 the few major oil tanker operators ordered $20 billion worth of ships (enough to double their tonnage within four years), assuming that the oil consuming countries would import rapidly increasing amounts of crude oil from the Middle East. A recent *Fortune* article[5] noted that "in any other industry, decisions on investments so huge would be wrapped in the full panoply of managerial science—economic forecasts, cash-flow projections, feasibility studies, and the like," while in the tanker business each fleet is treated as an extension of the top man's personality. One shipowner (who ran $30,000 up to $50 million in twenty years) says that his Harvard Business School graduate son is "too intelligent." Instead of using analysis, says the head man, "I use my nose."

Judgmental decisions are not necessarily bad, of course. But when the decision maker deliberately ignores other sources of assistance which could lead to sounder decisions, the heart is ruling the head. During the 1960s, ship operators did not normally order new ships without first having oil company charter contracts, but with the ordering spree of the early '70s the operators were insulated from systematic oil company planning and unknowingly deprived themselves of an important source of decision data. As a result, by the mid-'70s some oil company executives were predicting that before the end of the decade a quarter of the tanker fleet would be surplus.

quantitative approach

The *quantitative* category includes all the techniques listed in the *Fortune* magazine quote (i.e., economic analysis, scientific management, and systems analysis). A business executive can assemble all the available facts about a proposed venture into a "mathematical model" illustrating the approximate payoff that can be expected from various alternative plans of action. Quantitative methods do not manufacture facts, but they can help arrange facts into proper perspective so that the manager can see their significance more clearly than if they were simply considered independently.

payoff table

If a manager who is considering building tankers knows that a tanker under contract will earn $7 million a year and cost $4 million to operate, but an idle tanker will cost $2 million a year to maintain at anchor, that information can be used to create the following (highly simplified) "payoff table." The starred numbers in the table, although shown as profit, represent cases where demand exceeded available supply, so the manager lost money in terms of potential opportunity. If only two ships were on hand and four could have been chartered, the manager made $6 million—but could have made $12 million with two more ships. Such "opportunity cost" does not show up on the balance sheet, but it should.

Figure 7-7.
Payoff Table

	Number Available				
	1	2	3	4	5
1	3	1	−1	−3	−5
2	3★	6	4	2	0
3	3★	6★	9	7	5
4	3★	6★	9★	12	10
5	3★	6★	9★	12★	15

Number Wanted (rows)

EXPLANATION: If the manager builds three and only two are chartered, the two in use will earn ($7−$4) or $3 million each, and the one not in use will cost −$2 million for a total profit that year of $3 + $3 − $2 = $4 million.

238
MANAGEMENT PROCESSES

To decide how many ships to have available in a given year, the manager should make a careful study of expected demand for ship charters. If there is a 50% probability that two ships can be chartered, a 30% probability that three can be chartered, and a 20% probability that four can be chartered, the payoff table can be converted to an "expected value" table that will show the profit to be made from having two, three, or four ships available. (The manager need not consider one ship or five ships, since there is no chance of such numbers being wanted, so we reproduce only part of the payoff table.)

expected value

Consider the situation if four ships are stocked. There is a 50% chance that only two will be chartered (on which the profit would be $2 million), a 30% chance for three (and a $7 million profit), and a 20% chance for four (and a $12 million profit). An expected value calculation for this case would look as follows:

Table 7-1.
Expected Value Calculation

Number	Probability This Number Chartered	Profit if Chartered	Expected Profit
2	.5	$ 2	$1.0
3	.3	7	2.1
4	.2	12	2.4
Expected value of buying 4 ships			$5.5 million

A similar calculation for two ships and three ships discloses expected values of $6 million and $6.5 million for the year respectively. Therefore, when facing this estimated demand, the best strategy is to acquire three ships. This calculation holds true only for the one year, of course, and is an enormous simplification of the problem, but does illustrate an expected value approach to evaluating alternative courses of action.

Suppose the estimate of expected demand is changed somewhat, as follows: $P(1) = 10\%, P(2) = 20\%, P(3) = 30\%, P(4) = 20\%, P(5) = 20\%$. The expected values for various numbers of ships available would be as shown on the graph of Figure 7-8. Note that the expected revenue increases as each additional ship is added, up to four ships, and then drops. The "marginal" increase from four to five is negative; no additional ships, then, should be added. Techniques for calculating the "marginal" addition that an alternative course of action would contribute to profit (or to costs) fall within the methods of marginal economic analysis. They show what the enterprise would achieve with and without the addition. For example, if a new product is to be manufactured in a factory, the accountant will wish to charge to it a proportional share of overhead and machine rental, and *after* it has been put into production this approach is proper. But *before* it is added to the manufacturing line, the correct way to analyze its desirability is to see what the total costs and profits of the plant will be with it and without it. The present products are carrying all the overhead now, and the new product should be added only if it will produce a marginal increase in profit.

marginal profit

Suppose only one product is being manufactured now. It costs $30 in direct material and labor to manufacture, is charged $20 for plant overhead, and sells for $100. Now the new product is being considered; it will cost $40 in direct labor and material and will sell for $50. If we charge to it the same percentage of selling cost as overhead, or $10, it will show no profit. But since it will not add to the overhead expenses, which must be paid anyway if the first product is to be manufactured, it will in fact bring a profit of $50-$40 for every one made and sold. *After* it has been added to the line, overhead should be reapportioned between the first product and this one, but only the marginal (additional) costs and revenues should be considered in deciding whether to adopt it or not.

There are many ways to represent a company or a process in a mathematical form. Properly used, such models emphasize the essential factors and make it easier to see what effects result from what causes. The executive can use a "gaming model," which tries to capture all the important factors involved in strategic decisions when competitors are involved ("If we do this, what will our competitor do—and how will that hurt or help us?"). Or a "breakeven model" can be used to show what might happen to sales volume as prices are lowered, and just how much reduction in prices will be optimum. A "tradeoff model" will show the extent to which an increase in one sort of cost (e.g., buying labor-saving equipment) will produce a decrease in another sort (e.g., direct labor), so the best strategy can be determined. "Forecasting models" attempt to project some part of an operation (perhaps price of raw materials or volume of sales) into the future. The tanker fleet operators discussed earlier could make very good use of tanker charter price forecasts in

---

mathematical model

Which of these types of mathematical models do you think Jo was using? Explain.

Figure 7-8.
Expected Value Graph

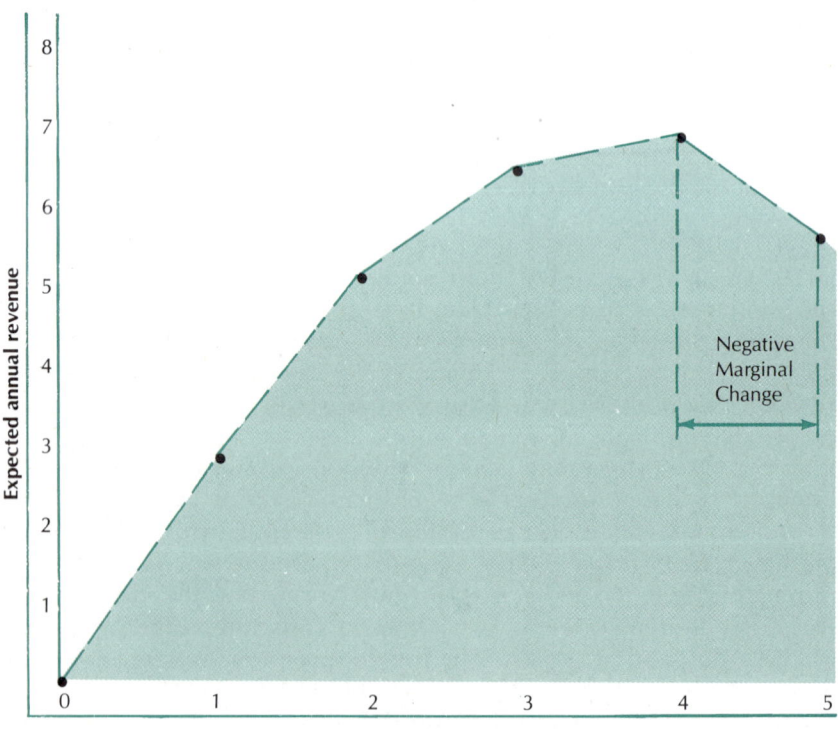

helping them decide what ships to build. Models of shipment and production costs of a product, for various factory locations, can help determine the lowest cost arrangement of factories relative to markets; this is a "transportation model." There are many other forms of decision models. Some are *operational* in nature and deal with a particular problem such as scheduling of machines in the plant. Others are *strategic* in nature, dealing with the whole corporate strategy in the face of changing conditions. A major oil company might use a strategic model in attempting to decide whether to lower prices in the face of consumer dissatisfaction with alleged high oil company profits.

Psychological theories try to look beyond the obvious factors of a decision situation to the human factors that will affect the outcome. If employees are highly dissatisfied in an organizational environment, their performance is almost sure to be poor, and the organizational output will suffer no matter how carefully the best course of action has been selected. A bad plan enthusiastically carried out can triumph over a good plan poorly executed by disinterested players. There have been cases in recent years of assembly-line manufacturing plants producing a high volume of rejects because of worker unhappiness, despite careful industrial engineering studies concluding that the process was efficient and well within the capabilities of workers on the line.

_{psychological approach}

Psychological factors with regard to *workers* (including subordinate-level managers) involve their need to feel they belong to the organization—even own it in part—and do rewarding and useful work. Decision making in such an environment would involve the maximum of advance discussion with all those likely to be affected, and reaching decisions that the organization can "live with." It would involve treating employees as individuals with personal rights and dignity, rather than as elements in an organizational machine. It would involve providing medical insurance, bonuses, vacations, and so forth as basic rights to which the employees were entitled rather than as gifts from a benevolent management.

Many companies whose managers feel their personnel practices are modern and enlightened go through a traumatic period when efforts are made to unionize. Despite the fact that union membership is a basic right protected by law, managers sometimes make it clear that employees who vote to affiliate with a union are acting in an almost traitorous way. An organizational environment that seeks to encourage participation from all the members must *accept* the actions of those members who seek to enhance their rights by joining unions or by taking any other legal and ethical actions.

With regard to *managers,* psychological factors involve the question of managerial drives and incentives. The old-line company with one autocratic boss who was also the owner has given way in most modern industrial settings to the large company whose managers are employees rather than owners and whose drives and motivations are markedly different from those of a sole proprietor. Earlier we discussed Simon's theory of the "satisficing" manager, who is content to find a satisfactory solution rather than the best. One reason for this approach is lack of time to find the best solution to each decision situation, but another may be that the manager's personal interests are served as long as decisions are good

The executive may be a "risk-avoider" who demands favorable odds before gambling on a course of action.

---

risk-avoider

When the partners decided not to merge, do you think they were thereby "risk-seekers"? Why or why not?

risk-seeker

---

enough to avoid criticism. The salaried manager has little inducement to take chances that will advance the company markedly if they work out but will produce disapproval if they do not. In a very large company, with responsibility spread among many executives, the pursuit of profits may be far down on the list of goals.

Economists tend to assume that executives are economically oriented, always taking the action that seems most likely to maximize the organization's profit, but this assumption ignores major individual differences in temperament and viewpoint. An executive may be a *risk-avoider*, who demands favorable odds or even an almost "sure thing" before gambling on a course of action—and since sure things are rare in the real world, this hesitation means avoidance of *any* new ventures. If you were downtown late at night with a dollar in your pocket for bus fare home, and someone offered to toss a coin for a dollar at three to one odds in your favor, the prospect of walking home if you lost would probably compel you to pass up this seemingly favorable gamble. A risk-avoiding executive may see the world from a similar viewpoint: things are going well now and there is no reason to "rock the boat." This attitude emerges in some government organizations. Employee unwillingness to make apparently sensible exceptions to routine, often defined as bureaucracy, is actually a form of self-preservation. On the other hand, an executive may be a *risk-seeker*, sometimes taking unreasonable gambles when the advantages of the possible payoff appear to outweigh the risk of failure. If a company is nearing bankruptcy, a risky venture may be justified because there is nothing to lose. But when only the executive is in trouble, expecting to be fired or transferred if performance does not improve, gambling with company funds in hopes of improving things is not a wise move. The separation of goals between the organization and certain of its salaried managers poses a constant dilemma for large organizations that does not exist when the owner is the manager.

Quantitative Aids to Judgment

As we have stressed all along, proper decision making need not be all one approach or the other. Good managers never forsake good judgment, but neither do they refuse to gather and heed numerical data when it is available. And they keep the personal equation constantly in mind, without letting the wish for organizational harmony override economic considerations.

Suppose you were in charge of the annual chest X-ray program for detecting tuberculosis conducted by your county health department, and it was up to you to establish guidelines for reading the films and determining which school students showed a positive result (that is, had signs of tuberculosis, requiring further examination in the hospital). To artificially simplify the situation, let's suppose that it has been found that the average student who actually has tuberculosis symptoms will have about six spots on the film, and the average student who does not will have about three spots on the film. But it isn't this simple, because each group has some variation. Some 16% of students with positive symptoms will have five spots or less, and some 2% will have four spots or less; no positive reaction students will have less than three spots on the film. On the other hand, some 16% of students with negative symptoms will have four spots or more, some 2% will have five spots or more, and no negative reaction students will have more than six spots. This situation is shown graphically by means of probability distributions in Figure 7-9.[6]

This situation poses a real dilemma. Say there are 10,000 students who do not have tuberculosis, and probably about 100 who do. Any students you call "positive" will go to the hospital for more careful study, but any you call "negative" will not be seen by a doctor until X-ray time next year (when, presumably, the situation will have deteriorated for students who actually have TB). What will you tell the film readers as to the number of spots to call "positive"?

Emotion would say to call three or more positive, so that you would not risk missing any student who really has TB. No one could criticize you. But what would be the result? Since half of the "negative" students have

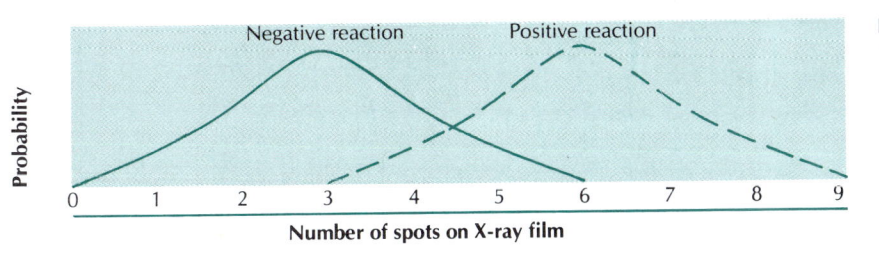

Figure 7-9.
Probability Distributions

three or more, you would be sending 5000 students to the hospital, worrying their parents and swamping the medical facilities to the point where no one would get a good hospital examination. How about four or more? 16% of the negatives have four or more spots, so 1600 of them would go to the hospital—and you would miss about two of the hundred positives. If you make the dividing line five or more spots, only 200 negatives would get sent to the hospital, which isn't so bad, but you would miss 16 or so of the 100 positives.

decision rule

In order to arrive at the best decision in this difficult problem, a management scientist would probably "price out" the costs in each case, to establish the tradeoff between the benefits of including more positives against the costs of including more negatives. Costs include the hospital examination, the worry and disruption caused by sending negatives to the hospital, and the danger of passing up positives whose conditions will deteriorate by the next year. Some of these costs are very difficult to determine precisely, but that is no excuse for not trying. Quite often, even though it seems impossible to establish a price for such intangible matters, the very effort to calculate a realistic cost sheds light on the problem. In this case, it may even show the public health authorities that some other medical procedure is necessary.

One problem facing the Federal Trade Commission is how to spend its limited enforcement resources in policing corporate suspects (for deceptive advertising, antitrust, and consumer protection in general). Still in the experimental stage is a computerized mathematical model that collects statistics on key measures of industries and companies, to estimate the benefit to society of directing an enforcement effort in one area against another. At present the Commission must rely on instinct and judgment, and hopefully a model will raise some flags that will select from the thousands of possible enforcement areas those which offer the most promise of uncovering some significant abuses—and of winning in court, which is just as important if the Commission lawyers are not to spin their wheels. Figure 7-10 lists some of the statistical measures that play a part in the model. There are contradictory effects that have to be handled by the model, making it very difficult to construct. For example, if the concentration ratio (proportion of sales by the top four firms) is high, it becomes probable that antitrusters should look into the industry. But if it is a rapid growth industry, competition may be less of a problem because growth will attract new competition. On the other hand, growth means the industry is increasingly important to consumers, who must be protected. And so on.

Improving Decision Making

public pressures on the manager

One of the benefits of the tremendous current increase in outside pressures on the manager—whether corporate executive or government official—is the new spotlight on how decisions are made and how executives manage. Previously, the more invisible executives could remain, the happier they were—and, they believed, the most effective. Today, like it or not, they must come out of their shells and plunge into a whole cauldron of outside activities that make their lives far more complex and harried than ever before. Chairman Roy Chapin of

American Motors says that "the added dimension of social responsibility...has now become so overwhelming that if I wanted to, I could spend my entire time being civically and governmentally not just active but hyperactive." Chairman Frank Nemac of Youngstown Sheet and Tube Company says, "It's an odd world we're living in. We're sitting on a volcano of conflicting interests." And Alonzo McDonald, managing partner of McKinsey and Company, adds, "Just a few years ago the chief executive of a big company spent 10% of his time on external matters. Today the figure is generally 40%."[7]

The inevitable result of this pressure is a search for new ways to spread the decision-making load. Harlan Cleveland, formerly a high governmental official and now president of the University of Hawaii, writes, "The organizations that get things done will no longer be hierarchical pyramids with most of the real control at the top. They will be systems—interlaced webs of tension in which control is loose, power diffused, and centers of decision plural."[8] John Hancock Mutual Life Insurance Company has an eight-member executive committee that makes corporate decisions by consensus; Chairman Gerhard Bleicken says he can't ever recall using his veto power. President James B. Farley of Booz, Allen and Hamilton believes that another reason for moving to consensus management is the need to involve the younger executives. "If the thirty-year-olds are going to commit themselves," says Farley, "you have to give them a forum in which to express their ideas."

This shift can be quite frustrating to chief executives. President A. W. Clausen of Bank of America says it leads to a "certain powerlessness on the part of the chief executive; you can thrust with all your weight and smarts,

spreading the load

How is Henry spreading the decision-making load? Is his method effective in freeing his time for more important or appropriate tasks?

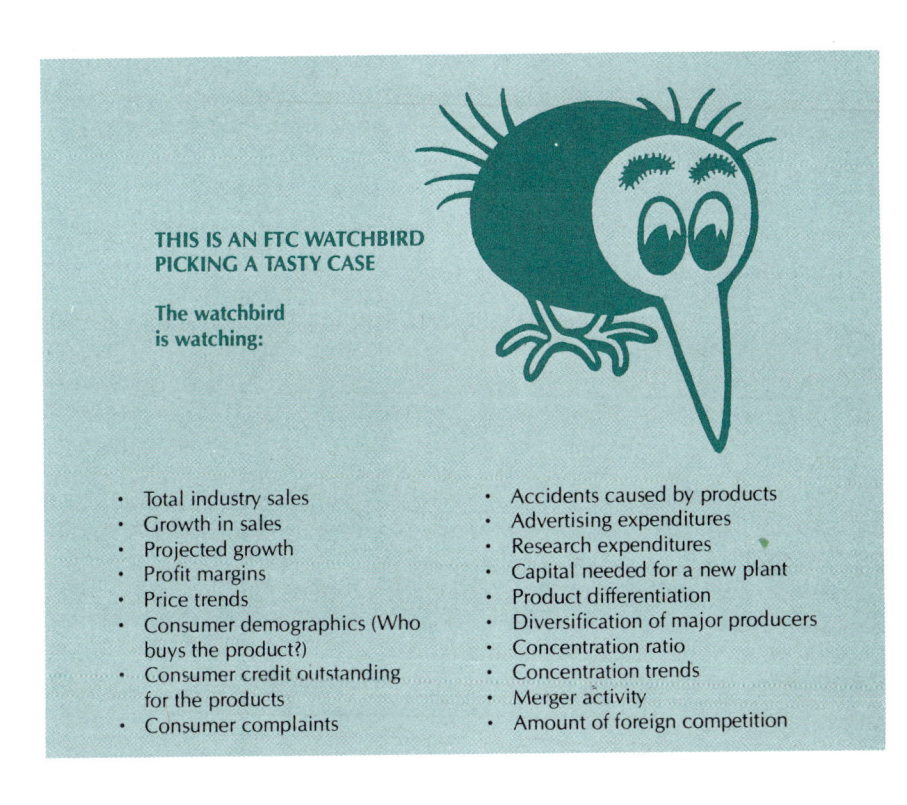

Figure 7-10.
Factors Used by FTC in Choosing Cases

THIS IS AN FTC WATCHBIRD PICKING A TASTY CASE

The watchbird is watching:

- Total industry sales
- Growth in sales
- Projected growth
- Profit margins
- Price trends
- Consumer demographics (Who buys the product?)
- Consumer credit outstanding for the products
- Consumer complaints
- Accidents caused by products
- Advertising expenditures
- Research expenditures
- Capital needed for a new plant
- Product differentiation
- Diversification of major producers
- Concentration ratio
- Concentration trends
- Merger activity
- Amount of foreign competition

and nothing moves." Moreover, by no means do all chief executives accept the legitimacy of consensus management. Former chairman Bob R. Dorsey of Gulf Oil Corporation said, not long before he left the company, that there is no way a chief executive can spend less time on operating problems: "Some of the disasters in this country have occurred when people decided they were going to take a lofty position, play the role of elder statesman, and turn over the operating responsibility to a group of other people."[9] A few years ago, when President Mills B. Lane stepped down as the presiding officer at Atlanta's Citizens & Southern National Bank, after a quarter-century of spectacular success, his successor set up a team organization. The new management has encountered more than its share of problems, and it is far from clear that the team operation is an improvement over the former arrangement where the boss was at the hub with everybody reporting to him.

Management by Persuasion

Whether the organization should be hierarchical or a team, it is clear that good managers in today's environment cannot ignore the desires, ideas, ambitions, and feelings of those who work for and with them. John Morgan, whose recent book[10] presents some serious truths in fable form, offers the following "nine principles of persuasion," based on the goal of managing by persuading others to do willingly what you want them to do:

principles of persuasion

1. Make it very clear just where you stand, and why.
2. Emotions persuade more effectively in the short run than facts.
3. Be patient in getting your ideas across; it isn't easy.
4. Make use of repetition—repeat the message many different ways.
5. Plan to encounter resistance, and be ready to deal with it.
6. Try to get your colleagues deeply involved personally.
7. Show that the desired action really is feasible—not just a dream.
8. Be perfectly frank in stating your motives—no "hidden agendas."
9. Be totally honest and believable—don't lose your credibility.

A Framework for Management

One of the corporate clients of Peter Drucker, dean of U.S. management consultants,[11] describes Drucker's deceptively simple approach as follows: "It's not specific advice so much, as that he gives you a framework in which to view your business, your markets—and your life." Drucker does not describe detailed techniques or "how-to" formulas—he leaves that to others—but rather backs off and looks at the goals of the organization, forcing you to consider the best ways to attain them. He is a philosopher of business, which he sees as the most typical (and influential) social institution in today's society. Profits, says Drucker, are not the "goal" of business (any more than breathing is the goal of man). Rather, they are the basic need without which there can be no business. Concord is not necessarily a requirement for management success, unless there is some specific need for it; indeed, conflict can be healthy. ("So your salesmen and your engineers fight? That is what they should do. God help you if they are in agreement.")

If an organization concentrates its resources, it has enormous capability, yet there are many things that even a large organization cannot do. One of the most difficult tasks is to focus the power of this monster so that its strength is used effectively. This is why time spent thinking about where your organization ought to be going, about the framework within which it should operate, and about the reasons that it does what it does, is never wasted. A useful and revealing framework can be constructed by identifying the decisions that have to be made at the top level and cannot be made anywhere else, the decisions that have to be made at the next lower level (and should not be made at a higher level), and so on. This procedure will reveal a great deal about the structure of the company, and will raise questions about the correctness of the present way of doing things.

An organization must be prepared for change, because change is inevitable. If your organization treats every new change as a crisis, there is something wrong with its underlying framework. How does an organization learn to treat change as normal? Perhaps by brainstorming all of the things that could change and considering the best organizational response to each. Suppose your major product was suddenly outlawed because a principal ingredient was deemed to be potentially harmful. Suppose young people suddenly took offense at your type of company, and none of them would come to work for you. Suppose a new technological development allowed a competitor to duplicate your leading product line at half the price. Suppose the cost of your raw materials suddenly zoomed out of sight—or they became totally unavailable. Considering how you would respond to these changes (all of them happen, and not infrequently) might shed a good deal of light on your organization.

back to fundamentals

Where is North Star going? What should be its operating framework? In your opinion, is it doing the right things?

preparing for change

An organization must be prepared for change, because change is a constant.

Keeping in Contact

people contact

Dramatic stories about computer terminals that will fill the manager in on events while he or she sits at a desk, so decisions can be made by watching the "scope" in the manner of a space shot headquarters at Cape Canaveral or Houston, downplay the constant need for managers to keep in contact with people out on the firing line. A computer provides information in numerical form, but the vitally important analysis—the why, the "yes, but" information, the amplifying facts that can put an entirely different interpretation on the figures—must come from people. Only people have judgment, to sense when a turning point is coming or when opportunity or danger lies ahead. Only people have ideas: new approaches that ought to be tried, situations that are deteriorating and should be treated, information that cannot be certified as positive but ought to be considered.

The manager who loses contact with the organization's members—their work, their problems, their objectives—will start making poor decisions. No manager is good enough to go it alone. Executives need the support of the whole organization to inform and guide them, to let them see the human impact of their plans and actions. And, if the executive is a real leader, he or she will show subordinates that their accomplishments and inputs are important, in the thousand little ways that spell morale.

Summary

Some see managers as systematic people who carefully review all alternatives and scientifically select the best; others see them as plagued with doubts and short of information, selecting any course of action that appears likely to work. The form of organization, and its expectations, have a good deal to do with how systematically and effectively its managers behave.

There are several levels of deciding. The simplest level is that where the information provides almost an automatic choice of decision. At the next level up in complexity, the decision results automatically from the manager's estimate or expectation of information. Then comes the case where different pieces of information must be weighed to determine their relative importance, and finally the most complex case, where the manager is uncertain both as to the facts and their relative importance. Structured decisions are those where the answer virtually suggests itself when the information is presented, but most management decisions have very little structure.

Deciding starts with determining the alternatives and tracing their implications. Usually a choice of one alternative affects actions in the future, and therefore is a broader decision than it appears at first sight. Managers don't always make "right" decisions, because they are operating under many pressures from their colleagues, who have weapons to influence the decision.

Programmable decisions are those with predictable elements, and most decisions contain some programmable elements. Usually there are key factors which affect the outcome, and decision makers should concentrate on these.

Decisions should be made at the lowest level where there is competence and impartiality, recognizing that decisions often have wide repercussions. Decisions made by groups are likely to be more acceptable, but not always as efficient. Seeking group consensus will lead to acceptable decisions, but seeking facts from the group may lead to a better decision. Decisions should not be made by managers with no responsibility for the outcome. Decisions involving more money usually are more complex decisions, and usually are made at a higher level in the organizational hierarchy.

Some decision makers lean heavily on collecting facts as a basis for their decisions. Others try to apply their own experience to situations. Some appear to decide intuitively, though experience is always a factor in such cases. Some set up a logical cost/benefit analysis, weighing importance and reliability of data, and trying to leave little to chance. Some try to consider the entire environment as a total system and to evaluate the effect of each decision on the whole.

The overall approach may vary, but certain systematic guidelines apply to all decision making: determine goals, evaluate the impact of the action on goals, analyze the results of the action, test the action in a small way, be consistent and carry through, and assess the results of the action.

The major theories of decision making—bureaucratic, scientific management, human relations, economic rationality, satisficing, and systems analysis—may all be reduced to judgmental, quantitative, or psychological approaches. Judgmental decision makers risk overlooking valuable inputs in terms of statistical information or impact on others. The numerous quantitative approaches reduce decision factors to mathematical terms. Psychological theories look beyond the question of which decision is "best" to which will be more acceptable, and pay major attention to human factors in the organization.

The actions and decisions of today's manager are publicized more than ever before, and the increased workload is encouraging some managers to seek help, sometimes via committee management. Whatever management approach you use, it must enable you to persuade others to work toward organizational goals. It is useful to establish a framework for management, by thinking about how the organization divides up its decisions, how it adjusts to change, and how it fits into society. No manager can be effective without maintaining personal contact with others in the organization.

Notes

1. James G. March and Herbert A. Simon, *Organizations* (New York: John Wiley & Sons, Inc., 1958).

2. In the early '30s a squadron of naval destroyers was proceeding up the West Coast in a fog. When the navigator of the leading destroyer thought he had passed Point Honda, which juts out from the California coast, he turned in to follow what appeared to be the in-turning coastline. His navigation was in error, and his destroyer ran on the rocks. Six other destroyers, turning in as he had done, also hit the rocks in one of the worst naval disasters in peacetime history. Following the leader is not always safe.

3. Charles G. Burke, "The Intricate 'Politics' of the Corporation," *Fortune*, April 1975, p. 109.

4. This school paid scant attention to worker inputs to decision making, or

the human side of management in general. Frederick W. Taylor, pioneer of the scientific management school, in his *Principles of Scientific Management* (New York, Harper & Row, Pubs., 1911), gave as one of the "first requirements" for a factory laborer "that he shall be so stupid that he more nearly resembles in his mental makeup the ox than any other type, and he must consequently be trained by a man more intelligent than himself before he can be successful."

5. "Betting $20 Billion in the Tanker Game," *Fortune,* August 1974, p. 145.

6. Imagine that either of these probability distribtuions is a side view of a pile of pennies you are tossing at a line from some distance to one side. You are aiming at #6 (in the right distribution); while the majority fall rather close to 6 there are some shorts and some overs. 16% of the pennies fall between 5 and 3, 2% between 4 and 3, and so on.

7. Comments quoted in "The Chief Executive Office," *Business Week,* May 4, 1974, pp. 37-86.

8. Harlan Cleveland, *The Future Executive* (New York: Harper & Row, Pubs., 1972.)

9. Quoted in "The Chief Executive Office," *Business Week,* May 4, 1974, pp. 37-86. Ironically, Gulf's board of directors fired Dr. Dorsey in January 1976 as a result of payment of questionable contributions, though he maintained that he had not authorized and was not aware of all of them.

10. John Morgan, *Aesop's Fables in the Executive Suite* (New York: D. Van Nostrand Co., 1974).

11. Drucker's encyclopedic new compendium, *Management: Tasks, Responsibilities, Practices* (New York: Harper & Row, Pubs., 1974), distills his 40 years of experience as a writer, thinker, and consultant in management.

Review Questions

1. What is the difference between optimizing and "satisficing" in making management decisions? Do you think satisficing is necessarily a poor technique?
2. Define the four levels of complexity in decision making. At which level do you think computers "decide"? Explain.
3. Think of an example of a decision in your daily life that will affect your ability to make a second decision later. How does this situation resemble a two-stage lottery (or a three-stage, or more)?
4. Is it more important to make a decision that is "right" or one that will be accepted by the organization? Explain.
5. Why is it important to select the key factors in a decision before deciding? Why not consider *all* the factors?
6. Who should make a decision that primarily affects one division, but has significant secondary effects in two other divisions in the same organization?
7. What are the disadvantages of group decisions?
8. Why is it not always enough to collect all the facts in order to make a decision?
9. What are the various "schools" of decision making? Which one do you favor? Why?
10. What is a "payoff table?" Why is it useful to managers?
11. Why are the motivations of managers important to the performance of a company? If you were boss, how would you try to make managerial motivation work for you instead of against you?
12. What would you consider the advantages and disadvantages of team management?
13. Why is it sometimes useful to try and establish a framework for your organization?

Discussion Questions

1. In the 50:50 coin example, do you think "don't bet" would be a better decision than "bet" if the coins were slightly "unfair" (say, a 55% chance of losing and a 45% chance of winning)? Or would this factor make no difference in your decision?
2. Is the manager who is influenced by organizational pressures to cut corners somehow dishonest or cowardly, or just practical? Why?
3. What are the "key factors" in deciding whether to buy a certain house? What are the less important factors, and why are they not as important?
4. Should new managers obtain experience in making the complex decisions that fall on the right side of Figure 7-6? How could the organization arrange for them to get this kind of experience without too much risk of costly errors?
5. Apply the eight decision-making guidelines to your house-buying decision (3, above).
6. If the tanker operators had used a quantitative approach, how might their attention have focused on points they would otherwise tend to overlook?
7. If you were the public health official in charge of TB X-rays, and you did price out the costs involved in making the dividing line 3, 4, or 5 spots, do you think you could sell your approach, and final decision, to the public? (E.g., if a cost-benefit analysis proved that 5 spots did make the best cut-off point, how could you justify the 16 cases who would not go to the hospital?) How might political opponents of the mayor (who appointed you) attack your actions? How would you respond? (This thought process is a form of "gaming.")
8. Have you ever tried thinking about your personal framework for management? Try it. Does it shed light on any strengths or weaknesses you may not have considered before?

North Star Case Study

In the prologue to this chapter, North Star received an offer from Barnhard & Walker Corporation to sell out for $500,000, but decided to reject the offer and continue in business on their own. Imagine that a year has gone by, and several changes have taken place. Jo Parnela has left the company to return full time to the university. Dick has been prevailed upon by friends in his home town to return and run for Congress, so will be leaving within the month; Bert had to go out and replace him on site, although he was very reluctant to do so.

At this time, Abner Jenkins (who had replaced Bert as Technical Director when the latter went overseas) came to Henry to say that B&W had offered to hire away the entire drafting room gang to set up a competing company for work such as the Natal job. While Ab didn't want to accept, some of the others did. They had agreed, however, that anything they did would be as a group: they would all go or stay en masse. What worried them was the fear that North Star would go under, and this was compounded by their feeling that they had no voice in seeing that it succeeded. If they were to stay, they wanted a larger voice in what was done, including a method for earning shares of stock in the company so that they would have the lure of potential ownership to make it more attractive as a long-time place to work.

1. If you were to structure this decision problem as a sequential lottery, how would you do it? What factors would you include that would affect future decisions?

2. What alternatives are open to Henry and Bert? What are the probable results of each alternative course of action? What are the probabilities? How about the positive and negative payoffs?

3. From the point of view of Ab Jenkins and the drafting room group, which is the nature of the decision problem? What are the alternate probabilities and payoffs involved in each?

4. Is there an outcome that will be best for both sides? Or is this a situation where if one side wins, the other side loses?

5. Is there any way that Henry could bring in the drafting room group to help make the decision on what to do? Or would this action violate the rule that an impartial decision maker is needed? In that case, who *is* an impartial decision maker in this situation?

Suggestions for Further Reading

Benton, J. B. *Managing the Organizational Decision Process.* Lexington, Mass.: Lexington Books, 1973.

Bridges, F. J. *Management Decisions & Organizational Policy.* Boston: Allyn & Bacon, Inc., 1971.

Brinkers, H. S., ed. *Decision-Making, Creativity, Judgment, and Systems.* Columbus, Ohio: Ohio State University Press, 1972.

Brown, R. G. *Management Decisions for Production Operations.* Hinsdale, Ill.: Dryden Press, 1971.

Brown, R. V.; A. B. Kahr; and C. Peterson. *Decision Analysis: An Overview.* New York: Holt, Rinehart & Winston, Inc., 1974.

Delbecq, A. L. *Group Techniques for Program Planning: A Guide to Nominal Group & Delphi Processes.* Glenview, Ill.: Scott, Foresman & Co., 1975.

Dewhurst, R. F. J. *Business Cost-Benefit Analysis.* New York: McGraw-Hill Book Co., 1972.

Drucker, P. F. *The Effective Executive.* New York: Harper & Row, Pubs., 1967.

Easton, A. *Complex Managerial Decisions Involving Multiple Objectives.* New York: John Wiley & Sons, Inc., 1973.

Fabrycky, W. J. *Economic Decision Analysis.* Englewood Cliffs, N.J.: Prentice-Hall, Inc., 1974.

Foster, C., et al. *Lessons of Maplin: Is The Machinery for Governmental Decision-Making at Fault?* London: Institute of Economic Affairs, 1974.

Johnson, R. J. *Executive Decisions.* Chicago: South-Western Publishing Co., 1970.

Jones, G. T. *Simulation and Business Decisions.* Harmondsworth, England: Penguin Books, 1972.

Lee, Wayne. *Decision, Theory, and Human Behavior.* New York: John Wiley & Sons, Inc., 1971.

Mack, R. P. *Planning on Uncertainty.* New York: Wiley-Interscience, 1971.

Moore, P. G. *Risk in Business Decisions.* New York: John Wiley & Sons, Inc., 1973.

Payne, F. T. *Strategy and Policy Formation: An Integrative Approach.* Philadelphia: Saunders, 1974.

Simon, H. A. *The New Science of Management Decision.* New York: Harper & Row, Pubs., 1960.

Vroom, V. H. *Leadership & Decision-Making.* Pittsburgh: University of Pittsburgh Press, 1973.

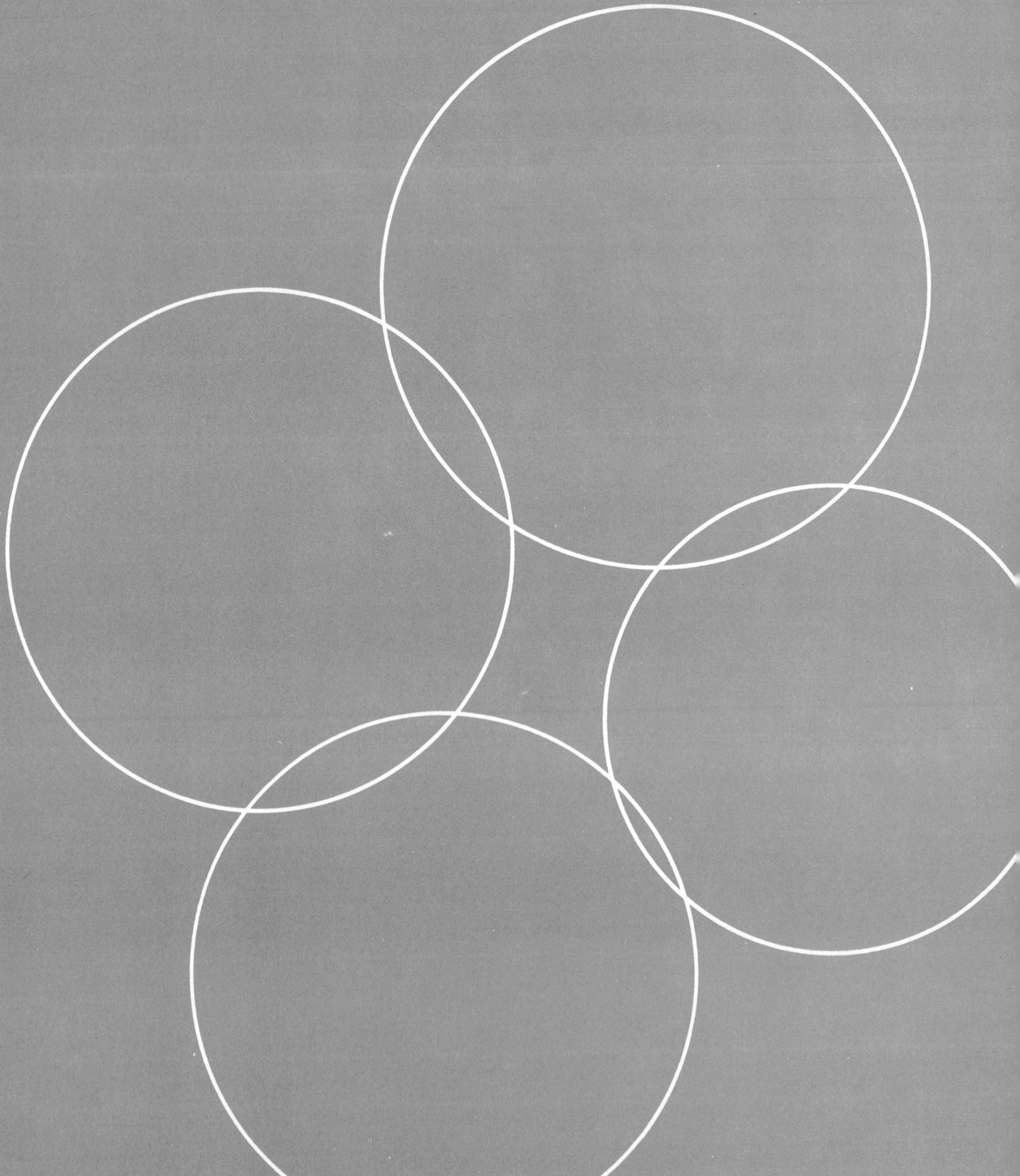

PART THREE

Managers at Work

Getting Things Done

8

North Star Prologue

North Star has successfully weathered the start-up of a new company, shift to new offices (involving problems with leadership), and preliminary murmurings of employee difficulties that suggested the establishment of a union (avoided by setting up an improved communications philosophy). The discovery that their job backlog was not sufficient to keep them profitable led to the establishment of a planning system. One of the most exciting events thus far was the offer of a merger with a major corporation—but on closer look they decided that it was not an attractive offer and turned it down.

One complication in the North Star organization chart was that in theory all four vice-presidents worked for Bert in his capacity as technical director (Figure 8-1). When Henry and Jo won a Bureau of Mines contract to do an underground coal mining systems study, a major argument erupted between Jo and Bert as to who would be in charge for technical matters—Bert, to preserve the organizational structure, or Jo, because she understood systems analysis. Henry was able to defuse the antagonism to a large extent by forming an ad hoc committee to review the organization in the light of numerous conflicts that had come up in recent months: Ab angry at Jim Pozzi, hired to prepare bid estimates and placed in charge of the library and plan files (though Ab's people made most use of them); Bert mad at Zeb for requiring that the technical department obtain advance approval for any book purchases; Zeb angry at Bert for not cooperating in budgeting; Bert mad at having to use the secretarial pool instead of having a personal secretary; Jo mad because she had not been granted top priority for use of the drafting room facilities when her work required it; and so on.

An effort to deal with these conflicts led to formation of an "organizational structure" committee, which turned out to be a very useful exercise. Bert brought Ab onto the committee, with the concurrence of the other members, and was chagrined to find out that he confirmed Zeb's comment about Pozzi's status being a thorn in the side of the engineers. Zeb learned about the organizational frustrations generated because all the secretaries worked for him. Jo was persuaded that there was merit in Bert's stand that all jobs should get centralized technical *management* (which she detested, and didn't plan to exercise in any case), provided that decisions on technical *substance* rested with the officer best equipped to make them. All hands agreed that the vice-presidents never really had worked for Bert, and that fiction should be laid to rest—but that there was merit in putting all the engineers and other professional people administratively under the chief engineer. And it was agreed that assignment of time for the back-room people should rest with Bert, though each of the partners would have control of technical decisions relating to jobs in his or her area. Thus, Jo would have full technical and professional responsibility for the Bureau of Mines job (something Bert had never wanted), but would keep Ab Jenkins apprised of what was going on and what drafting room help she required. Any part-time professors hired for the job would report administratively to Ab, but would take substantive direction from Jo. Indeed, Ab would be working for Jo in such a case, in effect.

As to the situation between Bert and Zeb, the latter agreed to assign two secretaries directly to the technical director, with Zeb responsible for their hiring and training, as well as for setting standards and procedures. And the two agreed that Bert had always been free to buy publications when needed, but in future he would see that such purchases were budgeted in advance insofar as possible, so that Zeb could plan his financial system with some sort of stability. The organizational structure they finally came up with is shown in Figure 8-2.

In some respects this new organization chart simply reflected an existing (but not always acknowledged, as indicated by the

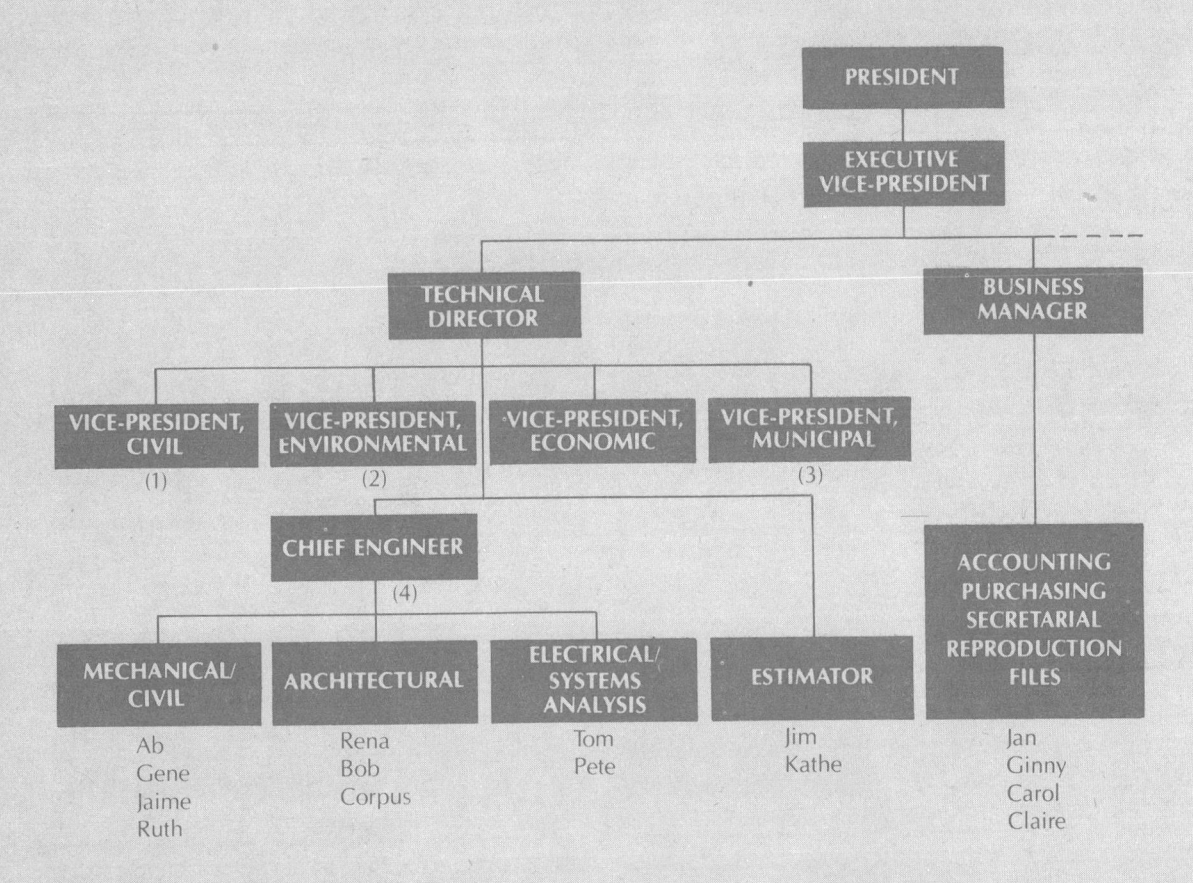

(1) Double-hatted as Director of Project Management (not shown)
(2) Double-hatted as Technical Director
(3) Double-hatted as President
(4) Double-hatted as Head of Mechanical & Civil Department

Figure 8-1. North Star Organization Chart

argument between Bert and Jo) structure. Pulling the officers out from under Bert made the chart correspond more closely to reality, as did establishing the broken lines of technical authority from Dick and Jo to Ab. The notation that the Executive Vice-President post was for overseas purposes only recognized the real purpose of this largely fictitious title.

In two respects, the new organization chart made some significant changes. One was the elevation of Zeb to vice-president—a senior officer on a level with the partners (though not an owner, as they were). This change had been proposed by Bert, feeling a bit sheepish at his rudeness in questioning Zeb's right to attend the "conflict conference." The other was the addition of marketing responsibilities to Zeb's billet. It was the first time anyone had specifically been charged with marketing duties, and reflected the need to put the firm on a more businesslike basis.

The separation of marketing from the group that would do the work once it was told called for resolution of a matter that had become increasingly troublesome: accurate estimates of what it would cost North Star to do a job. The municipal work, and much of the civil engineering and consulting work, was not billed on the basis of a bid but rather in terms of time actually used or a fixed fraction of the estimated construction cost. Work that was obtained competitively, such as the Bureau of Mines study, required a firm bid before the job started: a specific job had to be accomplished for a fixed price established in advance. This meant that the cost estimates were vitally important to the firm's profit and loss. When Zeb and Bert got together with Pozzi to discuss his procedure for making job

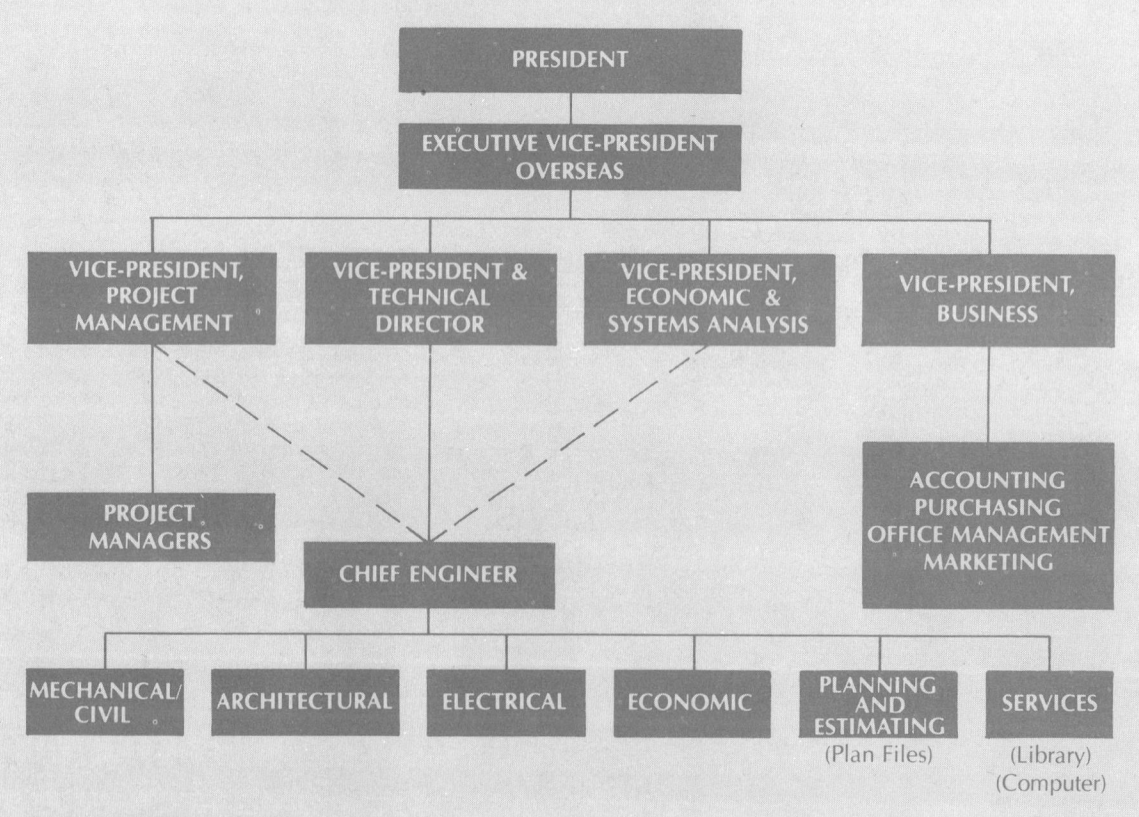

Figure 8-2. Revised North Star Chart

estimates, they were chagrined to learn that he never got any feedback on what a job had actually required in number of workdays per employee, but simply estimated on a judgment basis. His judgment was good, since he was an old-line civil and structural estimator, but many of the new jobs were in areas beyond his experience.

With Zeb's help (drawn from his experience on his previous job), Bert set up a manpower budgeting system for each job, and required the department head to concur in it before it was incorporated into an estimate; thereafter, the department was required to complete within plus or minus 10% of this estimate or make a variance request to Bert. This system worked fairly well, but it had two defects: one was a tendency for the departments to estimate high in order to cover themselves, which led to charges of padding by Jim Pozzi; the other was a tendency for design work to be slighted somewhat in the last stages of a job, when costs were beginning to press against the budgets.

What North Star Can Learn from Chapter 8

1. The desirability of a work plan (for jobs like the Bureau of Mines job)

2. The benefits of detailed work schedules in maintaining cost control

3. The need to understand the relationship between basic individual motivators and managerial attitudes—how attitudes affect motivation

4. The problems inherent in progressing work with and through parts of the organization where the manager has no direct supervisory authority

5. The elements of production, and how they can be utilized to improve the productivity of an organization

6. The role of controlling in monitoring cost control

Thus far, we have discussed the building blocks of management that enlarge an organization from one individual to a group and then to several different groups, and the fundamental management processes that make this enlargement possible. This chapter describes the management problems involved in taking an organization and making it produce something in four parts:

1. *Directing* – the manager's function in activating an organization and the nature of directing.
2. *Producing* – the process by which goods and services are created and the elements of the production task.
3. *Monitoring* – setting and meeting standards, scheduling and follow-up, incentives and productivity.
4. *Selecting* – picking the winners and retiring the also-rans, relating results to resources and opportunities, and identifying potential obstacles.

The big rewards go to the doers, who can enlist the energy and enthusiasm of employees to achieve the objectives of the organization and get results. Many managers believe that they are doing their jobs if they simply handle the work that comes their way, keep themselves informed about progress, and keep peace in the organizational family. But the really effective manager never loses sight of the real goal: to convert all the inputs of labor, material, and capital into outputs of higher value than the sum of what goes in. If this objective is not met, the finest communication, most careful planning, and best possible decision making will go for nothing, because it will not have been welded into an organization that produces.

Directing

directing

No matter how well a business is organized, how well the planners have worked out a strategy for action, or how well the personnel have been selected for their tasks, nothing happens until management directs all of this potential toward the targets that have been selected. The problem is analogous to that facing a breeder of racing thoroughbreds, whose stables are full of top-flight horses; nothing comes of all this investment and potential until the horses are put under competent jockeys and released from the starting gate. The secret of getting things done is effective direction of the whole organizational effort, by harnessing the strengths of all its employees toward a common goal. A new organization is no more than a lump of clay until its employees have been *taught* to do their jobs properly, and *motivated* to do their jobs *well*.

Directing involves *actuating*, or setting in motion, the men and women who make up the organization; *motivating*, or inspiring them to turn their energies and enthusiasm to the organization's tasks in pursuit of the common goal; and *achieving*, or actually reaching the goal being sought. The problems inherent in each of these tasks, and possible approaches to each, are discussed below.

Actuating

Six Actuating Principles

1. The first principle to follow in setting up a program to achieve a goal is to *select competent subordinates*—competent to perform the necessary tasks at their level in the organization. If people do not possess the basic competences, including the ability to learn, the enterprise cannot flourish.

2. The second principle is to *let them know what must be done*. It is surprising how many organizations somehow overlook the need for communicating ultimate objectives to their members; then management is surprised when subordinates do not live up to expectations they never understood to begin with.

3. The third principle is to *show them how to do their jobs*. Telling them what is to be done takes care of the "what," but not the "how." In a modern organization, buffeted by constant winds of change from within as well as without, the task of employee education is never done. In the early days of industrial enterprise, all training was left to the employee, but a modern industrial corporation could not survive if methods were left to chance in this way.

4. The fourth principle is to *give subordinates the resources they need*. This can mean proper tools and materials, a proper work environment, or proper authority to call for assistance when they need it. It is not unusual for an employee to be given a task, but not the necessary authority to do it efficiently. Thus, the worker must beg for assistance or take the long way around, with resultant inefficiency and a job poorly done.

actuating principles
selection of personnel

what to do

how to do it

How does Ab Jenkins show Pozzi "how to do his job" when his knowledge of estimating is more extensive than Ab's?

resource assignment

The fourth principle is to give them the resources they need.

job motivation

5. The fifth principle is to *motivate them to do the job*. This goal is the most difficult of all, because we know relatively little about what makes people want to achieve, or how to attain a close correlation between individual aims and organizational aims. It is more than happiness; employees can enjoy a job where little is getting done. It is a matter of harnessing basic human desires in a positive way so that people will work toward the objectives of an organization and in the process will achieve personal objectives. It is a matter of inspiring confidence that they can do the job, and enthusiasm for wanting to do the job.

removal of barriers

6. The sixth principle is to *remove barriers to the job*. Some work environments are so hemmed in with obstructing rules and hobbled with poor management that employee enthusiasm sickens and dies in vain efforts to surmount nearly impossible obstacles. If employees cannot believe management promises, if they see an atmosphere of unfairness, if managers appear to be out to serve their own selfish ends, if there is indecision or lack of managerial skill, they will give up the effort to contribute their part to the enterprise and become cynical and listless.

Methods of Actuating

actuating methods

In each of the following types of organizations, a different mechanism is at work to actuate the members.

group ownership

In a *commune*, everything is owned by the group and each member contributes according to personal abilities and utilizes according to personal needs. The Chinese collective farm and the Israeli kibbutz are examples, as were certain early religious settlements in the United States. In such a group, community ownership implies that each member is working for himself or herself; but group approval or disapproval is used to motivate.

fear

In an iron curtain *concentration camp* or exile settlement, the inmates are forced to perform work and are prisoners of the state. Here, the motivator is fear of deprivation; poor performance is punished by withholding of food or other privileges, and in extreme cases by death. The inmates are not even remotely happy, but productivity can be high nonetheless.

harshness

On a *hard-boiled construction crew*, when jobs are scarce and the foreman manages with iron fists, poor performance is met with immediate repressive action; management is interested in nothing more or less than a fair day's work. Despite the apparent lack of concern for group morale, such a work gang may develop a certain esprit born of the very ability to endure the hardships of the job.

salary

In a *piecework garment factory*, employees work in a loft or even in their own homes, and are paid for exactly what they deliver in the fashion of subcontractors. There is no job security and no concern with motivation, because the employees are simply selling a product and the price provides all the inducement needed.

needs satisfaction

In a *"senior citizen" enterprise*, retired people work at such undemanding tasks as envelope-stuffing for low wages, or perhaps on a volunteer basis with no wages at all. The purpose here is more to provide an atmosphere of companionship and mutual support than to achieve high production levels, and the incentive comes from the ability of the workplace to satisfy human needs for security and for being useful.

In a *government agency,* salaries are fixed by law and performance is graded by supervisors who make out periodic evaluation forms. There may be little or no probability of dismissal, and similarly no way in which the supervisor can reward performance with increased pay; but promotion comes largely as a result of performance evaluation reports, and these are prepared by the worker's immediate supervisor.

promotion

In an *informal work group* in a large industrial plant, members are drawn together by common skills and the accident of assignment to the same work tasks. Desire for group respect and recognition is an important motivator, but whether group approval relates to performance in support of organizational goals or to other concerns is determined by many factors (including the ability of management to recognize and deal with the group needs).

group approval

In each of these environments, some method of actuating is at work. Let us list them:

1. community ownership (self-interest);
2. fear;
3. harshness;
4. salary;
5. satisfaction of human needs;
6. prospect of advancement;
7. group approval.

As a basic condition, of course, people work for money. At a subsistence level (as in underdeveloped countries, where poverty and starvation always stalk the streets), money is a great inducement, and the offer of a job (or the threat of a lost job) is of paramount concern. As employees become relatively affluent, and their basic needs are met, they seek pay to satisfy other desires. An important need is for status or recognition (which may be as important to an employee in a promotion situation as the increased money). Another is the accomplishment of useful or interesting work. Job security may also be important, but other factors often outweigh it (as the University of Michigan survey described in chapter 4 suggests). Employees like good leadership, particularly employees with relatively little education and income. Employees are particularly anxious to realize their potential, but this desire can work both ways. On the one hand, a very competent person will not remain long in a post where he or she cannot advance to more responsible work. On the other hand, not infrequently an employee will refuse promotion or even request demotion if the conditions of the higher job are recognized as nerve-racking or beyond the employee's ability.

Which one or combination of these best fits the four partners? Which the drafting room group? Why?

Job Design

It is the task of management to define the job and to establish methods of work. In some organizations, jobs are defined in precise detail, down to the specification of which hand to use to pick up a part and to exact descriptions of how items are assembled. In part, such detail is necessary to acquaint employees with unfamiliar tasks (as the assembly of a new and intricate component); but it is also advisable because industrial engineering study often can produce a more efficient sequence of steps than the unaided employee or foreman. Thus Figure 8-3, an operation chart for a

job design

operation chart

simple assembly process in a factory, segregates the motions of the employee's hands into elements of "reach," "grasp," "carry," "hold," "position," "assemble," and "release," using principles of motion economy to work out the most effective way to do the task. In other organizations, job definition is left to the individual employee, sometimes because it is too simple for detailed planning but sometimes because management is shirking its job and improperly leaving this discretion to the employee.

the individual module

In a complex organization, each individual constitutes a module of four phases, as shown in Figure 8-4. He or she receives communications (as instructions or as information), decides what action to take, acts, and transmits communications (including feedback, which modifies the action).

job content

When the job is designed for an individual, the planner must determine *what the job is* and *how it is done*. The former element, job content, is based on the type of trained labor available, the possibilities for division of labor, the production processes suited to current technology, the product to be made, and the production facilities available. The latter

Figure 8-3.
Operation Chart for Assembly Process

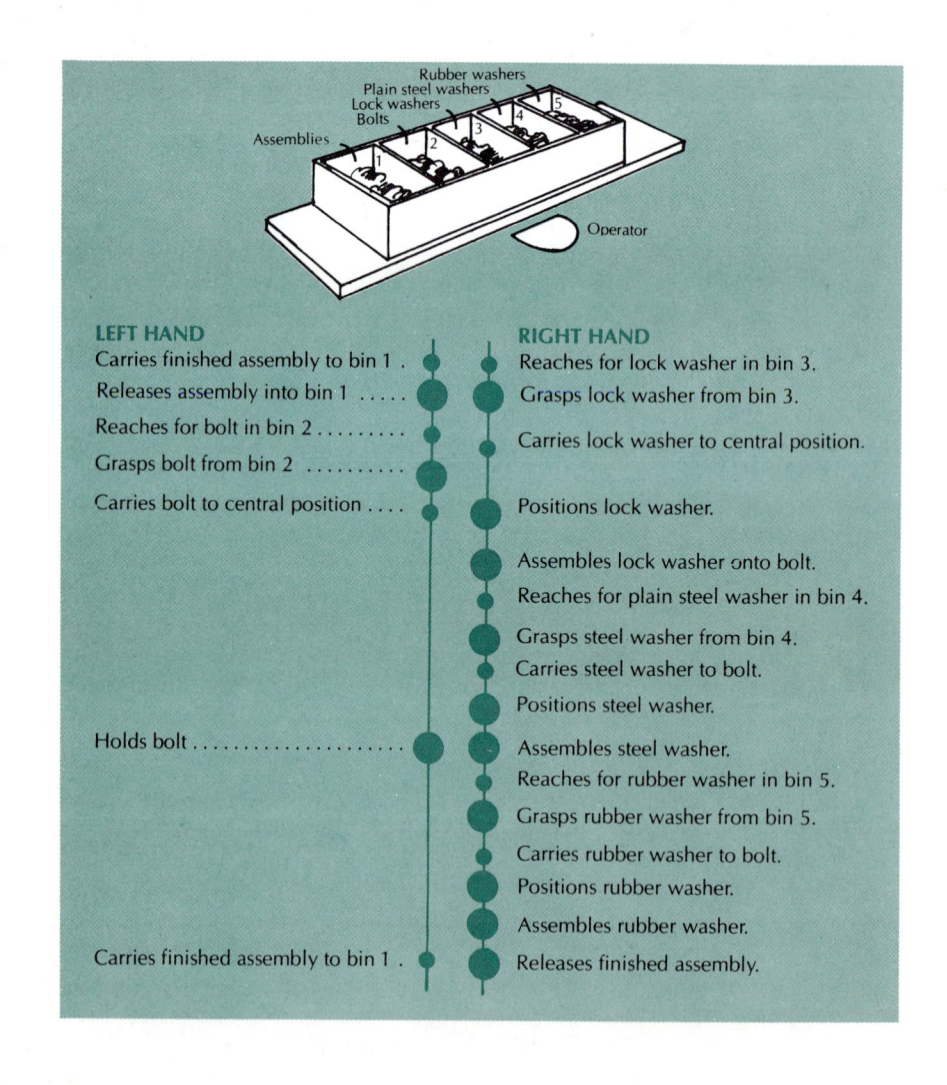

[Diagram showing bins labeled: Assemblies (1), Lock washers (2), Bolts (3), Plain steel washers (4), Rubber washers (5), with Operator position]

LEFT HAND	RIGHT HAND
Carries finished assembly to bin 1.	Reaches for lock washer in bin 3.
Releases assembly into bin 1	Grasps lock washer from bin 3.
Reaches for bolt in bin 2	Carries lock washer to central position.
Grasps bolt from bin 2	
Carries bolt to central position	Positions lock washer.
	Assembles lock washer onto bolt.
	Reaches for plain steel washer in bin 4.
	Grasps steel washer from bin 4.
	Carries steel washer to bolt.
	Positions steel washer.
Holds bolt	Assembles steel washer.
	Reaches for rubber washer in bin 5.
	Grasps rubber washer from bin 5.
	Carries rubber washer to bolt.
	Positions rubber washer.
	Assembles rubber washer.
Carries finished assembly to bin 1.	Releases finished assembly.

element, job procedure, is based on the flow of work through the plant, any physical limitations (in terms of available skills and facilities), the relative economics of worker and machine performance, and industrial engineering analyses. Job content might be defined as machine aluminum welding of material up to two inches thick. Job procedure would specify the type of machine, size of welding rod, voltage and current for the welding machine, speed of advance, type of inspection, and so forth. Normally, procedure contains far more detail than content, and management "gets the job done" by establishing detailed procedural specifications.

job procedure

Delegating

Since a manager cannot do everything personally, it is necessary to delegate some authority, so that subordinates will have the necessary power to make things happen. In Figure 8-2, the subordinate receives instructions, some of which convey the authority to transmit instructions—to act, in other words, on the basis of delegated authority.

delegating

Delegation has many pitfalls. If too little authority is delegated, the subordinate is denied the necessary tools for obtaining results, and cannot be blamed if performance is not up to par. If too much is delegated, the subordinate may act beyond his ability or knowledge, and improper actions may result. If delegation is too specific, the subordinate is needlessly and sometimes harmfully hampered. (A subordinate military commander may be empowered to call for air strikes if the enemy force *attacks*, but may lack the authority to do so when *intelligence is received* that the enemy is massing in preparation for an attack, since they have not actually attacked. Thus, the commander may lose the valuable element of striking first.) If delegation is broad, interpretation by a subordinate may be far afield from what the superior intended.

In a successful organization, delegation is essential, both to get work done intelligently and flexibly and to build experience in future managers. Different subordinates can accept different degrees of delegation, and usually subordinates can be delegated increasing responsibilities as

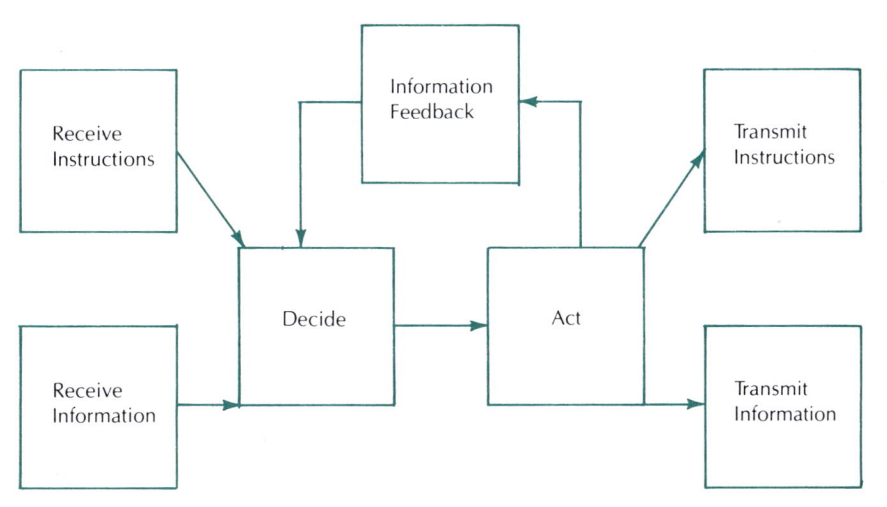

Figure 8-4.
The Individual's Process Module

they grow in experience and capability. When a superior has delegated responsibility for a task, relationships with the subordinate are rather delicate. On the one hand, the manager cannot constantly look over the subordinate's shoulder, because this approach destroys initiative (and wastes managerial time). On the other hand, the responsibility for delegated work remains with the delegator.

When a manager delegates authority to several subordinates, there are almost sure to be overlaps, where each of two or more subordinates tries to assume the responsibility for one task. This problem is particularly likely in the case of line and staff subordinates, where the former is authorized to specify the qualifications for a prospective new position and the latter is empowered to establish guidelines for personnel actions; or the former is responsible for developing shop processes and construction methods and the latter has the general task of specifying technical standards for work. Some managers view an overlap of responsibility among their subordinates as a healthy checks-and-balances system, to ensure that important jobs will not be overlooked.

> What are the advantages and hazards of Henry's delegation of responsibility and authority to Dick? Can you think of any changes he should make?

As essential as delegation is, there is a serious hazard inherent in any decentralization of authority. If there is only one boss who controls virtually all tasks, with all members of the organization reporting directly to him or her, that person can ensure that everyone understands the goals of the organization and the objectives of every undertaking. If top management must relay its orders through several levels, there is a strong likelihood that misinterpretations or intentional modifications will occur somewhere during the multiple transfer process.[1] In extreme cases, the changes en route may be so major as to reverse what the top executive had in mind, under the guise of simply "carrying out orders."

It must be remembered that delegation of authority includes the authority to make errors. The manager must accept the fact that errors will be made, as part of the process of learning. If the manager has been very thorough in transmitting *concepts* (the goals of the organization and the way they translate into group objectives) and *policies* (which practices and actions are generally acceptable and which are not), subordinates will have a sound basis for judging the correctness of their actions in carrying out delegated authority.

It is well to realize that the manager *cannot avoid* delegating some authority. No manager can control every machine all the time, or guide every choice of every subordinate. And it is well to recognize that the less a manager delegates, the less the organization will produce. This point is by no means accepted by all managers, but it is apparent that if subordinates have to check with the boss at every turn they will take valuable time from their work. Moreover, as we discuss below, their motivation will suffer if they must check with the boss for every little decision.

Motivating

> motivating

Admiral Hyman B. Rickover, father of the nuclear submarine, once stated that a competent person can do a job a hundred times faster than an incompetent one. He may have been right, but that is not the whole story. An incompetent but highly motivated person can do a job much more rapidly than a competent one who doesn't care. Indeed, the latter may not do the job at all if he or she is demoralized, with no interest in the organization. One of the most vital tasks of management, and one often neglected because in a technical sense it does not *have to* be performed, is to encourage subordinates by praise and attention and to show that the manager has their advancement and compensation (of many sorts) constantly in mind. No manager does the job alone; many subordinates contribute to each superior's good performance, and superiors must never lose sight of this fact.

Attitudes

We are concerned both with the attitudes of managers and the attitudes of subordinates—or, more specifically, how attitudes of managers form and develop the attitudes of their employees. Managers can fall into one (or more) of the following five categories, with respect to their attitude toward their subordinates.

attitudes

1. *Authoritarian.* These managers run a "taut ship," cracking down hard on any violation of their standards and delegating as little responsibility as possible. Production is obtained by posing a fear of the consequences of not producing—reprimands, suspensions, or dismissal. The word of the manager is final, and there is little chance for appeal. Managers of this sort seldom exist in pure form when the subordinates are educated and salaries are above the lower levels, but managers showing some of these traits can be found in a wide variety of organizations.

authoritarian

2. *Paternalistic.* These managers appear to have a strong concern for the employees, voluntarily providing employee benefits and perhaps paying wages far above the average, but they perceive such rewards as management gifts rather than as rights accorded to the employees—and in certain areas the employee privileges can be quite limited, depending on what the boss considers appropriate.[2]

paternalistic

3. *Conventional.* As the word implies, these managers walk the middle path. They are aware of theories of participation, and perfectly willing to make gestures toward employee involvement in decisions—but their main energies are devoted toward turning out the product, and they regard personnel matters as secondary. While their actions are not especially authoritarian or arbitrary, they are not characterized by any particular attention to the psychic needs of their employees; consequently, workers are likely to operate at less than full organization potential.

conventional

4. *Collaborative.* The modern manager of a progressive company is likely to fall in this category. Such managers make serious efforts to involve subordinates in decision making and to provide full information about pending activities. The rationale behind organization decisions is presented, though sometimes via a public relations approach that appears less than frank.

collaborative

5. *Developmental.* These managers devote attention to the development and progress of subordinates so that the latter are helped to reach their full potential. They delegate increasing authority, provide training, and take steps to support and encourage the instinctive desire of employees for professional growth. They accept the occasional mistakes that occur in the process of employee development as the unavoidable cost of constantly expanding the horizons and responsibilities of the organization members.

developmental

Which of these would Bert think fits his behavior with the drafting room?

Attitude Development

attitude development

People are not born with attitudes; they learn them through their life experiences. No one is born friendly or antagonistic or fearful; we develop such attitudes through our life encounters. Such early attitudes are likely to remain, however, unless conscious efforts are made to change them by the positive behavior of those around us.

Our attitudes can be changed by the impact of a social group or a work group, provided we accept the group's values and premises. Students who attend an undergraduate college where cheating is the norm, and then go on to a graduate school where the idea of "beating the system" has been replaced by a general standard of professional pride, will adopt the group attitude that cheating is both juvenile and "unprofessional." Similarly, certain undergraduate schools manage to convey such a high standard of institutional expectancy that new students soon take on the values of the institution and reject scholastic cheating as inappropriate.

group attitudes

A group attitude can be supportive or destructive of institutional goals. If the group has an informal standard that "four hours work for eight hours pay" is about right, it is exceedingly hard for management to get more work than this from the employees. On the other hand, managers who work positively to identify groups and match their goals with those of the enterprise can make group cohesiveness a significant supportive element.

attitudinal differences

Of course, inherent attitudinal differences derived from background and training will cause two people to see the same fact in entirely different lights. A professional soldier and a conscientious objector are bound to have different attitudes on the use of military force to repel an enemy attack; a doctor and a jail warden will have different attitudes on the need for medical attention by an inmate who has killed a guard and been injured in the process; a professor and a rural member of the state legislature will have different attitudes on demonstrations against the legislature by a student holding a state scholarship. What sounds entirely "reasonable" to a business executive may seem completely oppressive to a union member.

attitude change

Attitudes are never changed by argument. For one thing, people who hold certain attitudes may be *unaware* of these feelings, and when attitudes are lodged in the subconscious it is useless to combat them with conscious arguments. For another thing, people will not always admit to their *conscious* attitudes—say, as to race prejudice, need for status symbols, or feelings of inferiority. Here again, open argument will never address the real issues. People are bound to resist direct efforts to change their attitudes, because such efforts seem to strike at their very identities and personalities. (Witness the effectiveness of seemingly pointless commercials: "She knows who she is," "He knows he's a man," etc.)

Attitude change is a slow process, but there are steps a skillful manager can take to help it along. An executive can create an example that subordinates will seek to emulate, or provide unquestioned facts for employees to consider, or harness the efforts of the group in a new direction that builds a basis for collaboration (for example, soliciting their support for an organization's athletic team), or try to demonstrate that undesirable attitudes or actions damage the organization as a whole.

The following steps, incorporated into management behavior, will help to build effective employee attitudes:

steps that build attitudes

1. Treat people as individuals, which they are, rather than as elements of production.
2. Be generous in praise and recognition, but never when it is not merited, for the latter will be spotted instantly as insincere.
3. Include employees in decision making.
4. Keep employees informed as fully and honestly as possible.
5. Be sure that employees are paid for their efforts.
6. Initiate positive programs for helping employees to grow to their potential with the organization.
7. Give employees full opportunity to express themselves, positively or negatively (that is, when they have grievances to air or beneficial suggestions to propose).
8. Provide positive leadership, including training and development, so employees are conscious of effective supervision.
9. Delegate effectively, but with full recognition of individual differences in degree of authority that can be handled. (Do not give inexperienced subordinates enough rope to hang themselves.)

Motivating Attributes

Certain attributes will motivate the people who have them, but they are not constant in particular individuals because we are creatures of change. The prisoner condemned to life in a basement dungeon looks with longing at the thin shaft of sunlight stealing through his window and feels that freedom is an overriding psychological need. The constantly hungry person envisions a heaven only in terms of a place where there is plenty of everything to eat. As soon as one need is satisfied, other needs emerge. Fulfilled needs, it has been said, are never motivators. However, needs can be classified, as we noted in chapter 4, as follows:

motivating attributes

1. basic survival;
2. safety and security;
3. love;
4. esteem;
5. self-actualization.

Everyone does not experience these needs to the same degree, of course. Some people value esteem more than love (though perhaps because they feel the former is a gateway to "being loved"). Extremely able people may rate self-actualization above esteem. People of very low ability and ambition may not raise their inner targets high enough to see self-actualization as a need at all. In another vein, people who have never felt the lack of something may undervalue it out of ignorance (as a rich person may give little weight to survival or security, because these objectives have never been in question and seemingly never could be).

In an organizational situation, the same needs exist as potential motivators, but the environment is such that some of them are substantially met and hence no longer serve that purpose. In general, survival and security are satisfied already, so emphasis shifts to love, esteem, and self-actualization. These translate into the following attributes, with which management can and must deal:

organizational attributes

- *Respect of others,* including groups in the organization. People need the approval of their coworkers, and by bestowing or withholding this positive response the group can constitute a strong motivator to mold the individual's behavior into acceptable directions.
- *Achievement of one's own standards.* Esteem starts with self-esteem, and this arises from self-evaluation of one's performance on the job. There can be no esteem, regardless of what others may say, if the individual is failing to meet personal standards of performance.
- *Recognition by others of performance.* If we know we have done a good job, we seek recognition of that fact by others. Management has a priceless opportunity here to provide that recognition, both by verbal appreciation and by commonly recognized rewards for performance in the form of pay and advancement. Esteem is enhanced when the organization extends such recognition, and the individual begins to identify personal goals with those of the organization.
- *Assignment of responsibility.* A strong part of self-actualization comes from the assignment of additional responsibility, the delegation of authority that enables one to have increased control over one's environment and to succeed or fail in each project. Bestowing of trust by a supervisor indicates a shared collaboration in achieving the goals of the enterprise, and helps in identification with the organization, just as oversupervision connotes a lack of confidence.
- *Personal development.* It is not enough to delegate responsibility. Management must provide opportunities and training for advancement to jobs of greater responsibility and achievement. A well-run organization is in a constant state of change, with individuals encouraged to move as far as their innate abilities and drive will take them.[3]

Discipline and Morale

Morale is an indefinable quality that reflects an inner enthusiasm and confidence. It can exist in unpromising circumstances, and can be absent when an individual seems to be "on top of the world." The morale of a close-knit group in a prisoner-of-war camp can be higher than that of a victorious Olympic team, if the former is united in common opposition to extreme adversity while the latter is racked by disagreements.

Morale is affected by the quality of leadership in the organization. When leader and group are bound by dedication to a common goal, morale is high even if working conditions are extremely poor. Morale rises from common bonds in a compatible working group, and group members will go to extreme steps to avoid taking any action that is destructive of group goals.

Unfortunately, high morale can coexist with low productivity. The employees of an organization can be members of a close-knit group whose objectives do not coincide with those of the organization, and members can find themselves quite fulfilled in the work environment even though they are not turning out as much work as another group with lower morale. In this situation, the reward system in the former group is an

Unfortunately, high morale does not necessarily guarantee high productivity.

informal one, administered as group approval. It is the responsibility of management to see that the group goals are brought more closely into alignment with goals of the enterprise.

At first glance, it might appear that discipline runs counter to morale, but this is not so. An undisciplined group can become a disorderly group, with an environment that is unpleasant for many of the members, and the responsible members blame management for allowing things to come to such a pass that their work is interrupted or their well-being threatened. Moreover, they resent the spectacle of some members doing less than their share, or creating disturbances, without being called to account; it offends their sense of fairness, and they are likely to be even more upset with the offenders than is management (though the strong group norm against informing will usually prevent them from reporting the offenders directly).

discipline

The goal of management is to produce high morale with positive reference to the organization. Disciplinary techniques are crucial in developing positive morale. The old rule of "private reprimand, public praise" reflects the fact that employees want public recognition for their good performance but will become resentful and bitter if their shortcomings are exposed openly. Telling an employee to "get the hell into my office—I want to talk to you" doesn't constitute a private reprimand, because everyone can recognize the situation without hearing the dialogue inside the office. Public reprimanding tears down esteem, one of the major human needs, and should never be resorted to without compelling reasons.

Achieving

achieving

If actuating is setting a work plan in motion, and motivating is making the employees want to work toward organizational goals, achieving is getting results. The proof of the pudding lies in how effectively the organization achieves what it sets out to do. High morale leads to achievement, provided group and organizational goals are similar, because workers who are interested in getting the job done will compensate for managerial shortcomings by using their initiative to correct errors and omissions and to see that unassigned work is performed regardless. Alternatively, they will trade off resources with other groups to balance workloads without specific instructions to do so. But executives cannot and should not count on this sort of help, since its purpose is to prop up management which is not doing its job.

The Work Plan

There are four basic requirements for converting a new organizational task into an effective work plan:

the work plan

1. The task must be converted into work elements which conform to the organization's present practices, so that its initiation will not cause problems of jurisdiction or the need for unfamiliar skill divisions.
2. These work elements must be assigned to specific people who are on board or available, and these people must be made responsible for performing the work.
3. A scheme must be devised for coordinating all of the needed resources — personnel, materials, machines, money — so that this task will be completed properly, on time, and within the funds allotted.
4. Steps must be taken to insure that the spirit of the group will support the successful accomplishment of the task.

It occasionally happens that an organization of one sort takes on a task that fits another sort of organization, and, not recognizing the special nature of the task, overlooks some of the special requirements for success with this unusual assignment. For example, a company familiar with manufacturing industrial buildings is accustomed to going to the site with a nucleus of experienced men under a project superintendent, hiring the labor it needs in the local area, and making all decisions as they come up by drawing on the experience of the superintendent and two or three principal subordinates. It wins a contract to manufacture a large number of heavy structures for shipping coal by rail and waterway, sets out to accomplish this in its usual manner, and falls on its face.

Why?

Step one is the first problem. This company is not familiar with the requirements for repetitive production, where a product is shifted from one group to another during the productive cycle, and has not recognized that a change in practice will be required. Its unfamiliarity with assembly-line production leads to jurisdictional squabbles between supervisors as to who does what, lack of communication as to what has been done, and failure to understand clearly the great difference between one-time and repetitive production.

Step three is the next problem. Continuous production requires far more detailed work planning than a one-job project (as discussed under "Elements of Production," page 279). When multiple products are flowing through the plant there are frequent opportunities for interference, and machines must be scheduled in detail to make sure they will be available each time they are needed. While the person in charge can keep fairly good watch on all the processes of a one-product job, detailed planning and written schedules are essential for supervision of a mass-production job. Failure to recognize this fundamental difference insures constant small difficulties that contribute to a major foulup.

Does North Star have any problems of this sort with its job mix?

Giving Orders

Orders or instructions are an essential preliminary to getting things done. Work is not performed until someone directs subordinates to do something and advises how to do it. Orders are issued at all levels in the organization, from the chief executive officer talking to senior executives all the way down to the mechanic talking to a helper. It is not the tone or the words that determine whether a communication is an order, but whether or not the sender effects action by the recipient. Orders can be couched in request or suggestion form; for example, a manager might say to a subordinate, "I wonder if it would be a good idea to bring in a consultant on this job" or "Why don't you try reducing the price and see if it sells better?" A mechanic might tell a helper, "The supervisor wants us to get on that other job when we finish this, so maybe you ought to pick up the prints from the office." The fact that these orders are issued indirectly does not change the fact that the senior wants to have them followed.

giving orders

Many conditions must exist before an exchange is an order. In general, they are:

conditions for an effective order

- The issuer must be in a position of authority, delegated or assumed.
- The recipient must be a subordinate, at least in the area covered by the order.
- The order must relate to the business of the organization.
- The subordinate must be able to carry it out.
- The order cannot violate any strong standards or beliefs of the subordinate.
- The superior must be able to enforce it.

Nothing in this list tells *how* an order should be given, and there are many difficulties inherent in choosing the method. An order can be very specific ("Take the truck down to the garage, and bring the key back to me"), or quite general ("Get going on the new contract, and let me know if you have any trouble"). In general, the more rigid the order the less chance there is for confusion or misunderstanding — but the less opportunity the subordinate has to adjust matters if conditions change. Similarly, the more general the order, the more discretion the subordinate has to fit actions to circumstances — but the more chance there is of an undesirable or even an unethical action happening (possibly at the expense of the enterprise as a whole).

An order can be written or verbal. In some situations an order is verbal because time is too short to put it in writing, or writing it down would be absurd—in a football huddle, for example, or in a police emergency, or in a request to the messenger to bring a cup of coffee. In some situations an order is written because it is too complex for verbal transmission—as an order to a marketing manager calling for an elaborate advertising campaign. These are clear-cut, and the argument for making them verbal or written is compelling. But in other cases an order could be expressed either way, and the choice of which it should be is not always easy to make.

A verbal order between boss and subordinate implies a certain degree of trust, in that neither one will claim it was given in a different way if things should turn out badly. A verbal order implies a willingness to delegate details in many cases, since verbal instructions cannot include as much detail as written instructions. A written order issued in circumstances where a verbal order might be expected suggests to the subordinate that the senior is going "on the record," in case of unsatisfactory results or to prove at a later date that the subordinate got those specific instructions. Conversely, a subordinate may demand orders in writing when he or she disapproves of them, fears lack of support in case they turn out badly, or wants to be able to prove that the superior issued these orders in case they are questioned at higher level.

Sometimes written orders are used for other reasons. Perhaps they apply more to the position than to the particular incumbent, and the boss wants them to be standing orders that will apply to all holders of the job. Perhaps others need to know what the orders say—people in other departments who will be affected, members of the subordinate's work team who might otherwise question the instructions, service groups who will need to see the order before they will assist the subordinate. Perhaps the written details are necessary to prevent overlap with similar work in other departments.

Regardless of how the order is given, the manager must understand that issuing it is no guarantee that it will be carried out. For many reasons—procrastination, incompetence, laziness, forgetfulness, countermanding by a superior, or simply unwillingness to act—the subordinate may fail to carry out the order. Therefore, following up on orders is as essential as issuing them in the first place. Sometimes the subordinate is required to make periodic reports of progress; sometimes the superior asks how things stand at a later date or checks the scene of action to see if things are happening. The superior has a right and a duty to keep informed, so none of these actions necessarily connotes checking up or snooping—but there is a diplomatic and an undiplomatic way to do the checking.

However an order is given, it is important that it not surprise the recipient. The subordinate should feel that the order is consistent with overall plans for the group and with previous employee/employer discussions. If an order genuinely surprises a subordinate, the senior must ask what managerial omission contributed to this surprise, and determine how it could be avoided in the future.

Producing

Getting things done applies to all organizations, whether they make physical objects or provide services, but this section focuses on the former — getting things done in a manufacturing environment. We will not explore planning, design, and the other elements that must be handled in a manufacturing plant, but only production: getting things done.

making

The Production Process

Background

The earliest manufacturing was a one-person operation, where the individual craftsman performed every step in the process. Even when craftsmen drew together in guilds and work was done in groups, the process remained the same: each individual completed the whole job. We don't know what anonymous entrepreneur first organized a job into specialties, but the most articulate early writer on the subject was Adam Smith, who described in his *Wealth of Nations* (1776) how division of labor worked. He analyzed the operation of a pin factory, setting forth the following advantages of the division of labor that existed therein:

production

division of labor

1. It permits relatively unskilled employees to develop facility in performing a single repetitive task.
2. It saves in the changeover time required for an employee to shift from one activity to another.
3. It makes it economical to develop special purpose machines, because they will be in use full-time.

Nearly 150 years later, Frederick W. Taylor[4] found that things had not advanced a great deal. Conceptually, division of labor was perceived as it had been in Adam Smith's day, and management was not applying much skill or direction to the problem. Taylor, who effected a minor revolution with his techniques of job analysis, established four basic duties of management:

duties of management

1. Development of a science of production process analysis, which would replace the haphazard rule-of-thumb method then in vogue.
2. Development of scientific methods for selecting and training workers, which would replace the method of self-selection and catch-as-catch-can training on the job.
3. Development of a cooperative spirit between manager and worker, so the latter would complete tasks in conformance with scientifically designed procedures.
4. Proper division of work between manager and worker, with the former assuming proper responsibilities instead of leaving much of management to the worker by default.

Taylor's pioneering work broke the logjam, and within the next ten to 15 years the techniques of *work sampling* and *statistical quality control* had been developed. In large modern industrial plants these techniques have been applied extensively, along with more recent methods of industrial engineering.

Elements of Production

elements of production

The steps in a manufacturing process can be divided in many ways. One division often used is as follows: planning; organizing; implementing; controlling; supporting. Planning and organizing have been covered in chapters 3 and 6; the other elements are covered in this chapter, including controlling, though it is also explained in chapter 9. Controlling work output in a manufacturing process has a somewhat different meaning from controlling as an overall management function.

implementing

Implementing is the step of actually producing the product—the evolution toward which all the other steps and preliminaries are directed. There are many decisions to be made concerning how the product will be produced. First, will it be *mass-produced,* or run as a *unit production?* When we discussed the work plan a few pages back, the company in the example had been accustomed to the unit production method—turning out one product from start to finish before undertaking another—and was unfamiliar with the very different techniques of control involved in mass production, or running a series of products in various stages of completion through the shops at the same time.

Will the process be *continuous* or *intermittent?* In a continuous manufacturing process the product rolls through with no cycles or interruptions, like the production of taffy in a candy factory or soft drinks in a bottling factory. In an intermittent process the product comes in batches, like the production of fudge at home (where one pan is completed before another is started) or of beer in a brewery (where the brewing is done a vat at a time). The previous work plan example involved a shift from an intermittent to a continuous process as well as from unit production to mass production, making it a major change from that company's past practice.

Will the process be manufacturing *to order* or *for stock?* In the former case, customers have placed orders before the work starts, so the company knows exactly what is wanted. In the latter, the company is estimating what sort of products will be needed, and is speculating that it will be able to sell just what it makes. For some products, the distinction is meaningless; in a pencil factory, for example, there is no way you or I can order particular types of pencils to be manufactured. But in the house market, the distinction is crucial: a contractor who manufactures an expensive house on speculation, without a buyer, not only must guess at the taste of probable buyers but must also have enough money to finance the whole construction until the sale goes through. A company manufacturing water towers for municipalities obviously manufactures to order, just as a company making pickup trucks obviously manufactures for stock—and the processes are worlds apart.

Will the process be to *customer specifications* or to *standard specifications?* A 12-meter yacht built to compete for the America's Cup in international yacht racing obviously is built to precise and often highly secret specifications, with the aim of adding a tenth of a knot in speed, whereas the buyer of a 16-foot outboard runabout knows nothing about the complexities of naval architecture and must depend on the manufacturer to provide all the technical knowledge as to design and construction. A manufacturer who builds to customer specifications cannot set up any sort of assembly line or plan any work in advance, since each job is quite different from all the others, whereas standard specifications permit any necessary amount of advance planning and division of labor.

There are three steps in the process of getting things done, or implementing, in a manufacturing plant. They are *routing, scheduling,* and *dispatching*.

The first, *routing,* is the analytical part of the manufacturing process: planning what is to be done within the production phase, determining which machines will do which elements of the work, selecting the different human skills for the different parts of the job, and selecting the materials that will go into the product. Routing describes *how* the item will be manufactured, and insures that the shop capabilities mesh with the job requirements.

The second, *scheduling,* provides the *when* of the manufacturing process. It specifies when the item will proceed from one section of the shop to another, how long it will remain in each section, and how its manufacturing sequence will mesh with those of other items being produced simultaneously and competing with it for resources—personnel, machines, and so on. The aim of scheduling is to get all of the work done as close to the required dates as possible, with priority items given the first choice of facilities, but also to keep costly manufacturing facilities as fully utilized as possible. Accountants sometimes overlook the fact that a facility which isn't being used still costs its "rent" (the equivalent regular cost to the company to amortize its purchase price, upkeep, and the floor space it occupies). Thus, if a new process is worked out that doesn't need Machine A, so that the latter stands idle, some product has to bear the rental cost of Machine A, and it is no saving to avoid the use of an otherwise unused machine.

The third, *dispatching,* orders the *accomplishment* of the manufacturing process. It constitutes preparing the work orders of the various groups that are to work on the product, issuing the material requisitions that will insure arrival of the material when it is needed, arranging for preparation and issue of needed plans and specifications, and providing for related work such as inspection, packaging, and shipping of the completed product. In a small operation, dispatching is done by the line supervisors (in very small operations probably by word of mouth), whereas in a large manufacturing activity there may be a central shop planning group that specializes in the skills required for effective dispatching.

Chapter 9 discusses the control function in management operations as a whole. It should be mentioned at this point, however, that the manufacturing process itself includes a vital controlling function, which consists of monitoring *procedures, costs,* and *performance*. The line supervisors, principally the foremen directly supervising the job, have major responsibility for this control function. If a company allows any of these three to get out of control at the job level, it is in serious competitive trouble. Procedures are not sacred, and at times the workman can devise an improved method, but no employee should depart from specified methods for doing the job without good reason and it is the supervisor's responsibility to know about such changes and approve them. Cost

---

Of the four types of processes, which of the two categories (in each type) does North Star's work fall into? Would it be difficult for them to change any one of the four types to the opposite category?

routing

scheduling

dispatching

controlling

control means doing the job within the funds allowed, and performance control means doing a job of acceptable quality. In many plants, inspectors not responsible to the foreman (and at times not even responsible to the plant superintendent) monitor the work quality to insure that inadequate work is not allowed to leave the plant.

supporting functions

Many *supporting* functions are required to keep a manufacturing operation moving. Someone must buy and store the material required, keep the machines and buildings in good condition, constantly monitor the safety practices (which have a tendency to be neglected under the pressure of production), hire and train the new employees, and see to such personnel needs as counseling, grievance handling, health, and many welfare items. These support functions, while not directly within the line channel, are equally essential to a well-run organization.[5]

Analysis

analysis

Modern production is an exceedingly complex affair. Manufacturing plants do not just happen, nor does the manufacturer go to an architect and relinquish the task of construction and layout. Operating processes and sequences are not left to the foreman, who is a specialist in performing certain technical operations rather than meshing the various plant operations into an efficient whole. Special skills, principally those of the industrial engineer, are needed to set up a manufacturing line and bring it to smooth operation.

Arrangement

arrangement

In the earliest shops, the work stood still and craftsmen came to it. Since most tools were hand tools that could be transported easily, the question of proper shop layout seldom arose apart from matters of sufficient clearance and adequate light. Today the machinery is so large, and much of it is so special in nature, that all but the largest products are moved around to the machines rather than the opposite. Even in nonmanufacturing operations, proper layout coupled with selection of suitable handling equipment can effect great savings in operating cost. For example, an automated warehouse operated by the Great Atlantic Pacific Tea Company depends on an elaborate computer system that reads store orders, fills them, and directs a loading device to place cartons inside a delivery truck.

mockups

Many aids are utilized in devising such an arrangement. Companies use scale models of the machines—sometimes even three-dimensional models, when overhead clearance is important. For particularly important or complex installations, "mockups" are used, which essentially involve complete installation of all equipment in a simulated shop which resembles the real one in all respects except size and operability. Mockups are often built to quarter scale, so the completed "doll house" will be large enough for engineers to get in and try things for size and layout. In the most elaborate mockups, all piping and wiring is in place, conveyor systems actually work, and the entire scene is as realistic as the basement setup of an advanced model railroad hobbyist.

In earlier times, when power-driven machinery was expensive and scarce, layout was likely to be vertical, so that material could be lifted in one step to the top of the factory and thereafter lowered to successive work stations by gravity. This design was customarily used in flour mills, where the wheat could be raised once by the only piece of power machinery, and thereafter dropped vertically to the successive milling stages. Today, when ample power is available and the multiplicity of electric motors makes it easy to design separate conveyor systems, a plant is far more likely to be arranged horizontally.

With assembly-line production, all operations must fit an arrangement that meshes with the central assembly line. Subassemblies may have lines of their own, arranged to feed into the main line at just the point where the subassembly part is needed. It is not unusual for the inspectors to indicate defects by raising special levers on the part, thus switching the defective part off the main line at some junction point and sending it automatically to the repair section of the shop, after which it is returned to the line—much as a freight car might be sidetracked for loading and then returned from the spur line to the train.

When North Star designed the layout of their new building in the industrial park, they considered the need for smooth work flow by putting the drafting room group together in one section, and locating Bert's office nearby. Similarly all the officers were located in the same section to facilitate upper-level communication, and the stenographic pool was centrally located so it could serve the officers like the hub of a wheel (see Figure 8-5).

How important is layout for the North Star office, when material does not flow—only ideas?

Process Analysis

process analysis

Before a product can be manufactured, it must be analyzed in detail, to determine the choice of materials and processes—what it should be made of and exactly how it should be made. Even the simplest projects can be approached in more than one way, and it is not immediately clear which is best. Suppose that you are planning to frame your diploma, which measures 10½" x 13", and you find a frame 11" x 14" in the store. It will be too expensive to have the frame custom-made, so you decide to cut down the 11" x 14" standard frame. You go into your shop, pull the frame apart, mark the new dimensions, bevel the corners to your marks, and nail the frame together. Simple—but only after a lot of careful measuring and sawing.

Several of your friends see what you have done, and ask you to make frames for them. How do you tackle this job? Not as you did the single one, because too much measuring and adjusting would be required. Chances are you outline on a piece of plywood the frame you just cut down for yourself, and tack four pieces of wood on the plywood as a guide. Then you pull all of the frames apart, saving the nails. You mark all the frame pieces at the same time, lay them on a board and clamp them in place so the sawing is easy. Then you saw all of them at once. You then drill the ends for nails (avoiding the trouble you had with the first one with a tendency to split), lay them in the guide you made on the piece of plywood (an industrial engineer would have called it a "jig"), and discover you should have left openings in the guide for tacking in the small nails. You cut the openings and assemble the frames one at a time when all are ready. Then you get a glass cutter and another jig, and cut all the glass at once. And so on.

This relatively simple operation involved a good many steps, and the proper "process analysis" enabled you to work out an efficient way to perform the job. You can see how much more important it is when a product is relatively complex, and how unlikely the average worker is to come up with the most efficient way of doing the job without a great deal of study. That study is not the worker's job—it is the manager's job. Many managers fail to understand this.

The industrial engineer has a whole arsenal of tools for process analysis (including product analysis, which determines what goes into the product and how its parts fit together—a preliminary to deciding how to build it). These include *assembly charts,* similar to the "exploded" drawings that come with wagons and other items that are bought disassembled; *operation charts* that show what the worker does to put the parts together ("Put washer A and nut B on bolt C and screw down loosely," etc.); *flow process charts* that show the above assembly operations plus the transporting from one station to another and the idle time involved in the process;

process charts

Figure 8-5.
Spatial Schematic of North Star Office—Layout and Work Flows (Lines show paths of frequent interchange.)

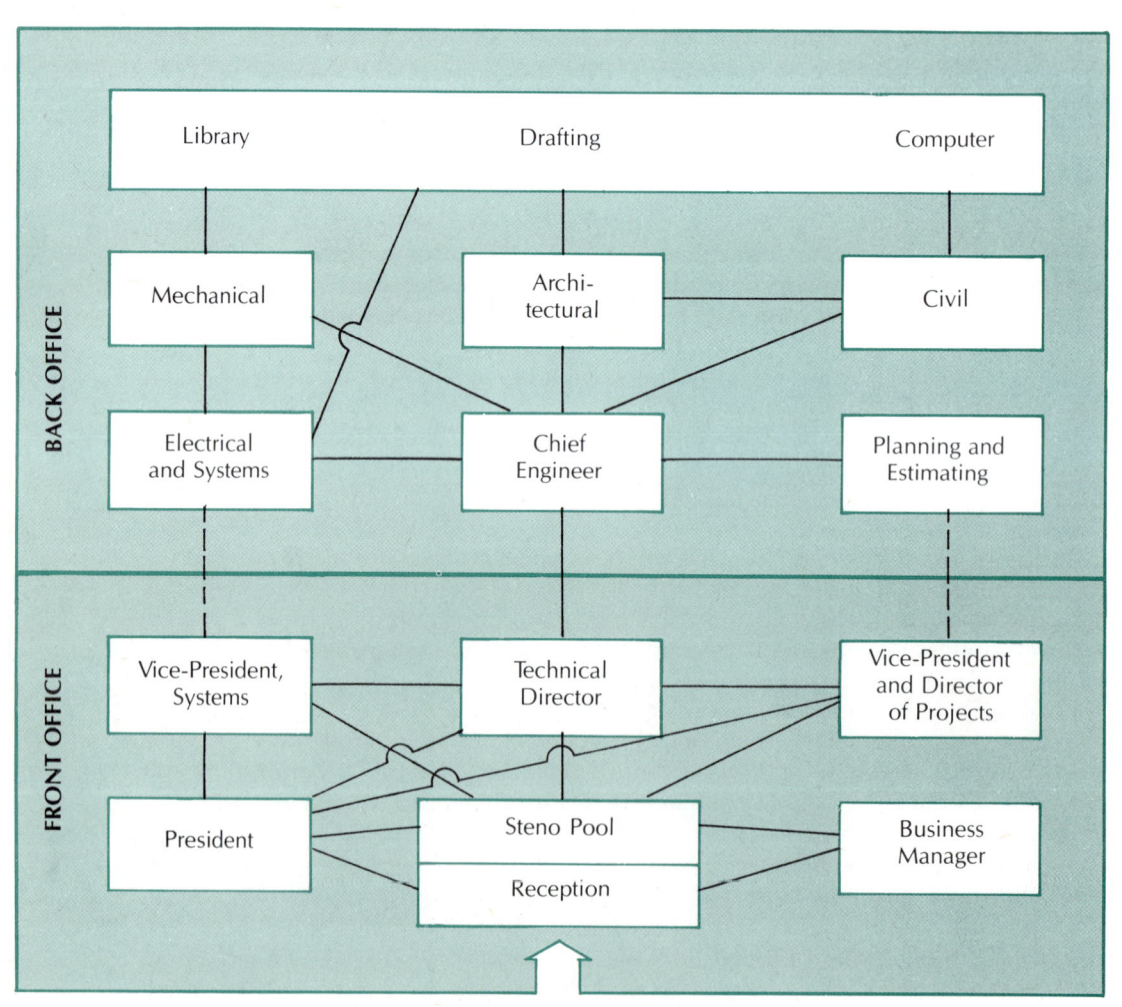

280
MANAGERS AT WORK

and *man-machine charts* that show the demands for various machines. When the importance of the process justifies it (as in manufacture of large quantities), *micro-motion charts* are prepared which show motions in extreme detail and timed to thousandths of a second.

Schedule Analysis

In the task of cutting down your picture frames, you probably had no need to schedule the activities, because you could see clearly enough what followed what and there was little chance that you would get things done in the wrong order. Since there was only one of you, moreover, the probability that "two" of you would want a machine at the same time was nonexistent. If you had charged for this job, however, you would have needed a schedule to estimate the labor time for each step in the process.

Two general types of charts are used for schedule purposes in manufacturing processes: *Gantt charts* and *network diagrams*. To illustrate these two types of charts, assume you have the task of manufacturing wren houses in quantity, and you are laying out the process. You have determined that the wren house, which looks like the sketch of Figure 8-6, will be manufactured by the following sequence of steps:

1. Saw out front, sides, back, roof, and floor.
2. Drill two holes in front, for entrance and perch.
3. Shingle roof.
4. Paint front and sides red.
5. Screw hook to back for mounting.
6. Paint floor and back brown.
7. Glue perch into hole in front.

schedule analysis

Gantt charts
network diagrams

The industrial engineer has a whole arsenal of tools for completing the process analysis.

8. Glue together front, back, sides, and floor.
9. Screw down roof.

On a Gantt chart, these steps would be as shown for the six work divisions (in a large plant, these would be separate shops or work centers) of sawing, drilling, shingling, painting, gluing, and screwing (Figure 8-7). On a network diagram, the same steps would be represented in a somewhat different way (Figure 8-8). Note that the network chart shows one thing that the Gantt chart does not—the operations that must be completed before a later operation can start. Thus in the second set of

Figure 8-6.
Manufactured Product

Figure 8-7.
Gantt Chart

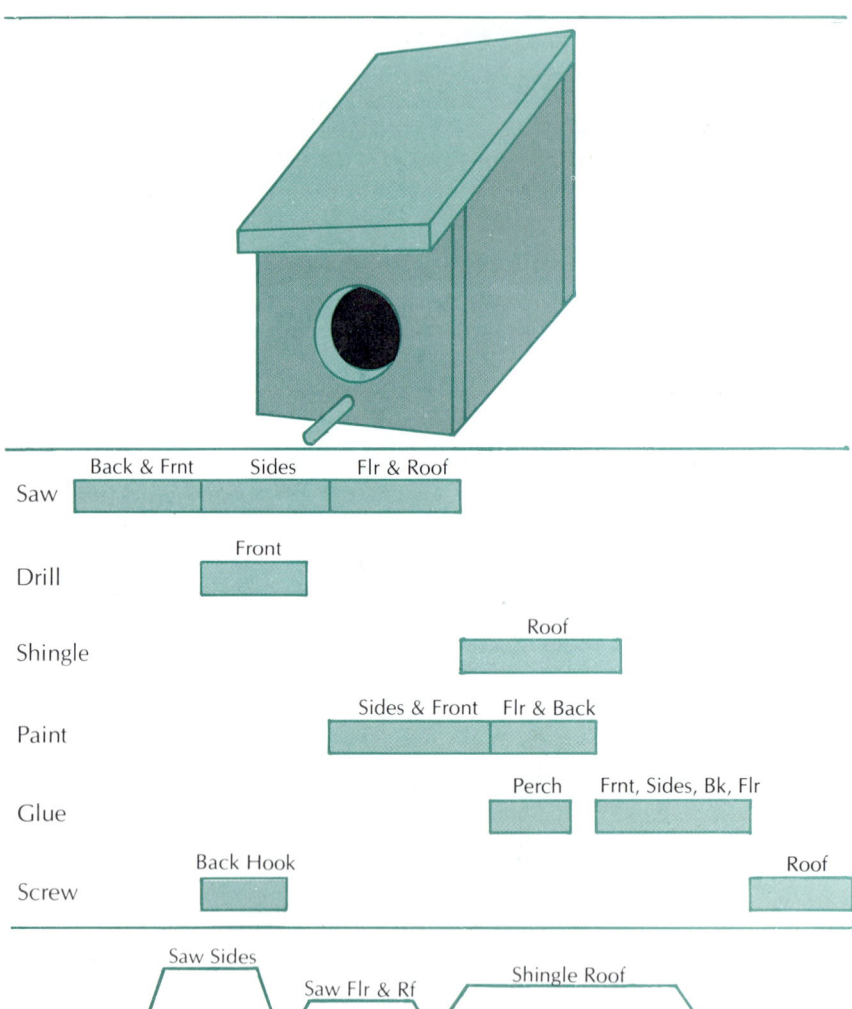

Figure 8-8.
Network Diagram

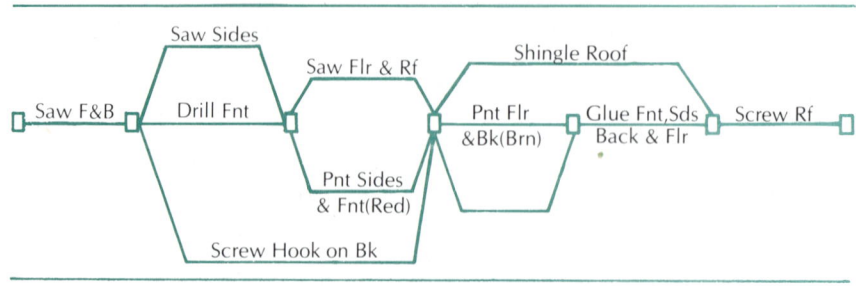

282
MANAGERS AT WORK

activities, the sides must be sawed and the front drilled before (1) the sides and front can be painted, and (2) the floor and roof can be sawed. In the former, items cannot be painted until previous operations on them are completed; in the latter, an operation cannot be performed in the sawing shop until an earlier operation is completed. Note that the Gantt chart shows by its length the elapsed time, and thus shows directly whether a work center is filled or has spare capacity; the network diagram, however, must state the elapsed time, because lengths do not necessarily indicate the elapsed time.

A special type of network diagram known as a *PERT network* (from "Program Evaluation and Review Technique") incorporates an additional feature: the probability of meeting any specified completion date. For each separate *activity* ("saw sides" or "shingle roof" are activities), three time estimates are provided: a shortest realistically possible time, the most likely time, and a longest realistically possible time. The system then makes the assumption (reasonably borne out in project management experience) that there is a 1/6 probability of the shortest time being sufficient, a 1/6 probability of the longest time being required, and the balance (4/6 probability) of the most likely time elapsing.

PERT

Refer to Figure 8-9, a two-activity network where the two activities are in series (one cannot start until the other one finishes). Each has a shortest realistically possible time (S) of 2 days, a most likely time (M) of 4 days, and a longest realistically possible time (L) of 6 days. The probabilities are taken to be 1/6, 4/6, and 1/6 respectively, as explained above. What are the times the whole job can take? If both the first and second jobs take 2 days, the overall time will be 4 days, but there is only one chance in 36 of that outcome (1/6 x 1/6 = 1/36). If the first job takes 2 days and the second 4, the overall time will be 6 days, with a probability of 4/36 (1/6 x 4/6). Similarly, if the first job takes 4 days and the second 2, the overall time will be 6 days with a probability of 4/36. We can calculate all possible times and their probabilities in this way, with the results as shown in Figure 8-9.

The tabulation of *cumulative probabilities* (probability of the job taking the indicated number of days or less) shows that, while the most likely duration of the job (the *expected time*) is 8 days, there is a 25% probability (1.000 – 0.750) that it will take longer than this. If it was vitally important to complete the job on time, it would be prudent to estimate that its completion time would be 10 days rather than 8, since we are some 97% sure it will make this date.

Figure 8-9.
Two-Activity Network (Series Elements)

Duration of total job (days)	Probability this No. of days	Probability this No. of days or less
4	1/36 (.028)	.028
6	8/36 (.222)	.250
8	18/36 (.500)	.750
10	8/36 (.222)	.972
12	1/36 (.028)	1.000

```
□  2 - 4 - 6  □  2 - 4 - 6  □
   1/6 4/6 1/6    1/6 4/6 1/6
```

When two or more jobs are parallel rather than in series, so that both must be completed before the next job in the series can start, as shown in Figure 8-10, the "expected time" for finishing the two jobs is longer than the most likely time (M) for finishing either one separately. Many project managers do not have a sufficient understanding of this phenomenon, and frequently lay out for themselves a schedule that they have very little chance of meeting. Assume that the two parallel events are the readying of the bride and the groom for a wedding by their various bridesmaids, ushers, and other attendants. The (S), (M), and (L) times for each are estimated as 2, 4, and 6 hours respectively, and we are trying to determine the expected time for both of them to be at the church so the wedding can proceed.

There is only one way in which the total time for both can be 2 hours—and that is if the bride takes 2 hours and the groom takes 2 hours. The probability of this is 1/36 (1/6 x 1/6). How many ways can the total time for both be 6 hours? There are five ways—bride 2 and groom 6, bride 4 and groom 6, bride and groom both 6, bride 6 and groom 4, and bride 6 and groom 2—and the total probability of all these is 11/36. By subtracting, we determine that the total probability of the total time being 4 hours is 24/36. You can see that there is far more chance of exceeding 4 hours than of beating it. Indeed, a properly weighted average of these times would give an "expected time" of 4.55 hours. That is, if the experiment were tried hundreds of times, the length of time would average to 4.55 hours.[6]

What system would be best for scheduling North Star's Bureau of Mines job? the nuclear power plant job?

Support

support

One of the most difficult things to manage in a manufacturing plant is the support functions. The division of labor concept makes it theoretically far more economical to centralize such service activities as maintenance, material procurement and storage, shipping, inspection, design and engineering, scheduling, job planning, and so on. But the line manager thereby lacks direct control over the tools of production, and must arrange for cooperation from other independent managers whose measures of performance are different.

For example, a central manager of stores may have responsibility for procuring, storing, issuing, and maintaining inventory of repair and manufacturing parts required by the line manufacturing managers. The manager is given this job as a specialist in materials management, an expert in the requirements of the task. But the probability is that the

Figure 8-10.
Two-Activity Network (Parallel Elements)

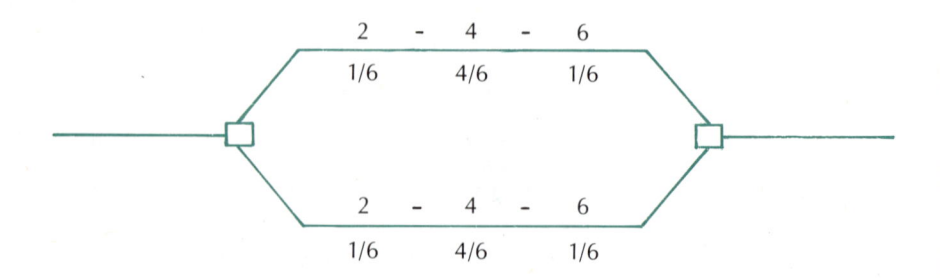

manager's performance is measured by such yardsticks as maintaining a low inventory, seeing that goods turn over frequently in stock (as few items in stock as possible which are issued very infrequently), and getting by with as few storekeepers as possible. Performance is not measured by how well the production jobs progress through the shop, how quickly material is issued after requested, or how seldom it is necessary to make a special order for material not in stock.

The maintenance manager is measured by how few assistants he or she needs, and how completely their time is occupied, rather than by how much (or little) time the line production managers lose because of machines not in service. (To measure in the latter way would be akin to measuring the performance of your doctor by how seldom you are sick—a system that has never caught on anywhere.)

As a result of these differing reward systems, there are built-in conflicts between the line and the support managers, and it takes a high order of negotiating skill and an inordinate amount of time on the line manager's part to cope with the support personnel whose help is so important. The problem is that the relationship is one-sided: the line manager needs them and they seldom need the line manager. Consequently, they occasionally play favorites, giving one manager a better break than another, and making the unpopular line manager look bad because their casual approach affects production levels.

The same thing is true to a lesser degree between production shops. A shop that typically comes early in the manufacturing process, such as a foundry that makes rough castings to be machined in later steps, always has the potential to hold up the later shops. When the date is finally missed, it may be some weeks or months later, and it is hard to focus the attention back on the shop that caused the delay in the first place.

One of the major problems is scheduling. When a service or support shop is somewhat late, or a shop early in the manufacturing cycle delivers the material to a later shop behind schedule, the later shop has to go on overtime or priority work in an effort to catch up. An important strategy for the later shop is to maintain very close relationships with the earlier shop, and attempt both to determine the status and progress of work in the earlier shop and to *influence* it by requesting high priority for the most urgently needed items. In this sort of situation, diplomacy is a very important skill, and the manager who has good personal contacts at many levels with related organizations is the one who gets the service.

In a new organization, managers typically underestimate the extent of difficulties that will develop between shops or groups, because these informal relationships have not had a chance to develop. Consequently, seemingly trivial factors cause jobs to be delayed excessively, and apparently no amount of top-level attention can cure the situation. The same thing is true, to a lesser degree, when a new product line is started, and support relationships have not had a chance to develop to fit the new work flows.

The most important lesson a manager can learn from this sort of relationship is the need to simply keep things moving. Almost more important than *internal* leadership functions are *external* "fixit" functions. When other groups seem to be failing in their responsibilities to the manager's group, it should be seen as a natural event, and the manager

external role of manager

must be geared to open the lines of communication with as little recrimination as possible.

Herbert Kaufman has described this phase of the manager's duties as follows: "A leader...devoting time to detection of situations [where routine breaks down] and to the issuance of messages that inhibit some actions, encourage others, slow some down, speed up others, change the directions and intensities of flows, open new channels, and so on, can often end blockages, prevent jams, and thus facilitate the vigorous performance of the basic process."[7] Certainly a manager who does not recognize the inherent tendency of the group to drift off course, and of support groups to work at cross-purposes to the manager, will miss the whole point of the job. A manager is not a member of a bureaucratic chain, whose sole task is to transmit orders down and information up. This aspect is a rather small part of the total function. More accurately, managers are fire-fighters whose main territory is the groups outside their own with which they and their personnel must deal.

Monitoring

monitoring

Work can be set in motion by means of the production control devices and procedures just discussed, but it will not stay on the track automatically. It needs to be monitored constantly to see that it is moving properly, and there must be effective feedback to correct the malfunctions before they become serious. These monitoring techniques include *setting and meeting standards, maintaining work flow,* and *scheduling and progressing the work.*

Setting and Meeting Standards

setting and meeting standards

The most important standard for the manager to set is the indefinable one of working for the good of the organization. In complex enterprises, with division of labor and many departments which are not directly concerned with delivering a product for a profit, there is so much difficulty in determining the productivity of a group that individuals can get away with destructive behavior almost unobserved. If these individuals are persuaded that the organization's success is closely tied to theirs, they will have less tendency to behave destructively. In the fall of 1974, when Pan American Airlines was in desperate financial straits and had appealed to the federal government for operating subsidies to tide it over, employees of the airline voluntarily donated funds to pay for advertisements seeking public support for the subsidies. Even granting that funds for the airline would help to protect their jobs, it would have made little difference in the case of *any one employee* whether he or she donated money or not.

In production processes, there is no objective way to set a standard. If management sets too low a standard through lack of thorough understanding of the process, foremen or experienced mechanics will raise the standard voluntarily if there is a healthy atmosphere in the group. On the other hand, if management sets an unrealistically high standard, either through ignorance or in a misguided effort to increase production, not only will the standard not be met but performance is likely to drop even lower than would otherwise be the case.

If a standard has been set, and the group continually fails to meet it, the situation cannot be allowed to continue. Either the cause for failing to meet it must be found and corrected, or the standard must be modified. Management looks ridiculous when it keeps in force standards that are not being met. Worse, it looks ignorant.

Where repetitive processes are involved, much care is taken in setting work standards. Processes that are repeated frequently in the plant can be studied by an industrial engineer or a time and motion specialist, and *standard times* can be established for such describable job segments as hacksawing a two-inch galvanized steel standard pipe or splicing a 100,000 CM armored electric cable. Jobs that consist of groups of job segments for which standard times exist can be placed on standard, and if the calculation is properly made there will be little dispute with the results. For certain processes, there are tables of *universal standard data* that apply in any plant. Where the job cannot be described in this manner, work sampling can determine how long a competent mechanic takes, with suitable allowance for rest, and a standard can then be established. Where jobs are so generalized or individual that these approaches are not profitable, it is still possible to take work sampling observations through the shop periodically in order to determine the percentage of time that workers are working productively or are idle. Not all the idle time is the fault of the worker, of course, and one purpose of such work sampling is to spot areas where enforced idleness exists.

standard times

universal standard data

How does all this relate to North Star's problem of maintaining design quality near the finish of a project?

Maintaining Work Flow

A manufacturing process is an incredibly complex set of interconnections. Look at Figure 8-6, which describes an exceedingly simple building job—a tiny birdhouse—and you will see that even here the failure of any element in the process will throw the remainder into confusion. Let the brown paint fail to arrive, let the wrong hanging hooks be received, let the saw department be temporarily overloaded, and the schedule falls apart. Managers function as essential expediters of this complex network by being spokespeople for, and leaders of, their groups. Imagine that the birdhouse construction is a repetitive process, with thousands of them being manufactured. Each of the six departments must have a manager who not only knows what is going on in the department but is also alive to signals from the other departments. Regardless of the number of jobs in progress, if each of the six managers needs only to contact one of the other five when trouble is brewing, the complex network becomes workable. The manager is the person who must make the work move, by receiving and acting on complaints from other groups (and by speaking accurately and authoritatively for his or her own group, which means readjusting priorities when necessary), and by registering complaints with other groups.

work flow

Consideration of this important duty of management will give a better understanding of what managers *really* do. The military model of management, with visions of the army commander issuing orders which fan out in all directions, flowing downward to be converted into action, is a misleading one. Top management gives very few orders. (Top management plans, sets policy, watches results, and so on—but does not issue day-to-day orders.) An organization starts at the bottom, where the work is done, and it exists to remove the obstacles that develop as that work proceeds. Top-notch managers don't have their heads in the clouds; they have their ears to the ground. A good manager is busy constantly; an idle moment is the signal to start worrying about parts of the job drifting away from their designed course without supervisory guidance.

The manager watches for deviations from and obstacles to the regular course of events. When one crops up, its seriousness must be determined and corrective action prescribed, if necessary. If action does seem appropriate, is it short-term or is an organizational change required? True, disorder is a fact of life, but if things are too disordered (so that emergency action must be taken frequently) a change in organization or procedure probably is indicated. It is the manager's job to decide what change is needed and then fight the battle to place the change in effect.

Scheduling and Progressing

scheduling and progressing

Earlier, we discussed the various types of work schedules. It is important to set up a good schedule, but it is more important to *make the schedule happen*. Some companies prepare very detailed schedules but somehow fail to issue them to the people doing the work—and then wonder why they are not followed. Schedules of the form shown in Figure 8-6 become extremely complex when the jobs are large: we find 8,000 activities for an electric power plant, 20,000 for a factory, and up to 50,000 for an aircraft carrier. No one person can keep track of a 20,000-activity schedule, or even understand it. Consequently, the schedule is subdivided; and the overall schedule for the whole project is likely to be a simplified network

The manager watches for deviations from and obstacles to the regular course of events.

that shows an entire subdivision (of hundreds of activities) as one activity (such as "install a 130-inch rolling mill").

Maintenance of the schedule requires knowing whether or not work is completed when it should be. Most firms that do complex scheduling have a progress group whose principal responsibility is to keep up with the status of work. (They have other responsibilities, such as chasing material, etc., but their principal role is information gathering.) At regular intervals (usually of a week), the progress personnel and the senior supervisors meet with the project manager, at which time the status of work is compared to the schedule with a no-holds-barred discussion of what went wrong and what must be done. Support and service supervisors should attend this meeting, because often it is their failures that have prevented the line supervisors from meeting their dates.

It is probably accurate to say that the average plant foreman or supervisor is far more concerned with technical matters than scheduling matters. Usually these managers came up through a trade, and their whole training is technical rather than managerial. Yet organizational failures are more likely to be failures to get work done on time than to get work done to proper quality. Consequently, the manager must redress this imbalance by giving extra attention to schedule performance. (It is a truism that if work is done on time, it will be likely to complete within cost, for delays and cost overruns are usually partners in crime.)

Selecting

Thus far we have talked about how to do what we are assigned to do. But selecting *what* we are to do is of vital importance as well. A company is not "getting things done" if it is doing the wrong things. Organizations fall in love with their routine, and imagine that what they are now doing well will always be worth doing. Examples abound of products that actually lose money every time one is sold, but the company cannot bring itself to abandon the item — probably because everyone knows how to make it and it generates so few internal problems.

selecting

A useful exercise for an organization is to make a *managerial audit* of its principal products, to find out what they actually cost, what they really earn, and which way they are headed. A company that does not have a few future stars being groomed among its products is a company headed for serious trouble.

managerial audit

Managers are paid to think in broad terms about what their groups are doing, because if they don't no one will. Particularly in a big organization, things are too complex and top management is too preoccupied with policy and outside contacts for individual departments and operations to get a very close look. A good viewpoint for meeting this objective is to ask, "If this department (this product, this service) were not in existence now, would we institute it, and if so, what would it earn?"

If you can ask that question of yourself, and come up with hard and thoughtful answers, you will be on your way toward managerial competence.

Summary

Only when management directs a business or public enterprise into action is there any payoff for all of the preliminary organization and planning. The employees must be both taught and motivated. Directing involves actuating (setting in motion), motivating (making workers want to achieve the organization goals), and achieving (actually reaching the goals).

There are necessary principles for actuating a program: selecting subordinates, telling them what to do, showing them how, giving them resources, motivating them, and removing job barriers. Some methods of actuating are: self-interest in outcome, fear, harshness, salary, meeting human needs, promotion, and group approval.

Management must design the job methods, rather than leaving this task to the worker. The design is built around the basic human module of receiving data, deciding, acting, and transmitting data. Job content describes what responsibilities the job entails, and job procedure defines the details of carrying it out.

Managers must delegate, since they cannot be everywhere at once, but delegation brings problems. If subordinates have too little authority, they will lack the necessary freedom to work efficiently; if too much, they can operate in ways counter to goals of the enterprise. Delegating is a way of training new employees.

Manager attitudes can be authoritarian, paternalistic, conventional, collaborative, and developmental. Managers can develop employee attitudes, working to change poor attitudes learned from past experiences or picked up from a work group. Positive changes are most likely to occur if the group will cooperate. Other steps for improving attitudes are to treat people as individuals, use praise, use participative decision making, pay them for their efforts, keep them fully informed, and help them develop their potential.

Basic needs of individuals are for survival, safety and security, love, esteem, and self-actualization; all of these can apply on the job. Morale is the quality of inner enthusiasm for the job, and is attained by helping workers to meet their needs. Discipline is important to morale, but while praise should be handed out in public, reprimanding must take place in private.

A work plan is needed to get results: converting tasks into work elements, assigning them to specific people, coordinating resources, and developing group spirit. The plan must fit the sort of work the company is familiar with. In production processes, management must plan, organize, implement, control, and support. The type of work must be defined: mass-produced, continuous, to order, to standard specifications, or the opposite of these. Implementing involves routing, scheduling, and dispatching.

Controlling is monitoring of procedures, costs, and performance. Supporting involves the assisting departments not in the actual production chain. Arranging the work place is of vital importance, as it determines the physical transport of the material from place to place. Process analysis involves setting forth exactly how the job will be done; schedule analysis specifies in what order it will be done and how jobs will mesh together in terms of time.

One of the manager's main tasks is obtaining support for his or her group with and from outside groups over which the manager has no real control, thereby keeping the productive processes moving.

Monitoring techniques include setting and meeting standards, maintaining work flow, and scheduling and progressing work.

Notes

1. Chairman C. Peter McColough of Xerox Corporation says he goes through memos and reports "pretty damn fast" because "I know that before I see them they go through fifteen hands, and I know what they do to them." Internal reports, in other words, will have been modified and adjusted so much in the process of being made satisfactory to each member of a large chain of subordinate executives that they are unlikely to express the sense of what the originator was trying to say—and they seldom will report anything that reflects unfavorably on anyone higher up in the supervisory chain.

2. Farah Manufacturing Company, an El Paso, Texas, producer of men's slacks, underwent a devastating strike and boycott by the Amalgamated Clothing Workers of America in 1972-74, despite an excellent physical plant and fringe benefits generally superior to union contract requirements: hospitalization, pensions and profit-sharing, free bus transportation, hot lunches below cost, and free turkeys at Thanksgiving. But the company reportedly overreacted to the union organizing drive, taking the view that any workers who joined the union were in effect knifing an old friend in the back, making it hard for organizers to gain access to some employees, and eventually firing a number of union supporters. The strikers didn't benefit in any material way from the strike—but they were reacting against what they saw as company harassment. (See "How the Union Beat Willie Farah," *Fortune*, August 1974.)

3. This encouragement can go too far. The modern corporation, constantly shifting executives from city to city in the process of enlarging their horizons, runs the risk of making their families rootless people who can never make enduring contacts. In the corporate environment, to refuse a move that brings advancement is to announce that one is lacking in dynamic ambition and perhaps unworthy of further promotion. Lately, there has been a corporate rebellion against such regular moves as the inevitable accompaniment to advancement.

4. F. W. Taylor, *Scientific Management* (New York: Harper & Row, Pubs., 1947).

5. In the McGraw-Hill Special Report, *Scenario for Survival (Business Week*, September 14, 1974), the deterioration of U.S. railroads is discussed. The report notes that the industry has survived "by cannibalism (stealing parts from one piece of equipment to repair another when material is not available), deferred maintenance, erosion of equity, and worsening safety..."

6. One time in every 36 the two would get there in 2 hours, 24 times in every 36 the two would take 4 hours, and 11 times in every 36 the two would take 6 hours (approximately, of course—not precisely), so the *expected time* is: 2 x 1/36 + 4 x 24/36 + 6 x 11/36 = 4.55 hours.

7. "Why Organizations Behave as They Do," *Interdisciplinary Seminar on Administrative Theory*, University of Texas, Austin, 1961.

Review Questions

1. What are the key principles involved in setting a program in motion?
2. What do we mean when we say management must "design the job," rather than letting labor design it?
3. What are some of the pitfalls of delegating too much authority?
4. What would be the characteristics of a manager with a developmental attitude toward his subordinates?

5. How do the five basic motivating needs of individuals fit into the usual organizational situation on the job?
6. What does a work plan do for an organization?
7. When should a verbal order be given? When should a written order be given?
8. Define routing. In what sort of job would routing not be necessary?
9. What is process analysis? How does it help management?
10. Describe the difference between Gantt charts and network charts.
11. In monitoring, what is the difference between setting and meeting standards, and scheduling and progressing work?

Discussion Questions

1. If you were designing a company to maximize incentives, how would you use the seven methods of actuating employees (salary, self-interest, etc.)?
2. Do you believe that it is impossible *not* to delegate authority? Explain.
3. If you knew you were changing your organization's type of task (as in the example of the industrial building company switching to heavy structures), how could you improve your chances of doing it successfully?
4. Think up an example of two companies: the products of one are mass-produced, continuous process, for stock, and to standard specifications; the products of the other are the opposite in each category. How would the requirements for managers in the two firms differ?
5. What problems do you think would arise in trying to ensure that a work group follows a schedule, when the group had no hand in preparing the schedule? How could you reduce the problems somewhat but still meet your required completion date?
6. Many workers resent the application of standards to their jobs, considering it to be a form of company speedup. How would you deal with this feeling?

North Star Case Study

Assume that North Star obtains a contract with the Home Builders' Association of America (headquartered in North Star's home city), to produce standard plans for houses of many different kinds. While North Star does have a contract, it is more on the order of a concession, in that it simply appoints North Star as exclusive representative for the Home Builders' Association. However, North Star takes all the risks that the plans will not sell. The arrangement is that member builders of the Association will buy the plans as they wish to, and the Association will get a share of the proceeds. The Association will advertise them in its monthly publication, but all other expenses (and all risk of producing plans that will not sell) are borne by North Star.

The contract requires that ten complete house plans and specifications be produced each month, and the total life of the initial contract is twelve months. So North Star is obligated to produce 120 individual house plans and specifications in a year.

1. What is the difference between the type of work North Star has been accustomed to in the past and this new assignment?
2. If the partners take this on as just another job, without any particular planning or recognition of the different nature of this job, what troubles would you foresee?

3. Recognizing that this task is quite different from what they have been doing, the partners want to plan in a way that will enable them to succeed in this contract. What sort of planning might they do to achieve this?
4. Do you think it would be better for them to turn the job down because it is out of their usual line? Or do you think the possibilities for expansion of this business justify the major effort needed to succeed on the contract?
5. Should this task be under Ab Jenkins, on the basis that it is preparation of engineering plans and specifications, or under the Project division, on the basis that it is a separate project? Why?
6. What kind of scheduling should be used to run this new contract? What will the scheduling do for the company? Should it be completely scheduled in advance, or only as they get to each part of the job? Why?

Suggestions for Further Reading

Brown, R. G. *Management Decisions for Production Operations.* Hinsdale, Ill.: Dryden Press, 1971.

Buffa, E. S. *Production Management.* New York: John Wiley & Sons, Inc., 1973.

Burnham, D. C. *Productivity Improvement.* New York: Columbia University Press, 1973.

Fleeman, R. K. *Productivity Bargaining: A Practical Guide.* London: Butterworths, 1970.

Gavett, J. W. *Production and Operations Management.* New York: Harcourt Brace Jovanovich, Inc., 1968.

Greene, J. M. *Production and Inventory Control Handbook.* New York: McGraw-Hill Book Co., 1970.

Groff, G. K. *Operations Management: Analysis for Decisions.* Homewood, Ill.: Richard D. Irwin, Inc., 1972.

Mayer, R. R. *Production & Operations Management.* New York: McGraw-Hill Book Co., 1975.

McBeath, M. G. *Productivity Through People: A Practical Guide to Improvement.* New York: John Wiley & Sons, Inc., 1974.

Mize, J. H. *Operations Planning and Control.* Englewood Cliffs, N.J.: Prentice-Hall, Inc., 1971.

Mockler, R. J. *The Business Management Process: A Situational Approach.* Austin, Tex.: Austin Press, 1973.

Starr, M. K. *Systems Management of Operations.* Englewood Cliffs, N.J.: Prentice-Hall, Inc., 1971.

Vollmann, T. E. *Operations Management: A Systems Model-Building Approach.* Reading, Mass.: Addison-Wesley Pub. Co., Inc., 1973.

Controlling

9

North Star Prologue

The North Star Company, learning from its initial contracts that it was deficient in a number of areas, gradually improved its organization and planning to a level more suitable to its increasing size and scale of operations. It survived some touchy communications and leadership problems within its own house, becoming more effective in the process. An offer to merge with a major corporation was rejected when careful decision analysis disclosed that it was not in North Star's best interests. As the company continued to get more work in several areas, arguments arose about the growing jurisdictional overlaps that grew out of this diversity of operations, and a reorganization was undertaken that would draw more precise organizational lines. The company embarked for the first time on fixed price contracts, which disclosed the need for more accurate cost estimates than had been made previously—and emphasized that North Star was deficient in many areas of financial and nonfinancial control.

The Bureau of Mines job came to North Star, and instead of a fixed price contract as they had expected it was a "time and material" job. This arrangement meant the Bureau would pay all allowable expenses, and the contracting officer would have to approve each item of work before any funds were obligated. Zeb told the others that this meant the firm would be audited: first there would be a pre-audit to establish North Star's actual overhead rate, which the Bureau would add to the labor costs in paying for the work; second, there could be a post-audit where the Bureau would be entitled to examine all the North Star books and personnel records to see if people really did work on the job as claimed. This meant the company would have to set up a record system, which Zeb thought it should have anyway for its own control purposes.

Henry was heartily in favor, and in fact wanted to add a few features of his own. For some time he had noticed that the weekly staff meetings frequently bogged down over questions of whether one job or another was on schedule, whether too much was being charged to one contract for the amount of work actually being done, or in fact what had been spent to date on the various jobs. When a client asked for an accounting, it always was a big effort to get the information together. What Henry needed was a weekly report that listed every job, along with the total amount to be spent and the completion date where one was established, and provided a running record of what had been expended to date. With such a record on his desk at all times, Henry need never fear a telephone call from a client but could always be reasonably well informed.

When he described his needs, Zeb said of

course that was a good idea and he would set it in motion, but it still missed the real concept of *control*. Henry's report would just *tell him* what was happening, when he really ought to be *having some managerial impact* on what was happening. The missing ingredient was some form of performance measure, so that the officers as well as the chief engineer (and indeed, every department head) could tell how well the departments were achieving their targets. The report, said Zeb, should provide a target each week for each job—a sort of running total of what ought to be achieved as of that date on the job, and what it ought to cost. The actual report of expenditures then should be coupled with an estimate of the percentage completion of each job. This information, properly presented, would enable the reviewer to see if the firm was on schedule and within its cost target. If more time or funds would have to be requested from the client, there would be an early warning to avoid last-minute pleas. And the same treatment, Zeb added, should be applied to the firm's overhead budget—the cost of running the office, buying supplies, travel, and so on.

When the time came to update the company plan, which had been done every six months on a rather haphazard basis, Jim Pozzi asked if they wanted him to participate. Bert explained that the feedback Jim was now getting on what jobs actually cost made him realize that another form of feedback was needed as well: there ought to be a more detailed forecast of worker availability, and the impact of each new job on this factor. Some of the problems in getting jobs completed, Jim said, occurred because far more work was scheduled for some weeks than the company could staff. The plan ought to include a composite manpower schedule, to keep the officers from promising more than they could deliver. Jim was given the job of developing such a manpower schedule and forecast, and it was agreed that it ought to be updated every three months. When the gist of this schedule was summarized on the weekly report, along with figures on how well North Star was meeting its manning forecasts and commitments, Henry felt for the first time that he was on top of what the firm was doing instead of just watching its operations from the sidelines.

One question still remained in Henry's mind. These various devices that they had installed to help control operations, and the various ideas on what ought to be controlled, had seemed to pop up on a rather impromptu basis from whomever the idea happened to strike. It seemed to Henry that in a well-run company (and he still wasn't sure that North Star merited that description) there ought to be someone whose specific responsibility it was to think of all these points and to know how to set up controls that would point out explicitly how they were doing. He thought about discussing with Bert the idea of giving Zeb such responsibilities, since the latter had the most experience in that area; but the innovations they had undergone to get the weekly report moving had taken a lot out of the group, and he didn't feel up to another brainstorming confrontation just yet.

Thus far the firm's accounting had been carried out more or less on a hand-to-mouth basis, with Zeb setting up the system and Jan Marovic, the senior secretary, doing the record-keeping and writing the checks in her spare time. With the new requirements for a weekly report, and for the data required by the Bureau of Mines job, it was clear that Jan would have to spend all her time on such records and relinquish her office management duties. Zeb recommended that they give her the title of bookkeeper (it didn't quite fit, but the level sounded all right), and that they recruit for a qualified office manager. Of the other girls in the office, Ginny had moved to the technical division and was entrenched as Bert's secretary, and she didn't want the responsibility of supervision. Neither Carol nor Clare was qualified to be office manager, and Kathe's special library skills made it necessary for her to stay on in the librarian spot.

Zeb recognized that the new office manager would have to be acceptable to everyone, even though she worked under him, because she would have the difficult task of supervising employees like Ginny and Kathe who actually worked for people in other departments. So he had the candidates interview with Bert, Jo, and Ab as well as with himself. A parade of candidates flowed through the office, and none was acceptable to all the interviewers. Zeb began to despair of ever finding a way out of this dilemma. He came to Henry to talk over what they ought to do, regretting that he had ever given the others a chance to review the candidates but acknowledging that it was too late now to change that.

The company was still trying to find an acceptable office manager when word came from overseas that Dick Boyer was coming home. He left behind a first-class project manager in Walter Shaver, who was the AID project director when the Natal job was under AID funding, and who came in with Dick when the AID phase terminated and the nuclear power plant job got underway. Dick had walked a fine line in monitoring the Barnhard and Walker job without upsetting them unduly, and had established such good relationships with the big electrical equipment corporation that they were hinting very broadly that he should get back to the U.S. to line up new jobs elsewhere in cooperation with B&W. He decided that the best move was to reestablish a U.S. base and seek to build up new large-scale projects with major corporations such as B&W.

What North Star Can Learn from Chapter 9

1. The general purpose of a control system
2. How to determine the sort of controls North Star needs
3. An approach to selecting good control indicators
4. The use of job standards (particularly in the drafting room)
5. The need to consider control requirements in drawing the organization chart
6. What sort of overall performance measures North Star needs
7. Some aspects of personnel control that might help to prevent unrest
8. An approach to controlling overhead cost
9. A philosophy for deciding what items to check on plans and specifications
10. How to look at marketing effort in terms of its payoff
11. The notion of management accounting as differentiated from financial accounting
12. A workable project control system

Controlling is the process of maintaining the desired standard of efficiency and quality in company operations. Products must be manufactured to specifications and delivered on time, expenditures kept within bounds, plans carried out as intended, sales and profit goals achieved, personnel administered equitably and effectively, plant and facilities kept in shape, laws and regulations obeyed; in short, the organization must live up to management and employee expectations. If some elements are controlled while others are neglected, the organization will function like a bird trying to fly with one wing.

In this chapter we will analyze controlling from three viewpoints:

1. *The control process* – principles of control, requirements and procedures for a control system, and organizational control structures.
2. *Types of control* – overall control at the top, functional control, and product control.
3. *Methods of control* – primarily budgetary or nonbudgetary, but including various types of management audits.

The popular notion is that the organization's "controller" is responsible for all these areas, but in fact the controller's main task is to keep tabs on where and how the funds are spent. True control—monitoring all aspects of the organization and acting to correct deficiencies—is the job of every manager.

The Control Process

Any operation must be held within certain limits if it is to achieve the intended results. In a small organization the need for control is not so apparent, since the aims of the enterprise are likely to be understood and shared by most of its members. Even a one-person organization needs some self-control, however; we do not always direct our energies along the most efficient paths, and we need desk calendars, reminder notes, and so on to help us control our affairs.

As the organization grows, its various members inevitably pull in different directions. Departments may become more concerned with competing than with cooperating. Specialty groups such as research, maintenance, personnel, and warehousing seek to build their own staffs, even at the expense of the overall enterprise. Individuals lose sight of organizational goals in the heat of promoting personal success. Some are simply dishonest, and misappropriate property or misapply time if not kept in check. Others, with the best of intentions, take improper steps through misunderstanding of company purposes or lack of guidance. Specific control actions are needed to prevent a large organization from drifting out of control.

In this section you will be introduced to *principles of controlling* an organization, *requirements* for a good control system, *procedures* for achieving effective control, and ways of organizing to facilitate control.

control process

Principles of Control

control principles

The fundamental principles for setting up control systems may be grouped under the headings of *why, what, how,* and *who*. We begin with why: the purpose of control.

Purpose of Control

purpose of control

A good management control system *stimulates action* by spotting the *significant* variations from the original plan and highlighting them *for the people who can set things right*. Controlling does not involve spying or trying to catch people breaking rules. Occasionally it uncovers improper or illegal action, but its purpose is to prevent rather than punish. It differs from financial accounting in this way: financial reporting shows what *has happened* for information purposes, whereas managerial controlling shows what *is happening* in time to set things right.

Control concentrates on variations that managers can do something about. If ski sales are down in a mild winter, financial reports will show the reduced income; but the control report doesn't highlight the problem, because the manager can do nothing about it. By contrast, if sales of one ski manufacturer are down while they are up for the industry, this fact is presented in the report with all possible supporting detail, so the manager can diagnose the cause and act accordingly.

Control systems should cover all parts of the company. Some firms establish detailed controls for production personnel, while assuming that overhead groups have no "product" against which to judge their performance. But a dollar spent on the library, or research, or personnel services represents no less of a drain on profit than a dollar spent on productive costs, so it is important to use imagination in finding ways to evaluate overhead performance. If no standards by which to measure an administrative operation can be devised, maybe the function is unnecessary.

Accounting figures must be accurate, even if they must be late as a result. A corporation does not publish its annual report until its independent accountants have certified it. With control figures, the reverse logic applies: they must be timely even if they are only approximately correct as a result. Telling a foreman that products are out of tolerance after the production run is over is like having a fire detection system report that the building just burned down, or a burglar alarm that the bank was robbed last night. The accounting department may require the complete story on a cost variation, but the manager needs an "early warning system" that reports before the variation becomes serious.

The purpose of control is to help the manager *respond* to a variation from plan, not simply to record it. It is not enough to say that something is wrong without gathering information on why it is wrong and where corrective action might be taken. If costs of a product are up from past levels, which part of the product is costing more, which department is responsible, and which supervisor is in trouble?

What to Control

A company that makes no profits will fail, and nothing else it does will make any difference, so top managers focus primarily on profits. But they cannot think only of current profits. Business must build constantly for tomorrow's profits, just as society constantly rears new generations. The control system cannot neglect the years ahead in its preoccupation with today's balance sheet.

Peter Drucker has described how profits should be analyzed to insure a successful tomorrow,[1] dividing the product line into the following categories (among others):

1. Present breadwinners
2. Future breadwinners
3. Repair jobs
4. Sleepers
5. Failures

product categories

Present breadwinners include those products that have made a profit in the past. Most present breadwinners are nearing the end of their useful life and may become liabilities before anyone admits it. Instead of taking them for granted, like privileged guests, the company should make them prove their continuing profitability each year—or retire them.

Future breadwinners are the profitable products of tomorrow; they are coming along, but have not made their reputations yet, so the strong men in production, marketing, and finance are reluctant to give them unqualified support. A good control system will identify potential breadwinners and provide them enough funding to develop, probably drawing support funds from present breadwinners in the process.

Repair jobs are so-so products that might pay their way if improvements could be made in design, materials, manufacturing, or marketing. Sometimes this approach works (e.g., the resurgence of Lincoln and Rambler models in recent years), but many "repair jobs" throw good money after bad. Management needs the ability to analyze such products objectively and withhold repair funds unless probability of success is high.

Sleepers are products that suddenly take off, usually because changes in market conditions make them very desirable. Levis were sleepers for several generations, until changing lifestyles caught up with their casual cut and old-fashioned durability. A control system for sleepers must sense the impact of developing shifts in tastes and markets.

Failures come in many forms: specialties that are supposed to enhance reputation but sell at a loss, monuments to company pride, favorites of top management, or products designed for a market that never materialized. The product review system must have enough discriminating power to determine the worth of these products and get rid of them before they become expensive white elephants.

Top management likes to focus on costs, because they are easy to measure. True, costs cannot be allowed to grow unchecked; but the purpose of an enterprise is to get results, not hold down costs. Sometimes a department undermines the company's future by failing to spend on such deferrable items as training, maintenance, or quality control. A good control system must not allow a shortsighted manager to starve vital areas in order to make a good short-term showing.

Positive results depend on a creative approach to organizational goals—and creativity usually costs money. A control system that hems in subordinates by jumping on every departure from guidelines, without analyzing where the operation is going, can reduce them to simple obedience—at a very low achievement level. Good workers need the freedom to disobey orders and violate rules when the gains justify such maverick behavior. A control environment that places rules first and achievement second will drag the organization down.

Record systems capable of reporting progress levels (and costs, when that is important) are useful to managers at all levels. For the largest and smallest units of a company—major divisions which are separate profit centers and individual job operations where work can be standardized— records can supply explicit performance information. But in less straightforward areas, useful performance measures are rare; overly general measures provide only crude or misleading signals. As an example, consider the use of overhead rate as a source of control data for an organization that works irregular overtime. Say a large machine shop spends $50,000 a week for direct labor employees turning out productive jobs, and $20,000 on shop clerks, schedulers, stock workers, and other overhead employees. Work is running behind, and the entire production crew (but not the overhead people) works Saturday at time-and-a-half. Thus, the overhead rate for this week drops from $20,000/$50,000 or 40% to $20,000/$65,000 or just under 31%. Top management notes the "improvement" in overhead rate and congratulates the shop superintendent on "getting the overhead under control."

deficient overall measures

Of course, many factors in these problem areas *are* legitimate candidates for control: the use of time, cost of products or particular overhead functions (absolute cost, not rate), use of labor, use of important equipment, quality, sales effort and results, amount of material in dead stock, advertising programs, maintenance plan, and so on. What *should be* measured is how well the function is being performed relative to standards for that sort of job. What *can be* measured often falls short of this ideal, because it is hard to evaluate performance at all times, even if standards can be established, and more often standards are unreliable or nonexistent. And what actually *is* measured can vary from nothing to factors that are insignificant at best and sometimes completely irrelevant.

How to Control

methods of control personal observation

Managers use many control devices. A *direct* approach is to visit the site in person. This technique works well when the operation involves something tangible such as building a house or painting a fence. No indirect reporting system could compete with on-site inspection in the latter case. But often there is no site to view—perhaps the assignment involves teaching new employees safety practices, perhaps the site is far away, or there are too many sites to visit, or the job is too complex for personal inspection to convey real understanding. Then, too, employees may interpret such a visit as management spying. Personal inspection, then, should be limited to small jobs or to a rather general overview of larger ones.

cost analysis

Perhaps the most *common* method of control is cost analysis. Sometimes actual costs may be compared with the original budget, as in evaluating the cost performance of an administrative unit. Sometimes unit costs may be compared with standard costs, as in checking the per-item price for a production group against the standard price

Reporting a product out of tolerance after the production run is like having a fire detection system tell you the building just burned down.

established for the item. Sometimes, as in flexible budgeting, expenditures may be related to the level of operations. For example, a medical unit may plan to spend a certain amount for the year, but if company operations expand and more physical examinations are required, the budgetary plan will provide for a higher budget target consistent with the increased operating tempo.

A seemingly *precise* control method is analysis of operating statistics. If the print shop's budget for the month is based on producing 500,000 items of printed material, then presumably a 400,000-item output would amount to 80% performance. But the number of items produced means little by itself; 500,000 report blanks or letterheads don't call for as much effort as 400,000 detailed specification sheets or assembly instructions. Quantitative statistical reports seem objective, in the sense that they present "facts," but they may measure the wrong factors or permit the wrong conclusions. Moreover, they cannot measure such vital elements as esprit, quality of ideas, customer satisfaction, and so on; as a result, managers leaning toward statistical analyses may overlook these things because they don't fit a quantitative framework.

operating statistics

Control can be *standardized* when applied to production or service processes for which standard times have been developed. If the steps in manufacturing a product can be divided into operations which can be precisely costed, management has an accurate guideline as to what the product ought to cost. Control is exercised by measuring performance

standard times

against that standard. Many industrial processes fall into this category, and the federal government is making some progress in developing standards for repetitive governmental operations.

As organizations grow, top management is tempted to guard against the increasing risk of large losses by trying to keep informed about more and more operations—and by bringing more and more control into the executive suite. The computer aids in this process, since it can collect and report massive amounts of data. This mechanical approach tends to emphasize budgetary control, since cost figures are most easily adapted to computer storage and reporting systems. The reduction in middle-level managerial authority tends to stunt managerial development and counter the decentralization that should accompany organizational growth. Some recent labor troubles have resulted from management overemphasis of numerical performance measures while slighting more subjective measures of employee motivation and well-being.

Which of these applies best to North Star? Why?

The controller can buck this centralization trend by concentrating on helping lower-level managers get the information they need to measure their own performance. Any variances should not be reported to upper management until these lower managers have received the information and taken what corrective action they can. Individual supervisors understand their jobs better than the controller, who sees only third- or fourth-hand financial reports; supervisors should help determine which records are more important than others. If managers at all levels can feel that the control department works for them, control will be more decentralized and more useful.

Who Should Do the Controlling

controller

The controller of a company or government agency is a staff officer who is not responsible for delivering the organization's product or service and commands no productive resources. Control records provide a superficial understanding of many departments, but the controller usually does not know how work really gets done or perceive the actual obstacles to successful performance. Control records offer partial *information,* but seldom indicate the *action* that should be taken. Since the line manager (not the controller) is held responsible for missing goals, only that manager has the authority to make line decisions.

Even within the line organization, control should be exercised as close to the scene of work as possible. Removing decision power from a supervisor damages morale, unless the reason for it is obvious. If a manager is relieved of the responsibility for deciding what corrective action to take, that manager will no longer feel accountable for the results. The management control system must place accountability squarely where it belongs and where it will produce the best results.

If lower levels of management are to control properly, they need as complete and timely information as possible. If jobs cannot be measured, managers tend to slough off responsibility. If they don't get information, they may not recognize deficiencies or understand that their operations are responsible. Ideally a supervisor should know the performance trend of every employee, the usage of material, and the time use of machines, and have access to information on other cost items. An awareness of the way each expenditure contributes to output will enable the supervisor to elicit maximum performance from workers, and management fails when it does not provide the necessary control information.

A control system operating at too high a level tends to measure the wrong factors, because a manager who is not on the scene must depend largely on records and reports. These tend to concentrate on (1) measures that are easy to evaluate quantitatively and (2) measures the manager is familiar with. A manager who came up through quality control, for example, unconsciously underplays other aspects of performance because they are less familiar. The supervisor on the job knows exactly what is important in that operation and what is not; thus, the supervisor should be consulted when the control system is set up.

Even if the upper-echelon manager avoids the pitfall of concentrating on the wrong factors, some factors must be isolated for measurement purposes. But as soon as the selection is made, subordinates will automatically concentrate on these factors, at the expense of all the rest. A manager known to be a bear on neatness will find everything freshly painted and shined for inspections, even if workers stole time needed for machinery repairs to clean up. A supervisor close to the job can spot such nonproductive shifts in priority, while a manager two or three levels up probably cannot.

Requirements of a Control System

A control system should stimulate action. It is not the *final* purpose of control systems to compare what is done with what should be done (in terms of costs, profits, production, and so on)—this comparison is simply the means to an end. It is no help to know that something is wrong unless we also *know what to do about it* and then actually *do* something about it.

control system requirements

Many control systems are based on accounting reports. Controllers often feel content if they develop reports that are *accurate,* and that *they can understand.* Suppose your doctor tells you after an examination, "You have obstreosis of the ductal tract." You don't know whether to laugh or cry, and you have no idea of how to make things right. Control reports must be understood by the managers who read them or they won't control anything.

Encouraging Decision Making

Since control systems that produce no action are useless, they must provide information for taking action. A typical decision situation consists of the following steps by management:

information for decision-making

1. Determine all possible courses of action.
2. Evaluate the costs and benefits of each course, and the probabilities that each course of action will be successful.
3. Select the "best" course of action (optimum combination of the possible payoff and the probability of its coming to pass).

In order for the control system to be helpful, it must be geared to the needs of the managers, at whatever level. Profit center managers need information before costs get out of line, and they need information on sales or receipts during the sales year or even earlier if possible. A "pro forma" (meaning approximated in advance) profit and loss statement shows the manager what the near future probably will look like, so that action can be taken in advance if necessary. A stock market analyst, commenting on the Allstate Insurance Company of Sears Roebuck, observed that "its budgeting and management systems are so good that the company could run itself." And the president of a rival insurance firm added that "Allstate is the only company in our business that knows now what its earnings are going to be not only this year, but next year, too." Granted that it is not easy to peer into the future, the decision steps can be greatly simplified if the control system embodies some elements of forecasting such as that credited to Allstate.

If the decision maker is a sales manager, the information must be keyed to the decisions that will be made: assigning salespeople to territories, deciding how territorial lines will be drawn, determining how much effort to allocate to each area, and assessing the level of promotion for each product. The control system for that manager must evaluate the factors that guide these decisions: how each salesperson is doing, what return a given sales effort produces for each territory and each product, and so on.

A foreman, in order to evaluate workers, needs to know how productive each individual is, whether each is becoming more or less productive, and whether the quality of output is up to par. In addition, in order to complete each job on time, this supervisor must know the progress of each job in comparison with the schedule; the status of needed materials; and what items are holding up the work. If the supervisor has cost responsibility, cost trends must be considered as well as time trends. Perhaps all of this information cannot be provided—but it is needed.

If control reports are evaluated on the basis of how well they encourage the appropriate managers to take decisive action, those which summarize after the fact and report status to the top managers would fail on two counts: they come too late for the managers concerned to take corrective action, and they are aimed so high in the organization that they miss the action managers.

Flexibility

control flexibility

Since the tasks of an organization change frequently, the control system must be flexible enough to respond accordingly. Perhaps on one job the need for quality is paramount, with cost almost no object provided the specifications are met. On the next, speed is the major requirement; on the next, it is most essential that the cost quotation not be exceeded; and on the next, nothing will count if the product cannot meet certain test specifications. The control system must shift gears and keep tabs on whichever element is most crucial.

The organization includes many types of people, and each type responds to a different control approach. On the production line, if piecework rates or other incentive systems are in effect, the workers understand the need for accurate production counts and labor time records; but in the research laboratory the employees would be up in arms if scientific production were assessed in the same mechanistic way. Salespeople may resent close time control, feeling that their sales volume is more important than their minute-by-minute work habits. Alert young managers will be very dissatisfied under the close supervision accorded timekeepers, and public relations people will chafe under the conflict-of-interest restraints that purchasing people accept as a fact of life.

The control system must conform to the different organization patterns that exist in the enterprise. In product-oriented segments, the cost system should report on product costs; in other segments, which perform certain work on many products, a system that tallies product costs will be meaningless (because those departments are responsible for only part of the costs on any product).

A company may have short-term and long-term jobs proceeding through the shops at the same time, and the time-response of the control system must be geared to fit the tempo of each. On a job that will take three years to complete, the "short fuse" cost reporting system of a two-day job is inappropriate, while a system that spots cost and time trends that signal overruns or other troubles far down the road is essential.

Most control systems are designed for double duty—providing information for the manager of the particular project, and providing oversight data for the manager's immediate boss and perhaps another echelon up as well. The idea is that control data should link each management level with the level above and the level below. From a plus standpoint, this approach keeps different levels of management in touch with the same developments and thus creates a system of checks and balances. From a minus standpoint, it is very hard to design a reporting and record system that provides enough detail for one level without also providing too much for the level above. Therefore, the system should have the flexibility to permit reading out *primary data* (the first level, with greatest detail), *data summary* records (a second level, of less detail), and *data summary analysis* (the highest level, with just enough detail to indicate which way the figures are moving and what is happening to the key ratios).

Focus on the Main Elements

There are two reasons why a single control system cannot incorporate every aspect of a company's operations. First, it costs far too much. Second, it will smother the managers with information. Kenneth Whipple, Ford Motor Company's finance staff systems analysis manager, described an approach to the recent 10% reduction in the 90,000 tons of paper used annually by Ford, citing an example of a daily report on parts shortages that had ballooned to 1000 pages: "It was just so damn big that nobody could possibly use it. That went into the wastebasket right away." Any report that is more than a few pages long will tax the ability of managers to read and digest. There is a sort of Parkinson's Law[2] at work on computerized control reports: they tend to expand to fill the capacity of the computer to turn them out, paying attention to what *can be done* rather than what *is needed*.

limiting control system coverage

If something is taking place in the organization that cannot be corrected by a particular manager, as a general rule that information need not be provided in any control report the manager receives. Out-of-control elements that are the province of a senior should not be reported to juniors. For example, information that the cash flow status of the company is becoming hazardous rightly goes to the treasurer, but there is no reason to send it to the plant superintendent, who can do nothing about it. Similarly, out-of-control elements that are the province of a junior should not be communicated to higher levels until the junior manager has had a chance to correct them. Thus, information that supplies are in danger of running out for a production line should not go automatically to the vice-president for manufacturing until it has gone to the material superintendent, who has a chance to set things right first. If the latter can take proper corrective action as the job demands, it would be a waste of time for the former to see the report. The few cases where such double and triple notification prevents costly variances are outweighed a hundredfold by cases where the senior managers are smothered by needless information.

The main requirements for any job, at any level, are to get assigned work done on time, within cost, and to proper specifications. These elements of *time, cost,* and *performance* are paramount; everything else is subordinate. Perhaps other elements must be controlled in order to keep one of these under control (such as seeing that employees check in on time and do not check out early), but unless they are clearly significant they should be ignored in control statistics. It may be interesting to know how much each employee spends each year on government bonds, how much is paid out to employees in the suggestion system, or who has given how much blood, but does anyone need the information? If not, don't publish it.

<aside>What would you use for performance measures on North Star's overseas job?</aside>

There are many elements that will measure performance *in some way*. The important thing is to select the ones that are *best*. This means picking measures that fit most closely with the goals (because the closer they correspond to the real goals of the organization, the less likely it is that employees can strive to meet those standards and still fail to meet organizational goals). It means picking measures that are easy to work with—preferably, measures that are already available from some other source. It means using measures that will show where the fault lies and who is responsible—and, hopefully, what to do to correct it.

Provide True Evaluation

Some control records provide information about the operation, but do not really indicate whether it is doing well or not. An example would be a report of jobs completed in a given period that did not indicate how many were *scheduled* for completion or a report on distribution of workers to different assignments that did not state whether personnel expenses fell within or over the budget. An almost sure sign of unsatisfactory performance is a progress report that describes problems surmounted, items started and completed during the period, material received or ordered, and all manner of information that cannot be compared with any standards.

<aside>prior period comparison</aside>

A very useful form of reporting is to compare performance for any period with a previous comparable period, so one can see at once whether things are better, worse, or holding their own. Another is to provide ratios which are carried over from one reporting period to another, to establish whether such ratios as *net sales to inventory, administrative costs to sales, current assets to current liabilities,* or *net profit to invested capital* are within acceptable range.

In boom times, a report showing an increase in sales may not be a true evaluation, because sales of competitors may be increasing faster. A better indicator is percent of market share, when this data can be obtained. In poor times, when decreasing sales suggest poor performance, a check against market share may show that the company is performing well considering the difficult conditions.

When a complex job is in its early stages, it is customary to compare the costs of completed tasks with their estimated costs, and carry this ratio forward to estimate whether the total job will come in under estimates. If tasks estimated at $100,000 are completed for $102,000, this approach would say that the total project will be completed at a 2% cost overrun. Experience shows, however, that the early jobs on such a large project are usually completed without difficulties (no design errors, material delays, or construction problems); thus, a project that is slightly over estimate during the early stages may have a substantial cost overrun by the time it is completed. Simple comparisons of this sort, that have not proven out in practice, must be avoided.

Standards and Procedures

This section covers the choice of standards for evaluating performance and procedures for establishing effective control of the organization. If there are no standards, opinions as to performance tend to be based on subjective or personal impressions and can vary widely. Even with good standards, if the control procedures are not explicit and mandatory there will be no policing of the standards and good performance will be just an accident.

Areas for Establishing Standards

Every manager is (or should be) aware of the applicability and availability of standards in manufacturing processes, and to a lesser extent in nonmanufacturing repetitive processes such as handling invoices, moving warehouse stock, performing janitorial functions, and so on. But there are many other areas where standards should be established if possible, even though the task is difficult and the manager may not entirely succeed.

applicability of standards

In personnel administration, most of the attention focuses on salary administration, probably because this factor is quantitative and thus amenable to close control. Very little attention is given to promotion standards (insuring that individuals are not promoted until eligible, setting fair but flexible eligibility standards, and determining realistic guidelines for probationary performance). Disciplinary rules in all but the largest organizations tend to be quite unstructured, so that the same offense may be met with a warning at one time and a discharge at another. There are few standards for obtaining various privileges which are important prestige items, yet the abuse of these privileges severely undermines employee morale. Personnel's promptness in dealing with employee grievances, reimbursements, reclassification, and similar matters is crucial to employees, yet the personnel department is seldom measured in terms of promptness and responsiveness; if any standard is used, it is likely to be the number of cases handled each month.

Ethical standards may be hard to measure, or to establish, but the area is of vital importance. If purchasing people are accepting meals and gifts from vendors, the fact will be known all over the organization in a short time, and it establishes an atmosphere of permissiveness and contempt for propriety that will tempt others to "get theirs" and spread an unfortunate shadow in many departments other than personnel. Top management must set the tone, because if managers casually divert company property or labor to their personal use they will not be able to hold their subordinates to a higher standard. (The broad question of ethics in business is discussed in chapter 16, "Management and the Public.")

Who are the in-house "customers" for Ab Jenkins' work? How can Henry use them to rate Ab's performance?

In service functions, such as maintenance or material issue, the "customers" in the organization have a very good idea of how well they are being served. In addition, the service supervisors know rather accurately what constitutes good and bad performance. Use can be made of these two evaluators, even though detailed standards cannot be established in the areas involved. Customers can be asked to rate the effectiveness of support, on a monthly basis, and these ratings will indicate whether the service work is tending up or down. Supervisors can set standards on a judgmental basis for the length of time needed for certain repair jobs, the number of issues a material clerk should be able to make per hour, and so on. If several different shops are involved, management will have several opinions to draw on. Because an experienced supervisor is proud of the department's accomplishments, an estimate of time needed for a job may fall below the standard management otherwise applies. It must be made clear, in this situation, that the standards are set primarily to develop control reports for the supervisor's use, not *about* the supervisor's abilities.

At higher levels in an organization, numerous kinds of standards may apply. Quantitative standards relate to costs, receipts, capital expenditures, physical production, return on investment, and various forms of expressing output in terms of input. Standards that are less definable (in that management may not know what constitutes "good" performance) can be measured in terms of relative performance compared with the past. Profit centers typically find their monthly performance compared with the same month a year ago (and when seasonally adjusted, *each* month can be compared with the *average* month to see which way it is tending). Each of several units can be compared with the unit norm (as sales of various company-owned service stations), or compared with competitor performance. Intangible factors such as morale, creativity, or cooperative behavior can be assessed by management audits, which seek to dig below the surface and elicit frank opinions and recommendations from the groups involved. When this action is taken, it must be clear to those being questioned that the information will be used in a positive way.

Application of Standards

when to use standards

There are times when standards should *not* be applied. If a supervisor is being asked to handle an urgent job on a rush basis, and must inspire superhuman efforts in the work team, there is an implied understanding that normal cost (and possibly normal quality) standards are out the window for the time being. Similarly, if the supervisor is asked to make a home for trainees, handicapped personnel, or problem employees, customary performance standards should be waived (though in some cases, particularly the second category, standards may well be met or even exceeded). If standards are developed on new or high-speed machines, and the supervisor is saddled with antiquated equipment, clearly allowances must be made.

Since the overall results are what counts, management really does not care what level of performance is achieved on partial segments of the job, provided it is made up elsewhere. The foreman may accept an overage in one work area to avoid waiting lines in a more costly area, to reduce material transport costs to a more efficient machine and back again, to eliminate an otherwise necessary operation, and so on. Perhaps this supervisor has found that if a piece of equipment is partially assembled on the work site (even though the work plan calls for delivering it disassembled), a costly shipment package can be avoided. *All* costs must be considered, not partial costs.

If original planning contemplated a large-scale operation, but operations had to be scaled back, the production-line standards will not fit the reduced production rate. In this case, new standards must be developed or judgmental standards applied. Conversely, if the estimates and standards are based on a certain output, and demand is higher than expected, the production team should be held to higher standards, since such costs as learning, set-up time, and tooling can be spread over a larger production run.

The principle of greatest payoff should be employed in applying standards. If a job is to be repetitive for a long period, it will pay to apply standards at the very start and throughout the operation, in order to gain the greatest saving. If it is one-of-a-kind, standards will not bring any results, because the work will be finished before they can be shaken down into accurate and workable form. If the machine rate pretty much establishes the standard and enforces it as well (the worker has to keep up with the machine, and can't possibly go any faster), any application of standards will be an exercise in uselessness.

How Control Is Effected

Some standards, particularly in manufacturing, take the form of allowable variations from a norm. If the norm is cost, the allowable variations are on the high side only (obviously it makes no sense to limit the amount by which cost can be under the standard). If the norm is in terms of specifications, as a designed dimension, the allowable variations (the "tolerance") will be above or below this dimension by a stated amount. Figure 9-1 shows a *control chart* for measuring the trend in dimensional variation (points connected by heavy solid lines) with regard to the design dimension (solid center line), within the tolerance limits (dotted lines).

control charts

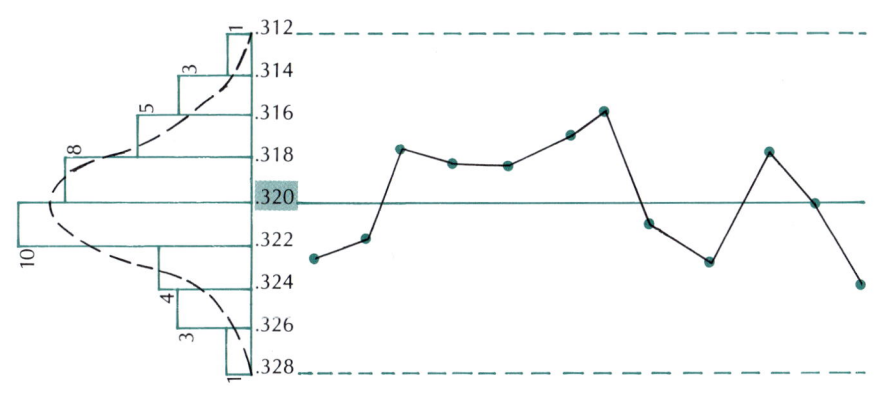

Figure 9-1.
Statistical Tolerance Chart

The bell curve at the end is a smoothed representation of the actual past manufacturing tolerances for a sample of 35 (shown on the *histogram,* or bar chart). The tolerance limits are spaced at three *standard deviations* on each side of the design dimension. (These limits represent the envelope within which over 99% of the manufacturing variability would fall if the manufacturing process were remaining *in control,* with no increase in the past average variability.) An inspection of the results in Figure 9-1 for 12 manufactured items shows none out of control and no appreciable trend toward growing variability.

When an item is very important (such as equipment involved in a major space program), every piece manufactured will be inspected, perhaps several times. When a failure would not have a catastrophic effect, only a representative proportion of pieces will be inspected. For the run shown in Figure 9-1, perhaps five out of every lot of 100 would be inspected; as long as this check shows that the manufacturing process remains in control, no further inspection is necessary. When variations start increasing from past norms, the number inspected will increase, thus imposing more stringent controls and seeking to catch the onset of defective production before many defective items are made.

applying job standards

When job standards are applied, most of the labor force must be able to meet them with reasonable effort. Figure 9-2 shows the result of a task performed by 76 workers. One person completed the job in the range of 170 to 180 seconds, five completed it in the 180-190 range, and so on as shown. The average time achieved by the group was 216 seconds, which was taken as the target time. Three people exceeded 250 seconds and one

Figure 9-2.
Job Duration Histogram

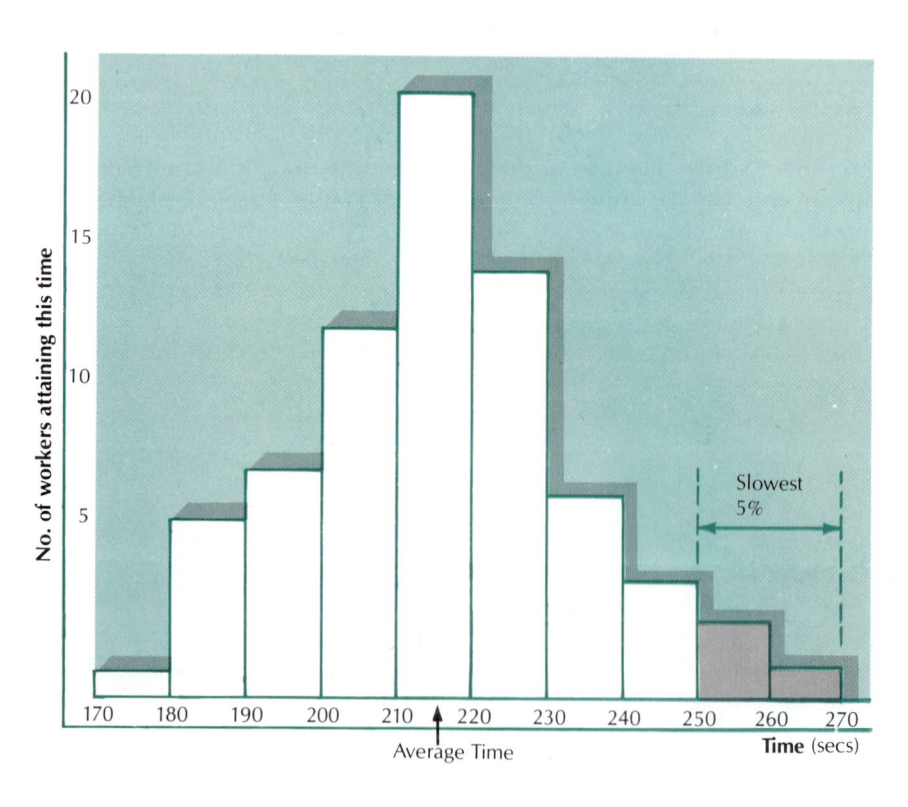

person exceeded 260 seconds. The *minimum standard* (time which approximately 95% of the force could better) was set at 250 seconds. Some managers are reluctant to set minimum standards, for fear that many of the force will ease up and seek only to beat this easily attainable standard. It may be preferable to set an *expected standard* (216) knowing that half the group can meet or beat it, and believing it to be a realistic incentive target for the other half. All hands will be required to meet 250 seconds.

Organization for Control

If the organization really means to operate on the basis of management control, there must be a philosophy of establishing objectives at all levels and of judging performance on the basis of meeting those objectives. Many organizations really have no stated objectives, and just blunder along as they have done in the past. In such enterprises, no one really is in charge. Each element in the organization runs its own show to suit its own goals—which may be diametrically opposed to those of the organization as a whole.

Operating by objectives means that the supervisor must understand the difference between administering and really managing. The administrator is a supervisor attempting to survive in the work environment: playing it cool, not rocking the boat, running things more or less as they have been in the past, and hoping to avoid criticism. The true manager takes charge of the work environment, changing it as necessary, imposing tough standards, and requiring subordinates and associates to produce in the interests of the organization's objectives.

organizational requirements for control

The administrator is a supervisor attempting to survive in the work environment.

We are all familiar with the traditional pyramid organizational structure, where a subordinate at one level manages the next lower level. Figure 9-3 shows such an organization. The chief executive (Level A) has three principal assistants (Level B). Tracing the line control path from manager B-1 through Levels C, D, E, and F, we reach a work team at Level G. The cross-hatched blocks represent the linking supervisors through which direction and control from the chief executive flows down, and performance reports flow up. Organizational theorists who advocate abolishing hierarchical structures forget that it is only through these essential linking supervisors in the hierarchical pyramid that control standards *supporting the organization's goals* are transmitted. If such standards are not transmitted through this linking path, employees do not really know what the organization expects of them, and they will relax into bureaucratic behavior where their own goals substitute for the organizational goals they do not know. Administrators who are not managers tend to assume that somehow the proper understanding of goals, and the proper imposition of standards and controls, will filter through to the working level even though they take no managerial action to make it happen.

One organizational hazard in an active *staff* organization (such as a controller group, which establishes standards and *records* performance against standards in its reports to management), is that supervisors will

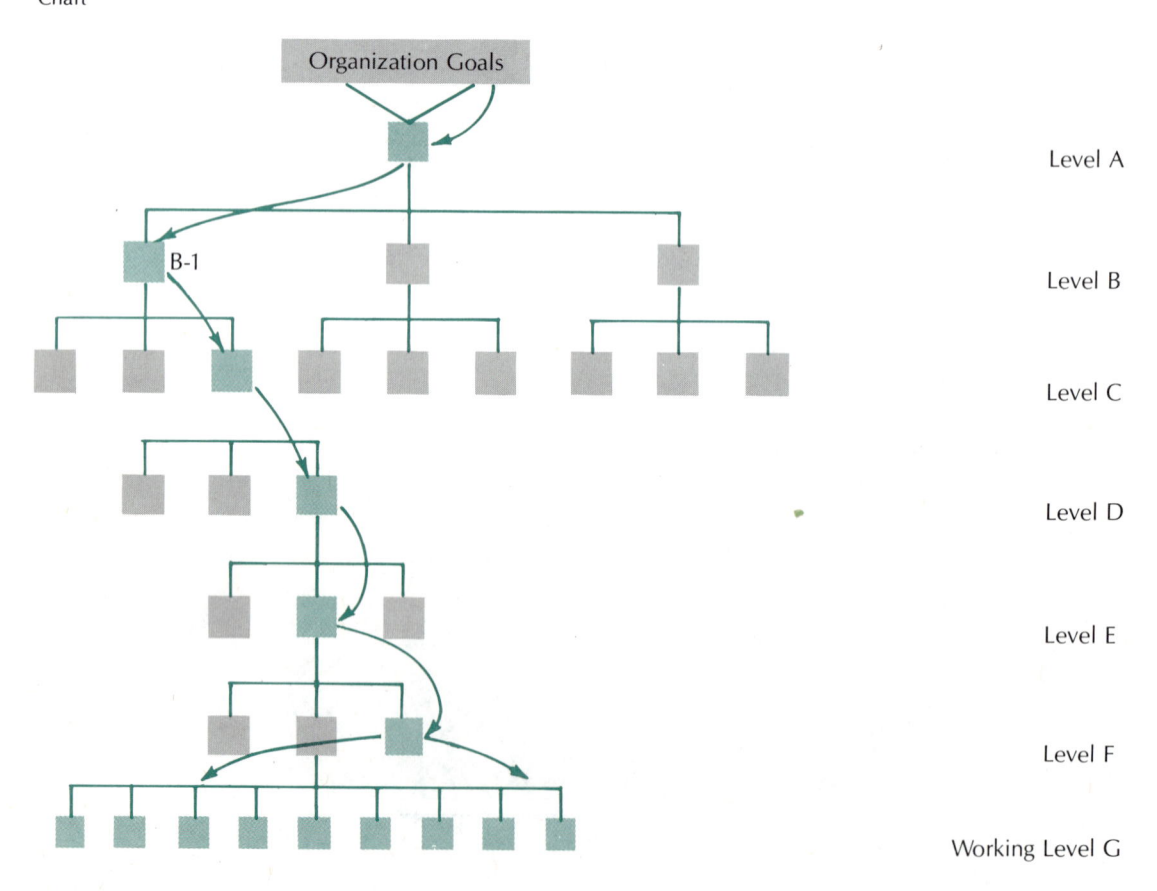

Figure 9-3.
Pyramidal Organizational Control Chart

tend to expect that group to *enforce* performance. A supervisor who labors under this misconception will consider it his or her job to "get the work out," with record-keeping left to the controller. True, the supervisor is paid to get the work out, but that includes doing it right and meeting proper performance standards which adequately support organizational goals.

An important organizational requirement is that no staff manager ever be able to insist on secondary goals that interfere with the primary goal of profitability. Some organizations concentrate so much energy on secondary issues—seeing that all positions are defined in writing, that bond sales are pushed, that personnel improvement courses are developed, that affirmative action programs are supported, and so on—that the harried supervisor forgets to monitor issues of paramount importance. All of the above-mentioned matters are important, of course, but profitability is essential, and the organizational structure must reflect and reinforce this priority.

One organizational device that aids in achieving overall control is the *centralized control unit*. The Watergate scandals so blackened the reputations of certain White House staff officials that the whole concept of an executive staff suffered in the public eye. Yet a busy top manager (whether the President of the U.S. or the chief executive of a large corporation or government agency) faces so many demands that a strong supporting staff can serve as an invaluable extension of his or her talents. Senior military commands have long had such an institution in the office of the Chief of Staff; several large corporations have experimented with an Office of the President unit. Such a unit, known to be acting for and as the chief executive, can review the performance of senior subordinates, conduct management audits, analyze inadequate performance, and recommend corrective steps. Members of the unit take no *action*, and all of their reviews and recommendations are understood to be directly on behalf of the chief executive.

centralized control unit

When a manager uses several subordinate units that are similar in composition and functions, it is possible to evaluate performance by using the key individuals from one unit to inspect another unit, as assistants to the overall manager. In the military, a unit commander with several ships or combat groups under him will schedule an inspection of ship or group A, and will designate individuals from ship or group B to accompany him on an inspection, during which specialist officers of B will inspect corresponding functions of A and report the findings to the unit commander. A unit manager of several similar supermarkets or other stores can do the same thing. This avoids the need for a large staff, and insures that the inspectors will be looking with a practical eye, since they are in the line part of the organization themselves and are aware of practical problems.

Is Zeb something of an "office of the president" for Henry? How?

Types of Control

The previous section examined the general requirements for a control system, the principles of control, and the factors to consider when establishing and enforcing standards. We discussed the importance of organization in helping the manager assert adequate control, and answered some of the questions about what is controlled, who does it, how it is done, and why we need to do it.

Now we will look into the different forms that control can take: *overall control* of the whole organization, as exerted by top management; *functional control* of the separate departments or functions of an organization; and *product control,* which cuts across departments if necessary and focuses on the organizational output.

Overall Control

control by top management

Overall control is exercised by the chief executive of the firm or government agency. Similar broad control may be exercised by the head of a major profit center—a principal division of such a firm. Since this control has to be exercised largely through written records, and since most of these are essentially quantitative, overall control usually means financial control. Top managers endeavor to find and use other forms of control, such as management audits and special reports. Some of the uses of outside consultants boil down to efforts by top managers to find out what is going on within their organizations.[3]

Control of Profit

profit and loss statement

If a firm's accounting practices are realistic, the *profit and loss statement* is an accurate summary of how well the firm (or profit center within a firm) has done over the past period covered by the statement—typically the past three months, six months, or year. Without the profit and loss statement, the manager of a large organization will have little or no ability to determine how well the organization has done, because there are so many diverse elements working at so many different tasks that no nonquantitative measures can possibly present any overall assessment. Even with the profit and loss statement, there are many opportunities for misleading data to creep in and give an erroneous picture. Consider a firm which is developing a new "breadwinner" product and has spent $10 million on research and development costs. Because the product is expected to sell

capitalizing costs

profitably for many years, it is appropriate to *capitalize* these expenses, charging only $1 million as operating expenses each year for ten years.[4] Now suppose the product seems to be turning sour, and management feels it should be abandoned because it is unlikely to make a profit. The remaining $9 million, which was to be expensed at a rate of $1 million a year over the next nine years as a charge against profits, is hanging there waiting to be assigned elsewhere. A profit center manager trying to show good performance next year may wish to keep things as they are, taking only the $1 million in expenses next year, rather than admitting that the product will never fly and charging the whole $9 million as expenses in one year. If the manager takes this approach, perhaps the department will show a $5 million profit for the year; if the product is written off, the department will certainly show a $3 million loss. When the pressure to be profitable is intense, managers are greatly tempted to arrange such figures in the least painful way, hoping the future will somehow take care of itself.

While the profit and loss statement deals only with the past, it can be extended into the future by a *pro forma profit and loss statement* which estimates sales, revenues, and costs on the basis of the best available forecasts, and computes what the profits will be if things worked out as estimated. While the results of this exercise are no better than the accuracy of the forecasts, it shows managers what they must achieve (in sales and revenues) and what ceiling they need to apply to costs.

When a company has different departments that service one another (warehousing, shipping, transportation, research, legal, etc.), a profit center may try to get a different department to provide services that would have to be bought otherwise, thereby increasing profits. To get around this bookkeeping problem, some firms have internal charging systems, where service departments "sell" their services to the user departments. As a rule, no actual funds change hands, but the bookkeeper levies the fees as a bookkeeping charge against profits. This system, although it sounds appealing, leads to problems. The using department may decide that the service is overpriced, and may go outside the company for service—a practice which contradicts the overall best interests of the company. Arguments arise as to whether the charge is excessive; since the using department generally has nothing to say about how much the charge should be, such arguments can go on interminably. Most companies find that this system is more trouble than it is worth.

Control Through Return on Investment

Profit is not the whole picture in many cases. If a company has two subsidiaries, and invests $50 million in capital in one subsidiary while investing only $6 million in the other, it would be unreasonable to expect the second to make as much profit as the first. Capital is always scarce,[5] and companies invest this scarce commodity in order to bring profits from its use. Since capital is expensive—borrowed capital can cost as much as 12% to 15% a year, and investment capital expects even more return than that if there is any element of risk present—it must bring in more than it costs or there is no point in using it.

To get around this problem, many companies assess overall performance on the basis of *return on investment* (ROI). The total investment in a profit center or overall company usually amounts to the total value of fixed assets less depreciation (though often certain intangible investments such as research are capitalized). This approach focuses on what many managers feel is the central goal: achieving the best profit from the available capital. There are many problems with such computations. One deals with how fast the return comes in: is a 25% return that promises to last a moderate length of time better than a 20% return that will keep up longer? Another deals with the total duration of payoff: since no investment lasts forever, how will the accountants treat returns that start to taper off a few years down the road? How fast should new capital equipment be written off? Should long-term leases be counted as the equivalent of capital investments? (Pan American Airlines reported a net loss for 1973 of $18.4 million, with $872 million in debt; but it has another $491 million of lease obligations, including 23 aircraft for which the $40 million a year rental lasts until 1990. If the lease obligations were treated as conventional capital debt, Pan Am would have shown a 1973 net loss of nearly $24 million.) Return on investment implies that money is the only

---

pro forma profit and loss statement

Looking back to the North Star story on planning, how did Zeb use this device?

return on investment

valuable factor; but certainly most companies have too little management, and a cost center provided with the best available managers in the organization should be expected to increase returns for that reason as well.

Despite its shortcomings, ROI is such a useful and practical measure that its use is likely to increase in the executive suite.

Control Through Management Audit

When all is said and done, top managers are supposed to know something about good and bad management that goes beyond studying the bottom line in profit and loss statements, or pondering the ROI ratio. All corporations are required to undergo *external audits* by independent public accountants, who certify their annual report and comment on any significant factors that seem to make them good or bad risks for public investment. While this audit is quite broad, and cannot be expected to uncover detailed management shortcomings, the courts are taking a more and more strict view about accounting firms' responsibility for finding serious performance problems, and the accountants are making strenuous efforts to find performance shortcomings if they exist. But the more detailed *internal audits,* which amount to management inspections and appraisals of their own company's performance, can provide detailed performance information that is not dependent on quantitative cost or production reports.

external audits

internal audits

Management audits look past actual costs to the reasons and payoffs. Productive costs should be allowed to grow if the increase buys more than it costs. Support costs should be viewed with constant suspicion, not so much to hold them down as to decide whether the support function is needed at all. One of the most useful things a management audit can do is to spot costs that are wasted: material standing idle in stock because too much is bought, machines that are underutilized, unnecessary movement of work about the shop, superfluous inspections (where a later one can take their place), too-late inspections (where a defective part wastes all the work done after the defect could have been discovered), using costly processes when cheaper ones are available, and so on. The technique of *value analysis* studies a process to determine whether more efficient ways of doing the job can be introduced.

value analysis

Wide-awake management audits can spot whole departments that should be abolished, and the major gains are made in this way. Within departments, such audits concentrate on key commonsense indicators to see if performance is up to par. For the purchasing office, a controller report might show the average time needed to process a requisition, the number processed a month, the average procurement time, and so on; the management audit would go to users of purchasing services and analyze examples of observed poor performance to see if any pattern is emerging. For the employment office, the management audit would determine whether all departments were getting the desired personnel and whether they were proving satisfactory. For the industrial engineering department, the audit would analyze new processes installed or new tooling devised, to see how well the users thought they had worked out and exactly what benefits had ensued. Every group in the organization has assigned tasks to carry out in support of overall goals; the management audit examines what the group has done in relation to these overall goals, and tries to decide if it could be done better.

Functional Control

The functional divisions of an organization are the groups that have specified functions: production, personnel, plant maintenance, material control, procurement, research and development, engineering, and so on. The meaning of *functional* will be clear if you consider two different ways a municipal public works department might handle its work. In one organization, it would handle every type of work with the same groups, whether the tasks involved streets, sewers, public buildings, or transportation equipment. There would be one engineering department for plans, one director of works to handle repairs and servicing, one set of planners and inspectors, and so on. In another organization there would be a streets division that handled everything to do with streets, a sewer organization to handle everything about sewers, and so on. The first is a *functional organization,* with one group handling the engineering function, another the repair and building function, another the inspection function, and so on. The second is a *product* or *project organization,* with each type of product having its own unit to perform all the functions for that product.

Production Control

Production control gets more attention in management literature than any other functional group, since production is the major purpose of industry and of many government agencies. It can involve *labor cost control, quality control, inventory control, maintenance control,* and *schedule control* (including machine assignment).

There are two parts to *labor cost control:* (1) evaluating job difficulty in relation to available labor skills to determine wage scales and (2) setting time standards for particular jobs to weigh worker performance against the standard. The first of these is of great importance, since a company or agency that overstates the skill requirements for a series of job positions will be paying for overqualified workers—and once the skill level is established there will be marked employee unrest if the job is reclassified downward. However, this evaluation takes place primarily in the initial stages of a new enterprise (or a new product line, or the emergence of a new technology), and any adjustments in skill level requirements are likely to be minor thereafter.

The second task, setting time standards, crops up every time a different product or subassembly is needed, including minor redesign of existing products. One method is to use past performance as the standard, if the product has been produced before; this approach does not imply that past performance was good or bad (it may have been quite poor, or outstanding), but it does provide a measure of whether performance is holding its own or getting better or worse. Another method is to use performance in equivalent situations, where the product has not been made before but the supervisor can draw on cases of similar work for

production control

labor cost control

which typical performance levels are known; this approach depends on the judgment of the supervisor and involves little quantitative content, but is useful nonetheless. A third method is to use unit standard costs (or times), where the time for doing a single pass of welding of a certain sort, or painting a square yard of surface, or laying a square yard of floor tile is well established from past experience in this and other companies (and may even be published in industry handbook form). To the extent that the process contains these standard evolutions, the standard may be applied directly. A fourth method is to study the detailed operations involved in the process, reduce them to elemental movements such as "grasp," "lift," "transport," and elemental processes such as "drill," "sand," "assemble," and build up the allowed time by summing these times and adding allowances for rest time and so forth. A fifth method is simply to time the performance of the particular job as a whole, under conditions where it can be determined that the worker is working efficiently, and use that time (with adjustment for rest times, set-up, etc.) as the standard thereafter.

Quality control can be a precise technique, with systematic sampling methods for taking exactly the proper number of samples and testing them; or it can be more general, with inspectors assigned to the plant but moved from one area to another as managerial judgment directs. In some production processes, where the foreman is quite familiar with the product, inspection by the fabricator or the supervisor is sufficient. Where the finished product is quite complex, or involves the efforts of many workers (so that no one feels responsible for overall quality), or is a new product for which workers do not fully understand the specifications, a separate inspection operation probably is needed. Where the product must pass performance specifications (as a container which must hold a certain amount of pressure for a stated period, a piece of machinery which must operate for a certain period without overheating, etc.), an inspector is needed to conduct and observe the test.

If inspection is important, it is wise to assign inspectors to a supervisor who is not in the manufacturing division, so they will feel independent of the pressures on the manufacturing manager to get out the work, at the expense of quality if necessary.

Sometimes a product that is produced in quantity does not fail to meet acceptance standards, but shows a larger number of units than usual which are somewhat outside the expected quality limits. Perhaps the item is packaged, with the desired quantity being 10 ounces but with allowable variation between 9½ and 10½ ounces. Statistical sampling can reveal a tendency for the filling process to increase in variability, though still within allowable limits, which is a warning to adjust the filling system before the variation reaches the point of rejects. This procedure is a variation of the acceptance sampling described earlier, which checks the products and takes only those within acceptable limits; the second type of sampling seeks to control the production process so that *no* bad parts are produced.

In an assembly-line process it is extremely important that the line not be stopped except for compelling reasons. Inspectors on an assembly line cannot stop the line when a defect is noted,[6] so they must direct the piece off the line to a repair area or tag it so that when it completes the line the defect is corrected. In the former method, the inspector may indicate a defect by setting a signal to divert the defective item to the repair area

---

quality control

Should the drafting room have any quality control system? How could it work?

automatically. Say it is a washing machine, and the inspector notes an unpainted area. The inspector sets a lever on the carriage which actuates an automatic switching device so that the piece is switched off the line at the proper place, and the carriage takes the piece to the repaint shop. After repainting, it is sent back to the proper place and continues on the assembly line.

Inventory control involves insuring that sufficient parts are in stock to meet manufacturing needs (or other needs) without carrying excess stock. Since parts are used at a measurable rate, and the reordering process takes an amount of time that can be determined, it is possible to set a "triggering" stock level at the *reorder point* such that the order will be placed and the new shipment will arrive just in time to keep the production rate from running the bin out of stock. There is a *safety stock* level over and above this quantity, to allow for faster use or slower replenishment than usual. For simple situations involving commonly used items, a reminder board can be placed in the bin with enough parts underneath it to take care of the reorder cycle time plus safety stock, just as the bank puts a reorder form in your checkbook with enough checks beneath it to tide you over until the new stock comes.

The question arises as to the *size* of a reorder. One order a year is cheaper to place than four orders of a quarter the size, because less clerical work is needed to place the order. Moreover, quantity discounts are more likely. On the other hand, the single order ties up more money in inventory, and requires more warehouse space. Simple techniques are available for computing the *economical order quantity* (EOQ) in any particular case.

Control of inventory is important, because it is not unusual for a manufacturing company to have a quarter of its capital tied up in material in the inventory. A popular control system is to compute the *turnover rate* for various types of material in the inventory, and to establish records which will provide the average turnover rate for a three-month period or other suitable period. If the total value of the material in stock at any one time is one-fourth the value of the total issues in a year, that stock has an annual turnover rate of four. (Imagine yourself a bicycle dealer, with a stock of three bicycles; every month you order another bicycle, and every month you sell another bicycle on the average—but you have some safety stock to insure that you never run out. Your turnover rate is four times your stock level.)

Turnover rate does not apply to *insurance items*, slow-moving items which you must keep in stock because when they are needed the failure to have them would be very costly. The stocking of such items must be on a judgmental basis, though past records are of some help.

Items that have failed to move because the need for them no longer exists are particularly troublesome, because they are hard to identify. The *usage rate* records are helpful for items that move, but when an item does not move it takes judgmental investigation to see if it is temporarily or permanently unneeded. In the latter case, it must be removed for two reasons. One reason is to save the cost of warehousing it. The other reason is an accounting one: it is being carried as an asset when in fact it is not, and thus it is inflating the value of the company assets on the books and giving a misleading financial signal.

inventory control

reorder point

safety stock

economical order quantity

turnover rate

usage rate

Maintenance Control

maintenance control

All of us who drive cars practice maintenance control. We decide when the car needs to be serviced, when the winter oil goes in, when the tires are ready for the scrap heap, and perhaps when it should go into the shop for a tune-up or inspection. Many states have inspection laws that provide some additional maintenance control: inspecting brakes, lights, and other essentials before they become dangerous and lead to larger repairs.

In a large organization, maintenance control reaches the level of a science. Machines are put on a lubrication and inspection schedule to keep them in shape and spot troubles while they are still small. Careful calculations are made as to the proper frequency for overhauls, to strike the lowest cost balance between overhauls so frequent that there are no unexpected breakdowns (an expensive procedure, including the high cost of taking the machine out of service frequently), and overhauls so infrequent that unexpected breakdowns and emergency repairs (plus the dislocation cost of an *unplanned* outage for repairs) more than match the cost of frequent overhauls.

The maintenance of a large rental car fleet is a complex business. Methods of inspection must be quick and inexpensive, but dependable enough to spot potential problems which would stall a rental customer out on the highway. There are rules as to how frequently to make certain replacements, even though the part has not yet failed, because of the significant probability that it will fail before the next inspection.

The other category of maintenance applies to items which fail without warning, when the significance lies not in *which one* fails but only in *what proportion* fail. The simplest example would be the fluorescent lighting tubes in the plant ceiling. Perhaps there are 100 tubes in the ceiling, and replacement of individual tubes is such a costly operation that the industrial engineer decides to replace all of them at one time. But what will the best time be? Table 9-1 shows the result of a life-to-failure test on 100 such tubes, indicating that by the end of the seventh week 60 are left and by the end of the eighth week 44 are left. From the probability information contained in this table, Figure 9-4 can be developed; it shows that although the longest-lived tube will last 15 weeks, by the end of the eighth week (with 44 still lighted), 88% of the total life in all the 100 tubes has been used up and only 12% of the life remains. The curve further tells us that, with 60 on the seventh Friday and 44 on the eighth Friday, there are only two days (the last Thursday and Friday) when less than 50 tubes will be lighted. If the cost of more frequent replacement (when they burn out) is over 12% more than the cost of this single-time replacement (and if the 50% illumination level is enough as a minimum), the single replacement every eighth Friday is the optimum relamping strategy. Whatever the desired replacement, this analysis will enable the maintenance people to calculate the costs of various relamping strategies.

Personnel Control

personnel control

In most organizations, whether public or private, people are the most significant element of cost. Moreover, this particular cost element tends to creep upward if nothing is done. It is easy and tempting to hire another person when workloads grow, but it is very difficult to lay that person off. Aside from the human aspect of depriving someone of a job, there is the empire-building instinct of the supervisor, who tends to equate prestige and importance with the number of people supervised. Some rating systems unconsciously reinforce this instinct by including number supervised in classifying job importance and pay.

Besides the growth in numbers, there is a similar automatic growth in wages. Where pay scales are negotiated with a union, this increase is in plain view and a great deal of attention is devoted to it. When wage administration is more casual, however, there is a tendency for salaries to increase for insufficient reason—as a reward for a small achievement, to

Table 9-1. Life-to-Failure Test Results

Week	Fail	Survive
1	1	99
2	1	98
3	2	96
4	4	92
5	7	85
6	11	74
7	14	60
8	16	44
9	13	31
10	12	19
11	8	11
12	5	6
13	3	3
14	2	1
15	1	0

Figure 9-4. Survival Curve for Fluorescent Tubes

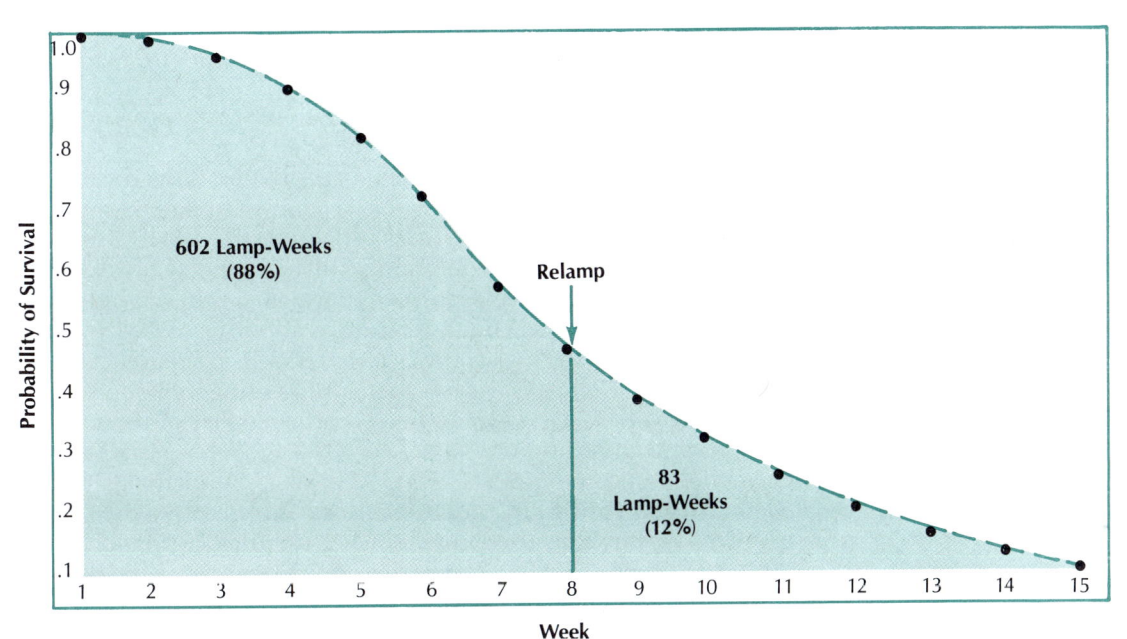

quiet a constant complainer, or just with the feeling that "Charlie hasn't had a raise for quite a while." One raise begets others, because people see it happen and want the same treatment for themselves. As in number of employees, it is far harder to reduce salaries than to increase them; in fact, it is virtually impossible except in time of dire emergency.

For these reasons, well-run organizations have a highly systematic and structured method of wage administration, with rigid promotion rules. This is one case where a closely controlled bureaucratic system is almost a necessity if salaries are not to get out of hand.

Control over the organization structure usually requires a personnel manual to describe organizational relationships, wage administration, promotion policy, and position descriptions for key or typical jobs. Any personnel or organizational changes must be reviewed by an administrative committee to insure that they mesh with overall policy. But there are problems with such a structured system: it tends to be inflexible and hard to change; it gets out of date, so that it represents the way things used to be instead of the way they are; and the effort to cover all situations in a permanent manual (even temporary adjustments for special problems) requires a bloated and complex publication unless pains are taken to avoid this problem.

Since it is not possible for a large organization to operate without a policy manual, and a rather specific set of corresponding procedures, top management must take a firm position in support of a good manual. It must be made clear that there are proper ways to do things, and that the organization will operate in this way. Procedures must be reviewed at regular intervals, and the goal should be to cancel a procedure for each new one that must be written. Procedures must be *necessary* if they are to stay in the manual. If conditions change, revise the applicable procedures or cancel them. If a procedure has become widely accepted standard practice, it need not be written down any longer in most cases. There should never be anything in the manual that the firm can get along without. In this way, all hands will accept the fact that the manual is current, and will consult and follow it regularly.

Administrative Cost Control

overhead cost control

One of the hardest things to control in an organization is overhead cost. Productive costs, as you will see in the next section, are related to specific products, and when they start drifting off target the fact is apparent immediately. But overhead functions are so diverse, and so unrelated to specific payoff, that it is nearly impossible to say what they ought to cost. Many accounting systems shelter overhead costs from review by "distributing" them to the various productive centers which theoretically use their services. Thus a light electric motor manufacturing shop might have

overhead burden

an *overhead burden* of 75%, meaning that for every dollar of direct labor spent in that shop an additional 75¢ of overhead labor charges are tacked on. When the electric motors are priced for sale, the factor of 0.75 is applied to all direct costs when the company starts computing the proper selling price. This overhead represents what the finance committee or comptroller or other group decides is that shop's "fair share" of the cost for running personnel, research, sales, warehousing, planning, scheduling, and all other groups that don't make a product to sell.

Now shift to the personnel division. In such a system its operating costs are "generated" from product sales, almost as though they came from heaven, and there is a tendency for top management to consider personnel as "free"—the customer is paying for them. And when the sale of light electric motors encounters some resistance because of high prices, the superintendent of the motor shop is called in and told to lower costs. No one sends for the personnel manager. Or the research director. Or the other overhead managers.

This situation is somewhat exaggerated, of course. But the point is that management must not consider that overhead *costs* are satisfactory as long as the overhead *rate* doesn't rise. Every overhead cost is a direct drain on profits, at a ratio of about four to one; it takes four dollars' worth of sales to make enough profit to fund one dollar's worth of personnel costs, and the quickest way to run up profits is to reduce *unneeded* overhead.

<aside>How would you say North Star handles overhead in setting its charges for overseas work? For municipal work? Should there be any difference?</aside>

What overhead is unneeded? This question must be answered by a hard process of examining each overhead function separately and in detail. No simple formulas or ratios will give the answer. Essentially, it calls for the technique of benefit-cost analysis, or cost-effectiveness, which examines each service of an overhead department and asks, "Is it worth what it costs?" You must analyze what would happen if the service were cut back or canceled entirely. How would the matter be handled without this service? What things would go wrong, and what indirect cost would ensue?

One effective way to spotlight overhead is to play the game of "If you want it, pay for it." Suppose that at present you have ten productive or direct labor activities, and all of the overhead activities are charged to those ten—perhaps eight overhead activities. For each of the ten productive activities in turn, ask yourself if it could do without the services of any or all of the eight overhead activities. If it could, stop charging it any overhead burden for such activity or activities. Make the productive activities that need overhead activity services share all of the overhead costs. Say Overhead Activity F, formerly charged to ten productive activities, is needed by only three, so those three—Productive Activities 5, 6, and 8—now must carry all of F. The burden on each of them for F has approximately trebled. Do they still need it, at three times the price? This sort of exercise forces a brutal reappraisal, and is likely to lead to some overhead cutbacks, if not eliminations.

Product Control

Product control (or project control) looks to the end purpose of the organization—to turn out particular products—and focuses management control on the cost, timeliness, and characteristics of the products. It need not involve a private business; a municipal sanitation department can focus on product control through centering its attention on the services it delivers and how much they cost, by measuring all of its efforts in terms of what they produce. Baltimore's Water Department recently undertook an overhaul of its services by establishing output measures and determining the units of effort that went into producing those outputs. The result was a major saving in costs.

<aside>product control</aside>

When control is directed at the product, many difficult questions become simpler. No longer is it a question of trying to decide whether engineering services are excessive, or comparing your engineering group with another to decide if it looks too large. Now you ask what engineering contributes to the product, how much it costs, and how much it brings in revenue. If output doesn't balance input, engineering services is not paying its way—and there is a call for management action.

Product Cost Control

product cost

The most direct of the product control points is in product cost control. The cost of products *within* manufacturing shops is handled rather effectively. Usually there is a breakdown of costs among the following:

1. engineering design direct labor cost;
2. manufacturing direct labor cost;
3. machine time cost;
4. material cost; and
5. shop overhead cost (shop schedulers, supervision, power, clerical, supplies, etc.).

It is the cost of products *outside* of the manufacturing shops that opens up areas of uncertainty. Usual accounting practice is to spread all of the plant overhead across the shops uniformly, more or less regardless of the use each shop makes. Thus a transportation department may have its costs absorbed in overhead by simply adding 5% to the direct labor cost in each shop—even though one shop uses transportation a great deal and another almost never. As discussed in the previous section, a close look at which overhead functions actually are used by which shops will disclose who ought to pay for what, and that is the way the overhead costs should be distributed. Concentration on the *product* as the unit needing each overhead function will make this allocation task easier.

Products cost money at points other than during their manufacture. They must be shipped, packaged, held in the warehouse, handled, tested, demonstrated, distributed—and occasionally taken back. All of these areas involve costs, sometimes higher than the outlay needed to make the products in the first place. It is more or less typical for the manufacturer of a product to get about a third of what the buyer pays for it, and in some lines far less than that. A not insignificant item involved in many of the above is interest on the money tied up in products and materials, which can be saved if they are moved faster through the cycle from initial material purchase to final product sale.

Table 9-2 shows an actual corporate income statement for a company manufacturing chemicals and pharmaceuticals. Note that the *direct* cost of the products is less than $32 million—a third of what the company sells the products for at wholesale. The *overhead* cost of the products is about $49 million—50% more than the direct cost. And this overhead cost excludes the two items of *depreciation,* which can be considered as rent for the plant and equipment, and *interest.* The latter item alone, at $2,270,000, is nearly half the net earnings of $4,790,000.

A similar income statement should be made for each major product or service, to establish just what the product is earning and what it is costing. Corporations follow this procedure for cost centers, but seldom do they break the accounting down into individual products. If they did so, making a determined attempt to assign the overhead costs accurately (on the basis of what the overhead services actually contribute to each product), costs would be highlighted and it would be clearer which products were paying their way and which overhead functions were out of control.

Product Quality Control

The purpose of quality control is to see that products meet the desired standards for performance, looks, safety, and other necessary characteristics (such as finish, weight, dimensions, etc.). Conceptually, quality control is the simplest and most direct form of control, because usually there is no doubt as to standards and no question about how to check them. But checking costs money, and the problem is to arrive at a reasonable level of quality control expenditure. In some areas, where public health or safety is an important ingredient, government agencies prescribe the inspections or tests, and often conduct the tests themselves or at least witness and certify them. In a meat-packing plant, for example, the U.S. Department of Agriculture inspector personally incises and inspects every animal for disease, and those that do not pass are discarded. In a canning plant such individual inspection would be impossible, so the government inspector keeps watch on the sterilization processes, samples batches, and in general conducts a process inspection. For ships at sea, the U.S. Coast Guard reviews the manufacturer's plans and specifications, and for critical items such as high-pressure containers, lifesaving equipment, etc., witnesses shipbuilder tests and conducts its own inspections.

Where no government control is required, there is wide variability as to how inspections are conducted. Some companies do no inspecting at all, relying on complaints from customers to point out where they are drifting out of control, and considering it cheaper to make individual adjustments than to set up costly inspection systems. Other companies (by far the majority) have internal inspection organizations to check work performance.

In most circumstances, particularly in large organizations where more than one person works on a product, inspection is a psychological necessity. The production force, pushed to get work out within cost and time constraints, naturally tends to be forgiving about its own minor errors; it takes an independent inspector, who is under no such pressures, to call them as he sees them.

product quality

Table 9-2. Corporate Income Statement

Net sales	$95,000,000
Cost of labor, material and supplies	31,816,000
Advertising, selling, administration, research	48,950,000
Depreciation	2,677,000
Interest	2,270,000
Earnings before taxes	9,287,000
Taxes	4,497,000
Net earnings	4,790,000

Quality control starts with establishment of standards, and this raises the question of how much quality really is necessary. Should a household appliance such as a toaster be screwed together for ease of disassembly and repair, or inexpensively crimped on the premise that repairs to such minor items are infrequent and it would be cheaper to provide replacements in such cases? Should an engineering report be expensively printed and bound, or mimeographed and stapled together? Once decisions are made on these policy matters, the question arises as to *when* to inspect: early in the production process, to avoid throwing good work after bad, or on completion, to reduce the work to a single inspection? There is the question of *what* to inspect: the items most likely to be defective, the items most important if they are defective, or the items cheapest to inspect. There is the question of *how often* to inspect: every one, every tenth one, every thousandth?

benefit-cost analysis

Table 9-3 shows a *benefit-cost analysis* of inspection strategy, for three components that are candidates for inspection in a manufacturing plant. For each of the three, the quality control division has estimated the following factors:

1. The probability of failure during the guarantee period.
2. The cost of making good the failure if it does fail (the "conditional cost" of failure).
3. The "expected cost" of failure. (For A, if 5 fail out of 100, so that the company is liable for 5 x $200 or $1000, this is an average of $10 each for the 100 products: 0.05 x $200 = $10.00).
4. The estimated cost of inspecting the item per product.

The purpose of quality control is to see that products meet the desired standards.

5. The ratio of expected cost of failure to unit inspection cost (a ratio indicating the dollars' expected benefit per dollar of inspection cost. (For A, $10.00/$3.00 = 3.33).

This table shows that, although item A has the highest probability of failure and item B has the highest cost if it does fail, a dollar of inspection effort expended on item C will bring the highest return in savings of guarantee replacements.

Quality control starts with training employees in the need for quality and establishing a quality consciousness throughout the organization. The best and cheapest quality control is that which prevents defects from happening in the first place. As a general principle, the further back in the production process that a defect can be caught or prevented the less costly it will be.

Sales Control

An expected value table can be constructed for sales effort, just as it can for quality control effort. The sales manager has a certain limit that can be expended on producing more sales, and in some districts a given level of effort will bring more returns than in others. By and large, it costs about the same to sell a $500 order as to sell a $50,000 order, and the records of the sales force can be used (if they are well kept) to find out how much return a given amount of effort has produced in each district and for each product in the past. This information can be translated into a sales strategy that will focus effort where it has shown to be best utilized in the past.

sales effort

Would it be a good idea for North Star to do this? How would they do it?

One of the most difficult tasks in marketing is to determine the value of a given level of advertising. Figure 9-5 shows the hypothetical relationship between the effort spent on advertising (input) and the net profit brought about by that advertising (output). The profit discussed here is meant to be profit that would not have been earned without this level of advertising—profit beyond the amount that would have come in otherwise. The difficulties of determining how much that profit is are obvious: essentially, each of the contributors to profit must be separated, and its independent contribution calculated. *Regression analysis*[7] is a statistical tool which has helped companies with good cost and expenditure records to estimate what their advertising has brought them, thus providing a systematic basis for analyzing this subjective question.

ITEMS	Probability of Failure	Cost if the Item Fails	Expected Cost of Failure	Estimated Cost of Inspection	Inspection Benefit/Cost Ratio
A	0.05	$200	$10.00	$3.00	3.33
B	0.01	$1200	$12.00	$2.75	4.36
C	0.006	$70	$ 0.42	$0.05	8.40

Table 9-3.
Inspection Benefit-Cost Analysis

product line

Product Line Control

Probably more important than any of the other control elements is the matter of *what* products to make. This decision really starts with a policy question: "What business are we in?" A petroleum company that acquires a chain of motels may decide "We are in the travel business," whereas another petroleum company that starts coal mining may decide "We are in the energy business"; and a manufacturer of amateur power tools that starts manufacturing tennis equipment and boats may decide "We are in the leisure item business." The choice of products should be based on a systematic analysis of "What can we do best?" This does not mean what the company can manufacture or design best, but what it can best sell, service, and *understand*. After World War II, many companies with war profits went into fields for which they were ill-equipped (as an industrial company entering the retail market, and trying to shift from making and selling $20,000 items for business to making and marketing $2 items for individuals).

On a more immediate level, constant control must be exercised over *how much* of a product to make. In the inflationary period of 1974, many executives read the rising prices as a sign of increasing consumer demand, and competed for raw materials at inflated prices to be able to build up their stocks of goods for sale. In fact, the rising prices came from other forces, and consumer demand was falling in resistance to the cost of goods; thus companies that had increased production were stuck with costly products that in many cases had to be sold at a loss. Even in normal times, products must be compared constantly with competitive items, to see if improvements in the latter make it wise to reduce production.

Control of quantity is a very difficult problem at best. The firm is buying material for many different products at the same time, some of which have short production times and others long. If the product goes to distributors who sell to stores that sell to the public, there may be a long "pipeline" that takes months to fill (thus, Christmas items must often be shipped by the end of spring). Moreover, when demands change, the

Figure 9-5.
Advertising Cost vs. Profit

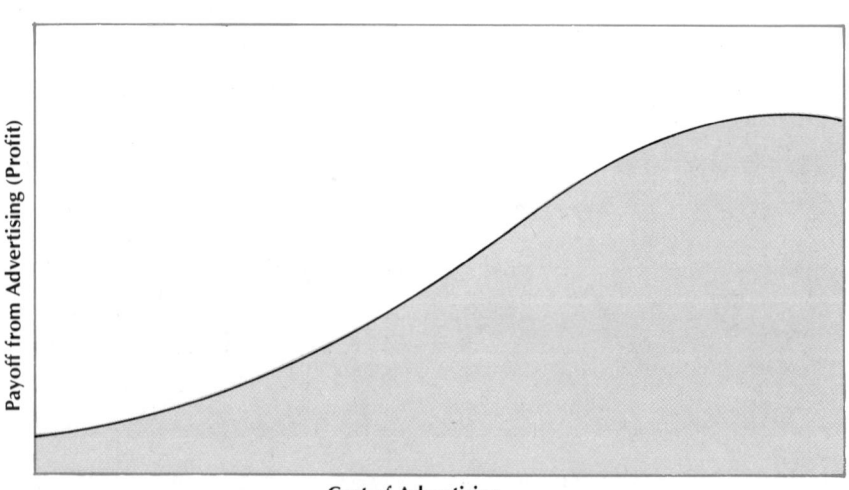

pipeline will be full of unsalable items unless close control has been exercised over what to make.

It is seldom that demand shifts overnight. Usually a product that is on the verge of losing public favor has been giving signals for some time, if any one is tuned in to listen. It has been getting harder to sell, requiring more sales effort per dollar of sales. Retailers have shown less willingness to handle it, and perhaps markdowns have been necessary to persuade them to continue ordering. New products appearing on the market have recognizable advantages over it. Oddly enough, the people who are closest to it, such as the sales manager, the product manager, and the production superintendent, know the product so well that they may interpret this increasing sales difficulty as just another problem to surmount as well as they can, instead of a sign that the item is becoming obsolete.

Methods of Control

The basic control methods can be divided into two principal areas: budgetary control and all other methods. Budgetary control has the convenient characteristic of being fueled by explicit cost and expenditure figures, which makes it very tempting as a control device, whereas nonbudgetary control systems have to search for other supporting elements and are correspondingly more difficult to design and implement.

methods of control

Budgetary Control

In recent years the controller, a post virtually unheard of a few generations ago, has become an essential executive cog in the management team. The bookkeeper has been a fixture in companies for centuries, but his purpose was always to keep the accounting records so that the profit on the firm's transactions could be known after the fact. The bookkeeper's financial records basically answered four questions about past operations:

budgetary control

1. How does the company stand at year's end (balance sheet)?
2. Which way did the company move during the year (income statement)?
3. Where did we make money and where did we spend it (source and application statement)?
4. How is the bank account (cash flow account)?

Those are important questions, but they concern *financial* accounting. The controller works in the area of *management* accounting, which seeks to answer questions like the following:

management accounting

1. Which effort brings which results?
2. How does each product or project affect profit?
3. How does each division contribute to profit?
4. What does each overhead item cost?
5. What are the indirect contributors to profit?

6. What are the marginal costs of products and projects?
7. How do the products we approve compare with those we reject?
8. How accurate are our past estimates of costs and revenues?
9. What are the social and environmental benefits and costs of our operations?
10. What management information of a budgetary nature does management need?

> Could North Star benefit from looking at these questions? How?

The list could go on. The controller is the person chosen by management to develop that sort of information, principally of a budgetary nature. It is the controller who points out what the projected new plant really will cost, what promotional costs are being expended on the pet new product, or how well (or poorly) each product line and cost center are meeting their budgeted goals.

The reason the budget is such a useful control device is that it is a *plan for future operations.* It commits managers, line and staff, to a specific course of action, with specific authorized expenditures, and in anticipation of specific forecast revenues. It says, "Here is what I am going to do, and here in dollars and cents is what I will bring in." If the manager is wrong, the budget will pinpoint the error, and this information may indicate the *reason* for the error. The budget involves numbers, not adjectives, and it is mercilessly explicit.

For top management, the controller produces a series of ratios that permit *ratio analysis*—comparing current financial performance both with the firm's own past performance and with generally reasonable performance. Some of the key ratios are as follows:

> ratio analysis

1. Net sales/working capital: Capital is what the owners put into a business, and if more capital cannot produce more sales there is a management problem (or the capital was not needed).
2. Net sales/inventory: Inventory is a necessary waste, and must be kept low. If this ratio is down, there is too much inventory.
3. Return on investment: See 1.
4. Output per employee (or output per labor dollar): Output is the "value added," that is the only reason for the firm's existence.
5. Quick ratio: This ratio of what the company can turn into cash on short notice to what it owes in the near future is a measure of short-term health if hard times should strike.
6. Administrative expense/sales: This is a crude overall measure that takes the overhead pulse to see if it is lean or bloated.

There are many other top management reports, some more popular in certain types of business (say retail sales) than others (say construction and engineering). All provide a quick measure of performance, to the extent that financial numbers can portray this information.

At other levels, budgetary control can be exercised by graphing trends in revenues, sales, marketing costs, and production costs, with more detailed breakdown for areas where the trends are unfavorable. If costs are going up or revenue coming down, the controller should find the particular department or section that is "out of control" and highlight the circumstances with as much detail as possible. Overhead costs are singled out particularly for budgetary reporting, since they cannot be controlled through product profitability analysis as can direct labor costs. Here the controller should indicate both trends in overhead cost and ratios of overhead compared with other parts of the firm or other firms.

Marginal costs should be reported, so management can see what good it does to add that last unit of production. When industry is working to capacity, it sometimes happens that the last increments of production (which are attained by using inefficient facilities, less-trained workers, and overtime) actually are unprofitable—though usual accounting practice will not reveal this situation, since it lumps all production together.

Nonbudgetary Control

As useful as budgetary reports are, it is not possible to capsule all key events and activities in a company in terms of what they spend and what they take in. Management needs a good deal of statistical data that cannot be reduced to financial terms. When a new project is getting under way, but has not reached the point where it is profitable, management must obtain information as to its progress and prospects from nonfinancial reports. Many elements in a business are vitally important to it, but do not translate directly into profit and loss terms: state of worker training, absenteeism, rate of separation from the company, accident rate, amount of damage and waste, number of patents granted, machine out-of-service time, progress of new construction, sales trend of new products, share of market, and many more. nonfinancial control

In some companies, the controller is responsible for such reports, financial or nonfinancial. In other companies, there is no systematic responsibility for developing such information, or responsibility is spread through the organization. When the latter situation exists, it is probable that the subordinate managers involved will generate the report data themselves. While this is useful, such managers do not have the detachment to be able to prepare critically objective reports, as a staff office similar to the controller's office would.

A very useful analytical tool for looking at new proposals is the *breakeven analysis*. Figure 9-6 shows the form of a breakeven chart. There are fixed charges which continue whether any production takes place or not, variable charges which increase with volume of production (initially they rise steeply, reflecting start-up inefficiencies, then level off, then curve up again as the plant presses against its capacity limitations), and revenues which increase in straight-line relationship to number sold but later turn down as additional marketing effort is needed to make the sales. These relationships show the volume range within which the operation will be profitable. breakeven analysis

When a firm is working on many projects, and drawing on various departments and groups for each, control is likely to weaken, including the ability to forecast performance and promise realistic completion dates. Figure 9-7 shows a project control system of the sort that North Star might have set up. Each project manager makes up such a project planning sheet for the projects he or she controls, showing the budget by months for his or her own personnel, and separately for personnel under other managers. Thus Dick Boyer might make up such a planning sheet for six months ahead, showing all of the projects under his jurisdiction project control system with his workers assigned by months and by project (left-side entries) from each of his departments (top entries, under "OWN RESOURCES," "PERSONNEL"). The additional personnel he would need from Bert he would show similarly ("RESOURCES OF OTHERS," "PERSONNEL"). These entries are in the upper half for the projects Dick is responsible for. In the bottom left of the sheet, labeled "PROJECTS OF OTHERS," would be the assignment of Dick's workers (if any) to projects under Bert, Henry, and so forth. Jo would do the same for her projects. Bert makes up a similar sheet for *his* projects, and on his sheet he also shows the assignment of Dick's or Jo's workers to his projects, only in the upper half under "RESOURCES OF OTHERS." It is, in other words, a "double entry" employee bookkeeping system that sets up both personnel and fund requirements six months in advance by project and by providing department. The bottom right blocks are for a cumulative report of project status.

When a new product is being introduced (one of the major nonrecurring tasks of companies), during the whole process of planning (setting time and cost targets, laying out marketing strategy, doing the tooling and production scheduling, and seeing that the project is on schedule) it is vitally important that control reports come to the responsible managers in time for them to clear roadblocks and take all necessary corrective action. Obviously this is not a matter for budgetary controlling, except in minor aspects.

In the important area of marketing, buyer research, promotional activities, and analysis of sales effort, timely reports are necessary to spot trends in a welter of complex information. A product manager who gets up-to-date information on such events can take corrective promotional action, or even make product changes as a result of preliminary marketing studies and convert a sluggish marketing campaign into a successful one.

Figure 9-6.
Breakeven Chart

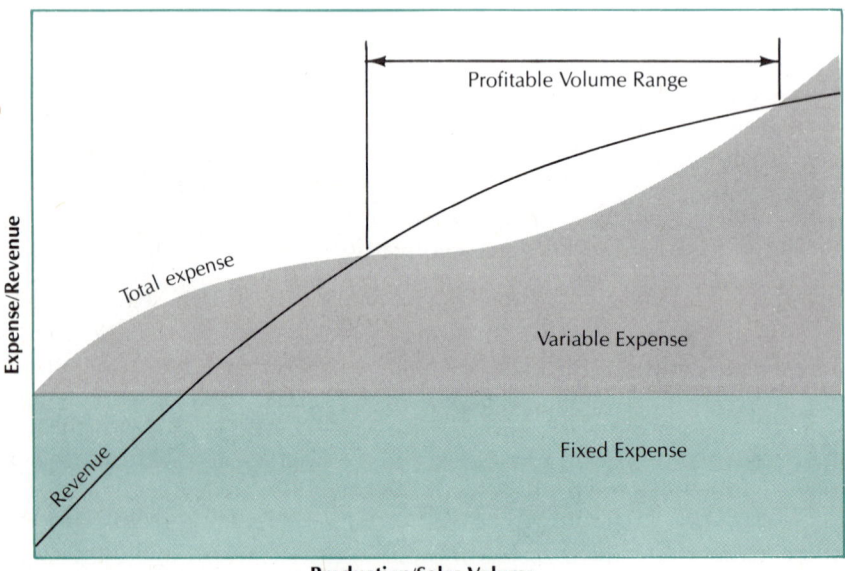

Management Audits

Most of the control reports we have been discussing are numerical in nature: reporting receipts, sales, costs, profits, or numbers of events that take place. But such numbers often miss the essence of performance

management audits

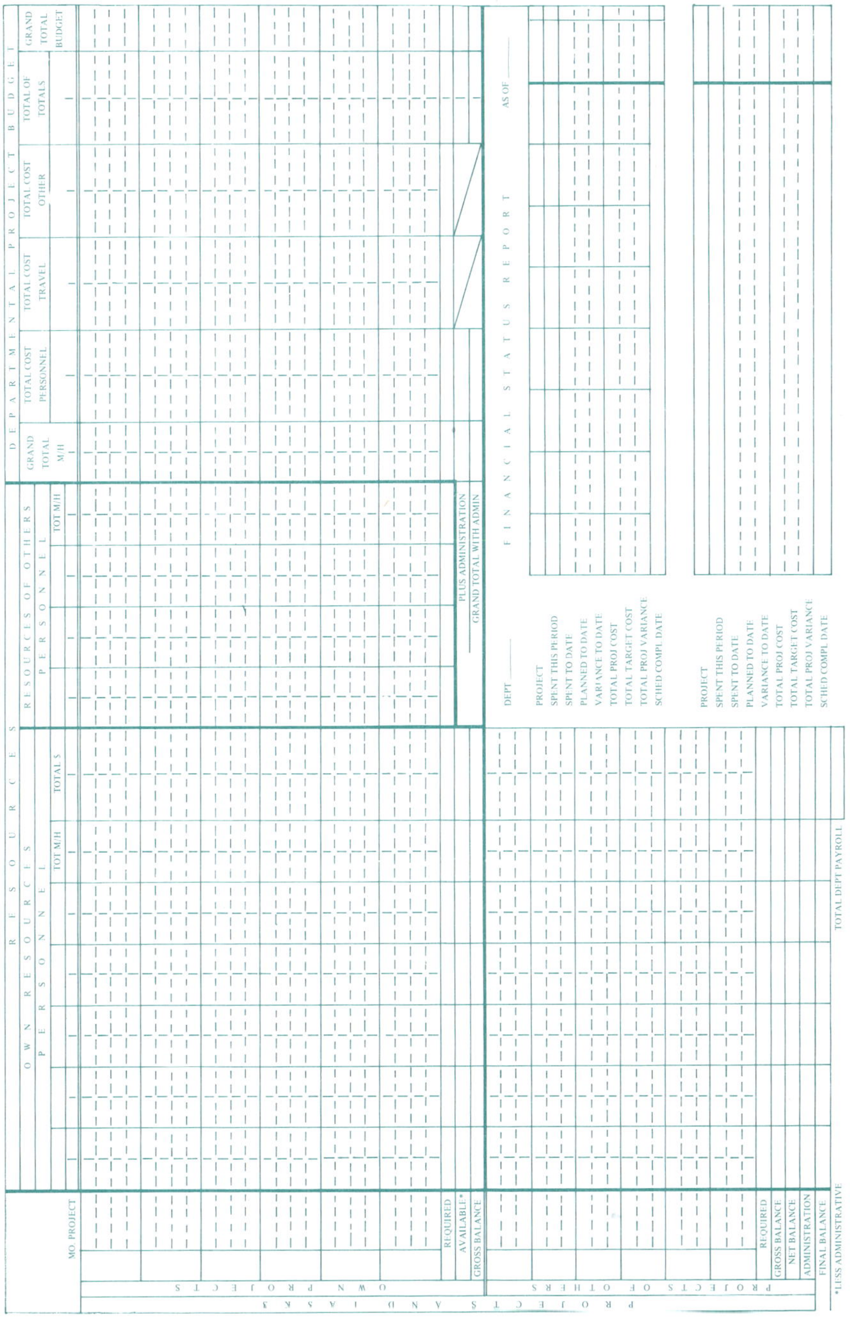

Figure 9-7.
Project Control System

analysis, in that they cannot measure a situation which gives subjective signs of progress despite unpromising numerical data. Perhaps extensive spadework has been done, which has not paid off but is about to do so. Perhaps a project which is behind schedule nonetheless is better off than those of competitors which are *further* behind. Perhaps a manager has been bleeding a market area dry to show good numerical reports, overstocking wholesalers and building up hard times ahead for the department or the company. There are a hundred such "perhaps" situations where numbers give inadequate control information.

There is no substitute in such situations (indeed, in almost any managerial problem), for on-the-spot analysis by an alert and informed representative of management, who can look beneath surface reports and understand the whole environment in which the organization operates. The control responsibilities of management cannot be discharged by simply checking budgetary or statistical data and pinpointing variances. Would that it were so simple. The manager needs to understand what must be controlled and monitor performance levels constantly.

Summary

In all organizations except very small ones, specific action must be taken to keep costs and performance on the track toward achieving the organizational goals. Control systems should stimulate corrective action and should apply to all parts of the organization. In a business enterprise profits are most important, since the firm would fail without them, but this means long-run as well as short-run profits. There is danger of paying too much attention to products or services that have made profits in the past, and too little to new items that will make future profits.

Some record-keeping systems deal with the wrong issues, and workers striving to look good on the record tend to emphasize what is being recorded rather than what will make the enterprise prosper. Useful control methods include: direct observation, cost analysis, evaluation of operating statistics, comparison with standard costs or times, and centralized control. The latter can sap initiative, however, if control records always go to top management instead of the supervisors directly responsible for setting things right.

Control systems need to indicate variances from plan while there is still time to correct them. Therefore, they must be timely, but they must also be understandable to the people who will take action. Moreover, they should include as much detail as possible, so the supervisor will know what has gone wrong, where it took place, and who was responsible.

Control systems must be flexible enough to change with organizational changes, to fit short-term and long-term jobs, to provide control of different organizational departments and functions, and to provide information about the same situation to different management levels.

Control reports should cover only matters that managers can do something about. In general, managers should control cost, time, and performance. While many measures provide information about these areas, a good control system concentrates on the measures that are economical, comprehensive (showing where the fault lies as well as what is wrong), and appropriate to organizational goals. A good system should guard against giving information that does not really measure performance against standards. When exact job standards are not obtainable, it is useful to compare against the organization's own past performance or that of similar organizations. This approach may involve ratios such as net sales/inventory or net profit/capital invested. In administrative operations, standards are hard to establish, but close study of what the activity should accomplish usually will suggest some measures of performance.

Control charts can be used for setting quality control standards. Actual performance of a labor force can be used to set job standards, by insisting on maintenance of or a moderate improvement in past performance.

A good organization can assist control by insuring a chain of linking supervisors to transmit top management goals to the work force. Overall control by top management usually means financial control, though special reports and management audits are essential as well. The profit and loss statement is useful for measuring past performance, and a pro forma P&L can be used to estimate future direction. Return on investment is an important measure, since it assesses how well invested capital is employed. External audits are helpful, but internal audits include more detail.

Two major *types* of control are: functional (by department) and product (by what is produced). Production control is the best developed of the functional systems, involving labor, quality, inventory, maintenance, and schedule control. Personnel and administrative cost control are less well-developed but no less important. Product control involves control of product cost, quality, sales, and product line (what is made, and how much).

Two major *methods* of control are budgetary and nonbudgetary. The controller concentrates mainly on developing budgetary measures and reports. What is needed is management accounting data, which differs from financial accounting in showing what actions have brought what results. The budget is a very useful control device because it is a plan for the future against which results can be measured. Many controller reports are in ratio form, so one can see at once whether things are getting better or worse. Many valuable reports are not in budgetary form, particularly those on new projects which have not generated any cash flow yet and must be judged in other ways. Many elements of business health don't have a price tag: morale, training, absenteeism, share of market, etc. A project control system is an essential nonbudgetary device for keeping control of multidepartmental operations.

Management audits, though difficult to carry out, bring a depth of information not available in any quantitative reports.

Notes

1. Peter F. Drucker, *Managing for Results* (New York: Harper & Row, Pubs., 1964).

2. The notion that "work expands to fill the available time," proposed by C. Northcote Parkinson in *Parkinson's Law* (Boston: Houghton Mifflin Co., 1957), a tongue-in-cheek treatise about the organizational tendency to add superfluous personnel and the resulting drop in efficiency.

3. The author once was retained as consultant by the top management of a large subsidiary corporation to visit a division in a distant city. While the assignment was to work with the division in developing a work plan for a government contract, the important unstated purpose was to assess for top management how effectively the division was moving on the contract, and what action should be taken to improve divisional performance. Such assignments are not at all unusual.

4. Similarly, an individual buying a house would not consider that the whole purchase price was chargeable as rental cost in the year the house was bought, but would mentally "charge off" the mortgage payments as rent for the next twenty years, since the house will be used as lodging during all that time.

5. James Needham, Chairman of the New York Stock Exchange, estimates that business needs $50 billion a year in new capital, whereas the equity markets in stocks and bonds provide only $10 to $15 billion a year in good years—and much less when public confidence is down. It can be expected that the corporation will pay much more attention to efficient use of capital (and such performance measures as ROI) in the future than in the past.

6. If the process is running outside of tolerance, and generating repeated unacceptable products, the inspector must stop the line at once.

7. This technique involves using past records to establish a mathematical relationship between the *causative* factor or factors (here, the cost of advertising) and the *resultant* factor (here, the net profit, presumably influenced in part by the level of advertising).

Review Questions

1. What is the purpose of managerial controlling, as distinguished from financial accounting?
2. What are some different control devices?
3. Why is the controller not the right person to control the organization?
4. Why should control reports go to the lowest action level?
5. What do we mean by flexibility in the control system?
6. Think of your own example of a control record that provides information but gives no real measure of performance.
7. What sort of standards are used at upper levels in an organization?
8. What is a control chart and how is it used to control quality?
9. What is meant by "linking supervisors" in an organization chart designed for good control?
10. Why is profit control the principal control measure at top levels?
11. What is the purpose of a pro forma profit and loss statement?
12. What is the difference between functional and product control?
13. What are the two elements in labor cost control? Which is more important, on a day-to-day basis?
14. What is the meaning of "economical order quantity"?
15. What is an approach to deciding what overhead can be reduced or eliminated?
16. What do we mean by a "benefit-cost" approach to quality control strategy?
17. Why is product quantity control important?
18. What are four major questions answered by financial reports?
19. What is ratio analysis? Why is it useful?
20. Why is budgetary control insufficient for some organizational performance measures?
21. What is breakeven analysis?

Discussion Questions

1. If you were in charge of building a house, which control device(s) would be best? Suppose you were building 1000 homes, at 20 different sites?

2. Some managers set one standard until the workers all improve to the point of meeting or beating it, and then set a tighter standard. What do you think would be the good and bad points of doing this?

3. Under what circumstances would control through management audit be preferable to control through profit?

4. Suppose you, as a manager of a plant making radio and TV sets, had a material superintendent who told you more staff was needed to keep better control of ordering and stocking parts. How would you evaluate the need for more staff?

5. What would an expected value table for sales effort look like?

6. How would you find out if a company manufacturing 5000 items a week was making money or losing it on the last 500? Refer to the breakeven chart, Figure 9-6.

North Star Case Study

You remember from the North Star story at the start of the chapter that Dick Boyer has been urged by Barnhard and Walker to return to the U.S. and try to line up a new large-scale project that can be carried out with B&W. Suppose that he has found such a project: designing a new rapid transit system for the headquarters city, with North Star doing the engineering design and with B&W handling the construction as well as building the advanced technology rail cars and electronic control system.

The project gets under way, and North Star finds it will be turning out literally thousands of engineering drawings and construction specifications. Some of these are simply taken from equipment manufacturer drawings, checked hastily for overall applicability, and reissued. Others are B&W plans for the rail cars and electronic control system, which North Star must reissue and for which it is fully responsible as to correctness and workability. Still others are plans prepared from scratch by North Star. The task includes preparing instructions for a large number of tests to check the correctness of construction, performance of various parts of the system, and so forth.

Dick Boyer realizes that control of this huge multiyear project will make the difference between success or failure. He perceives that the company will get hopelessly fouled up if he doesn't get on top of things quickly. He seeks to design a good control system.

1. What should he do to control the performance of his design group as far as the quantity, or productivity, of what they turn out?

2. What system or concept should he use to see that the plans drawn by B&W for the cars and electronic system are technically accurate and are compatible with the construction plans he will draw—without incurring the huge engineering costs of rechecking and recalculating everything?

3. How will he decide what items to prepare detailed tests on? Are there any general concepts to guide him in answering this question?

4. What method will he use to see at regular periods whether he is on

schedule or not? whether he is within budget on his costs or not? whether the overall project is within its budget on costs or not (for construction of the whole system, including all B&W work)?

Suggestions for Further Reading

Albanese, R. *Management: Toward Accountability for Performance.* Homewood, Ill.: Richard D. Irwin, Inc., 1973.

Anderson, D. R. *Practical Controllership.* Homewood, Ill.: Richard D. Irwin, Inc., 1973.

Bacon, J. *Managing the Budget Function.* New York: National Industrial Conference Board, 1970.

Benjamin, R. I. *Control of the Information System Development Cycle.* New York: John Wiley & Sons, Inc., 1971.

Leonard, W. P. *The Management Audit: Appraisal of Management Methods and Performance.* Englewood Cliffs, N.J.: Prentice-Hall, Inc., 1962.

Luck, D. J. *Product Policy and Strategy.* Englewood Cliffs, N.J.: Prentice-Hall, Inc., 1972.

McKeever, J. M., and B. Kruse. *Management Reporting Systems.* New York: John Wiley & Sons, Inc., 1971.

Plossel, G. W. *Manufacturing Control: The Last Frontier For Profits.* Reston, Va.: Reston Pub. Co. 1973.

Rossel, J. H., and W. W. Frasure. *Managerial Performance Standards.* Columbus, Ohio: Charles E. Merrill Pub. Co., 1964.

Rowland, V. K. *Managerial Performance Standards.* New York: American Management Association, 1960.

Sayles, L. R., and M. K. Chandler. *Managing Large Systems.* New York: Harper & Row, Pubs., 1971.

Siegman, J., et al. *Control Mechanisms in the Idea Flow Process: Model and Behavioral Study.* NASA document, 1966.

Skousen, K. F. *Contemporary Thought in Accounting and Organizational Control.* Encino, Calif.: Dickenson Pub. Co., Inc., 1973.

Thomas, W. E. *Readings in Cost Accounting, Budgeting and Control.* Cincinnati, Ohio: South-Western Pub. Co. 1973.

Personnel Management   10

North Star Prologue

As North Star continued to grow, the continual need for improvement in its management style became evident. Obviously it had done something right, or it wouldn't have expanded. As the company embarked for the first time on fixed-price contracts, the officers fashioned a badly needed control system which included manpower scheduling as well as financial controls. Now that a system was set up which could more effectively monitor organizational performance, the officers turned their attention to personnel administration. The company had no staff person to handle personnel; to top it off, Dick Boyer, who had returned from overseas, was proposing to create three new positions to handle his affairs. There was no doubt that with the large component of North Star overseas and the increasing number of contracts at home, North Star could no longer survive with its haphazard system of personnel management.

Dick's return kicked off a wholesale reshuffle at North Star. In addition to providing physical space for the project management office, it was necessary to staff the new office. The first was achieved by doing at long last what Bert had expected them to do when they first moved into the new building—breaking up the high-ceilinged shop section in the back by adding a deck and moving the drafting room to the second floor, which freed space on the first floor for adequate offices for Dick and Jo and made extra space for conference workrooms and the small computer they rented. The second task introduced problems of secretarial distribution and the question of what staff Dick would need for his new stateside responsibilities. He said he had definite need for a proposal writer to help get new projects, a progress engineer to monitor the status of projects since he would not be on site to handle that himself, and a personnel expert to maintain overseas staff and handle the recruiting and other arrangements for his overseas project people—who now numbered nearly 50, and could be expected to increase as he was able to get new projects.

Henry considered this approach the most flagrant sort of empire-building, and called in Zeb for advice and commiseration. He was extremely reluctant to try to check any of Dick's enthusiasm, for several reasons. One was the simple fact that Dick probably didn't wholeheartedly endorse the idea that Henry was president in fact as well as form, and another was a lingering holdover from the period some 12 years back when Lieutenant Boyer had been his Division Officer in the SeaBees. But the most important reason was that Dick Boyer's side of the company still brought in the majority of its revenues, and nothing in his performance to date indicated any lack of solid business judgment. Still, Dick was entering a new phase in his operations which required him to get out and drum up new business (Henry wondered in passing if Dick would accept the idea that "marketing" was under Zeb), and if he didn't succeed in that new venture the company would be saddled with lots of new overhead that wasn't paying its way.

Zeb suggested an out that would solve two problems at once. North Star would establish a personnel division, with responsibility both for staffing and for office management. It could be under him or a separate office under the president (he preferred the former). The personnel director could take over Dick's project personnel problems, as well as those of the rest of the company, and he could be the office manager whose qualifications they had not been able to agree on. Moreover, if they got a professional with some experience in firms like North Star, he or she could also handle the problem of establishing qualifications for all North Star nonprofessional jobs and could prepare position descriptions for them. And he or she could see that North Star's patchwork system for employee benefits—health insurance, overtime and compensatory time systems, retirement plan, and so on—were put on a sound basis. The personnel director could establish proper policies for vacations, sick leave, promotions, and several other issues that had been handled on an ad hoc basis or not at all thus far—in short, could shore up a weak area in the North Star structure. Still left was the question of how many new employees Dick would hire and when they would come on board (whether right away, or not until his selling program had begun to bear fruit), but at least Dick would have to take sufficient stock of his actual needs to work with the new personnel specialist in preparing specific position descriptions for anyone he wanted to hire, and that process would induce useful second thoughts.

There were no real objections to the new personnel billet. Dick was most enthusiastic, probably because he understood better than anyone how disorderly the personnel management of his project staff had been. Bert had a lukewarm response to the idea, but when he saw that Ab was in favor of it, he went along too. Even Jo, surprisingly, liked the idea—probably because she preferred to have personnel decisions made more professionally than they had been at North Star. Henry was deputized to work up requirements for the job (which he did by stealing a position description from the personnel director at the university and splicing some office management duties onto it), and Zeb was given the job of recruiting for the post, with the understanding that the person selected would be acceptable to both Dick and Bert.

The person selected turned out to be a surprise all around, not being strictly a personnel manager at all. She was Barbara Newman, the training director for a large and somewhat tired corporation that really didn't believe in training at all. Originally, Barbara had worked for a personnel placement firm (a "body shop," she scornfully called it), and later had written position descriptions and done job classifications for the tired corporation's captive (and equally tired) research laboratory. She was sick of the musclebound bureaucracy where she worked and when she heard through one of North Star's engineers who was in her bowling club that this post was being established she came roaring over and sewed up the job before Zeb got around to advertising it.

Her sales pitch was that personnel administration was important, but the keystone of it all was personnel development. That meant training, and inspiring employees to *want* training to improve themselves at every opportunity and in every way so that they could move up in the company. She made the point that a static company was a dead company, and that as they grew larger they would expect constant personnel turnover. The point was for them to control the turnover, indeed to stimulate it, by seeing that the people who grew overqualified for their present jobs were not lost to the company, but moved on within the firm to other jobs where their knowledge and loyalty could still benefit North Star. She told them how important performance appraisal was—telling employees where they fell short and where they did well, and helping them with training to correct their shortcomings.

Barbara was an immediate hit. She had a disarming bluntness that let her speak the truth without being in the least offensive. Barbara eliminated both of Dick's proposed hires by asking him directly where he was going to get the money to pay them with no jobs on the books—and by persuading him to use Zeb's marketing help instead of writing longwinded proposals that the corporations wouldn't read anyway. She brought the personnel manual from her former company along, and after telling everyone that it was no damn good she enlisted their help in adapting it to North Star's needs and establishing personnel practices on a systematic basis. She set up the policy that North Star would pay tuition for any employee who went to school after hours to improve professionally, and then bullied and chivvied the drafting room crew until the majority of them were taking night courses at the university and updating their skills in sorely needed areas. And she made a start at exploring methods for profit-sharing that would give every member of the staff a stake in North Star's financial success.

What North Star Can Learn from Chapter 10

1. The various components of a personnel system and their interrelationships
2. The fact that personnel management involves the joint effort of both operating managers and personnel staff
3. The role of the personnel department and the alternative structural formats by which a personnel division can be arranged
4. The importance of manpower planning in determining the future of organizations
5. The various steps an organization must take to establish a job classification system, promotion scales, appraisal systems, recruitment procedures and selection criteria
6. The fact that motivation and managing conflict are essential elements of personnel management
7. The impact of technological developments and value reorientations on personnel administration

In this chapter we discuss the vital functions involved in managing the organization's human resources. Managing personnel includes the recruitment, placement, development, appraisal, compensation, and discipline of employees, as well as the maintenance of harmony and coordination among the various groups and individuals in the organization. Because prospective employees make their first contact with the enterprise through the personnel division, they tend to think of personnel management solely in terms of administering paperwork and screening out misfits from the employment stream. Although the personnel division does indeed process the paperwork, the job of personnel officer extends well beyond such routine matters, and indeed beyond the personnel department proper. Every manager in the organization is a personnel manager: dealing directly with employees, specifying job requirements, making final hiring decisions, doling out rewards and discipline, and implementing the guidelines or suggestions of the personnel officer.

This chapter is divided into four sections:

1. The role of line and staff in personnel management—effective personnel management requires a cooperative division of labor between line and staff, accepting the vital role of each and appreciating the necessity for a close working relationship.
2. The functions of personnel management—the close interactions among recruitment, placement, evaluation, and development.
3. Managing conflict in the organization—negotiating with unions, handling grievances, mediating disputes, and effecting disciplinary action.
4. The changing scene in personnel administration, in response to changing societal values and rapidly evolving technology—the important role personnel management will continue to play in future organizations.

Personnel management serves as a coordinating mechanism to facilitate a harmonious work place, ensures that employee planning is not left to chance, and assists management in specifying the numerous personnel policies that affect worker and supervisor alike. Throughout this book we have emphasized the importance of effectively motivating employees to fulfill organizational goals while making the task at hand intrinsically satisfying for the worker. In this chapter, we shall examine the various formal processes developed by organizations to accomplish this objective.

The Role of Line and Staff

The Need for Staff

As North Star was getting organized, the four partners thought little about establishing a staff position to advise them in personnel matters. Indeed, they did not give a thought to personnel concerns. All were too busy trying to meet production deadlines and to line up new work. A young company is totally preoccupied with matters of survival, leaving no time for organizational and procedural aspects; thus, the establishment of firm company policies on pension plans, retirement benefits, and other "fringes" may seem incidental to the job at hand. The managers do not draft job descriptions or take the necessary time to record policies and procedures; if they consider this oversight at all, they probably rationalize that flexibility takes precedence over structure. In short, they are just too busy for such "red tape"—and there is usually no one on the start-up team who is trained in such matters, anyway.

As a company takes on more employees, however, such an informal situation becomes unworkable. Although we saw in chapter 4 that workers are not motivated solely by such factors as wages, fringe benefits, incentives, and security, these amenities nevertheless are important to them (they are the main focus of most union efforts), and generally they are unwilling to accept ambiguity in the matter of benefits. Yet line executives, though they are attuned to the importance of "managerial" personnel administration (monitoring and supervising workers to do the task at hand), are almost always too busy to consider "routine" personnel matters. This situation calls for a staff position to provide expertise in the vital matters which the line views as incidental, coordinate policies across all departments so the company speaks with a single voice, and establish rules to serve as precedents for future personnel actions. Unless such a coordinating section is set up rather soon after an organization gets under way, the managers will have to formulate hasty policies on matters they know little about, resulting in a patchwork quilt of uncoordinated and often inconsistent policies. The sum total may not only vary from department to department but also conflict with the goals of the enterprise.

This situation has developed in many city governments, as public workers have begun to win lucrative pension benefits for future payment. City budgeters are awakening to the disconcerting fact that such pension obligations create large fixed costs in future budgets and eliminate a great deal of flexibility in city planning. The problem has grown slowly, reflecting the administrators' lack of real experience in such matters; and it is compounded by the fact that line decision makers in many municipal governments are relatively short-term politicians who look toward tomorrow's election rather than potential financial crises years in the future.

In chapter 3, "Design and Development of Organizations," we saw that the "line" is composed of managers on the firing line, doing the job the organization was built for. Staff plays an advisory and service role, keeping the line people supplied with the ammunition they need to carry on the fight. The dividing line between these seemingly clear-cut functions is often blurred, however, creating confusion as to which group does what.

line
staff

Role of the Line

Imagine that you manage one of six supermarkets in a large chain in your city. You are a member of the "line." What personnel responsibilities do you carry, as compared with the chain's personnel department, headed by the vice-president for personnel?

job description

First of all, you are responsible for determining job descriptions and selecting qualified applicants to work in your store. It is your job to determine what duties need to be performed and to prepare written specifications setting forth these duties (except with standardized jobs, to which the same specifications apply for all stores). You will interview potential candidates sent to you by the personnel department (or if the job is a minor one, you may do the advertising for candidates yourself), and will make the final decision as to which of the qualified candidates you will hire.

Every new employee needs to learn how to carry out the duties of his or her position, and it is your job to provide this training, in terms of proper performance of the particular job and information necessary to survive in the organization. In addition to training for the immediate present, you must look ahead and predict future training needs so your present employees will be prepared to cope with future tasks. As we shall see in the following sections, training for future needs (employee development) may consist of in-house training courses, training in outside schools or colleges, or consultant-based training. Training for present needs most frequently involves on-the-job training, though for complex tasks more formal training is required.

types of training

The manager is responsible for employee evaluation and promotion. As a line manager, you are obliged to review your employees' performance and provide a fair appraisal of progress to date. If you are innovative, you may employ *management by objectives* or *management by results* techniques to carry out this task. As positions become available, it is your job to decide what individuals deserve promotion within your sphere of operations.

Probably your major role as a line manager is to instill morale into your employees—to make them want to work for you. As their immediate supervisor, you are their first major contact with the organization (they view their fellow workers as "peers," not as "the company"). Thus, your behavior will have a major impact on how your workers behave and on their attitude toward the company. Your management style is an important factor in determining the effectiveness of the organization's human resource skills. You are the bestower of rewards and discipline; although company policies exist that spell out incentives and punishments, you implement those policies and thereby control their operation. If they are wise, you must defend them; if they are poorly conceived or unjust, you must seek to change them. You are the grantor of certain privileges and benefits, such as choice of those who work overtime, approval of sick leave, confirmation of vacation schedules and other absences, control of working conditions, procurement of better equipment, and so on.

Safety and health are important issues in every organization, and here again it is the line manager who is responsible for insuring that company policy is carried out. It is the immediate supervisor's duty to familiarize his or her workers with safety rules, and to develop in them a sense of responsibility for carrying them out.

The line supervisor plays a vital role in the labor relations area, as the person who establishes day-to-day contact with representatives of the union local. Although there is a role for staff to play in the negotiation process, the line must be intimately involved, for line supervisors implement the resultant contract provisions, deal with grievances, and strive to make labor-management relations a positive force for attaining organizational goals.

Functions of Staff

By examining the personnel roles of our supermarket manager, we see that the line has many duties in the personnel area. However, our manager directs only one of many supermarkets owned by the chain. Clearly, if policy is to be uniform across the company, some central personnel department is necessary to provide both coordination and expertise. In each of the personnel areas where line has a responsibility, so too does the staff—the personnel director and his or her associates. For example, it is the personnel director who does the recruiting, seeking to attract the most qualified candidates for each job specified by the line. Unless a job to be filled is one requiring few skills, with many applicants, a central recruitment operation can cover the labor market more efficiently than any one store. The personnel department is the gateway to the company, as nearly all applicants are screened first by this office. After applicants have completed interviews and any necessary testing, the personnel department selects qualified candidates (often in priority order, based on qualifications), and sends them to the line manager for further interviewing. The line makes the final decision, but the choice is confined to candidates certified as qualified by the personnel department. For more senior posts, there may be a company rule requiring the line manager to select one of the top three candidates on the personnel department priority listing.

personnel department

Personnel departments, often to the chagrin of the line, are experts on the organization's policy, and apply it in classifying positions. Thus, if a line manager wishes to offer a prospective employee a particular salary, the personnel office must certify that job specifications are in line with the salary recommended. If they are not, the salary must be adjusted according to company policy (bearing in mind the competitive conditions of the labor market). If this adjustment were not made centrally and impartially, there would be a tendency for individual departments to offer salaries out of line with those in other departments, leading to a chaotic salary structure with the same job earning different rates in different departments. Similarly, the personnel department is familiar with federal and local regulations regarding hiring procedures. In the past, sources of employment discrimination have ranged from flagrant prejudice to more subtle rationales such as biased testing procedures, slanted job qualifications, and prejudicial recruitment procedures. Recent federal legislation (such as the Equal Opportunity Act of 1964 and the Occupational Safety and Health Act of 1972) and court decisions have provoked many changes, and the personnel department performs a watchdog function to ensure that both line and staff departments observe the established guidelines. Personnel maintains similar surveillance over such areas as overtime rules, minimum wage standards, pensions, and so on.

The personnel department assists all other departments in training and development, seeing that the employees get the training needed to keep them from growing stale. One route to company vitality lies along

supervisory development

the path of continual sensible training and development programs. Tomorrow's top managers are today's lower level employees, and most firms of any size (including governmental agencies) have continuous educational programs to prepare their employees. Changing technology imposes demands for entirely new skills, which must be developed either by bringing in and training new employees or by "retreading" present employees with somewhat similar jobs. Although the department needing the trained workers has a major input into training curricula, the personnel department has the prime responsibility for arranging the courses and for suitable liaison with the department. Personnel has the follow-up task of determining how effective training programs have been and planning future directions for training. In the broad field of "supervisory development," concentrating on leadership topics as opposed to specific technical training, personnel has the overall responsibility and may require (through top management) attendance by line supervisors at such training programs.

Other personnel department functions include:

- Maintaining formal employee files, frequently important for legal purposes
- Establishing the system for employee evaluation, and requiring the line supervisors to conform to it
- Preparing a schedule of offenses and of authorized disciplinary action, for administration by the line
- Insuring that employees are aware of, and are given, their full rights in grievance and disciplinary appeal cases
- Establishing promotion rules (time in grade, eligibility, number of steps, etc.)

Changing technology demands entirely new skills.

- Establishing salary and wage schedules, where these are not matters of union contracts, often by conducting wage surveys of firms utilizing similar skills
- Advising supervisors of personnel regulations and policies, and occasionally providing professional counsel to supervisors when faced with a grievance case where the employee is represented by private counsel or union counsel

Although managers have primary responsibility for dealing with their workers, some fail to recognize (or acknowledge) the need for human relations skills in that area. By contrast, personnel department specialists often *are* human relations-oriented; a dissatisfied employee will go to the personnel specialist with many work-related problems, casting the personnel officer in the role of mediator between supervisor and employee to ensure that company policy is carried out. If this task is well performed, the supervisor's understanding of human relations skills may be improved; if badly performed, disharmony between personnel and line departments may result.

In labor-management dealings and negotiations, personnel officers utilize their human relations skills to diagnose the underlying sources of difficulty and work with line management to alleviate tension spots and build positive relations. Actual negotiations are handled in different ways in different companies, but the personnel specialist always has a key role to play. Although the personnel officer is always attuned to human relations, he or she should not allow this concern to mask the realities of the situation at hand. The personnel representative should view the situation objectively and offer advice based on the facts, rather than always siding with the workers.

When the municipal employees of a small California coastal city demanded cost-of-living raises on a par with those accorded city employees in Los Angeles and San Francisco, the city managers responded by calling in an outside personnel specialist as mediator. Instead of simply pointing out that both living costs and tax revenues were considerably higher in the larger cities, a sarcastic approach that could only have angered the workers, the mediator took a different tack. First, job descriptions for each level in the city wage structure were carefully analyzed. Next, current wages were compared with those earned by workers at the same levels in cities of a similar size. Finally, the percentage increases recently awarded those workers by their cities were calculated. When this information was laid before the labor representatives, it was clear to them, as to the city managers, that cost-of-living raises were certainly indicated—but on a somewhat smaller scale than labor had originally demanded. Angry rhetoric was avoided on both sides; the statistics told the story. Such an approach clearly demands not only an understanding of human behavior and a grounding in human relations techniques, but a proper perspective on labor-management relations as well. This balanced viewpoint can serve as the basis for fair and objective personnel policies.

One of the most useful functions performed by the personnel department is research on all areas of human resource management. In virtually every area we have discussed thus far, research for the purpose of

human resource management

evaluating and predicting must be conducted. How does our organization compare to competitors' in terms of opportunities for promotion, advancement, and training? How are we doing in terms of salary? In general, do people enjoy working for us? Is the company meeting federal guidelines for employment? How well are current staffing and training efforts fulfilling present and future company goals? What benefits are we getting in return for current expenditures on human resources? Are we developing a dependable supply of replacements for skilled employees who will retire or quit? Many other questions will occur to the alert personnel officer, and if the answers are unsatisfactory, there is work to be done.

After Barbara Newman was hired, what were the roles of line and staff in the area of personnel? What were the areas of line and staff cooperation?

Interaction Between Line and Staff

Back to the supermarket again. Suppose it is different from the other stores in the chain, because it is located in a large Cuban refugee colony. As manager, you decide that it would be a wise competitive move to provide a consumer advisor who can communicate with the customers in their own language and can assist them in buying and preparing American dishes to suit their tastes. To create such a position, you need both the approval of higher management and the assistance of the personnel department. You write up a justification for the position and a description of duties, and send them to the personnel department for classification and review. The personnel department must set a salary schedule, review the job specifications, and determine the qualifications required. Personnel takes this task seriously, for precedent is being set for the company's future hiring and classifying of consumer advisors in any store in the chain. The process is often lengthy, and sorely tries the patience of the line operator, who becomes frustrated by all this "red tape."

recruitment

Assuming all these hurdles are cleared, the next step is recruitment. Personnel advertises within and outside the company for qualified applicants, and screens them. It then sends those who are approved to you, the line manager, for final interviews and selection.

employee records

Once the individual is hired and on the job, interaction continues between line and staff in many areas: maintenance of employee records, any disciplinary action, employee benefits, any future training, labor relations, safety inspections, communication services (such as house organs, training manuals, photographs, speech releases), and personnel evaluation and promotion. Figure 10-1 shows some of the areas where the personnel department works with line employees.

Conflict Between Line and Staff

What are possible areas of conflict between North Star's new personnel director and the old-timers?

In any situation where there are two managers who exert some influence over the same division of an organization, there is bound to be some potential for conflict. The situation is made even more troublesome if the priorities of the two managers are different, as in the case of the personnel manager and the line manager. The former is preoccupied with procedures, and has very little interest in line productivity (not because he or she does not wish to see the venture prosper, but simply as a result of lack of information about line tasks). The latter is interested predominantly in productivity, and any procedures which interfere with that are a nuisance or worse.

Since the personnel specialist and the supervisor view the organization from different vantage points, the ensuing divergent perspectives create an atmosphere of conflict. The primary complaints of the line in dealing with personnel staff are:

- Personnel holds up progress with its red tape.
- New procedures upset the routine.
- Affirmative action is all very well, but there is a limit.
- Transfers break up existing smooth-running teams.
- New hires are not qualified.
- Training programs are nonresponsive and ineffective.
- Supervisory development training is a bunch of nonsense; if they had to run a job they'd see how silly it was.
- Such rules as restriction on unscheduled overtime are unrealistic.
- Personnel refuses to classify jobs the way they ought to be.
- Personnel actions are always being reversed because of some little loophole (such as disciplinary actions awarded by line supervisors).

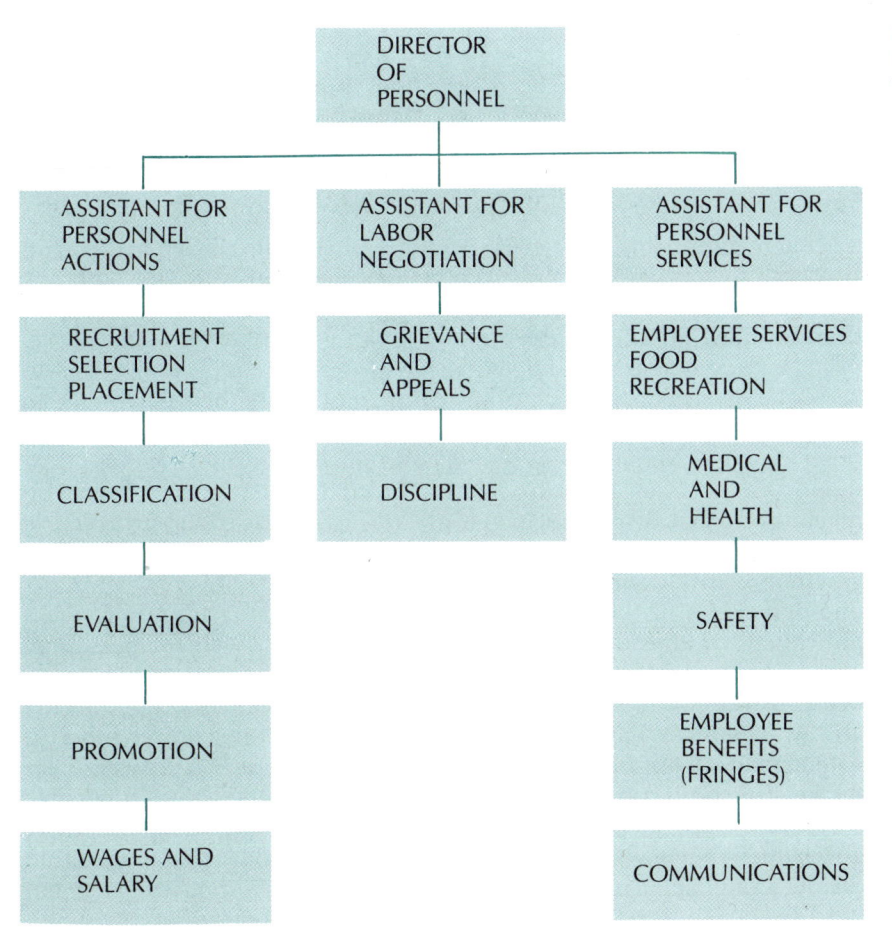

Figure 10-1. Personnel Department Organization Chart

```
                    DIRECTOR
                       OF
                    PERSONNEL
         ┌─────────────┼─────────────┐
  ASSISTANT FOR  ASSISTANT FOR  ASSISTANT FOR
   PERSONNEL        LABOR       PERSONNEL
    ACTIONS      NEGOTIATION     SERVICES
        │             │              │
  RECRUITMENT     GRIEVANCE    EMPLOYEE SERVICES
   SELECTION        AND             FOOD
   PLACEMENT       APPEALS       RECREATION
        │             │              │
                                  MEDICAL
  CLASSIFICATION  DISCIPLINE       AND
                                  HEALTH
        │                            │
   EVALUATION                      SAFETY
        │                            │
                                 EMPLOYEE
   PROMOTION                     BENEFITS
                                 (FRINGES)
        │                            │
  WAGES AND                    COMMUNICATIONS
   SALARY
```

349
PERSONNEL MANAGEMENT

- Personnel won't back up the supervisor in grievance cases.
- Personnel actions by the personnel department take too long.
- The company newspaper is a bunch of hogwash.
- Safety rules are too strict, particularly where it is a question of enforcing a rule when there is no real hazard at all.
- Personnel puts out instructions without checking with the line supervisors or other managers first, so they are unworkable.

Personnel specialists, on the other hand, often feel that the line supervisors are too parochial and stubborn in their views. They have the following complaints against the line:

- They never follow instructions or procedures.
- Every case is always an emergency.
- They are insensitive to human relations.
- They don't see the need for establishing policy and standardization of procedures.
- They take disciplinary action on insufficient grounds, and then want personnel to back them up in no-win situations.
- They try to "cheat" on all the rules whenever they can.
- They won't cooperate with personnel in following requirements.
- They always want jobs classified too high.
- They are reluctant to prepare position descriptions for jobs, and when they do the descriptions are poorly and incompletely written.
- They don't see the need for supervisory development training, although by and large they are all grossly in need of it themselves.
- They will not assist personnel in preparing training programs for their employees—and then gripe at how bad the training is.
- Senior managers try to "pull rank" on personnel.

Such complaints are typical of line and staff in all departments in practically every organization. There is some truth to what both are saying, but many of the complaints are the result of mutual misunderstandings. The tasks performed by both groups are essential to the organization, and top management must exert a continuous effort to reconcile divergent interests. Some companies rotate their personnel, to give line and staff an opportunity to see if the grass really is greener in the other pasture. Management should also encourage more contact and interaction between the two groups through scheduling of luncheon meetings and informal discussion groups, as well as structuring more formal interaction on the departmental level.

personnel director

In a relatively small company, the personnel director may be simply one person (as in the case of North Star). What is needed here is an individual who has the professional knowledge required for personnel management *and* the time to concentrate on personnel matters without being distracted by "higher priority" matters as the line managers always are. As a company gets larger the personnel function requires subordinate managers, but in all probability the director of personnel will retain the key functions, or at least some of them. Figure 10-4 shows a possible organization for such a medium-sized company. A large corporation or government agency would have directors of individual branches within the personnel department, as shown in Figure 10-5, with the department head free to concentrate on whatever area was important at any time.

What structure is most appropriate for North Star's personnel department?

Some organizations have gone so far as to split up the functions of personnel and labor relations under two separate managers who report separately to the chief executive. One very large corporation, United States Steel (which negotiates with the United Steelworkers for a number of steel companies in concert), has given its chief labor negotiator the post of vice-chairman, which in a sense puts him on a level with the president of the corporation. The personnel function, however, is handled at a level below the president. The advantage is that the labor relations manager can concentrate on his important task unhindered by personnel duties; the disadvantage is that he is not as well informed on personnel problems as he should be.

labor relations manager

A Systems View of Personnel Management

We have seen that the personnel function applies to many aspects of dealing with the people in an organization: recruitment, selection, appraisal, training and development, promotion, compensation, and on-the-job relations with employees. In the following paragraphs we shall consider some of the details of how each one is handled within an organization. One of the first things the manager must recognize is that all are very closely interrelated. Figure 10-6, for example, illustrates functional overlaps among what Richard Beatty[1] calls the selection, evaluation, training, and motivation subsystems.

subsystems of personnel

Let's begin with the selection subsystem, to see where the overlaps lie. This system is quite dependent on the evaluation and training programs, for it is in these systems that the relevant selection criteria for the position

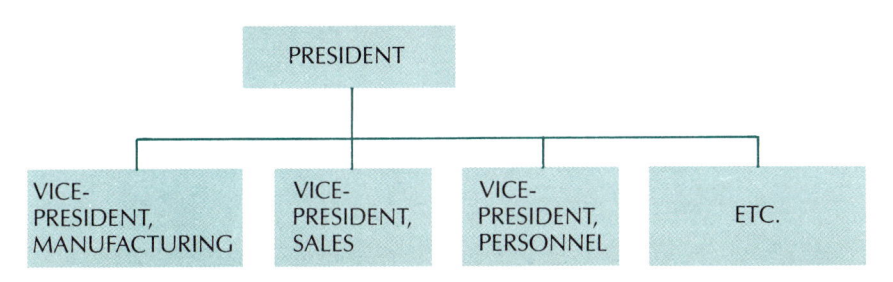

Figure 10-2.
Alternative Personnel Organization (A)

Figure 10-3.
Alternative Personnel Organization (B)

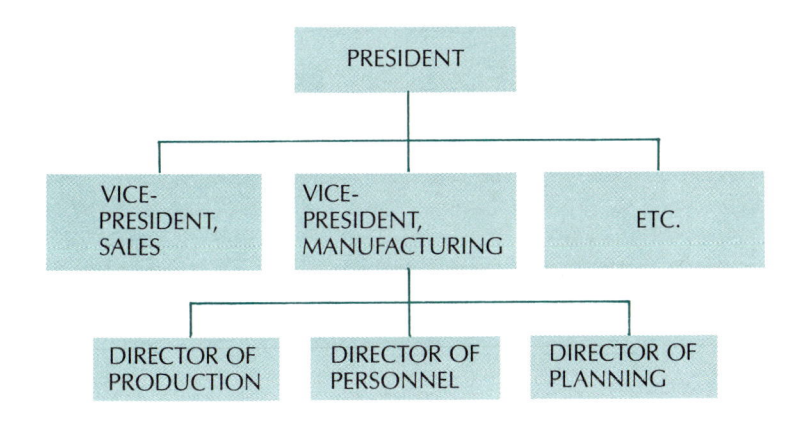

351
PERSONNEL MANAGEMENT

are grounded. Once appraisals of existing candidates are made, personnel staffers can determine both whether the existing criteria result in good performance and whether the positions can be filled by inside transfers. Similarly, an analysis of the training programs required for newly hired employees illustrates the necessary qualifications for the programs. Selection, on the other hand, determines the directions of the training program by establishing the characteristics of the raw material to be trained.

Personnel planners forecast future needs by examining the type of training and development programs which exist currently. Are the programs preparing present employees for the future needs of the company? The answer to this question will determine future selection criteria. Training programs, of course, influence appraisal systems by enabling employees to improve their on-the-job performance. The performance evaluation acts as a feedback system to indicate whether training programs have been successful and how they should be changed.

Each of these areas clearly influences employee morale. As we shall see below, appraisal systems can be designed so they involve the employee actively (management by objectives). Selection systems have a large impact on employee behavior. Talented young employees will be watching the promotion and reward practices of a company closely, and if not satisfied will look elsewhere for greener pastures. Similarly, seniority in job placement has been an important negotiating point with unions, for it provides essential security for older employees. Training programs affect employee morale in a number of ways. If employees see that the program improves their general skills and thus makes them more employable in other companies, they will have a favorable reaction. If they can see that the program is administered impartially, the morale effect will be good. Particularly bad is the sort of employee development program which

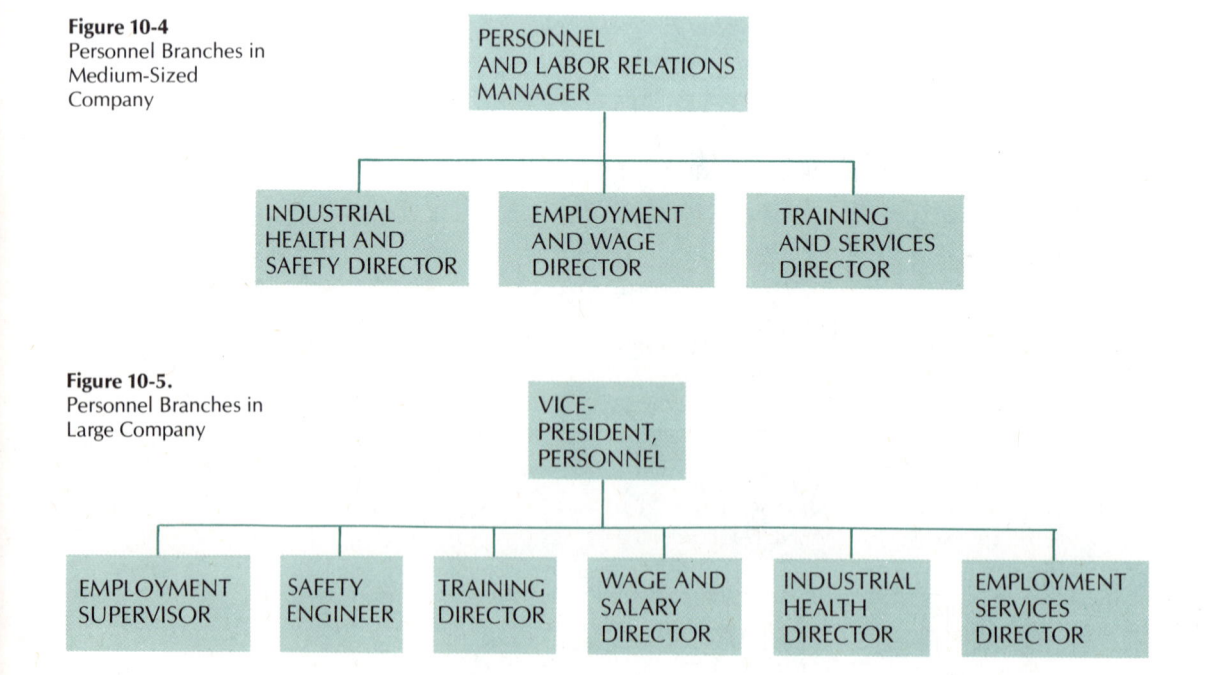

Figure 10-4
Personnel Branches in Medium-Sized Company

Figure 10-5.
Personnel Branches in Large Company

MANAGERS AT WORK

signals to employees that the fortunate ones selected for training have in effect been preselected for future promotion.

The personnel system of an organization is dynamic and interactive. Each of its parts, while important in itself, takes on additional significance for the company's success when viewed as a part of the whole. The best of wagons is useless without horses, and a company with superb physical facilities and equipment cannot stay afloat without both *capable* and *contented* employees. A properly functioning personnel system is vital insurance to help attain both of these goals.

Personnel Planning

In chapter 6 we saw that an organization must plan if it is to keep its head above water. Personnel planning is a critical necessity, but many managers have their eyes on other types of planning and overlook it. It cannot be postponed with safety, for it takes many years to develop a skilled work force, especially for managerial positions. In 1974, the Westinghouse Electric Corporation put into effect an early retirement system for its five most senior executives, placing them in a nonline consultative role at age 60. Thus, the company ensured an orderly progression of promotion in top managerial ranks without the need to retire a large number of executives at once with no chance for their replacements to get on-the-job training. It was an expensive move, for the semi-retirement salaries of the five probably ran about $750,000 a year, but apparently it was considered well worth this price for the valuable training it would provide the lower managerial echelons. Personnel planning involves assessing both external and internal factors to determine how the organization can be aligned to cope with the future. Although certain external factors such as the

personnel planning

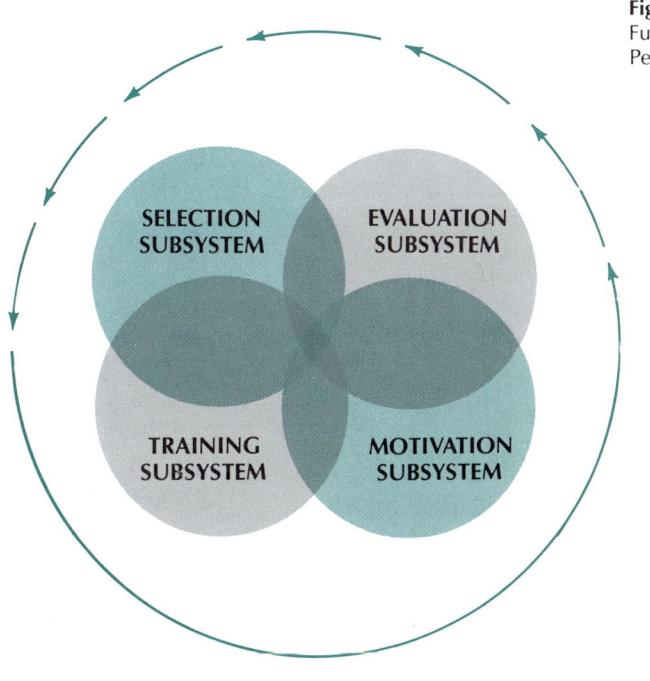

Figure 10-6.
Functional Overlap of Personnel Systems

<aside>Is a personnel planning program feasible in a new company such as North Star? What direction should such a program take?</aside>

unemployment rate or new technological developments are unpredictable, the personnel department should be cognizant of more reliable cues such as job market trends toward service and away from industrial orientation, foreseeable technological change, trends in market tastes, geographical and locational factors (shift of urban poor to the cities, etc.), and so on. A critical personnel task involves analyzing the impact of these factors on worker demand and supply levels. A forecast of internal trends such as forthcoming retirements or other terminations, personnel obsolescence because of changing product mix, restructuring of departments, and plant openings or closings, must be fed into the hopper as well. Such planning is facilitated by the growing use of the computer for management purposes.

Personnel planning is central to all of the components of the personnel system, particularly selection and training. In recent years much emphasis has focused on the managerial level, probably sparked by the unanticipated shortage of skilled executives after World War II. Planning for executive positions clearly extends beyond the counting of heads and listing of openings. Studies have shown that different management slots demand different sorts of people, with different values, backgrounds, and personalities. Indeed, some companies will change an organizational structure to fit the available person, rather than try to squeeze a square peg of a manager into a round hole of an executive slot. Solid personnel planning helps counteract the "Peter principle," whereby an employee is promoted step by step until reaching the maximum "level of incompetence."[2]

<aside>Peter principle

level of incompetence</aside>

Personnel planning is a vital key to an organization's future. An organization which is conscious of the importance of planning for worker

<aside>A company with superb physical facilities cannot stay afloat without capable and contented employees.</aside>

MANAGERS AT WORK

demand down the road will focus upon the development of appropriate training programs which will satisfy this demand. Through such planning, management avoids being caught with an organization full of fish when the situation calls for fowl.

Selection of Personnel

The selection subsystem of the personnel system involves the matching of jobs and individuals by means of job analysis and description, recruitment, and the final selection process.

selection subsystem

Job Analysis

Many organizations hire analysts to examine the various tasks performed in the company, in order to gain a clear idea of exactly what each task involves. Sometimes a verbal description by a supervisor of what workers do differs considerably from the job itself, as observation of an individual doing the job discloses. When Frederick W. Taylor performed his famous studies of laborer tasks involving shoveling, one of the key elements of the task was the selection of the proper shovel. No doubt a foreman, describing this task performed by laborers under his jurisdiction, would consider it simply *shoveling;* but Taylor found that the time for a given task could be halved by selection of the proper shovel. Since the selection was left to the laborer (who was not a critical analyst of the effect of shovel capacity on job duration), shovels of the wrong size were usually selected. A skilled analyst is trained to watch for these nonobvious elements in apparently simple tasks, and such job analysis enables the personnel department to classify positions, determine qualifications, and select measurement criteria for selection and appraisal.

job analysis

Job Specification

Job specification is the procedure whereby jobs are described and classified. Job description explains what the employee does; job classification indicates where the job falls in the ladder of organizational positions. It is not a simple task to write job descriptions and classify jobs, for the whole system on which the company bases evaluation, compensation, promotion and benefits is at stake. The employee is critically concerned, because the description is a worker's blueprint for employee action and management expectations. Time and again employees will refuse to perform certain tasks which are "not in the job description."

job classification

It appears easy to classify jobs. After all, this person is a bricklayer and that person is a house painter. The hard part comes in differentiating within a particular classification. How many classifications lie within the overall title of office worker or welder or computer programmer? Obviously, the clerk-typist turning out routine letters does not approach the polished skills of an executive secretary, who may research and compose top-level reports and organize major business conventions. Obviously, the tack welder attaching temporary lifting eyes to a steel beam for raising it into position doesn't face the exacting requirements of the craftsman who welds the high-tensile steel joints in the pressure vessel of a nuclear reactor. Between these two pairs of workers are many shadings of relative skills and judgment demanded by the many different sorts of jobs in a complex organization.

Some of the main issues involved in job classification and description are the following:

- How many positions should we have?
- What degree of discretion should be allowed, compared with the need for precise specification within the job description?
- How can a balance between too broad and too narrow be obtained? (If the former, it's hard to specify particular skills; if the latter, there are too many skills for any one employee.)
- How much technical detail should be included (realizing that technical processes change rapidly and the description may become outdated if too specific)?
- To what extent should employees in different departments but in similar work be classified together or separately (should an electrician in the power plant, handling heavy equipment, be in a different classification from an electrician in the maintenance shop, who troubleshoots problems with production equipment of all sizes)?
- What should hazardous or unpleasant working conditions do to the classification (is a steelworker who erects steel high in the air different from one who does the same thing on the ground, and if not, how will the differences be recognized and compensated)?

What steps must Barbara take to set up a classification system for North Star? What degree of flexibility should be built into North Star's classification system?

Recruitment

Recruitment is the process of attracting employees to the organization. In today's world, this involves more than simply filling a job with a person—even with a qualified person. Many laws describe just what you must do and not do in order to be a legal employer. Figure 10-7 shows guidelines drawn up by a major California company to guide its personnel specialists and supervisors in employment interviews. Title VII of the Civil Rights Act of 1964, as amended in 1972, prohibits discrimination in hiring on the basis of race, color, national origin, religion, or sex. Its provisions have been clarified by court cases which have awarded both blacks and women large damages for discrimination. (In *Phillips* v. *Martin Marietta Corp.*, it was labeled discrimination when a woman was denied an assembly line position because she had young children. In *Weeks* v. *Southern Bell Telephone Co.*, a woman denied a switchman's job because work was too heavy was granted legal expenses plus $31,000 in back pay and overtime earned by the man who got the job.) The Equal Employment Opportunity Commission (EEOC) was set up to enforce these statutes, initially under the guidance of the Justice Department, but now on its own. The EEOC has taken its job seriously and closely monitors the hiring practices of both public and private organizations.

Equal Employment Opportunity Commission

Grandpa (or Grandma) may not be on the shelf after all. Among other provisions, the Employment Act of 1967 prevents discrimination in hiring of those between 40 and 65. Airlines that were laying off their older stewardesses (or cabin attendants—who now include both men and women) have beat a hasty retreat. At the other end of the spectrum, the Fair Labor Standards Act prohibits child labor that is "oppressive," and state laws amplify these limitations.

Hiring the handicapped is not mandatory, but the federal government established a national committee years ago to encourage and assist firms in hiring disabled workers. A handicapped worker who is excluded unreasonably from a job because of a physical requirement can obtain legal relief. On the other hand, some state laws involving "aggravation of preexisting physical condition" may make it legally hazardous to hire certain types of handicapped individuals. One of the most frequently occurring issues in unemployment compensation cases is whether a disability was caused by conditions of work. When the disability is of a psychiatric nature, the employer is in a particularly tough spot; some studies show that individuals with psychiatric problems have a higher incidence of tardiness, absenteeism, and work disputes, yet such a problem may not in itself disqualify the person for the job.[3]

Recruitment takes many forms, and depends a great deal on the type of position available, current employment conditions, and the company's current situation. Some jobs (e.g., dishwasher) call for little skill and are filled virtually by walk-in applicants. Most jobs involve more qualifications, however, and recruiters must try to tap the right sources to reach qualified people, by posting on company bulletin boards; distributing position announcements in the company paper; listing through union media; running newspaper want ads; using state employment services;

recruitment techniques

Subject	Can Do or Ask	Cannot Do or Ask
Sex	Notice appearance.	Make comments or notes unless sex is BFOQ.*
Marital status	Status after hiring, for insurance purposes.	Are you married? Single? Divorced? Engaged? Living with anyone? Do you see your ex-spouse?
Children	Numbers and ages of children after hiring, for insurance purposes.	Do you have children at home? How old? Who cares for them? Do you plan more children?
Physical data	Explain manual labor, lifting, other requirements of the job. Show how it is performed. Require physical exam.	How tall are you? How heavy?
Criminal record	If security clearance is necessary, can be done prior to employment.	Have you ever been arrested, convicted or spent time in jail?
Military status	Are you a veteran? Why not? Any job-related experience?	What type of discharge do you have? What branch did you serve in?
Age	Age after hiring. "Are you over 18?"	How old are you? Estimate age.
Housing	If you have no phone, how can we reach you?	Do you own your home? Do you rent? Do you live in an apartment or a house?

*BFOQ = bona fide occupational qualification

Figure 10-7.
Personnel Recruitment Guidelines

using private employment services which charge fees to the employee or employer; and reviewing current lists of available people from the "register" of those who have applied in the past and been found qualified.

College recruiting is a common approach for professional and managerial posts, with company representatives visiting college campuses to provide information about the company and the job environment, and to make a preliminary assessment of candidates. Those who pass the first screening are invited to the company's headquarters or a plant. Many companies have established internship programs which bring in a number of candidates each year; the candidates spend the first year or so touring various departments and plants, with the aim of creating the best fit between candidate and job as well as providing a good training school in the company's business. Organizations assess the results from various recruiting approaches, and drop those that don't pay off. During the 1974-75 recession many companies cut back sharply on college recruiting, and newspapers reported long lines at recruiting stations.

Professional and managerial posts of more seniority often are recruited at professional conferences; generally there is a bulletin board full of notices announcing openings and soliciting interviews, and many conferees attend largely for the purpose of seeking new positions. Top management posts outside the company are filled by personal references from board members who know promising candidates, by word-of-mouth recruiting, or by "head hunting" (employing an executive search firm to solicit applications from successful executives in other firms). One company who sent its middle-level managers on a recruiting trip to professional society meetings during the period of candidate shortages did not get a single new recruit—but lost two of its managers to other recruiters. Government officials, particularly in policy positions, are attractive candidates for senior spots with major corporations, since the latter are so intimately involved in government projects and subject to government dictates. As long as a conflict of interest (where a government official influences some decision in favor of a company and then takes a job with the company) does not arise, this approach can be beneficial all around, since it broadens the perspective of the companies and increases their knowledge of government policies and practices.

The ability of an organization to attract top-notch people depends not only on its recruiting efforts but also on what it has to offer. Its reputation for professional excellence, social consciousness, and good personnel policies gets around, and unfavorable reports in this area can nullify any recruitment efforts. Moreover, it helps to be a company known to give young people some real opportunity for decision making, even if the company is also known to crack down on failure.

The Selection Process

Establishing criteria. Many elements are involved in the selection process. Once job qualifications are set down, through job analysis, it is important to establish criteria to measure a candidate's ability to do the job. Companies not only need to attract their share of good people, they need to know which are the good ones. Companies traditionally have laid down criteria such as graduation from high school (or college) and ability to pass a battery of tests designed both to let in qualified workers and to screen out unqualified ones. (Many companies, when charged with using these procedures maliciously to exclude certain kinds of people, were indignant. They hadn't consciously done anything of the sort—but neither had they reflected that many of their own well-qualified old-timers could not have survived such screening.) The problem with this method is that organizations cannot be sure that such criteria appropriately measure ability to do a job. A test must be both *reliable* (capable of measuring consistently) and *valid* (capable of measuring what you want to measure). Thus, a test may reliably measure mathematical ability, but the question is whether math is a valid requirement for the job.

reliability
validity

The EEOC has successfully challenged such testing procedures in court. In a significant case, *Griggs* v. *Duke Power Company* (1971), the right of management to require a high school diploma and to utilize the Wonderlic Personnel Test and the Bennett Mathematical Aptitude Test as conditions of selection was successfully challenged, since these tests did not measure the ability to learn or perform a job or a category of jobs. The Griggs case resolved four issues:

- Screening devices, whether tests or application questions, must be related to job performance, with the burden of proof on the organization.
- Verbal statements of good faith carry no weight as defense against use of tests which adversely affect employment of minorities or women and have no job relatedness.
- Neutral tests cannot be maintained if they operate to freeze the status quo of prior discriminatory practices.
- While screening devices are not discriminatory per se, the organization must be able to prove that the test is used solely to measure ability to do the job and is not used to reject people unfairly for employment.

Applying for the position. Basic information needed by the organization is requested on the *application form:* education, past employment, demographic background, interests, experience. A *personal history statement* is useful to supplement the information above.

application form

The initial screening process may involve an interview or simply a review of the written application, or both. Some jobs require the applicant to report in person, whereas others handle the whole thing by mail. Once it is determined that a person is a qualified candidate, the testing process starts, to determine whether he or she will be offered the position or be put on the "register" from which candidates will be selected from time to time as openings develop.

Entrance criteria. Every employer wants to know the qualifications and potential performance capabilities of a prospective employee before a commitment is made for hiring. One of the methods most frequently used to predict candidate abilities is testing. Advocates of testing cite the objectivity of the questions as an asset, for a written or mechanically oriented test screens out such subjective factors as personal appearance and other individual characteristics which can prejudice an interviewer against a well-qualified candidate. References from previous employers are sometimes as untrustworthy as the personal interview for a number of reasons: (1) previous bosses may have unfounded personal biases against the applicant; (2) poor applicants may end up with praiseworthy references because their previous employer felt sorry for them; and (3) a present employer may want a poor employee to leave and therefore provide a glowing recommendation. Given these shortcomings of subjective judgments, testing has been employed by numerous companies as a primary mechanism to guide hiring practices.

The Griggs decision cited above, however, established stringent guidelines for the use of testing. A recent study of 2,500 companies showed that 36.5% of those queried do not test at all, although it was not determined how many used tests prior to the court's decision. Of the remaining companies still using tests, three of four have reduced their use, and nearly 14% said they soon intended to stop completely, citing actual or potential problems with the EEOC as the primary reason.[4] Validation of tests is expensive (ranging from $5000 to $20,000 per study) and these companies apparently have decided that the cost simply isn't worth it.

But many larger companies, especially blue-chip companies including Exxon and AT&T, feel differently. They have found testing so valuable that they have taken the time and expense to validate what they are doing. The Personnel Research Coordinator for Exxon, a company with a continuous history of test validation, remarked: "The cost is very, very low compared with a large number of bust-outs in training programs." Considering that it costs Exxon $8,000 to train one refinery worker, the payoff of developing and validating a test that will predict employee success in the program is significant.

testing procedures

A number of tests may be used as entrance requirements, though (as noted above) many of the standardized tests are currently the target of careful scrutiny. One category of test directly measures the candidate's skill to perform on the job. For example, clerical tests are designed to measure ability to type (accuracy and speed) and to take shorthand, while welding tests measure the candidate's skill at welding. Another category of test assesses the applicant's intelligence and personality. Frequently used standardized tests for these purposes are: the Otis Quick Scoring Mental Ability Test, the Weschler Adult Intelligence Scale, the Wonderlic Personnel Test, and the Minnesota Multiphasic Personality Inventory (MMPI).

Some companies have used polygraph tests ("lie detectors") to determine whether candidates have stolen from previous employers. However, there is much criticism in recent years of such tests. They are unlawful in eleven states. The objections center around the fact that they imply self-incrimination, which is outlawed by the Fifth Amendment, and they constitute an invasion of privacy, which seems to violate the Fourth Amendment. In rebuttal, companies claim that they have a right to know whether candidates are demonstrably dishonest, since they are running a serious risk if they hire thieves.

assessment techniques

Assessment centers. Assessment centers are used mainly to select candidates for managerial posts. They involve comprehensive, standardized procedures in which multiple assessment techniques such as situational exercises, interviews, business games, tests, discussion groups and a variety of situations are used to evaluate individual employees or candidates. First introduced in the 1950s, they are being used increasingly both by the federal government and by private companies.

The growing use of assessment centers has created much discussion in management circles over their relative usefulness. Advantages of these centers include:

- They represent a systematic effort to avoid the "Peter Principle" by keeping candidates out of jobs they cannot perform well.
- They are sounder and fairer than traditional methods, because they simulate the actual job environment.
- They do not seem to be unfair to minorities or women.
- They prescreen potential candidates for development, and thus aid in personnel planning.
- The intermingling of candidates and assessors provides for more time to interact and thus a better assessment.

Disadvantages include:

- They are costly and time-consuming.
- The result, for a candidate who does poorly, may be permanent disbarment from future advancement (gets cataloged early).
- They are not inherently job-related.
- The approach runs counter to current ideas on how business, ideally, should operate.

Some assessment techniques are brutal, attempting to strip candidates of their defenses and place them in extraordinarily stressful situations to see if they have the resources or capability to rise to the problem. While the approach is praiseworthy in its attempt to cut through sham and see the real person underneath, it may unfairly judge a manager under circumstances not likely to be repeated on the job. There is division of opinion on the merit of some of the more rugged assessment techniques, but there is little doubt as to the overall contribution of the assessment center if the importance of the job justifies the expense. One northern state conducts a wilderness guide examination which includes a three-day survival test in the woods, beyond doubt separating the sheep from the goats.

Physical examinations. Most companies give physical examinations prior to hiring, although an increasing number do not. When the work is arduous, physical examinations are advisable, since employees will be able to sue companies who put them in job situations where their health or safety are endangered. Most companies who give such examinations are trying to uncover preexisting conditions and document them, so that at a later date the employee will not be able to claim that the condition developed on the job. If an employee willfully submits a fraudulent statement about his or her physical condition, this can be a cause for removal.

Choosing the Applicant

After all the tests and applications have been completed, and a list of eligible candidates has been developed, what then? Usually the candidates are interviewed, either in the personnel office or in the line manager's office, to pick out those elements that did not emerge from the other screening processes. This check determines whether the qualifications actually exist, evaluates personality and manner when these are important (from the study of groups, you can see that they almost always are), analyzes personal interests to see if they are compatible with those of the organization (maybe he or she would not be happy under the particular corporate constraints, etc.), and determines whether the individual is willing to travel, transfer, and so on.

Final interviews are conducted by line management in all but the more routine cases, and sometimes even then. In large companies, where a call goes out for "50 welders" or the equivalent, it makes little sense to conduct interviews, but generally the employing office will want to have the right to exercise a veto if desired. The prohibitions shown in Figure 10-6 must be observed by line interviewers as well as by those in the personnel department.

Training and Development

training subsystem

We have been discussing these functions at various points throughout the chapter. The training and development process covers two areas: training for the present job and training for future needs. Many managers overlook the latter, but it is just as important as capital development (few managers neglect to plan their needs for future equipment), and if it is neglected the company may well be caught short in the future. If industry indicators signal a move from electronics technology to solid state, companies that ignore these trends and develop no skills in this direction will be very slow to respond when customer demands shift. In a well-organized company, the personnel department works with top management to keep constant track of the skills inventory, to see where they might fit in and where the gaps are developing.

Figure 10-8 shows a training ladder, including various types of courses and the corresponding employee competences. Management training needs, in particular, are difficult to predict and fulfill; large organizations require an information system that can keep up with the changing needs in this area (discussed at length in a later section).

A recent development, arising from the combination of recession and previous overhiring of managers, is a glut of young managers in many corporations. This excess of talent has slowed the previous rapid pace of managerial advancement and created intense frustration for young people conditioned to expect a "fast track." Some companies are awarding impressive titles without any real promotion or salary raise. Others, probably more effectively, are arranging lateral transfers so the young managers can expand their horizons and gain more experience even though promotion is not in the cards.

Appraisals

evaluation subsystem

It is necessary for employees to know how they have performed, in order to correct improper habits and avoid misconceptions about work accomplishments. The supervisor closest to the employee is best qualified to do this, but the personnel department must establish appraisal standards to assure fair treatment across the board. Sometimes appraisal is handled by a board, so that individual prejudices are balanced out.

The employee is evaluated on performance in meeting specific job objectives, usually once or twice a year. Sometimes the organization establishes criteria, and sometimes the employee is involved in jointly setting the criteria he or she must meet. Under the *management by objectives* arrangement, the employee and supervisor together determine what the employee's targets will be and evaluate success in reaching them. This system tends to heighten employee involvement and thus to increase motivation. *Management by results* evaluates the employee in terms of what is actually being produced. This technique assumes that the goals are self-evident and that all the supervisor needs to do is see how well they are being met.

management by objectives

management by results

Regardless of the method, the employee should understand clearly what criteria are being used for evaluation. It is very poor (though common) managerial practice to come up with an evaluation at year's end based on criteria that the employee did not understand or appreciate. It is equally poor to award an unsatisfactory mark at the end of a period and have it come as a complete surprise to the employee, who thought all along that the work was satisfactory. These techniques reflect both managerial failure in appraisal and a general lack of communication.

Employees are appraised to provide feedback to the company and feedback to the employee. The former suggests how well recruitment and training programs are working, helps the manager arrange employees in some priority order for future promotion, compares departments in terms of their effectiveness in developing good employees, and provides an assessment of overall employee strengths. The latter apprises workers

Type of Training	Shop Track	Office Track
On-the-job	Top management	
Management seminars	Managerial upgrading	
External study courses	Professional upgrading	
Company indoctrination	Management intern	
College or university	Professional/manager	
Supervisory development	Supervisor	
Technical trade school	Technician	Computer operator
Apprentice school	Journeyman	Planner
Shop/office training	Sub-mechanic	Draftsman, estimator
Commercial high school	Mechanic helper	Stenographer, bookkeeper
On-the-job	Machine operator	Clerk
None	Laborer	Messenger

Figure 10-8.
Training Ladder, Shop and Office Jobs

of their shortcomings so they can work on these problems and motivates them to achieve good performance.

Many problems arise with appraisals. Supervisors do not like to lose good workers, and may tend (often unconsciously) not to report any special skills that could lead to promotion and transfer. Appraisal is a touchy process at best and may lead to ill will, which most humans wish to avoid. Many supervisors dislike playing the role of judge, and the appraisal task becomes a heavy burden to be cast aside whenever possible. Some supervisors feel that a poor report can lead to a grievance by the employee, so that they will have to "defend" the report—which they do not want to do. Sometimes supervisors do not know their people well enough to give an accurate appraisal, so they hedge with a noncommittal report. Appraisals are "red tape," which nobody likes. And finally, it is very hard to do a good job of appraising: it involves setting up criteria, comparing with others, thinking hard about each employee, and recalling good examples, among other difficult operations.

Promotions

Promotion policy is a crucial aspect of every personnel system. This policy plays a large role both in determining who will govern the organization and providing cues to young workers on how far up the organizational ladder they can expect to climb. A frequently used guideline calls for "promotion from within," an approach in which the advantages do not always outnumber the drawbacks. Positive features include retention of employee interest and morale, keeping the best employees with the company, insuring that those at upper management levels have had long experience with the company (and its problems), and reducing training time for new job holders. Promotion from within facilitates personnel planning because promotable employees can be channeled into the appropriate training and development programs well in advance of the promotion. Among its disadvantages, the policy means a lack of new blood and therefore of new ideas and skills—with a corresponding failure to recognize the value of new philosophies and procedures. In addition, the competence of some outside people may surpass that available within the firm.

What do companies look for in promoting an employee? There are many problems, because it is not easy to single out the most important skills for a given job. Is it better for someone to be articulate or energetic? How important are various character traits, and how can you measure them? A person might be promotable to one type of job but not to another—so clearly it is not correct to say that someone is "promotable" at a particular time without saying to *what*. Sometimes a person can do a fine job, but is stuck in a dead-end department. Some people seem to be ready for promotion, but say they do not want it.[5]

Since promotion is the choicest plum the organization has to offer, nothing can drag down morale quicker than mishandling of promotion policy. Management must be aware of the fact that all supervisors are not immune to favoritism or nepotism, and that the promotion system must not reflect such offenses if it is to be effective.

Compensation

Despite valid theories about psychic rewards of work, compensation remains the chief reward. It consists of direct salary or wages, incentive pay where applicable, opportunity for overtime, and fringe benefits which have a financial equivalent. Employees may be on a wage or hourly basis (compensated for each hour they work, with premium pay for overtime), or on a salary or annual basis (with no compensation for overtime, but an understanding that there may be some from time to time). They may also receive piecework or incentive pay, based on what the employee produces, and profit-sharing benefits, based on what the whole company does. The federal government applies strict limitations on the form of profit-sharing system a company may have, essentially saying that it cannot be limited to just a select few of the top employees. When times are such that unions find it inexpedient to push for large wage increases, they try to increase the fringe benefits (future wages).   *fringe benefits*

Companies have elaborate classification systems for setting up compensation scales. In the civil service, state or federal, there are carefully defined "grades" that call for specific salary ranges. An employee who attains a certain grade finds an applicable schedule of wages or salary, and moves up based on time in that grade; but the employee can move out of this schedule only by means of promotion or reclassification.   *compensation scales*

The "point system" assigns points based on amount of skill, physical or mental effort, dangerous or unpleasant work, and the responsibility the job demands. A typical system will evaluate some ten aspects of a job, assign weights to each, and add up the total, which translates into a salary grade.   *point system*

Individual Motivation

This question, discussed in detail in chapter 4, is one of the major personnel responsibilities of the supervisor, with assistance from the personnel officer.

Job enlargement is a reversal of the trend to specialization that came in with the industrial revolution, but has been the butt of much criticism dealing with "mindless" or "meaningless" work. The theory is that a broader and more rewarding job will call on more resources and induce more interest, will be more challenging, and accordingly will increase productivity. Chapter 2 discusses the use of the team system as applied at Volvo.   *job enlargement*

Job rotation, as discussed above, moves workers around and thus lessens boredom. It cannot be carried to the point of putting people in jobs they cannot handle, but properly managed it creates interest and broadens each worker's knowledge of the whole plant.   *job rotation*

Job enrichment consists of somehow making the job more meaningful, by enlarging the worker's discretion in organizing and controlling the job. If the worker plans the job, inspects it, and schedules it, this increased responsibility hopefully increases job satisfaction. For this approach to succeed, however, it requires wholehearted commitment from management, or the employee will consider it only a meaningless gesture.   *job enrichment*

Managing Conflict

As noted in chapter 2, conflict is almost inevitable in any organization. All members do not have the same aims; if one individual gains, another may have to lose. Personnel management is heavily involved in the management of conflict situations. The labor specialists primarily handle the formal union-management conflicts and questions, but they also get involved in dealing with the day-to-day small differences which develop, many of which fall outside of the provisions of the union contract. Conflict management is a primary line responsibility, of course, as are all matters of morale, but a personnel department that includes human relations specialists can be of great assistance.

Union Negotiations

This topic is discussed in detail in chapter 15, "Labor-Management Relations." For our purposes here, it will suffice to say that this area is a prime source of conflict. The employer must constantly take actions, any one of which the union may interpret as a violation of the contract. Even if the employer consults the union in advance about desired actions, the union may disagree and the employer may take the action anyway. In this case, the union may file charges with the National Labor Relations Board, thus formalizing the conflict.

Most negotiations between labor and management end in settlements that do not invoke the ultimate weapon—the strike. In each such negotiation the two sides are "doing what comes naturally," and there is no real conflict until the union takes strike (or boycott) action or the employer invokes a lockout.

Mechanisms used to settle these disputes include labor courts, arbitration, compulsory arbitration, inclusion of workers on management boards, union-company committees, and cooling-off periods. These will be discussed in chapter 15.

Handling Grievances

There are two sides to the labor-management relationship in the area of rights. The company has "rights," and when the employees violate these, management takes disciplinary action. The employee also has "rights," and when the company violates these the employee files a grievance. The usual basis for a grievance is apparent violation of a contract provision, although employees often come to management with informal grievances not specifically tied to the labor contract. Thus an employee might complain that his or her work place is in the hottest part of the building, or that the tools being used are obsolete, or that materials must be carried by hand to the job site instead of by truck. None of these issues may be covered by the contract, but each could still be a perfectly valid complaint that management should investigate.

Most grievances, however, are specific charges of violating some provision of the union contract. Chapter 15 describes in detail what happens when a grievance is filed. Essentially, the following steps are followed:

- The employee confers with the supervisor (and sometimes with the union steward as well).
- The employee and the union representative present the grievance in writing to the next higher authority—general foreman or superintendent.
- The employee and perhaps the union business agent take the complaint to top management.
- The matter goes to arbitration or conciliation.
- The NLRB hears the case and makes a decision.

Discipline

Discipline is the other side of the equation described above: where the company feels that its rights have been violated. In every case there must be a rule, and the employee must reasonably be expected to know the rule, or there is no violation. The union contract usually provides that management shall establish company rules, and often lists the accepted causes for disciplinary action, such as insubordination, stealing, fighting, skylarking, drunkenness, or violation of stated shop rules. The contract may go so far as to specify the form of punishment for various offenses. Figure 10-7 categorizes common employee behavior rules.

Discipline involves enforcing rules, and it is a job for everyone in the organization. There is almost never an excuse for overlooking a clear violation of the discipline code. If the rule is a bad one, it should be countermanded. If there are mitigating circumstances, or even a complete justification (as when safety rules are violated in an emergency situation, to save a life), the whole situation should be brought out.

disciplinary action

The contract may go so far as to specify the form of punishment for various offenses.

Figure 10-9.
Typical Employee
Behavior Rules

Directly Related to Productivity
1. **Time rules** 　Starting and late times 　Quit-work times 　Maximum break and lunch times 　Maximum absenteeism
2. **Prohibited behavior rules** 　Sleeping on the job 　Leaving workplace without permission 　Drinking on the job 　Using drugs 　Limit to non-employer action at work
3. **Insubordination rules** 　Refusal to obey supervisors 　Slowdowns or sitdowns
4. **Rules related to laws** 　Theft 　Falsification
5. **Safety rules** 　Smoking rules 　Safety regulations 　Sanitation requirements 　Fighting 　Dangerous weapons

Indirectly Related to Productivity
1. Moonlighting 2. Gambling 3. Selling or solicitation at work 4. Clothing or uniform regulations 5. Fraternization at work

Inexperienced managers sometimes feel that they will gain favor with their employees if they let them get away with a violation of the rules. They are wrong. The workers will have contempt for them as easy marks, and discipline will suffer as a result.

When disciplinary action is taken against any employee, the manager must remember that the entire organization is being disciplined: the one action will serve as an example to all. The entire organization must be made to see that, while disciplinary action is impartial, it is not callous or impersonal. A warning is perfectly appropriate for a first offense, or for an offender who clearly broke a rule inadvertently, whereas a warning might not be sufficient for an habitual offender. The manager must remember that, generally speaking, discipline depends on a confident assumption that a warning or more serious punishment is *deserved.* The manager who displays such confidence—tempered by a sense of justice and fair play—will be obeyed.

When a worker must be disciplined, it helps to remember that most employees want to abide by the rules, because they want the work place to

warning

be an orderly environment. Thus, they wish to see offenders brought up short; they would not appreciate a soft manager, though they would never admit it.

Bradford Boyd[6] has advanced the following rules for establishing a good disciplinary climate in an organization. Essentially, they are common sense, but it is well to remember them nonetheless (common sense can be a rare commodity):

- Make sure the employees understand the rules.
- Enforce the rules consistently.
- Make the disciplinary action fit the offense.
- Make certain the actions correct rather than punish.
- Remember to give credit as often as you give blame.

The punitive approach sometimes is the only recourse, but a manager should never take it without *listening* first; the employee's viewpoint may have considerable merit. Below is a typical range of penalties, more or less in ascending order:

1. Verbal warning and counseling, with no record in the file
2. Same, but with incident entering into personnel file
3. Transfer to another job or department
4. Suspension without pay
5. Suggesting that individual seek another job (Glueck calls this "dehiring")
6. Firing

The supervisor is the party who initiates the disciplinary action, but the personnel department is always implicitly involved, because discipline has implications for the entire company. A minor disciplinary action may affect the general morale (if an action is considered wrong in one department and acceptable in another, serious problems can develop) and an employee may appeal disciplinary procedures, thus creating union-company problems. The role of the personnel officer is to ensure that disciplinary action conforms to company standards, in regard to the severity of punishment and the impartiality and uniformity of application.

The Changing Scene in Personnel Management

The late 1960s and the 1970s have seen widespread changes in personnel administration. We have discussed how laws and court actions have compelled employers to follow a fair employment policy. This trend has raised some interesting questions for management: what sort of criteria should be set up to measure employee performance? Changes in technology have also generated new personnel practices, in response to changing employee demands and occupations. But technology has been of assistance as well, helping management to cope with these new demands by providing better information processing systems able to predict future employment needs.

On the minus side, technological advance has encouraged managerial obsolescence. An engineering supervisor, after supervising a project team on a particular project for two or three years, will be woefully out-of-date professionally and may actually need some training courses to fill in the gaps.

Worker discontent, produced by the monotony of the assembly line, is a phenomenon that managers a generation ago would have thought incredible. An older supervisor, facing open rebellion or less open work slowdowns and sabotage, is ill-equipped to face the employees' need for greater job satisfaction.

Despite these vexing and sometimes apparently insoluble personnel problems, the latter half of the twentieth century has been and will continue to be an exciting and challenging period for managers. As the crucial importance of personnel becomes more and more evident, human resource accounting systems will assist management in measuring the value of intangible personnel resources and developing them to maximum potential.

Affirmative Action

Prior to passage of the Civil Rights Act of 1964, minority groups held few responsible positions in organizations. Pressed by the EEOC and court cases, as discussed above, organizations have been launching aggressive programs to recruit and train minority employees. A major problem has been that, because of past overt and covert (and some unintentional) discrimination, few minority individuals were trained for managerial positions. Additionally, the lack of motivational support from secondary schools in poor neighborhoods created problems for minorities seeking high-ranking blue-collar positions. However, the onus has been on industry to recruit and train minorities nonetheless. Many industries have participated in programs for training hard-core disadvantaged workers, but the primary focus has been on providing basic skills. There must be motivation as well; past experience has made such employees insecure, and imparted a sometimes disconcerting (to supervisors) attitude toward society and the traditional work ethic. Thus these programs have not always been as effective as they might have.

Union Carbide has been quite successful in training the disadvantaged. The company worked with the University of Tennessee in a Training and Technology program (TAT), teaching skill development and technical theory in six areas: mechanical drafting, machine shop practice, welding, industrial electronics, laboratory glassblowing, and physical testing and quality control. Such skills have not been part of the life environment of ghetto residents; thus, the programs have included a great deal of basic indoctrination. Union Carbide had to insure (as all companies involved in such programs must) that testing procedures would avoid culturally biased tests, where results reflect the nature of one's life experiences. And they had to instill proper attitudes on the part of employees who would work with minorities, to counteract the natural feeling that these new hires were taking the "easy path," not having to work as hard or go through a preparatory period as many of the old employees did.

affirmative action

Affirmative action applies also to female workers and older workers. Many companies feel that older workers have lost their zip and cannot change or learn new skills, but studies have shown that older people can learn effectively (possibly not quite as fast, but with a higher degree of retention). Also, it may be more expensive to hire older workers, particularly if they pick up pension entitlements when they come on the payroll. (Pension law changes to correct this problem are in the works.) Women have been discriminated against in managerial positions in the past, but, through cases brought by EEOC, courts have awarded large sums to women who allege that they have been denied equal pay and treatment in the case of promotion to managerial posts.

True affirmative action cannot be fully attained overnight, since there are many deep-rooted misconceptions to dispel and much training to be accorded to minorities denied such attention in the past. In general, major corporations have positive action under way in the affirmative action area.

Human Resource Accounting

Until comparatively recently, there has been no attempt to include human beings on the corporate balance sheet. Yet funds spent on training and development programs and other personnel needs are no less a "capital investment" than funds spent on research or facilities, and should be included in the company's balance sheet—or at least in any comprehensive report of its condition. When a professional football team spends several million dollars to buy the rights to an outstanding athlete for several years, no one questions that the individual will be a tremendous asset to the team's future, but the same philosophy has not been recognized in business. Human resource accounting represents an attempt to price out the future benefits of training and other personnel costs, rather than simply treating them as current expenses.

capital investment

human resource accounting

Rensis Likert, of the University of Michigan's Institute for Social Research, believes that most leadership styles encourage the long-run liquidation of human assets in exchange for immediate increases in earnings. Likert has attempted to price out these effects—to place a dollar value on the income statement, either as an addition or deduction in terms of "net income." If the long-run effects of leadership styles, promotion policies, training programs, etc., can be determined and then converted to dollar terms, management might perceive that the short-term increase in profits or savings garnered by an overly authoritarian leadership style, a cutback in training and development programs, or a freeze on promotions is not necessarily worth the price in the long run.

One of the first companies to employ a human resource accounting system for personnel resources was the R. G. Barry Corporation. The first step, as described by Lee Brummet and his colleagues,[7] was to identify human resource costs and separate them from other costs. Then these costs were divided into "asset" costs (those which produce some enduring value) and "expense" costs (those which are essentially used up by the time they have been paid for). Finally, the asset cost items were classified into such functional categories as recruiting, hiring, training, development, and familiarization. Having thus developed the "capital costs" of human resources, rules had to be formulated as to how fast to write off the costs (how much of these capital costs to "expense" each year in the future). Some 90 different members of the Barry Corporation management team thus were debited with "Capital Invested in Human Resources," which then became an asset on their particular balance sheets.

Figure 10-10 shows Barry's 1970 balance sheet and income statement, including human resources, as compared to conventional statements, which omit the human factors. (Figures involving human resource investments and amortization are unaudited.)

The purpose of the human resource accounting system is to measure human resources in terms of what they cost originally, what it would cost to buy them at today's prices, and what they are worth. And why is all this

Figure 10-10.
Typical Balance Sheet and Income Statement

"THE TOTAL CONCEPT"
R. G. Barry Corporation and Subsidiaries
Pro-Forma
(Conventional and Human Resource Accounting)

Balance Sheet	1970 Conventional and Human Resource	1970 Conventional Only
Assets		
Total Current Assets	$10,944,693	$10,944,693
Net Property, Plant, and Equipment	1,682,357	1,682,357
Excess of Purchase Price of Subsidiaries over Net Assets Acquired	1,188,704	1,188,704
Net Investments in Human Resources	942,194	—
Other Assets	166,417	166,417
	$14,924,365	$13,982,171
Liabilities and Stockholders' Equity		
Total Current Liabilities	$ 3,651,573	$ 3,651,573
Long Term Debt, Excluding Current Installments	2,179,000	2,179,000
Deferred Compensation	77,491	77,491
Deferred Federal Income Taxes Based Upon Full Tax Deduction for Human Resource Costs	471,097	—
Stockholders' Equity		
Capital Stock	1,082,211	1,087,211
Additional Capital in Excess of Par Value	3,951,843	3,951,843
Retained Earnings		
Financial	3,035,053	3,035,053
Human Resources	471,097	—
Total Stockholders' Equity	8,545,204	8,074,107
	$14,924,365	$13,982,171
Statement of Income		
Net Sales	$28,164,181	$28,164,181
Cost of Sales	18,252,181	18,252,181
Gross Profit	9,912,000	9,912,000
Selling, General and Administrative Expenses	7,546,118	7,546,118
Operating Income	2,365,882	2,365,882
Other Deductions, Net	250,412	250,412
Income Before Federal Income Taxes	2,115,470	2,115,470
Net Increase (Decrease) in Human Resource Investment	(43,900)	—
Adjusted Income Before Federal Income Taxes	2,071,570	2,115,470
Federal Income Taxes	1,008,050	1,030,000
Net Income	$ 1,063,520	$ 1,085,470

information useful? Because it helps in making managerial decisions that "use up" human resources. If a new project requires the employment of certain highly trained personnel for its success, that need ought to be considered in its capital cost. Furthermore, this system helps in making decisions about training and other investments. If capital costs are incurred in this way, and departments decide against taking trained people if their books are going to be charged with the training costs, the training would not seem to be of much value. Finally, resource accounting provides management with data on current costs of developing personnel resources, so these costs can be incorporated into future planning.

The other half of the equation, of course, involves likely earnings resulting from this expenditure for human resource capital. Of course, the present value of its cost may exceed the present value of future *marginal* earnings (what it will add to the amount that could have been earned without it). In that case, the human resource capital item is not worth buying. It is very difficult to estimate such earnings, but it must be attempted.

marginal earnings

Impact of Technology on Personnel Systems

Managerial Obsolescence

Obsolescence exists when a person holding a managerial job no longer performs effectively. This can happen in several ways: the job itself is no longer necessary; other related jobs have changed, and the manager no longer adjusts to new requirements; or supervisory techniques have changed and the manager is being overtaken by managerial technology. How does this happen, and what is the cure?

It happens, often enough, because people fear change. The older an individual manager becomes, the greater his or her vested interest in retaining old procedures and philosophies. In recent years, many organizations have installed word processing systems as a means of gathering, analyzing, and communicating much of the information needed to pursue key objectives. Previously, a certain manager might have been responsible for supervising the preparation of major progress reports, research projects, condition statements, and so on. Now the same function is carried out by a combination of computerized data banks, programmers, technical writers, typists, and similar personnel. While each segment of the new system reports to one supervisor or another, no one individual retains full control over the operation. This arrangement may well produce higher quality materials at a more efficient rate, but the original manager is likely to resist the innovation as forcefully as possible.

Nonetheless, people can change. Experienced managers have a tremendous advantage in adapting to new techniques if they will make the effort, because they have a good understanding of the environment in which the technique is to work and what it must achieve. The organization can speed the process if it bears in mind that senior managers must be "sheltered" to some extent—not thrown in with new and younger managers to learn about new techniques and technologies, but given special attention and training sessions designed to fit their needs and apprehensions. When the computer came into general use in college teaching, some of the older faculty were reluctant to learn how to use it; some schools set up indoctrination courses designed specifically for this group and achieved good results.

Effects on Individual Workers

In the previous sections, we discussed job enlargement and enrichment. As machinery is introduced, it can lead to more mechanization of the job and consequent disenchantment, or it can shift some of the backbreaking work to a machine and ease the worker's burden. Although the choice of mechanical systems is not the province of the personnel department, the impact of machinery certainly is, and it is the duty of the personnel officer to point out to line management how these factors can influence labor peace.

Sometimes the introduction of machinery or the adoption of new technology will make employees obsolete—they simply aren't needed any more, because the machine has usurped their function. Whether or not union contracts provide safeguards against this eventuality (and many of them do), a farsighted management will try to keep such developments from actually forcing employee dismissals. Every effort should be made to retrain the workers, starting as far in advance as necessary, so that they can be usefully employed in other jobs that are not going to be phased out.

Another change is early retirement. For wage workers, the union contract may provide for optional early retirement at a somewhat lower retirement pension. For managerial workers, the company may be in a period of recession and dictate mandatory early retirement as a cost-saving measure. Sometimes, when work is slow, workers must be laid off for extended periods, in a share-the-work measure. In all such cases, although the company has no real responsibility, an enlightened personnel policy calls for guidance in making wise use of the unaccustomed leisure time.

impact of technology

Technology should not be viewed as a threat because in the long run it is the company's salvation, keeping it competitive. But the personnel department must be alive to the impact of technology on human values and perceptions, and guide its programs accordingly.

Personnel Information Systems

personnel information system

The greatly expanded personnel problems resulting from social, economic, and technological changes over the past decade have created the necessity for automated personnel systems in the larger organizations. Earlier we discussed the interrelatedness of personnel systems; an effective information system can do a good deal to integrate these various systems so that the effect of each on the others and the whole is more readily apparent. What impact does training have on future capabilities? What promotion systems are best for future needs? How might current personnel trends place us in some undesirable future situation?

Information systems are good for simulating various possible futures, to see what might happen *if*. How will it affect our personnel situation ten years down the road if we terminate our apprentice program, which is quite expensive? What if we start an in-house training school for welders, drawing from the supply of laborers and others? If we need to retrain electronics mechanics, would it be better to bring in people from the outside, or use people we have (and then find it necessary to retrain still others for *their* jobs)? If the system has all the information on all employees, it can respond immediately to such queries, and provide valuable decision guidance. It can aid in matching future candidates with future positions, by feeding in the job qualifications to your computer system. It can forecast possible technological futures and simulate varying personnel arrangements. It can evaluate the potential impact of various union contract proposals and predict possible difficulties you might not consider otherwise.

How would a personnel information system be helpful to North Star?

The fact that all employee information is contained in the automated system makes it possible to carry out better and faster research on turnover rate, absenteeism, relationship between type of recruitment and employee performance, effects of varying training programs, individual characteristics of the work force and how these are changing, affirmative action responses, and so on.

The Navy has instituted a Personnel Automated Data System (PADS) capable of handling problems such as the following. Suppose there is a major reduction in force throughout the Navy's huge industrial shore establishment (shipyards, arsenals, supply depots, etc.). As the reduction in force notices go out around the country, various employees whose jobs are no longer needed have "bumping rights" (they can displace similar employees of less seniority in other locations) or "retreat rights" (they can fall back to lower seniority jobs from which they were promoted in the past, displacing the employees in those jobs). In the latter case, the displaced employees can do the same with jobs from which *they* were promoted in the past—and on and on. Where will it all end? And what will be the shape of the organization ultimately, when all this bumping and retreating ends? PADS is able to simulate such complex chains of events on the computer, and provide a picture of what the whole operation will look like when it finally comes to rest. In the other direction, when new technology creates a need for people with new specialized skills, PADS can indicate what will happen when the people to be trained are pulled from existing labor pools, then replaced with others who have to be trained for the jobs they left, and so on.

Such systems give top managers an invaluable picture of the whole company and the effects of various innovations. Indeed, a large organization would be substantially handicapped in its executive decision making without such systems—as would day-to-day personnel administration.

Summary

One of the most important facets in any organization is personnel management. The task of managing personnel permeates the organization and includes: finding capable employees to work for the organization, keeping them motivated and happy on the job, and ensuring that personnel policies contribute to efficient and effective performance. Responsibility for establishing a coordinated personnel policy for the organization rests with the personnel department in consultation with top management. Line managers too have personnel duties. After all, employees deal with their immediate supervisor on a daily basis and thus look to this person as a source of support, doler of rewards, evaluator of performance, and enforcer of company rules. The supervisor represents the voice of the company to the vast majority of workers; thus, it is very important that the line and staff cooperate on personnel matters. Top management should encourage frequent interaction and discussions between the line managers and personnel staff to alleviate many of the tensions which inevitably spring up between the "doers" and the "advisers."

Personnel management can be viewed from a systems perspective with four interacting and dependent subsystems: selection, training, evaluation, and motivation. Selection of qualified candidates depends upon the criteria generated by the evaluation, training, and motivation subsystems, while evaluation depends upon the quality of the candidates selected as well as the type of training, the degree of employee motivation, and so on. Among the various functions of a personnel system are: personnel planning, recruitment, selection, training and development, appraisal, promotion policy and compensation, motivation, and managing conflict. The ultimate goal of any personnel system should be to facilitate a meshing of individual and organizational goals in order to achieve individual and organizational performance of a high quality. By viewing personnel as a total system with this goal in mind, management is better able to gain a total perspective on the policies which set the pace between workers and management and to fashion policies that will promote harmony within the organization.

The past decade has seen many changes in personnel functions, especially as various minorities have vociferously asserted their objections to policies which denied them equal work opportunities. A number of court cases have successfully challenged such entrance criteria as invalid tests and unwarranted education requirements which previously barred many qualified candidates from certain types of employment. Federal laws have established affirmative action requirements and many federal programs offer incentives for businesses to hire the hard-core disadvantaged or physically handicapped employee.

Managing organizational conflict is an important area of personnel. Large companies often employ a labor specialist to deal with unions, but in many companies this task is the duty of the personnel department. Of course, managing conflict is a task which must be assumed by all managers, but often personnel specialists can be of assistance in dealing with employee representatives, mediating employee-supervisor disputes, or handling disciplinary actions. A cardinal rule of conflict management holds that a certain amount of conflict is healthy for an organization. A manager must know when the balance has been tipped and prevent conflict from disrupting the organization.

The technological developments and value reorientation that have occurred throughout the last half of the twentieth century have greatly reformed personnel thinking. Managerial obsolescence, affirmative action, job enrichment, job enlargement, management by objectives, and automated personnel information systems—phenomena unknown to our managerial predecessors—are playing a significant role in today's personnel management. The thrust of personnel administration has been change, and attention has been directed toward making the organization more adaptive to environmental changes and more responsive to employee demands for greater job satisfaction and self-fulfillment. The focus of personnel management in the future will continue to be in these areas, as managers strive to attain organizational effectiveness without neglecting their obligations to employees.

Notes

1. Richard W. Beatty, "Personnel Systems and Human Performance," *Personnel Journal*, April 1973, pp. 307-12.

2. Laurence Peter and Raymond J. Hull, *The Peter Principle: Why Things Always Go Wrong* (New York: William Morrow & Co., Inc., 1969).

3. One of the authors, when manager in a heavy industrial plant, was faced with a grievance by an employee who objected to being taken from a certain section of the machine shop when workload shifted. During the discussion he announced that the machines in his former section "liked him," but in the new section they were "unfriendly." This man had been gainfully employed for some 30 years, despite an obvious disability, and his record showed him to have been an excellent worker. He was returned to the section with the "friendly" machines.

4. *Wall Street Journal*, September 3, 1975, p. 1.

5. Management should probe such situations carefully, to determine whether this decision is really the worker's or that of a supervisor who wishes to promote someone else and has threatened the worker with a "hard time" if the promotion is accepted.

6. Bradford Boyd, *Management-Minded Supervision* (New York: McGraw-Hill Book Co., 1968).

7. R. Lee Brummet, Eric G. Flamholtz, and William G. Pyle, "Human Resource Measurement—A Challenge for Accountants," *The Accounting Review*, April 1968.

Review Questions

1. What are the functions of a personnel manager?
2. What are the functions of the line manager in the area of personnel?
3. What are some sources of conflict between line and staff in personnel matters?
4. What are some alternative structural arrangements for the personnel department? What are the advantages and disadvantages of each?
5. Why should personnel management be studied from a systems view? What are the subsystems of the personnel system?
6. What are the main issues involved in determining job classifications and job descriptions?
7. What are the various methods of recruitment used by organizations?
8. What is meant by reliability of a testing procedure? Validity?
9. What is an assessment center? What are the advantages and disadvantages?
10. What is personnel planning? How does this relate to the various types of training and development courses available?
11. What is management by objectives? Management by results?
12. Why are employee appraisals necessary? What are some problems which are inherent in any employee appraisal system?
13. What are some rules for establishing a good disciplinary climate in an organization?

14. What is meant by affirmative action? What laws and court decisions have recently contributed to establishing an equitable system of employment?
15. What is human resource accounting?
16. What steps can an organization take to avoid managerial obsolescence?
17. What are the advantages of rapidly advancing technology for organizations? What are the disadvantages? What steps can management take to alleviate the disadvantages?
18. What is a personnel information system? What role will personnel information systems play in the future of personnel management?

Discussion Questions

1. Many companies feel that personnel planning is a waste because money is spent training people for competitors to hire. What are the pros and cons of this point of view?

2. What are the arguments for always advertising all new jobs in cases where several employees are qualified but management feels that one is clearly superior?

3. Suppose a foreman position is available. The shop superintendent wants to choose an experienced mechanic who frequently helped the former foreman but does poorly on written exams. What arguments might the personnel officer put forward to include the written exam as part of the testing criteria in the competitive testing process?

4. What are the arguments for having supervisory training carried out by the supervisor? By a party outside the shop structure?

5. When an employee files a grievance, do you think the circumstances and findings should be private or publicized to the employees as a whole? Why?

6. IBM recently decided to drastically cut the information kept in employee records, leaving out such facts as marital status, police records, etc. What do you think of this action? What information should be kept in employee files?

North Star Case Study

Assume that North Star employed a group of hard-core disadvantaged workers to perform mechanical duties and to train in the drafting room. While these workers adjusted to their new environment, Henry, president of the company, decided that company rules should be applied flexibly, especially in case of tardiness and absenteeism—difficult areas for the disadvantaged to adjust to. A problem arose, however, when Ab (drafting room chief) invoked disciplinary proceedings for excessive absenteeism against Stu Jones, a young employee who had worked for the company for almost two years. Jones protested Ab's action, saying that he had missed fewer times than the disadvantaged workers, and the other workers in the drafting room supported Jones, saying they were tired of being the underdogs because of affirmative action. They wanted equal treatment of all workers, and they wanted it now!

1. How should the company officers deal with this thorny situation?
2. Should Ab have taken disciplinary action against Jones?
3. How could have this situation been forestalled?
4. Should a company make an extra effort to hire workers from the disadvantaged and/or handicapped?
5. What can be done from this point onwards to create a more amicable and desirable situation in the company?

6. Which of the following groups is most ideally suited to effect a desirable solution: the union (if it exists)? informal employee groups? management? outside arbitrators?

Suggestions for Further Reading

Beach, D. S. *Personnel: The Management of People at Work.* 3d ed. New York: Macmillan Pub. Co., Inc., 1975.

Byham, W. C., and M. E. Spitzer. *The Law and Personnel Testing.* New York: American Management Association, Inc., 1971.

Finnegan, J. *The Right People in the Right Jobs?* London: Business Books, 1973.

Flamholtz, E. *Human Resources Accounting.* Encino, Calif.: Dickenson Pub. Co., Inc., 1974.

Foulkes, F. K. "The Expanding Role of the Personnel Function." *Harvard Business Review,* March-April 1975.

Glueck, W. *Personnel: A Diagnostic Approach.* Homewood, Ill.: Business Publications, 1974.

Hacon, R., ed. *Personal and Organizational Effectiveness.* New York: McGraw-Hill Book Co., 1972.

Luke, R. A., Jr. "Matching the Individual and the Organization." *Harvard Business Review,* May-June 1975.

Martino, R. *PMS—Personnel Management Systems.* Wayne, Pa.: Management Development, 1969.

Matteson, M.; R. Blakeney; and D. Domm. *Contemporary Personnel Management: A Reader on Human Resources.* San Francisco: Canfield Press, 1972.

Odiorne, G. S. *Personnel Administration by Objectives.* Homewood, Ill.: Richard D. Irwin, Inc., 1971.

Pigors, P. J., and C. A. Myers. *Personnel Administration: A Point of View.* New York: McGraw-Hill Book Co., 1973.

Pigors, P.; C. A. Myers; and F. T. Malin. *Management of Human Resources: Readings in Personnel Administration.* 3d ed. New York: McGraw-Hill Book Co., 1973.

Shafritz, J. M. *A New World: Readings on Modern Public Personnel Management.* Chicago: International Personnel Management Association, 1975.

Strauss, G., and L. Sayles. *Personnel: The Human Problems of Management.* 3d ed. Englewood Cliffs, N.J.: Prentice-Hall, Inc., 1972.

Yoder, D. *Personnel Management and Industrial Relations.* 6th ed. Englewood Cliffs, N.J.: Prentice-Hall, Inc., 1970.

Managing Finances

North Star Prologue

North Star Associates, starting as a small two-person firm, evolved into an effective organization, improving its planning and communication skills as it expanded. After it considered and turned down the offer to merge with a multinational company, it reorganized in order to sharpen organizational responsibilities and improve efficiency. The move to fixed-price contracts required North Star to set up formal control systems, including a worker forecasting and status system that would prevent their biting off more work than they could chew. Dick Boyer's return from overseas kicked off a personnel reshuffle, and pointed to the need for marketing and personnel to become two separate areas of responsibility. Zeb took the former, and a new personnel director was hired, who proceeded to revamp personnel and training practices—a move that apparently was long overdue.

With Barbara Newman capably handling the office affairs and personnel arguments—and with the other members of North Star practically eating out of her hand—Zeb had time to turn his attention to a sorely lagging area of the company's operations. The installation of the weekly report, and Jim Pozzi's new manpower schedule, had highlighted the shortcomings of the company's financial system. The problem, simply stated, was that North Star didn't have a budget. Its growth had been steady, and there had always been income to meet the costs incurred, but these blessings derived more from good luck than from good management. What they needed, and what Zeb set out to install, was a budgetary forecast that projected receipts and expenditures a full year in advance, with provision for updating the budget every three months. He recognized that no forecast of income could be entirely accurate for a company that often obtained new work on short notice (such as the municipal jobs that came up in Blackridge or other municipalities), but North Star had enough experience by now to make fairly good estimates of what work probably would come in. The forecast would show, for all contracts they had in hand, when the progress payments were expected and how long the payments would continue over the life of the contract.

Zeb ran into surprising resistance in putting the budget into operation. Dick was a supporter of the proposal, because his past experience both in the Seabees and overseas had shown him the value of knowing where he stood with respect to funds. Ab Jenkins and his people in the drafting room, never having faced the problem of paying bills, thought it was one more piece of red tape from the business manager, and said they didn't have the time or the information to provide the needed data. Jo said someone else would have to do it for her area; she was no administrator. Bert saw some benefits, but was inclined to go along with his people. Even Henry told Zeb he thought the gang was pretty punchy from setting up so many new systems, and perhaps they ought to have a respite before anything more was imposed on them. Zeb was wondering how he could proceed in the face of so many objections to budgeting, when an event took place that made his task easier.

It was not so much a single event as a pyramiding of separate events whose effects coincided in time. One event dealt with the computer: Jo had been authorized to lease an automatic plotter for work she was doing, but when the demonstrator showed her how much the company would save over the long run if they bought it instead, Jo said okay—but forgot to let anyone know until the bill came in. Bert was responsible for another event: he carried the building modification a good deal further than was strictly necessary, before the partners changed their minds—and even he was a bit staggered when he learned the total cost of what had been done. Dick had been pursuing a project management contract for a new nuclear power plant in an Asian country, and had spent heavily on trips to the site, taking no chances on letting the contract slip away. On the last trip the Asian Development Bank had approved the funds and the contract had been signed—with Barnhard & Walker again, in a joint venture with an Asian firm—but the work would not start for five more months. To compound matters, Dick had grabbed office space on site while he had a chance and had hired a local representative—and the bills for both were coming in. Henry had totally forgotten, until Zeb reminded him, that the final payment on the power plant job with Natal would be held up until completion of full power trials, which had been delayed twice and were still not firmly scheduled.

The overall result of these events was a severe and unanticipated cash crunch. The company did not have enough funds in the bank to meet its obligations, and could see no relief for this situation for four or five months. Zeb had arranged a line of credit with their bank when the first AID job was signed, and this had been increased when the power plant contract came along, but North Star had drawn on this to its limit; now there was no new business whose start-up justified going for an expansion in the line of credit. The only reason for more credit was bad management, and the bank was not likely to appreciate the logic of *that* situation. Dick approached B&W for a loan, but was rebuffed; they'd be glad to reconsider a merger, they said, but it was against corporate policy to lend to independent companies.

They got out of the situation by taking a number of steps. Jo was able to convert the plotter purchase back to a rental, though there was a penalty involved in doing so. Bert arranged to pay the builder on installments, with the latter using his bank credit to tide them both over. And, through Natal's help, Dick was able to get a loan secured by the balance due after the full power trials, although the foreign bank charged its usual 15% interest on the transaction. The partners thought they might have to forego a payday for themselves, but they were just able to get by without doing so. Even so, the experience was a shocker for them all, and when Zeb again proposed that he set up a detailed performance budget and cash flow forecast there were no voices raised in opposition.

The budget he established required each "profit center" to forecast its revenues and expenditures for a year ahead in general terms, and to make a detailed forecast by individual job for three months ahead. It also required that at the end of each three-month period a comparison be made between the forecasts and the actual outcomes, with a justification of the differences. For profit centers Zeb went back to the original partnership divisions, because these were the categories within which jobs were most likely to fall: environmental, municipal, economics, and civil/mechanical. Thus each of the original partners constituted a profit center, and each was required to estimate the amount of work that would develop within his area.

The system worked as follows. Henry, for example, was the profit center manager for municipal jobs, with Blackridge as the original client and some 15 other municipalities making some use of the company's services. (Even if the work was environmental in nature, if it came in from this route it came under Henry's profit center.) He estimated the level of work for the next three months and the number of workers needed to accomplish this work (with Jim Pozzi's help). Simultaneously, Bert was estimating whether he would have enough people with the right skills to satisfy his demands; if he did not, it was up to him to find part-time or subcontract labor. In a separate part of the budget, the "cash flow" section, Henry also estimated when payment for the work would come in. Jo was estimating similarly for jobs in the economics and systems analysis area (including the new field of market surveys and locational analysis, where she had gotten some work and was building up a competence); Dick was doing the same for the Asian power plant project; and Bert for the water treatment and air pollution control work which fell in his special area (though in many cases Henry and Zeb actually had sold those jobs). The system seemed to show promise, and Zeb stated that for the first time since he had joined North Star he could actually see where they were going.

What North Star Can Learn from Chapter 11

1. What the financial manager does for a company
2. How a financial analysis is done, in the short term and long term
3. The concept of management audits
4. Planning for funds needs
5. The need for, and techniques of, cash management
6. The interaction between liquidity and profitability
7. How to raise funds, and what the lender will be looking for
8. How businesses are valued, and the implications of this for the way North Star conducts its business
9. Capital budgeting approaches
10. The concept of program budgeting

Thus far in part 3, "Managers at Work," we have discussed *getting things done, controlling,* and *staffing*—specific operational areas that the manager must cope with to keep an organization moving. In this chapter, we will explore the financial manager's role and the important link between financial analyses and the effectiveness of the enterprise. Financial management includes four primary tasks:

1. *Financial planning*—how the financial manager uses financial analysis to predict future expenditures and funding needs.
2. *Managing funds*—the constant tradeoff between liquidity and profitability, management of cash and accounts receivable, and management of inventory and fixed assets.
3. *Raising funds*—how businesses acquire short-term, intermediate-term, and long-term capital, and how businesses are valued.
4. *Investing funds*—primarily, the problems of choosing among capital equipment alternatives within the business.

It is apparent from what has gone before that the process of attaining organizational goals can be reduced to five steps: planning, choosing, activating, evaluating, and controlling. Financial management influences each phase: *planning* the need for funds, *choosing* how the firm's assets should be expanded for orderly growth, *activating* plans by obtaining funds on the most advantageous terms, *evaluating* capital investment alternatives, and *controlling* the receipt and expenditure of funds and merchandise in the interest of honest and effective operations. In addition, and in a larger sense, the financial manager evaluates the entire enterprise through financial analysis and establishes the records and procedures through which outside agencies and the general public may judge the soundness of the enterprise (i.e., of its stock).

Financial Planning

In some respects, all organizational planning is financial planning, because it takes money to do anything significant. Therefore, no serious planning can take place for very long without bringing in the question of how much money will be needed, when it will be needed, where it will come from, and what other action will be deferred to free funds for the planned action. For this reason, in most corporations, the senior financial manager reports directly to the chief executive—and the chief executive too must be something of a financial professional. In recent years, as the cost of funds has risen spectacularly, many firms have found it increasingly difficult to get outside funds on any reasonable terms whatever; and the financial aspect of planning and operating has assumed great importance.

Role of the Financial Manager

In the simplest form of company, the one-person proprietorship, the key financial decisions are external ones. Suppose a young woman teaching in a business college believes there is a demand for machine preparation of multiple letters and wishes to get automatic typewriting equipment to go into business for herself. Since she is talking about an initial investment of perhaps $5000 (or a firm lease, which amounts to the same thing) and a sufficient additional bank account to meet rent and other costs for the first several months, she must go outside her own resources to find the money.

At this point an external individual or organization will engage in some financial analysis. Perhaps it is a bank, where she is seeking an unsecured loan. Perhaps it is an individual who is willing to be a *silent partner,* sharing the liability for future debts but not becoming involved in active management; or perhaps a *limited partner,* who puts up some investment funds but will not assume future debt liability. Perhaps she can find a full partner, who shares with her the costs, liabilities, profits, and management chores. In any case, it doesn't matter what decisions she has made—the individual or organization supplying funds will make its own independent decision on whether to invest, and on how the money can be used if the decision is favorable.

Once the enterprise gets under way, key decision making shifts to another actor: the customer. If the new businesswoman sets her price too high, the customer will not come. If she offers some wanted and some unwanted services, the customer will inform her promptly which she can continue and which she must forget. Every decision she makes henceforth is determined by market considerations; she can't stray very far from reality because her customers are setting her straight every day, telling her promptly whether her decisions make sense in terms of the marketplace. Similarly, her suppliers are telling her what to buy by the prices they offer.

In a large company, these external mechanisms operate belatedly and

silent partner

limited partner

Does North Star have any silent or limited partners?

If the price is too high, the customer will not come.

384
MANAGERS AT WORK

confusingly. When a corporation borrows $50 million in new funds, the president must decide who gets the money: the sales manager, the production manager, the research director, the employees, or someone else. Market forces can't signal the correctness of these decisions because so many other factors are at work. Neither will the outside banker or investor help with these detailed decisions—they expect management to handle such internal matters. The *financial manager* is the focus of these internal decisions, pointing out what financial decisions are necessary and providing technical expertise in the data and tools that will help those making the decisions.

financial manager

The financial manager's principal responsibility is to be sure that cash is in the bank to meet the bills. Beyond that, this manager assists the chief executive in handling funds to produce the optimum blend of profitability and security.

Financial Planning
The financial manager must participate when plans are made for expansion or major replacement, in order to estimate how much cash will flow out to pay the bills and how much will flow in as a result of the hoped-for improvements. The manager's ear must be tuned to possibilities of economic turn-downs, market shifts, or changes in material costs; and contingency plans must be prepared so these events will not sink the ship if they do occur. Potential sources of funds must be considered in terms of the advantages and disadvantages of each, insofar as this data influences the decision on what to spend and when.

financial planning

Financial Control
When operations are under way, the financial manager must ride herd on the receipt and expenditure of funds to see that the intent of management is being carried out. A family of reports must be developed that will compare actual with planned expenditures and receipts, check the status of inventories and the receipt of purchased items, and safeguard company funds. The control system must be designed to spot variances and unusual circumstances, and to invite management attention to situations that appear improper. Broadly speaking, the financial control system is set up to insure that organizational goals set by management are being pursued effectively.

financial control

Fund Raising
All enterprises need funds at times. Small companies are more bedevilled by fund-raising problems than are large companies. Growing enterprises find their very success accompanied by an increasing need for external supplies of cash. Seasonal companies need cash at certain times but can return it at other times. Different needs are met by different sources of funds, and every funds supplier establishes different conditions for assigning money. The financial manager must be able to relate internal operations to the appropriate external source of funds, and to drive the best possible bargain for the firm.

Fund Investing
Everything the company buys is an investment. This includes the raw material and parts needed to make the product, labor costs, fixed

How does North Star handle investment decisions? Is someone given responsibility for them?

assets—even the credit granted to customers by the company to induce business. When a credit policy is relaxed, to bring in more customers and sell more goods (but to write off more accounts as bad debts), the bad debts are an investment in increased sales. Investment analysis is a skilled trade, and planning how and when the company will invest its own funds in itself is a major element of the financial manager's job.

Financial Analysis

The modern financial officer has broader responsibilities than the traditional bookkeeper or keeper of the purse. In many business corporations and government agencies, financial responsibilities extend to management auditing of the sort described in chapter 9. That is, they go further than recording *where* the funds were spent, and develop information on *how well* they were spent. This task often falls upon the financial manager's shoulders. In this chapter, we will consider only those audit activities that relate closely to the expenditure of funds, or that are measured primarily in financial terms.

Management Auditing

management auditing

The financial manager's duties in this area include "the work of assembling, analyzing, and interpreting the essential dollars-and-cents information about the operations of an organization, to supply the facts *and the interpretations* which the organization must have in order to plan and control its operations effectively."[1] Such an audit would not only

receivables

report the size and age of *receivables* (sums owed the company for goods or services delivered), but would also compare current income with industry standards and the firm's past records. Thus, the audit would suggest the economic rationality of the *discount terms* offered (reductions for prompt payment) or the benefits and hazards of existing credit policy. It would go past the dollar value of material in inventory to comment on the possible benefits of carrying a larger or smaller stock, the dangers of obsolescence, potential cost increases, hazards of damage or deterioration in storage, and so on. It would report not only the depreciated value of fixed capital equipment, but the economics of its current utilization and possible benefits of making other arrangements (disposing of rarely used capital items and contracting out the occasional job, perhaps leasing instead of owning, etc.). In reviewing financial transactions, the audit would not be confined to checking for dishonesty but would determine whether the most economical lot sizes were being ordered, whether the systems for checking amounts received were unduly detailed (spending $2 to save $1), and whether the checking itself was being done efficiently.

The management auditor starts with cost statements, but uses them mainly as guideposts to probable paydirt within the operational side of the organization. For example, if records indicate an increase in material procurement for a department, this finding raises such questions as: Is there an increasing pattern of damage or waste? Are individuals trying to stockpile unreasonably to avoid a remote chance of job holdups, are thefts occurring, or are we buying things that it would be more profitable for us to make?

This operational audit function is not entirely welcome in many organizations. The financial auditor is considered incapable of forming judgments in unfamiliar technical areas. In fact, of course, while auditors are not experts in the technical processes, they *are* experts in comparing what they see with what is specified, or what is typical, or what they were told they would see. They are, or ought to be, experts in comparing the planned framework for an operation with the way it seems to work out in practice. They bring an inquiring mind to bear on the practices they are observing, and raise questions that line management should answer.

Short-Term Analysis
Many short-term financial reports and ratios serve double duty: they inform management as to the company's progress, and they provide information to outsiders who need to know something of company performance. The most crucial report by all odds is the *income statement* (sometimes called the profit-and-loss statement), because it cuts through all the details of other reports and states baldly whether or not the enterprise is making money. The income statement shown in Table 9-2 on page 325 shows net earnings of $4,790,000 on sales of $95,000,000, for a *net margin* of:

<small>income statement</small>

<small>margin</small>

$$\frac{\$4,790,000}{\$95,000,000} = 5.04\%$$

Every dollar of sales brought the company 5¢ in profits after taxes. Is this good performance? To answer that, we must ask several questions. What are the earnings trends in recent years and recent months: up or down, and by how much? What does this profit represent in terms of money invested—how much are the stockholders earning for each dollar they have in the company? And how do these figures compare with the performance of other companies in the same business?

Figure 11-1 compares the performance of several companies in various industries. Looking at the airlines, you might check the figures for Delta and Eastern. Second quarter sales were similar ($343 million and $384 million), but Delta's second quarter profits were $29.1 million for an 8.5% margin while Eastern's were $9.7 million for a 2.5% margin. (The industry composite margin was 5.5%; Eastern is well below this, while Delta is well above it.) What did these airlines earn for their stockholders (return on *common equity*, consisting of common stock, capital surplus, and retained earnings) for the past year? Delta made 23.8¢ on the dollar, while Eastern (thanks to some losses in earlier months) lost 10.6¢ on the dollar. Delta has a *price-earnings ratio* of 9 (value of a share of stock as of July 31 divided by dollar earnings for the year); Eastern's price-earnings ratio is of course not meaningful, since there were no earnings. The earnings per share shown for Delta in the last column were $4.56, which indicates that Delta stock was selling for about $41 a share (9 x $4.56).

<small>price-earnings ratio</small>

And what were the earnings trends? In the last quarter, Delta's sales were up 20% and profits were up 40% from the same quarter a year earlier; profit margins rose from 7.3% to 8.5%. All in all, a very healthy performance. If you were a banker, you would not hesitate to make a commercial loan to Delta. If you were a stockholder, you would not vote the present management out at the annual meeting. And if you were management, you would decide you must be doing something right.

Figure 11-1.
Corporate Financial Performance (Quarterly Report)

COMPANY	SALES 2nd Qtr. 1974 $ Mil.	Chg. From 1973 %	6 Mo. 1974 $ Mil.	Chg. From 1973 %	PROFITS 2nd Qtr. 1974 $ Mil.	Chg. From 1973 %	6 Mo. 1974 $ Mil.	Chg. From 1973 %	Margins 2nd Qtr. 1974 %	2nd Qtr. 1973 %	Return Com. Eqy. 12 Mo. Ending 6-30	P-E- 7-31	12 Months Earnings Per Share
AEROSPACE: Airframes, general aircraft, and parts													
Beech Aircraft (3)	71.8	39	129.1	27	3.2	23	6.1	21	4.4	5.0	20.2	5	1.61
Boeing	968.7	-1	1810.1	13	18.4	27	36.0	43	1.9	1.5	6.9	6	2.92
Cessna Aircraft (3)	111.0	12	208.2	7	6.3	1	12.1	-1	5.7	6.3	17.8	5	2.88
Curtiss-Wright	67.0	2	134.4	9	2.6	19	4.6	21	3.8	3.3	5.5	8	1.08
Fairchild Industries	71.2	23	129.1	15	1.6	289	3.2	NM	2.3	0.7	6.1	8	0.74
McDonnal Douglas	947.7	4	1785.7	3	37.0	-9	66.5	-11	3.9	4.4	13.2	4	3.09
Northrop	210.4	35	399.5	39	4.7	102	7.2	77	2.2	1.5	9.4	6	3.84
Rockwell International (3)	1224.3	47	2207.8	35	40.8	15	78.5	13	3.3	4.2	13.7	5	4.72
Rohr Industries (5)	114.7**	16	225.8	14	1.9	49	3.9	37	1.7	1.3	9.0	7	1.82
Thiokol	78.8	20	150.1	11	4.8	52	9.8	58	6.1	4.8	17.0	5	2.87
United Aircraft	891.9	50	1713.1	51	29.9	82	57.1	84	3.4	2.8	14.5	4	5.94
Industry Composite	4757.4	22	8892.9	23	151.2	21	285.0	23	3.2	3.2	11.8	6	3.31
AIRLINES													
Allegheny Airlines	99.2	18	179.4	15	8.6	93	6.7	552	8.7	5.3	22.7	3	1.81
American Airlines	408.5	12	767.3	12	13.1	NM	2.6	NM	3.2	NM	-1.9	NM	-0.36
Braniff International	137.3	29	263.0	29	7.8	10	13.5	22	5.7	6.6	20.5	6	1.27
Continental Air Lines	114.6	18	214.1	17	5.4	NM	6.0	NM	4.7	0.3	4.1	13	0.46
Delta Air Lines (6)	343.0	20	657.6	19	29.1	40	50.4	45	8.5	7.3	23.8	9	4.56
Eastern Air Lines	384.8	19	754.4	16	9.7	NM	8.1	NM	2.5	NM	-10.6	NM	-1.86
Frontier Airlines	37.3	13	74.8	20	2.7	13	6.5	100	7.2	7.2	72.2	4	1.34
North Central Airlines	38.7	23	72.3	22	2.3	54	3.3	117	6.0	4.8	22.1	4	0.66
Northwest Airlines	194.3	37	362.3	39	19.6	63	33.5	68	10.1	8.5	12.5	7	3.03
PSA	36.0	13	66.9	11	2.6	120	2.7	267	7.2	3.7	3.3	7	0.78
Tiger International	81.9	20	154.2	19	5.4	-31	7.9	-42	6.6	11.4	15.6	5	2.28
Trans World Airlines	473.1	15	803.5	1	21.5	-1	-25.8	NM	4.5	5.3	3.1	9	0.94
UAL	606.6	18	1128.9	18	35.1	111	45.1	537	5.8	3.2	12.5	6	3.56
Western Air Lines	123.6	23	238.9	22	5.2	17	12.9	77	4.2	4.4	23.7	5	1.78
Industry Composite	3078.8	19	5737.5	16	168.0	92	173.6	177	5.5	3.4	9.0	6	1.52
APPLIANCES													
Maytag	57.2	9	114.0	7	6.5	12	12.4	-1	11.4	11.2	28.8	10	2.18
Singer	673.8	9	1334.9	12	15.1	-29	31.8	-25	2.2	3.5	10.0	5	4.65
Tappan	58.1	-5	113.6	-11	-0.3	NM	-0.6	NM	NM	1.6	1.6	15	0.36
Whirlpool	436.7	-6	824.9	-2	11.0	-53	20.8	-50	2.5	5.0	17.3	13	1.83
Industry Composite	1225.8	2	2387.4	5	32.4	-37	64.4	-35	2.6	4.3	13.1	11	2.52
AUTOMOTIVE: Autos, trucks, equipment, and parts													
Arvin Industries	60.9	15	104.8	-1	0.4	-81	0.5	-87	0.6	3.8	5.4	13	0.65
Bendix (3)	659.0**	8	1260.0	8	20.5	13	38.6	11	3.1	3.0	10.6	6	4.59
Budd	204.4	3	398.2	3	5.5	-25	9.5	-33	2.7	3.7	10.6	3	2.92
Champion Spark Plug	112.6	3	226.0	7	13.3	14	25.4	13	11.8	10.7	22.0	8	1.36
Chrysler	3019.8**	-5	5713.4	-6	27.8	-74	29.4	-85	0.9	3.4	3.3	9	1.59
Cummings Engine	213.6	22	399.7	21	7.6	14	12.8	12	3.6	3.8	13.5	7	3.82
Dana (4)	284.0	5	532.9	4	18.1	8	32.4	5	6.4	6.2	17.3	5	4.11
Eaton	453.2	12	862.4	11	29.4	11	50.1	1	6.5	6.6	16.0	6	4.96
Federal-Mogul	91.3	5	179.4	8	4.6	16	7.5	4	5.1	4.6	10.3	7	2.52
Ford Motor	5977.5	-5	1144.00	-8	168.0	-57	291.6	-61	2.8	6.3	7.1	10	4.60
Fruehauf	337.1	105	657.7	104	11.5	34	22.0	32	3.4	5.2	14.5	5	3.94
General Motors	8330.6**	-13	15269.3	-20	305.3	-62	425.7	-74	3.7	8.3	9.9	10	4.18
Gould (6)	190.5	7	382.1	13	8.5	29	16.8	29	4.5	3.7	13.4	6	3.51
International Harvester (2)	1253.6	14	2249.7	15	37.3	10	60.6	35	3.0	3.1	9.6	5	4.41
Libbey-Owens-Ford	169.0	-6	320.2	-10	9.1	-45	16.2	-54	5.4	9.1	11.8	7	3.45
Maremont	73.5	6	126.2	0	2.5	-38	3.1	-42	3.4	5.9	11.3	5	1.97

(1) Second quarter ending May 31; (2) Second quarter ending Apr. 30; (3) Third quarter and most recent six months ending June 30; (4) Third quarter and most recent six months ending May 31; (5) Third quarter and most recent six months ending Apr. 30; (6) Fourth quarter and most recent six months ending June 30; (7) Fourth quarter and most recent six months ending May 31; (8) Fourth quarter and most recent six months ending Apr. 30; (9) First quarter and most recent six months ending June 30; (10) First quarter and most recent six months ending May 31; (11) First quarter and most recent six months ending Apr. 30; * Sales include excise taxes; ** Sales include other income; *** Sales include excise taxes and other income; NA, not available, NM, not meaningful. Data: Investors Management Sciences.

All-Industry Composite													
278039.1	28	532367.8	25	16504.2	24	30929.0	20	5.9	6.1	14.2	8	3.45

Looking at the *industry composite* at the bottom of the airlines listings, Delta's margin of 8.5% compares very well with that of the airlines as a whole (only 5.5%) and that of all industries as a whole (only 5.9%).

Returning to our new letter shop enterprise, now in its fifth year and doing a good business, note its *balance sheet* (Figure 11-2.). How is the company doing? Let us use some ratios for analysis. A figure of great interest to banks and suppliers (in deciding if you have the financial strength to repay them for loans or material) is the *current ratio*: the ratio of current assets to current liabilities. For the letter shop, this ratio is:

current ratio

$$\frac{CASH + ACCTS.\,RECEIVABLE + INVENTORY}{ACCTS.\,PAYABLE + NOTES\,PAYABLE + TAX\,LIAB.} =$$

$$\frac{2{,}500 + 15{,}400 + 7{,}300}{10{,}600 + 5{,}000 + 1{,}700} = 1.46$$

An even better indicator of the letter shop's ability to pay its creditors in the event of sudden business termination (as in a fire) is the *quick ratio* or *acid test ratio*, which omits current assets such as inventory that the owner perhaps could not liquidate (turn into cash) in a crunch. The letter shop's quick ratio is:

quick ratio

$$\frac{2{,}500 + 15{,}400}{10{,}600 + 5{,}000 + 1{,}700} = 1.03$$

Are these figures good? For a struggling new business, they're not bad, but for an established enterprise they would be close to the line.

Another significant ratio is that of *debt to net worth*, which compares how much capital the creditors have advanced with how much the owners have invested, excluding intangible assets. From the balance sheet

debt to net worth

BALANCE SHEET—Letter Shop (fifth year)

Cash	2,500	
Accounts Receivable	15,400	
Inventory	7,300	
Total Current Assets		25,200
Equipment	6,100	
Other Assets	1,700	
Total Fixed Assets		7,800
Allowance for Depreciation	1,600	1,600
TOTAL ASSETS		34,600
Accounts Payable	10,600	
Notes Payable	5,000	
Reserve for Taxes	1,700	
Total Current Liabilities		17,300
Equipment Mortgage	4,500	4,500
Proprietors' Capital	12,800	12,800
TOTAL LIABILITIES		34,600

Figure 11-2.
Balance Sheet for Beginning Business

How would you calculate North Star's debt to net worth ratio?

figures, creditors have advanced a $5,000 note and a $4,500 mortgage, and proprietor's capital of $12,800 less $1,700 in other assets (good will) making this ratio come to:

$$\frac{5,000 + 4,500}{12,800 - 1,700} = \frac{9,500}{11,100} = 0.86$$

Thus, business can claim more invested money than owed money, and banks will find this reassuring, as will merchants who are asked to ship goods on credit to the young company.[2]

Another important ratio for internal control is the *inventory turnover*, or measure of how rapidly goods flow through the inventory pool. If the turnover rate is only 2, meaning the amount used in a year of paper and other supplies is only double the amount on hand at any given period, this probably means excessive capital is tied up in inventory. The ratio is:

inventory turnover

$$\frac{\text{COST OF GOODS SOLD}}{\text{AVERAGE INVENTORY}}$$

We don't see the income statement for the letter shop, but let's try to approximate this ratio. Suppose we assume the shop does as well as the average industrial firm (see bottom line of Figure 11-1). The proprietor's capital is $12,800, and if the return on equity is 14.2%, this gives a return of:

$12,800 x 14.2% = $1,818

If the margin is 5.9%, then 5.9% of sales equals the return of $1,818, or:

Sales = $1,818/5.9% = $30,813

Since the letter shop is a high *value-added* operation, we can estimate the selling price of the product as perhaps three times the cost price of the materials.[3] This would make the cost of goods sold come approximately to:

$30,813/3 = $10,270

If this is anything like correct, the turnover rate would be well under 2:

$10,270/$7,300 = 1.41

which seems far too high an inventory for this shop to carry.

Another short-term analysis which banks and tradesmen often make is a statement of balance sheet changes, which establishes the company's *profit trend*. With regard to the letter shop, this analysis would consist of placing the fourth-year balance sheet beside the fifth-year balance sheet and tabulating the changes over the year. Figure 11-1 shows changes in sales, profit, and margin for major U.S. firms compared with the previous year; for a more thorough analysis, changes in such factors as inventory, fixed assets, and accounts receivable and payable would be included as possible indicators of worrisome trends.

Long-Term Analysis

Just as short-term creditors are interested in your short-term status (and really don't care about your long-term prospects), so long-term creditors are interested in your viability over a period of several years. You might have the finest prospects of any business in the city over the years, but short-term creditors don't want to wait for you to build up retained earnings to pay off their 30-day accounts. For the individuals or institutions who loan or invest in your business for ten or 20 years, the analysis is quite different; money in the bank and current assets are not nearly as important as other concerns.

One such concern is the company's *income/dividend* ratio. Is the organization earning enough on a continuing basis to pay dividends on its *senior* stocks and bonds? (If there are two classes of stock, the one with first call on any dividends is the senior stock; if stocks and bonds are both outstanding, generally the bonds have first call on earnings, until their required payments are met in full.) What is the return on *residual equity* (on those stocks which have no preferred claim on earnings)? This ratio may be defined as:

_{income/dividend ratio}

_{residual equity}

$$\frac{\text{EARNINGS AFTER TAXES \& PREFERRED DIVIDENDS}}{\text{COMMON STOCK PLUS SURPLUS}}$$

Not only must the level of earnings be adequate for dividend payments, it must also be maintained. If it is falling, the creditors will want to examine the composition of earnings, to determine why and where. Perhaps cost of goods sold has gone up in relation to total selling receipts. Perhaps total sales have not fallen—they may even have risen; but the margin is falling, and if so the creditors want to know why.

With a sizable company, *market share* is an important long-term measure, as it tells us whether the company is gaining or losing ground relative to its competitors. Are special circumstances affecting the economy (inflation, rising unemployment and resulting shifts in consumer buying patterns, conflicting environmental and energy priorities, and so on)? It is important to know whether the company can prosper in such circumstances.

market share

Is the company using short-term debt for long-term purposes—that is, buying fixed assets that will take many years to pay for themselves and using money that will have to be repaid in two or three years? And what is the trend in the *debt-equity ratio*? If more and more of the company is financed by outsiders, a reduction in the value of assets could reduce net worth to a point where almost the whole company is pledged to creditors. A mounting debt-equity ratio is a danger sign.

Planning Funds Needs

Figure 11-3 shows the cash flow situation for the company whose income statement is given in Table 9-2 on page 325. Of the $95 million in receipts the company gets for sales, only $5,467,000 stays with the company in cash (and $2,677,000 of this is reserve for depreciation, so eventually the company must pay it out for replacement of fixed plant and equipment). In what other ways are funds generated and spent by the business? Since the first duty of the financial officer is to see that there are sufficient funds on hand to keep operating, this question is a critical one for any company. Figure 11-4 shows funds flowing into and out of the corporate bank account, starting with the *depreciation reserve* and *retained earnings* of Figure 11-3. The company can keep some of the profits as retained earnings. It can keep some cash as depreciation reserve, but eventually must pay out for new plant and equipment. It can issue stocks or bonds, bringing in long-term funds (equity or credit respectively), and it will pay out funds if it retires bonds or buys back any of its stock. It gains funds when it buys on credit, and it becomes short of funds when it sells on credit. It can borrow from the bank, but ultimately it must repay these loans. (And banks will not allow companies to keep constant short-term loans outstanding by repeatedly renewing them; rather, they will require that continuing or long-term needs be met by long-term credit instruments.) It can have temporary use of funds when it accrues for taxes (or withholds taxes from employee salaries), but at tax time it must pay out these taxes—and the continuing trend of the Internal Revenue Service is to shorten the period during which tax accruals may be held.

Only retained earnings really stay with the company, and since they are actually earnings on stockholder equity that were withheld from the stockholders (not paid in dividends), they are properly considered as an increase in stockholder equity.

Controlling cash flow is a matter of timing. Figure 11-3 shows an excess of cash from the sales transactions, but what it does not show is that most of the expenditures required to make those sales were incurred well before the receipts rolled in. If we assume (1) that the sales were spread equally throughout the year at about $8 million a month, (2) that the

Figure 11-3.
Cash Flow Funnel

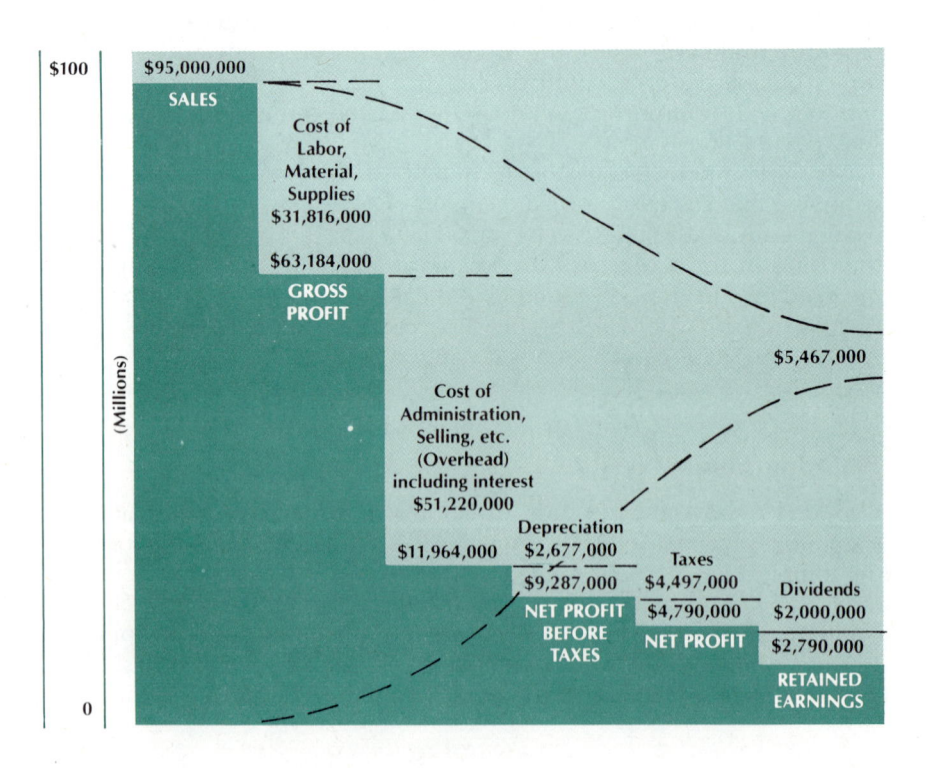

manufacturing process averaged a month, and (3) that payment was made about a month after delivery, then two months' worth of direct costs

$$\frac{(\$31,816,000)}{6}$$

and two months' worth of indirect costs

$$\frac{(\$51,220,000)}{6}$$

totalling about $13,840,000, would be required in working capital to keep this train of making-and-selling in motion. If volume were to go up 50%, then about 50% more working capital would be needed, or $20,760,000. You can see that if business expands in this way without the financial officer planning for it, the enterprise is going to run out of cash precisely because of its success.

Bear in mind that this $14 million or so is not needed just for some particular period; it is needed forever. And if this company is thought a poor credit risk and must pay a heavy 12% interest rate for its money, the interest would amount to $1,680,000 a year—more than a third of the entire net profit for this item alone.

A huge firm such as Sears Roebuck and Company reportedly has over $1 million in postage stamps, $10 million in cash register change, over $170 million in bank balances with 1,400 banks, and fully $10 million just flowing between banks at all times.

How does the financial manager plan cash needs? The following lists the steps involved in preparing a *cash budget:*

1. Estimate monthly sales.
2. Based on this figure, allowing for billing period, estimate monthly receipts.
3. Estimate monthly expenditures (based on sales forecasts and hence corresponding production volumes).
4. From 2 and 3, estimate end-of-month cash balances each month.
5. For months where balance is negative, forecast amount and timing of financing required.
6. For months where balance is excessive, forecast extra cash to be utilized (invested in short-term paper).

cash budget

When did North Star first do this? What effect did it have?

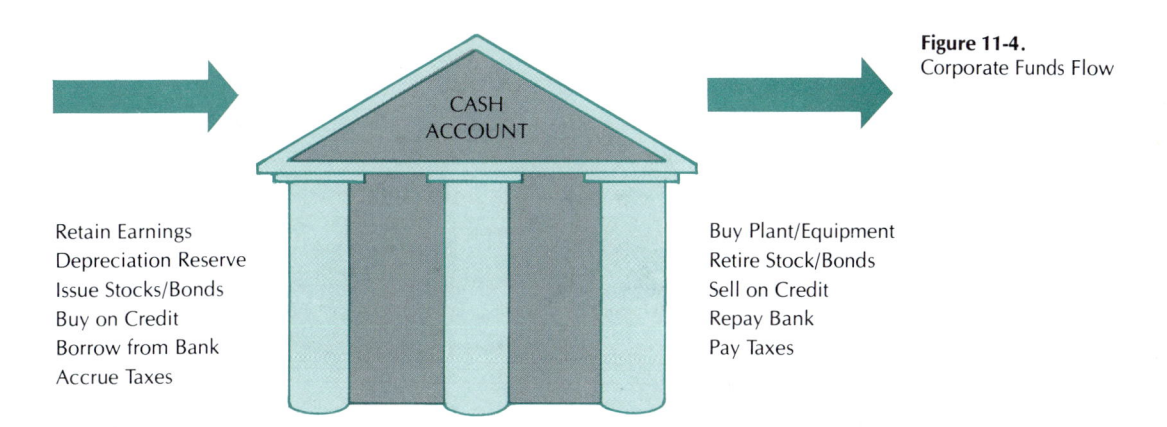

Figure 11-4.
Corporate Funds Flow

Retain Earnings
Depreciation Reserve
Issue Stocks/Bonds
Buy on Credit
Borrow from Bank
Accrue Taxes

CASH ACCOUNT

Buy Plant/Equipment
Retire Stock/Bonds
Sell on Credit
Repay Bank
Pay Taxes

In all of these estimates it will be necessary to estimate the "velocity" of funds—how long it takes for deposits to clear so they can be used, how much money it takes to fill the organization's pipeline, how fast receivables become cash, what fraction will pay early to get discounts, etc.

Profit Planning

Most companies use one or a combination of the following approaches:

1. Forecasting by causative factors
2. Forecasting by trend analysis
3. Use of profitable-volume analysis

Causative Factors

Probably the most sophisticated method of profit planning is to determine which elements in the economy and the industry environment have *correlated* with sales volume in the past, and estimate the combination of those elements that may exist during the next year. This calculation can be very simple: more skis and road salt are sold if the winter is snowy; more air conditioners sell in a heat wave; and more coal sells if there is a shortage of petroleum. For the usual business, however, a more complex analysis based on mathematical correlation is necessary to sort out the separate impacts of circumstances that lead to increased or decreased sales. Recession periods are viewed as sales depressants, but when money gets tight certain lower-cost items may actually enjoy a sales increase—staple foods, for example, which supplant the luxury cuts of meat when times are hard.

Chapter 7, "Decision Making," discusses some of these analytical methods. Page 227 describes an approach to relating net profit to amount of advertising, which can be extended to analysis of other causative

correlation or factor analysis

The cash flow problem is a matter of timing.

Year	Volume	Increase	+12% Volume
−10	100.00		100.00
− 9	117.12	17.12	112.00
− 8	133.77	16.65	125.44
− 7	150.04	16.27	140.49
− 6	165.82	15.78	157.35
− 5	180.96	15.14	176.23
− 4	195.62	14.66	197.38
− 3	209.59	13.97	221.07
− 2	222.77	13.18	247.60
− 1	235.07	12.30	277.31

Table 11-1. Growth in Sales Volume

Table 11-2. Projected Growth Rate

factors. Pages 238 and 239 describe a similar approach for forecasting profit from tanker operations. Every business has key factors (see page 228) on which sales and profit results primarily depend. This approach uses statistical techniques to relate past performance to the behavior of these key factors, and to forecast that past causation patterns will continue to operate in the future.

Trend Analysis
This method of profit planning, the most common in industry and government, assumes (unless the evidence suggests otherwise) that past trends in sales, market shifts, commodity and material prices, labor costs, etc., will continue. Unfortunately, it is not always easy to interpret the evidence. Any single trend you observe may in fact be a complex mixture of several trends, moving in different directions at different rates and with different degrees of strength. Today one particular trend may be in the ascendancy, tomorrow another. To sort them out requires a good understanding of the environment of your enterprise.

Suppose you are endeavoring to plot the sales volume for your company in a given community for the next 12 years. You have as raw data the sales figures for the past ten years, as shown in Table 11-1 (in thousands). The rate of increase is dropping a bit, but you are continuing to grow in an apparently healthy way. You decide to plot a trend line for the above figures and extend it 12 years into the future in a continuation of the pattern. You do this (in Figure 11-5), and the line forecasts a sales volume of $360,000. So you decide to plan your expansion based on that future volume.

Before you do this, however, you stop to theorize. Your neighborhood is growing at 12% a year, and your product is used by the general population, so that would suggest a 12% growth rate, corresponding to Table 11-2. Moreover, a survey last year reported that overall community acceptance of this product was going up about $10,000 a year, as regularly as clockwork—making the Table 11-2 figures even higher (adding 10 more to the −9 year, 20 to the −8 year, 30 to the −7 year, and so on).

If these two factors were operating, the growth rate in sales would not be turning down as in Figure 11-5. Instead, it would take off on a continuously increasing path. Figure 11-6 shows how each of these two effects would occur, from ten years ago to 12 years in the future, if in fact they were the only two effects operating. And since they are additive, you would expect the sales volume for year −1 to be 277.31 +90 or 367.31, instead of only 235.07.

What's wrong? There must be some third factor that is operating, adding to community growth and product acceptance (a +12% *rate* growth and a +10 per year *constant* growth); and there is. You calculate that this third factor is causing a 4% compounded negative growth rate (4% first year, 8% next, 12% next, and so on)—and if *that* continues, your firm's sales for the next 12 years will turn down in a sickening plunge, as shown in Figure 11-7.

You look for the culprit and find it in your competitor, who is taking a larger share of the total business each year. As of year −1 this competitor's share has risen to 36%, and by year +12 it is a huge 88%. Your company is going down the drain, and trend analysis can reveal if all the factors have been included. It is essential that you take prompt action.

Profitable-Volume Analysis

profitable-volume analysis

The previous two profit-planning methods seek to forecast the future, so you can calculate what this will mean in profit terms. *Profitable-volume analysis* (or breakeven analysis) calculates what volume is required to be profitable, so you can see if it is reasonable to expect this much business. Figure 9-6 on page 332 shows a breakeven chart for a given production process, which tells management how large a volume will be necessary if the product line is to be profitable—and how profitable it will be for different volume levels. Armed with this information, management can

Figure 11-5.
Graph of Overall Growth Rate

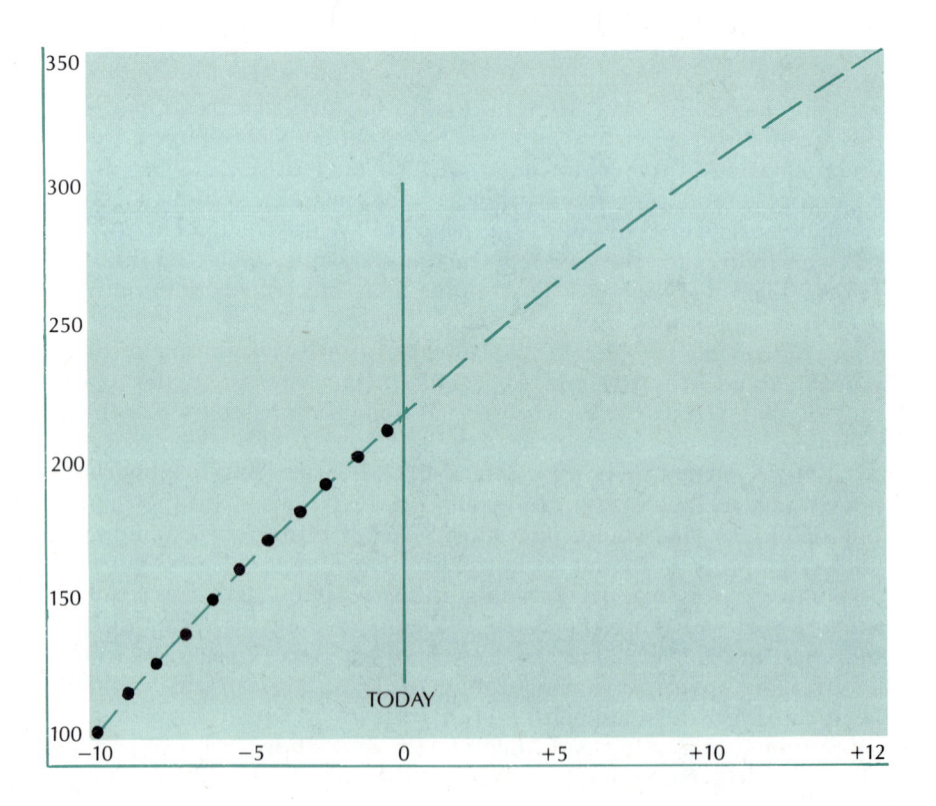

evaluate the market to see if operation within this profitable range is feasible. Some estimate of sales volume still is required, but this method puts bounds on the sort of information that is needed. Often it will be found that the breakeven point is higher than it is reasonable to expect volume to be, and the project can be put out of mind at once.

Which of these three do you think fits North Star's kind of operations best? Why?

Managing Funds

Managing funds once constituted the financial specialist's entire job. The owner raised funds, made the decisions as to their disbursement, and managed the undertakings in which they were spent. The bookkeeper or accountant simply recorded how they were received and spent and checked to insure that they were handled carefully and honestly. Today, not only has the financial manager's function expanded beyond the

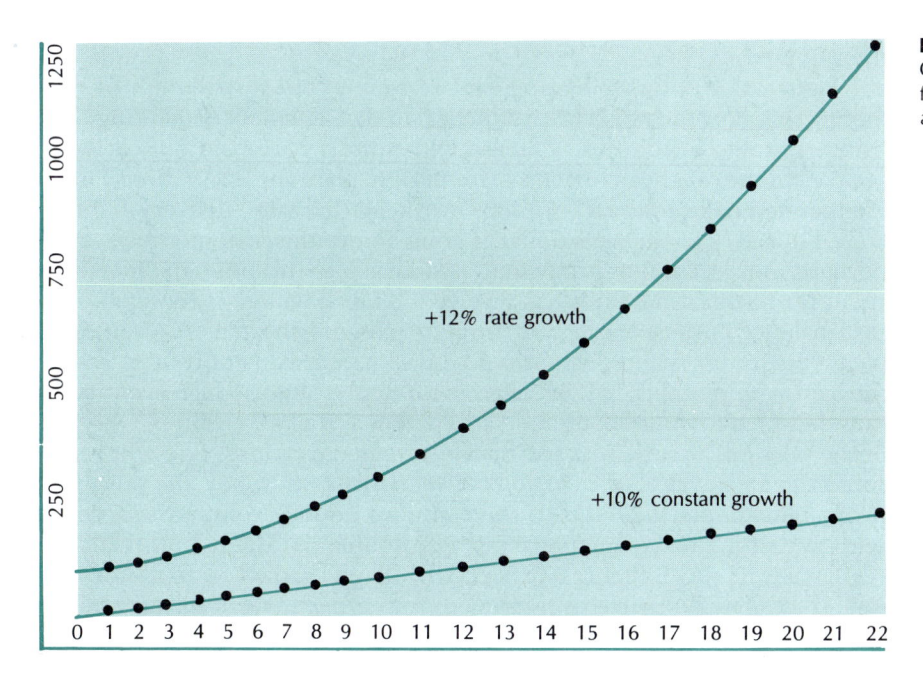

Figure 11-6.
Growth Component from Population Growth and Product Acceptance

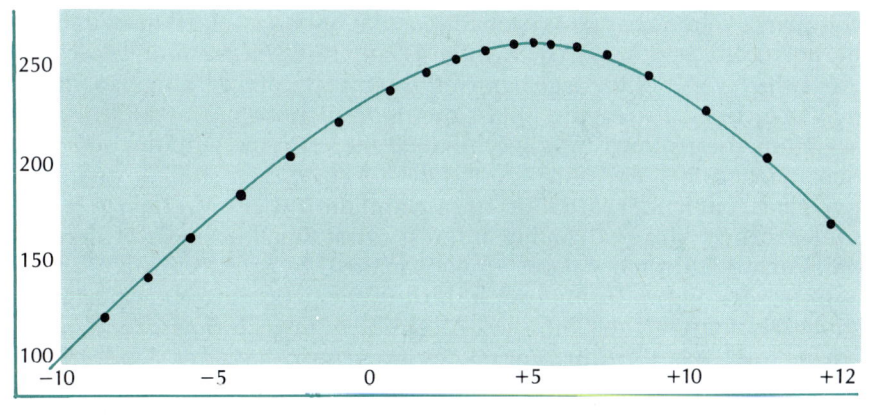

Figure 11-7.
Growth Component from Corporate Performance

397
MANAGING FINANCES

management of funds, but it has enlarged within this managing area to encompass analysis of the optimum compromise between liquidity and profitability, as well as to deal with managing cash, receivables, inventory, and capital items.

The Liquidity-Profitability Tradeoff

It is easy to have a fine record on library book security or aircraft readiness—don't loan out any books and don't make any flights. That way you have no thefts of books and no aircraft breakdowns; but your library and your airline are useless. At the other extreme, if everyone has free access to your shelves, and you make a flight whenever anyone wishes, your library and airline will come apart at the seams—and again, they'll be useless.

liquidity

The situation is the same with liquidity. Since businesses have to spend money to make it, every potentially profitable venture impairs liquidity to a degree, but without such ventures the businesses would earn nothing on their equity.

Figure 11-8 shows the approximate timing and distribution of the money that flows around the production-and-sales circuit, excluding any prior capital expenditures. Material expenditures are paid out early, as are part of the overhead expenses (for design, planning, etc.); direct labor is expended next, followed by more overhead (for sales, delivery, billing, etc.). Thus, 87¢ of the sales dollar is gone before the customer pays, and perhaps more than that if payment is slow. Up to this time, the firm has spent far more cash than it has received. After payment is received, the cash balance *for that transaction* shifts briefly into the plus column, but payments for taxes and dividends go out shortly, leaving only 6¢ to reach the bank—and of this, half is a reserve for depreciation, which eventually must be spent to replace outdated equipment and plant facilities. Only 3¢ of the sales dollar stays with the firm as retained earnings. These figures, subject to a good deal of variation between firms, show how the push for profitability impairs liquidity. If this company doubles volume, its 87¢ net outflow before receiving payment will double to $1.74, but retained earnings (one way to get this extra cash) will go up only 3¢ to 6¢ for the sale. If the company turns over its goods four times a year, it will take more than seven years for retained earnings to generate the amount of cash needed to handle this doubled net outflow—and by that time the company's volume has gone even higher, if it is successful. If the 87¢ must be borrowed at 9% for three months, interest will amount to nearly 2¢—which wipes out a large part of the extra retained earnings, so that it may take 15 or 20 years to amass the needed funds in this way.

In times of short funds and inflated interest rates, a double squeeze hits the business executive. Not only do customers slow down their payments, but lenders are short of cash and the owner must turn to other sources who charge far higher interest rates. Small business owners in particular (who number about 9 million in the U.S., constituting 95% of all enterprises and producing over a third of the nation's total output) find shortage of funds their most critical problem in such times, sometimes having to spend 18% to 20% for money just to keep operating. Under such conditions, expansion may have to go by the board—and with it, increased profitability—so that firms may remain sufficiently liquid to meet their pressing obligations.

Cash Management

On page 393, under "Planning Funds Needs," we listed the six steps by which the financial manager plans cash needs. Note that the normal business has two situations to deal with: months when cash is low and loans are needed, and months when excess cash is available that must be made to earn interest.

For the borrowing months, the financial manager must make advance arrangements with the bank, to avoid having to raise funds on very short notice and possibly to accept very poor interest terms as a result. In addition to giving the manager time to make the best arrangements possible, this planning signals a well-run business to the bank and increases the chances of a loan.

For the months when excess cash is available, it should be put out at interest, but in a place where the principal is safe and the manager can get it back when it is needed. Unless the business is *formed* to speculate (i. e., that is its *purpose*), financial managers should never speculate with their working capital. (The 1974 failure of the Franklin National Bank, then the

cash management

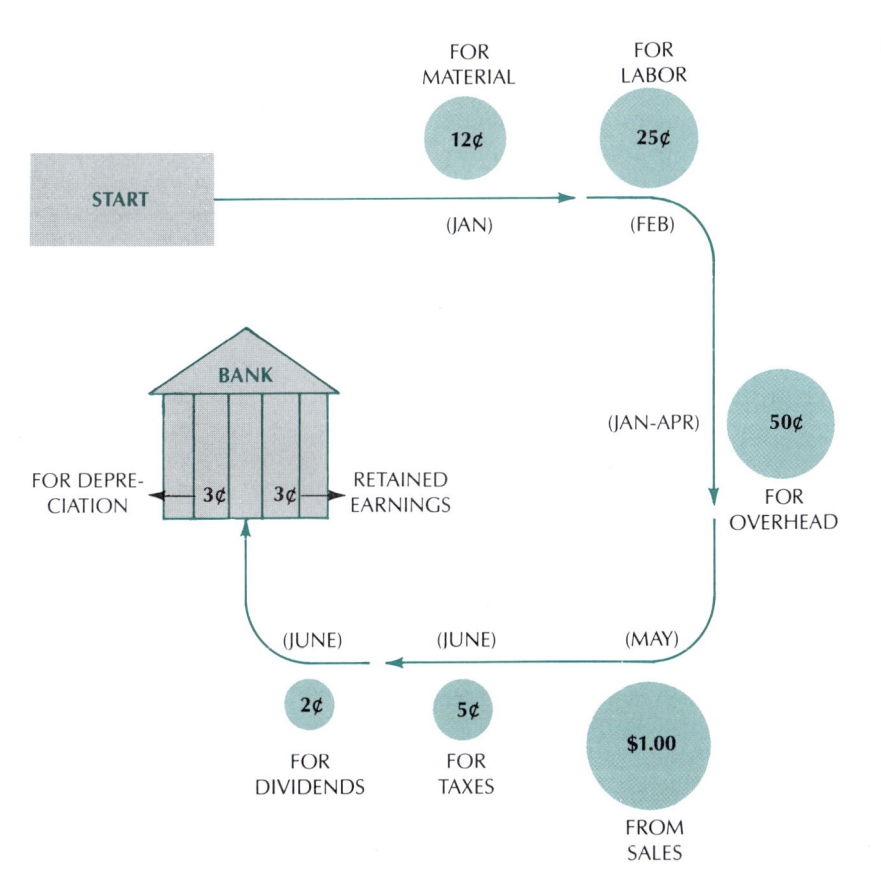

Figure 11-8.
Timing and Distribution of Cash Flow

twentieth largest in the U.S. with deposits of nearly $3 billion, was traceable in part to heavy and rather reckless speculation in foreign exchange. The banking community was shocked when, in May 1974, the Franklin suddenly announced foreign exchange losses of $40 million.)

An important element of cash management is making available cash go as far as it can. Many companies give a small discount, sometimes 2%, for payment within ten days, and specify that the full price will apply for payments made within 30 days. The prudent financial manager will hold off payments as long as possible—taking the 2% discount by paying on the ninth day if possible, otherwise waiting until the thirtieth day. When times are hard, of course, many companies improperly take far longer than 30 days to pay their due bills. Indeed, the normal lag in bill payments is about 45 days, and in the 1975 funds squeeze customers typically stretched this to 70 or 80 days—making the seller an unwilling lender who is not even paid interest on the overdue funds. When giving consumer credit, merchants customarily charge interest at 1½% a month (18% a year) on bills which are unpaid after 30 days.

> When Zeb was first hired, he said he was used to doing this. How do you think he did it?

Cash management includes prudent handling of incoming funds: seeing that different individuals open payment mail, post the receipts in the company ledgers, and deposit the checks in the bank. If a single individual does all three things, it is easy to embezzle funds and to falsify the records so that it will not be discovered until well after the fact. Cash management includes keeping watch on outgoing funds, separating functions similarly in order to prevent dishonest employees from paying nonexistent suppliers and certifying receipt of nonexistent goods.

Large companies, which send bills all across the country, may have to wait several days for checks mailed in one region to reach their home office in another region. For example, say a company billing $4 million a day (which would make it about one-twentieth the size of General Motors, and about the size of Boise Cascade Lumber Company, Bristol-Myers Drugs, Texas Instruments, or H. J. Heinz), figures its working capital is worth 12% and faces a five-day delay in receiving checks because of mail transit time. That company loses $2,400,000 a year in interest from this factor alone. In order to reduce this figure, sometimes to less than half, many companies use *lock-box billing* systems: they rent lock boxes in major cities around the country and have payments sent to the lock box nearest the customer. A local bank picks up and deposits these payments daily, thus getting them on deposit earlier and reducing the amount of additional cash the company would have to borrow otherwise.

> lock-box billing

Accounts Receivable Management

Figure 11-8 shows the small fraction of the sales dollar that returns to the company as retained earnings. And this figure can shrink even more if the sales dollar itself doesn't come—if the customer defaults on payment. A major responsibility of the financial manager is to see that bad debts are kept strictly under control by a careful scrutiny of prospective charge customers before they are granted credit. In consumer selling, sales are for cash unless credit has been arranged, but in commercial transactions it is unusual for a sale to be for cash. In fact, the only customers required to pay before delivery are usually those with such a poor credit record that no supplier will deal with them in any other way.

Dun and Bradstreet, Inc., is a national organization that for many years has investigated the great majority of businesses in the U.S. to keep tabs on their credit-worthiness—information Dun and Bradstreet then sells to suppliers. With services such as this available, there is little excuse for a company to extend credit to customers with a poor credit rating. Many credit losses occur when a customer with a good record suddenly falls on hard times, and credit reports have not had time to catch up with the current situation. Therefore, the financial manager must be particularly alert for any signs that a customer who usually pays promptly is delaying, that the customer's amount of credit is increasing, and so on.

Another problem in receivables is the question of how much credit to give. Some consumer businesses, notably drug stores and supermarkets, extend little or no credit.[4] Others, particularly those selling "big ticket" items such as cars or major appliances, would make very few sales if they did not grant credit. Since credit is extended as an inducement to buy, the financial and sales managers must make a joint decision on credit policies. If a 2% discount is granted for payment in 10 days, compared with no discount for "30 days" (which typically means 45 days), the company is making a 2% payment for 35 days' use of money. In effect, the company is charging itself a yearly interest rate of over 20%. Perhaps that seems an excessive reward to customers for their promptness. But there is more involved; customers who pay promptly always pay, whereas those who delay sometimes do not. Moreover, those who take the discount constitute a list of "gold-plated" credit risks, and this information gives the credit manager a useful reading on changes in credit worthiness.

If a potential customer seeks a large *line of credit* (amount that can be owed at one time without repayment on account), the financial manager is interested not only in willingness to pay but also in *ability* to pay. The latter is suggested by many elements of the customer's financial statements—current ratio and acid test ratio (page 389) will indicate whether assets are dwindling with respect to debts. *Turnover of receivables* (amount of credit sales relative to the size of receivables—measures the fraction of total volume that is still owed) and *turnover of inventory* (amount of material bought relative to the average amount on hand—measures quantity of obsolete material in warehouses) are also important. Changes in these ratios over time must also be considered; are things holding firm or sliding downhill?

<small>line of credit</small>

<small>receivables turnover</small>

A final comment on receivables management: it is not necessarily bad business to sell to poor credit risks if it is done knowingly and if they constitute only a small part of your total customers. Consider the situation of Figure 11-8:

Costs	Depreciation	Profits pretax	Taxes	Profits posttax
$0.87	0.03	0.10	0.05	0.05

Now sell another $1 of products to poor credit risks, with 5% defaults:

| $0.87 | 0.00 | 0.08 | 0.04 | 0.04 |

Depreciation was zero for the additional sales, since it is based on a given amount of write-off per year. The doubled business, even with 5%

defaults, brought in $0.95, and dropped profits only 1%. In this case, it is a question of trade-off—are the increased sales worth the increased defaults? The financial manager must calculate the breakeven point in detail to determine the proper credit strategy.

Inventory Management

working capital

Since it is not unusual for a company to have a quarter or more of its working capital tied up in inventory, management of these assets deserves close attention. Note from Figure 11-1 that the money invested in inventory must be spent earlier than the other costs—which means that it ties up more money in proportion to the total cost of material and other costs involved in the product. While material must be on hand *at the latest* by the time labor begins, it is usually on hand a good deal earlier than that. The reasons are related both to "insurance" (few production expenses are as great as those caused by waiting for needed material or making do with a substitute) and to economies of scale (savings from buying material in quantity).

cost of stocking
cost of ordering

The costs of material divide into two groups: the *cost of stocking* and the *cost of ordering*. These costs are tabulated below.

1. *Costs of stocking*
   a. *Interest on tied-up funds* (cost of inventory, cost of handling equipment, cost of warehouse space)
   b. *Maintenance of inventory* (heat, light, custodial, repair, taxes)
   c. *Operations on inventory* (stockworkers, receiving, record keeping)
   d. *Inventory losses* (pilferage, casualty losses, obsolescence, change in value[5])
2. *Costs of ordering*
   a. *Clerical* (order writing, checking, paying, follow-up)
   b. *Shipping* (common carrier rates)
   c. *Price* (related to quantity of orders)

As a general rule, the more orders there are in a given year the higher the order costs will be and the lower the stock costs will be. If your company needs 1200 items a year, and orders 100 a month (assuming regular delivery on schedule), it will need to stock only 100 items, but it will write and service 12 orders and receipts a year and will pay for 12 shipments. At the other extreme, if it orders 1200 at a time it will need a warehouse capable of holding the entire 1200, and will have that much tied up in interest, but will service only one order and receipt a year. Moreover, it will enjoy quantity reductions in both material cost and shipping charge.

It is beyond the scope of this book to explore the techniques for solving this trade-off problem, but they are quite straightforward, and the financial manager must be prepared to deal with them constantly.

Fixed Assets Management

The final section of this chapter, "Investing Funds," discusses the problems and techniques involved in capital budgeting—the acquisition of fixed assets. This section discusses the management of these assets after they have been acquired.

One important element of management, whatever the field, is getting the facts. After a major piece of equipment has been acquired and placed in service, management needs to know whether it has a gold mine or white elephant. The way to find this out is to see what the equipment is used for and how much it earns. It is important, therefore, that costly equipment charge "rent" to whatever jobs are using it, and that this rental be recorded so management can see what equipment is paying its way. Any items that are not earning enough rent to amortize their purchase price should be sold and the space made available for something else.

A major piece of equipment in a plant cannot be treated like a family's big color television set—just set down and promised a home for life. Let us consider what it costs:

- *Interest on tied-up funds* (the equipment cost, its kit of tools and related items, special facilities such as air conditioning, etc.)
- *Interest on tied-up space cost* (all the costs of plant construction, maintenance and operation for the square footage required)
- *Maintenance of the equipment* (repairs, upkeep, adjustment, cleaning)
- *Operation of the equipment*
- *Aging and obsolescence* (risks that a new model will come along and outdate this model, normal depreciation, change in value from economic forces—which could increase, but usually decreases)

Against all of these, what it earns is the rent it can charge to productive jobs. It is the financial manager's job to see that this equipment is *not* treated like the home color TV but is made to prove its worth every day of its life or cast out.

Raising Funds

A few years ago, a text on financial management would have discussed the raising of funds in rather routine terms: there are several methods, and the financial manager should consider the pros and cons of each in making recommendations, much like the diner at a smorgasbord decides among the ham and beef and chicken (or perhaps a bit of all three). Today the environment is profoundly different; financial managers are giving serious thought to the health of the U.S. capital market, and the ability of U.S. corporations to raise necessary funds in the stock and bond markets is being questioned as never before. In the short run, government efforts to combat inflation include raising the interest rates and decreasing the money supply, which makes short-term loans both more costly and harder to obtain.

In the automobile dealership business, *floor planning* is the term for loans that dealers use to buy cars from the manufacturers; it refers to the funds advanced by the bank until the car is sold and a satisfactory purchase contract worked out with the buyer. For years this money was available pretty much on demand at around 6% interest, since banks considered this a relatively low-risk operation. During the cash squeeze of 1974-75, however, not only did the interest rates double, but many banks

floor planning

worried that the cars might not sell and began backing out of this business except for the more gilt-edged dealerships. The dealers found that their internal practices were no longer simply their own business, but were of great importance in determining whether the bank considered them good risks.

Short-Term Funds

There are essentially four types of short-term funds; each will be discussed below.

Trade Credit

trade credit

Trade credit is simply the sale of material on 30-day terms. As short as this period is, it is an extremely important type of credit for small businesses, who use it to a much larger extent than large businesses. At the end of World War II, the long-repressed consumer demand for goods coupled with large individual purchasing power enabled some new businesses to order wholesale stock on trade credit, sell it at retail for cash, and pay their wholesale bills with the proceeds from retail sale of the same stock. In normal times, this procedure would be highly impractical.

Usual trade credit terms are sale on open account, with monthly billing and 30-day terms. As a company's credit reputation begins to appear dubious, sellers may demand a promissory note, may send COD, or may even demand cash before shipment. In some industries it is customary to place goods in retailers' hands on consignment (periodicals are sold this way through newsdealers, and real estate is almost invariably sold in this way). Since small businesses can get away with delaying

It is important that costly equipment charge "rent" to whatever jobs are using it.

payment for periods up to 60 days and perhaps even longer if suppliers are extremely anxious to sell to them, this constitutes a valuable and easily available source of short-term funds that keeps many businesses solvent. It would be a rare business, whatever its size, that would not find it somewhat embarrassing to have to pay all of its accounts payable down to zero (partly, of course, because so many of its assets are tied up in its own accounts receivable).

Bank Credit

The smaller the company, the larger its bank credit as a percentage of its total assets. The local bank is the cornerstone of business enterprise in any community, and there are few businesses that would not be severely hamstrung (or even thrown into bankruptcy) if the bank suddenly called in all of its outstanding loans.

Short-term bank loans must be acquired for legitimate short-term purposes—usually to build up seasonal inventory or to finance a large contract in anticipation of payment. Since the loan is for such a specific purpose, the bank probably will insist on a *cleanup* of the loan as the stated purpose comes full term: either seasonally, if for inventory, or as payments come in, if for a large contract. As a condition of such a loan, the bank may take title to the inventory or require that the contract payments be tendered through it. Banks are particularly attentive to any indication that short-term loans are being used to build up fixed assets or to cover a deteriorating profit situation, or for any other purpose that casts doubt on the ability of the business to repay them when due. loan cleanup

The banker will require the business to disclose full details of its operations and, if it is new or small, of its principal officers as well. Indeed, the bank will reach right through a small business and deal with the owner or owners. Thus a new business that is incorporated will be unable to secure short-term bank credit unless the note is countersigned and guaranteed by individuals. The banker will want to know the purpose of the loan, will want some assurance that the funds are used for this purpose, and will want to see a believable repayment plan.

Secured Loans

Most bank loans are unsecured, since the last thing banks wish or need is to take possession of some physical collateral in event of default and then be saddled with managing or disposing of it. Many specialized finance companies will make secured loans, however, and develop experience in dealing with the types of collateral usually involved. Security may be inventory, accounts receivable, fixed assets, or real estate. When the inventory is in the borrower's possession, it is secured by a *trust receipt,* which prohibits the borrower from transferring ownership without the finance company's agreement. A *warehouse receipt* signifies inventory that, while on the borrower's premises, is secured in a warehouse tended by a representative of the lender. In rare cases the inventory may be in the lender's custody, though this is clumsy to administer. Installment loans are secured loans, in that the property purchased does not transfer to the buyer's ownership until it is paid off; the business buys its equipment just as the consumer buys a car.

margin notes: secured loans; trust receipt; warehouse receipt

Unsecured Loans

unsecured loan

When the business cannot get an unsecured bank loan and has no collateral suitable for a secured loan, the owner may be able to get an associate or relative to *endorse* or *guarantee* the note; if the owner defaults, the endorser is obligated to pay it in full. At the other end of the spectrum, the largest and most powerful corporations obtain unsecured loans in the form of *commercial paper*. Thus General Motors Acceptance Corporation may issue an *acceptance,* offering to pay interest somewhat higher than the going bank rates for short-term money. It does this because its needs are greater than any one bank is willing to meet. Since its credit is unquestioned, it attracts investors who want to put funds to work for one or a few months at attractive rates.

commercial paper
acceptance

When North Star got in a cash bind, which of these four types of short-term credit did they use?

Suppliers of equipment often will make unsecured loans to buyers as a marketing inducement. These may take the form of deferring to spring payment for any items bought during the fall, waiving any interest payment, and so forth.

Intermediate-Term Funds

Whereas short-term loans are generally used to pay for items that will be turned into cash shortly (and the source of repayment is the receipts from such sale), intermediate-term loans are generally used for plant and equipment, and the source of repayment is profit before taxes and depreciation. The assumption made by both borrower and lender is that the borrowed funds will be put to work in a way that will make sufficient profit to gradually replace the loaned funds with earned funds—owner's equity.

Why do borrowers seek intermediate-term funds—loans for periods of up to ten years and sometimes twice that long? One basic reason is that loans do not transfer any ownership, and hence control, of the enterprise. If a corporation has $500,000 in stock that has been issued previously, and acquires an additional $250,000 by issuing additional stock, this means that an individual who initially had control by owning $250,000 worth (50%), now has only 33% interest and has lost control (assuming all issues were at the same price per share). A 33% interest in a large company would be effective control, because of the difficulty of marshaling all the thousands of small stockholder votes in opposition, but in a small company a majority ownership might be required to insure control.

dilution of ownership

In addition to this *dilution of ownership,* there is the problem that interest on debt (loans or bonds) comes before taxes, whereas dividends on stocks come after taxes. Suppose a company needs $100,000, on which it will be able to earn $20,000 a year before taxes. The taxes on this increment will be approximately $10,000 if the money is raised in the form of stock, and only $10,000 will be left for dividends plus retained earnings. Suppose the management decides to pay out $8,000 in dividends and retain $2,000; this amounts to an 8% return to the stockholders. By contrast, if the $100,000 was borrowed, 16% interest could be paid, leaving $4,000 in profits to divide between $2,000 for taxes and $2,000 for retained earnings. It is easy to see why debt issues can pay larger interest rates than equity issues for the same ultimate profit after taxes.

Why, then, don't companies issue nothing but debt issues, and why don't loaners flock to this sort of investing rather than stocks? The answer is that, at times, they do. When profit dips are expected, investors expect lowered stock dividends and move into bonds or loans. In the past few years public utilities have found it very hard to sell stock, and major corporations have filed big debt issues: DuPont announced a $500 million debt issue in late 1974; Xerox filed with the Securities and Exchange Commission a late 1974 sale of $150 million in 25-year debentures plus another $150 million in 8-year notes; Caterpillar Tractor and Continental Oil Company filed similar announcements shortly before.

But there is a limit, and when banks make loans that will take many years to pay off they take a far greater interest in the firm's operations than when they simply make short-term loans. For one thing, they want to ensure that the ratio of debt to equity does not rise so high that the owners' interest is far less than the bank's—in which case the owners might simply walk away when things got tough and leave the bank with the mess to untangle. Banks insist on maintaining some minimum floor on *working capital* (current assets minus current liabilities), some minimum current ratio, and so forth. They are likely to insist that no fixed assets or accounts receivable be sold, and perhaps that there be no executive salary raises above a certain annual rate. They will also insist on quarterly reports of performance, that lives of key officers be insured in their favor, and that no major expenditures be made for fixed assets. In short, when a company makes a major loan commitment with a lender for an extended term, the lender becomes in a sense a partner in the operation. working capital

Finance companies often make intermediate-term *equipment loans,* usually at higher interest rates than typical bank or bond rates. A variation on equipment loans is the practice of leasing, in which a leasing company buys the equipment (sometimes from the very company it will lease back to), and rents it to the operating company over a long period of years. There are several advantages. One is the fact that there is a loan involved—the operating company does not have to pay out the cash to buy the equipment. Another is the fact that the operating company can "expense" the entire rental as a cost and thus reduce taxes during the early years of the contract. A third might be that the operating company has a prior loss from an extraordinary event (such as the Chilean government's expropriation of Anaconda Copper's mines, resulting in a $356 million write-off), which makes tax write-offs that accompany large capital purchases (accelerated depreciation and investment tax credits) relatively useless. It then becomes advantageous to transfer these benefits to the leasing company, which can make the rental lower. Figure 11-9 shows such a lease deal, put together for Anaconda's new aluminum reduction mill. First, Kentucky Trust Company holds the property in the banks' names; First Boston arranged 65% of the funding from three insurance companies who will earn 9 1/8% on their money. Thirty-five percent is equity capital, put up by six banks and Chrysler Corporation, who will own the plant and get to use the investment tax credit and depreciation credits. Anaconda estimates that over the 20-year term of the lease its "rent" will be about $74 million less than the cost of interest on bonded debt if it had gone that route. equipment loans
leasing

Sometimes leasing, though the only way out for a small company, is a very costly alternative. An example is a small Pittsburgh machine shop

407
MANAGING FINANCES

which needed new machines for a profitable contract. The only way the shop could get them was to buy them on credit, sell them to a leasing company for $20,000 (paying off the seller with the proceeds), and lease them back for $500 a month over five years—a total of $30,000. At the end of five years, the shop will own the machines again, and will have paid the equivalent of 20% interest on the loan.

Long-Term Funds

Long-term funds refer chiefly to stocks and bonds, and they are raised either by floating new issues in the stock market or by arranging for an investment banking firm to underwrite the issues (buy them outright, and resell them to the general public and other investors). Figure 11-11 shows announcements for some typical offerings of longer term securities.

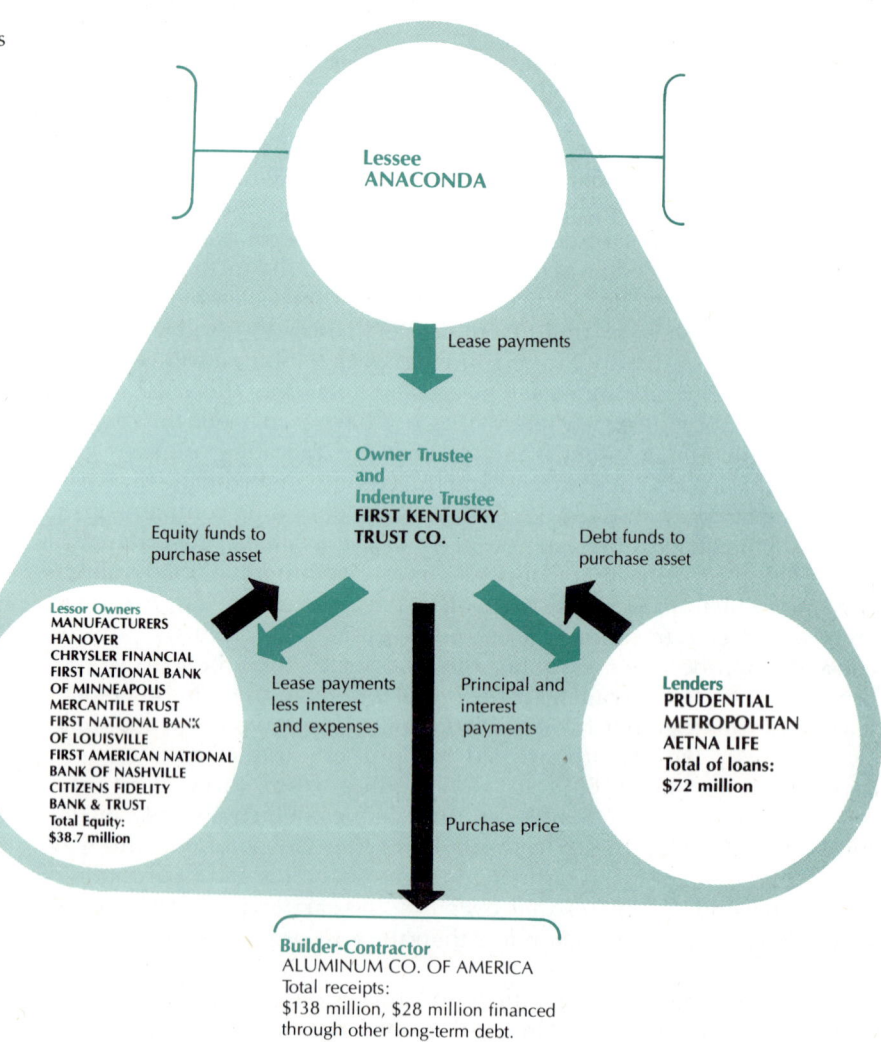

Figure 11-9.
Financial Implications of Capital Leasing

Lessee
ANACONDA

Lease payments

Owner Trustee and Indenture Trustee
FIRST KENTUCKY TRUST CO.

Equity funds to purchase asset

Debt funds to purchase asset

Lessor Owners
MANUFACTURERS HANOVER
CHRYSLER FINANCIAL
FIRST NATIONAL BANK OF MINNEAPOLIS
MERCANTILE TRUST
FIRST NATIONAL BANK OF LOUISVILLE
FIRST AMERICAN NATIONAL BANK OF NASHVILLE
CITIZENS FIDELITY BANK & TRUST
Total Equity:
$38.7 million

Lease payments less interest and expenses

Principal and interest payments

Lenders
PRUDENTIAL
METROPOLITAN
AETNA LIFE
Total of loans:
$72 million

Purchase price

Builder-Contractor
ALUMINUM CO. OF AMERICA
Total receipts:
$138 million, $28 million financed through other long-term debt.

Investors evaluating the prospects for stocks or bonds in new issues will look at the long-term promise of the company and the industry, as discussed in the next section, "Valuation of Businesses." It happens, however, that emotion plays a much larger part in stock market transactions than in the financial dealings we have discussed thus far, and the general public is likely to value issues much too high or much too low (depending on the circumstances). In a "two-tier market," a few popular stocks are overpriced and many stocks not popular at present are absurdly underpriced. Some feel this situation is caused by bank trust departments, which are under pressure to buy only growth stocks with high price-earnings ratios. Whatever the cause, it injects an element of uncertainty into stock selling and makes planning difficult.

Valuation of Businesses

No manager can afford to ignore the vital indicators of the business's credit status, because without credit the company is likely to go under, or at best to grow at a snail's pace. In boom times, when public optimism is high and investors are looking for "go-go" stocks which they expect to increase many times in value, new issues may sell with only the skimpiest justification. But in more normal times, investors assume their customary prudence and look for more substantial measures of future performance.[6]

There is a standard mathematical formula used on Wall Street to estimate what a company's stock ought to be worth. It requires the prospective purchaser to estimate the growth rate (g) expected each year for the dividend payment (d is this year's dividend), and to decide the discount rate (the expected interest rate plus an allowance for any risk the company seems to offer—r). The formula for stock value (V) is:

$$\frac{d}{1+r}\left[1+\left(\frac{1+g}{1+r}\right) + \left(\frac{1+g}{1+r}\right)^2 + \left(\frac{1+g}{1+r}\right)^3 + \left(\frac{1+g}{1+r}\right)^4 + \left(\frac{1+g}{1+r}\right)^5 + \left(\frac{1+g}{1+r}\right)^6 \cdots + \cdots \left(\frac{1+g}{1+r}\right)^7\right]$$

If, as an example, we are valuing a stock that paid an $8 dividend, and we estimate its growth rate $g = 4.5\%$ a year and the discount $r = 10\%$, this becomes:

$$\frac{8}{1.10}\left[1 + (.95) + (.95)^2 + (.95)^3 + (.95)^4 + (.95)^5 + \cdots\right]$$
$$= 7.27 (1 + .95 + .9025 + .8774 + .8145 + .7738 + .7351 + .6983 + \cdots)$$
$$= 7.27 (20.00) = \$145.45 \text{ Value of Stock}$$

(This can be simplified to: $\frac{d}{r-g}$ if g is constant—which it was in our example.

Thus $8/(.10-.045) = \$145.45$, the same result.)

Could Jo Parnela have used a system like this to evaluate the worth of North Star when the merger offer was made? How?

In this example, the price-earnings ratio would be $145.45/$16, if we assume that half of the earnings are being paid out in dividends, or 9—just the PE ratio of Delta Airlines in Figure 11-1. This suggests that the stock-buying public is anticipating a growth rate for Delta of about 4.5%, if our discount figure of 10% is realistic.

The general public must make its decisions on the value of businesses from rather general information, chiefly comparative reports in business journals (such as Figure 11-1), stock analyses by brokerage houses, and annual report data. Figure 11-10 shows balance sheet information of the type that would appear on the annual report for a major leasing corporation. If you were a short-term creditor you would note the quick ratio of $169,947,000/$263,802,000 or 0.64. If you were a longer-term creditor, you would be more likely to look at the debt-equity ratio of $309,057,000/$117,758,000 or 2.62. And of course, you would compare this balance sheet with last year's, to see the trend.

Banks and other lending institutions generally divide their analyses into *solvency tests* (important for short-term loans) and *profitability tests* (important for longer-term investments). The former deal mainly with access to sufficient cash: current ratio, quick ratio, cash on hand, working capital, and cash flow. The latter deal with prospects: net profit after taxes, rate of return on stockholders' equity, rate of return on assets, dividends paid, price-earnings ratio—and, more significantly, whether these prospects are turning up or down.

solvency tests
profitability tests

Do you have any feeling for how well North Star would fare on a solvency test? Do you think the partners have a good feeling for this?

Figure 11-10.
Combined Leasing Companies Balance Sheet

	June 30, 1974 (unaudited)
Assets	
Cash	$ 45,078,000
Accounts receivable, less allowances of $1,891,000	13,111,000
Finance Lease Receivables:	
Aggregate future rentals	129,306,000
Estimated additional amounts at end of lease terms	7,431,000
Total	136,737,000
Less unearned income to be included in future gross revenues, and allowances of $2,229,000	(24,979,000)
	111,758,000
Systems/360 and other computer rental equipment— at cost, less accumulated depreciation and unamortized investment grants of $136,106,000	123,380,000
Systems/370 computer rental equipment—at cost, less accumulated depreciation $14,548,000	63,927,000
Container rental equipment—at cost, less accumulated depreciation of $27,727,000	61,665,000
Real estate, furniture, fixtures and other equipment—at cost less accumulated depreciation of $590,000	1,809,000
Other assets	6,085,000
	$426,813,000
Liabilities and Stockholder's Equity	
Notes payable	$225,890,000
Accounts payable and accrued expenses	18,545,000
Accrued income taxes	7,397,000
Advances from parent and affiliates	11,970,000
	263,802,000
Subordinated debentures and secured notes	32,436,000
Subordinated debt due to parent and affiliates	12,819,000
Stockholder's Equity:	
Common stock	12,000
Additional paid-in capital	78,141,000
Retained earnings	39,603,000
	117,756,000
Commitments and contingencies	
	$426,813,000

Investing Funds

Thus far we have been preoccupied mainly with how the corporation gets funds, but a matter of equal importance is what it does with the funds when it gets them. When a relatively new company such as North Star *goes public* by selling stock to the general public, it has entered an entirely new phase. Prior to this, the owners were the principal officers, and their interests covered a broad range: professional interest in the work, pride in what they were building, employment of themselves, liking for the employees whose fortunes were being furthered by North Star's prosperity, and future earnings from their equity. After going public, the new owners were interested only in the last factor—how much they would earn on their investment. If they thought North Star was a risky affair, they would add a substantial amount to their expectations for the risk. If the basic interest rate was 10% at the time, the stockholders might expect an equivalent annual return of double this, or 20% (in dividends and retained earnings equity). This means that *North Star had better not take this money unless it can earn that much on it after taxes,* or it will be building up expectations among the new owners that it cannot realize, and the officers are likely to be thrown out of office for not producing.

The financial manager realizes that capital is a precious commodity, and that it must be invested so that it will earn what it costs. When projects are viewed in this light, prestige items such as a new building, landscaping, interior decorating, and so on assume a rather low priority. If they don't earn anything, in some sense (perhaps prestige or public image translates into earning power indirectly), they should not be undertaken. A current phenomenon is the tendency for major companies to move to low-cost buildings, even old warehouses, in unstylish parts of town, in order to save capital. The financial manager's task—in some companies, the principal task—is to analyze investment alternatives in-house, and pick the winners.

Capital Budgeting

When a company or a government agency is evaluating candidates for investment—say a bridge in the case of a state government, a machine tool in the case of a corporation, or a weapon system in the case of a national government—there are three general approaches to assessing the return in relation to the cost: *present value, discounted rate of return,* and *payback period.* Each of these will be discussed below.

Present Value

When you go to the bank and promise to pay them $100 a month for three years if they will advance you the funds to buy a used car now, they do not give you $3600, because the present value of $100 a month for 36 months is much less than $3600. The reason, of course, is that there is a rental cost for money just as there is for things money can buy. If I borrow $1 today, and agree to pay it back one month from now together with 1% interest, I will owe: $1 x 1.01 = $1.01, or in equation form:

Loan x (1 + Rate of Interest) = Repayment

If I agree to repay $1 at the end of the month, the amount the bank will give me is, from the same formula rearranged:

$$R = \frac{L}{l+r}$$

If I repay after two months, this becomes $R = \frac{L}{(l+r)^2}$, and so on.

So the amount the bank will loan me if I agree to pay $100 a month for 36 months is calculated as follows:

$$L = \frac{L}{l+r} + \frac{L}{(l+r)^2} + \frac{L}{(l+r)^3} + \cdots + \frac{L}{(l+r)^{36}}$$

$$= \$99.01 + \$98.03 + \$97.06 + \$96.10 + \$95.15 \cdots \text{etc.} \cdots = \$3010.75$$

When you calculate the value of a machine tool, its future earnings (the "rent" we discussed earlier, charged to each job that uses it) must be treated the same way. Thus if you expected a machine tool to earn $100 a month for three years, and then to have a salvage value of $800, its present value would be $3010.75 + $800 = *$3810.75* at a discount rate of 1% a month. If it costs more than that to buy, and if 12% a year is your standard discount rate, you should not buy it.

Rate of Return

rate of return

While this approach is conceptually the same as the one described above, its form is different. We are measuring earnings as a percentage of the amount invested. Table 11-3 shows the equivalent interest rate to pay off the principal and interest of an initial $100 investment in the number of years *(N)*, if the return per year is as shown in the body of the table. Suppose we make a $100 investment and it has a stream of earnings amounting to $19.25 per year for 12 years, at which time the equipment is of no further value. Going over the 12-year line, we find $19.25 falling about one third of the way from 15% to 18%, so the rate of return for this equipment, discounted, amounts to 16%.

original cost basis

On the rather simplistic *original cost basis,* we would say that its net earnings are first cost less gross earnings, or $100 ($19.25 x 12) which equals $131.00 in total or $131/12 = $10.92. Since this is 10.92% of the $100 cost, we say its earnings rate is 10.92% a year.

Table 11-3.
Discount Table

N	6%	9%	12%	15%	18%
2	54.54	56.85	59.17	61.51	63.87
4	28.86	30.87	32.92	35.03	37.17
6	20.34	22.29	24.32	26.42	28.59
8	16.10	18.07	20.13	22.29	24.52
10	13.59	15.58	17.70	19.93	22.25
12	11.93	13.92	16.14	18.45	20.86
14	10.76	12.76	15.09	17.47	19.97
16	9.90	11.94	14.34	16.80	19.37
18	9.24	11.32	13.79	16.32	18.96
20	8.72	10.84	13.39	15.98	18.68

The *average cost basis* allows for the fact that the machine is depreciating over the 12-year period, with a value at the start of $100 and a value at the end of zero, or an average value over the period of $50. It makes the same calculation as for the original cost basis, but applies the $10.92 yearly earnings to a $50 investment cost, rather than to $100, giving an average cost earnings rate of 21.84%.

Note that the discounted cash flow method shows a rate about midway between the other two methods.

average cost basis

discounted cash flow basis

Payback Period

This method, conceptually the weakest from the point of view of analytical accuracy, simply takes the undiscounted earnings and computes how many years it will take for them to pay back the initial investment. This system does not consider how long an investment will continue to pay off; a piece of equipment earning 20% a year for five years with no earnings thereafter would be rated above another piece of equipment that could earn 18% a year for 100 years. Nonetheless, when the general life of investments is relatively the same in a given company, this method is of some validity. Generally it serves in most companies as a rough screening system to throw out clearly unattractive proposals before much effort is devoted to analyzing them.

payback period

Evaluation of Risk

None of the above methods has considered the question of relative risk, except to the extent that this is incorporated in the discount rate we demand. Actually, risk should be considered separately from interest cost for money and required earnings rate on money. Chapter 7, "Decision Making," describes on pages 238 and 239 an expected value approach to incorporating risk into the estimate of payoff. This method should be used in estimating the expected return from capital investments. One important element that should be included is the corporate *utility function* for investments. This is a measure of how the company feels about the change in odds it demands when the investment gets large relative to its total working capital.

Consider an example. If you toss coins with a friend for $1 stakes, chances are the friend will settle for 50:50 odds. Make it $10 and your friend is less interested in playing, but 60:40 odds in his favor will change that. Raise the stakes to $100, and your friend won't want to play at all; but if you offer 70:30 odds, you finally persuade him to chance a toss. But when you talk $1,000, he's out of the game; whatever the odds, he simply can't risk the loss of $1,000. Companies have the same utility function, though of course the amounts vary with the company. Thus North American Rockwell spent $25 million a few years ago to prepare a proposal for the B-1 bomber weapon system contract. They estimated that the contract would bring in $8 billion for whomever got it; in effect they were gambling $25,000 for a payoff of $8 million, or $25 for $8,000. No matter what the odds, however, most companies just can't chance $25 million on anything short of a sure thing. It is well for the financial manager to understand this utility function and be prepared to up the required odds for success as the scope of the investment goes up.

If you want to toss coins with a friend for $100, chances are you'll have to give favorable odds or your friend won't be interested.

HEADS I WIN, TAILS YOU LOSE...

Project Investment

Could this approach be used to determine whether North Star should accept small engineering jobs from municipalities? How?

Not all capital budgeting involves the purchase of equipment. Some focuses on new research programs, which may pay off in terms of new products or processes. Some is devoted to speculative exploration, as with the oil companies, in hopes of striking a new raw materials find. And some provides for new projects, such as the Westinghouse breeder atomic reactor, which can turn into a profitable product in years to come. Sometimes the project is one which cannot be exploited by a small company, since the costs are too large, but falls within the "utility function" envelope of a larger company.

Such a case was Gillette's acquisition of S. T. Dupont, a French manufacturer of disposable cigarette lighters. The small company had a hot product but insufficient money or marketing network to exploit it properly so Gillette bought a controlling interest in Dupont, and now the Cricket disposable lighter is Gillette's fastest growing product. The 7 million lighters Dupont sold in 1970 burgeoned to 41 million in 1973 and sales continue to grow at a rapid rate.

One important aspect of capital budgeting is the tax treatment. For example, if research costs related to a possible new product are expensed when incurred, immediate taxes will be less than if these costs are capitalized and depreciated over the years. The latter is the more accurate approach in terms of management analysis, however, since the costs are associated with the product during its earning life (instead of being charged to current products, which do not benefit from the research).

It must be remembered, when capital projects are being considered, that whatever incremental working capital they require is properly chargeable against the capital investment. If a machine costs $100,000, but will tie up $30,000 more or less permanently in working inventory or parts, the proper sum to consider is $130,000.

Program Budgeting

This technique, developed with a good deal of fanfare by the military a few years ago, seeks to assign to a project or profit center all of the charges that properly belong to it. The advantages of this method seem too obvious to mention, but it is not always employed. If a warehouse is used for assembling a new product, and changes are required to make it weathertight and heated, these expenses should be charged to the product because they would not have been needed otherwise. Even so, some firms might put the costs on general overhead and make all products pay a pro rata share—hardly a valid procedure. Similarly, suppose product A, for which a costly machine tool was bought, shifts to another process and no longer requires the use of that tool. Product A should still be charged for the costs of the tool until some other product takes the tool over—because product A was responsible for that cost being incurred in the first place.

Retained Earnings

One of the principal sources of funds for capital investment is retained earnings—that part of profits after taxes which is not distributed to the stockholders. It must be remembered that this money belongs to the stockholders, and it should not be retained unless they are agreeable. Since they cannot be polled in each case, earnings should not be retained as a general rule unless they can earn as much as they would if distributed to the stockholders. If the stock is now at $150 and pays $12, or 8%, earnings should not be retained unless they can promise earnings of at least this much (neglecting taxes). When estimating the cost of capital, the cost of retained earnings should be calculated in this way.

Summary

Financial management involves planning funds needs, choosing how to expand assets for growth, activating plans by obtaining funds, evaluating investment alternatives, and controlling funds management. In a very small company, decisions are promptly checked by the market forces, but in a large company the market cannot reflect the wisdom of individual funds decisions because the firm is too complex for any single decision to be detected in the marketplace.

The financial manager participates in financial planning and control, and in raising and investing funds. In most companies, the manager has some management audit functions that go beyond financial matters (though often the need for management review is suggested by unusual values on financial reports).

The key report for short-term analysis is the income statement, which shows whether the firm is profitable, what margin it makes on its sales, what the overhead ratio is, and several other key figures. Another important report is the balance sheet, which shows the ratio of assets to liabilities, and particularly the company's ability to pay debts promptly. It also shows the debt to equity ratio, which tells whether too much of the total assets are owed to others (and too few are owned by the owners).

For long-term analysis, the income-dividend ratio, return on equity, and market share all indicate the long-run strength of the company. Long-term analysis seeks to determine whether the company will continue earning for several years, so is concerned with developing trends rather than current bank accounts.

Cash planning is important apart from profit planning, to keep the company from running out of cash. Figure 11-4 shows how funds flow in and out of the company. If business expands, the firm needs more funds immediately, though it will not start earning until much later; so expansion means more debt.

For profit planning, most companies use correlation or factor analysis, trend analysis, or profitable-volume analysis. Probably a combination of the three is most useful. Liquidity and profitability are opposed in a sense, in that the push for more profits impairs liquidity immediately: the increased costs occur before the increased profits, and operating funds needs go up much faster than retained earnings.

Cash management consists of making available cash go as far as it can, by judiciously deciding when to pay bills, by planning ahead for obtaining loans on the best possible terms, by closely monitoring incoming and outgoing cash, and by expediting cash collections. Accounts receivable management involves careful management of credit and analysis of credit customers. Inventory and fixed assets management involves recognition of the costs of storing needed items and costs of ordering or using them.

Raising funds has become one of the vital parts of the financial manager's job. There are four types of short-term credit: trade credit, bank credit, unsecured loans, and secured loans (the latter two from institutions other than banks). Trade credit is a key factor in small businesses, but all businesses run on credit. Short-term credit is for short-term purposes, and banks will react negatively to use of short-term credit to buy fixed assets or prop up the financial structure in other ways.

Intermediate- and long-term credit should be used to obtain fixed assets or to fund a permanent expansion in operations. The important factor is ability of the company to demonstrate long-term profitability and good management. Service on bonds and long-term loans is tax deductible, whereas dividends on stock come from after-tax profit, so the former can attract larger interest except when business is booming; in poor times, stock issues are hard to sell. An alternative to such credit is long-term leasing, which has advantages for tax purposes under certain conditions—though it usually is more costly than buying on a before-tax basis.

Investors value stock on the basis of their estimates of future dividend earnings and future risk; there are formulas to convert these factors into numerical estimates for stock value. However, certain stocks popular with institutional investors are chronically overvalued on this basis.

Capital investments are analyzed by present value, rate of return, and payback period, or a combination of these. In addition, risk can be evaluated by expected value techniques. Capital investment includes research, project investment, and even acquisitions. Program budgeting is used to be sure that each capital item pays its correct share. The principal long-term source for capital investments is retained earnings (or increased sale of equity).

Notes

1. G. A. Gustafson, "Managing Type Auditing," in *The Internal Auditor* (November-December 1970). Italics added.
2. In late 1974, when Pan American Airlines was in serious financial trouble, senior vice-president Willis Player said, "Our debt-equity ratio is 70:30...going into 1975 it could be 85:15 or 90:10, at which point we're just on the verge of blowing away." With a 90:10 ratio, a 10% decline in value of assets brings the business to the point of insolvency.
3. As compared with a company that simply assembles purchased components (e. g., some electronics equipment vendors), where the selling price could be as low as one and a half times the cost of materials.
4. This may be changing. A Chicago supermarket chain now accepts credit cards and others are following suit. One reason is that a smaller discount is applied to supermarkets (who operate on low margin) than to other retailers.
5. Inventory does not necessarily drop in value over time. During periods of inflation, durable inventory appreciates in value. When a strike is anticipated for such staples as coal or steel, companies typically stockpile in advance.
6. Say you could invest $100 in government bonds (representing complete safety) and earn $6 (6%). If you invest $1 each in 100 identical companies, each with a 2% chance of failure during the year, you will have only $98 of your principal left at year's end because on the average two will fail. Thus you want to earn at least the base $6 you could get from government bonds, plus repayment of the $2 for your lost principal, or a total of 8%.

Review Questions

1. What are five steps in attaining organizational goals, and how does the financial manager participate in each?
2. Why do external market mechanisms help a large company with investment choices less than they do a very small company?
3. What is management auditing, and how does it interface with financial auditing or accounting?
4. What is the difference between *current ratio* and *quick ratio*? What is the latter used for?
5. Why is management interested in inventory turnover?
6. What does the market share tell us, and is this information of more interest to short-term or long-term lenders? Why?
7. How does money flow into a company? Out of a company? Which of the incoming flows stays with the company?
8. How does the financial manager prepare a cash budget?
9. Briefly describe the three approaches to profit planning.
10. What do we mean by the "liquidity-profitability tradeoff"?
11. What aspect of cash management deals with keeping employees honest? With faster banking of incoming payments?
12. Why is it sometimes profitable to extend credit to doubtful credit risks?
13. What do we mean by the "cost of stocking" and the "cost of ordering"?

14. Describe the four types of short-term funds sources.
15. What is the difference between what a short-term and a long-term loaner look for in a company they may loan to?
16. Why may leasing be profitable to a company instead of buying equipment?
17. What factors are included in the formula used by Wall Street to estimate the value of a common stock?
18. How can the financial manager determine what equity money ought to earn when put to work in the business? What retained earnings ought to earn?
19. What are the three general approaches to estimating the payoff of capital investment projects? Explain briefly what each one does.

Discussion Questions

1. If you were conducting a management audit in a technical area unfamiliar to you, what approach would you take to minimize friction but still get your job done?
2. Look at Figure 11-4. Draw a parallel between this figure for a business corporation and the same elements for a private family. Which elements have parallels in the family budget? Are there any elements which do not have parallels in the family budget? Why?
3. In forecasting the future market for coal for your company (a large oil company which has subsidiary companies in the coal mining business), which of the three profit planning methods would you use—or which combination of the three? Explain.
4. Make an analysis of your automobile or your family automobile by listing the cost elements described on page 403 and stating to what extent each of these applies to the car. How would you determine the costs of each element?
5. What do you see as the advantages and disadvantages of each of the four types of short-term credit explained in this chapter? When would the proprietor of the letter shop described at the start of the chapter make use of each of these?
6. After reading the section "Valuation of Businesses," are there any things you would look for in deciding whether to buy a stock that you would not have looked for before? What are they, and where would you get the information?
7. Try to draw your utility curve for bets. Draw a graph with the size of the bet along the bottom line and the odds up the left side. Start the odds at 50:50 at bottom, going up to 1:0 (certainty) at top. Try to draw your curve for all values. Does it ever turn down as you move to larger bets? Does it ever flatten out? Is this pattern logical?

North Star Case Study

Assume that North Star has been operating at a volume of $2 million a year, with an average net profit of $200,000 before taxes, or about $110,000 after taxes. It distributes $60,000 in dividends and keeps the $50,000 balance as retained earnings. Its net margin thus is figured at $110,000/$2,000,000 or 5.5%.

Its jobs are usually billed monthly and paid for about 30 days later. Figuring that the labor for any job is spread evenly over the previous month, this means the company needs only about 50 days of working capital. Since its costs are approximately its total volume less profit before taxes, this amounts to $1,800,000 per year in costs: $150,000 a month, or $250,000 working capital needed for the 50 days. The fact that North Star can get trade credit for some of its expenses, such as travel and supplies, reduces the effective working capital needs to $200,000. It is increasing the working capital by the $50,000 a year of retained earnings.

Zeb wants to know how fast the company can expand in case they get a chance to increase volume by 25% or 50%, and what cash needs this will bring about, so he decides to make a pro forma cash flow budget for increases of these amounts.

1. From what you have been told above, and using Figure 11-8 as a guide, make up an approximate income statement similar to that shown in Table 9-2 on page 325. (Neglect depreciation, which will not be large in any case for a company like North Star.)
2. Making your own estimates of costs in various categories, show how the working capital of $200,000 is utilized by making a dated diagram similar to Figure 11-8.
3. If business expands 25%, how much additional working capital will be needed? How much if it expands 50%?
4. For the 50% expansion, assuming interest on the additional working capital costs 8%, estimate how long it will be until retained earnings at a 5.5% net margin enable North Star to pay back the money borrowed for expansion. Remember that the increased volume will bring increased dollar profits, and that as loans are paid back interest drops.

Suggestions for Further Reading

Bernstein, L. A. *Financial Statement Analysis*. Homewood, Ill.: Richard D. Irwin, Inc., 1974.

Bierman, H. *Financial Policy Decisions*. New York: Macmillan Pub. Co., Inc., 1970.

Falcon, W. D. *Reporting Financial Data to Management*. New York: American Management Association, Inc., 1965.

Golembiewski, R. and J. Robin. *Public Budgeting and Finance*. Fasca, Ill.: F. T. Peacock, 1974.

Goodman, S. R. *Financial Manager's Manual and Guide*. Englewood Cliffs, N.J.: Prentice-Hall, Inc., 1973.

Kempster, J. H. *Financial Analysis to Guide Capital Expenditure Decisions*, Research Report #43. New York: National Association of Accountants, 1967.

Levine, S. N. *Financial Analyst's Handbook*. Homewood, Ill.: Dow Jones-Richard D. Irwin, Inc., 1975.

Lines, J. *Beyond the Balance Sheet: Evaluating Profit Potential*. New York: John Wiley & Sons, Inc., 1974.

Shuckett, D. H. *Financing for Growth*. New York: American Management Association, Inc., 1971.

Steiss, A. W. *Public Budgeting and Management*. Lexington, Mass.: Lexington Books, 1972.

Teague, B. W. *Financial Planning for Executives*. New York: National Industrial Conference Board, Inc., 1973.

Van Horne, J. C. *Financial Management and Policy*. Englewood Cliffs, N.J.: Prentice-Hall, Inc., 1971.

Wilson, R. M. *Financial Control: A Systems Approach*. New York: McGraw-Hill Book Co., 1974.

Handling and Using Information

12

North Star Prologue

North Star started as a two-person company, but grew steadily as it learned more about planning, communications, leadership, and organization. It rejected a merger offer, and soon after found the need to set up a formal control system to keep it from running out of funds or inadvertently overcommitting itself in other ways. It went through a personnel reorganization, including separation of marketing and personnel administration, and established more enlightened personnel practices. The experience in cash flow problems indicated the need for a systematic budget, and management designed one that incorporated elements of a job status and financial control system as well.

Not long after the installation of the North Star budgeting system, Zeb came to Jo with the news that the U.S. Department of Housing and Urban Development was circulating in various cities a request for proposals to set up an "urban management information system" that could be used as a model for such systems all over the country. Four cities were to be selected and given contracts. The interesting part was that each competing city was to submit a proposal jointly with a consulting firm and a computer manufacturer, so that the proposal would have the best combination of expertise. In short order they called in Henry, because of his municipal experience, and the three of them decided to enter the competition in the small city category, in collaboration with Blackridge and with Barnhard & Walker.

They called a meeting with their prospective joint venture partners, and Jo sketched out what such a system might include and could achieve. It would tabulate police patrol practices and the effect on crime rates, keep crime information by offender (crime, sentence, repetition), by type of punishment (sentence, parole, suspension), by city district, and by time of day or time of year. It would keep similar records on fires, providing information that could help in prevention measures or fire station relocation. It would consolidate the data presently kept by the school board, health agencies and hospitals, city planning department, census district, and chamber of commerce. And, added Henry, it could include such public works information as type of public utility failure in relation to type of material and time since installation, maintenance practices on vehicles and operating equipment, solid waste collection and disposition operations, and street maintenance in relation to type of surface and repair schedules. The Blackridge city manager said it ought to have a section on urban renewal and on economic development. And the B&W man said the whole thing could be carried on a time-sharing computer system similar to the

B&W telecomputer system that currently linked all their company operations in a common net. The enthusiasm of the group was high, and they prepared and submitted a proposal to HUD.

Two months after the submission, they were called to Washington for a conference at HUD. The negotiating officer said they were one of the finalists in the small city group, and he wanted to ask them some questions. His first question was what sort of management information system was in use in their companies. Henry was caught flat-footed, wondering how he could answer, when the B&W representative picked up the ball and described in detail the elaborate system used in his corporation. The HUD man was clearly impressed at the scope of the B&W system, and then turned to the North Star trio. Zeb spoke up at once, before Henry could speak; he described in detail their weekly report, their manpower scheduling system, and their new budgeting system, making it all sound surprisingly systematic and effective. Henry had a fleeting thought that it sounded as though it were a computerized system. Perhaps the HUD man thought so; in any case he seemed quite satisfied, for when Zeb finished he said their group would be given the small city contract if they could work out the details of cost and overhead rates satisfactorily.

On the way back on the plane, as they were talking over the session and savoring the triumph, Henry asked Zeb if he thought the HUD man had gotten the impression that North Star had a computerized system. Zeb said of course he had—and what was more, they'd better set up such a computerized system without delay. In some respects, he added, this contract would provide them the learning experience they needed to set up their own system at relatively little cost, and they certainly should take advantage of the opportunity.

Jo was in charge of the Blackridge MIS contract, and she also took responsibility for setting up the North Star MIS. It was the first time any of them had seen Jo dabble in administrative matters, and Henry was doubtful that she would keep at it, but apparently the project intrigued her and she kept at it tirelessly. Indeed, the partners saw a new side of Jo, for she pursued with them relentlessly the question of whether they needed a piece of information, and whether it was really worth what it would cost to put it on the computer and keep it accurate. She reminded them sternly that it wasn't enough simply to *be able* to get information—they had to *need* it. She developed a crude price list of individual bits of information, and had each profit center and administrative unit certify that it was worth at least this much to get this bit of information. She worked incessantly with the output format, until the final product appealed to every user. Indeed, the others got so tired of the interminable questions and reviews of slightly different formats that Dick finally said if he had to look at another dummied-up report he was going to abandon the whole idea as far as project management was concerned.

The final report on the Blackridge system was almost an anticlimax compared with the first "flight" of the North Star system. Jo had incorporated personnel needs, manning schedules by department, job cost reports of jobs in progress, estimates of revenue and profit, cash flows, status of work progress by job or project—even information Barbara had persuaded her to include on status of training and personnel development. She had the payroll, with number of hours worked matched to manpower reports by jobs, with all pay deductions included, and even with a system to write the checks. And the best part of it, she said, was that it emphasized economy of operation. As a matter of fact, she added, her real interest in the North Star system was as a prototype for a small-company business system that she could dress up and sell to other companies. And she proceeded to do just that.

What North Star Can Learn from Chapter 12

1. What the needs of management are for information
2. The components of a management information system
3. How employees can fudge information to forestall providing data that seems to threaten them in any way
4. Some of the accounting variations that can affect the apparent performance of a business, and how to deal with them
5. Some thoughts on the value of information relative to its cost
6. Project control information design and needs
7. Fundamentals of data processing and of computer systems
8. Some approaches to management systems

In chapter 5, "Communication," we described the obstacles to clear and specific communication within an organization, and the ways to overcome them through formal and informal communication channels. This chapter discusses the *content* of what is being communicated. Even when a communication channel is free of "noise," or interference, there is no guarantee that the information being transmitted is worth the effort. This chapter explains how to collect, disseminate, and use the intelligence that managers and others need to do their jobs, from four viewpoints:

1. *The concept and purpose of information*—theory of information content and the use of computers to handle information
2. *Information needs*—both internal (data for management decisions) and external (data for evaluation and appropriate control of the organization by stockholders or the public)
3. *Information systems*—from formal data processing systems to more specific applications for a variety of purposes
4. *Information problems*—both internal (communication gaps within and among different organizational levels) and external (invasion of privacy or disclosure of privileged information)

Organizations have grown so complex that they cannot be managed effectively without carefully designed and often highly elaborate control systems, which feed on a steady diet of information. Most information systems are simple enough in concept, but the volume and diversity of their operations makes them extraordinarily elaborate in practice. More and more, information means the computer. A central problem for organizations is to provide sufficiently versatile information systems without turning over management functions to the programmers who must make these systems work. To avoid this delegation of responsibility, managers must learn to understand the basic principles of computer programming.

The Concept and Purpose of Information

When the city manager is asked to provide funds for a special police patrol in the city's X section, the decision depends on certain information: whether crime there is up compared with the rest of the city, how effective special patrols are in terms of arrests made or crimes prevented, and what the total costs of the decision are likely to be. When the plant superintendent is asked to authorize overtime to get product Y out on time, other questions arise: what the cost will be of delaying this production until the next open regular shift, what overtime will cost, and why the shop lacks adequate production resources to make Y on straight time. When the portfolio manager in the bank is considering investing trust funds in the stock of company Z, the necessary data include its continued earning power, prospects for getting into financial trouble, and the likelihood that it will pay the sort of dividends the trust account requires. When the regulatory officer of a government agency looks at corporation W, information must be obtained on its financial performance, its environmental behavior, or its actions with regard to collusion, restraint of trade or action in the public interest; and these data must be compared with legal standards for evaluating the corporation.

Not all data contains *information,* in the sense of facts adding to the recipient's store of knowledge. When you pass a friend on the street, and offer the stylized greeting "How are you?" the friend replies, "Fine." No real information has been transmitted; the friend may just have learned that he or she needs an operation, but neither of you expected your question to elicit specific information about your friend's state of health. If you hear on your car radio that city hall has burned down, and arrive at home to find that the evening paper carries the fact in banner headlines, no information has been transmitted by the headline because you knew the fact already. The young shepherd boy in the fable, who enjoyed crying "Wolf!" from time to time so he could see the townspeople scurry out to help, transmitted no information when he cried "Wolf!" in earnest, because by that time no one took him seriously.

Some data contains no information because it is foreign to your needs. Suppose you send a market analyst to a distant town to see whether it would be advisable for you to open a retail lumber business there. If the analyst returns with full date on the number and denomination of churches, the principal crops raised in the area, and the win-lose record of the local baseball team, these facts are not "information" in the sense you had in mind, for they cannot guide your decision at all. If you want to know whether the new management of a company is better than the previous management, an income statement and a balance sheet for the current year do not provide information relative to your needs because they are static reports (usually) and give no comparisons of the sort you need. A statement of changes in financial position does give some information, but many other factors affect the usefulness of this data, such as a change in the state of the economy; and the statement must be weighed accordingly.

The Manager as a Response System

managerial response system

Information can be in the form of passive data, instructions, requests, or feedback resulting from action taken earlier (as a result of previous information). Figure 12-1 shows the manager as a simple response system, receiving information, interpreting it, determining action to be taken, transmitting information that sets that action in motion, monitoring the action by evaluating the response information that arises from it,

Figure 12-1. Manager as Response System

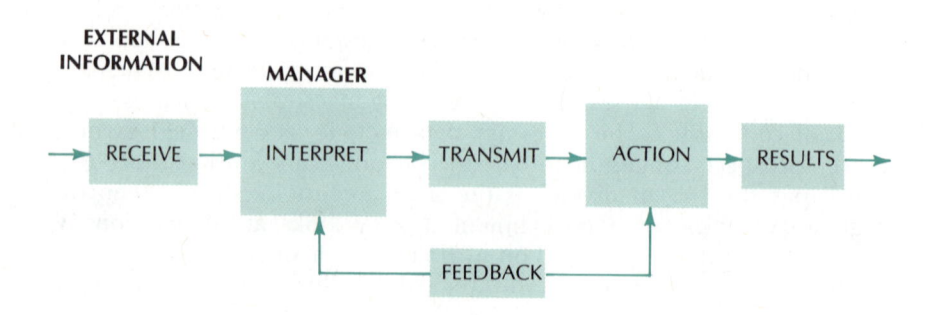

EXTERNAL INFORMATION → RECEIVE → [MANAGER: INTERPRET → TRANSMIT] → ACTION → RESULTS

FEEDBACK

424
MANAGERS AT WORK

modifying the information transmission to change the action if necessary, and ultimately achieving the results desired. This illustration portrays an idealized system, for the information reaches its designated target and takes effect without any obstruction. In actual cases, it would not be nearly so clear-cut. Figure 12-2 shows the impact of "noise" in the system, interfering with the flow of information, filtering out much of it, or misdirecting it. As a result, the manager does not get full and complete information from external sources as to what is desired (such as the market needs of the company's customers); clear information is not transmitted to all the parties who are responsible for taking action (manufacturing, sales, advertising, procurement, design, etc.); and when action is taken, the manager does not receive clear feedback on how well the action is progressing or what it is costing. Consequently, results fall far short of what would be attained with perfect communication.

In this drawing, the management information system (MIS) is shown in the feedback loop only, because that is the most important function of such an information system—collecting data about the operations and passing them on to management for analysis and decision. More precisely, every transmission path for information could be considered as part of the overall information system.

Entropy and Redundancy

In information theory, two useful concepts should be explained. One is *entropy*—borrowed from thermodynamics, where it is a measure of the unavailability or dissipation of heat energy. In information theory, it measures disorder of data, from which no information is obtained—just as a radio signal composed of nothing but random static conveys no intelligence to the listener. The other is *redundancy*—the notion of duplication or backup. In the NASA space program all vital components incorporated redundant systems so that if one should fail another was available,[1] and in an organization there are standby methods of handling essential jobs if the primary methods should be unusable.

entropy

redundancy

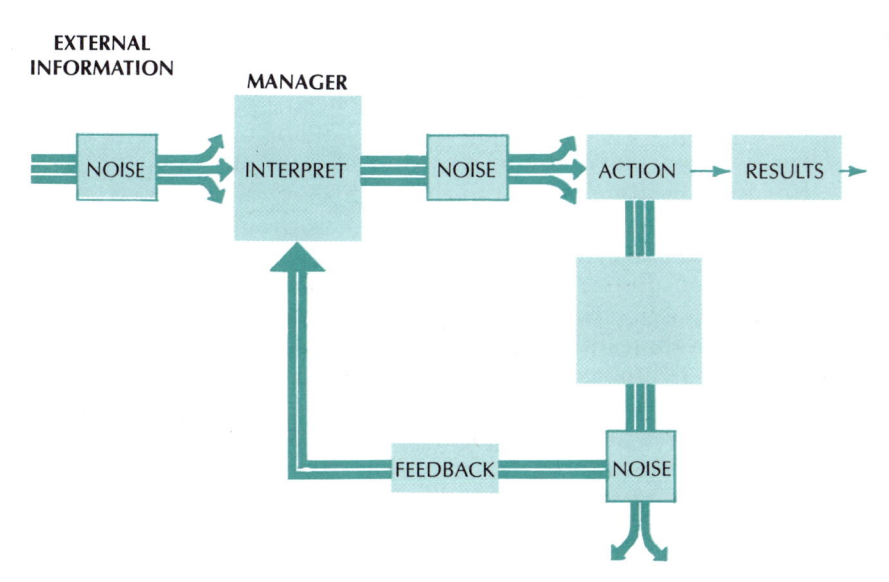

Figure 12-2.
Response System with Noise

In management information systems, entropy is analogous to the noise or random content of the information chain, and redundancy to the existence of alternate check systems to insure that an erroneous report will not go unchallenged. Let us consider each of these in turn.

Noise

noise

Chapter 9, "Controlling," stated that some control records provide information about the operation but do not really indicate whether it is going well or not. Thus, an almost sure sign of unsatisfactory performance is a progress report describing problems surmounted, items started and completed, material received and ordered, distribution of personnel to various projects, and so on—all with no information on scheduled objectives against which these accomplishments could be compared. Particularly in a situation where a periodic report is required, perhaps every week or every month, such random information is designed to give the appearance of activity and fill up space without disclosing any unsatisfactory performance—somewhat like the impromptu speaker who decided to "talk until he could think of something to say." Such a report endeavors to give the impression of *activity*, but it is not possible to say whether it is *directed activity*. When water is heated in a kettle and begins to change into steam, the molecular particles are in frenzied motion in every direction, but the total body of water isn't going anywhere at all. Let this teakettle be a steam boiler and direct the steam through a nozzle onto the blades of a turbine, and all this hullabaloo is converted into useful work.

The only facts that really constitute management information are those that evaluate performance (or nonperformance) against some specified and measurable standards. The rest is mainly noise.

Backup

To guard against the danger that noise will blank out a set of information, or that data will be erroneous, the manager must have duplicate sources of information as a check. It is foolhardy to depend on a single source when information is important, because the likelihood of error is so high. If the information deals with charging employee time to jobs, accidental error can occur in charging to the wrong job, charging an employee on leave to both the leave and the job account, holding up a charge awaiting information from the plant supervisor and neglecting to clear it up, and so on. Intentional error can occur in charging labor to job B when job A is running over budget, doing unauthorized work and charging to authorized jobs, falsely charging absent employees to jobs so they will be paid, and so on. Just as the accountant must have systems for checking funds control (as in seeing that receipt, deposit, and posting of payments are handled by three different units), so the information systems designer must provide redundancy to insure accuracy as far as possible.

What is the inherent backup in a company like North Star?

Certain elements of the information system are inherently reliable because of the way they are derived. For example, any system that stems from employee pay records is quite reliable because all of the employees are unofficial monitors of pay record accuracy: if they are underpaid, they are sure to report the fact, and if they are overpaid they are almost as sure to report it because they anticipate a later review and deduction. Other

It is essential for the manager to have duplicate sources of information as a check.

elements are inherently unreliable, because they are generated by people submitting reports or recording data that is a nuisance, or involves self-incrimination, or is not ingrained in habit patterns. Consider, for example, the instructions at an untended copying machine for every user to record the number of copies made and sign his or her name. (Another example is the effort at some state universities to have each faculty member fill in a form at the end of the term stating how many hours a week he or she worked and on what tasks—a requirement stemming from an investigation by the legislature of the charge that workloads are too light.)

Information Handling and the Computer

Since it is almost mandatory to use a computer for an information system of any size, it is well to understand how a computer does its job. Any information system contains the following elements:

- *Input,* where the data required for record keeping and decision are received initially into the system (in whatever coded form the system requires).
- *Storage,* where the data are kept until used (and in some information systems, of course, are kept long after they are of any use); the important feature is to have them in some form that makes them retrievable when needed.

computer components

- *Control,* where the data are managed—sent to the proper places, brought out when needed, and so on.
- *Processing,* where the various elements of data are combined so that they will be meaningful to the users. At this point all analysis of the data takes place, including necessary decision making based on the data.
- *Output,* where the information and orders are sent out from the system to set actions in motion in accordance with the wishes of management.

Any computer includes the same five elements. Since a computer essentially is a very rapid adding machine, with the ability to make comparisons between numbers and act on these comparisons, it speaks in a rather basic language. Much of the computer's internal capacity is taken up in translating the language of the human programmer into the language of the computer. Input rules govern the exact form in which the programmer must speak. The control component of a computer is the internal traffic cop that governs the way data are transmitted within the computer system. The processor is the computer's brain, where the desired calculations and comparisons are made. And the output unit retranslates the computer-language results into some programming language (or "formula translation") so the programmer can decipher it.

basic computer language

formula translation language

Appendix A to this chapter compares the way a computer handles information and the way a factory handles manufacturing. The detailed processes within different computers differ, but in concept every computer has to accomplish the tasks shown in the appendix in the manner shown.

The Purpose of Information

Management operates on the basis of information. Despite the reputations of some top-flight managers, implying that their fine judgment enables them to make decisions in the absence of complete facts, most managers would be absolutely lost if they could not count on reasonably accurate information on markets, prices, costs, production rates, and a host of other matters. Senior executives could not place their policies in effect if their subordinates were deprived of the information contained in budgets and planning documents. Project managers could not meet time and cost targets as well as they do (which often is far from perfect), if they did not have the benefit of continuous feedback on the effects of their actions to date.

The money markets live on information. Banks would not loan to companies without facts on performance as detailed in chapter 11, "Managing Finances," and most stockholders would not buy stocks without information on key ratios and parameters of the sort detailed in Figure 11-7.

Government regulators demand information to determine whether companies are complying with regulations in a wide variety of areas pertinent to the public interest: restraint of trade; collusive or deceptive practices; responsiveness to public needs; compliance with pricing, packaging, labeling or health standards; and so on.

Federal, state, and municipal tax officials require detailed revenue information in connection with levying taxes on operations, in addition to many transactional taxes.

The Different Faces of Information

Unfortunately, the same message often conveys different information (perhaps vastly different) to different recipients. To get around this problem, a common *language or set of symbols* must first be devised. In designing an operation process in a manufacturing shop, the symbols shown below have the following meanings:

symbols

◯ = OPERATION, ▢ = INSPECTION, △ = STORAGE, and ▷ = TRANSPORTATION.

None of these symbols means anything at all, however, unless the reader knows the language. Transmission will occur, but no information will be conveyed.

Second, the receivers must *perceive* the message as the sender intended, an occurrence which can by no means be taken for granted. Chapter 4, "Leadership," pointed out that the leader's perceptions may be quite different from those of the group; thus the Marine drill sergeant perceives his rigid discipline as simply an appropriate approach to positive military behavior, whereas new recruits are likely to perceive it as a serious threat to their security and sometimes even to their physical safety. Perceptions differ radically with age, economic status, education, ethnic or regional background, organizational position, sex, race, and personality. A productivity measurement information system, perceived by management as a tool to assess the benefits of various production techniques, may be perceived by the workers as a weapon to use for firing laggards.

perception

Can you think of any cases where there were basic differences in perceptions on the part of North Star people?

Third, there are *semantic* differences in interpreting the meaning of what was transmitted. An American manager in an Asian plant may ask the Asian subordinate, "You didn't get those orders shipped, did you?" and receive an answer of, "Yes." Later, when the manager discovers the orders are still unshipped, the subordinate is bawled out—and is totally bewildered, because the message being sent was "Yes, I didn't get the orders shipped." A manager who says, "Why don't you get a bigger chain fall from the tool room?" and really means "*Get* a bigger chain fall from the tool room!" may be unjustly irritated at the employee's "insubordinate" response—when the employee thought the boss was saying, "Do you think you need a bigger chain fall, or not?" Perhaps you remember the forest animals in the Uncle Remus story who were horrified at the new sign posted in the woods, "NO HUNTING ALLOWED." They interpreted it as "NO HUNTING ALOUD," and thought future guns would be far more threatening because they would be noiseless. Words that seem quite reasonable to one group may be violently inflammatory to another group because of semantic differences in interpretation—and neither side really knows what the fighting is about.

semantics

The Limitations of Information

Some information documents are not as complete as they might be, and the recipient is left to fill in the blanks. Budgets are quite specific in saying *what* spending limitations are imposed, but do not say *how* the results are to be achieved. In restricting a departmental budget, perhaps top management hoped to achieve a reduction in personnel level, cancellation of overtime, a moratorium on maintenance, and so on. But the department head affected by that budget may conclude that top management wanted to cancel out a program entirely, when that is not at all the case. Accounting records explain *where* we stand for the accounting period involved, but not *why* we got these results—which may lead executives to draw unjustified conclusions about the efficiency of profit center management.

When information is in numerical form, it can report only on those elements which can be represented quantitatively, and of course many factors cannot be so represented. In chapter 8, "Getting Things Done," we described how a shop supervisor who works a good deal of overtime automatically drops the overhead rate (by spreading the relatively fixed overhead costs over more direct labor costs), so that records of shop overhead will make the unit look good. This "improvement," of course, actually reflects inability to finish a job within the estimated cost and time limits.

The Principle of Easing the Pain

If you are sitting on a dilapidated old couch with springs coming out here and there, you will shift your position automatically to the one that gives you the least discomfort from protruding springs or other lumpy items. Employees will do the same, almost as automatically, to minimize the unpleasant impact (or the expected unpleasant impact) of information systems. Highway engineers in backwoods areas who put electronic traffic counters on the country roads to measure traffic volume sometimes find them shot full of holes, because residents suspect they are spying devices of some sort. Junior managers who walk through an industrial plant with portable cassette dictating machines to take notes of items needing managerial action are surprised to learn that the workers suspect them of tapping in on conversations in the plant and respond by raising the noise level.

Similarly, management may wish to collect information on costs compared with estimates, to assess the cost status of a project and determine whether it is likely to overrun. But if employees think this fact-gathering effort is an excuse to monitor their productivity, they will do everything in their power to make the information erroneous and incomplete, and thus meaningless. If a plant supervisor knows a score is being kept on the *percentage* of jobs on which each supervisor overruns the estimate, and expects to overrun slightly on three of five current jobs, he or she may shift the charges so that all the overrun is concentrated on one of the five, producing a score of 80% instead of 40% for jobs completed within estimate. The fact that records are distorted thereby may strike the supervisor as unfortunate, but much less important than his or her perceived need to take survival action. Whichever job offers the supervisor the best chance for defending an overrun, by pointing out design or planning deficiencies, will be overcharged. And management very probably will be doubly fooled, and will waste time investigating the engineering or planning groups to find out why they did such a poor job.

Since management information systems cannot measure *everything*, the people measured will take any steps they can to make those measures look good, at the expense of everything else that is not being measured. Ask yourself if you slow down automatically when you see a highway patrol car ahead, or virtuously maintain your present speed whatever it may be. Designers of information systems must allow for this self-preservation instinct in developing their data systems.

<small>nullifying information measures</small>

Information Needs

Business needs information about itself in a number of areas: the performance of labor and of management, the status of work in process, the handling of accounts with customers and suppliers, the profitability of the enterprise in all its aspects, the establishment of corporate strategy, and so on. The public needs information about business, both to determine the wisdom of business investments and to ensure governmental control of the public interface of business. And the public needs information about its public enterprises and itself in a hundred areas, from crime to public health to land use to census information. In the following sections we will discuss each of these needs, and in later sections we will describe systems that can provide information to satisfy them.

The Internal Needs of Business

The simplest example of the private business is the newsboy or girl. Consider some of their information needs. First, they need to evaluate their performance on some level, because if they aren't making enough to pay for their time they might as well quit and get into something else. They need marketing information to tell them where papers sell best. They need information on costs and receipts to tell them how much they are making. They need information on accounts receivable to know where to collect and how much. They need inventory information to know how many papers they must hold back for regular customers and how many they can sell to transients. They need information on accounts payable to check what the newspaper company says they owe. They need cash flow information to be sure they can meet their bills on time.

Most of this information can be obtained rather directly. But some written information is essential to keep accounts straight. If they lose their accounts receivable figures, for example, customers will not automatically pay. As business gets larger, the information needs multiply agonizingly. An army may march on its stomach, as Napoleon said, but a business moves on information.

Business Performance

At the top of the list for business information is data on the *overall performance* of the enterprise. For the most part, this is accounting information—the sort the business has been gathering for the longest period. The various overall measures of business profitability and health are discussed in chapter 11, "Managing Finances." By and large, this information is easy to gather, since procedures for accounting analysis

<small>overall performance data needs</small>

have been refined in most companies. Figure 12-3 shows a typical five-year income and earnings analysis (for Communications Satellite Corporation), including representative market data. Since all companies are required to collect and publish data of this sort, and since independent public accounting firms must certify the validity of the data, it would be surprising indeed if such information were not standardized and easy to collect.

Even information as standardized and subject to outside scrutiny as that in the annual report can be presented in different ways—reflecting markedly different pictures of the company's health. One important option, which can have a major effect on stated profits during inflationary periods, is whether to value inventory used in manufacturing on a "first-in-first-out" (FIFO) or "last-in-first-out" (LIFO) basis. If a company bought ten items of raw material during an inflationary period, paying in sequence $1 for the first, $2 for the second, and so on to $10 for the tenth, under a FIFO accounting system it would charge $1 in cost for the first one it used, $2 for the second, and so on. Under LIFO it would do the reverse: $10 for the first one used, $9 for the second, and so on. Companies never run their inventory down to nothing. Thus, assuming a LIFO company keeps on buying raw material at $10 an item, with ten items always in the warehouse, it will never charge itself less than $10 for a material item until outside prices for material fall. For large companies that carry huge

first-in-first-out (FIFO)
last-in-first-out (LIFO)

Figure 12-3.
Five-Year Income and Earning Analysis

FIVE-YEAR STATISTICAL REVIEW

(All dollar figures, except per share amounts, are expressed in thousands)

Income and Earnings Years ended December 31	1973	1972	1971	1970	1969
Operating Revenues	$119,291	$105,965	$88,385	$69,598	$47,034
Operating Expenses					
Operations and Maintenance	28,522	30,540	30,808	27,727	25,067
Depreciation and Amortization	31,264	32,047	23,838	19,968	17,481
Income Taxes	30,081	21,950	17,320	11,423	2,654
Total Operating Expenses	89,867	84,537	71,966	59,118	45,202
Net Operating Income	29,424	21,428	16,419	10,480	1,832
Other Income (Net of Income Taxes)	6,875	3,539	6,118	7,021	5,297
Net Income	$ 36,299	$ 24,967	$22,537	$17,501	$ 7,129
Earnings Per Share	$ 3.63	$ 2.50	$ 2.25	$ 1.75	$ .71
Dividends Per Share	$ .62	$ .545	$ .50	$ .125	$ .00
Retained Earnings	$113,310	$ 83,211	$63,694	$46,158	$29,907

MARKET DATA *(per Common Share)*

	1973	1972	1971	1970	1969
Earnings	$ 3.63	$ 2.50	$ 2.25	$ 1.75	$ .71
Dividends Paid	.62	.545	.50	.125	0
Dividend Payout Ratio	17%	22%	22%	7%	0
Book Value (End of Year)	30.85	27.84	25.89	24.14	22.51
Market Price—High	64½	75⅜	84½	57¾	60⅞
Market Price—Low	37⅛	52	49⅛	25	41¾
Price/Earnings Ratio High-Low	18-10	30-21	38-22	33-14	86-59

MANAGERS AT WORK

inventories, the difference in the short run can be great. B. F. Goodrich Company showed an 81% gain in third quarter 1974 earnings (a period of heavy inflation) using FIFO inventory accounting, but a switch to LIFO cut the profit gain to 15%. Firestone estimated that a 1974 switch to LIFO increased their cash flow some $46 million for the year. DuPont's change to LIFO accounting revised its first-half 1974 net earnings from $6.27 to $5.10 a share, and Celanese found that a similar change reduced its per-share income from $2.40 to $1.53.

Such an adjustment does not mean no taxes are paid; they are simply deferred to the time when the company actually uses up the lower-cost inventory. Many economists feel that a company which figures the cost of its raw materials at the low preinflation price (much lower than replacement costs during an inflationary period) is greatly overstating its profits. Economist Henry Wallich of Yale, a Federal Reserve Board member, estimated that $17 billion of stated industry profits in 1973 were "illusory inventory profits" which the companies would not be able to repeat.[2] It is quite misleading for a company to show as profits such "windfall" gains which do not result from efficient operations and cannot be repeated.

Another distortion, potentially even more misleading when inflation has continued over a period of years, involves charging depreciation for capital assets bought many years ago in terms of the same old dollars that were used to buy them. Robert T. Sprouse of the Financial Accounting Standards Board (a policy group for the public accounting firms which audit corporations) recently stated that "there is a serious question of whether you get a meaningful measure of income by deducting 1940 dollars from 1974 dollars."[3] If a large production machine which cost $100,000 in 1940 would cost $300,000 today, and is being depreciated at an annual rate of 1/40th or $2,500, replacing it with a machine at today's prices would up the depreciation to $7,500 a year. The $5,000 difference gives the impression that costs are $5,000 lower than they actually are—as the company will discover when old faithful finally expires and must be replaced at current machinery prices.

The public accounting fraternity has been pushing for a shift to "general price-level accounting," which the FASB states would equalize all dollars in such depreciation calculations by converting them to dollars of current purchasing power. For example, a $100,000 plant purchased in 1964 would be restated on a 1973 balance sheet by multiplying the actual cost by the ratio of the 1973/1964 price index figures, or 158.36/108.90, which would raise the cost of the plant to $145,400 for price-level accounting purposes. The accounting association's board approved such accounting for companies on a voluntary basis a few years ago, and Indiana Telephone Corporation published the effects of such an accounting change (Figure 12-4) compared with profits under conventional accounting. The profits would have appeared to be 50% higher, misleading both management and investors as to the performance of the company in reality.

price level accounting

In order to explore the effect of such adjustments on companies over a wide range of conditions, the Washington Survey (a Legg Mason institutional research affiliate) conducted a study in the summer of 1974 of 30 industrial companies included in the Dow Jones index. Adjusting their stated profits for depreciation charges only would have reduced reported earnings an average of 27.3%. Adjusting for all balance sheet items would have reduced reported earnings only 8.1% overall: some companies, though profits were reduced via the increased depreciation charges, actually gained because they had a high level of debt relative to cash. This 8.1% average, however, included a broad spread: General Motors would have reported an estimated 36% less profit, while Woolworth would have reported an estimated 39% more.

Whether or not such techniques are used to report profits on the balance sheet and income statement in the annual report, top management must take these elements into consideration, or they are likely to view their profits during an inflationary period as far higher than they actually are. Actual, meaningful *information* on performance requires full allowance for inventory profits, depreciation profits, and other price-level "windfall" effects which do not result from good management and are not likely to be repeated.

Since North Star has no real capital assets, and does not depreciate anything, is it immune from these errors due to price level changes?

Individual Performance

labor performance measurement

Many management information systems attempt to measure the productivity of individual workers, or supervisors in charge of individual work groups. The basis for all such systems is comparison against some previously determined standard. Usually the standard is the length of time a job ought to take, based on engineered estimates or a summing of standard times discussed briefly in chapters 8 and 9. Sometimes it is derived in another way, such as the proportion of the workday actually

Figure 12-4.
Impact of Price-Level Accounting on Balance Sheet

INDIANA TELEPHONE CORP. • STATEMENT OF INCOME 1973

	Historical Cost	Price Level
	Thousands of Dollars	
Operating Revenues	$12,495	$12,834
Operating Expenses		
Depreciation	2,395	3,033
Taxes	2,686	2,759
Other expenses	4,467	4,688
Operating Income	2,947	2,354
Deductions and Credits		
Interest	(892)	(917)
Other	235	238
Normal gain on retirement of long-term debt	16	17
Price-level gain on above	—	50
Normal gain on retirement of preferred stock	6	7
Price-level gain on above	—	18
Price-level loss on other monetary items	—	(209)
Net Income	$ 2,312	$ 1,558
Earnings per Common Share	$4.55	$3.00

Many management information systems attempt to measure the productivity of individual workers.

spent in producing (welders often are evaluated on the basis of proportion of "arc time" to total). Instead of times, costs can be used, by comparing actual direct labor costs with estimated labor costs for the job. The problem is that the estimates themselves often are subject to indeterminate variations. A *job shop* (where there is little repetitive work, and each job is more or less individual) is particularly difficult in this respect, for employees are being measured with a rubber yardstick.

Design of management information systems for measuring individual performance in a job shop, where standards are not precise, can lead to the following contradictory situation. The estimator estimates job costs and durations, which become standards for the shop. If the foreman of the group exceeds the estimate by 20%, for example, the production superintendent calls him on the carpet for being at variance with the estimate. Meanwhile the planning superintendent is calling the estimator on the carpet because the job was underestimated in view of the actual cost. The production superintendent is taking the estimated cost as a standard, and the planning superintendent is taking the actual cost as a standard. Both cannot be legitimate, but this kind of conflict is inevitable with information systems that try to evaluate everything.

Despite the difficulties, however, performance evaluation should be as detailed as possible. If it is not presented in punitive terms, the worker is just as anxious for a performance measure as is the supervisor or top management—but workers are also quick to spot any measure that is defective, and can manage to sabotage it without difficulty.

managerial performance measurement

Some management information systems attempt to measure managerial performance. When the manager is responsible for a profit center, this is not difficult, although there are problems with assignment of indirect costs (as discussed in chapter 11). But most managers are not responsible for profit centers, and assessing their performance in any systematic or quantitative way is extremely difficult.

An innovative system for subjecting executives to the same time and motion studies they have imposed on hapless workers, but in a form they are able to tolerate, is the "Data-Chron" (originated in Sweden as the Frekvensor). This device beeps at random intervals throughout the workday and asks the executive to punch onto a computer card or dictate onto a tape exactly what he or she is doing at the moment. A consultant analyzes the report (which usually records about 30 events per day), and sends the executive a private analysis of how effectively work time is being used. A study of Volvo retail sales managers covered the following areas:

1. What are you doing now, and on whose initiative?
2. To whom are you reporting?
3. How are you communicating?
4. How are you doing the job (reading, writing, meeting, traveling)?
5. What is the object of the job (sales, service, handling orders, budgeting, handling personnel)?
6. With whom are you in contact (customer, workshop, superior, spare parts shop, salespeople)?

Executives are usually surprised to see how inefficiently they are using their time: spending too much time on day-to-day problems and too little on long-range planning, doing too many tasks subordinates could handle, traveling too much, spending too much time at meetings, spending too much time alone and too little with their staff, and not working enough with management problems in their own departments. Executives may tend to cheat at first, self-consciously, but they don't keep it up; after all, the results will be referred only to themselves.

Managers for whom no realistic information system standards can be devised can find some variation of the Data-Chron a useful way to analyze their own performance. Results of such approaches show that the manager gets a new look at performance, and usually is dissatisfied with it to the point of making significant changes in behavior—precisely the goal of an effective MIS.

Status of Work

One of the most difficult points to determine with certainty in a large manufacturing operation is the status of completion of the thousands (perhaps millions) of items in the process of manufacture. Modern large-scale manufacturing must be scheduled very closely if facilities are to be used efficiently, but it does no good to schedule unless steps are taken to see that the schedule is met.

In a production shop, schedules are prepared to provide for meeting the required date for each job that goes through the shop, and at the same time for loading departments and machines to capacity as far as possible. This operation becomes very complex when numerous jobs and machines are involved, even if each job proceeds exactly on schedule. Consider a very simple case, where there are only three jobs to be done (I, II, and III) and each job must take its turn with each of three departments (A, B, and C). There are six different ways to schedule the set of jobs, as shown in Table 12-1. If there are two machines in each of the three departments— A1, A2, B1, B2, C1, and C2—there are 6 x 6 = 36 different ways to schedule the three jobs, as shown in Table 12-2. Make the situation a bit closer to reality by assuming that there are four jobs to be done, and four departments that each has to go to, and three machines in each department. In this case, the number of different sequences that can be scheduled has inflated enormously: there are 3,652,034,728,000,000 different ways to schedule the four jobs!

The situation is infinitely more complex in an actual shop, of course, because the minute any one job on any one machine slips behind schedule, the entire schedule begins to be in jeopardy. Obviously management cannot cope with anything like this number of different schedules; but consider the different priorities that apply to the different jobs, and management's need to readjust schedules in the least harmful way when any delay occurs—and you can see the need for prompt and complete information on work status.

Management cannot hope to analyze each scheduling system when so many different sequences are possible. But it can set up mathematical models simulating the various ways that work can be scheduled, and analyze the effects by simulating thousands of runs to see the average outcomes.

One of the earliest large-scale simulations of job shop scheduling was handled by A. J. Rowe at the General Electric Company in 1959. He tried six general decision rules for establishing schedules, as follows, and analyzed their effects on completion time relative to the scheduled time, labor utilization efficiency, and carrying cost of inventory.

schedule simulation

1. First come, first served.
2. Three priority classes based on dollar value of jobs, and first come, first served within each class.
3. A complex algorithm designed to consider a number of cost and scheduling factors.
4. First priority to shortest jobs.
5. First priority to longest jobs.
6. Priority on basis of job start dates, earliest first.

Rowe's simulation covered four months of operations, and was run separately for medium and heavy load conditions. The *distribution of completion times*—the probability of early or late completion under each of the six rules—is shown in Figure 12-5. Looking at the distributions, you can see that Rule 4 gives a rather high probability of early completion; in fact, under heavy load conditions 14% of the jobs will finish six days early. At the same time, Rule 4 produces a significant probability of late jobs, and is the only rule producing jobs as late as four days.

As to the other two factors, Table 12-3 shows how effective they are in

JOB I	JOB II	JOB III
A	B C	C B
B	A C	C A
C	A B	B A

Table 12-1.
Scheduling Alternatives

JOB I	JOB II	JOB III
A1–A2	B1–B2 B1–C2 C1–B2 C1–C2	C1–C2 C1–B2 B1–C2 B1–B2
A1–B2	B1–A2 B1–C2 C1–A2 C1–C2	C1–C2 C1–A2 B1–C2 B1–A2
A1–C2	B1–A2 B1–B2 C1–A2 C1–B2	C1–B2 C1–A2 B1–B2 B1–A2

JOB I	JOB II	JOB III
B1–A2	A1–B2 A1–C2 C1–B2 C1–C2	C1–C2 C1–B2 A1–C2 A1–B2
B1–B2	A1–A2 A1–C2 C1–A2 C1–C2	C1–C2 C1–A2 A1–C2 A1–A2
B1–C2	A1–A2 A1–B2 C1–A2 C1–B2	C1–B2 C1–A2 A1–B2 A1–A2

JOB I	JOB II	JOB III
C1–A2	A1–B2 A1–C2 B1–B2 B1–C2	B1–C2 B1–B2 A1–C2 A1–B2
C1–B2	A1–A2 A1–C2 B1–A2 B1–C2	B1–C2 B1–A2 A1–C2 A1–A2
C1–C2	A1–A2 A1–B2 B1–A2 B1–B2	B1–B2 B1–A2 A1–B2 A1–A2

Table 12-2.
Large-scale Scheduling Model

labor utilization and in holding down the cost of carrying material in inventory longer than needed. Rule 4 has the best labor utilization, but a very poor inventory cost ratio. All in all, Rules 2 and 3 appear to be the best when all three factors are considered.

This simulation assumes that schedules will be met, but quite often they are not. Machines break down, material is delayed, jobs take longer than expected, and other jobs have to be put into the schedule unexpectedly. The only solution, with thousands of jobs going through the system, is to get prompt feedback to the scheduling department whenever jobs are delayed. Usual methods of message handling in a plant are likely to be far too slow, and since the secret of effective rescheduling is prompt receipt of information (to permit prompt response), the best systems are those incorporating teletype reporting directly into the computer.

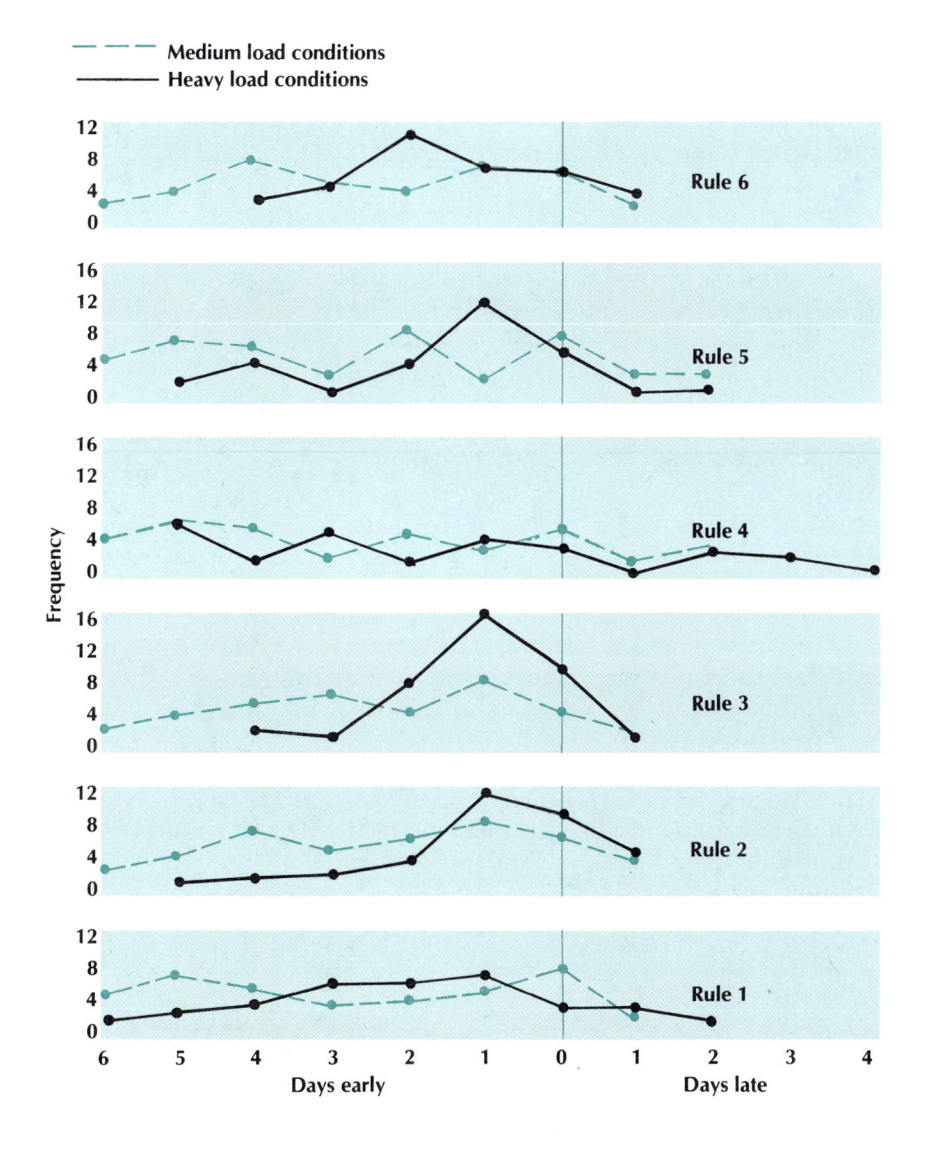

Figure 12-5.
Distribution of Completion Times

Table 12-3.
Impact of Scheduling Rules on Labor and Inventory Costs

Decision Rule	Labor Utilization	Inventory Cost Ratio
#1	85.6%	70.1%
#2	85.6%	41.9%
#3	88.2%	42.4%
#4	88.6%	72.4%
#5	76.9%	53.6%
#6	85.6%	51.1%

Handling of Orders and Accounts

integrated order handling systems

Information on the status of work in process is not desired solely to permit more efficient scheduling. It is needed also to keep customers up-to-date on the status of their orders. A truly integrated system will receive a customer order, search the computer memory to find where the item is available in stock, select the closest location, adjust the inventory to show a reduction by the amount of the order, issue shipment instructions to the warehouse, search the memory for information on the line of credit and discount level for the particular customer, prepare an invoice billing the customer and increasing the accounts receivable records—and, if the stock level is brought below a predetermined point, write a manufacturing order to replenish the stock. If the material is not available in stock, the manufacturing order will be issued on a priority basis, and the customer will be advised of the expected delivery date from manufacturing rather than from stock. Such a system, when it works well, saves both time and labor costs involved in a manual system, and ensures that the company will not promise material that is unavailable or lose valuable time in replenishing stock. Since it takes a tremendous amount of design effort to build such a system and work out the bugs, companies sometimes find their information systems generating incorrect actions such as replenishing stock that is available in excess or shipping material to the wrong customers.

Strangely enough, systems of this sort, originally promoted on the basis of the money they will save, often cost as much as the manual systems they replace—because management tends to want every possible feature in an information system, needed or not. Since *any* information is of *some* value (even if marginal), it is hard to draw the line and say, "This additional information is not worth what it will cost, so we will do without it." The principle involved concerns the *value of information.* As a general rule, the first increment of information that is collected both costs the least and contributes the most. Subsequent increments of information are increasingly expensive and have less and less effect on managerial operations. Consider the analogy of buying a house. The easiest bit of information to collect is the price of the house (through a telephone call), and this information probably has the greatest value to the prospective buyer in deciding if it will be suitable. Additional information can be obtained rather easily by inspecting the house to see the floor plan and size of rooms. Further inspection will reveal the overall quality of the house. Still more detailed inspection would involve taking out a section of pipe here and there to check the corrosion, cutting holes in the foundation to check for termites, and removing a section of roof to inspect for rot. Detailed study can be made of the neighborhood to ascertain trends in property values in the area. In general, however, the more thorough inspection and investigation, expensive though it is, will not add very much useful information to the facts about the price, the floor plan, and the general condition.

Figure 12-6 shows this relationship symbolically. While it is not easy to calculate the value of information, the relationship should be kept in mind; additional information should not be collected simply because it is possible to do so. There must be a hard-headed appraisal of what the information will do for management, and if no valid contribution is anticipated, the information should be forgotten.

Planning and Forecasting
The annual budget is the document that converts plans to action, and budget information is extremely useful in management. Some budget information is precise, and its meaning cannot be interpreted differently by different members of the organization; but other budget information is subject to interpretation, and may convey meanings in the organization that are not intended by top management.

A budget that deals with the rate of expansion in a given area usually is quite specific. It may describe a new plant that will be used to manufacture a new product or to change the scale of production, in which case it will indicate how fast the organization will get the new enterprise going and what level of personnel it will support. Capital budgets are clear in their meaning, and provide the funds to support the new project at the rate that capital equipment is intended to be installed. Since the entire project is new, there are no individuals or groups with an important stake in the status quo, and few chances to look for hidden meanings or policy shifts.

By contrast, a budget that increases the support of one department but not that of a competing department can be misinterpreted. The recipient may conclude that the latter department will be phased out soon, when in fact top management was simply providing additional funds for a special expense incurred by the former department. A budget cut may reflect a change in responsibilities, or it may simply represent a different way of financing the same activities. For example, a department that formerly paid for services within the company may have its budget reduced because these services will be funded by the supplying department henceforth. An objection to this cut by the department head would serve no useful purpose, and could initiate conflict that would reduce efficiency.

problems with budget interpretation

When budgets are reduced unreasonably, in an effort to cut costs without any real managerial analysis of the situation, the tendency is to ignore the budgets and almost deliberately overspend. When a top manager is faced with such action by subordinate managers, he or she must determine whether the budget has put the offending department into an impossible situation by imposing unrealistic limitations. If departments are asked to participate in budget preparation, this sort of problem can be avoided.

Figure 12-6.
Cost and Value of Information

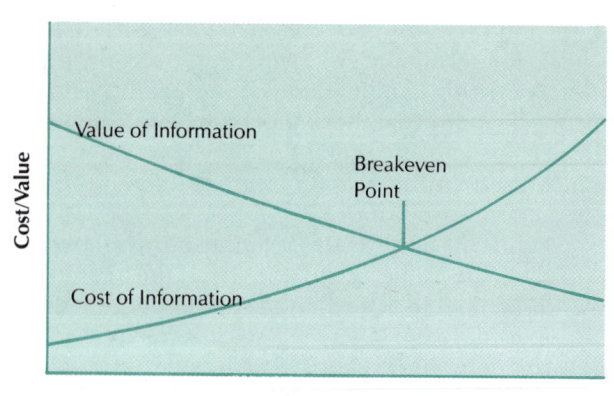

Once the budget is adopted, it becomes a major element in the management information system. Budget summaries should be distributed frequently, and variations from the target figures should be questioned immediately. If a subordinate is able to say, when budget reports are distributed, "Yes, but this and that have been omitted, so the figures are not correct," the budget information will not be a valid management tool. The information must include what it purports to include, and must be accepted by everyone in the organization as factual. If a budget covers routine operations, the control system is relatively simple: a certain proportion should be expended by a certain point in the budget period, and if expenditures are above this point the costs are going out of control and must be curtailed. If the budget is designed for a specific project, the problem is more complicated, because expenditures do not vary with time but rather with progress of the work—and that must be estimated in order to determine whether expenditures are in control or not.

project control information

Management information for project control consists of three control devices:

1. physical progress vs. scheduled progress over time;
2. actual expenditures vs. scheduled expenditures over time;
3. costs for work actually done vs. estimated costs for that work.

For a sample project, Figure 12-7 shows scheduled expenditures over time, together with a plot of actual expenditures to date. Since the latter is below the former, the first impression is that costs are running under estimates. But Figure 12-8 shows that actual work progress to date is well below scheduled progress; since we are behind schedule, we *should* be under our expenditure curve. Figure 12-9 shows, for those individual job items which are completed, the estimated costs and the actual costs; we can see that the actual costs are running over. Going back to Figure 12-8, an extension of the actual work progress line suggests that by the time we hit 100% completion we will be six months over the scheduled time. If we extend the estimated and actual cost lines in Figure 12-9 out to the same date, we have a crude estimate of the probable total overrun in cost. It is clear that immediate action must be taken to avoid both a major delay and a substantial cost overrun (problems that often go together).

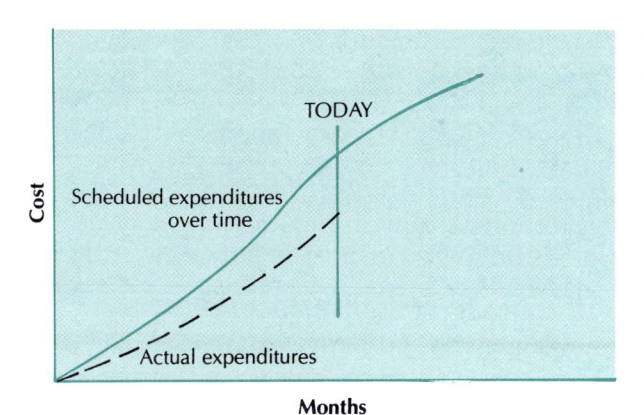

Figure 12-7.
Actual vs. Scheduled Expenditures Over Time

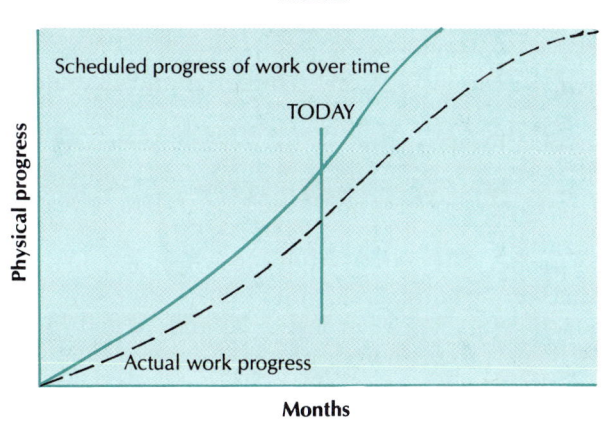

Figure 12-8.
Actual vs. Scheduled Work Progress

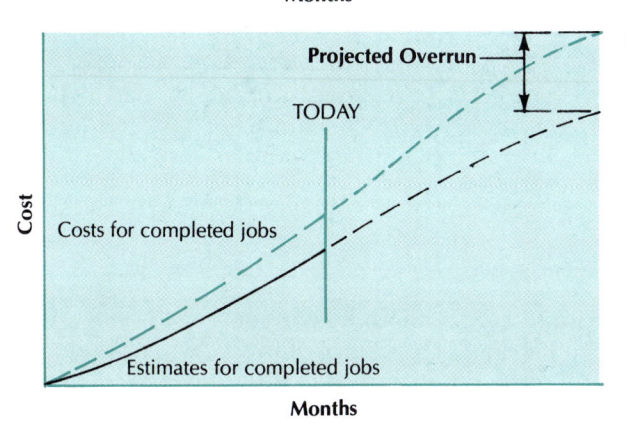

Figure 12-9.
Actual vs. Scheduled Job Costs

Some project control systems simply use expenditures as a measure of physical progress, assuming that if 35% of the funds are spent, then 35% of the work must be done. This assumption is fine if there are no cost overruns, but it lays a trap for management if costs actually are running over the estimates.

Clearly, a detailed method for estimating progress is required for a good project control system, however difficult it may be to devise such a method.

To forecast actual sales and obtain information on future markets,

Describe how North Star might use this system for the Bureau of Mines job.

443
HANDLING AND USING INFORMATION

pricing information systems

management uses the forecasting techniques described in chapter 6, "Planning." During inflationary conditions, the information system must be particularly detailed to permit management to set its prices properly. Donald W. Fuller, president of Microdata Corporation, described the pricing problem in such times with the following remarks (delivered in 1974): "Lead time on components we buy used to be 30 days; now it is a year. Because of component shortages, our inventories have doubled in the last year, while sales are up only 30%. To price a contract under these conditions, we have to double- and triple-check everything. A year or so ago, we budgeted every six months, made cash projections quarterly, and used the computer only for payroll. Now we budget quarterly, make cash projections weekly, and plug virtually every pricing factor into the computer." Companies that have developed information systems that will permit them to respond energetically to such conditions will be able to ride out such inflationary times; but those whose management data is insufficient will find their operations severely hampered and may not survive adversity.

Pricing can go in the other direction, too. In 1971, portable electronic calculators sold for $240; four years later the same items were selling for under $10. Small-signal transistors sold for $0.37 in 1970, and three years later were going for $0.02. Dacron was introduced at $2.25 a pound in 1953; 20 years later it had dropped to $0.40, despite all the inflation of the intervening years. One marketing authority, commenting on the shift in pricing responsibility to senior management levels, recently noted that whereas "pricing used to be part of the budget ritual, since it was almost impossible to keep track of the factors going into price, any good company now has an information flow system that allows prices to be reviewed at least weekly, if not daily." Marvin Rubin, group vice-president of Zale Corporation, a national retail jewelry company, says, "We are constantly looking for flags that tell us costs have gone up and we had better reexamine our margins"; one of Zale's principal tools is a daily computer printout that shows the current relationship between cost and profit margin on every item in the inventory.

Public Information Needs

With respect to business operations, the public is concerned both with *performance* (to evaluate the profit performance of business as a potential investment or loan, or to assess the health of existing investments and perhaps make a change in management) and with *behavior* (to see if business is conforming to regulatory standards). With respect to public enterprise, the public is concerned with proper management and responsiveness to public needs. And with respect to public statistics, the public is interested in knowing what is taking place in its environment. Each of these concerns requires information.

Evaluation of Business Health

Every corporation of any size in the U.S. is required to prepare an annual statement, and to have it audited by a public accounting firm which makes an independent investigation of its accuracy and completeness. In addition, corporations prepare quarterly statements of their corporate progress and health in the same format. Although companies may select various accounting techniques that can change the stated profits for a given period, the accounting rules require that such choices be explained in the notes accompanying the statements. Moreover, this option is limited by the requirement of certification by the accounting firm.

Figure 12-10 shows a quarterly *income statement* of Tiger International, (formerly Flying Tiger Corporation), and Figure 12-11 is a quarterly *balance sheet*. From these statements, the public will be able to see the general health of the company, and lending agencies will have a yardstick to determine the prudence of making loans. Looking at Figure 12-10, we can see that revenues for the nine-month period of 1974 have gone up from $207 million in 1973 to $242 million. At the same time, however, costs (particularly interest and fuel costs) have gone up from $166 million to $222 million, so that net income dropped from $23 million to $14

Figure 12-10.
Quarterly Corporate Income Statement

Consolidated Statements of Income
For the Three Months and Nine Months Ended September 30, 1974 and 1973 (unaudited)

	Three Months Ended September 30		Nine Months Ended September 30	
	1974	1973	1974	1973
	(expressed in thousands)			
Revenues:				
Common carriage—domestic	$19,343	$19,089	$ 55,065	$ 49,247
—international	25,218	23,178	67,158	60,349
Military Airlift Command	4,601	4,568	11,194	12,235
Leasing and related services	35,526	26,727	100,178	75,299
Other	4,059	3,997	9,349	10,486
	88,747	77,559	242,944	207,616
Costs and Expenses:				
Airline operations	39,452	29,451	108,851	81,546
Leasing operations	6,261	4,996	17,285	12,436
Selling, general and administrative	11,146	10,076	31,092	26,173
Depreciation and amortization	9,258	7,037	27,474	23,453
Interest, and preferred dividends of subsidiary	14,706	8,640	38,180	23,139
	80,823	60,200	222,882	166,747
Income Before Income Tax Provision	7,924	17,359	20,062	40,869
Income tax provision	1,773	7,348	6,019	17,209
Net Income	$ 6,151	$10,011	$ 14,043	$ 23,660
Primary Earnings per Share	$ .49	$ .78	$ 1.12	$ 1.87

Figure 12-11.
Quarterly Corporate
Balance Sheet

Consolidated Balance Sheets
September 30, 1974 and 1973 (unaudited)

Assets	1974	1973
Current Assets:	*(expressed in thousands)*	
Cash	$ 21,474	$ 46,766
Receivables (net)	51,307	48,898
Other current assets	35,800	23,117
Total current assets	108,581	118,781
Finance Lease Receivables:		
Aggregate future rentals (net)	277,978	149,426
Estimated residual value of leased equipment	15,925	10,993
	293,903	160,419
Less: Unearned income	98,575	72,454
	195,328	87,965
Property, Plant and Equipment:		
Equipment for lease or under operating lease	760,449	662,684
Equipment used in airline operations	172,451	132,759
Buildings, facilities and other	52,125	40,033
	985,025	835,476
Less: Accumulated depreciation and amortization	291,293	254,013
	693,732	581,463
Other Assets:		
Costs in excess of fair value of new assets of acquired business	15,835	15,886
Other	18,008	11,438
	33,843	27,324
	$1,031,484	$815,533

Liabilities and Stockholders' Equity	1974	1973
Current Liabilities:		
Current portion of senior and subordinated debt	$ 25,533	$ 16,825
Accounts payable and accrued liabilities	61,385	42,081
Total current liabilities	86,918	58,906
Senior Debt	605,351	437,204
Subordinated Debt	18,311	30,602
Deferred Credits, principally deferred income taxes	104,875	92,813
Minority Stockholders' Equity:		
North American Car Corporation $3 Cumulative Preferred Stock; $50 stated value	6,952	7,210
Tiger International, Inc. Stockholders' Equity:		
Common Stock, $1 par value	12,431	12,422
Additional paid-in capital	121,430	121,073
Retained earnings	75,216	55,303
	209,077	188,798
	$1,031,484	$815,533

A company's debt situation is an important piece of financial information.

million. Since these two cost elements clearly are not controlled by management, we would be inclined to blame the reduced earnings on general economic conditions.

An important piece of financial information is each company's debt situation. Is it borrowing more short-term funds than usual (which must be paid back soon), is it earning enough to pay interest on loans (which as of 1974 were rising rapidly), and is the ratio of debt to equity rising? Figure 12-12 shows this information for some selected major corporations.

Look at American Airlines, where short-term debt has gone up from an average 3.1% of total debt over the past ten years to 5.5% of total debt here. (However, debt as a percentage of equity has dropped from 158% to 95%—a good sign that the owners have put in more funds relative to what they owe.) A rather alarming figure is the *coverage ratio,* which is a measure of the company's ability to pay its interest and other mandatory payments; this has dropped from 2.4 to 0.7. The current ratio, or ability to pay all outstanding bills from current liquid assets, has dropped from 1.4 to 1.1, which is approaching the danger line. And *working capital ratio,* which measures net current assets as a proportion of long-term debt, is at a minimal 0.04—down from an average 0.15. Clearly this airline is going through a difficult time (as were many airlines during the same period, with a combination of overcapacity and vastly increased fuel charges).

Do you see any sign that North Star has run up against the coverage ratio?

HANDLING AND USING INFORMATION

Figure 12-12.
Debt Status of Selected Corporations

SURVEY OF THE LARGEST NONFINANCIAL CORPORATIONS

COMPANY	SALES 1973 $ Mil.	DEBT Total 6/30/74 $ Mil.	Short Term As % Total Debt 6/30/74	Avg. Short Term As % Of Total Debt 1964-73	Debt As % Of Equity 6/30/74	Avg. Debt As % Of Equity 1964-73	Int. Covge. Ratio Pretax 6/30/74	Avg. Int. Covge. Ratio Pretax 1964-73	Total Fixed Charge Covge. Ratio 6/30/74	Avg. Total Fixed Charge Covge. Ratio 1964-73	Work. Cap. As % Of Long-Term Debt 1973	Avg. Work. Cap. As % Of Long-Term Debt 1964-73	Current Ratio 1973	Avg. Current Ratio 1964-73
Albertson's (2)	852.5	24.1	6.2	6.0	45	27	11.3	25.5	11.3	25.5	1.10	1.67	1.5	1.6
Alco Standard	777.7	115.1	17.0	30.5	72	80	5.7	8.3	4.5	5.5	1.49	2.04	2.3	2.1
Allegheny Ludlum Industries	763.0	161.6	16.4	13.1	55	48	6.0	10.2	3.3	6.7	1.25	1.60	2.2	3.2
Allied Chemical	1664.6	426.7	1.8	4.9	44	54	8.2	6.8	8.2	6.8	0.89	0.74	2.5	2.5
Allied Stores (2)	1598.3	454.9	16.4	18.1	134	134	2.8	3.7	2.8	3.3	0.85	0.91	2.2	2.2
Allied Supermarkets (3)	1035.9	74.1	5.9	6.0	173	168	1.2	5.3	1.2	6.6	0.53	0.57	1.7	1.8
Allis Chalmers (3)	1166.4	231.9	39.5	35.4	64	61	1.6	2.5	1.5	2.5	1.50	1.98	1.7	2.3
Aluminum Co. of America	2157.3	888.9	2.2	4.0	63	71	5.3	5.4	5.0	4.8	0.68	0.62	2.9	3.1
AMAX (3)	1336.8	440.3	3.3	6.8	51	48	5.0	10.4	3.7	7.8	0.94	1.37	2.6	3.2
Amerada Hess	1896.4	567.0	5.6	8.1	67	85	12.5	9.3	6.2	2.8	0.75	0.46	1.8	1.5
American Airlines	1482.0	519.1	5.5	3.1	95	158	0.7	2.4	NM	NM	0.04	0.15	1.1	1.4
American Beef Packers (6)	896.9	61.5	65.5	57.9	272	206	2.4	2.5	2.4	2.5	0.28	0.53	1.1	1.2
American Brands	1864.7	765.1	52.2	37.2	80	56	5.9	19.3	4.8	12.6	1.41	3.68	2.1	3.3
American Broadcasting	880.5	109.9	3.2	7.4	35	73	15.2	8.7	15.2	8.7	2.26	1.36	2.6	2.4
American Can	2181.6	432.1	16.3	5.3	63	50	8.2	9.3	6.5	6.6	1.16	1.04	2.4	2.6

GLOSSARY

Sales
Total net sales as of the end of the company's latest fiscal year ending between June, 1973, and May, 1974.

Total debt
Long-term plus short-term debt.

Debt as percent of equity
Total long-and short-term debt as a percent of common equity, which includes common stock, capital surplus, retained earnings.

Interest coverage ratio
Pretax income plus total interest expense divided by total interest expense.

Total fixed charge coverage ratio
Net income plus total interest expense (adjusted by tax rate) divided by fixed charges (adjusted by tax rate) plus preferred dividends paid.

Working capital as percent of long-term debt
Total current assets less total current liabilities divided by long-term debt, as of the end of the company's latest fiscal year ending between June, 1973, and May, 1974.

Current ratio
Total current assets divided by total current liabilities as of the end of the company's 1973 fiscal year.

Information of this sort, available to investors and lenders, greatly improves their understanding of the health of listed corporations.

With the validity of this information heavily dependent on the adequacy of the review by public accountants, it is important to know whether their work is as accurate and complete as it might be. A survey done for Arthur Andersen and Company, a major public accounting firm, by Opinion Research Corporation, and completed in the fall of 1974, indicates that many investors feel they could be getting more and better information. Figure 12-13 shows the preliminary results of this survey, indicating that 31% feel the financial statements are biased and inaccurate to some degree, 39% feel they do not provide enough information, and nearly half feel that financial statements are difficult to understand.

A recent trend toward lawsuits or government actions against public accounting firms for failure to take all possible action to represent the public interest (even though most investors and other users of corporate statements rate the accountants high on integrity) probably presages even more surveillance of corporate accounting practices in the public interest.

evaluation of public accountants

Figure 12-13.
How Shareholders Rate Accountants

HOW SHAREHOLDERS RATE ACCOUNTANTS

MANY QUESTION THE ACCURACY OF FINANCIAL STATEMENTS...

Are financial Statements objective and accurate?

Entirely objective and accurate	7%
Mostly objective and accurate	56%
Rather biased and inaccurate	28%
Very biased and inaccurate	3%
No opinion	7%

...AND A LARGE MINORITY WANTS MORE CORPORATE DATA...

Do accountants provide enough corporate information?

More than enough	9%
Enough	46%
Less than adequate	32%
Much less than adequate	7%
No opinion	6%

...BUT ACCOUNTANTS RANK HIGH AMONG THE PROFESSIONS..

Percent of shareholders favorable to professionals' ethical and moral practices:

CPAs	74%
Bank executives	74%
Stockbrokers	51%
Lawyers	48%
Corporate executives	46%
Insurance agents	45%
Federal regulators	35%

Regulation of Business

regulatory impact on business accounting

The Securities and Exchange Commission, which has broad regulatory power over corporations listed on securities exchanges (such as the New York Stock Exchange), has been moving in recent years toward even more required disclosures to amplify the annual reports. Corporations must file special "10-K" reports with the Commission each year, and in 1973 and 1974 the Commission applied much stricter standards for these reports. A major change requires companies to disclose in detail their leasing arrangements (which tend to substitute for capital investments, as you saw in the discussion of Pan American Airlines in chapter 11, "Managing Finances") and their effect on projected earnings. Another requires companies to explain any differences between the depreciation and similar allowances that they use for tax purposes and those that they use to estimate profits for their stockholders. (A corporation may depreciate a large capital asset fast for tax purposes, to reduce present taxes, but may depreciate it more slowly on its books, both because it believes the life will be greater than the IRS-allowed life and also because it wishes to show as large a profit as it can.) Other requirements involve explaining taxes in detail, describing any agreements with lenders that limit how balances can be used, and other technical matters. Special industries such as insurance, land developers, franchisers and others will have stiffer new requirements. Other rules now under consideration and likely to be adopted soon require mining industries to show their reserve figures, require all companies to disclose their "inventory profits," and require companies to show the impact of any accounting changes they make. The public accounting firms are being pushed to move faster on various disclosure rules (such as a definition of what corporate events must be publicized promptly).

regulation of banks

Banks are essentially public institutions, because they play such an important role in maintaining the financial health of the community, and they are heavily regulated—by the Comptroller of the Currency, the Federal Deposit Insurance Corporation, the banking departments in the states, and the Federal Reserve Board. But the failure in recent years of two large U.S. banks—U.S. National and Franklin National—has brought pressure for a better "early warning system" to catch a bank in trouble before things become hopeless. Since the Franklin National Bank's failure was triggered by massive foreign exchange losses, new regulations now require banks to report their foreign exchange positions weekly. Since the Arab countries have started putting massive short-term deposits into U.S. banks, and since the only way a bank can make profits on its deposits is to loan them out (primarily on longer term loans), banks are tending to support more and more of their loans with "hot money": short-term deposits that might have to be paid out well before the long-term loans are due. Clearly, if a bank uses short-term funds to make long-term loans, it is taking a serious risk.

As a start on building a management information system for regulation of banks, the Comptroller of the Currency recently sent a survey to the 200 largest U.S. banks, attempting to design a computer model of conventional bank behavior against which each bank's operations could be judged. In fact, the New York bank stock firm of Keefe, Bruyette and Woods already has such a model, into which it recently plugged all 14,000 U.S. banks; its model immediately selected Franklin National as submarginal.

What worries bank regulators is that banks which are holding companies for other enterprises (a practice now permitted) may be tempted to use bank funds to bail out ailing subsidiaries. Indeed, First Wisconsin Corporation rescued a real estate investment trust that it sponsored by buying from it nearly $15 million in loans, and by taking certain other rescue actions. President George F. Kasten stated at the time that the bank felt strong legal and moral responsibilities to bring about this agreement for the shareholders' protection.[4]

An official of one bank regulatory agency summed up the need for more information as follows: "Those guys in Franklin were buying their way out of trouble, doubling their bets. We ought to have a process that picks up things like that—continuous monitoring, not concentrating upon a single exam, going into the dark corners to check the bonds once a year. It means more staff and more computers. It means a lot more reports from the banks."[5]

And it means a more complex and systematic management by bank regulators.

Management of Public Enterprise

The U.S. is a capitalist country, perhaps the most capitalistic of any nation in the world. But even so, we have a great deal of public enterprise. The Tennessee Valley Authority, the Port of New York and New Jersey Authority, the Atomic Energy Commission (now part of the Energy Research and Development Administration), the Federal National Mortgage Authority, the National Aeronautics and Space Agency, the Federal Deposit Insurance Corporation, the Maritime Administration, the Commodity Credit Corporation, the Small Business Administration, the Postal Service, Amtrak, Conrail, and so on operate to some extent as private businesses; and there are many state and local enterprises such as electric and water companies, airports, sewage plants, transportation companies, and various public "authorities" that do the same. Their need for management information parallels that of industry, and the complexity of their operations rivals that of major corporations.

Sometimes, indeed, they are even more complex. When the Patent Office decided a few years ago that an automated system was needed to deal with its 3.8 million patents, some dating back to 1800, it spent three years studying a scheme for installing automatic data processing equipment, only to have a National Bureau of Standards study conclude that existing information retrieval could not do the job in a single integrated package. The need is intense: the Patent Office handles 450 applications a day, and takes 22 months to award a patent; even then the search is not thorough enough, for about 60% of all patents contested in federal court are ruled invalid. The automated information system was intended to incorporate the 92,000 terms used to classify an invention into a retrieval system that each examiner could call up at a keyboard terminal by punching in a description of the invention's purpose. Reportedly, the 1200 patent examiners are not completely receptive to automated information technology—an additional hurdle for any new system, which undoubtedly would require loving care and tolerant understanding

public enterprise management

during its installation period when all sorts of growing pains could be expected. At present, the prospects for such an MIS at the Patent Office are unclear. The most likely course is that a relatively simple category will be used to start a system, and it will be moved gradually into other systems as its development proceeds.

Public Statistics

Probably the most elaborate information system in existence is used every ten years (and at intervals in between on a different scale) by the U.S. Census Bureau. A major industrial nation such as the U.S. desperately needs census information for all sorts of public and private decisions, and the census is a trailblazer in terms of survey techniques. A crippling problem facing some underdeveloped nations is their lack of a complete and accurate census; legislators and policy makers must operate by guesswork, and businesses are deprived of essential information about the buying public. In addition to the Census Bureau, a huge array of agencies collects information on every conceivable subject. The Bureau of Labor Statistics collects information on employment and other personal data and forecasts employment trends under a wide variety of conditions. The Department of Commerce "input-output model" of interrelationships in the U.S. industrial economy forecasts the impact of changes in any one industry on activity in other industries. The Federal Aviation Administration collects information on air travel at all airports in the U.S. (together with the Civil Aeronautics Board). So extensive is this government information-gathering procedure that in 1970 the president established a Commission on Federal Statistics to set up some federal guidelines for obtaining and processing raw information.

Commission on Federal Statistics

The study found that federal *statistical agencies* (which generally collect and prepare statistics about private individuals, organizations, and activities) perform creditably; but that federal *statistics* (about the government's activities) come generally from operating agencies, and are poor. It recommended that the Statistical Policy Division of the Office of Management and Budget take responsibility for all statistical data in the government, with a view to improving the application of statistical methods in all federal programs, as well as improving collection and distribution. It considered the question of the public need for statistics versus the individual's right to privacy, and recommended an independent advisory board of outstanding citizens to review policies on confidentiality, investigate possible breaches, and publish each year an appraisal of the problems and the performance of federal agencies in respecting privacy and confidentiality.

Federal statisticians have pioneered in improving ways of collecting, processing, and analyzing data. Examples are: the current population survey (conducted monthly to gather data on many features of our society), the national health survey program, automated geographic coding of census data to make it far more useful by unlocking valuable stores of local data for communities, the selective service lottery (which has never been questioned for complete statistical impartiality), the consumer price index on which many organizations rely for important decisions, and congressional redistricting (a highly charged problem, but not in terms of the accuracy of the relevant census data).

Information Systems

Every enterprise has some sort of *data processing system,* whether complicated or elementary. It might be as simple as that used by your newsboy or girl, by having a card for each customer with tear-off receipts for each week: a chit not torn off indicates an "account receivable" and a gap where a chit has been torn off indicates a payment. It might involve old-fashioned handwritten ledgers (Figure 12-14 shows some explanatory notes from a Reeves & Whittaker Company ledger, corresponding to an annual report of April 1, 1853). Or it might be a fully computerized reporting system, where all of the information is entered into the computer and can be extracted in any form or combinations desired. If a simple system will suffice, there is no justification for an elaborate system. But often the simple system will not suffice.

This section will discuss data processing systems in general, as well as management systems that extend beyond data processing concepts, and the applications of minicomputers and automation to information systems.

data processing system

Data Processing Systems

Data Processing Fundamentals

Until *data* are processed, they are unorganized facts. The processing operation is intended to put them in a form useful to management. The term "unorganized" does not mean that they are disorganized, for this is seldom the case. They were collected by someone with a purpose in mind, and are organized with respect to that purpose, but a reordering is necessary to achieve the goals of the particular management operation involved. The data may cover expenditures by a company for a three-month period. If information on capital expenditures is required, those entries must be extracted from the total of all expenditures, and the remainder disregarded. If information on allocation of funds is required, expenditures must be ordered by payees and purposes. If information on profits is required, expenditures must be put in categories depending on whether they were made to buy goods that will be sold, to finance administrative costs, to pay interest on loans or repay loans, and so on.

Information represents the transformation of data to tell a story. Some data will provide information for a given purpose, and other data will be needed for other purposes.

The *information system* transforms data into information. In data processing, the system involves the five activities described earlier: *input, storage, processing, output,* and *control.* The data processing system selects source data, records it in a form that will fit the system in use, classifies it into the desired categories, performs operations of sorting, comparing, and analyzing, summarizes the results, and distributes them as needed. Let us discuss each of these.

Selecting source data involves deciding which of the routine operations of the business will be recorded. These might be labor hours on each job or job category, payments for each category of expense, receipts by

information system

In chapter 11, North Star developed a budget (probably modeled on the one shown in Figure 9-7). How does that do each thing a data processing system is supposed to do?

selection of data

453
HANDLING AND USING INFORMATION

Every enterprise has some sort of data processing system.

categories, shipments of finished goods, orders for goods, and so forth. In general, each of these is a transaction that would be recorded in any case by the department concerned, as recording the completion of a transaction.

recording of data

Recording data involves placing selected information in a suitable form for incorporation into the information system. In a computerized system, this usually means putting it on a punched card or the equivalent (paper tape or magnetic tape). Sometimes this is a specific transfer, but sometimes the original transaction can be recorded at the time it occurs, such as with cash register transactions that are connected to a central computer and thus effect "real time" entries.

classifying of data

Classifying data involves separating the recorded data into categories corresponding to the analyses you wish to make—perhaps by product line, or territory, or profit center, etc. It does not change any data, but simply looks at it in different groupings.

sorting, comparing, analyzing data

Sorting, comparing, and analyzing involves putting the data into the particular form that will tell a story to management. Sorting might involve pulling out all sales during July, or all employees hired in the past quarter, or all transactions in a given area immediately following a particular advertising campaign, or all machine failures from those using various kinds of lubricants. Comparing is reading performance for a given month against the same operation for the average month, or placing profits of all profit centers against each other, or looking at our sales versus industry sales. Analyzing is relating these various factors in a way that will tell a story: perhaps dividing profits by equity to calculate return on investment, or subtracting cost of sales from sales revenue to get net revenue.

Summarizing results involves putting them in the form that will be most understandable to the users. This involves the method of presentation, or omitting less important material so the vital information is

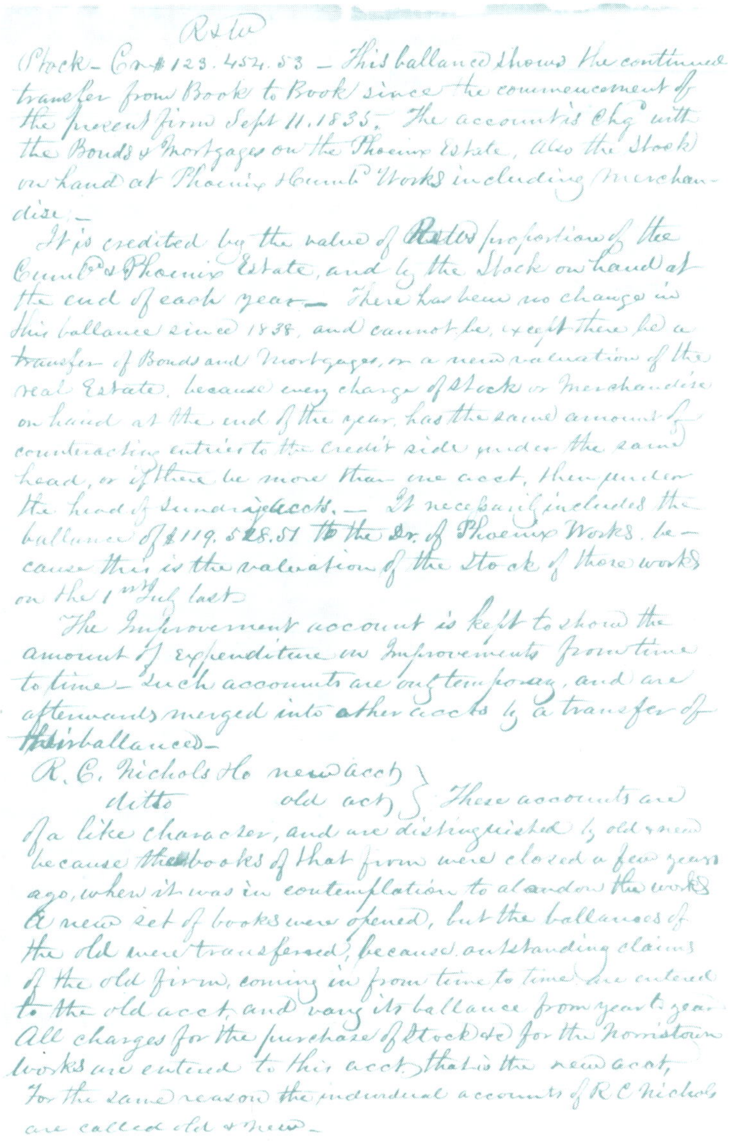

summarizing results

Figure 12-14.
Handwritten Annual Report Notes (1853)

HANDLING AND USING INFORMATION

highlighted, or grouping results in the way that the users normally would think of the problems. The more senior a manager, the more concise the summary.

distributing information

Distributing is an obvious operation, but one that cannot be done in a thoughtless manner. Many information systems deluge the users with so much in the way of printout pages that they almost wallow in numbers, and the tendency is for them to overlook all of it. Perhaps the information should be distributed more selectively—to fewer people, or less frequently, or smaller parts to each person. Distribution involves questions of whether the responsible person alone should get information, or that person and his or her immediate superior, or the competitors of the person (for comparative purposes).

storage of data

This listing omits the important question of *storage* of data, so that it can be retrieved at will. It is important to retain information that will be required later, but it is equally important to dispose of unneeded records (particularly if their gist has been saved in summary form) so that the data files are freed for more current uses. The great strength of a computer system is its ability to store large quantities of material and permit their retrieval on short notice at will; but its capacity is far from infinite.

The Common Data Base

An effective data processing system provides information for the various users—purchasing, manufacturing, accounting, sales, research, personnel, and so on—from a common data base. The key issue here is the kind of data that should be collected, because data in the right form for one user may be in a poor form for another. In companies that do not have a common data base, each department may collect essentially the same sort of data, but the form differs among departments so that the data are not compatible. This is particularly true in public data systems, where the school board collects by school grade, the health department by name, the water and sewer department by development unit of the city, the tax collector by lot and plant number, the census enumerator by census tract, the postal supervisor by zip code, the telephone company by exchange, and so on. Each agency has valuable information, but its files are virtually useless to other agencies because of the lack of a common data base. This duplication of effort can be avoided by careful consideration of what the common data base should contain, how it should be cataloged, what each agency's needs are and how they can be met, and so on.

common data base

Even if there is a common data base, it may not collect the information that would be required to improve management at a later date. The police department may have records of every offender, but probably not in terms of what sort of parole treatment they received after previous convictions, or how much education they have, or what kind of home environment they have, or other factors that may be valuable in making a study of the causes of crime in an effort to take action to reduce it.

The advantage of a common data base, in addition to questions of economy, is that every user has a stake in maintaining its accuracy; thus, there are many more "inspectors" checking the accuracy and completeness of the file than if each agency used its own.

Computerized Information Systems

When companies began to use computers, they were viewed as improved accounting systems, and usually were brought in under the accounting or bookkeeping department to accomplish specific tasks that were previously done manually. A study conducted by Avner Porat as part of his doctoral dissertation at the University of Pittsburgh evaluated the way in which computers were introduced into 30 small banks; he found that the initiative came generally from computer salesmen, and that computers were generally purchased for accounting purposes, with anticipated short-term benefits. Later on, when the computer's potential contribution to bank management became apparent (through evaluation of loan candidates, assessment of portfolio quality, and so on), the computers were under the jurisdiction of the wrong departments, and innovation of these broadened applications was slowed considerably.

computer information systems

The proper way to institute a computerized information system is to analyze the needs of the entire organization for management information. This study may be carried out through a series of weekly meetings, extending over perhaps a year or more, at which each department presents current information needs and a computer committee attempts to incorporate these into a constantly evolving system. At each meeting, the needs set forth from the previous meeting are put into rough presentation form, and department heads respond to these at the next meeting. The situation is a constantly changing one, as conferees see what can be done and modify their initial requirements in the light of what others have requested. Throughout such a session it is necessary to emphasize the *cost* of information systems, weighed against the projected benefits. It may be found that while one department cannot justify the cost of information it needs, other departments want the same information, and together they can justify the cost.

At some point during this process, the computer committee gets on the road and visits other organizations that have information systems, to compare what they have achieved with what the organization needs. There is an unfortunate tendency for organizations to exaggerate the achievements and benefits of their systems, discussing sometimes what they wish they were doing rather than what they actually are getting done. Thus, the committee should take every claim with a grain of salt unless they can see it in operation.

A particular manager who gets a weekly output and describes the wonderful things it does for him should be asked to pull out the most recent copy of the printout and show how it has been used—penciled underlinings, check marks, notes accompanying the printout, and so forth are helpful indicators. A neat 100-page weekly report without a mark has probably been examined for the first time when the visitor asks to see it.

Computer system designers may not be programmers in the strict sense of the word (i.e., in that they write detailed programs). They will do their work in block diagrams, and the programmer will write the formal programs to make things happen. It is necessary for them to break the systems into subsystems that cover different aspects of the total information system task. Figure 12-15 shows a file organization subsystem for an automated police information system. This example was developed by

police information system

Paul M. Whisenand of the School of Public Administration, University of Southern California, for the Office of Civil Defense.

Most companies have found that their computer systems divide naturally into specific subsystems, as follows (an incomplete but typical list):

- Budgetary and accounting system
- Production management system
- Material and inventory control system
- Personnel control system
- Marketing and sales system
- Economic and industry conditions system

These systems use a common data bank to the maximum extent possible, but still require a number of individual inputs for each system. New computer system applications, including problem-solving and decision-making computer models, are evolving almost daily.

Management Systems

While all of the above systems are "management systems" in a sense, they involve a high degree of routinized operations. After all, the computer was adopted initially to take over routine work and free personnel for more creative tasks (in addition to handling certain highly routine tasks

Figure 12-15.
File Organization for Police Information System

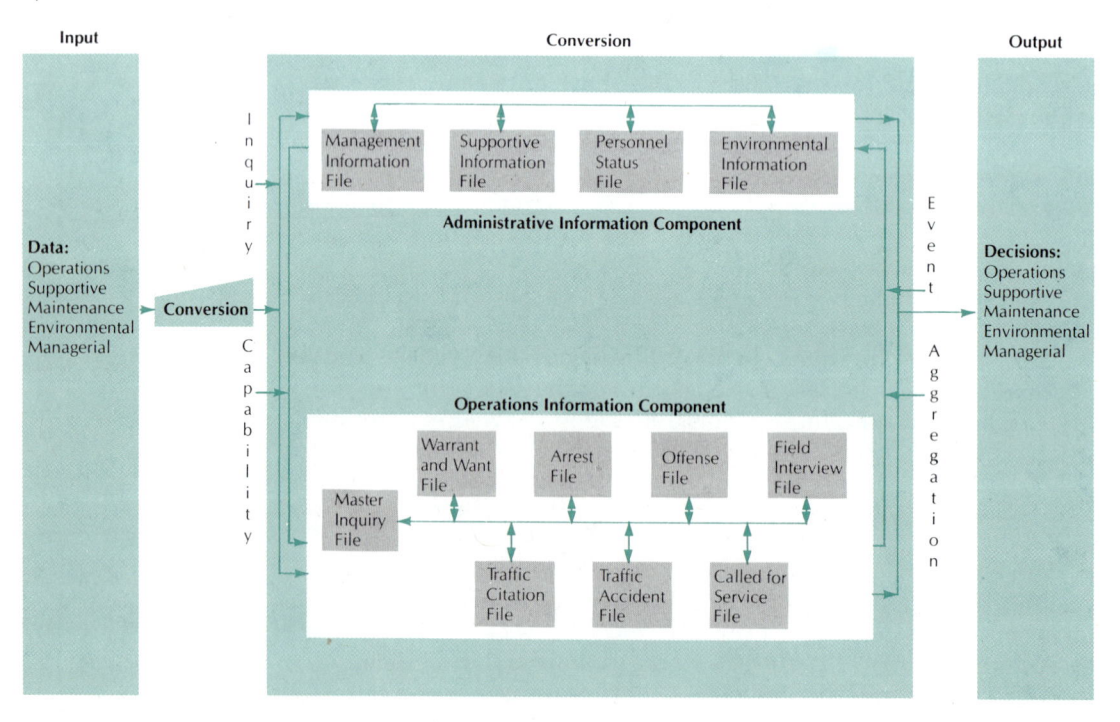

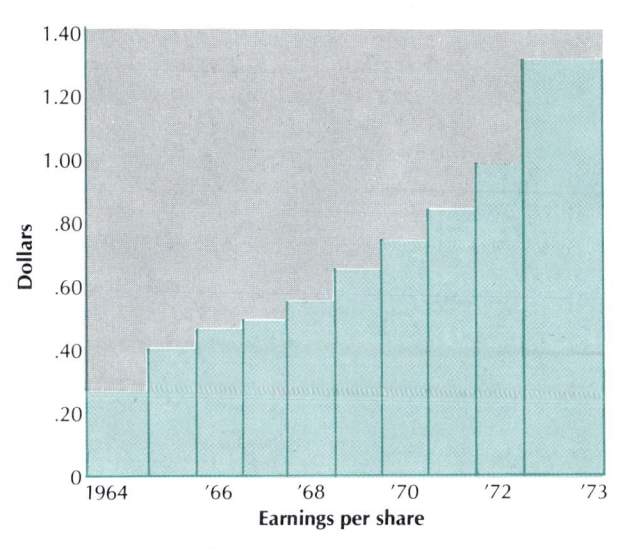

Figure 12-16.
Ten-Year Earnings Growth

Restated for three-for-one stock split in 1967 and two-for-one splits in 1971 and 1973

far more rapidly than humans). This section would be incomplete without a discussion of some systems designed entirely to provide management decisions.

Such a one is the "Holes Committee" established at Mallinckrodt Chemical Works, a pharmaceutical and chemical manufacturer. Mallinckrodt had a 33% sales increase and a 36% profit increase in 1973, capping ten years of uninterrupted growth in both sales and profits; and chairman Harold E. Thayer gives much of the credit to its meticulous system of internal information and control. "One of the principal challenges to management is to avoid being surprised," he says, and Figure 12-16 shows how successful the company has been in meeting this challenge.

Instead of a monthly report on sales and profits, typical of most companies, Mallinckrodt reads out a sales report for each division every five days, along with a readout of income compared with the budgeted plan. Billing reports are made daily, and each division reprojects its budget every 90 days. Overseeing all the information reports is the Holes Committee, which watches for "holes through which profits can leak"; its job is to study the information generated by the MIS (management information system), to make sure that "someone is listening," and it has unlimited authority to go into any of the 12 operating divisions and investigate anything that looks suspicious or out of line.

This concept of being sure that someone is listening to the MIS is extremely important, and without doubt a major source of the success of the Mallinckrodt system. A busy manager, pushed by all the daily press of work that will not wait, is tempted to put the MIS aside and look at it when "time permits." With the Holes Committee ready to look over managers' shoulders at the drop of a hat, they *make* time.

Campbell Taggart, Inc., gives its computer information system high

How would you say North Star discharges the functions of a "Holes Committee," if at all?

459
HANDLING AND USING INFORMATION

marks for its record earnings. During the early 1970s, the baking industry was hit in succession by the Russian wheat sale that quadrupled the cost of flour, the energy crisis that made baking costs soar, and skyrocketing costs of sugar ($15 to $70) and lard ($12 to $38) within a year's time. While the nation's three other major bakers saw profits virtually disappear, CT's profits actually rose 3% during this period. Campbell Taggart's secret is a control system that monitors costs and pricing so closely that cost increases can be passed along before they eat into profits. The information system provides daily cost data and a weekly profit-loss analysis for each of the firm's 70 plants. Key efficiency indicators disclosed by the system include number of pounds sold per product sales route and amount of stale bread returned; and the computer saves each of the firm's 3,600 salesmen an hour a day by calculating for them the sales figures for each of the 200 products they handle. Chairman Bill Mead says, "We can spot trouble before it hurts us. It takes other companies a month or more to get the figures, and by that time you may be dead and not know it." And President Connie Lane says of the firm's information system during these difficult periods, "Controls have never been this important; we live by them."

Hercules, Inc., is another company that makes top management use of its management information. Originally a DuPont subsidiary, Hercules was "spun off" in 1912, and from that date to 1970 its growth rate was only 7.5%. During the last few years of that period, it grew at only 5% a year, and seemed to be reaching a point of near-stagnation. When Werner C. Brown came in as president in 1970, his first task was to map out a growth plan for Hercules, and he spent nearly a year developing computer programs to test various strategies. The company came up with a measure of asset utilization called "total resource productivity"—a system to measure the productivity of labor, marketing, capital, know-how, and everything else that goes into adding value. This program required precise information on growth rate, rate of return on investment, the cost of capital and labor added per revenue dollar, the cost of material per revenue dollar, and so on—a mass of information not required before but now crucial.

Availability of this information—plus a clear management commitment to making use of it—enabled the company to enter growth areas never before considered and to find ways for the new growth products to start earning their way early. The key to their success has been *ability to measure the efficiency of both old and new businesses,* so they can make accurate decisions on where and how to expand.

Automated Information Systems

automated information systems

It has been estimated that technology's greatest contribution to industry in the next decade will be the ability of tiny computers to analyze production information and make immediate adjustments at the point of use. Over 100,000 minicomputers are at work in the U.S., and in the early 1980s this number is expected to grow to between one and two million—half in factories and half in offices. The cost of such a computer will be less than $100.

hierarchical minicomputers

Most sophisticated of the machines are the "hierarchical" type, which collect and analyze factory data, modify design, and control machines. A central computer supervises the minis, and each mini controls its group of mini-minis (or micros) which run individual machines. Any one mini can operate on its own, sending information up and getting back instructions in return.

In offices, it is expected that both executives and secretaries will have individual terminals with TV screens, combining the functions of telephone, transcriber, copier, and calculator. Typewriters will be centrally connected (in some offices this feature virtually exists today), and words can be edited centrally if desired. Already installed at Sperry Rand's Univac Division plant in Roseville, Minnesota is a "personalized information" system, where managers and supervisors have their individual terminals over which they can operate their private information systems. A manager can draw on the central information file for necessary data, or can instruct it to alert him or her when some event happens or some value goes over a given figure. Soon to come will be electronic mail, where a letter will go directly from the secretary's terminal to the recipient's screen—and the latter can file a printed copy simply by pressing a button. Western Union already is testing the concept in Chicago.

On the factory floor, numerical control of machine tools came into use in the late 1960s, using a large computer to run as many as 260 machine tools. This item was expensive to program, and a computer shutdown idled all the machines. The hierarchical minicomputer changed this; today more than 90% of the 40,000 computer manufacturing-and-design installations are under four years old, and more than half of these are less than two years old. Not only do these minis do specific jobs (adjusting carburetors for General Motors, controlling color negative film for Polaroid, blending tobacco for Philip Morris), but they generate information as they go: number of defective parts, material utilized and remaining, production rate. This information is passed up the line to computer "supervisors" which assemble and analyze it, and ultimately to the central factory computer that reorders parts and calculates production costs and schedule changes. Even the overall accounting information can come from these sources.

Such a factory will soon be operating in Richmond, Virginia, where Philip Morris is building a plant that integrates production, planning, and operations more completely than any plant now in existence. At the start, each mini will stick to its own department. But the potential is there for an integrated system, and when the company has sufficient experience to work out the bugs there is little doubt that it will come.

Information Problems

One of the enduring worries spawned by the information age is that more and more information will be gathered about people—and used by companies for their own nefarious ends. This fear is not confined to business: the existence of automated police information systems suggests that some police data are too sensitive to keep in files where improper use can be made of them.

The problem really strikes home at Retail Credit Company, the

computer files on individuals

largest company in the business of investigating private citizens for insurance companies, stores thinking of granting credit, and potential employers. In 1973, after a good deal of prior discussion, the Federal Trade Commission filed a formal complaint against the company for allegedly violating the Fair Credit Reporting Act of 1971. Senator William Proxmire, chairman of the Senate subcommittee on consumer credit, is pushing for a law giving people access to their own files. Retail Credit says if that happens the sources of information will "dry up," because no reference will be willing to provide information knowing that the person concerned can see it. The Fair Credit Reporting Act requires that companies report "the nature and substance" of data on individuals but not the identity of people who have provided it. Within three days after an investigation begins, the company ordering it must notify the individual. If that person is denied any benefit based on the report, he or she must be told. If the report is contested, Retail Credit must reinvestigate, and the individual may insert a statement explaining his or her side.

A similar problem is coming to a head with the law initiated by New York's Senator James Buckley, requiring individual files in educational institutions to be open to students within 45 days of any request to see such files. The problems revolve around the fact that most letters of recommendation in the files were collected under a guarantee of privacy, and now the student can see them without permission from the writer. This legislation has given rise to many questions of ethics and propriety that are still unanswered.

computerized salary information

Another computer area that smacks of "big brother" and machines taking charge of human destinies is that of salary administration (see Figure 12-17). With the growing size of companies, and the increasing number of managers at various levels, the chief executive can no longer hope to keep up with the various salary needs and entitlements of the company's employees. The move is toward administered salaries based on formulas, with an annual review and raise (if justified). The old cartoons about walking into the boss's office for a raise are becoming outdated. Indeed, it may be difficult in such a case to find anyone human to talk to.

computer "incompetence"

Other problems with computer information systems relate not to invasion of privacy, but to incompetence. A computer gives the impression of precision. Its numbers come spewing out so automatically and in such tidy rows that it takes an effort to remind ourselves that they were developed from the same old imperfect and error-prone numbers (or the lack of numbers) used in the old manual systems. A system that has been designed with imperfect logic will develop analyses that are in error, but with the logic buried somewhere in the programming library the users cannot see how the figures were dreamed up. Of course, a thorough understanding of the information system will counteract this problem—but that thorough understanding rarely exists.

When a computer reorders material that is running out of stock, what is to prevent it from taking an erroneous factor and ordering ten times too much, or a hundred times, or a thousand? A human inventory clerk would smell a rat, but computers have no sense of smell. Information systems need something akin to Mallinckrodt's "Holes Committee" to guard against the Big Lie, told by a computer with no sense of proportion that simply got its inputs crossed.

Figure 12-17.
A Computer May Be Deciding What You Get Paid

Summary

Data become information only when they provide needed facts. The manager is a response system with feedback, but noise interferes with the information flow. Information is characterized by entropy (disorder) and redundancy (backup).

The five components of a computer information system are input, storage, control, processing, and output. Computers are programmed in basic language, or in a formula translation language.

All of humanity requires information. In order for information to flow, there must be a common language, common perceptions, and common semantic understanding of meanings. Often, however, these conditions are not met, and the result is inaccurate or incomplete transmission of information.

Human beings seek to modify their actions to minimize pain or undesirable results. If an information system appears to be gathering data that will cause unpleasantness, humans try to circumvent the process. Systems must be designed with this tendency in mind.

Business needs information in many areas about its own performance; the public needs information about business; and the public needs information about public operations. The principal business information need relates to overall performance—i.e., accounting information. Although this is relatively straightforward, since businesses have been collecting such information for so many years, there are optional ways of allowing for depreciation and inventory use which can change profit margins substantially. General price level accounting seeks to level out the effects of inflation or deflation.

Individual performance of labor or management is sought in some forms of management information systems, but there are many measurement problems that make these assessments imperfect, unless there are precise job standards against which to compare. One management assessment system is a personal "time and motion" study conducted by the manager.

Status of work is an important contribution of a good MIS. When there are many jobs moving through a shop, it is almost impossible to know the status of each without a systematic reporting technique.

Some systems for handling orders are almost completely computerized, with orders being filled and customers billed entirely by computer. Often such systems do not actually save money, because of the tendency to obtain information regardless of its value. The concept of information value should be applied, to ensure that the information obtained will be worth what it costs.

Budgets contain information, but they are subject to misinterpretation if not completely clear. Project management systems seek to control both the expenditures against estimates and the progress against time. For a major project, a detailed information system is a must.

Public information on business performance is contained chiefly in annual reports. These are monitored by independent public accounting firms, and the Securities and Exchange Commission establishes strict rules for guidance on how such reports must be made out. Comparative figures on corporations are useful in determining coverage ratio, debt-equity ratio, and current ratio—all measures of financial strength. Recently public accounting firms have been held more responsible for complete and timely disclosure of the problems of corporations they audit.

Banks are particularly important financial institutions, and the present information systems on their health are deficient. A number of improvements are being placed in effect by bank regulating agencies.

Public enterprises require good management systems just as private businesses do. As an example, the patent office is urgently in need of an improved system, but to date none has been developed.

The federal government collects a vast quantity of statistics on all manner of subjects, and much of this collection is overlapping and redundant. The President recently appointed a Federal Statistics Commission, which studied the huge body of this data and recommended steps to simplify the government's approach.

Data processing systems select source data, record and classify data, sort and analyze data, summarize it into useful categories, and distribute it to users, as well as storing it for future use. A common data base offers opportunities for economies of use, provided different departments of a business or government can reconcile their different needs.

Computerized systems provide opportunities for economies of operation and various other advantages. Typical computer subsystems for information are budgetary, production, material, personnel, marketing, and economic. Some companies have developed management systems which are particularly effective, involving the selective and analytical use of information.

Automated information systems involving hierarchical minicomputers offer perhaps the greatest potential contribution of technology to management. Inexpensive computers can handle process control and at the same time collect management information and transmit it to larger computers.

Invasion of privacy problems arise with large information systems, and some of the credit investigation firms are themselves under attack for unwillingness to disclose their files completely to those they investigate. The trend is for more disclosure. In a related development, salaries are being established more and more on a systematic basis, using computers.

Appendix: Manufacturing Analogy

There are five components to a computer system (or an information system): *input, storage, control, processing,* and *output*. Let us see how these same functions exist in the manufacturing process, and for essentially the same purposes.

Refer to Figure A-1, top: "Manufacturing Process." This diagrams a process involving working on a small truck (perhaps a jeep), and then installing a radio system; then working on a trailer, and installing a generator in the trailer; then assembling the two and working on the pair to align radio and power supply; and finally sending them to shipping for delivery to the customer. These will be manufactured in quantity, and each truck and trailer will require somewhat different overhaul before the radio and generator are installed. The figure shows a "run-through" to see if the process will work. Shop Planning, carrying out its function of scheduling, routing, and dispatching (chapter 8, "Getting Things Done"), issues the following instructions:

1. Receive radio, send to parts warehouse, bay P1.
2. Receive generator, send to parts warehouse, bay P2.
3. Receive first truck, send to manufacturing shop.
4. Overhaul truck, install foundations for radio.
5. Ship radio from bay P1 to shop, mount on truck.
6. Ship completed truck with radio mounted to finished warehouse, bay F1.
7. Receive first trailer, send to manufacturing shop.
8. Overhaul trailer, install foundations for generator.
9. Continue work on trailer, install wiring and control system.
10. Ship generator from bay P2 to shop, mount on trailer.
11. Ship completed trailer with generator to finished warehouse, bay F2.
12. Ship truck/radio from bay F1 to manufacturing shop.
13. Ship trailer/generator from bay F2 to shop, connect to truck/radio.
14. Align and test truck/trailer unit, perform final inspection.
15. Ship completed truck/trailer unit to shipping bay.

Now refer to the bottom part, "Computer Process." The calculation carried on there is analogous to the above manufacturing process, to calculate $\sqrt{2x^2 + 4y^3}$ where 2 and 4 are the radio and generator, the square and cube operations are shop work on truck and trailer, "2 times x^2" and "4 times y^3" are installing radio and generator, "+" is connecting truck and trailer, and "square root" is aligning and testing the truck/trailer unit. "R" is the input unit, "M" the processing unit, "S" the output unit, and "F1, F2, P1, P2" the storage units. The instructions are handled in the control unit. The computer process is as follows:

Figure A-1.
Analogies Between Manufacturing and Computer Processes

CONTROL	INPUT	PROCESSING	OUTPUT	← STORAGE →		
MANUFACTURING PROCESS							

Shop Planning	Receiving Bay	Manufacturing Shop				Parts Warehouse Bay P1	Bay P2
1	Radio to P1					Radio	
2	Gen. to P2						Gen.
3	Truck to M	Truck		**Finished Goods Warehouse**			
4		(Truck)^W		Bay F1	Bay F2		
5	Radio to M	Rdo(Truck)^W					
6	R.T$_K$^{W} to F1			R.T$_K$^{W}			
7	Trailer to M	Trailer					
8		(Trailer)^W					
9		(Trailer)^W					
10	Gen. to M	Gen(Trlr)^W					
11	G.T$_L$^{W} to F2				G.T$_L$^{W}		
12	R.T$_K$^{W} to M	R.T$_K$^{W}	Shipping Bay				
13	G.T$_L$^{W} to M	R.T$_K$^{W}+G.T$_L$^{W}					
14		(R.T$_K$^{W}+G.T$_L$^{W})^W					
15			(R.T$_K$^{W}+G.T$_L$^{W})^W				

COMPUTER PROCESS

Instrs	R	M	S	F1	F2	P1	P2
2 → R → P1	2					2	
4 → R → P2	4						4
x → R → M	x	x					
R × M	x	x^2					
P1 → R × M	2	$2x^2$					
M → R → F1				$2x^2$			
Y → R → M	y	y					
R × M	y	y^2					
R × M	y	y^3					
P2 → R × M	4	$4y^3$					
M → R → F2					$4y^3$		
F1 → R → M	$2x^2$	$2x^2$					
F2 → R + M	$4y^3$	$2x^2+4y^3$					
M √		$\sqrt{2x^2+4y^3}$					
M → R → S			$\sqrt{2x^2+4y^3}$				

466
MANAGERS AT WORK

1. Enter 2 into input unit, and send it to storage register P1.[6]
2. Enter 4 into input unit, and send it to storage register P2. (Note: 2 and 4 are constants, to be used over and over again.)
3. Enter variable x into input unit, and send to processing register M.
4. Multiply the content of R (which is still x) by content of M, and leave the result in M.
5. Send content of P1 (which is 2) to M, multiply by content of M, and leave the result in M. (Note that it went first to R, displaced the x which was still there from step 3, and then went to M—but still remained in R also.)
6. Send result of above calculations ($2x^2$) to storage register F1.
7. Enter variable y into input unit, and send to processing register M.
8. Multiply the content of R (y) by content of M, and leave result in M.
9. Repeat step 8 (content of R is still y, so this is $y \times y^2 = y^3$).
10. Send content of P2 to M, multiply by content of M, leave result in M.
11. Send result of above calculations ($4y^3$) to storage register F2.
12. Send content of F1 to M, via R.
13. Send content of F2 to R, add to content of M, leave result in M.
14. Take square root of content of M, leave result in M.
15. Send final desired result from M to storage register S (output).

The above sequence corresponds to a basic computer process, and is very close in procedure to what happens when a programmer writes a program in some "basic" language (or "compiler" or "assembler" language). While this language can be very efficient in its use of computer time and storage space, it usually is quite wasteful of the programmer's time, since every little step must be spelled out. Consequently, there are many "formula translation" languages which write these basic operations out, and allow the programmer to call a whole set of such basic sequences, or "modules," with a single instruction. Such a language is FORTRAN, in its various forms. When a computer programmer learns a language such as FORTRAN, he is not strictly programming the computer itself, but is writing simplified instructions that can be translated automatically by any computer which "speaks FORTRAN," so that it knows what he means and rewrites his program into the necessary basic steps and then executes what it has written. If a management information system is to be used repeatedly and it is desired to accomplish the process using as little computer time as possible, usually it is preferable to write the program in the most economical form, which would be a basic language such as the example above.

Notes

1. A few years ago a computer manufacturer designed a computer with an open back, and invited spectators to start cutting wires while it was operating. Many wires could be cut without interfering with accurate output, because the computer had redundant circuits which provided alternate paths, combined with a system of checking the integrity of a path before it was used—and not using it if this check disclosed that wrong answers would result.

2. Henry G. and Mable T. Wallich, "Profits Aren't as Good as They Look," *Fortune,* March 1974, pp. 126–129.

3. Ibid.

4. Quoted in "Are the Banks Overextended," *Business Week,* September 21, 1974, pp. 52–56.

5. Ibid.

6. When a computer instruction calls for taking a number from one register to another, it actually goes to the first register, *reads* what is there without disturbing it, then goes to the second register and copies it there, displacing whatever is in the second register. The number formerly in the second register has no place else to go, so it is erased from memory.

Review Questions

1. What are the elements in the "manager response system"?
2. What is entropy? What is redundancy?
3. Why can the same information transmission convey different meanings to different people?
4. What does the principle of "easing the pain" mean in information systems?
5. Why do FIFO and LIFO give different net profit results? Which produces the lower net profit figure?
6. Why is job shop scheduling so complex?
7. What is the meaning of the "value of information" concept?
8. Why are budgets sometimes misunderstood?
9. Explain the three control devices for project management. How are they related?
10. What do income statements and balance sheets show? What do they omit?
11. What is "coverage ratio" and why is it important?
12. What is an "early warning system" for banks? What would it show?
13. What does the data processing system do?
14. What do we mean by a "common data base"? Why is it desirable?
15. What are some typical subsystems for computer information systems?
16. What is a hierarchical minicomputer?
17. Discuss the problem of privacy for reference sources versus the individual's need to know what is in his or her credit file.

Discussion Questions

1. Try using the approach of Figure A-1, bottom ("Computer Process") to write a program (add as many "F" registers as you need) to solve the following formula:
$$\frac{-b + (b^2 - 4ac)^{1/2}}{2a}$$

2. What would be some ways to make data systems proof against this tendency?

3. Can you think of any better way to measure planning performance than against uncertain and unreliable costs of actually completing the job that was being estimated?

4. Can you think of a personal example in your experience involving the value of information?

5. Does the Tiger International Balance Sheet show any other interesting data besides those mentioned above (revenues, fuel and interest costs, and net income)?

6. Imagine that you hire a number of newsboys or newsgirls, and run a business with them as subcontractors, paying them a fixed wage per hour. How might you carry out each of the above elements (selection, recording, classifying, comparing, and summarizing), even though you use a manual system?

7. What did chairman Harold E. Thayer of Mallinckrodt mean when he said that a principal challenge was to "avoid being surprised"?

North Star Case Study

If North Star had merged with Barnhard & Walker, it would now be a subsidiary of that corporation. Suppose it were to open an office in a Latin American country, and you were the manager of that branch. One day you get a letter from B&W outlining the requirements of a new management information system being placed in operation. One of the requirements is for you to report weekly the amount of time you, as manager, spend on marketing, administration, technical work, personnel guidance, and other areas. Another requirement is to show each week the number of jobs that are ahead of schedule, on schedule, and behind schedule. A third requirement is to show each week any jobs that have finished, stating whether they came in over budget, on budget, or under budget. And a fourth requirement is to show on a cumulative basis for the year to date what was budgeted in terms of sales and what is being achieved in terms of sales. The letter states that these requirements are being put in effect on a trial basis, and that comments as to changes in the system are being solicited. The corporate comptroller will visit the branch office sometime within the next two months, and will hear recommendations and comments then.

You have a strong feeling that this system is more appropriate for a manufacturing operation (which most B&W subsidiaries are) than for an engineering design firm, but you do not wish to appear obstructionist.

1. What do you think is the basic purpose of the information system for B&W?
2. Do you think there are any "hidden purposes"?
3. What do you think they are trying to get at with the first requirement (a detailed report on your time)?
4. You have been in the habit of working "tropical hours" (7:00 AM to 1:00 PM), along with the rest of the community. This will show up as only 6 hours a day, however. What will you do about this?
5. You don't really have any "schedule" for jobs you are doing, so it will be hard to report the status relative to a schedule. What will you do about this?
6. You did not make up a sales budget when you opened the branch. As a matter of fact, though, sales have far exceeded your expectations, and those of the North Star home office. How will you deal with the requirement to report sales against the budget?
7. What are you going to suggest about changes in the MIS procedure? And what does the MIS procedure suggest to you in terms of changing any of your practices?
8. Do you think the procedure outlined on page 457 is applicable here? Why or why not?

Suggestions for Further Reading

Benjamin, R. I. *Control of the Information System Development Cycle.* New York: Wiley-Interscience, 1971.

Bower, J. B., ed. *Financial Information Systems.* Boston: Houghton Mifflin Co., 1968.

Canning, R. G., and R. L. Sisson. *The Management of Data Processing.* New York: John Wiley & Sons, Inc., 1967.

Dierdon, J.; F. W. McFarlan; and W. M. Zani. *Managing Computer-Based Information Systems.* Homewood, Ill.: Richard D. Irwin, Inc., 1971.

Fertig, P. E. *Using Accounting Information: An Introduction.* New York: Harcourt Brace Jovanovich, Inc., 1971.

Hartman, W., et al. *Management Information Systems Handbook.* New York: McGraw-Hill Book Co., 1972.

Hodge, B. *Management and the Computer in Information and Control Systems.* New York: McGraw-Hill Book Co., 1969.

Kanter, J. *Management-Oriented Management Information Systems.* Englewood Cliffs, N.J.: Prentice-Hall, Inc., 1972.

Mesthene, E. G. *Technological Change: Its Impact on Manual Society.* Cambridge, Mass.: Harvard University Press, 1970.

Morton, M. S. *Management Decision Systems: Computer-Based Support for Decision Making.* Boston: Harvard University Graduate School of Business Administration, 1971.

Westin, A. F., ed. *Information Technology in a Democracy.* Cambridge, Mass.: Harvard University Press, 1971.

PART FOUR

Management and Its Environment

Facing the Market 13

North Star Prologue

After North Star, which grew from a two-person engineering consulting firm to a successful small firm with four partners, was offered the chance to merge with a multinational corporation and turned it down, it set one area after another in its internal affairs to rights: setting up a formal system for controlling its operations, establishing effective personnel practices, and designing a financial control system. The occasion of performing a contract to establish a municipal management information system made the partners realize that they had no effective in-house information system, and they established one. With this done, they had fulfilled most of the requisites for management of a successful organization.

One day when Henry was calling on the Blackridge city manager, to deliver final plans for a modification of the municipal incinerator, the latter told him of an opportunity facing the city and asked if North Star was the right company to help. A large trucking terminal located in Blackridge was shifting its facilities further from the city, and approximately 30 acres of land were becoming available. Since Blackridge was shifting from a manufacturing and industrial center to more of a suburb for the large university city which it bordered, he thought it might be inappropriate to try to attract a replacement industry. Instead, he was playing with the idea that Blackridge might acquire the land itself and develop a combination shopping center and civic center on the site. Undoubtedly there would be a tremendous uproar from the present merchants, who were mainly congregated in rather outdated shops in a strip development along Blackridge's main thoroughfare, but if proper opportunity were given the existing stores to have first choice at the new site this problem could be resolved. The lack of modern shopping facilities in Blackridge was causing the residents to take most of their shopping outside the city to nearby centers, and Blackridge was losing a large share of sales tax revenue as a result. Perhaps the city offices and the public library, now in deteriorating quarters and in a location that shifting residential patterns made inconvenient for public use, might be put there as well.

Henry said this matter required exactly the sort of market analysis North Star had done many times for discount department stores, lumber companies, and other retail establishments, and that he would bring Jo over to discuss the project. He pointed out that there was no difference in essence between a market analysis for a retail business such as a department or hardware store and a public "retail business" such as a free library. Both have a market area from which they attempt to draw in competition with other attractive institutions, and both serve retail customers whose consumption habits are a matter of statistical record. He stated that North Star would be able to forecast the volume of use such a center would get to an accuracy of plus or minus ten percent.

Jo undertook the project with enthusiasm because, although she agreed with Henry as to the universality of market survey concepts for both private and public sectors, in actual fact she had never attempted a market survey for a public service facility such as a library and would have to learn how as she went along. For retail establishments such as supermarkets or discount and specialty stores the approach was rather cut and dried; the area around each such potential site was divided into segments, and every household in such a segment was analyzed to determine its income and where it now bought those items the new store would offer. There was little question about Family A, with X members, buying a virtually known amount of groceries or clothing; the only problem was to decide which of several competing retail centers would get its business, and the approach was quite straightforward. But in the changing cultural environment of the day, it was not at all clear that people deprived of library books in one location would hunt for a library elsewhere; perhaps they would substitute more television, or paperbacks at the drug store, or more outdoor sports, or any of many other forms of leisure activity. If the Blackridge population, which had been moving to its new developments in recent years, had found the present library inconveniently located, perhaps it had permanently discarded the library habit.

Jo undertook a three-pronged approach. The first was a door-to-door survey. When an interviewer asked the householders where they bought their last purchase of $5 or more, and their last nonfood purchase of $30 or more (to develop the present buying distribution for retail products), the next question was how many times a week they would come to a library in the center, and what they would give up to find time for more reading. The second was an analysis of national library use trends, obtained from material that the university librarian found for Jo. The third was a study of three areas similar to Blackridge, where new library branches had been installed in recent years, to determine what trend back to library use developed there. From these sets of overlapping intelligence, Jo was able to forecast that a library was perhaps the most desired public recreation facility of all for the Blackridge population.

The completed survey made a very strong case for Blackridge Center, and the forecast of substantially increased tax revenues was one the city council could not resist. The library was not a moneymaker, of course, but the shopping center revenues would carry it and still give the city a handsome surplus. The city made the decision to go ahead, and Jo turned Henry and Zeb loose on the job of trying to get the contract to design it. But Zeb had other fish to fry as well. He had watched with intense interest as Jo ran her market survey for the center, and when the project was completed he asked Jo if there wasn't a lesson here for North Star. Jo asked what he meant, and Zeb said it seemed to him that North Star needed a dose of the same sort of market research: an analysis of what firms there were in the area that did the same sort of engineering work North Star did, combined with an analysis of what the market demand was. In that way it ought to be possible for North Star to see what facilities it should add for which there was a latent demand (like the free library in Blackridge Center), and to see which of its capabilities were surplus or in relatively little demand.

Jo liked the idea, and they budgeted a study for themselves for the next quarter. It showed some expected things and some unexpected things. One of the unexpected things was the fact that fully 75 of the 110 municipalities in the region were completely locked in with the same engineering consulting firm—one which Bert and Henry agreed was far behind the times both in municipal practices and engineering talent. Another unexpected thing was that 90% of the companies doing market studies skipped the local talent completely and turned to absentee companies in New York—which meant that market segment was woefully undeveloped. And a third unexpected discovery was that the major corporations based in the city were constantly running sizable projects for themselves or clients—but none had ever heard of North Star's work in conjunction with Barnhard & Walker, or had any idea that North Star had such capabilities.

As Zeb pondered the survey findings, and began to lay plans for plugging the gaping marketing gaps it had shown, he smiled a wry smile to himself at his gall in calling himself a marketing director, just because he had some elementary skills at closing a job when it was practically ready for the plucking. What a heck of a lot he had to learn about marketing. But he was learning.

What North Star Can Learn from Chapter 13

1. Why the cost of providing a service is not nearly as important in selling as how badly the customer wants the service
2. The different ways of organizing the marketing effort, and the advantages of each
3. The impact of locational factors (including library location)
4. The availability of marketing data from various sources (including the Census Bureau)
5. The life cycle of a product or service, and what is necessary to accomplish a "repair job" and revitalize it
6. The uses of market research
7. The meaning of a "total cost envelope" in developing new products or services
8. The application of product differentiation and market segmentation to a business
9. Some of the governmental regulation areas as they apply to business

Thus far in the book we have discussed the basic building blocks of organizations, the primary management processes, and the fundamental tasks of management *within* the organization. With this chapter we start to look at those management tasks that deal principally with the *external* environment. A key external element—in most business organizations, probably *the* key element in terms of profitability and survival—is marketing. The old fable that a man who builds a better mousetrap will find the world beating a path to his door is a gross distortion of reality—unless he has an effective marketing program that makes sure it is the kind of mousetrap the public wants at the right price, that sees it distributed properly to where the consumers are, and that tells the public all about it when buying decisions are being made.

This chapter will look at the market from the following perspectives:

1. *Organizing the marketing function* to answer the key questions of what and how much to make, how to distribute, and how to price and promote.
2. *Determining public needs,* which includes market research and other methods for analyzing market behavior.
3. *Dealing with public needs:* demand analysis, product strategy, distribution strategy, promotional strategy and pricing strategy, as well as market planning.
4. *Today's consumer,* which deals both with current marketing trends and with the "new consumerism."

Marketing is considered by some to be a sign of social waste. In the ideal society, people would produce only what was wanted, and there would be no need to "persuade" consumers to accept the products. Advertising would be limited to the bare transmission of product information, selling to the simple taking of orders, and distribution to the direct transfer from maker to consumer. In the simplest commune society, where everyone is in direct contact with everyone else, the "bridge" function of marketing is not necessary. But in any sort of complex society marked by division of labor, it is most unrealistic to assume that the right goods will be produced and properly distributed without any attention to the function that makes this happen. This chapter discusses the dimensions of this function.

Organizing the Marketing Function

The notion of "marketing" as persuading the consumer to buy *your* products is out of date. It has been replaced, in most successful companies (and government bodies, though to a lesser degree) with the realization that you must redesign your products to meet the *consumer's* needs. True marketing starts and ends with the consumer. Demand analysis studies the extent and diversity of consumer wants, and observes buying behavior so that the company's program may be consistent with that behavior. Product development then generates products which meet the observed demand. Distribution systems put the right products in the right place at the right

marketing and the consumer

time. Pricing policy endeavors to match what consumers will pay with what the item costs to produce. Inventory policy attempts to determine the duration of demand and to have enough products on the shelves to meet it. And advertising seeks to inform the consumers of product characteristics and availability. Even after the sale, marketing continues, with warranties or service agreements, replacement parts, and product recall if needed.

There is much more to an organization than marketing, of course—but marketing runs through the entire organization. Even credit policy is a marketing as well as a financial element; some products, such as large appliances, automobiles, and houses, would scarcely sell at all unless the consumer's need for credit were met. Product design is an engineering element, but marketing plays a strong role in seeing that the design is what the consumers want and need.

Marketing and the Organization

When a new entrepreneur takes the brave plunge and goes into business, he or she learns something that may have been only a suspicion—that the whole enterprise revolves around marketing. This comes as a shock, because people don't start businesses in order to market. They start because they have a novel product, or a special skill, or a particular location, or some persuasive advantage that tells them their chances of success are high. In the case of North Star, the two original founders had training in civil and environmental engineering which they thought added up to a worthwhile professional package, and they decided to team up. It is highly unlikely that they saw themselves pounding the pavement

Marketing is sometimes considered a social waste.

to acquaint prospective customers with their capabilities: rather, they envisioned themselves as working industriously on interesting projects that somehow had floated in over the transom. Once started, however, the operators of an enterprise learn that a major share of their efforts must go to facing the market, so that they will have work to perform.

Robert J. Keith has described the metamorphosis of the Pillsbury Baking Company's viewpoint from making to marketing, and how thoroughly it is ingrained in the latter today.[1] Its initial point of view, born with its founding in 1869 and continuing more or less into the 1930s, was toward *production:* the very idea for Pillsbury's formation came from the availability of high quality wheat and the proximity of water power, rather than from any availability of market areas or any demand for better flours. In the 1930s, its viewpoint shifted toward *sales:* the need for an organization that could dispose of all the products it could make. In the 1950s, the swift growth of consumer business tied to baking mixes made Pillsbury realize that it needed a way to select the best new products from the hundreds it could be producing—and the company's viewpoint shifted toward *marketing* at last. The goal was not to mill flour, nor to make a wide variety of baking products, but to satisfy the present and potential needs and desires of its customers.

But this wasn't the final shift. Today Pillsbury has shifted from a company with a marketing concept to a *marketing company.* Marketing sets operating policy now, and is influencing long-range policy more and more. Procurement, production, research, inventory control, capital investment, and profit planning all dance to marketing's tune. As consumer tastes shift, the company shifts with them. Marketing is becoming the basic motivating force of the entire corporation, as almost every activity of the corporation is aimed at satisfying the needs and wishes of the consumer.

> a marketing company
>
> What would North Star have to do to become a "marketing company"? Would it be a worthwhile effort?

The Marketing Concept

Thirty years ago two young men built the first prototype models of a patented baby carrier which since has become nationally known as the "Infanseat." They carefully calculated their costs, and went with the sample to see a wholesaler familiar with such items. He examined it, listened to their description of its merits, and said, "That's a $5.95 item." When they attempted to tell him its production cost, he said, "That's got nothing to do with it. This will sell for $5.95, and by the time you cover distribution costs, wholesaler profit, and retail markup, you will have to make it cheaply enough to sell it to the wholesaler at $2.00. If you can't meet that price, forget it."

This lesson is a difficult one for many to learn, because the logic seems to move backwards. One would think that a price should be set by determining the item's cost to produce, adding a reasonable profit, and taking care of distribution costs. This may be a reasonable approach for selling a few items, because some consumers will buy an item at almost any price (witness the sale of such luxury items as elephant-foot ashtrays or gold toothpicks), but for volume sales the price depends entirely on whether enough consumers would rather have your item than all the other things available for sale at the same price. If you can't produce profitably at that price, the item is not salable.

Henry Ford understood this point very well. In his early days, the motor car was a costly curiosity purchased by the affluent few. It was he who brought it to the public, by recognizing that the consumer sets the price. He showed how well he grasped this much-overlooked principle in his autobiography:

<small>Henry Ford and price policy</small>

> Our policy is to reduce the price, extend the operations, and improve the article. You will notice that the reduction of price comes first. We have never considered any costs as fixed. Therefore we first reduce the price to the point where we believe more sales will result. Then we go ahead and try to make the prices. We do not bother about the costs. The new price will force the costs down. The more usual way is to take the costs and then determine the price, and although that may be scientific in the narrow sense, it is not scientific in the broad sense, because what earthly use is it to know the cost if it tells you that you cannot manufacture at a price at which the article can be sold? But more to the point is the fact that, although one may calculate what a cost is, and of course all of our costs are carefully calculated, no one knows what a cost ought to be. One of the ways of discovering [this] is to name a price so low as to force everybody in the place to the highest point of efficiency. The low price makes everybody dig for profits. We make more discoveries concerning manufacturing and selling under this forced method than by any method of leisurely investigation.[2]

Ford became famous for mass production, turning out over 15 million of his famous "Model T's," but the mass production was a *result* of searching for a way to meet the selling price he knew would build volume. His first cars were priced around $2500, which was within the reach of few prospective motorists. When the first Model T was announced, in October 1908, its price was knocked down to $850, and subsequent reductions brought the price as low as $240. Even Ford's revolutionary setting of a magnanimous $5 daily wage was a marketing step—a move to insure loyal and hence experienced workers who could help him attain a true "market price."

<small>product-oriented vs customer-oriented</small>

There is more than price to the true marketing concept. Theodore Levitt has said that railroads are in trouble because they are product-oriented and not customer-oriented. While the need for passenger and freight transportation grew, the railroads let others take business from them because they saw themselves as being in the *railroad* business instead of the *transportation* business. Similarly, Hollywood was virtually strangled by television because it saw itself as being in the *movie* business rather than the *entertainment* business. In recent years Detroit became so preoccupied with big cars and the annual model change that it permitted foreign manufacturers who read consumer desires more accurately to grab off a large slice of the small car market. Even today Detroit sees itself more as a manufacturing than a marketing organization, paying little or no attention to the customer after or even during the sale. Arthur E. Sindlinger, long-time consultant on automobile consumer sentiment, in discussing the 1974 automotive slump, says the auto makers "totally misjudged the market. They overproduced and overpriced." He added that "the U.S. auto makers think they manufacture and sell cars. I say they manufacture cars and take orders for them." In fact, a new theme was heard in Detroit when the slump began to take hold: "It's time to get back to selling basics, and sell our way out of this."[3]

Some marketing professionals think a company that emphasizes product research and technological improvement, as important as that is for progress, may run the danger of thinking that a wonderful new product will sell itself. The new Polaroid SX-70 instant camera, introduced late in 1973, embodies the most advanced design ever conceived for a camera of its type—it automatically produces a finished color photo when the user presses the shutter—but its sales during the initial year were so unspectacular that Polaroid's stock dropped from 143 to 20. Basically oriented to research, Polaroid faces a serious marketing challenge. As the company's I. M. Booth stated, "What we need now is volume; we have all that capacity staring us in the face."

Marketing Goals

It is almost axiomatic that the primary goal of a business is to make a profit. Since this can be taken for granted, it is not much help in giving direction to the organization. Neither are statements such as "utilize efficiently all human, financial, physical and natural resources," or "provide quality products and services within the competitive limits of each product line," or "strengthen and expand marketing capabilities in company divisions to enable each business to become fully competitive"; these too are policies that any management would expect to embrace almost automatically.[4] These statements, from a Potlatch Corporation publication, could be made by virtually any corporation in any line of business. However, President Richard B. Madden's statement from the 1973 Potlatch Annual Report that "we are tree farmers and wood converters" reveals a great deal about the corporation's direction and purpose.

It is interesting to see how Potlatch has followed the market into new product areas. Founded in 1903 as a logging company, it moved into sawmill operations in 1906, built a railroad in 1908, and started its first retail yard in 1916. It moved into sawdust byproducts in 1930, into veneers in 1949, pulp and paperboard in 1950, plywood in 1952, and napkins and fruit and food wraps the same year. In the late 1950s it started producing laminated decking, in 1957 milk cartons, in 1958 paper plates and meat trays, in 1959 folding cartons, and in 1962 tissue products. In 1963 it entered the corrugated container field, in 1964 started a broad line of quality printing papers, and in 1965 expanded into a broad line of dimension lumber and siding. In 1965 it built a hardwood mill, in 1966 it acquired a setup box firm, and in 1971 expanded into Western Samoa. That same year it replaced its log drive with a truck and rail system on the Clearwater River. During the past decade Potlatch made some 24 acquisitions. Its future lies with improved utilization of its fiber resources—a long road from a logging operation in Potlatch, Idaho.

Marketing goals appear relatively unambiguous. Surely they would be attained by meeting customer needs and desires through maximum sales of the company's products at a satisfactory profit. But these goals are not as clear-cut as they appear. For one thing, there is the tradeoff between profits now and profits later: continuing an aging product line may help sales today but cripple them tomorrow when a new product should be ready to meet the competition. Second, profit is not everything: it may conflict with environmental requirements or create public resentment

goals of marketing organization

which can store up future trouble that outweighs the profit.[5] Profits may be "satisfactory" now, but perhaps they could be a great deal better with a changed product line or even a radically different business direction. Maybe the attainment of profits and sales requires an inordinate amount of capital investment, which (even though it is properly depreciated and charged as expense) requires the company to incur a larger debt than is prudent. Maybe the present products are so pedestrian that they are causing promising young managers to desert the company, which bodes ill for the future. Perhaps the present customers, though well pleased, represent a vanishing class of consumers, and thus the market eventually will dry up.

How do North Star's "marketing goals" compare with its overall goals? Should this be so?

In many respects, marketing goals are synonymous with overall goals, if they are properly conceived. Since the overriding focus of the company must be on its customers, anything that focuses on the profitable enhancement of customer relationships, with a proper balance of short- and long-term factors, is a marketing as well as an overall goal.

Marketing Strategy

As in all business strategy, marketing tactics are influenced by internal variables within the control of the marketing executive (or other executives in the firm) and by external variables beyond the firm's control. The marketing performance of the company depends on three sets of factors, as shown in Figure 13-1:

1. The company's basic performance, reflecting the nature of the business and the company's inherent strengths (in meat packing, for example, the business is old-line and mature, and margins are not large for any packer; but Oscar Mayer typically emphasizes the packaged segment and thus usually outperforms Armour and Swift in profit margin).
2. The controllable corporate strategy, consisting of the conscious actions taken by management to enhance performance.
3. Uncontrollable external factors, such as the state of the economy or performance of competitors, which affect market strength.

Figure 13-1.
Factors that Determine Market Performance

| BASIC STRENGTHS | + | INTERNAL STRATEGY | + | EXTERNAL VARIABLES | = | MARKET PERFORMANCE |

Some internal strategy elements are directly under the control of the marketing department, such as amount and type of advertising, use of other promotions, pricing structure, credit policy, and distribution patterns. Others are controlled by the firm but not usually by the marketing executive, such as amount and direction of new product research, product design and quality, production schedules, capital investment, corporate acquisitions to round out product line, and profit planning.

External variable elements include those imposed by a capricious fate, such as the economic climate, strikes, wars, and other disasters; those mandated by government, such as laws on price discrimination, packaging and marking standards, regulatory requirements, "truth-in-advertising," "exclusive dealing" compacts, safety and recall laws, and so forth; and those related to the consumer and the competition, such as buying patterns and the offerings of other manufacturers. While these are not under the market executive's control (except competitive actions to a limited degree, in the context of competitive "gaming"), he or she can to some extent forecast their effect and hence determine the internal strategy required to counter any unfavorable effects.

The internal strategy variables which add up to marketing strategy are:

1. product characteristics;
2. price structure;
3. distribution channels;
4. promotional plan; and
5. customer services.

elements of market strategy

Product Characteristics

Although products are designed in engineering, based on input from research, and are built by production to construction specifications that may depart from the original engineering performance specifications, they must be considered controllable. In a responsive company, marketing input concerning product characteristics (design, quality, durability, safety) is a vital necessity. In the early part of this chapter, when we discussed the current philosophy of the Pillsbury company, the idea of a marketing company came through clearly—the consumer is at the center, and what consumers want is what the firm must produce.

product characteristics

Perhaps the product should be changed in minor ways: if most battery-driven devices require two cells, a packaging change from three to two for replacement batteries is a significant marketing improvement; if the product will be carried outside of its case, a hand-strap will significantly increase its convenience; if kitchen shelves are spaced at intervals of 11 inches or less, reducing the height of a grocery product from 11½ to 11 inches can improve its acceptance tremendously. Perhaps the changes are significant: changing the case to stainless steel to prevent corrosion; increasing the power to prevent overheating in usual service; or providing replaceable components to permit repairs. In any case, the production manager has no way to determine whether consumers will accept the product; the marketing manager must obtain customer feedback and change the product to keep it competitive.

Price Structure

Price structure involves more than price—it means insuring that there is a full line of goods to match the financial capabilities of the entire market. Alfred P. Sloan understood this well when he provided General Motors with a variety of automobiles that completely covered the price spectrum (including the decision that the lowest end of the range would be taken care of by used cars and thus would provide a way for new car buyers to dispose of their present vehicles). Detroit manufacturers often seem in danger of forgetting this requirement today, since for years they vacated

price structure

the lower end of the scale and permitted small foreign cars to have the "mini" market to themselves.[6]

Within a given model line, price is very important because of the effect it has on volume. Figures 13-2, 3, and 4 show a determination of optimal price strategy for a particular product. Figure 13-2 shows the increase in *unit profit* for an item which costs $12 when the selling price is raised through increments from $12 to $17. Figure 13-3 shows (based on a market survey, past experience, or judgment) how *volume* of sales decreases as the price is raised, solely from the price effect. Figure 13-4 combines these two sets of data to show the effect on *total profit* of changing the price. When the price is $14, unit profit from 13-2 is $2, volume from 13-3 is 32, so total profit in 13-4 is 32 x $2 or $64 (the optimum). At a higher or lower price, total profit will be less than at a price of $14.

total profit analysis

This analysis is quite simplified, of course. It makes no allowance for the actions of competitors, who may move to lower their prices and perhaps capture some business from you, or for new businesses attracted by the volume. But in general it is a valid representation of the relationship between price and volume, and hence of total profits, because of the increase in demand following reduction in price, all else being equal.

Distribution Channels

When the two would-be entrepreneurs built the first infanseat 30 years ago, they had little choice of distribution methods. Since their price was too high to be feasible under low production-rate methods, they had to bring it down by higher volume production, and thus needed a rather large volume of sales. This meant they would have to affiliate with a wholesaler who already had a sizable distribution setup and was willing to handle the new item.[7] A larger company with some financial resources has

Figure 13-2.
Increase in Unit Profit

Figure 13-3.
Decrease in Sales Volume

Figure 13-4.
Effect of Price Change on Total Profit

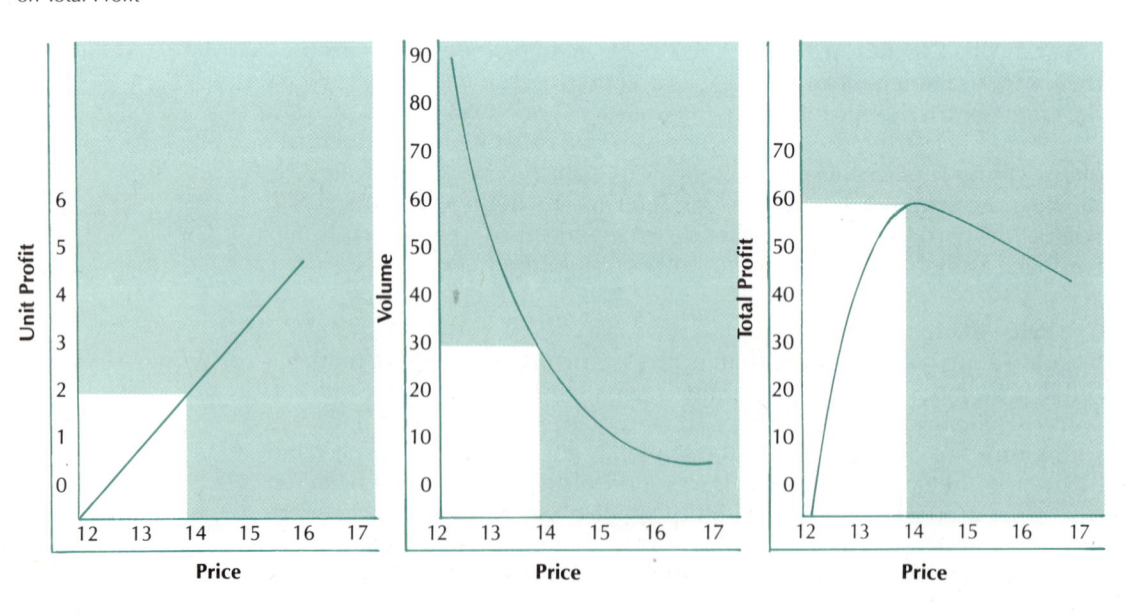

484
MANAGEMENT AND ITS ENVIRONMENT

more of a choice. It can elect to use regular distribution channels through wholesalers or manufacturers' representatives, or can establish its own sales force and sell direct to stores (or even, as in the case of Avon Products, direct to consumers through part-time "community salespeople"—a business which has been built into a billion-dollar annual volume).

If a company uses middlemen, it gives up a certain measure of control, because the middleman carries many products and will not push the company's products more than those of competitors. It also gives up access to information, because the middleman is the one who makes customer contacts and learns the feedback facts that can be acquired only on the "firing line." If there are faults with the product that decrease acceptance, the company must find this out at second hand through the middleman. On the other hand, it does not need to set up an expensive sales and distribution network to sell just its own line of products, but can take advantage of an existing network used by the middleman, who reduces costs by carrying many products.

With middlemen, a company can be very slow to learn that demand for its product has turned down; sales may be zero at retail levels, but its last sale at wholesale was some time ago, and it is still producing at its regular rate for a market that is not there any longer. With its own salespeople, this will show up much more quickly. With middlemen, the products go only to the outlets that they service, which may not be exactly right for the company's line.

What is North Star's distribution system? Has it ever received any help in getting work?

Traditionally, in the U.S. marketing sphere, firms have moved toward operating their own outlets and doing their own distribution as they built financial strength. As John Y. Brown, who took Kentucky Fried Chicken to national prominence, puts it: "Ideally, you'd like to have all your outlets company-owned. That's where the money is. But franchising is the only way to build a nationwide base quickly." In a more recent trend, manufacturers of basic components have begun to make the consumer products fed by the components. In pocket calculators, Bowmar Instrument Corporation (the "Bowmar Brain") started the industry, but bought its semiconductors from manufacturers. Since semiconductors amount to 70% of the manufacturing cost, this was a clear invitation for manufacturers to go the whole way. Texas Instruments, which manufactures semiconductors, now is the leading pocket calculator maker, and giant Rockwell International came into the market in a big way in 1974; Bowmar tried to go into semiconductors itself in order to compete, but it was too late.

The same trend is taking place in international marketing, as multinational companies broaden their foreign business. GAF Corporation shifted from foreign distribution channels to doing its own distribution in Germany, and its German chemical-product sales went up more than tenfold. Some 80% of this increase came from more business (GAF promoted harder than its distributor), while the balance came from distributor profits formerly handed away. General Foods Corporation is moving to centralize its overseas operation, particularly in product and market research.

The *horizontal structure* of distribution reflects the number of salespeople or wholesalers at each level. For a major distributing firm such as

horizontal structure of distribution

H. J. Heinz, which sells canned and bottled goods nationwide, the problem is one of minimizing costs. The more warehouses it has, the higher the warehouse costs but the lower the shipping costs. Figure 13-5 shows the trade-off in these costs (with only one warehouse, for example, shipments would travel long distances, but warehouse costs would be at a minimum). There is some number of warehouses at which total cost reaches a minimum and distribution expenses of a physical nature are optimum, as shown.

Promotional Plan

promotional plan

One of the most difficult tasks in marketing is to determine just what payoff is achieved through advertising and other promotions. Direct selling can be analyzed more precisely, because the sales of a particular individual can be compared with the direct and indirect costs incurred by that salesperson, and some relationship can be adduced. (Even then, indeterminate factors enter in: did the seller have a goldplated territory where any fool could makes sales, or the assistance of a recent advertising campaign, or has the competition recently become more or less intense in the area?) But advertising is so confounded with other factors that contribute to sales volume, and is so uncertain as to the relative time of its impact, that many market researchers virtually throw up their hands and try to settle for secondary effectiveness measures, such as recognition level after an ad campaign as shown by sample surveys.

Furthermore, there are so many forms of advertising: newspapers, radio, TV, billboards, magazines, direct mail, ad cards in buses and trolleys, displays in stores, etc. And each of these can be used in so many different forms: coupled with sales, associated with premiums or giveaways, spot or continuing, separately or in conjunction with a complementary product, concentrated or widespread over many media choices, and so on. Some advertising is institutional in nature, and doesn't even mention any of the perhaps hundreds of products the company sells. Some is for items so costly that no one ad or series of ads could be expected to do the selling job all alone, but must be coupled with extensive high-level executive selling. Some is designed not to sell a product directly, but merely to remove some undesired reputation or point out how the company is complying with regulatory mandates or persuade the public to favor some legislation important to the company. Some seems to be little more at times than a monument to executive ego.

Nonetheless, the marketing director must do as much research as possible to decide where promotional funds can be spent to best effect, and whether the promotional budget should be raised or lowered.

Customer Services

customer services

The sale does not end when the customer pays and walks out. Sears Roebuck has built a huge business on the slogan "Satisfaction Guaranteed or Your Money Cheerfully Refunded," first instituted in a day when most merchants thought such a ridiculous policy signified softness in the head. The snake-oil peddler who makes a quick sweep of the community and then leaves town need not worry about repeat orders, but most businesses have somewhat more permanence than this, and customer satisfaction is important to them. If the customer is convinced that redress can be obtained without a lot of argument if something goes wrong, at least this

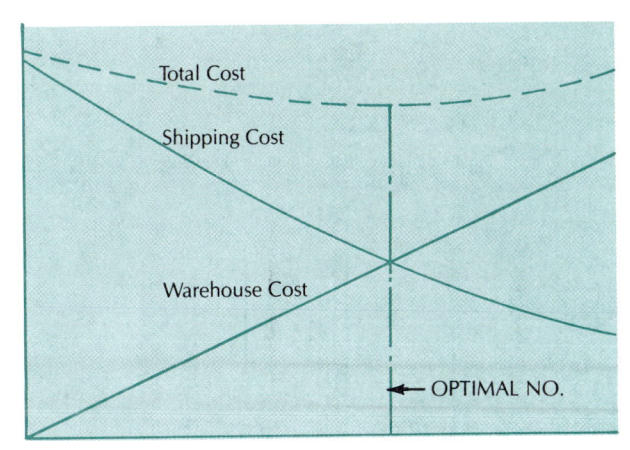

Figure 13-5.
Breakeven Analysis of Distribution Costs

obstacle to the sale is removed. The old motto "caveat emptor" ("let the buyer beware") is going out of style among businesses of any substance, but companies go to many different lengths in adopting a policy of cheerful customer attention.

Another Sears motto that inspires confidence is the one painted on every Sears truck: "We service what we sell." The advantages of this approach are obvious, but not all companies are in a position to deliver on such a promise. When Japanese consumer products first hit this country in volume, it was essential for the U.S. distributors to establish convenient and dependable service facilities. By and large, the products that had good service networks were the ones that survived.

Organizational Conflicts

Unfortunately, the very necessity for the marketing manager to exercise some control over many parts of the organization brings about almost inevitable conflict. The reason for this is the difference between individual departmental aims and overall company aims. The customer is king to the marketing department, but to departments more internalized within the company the customer is a terrible nuisance. The fact that customers are essential to the company—the very reason for its being—doesn't change this.[8] Customer demands upset the orderly tenor of their ways, impose changes on plans, necessitate constant review of operations, and so on.

Production wants products that are easy to make, standardized for production economy, planned long in advance, and set up for long production runs (which means few changes). Engineering wants functional designs, with no items added for style that will increase complexity, utilizing standard parts and with ample strength and durability (which sometimes operate contrary to dramatic design features that make a product desirable to consumers); moreover, it wants plenty of time to make designs, and with no last-minute changes. Purchasing wants to buy all needed materials and parts at the start of the year, with large orders for economy, and with no variation in components such as marketing would want to appeal to different customers. Research wants to get its teeth into "real" research involving technical matters, avoiding such "trivia" as

interdepartmental conflict in marketing

Can you recall any conflicts of this nature within North Star? Were they unavoidable?

research on consumer preferences. Finance wants to grant credit only to credit-worthy buyers, whereas marketing wants to make more sales by granting credit even to people with poorer credit ratings. And so on.

When marketing is successful, it may be by forcing other departments to be less successful according to their lights and in their frames of reference. The possibilities for organizational conflict under these conditions are obvious.

Organizational Models

In chapter 3, "Design and Development of Organizations," we saw that enterprises may be organized by territory, customer, product, or process. The same is true for the marketing organization, which is the major element of the company that meets the public. (Indeed, the structures of the marketing department can guide the structure of the entire company in this respect.) It is not likely that the marketing department would be organized by process, since that is an internalized concept, but organization by *territory,* by *customer,* and by *product* is typical for marketing groups. Under a territorial organization, shown in Figure 13-6, the marketing vice-president has divisional managers for principal assistants, depending on the major territorial subdivisions where the company is active. If the company is multinational, it is almost sure to have a foreign marketing organization (if, indeed, it does not have a completely independent foreign subsidiary). The vice-president of marketing will have staff assistants for research and advertising on his or her staff, and these assistants service the divisional managers (who may have similar assistants on *their* staffs, under their line control but looking to the directors of advertising and research for technical liaison). The products sold in each division are virtually the same, and the only reason for the shift is geographical convenience.

organization of marketing department

territorial marketing organization

Figure 13-6. Territorial Marketing Organization

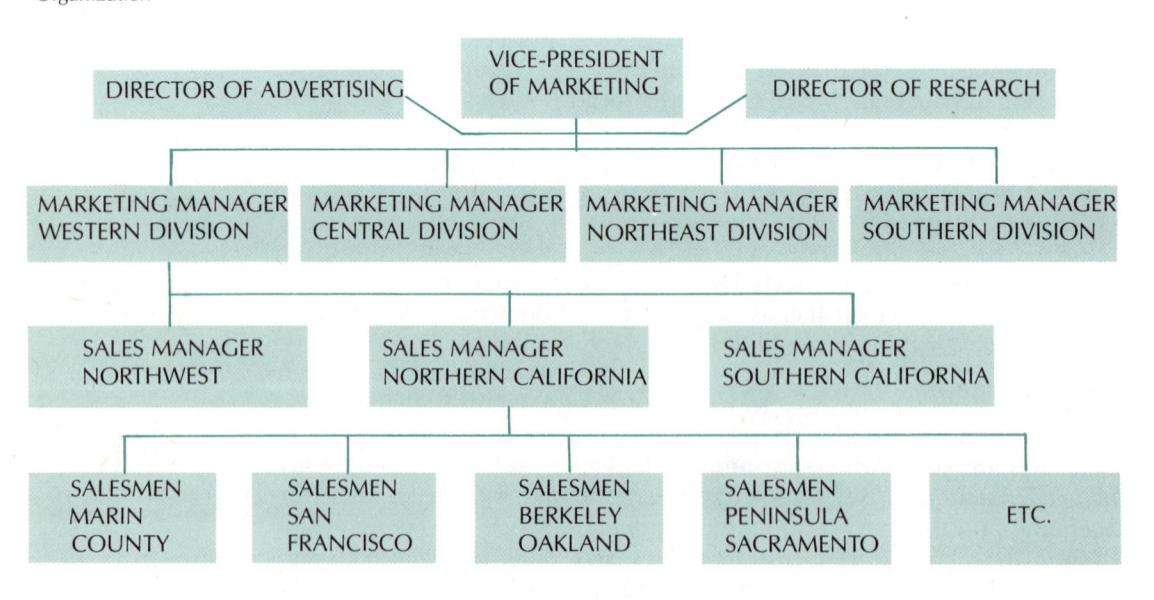

Figure 13-7 shows a customer marketing organization. In this case, the products are likely to be highly differentiated, to the point where each customer manager may supervise directors of advertising and research. The vice-president may have similar staff assistants as well.

customer marketing organization

Product Line Operating Management

One reason for conflict between marketing and manufacturing is that the former is organized by product while the latter is not; consequently, the marketing vice-president who wishes to discuss a particular product line finds no counterpart in manufacturing. In the plant, one executive is responsible for all production facilities, even though they turn out several highly distinct product lines. To the executive, the particular problems of an individual product line are of little consequence. Thus, marketing management is product-line oriented, but operations management is facilities oriented.

Golconda Corporation of Chicago has established a "product line operations manager" organization to bridge this manufacturing-marketing gap. Depicted in Figure 13-8, it shows functional supervisors reporting directly to the product line operations managers. In effect, Golconda has four general managers to run sections of the plant, so supervisors on these lines now answer directly to one executive, and don't face four different marketing managers begging for priority for their products.

product line marketing organization

Market Orientation of R&D

A 1973 Industrial Research Institute study disclosed that industrial communications between corporate research and marketing departments are very poor. The study noted that communications between these two departments *should* be particularly good, if the product is to move out of the lab and into a profitable home in the marketplace. Donald W. Collier, vice-president of research for Borg-Warner Corporation, commented on the steps being taken to combat this communication gap. "Many companies," he said recently, "are now organizing their R&D departments along broader concepts, so that they are responsible for innovation [moving the product into application and use] rather than just invention.

Figure 13-7.
Customer Marketing Organization

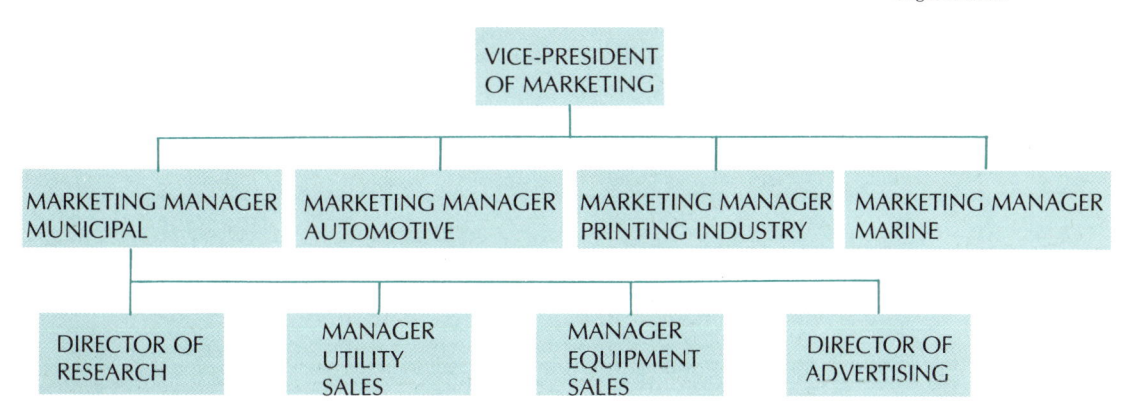

That is, they must develop the business system in which the new product or service is to operate, rather than simply the product itself. This organization must be strongly market oriented." Citing Borg-Warner's teaching machines, he said, "At our research center we worried not only about developing the machines and software, but also about how to integrate these into the teacher's normal classroom teaching, what sort of distribution system we would need to deal with people making the buying decisions in schools, and what specific benefits we would be selling."

Minnesota Mining and Manufacturing Company, maker of Scotch Tape, has been called the nation's most innovative enterprise, to a large degree because of its close linkage between R&D and marketing. When a laboratory scientist develops a new product, he or she often takes the product out into the field and becomes the product manager. D. W. Maher, vice-president for marketing, says, "The guy who creates a product has a right to be involved in all aspects of it." When an engineer conceives a product, he or she is encouraged to make a working model before talking it up. Robert M. Adams, vice-president for research, says, "We want research people to take their ideas beyond the idea stage, because a raw idea is awfully hard to sell to the next guy on the ladder. But if an engineer can say, 'Look what I can make for 50¢ each,' he may have something."[9]

It is rare for R&D and marketing to collaborate in this way, but it is extremely important for effective marketing performance.

Regional and Special Market Organizations

trade fairs

A growing phenomenon in selling is the *trade fair*, where sellers can reach many buyers at one time, and buyers can compare the products and prices of competing sellers conveniently. They may vary from the tiny commun-

Figure 13-8.
Product Line Manager Organization

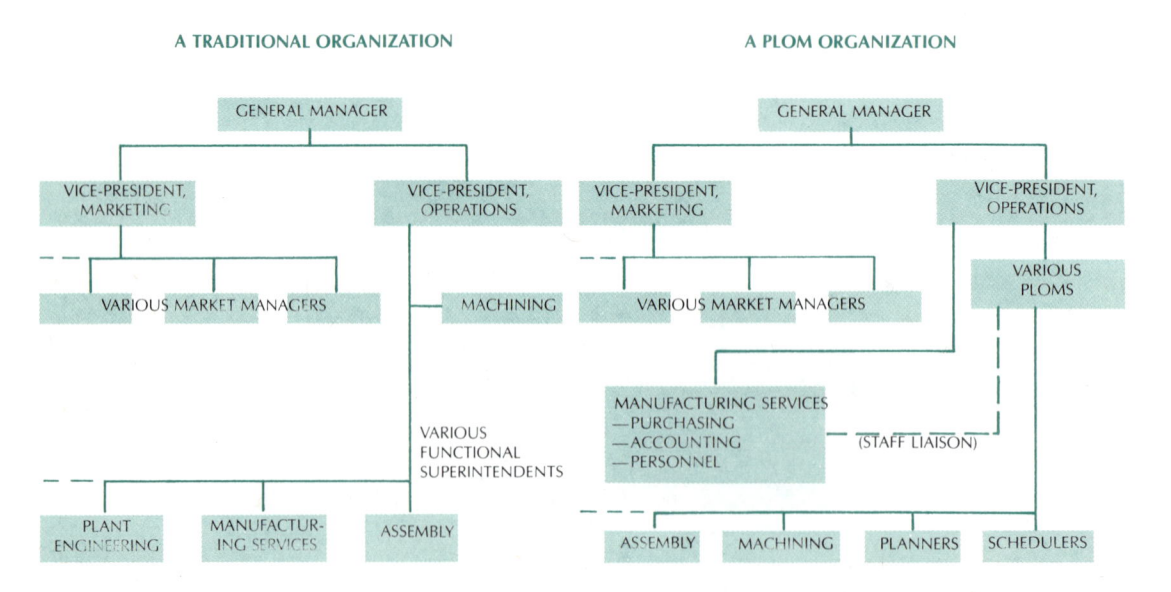

ity "craft fair" run by a local church to the American Pet Products Association Products Show in Atlanta, the Oyster Industry Equipment Show in Bordeaux, France, or the American Public Works Association Equipment Show, held in different cities. There are the great general trade fairs such as the Leipzig Fair in East Germany, held every March and September (a tradition for over eight centuries), the great April and October Canton Fair, where over half of China's $3 billion in exports are sold, and the famous Paris Air Show, which has been held 30 times. There are specialized trade fairs, such as Japan's Graphic Arts Show in Harumi and Canada's Annual Winter Boot Fair in Montreal.[10] Thirty-six U.S. companies exhibited at Japan's graphic arts fair.

Growing institutions for marketing of regional equities are the nine *regional stock exchanges,* which supplement the huge New York Stock Exchange, the American Stock Exchange, and the Over-the-Counter market in New York. In 1973 they did some 12% of all stock trading in the U.S., up from some 7% in 1967. Largest is Chicago's Midwest Stock Exchange, which has absorbed exchanges that formerly operated in Cleveland, Minneapolis-St. Paul, St. Louis, and New Orleans. The other large regional exchanges are those in Philadelphia (the PBW Stock Exchange—named for Philadelphia-Baltimore-Washington, and with trading floors in Pittsburgh and Miami), and San Francisco (the Pacific Stock Exchange, with an additional facility in Los Angeles). The others are at Boston, Spokane, Salt Lake City, Cincinnati, Detroit, and a tiny ten-member exchange in Honolulu.

In addition, there are *commodity exchanges,* of which the principal ones are the Kansas City Board of Trade, the Chicago Board of Trade, the New York Cotton Exchange, the Minneapolis Grain Exchange, and the London Metal Exchange. Dealing in materials rather than equities, such as fats, fibers, foods, grains, metals, oils, and textiles, one of their important roles is to permit firms requiring a guaranteed source of raw materials to buy on *futures* (an agreed-upon price today for materials delivered at some specified time in the future).

Marketing Structures

Although process organization of marketing is infrequent, the *task force structure* is becoming more popular in high technology markets. For example, Raybestos-Manhattan, Inc., which manufactures friction products (and did not even have a marketing department until 1970), recently closed its largest contract—$7 million for emission-control equipment on 1975 Fords—through a task force approach. It disbanded its force of Detroit salespeople, and its task force (the research directors of five R-M labs) began working under a marketing manager, with responsibility for contacting all purchasing sources and analyzing the total market. Xerox has shifted to a similar *vertical market structure,* where the salesperson no longer covers a geographic territory but specializes in a technical area (such as ACE, for architecture, construction, engineering). In 1974, National Cash Register (whose founder, John H. Patterson, used to say to his salespeople: "Don't talk machines. Don't talk cash registers. Talk the customer's business.") put its founder's customer-oriented philosophy into practice by following Xerox into a vertical market structure rather

If an engineer can say, "Look what I can make for 50¢ each," the product manager may sit up and take notice.

What is North Star's marketing structure? Explain.

than selling separate products as before. General Foods, IBM, and Addressograph-Multigraph are among major companies that have made similar shifts.

In addition to such shifts, other innovative marketing trends are developing. Colgate-Palmolive Company, a $2.2 billion company in sales, has started using its marketing and distribution system to sell other companies' products. It sells Mobil's Baggies, DuPont's Reveal roasting wrap, Chicopee Mills' Handiwipes, Wilkinson's razor blades, Henkel's Pritt Glue Stick, and Weetabix's Alpen cereal—to name a few. The reason is economy: Colgate's distribution system goes into the stores anyway, and it costs little to add more products, whereas the individual manufacturers would find it exceedingly expensive to set up a distribution network for one or a few products.

New advertising techniques are being tried across industries. Film producers have started advertising heavily with former arch-enemy TV—$43 million worth in 1973, and increasing each year. (Broadway shows are doing the same.) Theaters are substituting for the vanishing "short subject" films institutional releases from such companies as DuPont, AT&T, Univac, and General Dynamics. Association-Sterling Films, a large distributor, charges industrial customers $10 per theater per week for a ten-minute film, or about $5 per thousand audience reached.

pooled marketing

Pooled marketing is another new practice, where companies deal in the

492
MANAGEMENT AND ITS ENVIRONMENT

products of others for promotional purposes. Stokely-Van Camp., Inc., has offered a Tyco Industries train set at a discount for three labels, and Polaroid has offered a Hobby train set at a discount for three Polaroid film packages.

Franchising (licensing operators to run retail establishments using the franchiser's name and products for a fee) has reached high popularity in recent years, particularly in fast foods. In 1964, Nashville businessman Jack C. Massey and Kentuckian John Y. Brown bought Colonel Sanders's secret recipe for fried chicken done up with "25 herbs and spices," and by 1972 had boom sales up to $900 million; in 1971 the company was sold to Heublein, Inc. for $245 million. Brown then bought Lum's 53 company-owned stores and its franchise organization for $4 million, sold the company units for $6.3 million two weeks later, and has merged the ailing Lum's franchise units with a new "Ollie's Trolleys"; the only supplies sold the franchisees by the parent is a special sauce.

Born in the suburbs, fast food franchises (actually a mixture of franchised and company-owned stores) are starting a new move back to the cities. McDonald's (at $26 million net income, largest of the fast food companies), Burger King, Kentucky Fried Chicken, Dairy Queen, and A&W are all taking space in center city. A new Burger King opened across the street from the elegant Plaza Hotel on Manhattan's fashionable Upper East Side, and McDonald's has 16 units in Manhattan. Kentucky Fried Chicken's Times Square store, the chain's top unit, serves 300 people between 11:30 a.m. and 2:30 p.m. Instead of drawing from a two-mile radius, it draws from only a few blocks—but they are jam-packed blocks.

Locational Factors

A revolutionary market phenomenon is the development of monster shopping complexes removed from the center of our major cities and stealing their customers away. Catering to the public's automobile-propelled mobility, the centers sit astride major arteries leading to or around the city centers. Eastern Hills regional center in the suburbs of Buffalo, with over a million square feet of retail space, generates more sales volume than downtown Buffalo. The Galleria, on Houston's peripheral freeway, hums from breakfast to midnight, while downtown Houston becomes desolate after dark; it includes a 21-story hotel, a 22-story office building, ten air-conditioned tennis courts, two theaters, 14 eating and drinking spots, and 112 shops. Landerwood Plaza, in the suburbs of Cleveland, even includes a cemetery. The world's largest regional supercenter is the 2-million-square-foot Woodfield Mall, 25 miles from Chicago, with Sears' and Penney's largest stores, two office towers, and some 270 shops. As shown in Figure 13-9, the location pattern depends on the highway net and on population concentrations. Giant malls are recasting the urban structure. Urban planners consider that Washington, D.C.'s 66-mile Beltway is its real main street—some 800,000 new inhabitants settled along it in the past decade, and 12 regional shopping centers sprang up to serve them.

Strangely enough, countering this trend is another, for "suburban malls" to go back downtown where they started. Los Angeles's new Broadway Plaza, in the center of downtown, has a forbidding exterior without the trees and boulevard parking areas of the suburbs, but its roofed mall inside connects a hotel, office building, and some 30 stores in the same open style as its country cousins. Queens Center in New York City has a fully enclosed 640,000-square-foot center with some 70 shops. In Pittsburgh, Worcester, Salt Lake City, and Oakland, similar centers have moved in. Bruce A. Gimbel, who opened a new 12-story Gimbels on Lexington Avenue at 86th Street in New York City, says, "I think the city is being reborn." The city's first new major department store in more than a century, Gimbel's store has been emulated by Marshall Field in Chicago and Bullocks in downtown Los Angeles. These stores have recognized a shift in marketing (and lifestyle) patterns, and have moved to exploit it.

How does all this apply to the Blackridge shopping center study done by North Star?

Decision Systems

the computer in marketing

The computer and statistical handling of data are playing a more and more important part in marketing analysis and management. One of the major sources of market data, though surprisingly underutilized by many

Figure 13-9.
Regional Shopping Locational Patterns (Each dot is a shopping center.)

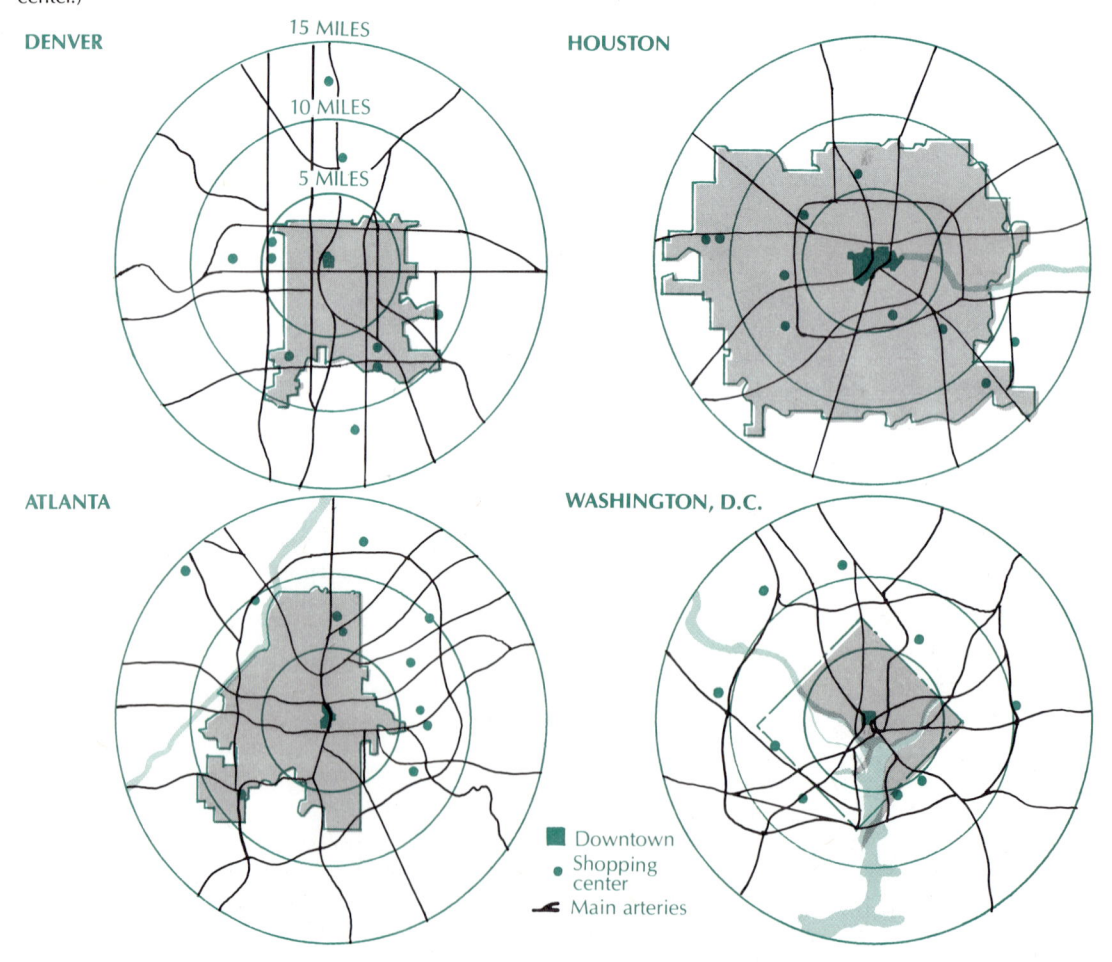

DENVER — 15 MILES / 10 MILES / 5 MILES

HOUSTON

ATLANTA

WASHINGTON, D.C.

■ Downtown
• Shopping center
⌒ Main arteries

494
MANAGEMENT AND ITS ENVIRONMENT

firms, is the Census Bureau. Its use is picking up: during the first half of the '70s, requests for census information quadrupled. Information is available in microfilm, computer tape, punch cards, and printed reports, and covers a wide array of topics. Hundreds of *Current Industrial Reports* provide information on production, stocks, and orders for 5,000 products (some 40% of all U.S. production), and are published weekly, monthly, quarterly and annually. Each month the Bureau publishes the *Current Population Survey,* giving household income by race, family size, occupation, and education, as well as the *Current Survey of the Retail Trades,* giving prices by product and brand in supermarkets, drug stores, and other outlets. Vincent P. Barabba, Director of the Census, calls it "the largest marketing research organization in the world." Its 1,100 reports contain more than 200,000 pages of data—on sales and payroll information for wholesale, retail and service businesses, import and export statistics, housing starts, and production and use of all important raw materials.

Since many companies use computerized market data, the Census Bureau organized the Data Users' Service in 1966. It has some 14,000 customers, and earns over a third of the Bureau's operating budget. Arthur C. Nielsen, Jr., president of the big market research firm of the same name, says that "census data are the keystones of all market research." He uses the Bureau's *Marital Status and Living Arrangements* report, together with its population estimates, to produce a detailed population profile that guides Nielsen's famous 1,500-household TV rating system. For another Nielsen report, he uses census data to guide his sample of 1,600 supermarkets and 750 drugstores in which he samples the performance of some 8,000 different retail products. Pepsi Cola is another example of a company drawing on census demographic data for its marketing research; Pepsi can determine by county all gas stations, supermarkets, drugstores, and eating establishments that might handle soft drinks.

Several companies combine census data with other statistics to compile their own special market reports and studies. CACI, Inc., updates census information between census years, serving such marketing giants as Penney's, Allied Stores, and Gulf when they hunt for new store locations.

Montgomery Ward, which nearly doubled its earnings while growing 22% in fiscal 1974 (outpacing both Sears and Penney's in the process), credits much of its marketing vitality to a computerized *sensitivity analysis* of catalog items. Each item is categorized by computer as to cost, merchandise return, catalog expense, and so on—and Wards can compute the sensitivity of sales and profits to the various elements. The program suggested that a small power saw advertised in a small space be given a page of its own and a $1 price cut; when this was done, sales leaped from $45,000 to $500,000 a year. Wards is computer-controlling its inventory, too, setting up a massive program that will link each store's electronic cash registers into a computer center so merchandise can be mass-reordered without delay.

McKesson and Robbins Drug Company, the largest U.S. drug wholesaler, puts portable electronic ordering terminals in drugstores so the manager can order directly from the warehouse computer. Along with this service, the store gets monthly computerized reports on profit mar-

and on shelf space effectiveness. In a similar system, steel customers can order steel products computer-to-computer, using the American Iron and Steel Institute's COMPORD code (for computer ordering).

The computer is used for checking credit card authorizations in gasoline stations, via a system Addressograph-Multigraph Corporation developed for National Data Corporation to spot stolen or over-limit cards instantly. Western Union combines the computer with its nationwide wire network to wire any of sixteen different gifts to a recipient in a distant city through any of 5,500 drugstores. And Amtrak solved its always-busy telephone problem with five computerized information systems containing a data base of 360,000 different fare possibilities, enabling it to handle most calls in six seconds.

Determining Public Needs

Behavioral Models of Buyers

The corner drugstore can analyze the customers face to face; the owner will hear their complaints if the store doesn't carry what they like, and can adjust stock accordingly. But large companies don't face their customers, and accordingly must utilize more subtle methods for analyzing what the public wants. Marketing analysts have developed theories of market behavior by the public, which guide the format of advertisements and the actual design of products.

Economic Consumer Theory

economic consumer theory

This theory presupposes that buyers use economic rationality, calculating more or less as corporate purchasing agents do what will bring the greatest satisfaction. This process involves *marginal utility theory:* after I have bought a certain number of one item—say clothes—my preference for the next purchase is for another item that initially I wanted less—say records; and I continue to buy each item until the cost of one more unit would exceed its usefulness to me.

On an economic basis, a raise in prices will reduce sales. A drop in the price of *substitute goods* (another make of TV set, say) will reduce sales of my goods. A drop in prices of *complementary goods* will increase sales of my goods (if I make outboard motors, a drop in the price of outboard boats will help sales of my motors). As real income goes up, sales of my goods (and everyone else's goods) will go up. The more I advertise, the more I sell. All very rational and businesslike. But do consumers always act this way?

Pavlovian Theory

Pavlovian theory

The Pavlovian says people are more complex than the economists suggest. While some behavior is clearly rational, other behavior is conditioned. The four central concepts in Pavlovian theory, are:

1. basic drives, such as thirst, fear, etc., which push us to action to satisfy these drives;

2. stimulations, such as a picture of a Coca Cola, which remind us of our drives and set them in motion;
3. responses, which are the steps we take to satisfy drives, ease pain or displeasure, etc.;
4. reinforcements, which are the good results we perceive from satisfying our drives, thus cementing the pattern of such action.

There may be little "economic rationality" in spending $2,000 for an elaborate burglar alarm system against the 1% chance that we will have a $5,000 burglary, but the peace of mind it brings against the fear of housebreaking may make the investment worth the cost. Security system advertisers cannot argue economically (particularly as most home owners are covered by insurance for at least part of the loss); so they show pictures of burglars sneaking into our castle, playing on this instinctive fear of intruders.

Freudian Theory

The Freudian says that people act to maximize their desires and minimize shame or guilt feelings. The middle-aged man who buys a racing sailboat which pulls him out on the ocean and makes him cold, seasick, and generally miserable (as well as a good deal poorer) has several levels of gratification:

1. *Overt level:* sailing is glorious fun!
2. *Subliminal level:* I will impress others; they will think I am a sport and will admire my professional seamanship.
3. *Subconscious level:* This will make me more manly; the hardship and modest danger will substitute for my unrealized sexual desires (and in some way may even help to gratify them).

Advertisers seeking to appeal to these motivations will advertise common personal toiletries such as deodorants and after-shave lotions as though they have magical aphrodisiac powers that will make their users irresistible.

Freudian theory

Veblen Theory

The Veblenian social-psychologist says that the consumer is a creature of his or her society, who constantly seeks to enhance prestige with the purchase of goods ("conspicuous consumption"). We are pushed to the marketplace by the pressures of our culture, our social class, our heroes or heroines, and our immediate groups. If our culture dictates a large automobile, as it did until the last few years, there are tremendous pressures on us to buy such a car rather than a far more economically sensible subcompact car. If our social class favors hunting and fishing, there are pressures for these to be our pleasures (and to guide our purchases), even though we don't really enjoy either sport. If the celebrities we admire endorse certain products, we feel a marked drive to buy those products ourselves. And if the group we see every day adopts certain styles in clothing, music, cigarettes, or entertainment, we are likely to favor those styles in our own buying. Advertisers subscribing to the Veblen theory will emphasize what celebrities use, or will show our contemporaries using certain products, to persuade us to do the same.

Veblen theory

Effect of Social Level on Buying Patterns

social levels in market theory

There are five social levels of interest to advertisers: lower lower, upper lower, lower middle, upper middle, and upper. The market preferences of each level vary, and advertisers must cater to these different tastes.

Lower Lower

These people tend to live in low quality housing, typically rental or public housing. They are less interested in their homes than in clothes and cars, which make it possible to present a superficially flashy exterior without large expenditure. They are less likely to buy for good value than for superficial appearance, and are inclined to make uneconomic purchases of nondurable articles.

Upper Lower

This social class has made its escape from the "lower lower" trap, and is determined to maintain the advantage. The home is far more likely to be owned rather than rented, and is an important status symbol. Permanent items for the home, such as refrigerators, washers, TV, furniture, etc., are significant purchases. This group is not flashy; the car is likely to be a durable one and kept for a long time, primarily for transportation rather than status. Members of this group will not buy any flashy clothes; the man is likely to have one good suit—his "laying out clothes," as his colleagues in the plant will call them, if he is so bold as to wear them on the job for some presentation or other ceremony. Group values are blue-collar values.

Lower Middle

This group incorporates the lower end of the white-collar culture. In 1953, Seymour Lipset and Reinhard Bendix noted that "the split between manual and nonmanual work is basic in American society."[11] While many in this class will not have gone to college, their ambition will be for their children to go (particularly the boys). They seek respectability, rate savings as important, and their homes are quite important to them. Items bought by the lower middle class contribute importantly to social respectability. The *Chicago Tribune* study of the Park Forest suburb described how families would make sacrifices to purchase certain items for the home that "everybody had," almost without regard to whether they really wanted them or whether they were useful.

The *Tribune* analysis of Park Forest middle-class purchases states that they "had no hesitancy in buying refrigerators and other appliances in discount houses and bargain stores because they felt they could not go wrong with the nationally advertised names. But taste in furniture is much more elusive and subtle because the brand names are not known; and therefore one's taste is on trial. Rather than commit a glaring error in taste which would exhibit an ignorance of the correct status symbols, the same individual...generally retreats to a status store for buying furniture to gain the support of the store's taste."

Upper Middle

These are the individuals who have made it, often in professional fields, and consequently have a great deal of confidence in their own judgment.

They pay much less attention to the social acceptance of purchases, and are more likely to buy what appeals to them as individuals. Thus in a given neighborhood will be found neighbors who spend for totally different things—one for a boat, another for travel, another for art, and still another for costly vacations. While they have nice homes and goods, these items are not bought for conformity purposes. Their spending often is for transitory things such as hobbies or travel rather than for artifacts, as with upper-lower and lower-middle-class families. Some of the upper-middle-class families are in positions requiring them to give frequent parties or to spend conspicuously. If professionals, they may be on the way up, with a certain pattern of social behavior required of them to some extent by the corporations for which they work. They are well-educated in general, and their children attend college as a matter of course.

Upper Class

There is no formal class structure in the U.S., but there is an upper class. Its members consist of top corporate officers, members of families with hereditary wealth, prosperous members at the top of their professions such as doctors, lawyers, etc., owners of moderate-sized businesses, and some celebrities. They are canny buyers, and little affected by most forms of advertising. Many of this group are taken in by the collapse or poor performance of various types of "tax shelter" investments. There are particular industries which advertise to this group, such as the yachting industry. (Dufour Yachts, after reminding the reader of J. P. Morgan's oft-quoted remark that "if you have to ask the cost of yachting, you probably can't afford it," and stating that we are in a similar era today when quality and tradition are more important than price, tells the reader that the Dufour 34 costs about the same as 62 cases of Chateau Lafitte 1966—but comments that "if you relate to the ultimate, price is of little consequence.") In general, however, this specialty market is of little importance to most consumer products companies, and most advertisements are not aimed at this class.

Market Research

Purpose

There is a short-term purpose for market research: to help in deciding what market action to take. There is also a long-term purpose: to better understand the market mechanism as a policy guide for all company actions. In the short term, the marketing organization is interested in finding if a product will sell and how well, if changes in the product will be worthwhile, if the market is just opening up or is starting to turn down, and so on. In the long term, it is interested in finding what makes people buy, how to change the image of the company and its products to fit public tastes, what emerging trends in consumer preferences may call for changes in the company's product line or even its overall direction, and so on.

When a company is considering a new product (a prepared food, a subcompact car, a new laundry product, a motorized snow vehicle, a

purpose of market research

Was the research Zeb set in motion for North Star short-term or long-term? Why?

restyled bathroom, a new type of refrigerator), it would be very hazardous to incur all the costs of developing the new product line and putting the product in the hands of retailers without any study of whether the public wants it. When a developer is considering spending the millions of dollars necessary to put up a major shopping center, or a store operator is deciding whether to open in a given area, it is easy to be fooled about how much business will be drawn; and if too little business comes, the enterprise fails. A market analysis is essential before such expenditures are committed.

Figure 13-10 demonstrates how common a phenomenon market research has become. The table shows, for the number of companies surveyed in each research category, what percentage perform research in that category.

Many governmental and nonprofit organizations perform market research. The Survey Research Center of the University of Michigan conducts a well-used "Quarterly Survey of Change in Consumer Attitudes." The Bureau of Labor Statistics publishes the Consumer Price Index, the Office of Business Economics puts out quarterly National Income Components, and the Commerce Department publishes a complex Input-Output Table for the U.S. economy, as well as an Export Expansion Program. Housing and Urban Development conducts studies of the Retail Structure of Decaying Central Business Districts, and Agriculture conducts the Agricultural Marketing Service. The National Planning Association publishes national forecasts not paralleled by any federal office. And so on, over a very wide range of topics and agencies.

Types of Research

Figure 13-10 lists some widely used types of market research. A major area for market research, since the company's fortunes are connected so intimately with it, is *sales forecasting*. While there are many kinds of forecasts, in general they divide into *short-term, annual,* and *long-term*. Short-term sales forecasts are usually made on a monthly basis, and sometimes even more frequently. (In chapter 12, "Handling and Using Information," you saw that some companies recap their performance each week.) Annual forecasts form the basis of the annual corporate budget. Long-term forecasts indicate which items are growth products and which are maturing. The short-term forecast sets production schedules, guides ordering of material, and forecasts cash flow. The short-term incorporates cyclical and irregular events such as holidays,

sales forecasting

Figure 13-10.
Research Distribution for Various Industry Categories

Type of Research	Total Companies	Manufacturing Consumer	Companies Industrial	Non-Manufacturing Companies
Market	99	100%	99%	100%
Sales	99	100%	99%	100%
Corp. Growth/Dev.	97	93%	98%	97%
Products	96	100%	96%	91%
Advertising	93	98%	91%	94%
No. responding	237	61	141	35

seasons, and special situations. The annual forecast considers the forthcoming state of the economy (trends in unemployment or overproduction, change in Gross National Product, taxes, etc.), and ties in with the short-term forecast, but extends it by different forecasting techniques. The long-term forecast must consider the entire life cycle of each product, as shown in Figure 13-11. Almost any product has an initial period of growth (if it is successful), then a middle period of good sales volume but reduced or zero growth, and finally a period of decreasing sales that is the prelude to death of the product. In chapter 9, "Controlling," you learned about "present breadwinners" and "repair jobs" (page 299). Product A of Figure 13-11 is a present breadwinner during the middle section of the curve. Perhaps its potential is such that it can be modified for some other use (a repair job) and be revitalized, as in A-1; and perhaps this process can occur again, as in A-2. Nylon is a classic example of a basic material that was introduced for one application, but was continually modified and applied to other uses. Its maturity point for one application coincided with its innovation point for others, and it continued its upward path as though there were no tomorrow (Figure 13-12).

Another important type of research is *locational analysis*—deciding where to locate a retail establishment and predicting the volume of sales that will result from various locations. Figure 13-9 shows the pattern of location for regional shopping centers along the major arteries of a metropolitan area. Each of these locations was selected on the basis of a combination of factors, as shown in Figure 13-13. The basic location produces a certain amount of local volume, known as *franchise volume*, from the people who live near the center (or the store, if it is located by itself). There is *interception volume*, or business picked up from individuals driving along the feeder road toward the central business district. There is *attraction volume*—customers attracted to this store or center instead of a competing one because the "gravitational pull" of this store or center (combination of its size, closeness, and other factors) is greater than that of the competition. There is *interchange volume*, or business picked up by one store in a center from customers who were drawn to the center by another store but shop around when they get there. And there is *growth volume*, from the increase in the population in the area (of which this store or center gets its proportional share).

<small>locational analysis</small>

<small>franchise volume</small>

<small>interception volume</small>

<small>attraction volume</small>

<small>interchange volume</small>

<small>growth volume</small>

Each of these factors can work the other way, of course. A center at an intercepting location on an artery going to the central business district can have its customers intercepted in turn by another center located farther out. A center with good attraction volume can see it fall off because a large competing center opens nearby. Interchange volume will drop if the stores in the center change character and become noncomplementary (a clothing store and shoe store are very complementary, a restaurant and shoe store less so, a bowling alley and shoe store much less so, and a mortuary and shoe store not at all). And growth volume disappears if the area drops in population.

The research for locational analysis is done by counting all consumers in an area, determining from census information their disposable income for "shoppers' goods," tracking their transportation arteries, calculating the relative attractiveness of competing centers, calculating the interchange volume produced by neighboring shops in your center, estimating

Figure 13-11.
Product Life Cycle with Product Modification

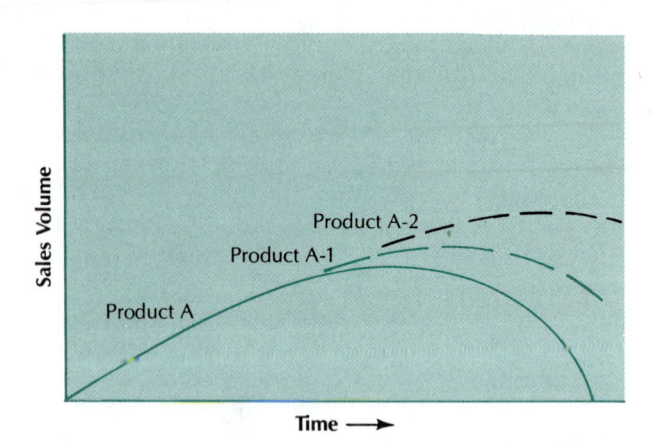

population growth, and putting all of this together into estimates of annual dollar volume.

The effect of *advertising and promotion* is difficult to determine, because there are many variables changing all at once, and it is hard to separate the effect of each. Figure 13-1 shows market performance as the result of basic strengths, internal strategy (such as advertising), and external variables (such as state of the economy). If the external variables hold relatively constant for a period, the expenditures for advertising in each month can be compared with the sales (or net profit) for the period immediately following the advertising, and some conclusions can be drawn. If external variables are changing during this period as well, the

Figure 13-12.
Product Life Cycle (Nylon)

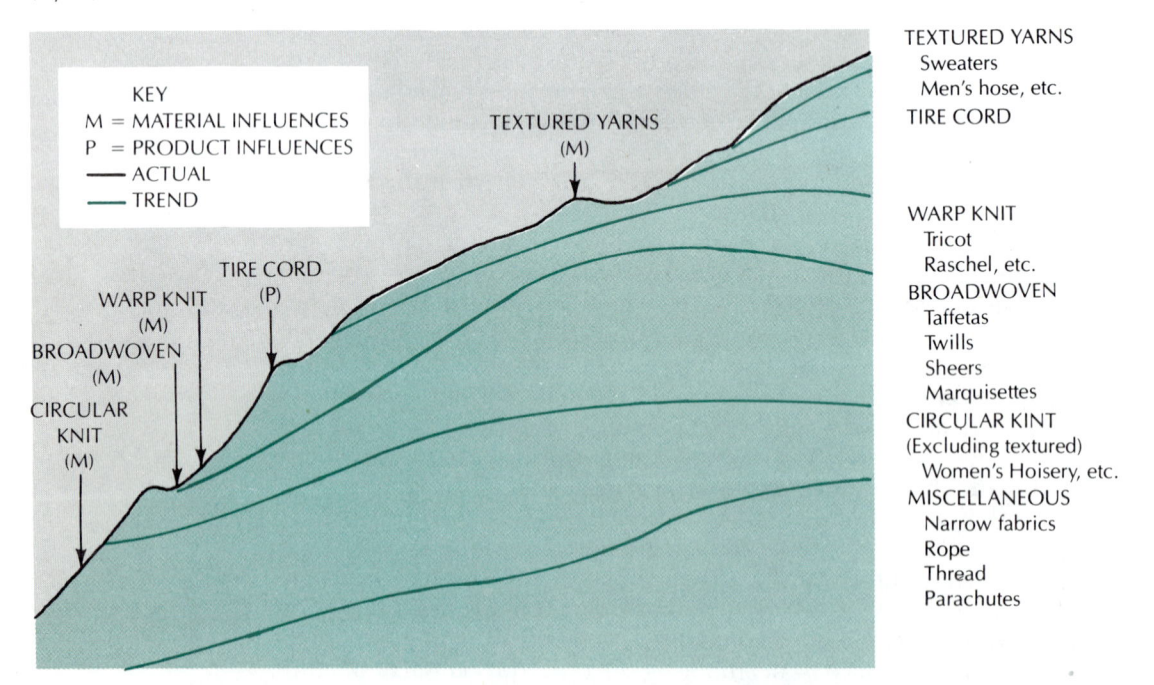

502
MANAGEMENT AND ITS ENVIRONMENT

problem is more difficult; but some analysis can still be performed, using the regression analysis techniques described in chapter 9 (see Figure 9-5).

Analysis of Market Research

Marketing Models

There are three basic categories of marketing models: *descriptive, systematic,* and *quantitative*. A descriptive model is a discussion of cause-and-effect relationships, from which conclusions can be drawn by the application of common sense. It is easy to develop, but there is danger of overlooking some of the interrelationships because it lacks any formal structure. There is the additional danger that the modeler with a particular interest in a certain outcome can slant the discussion so that it will favor that outcome, while seeming to be impartial. A systematic model sets out in block diagram form all of the possible events and attempts to connect them. The airport dispatcher model of chapter 7 (Figure 7-1) shows the general format of such a model. If it is properly prepared, all the logical outcomes of various actions and events can be seen. The analyst has only to assign probabilities in order to use the model. A quantitative model tries to determine mathematical relationships that describe the marketing

marketing models

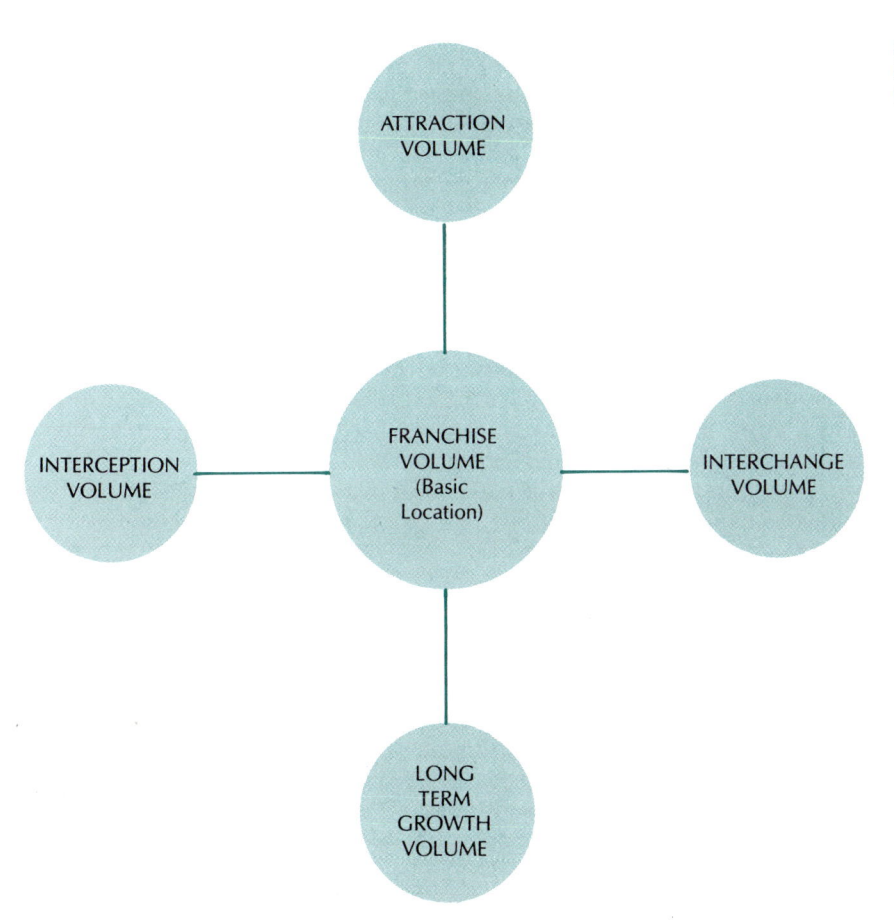

Figure 13-13.
Factors in Retail Location

process—leaving out the less important factors so the model will not be hopelessly complex—and to assign numbers to all of the values in the model. An example would be a regression model to forecast the net profit resulting from various levels of advertising and other promotions, in the face of various states of the economy and various behavior of competitors.

Models can be used to analyze some segment of a market, such as the probable sales of a particular product, or a broad market such as the forecast sales in a given industry. They can cover the current situation, or can be used to forecast changes in the market as various factors change. They can use specific estimated values of the variables (deterministic), or a range of values based on their probability (stochastic). They can be decision models, showing what will happen if certain actions are taken, or growth models, showing how a particular market will vary over time. They can be pilot or pre-test models (exploratory in nature, and giving only approximate answers), or full-scale. They can utilize personal interviewing, telephone interviews, or mail questionnaires—or a mixture of these.

Consumer Panels

consumer panels

Consumer panels were initiated by the late sociologist Paul Lazarsfeld in the late 1930s. They are continuing consumer groups, brought together to represent in miniature the behavior of all consumers with regard to a given type of product, so that from their recorded behavior predictions can be made about the behavior of the entire consumer public. They are convened for long periods, since their changing practices over time are of interest, and there are procedures for regularly changing a part of the panel to keep it up to date.

The Market Research of America panel studies consumer behavior changes over time in purchases of nondurable consumer products. It is a sample of 7,500 U.S. homes, selected to match national characteristics, and measures purchases of numerous products by price, region, type of store, etc. The Nielsen television panel consists of 1500 homes representative of the TV audience, each of which has an "Audimeter" wired to the TV receiver to record what channels were tuned in at what times; from these data Nielsen publishes a national TV index and a local station index. The Census Bureau has a national sample of 11,500 households, with one-sixth replaced each quarter, interviewed each quarter to determine the probability that they will make certain major purchases during the coming year.

Analysis Methods

trend analysis

A number of methods are used to analyze market data. Simple *trend analysis* can be worked out in freehand style, as in Figure 13-14, where a set of sales volume figures for various years in a "time series" is connected with the straight line that comes closest to all the points. This line, representing the general growth rate or tendency, can be extended to forecast the rate of future growth. More precise fits of the line can be made through such statistical methods as least-squares fit, moving averages, or exponential smoothing, but in each case the purpose is simply to interpret the information conveyed by the set of points as accurately as possible.

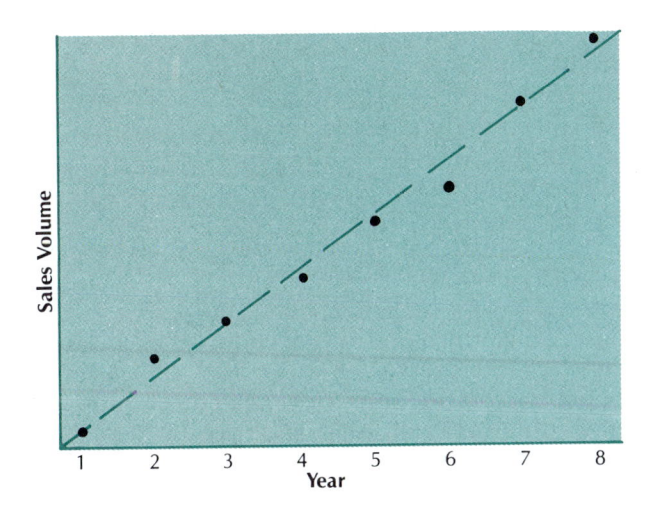

Figure 13-14.
Sales Volume Trend Analysis

Several methods are used to establish the relationships among variables (for example, the effect of advertising, unemployment rate, and competitive activity on net profit of a department store). *Regression analysis* finds the mathematical equation that best describes the relationship as it occurs in sample data the marketing staff has gathered over an extended period, and utilizes this equation to forecast future behavior. *Discriminant analysis* is similar to regression analysis but is used for classification; if a consumer responds to these three variables (advertising, unemployment, and competition) by buying a small amount, he or she is put in one class; if the response is to buy somewhat more, in a second class; if still more, in a third class; and so on. *Factor analysis* is a refinement of regression analysis; a large number of variables (such as those affecting size of purchase) is reduced to a smaller number of *key* variables by grouping each set that seems to have similarities and selecting the best variable in that set to represent the whole set.

regression analysis

discriminant analysis

factor analysis

Use of Market Research

Business executives are starved for accurate information about the market. They would like to know what prices to charge, what products to carry (or to manufacture), how to distribute their products, how to advertise (what media, what form of advertisement, how frequently), where to locate their store or stores, what hours to stay open, what credit terms to offer and to whom, how to change product design, and many other things. All of these questions are answered to some extent by market research, but a great deal is left to the judgment of the executive. Studies may show that price varies with quantity sold—the higher the price, the less the demand—but in many cases, an increase in price has led to more sales rather than less, because the consumer is a complex animal and responds to many apparently irrational motivations. When soap companies run test marketing campaigns in selected communities, they use the results to tell them whether to inaugurate the product nationally.

Sometimes research is used in the wrong way, as a justification for a decision that has been made *in advance of* the research. Vice-President

FACING THE MARKET

Stewart A. Smith of Lee Creative Research in St. Louis described a dialogue with such a product manager:[12]

Researcher: What if the test results are favorable?

Manager: Why, we'll launch the product nationally, of course.

R: And if the results are unfavorable?

M: They won't be. I'm sure of that.

R: But just suppose they are.

M: I don't think we should throw out a good product just because of one little market test.

R: Then why test?

M: Listen, Smith, this is a major product introduction. It's got to have some research behind it.

Long-term research is used to decide whether to enter a new product line or not, often involving hundreds of millions of dollars in capital investment. When Westinghouse Electric Corporation made the decision to proceed with the breeder nuclear reactor, it was committing close to $200 million on a long-term gamble that would not pay off for ten to 15 years; it based the decision on extensive analyses of energy demand and the prospects for competing energy sources before it proceeded. When the Ford Motor Company proceeded with the original Mustang, it based the decision on extensive sociological analyses of market preferences and changing tastes in cars; the decision was a good one, and the Mustang was an outstanding success. (An earlier market analysis which led to the decision to produce the Edsel was a disastrous mistake, as everyone knows—not because Ford did not do extensive market studies, but possibly because it focused more closely on *what kind* of a car the public wanted rather than broader trends such as whether large numbers of cars would be sold at all.)[13]

Businessmen are not the only users of market research. Urban planners use it to decide how to zone their communities and where to locate such facilities as schools, libraries, and fire stations as well as retail establishments. City managers, public works directors, and similar officials use market information to decide how to allocate such resources as street repairs, utility and sewage systems, trash collection equipment, municipal vehicles, parks, etc. Regulatory agencies use it to determine whether there are violations of free trade laws, price-fixing laws, etc.

Figure 13-15 shows excerpts from top-line demographic tables from three major syndicated research organizations, for a group of selected magazines. "Starch Elite" is a survey of 9,566,000 homes where the head of household is professional or managerial and makes over $15,000. "Target Group Index" and "Simmons" are more general surveys of total U.S. adults. This excerpt, from a *Newsweek* advertisement, presumably helps advertisers decide where to advertise in order to make the best contact with their most probable customers. The full studies run from 16 to 21 magazines, and provide more information than is shown here, but this is a representative crosssection.

The data cited by *Newsweek* concerns cost only, and by no means covers everything contained in the surveys. In addition to the cost of advertising (or any product or service) there is of course the matter of value, which is a little harder to get at. On January 10, 1975, the *Wall Street Journal* published an advertisement presumably in rebuttal to the previous *Newsweek* advertisement. Citing Starch Elite, W. R. Simmons, and Publisher's

Estimated Circulation, it ranked publications on the basis of subscriber attitudes. The rankings are shown in Figure 13-16. Both advertisements are partisan, of course, in that they show material generally favorable to the advertiser; advertising space buyers would have to weigh all of these points plus others contained in surveys to see which publication would fit their needs best.

Time chose still another approach. It brought suit in January 1975 against W. R. Simmons, charging that the study contained "biased and unreliable statistics," in that it showed *Time's* total reading audience dropping from 20,832,000 to 19,488,000 at the same time that *Newsweek's* audience rose from 13,984,000 to 19,013,000. *Time* questioned this finding in view of the fact that *Time's* guaranteed circulation is 4,250,000, while *Newsweek's* is 2,900,000. *Time's* suit said, in effect, that the 1974–75 Simmons figures were so at variance with those from 1962 to 1973 that one or the other set of figures was "the production of biased and unreliable figures."

Other rather massive shifts reported in the Simmons study were a

Starch Elite

	Household Heads (000)	Readers per $	Male HH Heads (000)	Readers per $	Professional/ Managerial (000)	Readers per $	HH Income 25M+ (000)	Readers per $
Newsweek	4,961	238	3,308	158	4,354	209	2,499	120
Time	5,359	179	2,904	97	5,108	170	3,156	105
U.S. News & World Report	3,084	210	1,949	133	2,695	184	1,439	98
Sports Illustrated	2,730	145	2,385	127	2,469	131	1,415	75

TGI (Midyear Report)

	Adult Readers (000)	Readers per $	Adult Males (000)	Readers per $	Professional/ Managerial (000)	Readers per $	HH Income 25M+ (000)	Readers per $
Newsweek	17,003	815	9,462	453	4,183	200	2,628	126
Time	18,673	623	9,759	326	5,176	173	3,386	113
U.S. News & World Report	10,255	699	6,115	417	2,399	164	1,784	122
Sports Illustrated	12,514	666	8,568	456	2,893	154	1,596	85

Simmons

	Adult Readers (000)	Readers per $	Adult Males (000)	Readers per $	Professional/ Managerial (000)	Readers per $	HH Income 25M+ (000)	Readers per $
Newsweek	19,013	911	11,075	531	5,545	266	3,713	178
Time	19,488	650	10,813	361	6,050	202	4,039	135
U.S. News & World Report	8,447	576	5,442	371	2,873	196	2,043	139
Sports Illustrated	12,132	646	9,570	510	3,479	185	2,209	118

Based on rates: P/B&W—1X, 1975

Figure 13-15.
Results of Magazine Readership Studies

showing that *Esquire's* male audience dropped from 5,469,000 to 2,749,000—almost an exact halving of coverage; and a showing that *Business Week's* total audience dropped from 4,573,000 to 3,410,000—a 25% reduction.

Dealing with Public Needs

Once the market research is completed, the enterprise must decide how it will react. What advertising or promotion will it conduct? What products will it make or modify? How will it distribute its products? How will it price them? And what will be the direction and thrust of its market planning?

Advertising Strategy

Advertising is not a clear-cut matter. Some advertising does little or no good. Some has been shown by test to help the competition more than the company doing the advertising. Some may be directed toward the wrong goals. Thus an advertisement for a car may get across very effectively the message that this is a high-performance status symbol, at a time when the consumer is shifting to economy and low maintenance costs; it is successful in convincing the consumer *not* to buy. Some ads are so outrageous that they turn consumers away from the product.

goals of advertising

The goals of advertising may be set forth in logical sequence: (1) brand recognition, (2) product recognition, (3) understanding of product advantages, (4) favorable decision as to product, (5) motivation to buy product, (6) actual purchase of product. (A further goal, repeat purchase of product, is a function of product quality and acceptability rather than of advertising effects, though advertising can help maintain product

Figure 13-16. Ranking of Attitudes Toward Publications

RANKING OF ATTITUDES TOWARD PUBLICATIONS

	FIRST TO INVESTIGATE, REPORT ON NEW DEVELOPMENTS	LOOK FORWARD TO READING ADS AS WELL AS ARTICLES	WELL WRITTEN	INCLUDES ARTICLES RELATING TO MY OWN SPECIAL INTERESTS	SOMETHING ABOUT IT GIVES ME CONFIDENCE IN COMPANIES THAT ADVERTISE IN IT	PEOPLE I KNOW OFTEN DISCUSS WHAT'S IN IT	HAS THE PRESTIGE TO BE INFLUENTIAL	LOOK FORWARD TO READING EVERY ISSUE	SAVE COPIES FOR FUTURE REFERENCE
BUSINESS WEEK	5	1	6	2	4	6	7	8	3
DUN'S REVIEW	8	7	3	2	7	8	4	2	2
FORBES	6	8	5	3	3	2	3	7	6
FORTUNE	7	3	1	4	2	4	1	4	1
NEWSWEEK	4	5	4	5	8	5	5	6	8
TIME	2	4	6	6	5	3	6	3	7
U.S. NEWS & W.R.	3	6	2	7	6	7	8	5	5
THE WALL STREET JOURNAL	1	2	4	1	1	1	2	1	4

508
MANAGEMENT AND ITS ENVIRONMENT

loyalty.) The choice of advertising methods must be based on studies of relative effectiveness, which include the following:

1. *Conscious response:* How many of a survey group were favorably motivated to purchase by the advertising, and will say so?
2. *Unconscious response:* How many respond to a questionnaire or test in a way that shows they associate the product with favorable qualities?
3. *Mechanical tests:* When flipping through a sample of various ads, how many linger at your ad, or show a high retention level for the subject matter of the ad?
4. *Post tests:* After the ad ran, how many more bought than were buying previously?
5. *Alternative post tests:* If two or more ads are run for different buying publics, which ad draws best?

In determining advertising budgets, one approach is simply to assign advertising a fixed percentage of the sales volume. This method puts things backwards, for presumably sales are caused by advertising rather than the reverse. A variation of this procedure, which makes more sense, is to give new products a heavier share in order to get them launched and to reduce advertising support as the product gets older. Another approach is to estimate through regression analysis or similar techniques what advertising level is required to attain a certain market share which corresponds to corporate goals. Figure 13-17 shows a study for the period 1947–1953 of the amount of advertising a company did relative to the competition (the advertising exchange rate) and the market share produced thereby. (Both sets of values are in logarithms, which is a technique to express a curved-line relationship as a straight line.) If other factors did not change during the period, or if they were allowed for statistically, this can be a valid analytical method. A third method, tested analytically by Green & Tull,[14] is to express in mathematical form the decisions actually made by executives deciding how to allocate advertising funds, and perhaps to use the formula to make automatic allocation decisions in repeat situations. While the formula may not actually be used in this way, this method has the useful feature of showing executives the implications of their subjective decisions, so they can reconsider them. The fourth method, of course, is to decide judgmentally, with the decision making left to the old hands who presumably have done well in the past. Its shortcoming is that no one can see which decisions worked well and which worked badly, even after the fact.

setting advertising budgets

Product Decisions

Product decisions involve choosing products (changing the product line) and modifying or developing products (improving the product line). When times are hard, companies are often forced to stay with the products they have because of the great expense of introducing new products; but in the long run, companies that do not innovate will not survive. In 1975, Chrysler was the only one of the major automobile companies that decided not to develop a subcompact car, almost certainly because of Chrysler's cash squeeze. Figure 13-18 shows, for 11 industries, estimates made by Booz, Allen, and Hamilton, Inc., in 1968 (in *Management of New*

changing the product line

Figure 13-17.
Regression Analysis of Advertising Impact

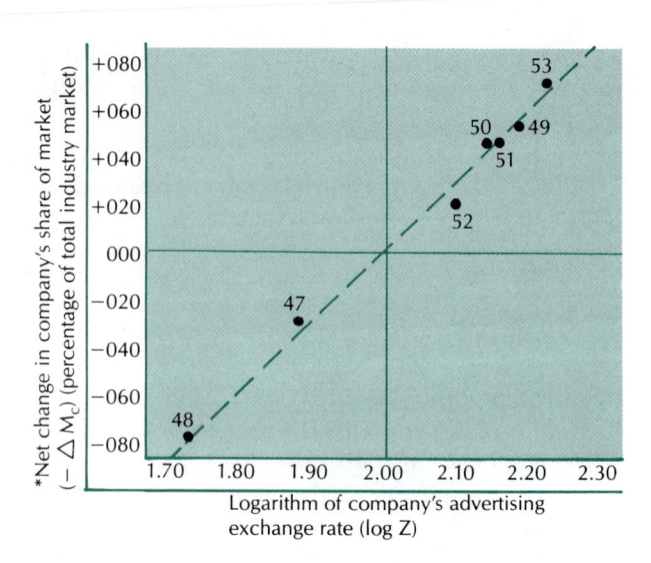

*Net change in company's share of market ($-\Delta M_c$) (percentage of total industry market)

Logarithm of company's advertising exchange rate (log Z)

Do these rules on new products apply to North Star, do you think? Explain.

Products), of sales increases during the period 1963–67, showing that an average of over 70% of the sales increases came from new products first introduced during the period. Companies simply must bring out new products to remain competitive.

Completely new products are rare (the first Polaroid self-developing camera was one), and the development period is longer than one might think. The National Science Foundation, in a study called TRACES (for

Figure 13-18.
Old and New Product Share of Sales

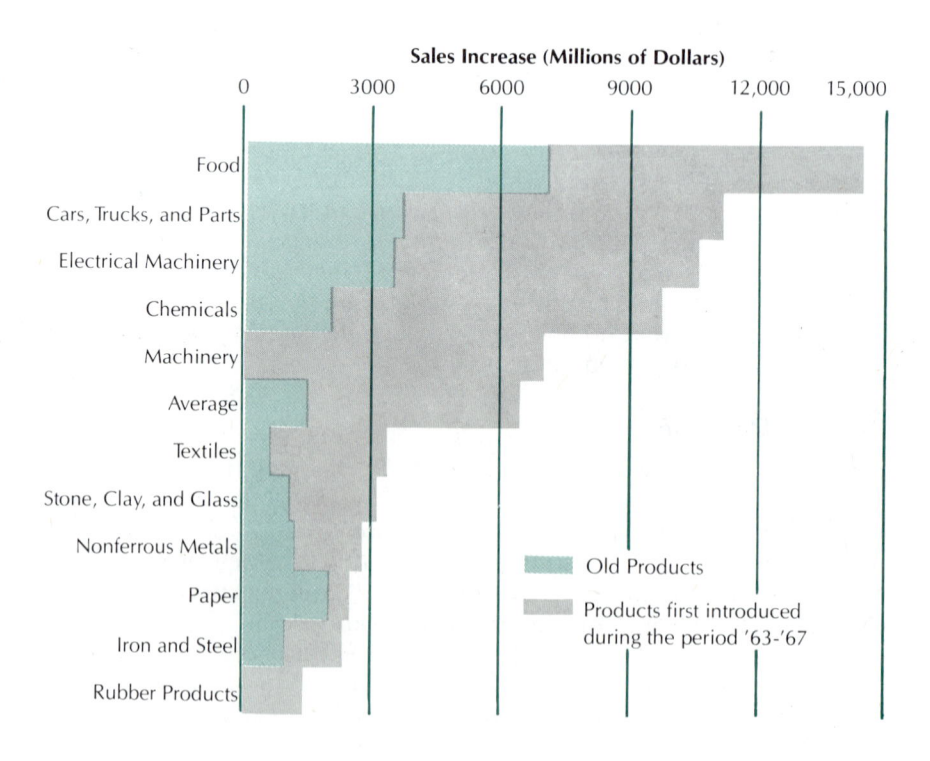

Sales Increase (Millions of Dollars)

Food
Cars, Trucks, and Parts
Electrical Machinery
Chemicals
Machinery
Average
Textiles
Stone, Clay, and Glass
Nonferrous Metals
Paper
Iron and Steel
Rubber Products

Old Products
Products first introduced during the period '63–'67

510

MANAGEMENT AND ITS ENVIRONMENT

"Technology in Retrospect And Critical Events in Science"), found that the research and development period is about 30 years to the point where workability is demonstrated, followed by about nine years to design and build a salable product and get it adopted in the marketplace. Figure 13-19 shows, for a fictitious new product where this period is seven years, what is involved in bringing out a replacement product. Note the additional nonreimbursed costs the company incurs for nearly the entire seven years. The new product must be more profitable than the old to repay this excess of costs, or there is no reason to bring it out.

total cost envelope for new products

Distribution

Goods flow from the original raw material, through parts and material *suppliers* to the *manufacturer*, through *manufacturers' representatives* to *wholesalers* (or chain buyers), and thence to the *retailers* for sale to the *consumers*. Trade channels look different to the manufacturer, the wholesaler, and the retailer, as shown in Figure 13-20. The manufacturer, dealing with several wholesalers, is in danger of forgetting that to each wholesaler the company is just another manufacturer, whose products can be promoted or neglected depending upon the benefits that accrue to the wholesaler. The retailer must deal with many wholesalers, and their approach determines in part how well the store will display and promote their products.

manufacturers' representatives

wholesalers

Marketing texts speak of the "four P's": Product, Place, Price, and Promotion. Distribution has a great deal to do with the second and fourth of these. Oddly enough, no one really *manages* the distribution channel in

"four P's" of distribution

Figure 13-19.
Total Cost Analysis, New Product Innovation

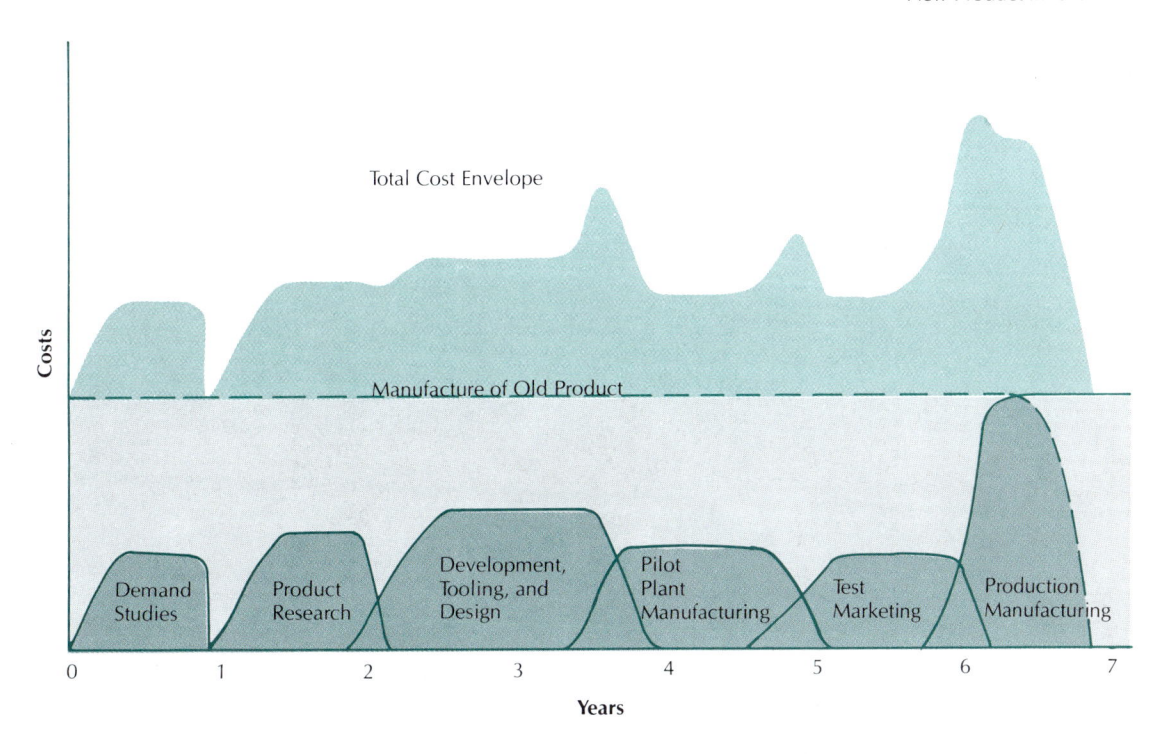

most companies. There is a feeling in some companies that manufacture products that everything is finished when the goods reach the shipping room. Other companies believe that the manufacturer is in charge of the distribution system. Still others think that the distribution system is for handling goods only. None of these is true. Certainly the battle is not over until the goods are sold to the consumer, because if consumers don't buy, the retailer will not restock. The channel is a cooperative entity, and no one institution runs it. And the distribution system is for transmission of *goods, ownership, money,* and *information*. Whether the manager is in manufacturing, wholesaling, or retailing, he or she must pay close attention to what is happening in the distribution system.

Promotion

Television advertisements have been called the "tribal rites of modern society" by anthropologist Merlin Myers of Brigham Young University. "Civilized people accuse tribal peoples of being superstitious in their rituals," he says. "But both utilize symbolism, mysticism and the value system of the culture... Just as the Swazi believe a certain dance will bring rain, American consumers [believe] a toothpaste will bring romance." The main difference is that tribal cultures are mainly concerned with production, whereas American society concentrates on consumption. "If a man can't get masculinity in society, he is made to believe he can get it in a mystical ritual way by smearing some commercial product all over himself." Dr. Myers concludes that the similarities between advertising and ritual far outweigh the differences. Both reflect cultural values and

Completely new products are rare, and the development period is longer than one might think.

needs, both are means of mass communication, both utilize people's superstitious beliefs, and both are necessary.[15]

Certainly advertising is necessary to the selling companies. A 1974 study by the American Business Press and Meldrum & Fewsmith, Inc., is the latest of three studies on the impact of advertising during five recession periods from 1947 to 1973. Covering the period from 1968 to 1973, it showed that companies that did not reduce advertising outlays in 1970 or 1971 had higher sales and income than those that did. The earlier studies reached the same conclusions. The gains were particularly marked after the recessions ended.

From an economic viewpoint (as compared to the ritual needs described above), advertising is a net gain to society if it increases production to the point where economies of larger-scale production (and consequent drop in price) outweigh the cost of advertising. Most of the mass-produced commodities we take for granted have dropped in price because economies of scale set in when public acceptance zoomed—and advertising must get much of the credit for massive public acceptance.

Product differentiation and *market segmentation* are ways to increase acceptance of your product. If your product is somehow different from all the others (even if the difference is highly intangible, and perhaps even imaginary), the price can be somewhat higher and still it will sell. Albert D. Lasker, the advertising genius who brought Lucky Strike cigarettes to undisputed sales leadership for two decades, coined the slogan "It's Toasted." Probably no one knew what it meant, or whether "toasting" improved a cigarette, but it made Luckies different, and that was enough. Market segmentation means trying to satisfy different sets of wants with different products, and concentrating heavily on promoting these differences. It can apply as well to industrial buyers as to private consumers; the salesman who knows the customer's needs in detail—who is oriented more toward *markets* than toward *products*—is in a position to tailor the product line to customer desires.

product differentiation
market segmentation

The 1960s saw a wave of "creativity" in advertising agencies, but today's managers with financial expertise have generated a shift toward efficiency. The huge growth in TV advertising budgets (from $10 billion in 1958 to nearly $20 billion in 1970) spawned many innovative agencies, but with the recession came an emphasis on more systematic marketing, with professionals schooled in pricing, distribution, packaging, and marketing

Figure 13-20.
Patterns of Wholesaler Representation

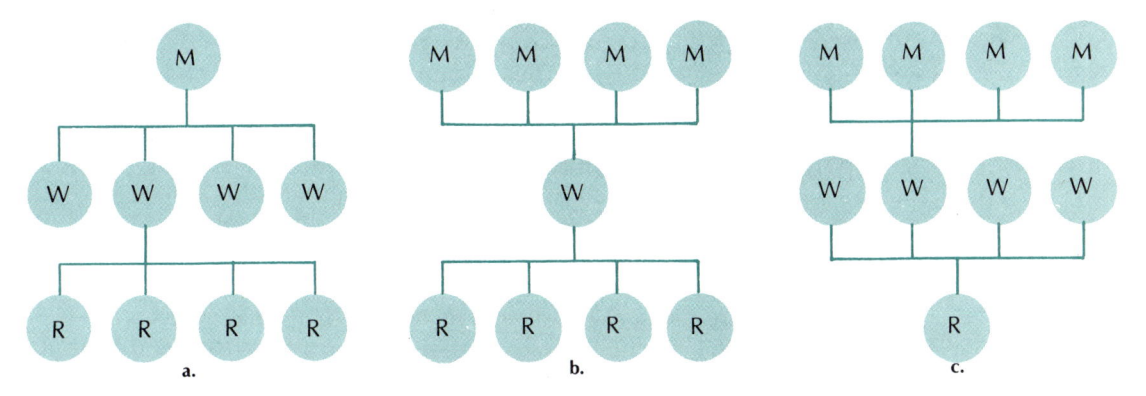

in general. Government inquiries into the accuracy and truthfulness of ads dampened enthusiasm for extravagant advertisements that sometimes strayed from the truth (as opposed to witty or novel ads, which can be at once accurate, creative, and effective).

Even the Postal Service has started to advertise. Its first nationwide advertising campaign began in 1975, using 365 newspapers in 323 cities. Postmaster General E. T. Klassen stated at the time that "if customers have a better understanding of mail services and how to use them, they will get better service, and the Postal Service can operate more efficiently." That goal, after all, is what advertising everywhere should be all about.

Pricing

When St. Marks Cinema in New York cut its admission prices from $2.00 and $2.50 to $1.00 flat in 1974, its gross went up 25%. Norman Levy of Columbia Pictures said of this price trend, "Theaters that have cut their prices to $1 have stayed alive where otherwise they might have died." Pricing is an exceedingly important element in marketing strategy. The huge discount store segment of the retail industry came into being on the philosophy that it is better to sell your stock ten times a year at a 20% markup than four times a year at a 40% markup. Today, oddly enough, the discount stores are starting to upgrade their stores and raise their prices—and a new discount area of *catalog discounting* is starting to emerge. Made up of many small chains, catalog discounting had become a $5 billion business by 1975.

Pricing strategy may backfire. When A & P touched off a supermarket price war in 1972 with its slogan WEO ("Where Economy Originates"), its sales reportedly rose 15%, but the effect on profits was questionable. In the food industry in general, supermarket profits declined sharply as other companies moved to match A & P's price cuts. Ultimately, A & P abandoned the strategy as unsuccessful.

Price cutting is not as popular among U.S. companies as nonprice methods of promotion. If a price cut does not work, it is hard to raise the price again, whereas a noneffective advertisement can simply be discontinued. There is a feeling that price cuts win customers only temporarily, whereas customers won by advertising or product differentiation are more enduring. In many lines, a few firms dominate the industry, and it is almost certain that a price cut by one will bring reactive cuts by the rest, leaving every firm worse off than before. In other industries, however, there is a two-tier retail market system: first-line stores which charge regular prices and may offer certain merchandising services such as delivery, charge accounts, and nice surroundings, and discount stores which charge lower prices but may lack the amenities of the first-line establishments. Buyers patronize one or the other depending on which they rate as more important—price or the intangibles. Sometimes the same company offers very similar items at different prices, such as Heublein's higher priced Smirnoff and lower priced Popov vodka, appealing to different markets with different lines.

Multinational firms (and to some degree firms solely within the U.S. that have wholly-owned subsidiaries) have been able to use *transfer pricing* (the price a company charges for an item sold by one division or subsidiary

transfer pricing

to another) to achieve nonmarketing aims. In 1974 a United Nations group listed some potential abuses of this practice:

- High transfer prices charged to a foreign subsidiary may reduce the subsidiary's apparent profits in countries with high taxes, and low transfer prices may increase subsidiary reported profits in low-tax countries.
- A parent company may drain profits from a subsidiary by charging unreasonably high prices for parts, when profits otherwise would be blocked or taxed by the host country.
- High transfer prices may make a subsidiary's profits look low when it is facing labor negotiations, enabling it to argue that it cannot pay higher wages.

When some oil-producing nations required oil companies to sell oil at the artificially high "posted prices" (now being phased out), the companies had to set up subsidiaries to buy oil at that price, and then sell to other subsidiaries at lower realistic prices—thus showing a regular loss every reporting period.

Many companies disagree violently with the idea that they use unrealistic transfer prices to achieve other aims, pointing out that foreign nations watch their pricing behavior closely. They add that it is difficult at best to prorate such things as research expense when pricing an item for overseas sale, and a price that is legitimate may look high. But several foreign countries are investigating transfer pricing, partly because of the huge sums involved: some $40 billion a year in transactions by U.S. multinationals within their own companies.

Today's Consumer

In recent years there have been marked changes in the American consumer. We are less impressed with status, and more inclined to simple living. We are more attentive to deceptive advertising, more ready to criticize faulty products, more preoccupied with safety. Robert Kennedy caught some of this in his book *To Seek a Newer World:*

> Distasteful to the young, as it has been to moralists for thousands of years, is the ethic that judges all things by their profit. They have seen high officers of the nation's largest corporations engage in conspiracies to fix prices. They have seen us send people to jail for the possession of marijuana, while refusing to limit the sale or advertising of cigarettes, which kill thousands of Americans each year. They have seen us hesitate to impose the weakest of safety standards on automobiles, or require that a...store or lending company tell the simple truth about the interest rate it is charging on loans. They think their elders have surrendered community values and personal excellence, in exchange for the tailfins and trinkets that Westbrook Pegler once called "a variety of dingbats for the immature."[16]

Government Impact on Marketing

New laws have been passed by the federal government in a wide area affecting marketing practices, coupled with growing emphasis on enforcing the laws now on the books. Some of this recent regulatory action has been sparked by the actions of so-called consumer advocate Ralph Nader, but much of it is a reflection of the times. Radio and TV stations are finding that they cannot present one side of a partisan position without providing time for opposing advocates to present their views; they must spend some time on local programming, even at the cost of giving up the network shows for certain hours; they cannot carry deceptive or misleading advertising; and their licences are subject to renewal hearings where their stewardship can be called into question by dissatisfied consumers. Companies are not nearly as free as before to make unsubstantiated claims about their products, and are required to give the consumers information about what is in the product or how strong it is, or details of its key specifications. The concept of *product liability* has been extended far past living up to specific written guarantees, and now covers responsibility for general good performance, even if not claimed. When goods are defective, the company is required to recall them and correct what is wrong, at the penalty of stiff fines or criminal action.

<small>product liability</small>

Recently the Federal Trade Commission brought a complaint against the four leading cereal makers—Kellogg, General Mills, General Foods, and Quaker Oats—on the grounds that extensive advertising by the four has created a "shared monopoly" in violation of Section 5 of the FTC Act. The FTC claims that these four, who sell over 90% of all cereals, advertise "wastefully" and thereby have increased cereal prices as much as 25%. But a study by economists William Comanor and Thomas Wilson in 1967 found that the cereal industry, more than any of the 41 consumer goods industries studied, was characterized by economies of scale in production (meaning that the 13% advertising expenditures paid their way in increasing volume and decreasing costs). The question of whether the FTC is a suitable judge of when product differences are important to consumers and when they are not is a touchy one, and bound to be explored extensively in the courts in the future.

<small>product recall</small>

Product safety, and the related *product recall* (requiring manufacturers to recall products to correct defects), have become important areas of federal action in recent years. General Foods' Quality Assurance Director David E. James has suggested that future marketing courses will include lessons in "reverse distribution"—getting the product back to the manufacturer from the customer. Since the Consumer Product Safety Act became law in late 1972, and a Consumer Product Safety Commission was set up in 1973, more and more manufacturers of TV sets, ovens, bicycles, and so on have been required to recall products for repairs, under penalty of fines up to $500,000. Automobiles have been under recall laws since the 1966 National Traffic and Motor Vehicle Safety Act; under one recall program, General Motors notified 6.5 million Chevrolet owners to bring their cars in for motor mount inspection (postage for the certified notices came to $3.5 million). Since the CPSA became law, there have been recalls for TV sets that might generate electric shocks, lawn mowers that might cause injury, ovens that might suffocate or shock, bicycles that might cause falls, and many other potentially harmful products.

Recall requires detailed product sales information, keeping track of where each batch goes through the distribution channel. Zenith Radio, which had to recall 23,000 TV sets to check a defect existing in less than 500, or Goodyear Tire, which had to recall a safe tire whose only defect was an inverted "6" (saying the tire would carry 1980 pounds rather than 1680), are typical of the companies which have had to incur heavy costs to make corrections of a rather minor nature. Other recalls have been so expensive that they have forced companies out of business.

Consumerism

"Consumerism" may be defined as increased attention to the protection of individual consumers from improper practices of marketers. The practices can be categorized as follows:

1. Clearly fraudulent or unsafe situations
2. Failure to provide needed or useful information (both as to technical specifications of products or food contents, or as to the weight and age of the products)
3. Protection of the environment against debris or byproducts that will not biodegrade or rust away into harmless residue
4. Protection of consumers from the results of their own carelessness or recklessness

The "lower lower" class consumers (in the jargon of social stratification demand studies) are likely to be treated badly in what they buy unless special preventive efforts are made. Confined to the ghetto by lack of convenient transportation, they often are limited to one or a very few inadequate stores, and don't realize the savings to be had by comparative shopping. Even though ingredients are printed on packages, they may have insufficient knowledge to interpret what they read—or insufficient motivation to read it. Used to being treated badly or at least indifferently by merchants, they do not know their merchandising rights under any of the new laws and are ill-equipped to insist on them. Many of the consumer activities stirring around them are passing them by. Consumer's Union, Consumer's Research, the Special Assistant to the President for Consumer Affairs, the Consumer Advisory Council, Ralph Nader, Warren Magnesun—all of these may as well not exist for any ghetto consumers, for all the practical good they do.

These consumers may not be able to get their money's worth, but there is a deep residue of resentment against what they feel are abuses. The National Commission on Civil Disorders reported as follows:

> Much of the violence in recent civil disorders has been directed at stores and other commercial establishments in disadvantaged Negro areas. In some cases, rioters focused on stores operated by white merchants who, they apparently believed, had been charging exorbitant prices or selling inferior goods. It is clear that many residents of disadvantaged Negro neighborhoods believe they suffer constant abuses by local merchants.[17]

The "new consumerism" even extends to the federal consumer organization itself. In 1974, when the White House demanded political clearance for the key figures in the Consumer Product Safety Commission (executive director, general counsel, and directors of Office of Public Affairs, Office of Congressional Relations, and Bureau of Compliance), chairman Richard O. Simpson refused "as a matter of principle" to permit it, maintaining that political clearance implied political control.

New Marketing Trends

Companies and products are changing, under the influence of the new consumer tastes, probably faster than at any time in the past. The fast food explosion is one example; so is the unexpected boom in wine sales (65% growth in the past five years, whereas distilled spirits have grown some 2.6% a year). Honda almost single-handedly changed the motorcyclist image from a guy with black leather jacket and studded boots to the suburbanite or suited business executive in need of transportation, leading the industry to sales of 1.2 million street vehicles (plus 500,000 recreational and racing bikes) in 1974—double the sales five years earlier. Detroit has been slow to hear consumer demands for smaller and more utilitarian cars—lighter, with more room inside and less under the hood, and greater economy—in effect, as Gerald C. Meyers of American Motors puts it, "setting people in the car first, and then building it around them." Between 1965 and 1973, almost the entire growth in the U.S. auto market was in small cars, but Detroit continued to build—and not sell—the long-hooded "status symbols" of an earlier day. Meyers thinks the American volume car of the 1980s will be "1,650 to 1,850 pounds, 1.4 to 1.6 liter engine (85.4 to 97.6 cu. in.)...the length will be 145 to 160 inches, the wheelbase about 86 to 96 inches, and it will seat at least four passengers." He has described a car very close to the Honda Civic.

The staid old bookselling business is changing to mass marketing, with chain buying and computerized retailing taking over from artistic achievement. Waldenbook Company and B. Dalton Booksellers are two in the new image, selling a whopping over $2 billion worth of books in 1973. Dr. Pepper, a prosaic old soft-drink company without much action, began advertising heavily on the basis that it was a "misunderstood" soft drink (and might appeal to young people who sometimes feel *they* are misunderstood)—and exploded into a 42% growth rate per year to become best performer among the nation's "Second 500" industrial firms (and third best performer of all leading U.S. firms). The booming leisure market has consumers now spending over $40 billion a year and is growing 9% to 12% a year, fueled by the young adults who today have the fastest-growing incomes in the population. Each 1% rise in disposable income seems to bring more than a 2% rise in leisure-time expenditures.

The garment trade, which once dictated fashion to U.S. women, realized with its failure to cram the midi down their throats in 1970 that women now are doing the dictating, and is starting to market systematically. Stewart G. Harris, former IBM executive who became president of Hers Apparel Industries, says, "All the way into the 1960s, many apparel companies were run purely on intuition. Their management techniques were clearly approaching insanity. Now they are doing much more with information systems and doing more marketing planning." Hers Apparel uses computerized reports from its nine subsidiaries to gather daily information on sales, inventory, and other marketing data. And the cosmetics industry, which has peddled art and mystique, is starting to change its sales channels radically, as sales move from the conventional department store to drugstore and discount chains.

Red Owl supermarkets, a 400-store chain, is offering refunds to shoppers who return containers for reuse (egg cartons, milk containers,

Companies and products are changing faster today than at any time in the past.

and even paper bags, as well as soft drink bottles), which both cleans up the environment and brings savings to the customers. The Metropolitan Transit Commission of Minneapolis-St. Paul is painting Duesenbergs, Volkswagens, and other cars on its buses and promoting the buses as the "Greater Metropolitan Car Pool," increasing ridership 13% to 15% a year. Even the staid old Social Security Administration is advertising its wares on TV. Toro Company's "Young Entrepreneur" program is teaching teenagers how to organize their own lawn-care businesses. The housebuilding business, typically a very staid area of marketing, is moving into buy-back plans, a six-month "rent-occupancy" period to enable buyers to accumulate the 5% down payment, free furniture, "California" styling and marketing including model home centers and custom designs—20-foot-high ceilings, kitchen counters extending onto patios, floor-to-ceiling glass, built-in planters, self-lighting fireplaces—and community pools, tennis courts, clubhouse, and putting greens.

The Postal Service is getting new competition from companies that carry the mail. Purolator Services, Inc., now does $64 million a year in postal services, joined by United Parcel, Wells Fargo, Brinks, Bankers Dispatch, and United Dispatch. Not only are the customers carrying their own mail, they are now designing their own products, through industrial *focus groups*. A time-tested marketing device whereby guests sit around and talk about how to improve the quality of magazines or dishwashers,

focus groups

> Could there be any new marketing trends in the engineering consulting business? What might they be?

the focus group has been converted to product design. Beckman Instruments, Inc., brought in a large group of industrial process-control equipment buyers for cocktails and a discussion session; the result was a completely new line of equipment that is reportedly designed by the customers themselves.

Summary

True marketing starts and ends with the consumer; the most successful companies are becoming "marketing companies." If a product cannot be made to sell at a price competitive with other goods, its production cost is unimportant; Henry Ford realized that setting a low selling price forced his firm to look for ways to reduce the production cost.

Marketing goals are very similar to overall company goals, since marketing pervades the entire company. Market performance is a composite of basic strengths, internal strategy (which the company can influence), and external variables (which it cannot influence); internal factors are product, price, distribution, promotion, and service. There is usually some price at which the optimum profit can be made. Middlemen help smaller companies, but their disadvantages have encouraged some larger companies to do without them. It is very difficult to determine the payoff from advertising, but one must try.

Marketing produces almost unavoidable organizational conflict because departmental goals and overall market goals are not always the same. Some marketing organizations function by territory, some by customer, and some by product line (the latter may help to minimize organizational conflicts).

Some special marketing organizations are trade fairs, regional exchanges, and commodity exchanges. Some special market structures are the task force and vertical structures. Franchising (licensing others to use your firm name) is becoming very popular, particularly in fast foods.

Location is of great importance. Huge shopping centers are locating around large cities, to take advantage of highway networks that bring them shoppers; a recent trend is moving such centers back to the city. Decision systems are important as well, and the computer is being used in many ways to assist the marketing manager with necessary data.

Large firms cannot meet their buyers face-to-face, so must use theories of buyer behavior to determine their wants and needs. There are behavioral theories of why buyers make buying decisions, based on economic factors, basic drives, insecurities and guilt feelings, and desires to conform to their cultures and social groups; different social groups have different market wants.

Market research can be short-term or long-term. New product introduction usually is preceded by a market analysis. Some types of research are sales forecasting, product analysis, and locational analysis. Research is done by using consumer panels which are models of the whole society in miniature. Trend analysis of past performance is used to forecast future developments. Decisions on new product lines are long-term, because of the time it takes to develop and introduce a new line.

Advertising strategy seeks to obtain product recognition, understanding of its benefits, favorable decision to buy, and actual purchase. Relative effectiveness of advertisements is evaluated by conscious or unconscious response to the ad, including recognition tests, or by analyzing the results after the ad has run. Some firms set budgets as a fraction of sales volume, and others seek to attain certain goals (such as a certain market share) and therefore set the amount of advertising that they think will achieve their purpose.

New products must be introduced, or the company will not prosper. The costs are high, and companies in a cash squeeze often cannot introduce new products despite the need to do so.

Distribution channels are important, but the manufacturer does not control them completely, and often no one in the company seems to be in charge of distribution. The distribution channel looks different to the manufacturer, the wholesaler, and the retailer.

Companies use product differentiation and market segmentation in efforts to carve out certain market areas exclusively for their products. Price strategy is used as well to increase sales; sometimes raising a price will raise sales, but usually the reverse is true. Large companies in oligopolistic situations (a few companies covering most of the market) hesitate to lower prices to increase sales, for fear that others will do the same. Multinational companies sometimes are accused of manipulating prices charged to their own subsidiaries in order to change their apparent profits and pay less in taxes.

There is great emphasis on consumerism in recent years—changing laws so that firms are required to pay more attention to consumer rights and protection. No longer is the transaction completed when the sale is made, for companies are being required to recall products that are unsafe or of inadequate quality. Firms are required to tell the consumer clearly what the ingredients and specifications of their products are. And there are many new trends in marketing, to match the changing consumer tastes and lifestyles.

Notes

1. Robert J. Keith, "The Marketing Revolution," *Journal of Marketing* (Jan. 1960): 35–38.
2. Henry Ford, *My Life and Work* (Garden City, N.Y.: Doubleday & Co., Inc., 1923), pp. 146–147.
3. "The Auto Slump Spreads," *Business Week*, December 14, 1974, pp. 58–64.
4. By contrast, Inland Container Corp.'s #7 of its seven corporate objectives for 1975 is clear-cut: "To have fun."
5. The huge 1974 profits of most oil companies resulted from an unusual combination of circumstances not likely to be repeated, and some analysts believe these profits were badly needed to fund the massive exploration expenditures required to improve our energy self-sufficiency. But they led to widespread resentment on the part of the public, and several initiatives in Congress to impose stringent profit curbs. (Senator Henry Jackson termed the profits "obscene.")
6. The petroleum shortage may have succeeded in forcing Detroit's attention on this unattended market sector; three of the "big four" quickly came out with contenders in this area—the first time since the short-lived Crosley that there has been a U.S. mini.

7. In fact, they rejected this alternative initially, and attempted to sell by direct mail and by calls to department stores—but with either method the costs were so high per sale that they soon realized their makeshift distribution system could not handle the problem, and fell back on making use of the wholesaler.

8. This phenomenon is most apparent at large universities, where some faculty feel that the most prestigious position is a research slot where it is unnecessary to see any students at all *as customers* (though they are highly acceptable *as employees*—that is, research assistants). Many top-notch professors are exceptions to this trend, however.

9. "How Ideas Are Made Into Products at 3M," *Business Week,* September 15, 1973, pp. 224–228.

10. Indeed, a shoemaker more interested in travel than in manufacturing could have attended 31 shoe fairs in 12 countries in the single year of 1973, starting with the Montreal fair and ending with the Tanners' Club Annual Symposim and Machinery Show at Woburn, Mass.

11. Seymour M. Lipset and Reinhard Bendix, *Class, Status and Power* (New York: The Free Press, 1953), pp. 454–65.

12. "Research and Pseudo-Research in Marketing," *Harvard Business Review,* March–April, 1971, pp. 73–76.

13. There was more to it than this, of course. The Edsel missed because of a complex mixture of shifting tastes, changing national economy, and actions of competitors—but good marketing should have gotten some hint of the impact of these diverse elements.

14. Paul E. Green and Donald S. Tull, *Research for Marketing Decisions* (Englewood Cliffs, N.J.: Prentice-Hall, Inc., 1966), pp. 427–430.

15. Summarized from Lidia Leszczynski, "TV Ads Called Tribal Rites of Modern Society," *Pittsburgh Press,* December 15, 1974, p. 2.

16. (Garden City, N.Y.: Doubleday & Co., Inc., 1967), pp. 6–7.

17. *Exploitation of Disadvantaged Consumers by Retail Merchants* (New York: Bantam Books, 1968), pp. 274–277.

Review Questions

1. What do we mean by saying a company is a "marketing company"?
2. What is wrong with the simple marketing goal of making the highest profit?
3. What variables affect internal marketing strategy?
4. What are the disadvantages of using a wholesaler or other middleman?
5. Why are there inherent conflicts between the marketing director and the heads of other operating departments in a company?
6. What is "product line operating management?"
7. Why are major shopping centers located outside of the city?
8. Explain the basic concepts of the Pavlovian theory of market behavior.
9. Why is it important for a marketing manager to know the social class of the customers for a product before designing a promotion plan?
10. What does the typical life cycle of a product look like? How can its life be extended?
11. What are the five factors producing sales volume in a given location?
12. How are consumer panels made up, and why?
13. What are some methods for measuring effectiveness of advertising?
14. Why must companies continually bring out new products?
15. Explain "product differentiation."
16. Why do some large companies hesitate to cut prices to increase profits?
17. Explain "product liability" and "product recall."
18. What do you think causes new marketing trends?

Discussion Questions

1. From your knowledge of corporations producing for the consumer market, how would you distinguish between a "marketing company" and a "production" company? Why?

2. In 1974–75, the Middle East oil producing countries started eliminating the middlemen and doing their own marketing. Why did they do this? Was it a surprising action, or in accordance with the way producers usually behave as they pick up strength?

3. Draw North Star's marketing organization as you understand it. Which of the three major organizational models—by territory, customer, or product—does it most resemble?

4. How does it happen that some shopping centers are moving from the city center and others are moving to the city center?

5. What would be the difference in the way you would advertise a car to a "lower-lower," an "upper-lower," and an "upper-middle-class" buyer?

6. If you were selecting a consumer panel to determine how a city election for mayor was going to come out, what factors would you consider in selecting the panel members?

7. One of the categories from the Starch Elite study not printed in Figure 13-15 (a *Newsweek* advertisement) is readers aged 50 to 64. In this category, *Time* (52 readers per dollar) and *U.S. News* (72 readers per dollar) fared better than *Newsweek* (49 readers per dollar). The figure also omits the *New York Times Magazine*, which came out higher than *Newsweek* in every Starch Elite category. Under what circumstances would these facts lead you to decide against *Newsweek* as an advertising medium?

8. Under what circumstances would advertising not be a net gain to society? (Assume we are talking about reasonably honest advertising—plenty of "puff," but no false statements.)

9. Try to think of an example of each of the four major consumerism practices.

North Star Case Study

When North Star completed the shopping center study for Blackridge, the partners were so convinced of the good prospects for its success that they decided to invest in it personally. The plan was to have a discount department store as the major draw, with about 75,000 square feet of sales area. There would be a number of specialty shops, plus the Blackridge public library and probably the municipal offices in the back. In addition there were discussions about adding a bowling alley, a movie theater, a skating rink and a motel. Volume forecasts for the discount department store suggested that it would be doing about $4.5 million in sales a year, or about $60 a square foot of selling space—a figure within the range of good performance for such stores. They assumed the others would do as well. The other stores, not including the bowling alley, theater, skating rink, and motel, would bring the total selling area to about 200,000 square feet.

They approached a friend of Dick Boyer's who had invested in building apartments in the past, because their funds were sufficient only for a fraction of what the center would cost (even though they planned to take out a mortgage for the majority of the cost). He showed some interest, and said he would be visiting the area within the month and would come by for an inspection and meeting. In order to prepare for this meeting, the partners reviewed the advantages and disadvantages of the project, and a number of questions came up. Some of the questions they might have asked are given below; how would you go about getting answers?

1. Basically, why would such a center attract any business away from other stores or centers?
2. What do you think about the benefits of a skating rink?
3. What are some of the dangers the future might hold, with other centers?
4. How would the social makeup of the Blackridge area affect the type of goods and stores that ought to be in the center?
5. A discount department store charges lower prices than a regular (junior) department store. Should the main draw be discount or not (what are the considerations)?
6. What kind of stores should the other stores in the center be? How about an automotive service station? A plumbing supply house?
7. How important is the existence of a major highway going by the center?

Suggestions for Further Reading

Alles, A. *Exhibitions: Universal Marketing Tools*. New York: John Wiley & Sons, Inc., 1973.

Boone, L. E., and J. C. Johnson. *Marketing Channels*. Morristown, N.J.: General Learning Press, 1973.

Cox, Keith K. *The Marketing Research Process*. Pacific Palisades, Calif.: Goodyear Pub. Co., 1972.

Cundiff, E. W., et al. *Fundamentals of Modern Marketing*. Englewood Cliffs, N.J.: Prentice-Hall, Inc., 1973.

Farley, J. V., ed. *Control of Error in Market Research Data*. Lexington, Mass.: Lexington Books, 1974.

Hopkins, D. S. *The Short-Term Marketing Plan*. New York: National Industrial Conference Board, 1972.

Hughes, D. G. *Demand Analysis for Marketing Decisions*. Homewood, Ill.: Richard D. Irwin, Inc., 1973.

Jolson, M. A. *Quantitative Techniques for Marketing Decisions*. New York: Macmillan Pub. Co., Inc., 1973.

Kollat, D. T., et al. *Strategic Marketing*. New York: Holt, Rinehart & Winston, Inc., 1972.

McKay, E. S. *The Marketing Mystique*. New York: American Management Association, 1972.

Miracle, G. E., ed. *Marketing Decision Making: Strategy and Payoff*. Ann Arbor, Mich.: Bureau of Business Research, University of Michigan, 1965.

Palda, K. S. *Pricing Decision and Marketing Policy*. Englewood Cliffs, N.J.: Prentice-Hall, Inc., 1971.

Perlman, R. *Theory of Markets*. Hinsdale, Ill.: Dryden Press, 1972.

Schening, E. E. *New Product Management*. Hinsdale, Ill.: Dryden Press, 1974.

Smykay, E. W. *Physical Distribution Management*. New York: Macmillan Pub. Co., Inc., 1973.

Weiss, E. B. *Marketing to the New Society*. Chicago: Crain Communications, 1973.

The Impact of Laws and Regulations

14

North Star Prologue

Starting as a two-person engineering consulting firm, North Star grew by taking on two more partners, and grew in size as it picked up additional work. One of its interesting relationships was with the large corporation, B&W, which proposed a merger that North Star turned down. As its overseas work reduced in overall importance, the partners found themselves facing various administrative problems: communications, handling conflict, a crisis in leadership, and problems with insuring an effective flow of information and effective budgetary management.

The above were primarily internal problems of good organization, but an important external problem was effective marketing. The accident of conducting a marketing study for a client led North Star to realize that its own marketing setup was deficient, and it reorganized the marketing function.

One of the new marketing areas disclosed by the in-house survey was one Bert really knew about, but hadn't taken the trouble to explore: technical assistance to firms being cited by the county health department for discharging contaminated water into the waterways of the region. One of Bert's first customers was a manufacturer whose process involved the discharge of 700 gallons a day of water contaminated with methanol and hydrochloric acid. Bert found him by following up on any condemnation or cease-and-desist actions of the county, and when he called on the telephone he found the owner in a state of enraged shock. The county inspector had showed up at his plant, put a padlock and seal on the discharge valve to the river, and effectively put his operation out of business. He had continued on a reduced basis by renting a 10,000-gallon railroad tank car, but that was buying him only two or three weeks at best, and he was very desperate for any solution.

Bert put on a crash effort in collaboration with faculty members from the university plus his own water treatment group, and they were able to find a way to convert the hydrochloric acid to lead chloride, which could be sent to a smelter for disposition, and to recover the methanol so the manufacturer could reuse it. The ending was a happy one, and Bert left the bemused owner in a state of wholehearted gratitude. But the event set Bert to thinking what amazing powers the government had; in this case it was able to deprive an individual of his personal property—the means by which he made his living—without any due process of law that Bert could see. He wondered what vulnerabilities North Star might have that could invite a similarly sudden and painful response.

As it happened, he didn't have long to wait.

One day soon after the water pollution episode, a representative showed up at the office and presented credentials indicating that he was from the Department of Labor. He asked to see the employee time records and interviewed several workers at length. At the end of his inspection, he told Henry that the firm was violating a labor law by not paying overtime to its secretaries—instead, North Star usually gave compensatory time off, which is not permitted. North Star was required to provide back payment for all the overtime shown on the records, and was given a stern warning to comply with the law hereafter.

At the next staff meeting, the conferees mulled over the question of what other regulations they might have been violating without knowing it. They decided to bring in a lawyer to look over their operations and give them an opinion—sort of a legal physical.

When the lawyer had completed his meetings with the various members of North Star Associates, which took place at individual sessions over a period of nearly a month, he met informally with the officers before submitting his report to summarize his general impression of the operation.

First, he said, the project management relationship with Barnhard & Walker smacked of conflict of interest, in that North Star and B&W were not exactly at arms' length (there had been the offer of a merger, there was the joint venture on the municipal information system, and they were jointly prospecting for new jobs since North Star had given B&W no trouble on the Natal job). Yet at the same time, North Star was representing itself to the Asian contractor and to other firms where they were soliciting jobs as able to conduct an independent monitoring operation of its huge friend. As further testimony to the special relationship the two firms seemed to enjoy, North Star had even asked B&W for a loan—the lawyer said it was a blessing that it had not come to pass, or a disgruntled joint venture firm could take the two of them to the cleaners in court.

Second—and this was downright illegal—North Star was paying no workmen's compensation and never had, although clearly required to do so by law. Third—another probably illegal action, although more subject to interpretation than the previous item—North Star was a corporation, and thus liable to corporate taxes, but had been in the habit of increasing the salaries of the principals as business increased in a way that resembled profit sharing, rather than simply establishing salaries as "suitable compensation" for services performed. The corporate tax laws imposed far more stringent control over compensation behavior than did the Uniform Commercial Code provisions of partnership laws which most states had adopted, for corporate taxes are an Internal Revenue matter. The fact was that the salaries actually were being set in order to keep pace with growth in profits, and the IRS would interpret this as an effort to evade corporate taxes. Fourth, and related: the bonuses paid members of the drafting room when the firm had a good year constituted a profit-sharing plan, and as such fell under rather restrictive legal provisions, including an upper limit, a requirement that all employees share at an equal rate, and a stipulation that IRS approval of the scheme probably was required.

Fifth, although this was quite controversial and many lawyers would disagree, the rigid fee structure and "gentlemen's agreements" which controlled the municipal consulting engineering practice in the area had many of the earmarks of price collusion and restraint of trade in violation of the antitrust statutes. Sixth, and also related, the lower rates that North Star had been charging Barnhard & Walker, while quite understandable as a consideration in return for getting work on a noncompetitive basis, were clearly a violation of the Robinson-Patman Act.

There probably were other violations, either of law or of public policy, which a bit more searching would disclose, said the lawyer. But these would do for a starter, he added with a smile. They shouldn't be too downcast about their legal peccadillos, he said—many managers violated one law or another unknowingly, to say nothing of those who broke laws or regulations intentionally. Quite often new companies, and some not so new, failed to obtain municipal or county permits to do business, neglected to pay required fees or taxes, or did not know that they had to get advance permission before they could operate in a certain way—such as the requirement for an engineer to have a state registration in many cases before approving construction plans. Companies who paid kickbacks or finder's fees often had a gut feeling that they were doing something against public policy, but might not know that it was a specific violation of federal law to pay brokerage fees to a purchaser or his agent when no services were rendered.

North Star had a bit of cleaning up to do, he said in leaving, and he would be glad to assist with that. But from what he saw, there was no intent to behave in a larcenous manner, and his experience was that public law was pretty reasonable when parties could convincingly argue that they had acted in good faith.

What North Star Can Learn from Chapter 14

1. The basic requirements of a business contract
2. The court structure, both state and federal, and what each handles
3. The meaning and implications of a class action suit
4. The trend in growth of legal problems from the "new consumerism"
5. The concept and application of administrative law
6. The various regulatory agencies, how they were formed, how they have evolved, and what they do today
7. The extent to which administrative agencies have taken over from the courts

The previous chapter, "Facing the Market," dealt with an important external factor for any organization: its relations with its customers. This chapter deals with another vital external factor: the pervasive control and regulation of business by government. In this chapter you will study:

1. *The elements of business law,* including legal systems that impinge on business operations, the principal elements involved in contracts, legal instruments, and various legal aspects bearing on property.
2. *Administrative law,* covering the powers and privileges of administrative agencies, which combine many of the legal aspects of the executive, legislative, and judiciary branches and have been termed the "fourth branch" of government.
3. *Regulatory agencies,* both independent commissions and arms of the executive branch, who more and more are replacing the courts as the principal adjudicative organs for business—what John F. Kennedy called a "chaotic patchwork" of uncoordinated law and bureaucracy.
4. *Consumer movements,* which have created their own set of regulators with a very different thrust from the conventional regulatory agencies, but with a no less overwhelming impact on industry and the economy.

communist system

socialist system

capitalist system

There are three kinds of governmental systems: the *communist system,* which abolishes private property except of a personal nature and assumes all ownership in the state; the *socialist system,* which nationalizes key industries but leaves much private property and provides free elections; and the *capitalist system,* which leaves most enterprises large and small in private hands, but provides controls to insure that the public interest is protected. In a capitalist system such as ours, it was inevitable that the increasing size and impersonal nature of corporations would lead to pressures for governmental agencies to deal with possibilities of abuse. When a company such as General Motors has one or two million "owners" who exercise no real responsibility for the company's actions, the public cannot tell "who is to blame" for unsatisfactory products, service, or conduct, and feels some outside authority must intervene to protect its interests. Alfred Sloan grasped this situation a half century ago:

> There is a point beyond which diffusion of stock ownership must enfeeble the corporation by depriving it of virile interest in management upon the part of some one man or group of men to whom its success is a matter of personal and vital interest. And conversely, at the same point the public interest becomes involved when the public can no longer locate some tangible personality within the ownership which it may hold responsible for the corporation's conduct.[1]

Indeed, many feel that a huge corporation is not "private property" at all, but rather a great public resource, whose profits go to individuals but whose conduct must be channeled in the public interest. Certainly, in view of their vast power, they must be subject to some sort of community control. Property rights are not paramount over the right to survival.

That is what federal and state regulation is all about. It may not do the job adequately—in fact Ralph Nader's task force report on the Federal

Trade Commission[2] called it a "self-parody of bureaucracy, fat with cronyism, torpid through an inbreeding unusual even for Washington, manipulated by the agents of commercial predators, impervious to governmental and citizen monitoring"—but that is its charter. Certainly it is an important force for business managers and public managers alike to understand, since its influence on our institutions and our well-being is so profound.

The Elements of Business Law

Business Relationships

The central element of business relationships is the *contract*. While a good many business dealings are the result of verbal agreements, ultimately most relationships of any size are reduced to writing in contract form. There are certain elements that must be present for a contract to be valid:

business contracts

1. Both parties (or all parties, if more than two) must be empowered to enter into a binding agreement (if you agree to sell the Brooklyn Bridge to your neighbor, the contract is not binding because you do not own it and the actual owners have not delegated to you the power to act on their behalf).
2. The transaction in question must be lawful (a written agreement to divide up the proceeds of a bank heist is not a valid contract, because dealing in stolen goods in unlawful).
3. All parties involved must enter into the contract of their own free will, without being coerced.
4. There must be some reasonable consideration that motivates both or all parties to enter the contract in the first place.

Individuals may not be entitled to enter into binding contract agreements if they are under age, mentally incapacitated, and so on. Corporation representatives are not competent to commit their corporations unless there is a specific delegation of powers in the bylaws that extends to them; perhaps it is a matter that only the board of directors can authorize, or perhaps according to the corporation's charter the stockholders must express themselves affirmatively before the agreement can be made. The legal doctrine of *estoppel* (which means that an entity cannot repudiate the acts and agreements of its representatives if a reasonably prudent person could conclude that they were acting within their authority) may lead the courts to decide that a valid contract exists even though the representatives were not in fact empowered to act. (No such doctrine operates in dealings with government agencies, however. If the local agent of the Federal Crop Insurance Corporation tells you your spring wheat crop is insurable against drought and accepts your application and premium, whereupon you lose your wheat and file a claim only to find that he was mistaken, the government is under no obligation to back up the agent's erroneous promise.)

estoppel

In business, a contract that commits the parties to an unlawful act, such as a merger that is prohibited under antitrust law, is not a lawful contract and hence is unenforceable. Agreements to discriminate in price, if they violate the Robinson-Patman Act of 1936, have no standing. In most business relationships, the respective corporate lawyers are well aware of such requirements, and hence are unlikely to enter into contracts in ignorance of the fact that they are unlawful.

If a contract is agreed to under duress, it can be broken. Suppose a small grocer signs a contract to handle a certain line of goods carried by a wholesaler, but does so under the threat that he will not get the usual price reduction on other items if he does not sign. The grocer can go to court and have the contract declared void if he can prove this chain of events.

consideration

Contracts are entered into for some *consideration,* usually money, but often other things of value such as franchise rights or assignment of sales territory on an exclusive basis. The contract should set forth what the consideration is. If there is no consideration on one side, the transaction is a gift. If there is no consideration on either side (nothing of value is being conveyed), the transaction is meaningless.

negotiable instruments

Negotiable instruments are the documents that carry out business relationships. When an individual or a business executive goes to a bank to borrow money, there may be an exchange of instruments: the bank hands the borrower a *bank check* or the equivalent, and the borrower hands the bank a *promissory note* or the equivalent (which promises to repay the loan and interest within a stated time and on stated terms). The borrower can transfer the check to another by endorsement, and the bank can convey the promissory note and its right to repayment on stated terms to another in a similar manner. (A bank that fails and is taken over by another bank would transfer its instruments in this way, or a bank may sell some notes to a collection agency or other investor.) Both of these instruments, then, are negotiable. The Uniform Negotiable Instruments Act requires that an instrument must be for a specific sum of money, must be unconditionally payable at a stated time to the payee, and must be properly signed and executed in writing.

transfers of property

Transfers of property take place when the contract terms of sale are fulfilled. Title to property may pass before payment, and the seller may take a note for the money due, or custody may pass to the purchaser but title remain with the seller (as with automobile installment sales) until payment is made in full. If a manufacturer sends goods to a retailer on *consignment,* title remains with the manufacturer until the retailer sells them; if goods are sent on approval, they are the property of the sender until the receiver accepts ownership in whatever way has been specified. Title during shipment may remain with the seller or the buyer, depending on the terms of sale. Sometimes conditional sales are made subject to a money-back guarantee or warranty if the buyer is not satisfied within a given period.

warranties

What sort of warranty would you say an engineering consulting firm gives as to the quality of the work it does?

Warranties may be *express* (statements of fact about the products) or *implied* (matters which the buyer has a right to assume automatically). An express warranty would be one stating that any damages to the power train of a washing machine will be repaired in full at manufacturer's expense for the first 90 days after sale. An implied warranty would hold that the fastenings for the weights of a set of barbells are strong enough for the use intended, and thus the weights are in no danger of breaking off under normal use. Some manufacturers' statements are neither, but are simply sales "puff," such as a claim that "our experts can come up with

If a contract is agreed to under duress, it may be broken.

the right answers every time." Since no expert can do that, the claim must be taken as an exaggerated way of representing that the experts are competent. It is unlikely that any legal action against the advertiser for shortcomings of the experts would be successful if predicated on the claim that the statement misled the buyer into thinking the experts were perfect.

Laws and Courts

The major distinction in law is between common law and statutory law. *Common law,* with its foundations in the U.S. going back to British roots, is the body of legal understandings and precedents that gradually gets established and confirmed by custom and repeated legal decisions. If a particular act omits some important basic guarantee that has been established by precedent, usually the act may be read as though the guarantee was included. *Statutory law* is all written law promulgated by government legislative bodies. It also includes the large body of regulatory law issued by various regulatory bodies who have been empowered by statute to issue such regulations with the force of law.

The two basic types of courts in the U.S. are *federal courts* and *state courts* (including municipal courts established under state jurisdiction). Cases involving violation of federal law or another federal issue are tried in federal courts; all other cases are tried in state courts. There is a great

common law

statutory law

federal and state courts

variety of state court systems; some separate criminal and equity matters while others combine them. In a given city, the first level of court is likely to be the *municipal court,* for minor offenses and small claims (generally, individuals can represent themselves in small claims court if the sum involved is low—not over $500 or $1000). One level higher is the *county court,* which has civil and criminal jurisdiction within certain limits; this court is sometimes known as the court of common pleas. At the next level is the *circuit court* or superior court, which includes all civil, criminal, or equity cases and sometimes serves as an appeals court for lower courts. The highest arbiter in state cases is the *state supreme court,* which is the court of final appeal if federal issues are not involved. Federal court systems include the *district courts, courts of appeals,* and the *United States Supreme Court.* The district courts, in their 88 judicial districts, have jurisdiction over all offenses against the United States; the courts of appeals, in their eleven judicial circuits, review the decisions of the district courts. The Supreme Court can strike down any state or federal statute that it decides runs contrary to the U.S. Constitution.

Business torts are offenses at law by one business against another, such as violation of contract, fraudulent acts, infringement of patent, etc. *Business crimes* are offenses by a business against the public, such as violation of consumer protection regulations, antitrust violations, selling of defective merchandise, etc. When one business initiates action against another for a tort, the former is the *plaintiff* and the latter the *defendant;* and the action is a *civil action.* A *suit at law* usually seeks money damages, while a *suit in equity* seeks to compel the defendant to perform the desired act or refrain from the act the plaintiff considers improper. When the government initiates action against a business (or any individual or group), the action is a *criminal action,* and the outcome following a conviction would be a fine or imprisonment.

The volume of business legal actions is increasing tremendously, as will be discussed below. Environmental and fair-employment suits are building from very low levels of activity just a few years ago (prior to 1972 there were virtually no fair-employment suits), and corporations are bringing antitrust actions against one another at a pace that seems to be mounting as much as 50% a year; securities regulation suits are increasing even more rapidly. Individuals are suing corporations, seeking damages for product liability (as buyers) and for harm to the environment (as citizens). Chairman William May of American Can Company stated in 1973, "I probably spend about 60% of my time on legal problems, more than twice as much as five years ago."[3] A lawyer specializing in securities law recently stated that "ten years ago, what a company said in its annual report was pretty much up to the public relations department; today what you say or fail to say, even in a press release, can be the basis for some monster lawsuit."[4]

Some of the large suits of corporation against corporation are new to the corporate scene: Control Data Corporation against I.B.M., Xerox against I.B.M., Litton Industries against Xerox, I.T.T. against General Telephone and Electronics, I.B.M. against Telex. A Department of Justice lawyer, commenting on this new development, said that ten years ago "it would have been like suing a member of your own club."[5] The trend is leading some lawyers to conclude that companies which cannot succeed in business are trying to make up for it in court. General Electric has a staff of 50 corporate lawyers headed by a senior vice-president, and they still remember their travails during the "great electrical conspiracy" of the early 1960s, when they were the largest of seven electrical manufacturers brought to trial for alleged price fixing. That trial, which found some senior officers of the companies guilty and actually sent some to jail, was a landmark case, and the corporate legal world has never been quite the same since.

Businesses as Lawbreakers

In subsequent landmark cases, business executives have been brought to trial for a multitude of actions that previously had not been prosecuted. The 1971 Campaign Financing Act turned the spotlight on campaign gifts, and increased the level of reporting above that required by the old Corrupt Practices Act. Coming on top of Watergate, it led to an investigation of political solicitation practices which revealed that many corporations had made illegal campaign gifts, sometimes thinly disguised as personal campaign gifts by the officers.[6] George Spater, chairman of American Airlines, after admitting that American had contributed $55,000 to the Committee to Reelect the President, reported that Nixon solicitor Herbert Kalmbach told him American Airlines was expected to give $100,000. American was only one of several corporate contributors which came forward to admit their illegal actions to presidential and congressional candidates of both parties, and who paid both corporate and personal fines as a result.

A relatively new development has been the "angry young public interest lawyers," who are not waiting for clients to bring specific problems but are seeking to ferret out failures of corporations and government agencies to protect the public well-being. They have forged a traditional legal tool, the *class action suit*—in which one plaintiff sues on behalf of all who have been injured similarly—into a deadly new weapon against corporate errors, using a 1966 Supreme Court ruling that each injured party can be included in the suit unless he or she specifically elects to stay out. A recent survey of corporations disclosed that two out of three were threatened by class action suits or defending against them at the time. The rules have been changed again, to make it less simple to include a larger group of people—and hence multiply tremendously the stakes for the company being sued—but the class action suit is still a technique of major importance in bringing pressure on corporations to guard against product or service deficiencies.

Five drug companies—American Cyanamid, Bristol-Myers, Pfiser, Squibb, and Upjohn—jointly were assessed damages of $117 million in the largest successful class action suit to date, for alleged overcharges dating all the way back to 1954. These class action suits (66 in all) were based on a Department of Justice antitrust suit related to price fixing of the antibiotic tetracycline.

Legal assistance groups, sometimes termed "poverty lawyers," many of whom are financed in large part by government programs, are now bringing legal services to a segment of the population that had never enjoyed that luxury before. They are suing businesses for consumer

class action suit

fraud, improper credit terms, excessive prices, and shoddy merchandise in stores available to the poor—and are suing government agencies as well for failure to deliver needed services. A parallel set of lawyers, often called "public interest" groups, sues to force corporations to put greater attention on safety, utility, and proper advertising and labeling, as well as bringing pressure to bear on reluctant or negligent regulatory agencies. Washington's Center for Law and Social Policy won a suit to force the Environmental Protection Agency to initiate actions against any products containing DDT; and the Sierra Club took similar action against the EPA in connection with maintenance of existing air standards in areas where federal air quality standards would have allowed some increase in air pollution.

In 1973, *Fortune* surveyed a cross-section of top U.S. corporations—65 in all—to ask what sort and amount of legal problems they were encountering. What came back was a picture of a vastly increased legal load, and far greater attention to these cases by the chief corporate executives. In the past six years, lawsuits have doubled (with environmental and fair employment just starting to pick up steam). The U.S. corporations have some 40,000 in-house lawyers, and it is estimated that they spend well over $3 billion a year in legal costs. Consolidated Edison, which pays out about $200 million in a year for environmental protection, finds itself defending legal actions brought by protesting citizen groups at every one of the seven sites it is exploring for generating plants. Since Con Ed must order machinery and start construction in a timely manner, yet is under the threat of being stopped at any or all of the sites selected, "it's conceivable that we may find ourselves with a half-billion dollars' worth of equipment that we can't use," says board chairman Charles Luce.[7]

In response to *Fortune's* question as to who generated most of the legal problems for the corporations, two-thirds of the companies responding picked the federal government. The major topics were: antitrust, securities and stockholder problems, consumerism, environmental problems, and fair employment practices. A great deal of the effort involves *preventive law:* planning corporate action in response to new regulations or court decisions. Complying with the letter of the regulation may put a corporation to heavy expense and sometimes serious competitive disadvantage; but failure to appear to be doing its best may subject it to a huge lawsuit. When two truck operators in California sued General Motors for replacement of allegedly defective wheels, the amount at stake for *their* trucks was negligible—but they sued "on behalf of" 200,000 other owners, and the total cost thus zoomed up to $90 million.

Corporations are suing other corporations far more frequently, and there is a new tendency for the company sued to be stuck with the legal costs of the one doing the suing. When Control Data won its suit against IBM, the latter paid $15 million of Control Data's legal fees (as well as an estimated $60 million of its own). And when public interest groups do the suing, the corporation may be made to pay even if it does not lose. In 1970, three environmental groups sued the Interior Department to compel it to prevent an oil consortium by the name of Alyeska from building a link of the Alaska pipeline. Alyeska intervened in the suit to protect its interests. The environmentalists failed to stop the construction, because Congress changed the law during the suit, but they asked Alyeska to pay half their legal fees. The U.S. appeals court ruled in their favor, saying that as "private attorneys general" they had stimulated a public debate and prodded Congress to amend the Mineral Leasing Act and Interior to abide by the National Environmental Policy Act. In an increasing number of civil rights and environmental cases, judges have been making business defendants pay the winning plaintiffs' court costs. When Chemical Bank of New York was sued by a customer in a truth-in-lending case, the customer won $100 in damages but Chemical Bank was assessed $20,000 in plaintiff legal fees.[8]

The volume of laws and regulations is tremendous, and it is difficult for business corporations to police all of their employees all the time, so they are always exposed to possible infringements. Companies find it almost impossible to comply faithfully with all the rules, even when they try—and, of course, they don't always try. But some perplexing situations arise. In 1973 the Ford Motor Company discovered that employees at its testing center had modified test engines to meet emission standards. Ford reported the tampering—no one from the government caught it—but the Environmental Protection Agency nonetheless levied a $7 million fine against Ford; EPA Administrator William Ruckelshaus said that EPA would not "condone unlawful practices by responsible employees at the operating level of the corporation."

An entirely different aspect of law applied to businesses was explored by the federal judiciary's second circuit, which includes New York, Connecticut, and Vermont. A study released in late 1974 explored the question of how differently the same offense can be treated by different judges. The 50 trial court judges in the second circuit were asked to assign sentences in 30 actual cases, with each judge getting exactly the same information. An independent business executive pleading guilty to one count of filing a false income tax return got sentences ranging from three months to three years. In a cargo theft case the sentences ranged from no jail at all (four years' probation) to seven and a half years in jail. The same judge who gave the most severe sentence in the income tax case let off a post office janitor who stole money with no jail at all and only 18 months' probation. The judge who sentenced a securities salesman conspiring to commit fraud to a year in jail and a $10,000 fine gave no jail and only two years' probation to a butcher passing counterfeit money. Chief Circuit Judge Irving R. Kaufman conducted the study in an effort to convince Congress of the need to "identify the purposes of sentencing, and to specify the criteria for determining the length and type of sentence." He added that "a system in which the length of an offender's sentence is determined by the random factor of assignment to a particular judge does not advance the ends of justice."

Table 14-1 shows the increase in recent years of various categories of court cases. Note the increase in the kinds of cases currently attracting the attention of poverty and public interest lawyers.

Administrative Law

Constitutional law deals with the grand structure and purposes of government: the separation of powers and the functions of the three main

constitutional law

branches of government. When President Nixon repeatedly stated that it was "constitutionally inappropriate" for him to turn over documents or tapes to Congress, or to allow certain of his aides to testify in the courts, he was enunciating a principle of profound importance, regardless of his immediate purposes. *Administrative law* deals with the legislative and judicial powers of administrative agencies established by statute: the way in which the federal government increasingly handles its responsibilities to provide for the general welfare, by delegation of its powers to commissions and agencies. And, as Louis Kohlmeier said in his discussion of the "watchdog agencies,"[9] there is a third type, *Parkinson's law,* which deals with the "predictability of the enlargement and convolution of government in its continuing pursuit."

administrative law

Administrative agencies (speaking generally of the regulatory agencies, but including also agencies that dispense public largesse) are given the authority to: (1) determine and order what can or cannot be done within the area of their dominion (a legislative act), (2) determine whether law has been violated and take action against the offenders (a judicial act), and (3) grant to certain individuals or groups privileges not granted to other similar individuals or groups without recourse (an executive act).

Administrative agencies are supplanting federal courts as law-giving bodies. Every year the regulatory agencies issue more than 100,000 rulings, far more than all the district and appellate courts put together. It might be said that the Federal Administrative Procedure Act of 1946 is now the basic statute in U.S. administrative law. The agencies are not legislative bodies; the Congress, having been delegated legislative authority by the Constitution, cannot delegate that authority to another body. What it does, however, is to draft "skeleton legislation," leaving the administrative agency to flesh it out with administrative decisions. Any penalties for violation of these rules must be lodged in the basic statute passed by Congress; and no regulatory agency can sentence any person to imprisonment, since that is the sole province of the courts.

skeleton legislation

In drafting one of the earliest legislative efforts to establish a regulatory agency, the Interstate Commerce Act of 1887, Congress did not quite have the hang of skeleton legislation. So the Act included such detailed procedures and instructions that the Interstate Commerce Commission has been forced to come back to Congress again and again for amendments to fit the changing times. By contrast, the Securities Exchange Act of 1934 was passed after Congress had become adept at broad delegation of powers (and probably swamped with other duties), and it is drafted in sweepingly general terms, simply employing such

Table 14-1.
Categories of Court Cases

Categories	1961	1966	1968	1970	1972
Environmental issues	—	—	42	140	268
Fair employment cases	—	—	—	—	1015
Antitrust law	420	480	707	929	1379
Security regulation	267	419	689	1211	1919
Trademarks, patents	1585	1832	1829	2150	2194
Labor law	2484	3336	3518	3999	4987

unspecific concepts as "information necessary for protection of investors," "manipulative or deceptive devices," "reasonable rates of commission," and "maintenance of a fair and orderly market," and leaving the rest up to the commissioners.

The great bulk of administrative decisions are made informally and by mutual consent, and hence do not reach the stage of formal procedure.

The Judicial Role

While the agencies dispense a form of justice, certainly more frequently than do the courts, there are some important differences. The very hallmark of our judicial system is separation of the functions of prosecutor and jury; equally vital is the existence of an impartial judge who stands apart from both prosecutor and jury, free to weigh the merits of the two conflicting parties.

It isn't this way at all when a regulatory agency conducts one of its administrative "trials." The trappings and appearances are the same: the party before the tribunal is represented by counsel, witnesses are sworn, written testimony is taken, and briefs are filed. But the commission before which the party appears is prosecutor, judge, and jury all rolled into one. The judge never takes sides, and is never a party to the dispute. But the commission usually *is* a party, and thus is in a position to be prejudiced at the outset. The commission presents the arguments for its side of the case; hears the evidence presented by the defendant; makes a determination of facts and findings; and decides on the penalty. In concept, this is a rather frightening situation. It would appear that the very guarantee of an impartial hearing and due process of the law promised by the Anglo-Saxon judicial system is denied. And that denial is even more significant when we consider that administrative agencies adjudicate many more cases, involving considerably more money in judgments, than do the federal courts.

Still other factors intensify the problem. A judicial opinion in a court of law will be guided by precedent, for the law is built on a body of precedent. That is what makes it possible for legal scholars to predict how the law will behave in a given situation—in short, to know what is legal and what is not. The function of a court of law is to find the appropriate law, determine the facts of a case, and then apply the law to the facts. But an administrative agency has no obligation whatsoever to find the facts and apply *legal precedent* to them. On the contrary, it applies *administrative policy*, and that can vary unpredictably with the winds of change. Thus, a regulatory agency can decide *for* a claimant one time, and, based on exactly the same facts, decide *against* that claimant another time.

This description makes it sound as if the companies hauled before the regulatory agencies are helpless creatures in the grip of a dictatorial monster. In fact, the picture is not quite that bleak, as will be seen.

We mentioned earlier that when an administrative agency's representative makes certain claims that are wrong, and an individual acts in good faith on this intelligence, the agency can reverse its representative and the individual has no recourse. Some agencies, however, have provided for relief in such cases, notably in labor law and price control areas.

declaratory orders

Suppose North Star joined with B & W in an arrangement where B & W always used North Star as its audit organization, even though the contracting organization (as Natal) did the actual contracting with North Star to do the schedule audit. What sort of declaratory order might B & W want to get from the Department of Justice?

Declaratory orders are useful devices for the individual. Congress has provided that an agency can make rulings of binding effect, which dispose of legal controversies in advance, and leave the party free to take the proper action secure in the knowledge that he or she is immune from prosecution because the agency has approved the course of action. Unfortunately, many agencies will not use these orders, notably the Federal Trade Commission and the Federal Communications Commission. Congress made the rulings permissable, but not mandatory.

Agency representatives make many regulations which interpret the law. While these interpretations have no statutory force, since the statutes themselves remain the only criterion for their meaning, they do indicate how the agency intends to press for prosecution, and hence they acquire something very close to the force of law. In most cases, they are accepted as final.

It must be remembered that the primary aim of administrative law is *not* justice; it is simply the execution of the legislative policy contained in the basic statute. Clearly this predisposes the agency in favor of certain outcomes when cases are before it. While private property rights are involved in every judicial action, cases are not brought either to protect or deny those rights, but to advance certain social policies that the framers of the statutes had in mind (or may have had in mind, since the ambiguity of the statutes make any details in this regard unclear). In a sense, every case against Individual D should be termed "*The Public Interest* vs. *Individual D.*"

The Public Interest Role

The earliest regulation was imposed by the states, to provide for such public benefits as the prevention of overcharging by ferries and toll bridges. In the 1800s, the rise of railroad power, with lines that crossed state borders, led to the need for a federal regulatory role. The first federal consumer law, passed in 1887 with the aim of preventing overcharging by the railroads, was the Interstate Commerce Act. While railroads were the major target, the legislators also envisioned a comprehensive transportation regulation agency, as evidenced by some of the language in the Act:

Interstate Commerce Act

> It is hereby declared to be the national transportation policy of the Congress to provide for fair and impartial regulation of all modes of transportation subject to this act, so administered as to recognize and reserve the inherent advantages of each; to promote safe, adequate, economical and efficient service and foster sound economic conditions in transportation; to encourage reasonable charges without unjust discrimination, undue preference or advantages, or unfair or destructive competitive practices; to cooperate with the States; and to encourage fair wages and equitable working conditions; all in the end of developing, coordinating, and preserving a national transportation system by water, highway and rail, as well as other means.

Interstate Commerce Commission

The Interstate Commerce Commission was formed in 1887, initially with five members, not over three of one political party. The president was given power to appoint but not to remove members, who served for fixed terms—the origin of the tradition of independent commissions beyond the power of the chief executive. Its purpose, as stated, was to regulate railroad transportation in the interest of the consumer, and its power grew until by 1906 it had the power to establish maximum rates. It has grown to 11 members, but retains its status as an independent agency with commissioners appointed for fixed terms. In 1910 it was given the additional power to regulate telegraph, telephone, and cable companies, both interstate and international.

In 1913, Congress started creating other agencies. Now there are over 50 such administrative bodies in the federal government dealing with consumer affairs in the broad context (44 are listed in Table 14-2.) Justice Robert H. Jackson of the Supreme Court said that the creation and expansion of these extralegislative and extrajudicial agencies was "probably the most significant legal trend of the last century."

Congress had the consumer in mind when it created the agencies. Its motivating concept was that natural monopolies are beyond the control of the free enterprise system, for how can a consumer cope on even terms with the railroad or telegraph when it is the only one in town? The Constitution bestowed on Congress the power to "regulate commerce," subject only to the limitations that no person be deprived of property without due process of law and that no property shall be taken for public use without just compensation. And Congress has made considerable use of that power. By the late 1800s, public anger at the big trusts had grown so strong that Congress passed the Sherman Antitrust Act in 1890, outlawing any contract, combination, or conspiracy in restraint of trade or commerce, private property or no. The Antitrust Division of the Department of Justice was formed in 1903, and ever since has been bringing antitrust suits in the firm belief that consumers get the best deal when there are a large number of competitors and maximum price competition. In 1907 the ICC made the pronouncement that "competition between railways as well as between other industries is the established policy of the nation."

Congress has two fundamental weapons in regulating commerce. It can regulate the prices and practices of producers, an activity known as *consumerism,* and it can promote commerce, an activity known as *industrial paternalism.* In the broadest sense, both functions benefit the consumer (on the premise that a healthy economy brings general prosperity), but in specific cases the two may be opposed. In the early history of the republic it made little difference, since the states regulated most commerce. But with the depression trauma and the New Deal, Congress and the president started taking it over, and they have been moving ahead vigorously on this track ever since.

The ICC started out with consumer protection in mind, and for many years it appeared that it would be the sole transportation regulatory agency. (Today it is one of some 30 agencies charged with some aspect of transportation regulation). One of its aims was passenger safety, and as a result it imposed speed limits, but this rule stifled technological advance. As a result, the speed record set June 12, 1905 by the Pennsylvania Railroad's Broadway Limited of 127 mph stood for 64 years—until broken by the Metroliners, which were built under government subsidy (after going to the Japanese for some technical reminders on how to engineer speed on the rails). The ICC's solicitude for the consumer caught the railroads in a squeeze between controlled rates and uncontrolled costs, and brought so many failures and near-failures that the federal government had to take over and operate them during World War I.

Federal Trade Commission

The Federal Trade Commission, established by the Federal Trade Commission Act of 1914, also started out with consumer protection in mind, chiefly the need to act promptly against combinations and monopolies. The Commission was to be a more efficient and thus more effective institution than the Justice Department, which "in most cases will take no cognizance of violations of the law until months or years after the violation occurs, and when the difficulty of awarding reparation for the violation is almost unsurmountable."[10] Its powers overlapped those of the Justice Department for antitrust (and still do). Initially its jurisdiction included meat packing, but this was transferred to the Department of Agriculture by the Packers and Stockyard Act of 1921. The concept of consumer protection was clearly central to the creation of both these administrative bodies.

Food and Drug Administration

The Food and Drug Administration, not an independent regulatory body at all but an arm of the Department of Health, Education and Welfare, was empowered by the Kefauver-Harris Drug Amendments of 1962 to regulate the pharmaceutical industry for the protection of drug consumers, enlarging its existing regulatory powers. The FDA was founded in 1931 and charged, together with the Department of Agriculture, with keeping an eye on the safety and nutrition of foods for the consumer. This agency was the subject of citizens' advisory committee studies in 1955 and again in 1962, empaneled by two different administrations to review what was seen as chronically poor performance, and was hauled over the coals by a Nader task force in 1969 on charges that it generally favored the interests of industry over those of the consumer.

The Industry Support Role

The Nader charges, while perhaps overdrawn, do raise a problem that has no simple answer. An agency that is charged both with *regulating* the industry in the interests of the consumer and *promoting* the growth and success of the industry is being asked to walk a tightrope. The situation is exacerbated by the fact that, while consumer representatives have not been much in evidence in the offices of the various commissions (at least until quite recently), industry representatives have been ever-present in Washington. The three major broadcasting networks have vice presidents in Washington, and the National Association of Broadcasters is headquartered there. Western Union and AT&T have vice presidents there. The Air Transport Association is headquartered there, and most major airlines have corporate officers there. The railroads, truckers, and barge lines have their trade association headquarters there. The American Petroleum Institute and National Coal Association are located there, as are the American Iron and Steel Institute, the Pharmaceutical Manufacturers' Association, and a good many more trade associations. It is easy for a commissioner to get an industry slant, without taking any bribes or doing anything more untoward than simply listening to the complaints and comments of the people who make it their business to call on commissioners.

There are two kinds of actions a regulatory agency takes, one specific and the other general. The specific kind responds to a complaint against or a request by an individual company: these problems are settled, like

An agency charged both with regulating an industry in the consumer's interest and promoting industry growth must walk a tightrope.

court trials, on a case-by-case basis. The general kind issues a ruling with the force of law to the entire industry or a major segment of it. The former kind upsets only the company involved (which, of course, can be traumatic enough: the last time the Department of Justice's Antitrust Division took on American Telephone and Telegraph Company, the proceedings took seven years; and the Federal Communications Commission's fundamental examination of AT&T's rates started in 1966 and is still going on). But the latter kind gets the whole industry aroused, and the pressures an industry can generate through its elected representatives can be intense. During President Kennedy's administration, Federal Power Commissioner Howard Morgan requested not to be reappointed, in a letter containing the following passage:

What might be an example of an industry-wide ruling that would affect North Star?

> Ordinary men cannot administer [administrative regulatory] laws today in the face of pressures generated by huge industries... The big problem in the regulatory field is not influence peddling and corruption... I have been approached only once with a veiled intimation that money or stock was available in return for a favorable decision, and that was at the state level...But abandonment of the public interest can be caused by many things, of which timidity and a desire for personal security are the most insidious. This commission, for example, must make hundreds and even thousands of decisions each year, a good many of which involve...hundreds of millions of dollars in a single case. A commissioner can find it very easy to consider whether his vote might arouse an industry campaign against his reconfirmation by the Senate.[11]

The members of a regulatory agency have constant contact with the industry. It cannot be otherwise, particularly where the agency's responsibilities include promotion as well as regulation. In recent times, when the airlines have had severe difficulties with both fuel costs and cut-throat competition in the face of overcapacity on international routes, it would be absurd for airline officers and CAB officials not to talk over their pressing problems in the interest of better understanding. When the railroads are edging ever closer to bankruptcy, and some have already crossed over the line, it is unthinkable that their officers could not confer with ICC commissioners to cast about for solutions. A commissioner or board member cannot afford to be ignorant of key industry developments, and one way to keep in touch is to maintain industry contacts.

In addition to these informal contacts, which inevitably involve social relationships as well as office visits and site inspections, there are the more regularized informal conferences at which individual cases are adjudicated "out of court," so to speak, or in which the agency and the company or industry representative confer prior to a more formal hearing and action. Since the agency is allowed a great deal of discretion, and since it is not committed to the straitjacket of legal precedent but more properly must follow the dictates of government policy, it happens that "policy" sometimes is read as that action which causes the least uproar in congressional committees. The stakes involved for the industry can be immense, and the pressures are correspondingly intense. When the president on January 4, 1975, signed a bill increasing allowable truck weights on the highways from 73,280 to 80,000 pounds, he commented that the lower speed limit put many truckers in an economic bind and stated that "this modest increase in allowable truck weights" should help gain productivity without threatening public safety. The increase was a controversial one, with the American Automobile Association and others contending that it *did* threaten public safety, but the approval was a political decision. Apparently the president had memories of the trucker strikes and "park-ins" fresh in his memory when he went along with the overwhelming will of Congress to authorize something probably quite alien to the desire of most consumers in the nation.

Even in an individual case the stakes are high. A route award to an airline, a television license grant to a station, or approval of a new drug of a pharmaceutical company, can be worth $50 million a throw. The company involved is likely to have its congressional representative contact the commission, and when the legislator is a member of an influential committee the pressure is undeniable. The FCC goes to the House Commerce Committee for its funds and for congressional action on its affairs, and any intervention by that committee on behalf of the broadcast industry is given serious attention. When it is recalled that the agencies are supposed to respond to governmental policy, if they should be contacted by the legislative committee that seems most appropriately to embody legislative policy it would be foolish to suppose that influence is not exerted.

Regulation often seems to be directly contrary to the best interests of the consumer. *Fair trade laws* (which have been passed by many states, forbidding retailers to sell certain "fair-traded" items below the price set by the manufacturer, or at least making it legal for the manufacturer to

fair trade laws

refuse to provide merchandise to retailers who do not conform) are not for the protection of the consumer, since they keep prices up, but for the protection of smaller businessmen. They specifically negate competition, and in some cases have been made possible only by specific repeal of federal antitrust laws. The Robinson-Patman Act of 1936 in effect extended fair trade to the national level. The economies of scale of chain grocers made it possible for them to underprice smaller grocers. The result was a law making it unlawful to sell at "unreasonably" low levels, be a party to a price discrimination so defined, or even to sell goods in one part of the country at a price lower than that charged elsewhere. Nowhere does the consumer interest in lower-priced merchandise enter the discussion.

Robinson-Patman Act

The Antitrust Division of the Department of Justice has been a consistent foe of combinations in restraint of trade, or moves taken in the interest of reducing competition, but Congress has circumvented the division on many occasions in the interest of protecting industry. For years the railroads have conferred openly on rates—a practice that would seem to be flagrantly in violation of antitrust statutes, and that would be prosecuted as collusive in many industries—but the ICC has shown no alarm. In 1944, the Department of Justice brought suit against the railroads; as a result the Reed-Bulwinkle Bill was passed in 1948, exempting rail, truck, and barge rate-fixing conferences from antitrust laws. Other antitrust immunity has been arranged by Congress, for labor unions, insurance companies, farm cooperatives, dairy farmers, vegetable growers, and a raft of others. A fourth of all our commerce is exempted from the antitrust laws, and is under no legal necessity to compete with lower prices or in other ways. The gainers, of course, are the industries—not the consumers.

Antitrust Division, Department of Justice

Reed-Bulwinkle Bill

The regulators have approved mergers in the interest of industry, when competition almost certainly was reduced thereby. The ICC approved a merger of the Atlantic Coast Line and Seaboard Airline Railroads, when it was clear that they had been competing vigorously in the same region of the Southeast. After the Comptroller of the Currency approved a spate of bank mergers that clearly reduced competition in the spirit of the Sherman Act—including the merger of two large New York banks, Manufacturer's Trust and Hanover Bank, in 1961—the Justice Department brought suit against the latter. The Chairman of the Senate Banking Committee put through a bill which became law in 1966, authorizing the merger and generally forbidding the challenge of future bank mergers on antitrust grounds.

Transportation management has been given abundant reason to understand that efforts to trim rates (and thus give the consumer a break) will be opposed vigorously, not only by the competing transportation lines (which is somewhat understandable), but by the ICC as well. The Southern Railway "Big John" grain cars were a classic example. Agricultural shipments by truck and barge are unregulated, because of the vagaries of the law, but rates are closely controlled for rail shipments. As a result, the truck and barge lines were undercutting the rails and getting most of the business. Southern designed an aluminum hopper car that could carry double the amount of grain of the standard steel boxcar and could be unloaded automatically. Ordering 455 of them, it petitioned to cut rates by 60% and 65% effective August 1961. The Commission

"Big John" grain cars

immediately suspended the rates for the maximum seven months allowed by law, and the fight started. The court of appeals granted a restraining order, and Supreme Court Justice Hugo Black extended the order. In April 1963 the Supreme Court ruled that federal courts do not have the power to enjoin rates, and the Southern cars started operating. In July 1963 the Commission ruled that the rates were "not adequately compensatory" (that Southern was losing money on the Big Johns, that is); it limited the cuts to 53.5%, saying this would "preserve for the barge lines the cost advantages they now enjoy" on grain shipments. In spring of 1964, a three-judge district court ruled that the decision was not supported by adequate findings, and the Supreme Court in early 1965 sent the case back to the ICC for further consideration. The ICC had had enough; this time it ruled that the 1961 rates were legal. Southern's grain revenues for the first full year of Big John use were 43% greater than before, and other rail lines bought Big John cars. The consumer benefit for this one innovation alone ran to millions of dollars a year. The Council of Economic Advisors estimated in 1966 that if the ICC would let rail rates "be appropriately geared to costs...on rail transportation alone, savings from possible rate reductions would come to more than $400 million a year." President W. D. Broznan of the Southern put it more strongly, claiming that the ICC's "witchcraft" was costing consumers "at least $1 billion a year through unnecessarily high freight rates."

The climate of maintaining high rates and suppressing competition through the same administrative law procedures initially set up to keep consumers from being overcharged makes the rail lines and the ICC almost instinctively oppose any effort to bring about reductions. Tom Hilt, a new college graduate whose father owned Hilt Truck Lines, was typing tariff rate schedules in March 1965 for some commodities which Hilt could carry profitably at 33¢ a hundred pounds. They had requested a reduction in the tariff from 50¢ to 42¢, but the railroads had protested that they couldn't possibly carry them for less than 50¢; and the ICC had suspended the rate cuts, putting the burden on Hilt of proving that they were legitimate. Hilt was not going to the expense of fighting the railroads, but Tom Hilt was mad enough to add a totally imaginary item to the proposed tariff: yak fat. He submitted a tariff offering to carry yak fat from Omaha to Chicago for 45¢ a hundred pounds, and waited for the automatic railroad reaction to *any* trucker's rate change, which he felt sure would come even on yak fat.

It came. The railroad's rate-fixing office protested the rate as obviously illegal, and enclosed an exhibit purporting to show that Hilt's "true" yak fat hauling costs were 63¢. The ICC's five-man Board of Suspension voted to suspend Hilt's yak fat tariff, saying that since it appeared that the yak fat rate "may be unjust and unreasonable in violation of the Interstate Commerce Act...it is ordered that an investigation be, and it is hereby...instituted."

The ICC could have prosecuted Tom Hilt, because unwittingly he had violated Title 18 of the U.S. Code in filing a fraudulent representation with an agency of the government. But since the ICC had clearly manufactured the hauling costs exhibit, it was too embarrassed, and Hilt was spared. Even so, his action shone a small light on a situation that bore little resemblance to what the legislators of 1887 had intended when they enjoined the new ICC to "encourage reasonable charges without undue preferences or advantages," and to "promote economical and efficient service."

The ICC may not be wholly to blame. In 1920 Congress passed the Transportation Act, encouraging rail mergers with immunity from antitrust in the interest of efficiency. It designed a system patterned on a public utility—except that by that time the railroads no longer had a monopoly. The artificially maintained rates caused the rails to lose even more business, and after 1920 they never grew as fast as the economy. In 1936, Congress put highway trucks under ICC rate control (and route control), and in 1940 barge transportation. And in 1940 the ICC admitted to Congress that its merger plan was not working, and the Transportation Act was repealed.

Transportation Act of 1920

Agricultural haulers were exempted from truck regulation and most bulk haulers from barge regulation, and since 1936 unregulated haulers have undercut the regulated rates. The result has been faster growth and better profits for the unregulated systems.

The "Fourth Branch" of Government

The tremendous power of the regulatory agencies, and the breadth of that power—covering, as it does, crucial elements of executive, legislative, and judicial jurisdiction—has led many to think of them as constituting an unintended "fourth branch" of government. By tradition, Congress recognizes a problem through committee hearings, and deals with it in the only way it knows—by legislating an agency to handle it. Since there is a mass of tiresome details in the administration of problem areas, and since Congress finds it hard to keep its attention on details in any effective fashion, it tends to assign sweeping authority to the agency and then to forget it. The agency is independent of the president because Congress sets it up that way—as an independent commission.[12] It is effectively independent of Congress (except for personal relationships with specific influential members) because the latter is not staffed with technical industry experts and tends to defer to its professional expertise. It is reasonably free from judicial interference by the courts, because they cannot take up any matters except those brought before them; if no one appeals to the courts, they are powerless to intervene. (In late 1974 the Supreme Court reaffirmed unanimously a position it has taken before: that federal courts are limited in their power to substitute their judgment in technical matters for that of the agency. It stated in the most recent case that "we will uphold a decision of less than ideal clarity if the agency's path may be reasonably discerned.")[13]

"fourth branch" of government

In addition, unfortunately, the agencies are effectively insulated from the consumers. Consumers do not come to hearings—indeed, they would have difficulty even finding out when and where the hearings are going to be held, and the informal hearings are closed-door affairs in any case. Since there is no tradition of "visitors in the gallery" as there is in Congress, individuals poking about the offices of a regulatory agency would be distinctly unwelcome.

Consider the powerful Federal Trade Commission, armed with the strongest investigative powers of any government agency in the business sphere. It can reach into any company and examine its corporate records, in what would be prohibited as a "fishing expedition" if attempted by the district attorney. It can call corporate officers into its hearing rooms at will to testify. It can register a formal complaint against any company whenever it finds what *in its own opinion* is "due cause"—something the district attorney must prevail upon the independent grand jury to do. It can charge a company with discriminatory pricing, false advertising, deceptive or misleading practices, shoddy products, and so forth. It can charge that a company's purchase of another company lessens competition to an illegal extent. And when it brings in the miscreant, it is prosecutor, judge, and jury.

Consider the Federal Trade Commission's study to determine the extent of competition in the U.S. It determined that the way to get the facts was to establish a "line of business" reporting program, requiring 345 of the largest U.S. corporations to disclose their detailed sales and profits within each line of business rather than giving company-wide figures as required by the S.E.C. The companies protested that disclosure of such information would cause them irreparable injury by laying bare their detailed performance and showing competitors where they were strong and weak, and what business steps had what success. Twelve companies brought suit in district court, pleading that the step was a violation of their Fourth Amendment right to privacy. The point is that a regulatory agency is not a protector of privacy, since it is not fundamentally interested in privacy or any other right of an individual or business, but rather in the furtherance of what appears to it to be administration policy. Initially the FTC promised to maintain the confidentiality of the data, publishing only aggregate figures, but subsequently the FTC

The agencies are effectively insulated from both industries and consumers.

chairman announced that he intended to ask the commission to release the names of the 345 companies and the information they filed in motions to the FTC to quash the program.

The Pervasive Influence of Law and Regulation

A random review of a single issue of the *Wall Street Journal* (for January 2, 1975) discloses 47 articles dealing with some aspect of law or regulation in action. This sampling suggests the extent to which legal requirements influence every aspect of the business world:

"Broadcasters Give In to Citizens' Demands on Program Content" (under pressure of FCC public hearings for station license renewals)
"Social Security Taxes Will Have to be Boosted"
"Local Service Airlines' Subsidy Rate Lowered by CAB" (which is also considering limiting expansion of service and cutting back flight capacity)
"Drug Pricing Practices of 12 Producers Found to be Discriminatory" (selling to hospitals at prices lower than to drug stores)
"Emission Standards for 1977 Cars May Be Extended One Year"
"Pacific Gas & Electric Receives Rate Rise"
"Financial Statements Would Have to Reflect the Effects of Inflation"
"Privacy Legislation Giving Individuals Greater Access to Information Passed into Law"
"Public Service Job Funds of $2.5 Billion Signed into Law"
"Unemployment Benefits Extended and Coverage Expanded to Three Million More People"
"Cities Getting Federal Job Funds Must Use Money Promptly or Lose It"
"Minnesota Mining Acknowledges Former Top Officers Face Criminal Prosecution in Connection With Secret Political Fund"
"Former Chairman of Westgate-California Charged With Causing Illegal Campaign Contributions To Be Made"
"Burmah Oil Company Yields Control over Wide Areas of Operation to Govt."
"New York Stock Exchange Chairman and Head of AFL-CIO to Meet on Capital Shortage Problems" (in connection with forthcoming government reorganization of securities market)
"Watergate Jury Returns Guilty Verdict Against Four Former Top Aides of Nixon"
"Federal Reserve Board Clears Joint Venture Proposal of Bradford Computer, Inc., and Crocker National Bank"
"Housing and Urban Development Department Cuts its Rate for Mortgage Subsidy Program"
"Chairman of Postal Rate Commission Resigns"
"National Vulcanized Fibers and Sharon Steel Hold Up Plans to Merge in Face of SEC Study"
"New Mexico Public Service Commission Approves Cost of Gas Adjustment Factor in Gas Prices of Southern Union Gas Company"
"Guyana Government Takes Over Reynolds Metal Bauxite Mine"
"French Boost Price of Almost All Energy"
"Chief Justice Burger Delays Pay Rules for States and Cities"
"Greyhound Loses Appeal of Conviction over Oregon Bus Case"
"Canadian Provincial Government to Provide $27 Million a Year to Oil Producers"
"IRS Temporarily Waives some Pension Plan Taxes"

"Greenland Residents Get Tax on Income This Year for First Time"
"Common Sense for Uncommon Times" (editorial dealing with regulation)
"Government Permits Gold Trading after 41 Years"
"SEC Proposes to Curb Broker-Dealers in Sale and Purchase of Gold"
"Generics Corporation Registers with SEC Shares for Distribution as Special Dividend"
"Open Letter from Building Industry Calling on President to Release Frozen Federal New Construction Funds"
"Clamor to Revive the Reconstruction Finance Corporation"
"Stimulating the Economy" (government steps, by cutting taxes or increasing the money supply)
"Moral Education Proposed by State-Directed Schools"
"Federal National Mortgage Administration Yields Fall"
"AT&T Registers Sale of Notes with SEC"
"Six Cities Register Sales of Tax Exempt Securities with SEC"
"National Stock Exchange Ends Trading"
"Tender Offer by Utilities & Industries Corp. for South Bay Corp. Approved by District Court, Being Reviewed by SEC for Approval"
"American Bancshares Agrees on Merger Plan with Combanks Corp., Subject to Approval by Regulatory Authorities"
"FAA Extends Rule Banning Fuel Venting to Propeller Planes"
"Indian Head, Inc., Sued: Alleged Fraud in Tender Bids"
"Grumman Corporation Receives Navy Contract"
"French Develop Capability to Make Own Nuclear Fuel Since AEC Refused to Release Information on 'Barrier' Technology"
"Amoco Oil Co. Attacks FEA Regulations" (requiring oil companies with more than 38% domestic low-cost crude oil to "buy the right" to refine it by paying other refiners with less than 38% domestic crude $5 a barrel—in short, paying $5 a barrel for the privilege of refining their own oil)

Ironically, the federal government is also competing with many of the same businesses it sets out to regulate. The abovementioned issue of the *Journal* also lists, on its stock market quotation pages, no fewer than 284 different issues of government securities for sale to private investors:

    55 different issues of Treasury bonds and notes
    22 different Treasury Bills
    49 different Federal Home Loan Bank issues
    25 different World Bank bonds
     9 different Bank for Coops bonds
     8 different Inter-American Development Bank bonds
    60 different Federal National Mortgage Administration issues
    38 different Federal Land Bank bonds
    15 different FIC Bank debentures
     3 different Government National Mortgage Administration issues

Regulatory commissions are created to perform a specific task in a limited field, and are given no mandate or charge to cooperate with any other commission. Since there is no institution overseeing their performance as a whole (except for specific challengers, and those not very frequently), they constitute a haphazard jumble of uncoordinated powers and in truth "irresponsible" agencies. They compete with one another in their efforts to get promotional funds for the industries they regulate. And they have neither the responsibility for considering, nor the inclination to consider, the needs and problems of the industries they do not regulate which are affected by their actions. Thus the FAA, in considering the funding of an airport project (typically it will pay half the cost of airport construction), gives little or no consideration to competition with other modes of transportation, or the need for feeder roads and transit lines. The Federal Highway Administration, in the Interstate Project (the government funds 90% of the interstate system and 50% of all streets and highways), gives no consideration to the deathblow it may be dealing to rail systems covering the same routes, which the ICC is trying to nourish back to life.[14] And the CAB, in assigning routes, gives no heed to availability of airport facilities (which are the responsibility of its sister agency, the FAA). Each agency fends for itself, and competes vigorously in the halls of Congress for funding (including subsidy and grant funds) with the other transportation mode agencies. Since they have large sums of money to hand out (besides acting in some degree as executive, legislator, and judge, the regulatory agency may take on the medieval role of *patron*), corporations and governments below the federal level court their favor and hardly dare to ask questions. If a community questions the plans for an expanded airport because feeder roads are not included, it risks cancellation of the matching grant. Roads are not FAA's worry (though they are the worry of FAA's parent organization, the Department of Transportation), and if the city is going to drag its feet over the matter of unbalanced transportation improvement, it can do without any improvement at all. For the same reason, the states scarcely dare question the FHWA's master scheme for interstates on grounds of throwing the transportation system out of balance, or they risk withdrawal of the interstate funds.

The Regulatory Agencies

What are these regulatory agencies whose power looms so large and who seem so difficult to control? Over the years since 1887, when the Interstate Commerce Commission was established, there have been 19 *independent* agencies. These are listed in Table 14-2, with their year of establishment and a brief notation of their purpose. There are 22 agencies within departments of the executive branch, and there are three in the executive branch that report directly to the President; these also are listed in Table 14-2. Those in the executive branch would appear to be under close control of the President, but in fact Congress put them there more for organizational convenience than to transfer control to the executive, and would be jealous of any sign that the President treats them as members of the executive family. Thus, although nominally under the President, they enjoy a good deal of the independence typical of their fellow agencies which are legally independent commissions.

Originally the commissions elected their own chairmen, but in recent years Congress has given the President the power to appoint chairmen. A chairman removed by an incoming President remains a commission member.

The New-Look Agencies

Two of the agencies listed in Table 14-2 do not have industry constituencies, so they are not thrown naturally into close contact with industry

Table 14-2.
Federal Regulatory Agencies

Independent Agencies

1887	Interstate Commerce Commission	Regulates rails, trucks
1913	Federal Reserve Board	Regulates banks, monetary policy
1914	Federal Trade Commission	Administers antitrust, packaging, advertising
1916	U.S. Tariff Commission	Investigates tariff and foreign trade
1924	U.S. Tax Court	Adjudicates federal tax cases
1926	National Mediation Board	Mediates labor disputes in air and rails
1930	Federal Power Commission	Regulates electricity and natural gas
1932	Federal Home Loan Bank Board	Provides credit reserve for home finance
1933	Federal Deposit Insurance Corporation	Insures deposits, supervises some banks
1934	Federal Communications Commission	Regulates radio, TV, telephone, telegraph
1934	Securities and Exchange Commission	Regulates securities industry
1935	National Labor Relations Board	Regulates unfair labor practices
1936	Federal Maritime Commission	Regulates foreign trade of steamships
1938	Civil Aeronautics Board	Regulates and promotes air travel
1946	Atomic Energy Commission	Regulates and promotes atomic energy
1952	Federal Coal Mine Safety Board	Hears appeals to Coal Mine Safety Act
1964	Equal Employment Opportunity Commission	Investigates discrimination charges
1970	Environmental Protection Agency	Monitors environmental matters
1974	Federal Energy Administration	Regulates energy production and use

Executive Branch Agencies

1824	Army Corps of Engineers	Builds and maintains rivers and harbors
1836	Patent Office	Administers patent and trademark laws
1862	Internal Revenue Service	Administers federal tax programs
1863	Comptroller of the Currency	Regulates national banks
1903	Antitrust division, Justice Department	Enforces antitrust laws
1915	U.S. Coast Guard	Regulates seaworthiness of ships
1916	Packers and Stockyards Administration	Regulates livestock and meat marketing
1922	Commodity Exchange Authority	Regulates commodity exchanges
1931	Food & Drug Administration	Regulates food and drug safety and labelling
1933	Bureau of Employment Security	Administers unemployment compensation
1933	Social Security Administration	Administers federal retirement programs
1933	Commodity Credit Corporation	Administers farm price support programs
1935	Rural Electrification Administration	Administers REA loan programs
1936	Maritime Administration	Promotes merchant marine
1951	Renegotiation Board	Renegotiates defense contracts
1953	Small Business Administration	Promotes small businesses
1958	Federal Aviation Administration	Regulates aircraft and air systems
1959	Oil Import Administration	Regulates petroleum imports
1963	Labor Management Services Administration	Regulates employee welfare and pensions
1964	Office of Economic Opportunity	Administers federal poverty/youth programs
1966	Federal Highway Administration	Administers road building and safety programs
1966	Federal Railroad Administration	Administers highspeed and safety programs
1966	National Transportation Safety Board	Investigates transportation accidents
1971	Occupational Safety & Health Administration	Issues and enforces industrial standards
1972	Consumer Product Safety Commission	Administers federal product safety laws

organizations: the Equal Employment Opportunity Commission and the Environmental Protection Agency.[15] Moreover, these two agencies came into being at a time when both minority rights and environmental considerations were exciting strong and emotional attention from the public and (naturally) the Congress. Consequently, both of these agencies came out strongly on the side of the consumer from the outset. Since both causes were popular, particularly with the young, devotees of environmental protection and of equal opportunity flocked to Washington and were added to the staffs of the two agencies. This has had two results—one undeniably good, the other more questionable. The former is that the agency staffs have been hard-working and remarkably devoid of the "torpor" and "cronyism" which Ralph Nader used to describe the typical industry-linked regulatory agency. The latter is that they have approached their work with a fervor which some believe has put them beyond the public and its real priorities.

Professor Irving Kristol, Henry Luce Professor of Urban Values at New York University and coeditor of the quarterly *The Public Interest,* has likened some aspects of the environmentalist movement to the "evangelical reform" movement against alcoholism—a crusade with praiseworthy objectives that may create more problems than it solves. He cites the EPA's venture into urban planning, trying to discourage suburban development because it implies more automobile use but at the same time appearing to discourage urban concentration because it locates many cars in a small area. EPA held up a low-income housing project for months because it perceived a threat of "noise pollution," as though the ills of urban slums (mugging, rats, junkie vandalism, despair) were of lesser consequence than a possible excess of rock music because of too many dwellings in too small a space. The environmentalists are adamantly opposed to offshore drilling, urged by the Federal Energy Administration to help break the Arab oil cartel, when the high cost of oil threatens the jobs of millions of Americans.

Similarly, when coal companies intensified their strip-mining efforts in the mid-1970s as a means of extracting more coal faster and thus alleviating the energy crisis, environmentalists protested that the areas involved would be subjected to severe erosion. But the coal had to be obtained somehow, and strip mining was much safer for the miners than deep mining—two facts the protestors overlooked. Partly as a result of their efforts, the law now requires coal companies to replant and restore strip-mined land, but some people continue to object. They assert that coal shouldn't be burned at all because it causes air pollution. This verdict, of course, bypasses the major issue involved: alternatives to oil must be fully utilized, and until "clean" energy sources can be developed, coal is one of the most efficient alternatives we have.

As with environmental protection, the philosophy behind equal employment is unquestionably a valid one. When the Equal Employment Opportunity Commission was established, Congress decreed a period of concurrent jurisdiction with the Civil Rights division of the Justice Department, which ended in 1974. During the two-year overlapping period, EEOC filed 160 employment discrimination cases, compared with 100 filed by the Justice Department during its nine years of jurisdiction. One of its celebrated initial cases was the steel industry-negotiated

Equal Employment Opportunity Commission

Environmental Protection Agency

settlement to give back pay as a redress of discrimination to 25,000 blacks, estimated at more than $40 million. Industry is under orders to live up to a consent decree for minority employment.

These steps are excellent, and the EEOC itself seems to be on a good course. But some federal enforcement of minority hiring has gone past the point actually required in the law, in effect establishing quotas for hiring women and blacks—despite the fact that any form of quota is prohibited in the legislation. And a New Orleans federal district court ruled in 1974 that Continental Can Company and a local of the United Steelworkers violated civil rights laws by using seniority as the sole criterion for laying off workers. The judge took the position that the low seniority of black workers was due to past failure to hire blacks; thus, "last hired, first fired" was discriminatory. The Labor Department's top attorney, William J. Kilberg, noted that this action does not help the specific workers hurt by discrimination—the blacks who could not get jobs at Continental Can during the 1940s and 1950s. Rather, it compensates other individuals simply because they fall in the same racial category. At the same time, it penalizes white employees with seniority, if they must be fired in order to rehire laid-off blacks. The judge specifically said the company should *not* take this action—leaving as its only realistic alternative that of paying the laid-off blacks until attrition opens up slots for them. Indeed, the judge specifically suggested this approach.

The Antitrust Division of the Justice Department, while not an "agency" in the sense of being independent of the executive branch, is similar in its behavior. It has pursued antitrust actions diligently since it was formed, and has never developed an industry "constituency" because there is no one industry which it regulates or monitors. Consequently, it has successfully maintained a reforming profile—sometimes to the extent of striking down concentrations of power that do not demonstrably decrease competition. One recent action of the division, seeking to split Western Electric and Bell Laboratories from AT&T even though the latter is a regulated monopoly in accordance with law, caused a substantial division of opinion on the part of knowledgeable observers.

Both the Occupational Safety & Health Administration and the Consumer Product Safety Commission are new agencies, without an industry constituency, and both came into being as a result of pressures for protection of individuals against the operations of business. The former deals with the individual in his or her capacity as an industrial worker, and the latter in his or her capacity as a purchaser of consumer products. (In that capacity, CPSC is setting standards for more than 10,000 consumer goods—something that has never been attempted on so general a scale before.)

A counter-movement, small but building in strength, asserts that the singleminded consumer agencies are falling into the same trap the older agencies did in concentrating on their particular mandate without counting the cost. Just as FAA, ICC, FHWA, and CAB disregard the need to coordinate all *transportation* resource and problems, so the new agencies with a mandate to protect their own particular resource fail to count all the costs involved. The Ford administration urged that all environmental and safety measures be subjected to *cost-benefit analysis,* to insure that "in doing these things that are so desirable, we do them in such a way that it is not going to destroy the economy." EPA now prepares new studies on the economic impact of its standards; OSHA and CPSC issue a cost analysis with every new rule.

When EPA issued national air quality standards, some areas had air that was cleaner than the standards, and EPA determined that industry could be allowed to pollute in those areas up to the limits. The Sierra Club and other groups sued to prevent any "significant deterioration" and won, in a case that went to the Supreme Court. The EPA issued "nondegradation guidelines," trying to comply with the court ruling without halting the construction of new industries in sparsely populated areas that do not want to remain rural. The plan utilizes three "air quality zones": Zone I, where no deterioration will be permitted; Zone II, where modest increases will be allowed; and Zone III, where pollution will be allowed up to the limits of secondary air quality standards (stricter than the primary standards, since they are designed to protect property and vegetation as well as health). The Sierra Club considers such regulations a copout, while several federal departments consider them too severe (the Commerce Department claims they will have adverse economic consequences; HUD that they will upset land use planning; HEW that they will force industry into heavily polluted areas, making them even worse). In the early days of the consumer oriented agencies, the choice was easy; with the economic turndown and the energy crisis, hard choices appeared, and the inevitable result was a compromise of some desirable goals in the interest of the overall public needs.

The Old-Line Agencies

Critics of the Interstate Commerce Commission, Federal Trade Commission, Federal Power Commission, Federal Communications Commission, Federal Maritime Commission, and Civil Aeronautics Board charge that these agencies are the willing tools of the industries they regulate. Undeniably their relationships are close; and such public-interest groups as Ralph Nader's Center for the Study of Responsive Law find that these old-line agencies tend to give industry needs priority over those of the public. (Some of the agencies have a dual responsibility both to *regulate* and to *promote* the industry, as stated earlier.)

Oddly enough, the old-line agencies started life as "new look" organizations, with public protection their primary goal. The ICC, as the dean of regulatory agencies in terms of age, is a good model to study. There was a populist movement in the 1880s, just as there is today, and under its urging Congress investigated the railroad industry, finding discrimination in rail freight rates and passenger fares. The Interstate Commerce Act of 1887 established the ICC to see that all users were treated equally and that rates were "reasonable and just." While its responsibilities expanded, its viewpoint remained essentially that of a consumer advocate up to World War I. At this point, since the ICC rates were not keeping up with rail costs, the railroads encountered financial problems, and the federal government had to take them over in order to handle the expanded wartime transportation demands.

The plight of the railroads gave Congress second thoughts, and it passed the 1920 Transportation Act which for the first time empowered

Many observers believe that ICC regulation has killed the railroad industry.

and instructed the ICC to establish *minimum* as well as maximum rates, with the aim of keeping the railroad industry healthy. Thus the ICC was directed to move in with the industry, so to speak, and it has never been the same since. This is not to say that its regulation has been *good* for the railroads; there are many observers who believe that regulation killed the industry. But its orientation shifted officially to that of a supporter of the railroads. The grand plan was to achieve mergers that would build a national railroad network, with rates designed to achieve a 6% return on investment. The grand plan failed, principally because the ICC was treating the rails as monopolies, and they actually had competition from trucks and barges. In 1940 the ICC told Congress that the plan had failed, and abandoned it. Since then, the ICC has endeavored to regulate the railroads, plus a large segment of the trucking and barge line industry, but its efforts to remove competition have not brought the transportation industry success; quite the contrary.

In recent years the ICC has come under unprecedented attack. In 1962 the Doyle Report proposed that it be merged into a single transportation agency, losing its identity. In 1970 the Nader-led "Interstate Commerce Omission" study repeated the proposal, stimulating bills in both House and Senate. President Nixon's Ash Commission on Executive Reorganization, his Council of Economic Advisors, and three executive departments all pushed for drastic revisions in the present situation. Stung by this unusual attention, the commission has been trying to pay more attention to the individual consumer.

The ICC may not know how to reform itself, however. In 1973 it handled 373,000 tariffs requiring review (it is not hard to see how a yak fat tariff could get through unnoticed) and heard 8,800 formal cases, or almost five per working hour. It is trying to make thousands of operating decisions that managements ought to be making, and in the process losing its policy sense in the welter of paper. Thomas Gale Moore of the Hoover Institute has estimated that ICC regulation of transportation in 1968 alone cost consumers more than $10 billion—a figure that probably rose to $15 billion by 1974. Moore calculated as follows: $2.9 billion for inefficient use of trucks, $2.4 billion for inefficient use of rail, and $2.9 billion lost in traffic that should go by rail going by truck. The Task Force on Railroad Productivity concluded in 1973 that in regulating trucking the ICC creates a local monopoly of an industry suited by its technology to being highly competitive. The American Trucking Association disagrees, contending that deregulation would create chaos. It is clear that uniform rates provide no opportunity for shippers who want better service to pay higher rates, and for those who can accept poor service to pay less. Thus, what could be a dynamic industry is smothered by a commission which, ironically, is only trying to help it. Professor George W. Hilton of UCLA, who has studied it closely for over ten years, says that "in the most literal sense, the ICC doesn't know what it is doing."[16]

Certainly no transportation expertise exists among the commissioners themselves, who are mostly political appointees. The commission has kept rates high, and thus kept inefficient modes of transportation in business, discouraging any technological improvements because there was no incentive. It has forced the railroads to keep operating money-losing facilities. Regulated truckers are losing more and more business to their unregulated cousins. Under its tight control, the railroads are facing the threat of wholesale bankruptcy. By almost any standard, the ICC is a failure. And the sands of time probably are running out for the ICC. The probability is good that the industry regulated in part by the ICC will shift gradually to deregulation, more competition, improved technology, and a dose of improved management once the ICC shackles are cut.

The oldest commission after the ICC (excluding the Federal Reserve Board) is the Federal Trade Commission, created in 1914 to facilitate antitrust actions by responding to "unfair methods of competition in interstate commerce"; its mandate was broadened in 1938 to include actions against "unfair or deceptive practices in interstate commerce." Unfortunately, it was given the conflicting task in 1936 of enforcing the ban on discriminatory pricing as defined in the Robinson-Patman Act, thus ending up with the dual job of stabilizing prices and promoting competition. Perhaps partly because of this dilemma, the FTC had a poor reputation for most of its first half-century. The turning point came with the report of an American Bar Association panel commissioned by the president:

> This Commission believes that it should be the last of the long series of committees and groups which have earnestly insisted that drastic changes were needed to recreate the FTC in its intended image... Further temporizing is indefensible. Notwithstanding the great potential of the FTC in the field

of antitrust and consumer protection, if change does not occur there will be no substantial purpose to be served by its continued existence....[17]

Change did occur. Casper Weinberger came in as chairman in 1970, and brought both good management and new programs to the commission. While he did not stay long, the impetus he gave was continued by his successor. The commission has moved against deceptive advertising, requiring proof of improbable claims and advertising to correct improper or misleading impressions arising from false advertisements in the past. A controversial case, initiated in 1974, pits the FTC against the four largest cereal manufacturers, alleging that it is illegal for four firms to advertise so massively that they garner 90% of the market and thus prevent effective competition. If the FTC succeeds, it will split the firms into more and smaller companies. The FTC is also seeking to end restrictive agreements involving soft-drink bottlers which divide the nation up into noncompeting areas. It has established consumer complaint centers in principal cities, which it shares with other agencies and local officials. It has started conducting public hearings on its own initiative. As Gilbert Burck commented in *Fortune*, "Inoculated with the New Consumerism, the fifty-seven-year-old commission is prancing around like an adolescent."[18] Certainly it is moving on consumer matters, which it did not do before. But its practices may be open to criticism. When the FTC thinks it has a case, it issues a "hot line" news release in advance, which gets the case in the papers before the proceedings with the company are under way, and before the company can study the complaint or present its side. This approach could not be used in court, where grand jury proceedings are secret until the jury decides that there is a case.

Despite this minor shortcoming, the FTC is performing a vigorous and useful role today as a consumer-minded regulatory agency, and no longer appears to be under the sway of the industries it regulates.

Civil Aeronautics Board

The Civil Aeronautics Board has the same dilemma as the ICC—trying to protect the consumer *and* promote the industry at the same time. And it has fallen into the same trap with the airlines that the ICC did with the railroads: it tells them where to fly and what to charge, but it cannot control the other costs or the competition. As did the ICC, it established a "fair return on investment," but only once since 1955 have the airlines attained it. Today the CAB guideline "fair return rate" is 12%, but the industry has never exceeded 6% since 1967. The airline management must share the blame for this, as they have rushed to buy fancy new planes which their business was not sufficient to fill, but the clumsy regulation of the Civil Aeronautics Board must share part of the blame, too. It has never followed a logical policy in awarding routes, but has tended to overaward with little thought of the economic consequences. At one time only United, Pan American, and Northwest served the U.S.-Hawaii run, but in 1969 the CAB let in five more lines for a total of eight. Today at least five of the eight regularly lose money on the run. The CAB commissioners have assumed that growing traffic will fill the added capacity they authorize, although it has failed to materialize at anything like the rate they anticipated.

The CAB is showing signs of change. It is receptive toward mergers that will save money, and is conducting a long-needed study of the entire air route system to analyze where there is too much competition and where there is too little. It is trying to establish a fare-setting formula that takes *present* costs into account rather than historic costs. (As recently as November 1973, in the middle of the oil cost push and soaring interest rates, the CAB still based its rate analyses on 6% money and historic fuel costs.) It is talking of abolishing discount fares, which probably cost the airlines money. And it is looking at route consolidations.

Most of the old-line regulatory agencies show signs of changing with the times, paying more attention to regulation that will help the consumer and less to support that seeks to help but may actually hurt the regulated industry. The FCC has been prodded into relicensing hearings that shake the existing station operators out of their disregard for the consumer and give some overdue clout to the wishes of viewers. (Indeed, so jumpy have broadcasters become about the possibility of losing their lucrative licenses that around the country they have been giving in to demands from citizen groups without even waiting for them to oppose the relicense applications.) The AEC (now incorporated into an umbrella federal energy research agency) is emphasizing its consumer safety role more than has been its practice in recent years (it, too, walked the tightrope of a dual role for both consumers and the industry). The FDA has been charged with some justice with being too susceptible to lobbying by food processors and growers, and with paying more attention to enforcement than to developing scientific competence. (When it warned of high mercury levels in tuna, the packers lost heavily; later it was shown that mercury levels had not changed in 60 years or more. Its banning of cyclamates after brief tests on rats caused some companies to incur heavy losses; when Abbott Laboratories petitioned the FDA to reinstate cyclamates, new tests indicated that cyclamates do not cause cancer in humans.)

Atomic Energy Commission

In December 1974 the House Interstate and Foreign Commerce Committee issued a 245-page report charging the FAA with "sluggishness" in ordering safety-related changes in aircraft and ground proximity warning systems. It described an alarming situation of divided authority, bureaucratic infighting, and favorable treatment of the airlines and the manufacturers who build their planes. The report cited the division of authority between the National Transportation Safety Board, which is charged by law with making safety recommendations, and the FAA, which must put them in effect. The report recommended that Congress separate the duty of monitoring safety (the consumer advocacy role) from the function of promoting air travel (the industry support role).

Consumer Movements

No section on the attention paid by regulatory agencies to the needs of the consumer would be complete without paying tribute to Ralph Nader and his tireless assaults against both business and government.[19] Some of his criticisms have been strident, some of his charges narrow and unfair, but he uncovered significant abuses and prodded Congress and the agencies to *respond* in a way they never had before he came on the scene.

Nader's concentrated assault on the agencies started in the summer of 1968, when a group of law and graduate students under his direction descended on the Federal Trade Commission and analyzed its shortcomings, described in *The Nader Report on the Federal Trade Commission* cited earlier. Their findings, in part, generated the ABA report discussed in the previous section, which caused an overhaul of the FTC with salutory results. Starting the following year, the law students associated with Nader's Center for the Study of Responsive Law began to file petitions for rule making or intervening before the FTC and other agencies. The accomplishment of these groups, using acronyms that expressed their aims dramatically, have been substantial:

SOUP (for Students Opposing Unfair Practices) intervened in a case the FTC was bringing against Campbell Soup, attempting to establish the principle of requiring corrective advertising after proof of deceptive advertising has been established.

SMASH (for Students Mobilizing on Auto Safety Hazards) pressed the National Highway Traffic Safety Administration to establish a performance standard for bumpers, which helped induce Congress to enact such legislation.

STATIC (for Student Taskforce Against Telecommunication Information Concealment) filed a petition with the FCC to require broadcasters to tell the listener at regular intervals what its obligations to the public are.

LABEL (Law students' Association for Buyers' Education in Labeling) petitioned the FDA for broader disclosure of ingredients on food and drink labels, leading to a court declaration that FDA did have such authority.

FLITE (Future Lawyers Investigating Transportation Employment) urged the CAB to examine minority hiring and promotion as a prelude to approval of route and rate change petitions.

For as long as large shopping centers have been commercially attractive, developers have induced the "major draw" stores to come in by giving them the right to restrict the leasing of space to competitive stores, and to control the floor space of smaller stores in the centers. In early 1975, the FTC moved against this practice—which denies consumers the lively competition that will bring down prices and provide merchandise variety—by ordering City Stores Co. of New York to stop entering into or enforcing leases that restrict competition at regional shopping centers. The order grew out of FTC charges that City Stores' Lansburgh division had such leases at Tyson's Corner, a major regional shopping center near Washington, D.C. The order was made applicable to City Stores' 38 department stores in various shopping centers. The order also forbade City Stores to negotiate contracts that would enable City Stores to determine the size of other tenants' stores, ruling that such contracts are anticompetitive. Previously the FTC had moved against May Department Stores Co. and Woodward and Lothrop, Inc., on similar grounds.

In its first case concerning sex discrimination against men, the Illinois Liquor Commission charged the Oxford Inn in Chicago with giving women reduced prices on drinks during a Tuesday "happy hour"—50¢ for the women versus 90¢ for the men. The owner agreed "not to differentiate in price between male and female customers."[20] In a more substantive discrimination case, a group of black homeowners won a case in the U.S. Court of Appeals in Chicago in 1974, which ruled that it was illegal to charge higher prices for houses sold primarily to blacks than for comparable houses sold in white neighborhoods.[21] A landmark decision, based on an 1866 statute giving blacks equal property rights with whites, it extends the reach of the law by defining exploitation as discrimination. Based on the case, black Chicagoans immediately petitioned the Illinois Insurance Department to cause Allstate and 11 other insurance companies to cease charging higher insurance rates for policies written in central Chicago. In the next step, financing will be explored, particularly the tendency of savings and loan associations to refuse loans in certain black sections of a city. In the house case, the plaintiffs are asking for damages to cover the difference between what they were charged and "fair" selling prices on some 1,000 houses.

For years the Department of Agriculture has applied the "prime" and "choice" labels to corn-fed beef possessing fat or "marbling" that is considered necessary to provide flavor and tenderness. But these grades require expensive feedlot stays, running up the cost to the consumer, and there may be a threat to health in that high fat and cholesterol are linked to heart disease. Nonetheless, many supermarket chains offer only choice and prime grades. The Department of Agriculture recently announced a revision of its long-time meat grading system, which would lower somewhat the amount of fat needed for meat to qualify for the highest grades.

Product liability has been greatly broadened in recent years. As to *negligence,* manufacturers formerly were not liable unless they sold direct to the consumer; today this does not apply, and the manufacturer is liable if the user can show carelessness that caused the injury. *Breach of warranty* now applies to implied warranties as well as express warranties (i.e., that the product is safe, usable, and fit for its reasonably intended purpose). *Product liability* formerly could be invoked only by proving that the manufacturer had been careless. Now, any manufacturer who places an article on the market knowing it will be used without inspection is liable if the article turns out to have a defect that could cause injury. The National Commission on Product Safety, established in 1967, reported that federal authority to curb hazards to consumer products was virtually nonexistent; as a result, the Consumer Product Safety Act of 1972 was passed, with wide enforcement powers over almost all consumer products.

The Securities and Exchange Commission has been expanding information disclosure requirements, which threaten public companies and their officers with substantial liability if they fail to disclose material corporate information promptly. The new SEC thrust is based on the following consumer protection concepts: (1) selected investors should not have access to important nonpublic information that gives them an advantage; (2) investors cannot be misled by false information; (3) investors are reasonably entitled to continuing information about companies which will help them with investment decisions.

The Employee Retirement Income Security Act of 1974—the "pension reform law"—comes after ten years of pressure for pension reform. Its purpose is to guarantee employees of companies with pension plans that the funds will be there when they retire, but it also gives employees more freedom to take pension rights with them when they change jobs. A Pension Benefit Guarantee Corporation is set up within the Labor Department, similar to the Federal Deposit Insurance Corporation which

pension reform law

insures bank deposits against loss. And the Act provides that company officers may be *personally* liable for making a wrong decision regarding benefit plans, which ensures careful attention to implementing the Act.

Esther Peterson, who has been the President's special assistant for consumer affairs, Assistant Secretary of Labor, and president of the National Consumers League, listed the following steps in the typical reaction of business to growing consumer awareness:[22]

1. When consumer groups make a charge, deny everything (accepting the legitimacy of consumerism involves a philosophical and emotional wrench).
2. If denying everything doesn't work, discredit whoever made the charge. (If business can't accept the sincerity of consumer groups, it questions their motives.)
3. When consumers get no redress and seek legislative action, oppose everything.
4. If legislation is passed...try to "defang" everything enacted by working against implementation and appropriations...
5. Do something about the problems. After repeated frustration, the awakening comes, and business realizes that service is its first obligation if it is to grow and prosper.

In furtherance of point 5, a survey of 3,418 managers by Stephen Greyser and Steven Diamond of the Harvard Business School indicates that they see the new consumerism as permanent, and moreover are optimistic about its effects on the marketplace. They support pressures to make advertising more factual and informative. Improvement of product quality and performance is the most constructive consumer route that companies can take.[23]

The most important force in pressing regulatory agencies to attend to the consumer's interests is to make the consumer presence at least as well felt as the industry presence has been in the past. Congress responds well to public pressures (far better than do the agencies, since Congress lives on people contacts), and although it will not maintain a constant level of attention it is alert to act when it sees a mandate. Ralph Nader's Center for the Study of Responsive Law has published a "comprehensive manual for citizen access to federal agencies," which summarizes his experience since 1968 in dealing with these organizations, and which is bound to stimulate many consumer groups to take action which will have useful results.[24] The agencies are waking up to their consumer responsibilities, and the companies are accepting the overdue need for attention in this area. The prospects for the future of consumerism are good.

Summary

There are three kinds of government systems—communist, socialist, capitalist—and all have the need to control products and services to some extent in the interests of the people. Capitalist systems use the regulatory agencies to monitor private business conduct.

A business contract must be between parties empowered to deal, must be for a lawful purpose, must involve free will on both sides, and must be for some consideration. Negotiable instruments are written documents that convey valuable considerations. Warranties may be express (specifically agree to guarantee certain performance) or implied (inherent in the nature of the product or service).

Common law is the body of legal precedent; statutory law is written law made by legislatures and their agents. The government takes its actions in federal court; all other legal action takes place in state courts. Business torts are offenses between businesses; crimes are offenses against government. Legal actions against and between companies are increasing greatly. A major consumer weapon against business is the "class action suit" in which one plaintiff acts on behalf of all with similar complaints (whether he knows them or not), often brought by "public interest" lawyers.

Administrative law is that made through rulings and regulations of regulatory agencies established by Congress. Many more cases are handled each year by these agencies than by the courts, and the total money value is far greater as well. Courts are guided by legal precedent, whereas agencies are guided by administrative policy (and do not dispense justice but seek to further the aims set forth by Congress in establishing them). Early years of most agencies find the public interest predominating, but agencies tend to become the tools of the industries they regulate, although this is changing under pressure of consumer advocates.

Although Congress supports free competition, and empowers both the Justice Department and the Federal Trade Commission to insure free competition with no restraint of trade, Congress moves again and again to void competition in specific industries, to the point that about a quarter of all industry is exempt from antitrust law. Industry support comes from the concept of helping infant industries to prosper, but tends to degenerate into protecting industry from competition. Paradoxically, such protection often proves debilitating to the industry regulated, sapping its competitive spirit and inhibiting managerial and technological innovation. As a rule, competitive industries perform best.

Regulatory agencies (and similar agencies within the executive department, to some extent) operate independently of Congress and the president, almost as a "fourth branch" of government, embodying the roles of legislator, executive, and judge (and prosecutor and jury), as well as that of patron. Often they are too well insulated from the consumers they are designed to protect. Agencies are given a mandate to operate within a narrow field, and too often do not cooperate with other agencies whose functions overlap: thus the CAB and the FAA do not cooperate with each other, though one assigns air routes and the other decides where airports will go. Within the same Department of Transportation, one agency is supporting feeder airlines and another is pushing highways that will put such airlines out of business.

The "new look" agencies, formed within the past few years when consumer interest and pressure have been high, tend to favor the consumer and the "public interest" more than some of the older agencies, partly because they have no easily recognizable industry constituency. Sometimes their enforcement is one-sided, giving too little heed to the potential harm that can be done in other areas. Thus EPA's environmental rules can work counter to the nation's need for energy self-sufficiency or for economic well-being.

The new consumer movement, which probably picked up its initial impetus in the late 1960s, is causing substantial changes in the old-line agencies, making them far more responsive to consumer interest. Such concepts as product liability are invoked more frequently, and with more teeth, thus forcing manufacturers to pay far more attention to safety and quality. The truth-in-lending and truth-in-advertising laws are bringing new frankness to these areas.

Notes

1. Quoted in Herman Drooss and Charles Gilbert, *American Business* (Englewood Cliffs, N.J.: Prentice-Hall, Inc., 1972), p. 264.
2. Cox, Fellmeth, and Schultz, *The Nader Report on the Federal Trade Commission* (New York: Richard W. Baron, 1969), p. vii.
3. Eleanore Carneth, "The Legal Explosion Has Left Business Well-Shocked," *Fortune,* April 1973, pp. 65-69.
4. Ibid.
5. Ibid.
6. The law forbids corporate giving to political campaigns, as an improper attempt to influence legislation or obtain special privileges. It is a vestige of our past business heritage, when many lawmakers were in the pockets of big business.
7. "Con Ed Makes Charles Luce Run," *Fortune,* September 1974, p. 171.
8. Paragraph based on "Making Losers Pay the Bills," *Business Week,* December 14, 1974, p. 88.
9. Louis M. Kohlmeier, Jr., *The Regulators* (New York: Harper & Row, Pubs., 1969), p. lx.
10. Report of the Senate Committee on Interstate Commerce of February 26, 1913, p. xv.
11. Howard Morgan, letter of January 23, 1963 to President John F. Kennedy, Washington, D.C.
12. There are exceptions to this rule. The Food and Drug Administration is part of the Department of Health, Education and Welfare, an executive agency. And in 1966 Congress engineered the largest expansion of executive authority ever when it organized the Department of Transportation, putting the FAA and the Federal Highway Administration under it and giving it the powers of the ICC and CAB to write safety regulations for rail, air, and trucking industries.
13. While the Administrative Procedures Act empowers a reviewing federal court to set aside arbitrary or capricious action by a regulatory agency, the Supreme Court, in a December 1974 review of a lower court case that found against the ICC, reversed the lower court, saying that it was not "empowered to substitute its judgment for that of the agency," even though the ICC's treatment of certain evidence was not "a paragon of clarity." It emphasized that the allowable scope of review of a court under the "arbitrary and capricious" standard is "a narrow one."
14. After the Connecticut Turnpike opened in 1958, traffic on the New Haven Railroad plunged from 45 million in 1957 to 30 million in 1960; it went bankrupt in 1961. Continuing in operation with government funding, it had dropped to 25 million in 1964. Interstate systems are slashing traffic on many feeder airline routes as well.
15. EPA is starting to pick up a constituency in all of the firms producing water, air, and noise pollution control equipment—a developing lobby against any relaxation of these regulations.
16. George W. Hilton, "Time to Unload the Regulators," *Fortune,* July 1971, p. 66.

17. Report of the American Bar Association Commission to Study the Federal Trade Commission (Chicago: American Bar Association, 1969), p. 3.

18. Gilbert Burck, "The Hazards of Corporate Responsibility," *Fortune,* June 1973, p. 114.

19. Many business executives would disagree vigorously with this accolade; in the end, historians will have to sort out the pluses and minuses.

20. "Lower Bar Tab Out for Women," *Pittsburgh Press,* March 1, 1974.

21. "The Price Can't Be Higher for Blacks," *Business Week,* September 22, 1974, pp. 72-73.

22. "Consumerism as a Retailer's Asset," *Harvard Business Review,* May-June 1974, pp. 91-101.

23. Stephen A. Greyser and Steven L. Diamond, "Probing Opinions," *Harvard Business Review,* September-October 1974, pp. 38-58.

24. James R. Michael, ed., *Working on the System* (New York: Basic Books, Inc., 1974).

Review Questions

1. What are the requirements for a valid contract?
2. What is the difference between an express and an implied warranty?
3. What is a "class action suit" and why is it assuming new importance?
4. What is the difference between business and administrative law?
5. What is the difference between legal precedent and administrative policy?
6. What was the common purpose in founding the ICC, the FTC, and the FDA?
7. Why does responsibility for regulating and promoting an industry bring problems?
8. How does the Robinson-Patman Act relate to "fair trade laws"?
9. Why do we call regulatory agencies the "fourth branch" of government?
10. Why does one transportation agency tend not to collaborate with others?
11. Why does Professor Kristol liken the EPA to "evangelical reform movements"?
12. Why can the "last hired, first fired" principle be discriminatory under certain conditions?
13. What new principle did the Transportation Act of 1920 embody for the ICC?
14. In what respect is the CAB like the ICC in its regulatory policies?
15. How has product liability broadened in recent years?

Discussion Questions

1. Think of an example of an express warranty, an implied warranty, and "puff" for the same product.
2. What sort of "preventive law" should an engineering consulting firm plan for?
3. Why might the FDA favor the interests of industry over those of the consumer?
4. How could the agencies regulating different transportation areas coordinate their independent actions? What sort of organization might be needed? What sort of direction and structure? (Bear in mind that the ICC is not under the Secretary of Transportation.)
5. If the EPA had a "constituency" in industry, which developed in time, can you think who or what it might be?
6. How could a company seek to avoid the initial negative responses to consumer awareness listed by Esther Peterson (page 560) before finally taking positive action?

North Star Case Study

When North Star performed the study for Blackridge to design the municipal shopping center, it followed its usual practice of estimating the number of worker days the job would take, and advising the city manager as a part of its proposal that the actual cost would be determined by the time it put on the job. This was acceptable to Blackridge, and the work was carried out on that basis.

Subsequently, suppose that Blackridge had asked North Star to submit a proposal to do the engineering design and construction supervision for the municipal building (city offices and library). In response to this request—which went to several other engineering firms in the city—North Star submitted a letter saying how it conceived of the municipal complex as being arranged, and stating that its fee would be the standard percentage for design (a fixed percent of the construction cost) and another standard percentage for construction supervision (some other fixed percent of construction cost). It stated in the letter that these percentages were established by the consulting engineers' association, and were standard.

Shortly after the bids were submitted, the city attorney brought an action against North Star and all the other bidders for "collusive action," in that all had submitted identical percentages; moreover, each had put in a statement saying this was in accordance with the consulting engineers association's standard fees.

1. Do you think the city attorney has a case at law against North Star?
2. If you were city attorney, what would you state as grounds?
3. If you were North Star, how would you defend your action?
4. What should North Star do?
5. Is there any difference between antitrust as applied to the professions and as applied to, say, tire manufacturers who all agree on a common price?
6. Is it in the public interest for professionals not to have standard rates?

Suggestions for Further Reading

Bailey, E. E. *Economic Theory of Regulatory Constraint.* Lexington, Mass.: Lexington Books, 1973.

Blumner, S. M., ed. *Readings in the Regulation of Business.* Scranton, Pa.: International Textbook Co., 1968.

Davis, K. C. *Administrative Law.* St. Paul, Minn.: West Pub. Co., 1973.

Estey, M. S. *Regulating Union Government.* New York: Harper & Row, Pubs., 1964.

Fox, S. *Management and the Law.* New York: Irvington Publications, 1966.

Jones, W. K. *Cases and Materials on Regulated Industries.* Mineola, N.Y.: Foundation Press, 1967.

Kohlmeier, L. M., Jr. *The Regulators: Watchdog Agencies and the Public Interest.* New York: Harper & Row, Pubs., 1969.

Lorsch, R. S. *Democratic Process and Administrative Law.* Detroit: Wayne State University Press, 1969.

McAvoy, P. W. *Regulation of Transport Innovation: The ICC and Unit Coal Transport to the East Coast.* New York: Random House, Inc., 1967.
Nizer, L. *The Implosion Controversy.* Greenwich, Conn.: Fawcett World Libraries, 1974.
Ostlund, H. J. *Fair Trade and the Retail Drug Store.* Chicago: Druggist's Research Bureau, 1940.
Redford, E. S. *Regulatory Process.* Austin, Tex.: University of Texas Press, 1969.

Labor-Management Relations 15

North Star Prologue

The four original partners formed North Star as an engineering consulting firm, with each partner bringing a different kind of expertise. They perceived the need to organize more formally as their work load grew, and successfully faced some problems arising from a challenge to their leadership and communication skills. The lack of advance planning threatened to create financial problems, and they found themselves deficient in problem-solving techniques; particularly troublesome was the growing potential for divisiveness and conflict within the organization. Despite a number of other problems, they had prospered, and reached the point where their outside contacts were assuming the major share of their attention. They set up a marketing structure, and suddenly found that they were in violation of administrative law in a number of areas; so they called in a lawyer and took a "crash course" in how to live with regulatory agencies.

The information from the lawyer was quite unexpected, and left the officers with the conclusion that they had some cleanup work to do. One of the steps they took was to review with Barbara Newman her earlier recommendation that the firm set up a proper profit-sharing plan, but the time did not seem ideal in view of their recent cash squeeze, so they decided to postpone its implementation. In the meantime, they canceled the bonus system for the engineers, informing them of the lawyer's comments regarding its illegality. This news produced a surprising amount of grumbling, and Bert noticed a sullen attitude in the drafting room that he had not encountered before; but he decided that it would pass in time, and determined to pay no attention.

A short time later, Dick advised Bert that the engineer he had hired nearly ten years earlier on the first Natal job (the one with the drinking problem) would be coming back to the U.S. soon upon completion of the Asian power plant project. Another nuclear project had opened up with B&W in Asia, but the combination of climate and alcohol was tearing down his health to the extent that the project manager had refused to allow him to stay. Bert wasn't delighted at the news, but Dick said if anyone in the engineering group had seniority Fred Zuba did, and Bert would have to make a place for him. He could continue to do the same work he had been doing, but it would have to be in the home office. When Zuba came in, Bert told Ab to put him in the Mechanical/Civil Department. The drafting room crew did not seem happy to see the new member, but nothing much was said.

Nothing was said, that is, until it became necessary six weeks later to lay off two engineers in the Mechanical/Civil Department, as a delayed result of the cash squeeze that had hit the company earlier. When that was announced, a delegation consisting of Gene Whitney and Ruth Mangeri from that department and Tom Heckathorn from Electrical came in to see Bert and demanded that Fred Zuba be let go before any of the regular home office team. Bert called in Dick, who said angrily that Fred had been with the firm longer than any of them, and he was damned if he was going to be a party to that sort of thing. Gene replied that Fred wasn't a member of the union, that he had been brought in from outside and stuck on top of the heap, and that they weren't going to sit still for that. Tom added that, while they were about it, the drafting room was damned sore about the sudden termination of bonuses, and they wanted to negotiate about that.

Dick said what did he mean "negotiate," and what was all this talk about the union? They didn't have a union shop at North Star. Gene said well, they could sure as hell remedy that; the way things were going with the bonuses, and never paying the engineers any overtime when they had to work late, and futzing around with vacation schedules, and not giving them any voice in policy matters, all they had to do was call for a union election and the company would find itself unionized overnight.

The discussion was beginning to escalate rapidly, with some rather bitter overtones, and Bert said they ought to call Henry in. When he heard the views of the opposing groups, he said Barbara Newman ought to be there too. Since she was out of the office, he suggested they terminate the discussions before they got out of hand, and let Barbara sum up things for both sides so they could start from there.

Barbara met with Gene and his group privately and at length. She would not let Bert or even Ab Jenkins sit in on her meetings with the engineers, because she said if her position was to be at all tenable she had to be a representative for the engineers as well as for management. Then she came in and laid the situation before the officers. North Star had no union, obviously, but most of the engineers had been union members when they came to work here, and the union still was a factor to consider in any negotiations. She had little doubt that Gene was not bluffing: if a union election were called in the present climate of mistrust it would carry and North Star *would* be a union shop. However, none of the engineers really wanted the union in, because in many ways it limited their freedom of action as much as it did management's. Moreover, they really thought of themselves as part of management—certainly, the department heads did.

Getting down to the gut issues, though, Barbara said everyone was going to have to give a bit. In the first place, clearly they were wrong about Fred Zuba; he had all sorts of seniority, and there was no way that he should be laid off before the new men. But he had been brought in pretty heavy-handedly, and Dick was at fault there. As to the bonuses, they were right; those had become accepted elements of the compensation package, and it was wrong for North Star to terminate those regardless of the IRS; moreover, that had been done clumsily, too. It could be straightened out legally if they would put in the profit-sharing system she had been promoting, providing a maximum of 15% profit share to every employee whenever the financial performance of the company permitted. She suggested that they tell the engineers immediately that the bonuses would be reinstated through this device.

As to the bag of other grievances, she suggested that the company act as though it were a union shop in such matters as vacation schedules, right to overtime pay, pay scales, and so forth. This could be done by informally adopting the practices of a large engineering firm that was unionized, and simply letting it be known that any significant benefits earned by the engineers of that company would be granted the North Star engineers. This would defuse the controversy completely, in her opinion, but would still leave the company and the engineers free of actual union involvement. She pointed out that this approach was a common one in many small companies; even if they were unionized, they would agree in advance to pattern their benefits on whatever the union won for the industry leader, thus saving themselves the stress and strain of negotiation and conflict.

It sounded great to Henry, and Bert agreed to go along, though with less enthusiasm. The drafting room group hung up for a time over the question of Fred, but finally agreed with the package as presented. When both sides had agreed to abide by the settlement, Barbara proposed that they all lay down their work and go out for a drink on her. The atmosphere brightened noticeably when they got their feet up on the bar, and Henry found himself talking with Gene and Rena and Tom and the others in a way he had never done before. Rena said it was a pleasure once in a while to be treated as people rather than as a "cost of production."

When they met later, Barbara told Henry North Star had been lucky to be introduced to the modern world of labor-management relations so gently. Many companies, she said, were not so sensible, and had to do it the hard way.

What North Star Can Learn from Chapter 15

1. The role which labor legislation has played in promoting unions during this century
2. The benefits which labor unions have gained for their members through the use of varying strategies and the goals of union members
3. The recent attitudes of blue-collar and white-collar workers toward their jobs, unions, and union leaders, and the inroads made by unions within these strategies
4. The role which recent Executive Orders have played in guaranteeing the right of unionization to public employees
5. The recent plight of various minority groups in the labor force
6. How organizations can deal with unions and employee demands

In chapters 13 and 14 we turned our attention to two of the main external forces affecting the enterprise: markets and government, law and regulation. In this chapter we will consider a third major constraint on management: the labor unions that represent employees in most large companies and an increasing number of large public agencies. Labor is a factor of production, like capital, equipment, and material; but unlike these factors, labor has an advocate in the form of a powerful union, and labor has emotions and desires and aspirations. In the early days of business, labor was treated as impersonally as equipment—hired when needed, fired when the need had passed, tossed aside when damaged or worn out, and considered to be a commodity without rights, preferences, or any voice in the operation. Today things are vastly different, and many of the gains can be credited to unions.

In this chapter you will look at four aspects of labor-management relations:

1. *The role of unions in society*—historical development, the evolution of labor legislation, the evolving strategy and goals of unions, and how unions fulfill worker needs.
2. *The work force*—blue-collar workers, the increasing white-collar segment as the U.S. shifts more to a service economy, public employees, and special groups (youth, women, blacks, and other racial minorities, and so-called "hard-core unemployed").
3. *Dealing with unions by management*—collective bargaining and other negotiating, working under the contract, handling grievances, and strikes or lockouts.
4. *The changing labor environment*—"no-strike" practices, technological change, worker alienation, industrial democracy, and the attendant problems in an evolving society.

Originally, workers banded together in unions because they needed the strength of solidarity to balance the power equation. Today the power is in balance: some believe the pendulum has swung in labor's favor. But increasingly labor is questioning the autocratic power of unions just as it did that of corporations, and we see the spectacle of strikes against unions and rank-and-file "takeovers." Many union leaders date from an earlier time, and they do not always understand the young workers who have become a sizable part of their constituencies. Workers are more highly educated, more questioning, and less willing to accept the necessity for monotonous or deadend work. Blue-collar workers are rebelling against the insecurity of automatic layoffs when work slackens. Minority workers are demanding equal rights, and perhaps something more than equality to redress past imbalance. And increasingly the government is interceding on behalf of labor, to force corporations to meet their obligations.

Role of Unions in Society

Historical Development

In chapter 2 we briefly described the medieval guilds, which in some ways resembled labor unions. However, their main thrust was to establish craft

collective strength standards and police the quality of work done by members of the craft; to a lesser extent they were self-help organizations, banding together for collective strength. Still earlier, the Chinese family organizations, with several generations living within one compound, took on some of the mutual support role of unions. But the guilds were too restrictive, the Chinese communes too family-centered, to be true unions in the modern sense.

unions In the U.S., worker associations predated the War for Independence, but their main purpose was to provide a vehicle for common discussion of problems. Associations occasionally struck against employers as early as the late 1700s, but they were not important forces—and moreover, they were not dealing with large employers. The waves of immigration that washed the shores of the new continent, starting about 1820, brought large numbers of new employees whose only wish was to find employment; as a result, the climate did not favor labor organization. Unions were formed during the 1800s, but their power waned during periods of depression, and it was not until the 1880s that unions became strong enough to weather the economic downturns.

Knights of Labor The Noble Order of the Knights of Labor, founded in 1869 by Philadelphia garment workers, gradually picked up strength and members until by 1885 it boasted 100,000 members. A successful strike against railroad tycoon Jay Gould brought it national recognition and an increase to 700,000 members before the year was out. However, its very success contained the seeds of decline, for it had brought in diverse elements including both skilled and unskilled labor, and their goals were so far apart that the more skilled trades left to form independent organizations with more singleminded aims. By the end of the decade their membership had declined to 100,000, and they gradually lost their influence, to disband entirely at the start of World War I.

American Federation of Labor The large craft unions of skilled trades which had left the Knights came together in 1886 to form the American Federation of Labor under the famous Samuel Gompers, often considered father of the American labor movement. Since this organization had formed specifically to deal with the problems of the skilled trades—operating as a *business union* to bargain for improvements in wages, hours, and working conditions—it continued to turn its back on the growing numbers of unskilled trades. Since the latter had no place to go, and since the AFL was moving slowly to open its doors to this important new segment of the industrial population, a dissident group of six AFL unions split off in 1938 and formed the Congress of Industrial Organizations. In 1955, the two powerful unions merged under the leadership of their respective presidents (George Meany of the AFL and Walter Reuther of the CIO) to form the AFL-CIO

AFL-CIO with Meany as president and Reuther as head of its large new Industrial Union Department.

The AFL-CIO boasts some 14 million members with its various affiliated unions, making it far and away the largest labor organization in the U.S., but some important unions are not members. The Teamsters, expelled from the AFL-CIO in the 1950s and now boasting over 2 million members, is the country's biggest union, and is an independent labor organization,[1] as are the railroad brotherhoods and the United Mine Workers (who have been affiliated and unaffiliated at several times).

The great scope and diversity of the American Federation of Labor and Congress of Industrial Organizations can be seen in the organization chart shown in Figure 15-1. It must be remembered, however, that it is a *federation* rather than a tight authoritative organization, and that the individual unions who are members have substantial autonomy to manage their affairs. Unions have left the central federations at many times, and could do so again for what they consider sufficient cause.

federation

Labor Legislation

The first labor legislation was directed against union activity, holding it illegal to organize (and thus "conspire" to seek higher wages). By the late 1800s this doctrine had been modified to the point where unions were judged under the common law doctrine of *restraint of trade* if their actions would tend to reduce competition in the classical sense. In 1890 came the Sherman Antitrust Act, and its passage heralded a series of court battles to see if union activities constituted a violation of the act. One of these, the Danbury Hatters case, found the Brotherhood of United Hatters guilty and a fine of $250,000 was levied. The anti-union interpretation of the Sherman Act prompted unions to press for clarifying legislation, and in 1914 the Clayton Antitrust Act specifically stated that nothing in the antitrust laws could be interpreted as preventing the organization of labor unions.

restraint of trade

Clayton Antitrust Act

Although the Clayton Act seemed to permit typical union negotiations, several court cases tended to weaken its thrust. It was not until the Railway Labor Act of 1926 that collective bargaining was explicitly authorized, and consequently this act has been considered a turning point in the power and recognition of unions before law. And in 1932 the

The medieval guilds were self-help organizations, banding together for collective strength.

LABOR-MANAGEMENT RELATIONS

Norris-La Guardia Act

yellow dog contracts

Norris-LaGuardia Act strengthened the hand of unions in three additional respects: it limited the power of employers to obtain court injunctions against strikes, picketing, and boycotts; it outlawed *yellow dog contracts* whereby employees had agreed not to join unions as a condition of employment; and it reiterated workers' rights to organize into unions and select their own bargaining agents without employer interference.

In 1933 the National Industrial Recovery Act was passed, reiterating and strengthening the government's support for collective bargaining, but it was declared unconstitutional by the Supreme Court because of its interference with a number of management prerogatives. Congress took heed of the objections to this act, and in 1935 passed the National Labor Relations Act (the Wagner Act), which held that employers could not:

Wagner Act

- interfere with or discriminate against workers for taking any authorized action under the act,
- interfere in any way, favorably or unfavorably, with union activities, or
- refuse to bargain collectively with unions selected by the workers.

Figure 15-1.
AFL-CIO Organization Chart

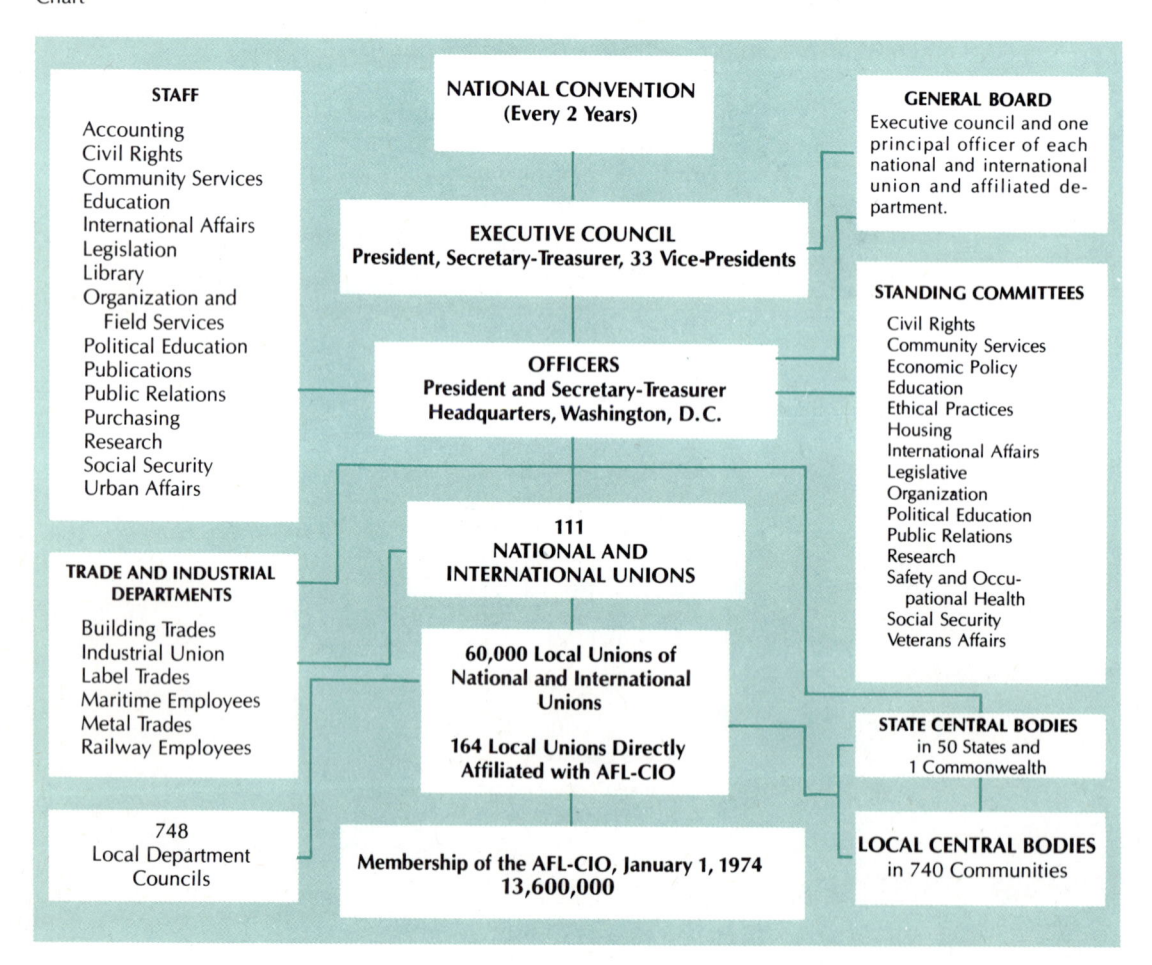

STAFF
Accounting
Civil Rights
Community Services
Education
International Affairs
Legislation
Library
Organization and Field Services
Political Education
Publications
Public Relations
Purchasing
Research
Social Security
Urban Affairs

TRADE AND INDUSTRIAL DEPARTMENTS
Building Trades
Industrial Union
Label Trades
Maritime Employees
Metal Trades
Railway Employees

748 Local Department Councils

NATIONAL CONVENTION (Every 2 Years)

EXECUTIVE COUNCIL
President, Secretary-Treasurer, 33 Vice-Presidents

OFFICERS
President and Secretary-Treasurer
Headquarters, Washington, D.C.

111 **NATIONAL AND INTERNATIONAL UNIONS**

60,000 Local Unions of National and International Unions

164 Local Unions Directly Affiliated with AFL-CIO

Membership of the AFL-CIO, January 1, 1974
13,600,000

GENERAL BOARD
Executive council and one principal officer of each national and international union and affiliated department.

STANDING COMMITTEES
Civil Rights
Community Services
Economic Policy
Education
Ethical Practices
Housing
International Affairs
Legislative
Organization
Political Education
Public Relations
Research
Safety and Occupational Health
Social Security
Veterans Affairs

STATE CENTRAL BODIES
in 50 States and 1 Commonwealth

LOCAL CENTRAL BODIES
in 740 Communities

MANAGEMENT AND ITS ENVIRONMENT

While the employer's responsibilities were set forth, the act was silent as to the union's responsibilities. Thus, there was a swing of power toward the unions; by implication, the act enabled them to refuse, to bargain, to engage in illegal picketing, and in some cases to discriminate against some workers in favor of others. As a result, managers prevailed upon Congress to correct the imbalance by passing the Labor-Management Relations Act (Taft-Hartley Act) in 1947. The National Labor Relations Board, set up by the Wagner Act to adjudicate complaints under the act, was continued, with an increase in its membership from three to five. As the Wagner Act had done for employers, the Taft-Hartley Act restricted the actions of unions, stating that they could not:

- interfere with or discriminate against workers for taking any authorized action under the act,
- to induce an employer to discriminate against any employee,
- extract payment from an employer for services not performed,
- require excessive initiation fees from new union members,
- engage in unlawful strikes or boycotts,
- refuse to bargain with an employer, or
- insist on the *union shop* (compulsory union membership for all employees after hiring) in states prohibiting it by *right-to-work* laws (which make union shop agreements by employers illegal).

The right-to-work laws, which have been passed by 19 primarily agricultural states, hinder union growth in those states, and the unions have made vigorous efforts to repeal Section 14B of the Taft-Hartley Act which authorizes them. In 1966 a bill to repeal Section 14B failed to pass in the Senate after having passed the House. It is certain that organized labor will continue its efforts to repeal this section.

To summarize, the Wagner Act placed restrictions on employers in dealing with unions, and the Taft-Hartley Act placed restrictions on unions in dealing with employers. But internal affairs of unions were not subject to governmental control, and there were examples of labor abuses and encroachments on individual rights. Consequently, in 1959 Congress passed the Labor-Management Reporting and Disclosure Act (Landrum-Griffin Act) to require unions to report and disclose certain of their internal affairs to the federal government. The principal features of Landrum-Griffin are as follows:

- Union members are given a "bill of rights" to nominate candidates, vote in union elections, participate in both union meetings and independent groups not sponsored by the union, and initiate civil action punishable by fine or imprisonment if the union fails to permit such action or threatens violence to interfere with them.
- Increases in dues or fees are prohibited unless democratically approved by the membership, and disciplinary action against a member by the union is surrounded by safeguards.
- Unions must adopt and publicize constitutions and by-laws, and must prepare and submit detailed financial reports, including payments to or from any employers.
- Elections must be held by secret ballot—every five years for national officers, every four for intermediate officers, and every

three for local officers. Each member must have an equal chance to nominate candidates, and no union funds can be used to promote any candidacy.

Various states have labor legislation to regulate firms operating wholly within the state, which in substance are similar to the Wagner Act and the Norris-LaGuardia Act. In addition, the states have unemployment compensation and workmen's compensation laws in areas not covered by federal law.

Equal Employment Opportunity Commission

In 1964, when Congress passed the Civil Rights Act, it established an Equal Employment Opportunity Commission to monitor compliance under the act, but in making compromises to achieve passage the commission was denied any enforcement powers. This was remedied in 1972 by the Equal Employment Opportunity Act, which gave the commission power to file a civil action in federal court against charges of discrimination, and to represent the charging party in the court action. Additionally it provided for injunctions against further discrimination, and for reinstatement and back pay in cases where charges were proven. The principal features of this act, incorporating elements of the 1964 Civil Rights Act, are as follows:

- Employment offers cannot discriminate against any individual on the basis of race, color, religion, sex, or national origin (except where such discrimination is a reasonable requirement for the job, as in an ethnic association or religious group).
- Unions may not exclude anyone from membership for the above reasons, or in any way deprive any such person from employment opportunity (which provisions have required unions to abolish segregated locals, merge seniority lines, etc.).
- Employers may not refuse to hire any such categories of persons or discriminate against them in any on-the-job situations on such a basis.
- State and local governments are covered by the act and federal government jobs are virtually covered, though not within the jurisdiction of the commission.

executive order

When federal contracts are involved, the Office of Federal Contract Compliance of the Labor Department comes into action, with an effect on minority hiring just as substantial as that of the EEOC. A 1965 presidential executive order on hiring of minorities and a 1967 executive order on hiring women were given teeth by a 1970 OFCC order and a 1972 OFCC revised order respectively. Applying to companies with a minimum of $50,000 in contracts and 50 employees, the orders establish affirmative action goals that require positive steps by both employers and unions.

Union Strategy and Goals

Unquestionably the major purpose of unions is to win improved wages, working conditions, fringe benefits, and other advantages for their members. It was not always so. The Knights of Labor had social goals high on its list of priorities—elimination of child labor, equal pay for women, the establishment of cooperative industries, and other social reforms—

and these led to an emphasis on political action rather than collective bargaining with individual employers. As a result, the Knights paid too little attention to the bread-and-butter issues, and ultimately disappeared from the labor scene. The American Federation of Labor got its start with the very dissident unions who favored collective bargaining, and it has never forgotten where it came from. As a result, it has concentrated mainly on being a *business union,*[2] and has grown to its present majority position by concentrating on what its members wanted most.

business union

Managers sometimes charge the unions with wanting to take over the "prerogatives of management." With few exceptions, the last thing union leaders want is to take on the problems of management. They are interested in the security and welfare of their members, and they may object to management practices that run counter to these goals, but they are not anxious to help with managerial problems. Unions bargain for rights, and they see that the resulting contract is enforced. They establish and enforce work rules and grievance procedures. For an individual company, the union rules become in effect the company rules in labor-management situations, since the union negotiates in effect for an entire category of workmen or even for an entire industry.

Welfare unions go a step further than business unions, seeking to help their members with community problems off the job as well as with job-related matters. Such unions sponsor health insurance plans, cooperatives, credit unions and recreational programs, and even adult education programs.

welfare unions

Union Goals

Unions cannot attract new members and hold the ones they have unless their goals mesh with the goals of their members. The primary goal of a union today, as when the AFL was formed, is the *economic welfare* of its members. This means primarily higher wages, but it extends to good overtime provisions, attractive fringe benefits such as retirement and paid vacations, and other financial matters such as paid health plans, work clothes, etc. It may also cover cost-of-living adjustments.

union goals

An important secondary goal is *job security*. This deals with such matters as seniority for older employees, the guaranteed annual wage where possible to cushion the ups and downs of the industry or the economy, rules governing discharges or suspensions, and unemployment benefits.

An increasing third goal is *working conditions*. At one time this meant protecting employees against hazardous or unreasonably arduous work environments, and this is still a major element in certain industries. The 1974 United Mine Workers' contract with the Bituminous Coal Operators aimed at reducing deaths of new workers from inadequate safety training. New miners must have four days of paid safety training and cannot be assigned to hazardous jobs for the first 90 days, and for the first time a miner can "refuse to work under conditions he has reasonable ground to believe to be abnormally and immediately dangerous," with the question settled by government inspectors in case of dispute. Today, however, with few work places as grossly hazardous or arduous as in the past, the thrust has shifted to clean and pleasant work environments. When the United Auto Workers met with Chrysler in their 1974 negotiations, UAW president Leonard Woodcock cited the Volvo plant as "light, clean, and a decent place to work," with the sunken assembly line "pit" where workers stand under the passing cars eliminated; and UAW's chief negotiater with Chrysler, Douglas Fraser, said the Chrysler facilities were "a disgrace, if you compare [them] with Japanese facilities."

A fourth goal, concerned perhaps more with union growth than employee welfare, is *political action*. Unions seek to involve their members in political and civic action, both to improve the union image as good citizens and to encourage legislation favorable to union goals. Unions contribute in various ways to assist congressional friends to get elected, and try to deliver the "union vote" on key matters (though with the secret ballot it is not always clear how effectively this can be achieved).

A fifth goal, though of lesser importance, is *cooperative benefits*, where the union uses its status as a cohesive worker organization to promote certain social or fraternal benefits—sponsoring adult education courses for temporarily unemployed, travel clubs for members, cooperative consumer buying programs, etc.

Union Strategy and Tactics

As union-management relations become more mature, the strike weapon is less of a major element in union strategy than it was in the early days of labor organizations. The strike is a two-edged sword, because it penalizes the workers as well as the company, and both sides usually lose in a long strike. Figure 15-2 shows the financial effect of a three-month strike, which results in a 20% salary increase, for a worker with an initial salary of $800 per month, discounted to present value—as compared with what the value would be with no strike and no salary increase, assuming a 10% interest rate for money. It is not until the twentieth month that the workers recover from the effects of the strike, and by the end of two years (from the start of the strike) the net gain for the workers is only 3.7%, rather than the 20% gain they won in theory.[3]

The net gain may be much lower than this at times. In the steel industry, customers have typically stockpiled supplies before contract talks, sometimes buying the extra steel from foreign producers. If no strike took place, customers had too much steel in inventory, and their buying took a slump after the settlement until they worked off the excess. If a strike did take place, they sought alternate sources of supply overseas, and some of these new contacts continued, hurting the steel industry overall. Recognizing the harmful effects of strikes for both company and union, the United Steelworkers and the ten major steel companies negotiated a no-strike contract bargaining plan (termed ENA, for Experimental Negotiating Agreement) in 1973. It provided that any unresolved issues in the 1974 bargaining be submitted to a five-person arbitration panel empowered to make binding contract decisions before the previous contract expired, and thus to settle differences without a strike. Although challenged by a small group of dissidents in the union, the agreement was worked out successfully, and in April 1974 the USW won one of its best contracts ever without any threat of a strike—indeed, despite an agreement not to strike. The president of the AFL-CIO, George Meany, has cited the steel plan several times as an example for other unions.[4]

One weapon unions are using with increasing frequency is the *boycott*. While labor boycotts are quite old (the Brotherhood of United Hatters used it against employers in 1901, and even before that the railroad brotherhoods used it against Pullman), until recently this tactic has presented legal hazards for the union. Favorable court decisions have made the boycott more useful as a substitute for expensive walkouts. Cesar Chavez won recognition for his union in the California grape vineyards with his celebrated campaign against buying grapes from that area, and in 1974 the Amalgamated Clothing Workers won union recognition by Farah Manufacturing Company after a 20-month picketing campaign (although it never shut down a single plant, it caused a 25% drop in profits). It is doubtful that most boycotts have much effect on consumers; the real impact is on retailers. One apparel manufacturer stated at the time of the Farah struggle, "All union officials have to do is call on local merchants and say 'I don't know what the boys are going to do

boycott

Figure 15-2.
Salary lost in Strike.

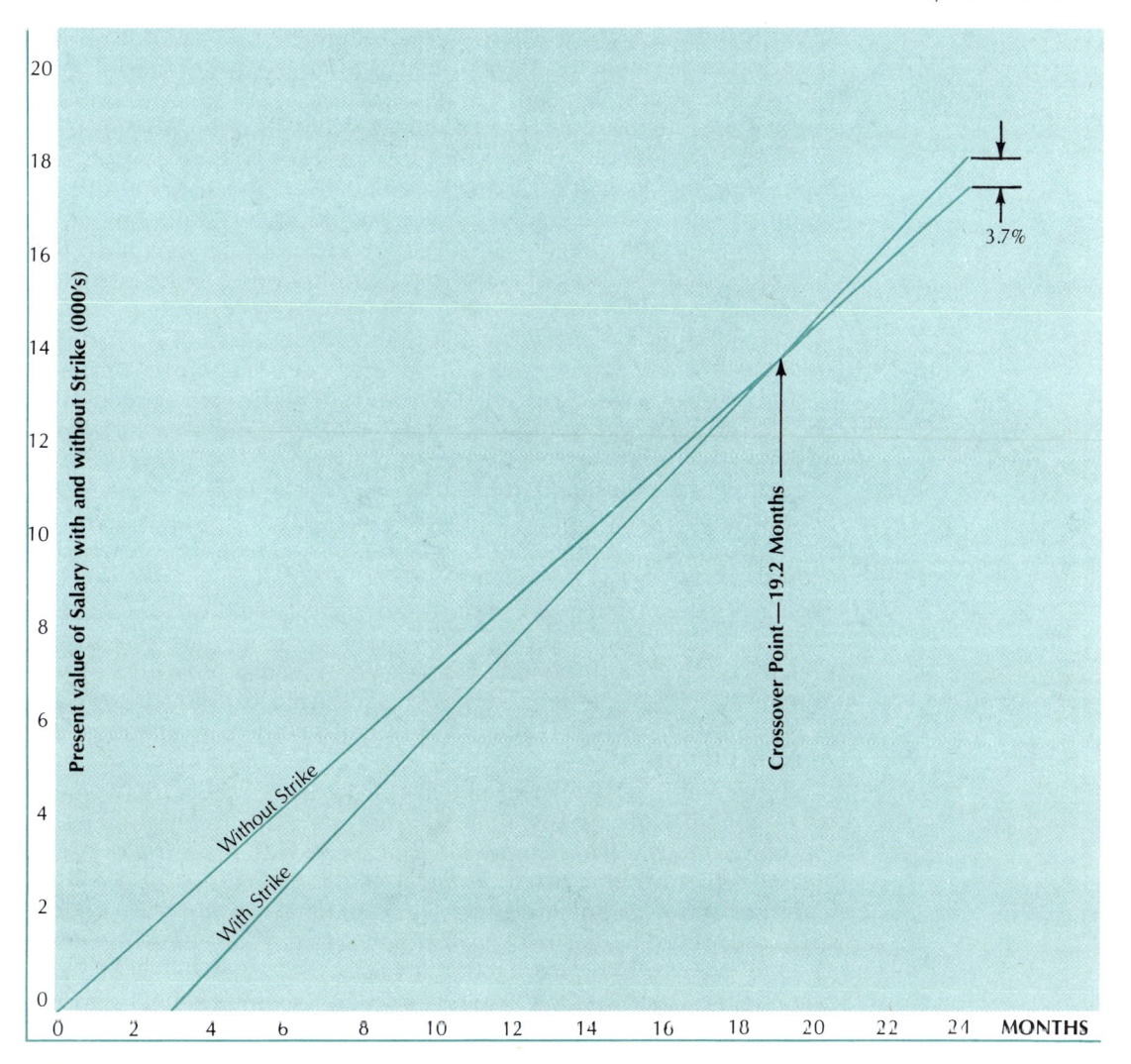

if you keep on handling these goods,' and the message is pretty clear." Unions hope that "informational" picketing outside a retail store will cause it to stop handling the boycotted products to end harassment. But there is a fine line between such "informational" picketing and an illegal *secondary boycott*—one aimed at shutting down an establishment not directly involved in the basic dispute. And boycotts are cumbersome for the union. Prior to the Farah case, the only major boycotts sanctioned by the AFL-CIO were the grape boycotts of the 1960s and the General Electric boycott during the 1969 strike.

A problem for the construction unions has been the growing loss of work to nonunion contractors, partly because such costly union practices as *jurisdictional strikes* have tended to make the union contractor's costs uncompetitive. In 1974 the AFL-CIO's 3.5 million-member Building and Construction Trades Department started a wholesale overhaul of costly practices that hamper union practices. President Frank Bonadio of the B&CT stated, "We're moving in the direction of total reform." One step was a thorough review of work practices that the late Walter Reuther (UAW president) said had "descended from the pyramids," and another was a draft agreement to allow the contractor to use any desired material or equipment and to ban any work rules that "limit or restrict" production. The draft agreement that evolved from the "total reform" review set procedures similar to the USW plan for binding arbitration of grievances, and included a ban on strikes over jurisdictional disputes (arguments over which trade or union should do a certain job).

During the inflationary climate of recent years, unions have been pushing for *cost-of-living* contracts that tie future raises to the living costs of members, usually based on the government's cost-of-living index; and some recent contracts have incorporated such wage escalation figures into basic salary on which pensions and other fringe benefits are computed.

In hard times, when jobs are scarce and layoffs threaten, unions often reach agreements with employers to take cuts in pay and working hours in order to stretch out the available jobs. During the 1975 recession, the International Brotherhood of Electrical Workers agreed with the Electrical Contractors Association in Chicago to work a four-day week and take a pay cut to effect the rehiring of 1,000 unemployed members. Newspaper Guild workers for the Washington *Star-News* voted over eight to one to take a 20% pay cut and go on a four-day week to avoid the dismissal of 100 colleagues. Rubber workers at Firestone's plant in Barberton, Ohio, willingly accepted a three-week closedown instead of a layoff of newer workers. and most clothing workers in Los Angeles, with the Amalgamated Clothing Workers Union, have chosen a 30-hour week rather than continued layoffs.

In the South, particularly in the textile industry (where unionism has had a tough organizing row to hoe), unions are attempting to persuade workers that they will have more job security and their pension funds will be safer if they are unionized. These are vulnerable areas for the textile manufacturers, which typically have only minimal pension plans in many cases, and where job security is at the pleasure of the company.

One major union effort today involves the organization of white-collar workers, including teachers, and public employees. The former traditionally refuse to become unionists, and until recently the latter have been prohibited by law from utilizing the union's most potent weapon: the strike. It is important for unions to make progress in organizing the white-collar "organizables" (excluding managers, proprietors, officials, etc.), because that group will continue to grow as the structure of U.S. society changes. Figure 15-3 shows the direction of employment for blue-collar, white-collar, and service segments of the work force deemed to be organizable over a thirty-year period. It is clear that the white-collar group represents a tempting target for labor union attention.

It is also clear that the unions will have to make inroads into the white-collar ranks if they are to retain their traditional strength in the labor movement. But the trends are not encouraging in this respect. While about 43% of blue-collar and service workers (excluding household workers) belonged to unions in 1968, white-collar membership dropped from 12.8% in 1956 to 11.2% in 1968. Table 15-1 shows this trend year by year for approximately this period. Note that in only one year did the gains in white-collar membership exceed the losses, and for the years as a whole the loss in absolute terms came to some 32,500 members, or about 35% more members lost in bargaining units than members gained. Clearly there is substantial resistance to white-collar unionism, and the unions must surmount this problem somehow if they are to retain their strength.

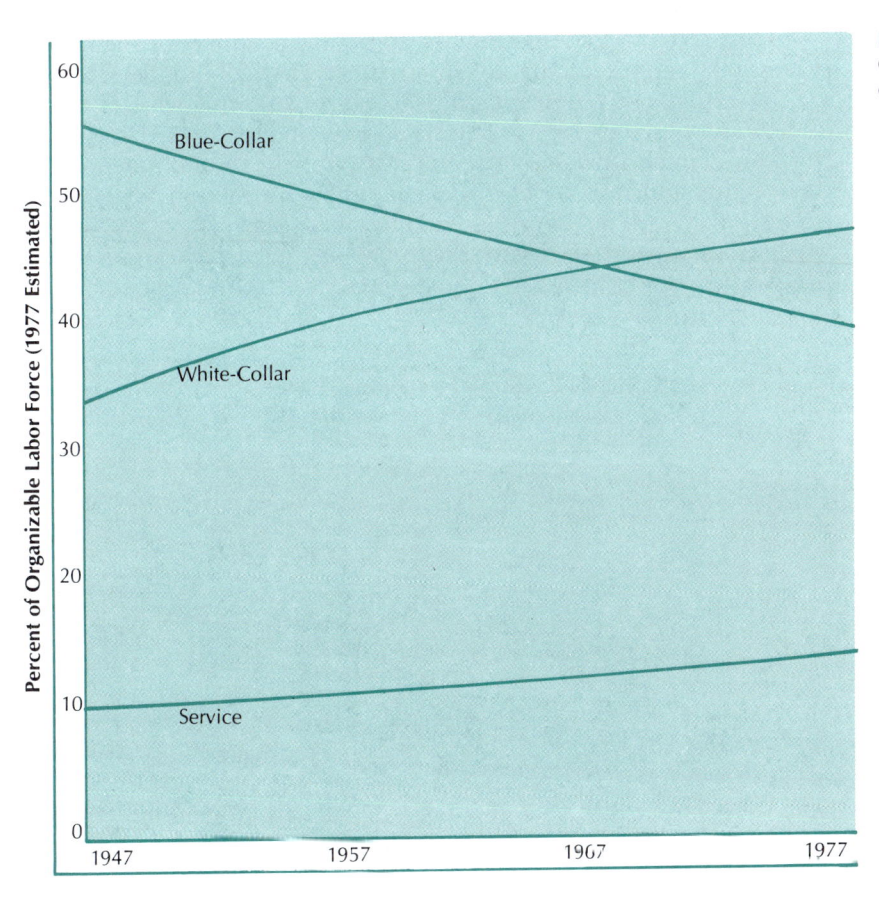

Figure 15-3.
Change in Composition of Work Force, 1947-77

In its other new organizing area, the union is doing much better. Membership rolls of civil service labor organizations are growing dramatically, and the AFL-CIO's new Public Employee Department, with 2 million members, is its fastest-growing segment. In the decade between 1964 and 1974, public employee union membership rose from less than 1 million to some 2.4 million; if the 1.6 million-member National Education Association and some other groups that are more social or professional in character than unions are included, the total would be about 5.5 million. The major union in the department is the American Federation of State, County, and Municipal Employees, with 700,000 members. Public unionism is hampered at times by prohibition in some sectors of public employee organizing, prohibition of striking legally, and restrictions on bargaining collectively; but in some celebrated public labor disputes, the law has been overlooked by both sides in their joint desire to settle the matter and get back to work.

Fulfilling Worker Needs

The major contribution a union makes to the individual worker is the strength that comes with numbers. An individual is virtually powerless to negotiate with a large corporation; as a member of a union which will come to the defense of any individual as though all were threatened, each worker's power is multiplied a thousandfold.

A less recognized but important additional need met by the union is professional representation. Even with the strength of numbers, workers are not experienced in negotiating a contract, knowing what to ask for, understanding labor law, or interpreting economic data that explains trends in the industry. In a grievance dispute, they will not be aware of their rights and how to obtain them. The contribution made by the professional staff of unions is so substantial that often the company supervisor is at a distinct disadvantage in an argument or hearing, because the worker is professionally represented and the supervisor is not.

Table 15-1.
Change in Union Strength, 1957-59

Year	Employees in bargaining units won by unions	Employees in bargaining units lost by unions	Percentage by which loss exceeds win
1957	5,500	7,000	27.3
1958	3,900	4,300	10.3
1959	3,660	6,860	88.8
1960	3,005	5,095	69.6
1961	4,660	6,845	59.8
1962	5,880	8,460	43.9
1963	6,495	15,250	134.8
1964	6,780	9,255	21.8
1965	7,605	10,125	33.1
1966	9,085	10,100	11.2
1967	15,090	11,940	(20.9) Gain
1968	11,175	15,900	42.3
1969	10,695	14,885	39.2
Total	93,530	126,015	34.7%

(Sometimes supervisors will be reluctant to press a legitimate charge for fear that they will be made to look foolish in an encounter; some companies establish legal representatives to assist the supervisor during such a grievance hearing, to restore the balance.)

In recent years, unions have pressed for fringe benefits that individuals might not think of demanding because of the inherent complexity of today's pension systems (including the right to have a *vested interest* in what has been paid in by the company and the employees, and to transfer it to another company if they change jobs), health plans, insurance, flexible rules on time of retirement, and other group benefits. Union economists can negotiate for valuable cost-of-living clauses, including some adjustment of retiree benefits to keep up with inflation.

vested interest

Unions probably have been weakest in coping with (or even understanding) the alienation of young workers who feel trapped in work their parents took for granted. A study of automobile workers by Eli Chinoy[5] describes how they hated their jobs and fantasized about leaving them. Many union leaders, being of an earlier generation, probably have difficulty really appreciating the distaste of the young workers for industrial work. With the early 1970s came the suggestion of a blue-collar revolt, reflected in rejection of centrally negotiated union contracts, proliferation of "local issues," and political strife within the unions themselves.[6] While unions are making a sincere effort to deal with these issues, it is not clear what they can do to fulfill deep-felt worker needs in this area.

In an indirect but important way, unions respond to worker needs when they help to promote productivity in the industries they represent. At one time, "productivity" was a dirty word to workers, because it meant the "speed-up" in which they simply were required to do more of the same operations with no increase in pay, or in which machines replaced men and total employment fell. In 1971, the United Steelworkers and the steel industry established a joint union-management advisory committee to devise means of improving productivity and promoting the use of domestic steel. In the words of USW president I. W. Abel, improved productivity means "better tools and modern technology, worker effectiveness, reducing equipment breakdowns, eliminating waste and negligent use of materials, using facilities and time more efficiently, and improvement of the plant safety experience."[7] The joint plant committees started to function in late 1972. In June 1974, the Bureau of Labor Statistics announced that steel was the one major industry that had a significant increase in productivity over the previous year: a 10.8% increase in 1973, compared with a 5.8% increase in 1972.

productivity

Unions support labor legislation deemed to be important to members. But more than that, they support a good deal of general legislation that could not be considered labor legislation at all. In the 92nd Congress, for example, the AFL-CIO actively lobbied in regard to many issues of general public interest, including: National Health Insurance, Veterans Educational Benefits, Older Americans Act, Consumer Protection Agency, School Lunch Program, Public Land Management, Water Pollution Control, Noise Control, Public Health Service Hospitals, Automotive Safety, Product Safety, Equal Rights Amendment, Campaign Reform, Radio Free Europe, Strategic Arms Limitation Treaty, and

Pesticide Control. AFL-CIO constituents stand to benefit from all these programs, of course, but as citizens rather than union members.

Pension Security Act — The unions lobbied energetically to get Congress to pass the Occupational Safety and Health Act of 1970, and the Pension Security Act of 1974. And they have gone further: in the 1974 Basic Steel settlement, the United Steelworkers contributed two million dollars to a joint Union-Company Research Committee to seek solutions to health hazards in steel-making, particularly in coke production operations.

Unions have become major institutions, and their efforts on behalf of their members have taken on an institutional cast broader than the narrow efforts of an earlier day to win fights with a belligerent industry.

The Work Force

Blue-Collar Workers

blue-collar workers — In June, 1970, the Secretary of Labor delivered to the White House a study by Assistant Secretary of Labor for Policy, Evaluation, and Research Jerome M. Rosow, entitled "The Problem of the Blue-Collar Worker." He noted that blue-collar workers earning between $5,000 and $10,000 a year, and constituting some 40% of all American families, are in an economic squeeze. Their wages rise more slowly than expenses when they reach the age where children come. They reach a plateau in earnings of a sort that other U.S. workers do not encounter. Since 1965, their wages rose some 20% but their real earnings hardly changed. They are sensitive about the low social status they see their fellow Americans according them.

The Rosow study was prompted by events a month or so earlier. On May 8, several hundred building construction workers in downtown New York took to the streets during noon hour, in what was a hastily planned but essentially spontaneous demonstration against some complex intangible issues that had been rankling for some time. It was tipped off by some students protesting for peace in Vietnam, grew into a march on City Hall where they forced the raising of a flag that had been half-masted by Mayor Lindsay in mourning for the Kent State student victims of National Guard fire, and expanded en route to chasing and attacking unsympathetic students or anyone else who seemed against what the marchers believed in.

According to the New York *Times,* this "was the wild start of two weeks of almost daily noon-hour, flag-waving, bellicose, damn-Lindsay...and praise Nixon countermarches through downtown New York,"[8] culminating on May 20 in a march of more than 100,000 blue-collar workers, mainly skilled building trades workmen, waving flags and singing patriotic songs. And on May 26, President Nixon received 23 leaders of New York's building trades and longshoremen's unions, who presented him with a symbolic hard hat to "stand as a symbol, along with our great flag, for freedom and patriotism to our beloved country."

The "hard hat" was born as a symbol of frustration for social and political standards apparently gone haywire, cherished values apparently scorned, and a society apparently over-permissive in tolerating the excesses of student and other protesters—by a newly recognized "silent majority" from "Middle America."

Who is this blue-collar American, and how is he different from any other American, if he is? What is the source of his discontent, and how is this unhappiness of interest to managers? What of Rosow's statement about the "economic squeeze"? Is he really harder up than other workers?

Yes, and no. During the 1960s, married blue-collar workers and their families increased their family income comparably to professionals, managers, and other white-collar workers; during the last half of the 1960s, their gains were one or two percentage points higher than those of the latter groups. But gains for workers aged 35-44 lagged behind for the blue-collar group: annual family income adjusted for the cost of living rose 46% in the decade for blue-collar workers, as opposed to 70% for professional and managerial workers in the same age group and 58% for clerical and sales workers.

And from the viewpoint of the white "hard-hat" worker, things are even worse. Gains by white manual workers lagged behind those of black manual workers during the decade. In the 1960s, blacks filled one-third of all added jobs for craftsmen and operatives that were held by married men. And median *individual* earnings for the blacks rose 42% during the decade, versus 25% for the whites. For blue-collar husbands between 30 and 40, individual salaries or wages went up only 33% in the decade. So while family income was maintained reasonably well for the blue-collar workers as a group, there was a distinct leveling off and some reduction in white gains in favor of black gains. Black earnings showed a higher percentage gain, of course, because they started from such a low base, but the white "hard hat" saw his relative progress slowing, at the same time that he experienced the plateau in his earnings in his middle years.

The middle-aged blue-collar worker experiences a leveling off in earnings just as his children are reaching the costly age. Essentially, since his wages are negotiated by the union for skill levels rather than worker ages, if he is not getting promoted to more demanding duties all he gets in raises is the cost-of-living adjustments which keep him standing still in living standards.

Rosow analyzed the problems of lower-income workers—the 20 million families (80 million individuals) whose incomes are above the poverty line but not sufficiently to support a moderate-income budget. In his report,[9] he described the "three-way squeeze" on these individuals.

- *The economic squeeze:* His wages don't keep up with his expenses, and in order to make ends meet he must moonlight, or his wife must go out and work, or both. Taxes are going up, and as inflation makes pay higher without any increase in living standard the progressive tax feature of the federal income tax takes an increasing share because he is in a "higher bracket" (though not in real income). And inflation is raising the costs of everything he buys; the fact that he has few discretionary expenditures (such as clubs, vacations, etc.) that he can forego makes the inflationary bite all but inescapable.
- *The work place squeeze:* He has less satisfaction on the job than his white-collar brethren. Health, safety, and attractiveness aspects of the work place are usually quite inferior to the white-collar environments. In large organizations there may be a lack of

The middle-aged blue-collar worker experiences a leveling off in earnings just as his children reach the costly age.

- promotion opportunities, with many workers locked into a large standardized work force. There is a lack of freedom, in that he is seldom free to leave the job (particularly in assembly-line tasks). And there are less fringe benefits, particularly the intangible ones.
- *The off-the-job squeeze:* He is likely to live in an urban area that is running down, probably in conditions of excessive pollution from nearby industrial plants. The increase in crime in his area, along with the fear of crime, inhibits the evening excursions to the movies or to visit friends that would add variety to his life. Home ownership is less and less available, with the average single-family house costing close to $35,000, and with an annual income of $18,000 required to buy and maintain such a home. Probably most important, he feels that society looks down on blue-collar jobs.

Rosow's article charts the location of this lower-middle-income worker in the blue-collar spectrum, as defined by the action of these three variables: economic variables, work place variables, and off-the-job variables, including a suggestion of how the next generation remains in this band or escapes it through moving upward or downward. Figure 15-4 is a reproduction of Rosow's chart.

Many blue-collar workers have "moved up" on the economic ladder: those from farm or laboring families, particularly rural blacks who have moved to the cities for industrial employment. But many have stepped down: the blue-collar son of a small-town preacher, town clerk, druggist, or educator has moved down socially though not economically; the college dropout from a professional household has moved down both ways. Starting salaries look attractive, but slow raises bring a financial squeeze later.

How does a blue-collar worker advance? If he or she goes through an apprenticeship, there is a good chance of moving up to management via the foreman route. Many enterprising blue-collar workers start their own businesses, thus becoming proprietors, though capital needs for starting an enterprise are substantial and the mortality rate is high. And in some industries it is possible to advance within the blue-collar framework to more skilled trades; a newcomer in the steel industry can start at $8,000, and there are avenues open to the most skilled and responsible trades where wages might come to $24,000 with overtime. It is not unheard of

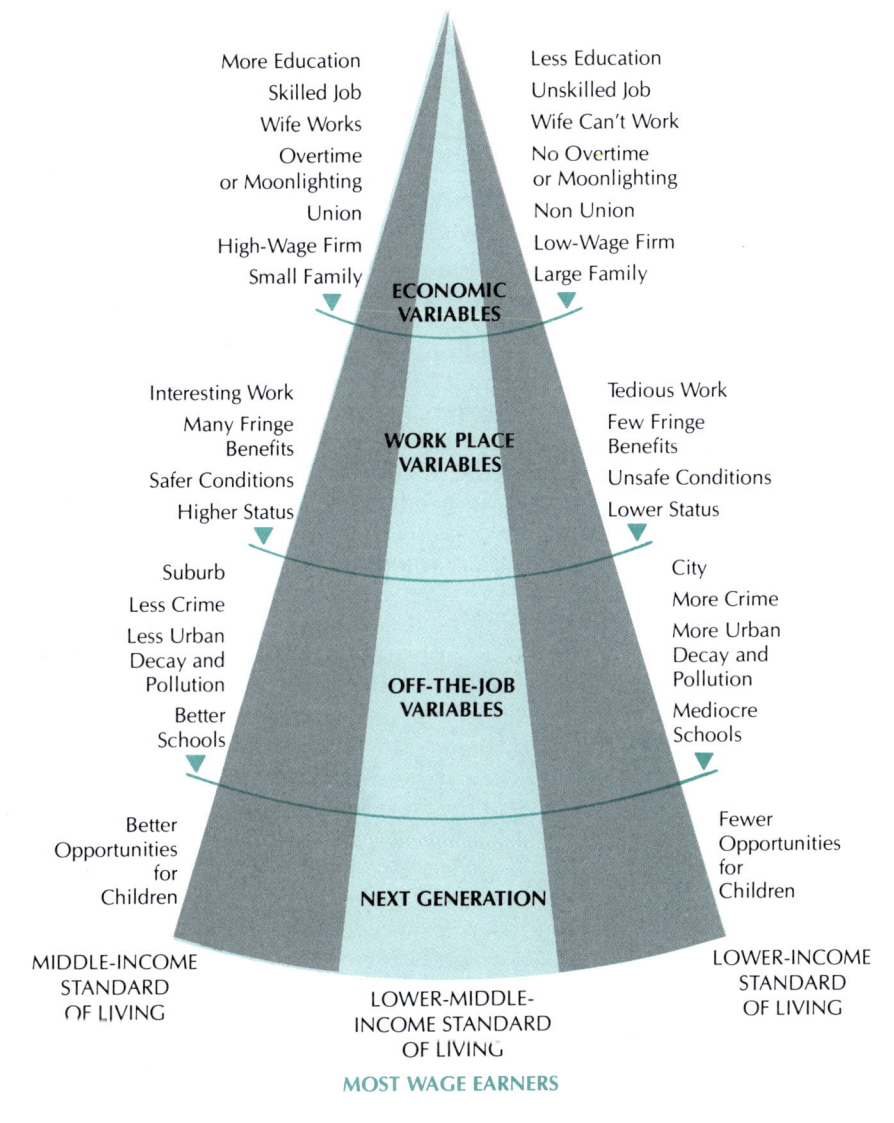

Figure 15-4.
The Lower-Middle-Income Worker

ECONOMIC VARIABLES
- More Education / Less Education
- Skilled Job / Unskilled Job
- Wife Works / Wife Can't Work
- Overtime or Moonlighting / No Overtime or Moonlighting
- Union / Non Union
- High-Wage Firm / Low-Wage Firm
- Small Family / Large Family

WORK PLACE VARIABLES
- Interesting Work / Tedious Work
- Many Fringe Benefits / Few Fringe Benefits
- Safer Conditions / Unsafe Conditions
- Higher Status / Lower Status

OFF-THE-JOB VARIABLES
- Suburb / City
- Less Crime / More Crime
- Less Urban Decay and Pollution / More Urban Decay and Pollution
- Better Schools / Mediocre Schools

NEXT GENERATION
- Better Opportunities for Children / Fewer Opportunities for Children

MIDDLE-INCOME STANDARD OF LIVING — LOWER-MIDDLE-INCOME STANDARD OF LIVING — LOWER-INCOME STANDARD OF LIVING

MOST WAGE EARNERS

for a husband-wife trucker team to take in $50,000 a year—but at the cost of sacrificing a normal home-and-family life.

What is the union doing about it? It is introducing health and welfare packages, pensions, and supplementary unemployment benefits to the collective bargaining table—items not in contracts 25 years ago, but becoming more important every year. It is pressing for more blue-collar training as a path out of the fixed-income trap, scholarships so children of employees can go to college, longer vacations, and even "sabbatical leaves" for longer-term employees. As the union contemplates the new blue-collar labor force, with its heavy fixed obligations for house and car payments, college tuition, and other expenses that rarely burdened the labor force in days past, it recognizes the need for a change in union thrust and strategies. In 1970, at a Labor Day address, President George Meany of the AFL-CIO said that this increase in blue-collar living standards makes for a very difficult situation when it comes to calling a strike, since workers with these fixed obligations cannot afford to forego the pay. He suggested that strikes might eventually give way to bargaining strategies that would make different, less painful demands on union members.

In some industries, particularly those with mind-deadening jobs, union-company committees seek ways to increase the variety of the tasks involved and to give employees more control over their job performance. Unions are joining with politicians to press for legislation such as the Occupational Safety and Health Act, which sets high standards for work place acceptability.

What can managers do about blue-collar unrest? One approach is to try and make jobs more interesting, with more decision power in the hands of the worker and less monotonous repetition. Only a few jobs are inherently varied, so that each day poses a different challenge. Many blue-collar workers find real fulfillment in the fact that they create: the carpenter can see the final product of a week's work, whereas the white-collar clerk may have only the memory of reports read and papers handled. The trick is to make the product more truly the worker's by requiring the use of imagination and direction as well as tools and hands. Another approach is to provide more training for upgrading skills, and to rearrange the organization so there is a pathway of advancement through increasing knowledge and ability. The union cannot make this change— only management can. And a third approach is to shift industry attitudes so that blue-collar employees work in the same sort of environment (where possible) as office workers: clean and modern bathrooms, lunchrooms, locker rooms, and workrooms. The machinist in the plant whose daughter is a typist in the front office should not find his work environment inferior to hers—but that is usually the case.

White-Collar Workers

white-collar workers

White-collar workers are the key to union growth, as they replace blue-collar workers in the labor force (Figure 15-3)—and white-collar workers are not joining the unions. Despite the growth in overall population in the U.S. between 1967 and 1974, AFL-CIO membership fell marginally (from 14,000,000 to 13,600,000) during that period. Union leadership anticipated this development. At the federation's 1961 convention, President Meany set forth the problem: "The greatest unresolved trade union problem remains...the essential task of organizing the [white-collar workers], where the benefits of union organizations are largely unknown." But no one seems to know how this might be accomplished. Walter Reuther, then president of the United Auto Workers, had some cogent thoughts one subject:

> You cannot appeal to a [white-collar worker] strictly on the basis of improving his salary or economic condition. I think the labor movement has to take on the character of a social movement. It is dealing more and more with the problems of the whole community, and will have to enlist these people, give them a sense of consciously participating in shaping the great issues that will determine the kind of society in which we are living.[10]

Perhaps a major reason why such white-collar employees as clerks and office workers do not join unions is that they identify more with management than with labor, and more with the middle class than with the "laboring class." Looking back in union history, deeply felt dissatisfactions have been the source of strong union membership in the past, and perhaps it will take such dissatisfaction for white-collar workers to get past the feeling that unionization amounts to reduced status and to embrace it willingly.

One thing that may generate such dissatisfaction would be a feeling on the part of white-collar "organizables" that they are locked into their jobs, with no chance to advance to management ranks. Some union leaders see the growth of automation as a potential frustration that could make office workers a prime target for organization. To the extent that automation reduces the need for white-collar skills, reduces job security, and reduces upward mobility, it could drive white-collar workers into unions.

Security

One of the original forces encouraging unionization of blue-collar workers was the need for some protection against arbitrary firing at the foreman's whim. White-collar workers hardly face such a problem today. One clear result of widespread unionization has been removal of the firing right from lower levels of management. Before a clerk can be fired, the action must be approved by the same personnel department that handles blue-collar removals (of unionized employees), and the same general safeguards and due process will apply. Thus the nonunion clerk or office worker is protected by the union to a high degree, even though he or she is not a member.

need for security

The past decade or two have been periods of relatively high prosperity and an expanding economy. Though automation has made substantial inroads (in banks, for example, where the paperwork revolution could not have been managed without widespread computerization of check accounting and handling), the clerks who might have been laid off have been needed to handle a growing clientele. Thus to date at least, automation has not brought about mass layoffs.

Automation has had its good side in the office suite. In the factory, the word implies machines that replace people (particularly the least skilled group, with nowhere else to go except welfare); but in the office, it implies machines that *assist* people (by taking over mindless, repetitive tasks and leaving more interesting and analytical tasks to the workers). The computer has created as many white-collar jobs as it has destroyed, and they are higher-level and higher-paid jobs. So while automation has taken over some low-level tasks that office workers once performed, it has opened a new avenue of upward mobility for the office worker with ability enough to master its intricacies.

In addition to the job security issue, white-collar workers must consider the matter of security in the union. White-collar members of a predominantly manual-worker union find that they are a decided minority, and their special problems may get very little attention. The unions that have had the greatest organizing success in white-collar organizing are those that are predominantly white-collar unions or those where white-collar members have received special powers out of proportion to their small representation.

<aside>What could a union have offered the North Star engineers? What disadvantages might accrue to them as a result of unionizing?</aside>

The retail clerks have done better than other white-collar unions, and the Retail Clerks International Association has over half a million members drawn wholly from the retail trades. Indeed, they have grown faster than the labor movement as a whole.[11] By contrast, engineers' unions have never been strong except during World War II, when thousands of engineers worked in plants under mass production conditions. Teachers' unions, among the first of the public employee unions, have been quite strong: the National Education Association has over a million members, and the much smaller American Federation of Teachers is growing vigorously.

<aside>teachers' unions</aside>

Public employees, though given the right to strike by the Lloyd-LaFollette Act of 1912, were prohibited from striking; the Taft-Hartley Act of 1948 reaffirmed that prohibition. But in 1962, Executive Order 10998 (though still forbidding the strike) extended formal, informal, and exclusive recognition of unions—the latter implying collective bargaining. The major union in the AFL-CIO's Public Employee Department is the American Federation of State, County, and Municipal Employees, with close to three-quarters of a million members.

<aside>American Federation of Government Employees</aside>

Special Working Groups

In this section, we will discuss four special groups: young people of various races and both sexes, women, blacks and other racial minorities, and so-called "unemployables" (or "hard-core unemployed").

<aside>special working groups</aside>

Youth

When employment turns down, the youth of the nation typically suffer first and most. Young people who are employed while in school or in their first jobs after leaving school are plagued by very high unemployment rates. The rates are higher for blacks and particularly for black girls.

Many reasons have been advanced for reduced youth employment, and particularly for the tendency for youth employment to show a long-term downward trend. One is the increase in the minimum wage and enlargement of its coverage; it is less attractive to hire untrained youngsters when they must be paid higher wages. Another is the increasing technical demands of all jobs, making it harder for untrained youth to qualify. A third is that typical "entry" jobs of the unskilled variety are being eroded by more mechanization. And a fourth is the inevitable results of the '50s "baby boom," with proportionately more young job-seekers than the workplace can absorb.

In fact, the number of employed youths has not decreased—it has gone up; but the number of youths in the population has gone up even faster. Between 1953 and 1957, the population of 16-19-year-olds went up only 8%. In 1957-60, 1960-63, and 1963-66, it went up 15%, 14%, and 15% respectively; the increase began to slow markedly in 1967. Table 15-2 shows the resultant fraction of youths aged 16-19 in the population. Between 1958 and 1967, teenagers in the work force increased from 5.7% to 7.6%. All teenagers need do from now on is hold their percentage in the work force, in the face of a falling teenaged population, and the unemployment "problem" should solve itself.

This fact does not mean that there will not be higher teenage unemployment than adult employment. The combination of minimum wage floors and union contracts that have the same effect for beginning and experienced workers will favor the hiring of more experienced workers if everything else is equal. In a recent year, median full-time earnings of teenage boys (girls) were 35% (41%) of all full-time male workers' earnings. (Full-time earnings of all full-time females were 58% of male earnings). Thus, teenagers are particularly likely to be bypassed when required minimum pay scales exist.

In recent years, numbers of teenage boys have been out of the labor force because they were awaiting induction. The number who are not in school, not awaiting induction, and not incapacitated, but still are not in the labor force is small; it runs about 2.8% for boys aged 16-19, compared with 1.8% for men aged 20-24. Among nonwhites, these percentages are somewhat higher—4% and 3.3% respectively—but not inordinately so.

Many statistics on teenage unemployment fail to take into account the period after the job-hunt starts and before the first job is found. The new job-seeker obviously takes longer to find the first job than would an experienced worker. Moreover, the intense pressure to find a job experienced by a household head does not bear on unmarried teenagers who live at home. How many youths look for work in a casual way, hoping to get their families off their backs more than to find an actual job? How many have unrealistically high goals, and initially refuse work that is beneath these goals?

Women

The concept of women as a "minority group" has gained public acceptance only since about 1971. After all, how can a group that constitutes some 52% of the nation be a "minority"? But the fact is that women have been paid less for the same work, kept out of certain lines of work entirely, and admitted only reluctantly to many others. In response to the women's liberation movement, Order No. 4 of the Department of Labor, previously covering only minority races, was revised to include women in the affirmative action required of government contractors; the Department of Health, Education and Welfare began vigorous enforcement in universities holding federal contracts; and Congress passed an Equal Rights Amendment to the Constitution (which has not yet been

Table 15-2.
Changing Teenaged Population

Year	Number of 16-19 age group in population
1953	7.7%
1967	10.5
1970	10.6
1975	10.7
1980	10.1

ratified by enough states to become law, however). The Equal Employment Opportunity Commission was extended shortly after this to include state and local government female employees.

Women represent some 40% of all U.S. workers, but only 15% of all managerial workers, 7% of all physicians,[12] and 21% of all other professionals (excluding education and health). The figures on female unemployment may be misleading in the opposite direction from those on youth unemployment: perhaps more women would work if there were opportunity, but as long as they are married to employed men they may not count as members of the labor force. Some 87% of all U.S. companies have 5% or fewer women in management above the first line.[13] Managers defend this unequal treatment with several rationalizations: women stay for a shorter period before they must quit to have babies; they are absent more frequently; they are more emotional and treat company matters in a more personal way; they cannot supervise other women well; their training is poorer. Few of these charges are true—probably only the last has any validity, and it rises in part from an earlier inequity which made it harder for women to enter professional schools.

Managers might experiment with part-time jobs that would permit wives (or husbands, for that matter) to work and provide home life for children at the same time. This option would undoubtedly raise the nation's productivity level: economists in Sweden and France have estimated that the national income (and thus the standard of living) would go up in their countries 25% and 35% respectively if women were fully utilized to the same extent as men. If both parents work, recent legislation permits the two to deduct up to $4,800 for child care *if* their gross income does not exceed $18,000—an odd limitation, since it reduces the incentive for both spouses to take jobs at any worthwhile salary level.

From a legal point of view, Title VII of the Civil Rights Act prohibits employers from discriminating in hiring or firing; in wages, terms, conditions or privileges of employment; in classifying, assigning or promoting employees; in extending or assigning use of facilities; or in training, retraining and apprenticeship—and it applies to any employer of more than 15 persons. But simply ending negative action is not enough, for there are many subterfuges (conscious or unconscious) open to those who hire and promote managers. Positive and conscious action is needed, based on self-interest, if women are to take their place alongside men in managerial posts.

There is some evidence of such activity. In a paper delivered at Columbia University's Conference on Women's Challenge to Management, held at Arden House in the fall of 1971, Dr. Phyllis A. Wallace quoted from the comments of several business school deans on the career patterns of recent women graduates:

> [T]here is a vast difference in the way they are received in the market today than was the case ten years ago. In the earlier 1960s, women were going into jobs which were traditionally women's jobs—retailing, research, personnel, etc. In the past five years this has changed drastically. True, women may have a harder time than men of equal ability, but they are now entering such fields as labor relations, consulting, product management, account executive work, public accounting, corporate finance, marketing, banking, etc., which had previously been closed to them. The Wall Street area is even beginning to take on women graduates in what has, up to now, been a male stronghold. In a year such as this, however, when jobs are tight, it is my feeling that women have to look much harder than do their male counterparts.[14]

Women are starting to make their way in unfamiliar fields, and in some companies they are so much in demand that they can bargain for starting salaries higher than those of their male counterparts. In 1973, for the first time, starting salaries of women engineers exceeded those of male engineers, on the average.

Married women are not as mobile as their husbands in our culture. A male manager is assumed to be ready to move when he and the company are "ready"; scarcely any business would assume that the wife would move

Some youths have unrealistically high goals, and initially refuse work that does not meet their standards.

for her job, thus taking precedence over her husband's job. (Some working couples, however, agree to give equal consideration to career advancement for each individual, even when the other may be uprooted in the process.)

Young working wives do leave their jobs to have and raise children, and this is a bar to their employment in higher-level jobs where they could not easily be spared. But this situation, too, is changing. Figure 15-5 shows that, whereas the 1940 working wife who left the labor force for childbearing did not return, and whereas the 1960 working wife returned but only after a substantial absence, by 1970 the number of women in the labor force was much higher throughout, and the drop in employment during the family years was far less. If this tendency increases, and management does not have to plan on the working wife leaving the job when she becomes a mother, women's working lives will become far more similar to men's than they have been in the past.

The graduating class of 1975 found the job market the worst of the entire postwar period, with a 4% decrease in job openings. But even in such bleak times, women (and minorities) found hirings looking up a bit from previous years. The College Placement Council estimated that employers made a third more job offers to women receiving bachelor's degrees than in the previous year.

Figure 15-5.
Women in Labor Force, 1940-70

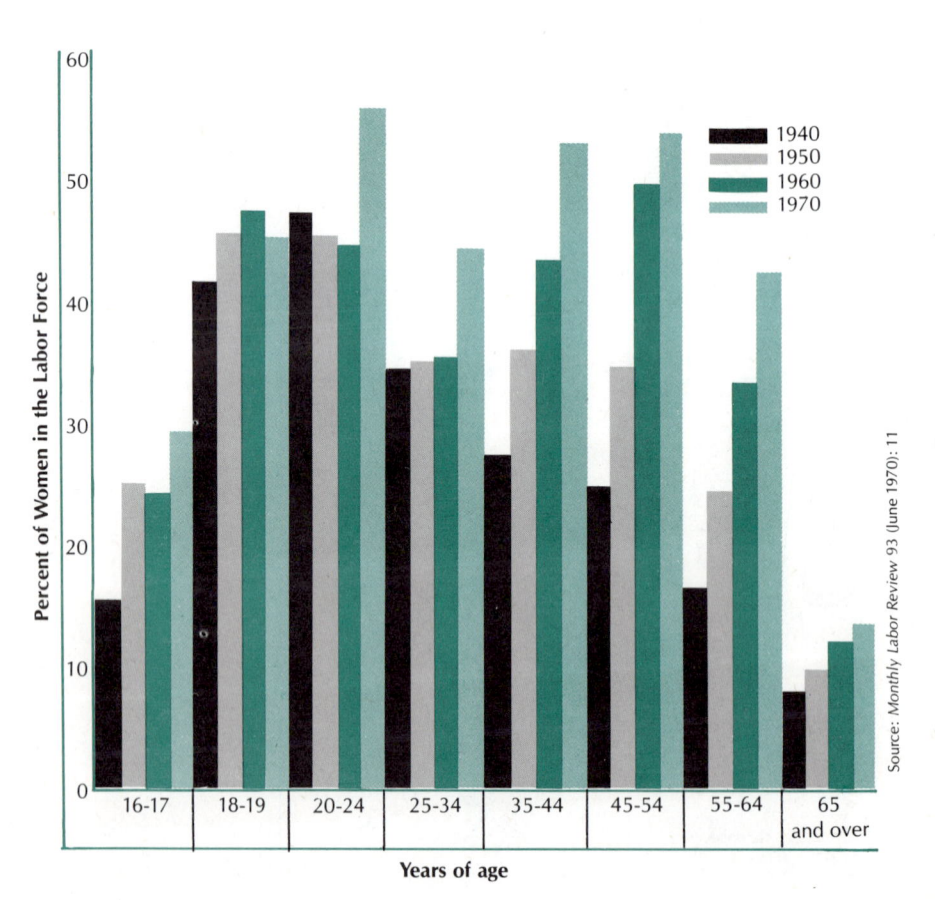

Source: *Monthly Labor Review* 93 (June 1970): 11

592
MANAGEMENT AND ITS ENVIRONMENT

Minorities

In principle, the government has been solidly against discrimination in employment for nearly half a century, starting with the Civil Service Act of 1883 which established the merit doctrine. The Unemployment Relief Act of 1933 and the National Industrial Recovery Act of 1938 inserted nondiscrimination clauses in their plans for grant-in-aid employment and low-rent housing. The Ramspeck Act of 1940 amended both the Civil Service Act and a subsequent Classification Act of 1923, by prohibiting "discrimination against any person, or with respect to the position held by any person, on account of race, creed, or color." But there was little enforcement machinery, and these acts included no standards to define discrimination.

With the outbreak of World War II, and the resultant boom in employment, President Roosevelt established a Fair Employment Practice Committee. It was overhauled in 1943 to cover all federal employment and all war contractors, but still had little enforcement clout. The committee died in 1946, until President Truman revitalized it with the Committee on Government Contract Compliance in 1951, replaced by President Eisenhower with a similar Committee on Government Contracts. None of these committees, however, had any power to enforce its recommendations.

In 1961, President Kennedy created the first agency with power to enforce nondiscrimination rulings against government contractors: the Committee on Equal Employment Opportunity. For the first time, contractors were required to do more than "not discriminate"; now they were required to take affirmative action to make the nondiscriminatory policy effective, including recruiting programs for minority group employees. During the later 1960s, the Office of Federal Contract Compliance was set up within the Labor Department and its powers broadened by several executive orders.

The impact of all the above laws and orders fell on employers, not on unions, but the National Labor Relations Board was taking up the same cudgels against discriminatory union acts, establishing the principle that it was the union's duty to represent all of its members equally and without discrimination. In 1945 the NLRB forced a union to give up the practice of having segregated locals, by threatening to revoke the union's certification. In 1964 (ironically, on the very same day that President Johnson signed the Civil Rights Act) the NLRB stripped a union of its certification as bargaining agent because it had segregated locals and a white local refused to handle a grievance for a black employee because of his race.[15]

The Civil Rights Act established the Equal Employment Opportunity Commission, but gave it few enforcement powers. This was corrected by the Equal Employment Opportunity Act of 1972, as stated earlier, by authorizing the commission to file an action directly in federal court.

Most states, except some in the deep South, have antidiscrimination laws. Even before the Civil Rights Act of 1964 was passed by Congress, half of the nation's nonwhite population was covered by state fair employment laws, applying generally to all unions, employers, and employment agencies in the states concerned. By the time the 1972 act was passed, 40 states had fair employment practices laws of broad application; the exceptions were Alabama, Georgia, Louisiana, Mississippi, North Carolina, North Dakota, South Carolina, Tennessee, and Virginia.

Despite these laws, minority hiring in unions has hit a number of snags. In 1969 the so-called "Philadelphia Plan" for minority hiring in the construction industry was instituted, under which mandatory quotas and timetables were established for minority hiring, after hearings with the contractors and unions involved. Similar plans were set up subsequently in St. Louis, Atlanta, San Francisco, Washington, Chicago, and Camden. These mandatory plans have not been as successful as had been hoped. In another approach, taken by the Nixon administration after the president and the "hard hats" made common cause during the 1970 congressional election campaigns, so-called "hometown plans" were set up in 62 locations. Audits of 31 of these, after a full year of operation, disclosed that less than a third of the unions had met their stated minority hiring goals (115 out of 372 local unions). Failure to meet the voluntary goals subjects the contractors to mandatory goals for all federally assisted construction, unless the craft concerned can show to the satisfaction of the Labor Department that it has made a "good faith" effort to meet the goals.

Another category of minority worker is an illegal one. Prior to 1964, the U.S. and Mexico had an agreement that would permit up to 450,000 Mexican "braceros" to work in the U.S. under temporary contracts; but under pressure from the AFL-CIO, the U.S. terminated the agreement. The U.S. Immigration Service seeks to apprehend the Mexicans who slip into the U.S. illegally, and does catch some three-quarters of a million a year. But some authorities estimate that as many as six or seven million Mexicans are living illegally in the U.S.—and, during economic downturns, taking work that would otherwise go to U.S. citizens. The solution to the bracero problem, given our long history of a relatively open border with Mexico, will not be simple.

"Unemployables"

hard-core unemployed

A problem demanding increasing attention by managers in recent years is that of the so-called *hard-core unemployed*—those who have such difficulty in finding (or reluctance to find) employment that they have been out of work too long to be counted in the labor force. The early attack on this problem—the War on Poverty mounted chiefly by the Office of Economic Opportunity—concentrated on job-training programs; but after the ghetto riots of the mid-1960s, the National Association of Businessmen established a cooperative program to create jobs for these individuals and train them on the job after they had been hired. Some 330,000 hard-core unemployed were hired by the numerous corporations taking part in this program. Although many felt that the program was not a success, it taught some interesting lessons about this previously unstudied group.

In general, the new hires had no unusual difficulty in learning the work, and in performing effectively on the job. These "unemployables," mostly blacks or Chicanos with little education, virtually no job training, and extensive arrest (not necessarily conviction) records, usually on drugs or alcohol, could become perfectly effective employees as far as the job tasks were concerned. It was the many other factors related to their change in status that tended to cause problems.

One such NAB program, in a San Diego aircraft plant, was studied in detail by Harland Padfield and Roy Williams.[16] A total of 28 trainees started the program. By the end of the first year 12 were fired, and ultimately only three successfully adapted to the plant—a 10% success score. The problems that led to this failure were both internal (shop-related) and external (home-related). Inside, according to the authors, the men tried to adapt to the factory society by using the techniques they had found effective in the ghetto society. "Seven reacted with the familiar bravado of the street corner male, an aggressive but careful risk-taking which resulted in high-level performance on the job but did not endear them to their coworkers. Seven were unable to control their aggression at the critical moment. Eight became 'dependents,' so beset by feelings of inadequacy that they could not cope with job success and opportunity for advancement."[17] Outside, troubles with the law and the rate of arrest tended to increase after the trainees were employed, because they had to live in two worlds: in the factory of conventional society and in the ghetto. The authors describe how these men, who needed cars to get to work, dealt with their transportation problems:

> To most of the hard-core, traffic was not a problem but a problem syndrome. If a trainee had one citation, he usually had several. In some cases, this resulted from the police making several charges simultaneously, a simple moving violation or a faulty equipment charge combined with a no-license, open alcoholic container, or concealed weapons charge. Sometimes, the emotional behavior of the trainees upon arrest...might lead to a charge of eluding the police, disturbing the peace, or resisting arrest...There was the tendency to compound the charges by such coping patterns as ignoring tickets, mutilating out-of-date licenses or forging new ones, or simply driving without one.
>
> There are numerous aspects of the hard-core situation which account for this mode of traffic behavior. One is their high exposure to traffic surveillance which comes from living in a high crime area. Another is their low economic standing. A hard-core...cannot afford accidents, expensive repairs, traffic fines, or attorney's fees.[18]

Ultimately, these difficulties lead to absence from work, which reduces the odds that a trainee will remain on the job at all.

The book reports the men's powerful effort to turn in good job performances and make the job central to their lives—probably working much harder at it than the average worker. But while the job had freed them from unemployment, it had not freed them from their lower-class society, and many of their former social partners hampered their ability to change old patterns. Wives, who formerly had ruled the roost because of their welfare payments, were now asked to take a back seat because the husbands were wage-earners—a change that did not come easily. In the plant, coworkers suffered from the job program to some degree (the hard-core trainees received privileges the regular workers did not, and were excused from transgressions for which the latter would have been penalized). The onset of training coincided with the start of the recession, and some older workers were laid off just as the trainees were hired. The union naturally (and not unsympathetically, for it did not want to hurt the trainees) felt the need to protect its older members first.

The U.S. economy cannot provide jobs to all in the labor force except in extraordinarily good times, so a recession is almost sure to limit such efforts to hire unemployables. The problem of ghetto unemployment remains, and efforts to hire such people will tax the skills of managers who come in contact with them, as well as the wisdom of unions who must mediate between the rights of senior workers and the need for compassion in giving losers a chance to win. Particularly in the middle are the foremen, who must set standards of work without requiring cultural and racial conformity, and who are at the cutting edge of worker suspicion and union rules, where their diplomacy and understanding can make the program or their lack of it doom the program to defeat from the start.

Dealing with Unions

Collective Bargaining

collective bargaining

Collective bargaining takes place between the union and the company. First, however, an election must be held among the employees and a certain union selected by majority vote as their exclusive bargaining representative. (Alternatively, the union may be recognized by the company as exclusive bargaining representative, even though it has not won such an election.) The unionized employees need not include all of the company's employees, but simply an appropriate bargaining unit (of employees with similar jobs, such as production and maintenance employees, truck drivers, etc.). The National Labor Relations Board conducts the election on request of 30% or more of the employees in the bargaining unit (the election's purpose can be to certify that the union represents the employees or to decertify a union that employees believe no longer represents the majority). Employers who have good cause to think that the union no longer represents a majority of the firm's employees can petition similarly for a decertification election. After the election, the NLRB issues a certification that the union has lost or that it is the bargaining agent.

What bargaining mechanisms did North Star employ? Were they successful?

The union takes the initiative by requesting the employer to meet in negotiating session, which often consists of negotiating from the basis of the union's standard agreement. If the contract is a renewal, notice must be given of any desire to amend or terminate the contract 60 days before the old contract runs out or automatically renews.

lock-out

If there is no agreement, the Federal Mediation and Conciliation Service may come in to assist, or the state mediation service where there is one. Failing agreement, the union may strike or the employer may *lock out* the employees, or both sides may agree to continue work pending agreement on a contract. Figure 15-6 shows the key terms of the USW agreement with the basic steel industry (the ten major steel companies), signed April 1974 as a result of the no-strike Experimental Negotiating Agreement. While most of the collective bargaining agreement items relate to financial or security benefits, as shown in the timetable, this contract contained other miscellaneous changes relating to supervisors working, garnishing of wages, contracting out, probationary period of new employees, apprenticeship rules, overtime, safety and health, etc.

Some contracts specify what areas are covered, and state that management has exclusive jurisdiction in areas not mentioned. Other contracts are quite specific in stating what management's rights are: to increase and decrease the work force, select products to manufacture, design them and determine work methods, take disciplinary action for cause, do all production scheduling, and in general operate the plant, provided that such acts do not violate any specific sections of the agreement or discriminate against any employee covered by the agreement.

Working under the Contract

Once the agreement has been signed, it constitutes a binding document for both parties. For the company, in particular, it has the force of standing instructions, and all managers must be thoroughly conversant with its provisions in their area of jurisdiction. First-line supervisors must be particularly familiar with the contract provisions, since it is at their level

Figure 15-6.
Timetable for Key Basic Steel Benefits

MAY 1, 1974
28c general wage increase.
.2c increment increase.
39c cost-of-living roll in.
15c quarterly cost-of-living adjustment based on new formula.

AUGUST 1, 1974
Sickness and Accident—improved benefits.
Supplemental Unemployment Benefits—improved benefits.
Quarterly cost-of-living adjustment.
Trade, craft and apprentice two-job classes in incentive calculation rate.
10c per hour non-incentive payment for production and maintenance workers in steel producing operations.
10c per hour increase in office and technical service bonus plan.

SEPTEMBER 30, 1974
$150 ENA bonus.

NOVEMBER 1, 1974
Quarterly cost-of-living adjustment.

JANUARY 1, 1975
Pay for holidays worked increased to 2½ times.

Vacation bonus increased to $30, $50 and $75.

FEBRUARY 1, 1975
Quarterly cost-of-living adjustment.

MAY 1, 1975
Quarterly cost-of-living adjustment.

AUGUST 1, 1975
16c general wage increase.
.3c increment increase.
New Pension Program.
Quarterly cost-of-living adjustment.
Annual cost-of-living roll in.
Doubling of shift differentials to 20c and 30c.
Sickness and Accident—improved benefits.
Prepaid dental program for active employees.
Medical care insurance for retirees.
Medical care improvements for active employees.

NOVEMBER 1, 1975
Quarterly cost-of-living adjustment.

JANUARY 1, 1976
Vacation schedule—4 weeks for 17 years for P & M.
—4 weeks for 15 years for O & T.

FEBRUARY 1, 1976
Quarterly cost-of-living adjustment.

MAY 1, 1976
Quarterly cost-of-living adjustment.

AUGUST 1, 1976
16c general wage increase.
.4c increase in increments.
Quarterly cost-of-living adjustment.
Annual cost-of-living roll in.
Sickness and Accident—improved benefits.

NOVEMBER 1, 1976
Quarterly cost-of-living adjustment.

JANUARY 1, 1977
Vacation schedule—5 weeks for 25 years for P & M.
—5 weeks for 23 years for O & T.

FEBRUARY 1, 1977
Quarterly cost-of-living adjustment.

FEBRUARY 16, 1977
Washington's Birthday holiday.

MAY 1, 1977
Quarterly cost-of-living adjustment.

that violations or alleged violations are most likely to develop and turn into grievances or walkouts. Management must hold briefing sessions to explain a new contract to supervisors, and must make personnel specialists available to interpret the contract whenever necessary.

shop steward

The union is represented in the shop by the *shop steward,* who is an employee but also a union spokesperson. Most contracts provide that the shop steward will have a certain amount of free time and such privileges as access to various records or managers in order to function effectively. If an employee feels that he or she has been treated badly, the steward is the first one to be contacted, and quite often the matter can be settled at that level. The supervisor and the steward should work closely together, since each is important to the other.

Consider the following case, in which both the supervisor and the shop steward played important related roles:

> Frank Marini was a skilled engraver working in the instruments section of an aerospace company. His job was to engrave the plastic instrument dials and covers for a wide variety of instruments. When he cut the plastic in the proper shape for the instrument, he collected the scraps, and instead of throwing them away as the other mechanics did, he put them in his lunch box and took them home, where he used them for hobby purposes.
>
> Ben Morell, the foreman, knew Frank did this, and did not entirely approve of it. He would grumble at Frank occasionally, calling him a "pack rat" or "magpie," but Frank simply said that he was saving them from the trash can. Ben never forbade Frank to take the plastic, and Frank continued to do it.
>
> One day the shop superintendent was in the shop to see Ben when the quit work whistle sounded, and as Frank got up to leave his lunch box came open and the shop superintendent saw the plastic, which included one or two rather large pieces that day. He asked Frank and Ben what was going on, told them that was company property which Frank could not appropriate, and directed him to empty his lunch box. When Frank left, the shop superintendent told Ben that they would take the main gate if it wasn't tied down.
>
> The next day Ben called Frank in, told him he'd been warning him about this for a long time, and gave him two days suspension without pay. Frank went to see the shop steward, Al Pasqual, who came in to see Ben about the case.
>
> Al Pasqual said that Ben had known about the scrap situation for a long time and had never taken any action before. It was unfair now to award a suspension without a warning. He agreed that it was wrong to take the scrap, even though the company was discarding it, because in fact there was a program for recovering scrap from the trash cans in the section and an old employee like Frank had to know about it. He suggested that Ben give Frank a written warning, but cancel the suspension, and to this Ben agreed. Both recognized that since the front office had discovered the situation, Ben was under real pressure to take some sort of action on the record.

In this situation the shop steward played a useful role. He served as a check on Ben, who probably knew he was being unfair to Frank but was on the spot himself. Both men, by their willingness to compromise, kept the incident from blowing up into a serious grievance that might have involved the whole company. Had Ben and Al not been on reasonably good terms, the compromise would not have been possible. The company benefited, because the final action was fairer than Ben's first impulsive action. Frank was in no position to object to the written warning, because he was enough of an old-timer to realize that his actions actually were improper.

Sometimes supervisors will unconsciously attempt to change the contract provisions, because they disapprove of them in some respects. If the contract allows time off for certain events such as medical appointments, the supervisor can make it as difficult as possible for the employee to get the time off, saying the schedule won't permit it or something similar. On the other hand, some supervisors more or less throw in the towel in complete surrender to the union, saying that if management wants to "give away the store" they won't try to stop it. If the employee comes for medical appointment time off, these supervisors will approve the request no matter what disruption it causes to the job; if called to account later, they will say that they were just going by the rules. A good supervisor will recognize that the contract must be interpreted reasonably, and that the union has no more desire than the company for unrealistic interpretations to harm the company (which is the source of jobs for the membership).

The shop steward is under all sorts of pressures from the workers in a union shop, many of which are unreasonable. A good shop steward shuts off many unjustified complaints, so that management never hears of them. Furthermore, the union representatives in the plant can be very useful to management, by presenting a legitimate management viewpoint to the membership in the plant, and by interpreting to management how the workers are likely to feel about projected rule changes. The employee who is a goof-off is as much a pain in the neck to the union as to the supervisor, and if relationships are friendly and cooperative the goof-off's unreasonable complaint will not get much attention. Sometimes the union steward cannot take a certain stand personally, for political reasons, but will not object if the supervisor takes such a stand.

Grievances

The case described in the preceding section, between Frank Marini and his foreman, would be considered a grievance in some union contracts simply because it was a dispute between an employee and the company. In other contracts, a grievance may be limited to matters involving application of specific clauses in the contract. In general, however, this case would represent the start of a grievance procedure.

grievances

If the shop steward (or union business agent, in plants having no shop stewards) could not settle the case with Al Pasqual, the next step would be a fact-finding session with Al's immediate boss, the shop superintendent. Some contracts provide a detailed procedure for handling such cases, while others do not. In all probability, the matter would be settled in the shop superintendent's office, with both Ben and Frank in attendance.

If settlement at this point proved impossible, the union would file a *grievance form,* and both the union and the company representatives would write on the form their versions of what took place at the meeting in the shop superintendent's office and before. The contract provides a time limit within which this form must be filed in order to be considered.

The employee cannot refuse to do the job assigned (if that is the subject of the grievance), since he or she could be fired for that even though the grievance subsequently was settled in a way indicating that the worker should not have been assigned the job. The union steward cannot leave work to handle the grievance unless the contract specifies that he may (which it often would). Until the grievance is settled, the company's orders must be carried out and the company's rules followed.

The procedure may be somewhat informal. In this case, the employee would next discuss the matter with the industrial relations department, where an official thoroughly familiar with contract interpretation would seek to defuse the issue and resolve the dispute. In larger companies, a more formal procedure would be followed. Step one of this procedure would be similar to the meeting between Al Pasqual and Ben Morell. Step two would be a meeting with a higher level of management. Sometimes this might involve a discussion between the shop steward or business agent and the foreman's immediate superior, in an attempt to settle the problem without a formal grievance filing. Sometimes the second step starts the formal procedure, in which a grievance form is filed, and a grievance committee meets with a designated member of management.

The third step would be a meeting between a senior union official or a union board and a senior industrial relations staff member or a senior company officer in the division involved. If no settlement is reached, the fourth step is submitting the matter to *arbitration,* in which a neutral arbitrator selected as provided in the contract hears the facts in the manner of an informal court procedure and issues a binding decision.

Arbitrators, usually members of the American Arbitration Association (but sometimes individuals listed with or part of the Federal

arbitration

Union representatives in the plant can be very useful to management by interpreting worker response to management actions.

Mediation and Conciliation Service or a corresponding state organization), are carefully selected for their ability to analyze a situation and issue a common sense decision. Sometimes the contract provides that union and management must agree on an arbitrator, or it may provide that a third party so choose. Since the arbitrator's decision is the final action in a sequence established by a valid union-company contract, it is enforceable, like any other contract provisions in civil law.

The arbitration process contains elements often insufficiently understood by managers. The judicial arbitrator endeavors to hand down the mutual intent of the disputing parties, but is not free to rely on common sense in reaching a decision. He or she is restricted to considering the terms of the basic collective bargaining agreement, the matters presented during the arbitration hearing, and resolution of the particular points raised in the agreement submitting the problem to arbitration. The latter is a particularly important restriction. Consider the following case.

Frank Kowalski was a pipefitter helper assigned by the foreman to segregate a pile of pipe fittings into various sizes. When Frank looked at the jumbled pile, he said "I'm probably going to need a crane to lift some of this stuff off the top," to which the foreman allegedly responded "Okay," and then left. Frank thereupon went in search of a crane operator to bring a portable crane to the site, but had to wait for the operator to finish another job. A half hour later the foreman checked and found Frank gone and nothing done, so he wrote him up for leaving the job without authority. The union submitted the dispute to arbitration, writing its submission as follows:

> Did Frank Kowalski have permission from the foreman to leave his job to obtain crane service at 8:30 A.M. on January 17, 1976?

Since this was the specific question raised, it was the only one the arbitrator could deal with, and the finding sustained the foreman's action because he had not in fact authorized Frank to leave the job to get crane service. In fact, as the union could have shown easily in a broadened submission, the company frequently authorized employees to act on their own initiative in advancing the completion of tasks, and almost never enforced the "leaving the job" provision of the contract in cases where employees were leaving for company reasons rather than personal reasons. By unwisely narrowing the scope of the arbitration, the union virtually guaranteed an unfavorable finding—even though the arbitrator was well aware of these other considerations and no doubt felt that Frank was in the right in the broad sense.

The preceding discussion on grievance procedure lists four steps, of which arbitration is the fourth. There can be as many as seven steps if the company is large or has many divisions, or if the problem that arises is a complex one.

While the above sequence sounds orderly, grievances that must be taken to a high level become costly, time-consuming, and damaging to personal relationships. It is far better if the supervisor does not allow a dispute to become a formal grievance. The most important thing is for the supervisor to determine what the real facts of the case are, and what is *really* bothering the employee. Quite often an employee knows that he is at fault, and is even willing to take the disciplinary action the foreman has meted out, provided that some related matter which is bugging him is brought out in the open and dealt with. In the case of hard-core unemployed brought into the plant as part of the NAB program, some cases of apparent insubordination—refusing to clean up the work site after a job was completed—actually reflected the hard-core employee's view that he was deliberately being assigned menial tasks as a slur on his minority status. The problem was something far more deep-seated than a simple refusal to carry out instructions, and even if the grievance had proceeded to its final resolution the basic issue would not have been resolved.

Sometimes a supervisor actually is acting improperly, but doing it in such a skillful way that employees cannot sustain a grievance against him in any particular instance. A flurry of grievance cases, even though not sustained, suggests that all is not well in the group, and the manager who supervises the foreman should try to determine the actual source of the unrest.

A supervisor investigating a case must take the position of an impartial judge. Some foremen or supervisors at higher levels cannot adopt an impartial role; they persist in seeing the grievance procedure as an adversary situation and the union as an opponent to be overcome if possible. With such a philosophy, they may win the battle but lose the war; an employee who is unfairly treated will find it difficult to let the matter rest without finding some way to retaliate.

The supervisor who is considering possible courses of action must be very mindful that this case is setting policy for all future cases. In all disciplinary actions, or grievance resolutions not involving such actions, each case will be cited by the union and the employees whenever similar cases come up in the future, and a poor decision will come back to haunt the supervisor.

Unfair Labor Practices

unfair employment practices

Did North Star engage in any unfair labor practices? Did the employees present unfair demands?

Section 8 of the National Labor Relations Act details the unfair practices which employers or unions may commit. These will be set forth briefly in the following paragraphs.

Unfair Employer Practices

Section 8(a)(1) *Interference with employees:* An employer may not "interfere with, restrain, or coerce employees in the exercise of rights guaranteed in Section 7 (those guaranteed by the Act)." Basically, these interferences are actions aimed at discouraging employees from joining unions or acting properly as union members.

Section 8(a)(2) *Assistance to union:* An employer may not "dominate or interfere with the formation or administration of any union, or contribute financial or other support to it." Just as he cannot discourage union membership, neither can he encourage it or conspire in any way with the union.

Section 8(a)(3) *Discrimination:* An employer may not behave any differently in any material way against an employee because he is a member of the union. This does not prevent the employer from discharging striking employees when there is a no-strike contract in force.

Section 8(a)(4) *Protection of petitioners:* An employer may not refuse to promote, or fire, or lay off (or take any other discriminatory action against) any employee who legally uses the NLRB machinery in connection with a charge of an unfair labor practice.

Section 8(a)(5) *Refusal to bargain:* An employer cannot refuse to bargain in "good faith" with the union that has been certified. Refusal would include not providing the union with basic necessary information such as job classifications and wage rates.

Unfair Union Practices

Section 8(b)(1) *Restraint and coercion:* The union cannot "restrain or coerce an employer in the selection of his representatives for the purposes of collective bargaining or the adjustment of grievances." Similarly it cannot "restrain or coerce" employees, by mass picketing which prevents them from entering premises, or threatening nonstrikers, or using discriminatory practices, or contracting with an employer when the union has not been certified as representative of the employees.

Section 8(b)(2) *Employment discrimination:* A union cannot "cause or attempt to cause an employer to discriminate against an employee in violation of subsection (a)(3)," which covers a wide variety of situations related to not favoring union members when nonunion members have equal rights, not forcing nonunion members in "right to work" states to pay union dues as a condition of employment, not trying to get employers to fire nonunion employees, etc.

Section 8(b)(3) *Refusal to bargain:* A union is subject to the same requirements as an employer in this area.

Section 8(b)(4) *Forcing independent contractors:* A union may not try to get a contractor doing company work to join the union, as though he were an employee. Another part of this section relates to prohibiting secondary boycotts (described earlier). Still another part relates to not coercing employees to join unions, to refuse to handle goods, etc. Other sections relate to excessive or discriminatory membership fees or dues, "featherbedding" (requiring pay for which no work was performed), or picketing to force an employer's hand where the union has not been certified.

Strikes

The strike is the ultimate weapon, and is not embarked upon lightly. Most union constitutions require more of a majority to vote a strike than to vote a contract, and more to vote a strike than to vote the ending of a strike. If local unions strike without the international union's authorization, in violation of its constitution, usually no strike benefits will be paid. While many unions require a secret two-thirds vote for striking, the NLRB does not have such requirements before the union strikes. If the employees strike as a group, the NLRB requires 60 days' notice to the employer, plus any time required by the collective bargaining contract.

Sometimes a union will strike one company and not others, as is customary in the automobile industry, seeking to put unbearable economic pressure on the company which thus loses all sales to its competitors. In the airline industry, the major airlines have a *mutual aid pact* whereby a struck airline is given revenues by the nonstriking lines to reduce such pressure. If a union strikes some but not all employees in a particular association (a so-called "whipsaw strike"), the employer may lay off the rest of the bargaining unit and bring in temporary hirees.

picket line

When there is a strike and a picket line, employees whose work is not that which is normally done by the striking employees usually can get the union *picketing captain* to authorize crossing of the picket line, even though employees concerned are part of the union.

wildcat strike

Wildcat strikes (those not authorized by the union following a regular vote, or those prohibited by the contract) occasionally take place when a particular union local decides to go out, even though the international union does not agree. The United Mine Workers have been particularly prone to such strikes, and in past years they have cost as much as 2.5% of total coal tonnage in lost production. In the current strike settlement between the UMW and the Bituminous Coal Operators, the union is attempting to curb wildcat strikes, hoping to offer the operators new stability in the mines in return for a good contract. Since 1968, the union has paid out some $10 million in court-awarded damages for this reason, and has lost an additional $5 million per year in recent years in its pension and welfare fund from lost royalties for unmined coal. Usually the wildcat strikes in the mines come from unsatisfactory safety situations, in the view of the strikers.

The Changing Environment

Worker Alienation

The German radical economist Karl Marx, celebrated as the "father of communism" in some circles, theorized that under capitalism the worker would find less and less job fulfillment while the employer found ways to pay lower and lower wages. Things did not turn out the way Marx predicted; the U.S. worker managed to get paid more and more, keeping up quite well with so-called *productivity improvements* (increases in productivity per worker, resulting in part from increased labor-saving equipment and in part from better work technology and methods). The sight of substantial automobiles filling the blue-collar parking lots was supposed to indicate that these workers could in fact enjoy the good life in materialistic terms. Work conditions improved dramatically, with better safety and health standards, various amenities, and markedly shortened hours of work at regular pay (with the excess paid at overtime rates).

worker alienation

But in the midst of plenty, there has been a recent spectacle of worker alienation: workers on the assembly line in occasional revolt against mind-deadening work and depersonalized surroundings, in which the worker finds little fulfillment because he or she is performing a hardly recognizable piece of the job. Michael Macoby puts it this way: "The alienated individual feels 'depersonalized' and cannot experience the full reality of himself. For example, the alienated person in this sense may be the one who adapts himself to mechanized work by cutting himself off from feelings of anger, becoming emotionally deadened and passive."[19] Macoby feels that revolt of some sort in this situation may be a healthy thing. As we noted earlier, it was hoped that automation would reduce this alienation by letting machines take over the most routinized tasks, but it does not seem to be working out entirely this way. The Lordstown assembly plant, manufactured by General Motors for the purpose of building the Chevrolet Vega, was intended to be the most automated plant yet; but it has been the site of celebrated work slowdowns, worker sabotage, and general demonstrations of dissatisfaction with working conditions, culminating in a widely publicized wildcat strike in 1971. Some feel that the (scarcely formulated) demands of the present generation for work that does not rob them of their identity may be very difficult to satisfy without radically altering the design of the work place and even our approach to work as such.

In their statistical portrait of the alienated worker, Harold Sheppard and Neal Herrick[20] present data from several studies and conclude that the young workers place these self-actualizing values (as discussed in chapters 4 and 8) higher on their priority list than their parents did, are far less willing to submit to authoritarian work places, and are more dissatisfied. But perhaps things are not as grim as some have presented them. A 1973 University of Michigan study shows that dissatisfaction levels have not increased significantly over a four-year period, and a review of this and other surveys by the Manpower Administration concludes that young people are more likely to be dissatisfied but this dissatisfaction is not getting worse.[21] There is no doubt, however, that job alienation is a problem with which private industry must deal energetically.

self-actualizing values

What mechanisms can North Star build into its organization to prevent worker alienation and promote self-actualization?

The unions are not immune from the new alienation and militancy. Arnold R. Miller, president of the United Mine Workers, was seated in office as a result of a rank-and-file takeover of the large union relatively unprecedented in recent times. Since Miller deposed W. A. "Tony" Boyle in late 1972, Miller and his colleagues have instituted a number of democratic reforms, but still lack political control.

In other unions, the top officers face pressures for change today as they never have in the past. Rebel movements, protected by the Landrum-Griffin Act of 1959, are gaining strength. The United Steelworkers, considered one of the most democratic unions, has come under Labor Department scrutiny several times in the recent past because of its referendum election procedures that conduct national elections at local polling places. In 1974, the International Association of Machinists was induced under threat of legal action to rerun its entire 1973 election of international vice-presidents.

Many of the young workers find union bureaucracy as stifling as corporate bureaucracy, with little to choose between the two. It will be interesting to see the impact on the unions if young people start to challenge union management of their affairs and turn the power of the unions in the direction of changing the quality and tone of the workplaces. Tony Zon, president of Local 1112 of the United Auto Workers, said during the 1973 negotiations with General Motors that his Lordstown (Ohio) workers "want to strike." There was just a bit of bewilderment in his tone. "They harass the hell out of us," he says of the company; and top union officials vowed that no contract would be signed with GM that did not guarantee an end to this "harassment," but neither the international nor local leaders could say exactly what the union wanted in the way of assurances. The chances are good that the union is just as uncertain as management what it is that is bothering the workers—or more to the point, just what to do about it.

Impact of Unions on Managerial Discretion

The law delegates to the NLRB the power to determine appropriate bargaining units, but does not specify what is a bargainable subject. The NLRB assumed an early role, subject to court review, in determining what compulsory bargaining subjects may be, and the group of mandatory topics has gradually been expanded. "Wages" have been interpreted to include incentive plans, overtime pay, shift differentials, paid holidays and vacations, severance pay, Christmas bonuses, pension plans, stock purchase plans, merit wage increases, company housing, meals and discounts, and so forth. "Other terms and conditions of employment" have expanded to include provisions for grievance procedure, arbitration, layoffs, discharge, workloads, health and safety measures, vacations, holidays, sick leave, plant rules, use of bulletin boards by unions, seniority, retirement, and union security. The question of right to subcontract has been controversial; in the case of Fiberboard Paper Products v. NLRB (1964), the court determined that the primary motivation for the decision to subcontract was anti-union sentiment, and thus the company had bargained in "bad faith." In Ozark Trailers, Inc. v. NLRB (1966), the NLRB specified that a company must negotiate with employees not only on the effects of decisions but also on questions of whether or not to close or relocate a portion of its plant.

The 1974 agreement between U.S. Steel and the USW contains a management rights clause giving the company "exclusive rights to manage the business and plants and to direct the working forces [including] the right to hire, suspend or discharge for proper cause, or transfer, and the right to relieve employees from duty because of lack of work or other legitimate reasons." But a later agreement at U.S. Steel's Clairton Works covers some traditional management prerogatives: arrangements to control coke oven emissions, crew arrangement, and equipment maintenance, rehabilitation, and control. The union and the steel companies have formed the Joint Committee on Productivity—certainly a prime managerial consideration—to work cooperatively in response to inroads of foreign steel imports.

In the public sector, collective bargaining was considered impossible until comparatively recently. In 1937, President Franklin D. Roosevelt expressed the view of public unionism which prevailed until the 1960s:

> All government employees should realize that the process of collective bargaining...cannot be transplanted into the public service...The very nature and purposes of the government make it impossible for administrative officials...to bind the employer...The employer is the whole people, who speak by means of laws enacted by their representatives in Congress.[22]

The Taft-Hartley Act of 1947 excluded the federal government, incorporating a strong antistrike provision, and Public Law 330 of 1955 reaffirmed this position. But the courts began to strike down anti-union provisions in various statutes in the late 1950s, and various state laws began to recognize such rights for public employees. President Kennedy's Executive Order 10988 of 1962 (the "Magna Carta" of public sector unionism) and President Nixon's EO 11491 of 1966 established the framework for labor-management relations in the public sector. Since that time, 34 states have adopted legislation permitting or requiring collective bargaining in public sectors.

How has this worked out with regard to management prerogatives? A 1972 Brookings Institution study found most urban executives stating that unions had almost no influence on work assignment and supervision—and most union executives agreed.[23] In the public sector as well as the private, unions have preferred to negotiate the traditional subjects of wages, hours, and working conditions, but to stay out of matters of work assignment, skill classification, production standards, and discipline—generally, to retain freedom of protest and avoid the crossfire of member criticism. Sometimes the unions may prevail indirectly in the latter areas, however. In a New York City case, the unions contested the city's decision to place one police officer rather than two in each car during safer times of day, and lost. But after the city had bought 300 cars suitable for one officer, union pressures were strong enough to prevent implementation. The situation with regard to teachers' unions has been slightly different, because in the classroom a teacher *is* a manager; but in a recent Pennsylvania decision, the courts upheld the conclusion of the state Labor Relations Board that 21 disputed items were "matters of inherent managerial policy" and hence not negotiable.[24]

Industrial Democracy

Perhaps one wave of the future is more power in the hands of the workers, though this will not come without a struggle. Yugoslavia has carried this philosophy to its furthest extreme; workers in each plant run the board of directors, elect the management, and have the power to fire for nonperformance. But Yugoslavia is not alone. Volvo recently built in Sweden what can only be called a plant for the workers. Certainly Volvo has found a different way to build cars, and U.S. automobile executives have visited the Kalmar plant in droves to study the company's methods. Volvo added about 10% to the cost of a conventional plant in innovations to eliminate the overhead conveyor belt and substitute silently running "carriers" guided by computer to bear body and engine assemblies about the plant. They tilt the bodies to eliminate the overhead work from the hated "pit," and workers operate in teams that to some degree can set their own pace (since the carriers are not an articulated assembly line that must move at one pace). Teams have their own coffee rooms and separate entrances, and plants are designed for industrial beauty and comfort. Subject to a given production goal, teams can take breaks or vary their pace as they wish.

Another Swedish innovation is addition of workers to the boards of some of Sweden's largest companies. Required by law for companies of more than 100 employees since April 1973, the new directors are being given a cram course by the Swedish Trade Union Confederation. The main thrust of the law is to involve unions in matters that affect their daily work, rather than to turn over top management to them.

industrial democracy

Germany has had worker directors for 20 years. In Germany's largest steel company, August Thyssen-Hutte, lathe operator Eberhard Sauerbier sits alongside Rudolph Leiding, managing board chairman of Volkswagen. Every coal and steel company must have equal numbers of labor and management members on its board. In every public company, one-third of the supervisory board members must be workers. Some say that the system works poorly, in that equally powerful, self-canceling factions of managers and workers result in nondecision of conflict cases.

Nothing of the sort has happened in the U.S., except voluntarily, and there are few signs that it is imminent. But the possibility exists, and today's managers would do well to carefully consider the pros and cons of such a development and its likely impact on labor-management relations in this country.

Summary

Union development in the U.S. really started in 1869 with the founding of the Noble Order of Knights of Labor, which rose to national prominence only to slump by the start of World War II because it did not appeal to the needs of the skilled trades. This group was replaced by the American Federation of Labor, which began to compete with the Knights in 1886 and ultimately merged with the Congress of Industrial Organizations in 1955. Today the AFL-CIO has some 14 million members.

Labor legislation initially was directed against unions, prohibiting them from organizing under the *restraint of trade* doctrine; not until the National Labor Relations Act of 1935 were unions finally freed to operate much as they do today. In fact, the pendulum swung too far, and the Taft-Hartley Act of 1947 placed restrictions on unions similar to those on employers.

The Equal Employment Opportunity Act of 1972 was the "bill of rights" for minorities and women in labor, imposing requirements on both management and unions to end various sorts of discrimination and providing the Equal Employment Opportunity Commission with the power to enforce the act.

Union goals include economic welfare, job security, good working conditions, positive political action, and cooperative benefits. Union strategy is changing as the strike becomes a costly effort for both sides; boycotts are used at times, but negotiation is becoming the more useful tool as labor-management relations mature. Unions are not having much success in organizing white-collar workers, and as a result their total strength in members is declining slightly.

Unions fulfill worker needs by providing collective security, professional representation, fringe benefits, and safety and health improvements, and occasionally working with employers to increase productivity and thus make the U.S. worker more competitive.

Blue-collar workers are currently experiencing an economic crunch because their wages reach a plateau just as their expenses are rising; in addition, they feel that society looks down on their work, and are alienated and vaguely dissatisfied. Unions cannot find much to do about these problems, particularly the social and work place alienations. White-collar workers are the key to union growth, and most of them are not joining unions—partly because they identify more with management than with labor, and partly because they feel that unionization implies a lowering in status. White-collar public employees are an exception to this trend.

Young people appear to suffer high unemployment rates, but in view of various special factors in their situations (time to find first job, youths who are not really searching for work, etc.), their unemployment rates do not seem abnormally high. Women are starting to make inroads in typically male job areas. Blacks are beginning to do the same, under the protection of the EEOA. Hard-core unemployed have been the subject of extensive retraining and job opportunity programs, but they still remain the least wanted employees, and their chances for employment still are quite low. Moreover, when they do get hired, many factors in their home environments operate against their keeping the jobs.

Collective bargaining is the process whereby the union and company argue out the terms of the agreement. A union must be certified by the NLRB after an election wherein a majority of the employees in the working group select the union. The Federal Mediation and Conciliation Service often helps to reach agreement. Once signed, the agreement is binding in law. The union usually has a shop steward (or business agent) to represent the employees, and the first-line supervisor usually represents the company for the first step of any disagreement over contract terms. If the disagreement continues, a formal grievance is filed, and union and company attempt to settle it; but if they cannot, the contract usually provides for arbitration by a neutral party.

Unfair labor practices forbidden by the National Labor Relations Act are as follows:

1. *For employers*—interfering with employees, assisting the union, discriminating in hiring, taking action against petitioners, and refusing to bargain.
2. *For unions*—restraining or coercing employees, coercing employers, discriminating in union membership, refusing to bargain, forcing independent contractors, sanctioning secondary boycotts, refusing to handle goods, featherbedding, and picketing when not certified.

The strike is the ultimate weapon of the union; since it is costly to the employees, it is used less than formerly. Wildcat strikes are those undertaken by locals but not authorized by the international, and may be prohibited by the contract.

Workers are responding negatively to deadening or repetitive work, and thus far neither employers nor unions know exactly how to deal with this. It appears that dissatisfaction levels, though high, are not increasing. Even unions are facing a new militancy in their membership.

A wave of the future is industrial democracy, where workers have more managerial control. Thus far, however, this movement has not really influenced labor-management relations in the United States.

Notes

1. And its principal officers are the nation's highest-paid union executives. In 1972, President Frank Fitzsimmons and Secretary-Treasurer Murray Miller drew nearly $246,000 between them—considerably more than George Meany's $75,000. Forty-three union officers received over $50,000 each in 1972.

2. Strictly speaking, a federation of many unions.
3. Not until the thirty-eighth month, if the raise is 10% rather than 20%.
4. If a strike goes on very long, both sides lose. Positions harden, and the situation becomes a fight and test of strength, where each side seeks to win rather than to work out a cooperative settlement that both can live with.
5. Eli Chinoy, *Automobile Workers and the American Dream* (Boston: Beacon Press, 1965).
6. See Stanley aronowitz, *False Promises: The Shaping of the American Working Class Consciousness* (New York: McGraw-Hill Book Co., Inc., 1973), and Jeremy Breecher, *Strike! The True History of Mass Insurgence in America from 1877 to the Present* (Greenwich, Conn.: Fawcett Publications, 1974).
7. "The USW's No-Strike Victory," *Business Week,* April 20, 1974, p. 6.
8. Richard Rogin, "Joe Kelly Has Reached His Boiling Point," *New York Times Magazine,* June 28, 1970, p. 14.
9. Jerome M. Rosow, "The Problems of Lower-Middle-Income workers," in Sar A. Levitan, ed., *Blue-Collar Workers* (New York: McGraw-Hill Book Co., Inc. 1971), p. 76.
10. Walter Reuther, "The Corporation and the Union," in *Interviews on the American Character* (Santa Barbara: Center for the Study of Democratic Institutions, 1962), p. 22.
11. In many cases, of course, retail clerks are only marginally "white-collar." The manual tasks a supermarket clerk performs, heaving heavy cartons about, trimming lettuce, and so on, hardly fit the label.
12. Of all the nations in the world, only three have a smaller proportion.
13. Bureau of National Affairs, American Society for Personnel Administration, "Bulletin to Management," March 5, 1970.
14. Phyllis A. Wallace, "Sex Discrimination: Some Societal Constraints on Upward Mobility for Women Executives," *Corporate Lib,* Eli Ginsberg and Alice M. Yohalem, eds. (Baltimore: The Johns Hopkins University Press, 1973), pp. 69-84.
15. Independent Metal Workers Union, Locals Nos. 1 and 2 (Hughes Tool Co.), NLRB, 1964, 56 LRRM 1289.
16. Harland Padfield and Roy Williams, *Stay Where You Were* (Philadelphia: J. B. Lippincott Co., 1973).
17. Ibid.
18. Ibid.
19. HEW Report, *Work in America* prepared by W. E. Upjohn Institute for Employment Research, James O'Toole, Task Force Chairman (Cambridge: Massachusetts Institute of Technology Press, 1973).
20. Harold L. Sheppard and Neal Q. Herrick, *Where Have All The Robots Gone: Worker Dissatisfaction in the '70's* (New York: The Free Press, 1972).
21. Robert T. Quinn, et al., *Job Satisfaction. Is There a Trend?* Manpower Administration Research Monograph No. 30 (Washington: Government Printing Office, 1974), S/N 2900-00195.
22. Patricia N. Blair, "State Legislative Control over the Conditions of Public Employment: Defining the Scope of Collective Bargaining for State and Municipal Employees," *Vanderbilt Law Review,* January 1973.
23. David T. Stanley, *Managing Local Government Under Union Pressure* (Washington, D.C.: The Brookings Institution, 1972), p. 90.
24. Donald H. Wollett, *The Law and Practice of Teacher Negotiations* (Washington, D.C.: Bureau of National Affairs, 1974), p. 49.

Review Questions

1. What are the landmark laws in the field of labor? What impact has labor legislation had in promoting unions? in hindering union growth?
2. What is a yellow-dog contract?

3. What are the main goals of unions?
4. What is the difference between a business union and a welfare union?
5. What are the major strategies generally employed by unions to gain their demands?
6. What are the contributions made by unions to their members?
7. What recent problems have blue-collar workers experienced? white-collar workers?
8. Why have unions made their greatest inroads among blue-collar workers? What factors have generated the recent interest in unions among white-collar workers?
9. Who are the members of the "special working groups"?
10. Who are the hard-core unemployed? Are there any solutions to their problem?
11. What is meant by collective bargaining?
12. What is the role of the shop steward or union steward? Why are good relations between the first-line supervisor and the shop steward important?
13. When does a disagreement become a formal grievance under the contract?
14. What are examples of unfair employer practices? union practices?
15. Why is the strike becoming less of an ultimate weapon for the union? What is taking its place?
16. Why are blue-collar employees becoming alienated? What can employer or union do about it?
17. What does "industrial democracy" mean?

Discussion Questions

1. It has been said that unions are getting "too strong," and that they are more powerful than management, so that they get their way more often than management and consequently contract settlements are too much in labor's favor. As the strike becomes less viable as a union weapon, do you think the balance will swing in favor of management? Discuss.
2. What kind of blue-collar job would be likely to bring job satisfaction, and why?
3. Do you think that automation might be going the other way: increasing the skill levels demanded of white-collar workers (say in a bank, where the computer does many accounting functions, review of eligibility of borrowers for loans, etc)? Discuss.
4. Some say that corporations have a social obligation to hire hard-core unemployed, even if to do so would require them to fire some well-qualified and trained employees. What might be an argument in support of this idea? against it?
5. Can you think of any possible disadvantages of Ben Morell, the foreman in the example on page 598, backing down on his decision to suspend Frank Marini for two days?
6. Can you think of anything the union and the automobile industry might do in cooperation to try to reduce the alienation problem of the blue-collar worker in this highly routinized industry (assembly-line work)?

North Star Case Study

Suppose that Barbara Newman had not been hired. Suppose also that when the lawyer told the partners they could not have the kind of bonus plan they had, they had canceled the bonuses and not reconsidered. In all probability that approach would have encouraged unionization of the engineers and possibly a strike.

So let us say that the drafting room *has* gone out on strike, and Gene Whitney has come in with a list of demands, as leader of the contingent, to say they will not come back to work until all the demands are accepted. At this, Henry calls Bert, Dick, and Jo together, and after a lengthy discussion they decide not to give in to the strikers' demands. Instead, they decide to hire more engineers, though it promises to be a traumatic effort (each of them will have to go back to the drafting board again), and their work will suffer for a time. But they all think the effort is worth it, to prevent the unionization of North Star.

The partners expect some of the engineers to return on those terms, but none do. Since all refuse to report for work, and since there is no union (and hence no valid union contract), North Star is within its rights to fire all of them for not reporting, and does so.

1. What are the pros and cons of such a decision by the partners, from a personal standpoint?
2. What do you think will be the reactions of customers, when North Star asks them to accept some delay in production, basing it on the important need for North Star to "maintain the integrity of its personnel process"?
3. What kind of personnel "climate" is likely to prevail in the new drafting room after the new hirees report, get settled in, and then are briefed by Gene Whitney and the others about what happened?
4. How would you have handled the confrontation with Gene Whitney?

Suggestions for Further Reading

Aronson, R. L. *The Localization of Federal Manpower Planning.* Ithaca, N.Y.: New York State School of Industrial and Labor Relations at Cornell University, 1973.

Blum, A. E., et al. *White-Collar Workers.* New York: Random House, Inc., 1971.

Editorial Research Reports on the American Work Ethic. Washington, D.C.: Congressional Quarterly, Inc., 1973.

The Equal Employment Opportunity Act of 1972. Washington, D.C.: Bureau of National Affairs, Inc., 1973.

Ginsberg, E., and A. M. Yohalem, eds. *Corporate Lib: Women's Challenge to Management.* Baltimore, Md.: The Johns Hopkins University Press, 1973.

Kalachek, E. *The Youth Labor Market.* Policy Papers in Human Resources and Industrial Relations no. 12. Detroit: Institute of Labor and Industrial Relations, 1969.

Labor Reform Law: The Landrum-Griffin Act. Washington, D.C.: U.S. Chamber of Commerce, 1960.

Lasson, K. *The Workers: Portraits of Nine American Jobholders.* New York: Grossman Publishers, 1971.

Levitan, S. A., ed. *Blue-Collar Workers: A Symposium on Middle America.* New York: McGraw-Hill Book Co., 1971.

Lokiec, M. *Labor and Technology in the Postwar Era.* Columbia, S.C.: Bobbin Publications, Inc., 1973.

Meyer, G. D. *Participative Decision Making: An Analysis and Review.* Center for Labor and Management Monograph Series no. 15. Iowa City: University of Iowa Center for Labor and Management, 1970.

Newport, G. M. *Labor Relations and the Supervisor.* Reading, Mass.: Addison-Wesley Pub. Co., Inc., 1968.

Padfield, H., and R. Williams. *Stay Where You Were: A Study of Unemployables in Industry.* Philadelphia: J. B. Lippincott Co., 1973.

Sheppard, H. L., and N. Q. Herrick. *Where Have All the Robots Gone: Worker Dissatisfaction in the '70s.* New York: The Free Press, 1972.

Wilson, W. M. *The Labor Relations Primer.* Homewood, Ill.: Dow Jones-Richard D. Irwin, Inc., 1973.

Management and the Public

16

North Star Prologue

North Star, formed as a simple two-person partnership, had grown into a large engineering firm by solving various managerial problems, starting with organizational, leadership, and communication roadblocks and later dealing with inadequate planning and decision-making procedures. The planning exercise disclosed the need for more marketing efforts; with these under way, the partners ran into labor-management differences that threatened to blow the company apart. At the same time, they were broadening North Star's markets and building up expertise and volume in different sorts of jobs. They were grateful that careful analysis by Jo Parnela had saved them from a tempting offer to merge with a large company and lose their identity. Thus far, however, except for a brief brush with administrative law (when they discovered that they had failed to pay overtime in accordance with Labor Department regulations), North Star's internal operations had not generated much outside response.

The year that followed North Star's "unionization" was a year of substantial change. Every profit center had expanded substantially, with the project management division growing most of all. Dick now was supervising three overseas projects with Barnhard & Walker, and had won a contract to manage the half-billion dollar installation of a rapid transit system in the university city. North Star's total employment, though admittedly swollen by temporary engineers who would not stay with the firm when their projects were completed, was over 300, and Zeb was projecting an employment of 500 in three more years. Henry thought back with pride and some amazement at what a flourishing enterprise they had created in 12 tumultuous and intensely exciting years.

Near the end of the year, an event occurred that put North Star into a brand new field. B&W had been a silent backer of a brilliant architect and sociologist who had conceived and started a completely new city nestled in the foothills and around a glacial lake some 60 miles from the university city. The enterprise had started well, and was proceeding toward its goal of 100,000 inhabitants and completely self-contained industry. Already it had 15,000 residents and two "village centers," and the conference center complex would be ready for use within the month. But some aspects of the grand design had turned sour: the designer whose concepts had been so inspired at the start was turning autocratic when the residents endeavored to wrest control of the civic life from him, and some ugly acts of vandalism had convinced the Barnhard & Walker board that they would have to replace the now embittered founder and assume direct control of the project.

George Barth, B & W's group vice-president of the civil systems group, which included the power plant division with whom Dick Boyer had now completed several joint projects, scheduled a meeting with North Star's board of directors—consisting of the five officers plus their lawyer and the vice-president for commercial banking of their bank. With every director present, he unfolded a proposal. The B & W board of directors wanted to assign to North Star the long-term responsibility for operating the new city—appropriately named Eldorado—and realizing the potential they were confident existed there, but there was one necessary and vital condition. The condition was that North Star would become a Barnhard & Walker subsidiary, retaining its name and corporate identity, but wholly owned by the parent corporation. He was not there to talk terms, but he was confident that the North Star stockholders would not find that B & W was undervaluing their excellent company.

It took six months for the North Star group to reach a decision, and then to arrange the terms of the merger after they had decided to go ahead. Again Jo presented the matter in decision theory terms, but this time the outcome was different. The opportunity for building the city of Eldorado was hard to turn down, and Jo pointed out that B & W had essentially invited North Star to make its own case for what the merger price ought to be. In her presentation, she made a carefully documented case for a $5 million price. When the merger finally went through, the price paid by B & W for North Star (in B & W common stock, with only modest restrictions on its resale) was $4,500,000.

Henry reactivated the executive vice-president billet and left the other North Star operations in Dick Boyer's hands as the holder of that title; he took Barbara Newman and Gene Whitney with him to Eldorado, and they started finding out what they had. It did not take long to discover that the founder had no city management structure whatsoever—every decision was made on an ad hoc basis by himself, and when he was otherwise occupied things came to a standstill. Henry went to seek advice from Roger Moore, the Blackridge city manager; instead of advice, he came back with Roger himself, eager to cast his lot with the new metropolis springing shakily to life in the country.

In order to announce the change in management, and to get acquainted with his new undertaking as quickly as possible, Henry scheduled a "town meeting" in the nearly completed conference center, and had Roger Moore preside. They asked the founder to attend, but he would have nothing to do with the enterprise, and departed before the time of the meeting.

It was a tumultous session. The residents had many things to complain about, and were far from shy in speaking out. Eldorado had been financing its city maintenance expenses by an annual maintenance charge agreed to by each resident when he bought or built his home, and the corporation had the right to raise the amount from time to time as needed—with itself being the sole judge of need. This arrangement had not seemed significant to homeowners when they bought, but had become particularly objectionable as they saw the founder make personal decisions on maintenance priorities without any input from those affected. He considered the bicycle paths which ran behind each house and linked homes with schools and village centers to be key elements in his open-air concept, and spent an inordinate amount on tending and beautifying them. On the other hand, he thought the snow was beautiful, and would scarcely spend a dime to remove it from the streets. A number of residents had refused to pay the maintenance fee any longer, and had banded together in a formal group that was depositing the fees into an escrow account while they sought to bring legal action to have a voice in how the funds were spent.

An equally bitter dispute had developed over the question of elective city government. Eldorado's initial charter called for it to be an unincorporated town and thus under county government, but the county commissioners had refused to grant the zoning permits needed to start the project until the corporation that managed Eldorado had agreed to provide funds for schools and other public amenities. Thus the residents paid taxes to the county, all incorporated into their home purchase mortgage contracts; but the county paid little attention to Eldorado except to provide a minimal amount of police protection—and award a generous quota of speeding tickets. The founder had established elective "village councils," but when it turned out that they were intended simply to advise him, with no power or real influence, the members resigned in a body.

Roger Moore was amazed at this litany of grievances, plus some others that came out in the meeting. It was incredible to him that a designer with such talent at creating urban beauty could be so inept at recognizing the need for residents to have control of their destiny. When he said he was sure North Star and B&W would agree with a plan to seek a town charter and establish a regular municipal government, he found that wouldn't quite do either. The residents had certain expectations from the new town corporation: they looked to it to provide certain facilities for which they did not wish to pay on their own. Each of the two village centers had a swimming pool, and a civic building for dances and other group affairs, and a greensward or park—and they felt that the corporation was obligated to make similar contributions in the future. Roger said they probably could not have it both ways: either they were in a protected environment with the corporate father doing the providing (but taxing them for the costs), or they were a conventional township with control over their affairs but responsible for finding the money therefor.

The meeting ended with a good deal less than full agreement, but at least a start had been made. One thing Henry picked up from the session was the wide variety of desires expressed by the residents, and the substantial number of different groups with varying and often opposing wishes. He began to see how much more complex this task was going to be than he had conceived when George Barth laid it out for him.

One of the first results of Barnhard & Walker's emerging into public view as the principal owner of Eldorado (or at least of the unsold land and the commercial establishments, for Eldorado itself had become a township and was owned by nobody) was a strong groundswell of approval from the populace for its advocacy of the civic reform that had taken place under North Star's guidance. This was accompanied by a feeling of pride in the image of "their" company for its worldwide enterprises and the innovative approach that had marked its entry into emerging fields such as (in addition to development of a new town) population control, health care delivery for the poor, and low-pollution incineration and waste disposal equipment.

It was also accompanied, as time went on, by a proprietary feeling in B&W's image and corporate conduct, so that when the corporation signed a contract with a country identified with colonial oppression and repressive political acts at home there were angry letters to B&W's board chairman and talk of picketing the annual meeting to force the corporation to put public members on its board.

North Star found that it was not immune from this attention. One day Henry came into the manager's office to find a delegation sitting there. Roger said it was really Henry they wanted to see. The spokesperson told Henry that, as the closest embodiment of Barnhard & Walker, he was being asked to give them some representation on his board. Henry pointed out that, as a subsidiary and wholly owned company, his board was a rather limited instrument: it consisted of himself, George Barth of B&W, and the B&W treasurer. In point of fact, it really amounted to an institutional extension of Barth himself, who was in a position to exercise sole control when and as he wished. That was just the point, said the spokesperson—one individual should not have the power to call the tune for a company like North Star which ran a town, involved itself in environmental problems, worked on public transportation systems, built (or collaborated in the building of) nuclear power plants involving undetermined health hazards, worked on urban systems involving maintaining secret police data on private citizens, and in general performed a great many of the functions normally assigned to municipal or county agencies and responsible to the electorate.

Henry was taken aback. He had to admit that this group had done its homework well; somehow it had learned a great deal about North Star. And from the citizen point of view, perhaps it did appear that North Star was acting at times like a public agency. But it was out of the question for him to take any action on their request, and he said as much. He told them he would pass their viewpoint on to George Barth, the chairman of his board. The spokesperson said this would be fine, and they would call on him in his office a week from that time to get their answer.

When Henry told Barbara Newman about the bizarre request, saying he would have to be some sort of fool to pass that sort of foolishness along to Barth, he was surprised to hear Barbara say it might be a half-good idea for North Star to do it. She said any corporation tended to become ingrown, and a bit of sincere outside advice could be a useful leaven at times, if it stopped short of absurdity or self-indulgence. From the way the session had gone, it sounded to her like this delegation was neither. She bet Henry that if he passed the request on to George Barth, along with a recommendation that one elected public member from Eldorado come on the North Star board, George would not think him a fool but would give it very serious consideration. She said a deluxe dinner with all the trimmings was riding on the bet, and dared him to take her up. But she added a word of advice; he should be ready with a thorough inventory of the pros and cons, for the inevitable questioning that Barth would level at him.

Henry lost the bet. Barth discussed the matter exhaustively with Henry, who called in Barbara to say her piece, and had further extended discussions with B & W's corporate public relations staff. When the delegation came in the following week, Barth was there with Henry, and questioned the group deeply and critically about their interest. Suddenly he told them he had heard enough: the city manager would poll all the residents, and if a two-thirds majority was in favor of it he would agree to have an elected Eldorado representative on the North Star board of directors as a public member. There was just one condition he would impose: in view of the public welfare nature of the innovation, and in order to remove any taint of self-interest, he would ask that the public member be disqualified from voting whenever a matter came up dealing with Eldorado.

The survey showed an overwhelming majority in favor of the move, and shortly thereafter Roger held the election and the director was elected. To Henry's surprise the delegation spokesperson who had first approached him was not a candidate: there were three men and two women, and one of the women—Gail Osterhaus—received a majority of the votes and was thereby voted onto the North Star board. Henry invited her to meet with him shortly thereafter, and explained to her that the board met every three months and that she would be paid $50 a meeting. She said fine, she would accept the $50 willingly because she intended to earn it—in fact the reason they had elected her was that she had free time to devote to North Star problems between meetings. Henry said he didn't know about that—they had agreed to have her be a director, not a member of management. She retorted that a director was all she would be, and she expected him to give her the same attention and provide the same sort of information that he would to any director of a corporation of which he was president.

She reminded Henry that directors had

legal obligations to the stockholders, and cited recent court actions holding directors responsible if they failed to keep themselves informed of the affairs of their corporate charge. She said she was sure Henry would not wish to make it difficult for her to carry out her legal obligations. Henry said that was the last thing he would wish, and with a smile he asked her what things she needed to know.

Gail Osterhaus was a persistent woman, and a very intelligent and well-informed one. At the outset she seemed to take an inordinate amount of officer time, asking them to explain things to her, but at times her questions raised issues that shed new light on matters or uncovered new facts that helped the officers to understand things better. They never were able to get Gail to take any interest in profits—she said she wasn't elected on that platform, and she was sure the other board members would pay sufficient attention to that aspect of North Star. They came to call her their corporate conscience, and occasionally they even contacted her for her view of a pending decision without her having to raise the question first. Henry thought once about offering her a job with the company, but something told him how she would respond to that, so he never did.

And in time, after she asked them if they really were afraid that she would abuse the situation, they removed the prohibition against her involving herself in Eldorado questions.

What North Star Can Learn from Chapter 16

1. What actions a small company should take to be a good corporate citizen
2. How to approach integration of the work force
3. The special problems of doing business in a large city
4. Requirements for public disclosure
5. Impact of business on youth; what youth is looking for in a job
6. What typical social activities business is entering into, and how
7. The meaning of a "social audit"
8. Environmental and consumer trends; invasion of privacy
9. The dilemmas facing multinational businesses

Thus far in Part Four, we have discussed three external forces that have major effects on the organization's policy and performance: the *customer*, whose market behavior dictates product lines and selling strategy; the *government*, whose regulations establish the legal environment within which the organization must operate; and the *worker*, who negotiates through the union to establish wages and working conditions. All of these are traditional constraints, and every manager recognizes from the start that they must be dealt with as surely as must the economic cycle or the weather. In addition, however, a relatively new force has materialized on the manager's horizon in recent years: something called the "public." It may not buy from or sell to the company, does not work for or control the manager, and has no legal hold over the company for the most part; but its needs and concerns are no longer remote from organizational activities.

In dealing with that upstart "public" which has come to dominate so much of the manager's life, we will explore:

1. *Management in the urban setting*—the development, renewal, and survival of cities and the role of organizations as equal opportunity employers, dealing with financial problems of cities and doing business in cities.
2. *The public as partner*—corporate disclosure and behavior in the public interest, various ways in which the public becomes a partner in the enterprise.
3. *Social responsibility of business*—its role in social reform, environmental considerations, consumerism, privacy and individuality, and the current climate in business as the present generation sees it.
4. *Ethics in business*—internal politics, efforts to influence government, institutional morality, and the growing dilemmas of the multinationals.

Much of this chapter concerns areas that are in a state of flux today. As an old order changes, under the pressure of many different societal elements, new ground rules come slowly and uncertainly. While some see the corporation as a form of "government," and require it to operate in the overall public interest, others disagree violently and consider any such demands as a rip-off of the stockholders whose money gets diverted for the benefit of total strangers. Some think a U.S. corporation in a foreign country should be guided by U.S. standards of conduct (such as not contributing to campaign expenses of local politicians), while others think the usual customs of the host country ought to govern. Some think companies operating in a particular city should help with urban management, while others favor a strictly hands-off policy. Solutions to these complex problems are hard to come by. This chapter, while not professing to offer specific answers, will explore the questions and present some of the solutions various companies have put into practice.

Management in the Urban Setting

What can or should business do in response to the "urban crisis"—the complex and frustrating problems that arise as our cities try to meet the

urban crisis

various goals of affirmative action, fiscal solvency, mushrooming costs of services, and urban development? From its own point of view, business recognizes (or should recognize) that social problems affect business, that a good community attracts and holds good employees, and that many of its markets are dependent on a healthy regional economy. From the "good corporate citizen" point of view, it might conclude that (1) corporations have many of the skills needed to solve urban problems; (2) overall, it might be less expensive to the public if corporations reduce dividends to provide the needed funds, rather than having public agencies increase taxes; and (3) many of the problems (such as that of the hard-core unemployed) simply can't be solved if corporations don't take on the job. This is not to say that private industry can do anything, or that it should offer assistance to the point of going bankrupt—but clearly the old laissez-faire attitudes are giving way, both among the general public and within many corporate board rooms, to a genuine belief that corporations must accept some responsibility for improving public welfare. In this section, we will try to see what corporations might do to meet these urban difficulties, and how many corporations are going about the task.

Urban Development

John Ruskin, in a perceptive and perhaps prophetic comment more than a century ago, told an Edinburgh audience that "it is chiefly by private, not by public, effort that your city must be adorned." From the mid-'60s through the mid-'70s, the U.S. seemed to abandon that traditional notion, as the Department of Housing and Urban Development poured millions of dollars into urban redevelopment schemes that produced all too little improvement in urban life. All across the land one can find cities, large and small, with "master plans" funded by public grants that seek to take development in the proper direction. There is no denying the evil this program tries to check, with helter-skelter uncontrolled development strewing ugly stores, apartments, and housing tracts along the commuter roads to blight the landscape and compound the problems of delivering effective city services. But too many of these plans lie unheeded in file cabinets for lack of actual volunteer development that would flesh out the ground designs, which are generally impractical in the first place.

urban redevelopment

Development takes private effort. Public development programs have been modest in overall scope, and many of them have failed signally. The most ambitious public developer, New York's $2 billion Urban Development Corporation, created by the city in 1968 to meet its housing and other urban problems, defaulted on some $130 million in bank loan and note obligations in 1975 and virtually destroyed itself as a public weapon against urban decay and suburban sprawl. The problem with public programs is the insulation of their managers from the overriding need to stay solvent, and their resulting temptation to undertake programs without careful preliminary analysis of their viability. (The problem with private programs, of course, is that they are not undertaken at all unless they promise a profit, thus ruling out many low-cost housing programs which would break even at best.)

Kansas City and Savannah are strikingly different examples of cities where private initiative is leading the way to urban health. The prime mover for Kansas City is Hallmark Cards, Inc., a major enterprise that turns out some 2 billion cards a year. For the past several years the Hall family has been converting 85 rundown acres in metropolitan Kansas City into Crown Center, a dramatic collection of offices, stores, and hotels surrounding a ten-acre plaza which is in effect a handsome city park. Hallmark has been willing to invest for far less than the normal short-term return, both to make a contribution to Kansas City and in hopes of a good long-term return. The total cost of Crown Center may come close to half a billion dollars. Clearly the Hall family is taking a very broad view of what is good for the Hallmark Company, in pouring this kind of money into its corporate neighborhood.

Savannah, Georgia, was founded nearly two and a half centuries ago, and laid out at that time with small city squares every few blocks apart, which now constitute 20 beautiful landscaped parks dotting the inner city. These parks came to typify the colonial charm of the city, but instead of government protecting them it posed the greatest threat. In the last 30 years four have been condemned by the city or the state highway commission. Since that date, private initiative provided funds to form and finance a preservation foundation, which bought old rundown buildings and resold them (often at a loss) for restoration. They have managed to designate a hefty part of the city's core as the nation's largest federal urban historical landmark, insuring that the parks are safe at last—not only from private developers, but from the greater threat of governmental developers with the scent of urban renewal in their nostrils.

A city with similar problems, on which the jury is still out, is St. Louis. A research report issued in late 1973 by the Rand Corporation, to the effect that the city's downtown area was dying, stirred its leading executives into angry action. While it is true that a $40 million apartment complex on urban renewal land went bankrupt in 1972, new construction begun or announced for center city during the year following the Rand study totaled $400 million, or $60 million more than the total of all such investments since World War II. The business leaders are aghast at the study's traditional solution: a massive federal spending program that would "turn the city into a kind of vast Indian reservation," in the words of director Norton Long of the University of Missouri's Center for Community and Metropolitan Studies. It remains to be seen if the activity of the business leaders can make this study a false prophecy, but the scope of private investment thus far suggests that the Rand Corporation may have underrated the strength of aroused corporate action.

The government has attempted to build "new towns," totally planned communities with a theoretically optimal mix of working, buying, and living facilities, and without the residential segregation typical of most existing communities. The Housing and Urban Development Department has approved loan guarantees for 14 such privately built new communities, but they have not prospered, and many will go under without further government aid. Some of the nation's best-known new towns are being developed without such government help, and although progress slowed during the economic turndown of 1974, by and large these projects are stronger than those backed by the federal government.

One of the major contributions made by private industry to urban development is the construction of office buildings and shopping malls.

new towns

North Star has the job of running a new town. What are the possible financial roadblocks?

In New York, the office-building capital of the world, builders have been overenthusiastic and banks overpermissive in recent years. Fifty-five million square feet of new office space went up between 1970 and 1973, and the recession at the end of that period converted 30 million of those square feet into surplus. It may be 1985 before this excess space is absorbed. The one benefit in such a situation is the reduction in rents, which tends to lure more corporations back to New York and thus check the corporate exodus which has been making New York, in the words of one writer, "a city destroying itself." Municipal government can do little one way or another in this sort of situation—the ball is almost entirely in the hands of private enterprise.

A new trend may be reducing corporate ability to help the cities. In 1973, Houston voters were considering a referendum to establish the Houston Area Rapid Transit Authority to solve the city's growing traffic problem, and sought business contributions to promote the campaign. Unfortunately, a state law passed the same year outlawing corporate contributions to a political cause scared executives away, not only from contributions (which probably would have been legal under this law) but even from saying anything that could be interpreted as political. Consequently, Houston voters vetoed mass transit three to one, and the intolerable traffic problems went unsolved.

Louisville, Kentucky, has been one of many cities watching helplessly as its downtown went downhill—until early in the 1970s, when business leaders joined with civic officials in a rejuvenation campaign. The result was a five-year, $2 billion redevelopment plan which has produced such major projects as a traffic-free shopping mall which is third largest in the nation, a riverfront park which has become a catalyst to spark other renewal on blighted land nearby such as office buildings, hotels, and shops, and an informal coalition of young and older business leaders that has updated the downtown plan and constitutes the driving force to make it happen. Most encouragingly, Louisville's new look is attracting visitors from Dayton, Memphis, Birmingham, and Flint, who want to see how their central city areas might be saved.

Equal Opportunity Employment

affirmative action/ equal opportunity

The federal program that is variously called "affirmative action," "equal opportunity," or "desegregation" has undertaken, first, the simple policy step of giving qualified women and minorities the same opportunities previously reserved for white males. Although this policy does require a change in managerial attitudes, it involves no sacrifice of profits or expenditure of managerial effort. Second, the program hopes to create employment opportunities (including training in both skills and attitudes) for a segment of the work force commonly considered as "unemployable." For both of these objectives, the government can legislate, but only managers can make it happen.

How does a corporation (or a government agency, for that matter) go about integrating the work force? At first glance, it appears that the available jobs do not fit the available unemployed, either because the skills demanded are not the skills possessed or because the jobs (usually manual tasks with unpleasant or degrading implications) are unattractive. At

Louisville has been watching helplessly as its downtown has gone downhill.

second glance, for companies that have taken the next step of waiving strict qualification requirements for hard-core unemployed, it seems that they just don't want to work—they show up late, with a high absentee rate, and may leave the job without authority.

The situation is not that simple, however, for those with the perception to understand it. Chrysler Corporation's experience with "unemployables" revealed many reasons why those who genuinely want to make it give the impression that they don't care. They may not be familiar with bus schedules, or maybe they can't read the bus signs. They arise late because they don't have alarm clocks and aren't familiar with their use. If they get cars, the cars may not meet inspection standards and thus be driven illegally, leading to brushes with the law that interfere with regular work attendance; or the cars may be so unreliable that they don't provide dependable transportation. Their ghetto environment provides many physical and cultural roadblocks that impair the incentive to work at a regular job, and although these can be dealt with, it takes time—during which the employee is missing work and getting on the foreman's list. Regular employees, who see the rules relaxed for the "unemployables" but not for themselves, eventually come to resent the situation and take covert steps to oust the newcomers.

unemployables

Companies who succeed in meeting "equal employment" requirements and hiring the hard-core have to work at it. They must discard such stereotyped ideas as the notion that customers won't accept blacks or women in sales and service of certain kinds, that blacks are "not dependable," or that productivity of white males will drop when they work in integrated or bisexual situations. They must make sure that high scores on their aptitude tests do not depend on exposure to a middle-class environment. They must have active recruiting programs to find qualified women and minority employees, since such individuals may not be discovered via the usual employment approaches. They must sell the equal employment concept to the existing labor force, many of whom see threats to their security in such programs. They must insure that promotion opportunities are color-blind, including training for promotable areas.

last hired, first fired

"Last hired, first fired" has been a great foe of equal employment, since any temporary turndown can remove the most recent hirees—the very people the equal employment programs have brought in. But a celebrated decision by U.S. District Court Judge Fred J. Cassibry in New Orleans, in March 1974, ruled that job seniority is an illegal basis for layoffs when it involves workers who owe their low seniority to past discrimination.[1] Since the judge also ruled that companies should not penalize longtime white employees by firing them to rehire laid-off blacks, he thus threw the problem directly in the laps of the company and the union. The particular circumstances of Judge Cassibry's ruling involved Continental Can Company and the United Steelworkers. As we noted in chapter 15, the U.S. Labor Department's top attorney, William J. Kilberg, commented that no previous ruling has moved so far from helping the specific blacks hurt by discrimination—those who could not get jobs at Continental Can during the 1940s and 1950s—toward compensation of entirely different individuals who are held to be in the same racial category. Since Judge Cassibry's decision holds that the companies should penalize neither the worker with seniority rights nor the new black employees, the brunt of finding a solution will necessarily fall on the company. Clearly, the judge reasoned that illegal racial discrimination created this seniority pattern and hence the problem was the fault of the company.

Civil Rights Act

The Cassibry ruling notwithstanding, the overwhelming majority of companies who made a choice during the 1974 turndown chose seniority. A Pittsburgh conglomerate that laid off 15% of its 30,000 workers by seniority notes that 26% of its black employees and even more of its women employees were caught in the layoff net. The reason, which applies to many companies, was that blacks in the work force had increased from 2% in 1965 to 11% in September 1974 when the layoffs started, and women had gone from 6% to 14%. Since recruiting and upgrading of blacks started in the late 1960s and of women in the early 1970s, the former had relatively low seniority and the latter had even less. Companies may be violating Title VII of the Civil Rights Act by these layoffs, but this is an unknown. The union's opposition to weakening of seniority rights is a certainty—they will fight it violently. A UAW local president stated the case for most union leaders: "There is no way I would stand for bypassing seniority. That's how the union was built." The UAW general counsel commented that "remedying past discrimination is hard enough without pitting worker against worker during a recession. That is not the way you make progress. You have to do it when the economy is expanding."[2]

In recent years, civil rights activists have adopted the tactic of arguing that the higher prices corporations charge to black customers constitutes discrimination just as unequal hiring policies do—and have made the argument stick in Chicago. In a case brought by a group of homeowners in 1974, the U.S. Court of Appeals ruled that it was illegal to charge higher prices for homes sold primarily to blacks than for similar homes sold in white neighborhoods, even though demand in the former market supports the markup. Similar cases apply to supermarket prices, insurance rates, and consumer financing. Evidence in the housing case showed that black families paid about 20% above the fair market value of similar homes in white areas, bringing the builders almost double the profits of builders in the white areas.

A growing number of black business executives are making it by themselves. A usual pattern of black business success is through Minority Enterprise Small Business Investment Corporation loans, guidance from white business executives, or other institutional aids for minorities. But many are moving up on their own. There are many examples of black business executives who have made it big, following the same hallowed path as white entrepreneurs. Herman Russell, who started as a plasterer in Atlanta, founded the H. J. Russell Construction Company and became a multimillionaire. John Small of New York quit an advertising agency to form his own, which grew to annual billings of $10 million. Alvin Boutte of Chicago used his pharmacist training to open a drugstore, expand it into a chain, and then branch out into a bank which has been one of the nation's fastest-growing banks, with some $60 million in assets. Curtis Sisco owns Rowell's, the nation's largest black-owned department store. And former activist Archie Williams of Boston started Freedom Electronics and Freedom Die Casting, which grew into a million-dollar annual volume business. These and other black business managers have demonstrated that the inherent ability to make an enterprise succeed is not a racial characteristic.

MESBIC

The Urban Financial Crisis

When the nation was treated to the spectacle in 1975 of New York City defaulting on its bonds and teetering on the brink of bankruptcy, there was a great deal of municipal criticism of the banks for refusing to continue their practice of bankrolling the city's deficits. In early 1975, New York State provided an advance of $400 million, but this was little more than a drop in the bucket compared to the city's needs for meeting its payrolls and servicing its debt. The banks now hold millions of dollars in city debt paper, and have reached the point where they fear any deeper involvement until they can see that New York has a reasonable plan for getting out of its financial hole. Critics point out that the banks hold millions of dollars in city deposits, and that in the past they have made a good deal of money as earnings on what they have loaned the city. The banks are afraid that a city bankruptcy, as unthinkable as that seems, may indeed be a possibility, and that it would drag down many of the banks with it. New York has made resolute attempts to cut its payroll by laying off thousands of municipal workers, but it started with some 340,000 employees in its work force, and it would take a tremendous cut to turn the trick.

Business critics suggest that New York City may simply be providing too many free services—far more than it can continue to afford. Its free City University is larger than the universities of 43 states. It has 19 public hospitals (Chicago has only one). If it paid for its welfare and social services at the same rate as Los Angeles, the bill would come to $125 million a year instead of the actual $2 billion. A look at Table 16-1, showing how New York's budget has risen in ten years with an average increase of 231%, plainly reveals the skyrocketing tendency of the cost of urban services.

On top of New York's $255 million bimonthly payroll, it has an overwhelming volume of other debts that exceed its capacity to raise funds through the usual channels. Moreover, investor fears about the city's ability to cut costs and live within its means have closed off New York's usual fund-raising channels. New York State's Municipal Assistance Corporation (Big Mac), faced with the task of rescuing New York City, prevailed on the union to accept a wage freeze while it endeavored to sell bonds by convincing banks and other investors that the city had turned over a new financial leaf and intended to live within its means. Steps taken by the mayor included substantial layoffs of public employees, raising of subway and ferry fares, and endeavoring to convince investors that the state would stand behind the MAC bonds. But the burden of short debt is crushing, as Table 16-2 shows—some $4 billion a year that must be "rolled over" or paid back. Ultimately, short-term federal loans were required to save the city from actual bankruptcy.

New York is not the only city with budget troubles, though its problems are by far the most pressing. When the revenue-sharing concept was introduced in 1972, many observers thought it would dampen the need for cities to go to the private investors with municipal bonds. The bond market had grown by 200% in the 1950s and another 125% in the 1960s. Indeed, as shown in Figure 16-1, there was a temporary dip at the time revenue-sharing funds hit the street, but it did not last long. Total borrowing turned up again in 1974. The reason is not hard to find: while revenue-sharing was intended to grow at a 3% annual rate, inflation grew at a rate closer to 8% during the period. It was more than inflation that

Municipal Assistance Corporation

Table 16-1.
New York City's Budget Growth, 1965-75

If you got a contract to analyze the trend in New York City expenditures, to see if the growth rates might parallel Eldorado's in the future, what would you look at in general? What would be the same and what would be different?

	1964-1965	1974-1975	Increase
Welfare	$ 416,000,000	$ 2,241,000,000	482%
Education	675,000,000	1,912,000,000	183
Debt service	470,000,000	1,435,000,000	205
Pensions	326,000,000	791,000,000	143
Police	236,000,000	734,000,000	211
Environment	144,000,000	330,000,000	129
Fire	120,000,000	307,000,000	156
All other	675,000,000	2,147,000,000	218
TOTAL	$3,355,000,000	$11,104,000,000	231%

Notes due on	Amount
Aug. 22, 1975	$741,000,000
Sept. 11, 1975	46,000,000
Sept. 15, 1975	400,000,000
Oct. 17, 1975	420,000,000
Nov. 10, 1975	250,000,000
Dec. 11, 1975	400,000,000
Jan. 12, 1976	620,000,000
Jan. 13, 1976	200,000,000
Feb. 13, 1976	290,000,000
Mar. 12, 1976	341,000,000
June 11, 1976	280,000,000

Figure 16-1.
Municipal Bond Market, 1965-74

fueled the increased demands for private loans to cities. Soaring city employee demands for salary hikes, plus demands for tremendous increases in pension and other fringe benefits, caused local government spending to rise 14% compared with an 8% rise in federal spending. The only source for this money is the capital markets, and municipalities are competing head-on with corporations in that area. In a sense, as the business climate recovers, the attractiveness of municipal bonds dwindles, so cities are closely involved in the business cycle whether they like it or not.

The new "block grant" provisions of the Housing and Community Development Act of 1974 means more undesignated funds for cities— money that can be spent for almost any purpose within wide guidelines—but some cities will end up with more while others get less. The amount is derived by a complex formula based on population, personal income, housing shortage, and similar social indicators. The 1975 forecasts of the Department of Housing and Urban Development, shown in Table 16-3, indicate the probable changes in federal funds awarded to various cities. The formulas boost some cities (Birmingham, Dallas, New York), cut others (Atlanta, Minneapolis, Seattle), and leave others substantially unchanged (San Diego, St. Louis). The cities need only submit broad plans setting forth how the funds will be used. Cities that have sought grants energetically in the past, such as Boston, will find their take reduced under the formula, while cities that have tended to shy away from federal funds, such as Dallas, will look forward to an increase.

block grants

Doing Business in the City

Cities are of interest to corporate managers for more reasons than the opportunity or demand they present for managers to assist in urban problems. The city is the environment of many corporations, and it is of compelling interest to managers that the city offer a good environment for doing business. What special knowledge must the manager have, and what special steps must be taken, to function successfully in the urban setting? What special opportunities does the urban setting offer?

One special opportunity is the opportunity to make a lot of money. Consider the example of Donald J. Trump, a New York City real estate

Table 16-2.
New York City's Short-Term Debt

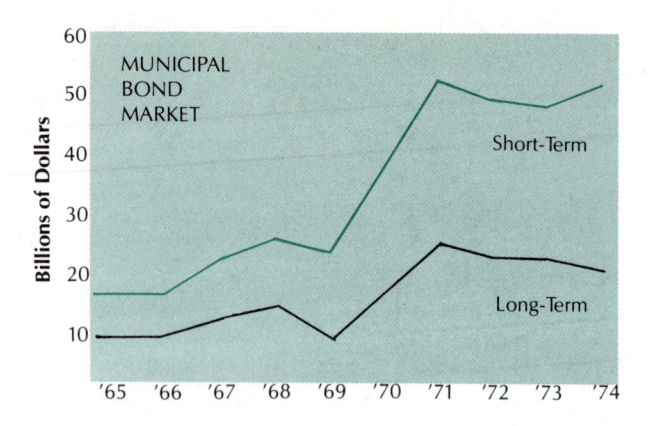

MUNICIPAL BOND MARKET

operator. The Trump Organization is a collection of 63 privately held corporations and family partnerships owning 22,000 apartment units. While these were developed with private money, the recent Trump approach is to launch major projects without any family investment at all. His technique is to finance development with the state and city, utilizing New York State's Mitchell-Lama Act which stimulates construction of lower-income housing by offering a mortgage at very low interest rates, and is the financing arm of the New York City Economic Development Administration. He promises to create jobs if the state and city will finance his projects, such as conversion of Penn Central's 144-acre switching yards along the Hudson River into an apartment and light industrial project—the former to provide some 30,000 apartment units to lure taxpayers back into the city, and the latter to provide them with jobs that would improve the city's tax base.

Businesses pay a hefty price for doing business in the cities, with the largest price paid by those who do business in New York City. Consolidated Edison, which generates New York's electricity, pays $360 million a year in state and local taxes, absorbing over 24% of its electricity operating revenues compared with about 10% nationwide. Its labor is more costly,

Table 16-3.
Changes in Federal Funding for Cities, 1975-80

	1975	1976	1977	1978	1979	1980
Birmingham, Ala.	$4.8	$4.8	$7.2	$7.3	$7.3	$7.3
Chicago	43.8	43.8	63.0	64.1	64.1	64.1
Dallas	4.0	9.7	14.8	15.0	15.0	15.0
Gainsville, Fla.	0.3	0.8	1.3	1.3	1.3	1.3
New York	101.1	101.1	153.9	156.5	156.5	156.5
Omaha	1.4	3.3	5.0	5.1	5.1	5.1
Atlanta	18.7	17.5	16.3	13.6	11.9	11.4
Boston	30.3	28.7	27.2	20.3	15.8	11.9
Minneapolis	16.7	15.9	15.0	11.6	8.4	6.3
Philadelphia	56.5	56.5	52.9	44.1	37.9	34.1
San Francisco	22.1	28.6	28.2	28.1	16.9	12.8
Seattle	11.5	10.5	9.4	7.3	6.9	6.9
San Diego	9.1	9.1	10.3	10.5	10.5	10.5
St. Louis	15.2	14.6	14.7	15.1	15.1	15.1

Source: Department of Housing and Urban Development

and that cost is rising faster than the national average. It has more buried cable than the rest of the industry combined (an amenity often demanded by city ordinances), and buried cable costs 20 times as much to maintain as overhead cable. Moreover, with the dense population, new plant siting involves bitter and protracted battles; Con Ed has given up on nuclear power, and local groups have delayed for more than ten years the pumped storage plant that most rural utilities could have built with little difficulty to ease peaking problems. And its ratio of unpaid bills is the highest in the industry—New York is a place where small businesses routinely open, run up big utility bills for three months, then fold without paying.

A new trend in urban cost-saving is the shift by businesses to cheaper and often very unconventional offices. When Christiana Companies was put off by the high cost of conventional office space, it renovated an old warehouse at a third the cost of competing office space; employees agree that the spacious and colorfully decorated new headquarters is "just one super place to be." Goodyear created corporate office space in an Akron factory built in 1898. Flair Merchandising Agency converted a rundown Chicago brownstone residence into a architectural showpiece. Sedco, Inc., restored an 1888 public school in Dallas for its headquarters, creating a distinctive interior with the original hand-carved woodwork. And Walter Landor Associates topped most converters for originality by taking over an old ferryboat at a San Francisco pier—getting among other advantages a breathtaking view.

Sometimes business executives band together to fight city hall for actions they believe will benefit the city. Atlanta, which has been proud of its race relations, elected a black mayor with much business support. When ties between business and city hall became shaky, many companies

A new trend in urban cost-saving has been the shift to cheap and unconventional offices.

considered moving out, prompting a downtown business group to present a list of demands to the mayor that centered on a commitment to downtown. The key problems involved were racial tensions, fear of crime, and lack of transportation and parking. Through joint meetings with the group, Central Atlanta Progress, and the mayor, attention was turned to the problems raised by the executives.

industrial revenue bonds

An intriguing new approach to public-private urban relations is the tax-exempt "industrial revenue" bond technique, whereby cities and states sell bonds to finance private industrial development. Allied Products Corporation of Chicago is an example of how the technique works. It planned an expansion program in its agricultural equipment business which involved building a facility in each of several communities. Since the community involved anticipated increased employment and tax revenues, it was in favor of the move. The community would issue industrial revenue bonds, which were tax-free and thus could obtain funds at about 6% rather than the 10% that corporate bonds would have paid. The funds would go to the company for building the desired facility. Utilities have done similar financing for pollution control bond issues, where the facility is deemed to provide a needed public good.

As retail costs rise, and profits are squeezed, department store managers in urban areas are getting more from the same space. J. C. Penney stores cast in the new mold get 15% more volume from the same space by tightening displays and putting more merchandise in front of the customer. Montgomery Ward closes 50 square feet of old and less productive urban space for every 100 feet of new store it opens, in contrast to the previous expansion approach that simply said more space would bring more profits. New K-Mart stores, which used to run 95,000 square feet, have dropped to 85,000 square feet but do the same job, and K-Mart puts 40,000-square-foot "minis" in many new locations. Penney's new Cumberland Mall store in Atlanta is 34% smaller than an older Penney store nearby, but gets 30% more sales.

no-growth

A new trend in urban centers is the "no-growth" mood that confronts builders and others wishing to expand with legal obstacles stemming from the public's perceived desire to limit development. Boca Raton, Florida, became the nation's first city to limit its ultimate size by putting an absolute legal limit of 40,000 dwellings in the city. San Jose, California, froze residential zoning in overcrowded school districts unless the builder would, in effect, provide temporary additional school buildings himself. Montgomery County, Maryland, forbade development unless the builder proved that adequate fire, police, sewer, and other services were available. Fairborn, Ohio, passed an ordinance requiring a builder to donate 8% to 20% of his land to the city for park and open space use, plus a third the value of the donated land in cash for maintenance. Fairfax County, Virginia, imposed a moratorium on new construction because sewers were up to capacity and the taxpayers did not want to vote bond issues for any more.

Petaluma, California, poses an interesting problem. Its controlled growth plan limits new housing to no more than 500 units a year, but one observer states "the fact is that Petaluma is producing more future citizens than 500 houses a year will handle." Builders and others interested in building wonder what would result if every community imposed growth limits similar to Petaluma's: "We would wind up with a surplus of people and no place to live." Ordinances such as these are bound to be challenged in the courts, raising the issue of whether cities really have the constitutional right to prevent citizens from residing within their boundaries.

Probably the most unusual of all cases involving business relations with an urban landlord involves the Anaconda Company and its "company town" of Butte, Montana. The nation's third-largest copper producer, Anaconda employs a third of Butte's labor force, pays close to two-thirds of the county's property taxes, and stimulates the economy to the tune of millions of dollars a year. But Anaconda's open pit copper mine is literally chewing up the city.

The Berkeley pit extends a mile in each direction and is over a thousand feet deep. Thus far it has swallowed more than 1000 homes, and the mine property covers nearly a fifth of the city. Fear that the pit may eventually engulf the whole city has contributed to urban decay. Anaconda has stated that it has no current plans to expand toward the city core (which it can legally do whenever it wishes), but has suggested that Butte build a new city center farther from the pit; it pledged to move its own offices there, and would consider participating with private developers. The proposal makes some citizens suspect that Anaconda wants to relocate cheaply. Butte is trying to attract new industry to lessen dependence on Anaconda, a move which the latter would welcome. All the residents are conscious of the potential for disaster if Anaconda exercised its right of eminent domain; the town of Bingham, Utah, once with a population of 10,000, was engulfed by Kennecott Copper's pit and now lies abandoned.

The Public as Partner

Recent legal and social developments have pressured corporations (and by implication government agencies) to become more "representative" of the people, to the point of taking public-interest representatives on their boards of directors. As a corollary, the public has moved to hold corporations "accountable" in a number of ways: for the quality and safety of their products, for their practices in advancing the nation's social goals, and for wide public disclosure of their financial and other operations. In short, the public is generally disillusioned with "business"—to some extent a valid change of heart, but also based in part on misunderstanding of the profit situation (one survey disclosed that most people thought business earned about 28% profit, when 6% to 8% would be more accurate).[3]

Another new direction involves business and government teaming up to achieve goals desired by both. From the corporate executive's point of view, all of this has meant an urgent need to "sell" the public on business, which means teaching more managers how to project a better image.

Corporate Disclosure

There are two opposing principles of the marketplace. One holds that the buyer is entitled to know all about a product before shelling out any

corporate disclosure

money. The other maintains that the seller is running a private business, and is entitled to privacy about business affairs. When the question is one of product safety, such as rating of automobile tires, few on either side question the public's right to know. When it deals with a food product, there may be a difference of opinion about the manufacturer's obligation to disclose the contents on the label; by and large, this issue has been resolved in favor of the consumer. But when it comes to buying a corporate stock, companies can become quite indignant about the need to disclose details of profitable and unprofitable operations on a product-line basis, alleging that this information tells competitors how well a manufacturing process is working out and the like. When the Federal Trade Commission demanded from several large companies such details of their profit experience by separate product line, several companies went to court to enjoin the FTC from obtaining these data.

Joseph B. Danzansky, president of Giant Food, Inc., has a battered hard hat hanging on his office wall, over a sign saying, "It ain't always easy being a nice guy." Danzansky's efforts to be a nice guy have made Giant Food an aggressive supporter of the consumer movement and the first major supermarket chain to adopt unit pricing, open dating, and ingredient labeling. He started his campaign by hiring Esther Peterson, former consumer advisor to Presidents Kennedy and Johnson, which some competitors said was like "inviting the cops to a burglary"—particularly as he told her that she would be the consumer's representative at Giant, not Giant's representative in battles with the consumer. The reforms instituted in the wake of Ms. Peterson's hiring have generated customer goodwill and may have helped Giant to increase its share of the Washington, D.C., market from 26% to 30%.

Disclosing information about foods or other products is quite different from disclosing information about the company itself, and the Securities and Exchange Commission has had to push hard to lay out disclosure rules that would provide potential buyers of stock with the information they need to make sensible choices. The SEC has worked to expand the information required in annual reports, stress the need for corporate insiders to disclose their trading in company stock, and require public disclosure of action taken by any company to acquire another. But in 1974 the SEC went a good deal further, in requiring that Mattel, Inc., turn over a majority of its board of director seats to executives with no former tie with the company. Moreover, the new outside majority must be approved both by the SEC and by the courts—and must make up a majority of the executive committee which is the immediate link with day-to-day operations.

This move, even in the view of some within the SEC, resembles a government takeover of stockholder rights in the name of protecting the public, for the time-honored procedure calls for the directors to be elected by majority vote of the stockholders who own the company. While the move was made at Mattel after the SEC felt that Mattel had inflated its financial reports, the precedent means that the SEC will be less reluctant to impose a similar requirement the next time. Many question the ability of outside directors to get involved deeply enough to uncover corporate shenanegans.

Membership on a board of directors is no breeze these days in any event. The increasing responsibilities and liabilities of being a board member are causing more and more designees to decline, even as stockholder pressure is forcing companies to go outside for black business executives, academics, environmentalists, younger executives, and consumer advocates. In addition to the demands on time, which are increasing as directors spend more and more hours preparing themselves for meetings, there is increased liability to being sued by stockholders or the SEC. Suits are more likely now for such lapses as absence from meetings, approval of expenditures considered improper, unwarranted payment of dividends, or accrual of personal profits. Directors can be sued for fraud if they could *reasonably* have known of the illegal situation, whether they *actually* knew or not. Even if a director sniffs fraud, and resigns the directorship, he or she will not be free from liability; the SEC says "the law will come down hard on directors who knew of pending fraud and did nothing."[4]

The accountant, hired by the company to certify its annual report but retaining mandatory independence of action, is the public's representative to insure that all pertinent facts about the company are disclosed. In 1974, the U.S. Court of Appeals in Chicago ruled that under certain circumstances auditors can be held liable to the investing public for not knowing what they should have known about a company. In the case at issue, a group of investors filed suit against Ernst & Ernst to recoup their losses from a fraudulent investment scheme, although they conceded that Ernst & Ernst had no knowledge of the fraud. The appeals court agreed with the investors that E&E should be held liable because a sufficiently detailed inquiry into the firm's affairs would have revealed the fraud. Seeking safeguards against such suits, accounting firms are taking such actions as the so-called "lawyers' letter," asking corporate legal counsels to describe any claims that might be brought against the company and evaluate their merits. This approach places the attorneys squarely on the horns of a legal dilemma, with the need for disclosure conflicting with the age-old prohibition against revealing client confidences.

lawyers' letter

Another area in which the SEC is pushing for disclosure is the corporation's impact on society. The SEC has traditionally been unwilling to seek nonfinancial data; but in 1975 a group of public interest law firms, led by the Natural Resources Defense Council, went to court to force the SEC to demand disclosure in the environmental and equal opportunity areas under the provisions of the 1969 Environmental Policy Act and the Securities Act of 1933. U.S. District Court Judge Charles Richey directed the SEC to reach an early decision on how it will respond. Prior to this decision the SEC had argued that "the securities laws were not intended nor expected to create a source of information for general public education," and in 1971 the Supreme Court held that the SEC could demand only that information wanted by "a realistic investor." The question posed by this recent decision is whether the SEC must take into account a new-style "ethical investor," who has corporate social responsibility as well as profit in mind.

A new force on the public interest horizon is Accountants for the Public Interest, a nonprofit organization that provides financial analysis to help consumer, environmental, and community action groups. It uses the volunteer service of accountants, some from major accounting firms (known as the "Big Eight"), to ferret out public issues such as utility rate hearings, airport expansion, low-cost medical service, and public acquisition of private facilities. API tries to demonstrate professional objectivity, not hesitating to turn down a public interest case when it thinks the plaintiffs are in the wrong. The main function of such an organization is to see that the pertinent facts, which often hinge on complex economic or financial issues, are made available for public scrutiny.

Public Partnership with Business

It is often said that large public corporations, such as U.S. Steel, Exxon, General Motors, etc., are approaching the status of public institutions. The term "public corporation" conveys only that members of the public own what is essentially a private enterprise; but the term "public institution" may mean that the corporation must serve public rather than private purposes. In Britain, this trend has resulted in nationalization of many important industries, with more to come. When the British government makes a decision to bail out an important company in financial trouble, as it did with Rolls Royce and British Leyland Motors, the most likely end result is either a strong minority government interest or outright control. The general consensus is that many of Britain's financial woes are due to her nationalized industry, and that government operation has not been as efficient as the former private operation.

public institution

In the U.S., events have not taken that turn, though it is not impossible that they could do so. An exception is the railroad industry, which is deemed to fall in the public utility category; the government's Amtrak Corporation was established to operate a passenger rail system that no private roads seemed able to continue. But the government has determined that it was in the public interest to effect many bailouts of private corporations, generally when the public had a major stake in the continuation of company operation. In 1973 Congress passed the Regional Rail Reorganization Act, Section 601 of which gives the Interstate Commerce Commission power to keep essential rail service going by requiring another railroad to take over an operation that is about to fail. The first railroad to utilize this provision was not the Penn Central, but the tiny Lehigh and New England Railway, which announced in January 1975 that it could no longer pay its bills; the ICC directed the Lehigh Valley Railway to take over a thirty mile section of the L&NE, serving primarily the cement industry. (Ironically, the Lehigh Valley was itself involved in bankruptcy proceedings, so the directive had to be approved by U.S. District Judge John P. Fullam, who is overseeing the LV reorganization as well as that of the Penn Central.) The Rail Reorganization Act provides for emergency loans to troubled railroads under certain conditions, but the L&NE did not quite fit this provision; all of its assets had been pledged by the Jersey Central Railroad to the government as collateral for a loan in default. Thus, in a sense, the government already owned the L&NE, though through no desire of the government. If the Penn Central finally goes under, it is this law that will probably keep essential segments running.

Amtrak

Regional Rail Reorganization Act

The Penn Central Railroad was probably the largest bankruptcy of an essential industry ever to hit the United States; as such, Congress has approved a series of grants and loans to keep it in operation. But the Penn Central is by no means the only freight-hauling railroad in deep financial difficulties, and Congress has bowed to the (apparently) inevitable by establishing the Consolidated Railroad Corporation (CONRAIL), an operating company largely federally financed, to acquire the Penn Central properties.

> Conrail

Lockheed Aircraft Corporation is a somewhat different case from the Penn Central since it performs no uniquely essential service, though it does represent an important defense and aerospace national asset, and moreover constitutes a major employer of people whose jobs would disappear if it went under. Lockheed was generally considered to be a strong and viable company that had seriously overextended itself in the process of jointly developing (with Rolls Royce of England) the L-1011 airbus. Consequently, in 1971 Congress agreed to aid Lockheed to the tune of guaranteeing up to $250 million of its bank debt. The rescue seems to have come off successfully, and it is probable that Lockheed (or a merger partner) ultimately will obtain a release by the banks of the government's guarantee.[5]

> North Star's parent company is as large as Lockheed. Under what circumstances would it be appropriate for the government to help it over a financial bind?

Seatrain Shipbuilding Corporation is another candidate for a federal bailout. The government was building two 225,000-ton tankers in its shipyard under a complex subsidy-guarantee program designed to support a U.S. flag tanker fleet. The government's quandary here is not only (1) whether it should invest further to complete the ships and salvage its investment, or write off the investment, but (2) whether it has a social interest in continuing a firm that has been very active in training and employing minorities in a depressed region.

Pan American Airlines has been in deep financial trouble and sought similar assistance from the federal government, but the aid was not forthcoming. It is not clear whether Congress and the administration see a fundamental difference between Lockheed and Pan Am (such a difference is far from obvious), or are wary of setting a precedent that appears to promise a bailout to any large corporation in trouble.

A broader question is whether the government will bail out the electric utilities. The cash pressures on utilities are severe, and are not likely to moderate. In recent years the combination of short money supplies and inflation in two digits has put power companies in a severe bind, to the point where many of them find it very difficult to raise the funds they need to keep up with electrical demand. When power companies tried to accelerate their depletion schedules to develop funds for expansion, regulatory agencies forced them to "flow through" the additional funds to rate reductions. Meanwhile, annual expenditure for new plants has grown alarmingly, nearly tripling from 1966 to 1974 ($7.4 billion to $21.5 billion), with the costs of nuclear plants leading the way. Now heavy new environmental expenditures for scrubbers and other equipment are coming on top of these inflated construction costs. While 60% of the funds for expansion came from internal sources in the early 1960s, by 1973 only 40% came from these sources—and the rest must be made up by issuing new stock or floating bonds. Rate relief is one answer, but increased rates already have slowed the growth of power consumption, and political opposition to more increases can be expected to intensify. Consolidated Edison already has asked the New York State

Power Authority to take over some of its nuclear plants, and other companies are proposing government-guaranteed or tax-exempt debt.

Hospitals may be the next major industry to form an involuntary partnership with government, as their own financial problems intensify. Of the 650 major voluntary hospitals, many are approaching bankruptcy. New York City's Columbia-Presbyterian Medical Center, largest voluntary hospital in the nation, started 1974 with $12 million in unrestricted endowment funds but ended it with nothing left of principal or interest. Other New York hospitals are in bankruptcy, or kept alive only by bank loans. Boston's University Hospital has exhausted all its unrestricted endowment and is running a $1 million deficit a year. Major urban hospitals are the main resource for treating the poor—and the poor cannot pay what it costs. The Vanderbilt Clinic at Columbia-Presbyterian spends $40 for each outpatient, charges $22, and tries to collect as much of the $22 as it can. The only answer, short of large-scale government aid, is closing or cutting back on the clinics—which will end hospital care for the poor. It is not politically probable that government will sit still and watch that take place.

On August 1, 1974, a mystery buyer started acquiring shares of Pacific Western Airlines, Canada's third-largest air carrier. By day's end the buyer held 79% of the outstanding shares, and was disclosed as the Province of Alberta, which spent $37 million to buy a private airline. The stated reason was to forestall a takeover by a Winnipeg transportation group which "threatens the continuation of PWA's capacity to expand and serve Alberta's growing needs." Certainly the stated situation was part of the reason for the purchase, but probably there was more to it. The purchase price was nothing much for a province whose oil royalties alone rose $1 billion in 1974. The province, anxious to reduce its dependence on oil revenues, and in a land-locked location far from population centers, doubtless hoped to capitalize on its potential as gateway to the Arctic North, with all the future activity that oil exploration there would bring. It is interesting that a conservative party, traditional representative of free enterprise, would make such a significant public investment.

Corporate Liberation

corporate lib

Not long ago, corporate personnel practices—hiring, firing, promotion, and training—were completely internal matters. Today, these issues arouse widespread public interest, with corporations required to justify everything they do to government agencies or private citizens. But faced with the Equal Employment Opportunity Act that requires them to hire more black and women managers, corporations are finding that there aren't enough to go around. Corporations are not reluctant to hire qualified women or blacks, but they do not want to hire people who are obviously unqualified simply to satisfy a government quota. Indeed, qualified applicants are in high demand, as starting salaries for women and minority professionals suggest.

Graduate-level business schools are trying to increase the supply of women managers; such top institutions as Harvard and Stanford are making all-out recruiting efforts to lure more women candidates to their programs. But some think that women need a special training approach.

Simmons College in Boston has designed a special graduate business program to prepare women for "male-dominated corporate organizations," taking into account their difference in outlook as to strategy, risk-taking, and achievement. And Pace University in New York City has a special program to prepare women liberal arts graduates for the business world.

With black MBAs, the competition is even more frantic. As an example, the University of Wisconsin conducted a program in 1974 in which executives from 90 top U.S. corporations spent three days looking over minority students who had not even entered business school yet, and thus wouldn't be on the job market for two more years. Most of the companies decided to help finance the students' schooling, in an effort to lock up their hiring in advance. Despite strenuous recruitment campaigns in the business schools, including financial and academic assistance, only 2% of their total enrollment is black. Blacks are beginning to enter management ranks in the large corporations, but many minority students are not enticed by the prospect of a corporate career.

Two university recruiting programs for bringing blacks and other minorities to the business schools are the Consortium for Graduate Study in Management (the universities of Southern California, Indiana, Wisconsin, Rochester, and North Carolina, and Washington University in St. Louis), and the Council for Opportunity in Graduate Management (Harvard, MIT, Wharton, Stanford, Columbia, Chicago, Carnegie-Mellon, Cornell, Berkeley, and Dartmouth). Business schools find that black students have been shortchanged in prior education and thus have weaker academic backgrounds than whites, though they generally follow the same curricula in business school. Two black organizations, the Association for the Integration of Management and the National Black MBA Association, sponsor seminars on problems and opportunities in management. For the black MBAs who make it, starting salaries are markedly above the overall graduating average.

The Equal Employment Opportunity Commission, after a transitional period during which the Department of Justice handled its court cases, got power to handle the cases itself in 1974. Since then it has moved aggressively on two fronts: a campaign to alter "broad systems of integration," and an ongoing policy of bringing plant-by-plant suits. With 240 civil rights lawyers, EEOC has a good deal of clout, though its power has been eroded by charges of internal mismanagement and financial irregularities.

EEOC

Selling Business

Chapter 4, "Leadership," discusses the alienation of young workers and their unwillingness to accept organizational patterns and goals without question as their fathers and mothers did. This alienation applies to blue-collar workers and managers alike. One reason for the lack of sympathy with business on the part of young collegians (who are the raw material for the managerial group in business) may be that they do not really know much about business. (Another reason, of course, could be that they know too much about it.)

Eugene Brown, personnel director of General Motors' Harrison

Radiator Division, knows more about the problem than he once did. In 1974 he spent a week living a student life in a coed dormitory at Bryn Mawr College for women. The visit was part of a program to acquaint college women and business executives with one another. Brown came to breakfast in his suit each morning, to find himself surrounded by bathrode-clad students discussing day-care centers, joint careers, dual appointments for husband-wife teams, and paternity leaves. He attended class faithfully, sometimes finding himself more or less *the* class as students grilled him on programs for hiring and upgrading women and minorities. Surprised to find that graduate social work students with strong opinions on assembly-line work had never seen an assembly line, he arranged for films of Lordstown's highly automated line. A colleague of Brown's in the program was "appalled by the abysmal ignorance of the business world even among girls whose fathers were businessmen."

Other companies are finding that apparently sophisticated students have little understanding of the environment of business: its rewards as well as its temptations, its opportunities to do good as well as commit fraud. When Senator George McGovern announced during his presidential campaign that 40% of U.S. corporations paid no income taxes, a group of graduate students in a professional school found little to question about the statement, and were uniformly surprised to learn that the typical business pays out about half its gross profits in taxes: the nonpaying 40% were generally those making no profits. Students who naively assume that all business people are somehow more selfish and less dedicated than people in the public service generally are surprised when thrown in close contact with business professionals to learn that their competence and dedication compares favorably with that of their counterparts in government.

In the 1960s, more than half the population thought of business with moderate or high approval, according to polls. In the 1970s, a majority of 60% held business in low esteem, according to Opinion Research Corporation polls. "Businessmen have been treated like folk heroes," in the words of Ralph E. Ablon, chief executive officer of Ogden Corporation. "The public thought of them as Horatio Alger characters when they didn't deserve it. Now people are finding out that businessmen have somewhat claylike feet, and are basically in the business of looking out for themselves." In a time when all institutions are under some attack, business looks too much like the power structure to be completely popular. The argument that a large corporation meets its payroll, thus helping thousands of people to earn a living, and pays dividends to thousands more stockholders, no longer has the old magic in days of product recalls, illegal campaign contributions, antitrust convictions, and similar highly publicized problems.

Some companies have convened outside panelists to evaluate corporate behavior. Strawbridge & Clothier, a nine-unit department store chain, has consumer advisory boards made up of shoppers, who criticize S&C's actions and make constructive suggestions such as child-care centers for shopping mothers and courses for community residents. Monfort of Colorado, Inc., a meat packing firm, has a Committee for the '70s to bring in outside views on its corporate performance as citizen; one result of the exercise was Monfort's decision to move a malodorous cattle feedlot operation away from Greeley, Colorado, at a cost of $5 million. Vice-President John W. Johnson of LTV Corporation in Dallas says that "enormous influence is wielded by professors, and I think business has dropped the ball for a long time in not maintaining close relationships with campuses."

Some businessmen take an optimistic view of the trends. Colorado's Monfort says "A person with a social conscience can make a greater contribution by being in business today than in the academic field or in labor. The challenge is probably as great as being in government itself." That message may be getting across to the new graduates, but it's not happening overnight. Probably a more typical viewpoint is that expressed by John H. Filer, chief executive of Aetna Life and Casualty Company, "You must operate your business with public acceptability, or sooner or later you aren't going to have any business to operate."

social consciousness

Social Responsibility of Management

How much can business institutions do to solve the problems of society? Certainly not everything that needs to be done. Business is better at some tasks than at others, and it makes good economic sense for institutions to do what they are best at. The most enduring contributions of business serve the interests of both business and society. For instance, it makes good economic sense for a business to enlarge its markets by selling without discrimination and by seeing that human potential is not wasted. Many problems of the disadvantaged can be solved without bypassing the profit motive. When business offers jobs in a spirit of charity, nobody benefits. How much better to have the individuals know they are being hired because business needs them.

social responsibility of business

Social Activities of Business

In 1974 the Clearinghouse on Corporate Social Responsibility analyzed the performance of 179 life and health insurance companies, representing some 86% of the total assets of all Clearinghouse companies, in six areas of corporate social responsibility. Figure 16-2 shows the level of investment in various sectors deemed socially desirable. It is not customary to think of insurance companies as having a social impact by means of their investments, but clearly this can be the case; it makes a difference whether funds are invested in desirable or undesirable products. The size of each piece of pie represents the fraction of total investments likely to benefit society.

Clearinghouse on Corporate Social Responsibility

In 1969, Henry Ford II, chairman of the Ford Motor Company, delivered a talk at Yale University on "Social Conscience and Profit." His theme, the question of how much business could and should do to solve the problems of society, was presented as follows:

> Like governments and universities and other institutions, business is much better at some tasks than at others. Business is especially good at all the tasks that are necessary for economic growth and development. To the extent that the problems of society can be solved by providing more and better jobs,

higher incomes for more people, and a larger supply of goods and services, the problems can best be solved by relying heavily on business.

On the other hand, business has no special competence in solving many other urgent problems. Businessmen, for example, know little about the problems involved in improving the education of ghetto children, the quality of ghetto family life, the relations between police and minority citizens, or the administration of justice. Solutions to problems such as these will be more effective if they are left to political, educational, and social agencies. In short, our society will be served best if each of its specialized institutions concentrates on doing what it does best, and refuses either to waste its time or to meddle in tasks it is poorly qualified to handle.

Ford went on to say that it is in the self-interest of businesses to enlarge their markets by selling without discrimination and by helping disadvantaged people to realize their full economic potential. Welfare, crime, disease, and waste of human talents are as costly to businesses as to other institutions. "The profit motive provides abundant incentive for businessmen to help solve the economic problems of the disadvantaged." With regard to hiring practices, Ford noted that minimum educational standards for jobs always discriminate against people (primarily minorities) who could meet the job standards but cannot meet the education standards. The answer is to develop innovative personnel practices that let applicants show what they can really do.

The most important changes ahead involve the relationship between business and society. As Figure 16-2 suggests, the terms of the contract are changing. Heretofore industry has served one narrow segment of society's needs, but now it is asked to accept an obligation to segments of society with which it has no formal contract to buy goods or sell products. It is being asked to contribute more to the quality of life than manufactured goods or services. The question here must always be, how much can business neglect one responsibility to serve the other?

Ford says it makes economic sense for business to bring more of the labor force into the ranks of the employed, and in the broad view that is true. But getting them there often entails a huge effort, which may not pay off in the short run for a given company. The hard-core unemployed are not used to coming to work on time or regularly, because nothing in their past experience has made these actions important. When they are given special treatment the other workers object; but if they are not, they will not last. By the same token, if they are paid for work they don't do, they will feel contempt for the company, which is a bad basis for a continuing relationship. They find it hard to believe that they really can find jobs, so often they refuse to respond to job announcements—not because they don't want regular work and the good things of life, and not because they won't work for them, but simply because they see the ads as more empty promises. Classroom training must be geared to the special needs of the hard-core, with the social-psychological side an important part. The teacher must balance respect for minority values and perspectives, and an appreciation for minority problems, with development of a stake in the economic system represented by business.

Harland Padfield, in a study of a National Alliance of Business training program in San Diego, funded in part through the Manpower Division of the Labor Department, made a systematic analysis of hard-core trainees to determine the reasons for their work interruptions and other problems. The following is a summary of his findings:[6]

Blacks predominate in the group. They have no effective education, tend to be in poor health and on welfare, and have often had serious contact with the law—an average of five arrests each. They are absent about one day in 17 to 20, compared with one day in 100 for the average employee. Reasons for their absences include: chronic and continuing trouble with public agencies (police arrests, court appearances for family violence, suspicion of illegal activities, traffic violations, child custody and support). Interruptions stem from self-indulgence (alcohol, narcotics, venereal disease, out on the town). Illnesses are half simple ailments, half those brought on by family strife. They do have middle-class aspirations, would like a meaningful steady occupation, and have middle-class attitudes in terms of family structure. Their material aspirations are typically middle-class, with first priority to furniture, appliances, and household improvements, second to clothes, and third to cars and accessories. But their present lives are based on a penny economy, and they are subject to the whims of an erratic credit structure. Significantly,

Figure 16-2. Corporate Investments for Socially Desirable Purposes

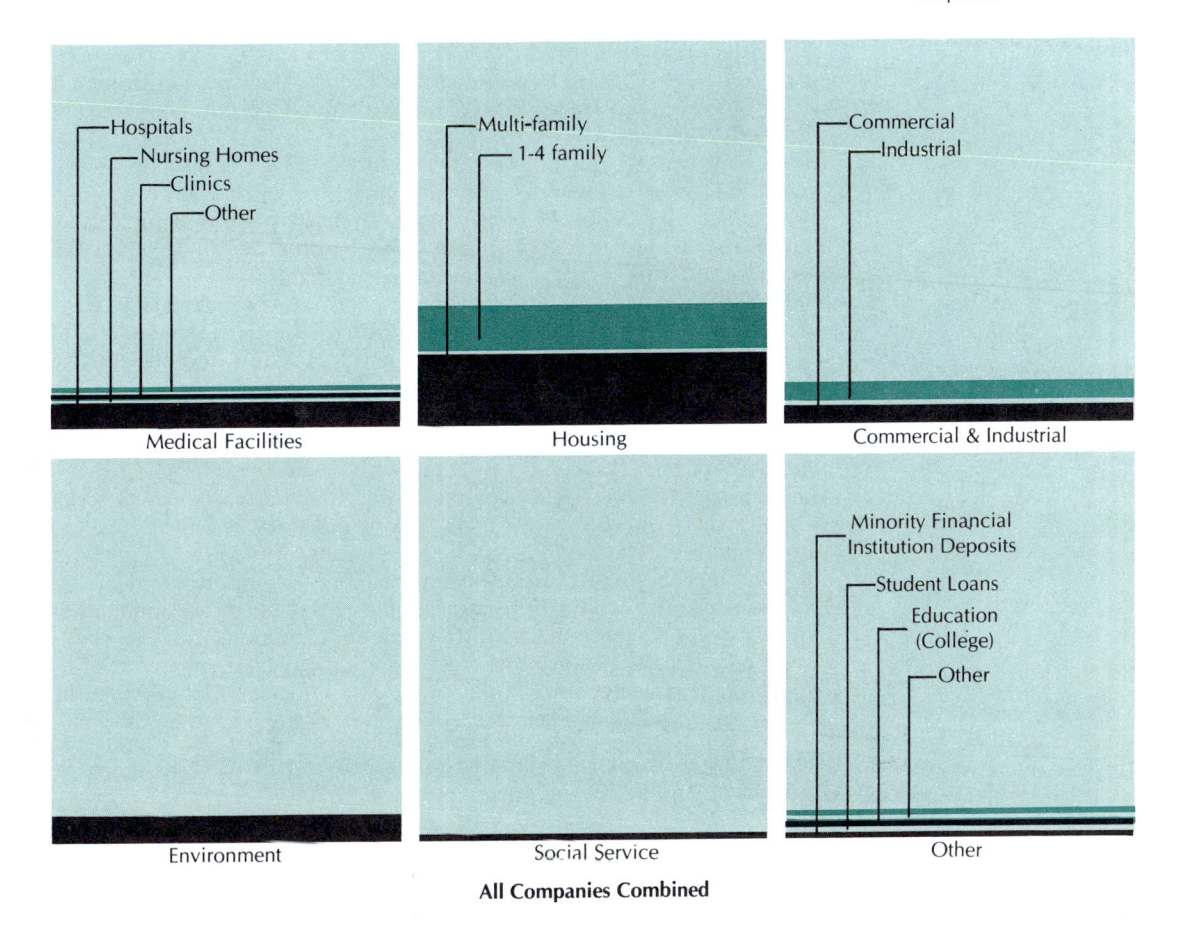

Medical Facilities — Hospitals, Nursing Homes, Clinics, Other

Housing — Multi-family, 1-4 family

Commercial & Industrial — Commercial, Industrial

Environment

Social Service

Other — Minority Financial Institution Deposits, Student Loans, Education (College), Other

All Companies Combined

they recognize other hard-core trainees as being irrational when they make decisions which threaten their job performance.

The Smaller Company

Conference Board

A report by the Conference Board, an independent nonprofit business research organization, summarizes the views of a panel of senior executives from typical U.S. and Canadian firms employing between 500 and 2,000, on the peculiar problems of smaller companies in the area of social responsibility. Some of the comments are summarized below, under topic headings:[7]

- *Debt to community:* In rural communities...our practice has been to make these plants a physical asset to the community and to have our staff very active in community affairs....In the metropolitan area...our participation is more indirect. Here our company supports community organizations [by] cash contributions, but with minimum inputs of time by its personnel.
- *Preservation of enterprise system:* A decaying society will result in a less viable business environment. Therefore a company must assume a position of good and active citizenship, not only in what it does...but also in providing some leadership in the direction society is moving. This will insure that its interests are at least considered....

  It has become increasingly clear that corporate officers and directors should be good citizens and that their corporations have civic responsibilities. Unless corporations and their officers take a more enlightened view as to their participation in community affairs, corporations will not survive for long....

  If corporations do not do what needs to be done [in terms of social problems], using stockholders' or consumers' money, it will be done by government with taxpayers' money. There are many reasons to think that a centralized political body often will get less value per dollar than the decentralized and results oriented business system.
- *Society's prior rights:* Corporate performance may soon be measured in areas of social responsibility, and particularly with reference to the continuing education and development of its people, product quality, and the effective solution of problems that industry itself creates [as pollution].
- *Limiting of social responsibility:* A company should accept only those responsibilities which are consistent with its role as a good citizen. It cannot unduly impair its competitive position.
- *Social responsibility and profit-making:* I do not think you can separate social responsibility from the performance of any company as a profit-making organization....A well-run company must be concerned with [it] in order to continue to succeed in its neighborhood, to be respected by its employees, and to conform to legislation....All of these are interwoven with its desire to continue as a profit-making institution....

  Any *good* company performs its social responsibility by the mere act of its existence; such a company not only provides employment but provides the public...with goods and services.

The conferees listed the following, in priority order, as valid areas for corporate involvement or support:

- Consumer concerns (product reliability, safety, etc.)
- Pollution abatement
- Education

- Charitable institutions
- Community activities
- Employment of disadvantaged
- Urban renewal and development

Social Audits

A social audit compares a business' results in the social responsibility area against the objectives set by the board of directors or management. Factors considered in preparing a social audit include the following:

social audits

1. The audit may be the responsibility of the board of directors, and not something that can be handed off to a committee or a consultant. It is too important to be treated lightly.
2. Without systematic checking of progress against goals, there will be no continuing program, particularly with something so foreign to normal corporation activities as social effort.
3. An auditing system is useful for educating middle managers in the goals and techniques of social action.
4. If it is undertaken by the company rather than an objective outside group, it may not be effective. ("Self-audits never are.")

Professor George Steiner of the Graduate School of Management of the University of California at Los Angeles defines the purpose of a social audit as identification of the social responsibilities a company hopes to fulfill and assessment of its progress in that regard. The audit can also determine whether the company is vulnerable to criticism by the public and impart a social awareness into managerial viewpoints. Steiner notes that an audit by outsiders would insure objectivity, but the groups must include people both socially and technically conversant in the particular business field; a valid in-house team might be a board committee, a group composed of industry experts, or a consultant brought inside. In any event, Steiner feels the audit should probably be publicized; the risk of blowing a small problem out of proportion is outweighed by the need to maintain credibility with the public. In conclusion, Steiner comments:

> There will be risks and opportunities both for corporations and society in attempts to measure the social performance of business—the corporation may be unjustly criticized either for omission or for commission. ...Society may be less well served if excessive expectations lead companies to do too much. On the other hand, there are opportunities for individual companies and society if acceptable criteria for guiding and limiting business and social performance can be hammered out.
>
> It may just be that by the social audit we may develop acceptable reforms which will make business stronger and more able to serve the social purpose.[8]

J. Irwin Miller, chairman of Cummins Engine Company, discussed the public responsibilities of business in a recent speech:

> The business community has very nearly as much influence as young people think it has. If business voluntarily, in the conduct of its affairs, accords the long-term public interest a priority equal to that assigned shareholders and demanded by organized workers, then the influence of such an example will be compelling.
>
> If businessmen go to their city councils, to their state houses, to Washington, and if they lobby there as hard and effectively for equal and adequate

education, improvement of the environment, solutions to transportation, health care, civil rights, and all the rest, and support the money and the changes required to make these possible—the country will turn around. Our example can be decisive.[9]

The Large Corporation

So what is a corporation's job? Charles Stabler's report on the activities of a number of major corporations in this area, cited below, at least suggests *their* perception of their task. The large corporation, with its thousands and sometimes millions of stockholders, may indeed be close to an arm of government. More and more of the major firms are acting as if they were:

- Standard Oil of Indiana recently contracted for an 80-story office building, with provisions requiring the contractor's work force to be 34% black, and a cancellation clause if the condition was not met.
- Sears, CNA Financial, and Standard Oil combined in a program in Chicago aimed at training 15,000 high-school dropouts who were considered hard-core unemployed. While the program was under way, 45,000 others dropped out, so the consortium is helping the community improve the schools to make dropouts less likely in the first place.
- Boise-Cascade teamed up with a black-owned construction firm to form Boise-Burnett Corporation, with Boise furnishing the financing but not the management. The ultimate failure of this project involved a $40 million loss, amounting to 72¢ a share.
- Grolier, Inc. (publisher of encyclopedias, Book of Knowledge) calls each customer back before the order is shipped to see if there are any problems with sales techniques or promises, and urges collect calls for complaints.
- General Electric plant managers are required to report regularly their percentage of nonwhite employees compared to the percentage in the area, and must submit five-year plans for increasing minority employment.
- Chase Manhattan Bank requires its young executives to make special efforts to counsel minority-owned businesses and community groups on financial matters.
- Atlantic Richfield instructs its managers to hire nonwhite job applicants ahead of equally qualified whites, and monitors a report showing the minority balance in all parts of the company.
- General Motors has appointed some of its directors to a public responsibility committee, and added a black activist to the board.
- CPC International (Skippy peanut butter, Karo syrup, Mazola margarine) named an outside group headed by Bruce Palmer, head of the Better Business Bureaus, as a committee on corporate responsibility to appraise the company's performance.[10]

The big corporations are appointing directors of corporate public affairs, though in many cases they are not in touch with top management. Some have installed toll-free telephone lines so that customers may call headquarters with complaints. They are providing far more detailed specifications on their products, and devoting substantially increased attention to product safety. Some corporations are approaching social goals with the same powerful tools of modern management they use for their profit-making work, and are fitting social responsibilities into their schedules of rewards and punishments.

The president of Quaker Oats, in a recent editorial, had this to say about his company's social posture:

> We expect to make a positive social contribution, as well as an economic contribution, wherever we go. Specifically, in the area of race relations we expect the communities we locate new facilities in to offer equal opportunities comparable to those we offer in our own employment. Thus, prior to our decision to locate a major food plant in Danville [Illinois]...we advised the city fathers that passage of an open-housing ordinance would impress us as an indication of the city's intent for social progress. The ordinance passed, and two days later we approved location of a new plant in Danville.[11]

The Committee for Economic Development, a nonprofit and nonpartisan group of 200 senior executives and academics, publishes a national policy statement on the social responsibilities of corporations and lists specific business activities that conform to this policy.[12]

Figure 16-3 sets forth graphically the three major areas of corporate commitment. In circle 1, the corporation sticks to its knitting; in 2, it operates with awareness of the social environment; in 3, it reaches out and exercises wider responsibilities of corporate citizenship. In recent years, more and more corporations have expanded their horizons to the outer circle.

Committee for Economic Development

What sort of public service would it be appropriate for a small firm like North Star to engage in, with special reference to Eldorado?

The Environment and the Consumer

For years, the promotional slogan "Keep Colorado Growing" was advanced by business executives, politicians, and private citizens in the nation's eighth-largest state, and one of its most beautiful. In recent years, this sentiment has been all but replaced by the antigrowth slogan, "Don't Californicate Colorado." Colorado's population is smaller than that of metropolitan Washington, D.C., and it has millions of acres of open plains and rugged mountains. The federal government owns more than a third of its land. So why should it worry?

Worry it does, as do Oregon, Wyoming, and Montana, and just about every state with enough open space to support substantial population increases. Its problems are few thus far, but Colorado can see them coming and is determined to avoid them. The problem is how to maintain economic growth without adding more people.

The controversy on land use in Colorado, with ranchers, farmers, and business executives opposed to statewide regulation that could stifle their prosperity, and city dwellers who head for the mountains to fish, ski, and play vehemently in favor of it, is taking place nationwide. Hawaii was first with a statewide land-use bill in 1961; since then Vermont, Maine, Florida, California, New Jersey, Delaware, and New York have started to climb on the bandwagon. Democratic Representative Richard Lamm of Denver was one of the major opponents of the 1976 Winter Olympics financing, which he said would have created an "environmental Vietnam"; the financing was defeated, and "Ski Country, U.S.A." did not host the

Figure 16-3.
Areas of Corporate
Social Commitment

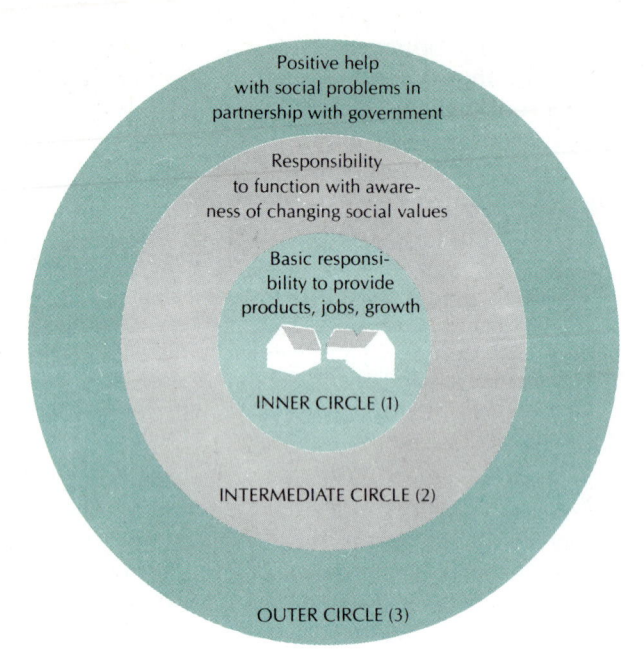

Positive help with social problems in partnership with government

Responsibility to function with awareness of changing social values

Basic responsibility to provide products, jobs, growth

INNER CIRCLE (1)

INTERMEDIATE CIRCLE (2)

OUTER CIRCLE (3)

Olympics. President Rex Jennings of Denver's Chamber of Commerce is in the other camp; he wants more jobs, and believes that "only when we are economically secure can we worry about the quality of life," claiming that stopping Denver's growth now would be irresponsible.

The industrialized East has environmental problems on a somewhat different scale. In Alloy, West Virginia, the Union Carbide plant was dubbed "the world's smokiest factory," emitting more health-endangering particles a year than the total for New York City. By installing the best available control technology, Union Carbide cut particulate emissions from 91,000 tons a year to 1,500—below the state compliance limits. The controls—precipitators to attract the fly ash and a combination of cooling towers and "vacuum cleaner" bags to catch the metallic emissions—cost $35 million and take as much land as the production facilities themselves, but they have done the job. The $3 million annual operating expense has raised Union Carbide's costs 15% and made it tougher to compete, but thus far Carbide has not lost any customers because of its higher prices. And in time its competitors will have to install similar facilities, which will equalize the cost structure.

scrubber systems

The Environmental Protection Agency has been pushing electric utilities to install scrubber systems to catch their sulfur dioxide emissions, and many hard battles have been waged by utilities who object both to the increased costs (perhaps $50 million additional for a new plant, and some 15% increase in operating costs) and to the problems with the relatively untested technology. Louisville Gas and Electric Company, first utility in the nation to develop a wet scrubber that appears to meet the tough EPA standards, illustrates the quandary represented by the scrubber situation. Having tested it in a small prototype installation near Louisville, and found it apparently successful, LG&E asked the Kentucky Public Service Commission for permission to spend $108 million on all nine of its coal-fired generating plants—which would mean raising rates 20%. This request set off a battle, with LG&E and EPA on one side and the Federal Power Commission and much of the utility industry on the other. Public Service Commission Chairman William A. Logan complained about "the tremendous expenditure in nonrevenue-producing plant."

Many companies in both the utility and steel industries face a similar dilemma with regard to the fate of obsolete plants. Many U.S. steel mills are nineteenth-century leftovers that are kept operating because of tight steel capacity and shortage of capital expansion funds. But these old mills are both the worst polluters and the most expensive to clean up. In the winter of 1973-74, three steel companies threatened to cut production drastically at several old mills in Youngstown, Ohio, rather than spend $150 million on pollution control equipment to meet the state's stringent water quality standards. Negotiations ended in a compromise, with the companies spending substantially less but still more than prudent management would dictate in the absence of environmental requirements. In Pennsylvania, Bethlehem Steel Corporation is accelerating the planned phase-out of its Johnstown works, because of air and water rules that would have cost an estimated $100 million. An EPA consultant has estimated that 11 old steel mills, employing 33,000 workers, might have to close if EPA's water pollution guitechnology" were applied. Proposed legislation would exempt plants with limited life from many of the environmental regulations, but environmental officials oppose such exemptions. Predictably, union officials tend to favor them; as Andrew Koban, a union leader in Johnstown, puts it, "I don't want to be the healthiest guy on the relief rolls."[13]

A worrisome development for business executives is a judicial trend toward having companies that lose environmental suits pay the winners' legal costs. In a 1970 case (discussed in chapter 14), three environmental groups sued to prevent Alyeska from building the North Slope-Valdez link of the trans-Alaska pipeline; Congress amended the law during litigation and in a sense vindicated the conservationist policy. When they asked that Alyeska pay half of their attorneys' fees, the U.S. Court of Appeals in Richmond finally, in 1973, ruled in their favor. Although many judges have ruled on the other side in such cases, it is an important precedent. Business executives are alarmed at such actions as the Chemical Bank assessment of $20,000 for plaintiff expenses, cited in chapter 15. Richard Godown, general counsel of the National Association of Manufacturers, says that such awards "would have an extremely punitive effect against private nongovernmental defendants, including industrial and business defendants."[14] The real worry is the probability that such awards will spur additional suits, as lawyers are able to take on cases that appear to have merit but where the clients have no money.

In the fall of 1974 a Pennsylvania couple stayed at a Holiday Inn in Philadelphia for a weekend that amounted to 48 hours of confusion because of a number of snafus with equipment, linen, and service. The angry letter they fired off to corporate headquarters in Memphis got an immediate response, which led shortly thereafter to an apology from the Philadelphia manager and an offer of two nights' free lodging. Holiday Inn, while not ready to give free rooms to every complainer, now has a consumer affairs setup that will listen to complaints—and act on them.

consumer affairs departments

Most corporations are making similar moves, not so much from a feeling of brotherly love as from recognition that a recession period is a good time to listen to consumer gripes. While consumer affairs people add another element of overhead cost, marketing managers are finding that they serve as a valuable listening post and data collector for marketing intelligence. In some companies the consumer affairs post is right up there in the executive corridor. Dianne McKaig, head of Coca Cola's consumer affairs outfit, reports directly to the president—and sports the title of vice-president herself. (She recently changed the Tab ad to read "less than one calorie per 1-oz serving," instead of the complicated "1/16 of a calorie per oz.") General Motors, who has been in this business since 1937, has 475 employees in its Owner Relations Department.

Carol Foreman, executive director of the Consumer Federation of America, charges that consumer affairs departments "are owned by the other side," and that she has never met a consumer affairs functionary "who gives me confidence that they can do anything." Many consumer advocates would agree. But Mona Doyle, consumer affairs director for Pantry Pride, thinks the company consumerist should seek to balance the demand of advocates and the "actual concerns" of the day-to-day customer. She has set up seven regional consumer boards of shoppers, and takes action on such suggestions as placing nutritional labels on the products.

Companies are now routinely sending their consumer affairs reports to marketing and quality control, and occasionally they find that the consumer complaint is the first indication that something actually has gone awry with the process engineering—as in the case of Scott Tissue, where investigation of letters complaining about smelly tissues disclosed

The average consumer has become far more aware of product value, safety, and contents.

an inadvertently opened valve in the plant which was letting the foreign substance in.

The average consumer has become far more aware of value, safety, content of products, and questionable sales practices. Unquestionably the consumer advocates stimulated this awareness; but it is there now, and the companies have no choice but to respond. Today, indeed, some observers feel that the companies are moving into the forefront of the consumer movement, and that corporate consumerism is a routine part of the scene.

Should North Star have a consumer advisor for its relations with Eldorado? Explain.

Invasion of Privacy

In the fall of 1974, 50 government and private agencies formed the National Commission on Confidentiality of Health Records. They were drawing a bead on practices such as those of the Medical Information Bureau of Greenwich, Connecticut, which files information about insurance applicants from some 700 health and life insurance companies and provides it to any of the 700 companies at 20¢ an inquiry. The Connecticut Civil Liberties Union wants the state insurance commissioner to order the past records destroyed, as private communications between applicant and insurance company.

invasion of privacy

Civil Liberties Union

The 1971 Fair Credit Reporting Act guarantees the credit seeker some protection from anonymous reports about credit worthiness and general character, which may lead to denial of credit to people who have never seen the charges against them or had a chance to refute them. Erroneous credit reports can be grounds for libel actions. An editor in St. Louis won $40,000 damages when he was refused auto insurance because of a report saying he used drugs and was subject to irrational behavior; the "information" was the flimsiest of neighborhood gossip for which the investigator was paid $1.45.[15] The Fair Credit Reporting Act is being used to charge the Retail Credit Company of Atlanta, a major collector of personal data, with violations of the act related to collection of retail credit material. Under present laws, people have the right to know what adverse information has been collected about them and to answer any charges they consider biased or misleading. Thus, in 1975 the Federal Trade Commission ordered Beneficial Corporation, a consumer finance company which also prepares tax returns, to cease using confidential tax information to determine the credit worthiness of consumer loan customers unless it gets written permission in advance.[16]

Fair Credit Reporting Act

Business and Ethics

There is always a case or two in the papers about some business fraud, and occasionally the cases assume vast proportions involving complex swindles that go down in history. But it is a relatively new phenomenon to have business in general connote questionable ethics. Probably the two major sources of such suspicions are the recent news media exposure of fairly widespread illegal corporate campaign contributions and the dubious overseas behavior of the multinational corporations. The troubling element in the recent situation is that the actions hitting the newspapers were taken or authorized (or at least not prohibited) by respected senior executives of blue-chip companies.

Those Multinational Corporations

In August 1975, the Lockheed Aircraft Corporation told the Securities and Exchange Commission that it would resist their efforts to keep it from paying bribes to promote foreign sales. Conceding that it had paid at least $22 million since 1970 to foreign officials and political organizations to solidify overseas sales contracts, while failing to disclose the payments to investors, it asserted that any bar to such payments would mean losing weapons and aircraft contracts to less scrupulous competitors. Such payments, Lockheed Board Chairman Haughton told the commission, "are consistent with practices engaged in by numerous other companies abroad, including many of its competitors, and are in keeping with business practices in many foreign countries." In addition, "future refusal or inability of Lockheed to conform to local competitive business practices could seriously prejudice the company's ability to compete effectively in certain foreign markets." And, he reasoned, disclosure of the overseas recipients of past payments "could have a serious adverse impact on several hundred million dollars of the company's present backlog," and "result in a material adverse impact with respect to the company's future operations" just when it is recovering from a perilous financial condition.

The Lockheed situation differs in one significant respect from a similar development earlier in 1975 involving the Northrop Corporation. The SEC charged Northrop with failing to keep proper accounts on some $30 million in payments to consultants and others, and it was disclosed that $450,000 was to be used to bribe two Saudi Arabian generals. Northrop consented to a court order barring further securities law violations, and apologized to the Senate Foreign Relations Subcommittee on Multinational Corporations for authorizing Adhan Khashoggi, its sales agent, to make the payments.[17] During the hearings, Northrop's board chairman said the company should have rejected bribery approaches "whatever the consequences," and added, "We are taking all necessary steps to assure that no payments for such purposes will occur in the future." Mr. Khashoggi also represents Lockheed, Raytheon, and Chrysler, getting commissions of 8% from Lockheed, 5% (and 15% on parts) from Raytheon, and 15% from Chrysler.

This dilemma is far from simple. Does a U.S. company operating overseas play by the rules of the parent company or the host country? Judged by the rules of the host country, neither Lockheed nor Northrop committed any ethical sin by conforming to foreign local custom (though they may have done so by failing to report the payments to stockholders and others). Indeed, there have been indications that Lockheed's ticklish position is winning some sympathy in the government, including the Senate multinationals committee. Senator Stuart Symington of Missouri, during the Northrop hearings, suggested that legislation to prohibit payoffs overseas could mean that American firms might be "automatically giving up an opportunity to get in this business." (He added that he wasn't judging the ethics of payoffs, but wanted to explore thhe consequences of prohibiting them "from a strictly theoretical standpoint.")[18]

On the other side of the coin, right is right, and payoffs are not proper in any country. Despite what the wise money says, it is by no means certain that payoffs in the Middle East do "conform to local custom." Certainly

multinational corporations

some companies do not pay them, and manage to survive. Companies such as Xerox and I.B.M. take the position that if they pay off a foreign political party secretly, the next party coming to power probably will find out and demand even more—all of which can be avoided by refusing in the first place. Boeing states that its products stand on their merits overseas, and that it refuses to resort to payoffs.

Gulf Oil Corporation made payoffs and gifts of over $450,000 in Bolivia; the new regime, which expropriated Gulf's holdings on coming to power, found out about the bribe and is threatening in retaliation to withhold the projected $57 million due Gulf in indemnification for the holdings. In Korea, Gulf secretly contributed $1 million to President Park Chung Hee's political party in 1966; in 1970 the party fund-raiser demanded $10 million. Aware of Gulf's $350 million investments in Korea, Chairman Bob R. Dorsey did not reject the offer, but talked the fund-raiser down to $3 million.

Why did Gulf do it? The South Korean government got U.S. Association for International Development (AID) funds to help it match Gulf's investments in oil and petrochemical partnerships, which should have given the U.S. government some clout in helping Gulf resist such demands; moreover, the U.S. had insured Gulf for $62 million against any loss from expropriation. Why didn't Dorsey report the demand to the U.S. ambassador? "It never occurred to me," he said. Senators who were cross-examining Dorsey pointed out that the U.S. has 42,000 troops in Korea helping to keep the country alive, and asked why U.S. pressure could not have been exerted with that leverage. Dorsey simply said, "Maybe I was basically ashamed of what was going on."[19]

In 1970, Del Monte Corporation began negotiations with United Brands to purchase some Guatemalan banana plantations that United Brands was forced to sell to comply with terms of an antitrust consent decree. It made a deal with United Brands, but in November 1971 Guatamala rejected the deal, saying it wanted the property bought by local interests. In May 1972 a Guatemalan representing himself as a businessman with good connections came to Miami and proposed that he represent Del Monte. The company explained, in a prepared statement, that "Del Monte recognized after over a year of unsuccessful effort that it needed the advice of an experienced Guatemalan businessman. He was extremely valuable in advising us on local customs and on what concessions we should offer the country in order to become a welcome guest."[20]

Indeed he was. At his suggestion, President Gordon of Del Monte wrote President Arana of Guatemala on Thursday, May 25, asking the government to reconsider, and a reply dated Monday, May 29, from a presidential aide said there was no "legal impediment" to the sale. After Del Monte paid the "consultant" nearly $500,000, events moved so swiftly that by summer the government reversed its former stand and approved the sale.

Del Monte, which charged the fee to administrative and general expense on the books of Panamanian shipping subsidiaries, says the fee was entirely legal and proper; the consultant assured Del Monte that none of the money went to any government officials, and shouldn't be compared to foreign bribes or illegal political contributions as paid by Northrop or Gulf.

International Telephone and Telegraph was very much in the news around Watergate time, with revelations of operations of a mysterious Dita Beard and news of shredding corporate documents. When I.T.T. decided that leftist presidential candidate Salvador Allende threatened its $160 million investment in Chile's national telephone company, it campaigned to get Washington to support his opponent. After Allende won, I.T.T. urged economic sanctions, and privately offered the CIA up to $1 million to finance a campaign against Allende—which the CIA did not accept. The corporation tried to get other U.S. multinationals to support it, but with little success. The Allende government did move to nationalize Chiltelco, and started negotiating with I.T.T. for compensation—until Jack Anderson broke the story about I.T.T.'s activities. The Senate said that I.T.T. "clearly overstepped the line of acceptable corporate behavior," though it broke no laws.[21]

The SEC pushes hard where securities law has been violated, but if "appropriate and complete disclosure has been made, the commission's role is, and should be, at an end," according to Chairman Ray E. Garrett.[22] Commissioner Alphonse Adam Sommer worries that complete disclosure might impair the competitive stance of U.S. firms; he would like to see disclosure of the payoffs and bribes but without identifying the country. In either case, there is no penalty for the payoff itself, since U.S. corporations are not required by any U.S. statute to refrain from violating laws of foreign nations.

Campaign Contributions

corporate campaign contributions

In the wake of Watergate, a number of U.S. corporations were found to have secret funds from which they made campaign contributions in violation of U.S. election law—and without disclosing the payments in their annual reports. George Spater, chairman of American Airlines, was the first executive to admit such illegal contributions. At the time, trying to win a merger with Western Air Lines, he was invited by Herbert Kalmbach to lunch; Kalmbach was counsel for President Nixon, but also for rival United Airlines. (He contributed $75,000 to CREEP, but the merger was never approved, and soon after Spater was fired.)[23] Braniff contributed an illegal $40,000 in 1972. It admitted before the Civil Aeronautics Board in 1975 that between 1969 and 1973 it issued unaccounted-for tickets for more than $300,000 which was used as a secret fund.[24] 3M Company was accused of hiding illegal transactions totaling over $600,000 in order to create a secret fund.[25] Ashland Oil Inc., after repeated prodding by the SEC, in August 1975 released the names of political candidates to whom it made largely illegal contributions totaling over $700,000 between 1967 and 1973. (It is illegal for companies to make contributions to candidates for federal office.) Ashland's most famous contribution was $100,000 to President Nixon's campaigns in 1968 and 1972, but the corporation contributed to a wide assortment of congressional and other candidates of both parties during the period. Cash was brought to a safe at headquarters in Ashland, Kentucky, from various foreign operations. Ashland also admitted to $342,000 in foreign payments, including $150,000 to Albert Bernard Bongo, president of Gabon, $52,000 to two of his government ministers, and $110,000 to prominent individuals in Libya.[26]

Price-Fixing

In December 1974, President Gerald Ford signed a tough new antitrust law, raising price-fixing from a misdemeanor to a felony, with a maximum jail sentence of up to three years and the maximum fine raised from $50,000 to $1 million. Companies that recently have pleaded "no contest," thus refusing to fight federal price-fixing charges without actually admitting guilt, are American Cyanamid, ARA Services, Armco Steel, Ciba-Geigy, Combustion Engineering, Diamond International, DuPont, Genesco, H. K. Porter, International Paper, Kaiser Gypsum, PepsiCo, Pet, and Sunshine Biscuits. A&P was hit with $32.7 million in damages for allegedly conspiring with other large chains to rig prices paid for wholesale beef. DuPont and eight other large dyemakers have paid $360,000 in fines for allegedly rigging prices, and face private damage claims similar to A&P.

But price-fixing is as old as merchandising and is extremely difficult to stop, particularly in a recession period. Price-fixers balance the risk of discovery against the assured profits. Some price-fixers don't think they are breaking the law, since they give competitors subtle hints rather than arranging overt conspiracies. Marketing director Lyle R. Johnson of Quaker Oats (which has never been indicted for price-fixing) says that "the overwhelming majority of businessmen discuss pricing with their competitors." David D. Dayton, vice-president of indicted ARA Services, says, "I don't see an end to price-fixing. People are people." And the indicted owner of a paper-label company says, "It's always been done in this business, and there's no real way of ever being able to stop it. It may slow down for a few years, but it will always be there."

price-fixing

Price-fixing is extremely difficult to stop.

A price-fixing law is something of a novelty worldwide. U.S. District Judge Charles B. Renfrew calls it "one of the anomalies of American society that price-fixing would brand one as a felon." He says, "I'm not familiar with any other country where a businessman is sent to jail for checking prices with the competition. In some European countries, you might even be branded as a slovenly competitor if you did not contact the competition." But that didn't stop Renfrew from prosecuting cases in the U.S. In one case, in addition to corporate fines of $10,000 to $50,000 and personal fines of $4,000 to $15,000, he ordered each of the accused price-fixers to make speeches before 12 business and public groups.

The price-fixing law is more pervasive than many businessmen realize. Alonzo R. Acosta, executive vice-president of Stecher-Traung-Schmidt Corporation, said, "I felt that I was discussing prices and market conditions with competitors, but that I was not reaching agreements with them." But such discussions may be enough to violate the law. *Business Week,* in a special report on price-fixing, lists ten dont's for those who want to avoid an indictment for price-fixing:

Which of these do you think North Star may have been doing with other engineering consulting firms?

1. Don't agree with your competitors to raise or maintain selling prices.
2. Don't coordinate discounts, credit terms, or conditions of sale with your competitors.
3. Don't talk prices, markups, or cost structure at trade association or other meetings.
4. Don't agree with your competitors to rotate low bids on contracts.
5. Don't arrange with competitors to issue new price lists on a uniform date.
6. Don't agree with competitors to uniformly restrict production or to shut down plants in order to keep prices up.
7. Don't conspire within your industry to lower prices in order to discourage customers from ordering substitute materials or product types.
8. Don't force suppliers to boycott price-cutting competitors.
9. Don't join with competitors in fixing maximum prices in purchasing from suppliers.
10. Don't agree with competitors to buy up distressed merchandise in order to keep prices from falling.[27]

This is by no means a comprehensive sketch of business frauds or complete discussion of business ethics. But it should be clear that the question of ethical behavior is becoming more pressing for business managers than ever before. The government is stepping up the drive on white-collar crimes. Not only do they want to catch major frauds such as the Funding case (where wholesale forging of insurance contracts was practiced over a long period), or grain-inspection scandals, but they hope to clean up the entire atmosphere of business.

Businessmen should not wait to be pushed. Ethical behavior in business ought to be an end in itself. It is not clear, in the long run, that unethical behavior really increases profits substantially; and it may establish in the organization an atmosphere of fraud and evasion that does more harm internally than an attractive balance sheet is worth.

Summary

In recent years, the American public has begun to exert control over the actions of corporations which were immune from public attention in the past. Some see a corporation as a form of government which should be required to act in the public interest, while others see it as a private enterprise owned by private stockholders whose funds should not be diverted to help others. The problem is particularly acute with the multinational corporations, whose overseas "commissions" (often the equivalent of bribes) are justified by some as a necessary adjunct to overseas business operation.

Business corporations are moving to help solve the problems of an urban society, often reducing their own profit by doing so. Some of these efforts are internal—changing hiring and promotion practices to redress past inequities, hiring and training marginal workers, and broadening internal practices. Others are external—assisting with urban renewal, contributing to educational programs, providing managerial help in urban problems, and so on. During times of economic turndown, the insistence of unions on seniority rules for layoffs conflicts with the affirmative action goals of redressing the balance from past hirings, since the "last-hired, first-fired" policy removes mainly the minority and women employees hired to achieve affirmative action goals.

Cities are encountering financial problems as costs rise faster than revenues, and in some cases are calling on business personnel to aid in managing these problems (notably in the case of New York City). Corporations are making an effort to respond to the changing urban environment: offering industrial revenue bonds for sale to investors, putting more people in less space, and coping in various ways with the new municipal resistance to uncontrolled growth.

Consumer groups, the SEC, and the courts are pressing corporations for more complete information on their financial situation and operating practices. Corporate directors are finding that they can be prosecuted for failing to act vigorously when they learn of improper acts, or even for being ignorant of acts that did occur. The public is becoming involved in corporate ownership, by bailing out financially troubled corporations or actually converting them to public institutions. It is not clear where the process will stop, though it is almost sure to continue in many troubled industries.

Women and minorities are finding corporate doors open to them, with schools instituting special programs to assist in this process and companies bidding against one another for qualified professionals from these groups.

Although there are differences of opinion as to the social responsibilities of business (inside and outside the company), companies are coming to accept the fact that their management skills can be of use to the public and that some of their resources should be devoted to social tasks. Corporations are being asked to contribute more to the quality of life than the goods and services they sell. The question is, how far can they go in this direction without weakening their main thrust as providers of goods and services?

Corporations are being attacked as despoilers of the environment, and are spending large sums to avoid this label by purifying industrial discharges into air or water, changing corporate practices with regard to product safety and responsiveness to the consumer, and revising plans for installations that could impair environmental values. Arguments between environmental groups seeking to preserve unspoiled areas and corporations trying to build power plants or refineries to meet public needs are bitter, and the matter often goes to the courts for resolution.

Business ethics, particularly in the areas of multinational operations and corporate political contributions, are under close scrutiny, and hearings by the SEC and Congress are bringing illegal or improper practices to light. Many business executives feel that ethical behavior in business is not bad for profits, and that companies that stand firm against such demands will not necessarily lose out competitively.

Notes

1. "'Last hired, first fired' Takes It on the Chin," *Business Week,* March 9, 1974, p. 166.
2. Ibid.
3. "Business Faces Growing Pressures to Behave Better," *Fortune,* May 1974, p. 314.
4. "Board Membership is No Longer a Breeze," *Business Week,* November 23, 1974, pp. 95-96.
5. Disclosures of massive secret foreign payments by Lockheed may weaken its overseas sales to the point of driving it into default, however. These disclosures, in early 1976, forced the resignation of Lockheed's board chairman and president.
6. Harland Padfield, "New Industrial Systems and Cultural Concepts of Poverty," in *Readings on the Current Social Issues in Business,* eds. Fred Luthans and Richard M. Hodgetts (New York: Macmillan Pub. Co., Inc., 1972), pp. 130-141.
7. James K. Brown, *Social Responsibility and the Smaller Company: Some Perspectives,* Conference Board Report No. 568 (New York: The Conference Board, 1972).
8. George A. Steiner, "Should Business Adopt a Social Audit?" The Conference Board Record, May 1972.
9. J. Irwin Miller, "The Public Responsibilities of Business," *Public Affairs Challenges of the '70s.* Public Affairs Conference Report No. 8 (New York: The National Industrial Conference Board, 1970), pp. 1-6.
10. Charles N. Stabler, "The Corporation's Job," in *Getting Involved: A New Challenge for Corporate Activists* (Princeton: Dow Jones, 1971, 1972), pp. 3–11.
11. *Social Responsibilities of Business Corporations,* Research and Policy Committee (New York: Committee for Economic Development, 1971).
12. Ibid.
13. "Steel: Clean Up or Close Up," *Business Week,* April 6, 1974, p. 72.
14. "Making Losers Pay the Bills." *Business Week,* December 14, 1974, p. 90.
15. "The Campaign to Protect Personal Privacy," *Business Week,* November 6, 1974, p. 86.
16. Ibid.
17. If, indeed, the money actually was passed on to any other parties.
18. Preceding paragraphs based on Senate Foreign Relations Committee hearings on multinational corporations (1975), as reported in "Lockheed Says It Will Resist SEC Efforts to Block It From Paying Bribes Abroad." *Wall Street Journal,* August 6, 1975, p. 6
19. "Payoff Is Not Accepted Practice," *Fortune,* August 1975, p. 124.

20. "Del Monte Corp. Finds a Foreign 'Consultant' Can Help a Great Deal," *Wall Street Journal,* July 14, 1975, p.1.
21. "The Further Misadventures of Harold Geneen," *Fortune,* June 1975, p. 113.
22. "Payoff Is Not Accepted Practice," *Fortune,* August 1975, p. 200.
23. Ibid., p. 124.
24. "Braniff Air Plans to Admit Violations of Laws to the CAB," *Wall Street Journal,* April 22, 1975, p. 13.
25. "Payoff Is Not Accepted Practice," *Fortune,* August 1975, p. 124.
26. "Ashland Names U.S. Foreign Recipients of Cash Contributions in Victory for SEC," *Wall Street Journal,* August 11, 1975, p. 2.
27. Preceding paragraphs are based on "Price Fixing: Crackdown Under Way," *Business Week,* June 2, 1975, pp. 42–48.

Review Questions

1. What did John Ruskin mean by saying that "it is chiefly by private, not public, effort that your city must be adorned"?
2. Why is the Hallmark Corporation willing to invest in an urban development that will earn it less income than it could earn in other investments?
3. What are the two parts to the program the government hopes to achieve in the equal opportunity employment area, and how are they different from the corporation point of view?
4. Why did New York experience an overwhelming financial crisis, while other U.S. cities remained relatively solvent?
5. What are some special problems a corporation encounters when it does business in a city?
6. What are the two opposing principles involved in corporate disclosure?
7. In what ways is the government increasing its "partnership" with business? Is this development likely to continue or reverse itself?
8. What has been the corporate experience with women and minority employees in the professional area? the university experience, in trying to assist corporations in this program?
9. Why should business become involved in outside societal problems? What are some ways that it might become involved?
10. Why is there a fundamental disagreement between environmental groups and business corporations?
11. What are the arguments for having a corporation's consumer affairs activities monitored by an inside or an outside reviewer?
12. What argument do the multinational corporations occasionally use to explain large commissions or bribes paid to secure business overseas? What do you think of this argument?
13. What are some corporate actions that appear relatively innocent but may violate the price-fixing laws?

Discussion Questions

1. Do you see any conflict of interest possibilities when a private firm has its chief executive sit on a committee that helps a city to plan its development? How might you avoid such problems and still help the city?
2. Do you think the "eminent domain" law that lets mineral companies in western states take urban properties (with fair compensation) is archaic and should be changed? What if the voters in those states do not think it should be changed? What are the considerations?

3. What might be the harmful aspects of having the government bail out a major company (not a public utility) that gets in financial trouble?

4. Suppose a company says it can't afford to hire hard-core unemployed, because they cost far more than they are worth. Can you think of any economic arguments to change their minds?

5. What do you think the Senate subcommittee on multinational corporations should decide on whether Lockheed should be made to divulge who had gotten "consulting fees" or "commissions" in the overseas countries? Bearing in mind that such payments are not a violation of U.S. law, do you think they should be, even if they make U.S. companies noncompetitive with other countries in getting such foreign contracts? Why or why not?

North Star Case Study

North Star was invited by the Agency for International Development of the U.S. Department of State to bid (along with other engineering firms) on a project to conduct a feasibility and master planning study for a projected airport in a small Asian nation. The request for the proposal, issued after approval by AID, contained a clause stating that the winning engineering firm would have to negotiate a subcontract with an economics consulting firm from the Asian country. Under this contract, the Asian firm would assist in obtaining financial, economic, and air travel data for the principal contractor; the payment to the Asian firm would be part of the approved expenses of the principal contractor.

North Star won the contract and negotiated a subcontract with the host country consulting firm for a sum amounting to 20% of the total contract. During its negotiations, members of the Asian government entered into the discussion and stated that the figure of 20% would be considered about the right amount. When North Star started work, and called on the consulting firm at its premises to request its assistance in getting the required data, it learned that the firm was actually a law office whose senior partner was the country's Minister of Aviation. Although the firm agreed to procure the necessary data, its performance was so poor that North Star had to do most of the data collection itself. As a result, its profits were lower than had been expected, and it appeared that it would lose on the contract.

When Dick gave the Minister of Aviation this news, the latter said that North Star should apply for an increase in the contract price. Dick requested a 10% increase, which was granted. Almost immediately, the consulting firm requested a 20% share of this increase; after a good deal of discussion, North Star gave in.

1. Do you think any of North Star's actions in this matter were unethical, or constituted the payment of bribes?
2. To what extent was the U.S. government involved in the payment of bribes or kickbacks in this case? Explain.
3. What do you think of the position that both AID and North Star were simply conducting business in the normal manner for the country concerned?
4. Given that the payment to the Asian subcontractor was required by the AID-approved request for proposal, what should North Star have done about this case?

Suggestions for Further Reading

Brown, J. K. *Social Responsibility and the Smaller Company: Some Perspectives.* New York: National Industrial Conference Board, Inc., 1972.

Flower, B. J. *Private-Sector Approaches to City Problems.* New York: National Industrial Conference Board, Inc., 1968.

Ford, H., II. *The Human Environment and Business.* New York: Weybright and Talley, Inc., 1970.

General Motors Corporation. *1973 Report on Progress in Areas of Public Concern.* Warren, Michigan: General Motors Technical Center, 1973.

Kobrak, P. *Private Assumption of Public Responsibilities: The Role of American Business in Urban Manpower Programs.* New York: Praeger Pubs., Inc., 1973.

Levitan, S. A., G. L. Mangum, and R. Taggart, *Economic Opportunity in the Ghetto.* Baltimore, Md.: The Johns Hopkins University Press, 1970.

Luthans, F., and R. Hodgetts, eds. *Readings on the Current Social Issues in Business: Poverty, Civil Rights, Ecology, and Consumerism.* New York: Macmillan Pub. Co., Inc., 1972.

Morgan, J. S. *Business Faces the Urban Crisis.* Houston, Tex.: Gulf Publishing Co., 1969.

Neuback, K. J. *Corporate Response to Urban Crisis.* Lexington, Mass: Lexington Books, 1974.

Odiorne, G. S. *Green Power: The Corporation and the Urban Crisis.* New York: Pitman Publishing Corp., 1969.

"Public Affairs Challenges of the '70's." Report on a conference at the Waldorf-Astoria. New York: National Industrial Conference Board, Inc., 1970.

"Why We Need the CIA." *Fortune,* June 1975.

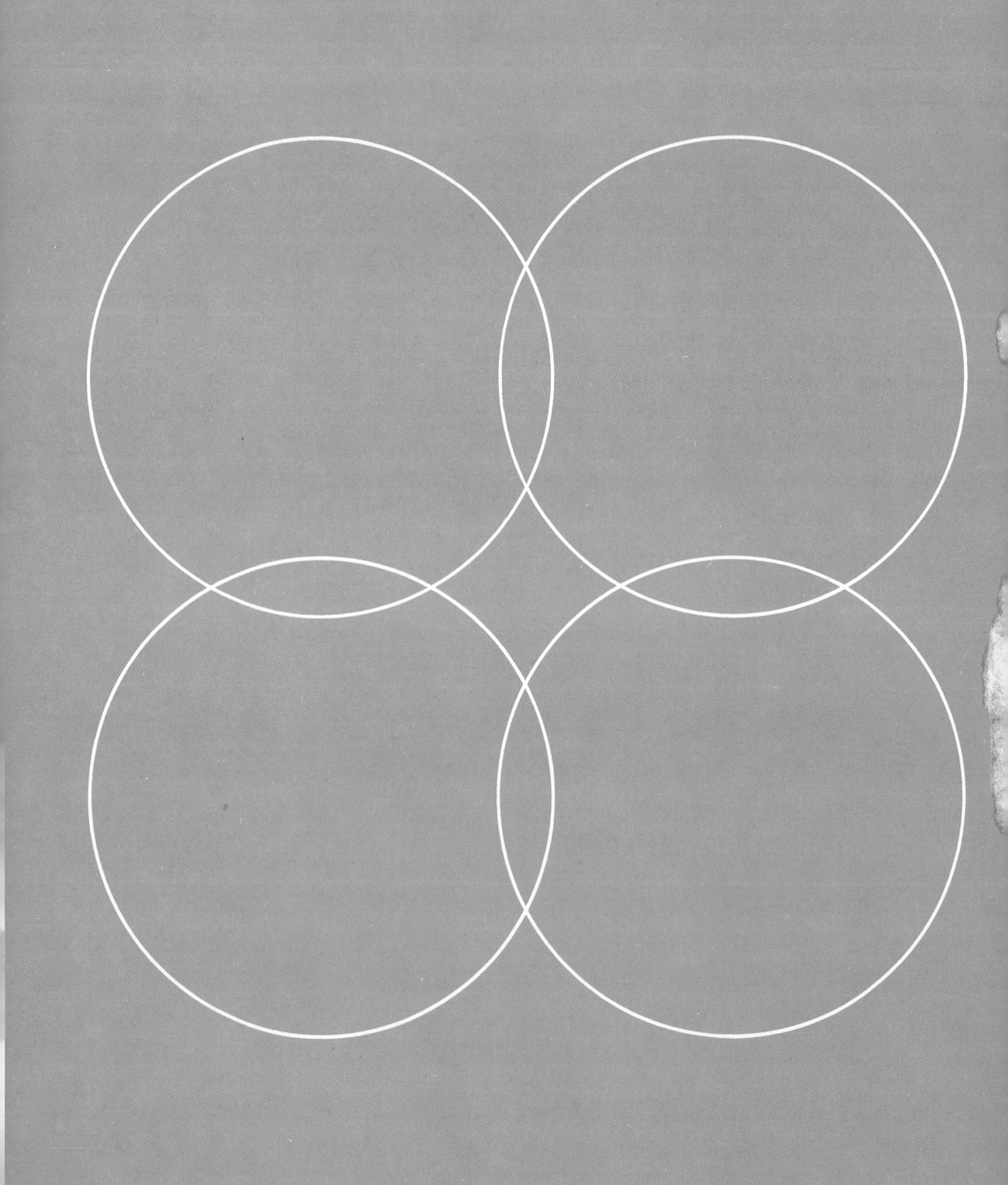

PART FIVE

Management Theory

Development of Management Theory 17

North Star Prologue

North Star, which had grown from a small, two-person engineering consulting team to a prosperous architectural and engineering firm with capabilities in economic and systems studies, encountered the usual growing pains in the areas of planning, budgeting, marketing, organizing, communicating, and handling conflict. It was quite surprised, however, to learn one day that it was in violation of a number of federal regulations without having realized that there were any laws in the areas involved. Correcting one of the problems (an unauthorized bonus plan) involved it in labor-management relations, almost bringing on a strike and a union. When this was settled, the company found itself managing a "New Town," without any prior experience in such matters. The pressures of the citizens for closer relations with North Star, and for a voice in what North Star did, brought on a confrontation involving citizen requests to be on the North Star board of directors.

The North Star experience in Eldorado, and the mind-expanding effect of Gail Osterhaus (aided and abetted by Barbara Newman at every opportunity), had left Henry with a humbling realization of how vast were his deficiencies in management as a science. Despite the fact that he was busy as never before, he decided to take the bull by the horns and go back to school for a graduate dose of management study. The state university had a branch campus in Eldorado—apparently the residents were intensely upwardly mobile, because the classes were attended far out of proportion to the size of the population—and Henry enrolled in its MBA program. The first term found him involved in a management principles course, and he was fascinated to trace the evolution of management thought down the years. Each period had its currently fashionable theory, and when the next period came along and a new approach developed it didn't replace the early notions but was spliced on as an additional set of concepts.

First came the scientific management movement, born in the steel mills and heavily engineering in its orientation, with the notion that men were so many resources to be spooned into the broth and heated just so. On top of this came the traditional management movement, with hardheaded industrialists and business barons stopping long enough to write down their maxims about how many subordinates a leader could control and so on. Next, and almost accidentally, came the human relations movement, when managers discovered to their surprise that workers behaved like real people with real hopes and fears, real pride and shame. Next, probably, came the motivation and informal organization school, deciding that there was more to a company or a society than how much the job paid or who was above whom on the organization chart. Then came the managerial accounting school, where the comptroller ruled and every in-plant group was made a profit center. And most recently came the systems analysis or management science movement, when managers concluded that all the complexities of a vast organization could be described reasonably well by reducing reality to mathematical models.

Henry wondered how on earth North Star could have done as well as it did without a single officer versed in such theories. As he pondered, it came to him that perhaps the accidental mix of people they had brought together embodied all of these schools and movements without even planning it so. How might such a division go?

Let's see. Perhaps Bert would be the scientific manager, with his overriding engineering interest, and his faith that the slide rule and the engineering computer conquered all. Certainly good solid Dick Boyer would espouse the traditional management notions, with his emphasis on form and on setting everything up systematically. Barbara Newman worked her human relations bit on both sides of the street, morning and night—and was bidding fair to convert them all. Henry looked at himself as dispassionately as he could, and decided that his middle-of-the-road approach and low-key attitude might come close to the motivation and informal organization technique. Zeb certainly deserved the managerial accounting crown, the way he had pressed them into keeping good records and seeing where they stood with the financial records. And surely Jo was the systems analysis and management science advocate par excellence.

Perhaps that was their secret. Perhaps all unknowingly they had stumbled onto an unbeatable managerial stew, incorporating the distilled wisdom of all the managers down the ages, so that they acted as a complex set of checks and balances, forever preventing excesses in any one direction, always steering the ship in roughly the proper direction. That is, assuming it had been the proper direction thus far. But on the other hand, how much better they might have performed if they had drawn on the best that management theory had to offer. And how much better they might do in the future, if they could be guided by the teachings and experience of management experts.

What would be the direction for the future? Now that their success to date had brought them a breathing spell, and they didn't have to spend every day earning the money they would need tomorrow, there was time to sit back and be deliberate, to plan exactly what their course ought to be. Henry resolved to develop a management plan for the new North Star, for the decade ahead. With a plan, they would not have to learn each step of the way by trial and error, as they had in the past—they could do it right the first time.

As he looked over the plan for the course he was embarked upon, and studied the syllabus and chapter headings of his first term books, it struck him that management consisted of some broad headings—planning, organizing, controlling, deciding—and a great number of specific disciplines provided by specialists—accountants, economists, industrial engineers, sociologists, management scientists, psychologists, computer programmers, market researchers, and a hundred more. The trick apparently was to know how and when to mix in doses of the specific disciplines to achieve the goals of the broad headings. There was nothing new in management, except the knowledge or intuition or both that told how to mix the standard ingredients to achieve extraordinary results.

But of course, he mused, that was all there was to music, or to painting, or indeed to any art: knowing how much of each ingredient to stir in. With a sigh, he decided it had to be done the hard way, and picked up his management principles book.

What North Star Can Learn from Chapter 17

1. The basic concepts of scientific management
2. The problems involved in getting employees to better their standard work pace, even with incentive systems
3. How to approach a job in terms of its basic elements ("therbligs")
4. The advantages of a bureaucratic organization, and the sort of environment where a bureaucratic system would work best
5. The implications of the relay room experiments in the Hawthorne plant
6. The basic action assumptions of the human relations school, and how they might be applied to the drafting room situation in North Star
7. How formal and informal organizations interplay
8. How problems change as organizations grow

Thus far, we have covered the elements or *building blocks* that go into management, how these are used to build up management *processes,* how managers draw on these processes in operating, and finally how managers harness their internal operations to face the external environment. This chapter discusses the origins of, and future prospects for, the management profession. Management is more than a pragmatic trade that is learned by doing; skilled managers have transformed experience into principles and assembled workable techniques into a theoretical framework so that students of management need not face each new situation as a totally new ballgame.

We will study the evolution of these principles in the context of the changing management environment by focusing on three topics:

1. The *background of management theory*—why the study of management became important and how it was approached by early management theorists.
2. The *principal schools of management theory*—particularly the classical school, the human relations school, and the structuralist school, with some attention to variations on these basic themes.
3. Some *current issues in management theory,* including a discussion of shortcomings in existing accepted theories and what management theorists are doing about them.

Background of Management Theory

In a sense, we have been using theory throughout this book, in analyzing the separate processes and operations with which the manager is involved. "Theory" is not a mysterious entity that is considered in a vacuum, without reference to the practical world it explains. When we discuss the task facing the manager in dealing effectively with subordinates, for example, we are discussing an important theory of interpersonal relationships, even if it is not specifically labeled as such. A theory simply offers reasons for the way events happen or the way an environment develops. Thus, we felt it made sense to explore the *environment* before presenting the *theories* that focus on that environment, instead of the other way around.

Of course, useful though theory may be, it is no substitute for skill and experience in making managerial decisions. But it can help to pull the various elements of this complex job into a unified whole, and thus reduce the amount of guesswork involved.

Preindustrial Origins

Management obviously has existed since the dawn of man, but management theory (or management as a profession) is a relatively new phenomenon. One can search Will and Ariel Durant's massive ten-volume *The Story of Civilization*[1] without finding in its copious bibliography-index (which in the tenth volume alone covers 125 pages of entries) a single mention of "organization," "management," or "administration." Why not?

There are many reasons for this seeming lack of attention to a field that helped produce a living standard under which most workers take for granted the cars, televisions, medicine, airplanes, watches, typewriters, air conditioners, cameras—and eight-hour day—that not even kings could enjoy in days gone by. For one, the ruling classes during much of history could neither read nor write. Not one of the powerful barons who forced King John to sign the Magna Carta could pen his own name—all had to attest the document with "X," even his Grace, the Archibishop of Canterbury. Thus, whatever "management skills" they learned in the process of running their feudal kingdoms they passed on by word of mouth, if at all. For another, specialization and subdivision of tasks is a relatively recent development; more typically, throughout history, groups of individual craftsmen have completed entire jobs on their own.[2] For a third, truly large organizations were rare: many "kingdoms" were hardly more than sizable towns, and most businesses involved very few workers. And for a fourth, management implies overhead costs and nonproductive work (which presumably, however, yield the desired profits), and civilizations struggling to eke out the bare necessities just this side of starvation could rarely afford the luxury of investing capital for future returns.

Even so, three organizations in preindustrial civilization displayed strong elements of management practice in their operations: the *guilds,* the *church,* and the *military* (in addition, of course, to the *state*). Sometimes the different organizations overlapped, and at various times each of the former three found itself involved in affairs of state.

The Guilds

Florence, Italy—city-state ruler of most of Tuscany in the fourteenth and fifteenth centuries, and for 100 years the center of culture for much of the civilized world—typifies the medieval city where guilds were interwoven with the state. She had seven Greater Guilds (Arti Maggiori), for clothing manufacturers, wool manufacturers, judges, etc., and 14 Minor Guilds (Arti Minori), for butchers, bakers, innkeepers, etc. No citizen could vote unless he belonged to one of these guilds; thus, guild membership was an essential prerequisite to any citizen power in affairs of state. Under the guilds were 72 workers' unions, but none of these had the vote. Still lower were thousands of day laborers, who were forbidden to unite in any organization at all. At the final and lowest level were the slaves.

In 1293 the business class had won out over the landowning aristocracy and had acquired effective power over the state in Florence and its surrounding cities and countryside. Today, this arrangement would be called a government by the managing class over the landlord class: the guilds effectively held the reins of government. In 1378 the wool carders revolted and actually seized the government for themselves, but they were ill-prepared to exploit their unexpected victory. Ironically, the same rift that brought down the Knights of Labor in the early twentieth century (between the "aristocracy" of skilled craftsmen and the left-wing group more interested in political reform) splintered the carders' movement and destroyed their supremacy in 1382.

Most powerful managerial clan of the period was the Medici. In 1428, Cosimo di Bicci de Medici boasted the largest fortune in Tuscany, with an empire that included banking, management of many farms, manufacture of silk and woolens, and trade networks linking Russia with Spain, Scotland with Syria, and Islam with Christendom. Although he did not hold formal state office, he controlled the strings that manipulated state affairs. He was renowned as a competent manager, though he left no treatises setting forth his managerial techniques.

The Catholic Church

The Catholic church has been cited by many management writers as an early example of a strong management organization, largely because of its early application of the staff principle. Ironically, for a 70-year period starting in 1378 it had great difficulty managing at all, for there were two competing popes—one in Rome, supported by England, Germany, Poland, Hungary, and Portugal, among other nations; the other in France, supported by Naples, Spain, and Scotland. Indeed, for a short time after 1409, there were three.

After the Great Schism was settled, the church underwent a rather uncertain period with many ups and downs. In 1492, Cardinal Rodrigo Borgia, who had served as vice-chancellor (head of the Papal Curia) to five popes over a 35-year period, was elected Pope Alexander. He was an unusually efficient manager, particularly during his earlier years. He inherited a budget badly in debt and brought it into balance within a few years; he also kept strict records and paid salaries promptly. In many ways, he was typical of the "manager-popes" who gave the Catholic church its historical reputation for strong bureaucratic management of a far-flung apparatus.

James D. Mooney, in his managerial study of the Catholic church,[3] describes its skillful use of line and staff concepts: "the staff principle is woven into the fabric of church rules and discipline, affecting every individual in every relation." There are no less than three staff concepts in operation: formal staff, informal staff, and "staff independence."

The formal staff system is represented by the Sacred College, which meets in conclave to elect the pope, and by the Curia Romana, which (through its several divisions) acts as a collective advisory council to the pope in his administrative functions. There are corresponding councils at the diocesan, provincial, national, patriarchal, or ecumenical level, consisting of various holders of high ecclesiastic office and special advisors.

The informal staff principle works within the line organization itself in a way that Mooney terms "compulsory staff service," whereby on vital matters each superior must consult all of his subordinates before making a decision. Thus the abbot must consult with the most junior friar in the abbey before making a key decision (though of course the subordinate's advice may be ignored—just as a line executive may ignore the advice of staff assistants).

The staff independence concept in the Catholic church is rather unusual in organizations. In some staff situations, the staff manager is not responsible to the person whom he or she advises, thus removing staff advice from the pressures of line supervision and dominance. (In a sense, this principle operates in modern companies, as in Figure 3-6 where the personnel director gives staff advice to the vice-president of Project B without being his or her subordinate; it would be even more analogous if a personnel staffer was part of the Project B organization, advising but not reporting directly to the vice-president.)

The Military

Frederick the Great, king of Prussia from 1740 to 1786, is the ruler whose name is most immediately associated with militarism, and not without good reason. When he returned to Berlin in 1763 from the Seven Years' War, he found affairs in disorder following his long preoccupation with military operations, and set about rebuilding Prussia. He watched the work of his ministers closely, dictated almost every move of policy, kept a close eye on the treasury, and most important of all, established the "Fiscal." This institution was a bureau of accounts, empowered to examine every government department at any time and instructed to report any suspicion of irregularity. (Our General Accounting Office, an instrument of the U.S. Congress, operates in the same way.) He punished malfeasance or incompetence rigorously. He arranged the laws of many provinces into a single code, built a network of roads, canals, and harbors, embarked on economic reconstruction, and developed industry in many ways, through loans, training, and importing key skills.

Actually, the most significant innovations in military management were made well before Frederick, by King Gustavus Adolphus of Sweden, who ruled from 1611 to 1632 and won much territory for Sweden. His efficient military machine earned him the title "Lion of the North." Each of his regimental headquarters staffs included a chief quartermaster, judge advocate, chaplain, surgeons, provost marshals, and clerks. His supreme army headquarters staff included the above, plus a chief of staff and various chiefs of arms: chief of artillery, chief of engineering, and chief of scouts. Gustavus Adolphus' innovations were adopted by the Prussians after their defeat by Napoleon at Jena in 1806, leading to the origination of the famous German General Staff. German military strategist Karl von Clausewitz enunciated the function of the general staff as follows: "to convert the ideas of the commanding general into orders, not only by conveying the former to the troops, but far more by working out all the necessary matters of detail, thus relieving the mind of the general from a great amount of trouble."[4]

The relative importance of the Prussian general staff, since adopted by most modern armies, is that it took far more than the usual passive staff role of advising. It served as a junior partner to the top commander, taking many line roles and exercising a great deal of authority, although in theory always acting in the name of the commander. Thus, a Chief of Intelligence would be careful to sign any general order "by direction," indicating that he was acting for the commander. In chapter 9, we describe the "centralized control unit" established by several large corporations. This concept was introduced by retired General Brehon Somervell, who had been Chief of the Army Services of Supply, when he became chief executive officer of Koppers Company after the war. As noted in chapter 9, the White House staff in President Nixon's administration operated in this fashion, though apparently within sufficient top-level review.

---

the "Fiscal"

military staff system

centralized control unit

Is there any individual or system in North Star who signs "by direction," in effect?

The Industrial Revolution

England was the natural birthplace for the industrial revolution in the mid-eighteenth century, for many reasons. England had fought (and won) many wars, but always on foreign soil, so there was little disruption of commercial life. Her command of the seas made her preeminent in commerce and accordingly receptive to ideas. Her overseas colonies provided a plentiful supply of raw materials. It was considered somewhat more acceptable for the nobility to engage in commerce and industry in England than it was in most other countries. Science instruction and related research in England emphasized practical results, and consequently did not scorn the task of helping to solve industry's problems. And government was friendly to industrialists and broadly based. Interest rates were quite low for the times, and banks were willing to loan to industrial borrowers.

The list of British industrial firsts is impressive. Blast furnaces were in vogue as early as 1754. The first major railway was inaugurated in 1763. The "spinning jenny" (named for inventor James Hargreave's wife), which could do the work of many spinning wheels, was put in service in 1765. And in 1765 came James Watt's famous steam engine, which released the world from the limitations of muscle power.

All the necessary components thus were present: fuel, power, materials, machines, and workers. But they produced most effectively when united under one organization and one discipline. It gradually became evident that the missing ingredient was management, and this the British proceeded to provide, with the "factory system" that came to flower near the end of the eighteenth century. This application of management to these tools of industry was the real industrial revolution.

The industrial revolution did not come painlessly. The half-century of transition from hand craft and home industry to factory, starting about 1760, was for the laboring class of England one of abysmal and sometimes subhuman working conditions, often worse than slavery itself.

Adam Smith, in many ways a management theorist ahead of his time (for his discussion on division of labor in the operation of a pin factory, see page 275), took issue with the eighteenth-century tradition of working employees until they dropped:

> Excessive application during four days of the week is frequently the real cause of the idleness of the other three....The man who works so moderately as to be able to work constantly not only preserves his health the longest, but in the course of the year executes the greatest quantity of work.[5]

But this view was by no means universal. A more popular opinion was that expressed by one J. Smith, Esq., during the same period:

> It is a fact well known to those who are conversant in this matter that scarcity, to a certain degree, promotes industry, and that the [manual worker] who can subsist on three days' work will be idle and drunk the remainder of the week. ...Upon the whole, we can fairly aver that a reduction in wages in the woolen manufacture would be a national blessing, and no real injury to the poor. By this means we might keep our trade, uphold our [revenues], and reform our people into the bargain.[6]

James Watt was more than an inventor; he was also an industrialist.

Initially he teamed up with John Roebuck, owner of an ironworks and mining interests, but in 1773 Roebuck became discouraged at production problems in producing the Watt engine and sold his share of the partnership to Matthew Boulton, an early industrial manager. Boulton had built at Soho (now Birmingham) in 1760 one of England's most extensive industrial plants, but was limited to waterpower. In 1775 the plant devised a hollow cylindrical boring bar that standardized the manufacture of Boulton and Watt engines of unprecedented power and quality; these engines soon gained popularity with manufacturers and mine operators across Britain. Social commentator James Boswell visited the factory in 1776, and described his reactions in his *Life of Samuel Johnson* (1787):

> Mr. Hector was so good as to accompany me to see the great works of Mr. Boulton...I wished Johnson had been with us, for it was a scene which I should have been glad to contemplate by his light. The vastness and the contrivances of some of the machinery would have "matched his mighty mind." I shall never forget Mr. Boulton's expression to me: "I sell here, Sir, what all the world desires to have—POWER." He had about seven hundred people at work. I contemplated him as an *iron chieftain,* and he seemed to be a father to his tribe.

A somewhat more analytical comment is found in the introduction to a comprehensive study of the management systems utilized in Boulton and Watt's factory:

> Neither Taylor, Ford, nor other modern experts devised anything in the way of plan that cannot be discovered at Soho (the Birmingham factory of Boulton and Watt) before 1805; and the Soho system of costing is superior to that employed in very many successful concerns today. This earliest engineering factory, therefore, possessed an organization on the management side which was not excelled even by the technical skill of the craftsmen it produced.[7]

The study detailed many managerial advances which seem remarkable even today. The managers determined the average time required to bore steam engine cylinders of different sizes and types, and used these "standard times" to set up an incentive payment system for cylinder borers. (When it is realized that methods-time measurement, or MTM, used widely by management today to establish such standard times for incentive purposes in industrial plants, was introduced only in 1948,[8] this early achievement seems all the more remarkable.) The company recorded the speeds of the various machines as a basis for time and cost estimates and listed all components of the manufactured items, with full documentation of manufacturing sequences (in the style of modern dispatching and routing systems). Complete job lists were maintained for all workers and work teams, suggesting the establishment of fixed "standard jobs." Production planning was based on market forecasts. Detailed management cost control records were utilized.

While these factories were operated by their owners, by and large, no factory could be successful unless the owners knew something about management. And not all wealthy investors were managers. The new emphasis on special-purpose machines and the increasing specialization of labor, all made possible by the prime movers and technical advances of the industrial revolution, led to an inexorable growth in the size of industrial firms. The day was at hand when partnerships would give way to corporations, so the large sums required to build and equip the big factories could be raised.

And the day was at hand when the owner-operator would step aside to make place for a new industrial phenomenon: the managerial class

Do you see any signs of this development of a managerial group separate from the owners in North Star? What is the relation of this group to the owners?

Schools of Management Theory

Management theory can be approached from two perspectives. One asserts that, as theorists build on the ideas and experiences of the past, their explanations become more and more valid and universally applicable. The other holds that times change; something that works for one period may prove inadequate for a later period. The major schools of theory—classical, human relations, and structuralist—generally combined both perspectives. In studying these theories, you should bear in mind, first, that they are not the final word—there is a good deal more to learn; and second, that many managers do not even use what we know now.

schools of management theory

The Classical School

This school includes two theories, which developed separately, at about the same period. One goes under the broad name of *scientific management*, and is concerned with the techniques of measuring work elements and of providing incentives based on financial rewards for measurable achievement. The other is concerned with the *structure of the organization* as a source of principles to serve as guidelines for the manager. Frederick W. Taylor, usually considered the father of scientific management, was born in 1856 and started developing his techniques in 1881. His first publication was a presentation to a technical society in 1903, and his first major book came out in 1911. Taylor's followers include Frank W. Gilbreth, a contemporary of Taylor whose publications spanned the period from 1909 to 1924 (and whose wife, Lillian Gilbreth, took over after his death), and Henri Fayol, who has been described as the father of management theory. Fayol was born in 1841, but his first major book was not published until 1916. Another important classicist, Max Weber, whose theories on bureaucratic organizations have been a point of departure for studies of organization structure and function for half a century, was born in 1864. Although Weber did a good deal of writing which has been reprinted in management anthologies, he left a major work uncompleted when he died in 1920. This list, of course, covers only the principal actors in a broad group of theorists.

classical school
scientific management

structure of the organization

Scientific Management

Frederick W. Taylor should have become an aristocrat. He was born in an exclusive Philadelphia suburb, traveled and studied in Europe as a boy, and prepared at posh Phillips Exeter Academy for entrance to Harvard. Although he passed the entrance examinations with honors, his poor

671

DEVELOPMENT OF MANAGEMENT THEORY

eyesight was further strained by studying, and in 1874 he abandoned higher education to become an apprentice machinist in a small firm. In 1878 his destiny took him to the Midvale Steel Company as a laborer, from which job he was transferred to lathe machinist and shortly thereafter became the gang boss. By 1885 he had been promoted to foreman, to master mechanic in charge of all maintenance and repair, to head draftsman, and to chief engineer. Meanwhile he had undertaken home study in engineering with the help of Harvard and Stevens Institute professors, earning a degree in mechanical engineering.

At Midvale, Taylor took note of what all industrial managers knew more or less at the time: that mechanics engaged in "systematic soldiering" on the job to limit their output far below what they could have achieved. He realized that careful analysis was needed to determine what constituted a legitimate day's work. In 1881 he started systematic time studies in the machine shop, and in 1903 he incorporated his findings from these and subsequent studies into a paper on shop management.[9]

Taylor's experience as foreman was not all smooth sailing. He showed the machinists that their output could be double or triple what it was, but to no avail. Then he decided on drastic action. He brought in some of the more promising laborers, promised to teach them a trade if they would turn out a fair day's work, and trained them in lathe work. When they caved in under the intense pressures from the other mechanics, Taylor cut their pay in half. He reported the results in his shop management paper:

> These men, of course, went to the management and protested that I was a tyrant...and for a long time they stood right by the rest of the men in the shop and refused to increase their output a particle. Finally they all of a sudden gave right in and did a fair day's work. ...Then they played what is usually the winning card. ...Every time I broke a rate or forced one of the new men to work...at a reasonable and proper speed, some one of the machinists would deliberately break some part of his machine as an object lesson to demonstrate to the management that a fool foreman was driving the men to overload their machines until they broke.[10]

Taylor had expected this tactic, and was ready. Every time a machine broke down he fined the operator, with no excuses whatsoever. He said to them: "I don't care if the roof falls in and breaks your machine, you will pay all the same."[11]

In 1898, Taylor went to the Bethlehem Steel Company to study the cause of low output in a large machine shop. Here he performed his famous study on loading of pig iron (walking 92-pound pigs up a ramp and loading into rail cars). The rate per man was averaging 12½ tons per day. Even though the task looked elementary, Taylor disagreed, saying "the science of handling pig iron is so great and amounts to so much that it is impossible for the man who is best suited to this type of work to understand the principles of this science."[12] He conducted a detailed study of the movements and the endurance of laborers; one of his findings was that the laborer would need to rest some 57% of the time in order to get the most production in an entire day. He selected a 130-pound laborer, whom he gave the pseudonym Schmidt, and predicted that Schmidt soon would be loading the amount indicated by his time and motion studies: 47½ long tons per day, or over 106,000 pounds. Schmidt

---

soldiering on the job

Do you recall any time when the North Star employees engaged in systematic soldiering? What steps did North Star take to deal with it? Do you think they could have taken more aggressive action?

did indeed meet and maintain this pace, and in short order other workers were asking to participate in this new incentive pace which had raised Schmidt's pay 60%.[13]

Taylor's studies produced many other victories, and by and large his new scientific management delivered on its promises. But he was more than an industrial engineer—he had firm thoughts on managerial organization of tasks. One of his firm principles was that *planning* should be separated from *operating:* the people on the firing line should have their work laid out for them in detail by planning specialists who were not distracted by the need to attend to the many job-related problems. Another was that foremen should be specialists in particular areas, rather than trying to be generalists. His major premise was that through scientific management workers would come to see how much improved their compensation was and would favor the adoption of his methods. He was confident that the extra pay would win over the workers; he thought managers would be the hard ones to convince, because in essence he was telling them their business, and at the same time laying out a much tougher role for them to play than they had been accustomed to in the past. He was telling them to *manage,* rather than just to be in charge:

organization of tasks (functionalism)

> It is only through *enforced* standardization of methods, *enforced* adoption of the best implements and working conditions, and *enforced* cooperation that this faster work can be assured. And the duty of enforcing the adoption of standards and enforcing the cooperation rests with the *management* alone. ...The *management* must also recognize the broad fact that workmen will not submit to this more rigid standardization and will not work extra hard, unless they receive extra pay for doing it.[14]

Careful analysis is needed to determine what constitutes a legitimate day's work.

Taylor has been criticized by modern management theorists on the grounds that he dehumanized work, making the workers into little more than automatons who had to do exactly what they were told, and that his ideas were not broad theories but simply practical tips at the shop level. Both of these charges are somewhat unjust. In the first place, Taylor showed more consideration for workers than writers have credited him with. (It is natural that he should have; he had been a laborer, a machinist, a gang boss and a foreman. His critics had been none of these.) J. Boddewyn claims that Taylor was indeed concerned that workers should get justice, and that the well-being of the work group was high on his list of priorities.[15] In the second place, Taylor's management theories *started* at the work place but encompassed a broad range of managerial responsibilities. He advocated a functional organization with trained specialists, separation of planning from doing, management by exception, clear job specifications, and training of managers for the specialty of management. He pioneered workable incentive systems, which spread through industry to the point where it is estimated that 30% of industrial jobs today follow some sort of incentive payment system. Modern human relations theorists, concerned with the "whole man," sometimes claim that compensation is low on the worker's priority list; but we seldom find unions (who work with workers at the grass-roots level) taking that position. Many of Taylor's concepts have found their way into later efforts to frame a general theory of management.

incentive systems

How would you go about putting in an incentive system in the drafting room? Do you think it would be feasible? Explain.

Taylor's disciples carried his work forward in several areas. Henry L. Gantt (who developed the Gantt Chart for scheduling and progressing work which is still in general use today—see Figure 17-1) improved Taylor's incentive approach through a system that, while it rewarded the superior achiever, did not penalize the average workman who could not match the high-output level. Frank Gilbreth carried Taylor's approach into the development of basic motions applicable to all tasks, and his work was the forerunner of modern methods-time measurement, the basic analytical method for the automotive industry, among others. He identified seventeen basic "therbligs" (Gilbreth spelled backwards with one minor shift), which are shown in modified form in Table 17-1. After Frank Gilbreth's death in 1924, his wife Lillian carried on his work, becoming a prominent industrial engineer. She was a trustee of the Maynard Foundation, the organization initially responsible for formalizing the modern form of methods-time management (MTM) in 1948. Figure 17-2 illustrates this adaptation and refinement of the original Gilbreth basic motions, expressed in time measurement units (TMU) equal to 0.00001 hour, as published by the MTM Association for Standards and Research in Ann Arbor, Michigan.

Gantt Chart

therblig

methods-time management (MTM)

Bertrand Thompson, another Taylor disciple, wrote on scientific management[16] and lectured at the Harvard Graduate School of Business Administration. By working closely with the union when he was installing the Taylor system in a company, Thompson was able to elicit union cooperation. Other pioneers in the scientific management movement were Harrington Emerson, who devoted much of his attention to improving railroad management and developed 12 general "principles of efficiency,"[17] and Morris L. Cooke, who worked at improving efficiency in municipal operations, including a tour as Director of Public

Works for Philadelphia from 1912 to 1916 during which productivity was greatly improved.[18]

Fayol's General Theory of Management

Henri Fayol, born in 1841 and trained as a mining engineer, was a practicing executive in France. In 1888 he became general manager of the mining firm of Commentry-Fourchambault and brought it from a condition close to bankruptcy to a healthy and flourishing state. He first presented his views on management at the International Mining and Metallurgical Congress in 1900; and like Taylor, he was speaking from the distilled experience of many years of practical management. Although he came from the mining and metallurgical industry, he represented his theories as applicable to all management. In chapter 3, we listed his five

Figure 17-1.
Segment of Gantt Chart for Nuclear Power Plant

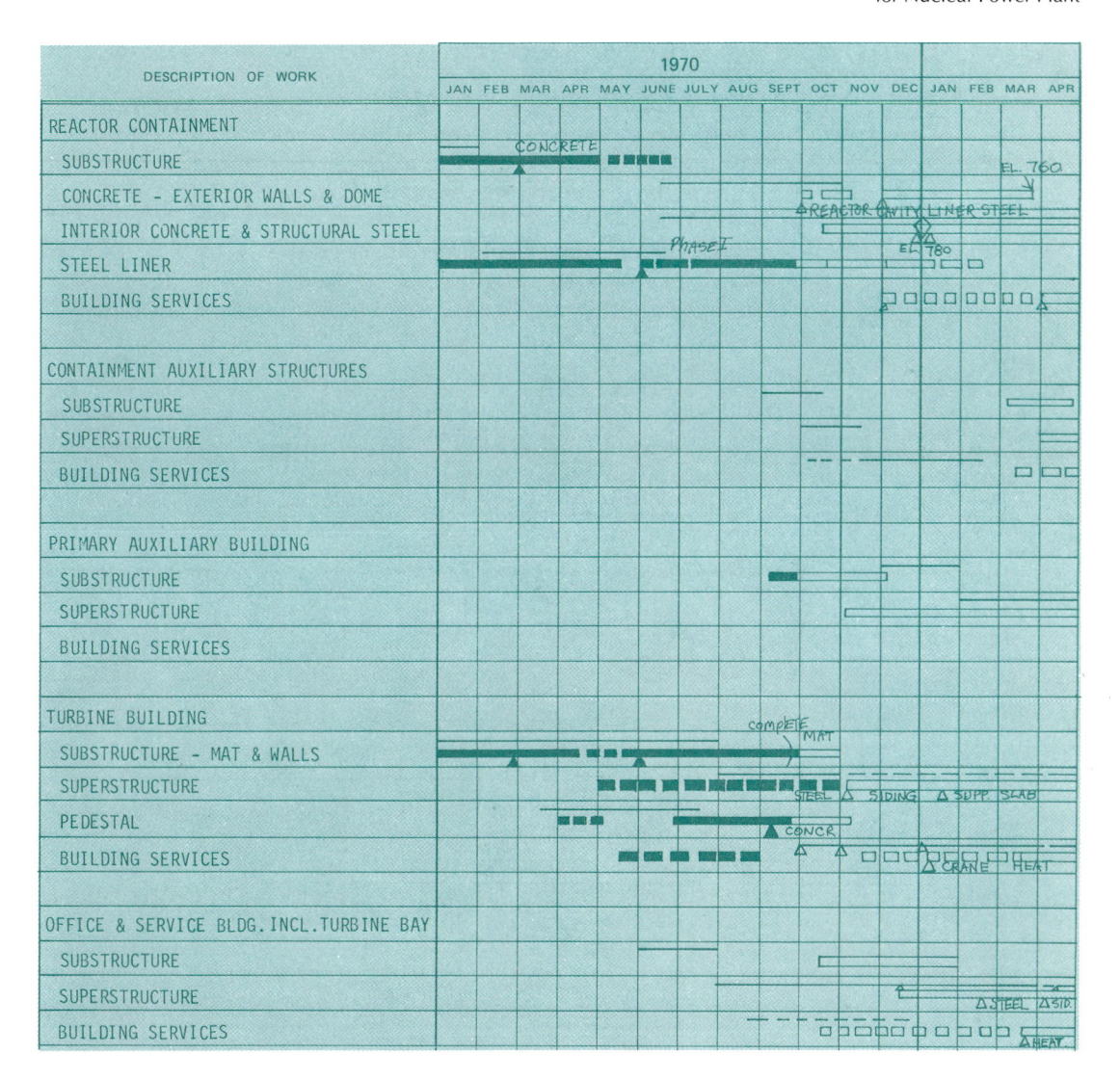

DEVELOPMENT OF MANAGEMENT THEORY

functions of administration (planning, organizing, commanding, coordinating, and controlling). He put great emphasis on the second function:

> To organize is to define and set up the general structure of the enterprise with reference to its objective, its means of operation, and its future course as determined by planning.... It is to give form to the whole and to every detail its place; it is to make the frame and to fill it with its destined contents.[19]

Fayol's 14 principles of administration

In establishing what he called his 14 "principles of administration," Fayol was careful to emphasize that they were not hard-and-fast rules, but had to be tempered in the light of the circumstances:

1. Division of work to make best use of individuals and groups
2. Authority to give orders and exact obedience
3. Discipline by competent superiors
4. Unity of command, so each employee has but one superior
5. Unity of direction for all activities with the same objective
6. Subordination of individual interest to group interests
7. Remuneration of personnel based on external and internal factors
8. Centralization to the proper degree for the tasks involved
9. Chain of command, with recognized levels that communicate with each other across different hierarchies (Fayol's "bridge")
10. An ordered organization, with a place for everyone and everyone in his place
11. Equity of treatment for all employees
12. Stability of personnel tenure
13. Initiative on the part of everyone, within limits of authority
14. Esprit de corps and morale

Consider these principles with reference to North Star. Are there any which you think do not apply? Why?

Fayol's "bridge"

Although Fayol believed firmly in the chain of command, he recognized the great saving in time and effort that could be achieved if hierarchical levels subordinate in different departments communicated with each other directly. Figure 17-3, from his book, demonstrates the operation of the "bridge," where F and P communicate directly. This bridge, Fayol explained:

> ...allows the two employees, F and P, to deal...with some question or other which via the scalar chain would pass through 20 transmissions, inconvenience many people, involve masses of paper, lose weeks or months. ...Is it possible that such practices [requiring F to go up through E, D, C, and B to

Table 17-1.
Modified List of Gilbreth Basic Elements

Group 1		Group 2		Group 3	
Reach	R	Change Direction	CD	Unavoidable Delay	UD
Move	M	Pre-Position	PP	Hold	D
Apply Pressure	AP	Search	S		
Grasp	G	Select	SE		
Position	P	Balancing Delay	BD		
Disengage	D				
Release	RL				
Examine	E				
Do	DO				

Source: Maynard Research Council, Inc.

676
MANAGEMENT THEORY

Figure 17-2.
Basic Elements in Methods-Time Management

TABLE I—REACH—R

Distance Moved Inches	Time TMU A	B	C or D	E	Hand in Motion A	B	CASE AND DESCRIPTION
½ or less	2.0	2.0	2.0	2.0	1.6	1.6	**A** Reach to object in fixed location, or to object in other hand or on which other hand rests.
1	2.5	2.5	3.6	2.4	2.3	2.3	
2	4.0	4.0	5.9	3.8	3.5	2.7	
3	5.3	5.3	7.3	5.3	4.5	3.6	**B** Reach to single object in location which may vary slightly from cycle to cycle
4	6.1	6.4	8.4	6.8	4.9	4.3	
5	6.5	7.8	9.4	7.4	5.3	5.0	
6	7.0	8.6	10.1	8.0	5.7	5.7	
7	7.4	9.3	10.8	8.7	6.1	6.5	**C** Reach to object jumbled with other objects in a group so that search and select occur.
8	7.9	10.1	11.5	9.3	6.5	7.2	
9	8.3	10.8	12.2	9.9	6.9	7.9	
10	8.7	11.5	12.9	10.5	7.3	8.6	
12	9.6	12.9	14.2	11.8	8.1	10.1	
14	10.5	14.4	15.6	13.0	8.9	11.5	**D** Reach to a very small object or where accurate grasp is required.
16	11.4	15.8	17.0	14.2	9.7	12.9	
18	12.3	17.2	18.4	15.5	10.5	14.4	
20	13.1	18.6	19.8	16.7	11.3	15.8	
22	14.0	20.1	21.2	18.0	12.1	17.3	
24	14.9	21.5	22.5	19.2	12.9	18.8	**E** Reach to indefinite location to get hand in position for body balance or next motion or out of way.
26	15.8	22.9	23.9	20.4	13.7	20.2	
28	16.7	24.4	25.3	21.7	14.5	21.7	
30	17.5	25.8	26.7	22.9	15.3	23.2	

TABLE II—MOVE—M

Distance Moved Inches	Time TMU A	B	C	Hand In Motion B	Wt. (lb.) Up to	Wt. Allowance Factor	Constant TMU	CASE AND DESCRIPTION
½ or less	2.0	2.0	2.0	1.7	2.5	1.00	0	
1	2.5	2.9	3.4	2.3				
2	3.6	4.6	5.2	2.9	7.5	1.06	2.2	**A** Move object to other hand or against stop.
3	4.9	5.7	6.7	3.6				
4	6.1	6.9	8.0	4.3	12.5	1.11	3.9	
5	7.3	8.0	9.2	5.0				
6	8.1	8.9	10.3	5.7	17.5	1.17	5.6	
7	8.9	9.7	11.1	6.5				
8	9.7	10.6	11.8	7.2	22.5	1.22	7.4	
9	10.5	11.5	12.7	7.9				**B** Move object to approximate or indefinite location.
10	11.3	12.2	13.5	8.6				
12	12.9	13.4	15.2	10.0	27.5	1.28	9.1	
14	14.4	14.6	16.9	11.4				
16	16.0	15.8	18.7	12.8	32.5	1.33	10.8	
18	17.6	17.0	20.4	14.2				
20	19.2	18.2	22.1	15.6	37.5	1.39	12.5	
22	20.8	19.4	23.8	17.0				**C** Move object to exact location.
24	22.4	20.6	25.5	18.4	42.5	1.44	14.3	
26	24.0	21.8	27.3	19.8				
28	25.5	23.1	29.0	21.2	47.5	1.50	16.0	
30	27.1	24.3	30.7	22.7				

TABLE III—TURN AND APPLY PRESSURE—T AND AP

Weight	Time TMU for Degrees Turned
	30° 45° 60° 75° 90° 105° 120° 135° 150° 165° 180°
Small— 0 to 2 pounds	2.8 3.5 4.1 4.8 5.4 6.1 6.8 7.4 8.1 8.7 9.4
Medium— 2.1 to 10 Pounds	4.4 5.5 6.5 7.5 8.5 9.6 10.6 11.6 12.7 13.7 14.8
Large— 10.1 to 35 Pounds	8.4 10.5 12.3 14.4 16.2 18.3 20.4 22.2 24.3 26.1 28.2

APPLY PRESSURE CASE 1—16.2 TMU   APPLY PRESSURE CASE 2—10.6 TMU

TABLE V—POSITION—P

CLASS OF FIT	Symmetry	Easy To Handle	Difficult To Handle
1—Loose No pressure required	S	5.6	11.2
	SS	9.1	14.7
	NS	10.4	16.0
2—Close Light pressure required	S	16.2	21.8
	SS	19.7	25.3
	NS	21.0	26.6
3—Exact Heavy pressure required	S	43.0	48.6
	SS	46.5	52.1
	NS	47.8	53.4

TABLE IV—GRASP—G

Case	Time TMU	DESCRIPTION
1A	2.0	Pick Up Grasp—Small, medium or large object by itself, easily grasped.
1B	3.6	Very small object or object lying close against a flat surface.
1C1	7.3	Interference with grasp on bottom and one side of nearly cylindrical object. Diameter larger than ½".
1C2	8.7	Interference with grasp on bottom and one side of nearly cylindrical object. Diameter ¼" to ½".
1C3	10.8	Interference with grasp on bottom and one side of nearly cylindrical object. Diameter less than ¼".
2	5.6	Re-grasp.
3	5.6	Transfer Grasp.
4A	7.3	Object jumbled with other objects so search and select occur. Larger than 1" x 1" x 1".
4B	9.1	Object jumbled with other objects so search and select occur. ¼" x ½" x ½" to 1" x 1" x 1".
4C	12.9	Object jumbled with other objects so search and select occur. Smaller than ¼" x ¼" x ½".
5	0	Contact sliding or hook grasp.

common superior A, and then down again via the other channel]...could be in current use? Unfortunately, there can be little doubt of it...it is insufficient executive capacity on the part of those in charge.[20]

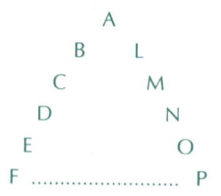

With regard to unity of command, Fayol's position was opposed to Taylor's concept of functional management, where an employee can have many bosses for different aspects of his work requiring different specializations. Fayol was sensitive to this difference in points of view:

> I do not think that a shop can be well run in flagrant violation of this [principle of unity of command]. Nevertheless, Taylor successfully managed large-scale concerns....I imagine that in practice Taylor was able to reconcile functionalism with the principle of unity of command, but that is a supposition whose accuracy I am not in a position to verify.[21]

Fayol's principles emphasized equitable treatment of employees, fair remuneration, organizational stability, and attention to morale, but the basic thrust of his philosophy was subordination of people to the organization, with the workers more or less interchangeable bits contributing to the all-important whole. He likened people in the organization to cells in the body:

> Man in the body corporate plays a role like that of the cell in the animal, single-cell in the case of the one-man business, thousandth or millionth part of the body corporate in the large-scale enterprise. ...The development of the organism is effected by the grouping together of elemental units [men or cells].[22]

Many management theorists built on Fayol's philosophy, though some of them were not familiar with his writings until several years after they had appeared in France (an English-language translation was not

---

unity of command

Figure 17-3. Fayol's Bridge

```
        A
      B   L
    C       M
  D           N
E               O
F ............. P
```

An ordered organization has a place for everyone and everyone in his or her place.

available in the U.S. until 1930). Experienced administrator Luther Gulick, in collaboration with Lyndall Urwick, codified managerial principles into the seven functions of "POSDCORB" (Planning, Organizing, Staffing, Directing, Coordinating, Reporting, Budgeting),[23] but departed very little from Fayol's basic framework. James Mooney and Allan Reiley, drawing on their experience with General Motors, agreed with Fayol in seeing work in a functional framework, with organizing clearly coming ahead of staffing. The worker thus became an interchangeable and disposable resource that performed by being dropped into pre-established slots:

> In every organization, there is a collective job to be done, consisting always of the sum of many individual jobs, and the task of administration, operating through management, is the coordination of all the human effort necessary to this end. Such coordination, however, always presupposes the jobs to be coordinated. The job as such is therefore antecedent to the man on the job, and the sound coordination of these jobs, considered simply as jobs, must be the first and necessary condition in the effective coordination of the human factor.[24]

Mary Parker Follett, one of the early classical theorists, shared Fayol's viewpoint, but to a different degree. She proposed four principles of organization, all emphasizing coordination:[25]

the coordination principle in organization

1. Coordination by direct contact of the responsible managers
2. Coordination in the early stages of an undertaking
3. Coordination as a two-way relating of all the factors in a situation
4. Coordination as a continuing process

Her first principle, although opposed to traditional hierarchical notions, supported the notion of Fayol's "bridge." Her third principle held that department heads could not realistically be expected to subordinate their departmental interests to a vague "good of the whole," but that frequent interplay between department managers would lead to a reconciling of divergent viewpoints into workable compromises. Her fourth principle says that organizations constantly change, and that no adjustment remains in effect for very long. She argued that authority automatically goes with the job and the situation, rather than the person; thus one worker is not really taking orders from another, but both are taking orders from "the situation." She was a vigorous advocate of the idea that "integration in organizational conflict" depends on reciprocal evaluation and adjustment of conflicting desires and needs.

Weber's Bureaucratic Theory of Organization

An important contemporary of Taylor and Fayol was the famous German sociologist Max Weber (1864–1920). He did not publish as extensively as some other theorists; his philosophies appear chiefly in reprints of works by other writers. At his death he left an unfinished work, *Economics and Society*, Part 1 of which has been translated by A. M. Henderson and Talcott Parsons.[26] Weber described organizations as bureaucracies and held that the well-ordered bureaucracy was the most effective form of organization; his views on this topic (summarized in his paper on "Bureaucracy") are paraphrased below.[27]

Weber's bureaucratic model

- *Characteristics of Bureaucracy*
    1. There is the principle of fixed and official jurisdictional areas:
        a. Regular activities (official duties) are distributed in a fixed way
        b. Authority to command is distributed in a stable way (defined by rules)
        c. Methodical provision is made for fulfillment of these duties by qualified people
    2. Principles of hierarchy means a firmly ordered system of supervision, with a regulated system of appeal
    3. Management is based on written documents (the "files"), and on separation of public and private duties and conduct
    4. Office management presupposes expert training
    5. Official activity demands the full working capacity of the individual
    6. Management of the office follows general stable rules which can be learned
- *Position of the Official*
    1. Office-holding is a vocation (acceptance of a specific obligation of faithful management in return for a secure existence). It does not establish loyalty to a person, but to impersonal and functional purposes.
    2. The position of the official is usually patterned as follows:
        a. He or she usually enjoys a distinct social esteem compared with the governed;
        b. is appointed by superior officers;
        c. holds the position for life—guarantees against arbitrary dismissal assure strictly objective discharge of duties free from personal considerations;
        d. receives a fixed salary based on status or rank rather than on the work done, with a guaranteed pension for old age security; and
        e. is set for a career within the hierarchical order.
- *Technical Advantages of a Bureaucratic Organization*
    1. Precision, speed, unambiguity, knowledge of the files, continuity, discretion, unity, strict subordination, reduction of friction and of material and personal costs are raised to the optimum point.
    2. Large modern capitalist enterprises are unequaled models of this classic bureaucratic organization, which develops best when the bureaucracy is "dehumanized" and when it eliminates from official business all personal and emotional elements. This is the specific nature and special virtue of bureaucracy.
    3. Once established, bureaucracy is one of the hardest social structures to destroy, so it is a power instrument of the first order for the one who controls the bureaucratic apparatus.
    4. The individual bureaucrat is chained to his activity. He is a cog in an ever-moving mechanism which prescribes a fixed route of march.
    5. The ruled cannot replace the bureaucratic apparatus of authority once it exists, for it rests on expert training. If the official is interrupted, chaos results, and it is hard to improvise replacements who can master such chaos.

Weber's theories have been picked up and amplified by later managers and management theorists, but not without a great deal of discussion and disagreement. He was describing the *formal organization*, and paying almost no attention to the informal and unofficial organization discussed in chapter 4. There is no doubt that many large corporations embody much of the bureaucratic structure, which enables them to continue functioning long after individual leaders have passed from the scene. But nothing in Weber's concept provides for revamping an organization that has ceased to grow or developed wasteful or destructive practices. Alfred P. Sloan, Jr., who reorganized the General Motors Corporation in the 1920s, combined Weber's feeling for structure with a design that would give capable subordinates the freedom of action to strike out in new directions. Sloan knew, as did Weber, that a great corporation (or large public enterprise) was too complex to be controlled by one man (as the brilliant William C. Durant, who put GM together, had attempted to do). So he built a corporate structure that would bring the most knowledgeable people into the decision process at the proper points, while still leaving them the discretion to move effectively within an orderly framework of policymaking.

While Weber still commands a good deal of respect for his insights, and while his model serves as a point of departure for many theories of organization and management, it is generally believed that his principles are not appropriate for a modern innovative enterprise that must be prepared to cope with change.

The Human Relations School

From the days of Adam Smith (quoted earlier in this chapter) and no doubt long before, managers have recognized the need for workers to rest if they are to produce their best. The need for rest is something that distinguishes us from the other "tools of production." It was exploration of this very human need for rest and recharging that linked the scientific management and behavioral schools, in a sense. The Gilbreths—members of the classical school—stated positively that experience had proven the increased output obtainable through short rest periods during the workday, and an experiment designed to test their assertion laid the foundation for quite a different theory of management.

human relations school

Mayo and the Hawthorne Experiments

Professor Elton Mayo of the Graduate School of Business Administration at Harvard was born in Australia in 1880, trained in psychology, and came to the U.S. in 1922 where he branched out into sociology. In 1927 he became part of a team that would conduct a long-term (until 1932) study at the Hawthorne Plant of the Western Electric Company in Chicago, initially designed to investigate the effect of fatigue on productivity.

Best-known of the Hawthorne studies was the one concerned with a group of six women who assembled telephone relays. This study, discussed in chapter 4, had several purposes, one being to explore the relationship between rest periods and productivity. Six women were drawn from a group of about 100 women working under an incentive plan

Hawthorne studies

where pay was based on group output. Payment of the six would be based on the production of their subgroup. After several weeks on this basis, rest periods were added to the daily schedule and eventually increased in length. As each change was made, production increased (with only minor exceptions).

After following this pattern for several months, rest periods were eliminated for 12 weeks. Output rose to a new level, and was maintained for the entire period. Then rest periods were again initiated, and output rose even higher. Indeed, during the entire experiment (conducted over several years), output continued its upward trend virtually independent of what changes were made. The sick record of the small group was three times better than that of the other workers, the women were enthusiastic and eager to come to work, and they required virtually no supervision.[28]

What did all this mean? The women themselves could shed little light on the question, except to say that they felt under less pressure and had no "slavedriver" boss. Rather, they dealt with a group of experimenters who explained the tests fully and patiently and solicited suggestions from the women in a way that undoubtedly made the latter feel they were participants.

Mayo's theory, arrived at after long consideration, was that workers did not necessarily behave as "economic" individuals, each attempting to serve his or her own self-interest (and thus each striving to earn the highest income under incentive systems, as Taylor postulated). Instead they behaved as members of social groups, and work groups were vitally important to their behavior. If work conditions reinforce this sense of belonging to a cohesive group, workers will experience job satisfaction; if not, they will be frustrated and inclined to complain about work conditions—and unable to do their best work regardless of personal incentives. In Mayo's words,

Recall in the case study to chapter 4 that the drafting room employees started running prayer sessions, and when Ab objected they began a slowdown. Was their response logical, nonlogical, or irrational? Explain.

[T]he responses of any adult individual to his surroundings are of three types:
  a. Logical...
  b. Nonlogical...actions may be adequate to the situation, but any intelligence they exhibit is socially and not personally derived...
  c. Irrational...symptomatic of social maladjustment, and shows all the signs of obsession...

The nonlogical response...in strict conformity to a social code, makes for social order and discipline, for effective collaboration...and for happiness and a sense of security.[29]

Human Relations after Mayo

The Hawthorne studies generated much interest and led to many other studies. There has been some criticism of their scientific validity: Alex Carey compared their findings and conclusions in detail and stated that the latter seemed almost entirely unsupported. He questioned "how it was possible for studies so nearly devoid of scientific merit, and conclusions so little supported by the evidence, to gain so influential and respected a place within scientific disciplines and to hold this place for so long."[30] But other studies came up with conclusions similar to those of Mayo and his colleagues. And by and large, industry has accepted the proposition that human factors influence output as do technical methods and machine capacities.

But *awareness* of the human relations dimension is a far cry from the ability to design management techniques that will take advantage of human relations theories and improve productivity accordingly. By and large, the scientific management school has improved productivity within its sphere of activity, but the same is not true of the human relations school. It has been said[31] that while early human relations theorists really had little impact on managerial practices, they did generate a noticeable change in managerial philosophy, toward less authoritative management and more consideration to workers as people.

Kurt Lewin and his colleagues did significant work in the late 1930s and the war years on the way leadership styles influenced attitudes and the impact of group discussions compared with authoritarian methods of changing practices.[32] In many respects, Lewin can be considered a major innovator in the field of group dynamics and sensitivity training. Another important early human relations theorist, Abraham Maslow, developed the "hierarchy of needs" discussed in chapter 4, pointing to the existence of higher-level needs such as status, esteem, and self-actualization which often supersede the basic needs for survival and economic well-being (though not when the basic needs themselves are in question).

group dynamics, sensitivity training

More recently, theorist Chris Argyris has approached the question of what motivates workers from the viewpoint of personality development over time, much as the child develops to the mature individual. He lists the following stages in this development:[33]

1. From passivity to activity (doing for oneself rather than relying on others)
2. From dependence to independence (exercising decision power rather than seeking direction)
3. From inflexibility to flexibility (ability to adapt to external conditions)
4. From superficial to significant interests (ability to find meaning in work for its own sake)
5. From short-term to long-term perspective (ability to see short-term means as paths to a longer-term goal)
6. From acceptance of subordinate role to demand for some autonomy (particularly with respect to one's own activity)
7. From lack of control to self-control (authority and ability to provide self-direction without external constraints)

Douglas McGregor, whose Theory X and Theory Y were discussed in chapter 4, proposed that managers accept the latter, based on these hypotheses:[34]

1. Work is a natural evolution, and may cause satisfaction or pain.
2. If workers are committed to objectives, they will control themselves.
3. Commitment comes from such rewards as self-actualization.
4. The average person can learn to seek responsibility.
5. A wide slice of the population has the imagination and creativity to solve organizational problems.
6. The intellectual potential of most workers is only partially utilized.

McGregor's propositions seem quite reasonable (indeed, in chapter 4 we discussed many approaches that were based on these assumptions). But it is one thing to accept these ideas about human nature and another to train managers so they can respond to employee aspirations in ways that will advance organizational goals. One problem, of course, is that a happy employee is not necessarily a productive employee. Another problem (the training problem) is that of teaching old dogs new tricks—changing managerial views that have become heavily ingrained. One training technique that has become exceedingly popular, sensitivity training, is discussed in chapters 4 and 10.

action assumptions of human relations school

William G. Scott has attempted to summarize what he calls the "action-designed assumptions" of the human relations school: those assumptions that are intended to guide managers in advancing organizational goals through improved employee relations. Scott's list represents a sort of consensus of the views of human relations writers:[35]

1. Good human relations call for managerial use of experience, intuition, and theory.
2. Employee participation generates greater human satisfaction and higher productivity.
3. Individual behavior arises from formal expectations (what the company demands) and informal expectations (what the work group demands).
4. Communication, essential to organizational effectiveness, is largely a human problem and subject to human foibles.
5. Teamwork requires agreement on goals by both manager and worker.
6. Employee work satisfaction is not entirely money-induced, but comes from a hierarchy of changeable needs (recognition, accomplishment, status, etc.).
7. The plant or office is a social system, and the executive must be a relationship expert to maintain its balance.
8. Executive skills in human relations can be developed.

The Structuralist School

structuralist school

In many respects, the so-called structuralist school is difficult to define; it is particularly difficult to isolate those theorists who adhere to it. Essentially, this school evolved as a compromise between two approaches to ideal management priorities: (1) first designing the organization and then pushing people into the slots, and (2) first developing meaningful roles for people and then finding some organization that could provide such roles. By this definition, anyone who sees good points in both scientific management and human relations would be called a structuralist.

The term was first suggested by Amitai Etzioni,[36] but the compromise position was building for some time before he suggested it, and in this discussion we are using it in a broader framework than he had in mind. William Scott criticizes the classical school as follows:

> It would not be fair to say that the classical school is unaware of the human problems which affect organization. They simply do not treat in any

systematic way the interplay of individual personality, informal groups, intro-organizational conflict, and the decision process in their conception of the formal structure. Additionally, the classical school has failed to incorporate in its theory the contributions of the behavioral sciences as part of a comprehensive explanation of human behavior in the organization. Classical theory...has relevant insights into the nature of organization which should not be discounted. But the value of this theory is limited by its narrow concentration on the formal anatomy of organization.[37]

Scott also criticizes the human relations school in several respects, drawing on the comments of several writers. He cites Peter Drucker as mounting a devastating attack on human relations for lacking an adequate focus on work; Drucker says it is not the job that determines employee happiness, but only relations to fellow workers. Scott criticizes studies showing that workers want things other than money, pointing out that some of them have been made during periods when wages were not subject to change ("man does not live by bread alone, once he has bread"), and that workers go out on strike because they want money, not because of Freudian reactions against authority. And he considers most human relations studies invalid because they focused on nonmanagerial behavior at low administrative levels (in the factory, the military, or the classroom), but their conclusions were applied to all management levels.

Barnard's Theory of Cooperation and Organization
Like Taylor, Fayol, Gulick, and Urwick (to mention some classicists), and unlike Mayo and other human relations advocates, Chester I. Barnard was a practicing executive. He obtained his managerial experience in the New Jersey Bell Telephone Company, of which he was president, and his experience led him to take a behavioral view. In chapter 3, we cited his four rules for getting an order (or other communication) accepted, which include structuring the order so that it is not incompatible with the recipient's personal interest. In the preface to his book, *The Functions of the Executive,* Barnard explains why he struck out in the behavioral direction:

> Nothing of which I knew treated of organization in a way which seemed to me to correspond either to my experience or to the understanding implicit in the conduct of those recognized to be adept in executive practice or in the leadership of organizations. Some excellent work has been done in describing and analyzing the superficial characteristics of organizations. It is important, but like descriptive geography with physics, chemistry, geology, and biology missing.[38]

In discussing the requirements for cooperation in organizations, he set forth the following principles:

1. The individual possesses a limited power of choice, so he selects a set of limiting factors, and tries to achieve his purposes by operating on these factors.
2. He has biological limitations, which he overcomes by cooperating with others, but this requires him to adopt a group purpose and brings in many other factors.
3. Social factors arise from cooperation. He must discover the process of interaction, which changes the motives and interests of participants.

requirements for organizational cooperation

4. Cooperation will persist as long as it accomplishes both the cooperative and the individual purposes.
5. Cooperation will become unstable if defects develop in either of these or in their combination. *The functions of the executive are those of securing the effective adaptation of these processes.*
6. An organization comes into being when persons able to communicate with each other are willing to contribute to a common purpose.

Barnard discussed the interrelation of formal and informal organizations (see our chapter 5) in terms of the following principles:

1. Personal interactions, when repetitive, become organized because of their effect on habits of action and thought.
2. Chain relationships among people generate uniform states of mind, which develop into customs and institutions.
3. Informal organizations thus give rise to formal organizations, which are necessary to any large informal organization.
4. Formal organizations firm up many informal attitudes and institutions, resulting in interdependence.
5. Formal organizations in their turn create more informal organizations.
6. Formal organizations must have informal organizations, as means of communication, cohesion, and protecting the integrity of the individuals.

Effectiveness vs. Efficiency

Barnard calls effectiveness the achievement of the cooperative purpose, and efficiency the satisfaction of individual motives. The structuralist

Cooperation will persist as long as it accomplishes both the group and the individual purpose.

would recognize that the cooperative purpose of the organization (not of the group) might have to take first place if the organization is to prosper. In chapter 4, discussing the Hawthorne experiments, we described a situation with a group of men in the bank wiring room: researchers found that they irrationally held down production and thus deprived themselves of incentive pay they could have earned with only modest extra effort. To the human relations theorist, this experiment confirms the importance of group feelings about the "priority motivators" (solidarity, group norms, etc.). The structuralist, however, might conclude that the men were in fact acting in their own economic best interest, in that they feared a reduction in piecework rates if they showed management that they could produce a great deal more.

The human relationist advocates that management pay as much attention to worker satisfaction as to getting the work done, on grounds that organizational goals are achieved by seeking to maximize individual goals. The structuralist is more cynical, believing that at times too much attention to worker goals may be harmful to organizational goals, and the latter must take priority.

Curt Tausky gives what he calls a dramatic and sad illustration of this dilemma.[39] In 1954, a human relations theorist glowingly described the enlightened worker relations in the Studebaker Corporation, which had been in business for over a century:

> An example of high worker satisfaction is found in the Studebaker company, which has an enviable record with respect to overt conflict...At the Studebaker company the union contract gives the stewards and the workers a real measure of control and power which the factory manager, the personnel manager, and the top foremen have in other plants. ...Yet this small company continues to compete successfully in the market with the giants of the automobile industry, and its workers are probably more involved and identified with the company than is true of most industrial organizations.

Tausky goes on to say that, while we may agree that the workers were more satisfied at Studebaker, the other companies still produce cars, whereas Studebaker closed its gates at the South Bend plant in 1963.

The structuralist gives far more importance to the formal organization structure, with the informal social influences seen as relatively insignificant. The employee pays close attention to those elements of his or her job that can be evaluated by superiors. The technical aspects of the job are primary factors, and it may be that jobs simply cannot be restructured so that they are meaningful and fulfilling, or so that the individual can have a high degree of self-control on his job.

Etzioni makes an interesting point about the primacy of organization structure and technology in terms of internal relationships. In a hospital, for example, line and staff are turned upside down in terms of authority:

line-staff reversal

> In full-fledged professional organizations the staff-professional line-administrator correlation...is reversed. [In such organizations] administrators are in charge of secondary activities; they administer *means* to the major activities carried out by the professionals.[40]

Would Erzioni's point apply to Zeb and Bert? Explain.

Etzioni defines three categories of influencing behavior in organizations: physical, material, and symbolic. Physical methods might be used in prisons, where actual restraint is applied. Material methods involve principally monetary rewards or the lack of them. Symbolic methods involve prestige or esteem, love or acceptance. Symbolic methods are the tools of the human relationists, whereas the structuralist recognizes that all of the categories apply to some types of organizations.

In 1952, Ernest Dale conducted a research study for the American Management Association, seeking to find how different U.S. firms used classical management theories in their actual work. He discovered that as firms grew in size, different organizational problems came to the fore (much as we are representing in the North Star story that runs through this book). Table 17-2 shows how Dale classified the problems at seven different stages of growth (using as samples different companies representative of such stages of growth), and the possible results that would flow from solving the problems.

Dale's study was a clear break with the classical school, yet did not embrace the human relations school. He showed that the stage of an organization's development had a great deal to do with the type of problems that were most troublesome at the time, but made it clear that classical considerations still were important regardless of size. He felt that the classicists were unwilling to deal with some important areas of organization which real managers were forced to face, and that any general theory ought to be capable of dealing with these. Dale also noted the need to study the interrelationships of personality and organization, to consider more deeply the meaning of social responsibility for managerial action, and to recognize that the manager cannot be inhibited by a network of organization theories.

Systems Analysis

closed system

Taylor thought of a company as a closed system, with all actions and reactions taking place within the confines of the work place. Mayo likewise thought of the company as a closed system; he sought to find causes for

Table 17-2.
Dale's Classification of Organizational Problems at Seven Stages of Growth

Stage of Growth	Size (no. of employees)*	Organizational problem and its possible sequences
I	3-7 (any size)	Formulation of Objectives: Division of work
II	25 (10)	Delegation of Responsibility: The Accommodation of Personalities
III	125 (50-100)	Delegation of More Management Functions: Span of Control
IV	500 (50-300)	Reducing the Executive's Burden: The Staff Assistant
V	1,500 (100-400)	Establishing a New Function (Functionalization): The Staff Specialties
VI	5,000 (100-500)	Coordination of Management Functions Group Decision Making
VII	465,000 (over 500)	Determining the Degree of Delegation: Decentralization

* Note—The first figure indicates the actual size of the company studied. The second figure in brackets indicates very broadly the size of the company when the particular organizational problem may arise for the first time.

behavior of the relay room women or the bank wiring room men entirely within the work environment, and if possible within the immediate confines of the work group itself. Taylor noted the difficulty that a worker would encounter if he or she attempted to "bust a rate" by higher output and lived in a neighborhood with other workers from the same plant. There is no evidence that the Hawthorne researchers took into account whatever attitudes the workers may have brought with them from outside (class consciousness, the role of unions, etc.); their studies have been criticized for this omission.

The structuralist attempts to consider the company as an open system, constantly interrelating with the elements of its environment—marketing, capital, public opinion, laws, raw materials, unions, and so on. The more mechanistic an organization is (Weber's pure bureaucracy), the less equipped it is to cope with a disordered external environment which forces it into frequent changes of direction. Mass production companies work best when the outside influences are moderated to a large extent; thus, Detroit was poorly equipped to sense the public need for a small car of low fuel consumption, and to respond rapidly by building and marketing such a car.

Systems analysis is a technique for dealing with open systems, and it would appear to offer a great deal of promise because of its capability for looking at a whole system and evaluating the interrelations among the subsystems. Unfortunately, systems analysis has chosen to tackle the small or "micro" problems, where fewer variables are involved and chances for success are higher. By and large, it has not worked at company level, so its capability for dealing usefully with the managerial problems of open systems remains untested. Some theorists believe that management and behavioral scientists will eventually collaborate in formulating a true systems approach for managerial and organizational analysis.

open system

Do you think North Star, as a small concern, is more likely to be an open system than a huge corporation like Barnhard & Walker, or the reverse? Why?

Current Issues in Management Theory

Some management scholars believe that the environment we live in today will build its own management theories. Just as Frederick Taylor was the right theorist for an industrial society seeking to harness new technology to improve productivity, and Mayo was the right theorist for an overly authoritarian society seeking ways to give a voice to the anonymous factory worker (and perhaps as Weber was the right theorist for a highly structured society with a very slow pace of change but a great deal of need for order and predictability), so some new savant will pull together the forces acting on us today and will find the right principles to mark the road we will travel.

What is that road? We can take the pessimistic view, and say we are in a new world of permanent scarcity, where resources are running out, and no-growth is the order of the day. We can agree with the environmentalists that we have paid too much for our material goods in terms of befouled air, polluted waters, and growing scrap piles. We can subscribe to the political notions about permanent mistrust in government institutions, which suggest an unwillingness to place our destinies in the hands of elected leaders. We can fall in with the systems people and the economists, and decide that central planning will be a fact of our coming life. We can decide that the large corporations will have to bow to some popular demand that they become instruments for social change, and perhaps give up some of their freedom and their profit motive in return for a guarantee of solvency. We can decide that the change in work expectations means that jobs will be designed to be more meaningful, with the assembly-line processes ruled out (and with them, no doubt, the low-cost mass-produced goods they made possible). We can decide that people are becoming nonmaterialistic, and will respond not to higher wages but to the more enduring humanistic values.

It would be dangerous to adopt any of these views, for we have so little evidence to go on. Perhaps there will be some movement toward greater consensus in management—there are trends in this direction already. Perhaps managers in the big corporations will have more administrative constraints placed on them by Congress—certainly, there is evidence of that trend. Perhaps there will be national constraints on use of scarce resources, so that a company will not be entitled to buy whatever it can afford. But the lessons of the past suggest that these tendencies will be modest, and that the managers of tomorrow will face many of the same problems they face today.

Organizational development promises to assume a greater role than it has in the past—but as a partner to classical management theories rather than a competitor. Its advocates promote it as a technology for managing change and for dealing with open systems.

Systems analysis should become a more important tool as it is adapted to deal with disorderly data and larger problems. This technique can be extremely useful in portraying a complex enterprise as a network of interrelating subsystems. As more managers are trained in the concepts of systems analysis and management science, their past reluctance to talk the language should disappear.

Improvements in communications and information technology may make it possible both to centralize and decentralize at the same time. The headquarters unit will have more information, enabling personnel to make policy decisions over a wider range of problems; but in order to free itself for true policy consideration, the unit may have to delegate more operating matters. Thus the future manager may have to consider far more than unit goals in making decisions.

Unions have a great deal more power than they had in the days when the management theorists we have been studying were developing and testing their ideas. Moreover, as we saw in the chapter on labor-management relations, unions are moving from bread-and-butter issues to increased concern with all sorts of fringe benefits. Industrial democracy, a philosophy that is gaining strength in some parts of Europe, involves workers in the decision-making process (in Sweden and Germany, for example, workers occupy up to half of the positions on what correspond to our corporate boards of directors). In Yugoslavia, workers actually hire the chief executive officer, and can fire him if he does not perform satisfactorily. This development may sharply reduce the inducements available to management; if worker participation is written into the union agreement, what more can managers do to increase "self-actualization"?

All these projected developments add up to very little in the way of guidance. The truth is, of course, that management theory is an uncertain matter at best, and managers must use pragmatic criteria in making their way through problem situations. Certainly most of the concepts that have worked in the past, as embodied in existing theories that have stood the test of time, will continue to work in the future. In a sense, the famous line used to describe the city of Paris could also be applied to management—the more it changes, the more it remains the same.

Summary

The notion of management as a profession is relatively recent. In earlier times, lack of reading (and hence studying) ability on the part of the upper classes, little task specialization of the type that called for coordinating management, the small size of most enterprises, and perhaps the unwillingness to spend scarce resources on an "overhead function" such as specialized management, all contributed to a lack of emphasis on this area. Nonetheless, several organizations made marked contributions to management methodology, notably the guilds, the church, and the military.

With the dawn of the industrial revolution came the "factory system," and some managerial skills were needed to consolidate the tools of production into large units. To some extent, the seeds of modern management skills were sown in the early factories. Management theories were first set down in writing at the start of the twentieth century, with the rise of the classical school.

Frederick W. Taylor, father of scientific management, was an early classicist, as were Henri Fayol, father of management theory, and Max Weber, author of the bureaucratic theory of organizations. Later theorists built on the work of these pioneers.

Elton Mayo, about 30 years after Taylor, was in charge of some research studies at the Hawthorne Plant of Western Electric Company in Chicago. His findings led to the formation of the human relations school, which emphasized the existence of motivators other than money, the power of the social group in the workplace, and the important impact of attitudes in generating interest in work. It was not clear that good human relations always meant an improvement in productivity, and the human relations school has been criticized for drawing conclusions from the Hawthorne studies that may not have been supported by the evidence. But other experiments have produced similar results, and the human relations movement has had important repercussions in changing managerial behavior.

The structuralist school found fault with parts of both the classical and the human relations schools, and used the most acceptable parts of each as the foundation of a compromise theory. The structuralist theory, essentially, evolved from the two earlier schools. Systems analysis should be a useful tool of the structuralists, but few systems analysts have chosen to work with large organizational problems, and their techniques are unproven in this context. The structuralists charge the two earlier schools with having treated the workplace as a closed system, with no attention paid to outside factors; they argue that it should be viewed as an open system, with both internal and external factors considered in testing various ideas about worker and managerial behavior.

What lies ahead in management theory? The future is difficult to project because so many variables are involved—scarcity, environmental worries, lack of confidence in institutions, energy problems, improvements in communications, and the changing role of unions, among others. It is hard to discern any firm trend, aside from anticipating closer ties between management science and behavioral science.

Notes

1. Will and Ariel Durant, *The Story of Civilization*, 10 vols. (New York: Simon & Schuster, Inc., 1954-1967).
2. With some exceptions—the Babylonians had division of labor, and the Chinese under the dynasties had an effective civil service and minimum wage rates.
3. James D. Mooney, *Principles of Organization* (New York: Harper & Row, Pubs., 1947), p. 116.
4. Bronsart von Schellendorf, "The Duties of the General Staff," in *Staffs of Various Armies* (Washington, D.C.: U.S. Government Printing Office, 1899), p. 9.
5. Adam Smith, *Inquiry into the Nature and Cause of the Wealth of Nations* (London, 1776; reprinted in Everyman's Library, vol. 1), p. 73.
6. Paul Mantoux, in *The Industrial Revolution in the Eighteenth Century* (London, 1955), p. 70.
7. From Erich Roll, *An Early Experiment in Industrial Organization*, summarized by Urwick and Brech in *The Making of Scientific Management* (London: Management Publications Trust, 1946), p. xv.
8. Though the principles had been applied many times since their initial introduction by Gilbreth, as discussed later in this chapter.
9. Frederick W. Taylor, "Shop Management," *Transactions of the American Society of Mechanical Engineers*, June 1903, pp. 1337–1480; reprinted in Taylor's *Scientific Management* (New York: Harper & Row, Pubs., 1947), pp. 83–84.
10. Ibid.
11. Ibid.
12. Ibid.
13. Making him a "high-priced man," as one story of the period termed him. But of course, it was not his wage rate that was important but rather how much he produced in proportion to what he was paid.
14. Taylor, "Shop Management."
15. J. Boddewyn, "Frederick Winslow Taylor Revisited," *Academy of Management Journal*, August 1961, pp. 100–107.
16. C. Bertrand Thompson, *The Theory and Practice of Scientific Management* (Boston: Houghton Mifflin Co., 1917).
17. Harrington Emerson, *Twelve Principles of Efficiency* (New York: The Carnegie Foundation, Bulletin No. 5, 1910).
18. Morris L. Cooke, *Academic and Industrial Efficiency* (New York: The Carnegie Foundation, Bulletin No. 5, 1910).
19. Fayol originally published his major work in 1916. It was translated much later by Constance Storrs as *General and Industrial Management* (London: Sir Isaac Pitman & Sons, 1949).
20. Ibid, pp. 35-36.
21. Ibid, p. 69.
22. Ibid, pp. 58-60.
23. Luther Gulick and Lyndall Urwick, eds., *Papers on the Science of Administration* (New Work: Columbia University Institute of Public Administration, 1937).

24. James D. Mooney and Allan C. Reiley, *Principles of Organization* (New York: Harper & Row, Pubs., 1939). By contrast, chief executive Dennis C. Stanfill of Twentieth Century Fox Film Corporation, who turned around the ailing film-maker by showing a profit every year since he was brought in in 1971, said in 1975 "I think of management structure in terms of the qualities of my executives. I don't make men fit the blocks; I make the situation fit the men."

25. Lyndall Urwick et al., eds., *The Collected Papers of Mary Parker Follett* (New York: Harper & Row, Pubs., 1942).

26. Max Weber, *The Theory of Social and Economic Organization*, trans. A. M. Henderson and Talcott Parsons (New York: The Free Press, 1964).

27. H. H. Gerth and C. Wright Mills, *From Max Weber: Essays in Sociology* (New York: Oxford University Press, 1958).

28. F. J. Roethlisberger and W. J. Dickson, *Management and the Worker* (Cambridge, Mass.: Harvard University Press, 1930).

29. Elton Mayo, *The Human Problems of an Industrial Civilization* (New York: Viking Press, Inc., 1960), pp. 92–93.

30. Alex Carey, "The Hawthorne Studies: A Radical Criticism," *American Sociological Review*, June 1967, pp. 403–416.

31. Reinhard Bendix, *Work and Authority in Industry* (New York: John Wiley & Sons, Inc., 1956), p. 319.

32. Kurt Lewin, Ronald Lippit, and Ralph K. White, "Patterns of Aggressive Behavior in Experimentally Created Social Climates," *Journal of Social Psychology* 10 (1939): p. 271-299.

33. Chris Argyris, "The Integration of the Individual and the Organization," in Chris Argyris et al., *Social Sciences Approach to Business Behavior* (Homewood, Ill.: Dorsey Press, 1962), pp. 57–98.

34. Douglas McGregor, *The Human Side of Enterprise* (New York: McGraw-Hill Book Co., 1960), pp. 33-43.

35. William G. Scott, *Human Relations in Management* (Homewood, Ill.: Richard D. Irwin, Inc., 1962), pp. 54–57.

36. Amitai Etzioni, *Modern Organizations* (Englewood Cliffs, N.J.: Prentice-Hall, Inc., 1964).

37. Scott, *Human Relations*, p. 121.

38. Chester I. Barnard, *The Functions of the Executive* (Cambridge, Mass.: Harvard University Press, 1938).

39. Curt Tausky, *Work Organizations* (Itaska, Ill.: F. E. Peacock, 1970), p. 58—quoting Daniel Katz, "Worker Satisfactions and Deprivations in Industrial Life," in Kornhauser, Dubin, and Ross, eds., *Industrial Conflict* (New York: McGraw-Hill Book Co., 1954), pp. 104-05.

40. Etzioni, *Modern Organizations*, p. 81.

Review Questions

1. Which activities in preindustrial civilization demanded some expertise in the practice of management?
2. What was the advantage of the "general staff" organization?
3. What elements of modern management were present in the Boulton & Watt company as early as 1800?
4. What are the three principal schools of management thought?
5. Why was Taylor's technique called "scientific management"? What was meant by "functional foremanship" in his system?
6. What is the purpose of methods-time measurement? Why would the manager need to understand this procedure?
7. Explain the advantages of Fayol's "bridge."

8. How does the bureaucratic philosophy of management perceive the individual?
9. What are the assumptions of the human relations school?
10. How is the structuralist school different from the classical and the human relations school? How does it borrow from each?
11. Explain Barnard's theories concerning the relationship between the formal and informal organizations.
12. What did the structuralists think was wrong with the human relations theory with regard to self-actualization and group motivations?
13. Distinguish between closed and open systems.

Discussion Questions

1. What sort of safeguards should an executive establish to avoid the staff taking action that the executive would not approve—without losing the benefits of speed and expertise that derive from the staff system?
2. Scientific management has been criticized as applying only to the "shop level" management, with no valid guidelines to offer for other levels. Do you think this is a fair criticism? Why or why not?
3. If Weber is right about bureaucracy being hard to break down because it is "a power instrument of the first order for the one who controls the bureaucratic apparatus," why did President Nixon, who controlled the FBI, the IRS, and other segments of the bureaucratic apparatus, lose control of his destiny?
4. Mayo concluded that the women in the Hawthorne relay wiring room were working not for money but to achieve some unspecified group goals; and he extended this conclusion to draw some broad generalizations about what makes people in general achieve. Can you think of any holes in his generalization (any elements present in his experiments with the relay wiring group that would not generally be present in other industrial situations)? Do you think the women really did not care much for money?
5. In a sense, the structuralist school is saying of the classical and human relations schools, "You're both right in some ways, and both wrong in some ways." Is it possible that Taylor was more right than wrong for his day (1900), and Mayo more right than wrong for his day (1930)? In other words, did times simply change, so that each was working on the principal problem of his day? Or do you think that each theorist actually was part right and part wrong?

North Star Case Study

As one of the intermediate steps in transferring of Eldorado to incorporated status and cutting it loose from the control of North Star and Barnhard and Walker, North Star was required to establish a working municipality, including a police organization, a public works maintenance group, a water and sewer crew, and so on. During the construction phase, the construction teams undertook whatever maintenance was required as part of putting the systems in service, but as construction was phased out, the maintenance and operating crew took over this function.

Henry had no experience with the question of productivity, or what constituted a "fair day's work" in such areas as vehicle maintenance, snow removal, street cleaning, and so on, and was unable to come up with useful guidelines by analyzing procedures in other cities. His studies revealed marked differences in the size of various work forces for cities of about the same population and area, and city managers and public works directors suggested that these differences negated the possibility of establishing standards on a comparative basis.

Henry brought in an industrial engineering team from B&W, and they told him that they could utilize the Gilbreth methods-time measurement approach to determine exactly how long each of the jobs in the maintenance and vehicle repair gangs should take. He then called in the public works employees and told them he planned to establish such standards. They objected strenuously, telling him that every job was different and standards would be impossible. The foremen agreed with the workers. Henry terminated the interview feeling uncertainty as to what he should do: continue with the establishment of uniform standards, select a test team and try out the standards on them, bring in and train a group from B&W to show the public works crew that it could be done, or abandon the whole idea of standards.

1. What would be the probable results if a test team was brought in from the outside? Would they be able to do the maintenance work in accordance with the standards set by the experienced industrial engineers?
2. If Henry decided to establish standards throughout, how should he go about it? Should be pick a special team like the Hawthorne relay room women? If he did, would they be likely to meet the standards? And if they did meet the standards, would that convince the rest of the public works crew?
3. Taylor would argue that the public works crew should not have a hand in deciding how the work ought to be done: the doctrine of separating planning from doing. Mayo would argue that the important thing would be to involve the people in work of their own design: in effect, lay out the tasks to suit the workers, making sure that all jobs were self-controlled. How do you think these two points of view apply here? What would happen if you did the first? The second?
4. How would a structuralist want to carry out the job analysis?

Suggestions for Further Reading

Argyris, C., et al. *Social Sciences Approach to Business Behavior.* Homewood, Ill.: Dorsey Press, 1962.

Barnard, C. I. *The Functions of the Executive.* Cambridge, Mass.: Harvard University Press, 1938.

Bendix, R. *Work and Authority in Industry.* New York: John Wiley & Sons, Inc., 1956.

Cyert, R., and J. G. March. *A Behavioral Theory of a Firm.* Englewood Cliffs, N.J.: Prentice-Hall, Inc., 1963.

Dale, E. *Management Theory and Practice.* 3d ed. New York: McGraw-Hill Book Co., 1973.

Durant, W. and A. *The Story of Civilization.* 10 vols. New York: Simon & Schuster, Inc., 1954-1967.

Etzioni, A. *Modern Organizations.* Englewood Cliffs, N.J.: Prentice-Hall, Inc., 1964.

Fayol, H. *General and Industrial Management,* trans. Constance Storrs. London: Sir Isaac Pitman & Sons, 1949.

Gerth, H. H., and C. W. Mills. *From Max Weber: Essays in Sociology.* New York: Oxford University Press, 1958.

Gulick, L., and L. Urwick, eds. *Papers on the Science of Administration.* New York: Columbia University Institute of Public Administration, 1937.

Kast, F. E., and J. E. Rosenzweig. *Organization and Management: A Systems Approach.* New York: McGraw-Hill Book Co., 1973.

March, J. G., and H. A. Simon. *Organizations.* New York: John Wiley & Sons, Inc., 1958.

Mayo, E. *The Human Problems of an Industrial Civilization.* New York: Viking Press, Inc., 1960.

McGregor, D. *The Human Side of Enterprise.* New York: McGraw-Hill Book Co., 1960.

Mooney, J. D. *Principles of Organization.* New York: Harper & Row, Pubs., 1947.

Rubenstein, A. H., and C. J. Haberstroh. *Some Theories of Organization.* Homewood, Ill.: Richard D. Irwin, Inc., and Dorsey Press, 1966.

Scott, W. G. *Human Relations in Management.* Homewood, Ill.: Richard D. Irwin, Inc., 1962.

─────. "Organization Theory: A Reassessment." *Academy of Management Journal* 17 (June 1974): pp. 242–54.

Sloan, A. P., Jr. *My Years with General Motors.* Garden City, N.Y.: Doubleday & Co., Inc., 1964.

Tausky, C. *Work Organizations: Major Theoretical Perspectives.* Itasca, Ill.: F. T. Peacock, Pubs., Inc., 1970.

Taylor, F. W. *Scientific Management.* New York: Harper & Row, Pubs., 1947.

Weber, M. *The Theory of Social and Economic Organization,* trans. A. M. Henderson and Talcott Parsons. New York: The Free Press, 1964.

Epilogue: A New Beginning

Although Eldorado was an incorporated town now, and Roger Moore accordingly worked for the town council rather than North Star, the relationships were not quite as clear-cut as that. The new town developer—Barnhard & Walker, a fact that put North Star on the firing line—was committed to expanding the city up to its planned size of 100,000. This task involved continued prospecting for new industries in the proper mix, while also enticing home builders to take a chance on constructing homes in a given price range—so the builders would need to draw on the labor pool provided by the town's new industries. It involved building shopping centers under very awkward circumstances: the major store that constituted the chief draw wouldn't come in until there was an adequate market of residents; the small satellite stores wouldn't sign until the major one did; and the homeowners wouldn't buy homes until they saw a shopping center they could count on. No one was willing to go first, and the developer had to exercise the skills of a pied piper to persuade them. It involved trying to decide what facilities ought to go in the parks, and whether to put in a concert hall or skating rink, and how to landscape the medians so the homes would be separated yet together at the same time—and all of this before the residents arrived, the only certain fact being that when they moved in they would want it different. It meant worrying over whether a multidenominational church with the separate sects taking turns on a Sunday would be hailed as a hallmark of the new ecumenism or dismissed as heretical nonsense and boycotted by all sects.

It meant many other things, but most of all it meant trying to manage a constituency over which Henry had no authority and no hold, and trying to get things done in an environment as foreign to traditional organizational hierarchy as he had ever seen or could ever imagine. North Star still paid a part of Roger Moore's salary, for example, but his real job was to serve as city manager of Eldorado, where he worked for the council and through them for the electorate. If Roger were fired by North Star, he would still have a job with the township. But it didn't work the other way, and Roger obviously knew it—if Eldorado fired him, there was no way North Star could keep him on. So Henry's hold over Roger was not very powerful; Roger was a decent person, however, and based on their past relationship Henry felt he would continue to cooperate.

In addition, both Henry and Roger were interested in doing a good job in Eldorado. That gave them a common objective that was perhaps more binding than any lines of authority could be. Indeed, Henry seemed to remember hearing something in class about the "legitimacy conferred by the environment" which provided an authority that could not be achieved in any other way. Perhaps that was the real cement that made this setup work.

One day Gail came in with a question about the hazards of a nuclear spill, something highly publicized at the time and a matter on which Gail frankly said she was quite ignorant. The discussion lasted until noon, and Henry suggested that she join him at lunch so he could pick her brains for a change. When they were seated and had ordered, he noted the philosophical complexity of "managing" a team as uncontrollable and diverse as the Eldorado residents, and asked her how she thought traditional management principles applied to such an offbeat environment. She replied that he hadn't seen anything: in the neighborhood group which she chaired (actually it was the village of Robin Hood Dell, which contained more than a third of Eldorado's population), she had no authority of any sort. Compared to her, he was a veritable despot, because he had the considerable power of being able to provide services and other community necessities, whereas she had only the power of persuasion on her side.

Perhaps, said Henry, her situation resembled "government by consent of the governed," which he had read about in his course recently. She served as long as her constituents thought she was doing a good job, but the moment they didn't like her she was out on her ear. That was exactly right, she said. She served for no specific term, and therefore could never be a "lame duck manager," with a guaranteed position for a given period no matter how well or badly she performed. In fact, said Henry, she was serving under a parliamentary system rather than a democratic system; like Britain's prime minister (and unlike the U.S. president), she was subject to removal any time a crucial question came up and she did not survive a "vote of confidence." That was about it, said Gail, and it was remarkable how that factor gave her the incentive to heed the day-to-day needs and wishes of her constituency. Henry wasn't in quite the same boat, because the Eldorado residents could not fire him whenever he failed to give satisfaction; but in the end they probably could work through B&W and get him replaced by someone else for that part of his job.

Afterward, Henry wondered what lessons this discussion held for him as a manager in general. In class, he had viewed the study of comparative management as a study of the different national systems: the British parliamentary system versus the French highly centralized system versus the U.S. democratic system with its broad powers assigned to the states and even the cities. Now he saw it differently: there were comparative ways to manage tasks even in a company such as theirs, depending on the environment of the job. Certainly the way he had to "manage" the other officers, during the early days when he was president in name only, was a far cry from the way Zeb could manage the secretaries, who knew they were replaceable on short notice and moreover suspected that Zeb knew